POGGIO AL TESORO

BOLGHERI·ITALIA

EXCELLENCE
HAS NEVER BEEN
SO YOUNG

SONDRAIA 2010

DEDICATO A WALTER 2009

DISCOVERING
THE SECRETS
OF THE BEST CHEFS
IS NOT SO DIFFICULT.
JUST TAKE A SEAT
AT THEIR TABLE.

THE FINE DINING WATERS

PITARS
Vigneti di famiglia in Friuli

CUSTODIANS OF
Authentic Passion

WWW.PITARS.IT

Pastificio dei Campi

GRAGNANO

www.pastificiodeicampi.it

GRAGNANO
CITTÀ DELLA PASTA

+40° 42' 26.04", +14° 30' 50.55"

CRUASÉ, TRADITIONAL METHOD
SPARKLING ROSÉ FROM OLTREPÒ PAVESE.

The word 'Cruasé' was formed by merging "cru" (selection) and "rosé", and adding an 'a' in the middle. The name of Oltrepò Pavese's new flagship wine (a DOCG traditional method rosé wine made from Pinot Noir grapes) came about while the Consortium was working on the concept of a "naturally rosé" wine made from red wine grape. This pink bubbly is a new point of reference for quality Italian classified sparkling wine. Created for the HORECA channel (hotels, restaurants and catering), it's also ideal for a sophisticated consumer who demands quality and a thrill from a wine that has been developed in respect of local history. Its strongpoint is value for money, within reach of the domestic market and exports. Cruasé is the new business card for a region that boasts quality and original wines.

Consorzio Tutela Vini Oltrepò Pavese
Via Riccagioia, 48 - 27050 Torrazza Coste (PV) - Tel. 0383.77028 - info@vinoltrepo.it - www.vinoltrepo.it

A world of Pinot nero

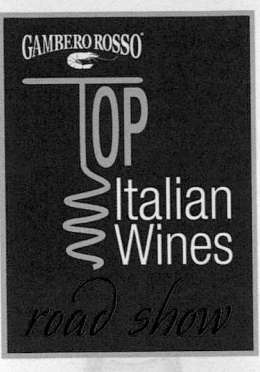

2013/2014

SEOUL
24 october 2013

OSAKA
28 october 2013

SYDNEY
10 march 2014

SINGAPORE
12 march 2014

SÃO PAULO
23 april 2014

MEXICO CITY
28 april 2014

Agricole Gussalli Beretta	Lunae Boson
Allegrini Estates	Marchesi di Barol
Arcanum	Masi/Serego Alighie
Baglio di Pianetto	Medici Ermete & Fig
Barone Pizzini	Il Molino di Grac
Bolla	Monte delle Vign
Cantina Produttori di Cormòns	Monte Schiav
Cantina Tollo	Nals Margrei
Cantine Due Palme	Ottel
Cantine Rallo	Provenza - Cà Mai
Casalfarneto	Ruggeri &
Castello di Cigognola	San Felic
Castorani	San Patrignan
Cavicchioli U. & Figli	San Salvato
Cavit	Santa Margherita Wine Grou
Colle Massari	Settese
Còlpetrone	Tenuta di Bibbiar
Cusumano	Tenuta Carret
De Stefani	Tenuta Uliss
Di Majo Norante	Tenute Rubir
Elvio Cogno	Tenute Sella&Mos
F.lli Giorgi	Torre Rosaz
Falesco	Torreven
Fattoria del Cerro	Valle Rea
Fattoria di Fèlsina	Velenc
Firriato	Vigne & V
Gaja	Vigne Surra
Gruppo La Vis	Vigneti Le Mon
iGreco	Villa Medc
Jermann	Villa Sar
Leone De Castris	Volpe Pas
Livon	

http://www.gamberorosso.it/

C.hianti ®

■━━━━ THE WINE ━━━━■

consorziovinochianti.it

A campaign financed according to EC Regulation n. 1234/2007

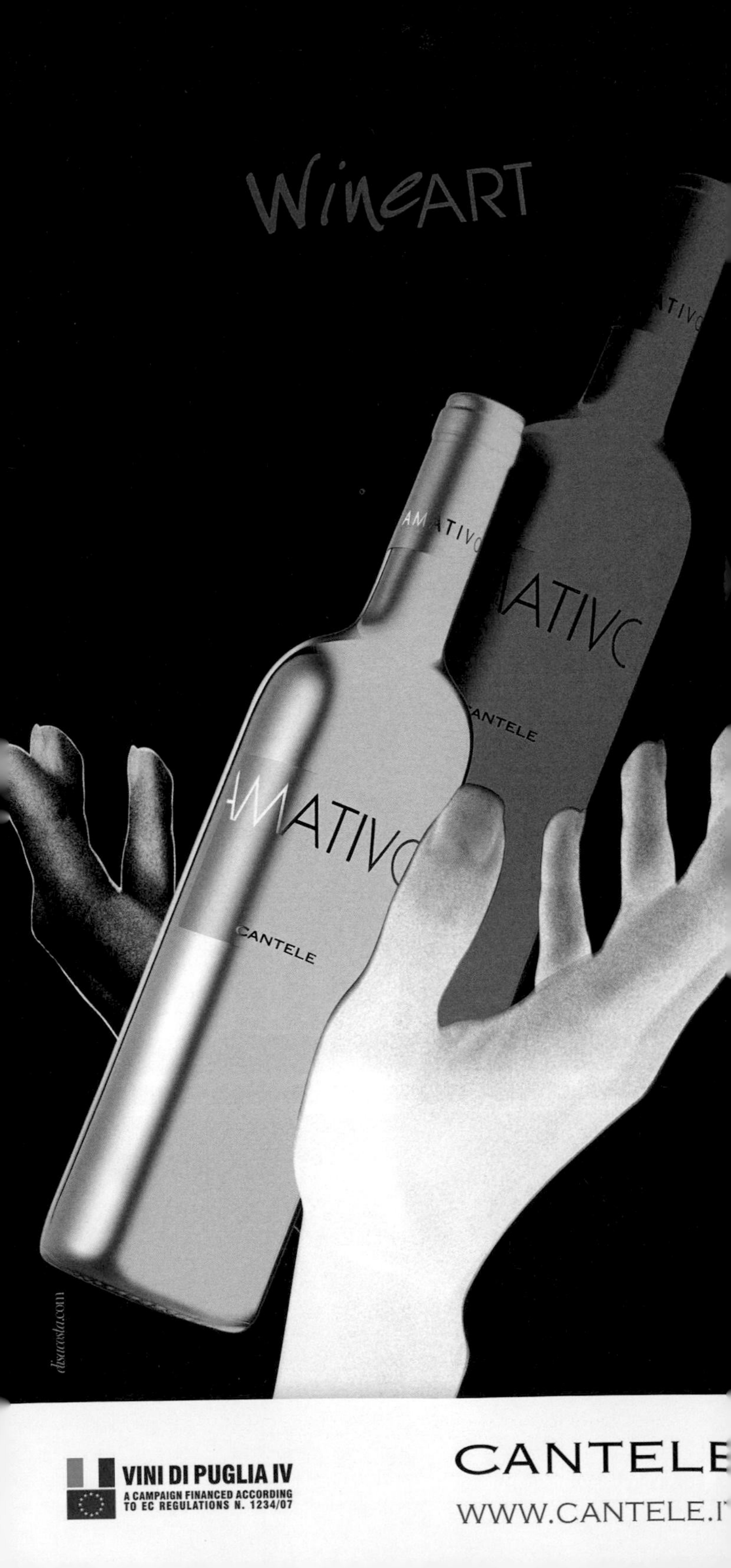

WineART

AMATIVO

MATIVC

AMATIVO

MATIVC

CANTELE

AMATIVO

CANTELE

CANTELE

WWW.CANTELE.I

2014

Italian
Wines

VINI D'ITALIA 2014
GAMBERO ROSSO®

Gambero Rosso Holding S.p.A.
via Enrico Fermi, 161 - 00146 ROMA
tel. 06/551121 - fax 06/55112260
www.gamberorosso.it
email: gambero@gamberorosso.it

Senior Editors
Gianni Fabrizio
Eleonora Guerini
Marco Sabellico

Co-editor
Giuseppe Carrus

Special Contributors
Antonio Boco
Paolo De Cristofaro
Lorenzo Ruggeri
Paolo Zaccaria

Regional Coordinators
Nino Aiello
Alessandro Bocchetti
Nicola Frasson
Massimo Lanza
Giorgio Melandri
Gianni Ottogalli
Nereo Pederzolli
Pierpaolo Rastelli

Contributors
Giovanni Angelucci
Francesco Beghi
Sergio Bonanno
Michele Bressan
Pasquale Buffa
Dionisio Castello
Francesca Ciancio
Enrico Melis
Giacomo Mojoli
Alessio Noè
Franco Pallini
Nicola Piccinini
Leonardo Romanelli
Giulia Sampognaro
Herbert Taschler

Other Contributors
Stefania Annese
Filippo Apollinari
Elena Bardelli
Enrico Battistella
Camilla Bianchin
Alexandre Bronzatto
Rossella Casula
Sergio Ceccarelli
Michele Cesarini
Claudia Cerchi
Goffredo D'Andrea
Mario Demattè
Matteo Farini
Maurizio Fava
Matteo Magnapane
Vittorio Manganelli
Andrea Marchetti
Leonardo Marco
Nicola Massa
Vanni Muraro
Renato Orlando
Gionata Ottogalli
Michele Palermo
Lina Paolillo

Antonio Paolini
Alessio Pietrobattista
Massimo Ponzanelli
Walter Pugliese
Carlo Ravanello
Maurizio Rossi
Ferruccio Sabiucciu
Cristina Sacchetti
Renato Sechi
Simona Silvestri
Andrea Sponzilli
Herbert Taschler
Cinzia Tosetti
Paolo Trimani
Vincenzo Verrastro
Stefano Zaghini

Editorial Secretary
Giulia Sciortino

Coordination and Layout
Marina Proietti

Managing Editor Books
Laura Mantovano

Graphics
Chiara Buosi

Commercial Director
Francesco Dammicco

Production
Elisabetta Di Fusco

Translation Coordinator
Angela Arnone

Translators and Revisors
Angela Arnone
Helen Donald
Juliet Hammond-Smith
Stephen Jackson
Sarah Ponting
Simon Tanner
Ailsa Wood

Publisher
GR USA CORP c/o CSC Services of Nevada Inc
2215-B RENAISSANCE DR
Las Vegas , NV 89119
email: gamberousa@aol.com

Distribution
USA nad Canada
by Antique Collector's Club, 6 West 18th Street -
Suite 4B, New York, NY 10011 - USA;
UK and Australia by Antique Collector's Club Ltd
Sandy Lane, Old Martlesham, Woodbridge,
Suffolk IP12 4SD - United Kingdom

The final edit of Italian Wines was completed on
11 September 2013

ISBN 9781890142230

Printed in Italy for Gambero Rosso Holding S.p.A.
in November 2013 by
Omnimedia s.r.l., Rome

3

SUMMARY

THE REGION

INDEXES

THE GUIDE

You are now reading the 27th edition of Italian Wines. The result of
another year of work by the great team of experts that Gambero Rosso
has been fielding for almost three decades. A team of 60 people who
spend months travelling Italy's wine trails, clocking up thousands of
kilometres, visiting all the wine regions and many hundreds of wineries,
sampling more than 45,000 wines, always as a panel and in strictly
blind tastings. Ours is a tried and tested method, and probably has no
equal in the world for the sheer volume of samples evaluated and the
size of the team. Work that makes up the Italian version and is then
translated into German and English, editions that have been published
from the start, now flanked by the recent addition of Chinese in its
third year, and this year Japanese is making its debut. No other wine
guide offers such a wide array of languages as ours and it remains
the primary information and study tool used by all lovers of Italian wine
worldwide. We are delighted that we are thus able to accompany the
growth of Italy's exports in international markets, a fact that appears
even more important considering the current economic crisis affecting
our country. Not to mention the number of international events, now
at 30 appointments around the globe, touching on every continent
and established and emerging market. Its success among wine
lovers, especially with professionals, is essentially due to two factors:
the independent classifications that are always unbiased, without
preconceptions, open to the new while attentive to tradition, and also
the completeness of information. We actually review 2,360 wineries
and more than 20,000 wines, offering plenty of facts about each estate
and its production, from whether they are open to the public, if there
are websites available, the type of viticulture practised, to the retail
price of each wine. In addition, of course, to the classic Un Bicchiere,
Due Bicchieri or Tre Bicchieri awards for each label tasted.
An immense task, which is performed with great care and skill by a
team of expert, enthusiastic tasters, handpicked over the years. We
have no ideological barriers and we move freely to voice our reviews in
a landscape as complex and fascinating as that of Italian wines, which
has no equals for richness and variety of climatic zones and cultivars.
A wine-growing scenario characterized by traditional native grapes
but where leading international varieties have made their homes and
express themselves with success. The proof of our labours this year is

represented by the 415 wines that have been awarded a Tre Bicchieri. All those we saw fit to reward because they passed the critical scrutiny of our panels and, subsequently, final tastings. Indeed, we do not believe it appropriate to insist that an ever-changing reality, conditioned by weather conditions and the arrival of new wineries, comply with predefined schema and figures. What you find in the pages that follow is the very best that the wines of Italy have expressed in the past year. Our special prizes sum up and illustrate all this, with a 2009 Calcarole Guerrieri Rizzardi Amarone elected Red of the Year; a 2012 Alto Adige Pinot Bianco Sirmian by the Nals Margreid winery is White of the Year; an Alta Langa Brut Zero Cantina Maestra 2007 from Enrico Serafino was chosen as Sparkler of the Year and, lastly, Barberani's Orvieto Classico Superiore Muffa Nobile 2010 is Sweet Wine of the Year. Our choice for Winery of the Year is Maremma's Colle Massari, owned by Maria Iris and Claudio Tipa, producing ace wines like the 2009 Montecucco Sangiovese Lombrone Riserva, but also leader of a group that has achieved true excellence both in Bolgheri with Grattamacco and in Montalcino with Poggio di Sotto. The Grower of the Year is Friuli's Alessandro Princic, the local Collio genius, while the Up-and-Coming Winery is Sardinia's Pala, fast becoming a reference point for the island's winemakers. Best Value for Money this year was an excellent Sicilian white, a 2012 Bianco Maggiore della Rallo. Our rundown of special prizes closes with our Award for Sustainable Viticulture to Montepulciano-based Salcheto: Michele Manelli has proved to be a compelling, charismatic character for the entire sector and we are happy to acknowledge that. In terms of sustainability and an ethical relationship with the environment, we are pleased to report that things are evolving positively. This year we restricted the Tre Bicchieri Verdi award to those wineries with official organic or biodynamic certification and there are 83, accounting for 20% of award-winning wines: a truly remarkable number. Besides this, our questionnaires revealed some interesting data on sustainability practices, with 463 companies adopting them at various levels, 336 applying UNI-ISO 14064 standards, and a respectable 522 businesses consuming at least part of their energy from renewable sources. Vineyard Italy, in short, is changing and evolving towards more environmentally friendly models. A complex, interesting picture that leaves us optimistic for the future of agriculture, viticulture and, in particular, our country.

Our thanks go to Bolzano EOS, Cagliari, Trento and Perugia chambers of commerce, the coordinators of Umbria's wine and oil trails, the Istituto Marchigiano di Tutela Vini (IMT) in Jesi, Vinea of Offida, Picenos – Consorzio Vini Piceni, ERSA Friuli Venezia Giulia in Pozzuolo, the Istituto Agronomico Mediterraneano of Valenzano, the Ente Vini Bresciani, the Centro di Ricerca Riccagioia, the Torrecuso Scuola del Gusto, and Ortovero municipal authority. Also, the protection consortiums for Chianti Classico, Brunello di Montalcino, Bolgheri, Vino Nobile di Montepulciano, Vernaccia di San Gimignano, Chianti Rufina, Colli Fiorentini, Cortona, Morellino di Scansano, Montecucco, Monteregio di Massa Marittima, Gavi, Nebbioli dell'Alto Piemonte, Vini Colli Tortonesi, Barolo Barbaresco Alba Langhe and Roero, as well as Franciacorta, Oltrepò Pavese, Lugana, Valtenesi, Valtellina, the wines of Valpolicella, Conegliano Valdobbiadene, and Samnium.

We also thank the regional wine cellars of Roero, Nizza Monferrato, Emilia Romagna of Dozza, Lazio, the Enoteca dei Vini della Provincia di Torino, the Cantina Regionale della Basilicata of Venosa, Cantina Comunale I Sörì of Diano, and the Bottega del Vino of Dogliani. We thank too the Carmignano and Arezzo wine trails. Among the private facilities, we remember La Réserve of Caramanico, the Calidarium of Venturina, the Carpe Diem restaurant of Montaione, the Due Sorelle of Messina, Millésimes of Collegno, Bottegaccia of Aosta, Caneva of Mogliano Veneto, the Fontanarosa Residence of Fontanarosa.

Last but not least, our thanks to the entire team that contributed to making the tastings, the notes and the volume a reality, with special thanks to Giuseppe Carrus, the Guide's irreplaceable co-editor.

We close remembering the figure of Stephen Rand Jackson, a longstanding contributor to the translation of the Guide: a talented wordsmith and a sterling human being.

Gianni Fabrizio, Eleonora Guerini, Marco Sabellico

7

TRE BICCHIERI 2014

Valle d'Aosta

Valle d'Aosta Chambave Moscato Passito Prieuré '11	La Crotta di Vegneron	27
Valle d'Aosta Chambave Muscat Flétri '11	La Vrille	31
Valle d'Aosta Chardonnay '12	Di Barrò	28
Valle d'Aosta Petite Arvine '12	Château Feuillet	26
Valle d'Aosta Petite Arvine '12	Elio Ottin	30
Valle d'Aosta Pinot Gris '12	Lo Triolet	29

Piedmont

Alta Langa Brut Zero Cantina Maestra '07	Enrico Serafino	165
Barbaresco Asili '10	Ca' del Baio	63
Barbaresco Camp Gros Martinenga '09	Tenute Cisa Asinari dei Marchesi di Grésy	84
Barbaresco Crichët Pajé '04	I Paglieri - Roagna	137
Barbaresco Currà '10	Cantina del Glicine	65
Barbaresco Gallina '09	Piero Busso	61
Barbaresco Pajoré '10	Sottimano	167
Barbaresco Rabajà '10	Giuseppe Cortese	93
Barbaresco Rabajà '10	Bruno Rocca	153
Barbaresco Rombone '09	Fiorenzo Nada	133
Barbaresco Roncaglie Ris. '08	Bel Colle	46
Barbaresco Ronchi '10	Albino Rocca	152
Barbaresco Serraboella '09	F.lli Cigliuti	84
Barbaresco Vign. in Ovello Ris. '08	Produttori del Barbaresco	147
Barbera d'Asti Montebruna '11	Braida	54
Barbera d'Asti Pomorosso '10	Coppo	90
Barbera d'Asti Sup. La Mandorla '10	Luigi Spertino	168
Barbera d'Asti Sup. Nizza Acsé '10	Scrimaglio	163
Barbera d'Asti Sup. Nizza Sotto la Muda '10	Paolo Avezza	43
Barbera del M.to Sup. Cima '07	Giulio Accornero e Figli	35
Barolo '09	Bartolo Mascarello	124
Barolo Arborina '09	Elio Altare	39
Barolo Baudana Luigi Baudana '09	G. D. Vajra	173
Barolo Bric dël Fiasc '09	Paolo Scavino	162
Barolo Bricco Fiasco '09	Azelia	43
Barolo Bricco Pernice '08	Elvio Cogno	85
Barolo Bricco Rocche '09	Ceretto	81
Barolo Brunate '09	Mario Marengo	122
Barolo Bussia '09	Giacomo Fenocchio	99
Barolo Bussia Bricco Visette '09	Attilio Ghisolfi	107
Barolo Bussia Dardi Le Rose '09	Poderi Colla	143
Barolo Ca' Mia '09	Brovia	60
Barolo Castelletto '09	Giovanni Manzone	119
Barolo Cerequio '09	Michele Chiarlo	82
Barolo Gavarini Chiniera '09	Elio Grasso	111
Barolo La Serra '09	Giovanni Rosso	156

Barolo Le Coste '09	Diego Conterno	87
Barolo Le Rocche del Falletto Ris. '07	Bruno Giacosa	107
Barolo Liste '08	Giacomo Borgogno & Figli	51
Barolo Marenca '09	Luigi Pira	142
Barolo Massara '08	Castello di Verduno	80
Barolo Monfortino Ris. '06	Giacomo Conterno	88
Barolo Monprivato '08	Giuseppe Mascarello e Figlio	125
Barolo Monvigliero '09	F.lli Alessandria	37
Barolo Ornato '09	Pio Cesare	141
Barolo Ravera '08	Flavio Roddolo	155
Barolo Rocche dell'Annunziata '09	Renato Corino	91
Barolo Rocche di Castiglione '09	Poderi e Cantine Oddero	135
Barolo Sarmassa '09	Marchesi di Barolo	121
Barolo Sottocastello di Novello '08	Ca' Viola	64
Barolo V. Cerretta '09	Ca' Rome' Romano Marengo	64
Barolo V. del Gris '09	Conterno Fantino	89
Barolo V. Lazzairasco '09	Guido Porro	145
Barolo Villero Ris. '06	Vietti	175
Carema Et. Bianca Ris. '09	Cantina dei Produttori Nebbiolo di Carema	133
Carema Et. Nera '08	Ferrando	100
Colli Tortonesi Timorasso Derthona '11	Luigi Boveri	53
Colli Tortonesi Timorasso Fausto '11	Vigne Marina Coppi	90
Dogliani Papà Celso '11	Abbona	34
Dogliani Sup. Bricco Botti '10	Pecchenino	139
Dolcetto di Ovada Sup. Du Riva '10	Luigi Tacchino	169
Erbaluce di Caluso La Rustìa '12	Orsolani	137
Erbaluce di Caluso Le Chiusure '12	Favaro	99
Gattinara '09	Torraccia del Piantavigna	172
Gattinara Osso S. Grato '09	Antoniolo	40
Gavi del Comune di Gavi Monterotondo '11	Villa Sparina	177
Ghemme Chioso dei Pomi '07	Rovellotti	156
Langhe Bianco Hérzu '11	Ettore Germano	106
Langhe Nebbiolo Costa Russi '10	Gaja	104
M.to Rosso Sonvico '09	Cascina La Barbatella	73
Montecitorio '11	Vigneti Massa	176
Nebbiolo d'Alba Cumot '10	Bricco Maiolica	58
Roero Bric Valdiana '11	Giovanni Almondo	38
Roero Mompissano Ris. '10	Cascina Ca' Rossa	69
Roero Printi Ris. '09	Monchiero Carbone	127
Roero Ròche d'Ampsèj Ris. '09	Matteo Correggia	92
Roero Sudisfà Ris. '10	Negro Angelo e Figli	134

Liguria

Cinque Terre '12	Samuele Heydi Bonanini	197
Colli di Luni Vermentino Et. Nera '12	Cantine Lunae Bosoni	202
Colli di Luni Vermentino Il Maggiore '12	Ottaviano Lambruschi	201
Riviera Ligure di Ponente Pigato '12	Maria Donata Bianchi	195
Riviera Ligure di Ponente Pigato Cycnus '12	Poggio dei Gorleri	204

Riviera Ligure di Ponente Pigato U Baccan '11	Bruna	198
Rossese di Dolceacqua '12	Terre Bianche	205

Lombardy

Brut Cl. '08	Monsupello	238
Franciacorta Brut Blanc de Noir '09	Le Marchesine	236
Franciacorta Brut Collezione Esclusiva Giovanni Cavalleri '05	Cavalleri	227
Franciacorta Brut Emozione '09	Villa	251
Franciacorta Brut Extrême Palazzo Lana Ris. '06	Guido Berlucchi & C.	217
Franciacorta Brut Nature '09	Barone Pizzini	215
Franciacorta Cuvée Annamaria Clementi Ris. '05	Ca' del Bosco	222
Franciacorta Extra Brut '07	Lo Sparviere	248
Franciacorta Extra Brut Vittorio Moretti Ris. '06	Bellavista	216
Franciacorta Nature	Enrico Gatti	233
Franciacorta Pas Dosé 33 Ris. '06	Ferghettina	231
Franciacorta Zero '09	Contadi Castaldi	228
Lugana Brolettino '11	Ca' dei Frati	221
Lugana Molin '12	Provenza - Cà Maiol	245
Lugana Sup. Sel. Fabio Contato '11	Provenza - Cà Maiol	245
OP Barbera Dodicidodici '11	Castello di Cigognola	226
OP Pinot Nero Brut Cl. 1870 '09	F.lli Giorgi	234
OP Pinot Nero Giorgio Odero '10	Frecciarossa	233
OP Pinot Nero Noir '10	Tenuta Mazzolino	237
Valtellina Sforzato Ronco del Picchio '09	Sandro Fay	231
Valtellina Sfursat 5 Stelle '10	Nino Negri	242
Valtellina Sfursat Fruttaio Ca' Rizzieri '09	Aldo Rainoldi	246
Valtellina Sup. Sassella San Lorenzo '10	Mamete Prevostini	244

Trentino

Carmenère '07	Tenuta San Leonardo	281
Fratagranda '10	Pravis	280
Granato '10	Foradori	276
Pinot Nero Rodel Pianezzi '09	Pojer & Sandri	280
Teroldego Rotaliano Pini '09	Roberto Zeni	283
Trentino Müller Thurgau Vigna delle Forche '12	La Vis/Valle di Cembra	277
Trento Brut Altemasi Graal Ris. '06	Cavit	271
Trento Brut Domini Nero '08	Abate Nero	268
Trento Brut Letrari Ris. '08	Letrari	278
Trento Extra Brut Perlé Nero '07	Ferrari	275
Trento Rotari Flavio Ris. '06	MezzaCorona	278

Alto Adige

A. A. Cabernet Sauvignon Lafòa '10	Cantina Produttori Colterenzio	292
A. A. Gewürztraminer Crescendo Aureus '12	Tenuta Ritterhof	310
A. A. Gewürztraminer Kastelaz '12	Elena Walch	319
A. A. Gewürztraminer Nussbaumer '12	Cantina Tramin	316
A. A. Lago di Caldaro Cl. Sup. Leuchtenburg '12	Erste+Neue	294

Montello e Colli Asolani Il Rosso dell'Abazia '10	Serafini & Vidotto	380
Recioto della Valpolicella Cl. '01	Giuseppe Quintarelli	373
Soave Cl. Campo Vulcano '12	I Campi	338
Soave Cl. La Rocca '11	Leonildo Pieropan	371
Soave Cl. Le Bine de Costiola '11	Tamellini	383
Soave Cl. Monte Alto '11	Ca' Rugate	337
Soave Cl. Monte Carbonare '11	Suavia	382
Soave Cl. Monte de Toni '12	I Stefanini	381
Soave Cl. Staforte '11	Graziano Prà	372
Soave Sup. Il Casale '12	Agostino Vicentini	388
Valdobbiadene Brut Rive di Col San Martino Cuvée del Fondatore Graziano Merotto '12	Merotto	361
Valdobbiadene Extra Dry Giustino B. '12	Ruggeri & C.	375
Valdobbiadene Rive di Farra di Soligo Brut Col Credas '12	Adami	322
Valpolicella Cl. Sup. Campo Casal Vegri '11	Ca' La Bionda	335
Valpolicella Cl. Sup. Camporenzo '10	Monte dall'Ora	362
Valpolicella Cl. Sup. Sanperetto '11	Roberto Mazzi	361
Valpolicella Sup. '09	Marion	358
Valpolicella Sup. Maternigo '11	F.lli Tedeschi	385

Friuli Venezia Giulia

Braide Alte '11	Livon	434
Breg Anfora '06	Gravner	429
COF Friulano '11	Davino Meroi	437
COF Friulano V. delle Robinie '11	Ronc Soreli	449
COF Merlot V. Cinquant'Anni '09	Le Vigne di Zamò	468
COF Pinot Bianco Zuc di Volpe '12	Volpe Pasini	471
COF Pinot Grigio '12	Torre Rosazza	463
COF Rosazzo Bianco Terre Alte '11	Livio Felluga	426
COF Rosso Sacrisassi '11	Le Due Terre	424
COF Sauvignon Zuc di Volpe '12	Volpe Pasini	471
Collio '12	Ronco Blanchis	452
Collio Friulano '12	Franco Toros	463
Collio Malvasia '12	Doro Princic	446
Collio Malvasia '12	Dario Raccaro	447
Collio Malvasia '12	Ronco dei Tassi	453
Collio Malvasia Miklus '10	Draga	423
Collio Sauvignon Ronco delle Mele '12	Venica & Venica	465
Eclisse '12	La Roncaia	450
Friuli Grave Pinot Bianco '12	Vigneti Le Monde	433
Friuli Isonzo Friulano Dolée '11	Vie di Romans	466
Friuli Isonzo Pinot Grigio Gris '11	Lis Neris	433
Malvasia '09	Damijan Podversic	444
Ograde '11	Skerk	459
Vintage Tunina '11	Jermann	430

Emilia Romagna

Albana di Romagna Passito Regina di Cuori Ris. '10	Gallegati	498

Chianti Cl. Fizzano Ris. '10	Rocca delle Macìe	623
Chianti Cl. Le Corti '10	Fattoria Le Corti	569
Chianti Cl. Ris. '09	Badia a Coltibuono	530
Chianti Cl. Ris. '10	Brancaia	539
Chianti Cl. Ris. '09	Castello d'Albola	550
Chianti Cl. Ris. '10	Castello di Volpaia	556
Chianti Cl. Ris. '10	Le Miccine	595
Chianti Cl. Vign. di Campolungo Ris. '09	Lamole di Lamole	587
Coevo '10	Famiglia Cecchi	557
Colline Lucchesi Tenuta di Valgiano '10	Tenuta di Valgiano	648
Cortona Syrah '10	Stefano Amerighi	525
Cortona Syrah Il Castagno '10	Fabrizio Dionisio	572
Dofana '10	Fattoria Carpineta Fontalpino	547
Fontalloro '10	Fattoria di Felsina	575
I Sodi di S. Niccolò '09	Castellare di Castellina	549
Le Pergole Torte '10	Montevertine	600
Montecucco Sangiovese '10	Montesalario	599
Montecucco Sangiovese Lombrone Ris. '09	Colle Massari	565
Morellino di Scansano Calestaia Ris. '09	Roccapesta	625
Morellino di Scansano Madrechiesa Ris. '10	Terenzi	640
Nobile di Montepulciano '10	Fattoria del Cerro	560
Nobile di Montepulciano '10	Il Conventino	568
Nobile di Montepulciano '10	Salcheto	627
Nobile di Montepulciano Nocio dei Boscarelli '09	Poderi Boscarelli	538
Oreno '10	Tenuta Sette Ponti	638
Orma '10	Podere Orma	604
Paleo Rosso '10	Le Macchiole	591
Poggiassai '10	Poggio Bonelli	614
Poggio ai Chiari '06	Colle Santa Mustiola	566
Poggio de' Colli '11	Piaggia	609
Rocca di Frassinello '11	Rocca di Frassinello	624
Siepi '10	Castello di Fonterutoli	553
Suisassi '10	Due Mani	573
Torrione '11	Fattoria Petrolo	608
Veneroso '10	Tenuta di Ghizzano	582
Vernaccia di S. Gimignano Campo della Pieve '11	Il Colombaio di Santa Chiara	568
Vernaccia di S. Gimignano Ris. '10	Fontaleoni	577
Vigorello '10	San Felice	629

Marche

Arshura '11	Valter Mattoni	701
Castelli di Jesi Verdicchio Cl. Crisio Ris. '11	Casalfarneto	687
Castelli di Jesi Verdicchio Cl. Il Cantico della Figura Ris. '10	Andrea Felici	694
Castelli di Jesi Verdicchio Cl. Plenio Ris. '10	Umani Ronchi	711
Castelli di Jesi Verdicchio Cl. San Paolo Ris. '10	Pievalta	704
Castelli di Jesi Verdicchio Cl. San Sisto Ris. '10	Fazi Battaglia	694
Castelli di Jesi Verdicchio Cl. V. Novali Ris. '10	Terre Cortesi Moncaro	710
Castelli di Jesi Verdicchio Cl. Villa Bucci Ris. '10	Bucci	684

Il Pollenza '10	Il Pollenza	704
Kupra '10	Oasi degli Angeli	703
Offida Pecorino Artemisia '12	Tenuta Spinelli	708
Rosso Piceno Sup. Roggio del Filare '10	Velenosi	712
Verdicchio dei Castelli di Jesi Cl. Sel. GG Ris. '08	Gioacchino Garofoli	696
Verdicchio dei Castelli di Jesi Cl. Sup. Ylice '12	Poderi Mattioli	700
Verdicchio di Matelica Collestefano '12	Collestefano	690
Verdicchio di Matelica Meridia '10	Belisario	682
Verdicchio di Matelica Mirum Ris. '11	La Monacesca	701
Verdicchio di Matelica Vign. Fogliano '10	Bisci	683

Umbria

Cervaro della Sala '11	Castello della Sala	725
Montefalco Sagrantino '09	Tenuta Bellafonte	721
Montefalco Sagrantino '09	Perticaia	735
Montefalco Sagrantino 25 Anni '09	Arnaldo Caprai	723
Montefalco Sagrantino Arquata '08	Adanti	720
Montefalco Sagrantino Colle alle Macchie '09	Giampaolo Tabarrini	738
Montefalco Sagrantino Colleallodole '10	Fattoria Colleallodole	727
Orvieto Cl. Sup. Campo del Guardiano '11	Palazzone	733
Orvieto Cl. Sup. Il Bianco '12	Decugnano dei Barbi	729
Orvieto Cl. Sup. Muffa Nobile Calcaia '10	Barberani	721
Torgiano Rosso V. Monticchio Ris. '08	Lungarotti	731

Lazio

Baccarossa '11	Poggio Le Volpi	752
Cesanese del Piglio Romanico '11	Antonello Coletti Conti	748
Ferentano '11	Falesco	749
Montiano '11	Falesco	749
Poggio della Costa '12	Sergio Mottura	751

Abruzzo

Montepulciano d'Abruzzo Cocciapazza '10	Torre dei Beati	776
Montepulciano d'Abruzzo Colline Teramane Adrano '10	Villa Medoro	779
Montepulciano d'Abruzzo Colline Teramane Neromoro Ris. '09	Bruno Nicodemi	772
Montepulciano d'Abruzzo I Vasari '10	F.lli Barba	762
Montepulciano d'Abruzzo Marina Cvetic '10	Masciarelli	771
Montepulciano d'Abruzzo Nativae '12	Tenuta Ulisse	777
Montepulciano d'Abruzzo Ris. '09	Castorani	764
Montepulciano d'Abruzzo Ris. '08	Contesa	768
Pecorino '11	Luigi Cataldi Madonna	765
Pecorino '12	Tiberio	775
Trebbiano d'Abruzzo '11	Valentini	778
Trebbiano d'Abruzzo C'Incanta '10	Cantina Tollo	776
Trebbiano d'Abruzzo V. di Capestrano '11	Valle Reale	778

Molise

Molise Aglianico Biorganic '11	Di Majo Norante	784

Campania

Aglianico del Taburno '10	Fattoria La Rivolta	805
Aglianico del Taburno Delius '09	Cantina del Taburno	789
Casavecchia Centomoggia '11	Terre del Principe	810
Falerno del Massico Rosso Et. Bronzo '10	Masseria Felicia	800
Fiano di Avellino '12	Pietracupa	804
Fiano di Avellino Pietramara '12	I Favati	796
Fiano di Avellino Selvecorte '12	Michele Contrada	791
Fiano Tresinus '12	San Giovanni	807
Greco di Tufo Cutizzi '12	Feudi di San Gregorio	797
Greco di Tufo V. Cicogna '12	Benito Ferrara	797
Ischia Biancolella Tenuta Frassitelli '12	D'Ambra Vini d'Ischia	793
Montevetrano '11	Montevetrano	802
Pian di Stio '12	San Salvatore	807
Sabbie di Sopra il Bosco '11	Nanni Copè	803
Taburno Falanghina '12	Fontanavecchia	798
Taurasi Coste '08	Contrade di Taurasi	792
Taurasi Fatica Contadina '08	Terredora	811
Taurasi Radici Ris. '07	Mastroberardino	801
Terra di Lavoro '11	Galardi	798
Trebulanum '10	Alois	788

Basilicata

Aglianico del Vulture Don Anselmo '09	Paternoster	828
Aglianico del Vulture La Firma '10	Cantine del Notaio	824
Aglianico del Vulture Re Manfredi '10	Terre degli Svevi	829
Aglianico del Vulture Titolo '11	Elena Fucci	827

Puglia

Castel del Monte Rosso V. Pedale Ris. '10	Torrevento	847
Gioia del Colle Primitivo 17 '10	Polvanera	842
Gioia del Colle Primitivo Et. Rossa '11	Plantamura	842
Gioia del Colle Primitivo Muro Sant'Angelo Contrada Barbatto '10	Chiaromonte	837
Masseria Li Veli '10	Masseria Li Veli	839
Merula '11	Carvinea	836
Primitivo di Manduria Dunico '10	Racemi	843
Primitivo di Manduria Es '11	Gianfranco Fino	838
Primitivo La Signora '10	Morella	840
Salice Salentino Rosso Ris. '10	Leone de Castris	839
Salice Salentino Rosso Selvarossa Ris. '10	Cantine Due Palme	837
Torcicoda '11	Tormaresca	847
Torre Testa '11	Tenute Rubino	845

Calabria

Cirò Rosso Duca Sanfelice Ris. '11	Librandi	859
Grisara '12	Roberto Ceraudo	858
Masino '11	iGreco	858
Moscato Passito '12	Luigi Viola	863

Sicily

Bianco Maggiore '12	Cantine Rallo	885
Contea di Sclafani Cabernet Sauvignon '10	Tasca d'Almerita	888
Contrada G '11	Passopisciaro	882
Etna Bianco A' Puddara '11	Tenuta di Fessina	875
Etna Bianco Arcuria '11	Graci	879
Etna Bianco Sup. Pietramarina '09	Benanti	871
Etna Rosso Feudo '11	Girolamo Russo	886
Etna Rosso Santo Spirito '11	Tenuta delle Terre Nere	889
Etna Rosso V. Barbagalli '10	Pietradolce	883
Frappato Carolina Marengo '11	Feudi del Pisciotto	876
Il Frappato '11	Occhipinti	881
Malvasia delle Lipari Passito Ris. '10	Hauner	880
Marsala Sup. Ambra Semisecco Ris. '85	Carlo Pellegrino	883
Noto Santa Cecilia '10	Planeta	884
Passito di Pantelleria Ben Ryé '11	Donnafugata	874
Rosso del Soprano '11	Palari	881
Sàgana '11	Cusumano	873
Saia '11	Feudo Maccari	876
Santagostino Rosso Baglio Sorìa '11	Firriato	877

Sardinia

Alghero Rosso Marchese di Villamarina '08	Tenute Sella & Mosca	912
Barrua '10	Agricola Punica	900
Cannonau di Sardegna Dule Ris. '10	Giuseppe Gabbas	905
Cannonau di Sardegna Mamuthone '11	Giuseppe Sedilesu	911
Cannonau di Sardegna Ris. '11	Pala	909
Cannonau di Sardegna Sileno Ris. '10	Ferruccio Deiana	904
Cannonau di Sardegna Vinìola Ris. '10	Cantina Dorgali	905
Capichera '11	Capichera	902
Carignano del Sulcis Is Arenas Ris. '09	Sardus Pater	911
Carignano del Sulcis Sup. Terre Brune '09	Cantina di Santadi	910
Semidano di Mogoro Sup. Puistèris '10	Cantina di Mogoro Il Nuraghe	908
Turriga '09	Argiolas	901
Vermentino di Gallura Sup. Sciala '12	Vigne Surrau	913

THE BEST

RED OF THE YEAR
AMARONE DELLA VALPOLICELLA CL. CALCAROLE '09 – GUERRIERI RIZZARDI

WHITE OF THE YEAR
A. A. PINOT BIANCO SIRMIAN '12 – CANTINA NALS MARGREID

SPARKLER OF THE YEAR
ALTA LANGA BRUT ZERO CANTINA MAESTRA '07 – ENRICO SERAFINO

SWEET OF THE YEAR
ORVIETO CL. SUP. MUFFA NOBILE CALCAIA '10 – BARBERANI

WINERY OF THE YEAR

COLLE MASSARI

BEST VALUE FOR MONEY

BIANCO MAGGIORE '12 – RALLO

GROWER OF THE YEAR

ALESSANDRO PRINCIC

UP-AND-COMING WINERY

PALA

AWARD FOR SUSTAINABLE VITICULTURE

SALCHETO

TRE BICCHIERI VERDI

Over recent years we have started to list Tre Bicchieri Verdi wines, those produced by wineries showing special environmental awareness. This year we decided to apply more selective criteria and the list includes only wines presented by cellars with official organic and biodynamic certification, the latter shown in red. This year we have 83 Tre Bicchieri Verdi wine awards out of a total of 415 overall, which means 20%. An important datum testifying how Italy's top wineries are now completely engaged in the environmental process. Italian vineyards, in short, are changing. We believe in that it is possible to achieve a better world, one that also passes through better viticulture. And we hope that in the future there will be increasing numbers of producers who use renewable energy sources as well as applying for certification with new sustainability protocols such as the UNI-ISO 14064 for greenhouse gases.

A. A. Gewürztraminer Nussbaumer '12	Cantina Tramin	**Alto Adige**
A. A. Moscato Giallo Passito Serenade '10	Cantina di Caldaro	**Alto Adige**
A. A. Terlano Pinot Bianco Eichhorn '12	Mancor	**Alto Adige**
Aglianico del Taburno '10	Fattoria La Rivolta	**Campania**
Aglianico del Vulture Don Anselmo '09	Paternoster	**Basilicata**
Aglianico del Vulture La Firma '10	Cantine del Notaio	**Basilicata**
Barbera d'Asti Sup. Nizza Acsé '10	Scrimaglio	**Piedmont**
Bardolino Cl. Brol Grande '11	Le Fraghe	**Veneto**
Barolo Bricco Pernice '08	Elvio Cogno	**Piedmont**
Barolo Bricco Rocche '09	Ceretto	**Piedmont**
Barolo Ca' Mia '09	Brovia	**Piedmont**
Barolo Rocche di Castiglione '09	Poderi e Cantine Oddero	**Piedmont**
Barolo V. del Gris '09	Conterno Fantino	**Piedmont**
Bianco Maggiore '12	Cantine Rallo	**Sicily**
Bolgheri Rosso Sup. Grattamacco '10	Podere Grattamacco	**Tuscany**
Bolgheri Sup. Campo al Fico '10	I Luoghi	**Tuscany**
Brunello di Montalcino Fornace '08	Le Ragnaie	**Tuscany**
Brunello di Montalcino Poggio al Vento Ris. '06	Tenuta Col d'Orcia	**Tuscany**
Brunello di Montalcino Ris. '07	Le Chiuse	**Tuscany**
Brunello di Montalcino Ris. '07	Poggio di Sotto	**Tuscany**
Cannonau di Sardegna Sileno Ris. '10	Ferruccio Deiana	**Sardinia**
Castel del Monte Rosso V. Pedale Ris. '10	Torrevento	**Puglia**
Castelli di Jesi Verdicchio Cl. Il Cantico della Figura Ris. '10	Andrea Felici	**Marche**

Castelli di Jesi Verdicchio Cl. San Paolo Ris. '10	Pievalta	**Marche**
Castelli di Jesi Verdicchio Cl. Villa Bucci Ris. '10	Bucci	**Marche**
Chianti Cl. '10	Fontodi	**Tuscany**
Chianti Cl. '10	Val delle Corti	**Tuscany**
Chianti Cl. Baron'Ugo Ris. '09	Monteraponi	**Tuscany**
Chianti Cl. Bugialla Ris. '09	Poggerino	**Tuscany**
Chianti Cl. Ris. '09	Badia a Coltibuono	**Tuscany**
Chianti Cl. Ris. '10	Castello di Volpaia	**Tuscany**
Colli Berici Carmenere Oratorio di San Lorenzo Ris. '09	Inama	**Veneto**
Colline Lucchesi Tenuta di Valgiano '10	Tenuta di Valgiano	**Tuscany**
Dofana '10	Fattoria Carpineta Fontalpino	**Tuscany**
Etna Rosso Feudo '11	Girolamo Russo	**Sicily**
Etna Rosso Santo Spirito '11	Tenuta delle Terre Nere	**Sicily**
Franciacorta Brut Nature '09	Barone Pizzini	**Lombardy**
Gioia del Colle Muro Sant'Angelo Contrada Barbatto '10	Chiaromonte	**Puglia**
Gioia del Colle Primitivo 17 '10	Polvanera	**Puglia**
Gioia del Colle Primitivo Et. Rossa '11	Plantamura	**Puglia**
Granato '10	Foradori	**Trentino**
Greco di Tufo Cutizzi '12	Feudi di San Gregorio	**Campania**
Grisara '12	Roberto Ceraudo	**Calabria**
Il Frappato '11	Occhipinti	**Sicily**
Malvasia '09	Damijan Podversic	**Friuli Venezia Giulia**
Masino '11	iGreco	**Calabria**
Masseria Li Veli '10	Masseria Li Veli	**Puglia**
Merula '11	Carvinea	**Puglia**
Molise Aglianico Biorganic '11	Di Majo Norante	**Molise**
Montecucco Sangiovese Lombrone Ris. '09	Colle Massari	**Tuscany**
Montepulciano d'Abruzzo Cocciapazza '10	Torre dei Beati	**Abruzzo**
Montepulciano d'Abruzzo Ris. '09	Castorani	**Abruzzo**
Moscato Passito '12	Luigi Viola	**Calabria**
Nobile di Montepulciano '10	Fattoria del Cerro	**Tuscany**
Nobile di Montepulciano '10	Il Conventino	**Tuscany**
Nobile di Montepulciano '10	Salcheto	**Tuscany**
Ograde '11	Skerk	**Friuli Venezia Giulia**
Orvieto Cl. Sup. Muffa Nobile Calcaia '10	Barberani	**Umbria**
Pian di Stio '12	San Salvatore	**Campania**
Pinot Nero Rodel Pianezzi '09	Pojer & Sandri	**Trentino**
Poggio della Costa '12	Sergio Mottura	**Lazio**
Primitivo di Manduria Dunico '10	Racemi	**Puglia**
Roero Mompissano Ris. '10	Cascina Ca' Rossa	**Piedmont**

Sangiovese di Romagna Longiano Primo Segno '11	Villa Venti	**Emilia Romagna**
Sangiovese di Romagna Sup. Limbecca '11	Paolo Francesconi	**Emilia Romagna**
Sangiovese di Romagna Sup. NatoRe '10	Maria Galassi	**Emilia Romagna**
Sangiovese di Romagna Sup. Ora '12	San Patrignano	**Emilia Romagna**
Santagostino Rosso Baglio Sorìa '11	Firriato	**Sicily**
Soave Cl. La Rocca '11	Leonildo Pieropan	**Veneto**
Suisassi '10	Due Mani	**Tuscany**
Taurasi Coste '08	Contrade di Taurasi	**Campania**
Terra di Lavoro '11	Galardi	**Campania**
Torcicoda '11	Tormaresca	**Puglia**
Torgiano Rosso V. Monticchio Ris. '08	Lungarotti	**Umbria**
Trebbiano d'Abruzzo C'Incanta '10	Cantina Tollo	**Abruzzo**
Trebbiano d'Abruzzo V. di Capestrano '11	Valle Reale	**Abruzzo**
Trentino Müller Thurgau Vigna delle Forche '12	La Vis/Valle di Cembra	**Trentino**
Valpolicella Cl. Sup. Campo Casal Vegri '11	Ca' La Bionda	**Veneto**
Valpolicella Cl. Sup. Camporenzo '10	Monte dall'Ora	**Veneto**
Veneroso '10	Tenuta di Ghizzano	**Tuscany**
Verdicchio di Matelica Collestefano '12	Collestefano	**Marche**
Vernaccia di S. Gimignano Campo della Pieve '11	Il Colombaio di Santa Chiara	**Tuscany**
Vernaccia di S. Gimignano Ris. '10	Fontaleoni	**Tuscany**

TABLE OF VINTAGES
FROM 1990 TO 2012

	BARBARESCO BAROLO	AMARONE	CHIANTI CLASSICO	BRUNELLO DI MONTALCINO	BOLGHERI	TAURASI
1990	▮▮▮▮	▮▮▮▮▮	▮▮▮▮	▮▮▮▮▮	▮▮▮▮▮	▮▮▮▮▮
1993	▮	▮	▮▮▮▮▮	▮▮▮	▮▮▮	▮▮▮
1995	▮	▮▮▮▮	▮▮▮▮	▮▮▮	▮▮	▮▮
1996	▮▮▮▮▮	▮▮▮	▮▮▮	▮▮▮▮	▮▮	▮▮
1997	▮▮▮▮	▮▮▮▮	▮▮▮	▮▮▮▮	▮▮▮	▮▮▮▮
1998	▮▮▮	▮▮▮	▮▮▮	▮▮▮	▮▮▮▮	▮▮
1999	▮▮▮▮▮	▮▮▮▮	▮▮▮▮	▮▮▮▮▮	▮▮▮▮▮	▮▮▮▮
2000	▮▮▮	▮▮▮	▮▮▮	▮▮	▮▮▮	▮▮
2001	▮▮▮▮	▮▮▮	▮▮▮	▮▮▮▮	▮▮▮▮	▮▮▮
2003	▮▮	▮	▮	▮▮	▮	▮▮
2004	▮▮▮▮▮	▮▮▮	▮▮▮▮	▮▮▮	▮▮▮	▮▮▮▮
2005	▮▮▮	▮▮▮	▮▮▮	▮▮	▮▮▮	▮▮▮
2006	▮▮▮▮	▮▮▮	▮▮▮	▮▮▮▮	▮▮▮▮	▮▮▮
2007	▮▮▮	▮▮▮	▮▮▮▮	▮▮▮▮	▮▮▮▮	▮▮▮
2008	▮▮▮▮	▮▮▮	▮▮▮▮	▮▮▮▮	▮▮▮▮	▮▮▮▮
2009	▮▮	▮▮	▮▮▮		▮▮▮▮	▮▮
2010	▮▮▮▮		▮▮▮▮		▮▮	
2011			▮▮▮			

	ALTO ADIGE BIANCO	SOAVE	FRIULI BIANCO	VERDICCHIO DEI CASTELLI DI JESI	FIANO DI AVELLINO	GRECO DI TUFO
2002	▯▯▯▯▯	▯▯▯▯▯	▯▯	▯▯	▯▯▯	▯▯
2003	▯▯	▯▯	▯	▯	▯▯▯▯	▯▯
2004	▯▯▯▯	▯▯▯▯	▯▯▯▯	▯▯▯▯▯	▯▯▯▯	▯▯▯
2005	▯▯▯	▯▯▯	▯▯	▯▯	▯▯▯	▯▯
2006	▯▯▯	▯▯▯	▯▯▯▯	▯▯▯▯	▯▯▯▯	▯▯▯▯
2007	▯▯▯	▯▯▯▯	▯▯▯▯	▯▯	▯▯▯	▯▯
2008	▯▯▯	▯▯▯	▯▯▯	▯▯▯▯	▯▯▯▯	▯▯▯
2009	▯▯▯▯▯	▯▯▯▯▯	▯▯▯	▯▯▯	▯▯▯▯	▯▯▯▯
2010	▯▯▯▯	▯▯▯▯	▯▯	▯▯▯▯	▯▯▯▯▯	▯▯▯▯
2011	▯▯▯	▯▯	▯▯	▯▯	▯▯▯	▯▯
2012	▯▯▯▯	▯▯▯	▯▯▯	▯▯▯▯	▯▯▯	▯▯▯▯

STARS

Stars are awarded to wineries that have won a Tre Bicchieri at least ten times. There are currently 177 "stellar cellars" across the Guide's 27 editions. These are the elite of Italian oenology, a ranking led for years by Angelo Gaja, who now has 51 awards under his belt, with an astounding average of achievements, almost two a year. Not so hot on his heels are Ca' del Bosco (38) and La Spinetta (37), Elio Altare (32), then the rest. We welcome nine new entries to the club of stars: Abbona, Azelia, Piero Busso and Villa Sparina from Piedmont, Podere Grattamacco and San Felice in Tuscany, Lungarotti in Umbria, Di Majo Norante in Molise, and lastly Pietracupa, Campania.

51

Gaja (Piedmont)

38

Ca' del Bosco (Lombardy)

37

La Spinetta (Piedmont)

32

Elio Altare (Piedmont)

★★

29

Allegrini (Veneto)
Castello di Fonterutoli (Tuscany)
Valentini (Abruzzo)

28

Fattoria di Felsina (Tuscany)

25

Giacomo Conterno (Piedmont)
Masciarelli (Abruzzo)
Tenuta San Guido (Tuscany)
Cantina Produttori San Michele Appiano
(Alto Adige)

24

Marchesi Antinori (Tuscany)
Bellavista (Lombardy)
Castello della Sala (Umbria)
Ferrari (Trentino)
Feudi di San Gregorio (Campania)
Jermann (Friuli Venezia Giulia)
Planeta (Sicily)

23

Castello di Ama (Tuscany)
Poliziano (Tuscany)
Tasca d'Almerita (Sicily)
Cantina Tramin (Alto Adige)
Vie di Romans (Friuli Venezia Giulia)

22

Domenico Clerico (Piedmont)
Livio Felluga (Friuli Venezia Giulia)
Gravner (Friuli Venezia Giulia)
Villa Russiz (Friuli Venezia Giulia)

21

Fontodi (Tuscany)
Bruno Giacosa (Piedmont)
Tenuta dell'Ornellaia (Tuscany)
Leonildo Pieropan (Veneto)

20

Argiolas (Sardinia)
Dorigo (Friuli Venezia Giulia)
Paolo Scavino (Piedmont)

★

19

Cantina Bolzano (Alto Adige)
Arnaldo Caprai (Umbria)
Cascina La Barbatella (Piedmont)
Isole e Olena (Tuscany)
Nino Negri (Lombardy)
Schiopetto (Friuli Venezia Giulia)

18

Barone Ricasoli (Tuscany)
Castello Banfi (Tuscany)
Michele Chi-arlo (Piedmont)
Matteo Correggia (Piedmont)
Falesco (Umbria)
Elio Grasso (Piedmont)
Mastroberardino (Campania)
Montevetrano (Campania)
Tenimenti Ruffino (Tuscany)
Tenute Sella & Mosca (Sardinia)
Venica & Venica (Friuli Venezia Giulia)
Elena Walch (Alto Adige)

17

Ca' Viola (Piedmont)
Cantina di Caldaro (Alto Adige)
Castello del Terriccio (Tuscany)
Cantina Produttori Colterenzio (Alto Adige)
Querciabella (Tuscany)
Tenuta San Leonardo (Trentino)
Cantina Terlano (Alto Adige)
Vietti (Piedmont)
Le Vigne di Zamò (Friuli Venezia Giulia)

16
Casanova di Neri (Tuscany)
Conterno Fantino (Piedmont)
Les Crêtes (Valle d'Aosta)
Romano Dal Forno (Veneto)
Gioacchino Garofoli (Marche)
Miani (Friuli Venezia Giulia)
Giuseppe Quintarelli (Veneto)
Luciano Sandrone (Piedmont)
Serafini & Vidotto (Veneto)
Franco Toros (Friuli Venezia Giulia)
Volpe Pasini (Friuli Venezia Giulia)
Fattoria Zerbina (Emilia Romagna)

15
Abbazia di Novacella (Alto Adige)
Roberto Anselmi (Veneto)
Ca' Rugate (Veneto)
Castellare di Castellina (Tuscany)
Aldo Conterno (Piedmont)
Cusumano (Sicily)
Lis Neris (Friuli Venezia Giulia)
Le Macchiole (Tuscany)
Montevertine (Tuscany)
Palari (Sicily)
Roberto Voerzio (Piedmont)

14
Brancaia (Tuscany)
Bricco Rocche - Bricco Asili (Piedmont)
Luigi Cataldi Madonna (Abruzzo)
Donnafugata (Sicily)
Massolino (Piedmont)
Cantina Convento Muri-Gries (Alto Adige)
Fiorenzo Nada (Piedmont)
Albino Rocca (Piedmont)
Bruno Rocca (Piedmont)
Ronco del Gelso (Friuli Venezia Giulia)
San Patrignano (Emilia Romagna)
Cantina di Santadi (Sardinia)
Sottimano (Piedmont)
Uberti (Lombardy)

13
Antoniolo (Piedmont)
Avignonesi (Tuscany)
Firriato (Sicily)
Foradori (Trentino)
Edi Keber (Friuli Venezia Giulia)
Kuenhof - Peter Pliger (Alto Adige)
Livon (Friuli Venezia Giulia)
Maculan (Veneto)
Masi (Veneto)
Monsupello (Lombardy)
Pecchenino (Piedmont)
Fattoria Petrolo (Tuscany)
Produttori del Barbaresco (Piedmont)
Ronco dei Tassi (Friuli Venezia Giulia)
Tua Rita (Tuscany)
Umani Ronchi (Marche)

12
Lorenzo Begali (Veneto)
Cav. G. B. Bertani (Veneto)
Bucci (Marche)
Castello dei Rampolla (Tuscany)
Cavalleri (Lombardy)
Cavit (Trentino)

Tenute Cisa Asinari dei Marchesi di Grésy
(Piedmont)
Tenuta Col d'Orcia (Tuscany)
Còlpetrone (Umbria)
Coppo (Piedmont)
Tenute Ambrogio e Giovanni Folonari (Tuscany)
Tenuta di Ghizzano (Tuscany)
Gini (Veneto)
Franco M. Martinetti (Piedmont)
La Monacesca (Marche)
Oasi degli Angeli (Marche)
Doro Princic (Friuli Venezia Giulia)
Dario Raccaro (Friuli Venezia Giulia)
Podere Rocche dei Manzoni (Piedmont)
Viticoltori Speri (Veneto)
Suavia (Veneto)
Velenosi (Marche)

11
Benanti (Sicily)
Biondi Santi - Tenuta Il Greppo (Tuscany)
Borgo San Daniele (Friuli Venezia Giulia)
Braida (Piedmont)
Le Due Terre (Friuli Venezia Giulia)
Poderi Luigi Einaudi (Piedmont)
Falkenstein - Franz Pratzner (Alto Adige)
Galardi (Campania)
Librandi (Calabria)
Malvirà (Piedmont)
Bartolo Mascarello (Piedmont)
La Massa (Tuscany)
Graziano Prà (Veneto)
Prunotto (Piedmont)
Fattoria Le Pupille (Tuscany)
Tenuta Sant'Antonio (Veneto)
Tormaresca (Puglia)
Tenuta Unterortl - Castel Juval (Alto Adige)
Vignalta (Veneto)
Viviani (Veneto)

10
Abbona (Piedmont)
Gianfranco Alessandria (Piedmont)
Azelia (Piedmont)
Piero Busso (Piedmont)
La Cerbaiola (Tuscany)
Di Majo Norante (Molise)
Marchesi de' Frescobaldi (Tuscany)
Podere Grattamacco (Tuscany)
Hilberg - Pasquero (Piedmont)
Tenuta J. Hofstätter (Alto Adige)
Dino Illuminati (Abruzzo)
Lungarotti (Umbria)
Monte Rossa (Lombardy)
Pietracupa (Campania)
Russiz Superiore (Friuli Venezia Giulia)
San Felice (Tuscany)
Villa Matilde (Campania)
Villa Sparina (Piedmont)
Conti Zecca (Puglia)
Zenato (Veneto)

HOW TO USE THE GUIDE

WINERY INFORMATION
ANNUAL PRODUCTION
HECTARES UNDER VINE
VITICULTURE METHOD

SYMBOLS
O WHITE WINE
⊙ ROSÉ
● RED WINE

RATINGS

GOOD WINES IN THEIR RESPECTIVE CATEGORIES
VERY GOOD TO EXCELLENT WINES IN THEIR RESPECTIVE CATEGORIES
VERY GOOD TO EXCELLENT WINES THAT WENT FORWARD TO THE FINAL TASTINGS
EXCELLENT WINES IN THEIR RESPECTIVE CATEGORIES

WINES RATED IN PREVIOUS EDITIONS OF THE GUIDE ARE INDICATED BY WHITE GLASSES (Y, YY, YYY), PROVIDED THEY ARE STILL DRINKING AT THE LEVEL FOR WHICH THE ORIGINAL AWARD WAS MADE.

STAR ★
INDICATES WINERIES THAT HAVE WON TEN TRE BICCHIERI AWARDS FOR EACH STAR

PRICE RANGES
1 up to 5 euro
3 from € 10.01 to € 15.00
5 from € 20.01 to € 30.00
7 from € 40.01 to € 50.00

2 from € 5.01 to € 10.00
4 from € 15.01 to € 20.00
6 from € 30.01 to € 40.00
8 more than € 50.01

PRICES INDICATED REFER TO AVERAGE PRICES IN WINE STORES.

ASTERISK *
INDICATES ESPECIALLY GOOD VALUE WINES

ABBREVIATIONS

A. A.	Alto Adige	P.R.	Peduncolo Rosso (red bunchstem)
C.	Colli	P.	Prosecco
Cl.	Classic	Rif. Agr.	Riforma Agraria (agrarian reform)
C.S.	Cantina Sociale (co-operative winery)	Ris.	Riserva
CEV	Colli Etruschi Viterbesi	Sel.	Selezione
COF	Colli Orientali del Friuli	Sup.	Superiore
Cons.	Consorzio (consortium)	TdF	Terre di Franciacorta
Coop.Agr.	Cooperativa Agricola (farming co-operative)	V.	Vigna (vineyard)
C. B.	Colli Bolognesi	Vign.	Vigneto (vineyard)
C. P.	Colli Piacentini	V. T.	Vendemmia Tardiva (late harvest)
Et.	Etichetta (label)	V. V.	Vecchia Vigna/Vecchie Vigne (old vine /old vines)
M.	Metodo (method)		
M.to	Monferrato		
OP	Oltrepò Pavese		

VALLE D'AOSTA

During the economic boom that followed
the Second World War much farmland was
abandoned, particularly in areas that were less
profitable or more difficult to tend. Viticulture in
Valle d'Aosta survived due to the stubbornness
and pride of its mountain folk, who would never have
allowed the plots under vine that had fed and quenched the thirst of their
ancestors to fall fallow. The first co-operative wineries were founded in the 1970s
and also played an important social function by buying up the grapes that the
owners did not want to or could no longer make into wine themselves. Today the
revival has been a success and the region is looking to the future, with vineyards
extending over an area of just under 400 hectares, from Morgex to Donnas, with
250 within the DOC zone. An important slice of production is controlled by the
co-operatives, which have always maintained high quality standards but need
to supply the market with a substantially unchanging range. The local wines are
very popular and practically enjoy a monopoly in the region, but they're still little
known in the rest of Italy and abroad, and it is certainly not by increasing the
amount of bargain-basement labels that the situation can be reversed. This is
clear to a young generation of producers still at the embryonic state, but slowly
and steadily growing. They have chosen to extend the plantings of the many native
grape varieties, particularly reds like vuillermin, mayolet and cornalin, in order
to establish an ever-closer bond with the terroir. This is an interesting approach,
particularly if the experiments are combined with a study that will connect each
area to the most appropriate cultivar. The only flaw seems to be the desire to focus
on red grapes: it is true that the region has always produced more red wine, but
outside its boundaries it is seen as a producer of whites for historical as well as
soil and climate reasons. While this year's array of prize-winners is without its
driving forces, as Les Crêtes and Anselmet are missing for the first time in years,
the performance of the wines provides important validation for the region. Year
after year Château Feuillet and Ottin prove their worth, while Crotta di Vegneron
and La Vrille offer proof of the area's ability to produce great dried-grape wines.
Marco Martin's Pinot Gris no longer comes as a surprise, while Di Barrò is back on
top with a magnificent Chardonnay.

Anselmet

FRAZ. VEREYTAZ, 30
11018 VILLENEUVE [AO]
TEL. 3484127121
www.maisonanselmet.vievini.it

CELLAR SALES
PRE-BOOKED VISITS
ANNUAL PRODUCTION 70,000 bottles
HECTARES UNDER VINE 8.00

Maison Anselmet embodies a family's passion over the generations for this territory, its fruits and deep-rooted traditions. It was Renato, in 1978, who decided to dedicate himself completely to producing wine that was not solely for family consumption, and in doing so established one of the region's best-known operations. Over time, there has been a careful selection of varieties, and the area under vine has been extended, with a consistent focus on quality. Some years back Renato handed over the reins of the winery to his son Giorgio, who has brought production levels to the current impressive level of 70,000 bottles. As always, we saw a range of stylish wines, starting with an intense, fruity Chardonnay Elevé en Fût de Chêne, with delicate apple and vanilla aromas over a fresh, harmonious palate. The impressive Petite Arvine 2012 followed a fruity nose with tangy freshness in the mouth. The superb, harmonious Pinot Gris offered a captivating nose of pears and mountain herbs.

○ Valle d'Aosta Chardonnay Élevé en Fût de Chêne '12	♟♟ 5
○ Valle d'Aosta Petite Arvine '12	♟♟ 3*
○ Valle d'Aosta Pinot Gris '12	♟♟ 3*
○ Valle d'Aosta Chambave Muscat '12	♟♟ 3
○ Valle d'Aosta Chardonnay '12	♟♟ 3
● Valle d'Aosta Fumin Élevé en Fût de Chêne '11	♟♟ 4
● Valle d'Aosta Pinot Noir Élevé en Fût de Chêne '11	♟♟ 4
● Valle d'Aosta Torrette Sup. '11	♟♟ 4
○ La Touche	♟ 3
○ Stéphanie	♟ 4
○ Valle d'Aosta Chardonnay Élevé en Fût de Chêne '11	♟♟♟ 5
○ Valle d'Aosta Chardonnay Élevé en Fût de Chêne '10	♟♟♟ 5

Château Feuillet

LOC. CHÂTEAU FEUILLET, 12
11010 SAINT PIERRE
TEL. 3287673880
www.chateaufeuillet.vievini.it

CELLAR SALES
ACCOMMODATION AND RESTAURANT SERVICE
ANNUAL PRODUCTION 30,000 bottles
HECTARES UNDER VINE 5.00

Leaving Aosta and heading north towards Monte Bianco, one of the first wine-growing areas you encounter is Torrette. In the heart of this microscopic region lies Chateau Feuillet, a small winery, but one of the region's most interesting. Maurizio Fiorano, the owner, lavishes great care on his plots, which are planted solely to native varieties, and capably runs this fairly recent operation, which dates back to the 1960s. The estate has grown from 5,000 square metres in 1997 to the current three hectares. Maurizio Fiorano's Petite Arvine thrilled once again. Showing bright straw yellow tinged with pale green, it boasts varietal finesse and a complex nose of mineral notes, apple and marked citrus aromas, with tangerine to the fore. On the palate, its evident youth does nothing to compromise its vibrancy and length. We really liked the Fumin, with its characteristic black berry fruit, and the Pinot Nero. The Torrettes and the Chardonnay are also recommended.

○ Valle d'Aosta Petite Arvine '12	♟♟♟ 3*
● Valle d'Aosta Fumin '12	♟♟ 4
● Valle d'Aosta Pinot Nero '12	♟♟ 3
○ Valle d'Aosta Chardonnay '12	♟ 3
● Valle d'Aosta Torrette '12	♟ 3
● Valle d'Aosta Torrette Sup. '11	♟ 3
○ Valle d'Aosta Petite Arvine '11	♟♟♟ 3*
○ Valle d'Aosta Petite Arvine '10	♟♟♟ 3*
○ Valle d'Aosta Chardonnay '10	♟♟ 2*
● Valle d'Aosta Fumin '08	♟♟ 3
● Valle d'Aosta Torrette Sup. '10	♟♟ 3*
● Valle d'Aosta Torrette Sup. '09	♟♟ 3

★Les Crêtes

Loc. Villetos, 50
11010 Aymavilles [AO]
Tel. 0165902274
www.lescretes.it

CELLAR SALES
PRE-BOOKED VISITS
ANNUAL PRODUCTION 200,000 bottles
HECTARES UNDER VINE 20.00

Costantino Charrère, heir to a 200-year tradition of wine-growers, has created a model winery, one of Italy's finest. But Costantino and his wife Imelda are not merely excellent entrepreneurs: Les Crêtes, which incidentally boasts one of Italy's most attractive, modern cellars, embodies a whole philosophy and vision of nature and wine making. Its owner is an influential figure. Eleonora and Elena, who grew up amidst the aromas of vines in blossom and must fermenting in the cellar, are now an essential part of the team alongside their parents. This year saw another excellent, well-balanced oak-aged Chardonnay, displaying a bright gold hue and elegant hints of fruit and spice. The outstanding Petite Arvine, straw-coloured with pale green tinges, offers citrus notes and mountain herbs on the nose, with finesse and length in the mouth. We were also taken by the intensely-hued, harmonious Fumin, with its spicy nose.

○ Valle d'Aosta Chardonnay Cuvée Bois '11	♟♟ 6
● Valle d'Aosta Fumin '10	♟♟ 4
○ Valle d'Aosta Petite Arvine '12	♟♟ 3*
○ Valle d'Aosta Chardonnay '12	♟♟ 3
● Valle d'Aosta Syrah Coteau La Tour '11	♟♟ 4
● Valle d'Aosta Pinot Noir '12	♟ 3
● Valle d'Aosta Torrette '12	♟ 2
○ Valle d'Aosta Chardonnay Cuvée Bois '10	♟♟♟ 6
○ Valle d'Aosta Chardonnay Cuvée Bois '09	♟♟♟ 6
○ Valle d'Aosta Chardonnay Cuvée Bois '08	♟♟♟ 6
○ Valle d'Aosta Chardonnay Cuvée Bois '07	♟♟♟ 6

La Crotta di Vegneron

P.zza Roncas, 2
11023 Chambave [AO]
Tel. 016646670
www.lacrotta.it

CELLAR SALES
PRE-BOOKED VISITS
RESTAURANT SERVICE
ANNUAL PRODUCTION 220,000 bottles
HECTARES UNDER VINE 39.00

Faithful to tradition, La Crotta di Vegneron has made the focus on native varieties its main aim. Its 120 growers bring the cooperative the fruits of their labours, farmed in a difficult territory, but one that is rich in tradition and can bring great satisfaction. The excellent results they have achieved are due to the dedication of the entire community of Chambave, a small village just outside Aosta. The traditional varieties, grown here with pride and expertise, and attentive vinification aimed at preserving local character, embody the spirit of the mountains surrounding the vineyards. Prieuré, a raisin wine from moscato, is this winery's champion. It opens with a beautiful, bright, intense golden hue and supremely elegant raisin aromas, while sweetness and great balance on the palate endow delightful, sumptuous elegance. The characteristic, well-typed Fumin, this region's iconic red, is a deep ruby, with aromas of fruit and spice, but still young. We also recommend the Nus Malvoisie, from an unusual clone of pinot grigio.

○ Valle d'Aosta Chambave Moscato Passito Prieuré '11	♟♟♟ 5
○ Valle d'Aosta Chambave Muscat '12	♟♟ 3
● Valle d'Aosta Fumin Esprit Follet '11	♟♟ 5
○ Valle d'Aosta Nus Malvoisie '12	♟♟ 3
○ Valle d'Aosta Chambave Moscato Passito Prieuré '08	♟♟♟ 5
● Valle d'Aosta Fumin Esprit Follet '09	♟♟♟ 3
● Valle d'Aosta Fumin Esprit Follet '07	♟♟♟ 3*
○ Valle d'Aosta Chambave Moscato Passito Prieuré '10	♟♟ 5
○ Valle d'Aosta Chambave Moscato Passito Prieuré '09	♟♟ 5
● Valle d'Aosta Chambave Sup. Quatre Vignobles '08	♟♟ 3*
● Valle d'Aosta Fumin Esprit Follet '10	♟♟ 3*
● Valle d'Aosta Fumin Esprit Follet '08	♟♟ 3

Di Barrò

LOC. CHÂTEAU FEUILLET, 8
11010 SAINT PIERRE [AO]
TEL. 0165903671
www.vievini.it

CELLAR SALES
PRE-BOOKED VISITS
ANNUAL PRODUCTION 20,000 bottles
HECTARES UNDER VINE 2.50

The winery name in local dialect means "from the barrels", and the small, unique wooden barrels in question were once used for transporting hand-pressed grapes from vineyard to cellar, or to hold for wine sold. At village festivals, for example, wine came directly from the barrel tap. The word is also an acronym of the first letters of Barmaz and Rossan, the winery's former owners, who ran the family vineyards back in the 1960s, and parents-in-law of the new owner. In 1985 the winery was one of the first to be awarded Torrette DOC status, and is in the heart of the traditional production zone. This year's outstanding Chardonnay justly took a Tre Bicchieri. This intense straw-yellow wine with pale green highlights combines apple and acacia blossom with a full, balanced palate, and a long finish. The winery is in the Torrette zone, as is evident in Di Barrò's version, whose ruby hue joins forces with elegant black berry fruit, while the full mouth comes with balance and great length. We also enjoyed the Syrah.

○ Valle d'Aosta Chardonnay '12	♟♟♟ 3*
● Valle d'Aosta Syrah V. de Conze '10	♟♟ 3
● Valle d'Aosta Torrette Sup. Clos de Château Feuillet '10	♟♟ 3
● Valle d'Aosta Torrette Sup. V. de Torrette '06	♟♟♟ 6
● Valle d'Aosta Fumin '10	♟♟ 4
● Valle d'Aosta Syrah V. de Conze '09	♟♟ 3
● Valle d'Aosta Torrette Sup. Clos de Château Feuillet '09	♟♟ 3
● Valle d'Aosta Torrette Sup. V. de Torrette '07	♟♟ 6

Feudo di San Maurizio

FRAZ. MAILLOD, 44
11010 SARRE [AO]
TEL. 3383186831
www.feudo.vievini.it

CELLAR SALES
PRE-BOOKED VISITS
ANNUAL PRODUCTION 40,000 bottles
HECTARES UNDER VINE 7.00

The recently established operation is the result of three 20-something friends investing in their dreams, and deciding in 1989 to produce quality wine at Sarre, a sun-kissed town just outside Aosta. With the passing of time, their transformation of untended plots into verdant vineyards has further fuelled their passion for wine-making and farming traditions. The whole range consciously focuses on native varieties. Feudo di San Maurizio also has accommodation for those wishing to stay for a holiday. Michel's wines are always a pleasure to taste, especially his sumptuous, stylish reds, which never fail to charm and excite with their depth and intensity. This year we particularly liked the well-typed, characterful Fumin, with its lingering finish, and the must-try Torrette Superiore. We were also won over by the basic version of the Torrette and the typical Petite Arvine.

● Valle d'Aosta Fumin '10	♟♟ 4
● Valle d'Aosta Torrette Sup. '11	♟♟ 4
○ Valle d'Aosta Petite Arvine '12	♟ 3
● Valle d'Aosta Torrette '12	♟ 3
● Saro Djablo '10	♟♟ 3
○ Valle d'Aosta Chardonnay '10	♟♟ 3
● Valle d'Aosta Cornalin '10	♟♟ 4
○ Valle d'Aosta Gewürztraminer '10	♟♟ 3
○ Valle d'Aosta Petite Arvine '11	♟♟ 3*
● Valle d'Aosta Torrette Sup. '09	♟♟ 4

F.lli Grosjean

VILLAGGIO OLLIGNAN, 1
11020 QUART [AO]
TEL. 0165775791
www.grosjean.vievini.it

CELLAR SALES
PRE-BOOKED VISITS
ANNUAL PRODUCTION 90,000 bottles
HECTARES UNDER VINE 10.00
VITICULTURE METHOD Certified Organic

The waters of the Beauregard dam in Valgrisenche lie over the old village of Fornet, from where in 1781, the ancestors of the Grosjean family would go down to Ollignan to stock up on wine and chestnuts for the long mountain winters. In 1969, Dauphin senior started bottling his wine, and presented it at the first edition of the Exposition de Vins de la Val d'Aoste. The winery lies on the border between the municipalities of Quart and St. Christophe, where the winery's best plots are also found. The varieties initially grown, alongside the traditional petit rouge, were gamay and pinot nero. Recent additions are the native varieties petite arvine, fumin, cornalin, prëmetta and vuillermin. This year's production, although well-managed, is not up to the winery's usual standard. Among the new entries, we should mention the Muscat Petit Grain, with its captivating, intense nose. Although not on a par with previous editions, the potent, warm Fumin is interesting, but needs more time to mature.

● Valle d'Aosta Fumin V. Rovettaz '10	♟♟♟ 5
○ Valle d'Aosta Muscat Petit Grain '12	♟ 2
● Valle d'Aosta Fumin '06	♟♟♟ 4
● Valle d'Aosta Fumin V. Rovettaz '07	♟♟♟ 5
○ Valle d'Aosta Petite Arvine V. Rovettaz '09	♟♟♟ 4
● Valle d'Aosta Fumin '10	♟♟ 5
● Valle d'Aosta Fumin V. Rovettaz '09	♟♟ 5
● Valle d'Aosta Mayolet '10	♟♟ 3
○ Valle d'Aosta Petite Arvine V. Rovettaz '10	♟♟ 4
● Valle d'Aosta Pinot Noir '10	♟♟ 3
● Valle d'Aosta Torrette Sup. V. Rovettaz '09	♟♟ 3

Lo Triolet

LOC. JUNOD, 7
11010 INTROD [AO]
TEL. 016595437
www.lotriolet.vievini.it

CELLAR SALES
PRE-BOOKED VISITS
ANNUAL PRODUCTION 42,000 bottles
HECTARES UNDER VINE 3.00

Marco Martin runs the Lo Triolet winery with his family at Introd, whose 17th-century premises are also home to a charming agriturismo. His adventure in the world of wine began as a viticultural technician with the regional council. Marco brought this experience to the family vineyards, where he focused on pinot grigio, an early-ripening variety that has brought him great satisfaction. New vineyards have been planted and production has risen from the initial 1,000 bottles to the current levels of 42,000. All the vineyards lie at elevations of between 600 and 900 metres, and consequently, above all thanks to light-handed vinification, give wines full of the essence of the mountain terroir. A Tre Bicchieri went to the base Pinot Grigio version, a bright straw-yellow wine, offering intense fruit aromas of pear and damson, plus great structure, extraordinary finesse and a long finish. Although also very pleasing, the barrique-aged version is less intriguing. We also liked the Coteau Barrage.

○ Valle d'Aosta Pinot Gris '12	♟♟♟ 3*
● Valle d'Aosta Coteau Barrage '11	♟♟ 4
○ Valle d'Aosta Pinot Gris Élevé en Barriques '11	♟♟ 5
● Valle d'Aosta Fumin '11	♟♟ 3
○ Valle d'Aosta Pinot Gris '09	♟♟♟ 3
○ Valle d'Aosta Pinot Gris '08	♟♟♟ 3*
○ Valle d'Aosta Pinot Gris '05	♟♟♟ 3*
○ Valle d'Aosta Pinot Gris Élevé en Barriques '10	♟♟♟ 5
● Valle d'Aosta Coteau Barrage '09	♟♟ 4
● Valle d'Aosta Coteau Barrage '09	♟♟ 4
○ Valle d'Aosta Pinot Gris '10	♟♟ 3

Elio Ottin

FRAZ. POROSSAN NEYVES, 209
11100 AOSTA
TEL. 016533487
www.ottinvini.it

CELLAR SALES
PRE-BOOKED VISITS
ANNUAL PRODUCTION 30,000 bottles
HECTARES UNDER VINE 4.00

Elio Ottin's great passion for wine is the driving force behind this winery, with strong links to the land, local traditions and mountain culture. Every bottle is a testimony to the hard work necessary to achieve the final result. His is a passion with its roots in the past, inherited from a family who have been growers in the mountains for generations. Elio has managed to make the most of these centuries of knowledge and expertise, and established this operation in the early 1990s, after studying at the Institut Agricole Régional and the Istituto Agrario di Verzuolo. Petite Arvine is one of Valle d'Aosta's most representative whites, and Elio one of its best interpreters. A Tre Bicchieri went to the bright, straw-yellow 2012, with mountain herbs on the nose leading to elegant apple and citrus in the mouth, for a harmonious, well-balanced whole. The Torrette Superiore and the Fumin both impressed. We are still waiting to see the effect of oak ageing on the Petite Arvine Nuances.

○ Valle d'Aosta Petite Arvine '12	♀♀♀	3*
● Valle d'Aosta Fumin '11	♀♀	3*
● Valle d'Aosta Torrette Sup. '11	♀♀	4
● Valle d'Aosta Pinot Noir '11	♀♀	3
○ Valle d'Aosta Petite Arvine Nuances '11	♀	4
○ Valle d'Aosta Petite Arvine '11	♀♀♀	3*
○ Valle d'Aosta Petite Arvine '10	♀♀♀	3*
● Valle d'Aosta Fumin '10	♀♀	3*
● Valle d'Aosta Pinot Noir '10	♀♀	3*
● Valle d'Aosta Torrette Sup. '10	♀♀	3
● Valle d'Aosta Torrette Sup. '09	♀♀	3*

Ermes Pavese

S.DA PINETA, 26
11017 MORGEX [AO]
TEL. 0165800053
www.vievini.it

CELLAR SALES
PRE-BOOKED VISITS
ANNUAL PRODUCTION 30,000 bottles
HECTARES UNDER VINE 4.00

At the foot of Monte Bianco, where the snow is a constant companion, tenacious vignerons manage to grow a unique variety: the still ungrafted native priè blanc, of which Ermes Pavese is a leading producer. Managing to create exciting wines in a cold, harsh environment such as Morgex is no mean feat, and deserves wider recognition and appreciation. The Pavese family comes from a long wine-making tradition, and is led by Ermes, a man of few words but great generosity. His passions are his vineyard and family, which explains why he has named his wines after his children. As he says, wine should be nurtured, loved and helped, just like a child. The new arrival this year is the sparkler: a well-structured Pas Dosé for demanding palates. The brilliant, intense Sette Scalinate shows a lively character, with focused aromas of apples and spring flowers, followed by a fresh, tangy palate with a long finish. The basic Morgex was characteristic and true to type.

○ Valle d'Aosta Vin Blanc de Morgex et La Salle '12	♀♀	2*
○ Valle d'Aosta Vin Blanc de Morgex et La Salle Le Sette Scalinate Carlo Pavese Ris. '11	♀♀	6
○ Valle d'Aosta Vin Blanc de Morgex et La Salle Pavese Pas Dosé '10	♀	3
○ Valle d'Aosta Vin Blanc de Morgex et La Salle Le Sette Scalinate Carlo Pavese Ris. '10	♀♀	3*
○ Valle d'Aosta Vin Blanc de Morgex et La Salle Nathan '10	♀♀	2*

Cave du Vin Blanc de Morgex et de La Salle

FRAZ. LA RUINE
CHEMIN DES ÎLES, 19
11017 MORGEX [AO]
TEL. 0165800331
www.caveduvinblanc.com

CELLAR SALES
PRE-BOOKED VISITS
ANNUAL PRODUCTION 140,000 bottles
HECTARES UNDER VINE 19.00

The first bottles of Blanc de Morgex et de La Salle were sold by individual vignerons, resulting in limited production, varying availability on the market, and inconsistent quality, factors which did nothing to promote the image of this wine. Subsequently, a sense of tradition and the centuries-old Alpine village custom of working in groups led to the creation of the Association des Viticulteurs. In 1983, the regional policy for supporting and developing viticulture in the Valle d'Aosta bore its first fruits, with the establishment of the Cave du Vin Blanc de Morgex et de La Salle, which subsequently took possession of the premises of the new high-tech headquarters at Morgex. The wide range of spumante and traditional wines all display mountain aromas of herbs and flowers, and are fresh, light, and well-balanced in the mouth. We recommend the Brut sparkler, the basic Morgex, and the Rayon, a version produced with selected grapes.

○ Valle d'Aosta Blanc de Morgex et de La Salle Brut M. Cl. '10	🍷🍷 4
○ Valle d'Aosta Blanc de Morgex et de La Salle Rayon '12	🍷🍷 2*
○ Valle d'Aosta Blanc de Morgex et de La Salle '12	🍷 2
○ Valle d'Aosta Blanc de Morgex et de La Salle Vini Estremi '12	🍷 2
○ Valle d'Aosta Blanc de Morgex et de La Salle '11	🍷🍷 2*
○ Valle d'Aosta Blanc de Morgex et de La Salle Blanc des Glaciers '10	🍷🍷 4

La Vrille

LOC. GRANGEON, 1
11020 VERRAYES [AO]
TEL. 0166543018
www.lavrille-agritourisme.com

CELLAR SALES
PRE-BOOKED VISITS
ACCOMMODATION AND RESTAURANT SERVICE
ANNUAL PRODUCTION 10,000 bottles
HECTARES UNDER VINE 1.50

Luciana Neyroz and Hervé Deguilllame live mountain life to the full. La Vrille is a small estate of four hectares, with one and a half under vine, but has everything, with chickens, sheep, a vegetable garden and a fine agriturismo. Situated at Verrayes, on a well-aspected site 650 metres above sea level, it offers views over Mount Avic and Mount Emilius. Last year the Chambave Muscat Flétri della Vrille was our Sweet of the Year. This year is no exception, with impeccable finesse and impressive structure in this deep gold wine, offering dried fruit aromas and elegant spice, with extraordinary balance and harmony in the mouth. The dry version is also impressive, displaying intriguing aromas of spring flowers and fruit, with peach and apricot to the fore. The appetizing, deep gold Fumin couples a nose of dried fruit and elegant spice with extraordinary balance and harmony in the mouth.

○ Valle d'Aosta Chambave Muscat Flétri '11	🍷🍷🍷 6
○ Valle d'Aosta Chambave Muscat '11	🍷🍷 4
● Valle d'Aosta Fumin '10	🍷🍷 5
○ Valle d'Aosta Chambave Muscat Flétri '10	🍷🍷🍷 5
○ Valle d'Aosta Chambave Muscat Flétri '07	🍷🍷🍷 4*
○ Valle d'Aosta Chambave Muscat '10	🍷🍷 4
○ Valle d'Aosta Chambave Muscat Flétri '09	🍷🍷 5
○ Valle d'Aosta Chambave Muscat Flétri '08	🍷🍷 5
● Valle d'Aosta Cornalin '09	🍷🍷 3
● Valle d'Aosta Cornalin '08	🍷🍷 3
● Valle d'Aosta Fumin '08	🍷🍷 4
● Valle d'Aosta Gamay '10	🍷🍷 3

Coopérative de l'Enfer

VIA CORRADO GEX, 65
11011 ARVIER [AO]
TEL. 016599238
www.coenfer.it

CELLAR SALES
PRE-BOOKED VISITS
ANNUAL PRODUCTION 50,000 bottles

● Valle d'Aosta Enfer d'Arvier '12	♀♀ 4
● Valle d'Aosta Enfer d'Arvier Sup. Clos de L'Enfer '11	♀♀ 5
● Valle d'Aosta Enfer d'Arvier Bio '12	♀ 3

D&D

VIA REGIONE BIOULA, 13
11100 AOSTA
TEL. 0165552687
www.maisonded.vievini.it

PRE-BOOKED VISITS
ANNUAL PRODUCTION 19,000 bottles
HECTARES UNDER VINE 2.60

● Valle d'Aosta Fumin '11	♀♀ 3
● Valle d'Aosta Pinot noir '11	♀♀ 3
● Valle d'Aosta Syrah '11	♀♀ 3

Caves Cooperatives de Donnas

VIA ROMA, 97
11020 DONNAS [AO]
TEL. 0125807096
www.donnasvini.it

CELLAR SALES
PRE-BOOKED VISITS
ANNUAL PRODUCTION 150,000 bottles
HECTARES UNDER VINE 26.00

● Valle d'Aosta Donnas Napoléon '10	♀♀ 3
● Valle d'Aosta Donnas Vieilles Vignes '09	♀♀ 4
● Valle d'Aosta Donnas '08	♀ 2

Les Granges

FRAZ. LES GRANGES, 8
11020 NUS [AO]
TEL. 0165767229
www.lesgrangesvini.it

CELLAR SALES
PRE-BOOKED VISITS
ANNUAL PRODUCTION 15,000 bottles
HECTARES UNDER VINE 2.90
VITICULTURE METHOD Certified Organic

○ Valle d'Aosta Nus Malvoisie '12	♀♀ 3*
● Valle d'Aosta Fumin '11	♀ 4
● Valle d'Aosta Pinot Noir '12	♀ 3

Institut Agricole Régional

LOC. RÉGION LA ROCHÈRE, 1A
11100 AOSTA
TEL. 0165215811
www.iaraosta.it

CELLAR SALES
PRE-BOOKED VISITS
ANNUAL PRODUCTION 45,000 bottles
HECTARES UNDER VINE 7.00

○ Valle d'Aosta Petite Arvine '12	♀♀ 3*
○ Valle d'Aosta Chardonnay '12	♀♀ 3
○ Valle d'Aosta Nus Malvoisie '12	♀♀ 3
● Valle d'Aosta Syrah '11	♀♀ 4

La Source

LOC. BUSSAN DESSOUS, 1
11010 SAINT PIERRE [AO]
TEL. 0165904038
www.lasource.it

CELLAR SALES
PRE-BOOKED VISITS
ANNUAL PRODUCTION 40,000 bottles
HECTARES UNDER VINE 6.00

○ Valle d'Aosta Petite Arvine '11	♀♀ 3
● Valle d'Aosta Torrette '12	♀ 3
● Valle d'Aosta Torrette Sup. '11	♀ 3

PIEDMONT

While its fame as a winemaking region derives from its great reds, these days it would be restrictive to consider these alone, for Piedmont has shown itself to be at the top of every sector. Just over a century and a half ago the region emerged as the cradle of Italian sparkling wines and today its great return is marked by the Sparkler of the Year award, won by one of the great Italian Metodo Classicos: Enrico Serafino's Alta Langa Brut Zero. Nor should we forget that Moscato d'Asti and Asti Spumante are renowned worldwide, and while the 2012 vintage did not offer ideal conditions for its return to our top accolade, Moscato remains a landmark of local wine-growing. Although the language of Piedmont is still nebbiolo, with 59 of its 77 Tre Bicchieris won by nebbiolo-based monovarietals and blends, we are certain that other grape varieties will carve out more space for themselves in the future. For now, the nebbiolo wines are followed by others made from barbera, with six Tre Bicchieri awards; dolcetto and timorasso with three each; erbaluce with two; and cortese and riesling, along with two blends, with one award each. These include four new names: Cantina del Glicine, Diego Conterno, Giacomo Fenocchio, and Rovellotti. A look at the award-winning vintages shows one 2004 wine and two from 2006, which are excellent years for cellar-worthy Nebbiolo; the rest run from 2007 to 2012. Hot, dry weather was the hallmark of 2007, which led to an early harvest. As always, this benefited the early-ripening and the hardier, more rustic grape varieties. Consequently it was a good Barbera vintage, while the Nebbiolos are soft and delicate. The following year, on the other hand, was colder and rainier, resulting in more difficult ripening conditions. The nebbiolo grapes were harvested between mid-October and early November, and far outclassed both the barbera and the dolcetto. The profile of the wines is more subtle, with low alcohol and high acidity. There were many similarities between 2009 and 2011. Both were fairly hot years with early harvests, making them excellent vintages for barbera and early-ripening grape varieties. The intervening year, 2010, was a very classic vintage, yielding nebbiolo with firm structure and focused tannins. Finally, the 2012 vintage was another late harvest and the early-ripening grape varieties suffered from a rainy late summer, while nebbiolo was harvested later, under the autumn sun.

★Abbona

LOC. SAN LUIGI
B.TA SAN LUIGI, 40
12063 DOGLIANI [CN]
TEL. 0173721317
www.abbona.com

CELLAR SALES
PRE-BOOKED VISITS
ANNUAL PRODUCTION 250,000 bottles
HECTARES UNDER VINE 45.00

This estate's superb new winery building blends well with the splendid landscape in this corner of Langhe long renowned for the excellence of its dolcetto grapes, of which Marziano Abbona has been an absolute master for many years. It currently offers a comprehensive range of wines, including a very good Metodo Classico, an array of whites, and Barolo. All the wines have a well-defined personality and faithfully reflect the dynamic versatility of the owner, who, over many years in the world of wine, has always stood out for his strong-mindedness and determination. Another Tre Bicchieri triumph for the Papà Celso 2011, a very leisurely Dolcetto with bags of fruity flesh. The Barolo Pressenda 2009 shows complex and layered with vigorous tannic texture and a fresh acid vein that protracts the finish. The lively, balsamic Barolo Terlo Ravera 2009 displays lovely balance between assertive tannins and supporting acidity.

● Dogliani Papà Celso '11	♛♛♛ 3*
● Barolo Pressenda '09	♛♛ 7
● Barolo Terlo Ravera '09	♛♛ 6
● Barbera d'Alba Rinaldi '11	♛♛ 4
● Dogliani San Luigi '12	♛♛ 3
○ Langhe Bianco Cinerino '12	♛♛ 4
○ Marziano Abbona Brut M. Cl.	♛♛ 2
● Nebbiolo d'Alba Bricco Barone '11	♛♛ 4
● Barolo Terlo Ravera '00	♛♛♛ 6
● Barolo Terlo Ravera '08	♛♛♛ 6
● Barolo Terlo Ravera '06	♛♛♛ 6
● Dogliani Papà Celso '09	♛♛♛ 3
● Dogliani Papà Celso '07	♛♛♛ 3
● Dogliani Papà Celso '06	♛♛♛ 3
● Dogliani Papà Celso '05	♛♛♛ 3*

Anna Maria Abbona

FRAZ. MONCUCCO, 21
12060 FARIGLIANO [CN]
TEL. 0173797228
www.annamariaabbona.it

CELLAR SALES
PRE-BOOKED VISITS
ANNUAL PRODUCTION 75,000 bottles
HECTARES UNDER VINE 12.00

Franco Schellino and Anna Maria Abbona are specialists in Dogliani, the iconic wine of this southern section of the Langhe, where the influence of the Ligurian Sea is palpable. We are at an elevation of around 600 metres, where dolcetto achieves depth and complexity, especially after a couple of years' bottle ageing, while at the same time maintaining its hallmark drinkability and intensely fruity character. In addition to four versions of Dogliani, the winery offers a fairly wide range, from Barolo and Barbera d'Alba to Langhe Nebbiolo, not to mention two whites from riesling and nascetta. The Barolo 2009 stands out for its focused nose and precise palate. The Dolcetto Sorì dij But 2012 is fresh and vibrant with notes of plum, blackberry and leather on the nose; the palate is succulent and eminently drinkable. The Dolcetto Maioli 2011 shows deep and complex with good balance between acidity and tannins.

● Barolo '09	♛♛ 6
● Dogliani Sup. San Bernardo '10	♛♛ 4
● Dogliani Sorì dij But '12	♛♛ 2*
● Dogliani Sup. Maioli '11	♛♛ 3
● Langhe Nebbiolo '10	♛♛ 3
● Langhe Rosso Cadò '09	♛♛ 4
● Langhe Dolcetto '12	♛ 2
○ Langhe Nascetta Netta '12	♛ 3
● Dogliani San Bernardo '06	♛♛ 3
● Dogliani San Bernardo '05	♛♛ 3
● Dogliani Sup. Maioli '10	♛♛ 3*
● Dolcetto di Dogliani Sorì dij But '11	♛♛ 2*
● Dolcetto di Dogliani Sup. '04	♛♛ 3
● Langhe Rosso Cadò '06	♛♛ 3

Orlando Abrigo

VIA CAPPELLETTO, 5
12050 TREISO [CN]
TEL. 0173630232
www.orlandoabrigo.it

CELLAR SALES
PRE-BOOKED VISITS
ACCOMMODATION AND RESTAURANT SERVICE
ANNUAL PRODUCTION 80,000 bottles
HECTARES UNDER VINE 21.00

The Abrigo estate in Treiso is owned by a family that have been growers for generations. Giovanni took over from his father Orlando, and his wines are made exclusively from his own carefully cultivated and selected grapes. In addition to the traditional wines, which include three fine Barbaresco selections, the range includes the classic Nebbiolo d'Alba, Barbera d'Alba and Dolcetto d'Alba. Over the years, Giovanni has also experimented with international grapes such as chardonnay, sauvignon and merlot, with excellent results. The wines are aged in a combination of large Slavonian oak casks and 225-litre French barriques. The Barbera d'Alba Mervisano 2010 is very balanced and convincing with ripe red berry fruit aromas exemplifying the deep, vibrant palate that is supported by a clear acid vein. The Barbaresco Rocche Meruzzano 2010 promises well but has yet to express its potential; its youth sees it in an interim phase.

● Barbera d'Alba Mervisano '10	♛♛♛ 3*
● Barbaresco Rocche Meruzzano '10	♛♛ 5
● Barbera d'Alba V. Roreto '11	♛♛ 2*
○ Langhe Bianco D'Amblè '12	♛♛ 2*
● Langhe Nebbiolo Settevie '11	♛♛ 3
● Nebbiolo d'Alba Valmaggiore '10	♛♛ 5
● Dolcetto d'Alba V. dell'Erto '12	♛ 2
○ Langhe Tres Plus '11	♛ 3
● Barbaresco Montersino '09	♛♛ 6
● Barbaresco Montersino '08	♛♛ 6
● Barbaresco Montersino '07	♛♛ 6
● Barbaresco Montersino '05	♛♛ 5
● Barbaresco Rocche Meruzzano '08	♛♛ 5
● Barbaresco Rocche Meruzzano V. Rongallo '07	♛♛ 6
● Barbaresco Rocche Meruzzano V. Rongallo '06	♛♛ 6

Giulio Accornero e Figli

CASCINA CA' CIMA, 1
15049 VIGNALE MONFERRATO [AL]
TEL. 0142933317
www.accornerovini.it

CELLAR SALES
PRE-BOOKED VISITS
ACCOMMODATION
ANNUAL PRODUCTION 100,000 bottles
HECTARES UNDER VINE 22.00

On the road from Vignale Monferrato to Casorzo, a signpost informs you that you are approaching one of Piedmont's most famous wineries. At the bottom of a steep hill you will find the family house surrounded by vineyards, where Ermanno and his family, with the oenologist Mario Ronco, embarked many years ago on a journey that has brought them widespread critical acclaim. The wines display excellent quality across the board. Ermanno thrilled us with an explosive range. The powerful, harmonious Cima is still evolving with gorgeous balsamic notes and a potent palate. The Bricco Battista and Giulin are complex, layered and very intriguing. We loved the Grignolino Bricco del Bosco, although once again it didn't net an award. The Bricco del Bosco Vigne Vecchie is refined and elegant.

● Barbera del M.to Sup. Cima '07	♛♛♛ 8
● Barbera del M.to Sup. Bricco Battista '10	♛♛ 5
● Grignolino del M.to Casalese Bricco del Bosco '12	♛♛ 2*
● Barbera del M.to Giulìn '11	♛♛ 3
● Casorzo Brigantino '12	♛♛ 2*
● Grignolino del M.to Casalese Bricco del Bosco V. V. '07	♛♛ 6
○ Fonsina '12	♛ 2
● M.to Freisa La Bernardina '12	♛ 2
● Barbera d'Asti Bricco Battista '97	♛♛♛ 5
● Barbera del M.to Sup. Bricco Battista '09	♛♛♛ 5
● Barbera del M.to Sup. Bricco Battista '07	♛♛♛ 5
● Barbera del M.to Sup. Bricco Battista '04	♛♛♛ 5
● Barbera del M.to Sup. Bricco Battista '99	♛♛♛ 5
● Barbera del M.to Sup. Bricco Battista '98	♛♛♛ 5
● M.to Rosso Centenario '06	♛♛♛ 5

Marco e Vittorio Adriano

FRAZ. SAN ROCCO SENO D'ELVIO, 13A
12051 ALBA [CN]
TEL. 0173362294
www.adrianovini.it

CELLAR SALES
PRE-BOOKED VISITS
ANNUAL PRODUCTION 120,000 bottles
HECTARES UNDER VINE 22.00

Even in a region like Langhe, where the pecking order and traditions are firmly established, there's always space for innovation and surprise. Witness the speed with which Marco and Vittorio Adriano have carved out a position for themselves in recent years. This brother-grower team operates in San Rocco Seno d'Elvio, a very densely planted village in the municipality of Alba. Their 22 hectares under vine are divided between barbera, dolcetto, freisa, sauvignon, and moscato, but not surprisingly it is nebbiolo that reigns supreme and expresses the personality of the Basarin and Sanadaive crus. Their Barbarescos are straightforward and direct, and offer very good value for money. Elegant notes of sweet tobacco, leather and violet and well-rounded tannins characterize the Barbaresco Basarin 2010, while the Barbaresco Sanadaive 2010 still has rather an edgy palate that bottle-ageing will help to smooth. The Sauvignon Basaricò 2012 is highly original with hints of sage and grapefruit giving it a distinctive, very attractive character.

● Barbaresco Basarin '10	♟♟ 4
● Barbaresco Sanadaive '10	♟♟ 4
● Barbera d'Alba Sup. '11	♟♟ 2*
● Langhe Nebbiolo '11	♟♟ 3
○ Langhe Sauvignon Basaricò '12	♟♟ 2*
○ Ardì '12	♟ 2
● Barbera d'Alba '12	♟ 2
● Dolcetto d'Alba '12	♟ 2
● Langhe Freisa '12	♟ 2
○ Moscato d'Asti '12	♟ 2
● Barbaresco Basarin '08	♟♟ 4
● Barbaresco Basarin Ris. '06	♟♟ 5
● Barbaresco Basarin Ris. '05	♟♟ 5

Claudio Alario

VIA SANTA CROCE, 23
12055 DIANO D'ALBA [CN]
TEL. 0173231808
www.alarioclaudio.it

CELLAR SALES
PRE-BOOKED VISITS
ANNUAL PRODUCTION 46,000 bottles
HECTARES UNDER VINE 10.00

This important Piedmont estate, headed by oenologist Claudio Alario, has made quite a name for itself over the years, particularly with its Dolcetto di Diano. In 1995 it also commenced production of two exclusive Barolo selections from its excellent vineyards in Serralunga d'Alba (Barolo Sorano) and Verduno (Barolo Riva). The Costa Fiore and Montagrillo selections of Dolcetto di Diano, aged exclusively in steel, have now been joined by the Pradurent, aged in oak. All of the wines have a very well-defined style and personality, which faithfully reflects the different terroirs from which they hail. The Barolo Sorano 2009 offers notes of tobacco, liquorice, quina and red berry fruit; the fresh palate is buttressed by balanced acidity and close-knit, assertive tannins. The Diano d'Alba Costa Fiore 2012 is still developing but shows juicy and very powerful. The Montagrillo 2012 is not as firm.

● Barolo Sorano '09	♟♟ 6
● Dolcetto di Diano d'Alba Costa Fiore '12	♟♟ 2*
● Barbera d'Alba Valletta '11	♟♟ 4
● Dolcetto di Diano d'Alba Montagrillo '12	♟♟ 2*
● Nebbiolo d'Alba Cascinotto '11	♟♟ 4
● Barolo Riva Rocca '09	♟ 6
● Dolcetto di Diano d'Alba Sup. Sorì Pradurent '11	♟ 3
● Barolo Sorano '05	♟♟♟ 7
● Barolo Riva Rocca '07	♟♟ 6
● Barolo Sorano '06	♟♟ 7
● Dolcetto di Diano d'Alba Costa Fiore '11	♟♟ 2*
● Dolcetto di Diano d'Alba Costa Fiore '10	♟♟ 2*
● Dolcetto di Diano d'Alba Costa Fiore '09	♟♟ 2*
● Nebbiolo d'Alba Cascinotto '10	♟♟ 4

F.lli Alessandria

VIA B. VALFRÉ, 59
12060 VERDUNO [CN]
TEL. 0172470113
www.fratellialessandria.it

CELLAR SALES
PRE-BOOKED VISITS
ANNUAL PRODUCTION 80,000 bottles
HECTARES UNDER VINE 14.00

This estate run by brothers Alessandro and
Gian Battista Alessandria and his son, the
skilled young Vittore, is at the top of its
game, one of the most accomplished and
reliable in Langhe. With the exception of a
little chardonnay, the approximately 14
hectares are planted to the zone's
traditional varieties: favorita, dolcetto,
barbera, and above all pelaverga and
nebbiolo. Monvigliero and San Lorenzo in
the municipality of Verduno, and Gramolere
in Monforte d'Alba are the Barolo crus.
They are bottled separately and their
expressive characteristics are enhanced by
the classic but certainly not retro style, with
ageing in 900-litre casks and 20- to
30-hectolitre barriques. The whole broad
range performs very well indeed, but it is
the Barolo Monvigliero that sweeps the
boards to take a Tre Bicchieri thanks to its
ideal terroir and well-balanced, elegant
interpretation. The Barolo Gramolere is also
excellent, showing fresh balsamic tones
and expressive power that will last for
many years.

● Barolo Monvigliero '09	♈♈♈	6
● Barolo Gramolere '09	♈♈	6
● Barolo S. Lorenzo di Verduno '09	♈♈	6
● Barolo '09	♈♈	5
● Langhe Nebbiolo Prinsiot '11	♈♈	3
● Verduno Pelaverga Speziale '12	♈♈	3
● Barbera d'Alba '12	♈	2
● Barolo Gramolere '05	♈♈♈	6
● Barolo Monvigliero '06	♈♈♈	6
● Barolo Monvigliero '00	♈♈♈	6
● Barolo Monvigliero '95	♈♈♈	6
● Barolo S. Lorenzo '08	♈♈♈	6
● Barolo S. Lorenzo '04	♈♈♈	6
● Barolo S. Lorenzo '01	♈♈♈	6
● Barolo S. Lorenzo '97	♈♈♈	6
● Barolo Gramolere '08	♈♈	6

★Gianfranco Alessandria

LOC. MANZONI, 13
12065 MONFORTE D'ALBA [CN]
TEL. 017378576
www.gianfrancoalessandria.com

CELLAR SALES
PRE-BOOKED VISITS
ANNUAL PRODUCTION 45,000 bottles
HECTARES UNDER VINE 7.00

This family-run estate, situated in Monforte
d'Alba, is a veritable gem, with just over
five hectares of vineyards. Gianfranco
Alessandria, with the aid of his wife Bruna
and daughter Vittoria, after whom his
famous Barbera d'Alba is named, has
meticulously and competently tended it for
years. Very low yields per hectare and
modern cellar equipment ensure top-quality
products. The wines, aged mainly in small
French oak casks, are generally
characterized by a close-focused nose and
ideal structure. Youth lends the Barolo San
Giovanni 2009 a lively palate with tannins
that are still well integrated and balsamic
nuances that promise well for the palate.
The well-made, elegant Barolo 2009 shows
nice balance between drinkability and
structure. A special mention goes to the
Langhe Nebbiolo 2010, very typical, fresh
and lively, and the harmonious, fruity
Barbera d'Alba Vittoria 2010.

● Barolo S. Giovanni '09	♈♈	7
● Barbera d'Alba '12	♈♈	3
● Barbera d'Alba Vittoria '10	♈♈	5
● Barolo '09	♈♈	6
● Langhe Nebbiolo '10	♈♈	3
● Barbera d'Alba Vittoria '98	♈♈♈	5
● Barbera d'Alba Vittoria '97	♈♈♈	4*
● Barbera d'Alba Vittoria '96	♈♈♈	6
● Barolo '93	♈♈♈	6
● Barolo S. Giovanni '04	♈♈♈	7
● Barolo S. Giovanni '01	♈♈♈	7
● Barolo S. Giovanni '00	♈♈♈	7
● Barolo S. Giovanni '99	♈♈♈	8
● Barolo S. Giovanni '98	♈♈♈	7
● Barolo S. Giovanni '97	♈♈♈	7
● Barolo '08	♈♈	6

Marchesi Alfieri

P.ZZA ALFIERI, 28
14010 SAN MARTINO ALFIERI [AT]
TEL. 0141976015
www.marchesialfieri.it

CELLAR SALES
PRE-BOOKED VISITS
ACCOMMODATION
ANNUAL PRODUCTION 100,000 bottles
HECTARES UNDER VINE 21.00

In 1990, the three San Martino sisters of San Germano decided to bottle their Barbera, thus creating Marchesi Alfieri. Since then, this estate has become a pillar of Asti wine-making thanks to its consistently high quality. In addition to barbera, which accounts for 60% of the area under vine, the estate also cultivates grignolino, nebbiolo and pinot nero. The oldest vines on the Quaglia slopes, planted in 1937, go to make the estate's flagship wine, Barbera d'Asti Superiore Alfiera. Production focuses on the richness of the fruit and the drinkability of the wines. A solid all-round performance from the Marchesi Alfieri. The Barbera d'Asti Superiore Alfiera 2010 presents notes of sweet spice and black berry fruit and a harmonious palate with good structure and acidity. The Barbera d'Asti La Tota 2011 has notes of peachy fruit and decent backbone. The Monferrato Rosso Sostegno 2011 from barbera and pinot nero is fresh and balanced with a long, pleasing finish.

● Barbera d'Asti La Tota '11	♟♟ 3
● Barbera d'Asti Sup. Alfiera '10	♟♟ 5
● M.to Rosso Costa Quaglia '10	♟♟ 4
● M.to Rosso S. Germano '10	♟♟ 5
● M.to Rosso Sostegno '11	♟♟ 2*
● Piemonte Grignolino Sansoero '12	♟ 2
● Barbera d'Asti Sup. Alfiera '07	♟♟♟ 5
● Barbera d'Asti Sup. Alfiera '05	♟♟♟ 5
● Barbera d'Asti Sup. Alfiera '01	♟♟♟ 5
● Barbera d'Asti Sup. Alfiera '00	♟♟♟ 5
● Barbera d'Asti Sup. Alfiera '99	♟♟♟ 5
● Barbera d'Asti La Tota '10	♟♟ 3*
● Barbera d'Asti Sup. Alfiera '09	♟♟ 5
● M.to Rosso Sostegno '10	♟♟ 2*
● Piemonte Grignolino Sansoero '11	♟♟ 2*

Giovanni Almondo

VIA SAN ROCCO, 26
12046 MONTÀ [CN]
TEL. 0173975256
www.giovannialmondo.com

CELLAR SALES
PRE-BOOKED VISITS
ANNUAL PRODUCTION 100,000 bottles
HECTARES UNDER VINE 16.00

The Almondo family has lived in this area for centuries. They established their own estate and started bottling wine in 1980, carving out a niche for themselves among the top Roero wineries. Over 60% of their vineyards are dedicated to arneis, which grows on the estate's sandier, higher plots at an altitude of 360 metres. The rest of the vineyards are home to nebbiolo, barbera and brachetto. The range offers fresh, elegant whites and modern reds that are more firmly structured but eminently drinkable. Yet another Tre Bicchieri for the Roero Bric Valdiana 2011, an extremely elegant wine showing flowery, fruity aromas, a firm, balanced palate, very refined tannins and a long finish. The Roero Giovanni Almondo Riserva 2010 also reached the finals with its notes of spice, toastiness and red berry fruit, full and pleasing. We liked the Barbera d'Alba Valbianchèra 2011 for its ripe fruit, tobacco and quina tones.

● Roero Bric Valdiana '11	♟♟♟ 5
● Roero Giovanni Almondo Ris. '10	♟♟ 5
● Barbera d'Alba Valbianchera '11	♟♟ 3
○ Langhe Bianco Sassi e Sabbia '12	♟ 3
○ Roero Arneis V. Sparse '12	♟ 2
● Roero Bric Valdiana '07	♟♟♟ 5
● Roero Bric Valdiana '03	♟♟♟ 5
● Roero Bric Valdiana '01	♟♟♟ 4
● Roero Bric Valdiana '00	♟♟♟ 4*
● Roero Giovanni Almondo Ris. '09	♟♟♟ 5
● Barbera d'Alba Valbianchera '10	♟♟ 3
○ Roero Arneis Bricco delle Ciliegie '10	♟♟ 3

★★★Elio Altare

FRAZ. ANNUNZIATA, 51
12064 LA MORRA [CN]
TEL. 017350835
www.elioaltare.com

CELLAR SALES
PRE-BOOKED VISITS
ANNUAL PRODUCTION 60,000 bottles
HECTARES UNDER VINE 11.00

Elio Altare has long been acknowledged as a beacon and pioneer of modern winemaking in Langhe, widening horizons and paving the way for an entire generation. The years have passed, but the estate philosophy has remained the same, almost always implemented by Elio himself, from cellar work to tending the vineyards. All the wines, commencing with the entry-level bottles, display a well-defined style and varietal purity, making them true benchmarks. At the beginning of the year we tasted a Larigi and a Barolo Arborina 2001, which were both still very fresh and youthful, reconfirming the soundness of their flavours, capable of withstanding unscathed the passage of time. The complex and elegant Barolo Arborina 2009 displays notes of red berry fruit, tobacco, spice and liquorice, and a layered palate supported by smooth tannic texture and refreshing acidity. A well-deserved Tre Bicchieri. The Langhe Larigi 2011 is complex and captivating with extremely pleasant drinkability.

● Barolo Arborina '09	♥♥♥ 8
● Barolo Cerretta V. Bricco '07	♥♥ 8
● Langhe La Villa '11	♥♥ 8
● Langhe Larigi '11	♥♥ 8
● Barolo '09	♥♥ 8
● L'Insieme '11	♥♥ 7
● Langhe Arborina '11	♥♥ 8
● Barolo Cerretta V. Bricco '06	♥♥♥ 8
● Barolo Cerretta V. Bricco '05	♥♥♥ 8
● Langhe Arborina '08	♥♥♥ 8
● Langhe La Villa '06	♥♥♥ 8
● Langhe La Villa '05	♥♥♥ 8
● Langhe Larigi '07	♥♥♥ 7
● Langhe Larigi '04	♥♥♥ 7

Antichi Vigneti di Cantalupo

VIA MICHELANGELO BUONARROTI, 5
28074 GHEMME [NO]
TEL. 0163840041
www.cantalupo.net

CELLAR SALES
PRE-BOOKED VISITS
ANNUAL PRODUCTION 200,000 bottles
HECTARES UNDER VINE 35.00

Breclema, Carella, Livelli and Baraggiola are just some of the Ghemme crus that make up the splendid Antichi Vigneti di Cantalupo estate. The lion's share of its 34 hectares is given over to nebbiolo spanna, with a small percentage of vespolina, uva rara, erbaluce, arneis and chardonnay. The range of wines it offers has always conveyed the characteristics of the morainic slopes of the province of Novara with consistency and stylistic maturity. Hats off to the Arlunno family and their production that aims to express the different varietals with ageing in in mainly Slavonian oak barrels or in barriques. The vintages of the two Ghemmes currently on the market exemplify this estate's style that has always favoured aromatic complexity and refined sensations on the palate. The Collis Breclemae 2005 offers notes of tobacco with coal tar nuances, and a still-austere palate. The Anno Primo 2007 is just as layered but already shows softer.

● Ghemme Cantalupo Anno Primo '07	♥♥ 5
● Ghemme Collis Breclemae '05	♥♥ 6
○ Carolus	♥♥ 2*
● Colline Novaresi Abate di Cluny '07	♥♥ 5
● Colline Novaresi Primigenia '10	♥♥ 2*
● Colline Novaresi Agamium '08	♥ 3
⊙ Mia Ida Brut	♥ 3
● Ghemme '05	♥♥♥ 4
● Ghemme Collis Breclemae '00	♥♥♥ 6
● Ghemme '06	♥♥ 5
● Ghemme Collis Breclemae '04	♥♥ 6
● Ghemme Collis Carellae '07	♥♥ 6
● Ghemme Signore di Bayard '05	♥♥ 6
● Ghemme Signore di Bayard '04	♥♥ 5

Antico Borgo dei Cavalli

VIA DANTE, 54
28010 CAVALLIRIO [NO]
TEL. 016380115
www.vinibarbaglia.it

CELLAR SALES
PRE-BOOKED VISITS
ANNUAL PRODUCTION 25,000 bottles
HECTARES UNDER VINE 3.00

With over 60 years of activity under its belt, Antico Borgo dei Cavalli is a historic name in the Novara growing district. Established as a small estate by Mario Barbaglia in 1946, it is run today by his son Sergio and grand-daughter Silvia. Their exploratory approach is evident in a range of wines that treads an admirable line between tradition and modernity. It's hard to single out the one big label. The Boca often represents one of their most interesting interpretations, but the monovarietals derived from nebbiolo, uva rara, croatina, vespolina and erbaluce hold their own, as do the three spumantes that comprise the Curticella line. In anticipation of a splendid Boca from the family's new vineyards, we enjoyed the 2009 version, impressive for the fullness of its aromas ranging from gentian to blood-rich meat, and its close-knit but never aggressive tannic texture. Sergio's skilled hand is also evident in the bottle fermentation, witness the exceptionally taut and leisurely Curticella Caballi Regis Dosaggio Zero.

● Boca '09	♟♟ 5
○ Curticella Caballi Regis Dosaggio Zero M. Cl.	♟♟ 5
● Colline Novaresi Nebbiolo Il Silente '09	♟♟ 3
○ Curticella Caballi Regis Brut M. Cl.	♟♟ 5
○ Colline Novaresi Bianco Lucino '12	♟ 3
● Colline Novaresi Croatina Clea '10	♟ 2
● Colline Novaresi Vespolina Ledi '11	♟ 3
● Boca '08	♟♟ 5
● Boca '07	♟♟ 5
○ Colline Novaresi Bianco Lucino '10	♟♟ 3*
● Colline Novaresi Croatina Clea '09	♟♟ 3
● Colline Novaresi Nebbiolo Il Silente '07	♟♟ 3
⊙ Curticella Rosé Brut Uva Rara	♟♟ 5

★Antoniolo

C.SO VALSESIA, 277
13045 GATTINARA [VC]
TEL. 0163833612
antoniolovini@bmm.it

CELLAR SALES
PRE-BOOKED VISITS
ANNUAL PRODUCTION 60,000 bottles
HECTARES UNDER VINE 12.00

San Francesco, Osso San Grato, Castelle, Borelle. If these splendid vineyards now rank alongside the most prestigious crus in the world, much of the credit must go to the work conducted with extraordinary determination and passion by the Antoniolo family. Signora Rosanna promoted and extolled the virtues of nebbiolo di Gattinara in the most challenging years, and her children Alberto and Lorella continue to fly the flag with the same vigour. Their wines give new meaning to the concept of purity and flavour and speak of evolution over decades, rendering debates about fermentation and ageing, tradition and modernity superfluous. The heavy hailstorms that hit the zone limited the number of Gattinara labels to two in the 2009 vintage. The Osso San Grato takes home the latest in a long line of Tre Bicchieri, displaying its usual magnificent structure and a softer, warmer character thanks to the heat of the growing year. The San Francesco shows its customary delicate texture.

● Gattinara Osso S. Grato '09	♟♟♟ 8
● Gattinara S. Francesco '09	♟♟ 7
● Coste della Sesia Nebbiolo Juvenia '11	♟♟ 4
⊙ Coste della Sesia Rosato Bricco Lorella '12	♟ 3
○ Erbaluce di Caluso '12	♟ 3
● Gattinara S. Francesco '08	♟♟♟ 7
● Gattinara S. Francesco '07	♟♟♟ 5
● Gattinara Vign. Osso S. Grato '06	♟♟♟ 6
● Gattinara Vign. Osso S. Grato '05	♟♟♟ 6
● Gattinara Vign. Osso S. Grato '04	♟♟♟ 6
● Gattinara Vign. S. Francesco '06	♟♟♟ 5
● Gattinara Vign. S. Francesco '05	♟♟♟ 6
● Gattinara Vign. S. Francesco '03	♟♟♟ 6
● Gattinara Vign. S. Francesco '01	♟♟♟ 6

Araldica Castelvero

V.LE LAUDANO, 2
14040 CASTEL BOGLIONE [AT]
TEL. 014176311
www.araldicavini.com

CELLAR SALES
PRE-BOOKED VISITS
ANNUAL PRODUCTION 8,000,000 bottles
HECTARES UNDER VINE 900.00

Following its merger with Antica Contea di Castelvero this year, Araldica VInI Plemontesi is now known as Araldica Castelvero. This co-operative produces no less than 43 labels, divided between four lines. Its wines derive from all of the most prestigious wine-growing zones in Piedmont with its relative DOCs, from Asti to Langhe, Roero to the zone of Gavi, all the way to Alta Langa. Above all, the winery seeks to produce accessible quality wines, with a keen eye to offering everyday products at affordable prices. A stunning performance from the Araldica Castelvero Barberas. We particularly liked the Barbera d'Asti Superiore Crocera 2011 with its cinnamon and blackberry aromas over hints of quina, austere, complex palate and very lengthy finish. The simple but balanced Barbera d'Asti Superiore Rive 2011 offers ripe cherry notes. The Merlot Soliti 2011 is not complex but still charming.

● Barbera d'Asti Sup. Crocera '11	♟♟ 3*
● Barbera d'Asti Sup. Rive '11	♟♟ 3
● Merlot Soliti '11	♟♟ 2*
○ Gavi '12	♟ 3
○ Piemonte Chardonnay Campo Fiorito '11	♟ 3
○ Riesling Fontanino '11	♟ 2
○ Alta Langa Alasia Brut '08	♟♟ 3*
⊙ Alta Langa Alasia Brut Rosé '07	♟♟ 3
● Barbera d'Asti Sup. Crocera '09	♟♟ 3
● Barbera d'Asti Sup. Rive '08	♟♟ 3
○ Gavi '11	♟♟ 3
● Langhe Nebbiolo Castellero '07	♟♟ 3

Tenuta dell'Arbiola

LOC. ARBIOLA
REG. SALINE, 67
14050 SAN MARZANO OLIVETO [AT]
TEL. 0141856194
www.saiagricola.it

CELLAR SALES
PRE-BOOKED VISITS
CELLAR SALES
ANNUAL PRODUCTION 100,000 bottles
HECTARES UNDER VINE 20.00

Tenuta dell'Arbiola, the Piedmont estate belonging to Saiagricola, sits on the hill of the same name on the border between Monferrato and Langhe. It lies in the municipality of San Marzano Oliveto where the estate's vineyards occupy a sandy limestone terrain. Accounting for 60% of the area planted to vine, barbera is king-pin and the estate obtains its flagship wine – Nizza – from vines planted over 60 years ago. The wines on offer are modern in style and very technically clean. They show natural concentration and fabulous richness of fruit. The intense, layered Barbera d'Asti Superiore Nizza Romilda XIV 2010 goes all the way to the finals, even if it doesn't bag top prize. The spicy entry on the palate leads into notes of plum and rain-soaked earth, taut almost to the point of austerity. The Barbera d'Asti Carlotta 2011 has a full, compact fruity nose and a complex, generous palate that has yet to balance out fully. The Nysus Rosé Brut Metodo Classico 2010 has flowery aromas and pronounced, pleasing acidity.

● Barbera d'Asti Sup. Nizza Romilda XV '10	♟♟ 5
● Barbera d'Asti Carlotta '11	♟♟ 2*
⊙ Nysus Brut M. Cl. '10	♟♟ 5
○ Monferrato Bianco Brandé '12	♟ 3
○ Moscato d'Asti Ferlingot '12	♟ 2
○ Nysus Blanc Brut '09 M. Cl.	♟ 5
● Barbera d'Asti Sup. Nizza Romilda XIV '09	♟♟♟ 5
● Barbera d'Asti Carlotta '09	♟♟ 2*
● Barbera d'Asti Carlotta '08	♟♟ 2*
● Barbera d'Asti Sup. Nizza Romilda VIII '03	♟♟ 5
● Barbera d'Asti Sup. Nizza Romilda X '05	♟♟ 5
● Barbera d'Asti Sup. Nizza Romilda XI '06	♟♟ 5
● Barbera d'Asti Sup. Nizza Romilda XII '07	♟♟ 5
● Barbera d'Asti Sup. Nizza Romilda XIII '08	♟♟ 4

L'Armangia

FRAZ. SAN GIOVANNI, 122
14053 CANELLI [AT]
TEL. 0141824947
www.armangia.it

PRE-BOOKED VISITS
ANNUAL PRODUCTION 95,000 bottles
HECTARES UNDER VINE 10.00

With the initial goal of focusing on the production of white wines from moscato, chardonnay and sauvignon, the winery of the Giovine family has for some time proposed a range offering all-round quality, with a series of excellent Barberas, recently joined by a Pinot Nero. The vineyards are situated at Canelli on limestone and clay soils, and at Moasca and San Marzano Oliveto on heavier, more compact soils. The modern-style wines express not only varietal characteristics but also territorial identity. What a superb array of wines from the Giovine family. The Barbera d'Asti Superiore Nizza Titon 2010 stands out for its notes of black berry fruit and full, powerful palate nicely buttressed by lively acidity. Still young, it will be worth the wait. Of the others, we liked the Piemonte Chardonnay Robi & Robi 2011, fairly complex and well balanced, and the Moscato d'Asti Canelli 2012, citrussy, elegant and agreeable.

● Barbera d'Asti Sup. Nizza Titon '10	♥♥ 3*
● Barbera d'Asti Sopra Berruti '12	♥♥ 2*
● Barbera d'Asti Sup. Nizza Vignali '07	♥♥ 5
○ Moscato d'Asti Canelli '12	♥♥ 2*
○ Piemonte Chardonnay Robi & Robi '11	♥♥ 3
● Piemonte Pinot Nero Dall'Alto '11	♥ 3
● Barbera d'Asti Sopra Berruti '11	♀♀ 2*
● Barbera d'Asti Sopra Berruti '10	♀♀ 2*
● Barbera d'Asti Sup. Nizza Titon '09	♀♀ 3
● Barbera d'Asti Sup. Nizza Titon '08	♀♀ 3*
● Barbera d'Asti Sup. Nizza Vignali '06	♀♀ 5
● M.to Rosso Pacifico '09	♀♀ 3

Ascheri

VIA PIUMATI, 23
12042 BRA [CN]
TEL. 0172412394
www.ascherivini.it

CELLAR SALES
PRE-BOOKED VISITS
ACCOMMODATION AND RESTAURANT SERVICE
ANNUAL PRODUCTION 240,000 bottles
HECTARES UNDER VINE 40.00

The approximately 40 hectares that make up the property belonging to the Ascheri family span three districts: Sorano in Serralunga d'Alba, Rivalta between La Morra and Verduno, and Montalupa in Bra, Roero, which produces the Syrah and Viognier of the same name. The broad and complex range aims to offer value for money and also graces the wine list of the Muri Vecchi inn, a stone's throw from the centre of Bra in the group of buildings that houses the cellar and a delightful hotel. We strongly advise a visit – it's the best introduction to this compact, harmonious style of Barolo that is a far cry from standardized commercial versions. Via the Sorano cru, the terroir of Serralunga plays a very influential role in the creation of a Barolo with enormous expressive power that displays the full force of its taste sensations in the 2009 vintage. The Barolo Pisapola 2009 is not quite so well defined and needs time to reconcile its tannic texture with the pulp and structure typical of the vintage. The Dolcetto Nirane 2012 is fresh, easy-drinking and well balanced.

● Barolo Sorano '09	♥♥ 5
● Barbera d'Alba Fontanelle '11	♥♥ 3
● Barolo Pisapola '09	♥♥ 5
● Dolcetto d'Alba Nirane '12	♥♥ 2*
● Dolcetto d'Alba S. Rocco '12	♥ 2
○ Langhe Arneis Cristina Ascheri '12	♥ 2
● Nebbiolo d'Alba Bricco S. Giacomo '11	♥ 3
● Barolo Sorano '00	♀♀♀ 5
● Barolo Sorano Coste & Bricco '06	♀♀♀ 5
● Barolo Pisapola '08	♀♀ 5
● Barolo Sorano '08	♀♀ 5
● Barolo Sorano '07	♀♀ 5
● Barolo Sorano '03	♀♀ 5*
● Barolo Sorano Coste & Bricco '07	♀♀ 6
● Barolo Sorano Coste & Bricco '04	♀♀ 6
● Barolo V. dei Pola '01	♀♀ 5

Paolo Avezza

REGIONE MONFORTE, 62
14053 CANELLI [AT]
TEL. 0141822296
www.paoloavezza.com

CELLAR SALES
PRE-BOOKED VISITS
ANNUAL PRODUCTION 25,000 bottles
HECTARES UNDER VINE 7.00

Paolo Avezza is at the helm of this family estate and was the driving force behind the renovation of the cellar in 2001. In just over ten years, his bottles have emerged as some of the most interesting in the area This goes for both the still wines – notably the Nizza – derived from plots in Nizza Monferrato, and the sparklers – led by the Alta Langa – that are obtained from vineyards in Canelli. The estate's style favours elegance and aromatic precision within the framework of a traditional, territorial approach. A Tre Bicchieri for the Barbera d'Asti Superiore Nizza Sotto La Muda 2010, sweetly spicy yet elegant with hints of cherry, a clear, harmonious palate and a long finish well supported by acidity. We also liked the taut, elegant Alta Langa Brut 2010, minerally with notes of damson and lime. The well-structured, tangy Moscato d'Asti Canelli La Commenda 2012 and the lively, juicy Barbera d'Asti 2012 are both pleasant.

● Barbera d'Asti Sup. Nizza Sotto la Muda '10	♟♟♟ 4*
○ Alta Langa Brut '10	♟♟ 4
● Barbera d'Asti '12	♟♟ 2*
○ Moscato d'Asti La Commenda '12	♟♟ 2*
● Barbera d'Asti Sup. Nizza Sotto la Muda '07	♟♟♟ 3*
○ Alta Langa Brut '08	♟♟ 4
● Barbera d'Asti '11	♟♟ 2*
● Barbera d'Asti '10	♟♟ 2
● Barbera d'Asti '09	♟♟ 2*
● Barbera d'Asti Sup. Nizza Sotto la Muda '09	♟♟ 4
● Barbera d'Asti Sup. Nizza Sotto la Muda '08	♟♟ 4

★Azelia

FRAZ. GARBELLETTO
VIA ALBA-BAROLO, 53
12060 CASTIGLIONE FALLETTO [CN]
TEL. 017362859
www.azelia.it

CELLAR SALES
PRE-BOOKED VISITS
ANNUAL PRODUCTION 80,000 bottles
HECTARES UNDER VINE 16.00

The wines made by this long-standing estate in Castiglione Falletto are undeniably elegant and sophisticated. Headed by Luigi, whose grandfather founded it in the 1930s, the winery remains a family affair, run with the aid of his wife Lorella and son Lorenzo. All the grapes are estate grown and the wines reflect a philosophy based on painstaking care in the vineyard and scrupulous cleanliness in the cellar. The Barolo selections are all very distinctive and characterized by carefully calibrated structure and a well-orchestrated palate. Vinification takes place in large barrels and small oak casks. The quality of Luigi Scavino's wines has achieved an enviable standard. Credit is partly due to the exceptional terroir that this year brings us a superb Barolo Bricco Fiasco 2009 of rare elegance and complexity, whose balsamic tones meld to perfection with nuances of morello cherry and tar. The San Rocco 2009 and the basic version are also excellent, full of personality and character.

● Barolo Bricco Fiasco '09	♟♟♟ 8
● Barolo '09	♟♟ 6
● Barolo S. Rocco '09	♟♟ 8
● Barbera d'Alba Vign. Punta '11	♟♟ 4
● Barolo Margheria '09	♟♟ 8
● Dolcetto d'Alba Bricco dell'Oriolo '12	♟♟ 3
● Langhe Nebbiolo '12	♟ 4
● Barolo Bricco Fiasco '01	♟♟♟ 7
● Barolo Bricco Fiasco '95	♟♟♟ 7
● Barolo Margheria '06	♟♟♟ 7
● Barolo S. Rocco '08	♟♟♟ 8
● Barolo S. Rocco '99	♟♟♟ 7
● Barolo Voghera Brea Ris. '01	♟♟♟ 8
● Barolo '08	♟♟ 6
● Barolo Bricco Fiasco '08	♟♟ 8
● Barolo Margheria '08	♟♟ 8

Osvaldo Barberis

B.TA VALDIBÀ, 42
12063 DOGLIANI [CN]
TEL. 017370054
www.osvaldobarberis.com

CELLAR SALES
PRE-BOOKED VISITS
ANNUAL PRODUCTION 20,000 bottles
HECTARES UNDER VINE 8.00
VITICULTURE METHOD Certified Organic

This excellent little family-run estate has strict principles concerning respect for the land and nature, hence its organic certification, which represents a genuine philosophy of life and work. Dolcetto, the traditional local grape variety, obviously accounts for the greatest area under vine, and is vinified in a very simple, authentic style. It is accompanied by nebbiolo and barbera, which produce equally pleasant and varietal wines. The price list is very reasonable and competitive in relation to quality. The very convincing Nebbiolo Muntajà 2011 is lively and dynamic with a deep, edgy palate. The fruity, zesty Dolcetto Valdibà 2012 is remarkably drinkable. The complex Dogliani Superiore Puncin 2011 is distinctive for its varietal notes of red berry fruit and forest floor.

● Dogliani Sup. Puncin '11	♥♥ 3*
● Nebbiolo d'Alba Muntajà '11	♥♥ 3*
● Dogliani Avrì '12	♥♥ 3
● Dogliani Valdibà '12	♥♥ 2*
● Piemonte Barbera Brichat '11	♥♥ 2*
● Barbera d'Alba Castella '11	♥ 3
● Barbera d'Alba Castella '08	♀♀ 3
● Dogliani Puncin '10	♀♀ 2*
● Dogliani Puncin '09	♀♀ 2*
● Dogliani Puncin '08	♀♀ 2*
● Dogliani Valdibà '11	♀♀ 2*
● Dolcetto di Dogliani Puncin '05	♀♀ 2*
● Nebbiolo d'Alba Muntajà '09	♀♀ 3
● Nebbiolo d'Alba Muntajà '08	♀♀ 3

Batasiolo

FRAZ. ANNUNZIATA, 87
12064 LA MORRA [CN]
TEL. 017350130
www.batasiolo.com

PRE-BOOKED VISITS
ANNUAL PRODUCTION 2,500,000 bottles
HECTARES UNDER VINE 107.00

Owned by the Dogliani family since 1978, Batasiolo is undoubtedly one of the greatest Langhe estates, thanks to its vineyards in Monforte d'Alba, Barolo, Serralunga d'Alba and La Morra, and the range of a line that showcases the area's great classic wines. Its vineyards include some of the very finest crus, such as Cerequio and Brunate. The grapes are vinified in traditional style, with ageing in large Slavonian oak casks, with the exception of the famous Barolo Corda della Briccolina, which is more modern, due to the use of French barriques. The very varietal Barolo Brunate 2009 with controlled tannins and notes of spice and quina on the palate dominates this broad range of wines of medium-high quality across various typologies. The whites give an excellent performance with the Gavi del Comune di Gavi 2012 taking centre stage, mineral and tangy with hints of tropical fruit and fresh sage.

● Barolo Brunate '09	♥♥ 7
● Barbaresco '10	♥♥ 5
● Barolo '09	♥♥ 5
● Barolo Boscareto '09	♥♥ 7
● Barolo Bussia Vign. Bofani '09	♥♥ 7
● Barolo Cerequio '09	♥♥ 7
● Barolo Corda della Briccolina '09	♥♥ 8
● Dolcetto d'Alba Bricco di Vergne '12	♥♥ 3
○ Gavi del Comune di Gavi Granée '12	♥♥ 3
○ Langhe Chardonnay Vign. Morino '11	♥♥ 5
● Langhe Nebbiolo '11	♥♥ 3
○ Moscato d'Asti Bosc dla Rei '12	♥♥ 3
○ Roero Arneis '12	♥♥ 3
● Barbera d'Alba '11	♥ 3
○ Langhe Bianco Sunsì '12	♥ 3
● Barolo Boscareto '05	♀♀♀ 7

Fabrizio Battaglino

LOC. BORGONUOVO
VIA MONTALDO ROERO, 44
12040 VEZZA D'ALBA [CN]
TEL. 0173658156
www.battaglino.com

CELLAR SALES
PRE-BOOKED VISITS
ANNUAL PRODUCTION 25,000 bottles
HECTARES UNDER VINE 5.00

Fabrizio Battaglino runs this small family estate with skill and passion. His philosophy of quality produces balanced, easy-drinking wines that express the characteristics of the terroir. The arneis and nebbiolo vineyards are located in Vezza d'Alba, very near the estate headquarters. They lie at an altitude of 350 metres on the sandy Colla slopes, with the young vines destined for Roero and those over 45 years of age for Nebbiolo d'Alba. The barbera plots are situated on the slopes of Montebello in Guarene, a zone that is particularly well suited to the cultivation of this variety. The generously fruity, faintly balsamic Nebbiolo d'Alba Colla 2011 shows lovely texture, elegant tannins and a pleasant palate. We also loved the Barbera d'Alba Munbél 2011 for its intense notes of red berry fruit and rain-soaked earth, and palate showing good mouthfeel and acidity. The Roero Arneis 2012 is balanced with notes of appley fruit and flowers and a nice long finish.

● Barbera d'Alba V. Munbèl '11	♟♟ 3*
● Nebbiolo d'Alba V. Colla '11	♟♟ 4
● Nebbiolo d'Alba '11	♟♟ 3
○ Roero Arneis '12	♟♟ 2*
● Nebbiolo d'Alba V. Colla '07	♟♟♟ 3*
● Barbera d'Alba Sup. Madunina '08	♟♟ 3
● Nebbiolo d'Alba '07	♟♟ 2*
● Nebbiolo d'Alba V. Colla '08	♟♟ 3
○ Passito Bric Bastia	♟♟ 4
○ Roero Arneis '11	♟♟ 2*
● Roero Sergentin '10	♟♟ 4
● Roero Sergentin '08	♟♟ 3*
● Roero Sergentin '07	♟♟ 3*

Bava

S.DA MONFERRATO, 2
14023 COCCONATO [AT]
TEL. 0141907083
www.bava.com

CELLAR SALES
PRE-BOOKED VISITS
ACCOMMODATION
ANNUAL PRODUCTION 500,000 bottles
HECTARES UNDER VINE 55.00

This estate belonging to the Bava family has been a feature of the Asti landscape for over a century. The various acquisitions of the last 30 years have made it a leading light in Piedmont wine-making. The estate's properties are located at Cocconato, Cioccaro and Agliano Terme in Monferrato, where barbera is the dominant variety, and at Castiglione Falletto in Langhe, home to nebbiolo and dolcetto. It also produces spumante at the Giulio Cocchi winery along with some excellent wine-based aperitifs, including Vermouth di Torino and Americano. The range of wines is very drinkable, pleasing and modern in style. A fine showing overall from Bava's wines. The Barbera d'Asti Libera 2011 is fresh, long and balanced; the Barolo Scarrone 2008 is balsamic and spicy; the Moscato d'Asti Bass Tuba 2012 presents notes of candied fruit and a fittingly sweet palate. We also enjoyed the Barbera d'Asti Superiore Nizza Piano Alto 2010 showing earthy and black berry fruit sensations, and the fruity Alta Langa Bianc 'd Bianc Brut 2007.

○ Alta Langa Brut Bianc 'd Bianc Giulio Cocchi '07	♟♟ 5
● Barbera d'Asti Libera '11	♟♟ 3
● Barbera d'Asti Sup. Nizza Piano Alto '10	♟♟ 4
● Barolo Scarrone '08	♟♟ 7
○ Moscato d'Asti Bass Tuba '12	♟♟ 3
○ Alta Langa Brut Toto Corde Giulio Cocchi '07	♟ 4
● Malvasia di Castelnuovo Don Bosco Rosetta '12	♟ 3
○ Piemonte Chardonnay Thou Bianc '12	♟ 3
○ Alta Langa Brut Toto Corde Giulio Cocchi '06	♟♟ 5
● Barbera d'Asti Sup. Nizza Piano Alto '09	♟♟ 4
● Barbera d'Asti Sup. Stradivario '07	♟♟ 6

Bel Colle

FRAZ. CASTAGNI, 56
12060 VERDUNO [CN]
TEL. 0172470196
www.belcolle.it

CELLAR SALES
PRE-BOOKED VISITS
ANNUAL PRODUCTION 180,000 bottles
HECTARES UNDER VINE 10.00

Founded in 1976, Bel Colle immediately made a name for itself with its production of the singular Pelaverga di Verduno. However, brothers Franco and Carlo Pontiglione also decided to invest in the wines classic to the Langhe: Barolo, Barbaresco, Nebbiolo, Barbera and Dolcetto. These have improved enormously in recent years, partly due to the precious aid of oenologist Paolo Torchio, who has drawn on his experience at other wineries, particularly local ones, to enhance their distinctive and highly personal style. They are undeniably traditional, although ageing in large Slavonian oak casks is combined with the limited and attentive use of small French oak casks for a modern touch. The Barbaresco Roncaglie Riserva 2008 presents an austere, aristocratic taste profile distinguished by notes of medicinal herbs, quina, eucalyptus and dark tobacco. The Barolo Monvigliero 2008 offers liqueur cherry aromas with faint balsamic nuances. The Nebbiolo Bricco Reala 2011 is wonderfully drinkable and fresh.

● Barbaresco Roncaglie Ris. '08	♟♟♟ 5
● Barolo Monvigliero '08	♟♟ 5
● Nebbiolo d'Alba Bricco Reala '11	♟♟ 3*
● Barbera d'Alba Sup. '11	♟♟ 3
○ Roero Arneis '12	♟ 2
● Verduno Pelaverga '12	♟ 3
● Barolo Monvigliero '07	♟♟♟ 5
● Barolo Monvigliero '06	♟♟♟ 5
● Barbaresco '08	♟♟ 5
● Barbaresco Roncaglie '07	♟♟ 5
● Barolo '07	♟♟ 5
● Barolo '06	♟♟ 5
● Barolo Monvigliero '05	♟♟ 5
● Barolo Monvigliero Ris. '04	♟♟ 6

Bera

VIA CASTELLERO, 12
12050 NEVIGLIE [CN]
TEL. 0173630194
www.bera.it

CELLAR SALES
PRE-BOOKED VISITS
ANNUAL PRODUCTION 140,000 bottles
HECTARES UNDER VINE 22.00

Thirty years have passed since Valter Bera transformed his family winery into one of the most interesting – and best known – operations producing Moscato d'Asti, not to mention a series of quality reds. The majority of the vines, boasting an average age of around 40 years, are situated in the hills near the winery, on soil rich in tufa, clay and limestone. Alongside moscato there are also plantings of dolcetto, nebbiolo, barbera, chardonnay and pinot nero, used to produce an Alta Langa. The Moscato d'Asti Su Reimond 2012 is one of the best of the typology. Intense and gorgeous notes of sage and rose lead into hints of lime and medicinal herbs; the palate shows fresh and elegant thanks to the lovely balance between sugars and acid element. The other wines are well made and a special mention goes to the Barbaresco 2009, elegant with smooth tannins, and the tangy, lingering Barbera d'Alba Superiore La Lena 2010.

○ Moscato d'Asti Su Reimond '12	♟♟ 2*
● Barbaresco '09	♟♟ 5
● Barbera d'Alba La Lena '10	♟♟ 3
● Barbera d'Asti Sup. '10	♟♟ 2*
● Langhe Nebbiolo Alladio '09	♟♟ 3
○ Moscato d'Asti '12	♟♟ 2*
○ Asti '12	♟ 2
○ Langhe Chardonnay '11	♟ 2
○ Alta Langa Bera Brut '06	♟♟ 3
● Barbera d'Alba '11	♟♟ 2*
● Barbera d'Alba La Lena '09	♟♟ 3
● Barbera d'Asti Sup. '09	♟♟ 2*
● Langhe Sassisto '09	♟♟ 3
○ Moscato d'Asti '11	♟♟ 2*
○ Moscato d'Asti Su Reimond '11	♟♟ 2*

Cinzia Bergaglio

VIA GAVI, 29
15060 TASSAROLO [AL]
TEL. 3484032968
www.vinicinziabergaglio.it

CELLAR SALES
PRE-BOOKED VISITS
ANNUAL PRODUCTION 25,000 bottles
HECTARES UNDER VINE 5.00

The tiny estate enthusiastically and
determinedly run by Cinzia Bergaglio covers
an area of just five hectares, entirely planted
to cortese. Its vineyards are located in the
municipalities of Gavi, characterized by very
clayey and calcareous soils, and Tassarolo,
on more tufaceous and iron-rich plots.
Grifone delle Roveri, aged in steel after brief
cold maceration, hails from the former,
while Tassarolo yields La Fornace, which
undergoes slow fermentation off the skins.
The estate concentrates solely on these two
wines, which share a very accentuated
fresh, delicate terroir identity, which often
boosts their vigour and complexity with
bottle ageing. As always, this estate offers
quality wines at reasonable prices. These
authentic bottles contain a fine
representation of the territory's
characteristics: elegantly vegetal aromas
hinting at grass and alpine flowers, and
fresh, sharp acidity to support the structure.
The new spumante makes a decent debut.

Nicola Bergaglio

FRAZ. ROVERETO
LOC. PEDAGGERI, 59
15066 GAVI [AL]
TEL. 0143682195
nicolabergaglio@alice.it

CELLAR SALES
PRE-BOOKED VISITS
ANNUAL PRODUCTION 130,000 bottles
HECTARES UNDER VINE 17.00

The wines made by the Bergaglio family
are constantly held up by those, ourselves
included, who believe that the finest Gavis
aren't simply summer whites to be drunk
within a few months, but wines capable of
surprising and exciting development even
after years. A good example is the Minia
selection, from cortese grown on the
Rovereto hill and aged in steel, which is
consistently linear and ageworthy. It is the
flagship of a small line, now produced by
Gianluigi Bergaglio with his son Diego,
which is completed by the basic Gavi di
Gavi, also vinified exclusively in steel.
Nicola Bergaglio's wines give their usual
fine performance, even if they don't take
top prize in the edition of the Guide. They
showed well but not exceptionally in the
selection stage, but gained weight and
character in the final tastings. A touch more
definition would have tipped the scales for
the magnificent Minaia.

○ Gavi del Comune di Gavi Grifone delle Roveri '12	♀♀ 2*
○ Gavi La Fornace '12	♀♀ 2*
○ Pulein Brut M. Cl.	♀ 3
○ Gavi del Comune di Gavi Grifone delle Roveri '11	♀♀ 2*
○ Gavi del Comune di Gavi Grifone delle Roveri '09	♀♀ 2*
○ Gavi del Comune di Gavi Grifone delle Roveri '08	♀♀ 2*
○ Gavi del Comune di Gavi Grifone delle Roveri '07	♀♀ 2*
○ Gavi del Comune di Tassarolo Fornaci '07	♀♀ 2*
○ Gavi del Comune di Tassarolo Fornaci '06	♀♀ 2*
○ Gavi La Fornace '10	♀♀ 2*
○ Gavi La Fornace '09	♀♀ 2*
○ Gavi La Fornace '08	♀♀ 2*

○ Gavi del Comune di Gavi Minaia '12	♀♀ 3*
○ Gavi del Comune di Gavi '12	♀♀ 2*
○ Gavi del Comune di Gavi Minaia '11	♀♀♀ 4*
○ Gavi del Comune di Gavi Minaia '10	♀♀♀ 4
○ Gavi del Comune di Gavi Minaia '09	♀♀♀ 4
○ Gavi del Comune di Gavi '11	♀♀ 3
○ Gavi del Comune di Gavi '10	♀♀ 2
○ Gavi del Comune di Gavi '09	♀♀ 3
○ Gavi del Comune di Gavi '07	♀♀ 2*
○ Gavi del Comune di Gavi Minaia '08	♀♀ 3*
○ Gavi del Comune di Gavi Minaia '07	♀♀ 2*
○ Gavi del Comune di Gavi Minaia '06	♀♀ 2*
○ Gavi del Comune di Gavi Minaia '05	♀♀ 2*
○ Gavi del Comune di Gavi Minaia '04	♀♀ 2*

Bersano

P.ZZA DANTE, 21
14049 NIZZA MONFERRATO [AT]
TEL. 0141720211
www.bersano.it

CELLAR SALES
PRE-BOOKED VISITS
ANNUAL PRODUCTION 2,200,000 bottles
HECTARES UNDER VINE 240.00

Bersano comprises no less than ten estates located mainly in Asti and Monferrato, and let's not forget the Badarina cascina at Serralunga d'Alba. It also buys in grapes from several of Piedmont's prestigious zones. The estate's philosophy is to produce quality wines in large volumes that are technically well made and obtained largely from local varieties with a strong territorial slant. The range of labels on offer is very broad and includes the production of Metodo Classico from pinot nero and chardonnay. Bersano proposes a very high quality range this year, starting with the two finalists. The Ruché di Castagnole Monferrato San Pietro 2012 displays the aromaticity typical of the variety with notes of rose and wild strawberries, deep and harmonious. The Barolo Badarina 2008 has an elegant complex nose of sweet tobacco and dried aromatic herbs, and an enveloping palate boasting velvety tannins.

● Barolo Badarina '08	🍷🍷 6
● Ruché di Castagnole Monferrato S. Pietro '12	🍷🍷 3*
● Barbaresco Mantico '10	🍷🍷 6
● Barbera d'Asti Sup. Cremosina '11	🍷🍷 3
● Barbera d'Asti Sup. Nizza Generala '10	🍷🍷 5
● Barolo Nirvasco '09	🍷🍷 6
● Barolo Ris. '07	🍷🍷 7
○ Moscato d'Asti Monte Olivo '12	🍷🍷 3
○ Gavi del Comune di Gavi '12	🍷 3
● Barbera d'Asti Sup. Generala '97	🍷🍷🍷 5
● Barolo Badarina '07	🍷🍷 7
● Barolo Ris. '06	🍷🍷 7

Guido Berta

LOC. SALINE, 53
14050 SAN MARZANO OLIVETO [AT]
TEL. 0141856193
www.guidoberta.com

CELLAR SALES
PRE-BOOKED VISITS
ANNUAL PRODUCTION 25,000 bottles
HECTARES UNDER VINE 10.00

Guido Berta offers a limited range, focusing on wines with a real sense of place. The vineyards are situated mainly in the district of San Marzano Oliveto, with some small plots at Agliano Terme and Calamandrana. The calcareous-clay soils are planted to vines aged between 25 and 50 years old, and the main variety, as always in this area, is barbera, accounting for over 60% of the vineyard holdings. The other grapes grown are moscato, chardonnay and nebbiolo. This year we particularly liked the Barbera d'Asti Superiore Nizza Canto di Luna 2010, one of the best of the DOC. Clear cherry and fresh plum aromas and captivating spiciness lead into a very structured palate showing bags of character supported by a long finish with marked acidity. The fresh, elegant Moscato d'Asti 2012 with sage and lime tones, and the Barbera d'Asti Superiore 2011 with more rustic hints of rain-soaked earth are also well made.

● Barbera d'Asti Sup. Nizza Canto di Luna '10	🍷🍷 5
● Barbera d'Asti Sup. '11	🍷🍷 4
○ Moscato d'Asti '12	🍷🍷 3
● Barbera d'Asti Sup. '09	🍷🍷 4
● Barbera d'Asti Sup. '08	🍷🍷 3
● Barbera d'Asti Sup. Nizza Canto di Luna '09	🍷🍷 5
● Barbera d'Asti Sup. Nizza Canto di Luna '08	🍷🍷 5
● Barbera d'Asti Sup. Nizza Canto di Luna '07	🍷🍷 4

♀♀♀ TRE BICCHIERI

Ca' Rome'
Barolo - Barbaresco
Strada Rabajà, 86/88
12050 Barbaresco (CN)
Tel. +39 0173 635126
Fax +39 0173 635175
www.carome.com
info@carome.com

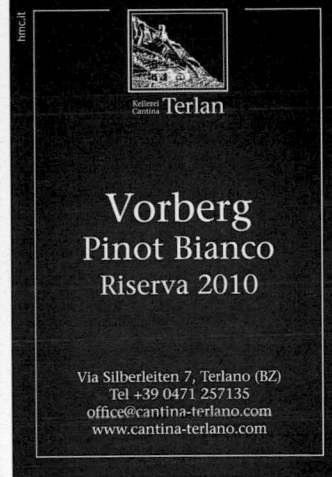

Via Silberleiten 7, Terlano (BZ)
Tel +39 0471 257135
office@cantina-terlano.com
www.cantina-terlano.com

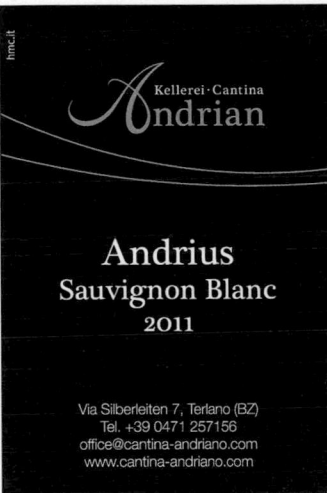

Via Silberleiten 7, Terlano (BZ)
Tel. +39 0471 257156
office@cantina-andriano.com
www.cantina-andriano.com

Altemasi di Cavit
Via del Ponte, 31 - 38123 Trento
Tel. +39 0461 381711
Fax +39 0461 381787
www.cavit.it - www.altemasi.it
cavit@cavit.it

Azienda Agricola Ferghettina
Via Saline, 11 - 25030 Adro (BS)
Tel. +39 030 7451212
Fax +39 030 7453528
www.ferghettina.it
info@ferghettina.it

Az. Agr. Lo Sparviere
Via Costa, 12
25040 Monticelli Brusati (BS)
Tel. +39 030 652382
www.losparviere.com
info@losparviere.com

♟♟♟ TRE BICCHIERI

I Stefanini
Via Crosara 21
37032 Monteforte d'Alpone (VR)
Tel. and Fax +39 045 6175249
www.istefanini.it
francesco@istefanini.it

Ronco Blanchis
Via Blanchis, 70
34070 Mossa (GO)
Tel. +39 0481 80519
Fax +39 0481 880816
www.roncoblanchis.it

Tel.+39 059 3163311
Fax +39 059310868
www.chiarli.it - export@chiarli.it

CAMPAIGN FINANCED ACCORDING TO EC REG. N. 1234/07

Azienda Agricola Carvinea
Via per Serranova 1
72012 Carovigno (BR)
Tel. +39 080 5862345
Fax +39 080 5322247
www.carvinea.com - info@carvinea.com

BISCI
Via Fogliano 120
62024 Matelica (MC)
Tel. and Fax +39 0737 787490
bisciwines@libero.it
www.bisci.it

The company was founded in 1980 and extends for approximately 80 hectares between the provinces of Macerata and Ancona. Set up according to criteria for the highest of quality, it boasts 19 hectares of specialised vines, 17 of which are cultivated for Verdicchio and 2 for Sangiovese and Merlot. The cellar, at the centre of the vineyard, is divided between modern buildings and ancient rustic buildings.
A leader in its qualified range, the Verdicchio di Matelica DOC is also available in the Vigneto Fogliano, Passito and Senex versions.

♀♀♀ TRE BICCHIERI

Cantine del Notaio
Via Roma, 159
85028 Rionero in Vulture (PZ)
Tel. +39 0972 723689
Fax +39 0972 725435
www.cantinedelnotaio.com
info@cantinedelnotaio.it

Az. Agr. Ceraudo Roberto
C.da Dattilo - 88815 Strongoli (KR)
Tel. +39 0962 865613
Fax +39 0962 865696
info@dattilo.it
www.dattilo.it

Barberani
Loc. Cerreto
05023 Baschi (TR)
Tel. +39 0763 341820
Fax +39 0763 340773
www.barberani.com
barberani@barberani.it

Cantine Sardus Pater
Via Rinascita, 46
09017 S. Antioco (CI)
Tel. +39 0781 800274
Fax +39 0781 83055
www.cantinesarduspater.com

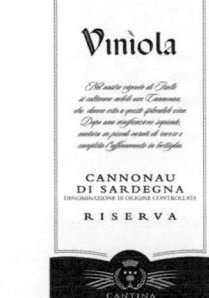

Cantina Dorgali
Via Piemonte, 11 - 08022 Dorgali (NU)
Tel. +39 0784 96143
Fax +39 0784 94537
www.cantinadorgali.com
info@cantinadorgali.com

Cantina Santadi
Via Cagliari, 78 - 09010 Santadi (CI)
Tel. +39 0781 950127
Fax +39 0781 950012
info@cantinadisantadi.it
www.cantinadisantadi.it

♈♈♈ TRE BICCHIERI

Podere Sapaio
Loc. Lo Scopaio, 212
57022 Castagneto Carducci (LI)
Tel. +39 0565 765187
Fax +39 0565 765945
www.sapaio.it - info@sapaio.it

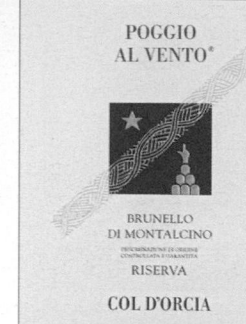

Col d'Orcia
Via Giuncheti
53024 Montalcino (SI)
Tel. +39 0577 80891
Fax +39 0577 844018
www.coldorcia.it - info@coldorcia.it

Società Agricola Fontaleoni
Loc. Santa Maria, 39
53037 San Gimignano (SI)
Tel. +39 0577 950193
Fax +39 0577 951691
www.fontaleoni.com - az.fontaleoni@libero.it

Az. Agr. Il Colombaio di Santa Chiara
Località San Donato, 1
53037 San Gimignano (SI)
Tel. and Fax +39 0577 942004
www.colombaiosantachiara.it
info@colombaiosantachiara.it

www.iluoghi.it

Azienda Agricola I LUOGHI di Stefano Granata
Loc. Campo al Capriolo 201 Castagneto Carducci Toscana

E&S

The best hotels,
restaurants and wineries
of the region...

www.eatandsleep.it

PERLA DEL GARDA

Via Fenil Vecchio 9
25017 Lonato del Garda (BS)
Tel. and Fax 030 9103109
info@perladelgarda.it
www.perladelgarda.it

Born from the ambitious idea of reintroducing vines to the company's morainic hills - rocky and arid but highly suitable for vine-growing - the Perla del Garda project is based on one criteria: wine starts being made from the vine, adapting to the climate of the year, with the attention and wisdom of country tradition without renouncing the concept of organic agriculture they have recently introduced and experimented on a part of the vineyards. Thus, the white Trebbiano di Lugana, Sauvignon, Riesling, Chardonnay, and Incrocio Manzoni and the red Merlot, Cabernet Franc, Sauvignon and Rebo grapes, all hand picked, bring forth some prestigious bottles for the most refined connoisseur.

GAVI
LA SMILLA

Close to the Ligurian Apennines, the **La Smilla** vineyards cover the DOCG [Controlled and Guaranteed Designation of Origin] of the Gavi and the DOC [Controlled designation of origin] of Dolcetto di Ovada. A charming winery in the historical centre.

Bosio (AL) - Piedmont - info@lasmilla.it - www.lasmilla.it

PRODUTTORI DEL GAVI

Tel. +39 0143 642786
Via Cavalieri di V. Veneto 45, 15066 Gavi AL
cantina.prodgavi@libero.it

E&S

The best hotels,
restaurants and wineries
of the region...

www.eatandsleep.it

Gambero Rosso
Vini d'Italia
tour 2013/2014

25 november 2013
ZURICH

27 november 2013
WARSAW

14 january 2014
STOCKHOLM

15 january 2014
COPENHAGEN

16 january 2014
OSLO

may 2014
MIAMI

june 2014
TOKYO

The Grand Tou
of Italian Wine

GAMBERO ROSSO

INFO: eventi.estero@gamberorosso.i

Bianchi

VIA ROMA, 37
28070 SIZZANO [NO]
TEL. 0321810004
www.bianchibiowine.it

CELLAR SALES
PRE-BOOKED VISITS
ANNUAL PRODUCTION 150,000 bottles
HECTARES UNDER VINE 21.00
VITICULTURE METHOD Certified Organic

This small estate run by Paolo Tealdi
Bianchi and his mother Eva has grown
slowly but surely over the last few years. It
practises organic growing methods and its
plots extend over 20 or so hectares that
span several of northern Piedmont's
historic DOCs, from Gattinara to Ghemme,
and the lesser known but equally
distinguished Sizzano. The style is more
than classic; we would go so far as to call it
contemporary in its quest for a pure, juicy
fruitiness as a foil to overabundant
toastiness. Yet again we failed to find
consistency in Paolo Tealdi's range of
wines. On one hand, it contains absolute
thoroughbreds to rival the best in Upper
Piedmont, such as the austere, aristocratic
Sizzano 2008 or the Gattinara 2008, full of
well-integrated tannins. On the other, we
have blue-blooded reds that are
over-evolved in style.

● Sizzano '08	♀♀	3*
○ Colline Novaresi Bianco Luminae '12	♀♀	2*
● Gattinara '08	♀♀	4
● Colline Novaresi Nebbiolo '12	♀	2
● Gattinara Vign. Valferana '08	♀	4
● Ghemme '09	♀	3
● Colline Novaresi Rosso Sanclemente '11	♀♀	2*
● Gattinara '07	♀♀	4
● Gattinara Vign. Valferana '07	♀♀	4
● Gattinara Vign. Valferana '06	♀♀	4
● Ghemme '08	♀♀	3
● Ghemme '07	♀♀	3
● Ghemme '07	♀♀	3
● Ghemme '05	♀♀	3
● Sizzano '07	♀♀	3

Enzo Boglietti

VIA FONTANE, 18A
12064 LA MORRA [CN]
TEL. 017350330
www.enzoboglietti.com

CELLAR SALES
PRE-BOOKED VISITS
ACCOMMODATION
ANNUAL PRODUCTION 100,000 bottles
HECTARES UNDER VINE 22.50

Commencing with the styling of their labels,
the Boglietti brothers made a name for
themselves from the outset as original
producers with plenty of personality and
imagination. Their range of wines has grown
over the years and the estate's vineyards
not only include several important plots in
La Morra, but also the Arione cru in
Serralunga d'Alba, and recent plantings in
the municipality of Roddino, dedicated
mainly to international grape varieties. The
wines show exuberant body and great
thrust, reinforced by the use of mainly small
oak casks, and require appropriate ageing
to achieve perfect balance. Although it
didn't hit the bullseye this year, Enzo
Boglietti's prestigious array of Barolos is
worthy of its fame. The Barolo Brunate
2009 is deep and intense with notes of
spice and sweet tobacco. The Barolo Fossati
2009 shows an exuberant fruitiness that is
part covers the darker nuances of tar and
forest floor. The complex Riserva di Barolo
2007 is still a tad oaky.

● Barolo Brunate '09	♀♀	8
● Barolo Fossati '09	♀♀	8
● Barolo V. Arione '09	♀♀	8
● Barbera d'Alba Roscaleto '10	♀♀	5
● Barbera d'Alba V. dei Romani '09	♀♀	6
● Barolo Ris. '07	♀♀	8
● Dolcetto d'Alba Tigli Neri '11	♀♀	3
● Langhe Nebbiolo '11	♀♀	3
● Barbera d'Alba '11	♀	3
● Barolo Case Nere '09	♀	8
● Dolcetto d'Alba '11	♀	2
● Langhe Cabernet V. Talpone '09	♀	6
● Barolo Arione '06	♀♀♀	8
● Barolo Arione '05	♀♀♀	8
● Barolo Case Nere '04	♀♀♀	8
● Barolo V. Arione '07	♀♀♀	8

Bondi - Cascina Banaia

S.DA CAPPELLETTE, 73
15076 OVADA [AL]
TEL. 0131299186
www.bondivini.it

CELLAR SALES
PRE-BOOKED VISITS
ANNUAL PRODUCTION 20,000 bottles
HECTARES UNDER VINE 5.00

In this year's profile there is some news to report. The designation of the Barbera Banaiotta and the Dolcetto di Ovada Nani has changed to table wine, even though the varieties used remain the same and, judging by the results, the Bondi family's commitment is unwavering. This was clearly a choice made solely to cut through the red tape that afflicts the winemaking sector. La Banaiotta reached the Tre Bicchieri finals. Ruby tending to black of opaque intensity in the glass, it shows fresh fruit aromas verging on jam and a palate magnificent in its concentration and freshness. Nani is a vibrant, highly complex Dolcetto whose balsamic notes offset the crunchy fruit. The dense, powerful palate contends with the alcoholic, tannic element.

Bongiovanni

LOC. UCCELLACCIO
VIA ALBA BAROLO, 4
12060 CASTIGLIONE FALLETTO [CN]
TEL. 0173262184
www.cascinabongiovanni.it

CELLAR SALES
PRE-BOOKED VISITS
ANNUAL PRODUCTION 40,000 bottles
HECTARES UNDER VINE 7.20

Vaunting a family tradition of winemaking dating back to 1950, Davide Mozzone continues to run his estate with great enthusiasm and competence. The success of Cascina Bongiovanni's wines is derived from a combination of meticulous care in the vineyard and innovative cellar techniques that nonetheless respect tradition. Their style focuses on expressive authenticity, and when young the wines sometimes show a little rough on the palate. However, they are destined to soften with ageing, becoming balanced and harmonious. The entire range is excellent value for money. Although it doesn't win any awards, Davide Mozzone's production is always very balanced with plenty of space and alternating fortunes for Piedmont's principal grape types. The Barolos – notably the Pernanno – focus on tannic strength and solid drinkability at attractive prices. The fruity, typical Dolcetto di Diano 2011 is very interesting.

● Banaiotta	▼▼ 4
● Nani	▼▼ 2*
● Ovada Sup. Duién '10	▼ 4
● Barbera del M.to Banaiotta '10	♈ 2*
● Dolcetto di Ovada Nani '11	♈ 2*
● Dolcetto di Ovada Nani '09	♈ 2*
● Dolcetto di Ovada Nani '08	♈ 2*
● Dolcetto di Ovada Sup. D'Uien '08	♈ 3
● M.to Barbera Banaiotta '09	♈ 4
● M.to Barbera Ruvrin Sup. '07	♈ 4
● Ovada D'Uien '09	♈ 3

● Barbera d'Alba '11	▼▼ 3
● Barolo '09	▼▼ 5
● Barolo Pernanno '09	▼▼ 6
● Dolcetto di Diano d'Alba '12	▼▼ 2*
● Dolcetto d'Alba '12	▼ 2
○ Langhe Arneis '12	▼ 2
● Langhe Rosso Faletto '11	▼ 4
● Barolo Pernanno '01	♈♈ 6
● Barbera d'Alba '10	♈ 3
● Barolo '07	♈ 5
● Barolo '06	♈ 5*
● Barolo Pernanno '08	♈ 6
● Barolo Pernanno '05	♈ 6
● Dolcetto di Diano d'Alba '11	♈ 2*

Borgo Maragliano

VIA SAN SEBASTIANO, 2
14051 LOAZZOLO [AT]
TEL. 014487132
www.borgomaragliano.com

CELLAR SALES
PRE-BOOKED VISITS
ANNUAL PRODUCTION 295,000 bottles
HECTARES UNDER VINE 21.00

The Galliano family's estate is located at Loazzolo in the Asti Langa area. It lies at an altitude of 450 metres in a zone rich in marl and sandstone and cooled by the breeze coming off the Ligurian Sea. Borgo Maragliano offers the classic moscato production in all of its various versions, and in 2011 it added to its line-up with brachetto cultivated in Bistagno, an area of the province of Alessandria particularly well-suited to this variety. It also presents a range of sparkling wines mainly Metodo Classicos, from chardonnay and pinot nero, whose complexity, elegance and aromatic fullness make them some of the most interesting not only in Piedmont but also beyond its borders. This year we were very impressed by the Dogma Blanc de Noirs 2010 from pinot nero, a complex, concentrated wine with notes of red berry fruit and toast, character and acid staying power. The rather dosed Giuseppe Galliano Brut 2009 has fruity notes with undertones of crusty bread, while the Giuseppe Galliano Brut Riserva 2006 is austere and leisurely. Both are obtained from 80% pinot nero with chardonnay.

○ Dogma Blanc de Noirs M. Cl. '10	♈♈♈ 5
○ Francesco Galliano Blanc de Blancs M. Cl. '10	♈♈ 4
○ Giuseppe Galliano Brut M. Cl. '09	♈♈ 4
○ Giuseppe Galliano Brut M. Cl. Ris. '06	♈♈ 5
⊙ Giovanni Galliano Brut Rosé M. Cl. '09	♈ 4
○ Chardonnay Brut	♈ 2
○ Moscato d'Asti La Caliera '12	♈ 2
○ Piemonte Chardonnay Crevoglio '12	♈ 2
○ Giuseppe Galliano Brut M. Cl. Ris. '01	♈♈♈ 4*
○ Francesco Galliano Blanc de Blancs M. Cl. '09	♈♈ 3
○ El Calié '11	♈♈ 2*
○ Loazzolo Borgo Maragliano V. T. '09	♈♈ 5

Giacomo Borgogno & Figli

VIA GIOBERTI, 1
12060 BAROLO [CN]
TEL. 017356108
www.borgogno.com

CELLAR SALES
PRE-BOOKED VISITS
ANNUAL PRODUCTION 110,000 bottles
HECTARES UNDER VINE 16.00

Andrea, the son of the world-famous Oscar Farinetti of Eataly, one of the most successful Italian businessmen of recent years, confidently runs this prestigious Piedmont winery with the competent assistance of his first-rate staff. Founded over 250 years ago, the cellar produces classic, traditional wines, all designed to be appreciated in their youth whilst promising rare ageing potential. A unique focus is represented by the extraordinary collection of old vintages, some with many bottles still available, which are often capable of offering unforgettable sensations. It is the little-known Liste cru in the municipality of Barolo that bags the top prize for an overall performance of absolute quality. The tannic texture of this Barolo 2008 is close-knit and powerful, but does not detract from the elegance and balance of the palate. Vibrant and fresh in its noble and elegant character, the Barolo Riserva 2006 also excels, along with the Fossati and Cannubi 2008.

● Barolo Liste '08	♈♈♈ 8
● Barolo Cannubi '08	♈♈ 8
● Barolo Fossati '08	♈♈ 7
● Barolo Ris. '06	♈♈ 7
● Barbera d'Alba Sup. '11	♈♈ 3
● Barolo '08	♈♈ 6
● Langhe Nebbiolo No Name '09	♈♈ 5
● Dolcetto d'Alba '12	♈ 3
● Langhe Nebbiolo '11	♈ 4
● Barolo Cl. '98	♈♈♈ 7
● Barolo Liste '07	♈♈♈ 7
● Barolo Liste '05	♈♈♈ 7
● Barolo V. Liste '06	♈♈♈ 7
● Barolo '07	♈♈ 6
● Barolo Ris. '05	♈♈ 7
● Barolo Ris. '04	♈♈ 7

Boroli

FRAZ. MADONNA DI COMO, 34
12051 ALBA [CN]
TEL. 0173365477
www.boroli.it

CELLAR SALES
PRE-BOOKED VISITS
ACCOMMODATION AND RESTAURANT SERVICE
ANNUAL PRODUCTION 2,500,000 bottles
HECTARES UNDER VINE 32.00

Two farms, one winery. On one side
Cascina Bompè, a few kilometres from the
centre of Alba, where the Madonna di
Como vineyard is planted to dolcetto
d'Alba; on the other, La Brunella at
Castiglione Falletto, with some of Barolo's
most famous crus, including Bussia,
Cerequio and Villero. Established in 1997
by Silvano and Elena Boroli, the winery also
boasts an attractive inn with rooms and a
restaurant. Several impressive wines make
for an overall fine performance led by a real
champion. The Barolo Cerequio 2009 has
complex notes of tar, liquorice and red
berry fruit, and a deep, complex, velvety
palate. The Barolo Villero 2009 is more
austere and introverted; the Villero
Riserva 2006 has bags of character and
tannic structure. Patience is the key. Hot on
their heels, the superb Barolo 2009 weds
freshness and structure with great
classicity and a long, delicately salty finish.

Francesco Boschis

FRAZ. SAN MARTINO DI PIANEZZO, 57
12063 DOGLIANI [CN]
TEL. 017370574
www.marcdegrazia.com

CELLAR SALES
PRE-BOOKED VISITS
ANNUAL PRODUCTION 40,000 bottles
HECTARES UNDER VINE 11.00

The Boschis family did not start bottling
fine wine until 1968, commencing with
Dolcetto. Today the work of Paolo and
Marco still focuses chiefly on the prince of
Dogliani grapes, with the consistently valid
Vigna del Prey, Sorì San Martino and Vigna
del Ciliegio selections accounting for a
good proportion of the estate's production.
The Dolcettos are traditional, interpreted in
a classic style, and only Vigna del Ciliegio
is aged in used oak. In addition to Dolcetto
di Dogliani, the estate also produces
Barbera d'Alba, Grignolino, Freisa and a
limited number of bottles of a singular
Langhe Sauvignon with excellent character.
We start our tasting notes with praise for
the Sauvignon Vigna dei Garisin 2012. It
presents exciting varietal tone recalling
tropical fruit, sage and aniseed that make
it captivating and unique. The Dogliani
Vigna dei Prey 2011 is juicy and fruity with
lovely balance between tannins and acidity.

● Barolo Cerequio '09	♟♟ 7
● Barolo Villero '09	♟♟ 7
● Barolo Villero Ris. '06	♟♟ 8
● Barbera d'Alba '11	♟♟ 2*
● Barbera d'Alba Quattro Fratelli '11	♟♟ 3
● Barolo '09	♟♟ 6
● Langhe Rosso Anna '11	♟♟ 2*
○ Moscato d'Asti Aureum '12	♟♟ 2*
● Dolcetto d'Alba Madonna di Como '11	♟ 2
○ Langhe Arneis '12	♟ 2
○ Langhe Bianco '12	♟ 2
○ Langhe Chardonnay Bel Amì '11	♟ 3
● Nebbiolo d'Alba '11	♟ 3
● Barolo Villero '01	♟♟♟ 6

● Dogliani Sup. V. dei Prey '11	♟♟ 3*
○ Langhe Sauvignon V. dei Garisin '12	♟♟ 3*
● Dogliani Pianezzo '12	♟♟ 2*
● Dogliani Sup. Sorì San Martino '11	♟♟ 3
● Langhe Rosso nei Sorì '10	♟♟ 4
● Dogliani Sup. V. del Ciliegio '10	♟ 3
● Dogliani Sorì S. Martino '09	♟♟ 2*
● Dogliani Sorì S. Martino '08	♟♟ 2*
● Dogliani V. dei Prey '10	♟♟ 2*
● Dogliani V. dei Prey '09	♟♟ 2*
● Dogliani V. dei Prey '08	♟♟ 2*
● Dogliani V. dei Prey '07	♟♟ 2*
● Langhe Freisa Bosco delle Cicale '10	♟♟ 2*
● Langhe Rosso nei Sorì '09	♟♟ 4

Agostino Bosco

VIA FONTANE, 24
12064 LA MORRA [CN]
TEL. 0173509466
www.barolobosco.com

CELLAR SALES
PRE-BOOKED VISITS
ANNUAL PRODUCTION 22,000 bottles
HECTARES UNDER VINE 5.00

Last year's performance, when we reported on a range of wines on outstanding form, has been confirmed this year in an equally impressive selection, resulting in a rightly earned full-length profile. This small, family-run operation, established by Agostino and run with his son Andrea and wife Carla, farms five hectares of vineyards. They are particularly proud of their two Barolo crus: Neirane, in the district of Verduno, and La Serra, the historic cru of La Morra whose soil is particularly rich in clay and limestone. Both of the Barolo selections reached our final tastings. The excellent Barolo Neirane 2009 combines elegant fresh fruity notes with sensations of tobacco and aniseed, a palate with big structure, solid tannic framework and a long, precise finish. More austere but just as fascinating, the Barolo La Serra 2009 has strong fruity aromas leading into quina and medicinal herbs.

● Barolo La Serra '09	♟♟ 6
● Barolo Neirane '09	♟♟ 5
● Barbera d'Alba Volupta '11	♟♟ 3
● Langhe Nebbiolo Rurem '11	♟♟ 3
● Dolcetto d'Alba Vantrin '12	♟ 2
● Barbera d'Alba Sup. Volupta '11	♟♟ 3
● Barolo La Serra '08	♟♟ 5
● Barolo Neirane '08	♟♟ 5
● Langhe Nebbiolo Rurem '10	♟♟ 2*

Luigi Boveri

LOC. MONTALE CELLI
VIA XX SETTEMBRE, 6
15050 COSTA VESCOVATO [AL]
TEL. 0131838165
www.boveriluigi.com

CELLAR SALES
PRE-BOOKED VISITS
ANNUAL PRODUCTION 70,000 bottles
HECTARES UNDER VINE 15.00

In a territory where wineries do without sales directors and marketing managers, a vigneron has to be a factotum. Luigi is no exception, and takes on these extra duties with great passion and willpower, helped by his wife Germana, until their children are old enough to lend a hand in the business. The results so far have been consistently flattering, and Luigi is clearly managing to keep on top of the workload. On his side he has the soil, which in this subzone of the Colli Tortonesi area is rich in limestone and gives the wines a marked mineral character. The two estate Timorassos dominate this range, the Derthona and Filari di Timorasso. This year our preference is for the Derthona, which presents splendid notes of appley fruit and greater freshness than its elder brother. Indeed, it takes home the highest marks our Guide awards.

○ Colli Tortonesi Timorasso Derthona '11	♟♟♟ 4*
● Colli Tortonesi Barbera Vignalunga '10	♟♟ 5
● Colli Tortonesi Barbera Poggio delle Amarene '11	♟♟ 4
○ Colli Tortonesi Cortese V. del Prete '12	♟♟ 2*
○ Colli Tortonesi Timorasso Filari di Timorasso '10	♟♟ 5
● Colli Tortonesi Barbera Boccanera '12	♟ 2
● Colli Tortonesi Croatina Sensazioni '10	♟ 4
○ Ramasco '12	♟ 2
○ Colli Tortonesi Timorasso Filari di Timorasso '07	♟♟♟ 3
● Colli Tortonesi Barbera Poggio delle Amarene '10	♟♟ 3*
● Colli Tortonesi Barbera Poggio delle Amarene '09	♟♟ 3*
○ Colli Tortonesi Cortese Vigna del Prete '11	♟♟ 2*

Gianfranco Bovio

FRAZ. ANNUNZIATA
B.TA CIOTTO, 63
12064 LA MORRA [CN]
TEL. 017350667
www.boviogianfranco.com

CELLAR SALES
PRE-BOOKED VISITS
ANNUAL PRODUCTION 70,000 bottles
HECTARES UNDER VINE 10.00

Gianfranco Bovio was an important figure in the Langhe restaurant scene, and the Belvedere at La Morra was for years a mecca for lovers of good food. The winery, established in 1976, has progressively grown also thanks to the qualities of Walter Porasso, who can count on the three historic La Morra crus of Gattera, Arborina and Rocchettevino, with and on Bricco Parussi at Castiglione Falletto. The style of these Barolos is fairly classic, with fruit to the fore and the oak barely perceptible in its first years in the bottle. The Barolo Rocchettevino 2009 is kingpin in this small but high-quality range of wines, offering intense aromas of tobacco, spice and light violet, with silky, non-invasive tannins. In its current phase, the Barolo Gattera 2009 is a bit rugged with tannic texture that has yet to smooth out. The Barolo Arborina 2009 has fresh notes, red berry fruit to the fore.

● Barolo Rocchettevino '09	♈♈ 5
● Barolo Arborina '09	♈♈ 6
● Barolo Gattera '09	♈♈ 6
● Barolo Bricco Parussi Ris. '01	♈♈♈ 6
● Barolo Rocchettevino '06	♈♈♈ 5*
● Barolo V. Arborina '90	♈♈♈ 6
● Barolo Arborina '08	♈♈ 6
● Barolo Bricco Parussi Ris. '04	♈♈ 7
● Barolo Gattera '08	♈♈ 6
● Barolo Gattera '07	♈♈ 6
● Barolo Gattera '06	♈♈ 6
● Barolo Rocchettevino '08	♈♈ 6
● Barolo Rocchettevino '07	♈♈ 5*

★Braida

S.DA PROVINCIALE, 9
14030 ROCCHETTA TANARO [AT]
TEL. 0141644113
www.braida.it

CELLAR SALES
PRE-BOOKED VISITS
ACCOMMODATION AND RESTAURANT SERVICE
ANNUAL PRODUCTION 600,000 bottles
HECTARES UNDER VINE 53.00

The Bologna family has run this estate with aplomb for more than 50 years, keeping it consistently at the top of the Piedmont wine-making tree. Production focuses on barbera, in particular barbera from the Rocchetta Tanaro vineyards, which are flanked by the plots located in Costigliole d'Asti, Castelnuovo Calcea, Mango and Trezzo Tinella from which the white wines of the Serra dei Fiori line are obtained. The Barberas on offer have always represented one of the most accomplished modern interpretations of this variety in terms of fullness, complexity and depth. A Tre Bicchieri for the Barbera d'Asti Montebruna 2011. Perhaps the less appreciated, it presents fabulous aromas of cherry, tobacco and quina, refined and complex, full yet harmonious, with refreshing acidity and extraordinary length. The Barbera d'Asti Bricco dell'Uccellone 2011 is also excellent, complex with a long finish. The Barbera d'Asti Bricco della Bigotta 2011 has chocolate nuances, big structure and acidity.

● Barbera d'Asti Montebruna '11	♈♈♈ 3*
● Barbera d'Asti Bricco dell'Uccellone '11	♈♈ 7
● Barbera d'Asti Bricco della Bigotta '11	♈♈ 7
● Barbera d'Asti Ai Suma '11	♈♈ 7
● Grignolino d'Asti '12	♈♈ 2*
○ Langhe Nascetta Regina di Fiori '12	♈♈ 3
● M.to Rosso Il Bacialé '11	♈♈ 3
○ Moscato d'Asti V. Senza Nome '12	♈♈ 3
○ Langhe Bianco Il Fiore '12	♈ 3
○ Langhe Riesling Re di Fiori '12	♈ 3
● Barbera d'Asti Bricco dell'Uccellone '09	♈♈♈ 6
● Barbera d'Asti Bricco dell'Uccellone '05	♈♈♈ 6
● Barbera d'Asti Bricco della Bigotta '07	♈♈♈ 6
● Barbera d'Asti Bricco della Bigotta '06	♈♈♈ 6

Brandini

FRAZ. BRANDINI, 16
12064 LA MORRA [CN]
TEL. 017350266
www.agricolabrandini.it

CELLAR SALES
PRE-BOOKED VISITS
ANNUAL PRODUCTION 70,000 bottles
HECTARES UNDER VINE 9.00
VITICULTURE METHOD Certified Organic

Although not indicated on the label, the wines produced by this interesting young estate in the municipality of La Morra are the product of certified organic agriculture. It is difficult to carve oneself out a distinct, well-defined niche on the very comprehensive Langhe wine scene, but the qualitative progress of the cellar's products, constituted by wines that faithfully respect their terroir, is truly noteworthy and they deserve to be known and placed alongside the finest of the area. Their great drinkability and reasonable prices are the winning cards of this estate just waiting to be discovered. Distinctive for its notes of spice and medicinal herbs, the Barolo Brandini 2009 repeats last year's magnificent performance with good tannic texture and balanced, harmonious structure. The other wines are show good quality and precise varietal definition, notably the characterful and very drinkable Nebbiolo Filari Corti 2011.

● Barolo Brandini '09	♟♟ 6
● Barbera d'Alba Sup. Rocche del Santo '11	♟♟ 3
● Barolo '09	♟♟ 5
● Langhe Nebbiolo Filari Corti '11	♟♟ 4
● Barbera d'Alba Rocche del Santo '10	♟♟ 3
● Barbera d'Alba Sup. Rocche del Santo '10	♟♟ 3*
● Barolo '08	♟♟ 6
● Barolo Brandini '08	♟♟ 6
● Langhe Nebbiolo V. Sant' Anna '10	♟♟ 4

Brangero

VIA PROVINCIALE, 26
12055 DIANO D'ALBA [CN]
TEL. 017369423
www.brangero.it

PRE-BOOKED VISITS
ANNUAL PRODUCTION 50,000 bottles
HECTARES UNDER VINE 9.00

Even though Marco represents the fourth generation of the Brangero family of growers at Diano d'Alba, the winery as a business really dates back to 1999 when under his drive, it began to bottle its wine. The family house is surrounded by eight hectares of their own vineyards, plus one more rented at Verduno. The classic range includes Dolcetto, Nebbiolo, Barbera and the whites of Langa, not to mention Barolo from the Monvigliero cru, in a vineyard around 45 years old. There is also a coastal offshoot under the Brangero brand and the La Ginestraia winery at Cervo, which has now earned an entry of its own in the pages dedicated to Liguria. The Barolo Monvigliero 2009 displays all of its fragrant youth in its aromas of red berry fruit, gentian, tobacco and quina, and full-bodied palate supported by assertive tannins. The typical Nebbiolo Bricco Bertone 2010 has fresh, fruity notes and a smooth, agreeable palate.

● Barolo Monvigliero '09	♟♟ 6
● Dolcetto di Diano d'Alba Sörì Rabino Soprano '12	♟♟ 2*
● Langhe TreMarzo '10	♟♟ 4
● Nebbiolo d'Alba Bricco Bertone '10	♟♟ 4
○ Langhe Chardonnay Vignacento '12	♟ 3
● Dolcetto di Diano d'Alba Sörì Rabino Soprano '11	♟♟ 2*
● Dolcetto di Diano d'Alba Sörì Rabino Soprano '10	♟♟ 2*
○ Langhe Chardonnay Vignacento '11	♟♟ 3
● Langhe Nebbiolo '10	♟♟ 3
● Langhe TreMarzo '07	♟♟ 3
● Nebbiolo d'Alba Bricco Bertone '09	♟♟ 3
○ Riviera Ligure di Ponente Pigato Via Maestra '11	♟♟ 3
● Riviera Ligure di Ponente Rossese Tramontana '11	♟♟ 3

Brema

VIA POZZOMAGNA, 9
14045 INCISA SCAPACCINO [AT]
TEL. 014174019
vinibrema@inwind.it

CELLAR SALES
PRE-BOOKED VISITS
ANNUAL PRODUCTION 150,000 bottles
HECTARES UNDER VINE 25.00

One of the area's historic estates, Brema
was among the first to bottle in these zones
when most growers made their living by
selling unbottled wine. The family continues
to promote the classic Asti cultivars, with
barbera in pride of place. The estate's
vineyards are scattered across the four
municipalities of Costigliole d'Asti,
Castelnuovo Calcea, Mango and Trezzo
Tinella, and are also home to dolcetto,
grignolino, brachetto, moscato and
cabernet sauvignon. The wines on offer
focus on the richness of the fruit and run
the gamut from the basic versions that are
more approachable and pleasing, to the
prestigious bottles that are more complex
and very typical. This year the Barbera
d'Asti Ai Cruss 2011 reaches the finals
thanks to its notes of tobacco and quina
with hints of damson, nice, full acidity and
long, tangy finish. The Barbera d'Asti
Superiore Volpettona 2011 is a bit under
par, with spicy tones and a toastiness that
tends to overwhelm the fruit. The Moscato
d'Asti Mariasole 2012 is pleasant.

● Barbera d'Asti Ai Cruss '11	♟♟ 2*
● Barbera d'Asti Sup. Volpettona '11	♟♟ 5
○ Moscato d'Asti Mariasole '12	♟♟ 2*
● Dolcetto d'Asti Montera '11	♟ 2
○ Gavi Gavise '12	♟ 2
● Barbera d'Asti Sup. Nizza A Luigi Veronelli '06	♟♟♟ 6
● Barbera d'Asti Ai Cruss '10	♟♟ 2*
● Barbera d'Asti Ai Cruss '09	♟♟ 2
● Barbera d'Asti Sup. Bricco della Volpettona '09	♟♟ 5
● Barbera d'Asti Sup. Nizza A Luigi Veronelli '09	♟♟ 6
● Barbera d'Asti Sup. Volpettona '10	♟♟ 5
● Grignolino d'Asti Bricleroche '11	♟♟ 3*
● M.to Rosso Il Fulvo '09	♟♟ 3

Giacomo Brezza & Figli

VIA LOMONDO, 4
12060 BAROLO [CN]
TEL. 0173560921
www.brezza.it

CELLAR SALES
PRE-BOOKED VISITS
ACCOMMODATION AND RESTAURANT SERVICE
ANNUAL PRODUCTION 80,000 bottles
HECTARES UNDER VINE 16.50
VITICULTURE METHOD Certified Organic

You can't really claim to know Langhe and
nebbiolo unless you have spent a few hours
at the Brezza family's inn and cellar. Here
you will be treated to the wonderful affability
and hospitality of Signor Oreste and can pay
tribute to the work of his son, Enzo, whose
Cannubi, Sarmassa and above all Bricco
Sarmassa Barolos are truly exemplary in
their classic style. With each harvest, they
simply become more complete and
imposing. These are wines that welcome
decades of ageing yet know how to appeal
with amazing consistency to the more
impatient among us as soon as they are
released. As is often the case with this
estate, it is the excellent Sarmassa cru that
offers the best results across this range.
The Barolo Sarmassa 2009 displays
complex notes of quina, ripe raspberries
and spice buttressed by tannins and an
acid vein that lends freshness and
personality. The Bricco Sarmassa 2009 is
still rather closed but promises very well.
The elegant Cannubi 2009 needs time in
the bottle to develop fully.

● Barolo Bricco Sarmassa '09	♟♟♟ 7
● Barolo Sarmassa '09	♟♟ 6
● Barbera d'Alba Sup. '11	♟♟ 4
● Barolo Cannubi '09	♟♟ 6
● Barbera d'Alba Santa Rosalia '12	♟ 3
● Dolcetto d'Alba '12	♟ 2
● Langhe Nebbiolo '12	♟ 3
● Nebbiolo d'Alba Santa Rosalia '11	♟ 3
● Barolo Bricco Sarmassa '08	♟♟♟ 7
● Barolo Bricco Sarmassa '07	♟♟♟ 7
● Barolo Cannubi '01	♟♟♟ 6
● Barolo Cannubi '96	♟♟♟ 6
● Barolo Sarmassa '05	♟♟♟ 6
● Barolo Sarmassa '04	♟♟♟ 6
● Barolo Sarmassa '03	♟♟♟ 6
● Barolo Cannubi '08	♟♟ 6

Bric Cenciurio

VIA ROMA, 24
12060 BAROLO [CN]
TEL. 017356317
www.briccenciurio.com

CELLAR SALES
PRE-BOOKED VISITS
ANNUAL PRODUCTION 45,000 bottles
HECTARES UNDER VINE 15.00

Bric Cenciurio is a very young estate among Barolo producers. In 1994 Franco Pittatore, oenologist at Marchesi di Barolo, decided to purchase vineyards in both Roero and Langhe, specifically in Castellinaldo and Barolo. Today the estate is run by his brother-in-law Carlo Sacchetto, his sister Fiorella and their sons Alessandro and Alberto. The style of the wines is undisputedly classic, and follows well-defined traditional lines, also due to ageing in large Slavonian oak casks. Barolo Costa di Rose is without a doubt the most representative wine of the range. Liquorice, tobacco and red berry fruit comprise the sensory profile of the excellent Barolo Monrobiolo di Bussia 2009, our pick of this range. The basic Barolo is already very evolved, while the Costa di Rose 2009 is still in a rather closed phase. The Langhe Nebbiolo 2010 is very interesting, fresh and agreeably drinkable.

● Barolo Monrobiolo di Bussia '09	♟♟ 5
● Barbera d'Alba Sup. Naunda '10	♟♟ 4
● Barolo '09	♟♟ 5
● Barolo Costa di Rose '09	♟♟ 6
● Langhe Nebbiolo '10	♟♟ 4
○ Roero Arneis '12	♟ 2
○ Roero Arneis Sito dei Fossili '11	♟ 3
● Barbera d'Alba Naunda '07	♟♟ 4
● Barbera d'Alba Sup. '10	♟♟ 2*
● Barolo Costa di Rose '08	♟♟ 6
● Barolo Costa di Rose '04	♟♟ 6
● Barolo Costa di Rose '02	♟♟ 6
● Barolo Costa di Rose '01	♟♟ 8*
○ Roero Arneis Sito dei Fossili '10	♟♟ 3
○ Roero Arneis Sito dei Fossili '08	♟♟ 3*
○ Roero Arneis Sito dei Fossili '07	♟♟ 3*

Bricco del Cucù

LOC. BRICCO, 10
12060 BASTIA MONDOVÌ [CN]
TEL. 017460153
www.briccocucu.com

CELLAR SALES
PRE-BOOKED VISITS
ANNUAL PRODUCTION 50,000 bottles
HECTARES UNDER VINE 10.00

The introduction of the DOCG and the expansion of the Dogliani production zone to absorb Dolcetto delle Langhe Monregalesi have given greater visibility to this scenic little-known corner of Langhe. Dario Sciolla's small winery is one of the area's many old-style estates that grow grapes and hazelnuts. Around Bastìa, the altitude and day-night temperature differentials give the wines character and originality. While Dolcetto is the mainstay, the range also includes other wines well worth discovering, all offering excellent value for the money. The Dogliani Bricco San Bernardo 2010 fails to repeat the performance of the 2009 vintage, but still achieves a fine level of quality. The nose is very complex, offering notes of ripe plum, black cherry and leather; the palate is fruity and leisurely. The Dogliani 2012 is very drinkable with dynamic freshness.

● Dogliani Sup. Bricco S. Bernardo '10	♟♟ 2*
● Dogliani '12	♟♟ 2*
○ Langhe Bianco Livor '12	♟♟ 2*
● Langhe Dolcetto '12	♟♟ 2*
● Langhe Rosso Diavolisanti '10	♟♟ 2*
● Dogliani Sup. Bricco S. Bernardo '09	♟♟♟ 2*
● Dogliani '11	♟♟ 2*
● Dolcetto di Dogliani '10	♟♟ 2*
● Dolcetto di Dogliani '05	♟♟ 2*
● Dolcetto di Dogliani Sup. Bricco S. Bernardo '01	♟♟ 3
○ Langhe Bianco Livor '11	♟♟ 2*
○ Langhe Bianco Livor '10	♟♟ 2*
● Langhe Rosso Superboum '09	♟♟ 2*

Bricco Maiolica

FRAZ. RICCA
VIA BOLANGINO, 7
12055 DIANO D'ALBA [CN]
TEL. 0173612049
www.briccomaiolica.it

CELLAR SALES
PRE-BOOKED VISITS
ANNUAL PRODUCTION 100,000 bottles
HECTARES UNDER VINE 21.00

Beppe Accomo's solid winery in this scenic corner of Langhe has deep roots, for it was founded in 1928. The subsequent generations gradually put together a first-rate estate, capable of supplying excellent fruit which forms the basis for top-quality wines. The range is very comprehensive, including both the typical local cultivars and several interesting versions of international varietals. Character and personality are skilfully integrated with the classic style of the different wines. The Nebbiolo d'Alba Cumot 2010 impresses with its clear aromatic thrust, presenting notes of red berry fruit, quina, tobacco and balsamic nuances. The palate is lively, tangy and fresh. A well-deserved Tre Bicchieri. The Barbera Vigna Vigia 2010 is juicy and complex, fruity in its aromas and supported by a marked acid vein.

Bricco Mondalino

REG. MONDALINO, 5
15049 VIGNALE MONFERRATO [AL]
TEL. 0142933204
www.briccomondalino.it

CELLAR SALES
PRE-BOOKED VISITS
ANNUAL PRODUCTION 80,000 bottles
HECTARES UNDER VINE 13.00

This winery at Vignale Monferrato was established in 1973, but only in the sense that this was when it started to bottle and sell its wines directly. Previously, the wine came onto the market through negociants or was sold unbottled. Production concentrates on native Piedmont varieties, of which the Gaudio family's extensive experience makes them excellent interpreters. The basic Grignolino is in fine form with its flowery, spicy aromas, and represents one of the best interpretations of this Monferrato classic. The Malvasia di Casorzo Dolce Stil Novo offers captivating, varietal characteristics. This sweet wine manages to balance the sugars with a good dose of acidity and a tannic note in the finish that takes you pleasantly by surprise.

● Nebbiolo d'Alba Cumot '10	♟♟♟ 4*
● Barbera d'Alba Sup. V. Vigia '10	♟♟ 4
○ Langhe Bianco Pensiero Infinito '09	♟♟ 6
● Diano d'Alba Sup. Sörì Bricco Maiolica '11	♟♟ 3
○ Langhe Bianco Rolando '11	♟♟ 3
● Langhe Merlot Filius '10	♟♟ 5
● Langhe Pinot Nero Perlei '10	♟♟ 5
● Langhe Rosso Tris '11	♟♟ 2*
● Barbera d'Alba '11	♟ 2
● Dolcetto di Diano d'Alba '12	♟ 2
● Langhe Nebbiolo '11	♟ 2
○ Langhe Sauvignon Casa Castella '12	♟ 2
● Diano d'Alba Sup. Sörì Bricco Maiolica '07	♟♟♟ 3*
● Nebbiolo d'Alba Cumot '09	♟♟♟ 4*

● Grignolino del M.to Casalese '12	♟♟ 2*
● Malvasia di Casorzo Dolce Stil Novo '12	♟♟ 2*
● Barbera del M.to Sup. '11	♟ 2
○ M.to Casalese Cortese L'Amor Cortese '12	♟ 2
⊙ M.to Ciarèt Zerolegno Rosé '12	♟ 2
● Barbera d'Asti Il Bergantino '07	♟♟ 3
● Barbera del M.to Sup. '09	♟♟ 2
● Barbera del M.to Zerolegno '09	♟♟ 2*
● Barbera del M.to Zerolegno '08	♟♟ 2
● Grignolino del M.to Casalese Bricco Mondalino '11	♟♟ 2*
● Grignolino del M.to Casalese Bricco Mondalino '10	♟♟ 2
● Grignolino del M.to Casalese Bricco Mondalino '09	♟♟ 2

Francesco Brigatti

VIA OLMI, 31
28019 SUNO [NO]
TEL. 032285037
www.vinibrigatti.it

CELLAR SALES
PRE-BOOKED VISITS
ANNUAL PRODUCTION 20,000 bottles
HECTARES UNDER VINE 6.50

Owner, oenologist and agronomist of the
estate that carries his name, Francesco
Brigatti is without doubt a rising star in the
district of Novara. He has always surprised
and intrigued us with his compact and
distinctive range of wines that are almost
unique in their ability to combine a deeply
rooted understanding of the territory with
forward-looking stylistic originality. The
estate's five hectares, plus one it rents, are
situated in the Colline Novaresi area.
Nebbiolo accounts for the lion's share, but
uva rara, vespolina, barbera and erbaluce
are also grown. The wines are aged in
casks of varying sizes but they all display
the same austere and agreeable traits. Still
a bit rugged and in thrall to their
oak-conditioning, the two house champions,
the 2010 Möt Ziflon and Mötfrei Nebbiolos
are deemed too young for release. Thus the
simpler wines step into the breach. The
Barbera Campazzi 2012 is fruity and
embracing, the Vespolina 2012, peppery
and acidulous. This year's protagonist is the
new balanced and measured Ghemme Oltre
il Bosco 2009.

● Colline Novaresi Barbera Campazzi '12	♥♥ 3
● Colline Novaresi Vespolina '12	♥♥ 2*
○ Ghemme Oltre il Bosco '09	♥♥ 4
○ Colline Novaresi Bianco V. Mottobello '12	♥ 2
● Colline Novaresi Nebbiolo MötZiflon '10	♥ 3
● Colline Novaresi Nebbiolo Mötfrei '10	♥ 3
● Colline Novaresi Uva Rara '12	♥ 2
○ Costabella Passito	♥ 5
● Colline Novaresi Nebbiolo Möt Ziflon '09	♀♀ 3
● Colline Novaresi Nebbiolo Möt Ziflon '08	♀♀ 3*
● Colline Novaresi Nebbiolo V. Mötfrei '09	♀♀ 3*
● Colline Novaresi Uva Rara '11	♀♀ 2*
● Colline Novaresi Vespolina '11	♀♀ 2*

Vitivinicola Broglia

LOC. LOMELLINA, 22
15066 GAVI [AL]
TEL. 0143642998
www.broglia.it

CELLAR SALES
PRE-BOOKED VISITS
HECTARES UNDER VINE 64.50

Founded by Bruno Broglia and now run by
his sons Gian Piero and Paolo, Tenuta La
Meirana is one of the most renowned
estates in the Gavi production zone. It
covers an area of approximately 100
hectares, mostly planted to cortese, which
is fermented exclusively in steel and forms
the basis for four different wines. Il Doge
and La Meirana are released a few months
after the harvest and are marked by a
stylish, racy style, while the Bruno Broglia
selection, which undergoes long ageing on
the lees, generally requires more time. The
range is completed by white and rosé
versions of the Charmat-method Roverello
Spumante, and the red Le Pernici, from
dolcetto and barbera. In the last few
editions of the Guide we have noted a
steady increase in the number of labels,
but the jewel in this estate's crown remains
the Bruno Broglia, an already harmonious
white with enormous cellaring potential. By
contrast, the heir apparent, the Gavi il
Doge, displays the fresh mineral character
of the territory.

○ Gavi del Comune di Gavi Bruno Broglia '11	♥♥ 5
○ Gavi Il Doge '12	♥♥ 2*
● M.to Rosso Le Pernici '11	♥♥ 2*
⊙ Roverello Brut Rosé	♥♥ 3
○ Brut M. Cl. Broglia	♥ 5
○ Gavi del Comune di Gavi La Meirana '12	♥ 3
○ Gavi del Comune di Gavi Spumante Roverello '11	♥ 3
○ Gavi del Comune di Gavi Villa Broglia '12	♥ 3
○ Gavi del Comune di Gavi Bruno Broglia '08	♀♀♀ 5
○ Gavi del Comune di Gavi Bruno Broglia '07	♀♀♀ 5
○ Gavi del Comune di Gavi Bruno Broglia '10	♀♀ 5
○ Gavi del Comune di Gavi Bruno Broglia '06	♀♀ 4

Brovia

via Alba-Barolo, 54
12060 Castiglione Falletto [CN]
Tel. 017362852
www.brovia.net

CELLAR SALES
PRE-BOOKED VISITS
ANNUAL PRODUCTION 60,000 bottles
HECTARES UNDER VINE 16.00
VITICULTURE METHOD Certified Organic

Brovia's wines have earned a permanent place on Langhe's Mount Olympus, above all for their unique and distinctive style. Today this historic estate is run by sisters Cristina and Elena with Alejandro Sanchez Solana. Its approximately 18 hectares are largely composed of vineyards like Villero, Rocche, Garblèt Sué in Castiglione Falletto and Cà Mia in Serralunga. These legendary crus are light and harmonious, undergoing fermentation in cement vats for 15-20 days and ageing in large barrels for around three years. The Barolos are peerless and esteemed by those who seek aromatic purity and don't mind forgoing a little structure and body. The Barolo Ca' Mia 2009 is distinctive for its dark notes of tobacco, liquorice and tar, and explosive yet non-invasive tannic texture. It wins our highest accolade to crown an overall performance of absolute excellence. The Barolo Villero 2009 is still rather reserved but promises great longevity. In this phase the Barolo Rocche 2009 is more expressive, showing power and fresh drinkability.

● Barolo Ca' Mia '09	♟♟♟ 8
● Barolo Garblèt Sué '09	♟♟ 7
● Barolo Rocche dei Brovia '09	♟♟ 8
● Barolo Villero '09	♟♟ 8
● Barolo Brovia '09	♟♟ 6
● Barolo Ca' Mia '00	♟♟♟ 8
● Barolo Ca' Mia '96	♟♟♟ 8
● Barolo Monprivato '90	♟♟♟ 8
● Barolo Rocche dei Brovia '06	♟♟♟ 7
● Barolo Villero '08	♟♟♟ 7
● Barolo Villero '06	♟♟♟ 7
● Barolo Ca' Mia '08	♟♟ 7
● Barolo Garblèt Sué '06	♟♟ 7
● Barolo Rocche dei Brovia '08	♟♟ 7
● Barolo Rocche dei Brovia '07	♟♟ 7
● Barolo Villero '05	♟♟ 7

Renato Buganza

loc. Cascina Garbinotto, 4
12040 Piobesi d'Alba [CN]
Tel. 0173619370
www.renatobuganza.it

CELLAR SALES
PRE-BOOKED VISITS
HECTARES UNDER VINE 10.00

Renato Buganza set up shop in Cascina Garbianotto on the hills of Piobesi d'Alba in 1978, and in 1996 purchased Cascina Gerbole, with a further five hectares under vine on grey marl soils, in crus such as Bric Paradiso. The varieties are those typical of tradition: barbera, dolcetto and nebbiolo for the reds, with vines aged between 40 and 50 years old, and arneis and some chardonnay for the whites. Since 2003, the winery has been a member of the Critical Wine movement. Buganza may lack a flagship bottle but the overall performance of its range is very solid. The Roero Riserva 2010 is a bit oak-dominated but has character and nice full flavour, with notes of spice, black berry fruit and roots. The full and complex Roero Arneis dla Trifula 2012 runs a gamut of aromas from wood resin to appley fruit; the Barolo 2009 is fruity and dynamic. The other labels are well made and agreeable.

● Barbera d'Alba Vija '10	♟♟ 5
● Barolo '09	♟♟ 6
● Langhe Rosso '09	♟♟ 3
○ Roero Arneis dla Trifula '12	♟♟ 3
○ Roero Ris. '10	♟♟ 3
● Barbera d'Alba Gerbole '09	♟ 5
● Barolo '07	♟ 6
○ Claudette Brut M. Cl.	♟ 3
● Nebbiolo d'Alba Gerbole '07	♟ 4
○ Roero Arneis dla Trifula '10	♟ 3
● Roero Bric Paradis '08	♟ 5

G. B. Burlotto

via Vittorio Emanuele, 28
12060 Verduno [CN]
Tel. 0172470122
www.burlotto.com

CELLAR SALES
PRE-BOOKED VISITS
ACCOMMODATION
ANNUAL PRODUCTION 60,000 bottles
HECTARES UNDER VINE 15.00

The estate owned by Marina Burlotto and Giuseppe Alessandria is charming and full of inspiration. Together wlth their son Fabio, they have given a new lease of life to the brand name established in the late 1800s by Commendatore Giovanni Battista. The original small property now comprises around 12 hectares, mostly dedicated to the cultivation of nebbiolo (Monvigliero, Neirane, Breri, Rocche dell'Olmo in Verduno, Cannubi in Barolo). The style is proudly traditional with ageing in barrels from 35 to 50 hectolitres. The crus vie for the title of flagship with the unique and highly distinctive Pelaverga. The wines obtained from barbera, dolcetto, sauvignon and freisa are also worthy of note. We were impressed by the wines we tasted. The Barolo Acclivi 2009 reveals faint balsamic nuances with undertones of forest floor and spice, assertive tannins and fresh acidity. The Barolo 2009 beguiles with its wonderful drinkability. The elegant Barolo Cannubi 2009 shows smooth, non-invasive tannins. A special mention goes to the excellent Sauvignons.

● Barolo '09	🍷🍷 6
● Barolo Acclivi '09	🍷🍷 6
○ Langhe Sauvignon Dives '11	🍷🍷 3*
● Barbera d'Alba Aves '11	🍷🍷 4
● Barolo Vign. Cannubi '09	🍷🍷 7
● Barolo Vign. Monvigliero '09	🍷🍷 7
● Langhe Freisa '11	🍷🍷 4
● Langhe Nebbiolo '11	🍷🍷 3
○ Langhe Sauvignon Viridis '12	🍷🍷 3
● Verduno Pelaverga '12	🍷🍷 3
● Barolo Acclivi '07	🍷🍷🍷 6
● Barolo Acclivi '08	🍷🍷 6
● Barolo Vign. Monvigliero '08	🍷🍷 6
○ Langhe Bianco Dives '09	🍷🍷 3*
○ Langhe Sauvignon Dives '10	🍷🍷 3*

★Piero Busso

via Albesani, 8
12052 Neive [CN]
Tel. 017367156
www.bussopiero.com

CELLAR SALES
PRE-BOOKED VISITS
ANNUAL PRODUCTION 45,000 bottles
HECTARES UNDER VINE 10.00

Great vineyards – just think of the estate's Barbaresco crus – and solid family management are the best way to sum up the winery owned by Piero Busso, who continues his steady rise towards the loftiest heights of Barbaresco with his wife Lucia and children Emanuela and Pierguido. Well known in Italy and abroad, their rigorous work is translated into a very reliable range of wines with a strong, unmistakable personality. The wines, matured in small and medium-sized barrels, are fairly enjoyable even while young, but express their full potential following appropriate ageing. The Barbaresco Gallina 2009 romps home with a Tre Bicchieri for a flawless performance. Its exceptional aromatic definition features notes of eucalyptus and sweet liquorice; smooth tannins and fresh acidity complete the impeccable palate. The Barbaresco Mondino and San Stunet 2010 are young as yet but have lots of personality and promise well.

● Barbaresco Gallina '09	🍷🍷🍷 8
● Barbaresco Mondino '10	🍷🍷 5
● Barbaresco S. Stunet S. Stefanetto '10	🍷🍷 7
● Barbaresco Albesani Borgese '10	🍷🍷 6
● Barbera d'Alba Majano '11	🍷🍷 3
● Dolcetto d'Alba V. Majano '12	🍷🍷 3
● Langhe Nebbiolo '11	🍷🍷 4
● Barbaresco Borgese '09	🍷🍷🍷 6
● Barbaresco Borgese '08	🍷🍷🍷 6
● Barbaresco Gallina '05	🍷🍷🍷 7
● Barbaresco S. Stefanetto '07	🍷🍷🍷 7
● Barbaresco S. Stefanetto '04	🍷🍷🍷 7
● Barbaresco S. Stefanetto '03	🍷🍷🍷 7
● Barbaresco S. Stefanetto '01	🍷🍷🍷 7
● Barbaresco S. Stefanetto '00	🍷🍷🍷 7

Ca' Bianca

REG. SPAGNA, 58
15010 ALICE BEL COLLE [AL]
TEL. 0144745420
www.cantinacabianca.it

CELLAR SALES
PRE-BOOKED VISITS
ANNUAL PRODUCTION 650,000 bottles
HECTARES UNDER VINE 39.00

A few kilometres from Alessandria, on a hillside site of great charm, we find Ca' Bianca, a winery that has been in business since 1954, and which skilfully manages various native Piedmont varieties. Their grapes of dolcetto, barbera, cortese and arneis are transformed in a cellar installed with the latest equipment, and the result is a range of stylish, elegant, long-lived wines. The winery, owned by Gruppo Italiano Vini, is currently run by Pierluigi Borgna, director and oenologist, assisted by Davide Mascalzoni on the commercial side. The wines on offer derive exclusively from Piedmont varieties and are balanced and interesting quality-wise. We loved the 2012 version of the Dolcetto d'Acqui for its refined fruity nose and powerful, harmonious palate. There are two 2011 Barbera d'Astis: the Chersì has personality, black berry fruit aromas and a very long finish; the Antè presents cherry and blackberry notes and a concentrated, balanced palate.

Ca' d'Gal

FRAZ. VALDIVILLA
S.DA VECCHIA DI VALDIVILLA, 1
12058 SANTO STEFANO BELBO [CN]
TEL. 0141847103
www.cadgal.it

CELLAR SALES
PRE-BOOKED VISITS
ACCOMMODATION AND RESTAURANT SERVICE
ANNUAL PRODUCTION 15,000 bottles
HECTARES UNDER VINE 12.00

Alessandro Boido's winery celebrates its 150th birthday this year, and this alone gives a clear idea of its crucial role in the world of Moscato. Almost all of his vineyard holdings are dedicated to moscato, and lie in a single plot around the winery on soils ranging from sandy to clay and limestone. The Moscatos proposed display great complexity, and contrary to popular belief, are long-lived, as shown by the aged version of the Vigna Vecchia selection, released after five years in the bottle. This year sees two quality Moscato d'Asti Vigna Vecchias. The 2007 offers very elegant notes of sage and candied fruit, and a full yet very refined, harmonious palate with a long refreshing finish. The flowery 2012 has sweeter tones recalling candied orange peel and honey. The attractive, lingering Moscato d'Asti Lumine 2012 and the fresh, citrussy Asti 2012 are both very good.

● Barbera d'Asti Sup. Antè '11	♟♟ 3
● Barbera d'Asti Sup. Chersì '11	♟♟ 5
● Dolcetto d'Acqui '12	♟♟ 3
○ Gavi '12	♟♟ 3
● Barbera d'Asti Teis '12	♟ 3
○ Roero Arneis '12	♟ 3
● Barbera d'Asti Sup. Antè '10	♟♟ 3
● Barbera d'Asti Sup. Chersì '10	♟♟ 5
● Barbera d'Asti Sup. Chersì '08	♟♟ 4
● Barbera d'Asti Sup. Chersì '07	♟♟ 4
● Barbera d'Asti Teis '11	♟♟ 3
○ Gavi '11	♟♟ 3

○ Moscato d'Asti V. V. '12	♟♟ 4
○ Moscato d'Asti V. V. '07	♟♟ 3*
○ Asti '12	♟♟ 2*
○ Moscato d'Asti Lumine '12	♟♟ 3
● Barbera d'Asti Cassinasco '11	♟ 3
○ Moscato d'Asti V. V. '11	♟♟♟ 3*
○ Asti '11	♟♟ 2*
○ Asti '09	♟♟ 2*
○ Asti Dolce '10	♟♟ 2*
○ Moscato d'Asti Lumine '11	♟♟ 3
○ Moscato d'Asti Lumine '09	♟♟ 3*
○ Moscato d'Asti Lumine '08	♟♟ 3
○ Moscato d'Asti V. V. '09	♟♟ 3

Ca' del Baio

VIA FERRERE, 33
12050 TREISO [CN]
TEL. 0173638219
www.cadelbaio.com

CELLAR SALES
PRE-BOOKED VISITS
ANNUAL PRODUCTION 100,000 bottles
HECTARES UNDER VINE 25.00

In terms of quality and consistency, few
estates can boast an array of Barbarescos
to rival that of Ca' del Baio, the historic
Langhe brand run by Giulio Grasso, his wife
Luciana and daughters Paola, Valentina and
Federica. Their crus, Valgrande and
Marcarini in the municipality of Treiso, Asili
and Pora in Barbaresco, wed a modern form
with classic substance. They are aged in a
mix of barriques, some new, 900-litre vats
and medium-sized barrels. The wines are
powerful, rich in fruit and spice, and tend to
require cellaring to achieve their full
eloquent harmony. We dedicate the latest in
a long line of great wines from this producer
to Federica, the last of three daughters to
join the estate full-time. The vivid, intense
Barbaresco Asili 2010 offers a fascinating
mélange of balsamic, spicy and liquorice
notes. The Pora 2009 has solid, elegant
character. The Valgrande 2010 rounds
off this truly excellent range of
Barbarescos. A special mention for the
debutant Riesling 2011.

● Barbaresco Asili '10	♥♥♥	6
● Barbaresco Pora '09	♥♥	6
● Barbaresco Valgrande '10	♥♥	5
● Dolcetto d'Alba Lodoli '12	♥♥	2*
● Langhe Nebbiolo Bric del Baio '11	♥♥	3
○ Langhe Riesling '11	♥♥	3
○ Moscato d'Asti 101 '12	♥♥	2*
● Langhe Nebbiolo '12	♥	2
● Barbaresco Asili '09	♀♀♀	5
● Barbaresco Asili '06	♀♀♀	5
● Barbaresco Pora '06	♀♀♀	6
● Barbaresco Pora '04	♀♀♀	6
● Barbaresco Valgrande '08	♀♀♀	5
● Barbaresco Valgrande '04	♀♀♀	5
● Barbaresco Valgrande '99	♀♀♀	5
● Barbaresco Valgrande '09	♀♀	5

Ca' Nova

VIA SAN ISIDORO, 1
28010 BOGOGNO [NO]
TEL. 0322863406
www.cascinacanova.it

CELLAR SALES
PRE-BOOKED VISITS
ACCOMMODATION
ANNUAL PRODUCTION 40,000 bottles
HECTARES UNDER VINE 10.00

This year sees the début in the main
section of the Guide for Giada Codecasa's
winery, established at Bogogno in 1996.
After leaving her job as a lawyer, Giada
threw her energies into the soils of the
morainic hills between Sesia and Ticino.
Her ten hectares under vine are situated
between Bogogno and Romagnano, and
planted mainly to nebbiolo, a variety that in
the Novara area displays elegance, balance
and pleasurable drinkability already in the
first years after bottling. The range includes
the various types of the Colline Novaresi, as
well as two metodo classico sparklers from
erbaluce grapes. The Ghemme 2007 offers
concentrated, elegant notes of tobacco and
gentian against a lovely backdrop of freshly
ground pepper. The full palate shows
tight-knit tannic texture, juicy and very very
long. The refined, complex Nebbiolo
Melchiòr 2007 has perfect acid support. A
special mention goes to the Extra Brut
Rosé, creamy in its yeasty notes and gutsy
in the finish.

● Ghemme '07	♥♥	4
● Colline Novaresi Nebbiolo Melchiòr '07	♥♥	3
⊙ Extra Brut M. Cl. Jad'Or	♥♥	3
⊙ Extra Brut Rosé M. Cl. Jad'Or	♥♥	4
⊙ Colline Novaresi Bianco Rugiada '12	♥	2
⊙ Colline Novaresi Nebbiolo Aurora '12	♥	2
● Colline Novaresi Nebbiolo Bocciòlo '07	♀♀	2
● Colline Novaresi Nebbiolo Melchiòr '05	♀♀	3
● Colline Novaresi Nebbiolo V. San Quirico '06	♀♀	4
● Colline Novaresi Nebbiolo V. San Quirico '05	♀♀	4
● Colline Novaresi Nebbiolo Bocciòlo '10	♀♀	2*
● Ghemme '06	♀♀	4
● Ghemme '05	♀♀	4

Ca' Rome'
Romano Marengo

S.DA RABAJÀ, 86/88
12050 BARBARESCO [CN]
TEL. 0173635126
www.carome.com

CELLAR SALES
PRE-BOOKED VISITS
ANNUAL PRODUCTION 30,000 bottles
HECTARES UNDER VINE 5.00

The presence of two crus of the calibre of Cerretta in Serralunga d'Alba and Rio Sordo in Barbaresco undoubtedly puts this estate among the ranks of the top producers. Barolo and Barbaresco are thus the flagship wines of this small but important winery. Romano Marengo favours a classic austere personality for his wines, to give them a traditional style that is not influenced by passing fashions or trends. In the cellar he draws on the precious aid of his children Giuseppe and Paola, engaged in the various tasks of running the estate. The choice to focus solely on nebbiolo grapes, with a small concession to barbera, is another interesting peculiarity. Of the many versions of the nebbiolo variety, we were particularly impressed by the Barolo Vigna Cerretta 2009. Its magnificent expressive power and superb taste balance win it our top prize. The Barolo Rapet 2009 and Barbaresco Rio Sordo 2010 are also extremely well made.

★Ca' Viola

B.TA SAN LUIGI, 11
12063 DOGLIANI [CN]
TEL. 017370547
www.caviola.com

CELLAR SALES
PRE-BOOKED VISITS
ACCOMMODATION AND RESTAURANT SERVICE
ANNUAL PRODUCTION 60,000 bottles
HECTARES UNDER VINE 10.00

The charming French-style villa that houses Cà Viola faithfully reflects the elegant, austere manner of its owner. Beppe Caviola is one of Italy's leading Italian oenologists and also runs this small but important Langhe estate. Its vineyards, with many old vines, are meticulously tended and the wines that they yield closely reflect the differences of the various terroirs and types. Several years ago nebbiolo was added alongside the mainstay varieties of dolcetto and barbera. The first-rate product range is topped by Barolo. From this year, the Dolcetto Barturot will age for an extra year, so we won't taste it until 2014. The Barolo Sottocastello di Novello 2008 is deep and complex, spunky and refined, a real cornucopia of sensory sensations that deserve a Tre Bicchieri. The Nebbiolo 2011 is very well made, typical, vibrant and rich.

● Barolo V. Cerretta '09	▼▼▼ 7
● Barbaresco Sorì Rio Sordo '10	▼▼ 6
● Barolo Rapet '09	▼▼ 7
● Barbaresco Chiaramanti '10	▼▼ 6
● Barbaresco Chiaramanti Ris. '08	▼▼ 6
● Barbaresco Maria di Brun '09	▼▼ 7
● Barolo Rapet '08	♀♀♀ 7
● Barbaresco Chiaramanti '09	♀♀ 6
● Barbaresco Chiaramanti '07	♀♀ 6
● Barbaresco Maria di Brun '08	♀♀ 7
● Barbaresco Maria di Brun '06	♀♀ 7
● Barbaresco Sorì Rio Sordo '08	♀♀ 6
● Barbaresco Sorì Rio Sordo '06	♀♀ 6
● Barolo Rapet '07	♀♀ 7
● Barolo V. Cerretta '06	♀♀ 7

● Barolo Sottocastello di Novello '08	▼▼▼ 7
● Barbera d'Alba Bric du Luv '11	▼▼ 5
● Langhe Nebbiolo '11	▼▼ 5
● Barbera d'Alba Brichet '11	▼ 4
○ Dolcetto d'Alba Vilot '12	▼▼ 3
● Barbera d'Alba Bric du Luv '10	♀♀♀ 5
● Barbera d'Alba Bric du Luv '07	♀♀♀ 5
● Barolo Sottocastello '06	♀♀♀ 7
○ Dolcetto d'Alba Barturot '07	♀♀♀ 3
○ Dolcetto d'Alba Barturot '05	♀♀♀ 3
● Langhe Nebbiolo '08	♀♀♀ 5
● Langhe Rosso Bric du Luv '05	♀♀♀ 5
● Langhe Rosso Bric du Luv '03	♀♀♀ 5
● Langhe Rosso Bric du Luv '01	♀♀♀ 5
● Langhe Rosso Bric du Luv '99	♀♀♀ 5

Cantina del Glicine

VIA GIULIO CESARE, 1
12052 NEIVE [CN]
TEL. 017367215
www.cantinadelglicine.it

CELLAR SALES
PRE-BOOKED VISITS
ANNUAL PRODUCTION 40,000 bottles
HECTARES UNDER VINE 4.00

One glimpse of the underground cellar built in the 1600s from brick and stone is enough to convince that a visit to Adriana Marzi and Roberto Bruno, owners of Cantina del Glicine, is worthwhile. But it's not just the splendid cellar; the production is also worthy of note. The wines on offer are the traditional Langhe bottles, restrained and terroir-true, and all offering good value for money. The jewels in the crown are undoubtedly the two Barbarescos obtained from the Currà and Marcorino crus. La Sconsolata and La Dormiosa are the two Barbera d'Alba selections. A magnificent overall showing and a first Tre Bicchieri. The protagonist is the Barbaresco Currà 2010, displaying a perfect marriage of structure and elegance, silky tannins and a fresh, vibrant palate. The very well-made Barbaresco Marcorino 2010 offers balsamic nuances and notes of tobacco. A special mention for the Barbera La Sconsolata 2011, fruity and very easy-drinking.

● Barbaresco Currà '10	♔♔♔ 4*
● Barbaresco Marcorino '10	♔♔ 5
● Barbera d'Alba Sup. La Sconsolata '11	♔♔ 2*
● Barbera d'Alba Sup. La Dormiosa '10	♔♔ 3
● Dolcetto d'Alba Olmiolo '12	♔ 2
○ Moscato d'Asti Nettare di Stelle '12	♔ 2
○ Roero Arneis Il Mandolo '12	♔ 2
● Barbaresco Currà '09	♔♔ 4
● Barbaresco Currà '07	♔♔ 5
● Barbaresco Currà '06	♔♔ 5
● Barbaresco Marcorino '09	♔♔ 5
● Barbaresco Marcorino '05	♔♔ 5*
● Barbaresco Marcorino '04	♔♔ 5
● Barbera d'Alba La Sconsolata '10	♔♔ 2*
● Barbera d'Alba Sup. La Dormiosa '09	♔♔ 3*
● Barbera d'Alba Sup. La Dormiosa '08	♔♔ 3

Cantina del Nebbiolo

VIA TORINO, 17
12040 VEZZA D'ALBA [CN]
TEL. 017365040
www.cantinadelnebbiolo.com

CELLAR SALES
PRE-BOOKED VISITS
ANNUAL PRODUCTION 250,000 bottles
HECTARES UNDER VINE 260.00

This important cooperative winery, set up in 1901 as Cantina Sociale Parrocchiale di Vezza d'Alba and re-established with its current name in 1959, today has 175 grower-members with vineyards situated in eight different municipal districts in Roero and the Langhe. Alongside their main variety, nebbiolo, they also vinify barbera, bonarda, dolcetto, freisa, brachetto, arneis and favorita. The wide range of wines shows a traditional style, with priority given to drinkability and aromatic focus. This year the Cantina del Nebbiolo earns a well-deserved place in the main section of the Guide with a range of high-quality wines. The Barbaresco Meruzzano 2010 has lovely notes of quina, liquorice and raspberry, medium structure but a first-class palate, delicate tannins and a characterful finish. The elegant Barbaresco 2010 is nicely complex and juicy. The other labels are very well made, notably the pleasant Barbera d'Alba 2011 and the tangy Roero 2010.

● Barbaresco Meruzzano '10	♔♔ 4*
● Barbaresco '10	♔♔ 4
● Barbera d'Alba '11	♔♔ 2*
● Langhe La Pranda '11	♔♔ 2*
● Nebbiolo d'Alba '11	♔♔ 2*
● Roero '10	♔♔ 2*
● Barbera D'Alba Sup. '10	♔ 2
○ Roero Arneis '12	♔ 2
○ Roero Arneis Arenarium '12	♔ 2
● Barbera d'Alba '10	♔♔ 2*
● Nebbiolo d'Alba Valmaggiore '08	♔♔ 2*
● Roero '09	♔♔ 2*
● Roero '08	♔♔ 2
○ Roero Arneis '10	♔♔ 2

Cantina del Pino

S.DA OVELLO, 31
12050 BARBARESCO [CN]
TEL. 0173635147
www.cantinadelpino.com

ANNUAL PRODUCTION 35,000 bottles
HECTARES UNDER VINE 7.00

Renato Vacca is a great interpreter of Barbaresco, and shows a sensitivity towards nebbiolo that first became evident when he was a member of the Produttori di Barbaresco winery, before starting out on his own to develop some old plots, among the most celebrated in the zone, at Ovello and Albesani. The cellar is spacious and functional, and the production style relaxed and modern, with long macerations and the use of small barrels, resulting in fruit-driven wines, that manage to conserve at the same time the tannic structure typical of this territory. His is a clearly recognizable style which over time has become a benchmark. It is the Barbaresco 2010 that convinces us the most at this time, typical, balanced and eminently drinkable. The estate's two 2008 Barbaresco crus, the Albesani and Ovello, are less harmonious than previous versions with an exuberance that bottle-ageing will soon tame. The Barbera d'Alba 2011 is juicy with enjoyable fresh fruity notes.

● Barbaresco '10	♟♟ 5
● Barbaresco Albesani '08	♟♟ 6
● Barbaresco Ovello '08	♟♟ 6
● Barbera d'Alba '11	♟♟ 4
● Langhe Nebbiolo '11	♟♟ 3
● Barbaresco '04	♟♟♟ 5*
● Barbaresco '03	♟♟♟ 4*
● Barbaresco Albesani '05	♟♟♟ 6
● Barbaresco Ovello '07	♟♟♟ 5
● Barbaresco Ovello '99	♟♟♟ 5
● Barbaresco '09	♟♟ 5
● Barbaresco '07	♟♟ 5
● Barbaresco Albesani '07	♟♟ 6
● Barbaresco Ovello '09	♟♟ 6
● Barbaresco Ovello '06	♟♟ 6
● Barbera d'Alba '10	♟♟ 4

Cantine Briamara

VIA TRENTO, 1
10014 CALUSO [TO]
TEL. 3358108781
www.cantinebriamara.it

CELLAR SALES
ANNUAL PRODUCTION 16,000 bottles
HECTARES UNDER VINE 4.00

Cantine Briamara was set up in 2012, thanks to the expertise that the two partners, Massimiliano Bianco and Claudio Cavi, acquired when producing Erbaluce at the Le Baccanti winery. Today, the two partners farm four hectares under vine, entirely dedicated to erbaluce. Exploiting a well-equipped cellar, with the help of the skilled oenologist Luca Caramellino, Briamara has managed to earn a fine reputation among the ranks of local producers. A special mention should go to their Passito, a raisin wine produced according to traditional dictates, with slow drying of the grapes, hung in the drying room, and long ageing in small oak. The two Passitos bowled us over, in particular the extraordinary Riserva 2001 whose residual sugars and acidity have had the time to harmonize in their long sojourn in oak. Of note, too, the stylistic perfection achieved by the Berenice spumante.

○ Caluso Passito Ris. '01	♟♟ 5
○ Caluso Passito Pescarolo '07	♟♟ 4
○ Erbaluce di Caluso Biancamano '12	♟♟ 2*
○ Erbaluce di Caluso Spumante M. Cl. Berenice '10	♟♟ 3
○ Caluso Spumante Berenice '05	♟ 4
○ Erbaluce di Caluso San Cristoforo '10	♟ 2*

La Caplana

VIA CIRCONVALLAZIONE, 4
15060 BOSIO [AL]
TEL. 0143684182
lacaplana@email.it

CELLAR SALES
PRE-BOOKED VISITS
ANNUAL PRODUCTION 100,000 bottles
HECTARES UNDER VINE 5.00

A small family-run estate founded by Guido
Natalino in the 1990s, La Caplana is one of
the most original producers in the Gavi
production zone, also due to its unique
position, which in many respects lies well
off the beaten track. It is in Bosio, a village
in the province of Alessandria, on the
northern slopes of the Ligurian Apennines
and the left bank of the Ardana river. This is
a border area, as is faithfully reflected in
the range composed of at least two main
lines: on the one side Gavi, on the other
Dolcetto d'Ovada, Barbera d'Asti and
Chardonnay Porfirio. In Bosio, a territory
that straddles white and red, cortese and
dolcetto, the Guido della Caplana family
excels in both typologies. Gavi and Dolcetto
are perfect representations of their
respective DOCs. Almond notes and acid
pressure are the hallmark of the Gavi di
Gavi; the Dolcetto Narciso shows black
berry fruit aromas and juicy tannins.

● Dolcetto di Ovada Narciso '11	♀♀ 2*
○ Gavi del Comune di Gavi '12	♀♀ 2*
● Barbera d'Asti Sup. '11	♀♀ 2*
● Barbera d'Asti Sup. Rubis '09	♀♀ 2*
○ Gavi Antico Podere di Vignavecchia '12	♀♀ 2*
● Dolcetto di Ovada '12	♀ 2
○ Gavi '12	♀ 2
○ Piomonte Chardonnay '12	♀ 2
● Dolcetto di Ovada Narciso '10	♀♀ 2*
● Dolcetto di Ovada Narciso '09	♀♀ 3
● Dolcetto di Ovada Narciso '08	♀♀ 2*
● Dolcetto di Ovada Narciso '07	♀♀ 2*
○ Gavi del Comune di Gavi '08	♀♀ 2

La Casaccia

VIA D. BARBANO, 10
15034 CELLA MONTE [AL]
TEL. 0142489986
www.lacasaccia.biz

CELLAR SALES
PRE-BOOKED VISITS
ANNUAL PRODUCTION 25,000 bottles
HECTARES UNDER VINE 6.70
VITICULTURE METHOD Certified Organic

The winery is based at Cella Monte, a
splendid location known for its buildings in
limestone, ideal, amongst other things, for
storing wine. This is where, some years
ago, the Rava husband-and-wife team,
both agriculture graduates, set out to
restore the family's viticultural tradition. In
the space of a few years they started to
produce an extensive range of labels,
above all the traditional wines of the
territory, with excellent results. We tasted a
balanced array of wines from this estate.
The big labels were absent from the line-up
but the basic wines show care and
attention. The Giuanin presents delicious
cherry tones and a first-rate palate. The
Grignolino is pleasing and the Freisa very
intriguing, faintly aromatic and spicy with a
very agreeable finish.

● Barbera del M.to Giuanin '12	♀♀ 2*
● Grignolino del M.to Casalese Poggeto '12	♀♀ 2*
● M.to Freisa Monfiorenza '12	♀♀ 2*
● Barbera del M.to Sup. Bricco del Bosco '10	♀ 2
● Barbera d'Asti Sup. Calichè '07	♀♀ 2
● Barbera del M.to Sup. Bricco del Bosco '09	♀♀ 2
● Barbera del M.to Sup. Bricco del Bosco '07	♀♀ 2*
● Grignolino del M.to Casalese Poggeto '10	♀♀ 2
● Grignolino del M.to Casalese Poggeto '09	♀♀ 2*
○ Piemonte Chardonnay Charnò '11	♀♀ 3

Casalone

VIA MARCONI, 100
15040 LU [AL]
TEL. 0131741280
www.casalone.it

CELLAR SALES
PRE-BOOKED VISITS
ANNUAL PRODUCTION 50,000 bottles
HECTARES UNDER VINE 10.00

The Casalone family has centuries of
history in Bricco Santa Maria at Lu
Monferrato, where they have always
farmed the land and grown grapes. Over
time, native varieties have been joined by
international cultivars, such as pinot nero
and merlot, not to mention the aromatic
malvasia greca, with which they are
achieving great results and which serves
as the raw material for three products: a
still white, a Metodo Classico and a
Passito. The range is limited but always of
excellent quality. The Bricco Morlantino is
in fine fettle with ripe fruit aromas and a
powerful, alcohol-rich palate. The wines
obtained from malvasia greca are very
interesting. The still Monemvasia is
aromatic and concentrated with lovely
fruity tones, and the Metodo Classico
shows elegant beading and wonderful
nose-palate balance.

Cascina Barisél

REG. SAN GIOVANNI, 30
14053 CANELLI [AT]
TEL. 0141824848
www.barisel.it

CELLAR SALES
PRE-BOOKED VISITS
ANNUAL PRODUCTION 35,000 bottles
HECTARES UNDER VINE 4.50

The Penna family winery, despite its limited
vineyard holdings, has for many years been
a leading name in the Monferrato area. The
vineyards surrounding the farmhouse are
fully south-facing, on highly calcareous soils,
and are planted to barbera, moscato and
dolcetto, while favorita is grown in a small
plot of just over half a hectare at San
Marzano Oliveto. It is worth noting that many
of the vines are between 40 and 60 years
old. The Barbera d'Asti Superiore La
Cappelletta 2010 is always at the top of its
typology. Intense and complex, it offers notes
of balsam and oak-derived spice, bags of
black berry fruit with undertones of cocoa
powder, a full-bodied yet elegant palate and
along, harmonious finish. The fresh, citrussy
Moscato d'Asti Canelli 2012, fruity, juicy
Barbera d'Asti Superiore Listoria 2011, and
simpler but pleasing Barbera d'Asti 2012
are all well made.

● Barbera del M.to Sup.	
Bricco Morlantino '10	♥♥ 2*
● M.to Rosso Rus '10	♥♥ 3
○ Monemvasia	♥♥ 2*
○ Monemvasia Brut M. Cl.	♥♥ 4
● Monferrato Rosso Arnest '09	♥ 3
● Barbera d'Asti Rubermillo '08	♥♥ 3
● Barbera del M.to Sup.	
Bricco Morlantino '09	♥♥ 2*
● Barbera del M.to Sup.	
Bricco Morlantino '08	♥♥ 2*
● Barbera del M.to Sup.	
Bricco Morlantino '07	♥♥ 2*
● M.to Rosso Rus '08	♥♥ 3
○ Monemvasia Passito '09	♥♥ 3
○ Monemvasia V. T. '08	♥♥ 3
● Piemonte Grignolino La Capletta '10	♥♥ 2*

● Barbera d'Asti Sup. La Cappelletta '10	♥♥ 4
● Barbera d'Asti '12	♥♥ 2*
● Barbera d'Asti Sup. Listoria '11	♥♥ 2*
○ Moscato d'Asti Canelli '12	♥♥ 2*
○ Enrico Penna Brut M. Cl. '09	♥ 5
● Barbera d'Asti '08	♥♥ 2*
● Barbera d'Asti Barisél '06	♥♥ 2
● Barbera d'Asti Sup. La Cappelletta '09	♥♥ 4
● Barbera d'Asti Sup. La Cappelletta '07	♥♥ 4
● Barbera d'Asti Sup. La Cappelletta '06	♥♥ 4
○ Moscato d'Asti '10	♥♥ 2*
○ Moscato d'Asti Canelli '11	♥♥ 2*

Cascina Ca' Rossa

LOC. CASCINA CA' ROSSA, 56
12043 CANALE [CN]
TEL. 017398348
www.cascinacarossa.com

Cascina Chicco

VIA VALENTINO, 144
12043 CANALE [CN]
TEL. 0173979411
www.cascinachicco.com

CELLAR SALES
PRE-BOOKED VISITS
ANNUAL PRODUCTION 80,000 bottles
HECTARES UNDER VINE 13.00
VITICULTURE METHOD Certified Organic

CELLAR SALES
PRE-BOOKED VISITS
ANNUAL PRODUCTION 320,000 bottles
HECTARES UNDER VINE 40.00

Now with the support of his son, Stefano, Angelo Ferro runs this estate with passion and dedication. Quality is his aim and he seeks to achieve it using organic and biodynamic methods. In addition to his most prestigious Canale crus of Mompissano and Mulassa, and Audinaggio, legendary for its steep slope and difficult working conditions but also for the quality of the wine it produces, Angelo has purchased and started to plant a new vineyard. It is also situated in Vezza d'Alba, on another very steep terrain. The wines he proposes are very authentic with bags of character and offer more in the way of elegance than power. The Cascina Ca' Rossa takes home another Tre Bicchieri for the Roero Mompissano Riserva 2010, a very refined wine with concentrated notes of forest fruits and spicy, flowery undertones. The palate is extraordinary for its full body, acidity and elegant tannins. The Roero Audinaggio 2011 lacks its usual elegance but has generous fruit. The Barbera d'Alba Mulassa 2011 is juicy and wonderfully fresh.

Brothers Enrico and Marco Faccenda have turned Cascina Chicco into one of the leading lights of Roero wine-making. They have greatly expanded both the estate headquarters and the area planted to vine. Their plots are situated in several of Roero's municipalities, including Canale, with the Mompissano cru, Vezza d'Alba, with the Valmaggiore cru, Castellinaldo and Castagnito. Also worth a mention is the Barolo produced by the Rocche del Castelletto estate in Monforte d'Alba that has five hectares of vines in the zone of Ginestra. The entire range is technically well made and rich in fruit. This has been a good year all round for Cascina Chicco. It saw two wines in our finals: the Roero Montespinato 2011 presents a full, complex nose and a taut, full-flavoured palate; the Roero Valmaggiore Riserva 2010 offers notes of flowers and forest floor, and a tight, leisurely finish. The Cuvée Zero Extra Brut Metodo Classico is also very pleasing, with lovely aromas of appley fruit and crusty bread, and a fresh, lingering palate.

● Roero Mompissano Ris. '10	♈♈♈ 5
● Roero Audinaggio '11	♈♈ 5
● Barbera d'Alba '12	♈♈ 3
● Barbera d'Alba Mulassa '11	♈♈ 5
○ Roero Arneis Merica '12	♈ 3
● Barbera d'Alba Mulassa '04	♈♈♈ 4*
● Roero Audinaggio '07	♈♈♈ 5
● Roero Audinaggio '06	♈♈♈ 5
● Roero Audinaggio '01	♈♈♈ 5
● Roero Mompissano Ris. '07	♈♈♈ 6
● Barbera d'Alba '09	♈♈ 2
● Barbera d'Alba Mulassa '10	♈♈ 4
● Roero Audinaggio '10	♈♈ 5
● Roero Audinaggio '09	♈♈ 5
● Roero Mompissano Ris. '09	♈♈ 4

● Roero Montespinato '11	♈♈ 3*
● Roero Valmaggiore Ris. '10	♈♈ 4
○ Arcass V.T.	♈♈ 4
● Barbera d'Alba Bric Loira '11	♈♈ 4
● Barolo Rocche di Castelletto '09	♈♈ 5
○ Cuvée Zero Extra Brut M. Cl.	♈♈ 3
● Nebbiolo d'Alba Mompissano '11	♈♈ 3
● Barbera d'Alba Granera Alta '12	♈ 2
○ Arcàss Passito '04	♈♈♈ 4
● Barbera d'Alba Bric Loira '98	♈♈♈ 4*
● Barbera d'Alba Bric Loira '97	♈♈♈ 4*
● Nebbiolo d'Alba Mompissano '99	♈♈♈ 3*
● Barolo Rocche di Castelletto '08	♈♈ 5
● Barolo Rocche di Castelletto '07	♈♈ 5
● Roero Montespinato '10	♈♈ 3
● Roero Valmaggiore '09	♈♈ 4

Cascina Corte

FRAZ. SAN LUIGI
B.TA VALDIBERTI, 33
12063 DOGLIANI [CN]
TEL. 0173743539
www.cascinacorte.it

CELLAR SALES
PRE-BOOKED VISITS
ACCOMMODATION
ANNUAL PRODUCTION 30,000 bottles
HECTARES UNDER VINE 5.00
VITICULTURE METHOD Certified Organic

If, as we are often told, value for money is
an intelligent parameter to guide us in the
highly fragmented world of wine, Sandro
Barosi and his small estate constitute an
example of rare consistency. Excellent
wines, produced using strictly organic
growing methods, painstaking attention to
the authentic expression of the various
grape varieties, and very attractive prices
are the pieces in this well-calibrated
mosaic. Dolcetto is the estate's flagship,
but its Barbera and Nebbiolo also display
excellent character and personality. This
intriguing picture is completed by the
friendliness, modesty and conviviality of
the owner. The Dogliani Superiore
Pirochetta Vecchie Vigne 2011 is deep and
layered with hints of ripe blackberry and
cocoa powder. The fruit, lingering palate
shows tannins in good harmony with the
acid vein. The vivid, vibrant Barbera 2011
is extremely drinkable, while the
Nebbiolo 2011 delights with crunchy fruit.

Cascina Cucco

LOC. CUCCO
VIA MAZZINI, 10
12050 SERRALUNGA D'ALBA [CN]
TEL. 0173613003
www.cascinacucco.com

CELLAR SALES
PRE-BOOKED VISITS
ANNUAL PRODUCTION 70,000 bottles
HECTARES UNDER VINE 12.00

The Stroppiana family of entrepreneurs,
who have made a name for themselves all
over the world, have roots in Piedmont and
own this handsome winery in prestigious
Serralunga Alba. Long-standing manager
Pierangelo Franchi attentively oversees
operations in the vineyard and cellar,
enabling the production of excellent wines
that, year after year, are carving out an
increasingly important place for themselves
among Langhe's very finest labels. In the
cellar, small barrels are flanked by large
casks in order to achieve perfect balance in
the various wines, all of which are well
defined and offer excellent value for money.
We were most impressed by the intense,
complex Barolo Cerrati 2009 with its notes
of tobacco, leather and spice, and good
balance between tannins and acidity. The
Cerrati Vigna Cucco 2009 is rather closed
on the nose but offers a very harmonious
palate with hints of red berry fruit that
blend with solid, vigorous tannic texture.

● Dogliani Sup. Pirochetta V. V. '11	♟♟ 3*
● Barnedòl	♟♟ 4
● Langhe Barbera '11	♟♟ 3
● Langhe Nebbiolo '11	♟♟ 3
● Dogliani '12	♟ 2
● Dogliani Vecchie V. Pirochetta '08	♟♟♟ 3*
● Dogliani Pirochetta V. V. '10	♟♟ 3
● Dogliani Pirochetta V. V. '09	♟♟ 3*
● Dogliani V. Pirochetta '07	♟♟ 3*
● Dogliani V. Pirochetta '06	♟♟ 3
● Dolcetto di Dogliani '09	♟♟ 2*
● Dolcetto di Dogliani '08	♟♟ 2*
● Langhe Nebbiolo '10	♟♟ 3
● Piemonte Barbera '09	♟♟ 3

● Barolo Cerrati '09	♟♟ 6
● Barolo Cerrati V. Cucco '09	♟♟ 7
● Barbera d'Alba Sup. '11	♟♟ 4
● Barolo Cerrati V. Cucco Ris. '07	♟♟ 8
● Barolo di Serralunga '09	♟♟ 5
● Langhe Rosso Mondo '11	♟♟ 4
● Barbera d'Alba '12	♟ 2
● Dolcetto d'Alba '12	♟ 2
○ Langhe Chardonnay '12	♟ 3
● Barbera d'Alba Sup. '10	♟♟ 4
● Barolo Cerrati '08	♟♟ 6
● Barolo Cerrati V. Cucco '08	♟♟ 6
● Barolo di Serralunga '08	♟♟ 5

Cascina Fonda

LOC. CASCINA FONDA, 45
12056 MANGO [CN]
TEL. 0173677877
www.cascinafonda.com

CELLAR SALES
PRE-BOOKED VISITS
ACCOMMODATION
ANNUAL PRODUCTION 100,000 bottles
HECTARES UNDER VINE 12.00

The brothers Marco and Massimo Barbero
passionately run this winery dedicated
almost completely to the production of
moscato, vinified in all the various types
envisaged by the production protocol. Two
thirds of the vineyard holdings, comprising
plants of between 35 to 60 years old, are
situated in the municipality of Mango, with
the remaining third at Neive, at an
elevation of around 450 metres with a
south-eastern aspect. The wines are
characterized by elegance, freshness and
pleasurableness rather than weight. This
year sees a fine overall showing from this
estate, starting with the Moscato d'Asti
Bel Piano 2012. It has notes of sage and
peach and fine acidity that renders the
palate balanced, elegant and very long.
The Moscato Spumante Tardivo 2011
presents musk and candied fruit aromas,
and a fresh, characterful palate. The
agreeable, lingering Asti Spumante
Bel Piasì 2012 is vibrant and citrussy with
nuances of lime and peach.

○ Asti Spumante Bel Piasì '12	♥♥	2*
○ Moscato d'Asti Bel Piano '12	♥♥	2*
○ Moscato Spumante Tardivo '11	♥♥	3
○ Brut M. Cl. '08	♥	4
○ La Tardja	♥	3
○ Asti Bel Piasì '11	♀♀	2*
○ Asti Bel Piasì '09	♀♀	2*
○ Moscato d'Asti Bel Piano '11	♀♀	2
○ Moscato d'Asti Bel Piano '10	♀♀	2
○ Moscato d'Asti Bel Piano '09	♀♀	2*
○ Moscato Spumante Tardivo '10	♀♀	3
○ Moscato Spumante Tardivo '09	♀♀	3
○ Vendemmia Tardiva '09	♀♀	3

Cascina Fontana

LOC. PERNO
12065 MONFORTE D'ALBA [CN]
TEL. 0173789005
www.cascinafontana.com

CELLAR SALES
PRE-BOOKED VISITS
ANNUAL PRODUCTION 20,000 bottles
HECTARES UNDER VINE 5.00

Mario and Luisa attentively and
enthusiastically run this small Monforte
estate, managing to express their concept
of quality through the production of a small
amount of very good wines. Barolo is of
course the star of the show, and
meticulous long ageing in Slavonian oak
casks produces a carefully calibrated
palate, which is simultaneously traditional
and highly drinkable. The reasonable price
tags of the entire portfolio, made from the
three main local grape varieties, help give
the estate an additional distinctive touch. A
fine showing from the Barolo 2008, fresh
and typical with notes of tobacco,
medicinal herbs, liquorice and spice. The
structure is well balanced and supported
by elegant, nicely integrated tannic texture.
The Dolcetto d'Alba 2011 is juicy,
pleasantly fruity and very drinkable. The
Nebbiolo 2010 is austere and leisurely.

● Barolo '08	♥♥	7
● Dolcetto d'Alba '11	♥♥	3
● Langhe Nebbiolo '10	♥♥	4
● Barbera d'Alba '09	♀♀	3
● Barolo Villero e Valletta '07	♀♀	5
● Langhe Nebbiolo '09	♀♀	3

Cascina Gilli

VIA NEVISSANO, 36
14022 CASTELNUOVO DON BOSCO [AT]
TEL. 0119876984
www.cascinagilli.it

CELLAR SALES
PRE-BOOKED VISITS
ANNUAL PRODUCTION 140,000 bottles
HECTARES UNDER VINE 21.00

Gianni Vergnano is without doubt one of the most passionate supporters and greatest interpreters of two native grape varieties that are as traditional as they are unusual: freisa and malvasia di Castelnuovo. His vineyards are situated on marly, clayey terrains and are also home to barbera and bonarda. It is freisa, however, that rules supreme and Cascina Gilli produces it in every version, from aged to semi-sparkling. The wines are expressive, authentic and surprising. This year we particularly liked the Barbera d'Asti Le More 2011, which shows good structure and notes of red berry fruit and tobacco. Also very well made, the Freisa d'Asti Arvelé 2010 has pepper and rose aromas and a long gutsy finish full of character. We also enjoyed the Freisa d'Asti Frizzante Luna di Maggio 2012, balanced and reasonably structured, and the Freisa d'Asti Il Forno 2011 with its peppery, flowery nose and long, rather austere finish.

Cascina Giovinale

S.DA SAN NICOLAO, 102
14049 NIZZA MONFERRATO [AT]
TEL. 0141793005
www.cascinagiovinale.com

CELLAR SALES
PRE-BOOKED VISITS
ANNUAL PRODUCTION 25,000 bottles
HECTARES UNDER VINE 7.00

Founded by Bruno Ciocca and Anna Maria Solaini in 1980, all of the vineyards of this estate, which focuses on barbera, are situated on the San Nicolao hill in the Nizza zone. The south-south-west-facing vineyards lie on sandy limestone soils and are mostly over 50 years old. Barbera accounts for the majority, although smaller amounts of moscato, dolcetto and cabernet sauvignon are also grown. The wines are distinguished by their rich fruit and focus on elegance rather than body. Cascina Giovinale presented just one wine this year, but it is their flagship. The Barbera d'Asti Superiore Nizza Anssèma 2010 goes all the way to our final tastings for its generous nose of spice, aromatic dried herbs and red fruit. The palate is rich and full-flavoured with fabulous tannic density and a long characterful finish.

● Barbera d'Asti Le More '11	♀♀ 2*
● Freisa d'Asti Arvelé '10	♀♀ 3
● Freisa d'Asti Frizzante Luna di Maggio '12	♀♀ 2*
● Freisa d'Asti Il Forno '11	♀♀ 2*
● Malvasia di Castelnuovo Don Bosco '12	♀ 2
● Barbera d'Asti Sebrì '09	♀♀ 3
● Barbera d'Asti V. delle More '10	♀♀ 2*
● Freisa d'Asti Arvelé '08	♀♀ 3
● Freisa d'Asti Arvelé '07	♀♀ 3
● Freisa d'Asti V. del Forno '10	♀♀ 2*
● Piemonte Bonarda Sernù '08	♀♀ 2*
● Piemonte Bonarda Sernù '07	♀♀ 2*

● Barbera d'Asti Sup. Nizza Anssèma '10	♀♀ 3*
● Barbera d'Asti Sup. '09	♀♀ 2*
● Barbera d'Asti Sup. '07	♀♀ 2*
● Barbera d'Asti Sup. '06	♀♀ 2*
● Barbera d'Asti Sup. Nizza Anssèma '09	♀♀ 3*
● Barbera d'Asti Sup. Nizza Anssèma '07	♀♀ 4
● Barbera d'Asti Sup. Nizza Anssèma '06	♀♀ 4*
● Barbera d'Asti Sup. Nizza Anssèma '05	♀♀ 4
● Barbera d'Asti Sup. Nizza Anssèma '04	♀♀ 4

★Cascina La Barbatella

s.da Annunziata, 55
14049 Nizza Monferrato [AT]
Tel. 0141701434
www.labarbatella.com

CELLAR SALES
PRE-BOOKED VISITS
ANNUAL PRODUCTION 22,000 bottles
HECTARES UNDER VINE 4.00

The Perego family took over Cascina La Barbatella three years ago and continue to follow the course piloted by Angelo Sonvico with passion and skill. The vineyards stand on limestone and sandy soils and radiate out from the estate's headquarters in three sections. Barbera with extremely low yields is cultivated in the Vigna dell'Angelo, while barbera and cabernet are grown in the Vigna di Sonvico, The wines are modern in slant and, in addition to the more traditional offering of high-quality Barbera, seek to enhance the marriage of indigenous and international varieties. A Tre Bicchieri for the Monferrato Rosso Sonvico 2009, a historic blend of barbera and cabernet sauvignon with cherry and tobacco aromas. Elegant and complex, it displays fine, harmonious body and a taut, lingering finish. Excellent, too, the intense, full Barbera d'Asti 2011, and the powerful Barbera d'Asti Superiore Nizza La Vigna dell'Angelo 2010 with lovely acid pressure.

● M.to Rosso Sonvico '09	🍷🍷🍷 6
● Barbera d'Asti '11	🍷🍷 3*
● Barbera d'Asti Sup. Nizza V. dell'Angelo '10	🍷🍷 5
● M.to Rosso Ruanera '10	🍷🍷 2*
● Barbera d'Asti Sup. Nizza V. dell'Angelo '07	🍷🍷🍷 5
● Barbera d'Asti Sup. Nizza V. dell'Angelo '01	🍷🍷🍷 5
● M.to Rosso Mystère '01	🍷🍷🍷 6
● M.to Rosso Sonvico '06	🍷🍷🍷 5
● M.to Rosso Sonvico '04	🍷🍷🍷 5
● M.to Rosso Sonvico '03	🍷🍷🍷 5
● M.to Rosso Sonvico '00	🍷🍷🍷 7
● M.to Rosso Sonvico '98	🍷🍷🍷 5

Cascina La Maddalena

fraz. San Giacomo
loc. Piani del Padrone, 257
15078 Rocca Grimalda [AL]
Tel. 0143876074
www.cascina-maddalena.com

CELLAR SALES
PRE-BOOKED VISITS
ACCOMMODATION
ANNUAL PRODUCTION 20,000 bottles
HECTARES UNDER VINE 4.00

Cascina La Maddalena is a small winery in the Ovada area, with products of a classic style that often display the somewhat rustic features of authentic wine, due to limited intervention at the cellar, aimed at preserving their personality. These are genuine products, and always excellently made, climate permitting, from dolcetto, barbera and merlot. The entire production process is managed on the premises, which also include a small bed & breakfast, as well as a tasting room for wine tourists. The 2012 version of the Bricco del Bagatto regales us with notes of black berry fruit, quina and cocoa powder. It is a vigorous wine with a compact, powerful palate. The basic Dolcetto has bags of character and personality, and generous, full-flavoured palate. The concentrated Rosso d'Ocra has lovely cocoa powder and sweet spice aromas that give it complexity; structure and harmony on the palate give way to a long, tannic finish.

● Barbera del M.to Rossa d'Ocra '11	🍷🍷 2*
● Dolcetto di Ovada '12	🍷🍷 2*
● Dolcetto di Ovada Bricco del Bagatto '12	🍷🍷 3
● Barbera del M.to '12	🍷 2
● Dolcetto di Ovada '11	🍷🍷 2
● Dolcetto di Ovada '10	🍷🍷 2*
● Dolcetto di Ovada '09	🍷🍷 2*
● Dolcetto di Ovada Bricco del Bagatto '11	🍷🍷 3
● Dolcetto di Ovada Bricco del Bagatto '09	🍷🍷 2*
● Dolcetto di Ovada Bricco del Bagatto '06	🍷🍷 3
● Dolcetto di Ovada Migulle '09	🍷🍷 4
● M.to Rosso La Decima Vendemmia '06	🍷🍷 5
● M.to Rosso Pian del Merlo '10	🍷🍷 3
● M.to Rosso Pian del Merlo '07	🍷🍷 3

Cascina Montagnola

s.da Montagnola, 1
15058 Viguzzolo [AL]
Tel. 3480742701
www.cascinamontagnola.com

CELLAR SALES
PRE-BOOKED VISITS
ANNUAL PRODUCTION 25,000 bottles
HECTARES UNDER VINE 10.00

Cascina Montagnola was a gamble taken by Donatella Giannotti way back in 1987, and turned out to be a winner. After purchasing this splendid estate in the offshoots of the Appenines and falling in love with the wines produced here, she began to bottle the wines from her own vineyards, and from the outset aimed for the highest possible quality. She initially focused on chardonnay for the whites, obtaining excellent results, but when she dedicated herself to the native variety par excellence, timorasso, her achievements were even more impressive. This time round a magnificent version of the Morasso came within a whisker of the Tre Bicchieri thanks to its intense notes of appley fruit and intriguing hints of pink grapefruit. The reds do well too. The Barbera Amaranto 2011 also reaches the finals, proving itself to be one of the most powerful Barberas in the entire territory of Tortona. The Rodeo 2010, an oak-conditioned Barbera, is also superb.

● Colli Tortonesi Barbera Amaranto '11	♟♟ 2*
○ Colli Tortonesi Timorasso Morasso '11	♟♟ 4
● Colli Tortonesi Barbera Rodeo '10	♟♟ 5
○ Colli Tortonesi Cortese Dunin '12	♟♟ 2*
○ Colli Tortonesi Bianco Alcesti '12	♟ 3
● Colli Tortonesi Rosso Donaldo '12	♟ 2
● Colli Tortonesi Barbera Rodeo '09	♟♟ 5
● Colli Tortonesi Barbera Rodeo '08	♟♟ 5
○ Colli Tortonesi Cortese Dunin '10	♟♟ 2*
● Colli Tortonesi Croatina Donaldo '11	♟♟ 3
○ Colli Tortonesi Timorasso Derthona '10	♟♟ 3*
○ Colli Tortonesi Timorasso Morasso '09	♟♟ 4

Cascina Morassino

s.da Bernino, 10
12050 Barbaresco [CN]
Tel. 0173635149
morassino@gmail.com

CELLAR SALES
PRE-BOOKED VISITS
ANNUAL PRODUCTION 20,000 bottles
HECTARES UNDER VINE 4.50

In recent years this small family-run winery has managed to carve out a place for itself among the top names of the highly diverse Barbaresco production zone. A tasting of the different wines produced by Mario and Roberto Blanco reconfirms the consistently high quality of their small production. The flagship wine is the Barbaresco from the Ovello cru, a terroir with excellent character and personality. Its style is harmonious and well calibrated, without any frills or extremes, but elegant and beautifully balanced. The Barbaresco Ovello 2010 presents notes of sweet liquorice, spice and medicinal herbs. Entry on the palate is exuberant and still in search of perfect balance; the tannins are clearly present but not invasive. The Barbaresco Morassino 2010 lacks expressivity as yet and needs time in the bottle to reveal its full potential.

● Barbaresco Ovello '10	♟♟ 6
● Barbaresco Morassino '10	♟♟ 5
● Barbaresco Morassino '09	♟♟♟ 5
● Barbaresco Morassino '05	♟♟ 5
● Barbaresco Morassino '01	♟♟ 5*
● Barbaresco Ovello '09	♟♟ 6
● Barbaresco Ovello '08	♟♟ 6
● Barbaresco Ovello '07	♟♟ 6
● Barbaresco Ovello '06	♟♟ 6
● Barbaresco Ovello '05	♟♟ 6
● Barbaresco Ovello '04	♟♟ 6
● Barbaresco Ovello '03	♟♟ 6
● Barbaresco Ovello '02	♟♟ 6
● Barbaresco Ovello '01	♟♟ 6
● Barbaresco Ovello '00	♟♟ 6
● Barbera d'Alba Vignot '07	♟♟ 4*

Cascina Pellerino

loc. SANT'ANNA, 93
12043 MONTEU ROERO [CN]
TEL. 0173978171
www.cascinapellerino.com

CELLAR SALES
PRE-BOOKED VISITS
ANNUAL PRODUCTION 50,000 bottles
HECTARES UNDER VINE 7.00

Cascina Pellerino's characterful wines with an unfalteringly modern style have made it a benchmark for winemaking in Monteu Roero for over 30 years. The vineyards, dotted over several municipalities, from Canale to Monteu Roero, Santo Stefano Roero and Vezza d'Alba, are planted with the typical local grape varieties of arneis, favorita, barbera and nebbiolo, alongside international ones, such as cabernet franc for the Langhe Rosso, and chardonnay and pinot nero for the Metodo Classico. This year two of this estate's wines reached our finals. The Barbera d'Alba Gran Madre 2011 shows notes of ripe fruit and spice, and a harmonious palate with good length and acidity. The Roero Vicot 2011 is full and complex with close-knit tannins and hints of black berry fruit. The Roero Vigna del Padre Riserva 2010 is also well made, intense and layered with balsamic, spicy aromas. The other labels are sound.

● Barbera d'Alba Sup. Gran Madre '11	♟♟ 5
● Roero Vicot '11	♟♟ 4
● Roero V. del Padre Ris. '10	♟♟ 5
● Barbera d'Alba Eleonora '12	♟ 3
○ Roero Arneis Atipico '12	♟ 4
● Barbera d'Alba Diletta '11	♟♟ 3
○ Brut M. Cl.	♟♟ 4
● Roero André '10	♟♟ 3
● Roero Vicot '08	♟♟ 5
● Roero Vicot '06	♟♟ 5
● Roero Vicot '05	♟♟ 4
● Roero Vigna del Padre '09	♟♟ 5

Cascina Salicetti

VIA CASCINA SALICETTI, 2
15050 MONTEGIOCO [AL]
TEL. 0131875192
www.cascinasalicetti.it

CELLAR SALES
PRE-BOOKED VISITS
ANNUAL PRODUCTION 25,000 bottles
HECTARES UNDER VINE 16.00

Cascina Salicetti is a classic family-run estate, led by Anselmo, who is now in charge of the viticultural side of the operation. Before coming back to work full time here, however, he earned his spurs in other local wineries, in particular at Gavi. This was an experience from which he benefited greatly, as became immediately evident in his outstanding white wines. The reds soon followed suit, and now display similar excellence. Our pick of the crop this year is the Timorasso Ombra di Luna 2011. In its best-ever version it romps home to win a place in our finals and just misses the Tre Bicchieri mark. Fresh aromas of citrus fruit with hints of flint, and taut, lively acidity are its winning cards.

○ Colli Tortonesi Timorasso	
Ombra di Luna '11	♟♟ 3*
○ Colli Tortonesi Cortese Montarlino '12	♟♟ 2*
● Colli Tortonesi Dolcetto Di Marzi '10	♟ 2
● Colli Tortonesi Barbera Morganti '10	♟♟ 2*
● Colli Tortonesi Rosso Risulò '10	♟♟ 2*
○ Colli Tortonesi Timorasso	
Ombra di Luna '10	♟♟ 3
○ Colli Tortonesi Timorasso Principio '10	♟♟ 3

Cascina Val del Prete

S.DA SANTUARIO, 2
12040 PRIOCCA [CN]
TEL. 0173616534
www.valdelprete.com

CELLAR SALES
PRE-BOOKED VISITS
ANNUAL PRODUCTION 55,000 bottles
HECTARES UNDER VINE 13.00
VITICULTURE METHOD Certified Organic

Surrounded by a splendid amphitheatre of estate-owned vineyards, at an altitude of approximately 200 metres, Cascina Val del Prete has become a solid winery offering consistent quality under the leadership of Mario Roagno. It was converted to biodynamic methods in 2005 and produces the classic Roero wines from arneis, barbera and nebbiolo. All the wines share firm structure and impressively rich fruit, particularly the nebbiolo-based reds. A low-key year for Cascina Val del Prete but it still goes all the way to the finals with the Roero 2009. Notes of brandied fruit, tobacco and dried aromatic herbs are the prelude to an austere yet juicy palate, very full and characterful. We also liked the Barbera d'Alba Superiore Carolina 2011 for its lovely notes of quina and spice with fruity undertones. The Roero Arneis Luèt 2012 has white pepper and tropical fruit on the nose but lacks verve in the finish.

● Roero '09	♥♥ 6
● Barbera d'Alba Sup. Carolina '11	♥♥ 5
● Barbera d'Alba Serra de' Gatti '12	♥ 3
○ Roero Arneis Luèt '12	♥ 2
● Nebbiolo d'Alba V. di Lino '00	♥♥♥ 5
● Roero '04	♥♥♥ 6
● Roero '03	♥♥♥ 6
● Roero '01	♥♥♥ 6
● Roero '00	♥♥♥ 6
● Barbera d'Alba Serra de' Gatti '10	♥♥ 3*
● Barbera d'Alba Sup. Carolina '10	♥♥ 5
● Roero '08	♥♥ 6
● Roero '07	♥♥ 6
● Roero Bricco Medica '09	♥♥ 5

Francesca Castaldi

VIA NOVEMBRE, 6
28072 BRIONA [NO]
TEL. 0321826045
www.cantinacastaldi.it

CELLAR SALES
PRE-BOOKED VISITS
ANNUAL PRODUCTION 10,000 bottles
HECTARES UNDER VINE 6.30

Francesca and Giuseppe Castaldi have the honour of flying the flag of Fara, one of the smallest appellations in Italy and the southernmost of those lying on the morainic hills of the province of Novara. Descended from one of the area's historic families, the brothers started replanting their over six hectares of vineyards in 1997 with nebbiolo and small amounts of vespolina and erbaluce. From these varieties they obtain a limited range of wines that, from the very first vintages, has been recognized for its clear, essential style and increasing aromatic and extractive definition. The 2009 growing year brings us a Fara with a refined nose and a palate that is still rather austere in its tannic progression but fortunately contrasted by extractive flesh and the tanginess typical of the zone's wines. The wines obtained from so-called lesser varieties – the peppery vespolina and Uva Rara with aromas of bark – are stunning in their simplicity.

● Fara '09	♥♥ 5
● Colline Novaresi Nebbiolo Bigin '11	♥♥ 3
● Colline Novaresi Uva Rara Valceresole '12	♥♥ 3
● Colline Novaresi Vespolina Nina '12	♥♥ 3
● Colline Novaresi Barbera Martina '11	♥ 3
○ Colline Novaresi Bianco Lucia '12	♥ 3
● Colline Novaresi Barbera Martina '10	♥♥ 2*
○ Colline Novaresi Bianco Lucia '11	♥♥ 2*
● Fara '08	♥♥ 3*
● Fara '07	♥♥ 3
● Fara '06	♥♥ 3*
● Valceresole '11	♥♥ 2*

Castellari Bergaglio

Fraz. Rovereto, 136
15066 Gavi [AL]
Tel. 0143644000
www.castellaribergaglio.it

CELLAR SALES
PRE-BOOKED VISITS
ANNUAL PRODUCTION 90,000 bottles
HECTARES UNDER VINE 12.00

Four generations of the family have tended this long-established estate in the Gavi production zone. Today, work revolves around Mario Bergaglio, particularly in the vineyard, and his son Marco, active mainly in the cellar and sales. Cortese di Gavi is the sole focus of the line, produced in seven different versions: the basic Salluvii; Fornaci and Rolona, which showcase the differences in soil and aspect of the vineyards in Tassarolo and Gavi; Rovereto, which is cold macerated; and Pilin, from the oldest vineyard, late-harvested and then aged in oak. Then there's the Metodo Classico Ardé and Gavium, made from partially dried grapes. With vineyards in the area's most prestigious crus, Marco Bergaglio maintains his excellent quality. Once again an elegant, fresh Rolona takes a Due Bicchieri, flanked this year by two very different wines: the approachable Salluvii and the complex, oaky Pilin 2011.

Castello di Gabiano

via Defendente, 2
15020 Gabiano [AL]
Tel. 0142945004
www.castellodigabiano.com

CELLAR SALES
PRE-BOOKED VISITS
ACCOMMODATION AND RESTAURANT SERVICE
ANNUAL PRODUCTION 100,000 bottles
HECTARES UNDER VINE 20.00

This year sees a full-length profile for Castello di Gabiano, which gives us a chance to provide some historical background. The Castle of Gabiano is a magnificent fort with a medieval town, which according to some documents dates back to the eighth century. In its long history, the property has been owned by various aristocratic families and has also undergone significant conservation work, thanks to which we are now able to appreciate its beauty to the full. Nor should we forget the breathtaking views over the River Po with the Alps in the background. A fine showing on its debut full profile. The Gabiano Riserva presents complex notes of red berry fruit, tobacco and cocoa powder, a powerful balanced palate and a long characterful finish. We tasted two Barbera d'Astis: the Adornes is a Superiore with great personality and balance; the La Braja is less complex but has superb nose-palate impact.

○ Gavi del Comune di Gavi Rolona '12	♥♥ 3
○ Gavi Pilin '11	♥♥ 5
○ Gavi Salluvii '12	♥♥ 2*
○ Gavi del Comune di Gavi Rovereto Vignavecchia '11	♥ 3
○ Gavi del Comune di Tassarolo Fornaci '12	♥ 2
○ Gavi Spumante M. Cl. Ardè '10	♥ 4
○ Gavi del Comune di Gavi Rolona '09	♀♀ 3
○ Gavi del Comune di Gavi Rovereto Vignavecchia '10	♀♀ 3
○ Gavi del Comune di Gavi Rovereto Vignavecchia '08	♀♀ 3
○ Gavi del Comune di Gavi Rovereto Vignavecchia '07	♀♀ 3
○ Gavi del Comune di Tassarolo Fornaci '10	♀♀ 2
○ Gavi del Comune di Tassarolo Fornaci '08	♀♀ 2
○ Gavi Pilin '06	♀♀ 4

● Gabiano Matilde Giustiniani Ris. '08	♥♥ 6
● Barbera d'Asti La Braja '11	♥♥ 2*
● Barbera d'Asti Sup. Adornes '09	♥♥ 5
● Grignolino del M.to Casalese Il Ruvo '12	♥♥ 2*
○ M.to Bianco Corte '12	♥♥ 3
○ M.to Chiaretto Castelvere '12	♥ 2
● Rubino di Cantavenna '10	♥ 3
● Barbera d'Asti Sup. Adornes '07	♀♀ 5*
● Gabiano Matilde Giustiniani Ris. '07	♀♀ 6
● Grignolino del M.to Casalese Il Ruvo '10	♀♀ 2*
● M.to Rosso Gavius '09	♀♀ 3
● Rubino di Cantavenna '09	♀♀ 3

Castello di Neive

VIA CASTELBORGO, 1
12052 NEIVE [CN]
TEL. 017367171
www.castellodineive.it

PRE-BOOKED VISITS
ANNUAL PRODUCTION 15,000 bottles
HECTARES UNDER VINE 27.00

In recent years we have systematically tasted several old vintages of Castello di Neive's Barbaresco during the extraordinary event, "The Tenth Anniversary of Nebbiolo", held at La Ciau del Tornavento restaurant, and we can guarantee the cellarability and soundness of these classic wines, which are always exciting and very terroir-true. Italo Stupino confidently runs this charming estate highly representative of the finest Langhe traditions, owned by his family for over 50 years. The solid, well-made Barbaresco Gallina 2010 has notes of spice and tobacco followed by good tannic texture and acidity. The Barbaresco Albesani Santo Stefano 2010 is a little more reserved but the right period in the bottle will bring out its full potential. A nod to the fine performance of the Pinot Nero Metodo Classico 2009 that shows character and an original palate.

Tenuta Castello di Razzano

FRAZ. CASARELLO
LOC. RAZZANO, 2
15021 ALFIANO NATTA [AL]
TEL. 0141922124
www.castellodirazzano.it

CELLAR SALES
PRE-BOOKED VISITS
ANNUAL PRODUCTION 150,000 bottles
HECTARES UNDER VINE 30.00

On the borders of the province of Asti, at Alfiano Natta the Olearo family have created a winery of great beauty. The headquarters are in a stately home dating back to the 17th century, converted to provide tourist accommodation, and offer views over the extensive vineyards surrounding the building. The extensive range of wines include many labels rooted in the territory, above all Barbera, in which the Olearo family excel, although they also use international varieties such as chardonnay, pinot nero and merlot. The prestigious bottles are absent from the ranks, but the overall quality is indisputable. The Grignolino Pianaccio is a concentrated, refined wine with a pepper and rose nose; the Leona is a balanced, harmonious Barbera d'Asti; the Cuntrà from merlot is an intense, elegant red with tobacco aromas over a hint of raspberry. The Barbera Campasso rounds off the range.

● Barbaresco Albesani S. Stefano '10	♟♟ 6
● Barbaresco Gallina '10	♟♟ 6
● Barbaresco '10	♟♟ 5
● Barbera d'Alba S. Stefano '10	♟♟ 3
● Barbera d'Alba Sup. '11	♟♟ 4
○ Langhe Arneis Montebertotto '12	♟♟ 2*
● Langhe Pinot Nero I Cortini '11	♟♟ 4
○ Piemonte Pinot Nero M. Cl. '09	♟♟ 5
● Barbaresco S. Stefano Ris. '01	♟♟♟ 7
● Barbaresco S. Stefano Ris. '99	♟♟♟ 7
● Barbaresco Gallina '08	♟♟ 5
● Barbaresco S. Stefano '09	♟♟ 6
● Barbaresco S. Stefano '08	♟♟ 6
● Barbaresco S. Stefano '07	♟♟ 6
● Barbaresco S. Stefano Ris. '06	♟♟ 7
● Barbaresco S. Stefano Ris. '04	♟♟ 8

● Barbera d'Asti La Leona '11	♟♟ 2*
● Grignolino del M.to Casalese Pianaccio '12	♟♟ 2*
● M.to Rosso Cuntrà '10	♟♟ 3
● Barbera d'Asti Sup. Campasso '10	♟ 2
● Barbera d'Asti Sup. Campasso '09	♟♟ 2*
● Barbera d'Asti Sup. Campasso '08	♟♟ 3
● Barbera d'Asti Sup. Del Beneficio '10	♟♟ 4
● Barbera d'Asti Sup. Del Beneficio '09	♟♟ 4
● Barbera d'Asti Sup. Eugenea '09	♟♟ 4
● Barbera d'Asti Sup. Valentino Caligaris '10	♟♟ 5
● M.to Rosso Cuntrà '09	♟♟ 3
○ Piemonte Chardonnay Costa al Sole '11	♟♟ 2*
● Piemonte Pinot Nero Onero '11	♟♟ 3

Castello di Tassarolo

Cascina Alborina, 1
15060 Tassarolo [AL]
Tel. 0143342248
www.castelloditassarolo.it

CELLAR SALES
PRE-BOOKED VISITS
ANNUAL PRODUCTION 130,000 bottles
HECTARES UNDER VINE 17.00
VITICULTURE METHOD Certified Organic

It is first and foremost a philosophical and cultural choice that has made Castello di Tassarolo one of the benchmarks for organic and biodynamic viticulture in the province of Alessandria. This decision was inspired and strongly encouraged by Massimiliana Spinola, the latest generation of an aristocratic family associated with the castle since 1300, with the fundamental aid of Henry Finzi-Constantine and Vincenzo Munì. The range is almost exclusively based on cortese di Gavi, with several wines produced without added sulphites, including Monferrato Rosso, a barbera and cabernet sauvignon blend, and Barbera Titouan. Given the number of wines and the frequency with which they feature in our finals, we are sure that this estate will eventually win its laurels. Vincenzo Munì is the oenologist. The Castello and Alborina, partly aged in oak, display personality and character. Hats off to the wines with no added sulphites, even if they have yet to develop.

○ Gavi del Comune di Tassarolo Alborina '12	♚♚ 3*
○ Gavi del Comune di Tassarolo Il Castello '12	♚♚ 2*
○ Gavi del Comune di Tassarolo Spinola '12	♚♚ 2*
○ Gavi del Comune di Tassarolo Sparkling Spinola No Sulphites '12	♚ 2
● M.to Rosso Cuvée '12	♚ 2
● Piemonte Barbera Titouan '12	♚ 3
○ Gavi del Comune di Tassarolo Il Castello '11	♙♙ 2*
○ Gavi del Comune di Tassarolo Spinola '10	♙♙ 2*
○ Gavi del Comune di Tassarolo Titouan '11	♙♙ 2*
● M.to Rosso No Sulphites '08	♙♙ 2*

Castello di Uviglie

via Castello di Uviglie, 73
15030 Rosignano Monferrato [AL]
Tel. 0142488132
www.castellodiuviglie.com

CELLAR SALES
PRE-BOOKED VISITS
ANNUAL PRODUCTION 90,000 bottles
HECTARES UNDER VINE 25.00

Simone Lupano is a veteran in the Guide, and his wines represent a guarantee of quality for his customers. Simone's ambition and ability, together with the pragmatism and clear-sightedness of his oenologist Mario Ronco have transformed the winery into an unstoppable force. The latest adventure of this dynamic duo is a Metodo Classico sparkler from 65% pinot nero topped up with chardonnay, that spends at least 36 months on the lees. The originality of this product and its ageing in the castle's tufa cellars, where temperature constantly remains at around 12° C, endow it with a perlage of great finesse. It's the revenge of the Grignolino. The San Bastiano reaches our finals to achieve the coveted title that still eludes the typology. The Le Cave, a new finalist, is complex and powerful in the 2011 version. We also liked the Extra Brut Metodo Classico Le Cave on its debut entry into the Guide. It displays impressive characteristics as well as a long, classy finish.

● Barbera del M.to Sup. Le Cave '11	♚♚ 3*
● Grignolino del M.to Casalese San Bastiano '12	♚♚ 2*
● Barbera del M.to Sup. Pico Gonzaga '10	♚♚ 5
○ Le Cave Extra Brut '09	♚♚ 5
● M.to Rosso 1491 '10	♚♚ 5
● Barbera del M.to Bricco del Conte '12	♚ 2
○ Bricco del Ciliegio Passito '09	♚ 5
○ Piemonte Chardonnay Ninfea '12	♚ 2
● Barbera del M.to Sup. Le Cave '09	♙♙♙ 3*
● Barbera del M.to Sup. Le Cave '07	♙♙♙ 3*
● Barbera del M.to Sup. Pico Gonzaga '07	♙♙♙ 4*
● Barbera del M.to Sup. Le Cave '10	♙♙ 3*
● Barbera del M.to Sup. Le Cave '08	♙♙ 3*
● Grignolino del M.to Casalese San Bastiano '09	♙♙ 2*

Castello di Verduno

VIA UMBERTO I, 9
12060 VERDUNO [CN]
TEL. 0172470284
www.castellodiverduno.com

CELLAR SALES
PRE-BOOKED VISITS
ACCOMMODATION AND RESTAURANT SERVICE
ANNUAL PRODUCTION 60,000 bottles
HECTARES UNDER VINE 10.00

It is hard to imagine a place with more history and charm than this corner of the world that is home to the Castello di Verduno estate. The magic lives on today in the prestigious wines produced harvest after harvest by husband and wife team Gabriella Burlotto and Franco Bianco. There are no chinks in their armoury of wines, but those derived from pelaverga and nebbiolo in particular testify to just how special these bottles are. Their austere and dazzling character is unrivalled and comes into its own with patience and oxygen. All the wines on offer are aged in large barrels. The Barolo crus are Massara and Monvigliero in Verduno, while Faset and Rabajà are in Barbaresco. The Castello di Verduno proposes a copious range that includes all of the crus and the Barolo and Barbaresco Riservas. This was an extremely difficult choice, especially given the majestic Barbera Bricco del Cuculo 2011 that holds its own with the nebbiolo-based wines. Our vote finally went to the aromas of the Massara 2008.

● Barolo Massara '08	♟♟♟ 6
● Barbaresco Faset '09	♟♟ 5
● Barbaresco Rabajà Ris. '06	♟♟ 6
● Barolo Monvigliero Ris. '06	♟♟ 7
● Barbaresco '09	♟♟ 5
● Barbaresco Rabajà '09	♟♟ 6
● Barbera d'Alba '12	♟♟ 3
● Barbera d'Alba Bricco del Cuculo '11	♟♟ 4
● Langhe Nebbiolo '12	♟♟ 3
● Verduno Pelaverga Basadone '12	♟♟ 3
○ Bellis Perennis '12	♟ 2
● Dolcetto d'Alba Campot '12	♟ 2
⊙ S-Ciopét Brut Rosé M. Cl. '10	♟ 5
● Barbaresco Rabajà '04	♟♟♟ 6
● Barolo Monvigliero Ris. '04	♟♟♟ 7

La Caudrina

S.DA BROSIA, 21
12053 CASTIGLIONE TINELLA [CN]
TEL. 0141855126
www.caudrina.it

CELLAR SALES
PRE-BOOKED VISITS
ANNUAL PRODUCTION 200,000 bottles
HECTARES UNDER VINE 24.00

Romano Dogliotti's winery is almost totally dedicated to moscato. It has 22 hectares under vine, on mainly calcareous marl soils in the municipality of Castiglione Tinella, with plants of between 35 and 45 years old. These provide the raw materials from which La Caudrina produces practically all of the types envisaged under the production protocols of the various designations. Barbera grapes meanwhile come from Nizza Monferrato. The various versions of Moscato always aim to express varietal character to the full, with great focus and aromatic definition. This year we preferred the basic Moscato d'Asti 2012 and its lovely notes of flowers and aromatic herbs, fabulous complexity and character, and very fresh, lingering finish, to the La Galeisa 2012 with its sweeter tones of citrus and cakes. The Asti La Selvatica 2012 is fluent despite marked sweetness in the finish. The two Barbera d'Astis are well made: the Monte Venere 2010 is taut and fruity; the La Solista 2011 is nicely typical.

○ Moscato d'Asti La Caudrina '12	♟♟ 3*
○ Asti La Selvatica '12	♟♟ 3
● Barbera d'Asti La Solista '11	♟♟ 2*
● Barbera d'Asti Sup. Monte Venere '10	♟♟ 3
○ Moscato d'Asti La Galeisa '12	♟♟ 3
○ Asti La Selvatica '11	♟♟ 3
● Barbera d'Asti La Solista '09	♟♟ 2*
● Barbera d'Asti Sup. Monte Venere '08	♟♟ 3
○ Moscato d'Asti La Caudrina '11	♟♟ 3
○ Moscato d'Asti La Caudrina '10	♟♟ 3
○ Moscato d'Asti La Galeisa '11	♟♟ 3*

F.lli Cavallotto
Tenuta Bricco Boschis

LOC. BRICCO BOSCHIS
S.DA ALBA-MONFORTE
12060 CASTIGLIONE FALLETTO [CN]
TEL. 017362814
www.cavallotto.com

CELLAR SALES
PRE-BOOKED VISITS
ANNUAL PRODUCTION 110,000 bottles
HECTARES UNDER VINE 23.50

Siblings Alfio, Giuseppe and Laura
Cavallotto are the fifth generation to make
wine at Tenuta Bricco Boschis, a monopoly
cru of around 25 hectares in Castiglione
Falletto on the geological border between
the white and yellow marl of Diano d'Alba
and the blue marl of La Morra. This
splendid single block of vineyards is
cultivated using natural agricultural
methods. The varieties grown include
barbera, dolcetto, freisa, grignolino, pinot
nero and chardonnay, but it is the Barolo
nebbiolos that dominate as always.
Fermented in rotomacerator tanks and
aged in large barrels, the fruit from the San
Giuseppe and Vignolo vineyards also goes
to make the Riservas in the best years.
Once again we have a first-rate overall
showing from this estate. The Barolo Bricco
Boschis 2009 is assertive and attractively
nuanced in terms of the variety, with
tannins that are still smoothing out and
refreshing acidity. The Vigna San Giuseppe
Riserva 2007 is less complete at this stage,
rather introverted on the nose. The Barbera
Vigna del Cuculo 2010 is very sound.

● Barbera d'Alba Sup. V. del Cuculo '10	♟♟	5
● Barolo Bricco Boschis '09	♟♟	7
● Barolo Vignolo Ris. '07	♟♟	8
● Barolo Bricco Boschis V. S. Giuseppe Ris. '07	♟♟	8
● Langhe Freisa '11	♟♟	3
● Langhe Nebbiolo '11	♟♟	5
● Dolcetto d'Alba V. Scot '12	♟	3
● Barolo Bricco Boschis '05	♟♟♟	6
● Barolo Bricco Boschis '04	♟♟♟	7
● Barolo Bricco Boschis V. S. Giuseppe Ris. '05	♟♟♟	8
● Barolo Bricco Boschis V. S. Giuseppe Ris. '01	♟♟♟	7
● Barolo Bricco Boschis V. S. Giuseppe Ris. '00	♟♟♟	7
● Barolo Bricco Boschis V. S. Giuseppe Ris. '99	♟♟♟	7

Ceretto

LOC. SAN CASSIANO, 34
12051 ALBA [CN]
TEL. 0173282582
www.ceretto.com

CELLAR SALES
PRE-BOOKED VISITS
CELLAR SALES
ANNUAL PRODUCTION 900,000 bottles
HECTARES UNDER VINE 90.00
VITICULTURE METHOD Certified Organic

Over the years, the Ceretto family has
developed a diverse portfolio of cultural and
food and wine projects. Here we will
concentrate solely on the jewels that make
up the crown of this brand that has played a
major role in the history of Piedmont wine.
The property includes vineyards in Bricco
Rocche in Castiglione Falletto and Bricco
Asili in Barbaresco, the plots around the
cellar in Alba and the estate in Santo
Stefano di Belbo, the nerve centre of I
Vignaioli di Santo Stefano that merits a
profile of its own. The broad and varied
range of wines features both traditional and
native grape varieties and has a decidedly
modern but evolving style. The intriguing,
complex Barolo Bricco Rocche 2009 reveals
clear notes of tobacco, eucalyptus and dried
flowers supported by close-knit, powerful
tannic texture. The Barolo Prapò 2009 is
solid and, although young as yet, expresses
all the power and depth of this fabulous
Serralunga d'Alba cru.

● Barolo Bricco Rocche '09	♟♟♟	8
● Barbaresco Bernardot '10	♟♟	7
● Barolo Prapò '09	♟♟	8
● Barbaresco Asij '10	♟♟	7
● Barolo Brunate '09	♟♟	8
● Barolo Zonchera '09	♟♟	8
● Dolcetto d'Alba Rossana '12	♟♟	4
○ Langhe Arneis Blangé '12	♟♟	5
● Nebbiolo d'Alba Bernardina '11	♟♟	5
● Barbera d'Alba Piana '12	♟	5
● Langhe Rosso Monsordo '11	♟	5
● Barbaresco Asij '97	♟♟♟	5
● Barolo Bricco Rocche '00	♟♟♟	8
● Barolo Prapò '06	♟♟♟	8
● Barolo Prapò '05	♟♟♟	8

Erede di Armando Chiappone

S.DA SAN MICHELE, 51
14049 NIZZA MONFERRATO [AT]
TEL. 0141721424
www.eredechiappone.com

CELLAR SALES
PRE-BOOKED VISITS
CELLAR SALES
ANNUAL PRODUCTION 35,000 bottles
HECTARES UNDER VINE 10.00

Every member of the Chiappone family is involved in the running of this small estate on the slopes of San Michele above Nizza Monferrato. The vineyards fan out around the cellar and the main variety grown is barbera, as dictated by the terroir. Vinified with a traditional approach, it is present in all of its versions, from fresh, current vintage labels to passitos and chinatos, all the way through to the most representative and heavyweight wine, the Nizza. The other varieties grown are dolcetto, cortese, favorita and freisa, proposed in an interesting aged version. In the absence of the Nizza Ru, we were thrilled by the Barbera d'Asti Brentura 2011. Intense and complex, gorgeous notes of quina and cocoa powder lead into a fresh, clear note of cherry, a dense, enveloping palate with character, and a long, tangy, harmonious finish. The Angel, a blend of chardonnay, cortese and favorita, is agreeable, faintly aromatic with hints of appley fruit.

● Barbera d'Asti Brentura '11	♀♀	2*
○ Angel	♀	2
● Barbera d'Asti Brentura '10	♀♀	2*
● Barbera d'Asti Brentura '09	♀♀	2
● Barbera d'Asti Brentura '08	♀♀	2*
● Barbera d'Asti Brentura '07	♀♀	2*
● Barbera d'Asti Brentura '06	♀♀	2*
● Barbera d'Asti Sup. Nizza Ru '09	♀♀	4
● Barbera d'Asti Sup. Nizza Ru '06	♀♀	4
● Barbera d'Asti Sup. Nizza Ru '05	♀♀	4
● Freisa d'Asti Sanpedra '05	♀♀	2*

★Michele Chiarlo

S.DA NIZZA-CANELLI, 99
14042 CALAMANDRANA [AT]
TEL. 0141769030
www.chiarlo.it

CELLAR SALES
PRE-BOOKED VISITS
ACCOMMODATION
ANNUAL PRODUCTION 1,100,000 bottles
HECTARES UNDER VINE 100.00

Michele Chiarlo and the history of Italian wine have trodden the same path over the last 50 years. Today this family estate possesses vineyards in some of Piedmont's most prestigious DOCs, from Barolo to Barbaresco, from Nizza to Gavi. The range includes some very famous labels, such as the Cerequio and Cannubi Barolos and Barbera d'Asti Nizza La Court, making this one of the very best wineries not only in Piedmont but also beyond, The determinedly modern style does not prevent the estate from offering the finest expression of its land of origin. Chiarlo proposes its usual impressive array of quality wines, this time with the Barolos to the fore. The Tre Bicchieri goes to the Barolo Cerequio 2009, a concentrated, layered wine with aromas of balsam, fruit and spice, harmonious with a long finish full of character. The Barbera d'Asti Superiore Nizza La Court 2010 shows typical notes of rain-soaked earth, liquorice and plum, and perfect balance between fruity sweetness and acidity.

● Barolo Cerequio '09	♀♀♀	7
● Barbera d'Asti Sup. Nizza La Court '10	♀♀	5
● Barolo Tortoniano '09	♀♀	5
● Barbaresco Asili '10	♀♀	6
● Barbaresco Reyna '10	♀♀	5
● Barolo Cannubi '09	♀♀	7
○ Gavi del Comune di Gavi Rovereto '12	♀	3
○ Moscato d'Asti Nivole '12	♀	2
● Barbera d'Asti Sup. Nizza La Court '09	♀♀♀	5
● Barbera d'Asti Sup. Nizza La Court '06	♀♀♀	5
● Barolo Cannubi '06	♀♀♀	7
● Barolo Cannubi '04	♀♀♀	7
● Barolo Cerequio '07	♀♀♀	7
● Barolo Cerequio '98	♀♀♀	7
● Barolo Cerequio '97	♀♀♀	7

Quinto Chionetti

B.TA VALDIBERTI, 44
12063 DOGLIANI [CN]
TEL. 017371179
www.chionettiquinto.com

PRE-BOOKED VISITS
ANNUAL PRODUCTION 84,000 bottles
HECTARES UNDER VINE 16.00
VITICULTURE METHOD Certified Organic

This solid and highly reliable Dogliani estate constitutes an unwavering beacon for lovers of genuine wines that respect the finest traditions. While the wines reflect the various vintages, they are always very consistent in their style and essence. They're not aged in oak, with the exception of a light touch for Langhe Nebbiolo, and are very smooth and enjoyable from a young age, with a classic palate. A veritable beacon for the entire zone, the charismatic Quinto Chionetti has made an important contribution to promoting the uniqueness and solidity of Piedmont's extraordinary heritage of wines. The Dogliani Briccolero 2012 has a complex nose of blackberry, chocolate and tobacco. The palate is elegant, a tad austere, and reveals good balance between tannic vigour and fresh acidity. The San Luigi 2012 is close-focused and forthright with lively, pleasant drinkability. The Nebbiolo 2012 displays the agreeable fruitiness of the variety.

● Dogliani Briccolero '12	♀♀ 3*
● Dogliani S. Luigi '12	♀♀ 3
● Langhe Nebbiolo '12	♀♀ 3
● Dolcetto di Dogliani Briccolero '07	♀♀♀ 3*
● Dolcetto di Dogliani Briccolero '04	♀♀♀ 3*
● Dogliani Briccolero '11	♀♀ 3*
● Dogliani S. Luigi '11	♀♀ 3*
● Dolcetto di Dogliani Briccolero '09	♀♀ 3*
● Dolcetto di Dogliani Briccolero '08	♀♀ 3*
● Dolcetto di Dogliani Briccolero '06	♀♀ 3*
● Dolcetto di Dogliani Briccolero '05	♀♀ 3*
● Dolcetto di Dogliani Briccolero '03	♀♀ 3
● Langhe Nebbiolo '10	♀♀ 3
● Langhe Nebbiolo '09	♀♀ 3

Cieck

FRAZ. SAN GRATO
CASCINA CIECK
10011 AGLIÈ [TO]
TEL. 0124330522
www.cieck.it

CELLAR SALES
PRE-BOOKED VISITS
ANNUAL PRODUCTION 100,000 bottles
HECTARES UNDER VINE 16.00

There are few estates – in Piedmont or other regions – that are capable of producing such a high level of quality across such a wide range of typologies as Cieck. Established in 1985, it takes its name from a farm in the village of San Grato in Agliè and is run today by Remo Falconieri and Domenico Caretto. Production focuses largely on Erbaluce. It includes two Metodo Classicos, the stainless steel-aged San Giorgio and the barrique-matured Calliope; three still Calusos, namely the standard-label basic, the vintage Misobolo and the oak-aged T released a year later; the Passito Alladium; the Canavese Rosso; and the Neretto, also available in a Rosé version. It doesn't repeat last year's stellar performance, but Remo Falconieri achieves gratifying results across all typologies and sees no less than three wines in the finals. The Passito Alladium 2007, flavoursome and very sweet, lacks the perfect harmony of the previous vintage. The Calliope Brut offers crusty bread aromas and creamy prickle. The Misobolo stands out for sheer loveliness.

○ Erbaluce di Caluso Calliope Brut '07	♀♀ 4
○ Erbaluce di Caluso Misobolo '12	♀♀ 2*
○ Erbaluce di Caluso Passito Alladium '07	♀♀ 5
● Canavese Nebbiolo '10	♀♀ 3
○ Erbaluce di Caluso S. Giorgio Brut '08	♀♀ 4
○ Erbaluce di Caluso T '11	♀♀ 3
○ Erbaluce di Caluso '12	♀ 2
⊙ Rosé Brut M.Cl.	♀ 3
○ Erbaluce di Caluso Passito Alladium '06	♀♀♀ 5
○ Erbaluce di Caluso Misobolo '11	♀♀ 2*
○ Erbaluce di Caluso Misobolo '10	♀♀ 2*
○ Erbaluce di Caluso S. Giorgio Brut '07	♀♀ 4

F.lli Cigliuti

VIA SERRABOELLA, 17
12052 NEIVE [CN]
TEL. 0173677185
www.cigliuti.it

CELLAR SALES
PRE-BOOKED VISITS
ANNUAL PRODUCTION 30,000 bottles
HECTARES UNDER VINE 7.50

In order to gain a full understanding of the essence and depth of this estate's wines, one must taste a few old vintages of Barbaresco Serraboella, which is capable of offering unforgettable sensations. The wines are the fruit of the fine vineyards and ageing in a combination of Slavonian oak barrels and small used casks. Renato Cigliuti, aided by his wife Dina and daughters Claudia and Silvia, has been at the helm of this important winery for many years, and his character and personality are reflected in the restraint and austerity that he has shown in modernizing it, as well as in the style of the wines and the production philosophy in general. The Barbaresco Serraboella 2009 brings home another well-deserved Tre Bicchieri to the house of Cigliuti. This solid, expressive wine possesses dark notes of morello cherry and quina, full flavour and length. The Barbaresco Vie Erte 2009 is also very good, showing nice balance between tannic texture and supporting acidity.

● Barbaresco Serraboella '09	♟♟♟	7
● Barbaresco Vie Erte '09	♟♟	5
● Barbera d'Alba Campass '10	♟♟	4
● Langhe Nebbiolo '11	♟	3
● Barbaresco '83	♟♟♟	6
● Barbaresco Serraboella '01	♟♟♟	6
● Barbaresco Serraboella '00	♟♟♟	6
● Barbaresco Serraboella '97	♟♟♟	6
● Barbaresco Serraboella '96	♟♟♟	7
● Barbaresco Serraboella '90	♟♟♟	6
● Barbaresco V. Erte '04	♟♟♟	6
● Barbaresco Serraboella '08	♟♟	7
● Barbera d'Alba Serraboella '09	♟♟	3*
● Langhe Rosso Briccoserra '08	♟♟	5

★Tenute Cisa Asinari dei Marchesi di Grésy

S.DA DELLA STAZIONE, 21
12050 BARBARESCO [CN]
TEL. 0173635222
www.marchesidigresy.com

CELLAR SALES
PRE-BOOKED VISITS
ANNUAL PRODUCTION 200,000 bottles
HECTARES UNDER VINE 35.00

Finesse and elegance: the domestic and international success of this estate, owned by the Gresy family as far back as 1797, can be summed up in these two words, which perfectly express the style of their classic Barbaresco. They began to sell their wines directly 40 years ago, thanks to Alberto Gresy, who created a clearly recognizable style which has remained constant over time, as has the outstanding quality of the wines. These results are achieved thanks to short macerations, a judicious use of oak and painstaking attention to detail in all the phases of production, starting with historic, renowned vineyards such as Camp Gros Martinenga, whose grapes are only vinified in the best years. The Barbaresco Camp Gros Martinenga 2009 gives an exemplary performance. Complex and noble on the nose, it offers faint hints of medicinal herbs, rhubarb and tobacco, and an austere palate that opens out savoury and long. The Barbaresco Gaiun 2009 is very drinkable and fresh on the palate.

● Barbaresco Camp Gros Martinenga '09	♟♟♟	8
● Barbaresco Gaiun Martinenga '09	♟♟	8
● Barbaresco Martinenga '10	♟♟	7
● Barbera d'Asti Monte Colombo '09	♟♟	5
○ Langhe Bianco Villa Giulia '12	♟	3
● Langhe Rosso Villa Martis '10	♟♟	3
● Langhe Rosso Virtus '07	♟♟	6
○ Langhe Sauvignon '12	♟♟	3
○ Moscato d'Asti La Serra '12	♟♟	3
● Barbera d'Asti '12	♟	3
○ Langhe Chardonnay '12	♟	3
● M.to Rosso Merlot da Solo '07	♟	5
● Barbaresco Camp Gros '06	♟♟♟	8
● Barbaresco Camp Gros '05	♟♟♟	8
● Barbaresco Camp Gros Martinenga '08	♟♟♟	8

★★Domenico Clerico

LOC. MANZONI, 67
12065 MONFORTE D'ALBA [CN]
TEL. 017378171
info@domenicoclerico.com

PRE-BOOKED VISITS
ANNUAL PRODUCTION 110,000 bottles
HECTARES UNDER VINE 21.00

From his shiny new high-tech cellar in Montforte d'Alba, Domenico Clerico continues to be one of the leading lights of Piedmontese viticulture, for the wines of this genuine, multitalented and very likeable man are renowned throughout Italy and the world. Their style is decidedly modern, and the cellar is dominated by 225-litre French oak barrels used for ageing the Barolo selections. All the wines exhibit plenty of body and fruit and are made in a distinctly recognizable style. The grapes are absolutely excellent, hailing from Domenico's enviable array of vineyards. Classic balsamic notes and hints of tobacco and liquorice are the hallmark of the superb Barolo Ciabot Mentin 2009, with close-knit tannins and a lingering finish. The Barolo Percristina 2005 profits from its lengthy ageing, revealing dried flower and tar aromas supported by a deep, austere palate.

● Barolo Aeroplanservaj '08	♟♟ 7
● Barolo Ciabot Mentin '09	♟♟ 8
● Barolo Percristina '05	♟♟ 8
● Barbera d'Alba Trevigne '11	♟♟ 6
● Barolo Briccotto '09	♟♟ 7
● Barolo Pajana '09	♟♟ 8
● Langhe Rosso Arte '11	♟♟ 5
● Langhe Dolcetto Visadì '12	♟ 2
● Langhe Nebbiolo Capisme-e '12	♟ 5
● Barolo Ciabot Mentin '08	♟♟♟ 8
● Barolo Ciabot Mentin Ginestra '05	♟♟♟ 8
● Barolo Ciabot Mentin Ginestra '04	♟♟♟ 8
● Barolo Ciabot Mentin Ginestra '01	♟♟♟ 7
● Barolo Percristina '01	♟♟♟ 8

Elvio Cogno

VIA RAVERA, 2
12060 NOVELLO [CN]
TEL. 0173744006
www.elviocogno.com

CELLAR SALES
PRE-BOOKED VISITS
ANNUAL PRODUCTION 70,000 bottles
HECTARES UNDER VINE 13.00
VITICULTURE METHOD Certified Organic

This estate is worth a visit for the beauty of the winery building and its natural setting alone; however, its entire line of wines is equally stunning. The progress made by Valter Fissore and his wife Nadia Cogno is plain for all to see, for the qualitative growth of their wines has been accompanied by their success on the leading international markets. The painstaking precision evident in visiting the estate can also be found in all the wines of the range, and work in the vineyards is carried out with the utmost respect for the terroir and without use of pesticides. The quality of this estate continues to march apace. It takes our top prize with a Barolo Bricco Pernice 2008 that is absolutely impeccable in its elegance and balance. The Barolo Vigna Elena Riserva 2007 is solid and compressed; the Ravera 2009 is more appealing and soft. A special mention for the Barbera Bricco dei Merli 2011.

● Barolo Bricco Pernice '08	♟♟♟ 8
● Barbaresco Bordini '10	♟♟ 5
● Barolo Ravera '09	♟♟ 7
● Barolo V. Elena Ris. '07	♟♟ 8
● Barolo Cascina Nuova '09	♟♟ 6
● Barbera d'Alba Bricco dei Merli '11	♟♟ 4
● Dolcetto d'Alba V. del Mandorlo '12	♟♟ 3
○ Langhe Bianco Anas-cëtta '12	♟♟ 3
● Langhe Rosso Montegrilli '11	♟♟ 5
● Barolo Bricco Pernice '05	♟♟♟ 8
● Barolo Ravera '07	♟♟♟ 7
● Barolo Ravera '04	♟♟♟ 6
● Barolo V. Elena '04	♟♟♟ 8
● Barolo V. Elena '01	♟♟♟ 7
● Barolo V. Elena Ris. '06	♟♟♟ 8

Colle Manora

S.DA BOZZOLA, 5
15044 QUARGNENTO [AL]
TEL. 0131219252
www.collemanora.it

CELLAR SALES
PRE-BOOKED VISITS
ACCOMMODATION
ANNUAL PRODUCTION 90,000 bottles
HECTARES UNDER VINE 20.00

Giorgio Schon's winery has begun a new era, with a new sales manager and a new oenologist, Piero Ballario, who works with various wineries both in the zone of Alba and in the province of Alessandria. We look forward to seeing how things develop, and in the meantime will continue to enjoy the excellent quality of his wines. Barbera d'Asti, Monferrato and the Albarossa Ray come from native cultivars, while the wider range from international varieties includes sauvignon for Mimosa, chardonnay and viognier for Mila, and cabernet sauvignon and merlot for Rosso Barchetta. In the 2011 vintage, this wine presents intense, elegant aromas of black currant and blackberry with spicy undertones of cinnamon. The Barbera Manora 2011 shows structure in a very fruity context, while the Albarossa Ray is concentrated and very leisurely. The Pais 2012 has good nose-palate harmony and very pleasant progression. The Bianco Mimosa 2012 displays the characteristics of the variety, while the Mila 2012 has yet to assimilate its ageing in oak, still evident.

● Barbera d'Asti Sup. Manora '11	♟♟ 3
● Barbera del M.to Pais '11	♟♟ 2*
○ M.to Bianco Mimosa '12	♟♟ 2*
● M.to Rosso Barchetta '11	♟♟ 3
● M.to Rosso Ray '11	♟♟ 3
○ M.to Bianco Mila '11	♟ 4
● Barbera d'Asti Sup. Manora '09	♟♟ 3
● Barbera d'Asti Sup. Manora '07	♟♟ 3
○ M.to Bianco Mila '10	♟♟ 4
● M.to Rosso Barchetta '09	♟♟ 4
● M.to Rosso Ray '10	♟♟ 3
● M.to Rosso Ray '07	♟♟ 3

La Colombera

S.DA COMUNALE VHO, 7
15057 TORTONA [AL]
TEL. 0131867795
www.lacolomberavini.it

CELLAR SALES
PRE-BOOKED VISITS
ANNUAL PRODUCTION 60,000 bottles
HECTARES UNDER VINE 20.00

Colombera's range has extended over the years, and now has many strings to its bow. This family winery is run by Piercarlo and his daughter Lisa, who has just become a mother. In addition to Timorasso Montino, which has won various prizes, there is in fact a wide range of labels that earn appreciation also for their excellent value for money. The winery's philosophy is based on the use of native varieties such as nibiò, a clone of dolcetto typical of the Tortona area, croatina, cortese and obviously barbera. One of the best of its typology, the Barbera Elisa 2010 goes all the way to the finals with its red berry fruit and tobacco aromas and faint salty nuance that makes it very interesting. Another finalist, the already cited Timorasso Montino, falls just shy of top prize. The 2011 version is notable for its enormous capacity to integrate the variety's typical mineral notes with fruitier sensations of white peach and bergamot.

● Colli Tortonesi Barbera Elisa '10	♟♟ 3*
○ Colli Tortonesi Timorasso Il Montino '11	♟♟ 5
○ Colli Tortonesi Timorasso Derthona '11	♟♟ 4
● Colli Tortonesi Barbera Vegia Rampana '11	♟♟ 2*
● Colli Tortonesi Rosso Suciaja '11	♟♟ 3
○ Colli Tortonesi Cortese Bricco Bartolomeo '12	♟ 2
● Colli Tortonesi Croatina Arché '10	♟ 4
○ Colli Tortonesi Timorasso Il Montino '09	♟♟ 5
○ Colli Tortonesi Timorasso Il Montino '06	♟♟ 4
○ Colli Tortonesi Timorasso Derthona '10	♟♟ 4
● Colli Tortonesi Barbera Elisa '09	♟♟ 3
● Colli Tortonesi Rosso Vegia Rampana '08	♟♟ 2*
○ Colli Tortonesi Timorasso Derthona '09	♟♟ 3
○ Colli Tortonesi Timorasso Il Montino '10	♟♟ 5

★Aldo Conterno

LOC. BUSSIA, 48
12065 MONFORTE D'ALBA [CN]
TEL. 017378150
www.poderialdoconterno.com

ANNUAL PRODUCTION 120,000 bottles
HECTARES UNDER VINE 25.00

Today Franco, Stefano and Giacomo uphold the reputation of the estate founded in 1969 by their father Aldo, who recently passed away. The family vineyards in the Bussia di Monforte area's Romirasco, Cicala and Colonnello crus, have yielded some of the most classic and ageworthy Barolos in history, commencing with the legendary Granbussia Riserva. This legacy has been preserved with a light restyling, resulting in Nebbiolos that have become more powerful and toastier over the years, despite ageing in large barrels. The estate is also home to other traditional grape varieties, such as barbera, dolcetto and freisa, and small amounts of chardonnay, cabernet sauvignon and merlot. Despite the absence of the Granbussia 2006, the overall range shows very well, consistent and distinctive in style. The complex, harmonious Barolo Bussia Cicala 2009 shows notes of tobacco, liquorice and spice, and vigorous tannins. The juicy, wide-ranging Barbera Conca Tre Pile 2010 is very drinkable.

● Barbera d'Alba Conca Tre Pile '10	♥♥	5
● Barolo Bussia Cicala '09	♥♥	8
● Barolo Bussia Colonnello '09	♥♥	8
● Barolo Bussia Romirasco '09	♥♥	8
● Barolo Bussia '09	♥♥	8
○ Langhe Bussiador '10	♥♥	5
● Langhe Nebbiolo Il Favot '10	♥♥	6
● Barolo Bussia Soprana '86	♀♀♀	7
● Barolo Bussia Soprana '85	♀♀♀	7
● Barolo Gran Bussia Ris. '01	♀♀♀	8
● Barolo Gran Bussia Ris. '95	♀♀♀	8
● Barolo Granbussia Ris. '05	♀♀♀	8
● Barolo Romirasco '04	♀♀♀	8
● Barolo Vigna del Colonnello '82	♀♀♀	8

Diego Conterno

VIA MONTÀ, 27
12065 MONFORTE D'ALBA [CN]
TEL. 0173789265
www.diegoconterno.it

CELLAR SALES
PRE-BOOKED VISITS
ANNUAL PRODUCTION 40,000 bottles
HECTARES UNDER VINE 7.50

The original nature of this young estate is eloquently expressed by the design of its unique and entertaining labels, which manage to convey the true spirit of its owner. Diego Conterno, aided by his son Stefano, has been at the helm of this important little gem for a decade, and during this short time has managed to make a name for himself with the balance and harmony of his entire line. The estate's vineyards are all very fine, crowned by the prized Ginestra and Le Coste crus. Medium-sized barrels are used in order to avoid overpowering oak flavours. Diego Conterno wins his first Tre Bicchieri with a big, deep Barolo Le Coste 2009 that offers a wide-ranging, inviting nose and compact, layered palate. He also proposes a very well-made Barolo 2009 with clear varietal definition and inviting drinkability. The fresh Barbera d'Alba Ferrione 2011 has red berry fruit notes.

● Barolo Le Coste '09	♥♥♥	6
● Barolo '09	♥♥	6
● Barbera d'Alba Ferrione '11	♥♥	3
● Nebbiolo d'Alba Baluma '11	♥	3
● Barbera d'Alba Ferrione '10	♀♀	3
● Barbera d'Alba Ferrione '07	♀♀	3
● Barolo '07	♀♀	6
● Barolo Le Coste '08	♀♀	6
● Barolo Le Coste '07	♀♀	6
● Barolo Le Coste '06	♀♀	6
● Langhe Rosso Mongùglielmo '07	♀♀	4
● Nebbiolo d'Alba Baluma '10	♀♀	3
● Nebbiolo d'Alba Baluma '09	♀♀	3*
● Nebbiolo d'Alba Baluma '08	♀♀	3*

★★Giacomo Conterno

LOC. ORNATI, 2
12065 MONFORTE D'ALBA [CN]
TEL. 017378221
conterno@conterno.it

Paolo Conterno

VIA GINESTRA, 34
12065 MONFORTE D'ALBA [CN]
TEL. 017378415
www.paoloconterno.com

PRE-BOOKED VISITS
ANNUAL PRODUCTION 60,000 bottles
HECTARES UNDER VINE 17.00

CELLAR SALES
PRE-BOOKED VISITS
ACCOMMODATION AND RESTAURANT SERVICE
ANNUAL PRODUCTION 70,000 bottles
HECTARES UNDER VINE 13.80

The estate's Barolo Monfortino is
deservedly considered among the most
famous wines in the world, a veritable
symbol of Italian oenological excellence,
although a careful tasting of its other labels
reveals the formidable overall quality of the
entire range. A few years ago the winery
added a plot in the important Cerretta cru
to its prestigious Francia cru, both in the
municipality of Serralunga d'Alba. The
wines have always been characterized by
their classic style, depth and crystal-clear
purity on the palate, along with their
extraordinary cellarability, underscoring the
uniqueness of this historic Piedmont
producer. The highly seductive Barolo
Monfortino 2006 takes top prize and with
its close-focused, typical, complex nose
and wide-ranging, extremely lengthy palate
confirms its status as a wine of absolute
quality. The entire range performs very well.

This interesting Monforte estate is situated
in the countryside, out of town, hinting at
the style of its wines, which are austere
and not in the least bit flamboyant. Indeed,
classicism is the guiding principle of the
determined Giorgio in his production. The
extraordinary Ginestra cru is the jewel in
the estate's crown, scrupulously tended to
ensure top-quality grapes. Today the
winery has finally started to enjoy
much-deserved international success. The
Barolo Ginestra 2009 shows its customary
balsamic freshness and dynamic palate,
but is a bit less assertive than in previous
vintages. The lovely Barolo Riva del Bric
2009 offers dried flower and spice
aromas. The fresh, typical Langhe Nebbiolo
A Mont 2011 is very convincing.

● Barolo Monfortino Ris. '06	♛♛♛ 8
● Barbera d'Alba Cascina Francia '11	♛♛ 5
● Barolo Cascina Francia '09	♛♛ 8
● Barbera d'Alba Cerretta '11	♛♛ 5
● Barolo Cascina Francia '06	♛♛♛ 8
● Barolo Cascina Francia '05	♛♛♛ 8
● Barolo Cascina Francia '04	♛♛♛ 8
● Barolo Monfortino Ris. '05	♛♛♛ 8
● Barolo Monfortino Ris. '04	♛♛♛ 8
● Barolo Monfortino Ris. '02	♛♛♛ 8
● Barolo Monfortino Ris. '01	♛♛♛ 8
● Barolo Monfortino Ris. '00	♛♛♛ 8
● Barolo Monfortino Ris. '99	♛♛♛ 8
● Barolo Monfortino Ris. '74	♛♛♛ 8

● Barolo Ginestra '09	♛♛ 8
● Barolo Riva del Bric '09	♛♛ 6
● Dolcetto d'Alba L'Alto '12	♛♛ 2*
● Langhe Nebbiolo A Mont '11	♛♛ 4
● Langhe Nebbiolo Bric Ginestra '10	♛♛ 5
● Barbera d'Alba Bricco '12	♛ 3
● Barolo Ginestra '06	♛♛♛ 8
● Barolo Ginestra '05	♛♛♛ 8
● Barolo Ginestra Ris. '06	♛♛♛ 8
● Barolo Ginestra Ris. '05	♛♛♛ 8
● Barolo Ginestra Ris. '01	♛♛♛ 8
● Barbera d'Alba Ginestra '07	♛♛ 3
● Barolo Ginestra '08	♛♛ 8
● Barolo Ginestra '07	♛♛ 8
● Barolo Ginestra Ris. '04	♛♛ 8

★Conterno Fantino

VIA GINESTRA, 1
12065 MONFORTE D'ALBA [CN]
TEL. 017378204
www.conternofantino.it

PRE-BOOKED VISITS
ANNUAL PRODUCTION 140,000 bottles
HECTARES UNDER VINE 26.00
VITICULTURE METHOD Certified Organic

Conterno Fantino is perched on a hilltop that dominates the old town of Monforte d'Alba. A delightful large tasting room overlooks the estate's vineyards where strict organic practices are followed, offering a perfect example of sustainable viticulture. Respect for the environment is the focus of the philosophy here, as demonstrated by a cellar that combines energy-saving techniques with the use of renewable energy sources. The involvement of the whole family allows Guido Fantino and Claudio Conterno to continue their high-quality production with pride. The excellent Barolo Vigna del Gris 2009 took our top accolade with soft minty nuances that mingle with notes of tobacco and Peruvian bark. Barolo Sorì Ginestra 2009 is deep and complex, while Langhe Rosso Monprà 2010 is exceptionally convincing, with vivid aromas of berry fruit and spice.

Contratto

VIA G. B. GIULIANI, 56
14053 CANELLI [AT]
TEL. 0141823349
www.contratto.it

CELLAR SALES
PRE-BOOKED VISITS
ANNUAL PRODUCTION 140,000 bottles
HECTARES UNDER VINE 21.00

With Giorgio Rivetti, the La Contratto winery at Canelli has returned to its roots, to focus entirely on the production of sparklers. The few labels are all vintages, with this year's Asti De Miranda produced using the long Charmat method, which takes 18 months. The grapes, almost 90% pinot nero, come from growers who have been working with the winery for decades, and from vineyards with an average age of over 40 years. For England Pas Dosé Blanc de Noirs 2009 has a nose of acacia blossom and damson on a citrussy background and a characterful palate that is potent and beautifully creamy yet balanced and dynamic. The alluring Asti De Miranda 2011 has classic notes of brioche and candied peel with floral hints, and perfectly calibrated sweetness on the palate, with a fresh, zesty finish. Blanc de Blancs Brut 2010 has honeyed appley notes, focusing more on opulent fruit than freshness.

● Barolo V. del Gris '09	♈♈♈ 8
● Barolo Sorì Ginestra '09	♈♈ 8
● Langhe Rosso Monprà '10	♈♈ 5
● Barbera d'Alba Vignota '11	♈♈ 3
● Barolo Mosconi '09	♈♈ 8
● Dolcetto d'Alba Bricco Bastia '12	♈♈ 2*
○ Langhe Chardonnay Bastia '11	♈♈ 5
○ Langhe Chardonnay Prinsìpi '12	♈ 2
● Langhe Nebbiolo Ginestrino '11	♈ 4
● Barolo Sorì Ginestra '07	♈♈♈ 8
● Barolo Sorì Ginestra '00	♈♈♈ 7
● Barolo Sorì Ginestra '99	♈♈♈ 8
● Barolo Sorì Ginestra '98	♈♈♈ 8
● Barolo V. del Gris '04	♈♈♈ 8
● Barolo V. del Gris '01	♈♈♈ 8

○ Blanc de Blancs Brut '10	♈♈ 4
○ For England Pas Dosé Blanc de Noirs '09	♈♈ 5
○ Asti De Miranda '11	♈♈ 5
○ Millesimato Extra Brut '09	♈♈ 4
○ For England Brut Rosé '09	♈ 5
○ Asti De Miranda M. Cl. '00	♈♈♈ 5
○ Asti De Miranda M. Cl. '97	♈♈♈ 5
○ Asti De Miranda M. Cl. '96	♈♈♈ 5
● Barolo Cerequio '99	♈♈♈ 8
● Barolo Cerequio Tenuta Secolo '97	♈♈♈ 8
○ Spumante M. Cl. Brut Giuseppe Contratto Ris. '96	♈♈♈ 5
○ Spumante M. Cl. Brut Giuseppe Contratto Ris. '95	♈♈♈ 5

Vigne Marina Coppi
VIA SANT'ANDREA, 5
15051 CASTELLANIA [AL]
TEL. 3385360111
www.vignemarinacoppi.com

★Coppo
VIA ALBA, 68
14053 CANELLI [AT]
TEL. 0141823146
www.coppo.it

CELLAR SALES
PRE-BOOKED VISITS
ANNUAL PRODUCTION 25,000 bottles
HECTARES UNDER VINE 4.00

CELLAR SALES
PRE-BOOKED VISITS
ANNUAL PRODUCTION 400,000 bottles
HECTARES UNDER VINE 22.00

Just as his grandfather Fausto sped up the rankings of cyclists, Francesco is rapidly earning a leading role among the growers of the Colli Tortonesi area and beyond. Although his decision to dedicate himself body and soul to the world of wine is a recent one, the results have already been extremely impressive. He initially focused on Favorita, and while achieving solid results, it is with Barbera and above all Timorasso that he has earned significant, widespread recognition. Once again the Fausto takes a Tre Bicchieri, with its bright hue, firm acid backbone and decidedly invigorating structure. The vibrant mineral nose has pleasant aromas of white-fleshed fruit and grapefruit. The red wines also performed splendidly, especially the two Barberas: the more powerful, extracted Castellania and particularly the delicious Sant'Andrea.

Since its foundation in 1892, this historic estate has been a benchmark for the zone's spumante production. Over the years, it has also built a reputation for the quality of its still wines. Most of its vineyards lie in Canelli, but it also has plots in the province of Alessandria and Langhe. The wines are modern in style and derived from local cultivars – mainly barbera – and international ones like pinot nero and chardonnay, used to make one of the most interesting and complex Italian wines based on this grape variety. Together, the latter two also form the base for the Metodo Classico sparklers. This year the estate's classics are flanked by some fine sparkling wines with good fullness and freshness. Barbera d'Asti Pomorosso 2010 won a Tre Bicchieri with its notes of dark berry fruit and pencil lead, elegant tannins and taut, caressing finish, while Piemonte Chardonnay Monteriolo 2009 confirmed its white Burgundian style in terms of complexity and behaviour.

○ Colli Tortonesi Timorasso Fausto '11	♆♆♆ 6
● Colli Tortonesi Barbera Sant'Andrea '12	♆♆ 3*
● Colli Tortonesi Barbera Castellania '10	♆♆ 4
○ Colli Tortonesi Favorita Marine '11	♆♆ 5
● Colli Tortonesi Rosso Lindin '10	♆♆ 5
○ Colli Tortonesi Timorasso Fausto '10	♆♆♆ 6
○ Colli Tortonesi Timorasso Fausto '09	♆♆♆ 6
● Colli Tortonesi Barbera Castellania '09	♆♆ 3*
● Colli Tortonesi Barbera I Grop '08	♆♆ 5
● Colli Tortonesi Barbera Sant'Andrea '10	♆♆ 3
● Colli Tortonesi Barbera Sup. I Grop '09	♆♆ 5
● Colli Tortonesi Rosso Lindin '09	♆♆ 5
○ Colli Tortonesi Timorasso Fausto '08	♆♆ 6
○ Colli Tortonesi Timorasso Fausto '07	♆♆ 6

● Barbera d'Asti Pomorosso '10	♆♆♆ 7
○ Piemonte Chardonnay Monteriolo '09	♆♆ 5
○ Piero Coppo Ris. del Fondatore M. Cl. '04	♆♆ 5
● Barbera d'Asti L'Avvocata '12	♆♆ 2*
● Barbera d'Asti Sup. Nizza Riserva della Famiglia '06	♆♆ 8
● Barolo '09	♆♆ 7
☉ Clelia Brut Rosé M. Cl. '09	♆♆ 5
○ Piemonte Chardonnay Riserva della Famiglia '07	♆♆ 8
○ Riserva Coppo Brut M. Cl. '07	♆♆ 5
○ Gavi La Rocca '12	♆ 3
● M.to Alterego '10	♆ 4
● Barbera d'Asti Pomorosso '08	♆♆♆ 6
○ Piemonte Chardonnay Monteriolo '08	♆♆♆ 5

Giovanni Corino

FRAZ. ANNUNZIATA, 24B
12064 LA MORRA [CN]
TEL. 0173509452
www.corino.it

CELLAR SALES
PRE-BOOKED VISITS
ANNUAL PRODUCTION 45,000 bottles
HECTARES UNDER VINE 8.00

The Barolos produced by Giovanni Corino and his son Giuliano have long been synonymous with consistent quality and an ideal balance of terroir character and personal touch. Their style is calibrated to offer a degree of drinkability able to satisfy even the most demanding palates, both in youth and after long ageing. Fruit, perfect structure and nicely restrained tannic weave characterize the Langhe estate's wines and their availability on some of the leading international markets has helped to make the winery a familiar name with a reputation for consistent, sound production. Barolo Vigna Giachini 2009 has a nose of sweet tobacco and spice, and a caressing palate with prominent tannins, while Barolo Vigneto Arborina 2009 focuses on dark notes of morello cherry and Peruvian bark. Barolo Vecchie Vigne 2008 is still rather oak heavy.

Renato Corino

FRAZ. ANNUNZIATA - B.TA POZZO, 49A
12064 LA MORRA [CN]
TEL. 0173500349
renatocorino@alice.it

CELLAR SALES
PRE-BOOKED VISITS
ANNUAL PRODUCTION 50,000 bottles
HECTARES UNDER VINE 7.00

The scenic location of this interesting little Langhe winery is characterized by the splendid backdrop of the famous Arborina vineyard. Renato Corino is an expert vigneron who for the past few years has been conducting his new winemaking adventure in a very well-designed cellar, calibrated for the production of small quantities but consistent quality. His wines are generally very generous and full bodied, with expressive power destined to accompany them throughout the entire ageing process. The estate's vineyards are home to many old vines, which ensure depth and character. A Tre Bicchieri went to the excellent Barolo Rocche dell'Annunziata 2009. It vaunts a close-focused nose, with notes of spice, tar and violet, and a deep palate well supported by a powerful tannic weave. We also liked the elegant, balanced Barolo Arborina 2009 and the tempting top-quality Barbera d'Alba Pozzo 2010.

● Barolo V. Giachini '09	♀♀ 7
● Barolo '09	♀♀ 6
● Barolo V. V. '08	♀♀ 8
● Barolo Vign. Arborina '09	♀♀ 7
● Barbera d'Alba V. Pozzo '97	♀♀♀ 5
● Barbera d'Alba V. Pozzo '96	♀♀♀ 5
● Barolo Rocche '01	♀♀♀ 7
● Barolo Rocche '90	♀♀♀ 7
● Barolo V. Giachini '89	♀♀♀ 7
● Barolo V. V. '99	♀♀♀ 8
● Barolo V. V. '98	♀♀♀ 8
● Barolo V. Giachini '08	♀♀ 7
● Barolo V. V. '07	♀♀ 8
● Barolo V. V. '06	♀♀ 8

● Barolo Rocche dell'Annunziata '09	♀♀♀ 7
● Barbera d'Alba V. Pozzo '10	♀♀ 5
● Barolo Arborina '09	♀♀ 7
● Barolo '09	♀♀ 5
● Barolo Ris. '07	♀♀ 8
● Barolo Vign. Rocche '06	♀♀♀ 7
● Barolo Vign. Rocche '04	♀♀♀ 8
● Barolo Vign. Rocche '03	♀♀♀ 8
● Barbera d'Alba V. Pozzo '07	♀♀ 5
● Barbera d'Alba V. Pozzo '06	♀♀ 5
● Barolo '06	♀♀ 5
● Barolo Arborina '08	♀♀ 7
● Barolo Arborina '07	♀♀ 7
● Barolo V. V. '04	♀♀ 8
● Barolo V. V. Ris. '05	♀♀ 8

Cornarea

VIA VALENTINO, 150
12043 CANALE [CN]
TEL. 017365636
www.cornarea.com

CELLAR SALES
PRE-BOOKED VISITS
ACCOMMODATION
ANNUAL PRODUCTION 90,000 bottles
HECTARES UNDER VINE 14.00

This estate owned by the Bovone family lies on the Cornarea hill, just outside Canale. Its vineyards form a single block and contain arneis – which accounts for over two-thirds of the vines grown – and nebbiolo. The terrain is limestone and clay with a large magnesium component. Cornarea was one of the driving forces behind the Arneis renaissance in the late 1970s and early 1980s, and an exceptional 1983 is still available for tasting. The estate proposes just a few labels, all excellent, which are traditional in style and aspire to express the personality of the grape variety and the terroir to the full. Roero Arneis 2012 is not quite as good as past vintages, appearing pleasant but rather predictable, with aggressive acidity. However, we very much liked Tarasco Passito 2009, also from arneis, which is complex and balanced, with notes of dried figs, coffee and walnut, and a very long, firm finish supported by good acidity. The fruity Nebbiolo d'Alba 2011 has good staying power.

○ Tarasco Passito '09	♛♛	5
● Nebbiolo d'Alba '11	♛♛	3
● Roero '10	♛	4
○ Roero Arneis '12	♛	3
● Nebbiolo d'Alba '10	♛♛	3
● Nebbiolo d'Alba '07	♛♛	3
● Roero '09	♛♛	4
● Roero '08	♛♛	4
● Roero '07	♛♛	4
○ Roero Arneis '10	♛♛	3*
○ Roero Arneis '08	♛♛	3*
○ Tarasco Passito '08	♛♛	5
○ Tarasco Passito '07	♛♛	5
○ Tarasco Passito '06	♛♛	5

★Matteo Correggia

LOC. GARBINETTO
VIA SANTO STEFANO ROERO, 124
12043 CANALE [CN]
TEL. 0173978009
www.matteocorreggia.com

CELLAR SALES
PRE-BOOKED VISITS
ANNUAL PRODUCTION 130,000 bottles
HECTARES UNDER VINE 20.00

The estate founded by Matteo Correggia continues to flourish. Today, Ornella Costa Correggia is joined by her son Giovanni. Most of the vineyards are situated in the municipalities of Canale and Santo Stefano Roero on the fine-grained Pliocene Asti sand soil typical of Roero. The plot that produces the estate's finest wine, Roero Ròche d'Ampsèj, is worth a special mention. Here the terrain is a mix of Asti and Tortonian soils. The wines display wonderful technical rigour and a modern style. They are Roero through and through. The elegant Roero Ròche d'Ampsèj Riserva 2009 has returned to take our top award, with notes of tobacco and aromatic herbs on a fruity background; fine-grained, juicy tannins; full flavour and good length. Roero La Val dei Preti 2011 is excellent, still young and dominated by fruit, but Barbera d'Alba Superiore Marun 2011 isn't quite up to past versions, showing potent but closed and stiff. The rest of the list is very reliable.

● Roero Ròche d'Ampsèj Ris. '09	♛♛♛	6
● Roero La Val dei Preti '11	♛♛	5
● Anthos '12	♛♛	2*
● Anthos Passito	♛♛	4
● Barbera d'Alba '11	♛♛	3
● Barbera d'Alba Sup. Marun '11	♛♛	5
● Langhe Rosso Le Marne Grigie '11	♛♛	6
● Roero '11	♛♛	3
○ Langhe Bianco Matteo Correggia '11	♛	5
○ Roero Arneis '12	♛	3
● Barbera d'Alba Bricco Marun '94	♛♛♛	5
● Roero Ròche d'Ampsèj '04	♛♛♛	6
● Roero Ròche d'Ampsèj '01	♛♛♛	6
● Roero Ròche d'Ampsèj Ris. '07	♛♛♛	6
● Roero Ròche d'Ampsèj Ris. '06	♛♛♛	6

La Corte - Cusmano

REG. QUARTINO, 7
14042 CALAMANDRANA [AT]
TEL. 0141769091
www.cusmano.it

CELLAR SALES
PRE-BOOKED VISITS
HECTARES UNDER VINE 50.00

Raimondo Cusmano successfully and passionately manages not only the agriturismo and the splendid Relais di Calamandrana, but also the winery. The vineyards, all lying at elevations of between 320 and 400 metres, are divided into various plots situated in various municipalities, such as Calamandrana, Canelli, Cassinasco, Castel Foglione, Momperone and Nizza Monferrato, mainly on calcareous marl soils. His love for the land is evident in his decision to produce wines from individual vineyards, in the pursuit of a marked territorial identity. Barbera d'Asti Superiore Nizza Archincà 2010 is among the best of the designation again, with top notes of cherry and raspberry, followed by Peruvian bark and juniper. The dense, balanced palate is long and full flavoured. Barbera d'Asti La Birba 2011 is also well made, showing fresh, dynamic and juicy, as is the more powerful and caressing Barbera d'Asti Superiore La Grissa 2011, bursting with spicy notes.

● Barbera d'Asti Sup. Nizza Archincà '10	🏆🏆 2
● Barbera d'Asti La Birba '11	🏆🏆 2
● Barbera d'Asti Sup. La Grissa '11	🏆🏆 3
○ Moscato d'Asti Preludio '12	🏆 2
● Barbera d'Asti La Grissa '09	🏆🏆 4
● Barbera d'Asti Sup. Historical '08	🏆🏆 5
● Barbera d'Asti Sup. Historical '07	🏆🏆 5
● Barbera d'Asti Sup. Nizza Archincà '09	🏆🏆 4
● Barbera d'Asti Sup. Nizza Archincà '08	🏆🏆 4
● Barbera d'Asti Sup. Nizza Archincà '06	🏆🏆 4

Giuseppe Cortese

S.DA RABAJÀ, 80
12050 BARBARESCO [CN]
TEL. 0173635131
www.cortesegiuseppe.it

CELLAR SALES
PRE-BOOKED VISITS
ACCOMMODATION
ANNUAL PRODUCTION 50,000 bottles
HECTARES UNDER VINE 8.00

Giuseppe Cortese, aided by son Piercarlo and wife Rosella, has focused on terroir and stylistic coherency to make a name for his little estate, earning it cult status in the Barbaresco production zone. Eight hectares in the heart of a legendary "lieu-dit" like Rabaja already make the difference, particularly when they inspire authentic, traditional wines, aged in large and medium-sized barrels of both Slavonian and French oak. The rest of the range is equally classic in style, from Barbera to Dolcetto, and includes two Chardonnays. Barbaresco Rabajà 2010 is an excellent interpretation of this great cru that unanimously won our top award. Its character and personality are already evident on the nose that is followed by a very long, vibrant palate. Barbaresco Rabajà Riserva 2006 is fresh and focused, while Barbera d'Alba Morassina 2011 is well crafted.

● Barbaresco Rabajà '10	🏆🏆🏆 5
● Barbaresco Rabajà Ris. '06	🏆🏆 8
● Barbera d'Alba Morassina '11	🏆🏆 3
○ Langhe Chardonnay '12	🏆🏆 2*
● Barbera d'Alba '12	🏆 3
● Dolcetto d'Alba '12	🏆 2
● Barbaresco Rabajà Ris. '96	🏆🏆🏆 8
● Barbaresco Rabajà '09	🏆🏆 5
● Barbaresco Rabajà '05	🏆🏆 5
● Barbaresco Rabajà '01	🏆🏆 5*
● Barbaresco Rabajà Ris. '01	🏆🏆 8
● Barbaresco Rabajà Ris. '99	🏆🏆 8
● Barbera d'Alba '11	🏆🏆 2*
● Barbera d'Alba Morassina '10	🏆🏆 3

Clemente Cossetti

VIA GUARDIE, 1
14043 CASTELNUOVO BELBO [AT]
TEL. 0141799803
www.cossetti.it

CELLAR SALES
PRE-BOOKED VISITS
ACCOMMODATION AND RESTAURANT SERVICE
ANNUAL PRODUCTION 700,000 bottles
HECTARES UNDER VINE 22.00

This historic Monferrato estate, property of
the Cossetti family, is living proof that quality
and quantity can go hand in hand. The
estate both ferments grapes it buys in and
has its own high-level production obtained
from its own vineyards in Castelnuovo
Belbo. Here, the soil is medium-textured
and rich in minerals and the vines have an
average age of over 30 years. Barbera holds
sway and goes to make several labels. It is
flanked by cortese, chardonnay and
dolcetto. The grapes bought from other
growers come from several zones in
Piedmont, including Langhe, Gavi and
Roero. Drinkability, fruitiness and
pleasantness are the main characteristics of
the wines on offer. Barbera d'Asti Superiore
Nizza 2010 is delightful, with spicy
cinnamon, flowers and dark berry fruit,
showing full flavoured and balanced with
fine-grained tannins. Barbera d'Asti La
Vigna Vecchia 2011 is also well made, with
a nose of rain-soaked earth and a supple
palate with good acidity, as is the pleasant
but atypical Grignolino d'Asti 2012.

● Barbera d'Asti Sup. Nizza '10	♟♟	4
● Barbera d'Asti La Vigna Vecchia '11	♟♟	2*
● Grignolino d'Asti '12	♟♟	2*
● Barbera d'Asti La Vigna Vecchia '07	♟♟	2*
● Barbera d'Asti Sup. Nizza '09	♟♟	4
● Barbera d'Asti Sup. Nizza '08	♟♟	4
● Barbera d'Asti Sup. Nizza '07	♟♟	4
● Barbera d'Asti Venti di Marzo '10	♟♟	3
● Barbera d'Asti Venti di Marzo '08	♟♟	2*
● Grignolino D'Asti '09	♟♟	2*
● Piemonte Albarossa Amartè '10	♟♟	3
● Ruchè di Castagnole Monferrato '10	♟♟	3

Stefanino Costa

B.TA BENNA, 5
12046 MONTÀ [CN]
TEL. 0173976336
www.ninocosta.eu

HECTARES UNDER VINE 7.00

Nino Costa's estate is one of the finest in
Roero. His vineyards lie on the
predominantly sandy terrains typical of this
region, most of them at an altitude of
between 350 and 400 metres in the
municipalities of Canale, Montà and Santo
Stefano Roero. Here he grows the classic
Roero cultivars: arneis, barbera, brachetto
and nebbiolo. The wines proposed are
nicely defined and balanced within a
traditional framework that expresses the
characteristics of the terroir. Roero
Medic remains the estate's flagship wine,
with the 2010 showing fruity with plenty of
flesh and fine-grained tannins, lacking only
a little structure. The balsamic Barbera
d'Alba 2011 has spicy notes of tobacco
and ripe berry fruit. Although still rather too
oaky, it has plenty of character. Roero
Vecchie Vigne 2009 isn't as good as the
previous vintage, offering notes of ripe dark
berry fruit and autumn leaves, but without
really shining.

● Roero Medic '10	♟♟	3*
● Barbera d'Alba '11	♟♟	3
● Roero V. V. '09	♟♟	4
○ Langhe Bianco Ricordi '11	♟	3
○ Roero Arneis Sarun '09	♟	3
● Langhe Nebbiolo '10	♟♟	2*
● Nebbiolo d'Alba '09	♟♟	2*
● Roero '08	♟♟	2*
● Roero Bric del Medic '09	♟♟	3*
● Roero Bric del Medic '07	♟♟	3*
● Roero Bric del Medic '06	♟♟	3
● Roero V. V. '08	♟♟	4

Daniele Coutandin

B.TA CIABOT, 12
10063 PEROSA ARGENTINA [TO]
TEL. 0121803473
ramie.coutandin@alpimedia.it

PRE-BOOKED VISITS
ANNUAL PRODUCTION 2,000 bottles
HECTARES UNDER VINE 0.80

It's certainly not its production figures that lead us to include this small winery near Pinerolo in the Guide, seeing that the wines of Daniele Coutandin and his parents Giuliano and Laura Pero are produced in medicinal quantities. We love the indisputable sensory qualities of their products and admire their courage, for farming the incredibly steep terraces at Pomaretto, aided by a monorail system built by the provincial council of Turin. They also keep alive rare native varieties such as avanà, averengo, chatus, becouet, lambrusca vittona and berla grossa, and above all have resurrected the Ramìe beloved of Richelieu. As the Barbichè is still ageing in the cellar, we'll concentrate solely on the Ramìe 2011. The exuberant fruity notes of blackberries and blackcurrants are tempered by hints of blood and quinine, while the long finish is enlivened by finely balanced acidity and tannins.

● Pinerolese Ramìe '11	🍷🍷 4
● Barbichè '05	🍷🍷 3*
● Pinerolese Ramìe '09	🍷🍷 4
● Pinerolese Ramìe '08	🍷🍷 4
● Pinerolese Ramìe '07	🍷🍷 4

Dacapo

S.DA ASTI MARE, 4
14040 AGLIANO TERME [AT]
TEL. 0141964921
www.dacapo.it

CELLAR SALES
PRE-BOOKED VISITS
ANNUAL PRODUCTION 42,000 bottles
HECTARES UNDER VINE 8.00
VITICULTURE METHOD Certified Organic

Founded in 1997 with the renovation of an old property at Agliano Terme, this estate owned by Paolo Dania and Dino Riccomagno produces a limited array of bottles that aims to express the characteristics of the terroir as fully as possible and in harmony with the environment. Barbera in several labels is kingpin, but nebbiolo, ruché, merlot, pinot nero and chardonnay (the basis of the estate's Metodo Classico spumante) are also present and go to produce wines that are eminently drinkable and traditional in style. The vineyards, planted with vines up to 60 years old, are situated on marly limestone terrain between Agliano Terme and Castagnole Monferrato. Barbera d'Asti Superiore Nizza Vigna Dacapo 2010 proved itself among the best of the designation again. Although still dominated by the sweet spicy notes of oak and rather stiff tannins, it is long, dense and fruit rich. Barbera d'Asti Sanbastiàn 2011, on the other hand, is pleasant and fresh, with notes of berry fruit.

● Barbera d'Asti Sup. Nizza V. Dacapo '10	🍷🍷 4
● Barbera d'Asti Sanbastiàn '11	🍷🍷 2*
⊙ Brut Rosé M. Cl. '09	🍷 5
● Barbera d'Asti Sanbastiàn '10	🍷🍷 2*
● Barbera d'Asti Sanbastiàn '09	🍷🍷 2*
● Barbera d'Asti Sup. Nizza V. Dacapo '09	🍷🍷 4
● Barbera d'Asti Sup. Nizza V. Dacapo '08	🍷🍷 4
● Barbera d'Asti Sup. Nizza V. Dacapo '07	🍷🍷 4
● M.to Rosso Cantacucco '09	🍷🍷 5
● M.to Rosso Cantacucco '08	🍷🍷 5
● Ruché di Castagnole M.to Bric Majoli '10	🍷🍷 3

Damilano

VIA ROMA, 31
12060 BAROLO [CN]
TEL. 017356105
www.cantinedamilano.it

CELLAR SALES
PRE-BOOKED VISITS
ANNUAL PRODUCTION 440,000 bottles
HECTARES UNDER VINE 48.00

Damilano is one of Barolo's legendary wineries. The first traces of the estate date from 1890, when Guido, Paolo and Mario's great-grandfather decided to embark on the adventure of making wine from its grapes. The vineyards, both estate-owned and leased, represent a highly prestigious credential. Several historic crus such as Brunate, Cannubi and Cerequio, along with the small but important Liste, contribute to forming a range of terroir-true wines with a well-defined style. The dynamic Paolo Damilano, along with brothers Guido in the cellar and Mario in the role of consultant, has given the wines a strong commercial boost on both the Italian and international markets. The overall quality of the wines tasted is more than convincing. Produced in large quantities, Barolo Le Cinquevigne 2009 is an excellent example of elegance and drinkability, while Barolo Brunate 2009 has a nicely focused nose and a very satisfying palate. The esterified Barolo Cannubi 2009 is sophisticated and Cerequio 2009 is powerful.

● Barolo Brunate '09	♟♟ 7
● Barolo Cannubi '09	♟♟ 7
● Barolo Cerequio '09	♟♟ 7
● Barolo Lecinquevigne '09	♟♟ 6
○ Langhe Arneis '12	♟♟ 3
● Langhe Nebbiolo Marghe '11	♟♟ 3
○ Moscato d'Asti '12	♟♟ 3
● Barbera d'Alba La Blu '11	♟ 4
● Dolcetto d'Alba '12	♟ 3
● Barolo Cannubi '04	♟♟♟ 8
● Barolo Cannubi '01	♟♟♟ 6
● Barolo Cannubi '00	♟♟♟ 6
● Barolo Brunate '07	♟♟ 7
● Barolo Cannubi '08	♟♟ 7
● Barolo Cannubi '07	♟♟ 8

Deltetto

C.SO ALBA, 43
12043 CANALE [CN]
TEL. 0173979383
www.deltetto.com

CELLAR SALES
PRE-BOOKED VISITS
ANNUAL PRODUCTION 170,000 bottles
HECTARES UNDER VINE 21.00

The Deltetto family's estate proposes a wide-ranging series of labels. It includes the classic Roero wines obtained from the traditional local cultivars like arneis, nebbiolo and barbera, the well-established spumante production derived mainly from chardonnay and pinot nero but also from nebbiolo, and Langa wines such as Barolo and Dolcetto d'Alba. The bottles on offer are technically well made and notable for their rich fruit and drinkability. Braja Riserva 2010 confirms its status as one of the finest Roeros around, with concentrated notes of redcurrants and blueberries. Although not powerfully structured, it's easy-drinking with fine tannins and a long finish sustained by refreshing acidity. After all, Deltetto's entire range is among the most reliable in the zone, as demonstrated by the elegant Roero Arneis San Michele 2012, with floral notes and fresh vegetal hints, and the various sparklers, which are all pleasant and well made.

○ Roero Arneis S. Michele '12	♟♟ 3*
● Roero Braja Ris. '10	♟♟ 4
● Barbera d'Alba Sup. Bramé '11	♟♟ 3
○ Deltetto Brut M. Cl.	♟♟ 4
○ Deltetto Extra Brut M. Cl. '09	♟♟ 5
☉ Deltetto Rosé Extra Brut M. Cl.	♟♟ 5
● Langhe Rosso Pinot Nero '11	♟♟ 3
● Barbera d'Alba Sup. Rocca delle Marasche '04	♟♟♟ 5
● Roero Braja Ris. '09	♟♟♟ 4*
● Roero Braja Ris. '08	♟♟♟ 4
● Roero Braja Ris. '07	♟♟♟ 4
● Barbera d'Alba Sup. Bramé '09	♟♟ 3
● Barolo Sistaglia '08	♟♟ 5
○ Roero Arneis S. Michele '11	♟♟ 3

Destefanis

VIA MORTIZZO, 8
12050 MONTELUPO ALBESE [CN]
TEL. 0173617189
www.marcodestefanis.it

CELLAR SALES
PRE-BOOKED VISITS
ANNUAL PRODUCTION 60,000 bottles
HECTARES UNDER VINE 12.00

Just a few wines, great passion and
excellent quality are the distinguishing
features of this wine-growing operation
situated in a pretty little village in one of the
most authentic and least-known areas of
Langhe. Marco Destefanis confidently
conducts the business of a family with
deep roots in the wine trade. Over the years
the estate's unwavering progress has been
accompanied by its expansion to include a
good array of first-rate vineyards. Dolcetto
reigns supreme in this area and the Monia
Bassa vineyard selection is constantly
among its finest expressions. Prices are
equally interesting and competitive in
relation to quality. The performance of
Marco Destefanis's wines confirms the
quality of his very convincing reds, fronted
by Dolcettos, for which Montelupo Albese is
an excellent terroir, and uncomplicated,
easy-drinking whites. Monia Bassa 2012 in
particular combines impressive structure
with enviable finesse.

● Dolcetto d'Alba V. Monia Bassa '12	♥♥ 3*
● Barbera d'Alba '12	♥♥ 2*
● Dolcetto d'Alba Bricco Galluccio '12	♥♥ 2*
● Nebbiolo d'Alba '11	♥♥ 3
○ Langhe Arneis '12	♥ 2
○ Langhe Chardonnay '12	♥ 2
● Alba '10	♀♀ 3
● Dolcetto d'Alba Bricco Galluccio '11	♀♀ 2*
● Dolcetto d'Alba V. Monia Bassa '11	♀♀ 3*
● Dolcetto d'Alba V. Monia Bassa '10	♀♀ 3*
● Nebbiolo d'Alba '10	♀♀ 3
● Nebbiolo d'Alba '08	♀♀ 3*

Gianni Doglia

VIA ANNUNZIATA, 56
14054 CASTAGNOLE DELLE LANZE [AT]
TEL. 0141878359
www.giannidoglia.it

CELLAR SALES
PRE-BOOKED VISITS
ANNUAL PRODUCTION 70,000 bottles
HECTARES UNDER VINE 8.00

In barely a decade the young Gianni Doglia
has managed to earn not only a leading
place among Moscato producers, but also
a reputation for outstanding reds. The
vineyards, situated mainly around the
winery at elevations of between 300 and
350 metres on calcareous soils, are
planted to moscato, which accounts for
more than two thirds of production,
alongside barbera and small plantings of
merlot. The winery style focuses on
highlighting finesse and drinkability. The
Moscato Casa di Bianca selection made a
very successful debut, showing original and
varietal, with fresh notes of sage and
aniseed to balance its enticing well-
calibrated sweetness. Moscato d'Asti is as
convincing as ever and Barbera
Boscodonne 2012 is very drinkable. The
production of Monferrato Rosso "!" 2010,
from merlot, is small but excellent.

● Barbera d'Asti Boscodonne '12	♥♥ 2*
○ Moscato d'Asti Casa di Bianca '12	♥♥ 3*
● M.to Rosso ! '10	♥♥ 5
○ Moscato d'Asti '12	♥♥ 2*
● Barbera d'Asti Boscodonne '11	♀♀ 2*
● Barbera d'Asti Boscodonne '10	♀♀ 2*
● Barbera d'Asti Sup. '10	♀♀ 3*
● Barbera d'Asti Sup. '09	♀♀ 3
● Barbera d'Asti Sup. '08	♀♀ 3
● Barbera d'Asti Sup. '07	♀♀ 3
● M.to Rosso ! '09	♀♀ 5
○ Moscato d'Asti '11	♀♀ 2
○ Moscato d'Asti '10	♀♀ 2

★Poderi Luigi Einaudi

B.TA GOMBE, 31/32
12063 DOGLIANI [CN]
TEL. 017370191
www.poderieinaudi.com

CELLAR SALES
PRE-BOOKED VISITS
ACCOMMODATION
ANNUAL PRODUCTION 250,000 bottles
HECTARES UNDER VINE 52.00

This estate is steeped in history and the sensation of the presence of its founder, Luigi Einaudi, can still be perceived very strongly. In 2001 the large-scale renovation of the winery was completed, transforming its outward appearance. Today, one passes through the entrance gate and sees the historic buildings, but the entire cellar is practically underground, equipped with the very latest technologies and preserving the charm of one of the handsomest and most charming Langhe estates. The portfolio features several wines: Dolcetto and Nebbiolo obviously account for the lion's share, with Dogliani and Dogliani Tecc, followed by the Terlo, Cannubi and Costa Grimaldi Barolo selections. All three Barolos are expressive and well typed, but we slightly prefer Terlo 2009, with fragrant notes of blackberry and cherry alternating with balsamic hints on the nose, and racy tannins combined with fresh acidity on the palate. Costa Grimaldi 2009 is still a little closed, but promises very well for the future.

● Barolo Costa Grimaldi '09	🍷🍷	7
● Barolo Terlo '09	🍷🍷	6
● Barolo Cannubi '09	🍷🍷	8
● Dogliani '12	🍷🍷	3
● Dogliani Sup. V. Tecc '11	🍷🍷	3
● Langhe Nebbiolo '11	🍷🍷	3
● Piemonte Barbera '11	🍷	3
● Barolo Costa Grimaldi '05	🍷🍷🍷	8
● Barolo Costa Grimaldi '01	🍷🍷🍷	7
● Barolo nei Cannubi '00	🍷🍷🍷	8
● Barolo nei Cannubi '99	🍷🍷🍷	7
● Barolo nei Cannubi '98	🍷🍷🍷	7
● Dogliani Sup. V. Tecc '10	🍷🍷🍷	3*
● Dogliani V. Tecc '06	🍷🍷🍷	4
● Langhe Rosso Luigi Einaudi '04	🍷🍷🍷	5

Tenuta Il Falchetto

FRAZ. CIOMBI
VIA VALLE TINELLA, 16
12058 SANTO STEFANO BELBO [CN]
TEL. 0141840344
www.ilfalchetto.com

CELLAR SALES
PRE-BOOKED VISITS
ANNUAL PRODUCTION 280,000 bottles
HECTARES UNDER VINE 38.00

In recent years Tenuta Il Falchetto has made a name for itself as a solid, reliable operation, not only for moscato but also for barbera. Today, the winery has no fewer than nine estates, situated between Alba and Agliano Terme, where 12 different varieties are grown, both native and international, led by moscato and barbera. The original core of the estate, planted to moscato, is situated in the hills of Santo Stefano Belbo. The wines proposed are modern in style, while also displaying clear territorial traits. The splendid battery wines includes two versions of Barbera d'Asti Superiore: the fruit-rich Lurëi 2011, with a nose of autumn leaves and rain-soaked earth, and a taut, close-knit palate, and Bricco Paradiso 2011, which still shows prominent oak and great concentration, but without any heaviness. Moscato d'Asti Tenuta del Fant 2012 is also very fine: fresh and harmonious with a complex nose of sage and lime and a very long, zesty palate with great character.

● Barbera d'Asti Lurëi '11	🍷🍷	3*
● Barbera d'Asti Sup. Bricco Paradiso '11	🍷🍷	3*
○ Moscato d'Asti Tenuta del Fant '12	🍷🍷	2*
● M.to Rosso La Mora '11	🍷🍷	3
○ Moscato d'Asti Ciombi '12	🍷🍷	2*
● Nebbiolo d'Alba Barbarossa '11	🍷	3
○ Piemonte Moscato Passito '11	🍷	4
○ Moscato d'Asti Tenuta del Fant '11	🍷🍷🍷	2*
○ Moscato d'Asti Tenuta del Fant '09	🍷🍷🍷	2*
● Barbera d'Asti Pian Scorrone '11	🍷🍷	3
● Barbera d'Asti Sup. Bricco Paradiso '10	🍷🍷	3*
● Barbera d'Asti Sup. Lurëi '10	🍷🍷	3
○ Langhe Chardonnay '11	🍷🍷	5
● M.to Rosso Solo '10	🍷🍷	5
○ Moscato d'Asti Ciombi '11	🍷🍷	2*

Favaro

s.da Chiusure, 1 bis
10010 Piverone [TO]
Tel. 012572606
www.cantinafavaro.it

CELLAR SALES
PRE-BOOKED VISITS
ANNUAL PRODUCTION 18,000 bottles
HECTARES UNDER VINE 3.00

Camillo Favaro has carved out a role for himself in the world of Italian wine that goes way beyond that of talented producer from the district of Canavese. Expert in communication and events, author and great aficionado of Burgundy wines, he now runs this estate founded by his father Benito at Piverone in 1992. His three hectares all lie on the magnificent morainic slopes of Serra and produce two Erbaluces: Le Chiusure matured in stainless steel, and the oak-aged 13 Mesi selection that is released on the market one year after harvest. Rounding out the range we have a series of unusual red table wines obtained from syrah, freisa and barbera. It's nothing new for Favaro's Erbaluce di Caluso to win a Tre Bicchieri, particularly considering the quality of the 2012 vintage, which offers a wealth of natural smoky notes and a perfect combination of firm structure, full flavour and freshness on the palate. As usual, the 13 Mesi 2011 scored well, but the surprise this year came from the reds, particularly Rossomeraviglia 2011, from syrah.

○ Erbaluce di Caluso Le Chiusure '12	▼▼▼	2*
○ Erbaluce di Caluso 13 Mesi '11	▼▼	3*
● F2 '11	▼▼	2*
● Rossomeraviglia '11	▼▼	5
● Basy '11	▼	3
⊙ Rosacherosanonsei '12	▼	3
○ Erbaluce di Caluso Le Chiusure '11	♈♈♈	2*
○ Erbaluce di Caluso Le Chiusure '10	♈♈♈	2*
○ Erbaluce di Caluso 13 Mesi '10	♈♈	3*
○ Erbaluce di Caluso 13 Mesi '09	♈♈	3
● Rossomeraviglia '09	♈♈	5

Giacomo Fenocchio

loc. Bussia, 72
78675 Monforte d'Alba [CN]
Tel. 017378675
www.giacomofenocchio.com

CELLAR SALES
PRE-BOOKED VISITS
ANNUAL PRODUCTION 80,000 bottles
HECTARES UNDER VINE 14.00

Bussia in Monforte d'Alba, Villero in Castiglione Falletto, Cannubi in Barolo: it would be hard to think of a more prestigious or better assorted trio of nebbiolo crus. The Fenocchio brothers interpret their personalities in an array of fluent, austere wines that offer a strong territorial character, good ageing potential and extraordinarily good value for money. Their Barolos are proudly traditional but never overly severe. They are created by long maceration and lengthy ageing in 35- to 50-hectolitre barrels of Slavonian oak. Barbera, dolcetto and freisa complete the offering. Balance, harmony, personality and depth are the distinctive characteristics of Barolo Bussia 2009, which earned Fenocchio its first Tre Bicchieri. Barolo Villero 2009 offers notes of tobacco and spice, combined with weighty yet discreet tannins for an impeccable palate. Barolo Bussia Riserva 2007 is very alluring.

● Barolo Bussia '09	▼▼▼	6
● Barolo Bussia Ris. '07	▼▼	7
● Barolo Villero '09	▼▼	6
● Barbera d'Alba Sup. '11	▼▼	3
● Barolo Cannubi '09	▼▼	6
● Langhe Freisa '11	▼▼	3
● Langhe Nebbiolo '11	▼▼	3
○ Roero Arneis '12	▼	3
● Barolo Bussia '06	♈♈	6
● Barolo Bussia Ris. '06	♈♈	7
● Barolo Cannubi '08	♈♈	6
● Barolo Cannubi '06	♈♈	6
● Barolo Villero '06	♈♈	6
● Langhe Nebbiolo '10	♈♈	3

Ferrando

VIA TORINO, 599A
10015 IVREA [TO]
TEL. 0125633550
www.ferrandovini.it

CELLAR SALES
PRE-BOOKED VISITS
ANNUAL PRODUCTION 50,000 bottles
HECTARES UNDER VINE 6.50

This estate has a magic that is inversely proportionate to the tiny size of the DOC that clings to the terraces carved out of the rock faces of Carema, the last outpost of a Piedmont that is practically Valle d'Aosta. Yet it produces some of the most characterful and thrilling Nebbiolos that an enthusiast could possibly imagine: real mountain wines that seem light and lean right from the colour, yet are virtually immortal. Much of the credit goes to the work of the Ferrando family, whose Etichetta Bianca usually comes out a year before the Etichetta Nera, produced only in the very best years. The 2008 vintage of Roberto Ferrando's Carema enhances the innate characteristics of this great red from the Ivrea area. Etichetta Nera offers a complex nose, where berry fruit and oak merge superbly, and beautifully orchestrated tannins on the palate. Etichetta Bianca 2009 is only slightly less full bodied, while La Torrazza Brut 2008 is still young.

● Carema Et. Nera '08	▼▼▼ 6
● Carema Et. Bianca '09	▼▼ 5
○ Erbaluce di Caluso Brut M. Cl. La Torrazza '08	▼▼ 4
○ Erbaluce di Caluso Cariola '12	▼▼ 3
● Carema Et. Nera '07	♀♀♀ 6
● Carema Et. Nera '06	♀♀♀ 6
● Carema Et. Nera '05	♀♀♀ 6
● Carema Et. Bianca '08	♀♀ 5
● Carema Et. Bianca '07	♀♀ 5
● Carema Et. Bianca '06	♀♀ 4
○ Erbaluce di Caluso Cariola '11	♀♀ 3*
○ Erbaluce di Caluso Cariola '09	♀♀ 3*

Roberto Ferraris

FRAZ. DOGLIANO, 33
14041 AGLIANO TERME [AT]
TEL. 0141954234
www.robertoferraris.com

CELLAR SALES
PRE-BOOKED VISITS
ANNUAL PRODUCTION 50,000 bottles

Established in 1923 by Stefano Ferraris, the nerve centre of this estate sits in Agliano Terme, in the heart of the historic Barbera d'Asti zone. Barbera is the main variety cultivated on this small estate, whose philosophy is to produce high-quality traditional wines through low yields, care of the old vineyards that are home to plants of more than 80 years old, and respect for this very wine-friendly area. Next to the nebbiolo, used for a Monferrato Rosso, there are smaller quantities of freisa, dolcetto and grignolino. Barbera d'Asti Nobbio 2011 has top notes of oak immediately followed by hints of cherry jam on the nose and a full palate with a very long finish refreshed by fine acidity. Other very pleasant wines are the nicely taut Barbera d'Asti 2011, with dark berry fruit, and Monferrato Rosso GriXa 2011, a very classic Nebbiolo with notes of roots and liquorice.

● Barbera d'Asti Nobbio '11	▼▼ 3*
● Barbera d'Asti '11	▼▼ 2*
● M.to Rosso Grixa '11	▼▼ 3
● Barbera d'Asti '10	♀♀ 2*
● Barbera d'Asti '09	♀♀ 2*
● Barbera d'Asti Nobbio '10	♀♀ 3
● Barbera d'Asti Nobbio '09	♀♀ 3*
● Barbera d'Asti Sup. La Cricca '09	♀♀ 3*
● Barbera d'Asti Sup. La Cricca '08	♀♀ 3
● Barbera d'Asti Sup. Riserva del Bisavolo '10	♀♀ 3*
● Barbera d'Asti Sup. Riserva del Bisavolo '09	♀♀ 3
● Barbera d'Asti Sup. Riserva del Bisavolo '08	♀♀ 3*
● Monferrato Grixa '09	♀♀ 4
● Monferrato Grixa '08	♀♀ 3

Carlo Ferro

REG. SALERE 41
14041 AGLIANO TERME [AT]
TEL. 0141954000
ferro.vini@tiscali.it

CELLAR SALES
PRE-BOOKED VISITS
ANNUAL PRODUCTION 25,000 bottles
HECTARES UNDER VINE 12.00

The Ferro family estate history spans over a century. However, as is often the case in this area, it only started bottling its wine about 20 years ago. It vaunts south-aspected vineyards with a density of 4-5,000 Guyot-trained vines per hectare. Barbera accounts for the lion's share, although smaller amounts of other local grape varieties like dolcetto and nebbiolo are also grown, along with cabernet sauvignon. The wines are traditional in style, distinguished by their elegance and drinkability. This year's battery of Barberas was as good as ever. The well-made Barbera d'Asti Giulia 2011 still has prominent charred oak, but shows good fruit on the nose and a rich, juicy palate with a long, characterful finish. All that's missing is a little aromatic focus. Barbera d'Asti Superiore Notturno 2010 is more clearly defined, but slightly less juicy, with notes of black pepper and tobacco and a balanced, fairly long palate.

● Barbera d'Asti Giulia '11	♟♟ 2*
● Barbera d'Asti Superiore Notturno '10	♟♟ 2*
● Barbera d'Asti '12	♟ 1*
● Barbera d'Asti Giulia '10	♟♟ 2*
● Barbera d'Asti Giulia '09	♟♟ 2*
● Barbera d'Asti Superiore Notturno '09	♟♟ 2*
● Barbera d'Asti Superiore Notturno '08	♟♟ 2
● Barbera d'Asti Superiore Notturno '07	♟♟ 2*

Fontanabianca

VIA BORDINI, 15
12057 NEIVE [CN]
TEL. 017367195
www.fontanabianca.it

CELLAR SALES
PRE-BOOKED VISITS
ANNUAL PRODUCTION 60,000 bottles
HECTARES UNDER VINE 14.00

Aldo Pola and Bruno Ferro run this handsome estate that has been focusing on quality for many years. Their respective parents purchased the vineyards and cellar in 1969 and since then much progress has been made, particularly in the production of the various Barbaresco crus. The style of the wines is well calibrated, allowing the estate to cater to different tastes, for example the extroverted modern Barbaresco Bordini and the more classic Barbaresco Serraboella, aged in Slavonian oak barrels, which requires long ageing in order to express itself to the full. Barbaresco Serraboella 2010 has a nose of berry fruit and sweet tobacco, followed by a mouthfilling palate with a fine tannic weave. Barbaresco Bordini offers dark notes of rhubarb, quinine and tar and a long, supple palate, while the Barbaresco 2009 is distinguished by its exceptional drinkability.

● Barbaresco Serraboella '10	♟♟ 5
● Barbaresco '09	♟♟ 5
● Barbaresco Bordini '10	♟♟ 6
● Barbera d'Alba Sup. '11	♟♟ 3
● Langhe Nebbiolo '11	♟♟ 3
● Dolcetto d'Alba '12	♟ 2
● Barbaresco Serraboella '06	♟♟♟ 6
● Barbaresco Sorì Burdin '05	♟♟♟ 6
● Barbaresco Sorì Burdin '04	♟♟♟ 6
● Barbaresco Sorì Burdin '01	♟♟♟ 6
● Barbaresco Sorì Burdin '98	♟♟♟ 7
● Barbaresco Bordini '09	♟♟ 6
● Barbaresco Sorì Burdin '07	♟♟ 6
● Barbera d'Alba Brunet '07	♟♟ 3

Fontanafredda

VIA ALBA, 15
12050 SERRALUNGA D'ALBA [CN]
TEL. 0173626111
www.fontanafredda.it

CELLAR SALES
PRE-BOOKED VISITS
ACCOMMODATION AND RESTAURANT SERVICE
ANNUAL PRODUCTION 8,000,000 bottles
HECTARES UNDER VINE 90.00

It would be a Herculean task to do full justice to what has developed into the Fontanafredda estate in these few short lines. The new company set up by Luca Baffigo, Oscar Farinetti and Eataly has relaunched the image of a producer of everyday wines made in line with current trends: natural viticulture, biodiversity and energy saving. However, we are mainly interested in the nebbiolo selections released under the Casa E. di Mirafiore brand: Vigna la Rosa, Lazzarito, and Vigna la Villa, a rigorous, essential Barolo that is the pleasing result of ageing in a combination of medium-sized barrels and partly new barriques. It's increasingly hard to keep track of the winery's extensive range, what with new labels, changing designations and products switching between lines. However, its sure-fire wines never change: the Barolo vineyard selections and Riservas and the Alta Langas. We particularly liked the power of Paiagallo 2009 and the drinkability of the Riserva Mirafiore 2007.

● Barolo Ris. Mirafiore '07	♟♟	6
● Barolo Paiagallo Mirafiore '09	♟♟	6
○ Alta Langa Brut Contessa Rosa Ris. '08	♟♟	5
○ Alta Langa Extra Brut '08	♟♟	4
● Barolo Lazzarito Mirafiore '08	♟♟	6
● Barolo Serralunga d'Alba '09	♟♟	6
● Diano d'Alba La Lepre '12	♟♟	3
● Langhe Nebbiolo Mirafiore '10	♟♟	4
● Nebbiolo d'Alba Marne Brune '11	♟♟	3
● Barbera d'Alba Sup. Mirafiore '10	♟	4
● Dolcetto d'Alba Mirafiore '12	♟	3
○ Langhe Bianco Marin '10	♟	3
○ Roero Arneis Pradalupo '12	♟	2
● Barolo Casa E. di Mirafiore Ris. '04	♟♟♟	8
● Barolo Fontanafredda V. La Rosa '07	♟♟♟	7
● Barolo Lazzarito V. La Delizia '04	♟♟♟	8

Forteto della Luja

REG. CANDELETTE, 4
14051 LOAZZOLO [AT]
TEL. 014487197
www.fortetodellaluja.it

CELLAR SALES
PRE-BOOKED VISITS
ANNUAL PRODUCTION 55,000 bottles
HECTARES UNDER VINE 9.00
VITICULTURE METHOD Certified Organic

Respect for the environment, extending far beyond the mere protocols prescribed by organic production, is a way of life for Silvia and Gianni Scaglione, the owners of this handsome Langhe winery in the province of Asti that became a WWF-affiliated reserve in 2007. Its vineyards are situated at an altitude of around 500 metres, in marly limestone soil and are planted with native grape varieties, principally moscato, but also barbera and brachetto, along with pinot nero. They yield traditional-style wines that are nevertheless highly original, with great character. The estate's range is solid and reliable. Moscato d'Asti Piasa San Maurizio 2012 has notes of candied fruit and orange peel, showing soft but with good character and impressive structure. The pleasant Barbera d'Asti Mon Ross 2012 is relatively light bodied and balanced, offering fruit with slight vegetal hints and attractive spiciness, while Loazzolo Vendemmia Tardiva Piasa Rischei 2009 is complex and well orchestrated.

● Barbera d'Asti Mon Ross '12	♟♟	2*
○ Loazzolo V. T. Piasa Rischei '09	♟♟	6
● M.to Rosso Le Grive '11	♟♟	4
○ Moscato d'Asti Piasa San Maurizio '12	♟♟	2*
○ Loazzolo Piasa Rischei '97	♟♟♟	6
○ Loazzolo Piasa Rischei '96	♟♟♟	6
○ Loazzolo Piasa Rischei '95	♟♟♟	6
○ Loazzolo Piasa Rischei '94	♟♟♟	6
○ Loazzolo Piasa Rischei '93	♟♟♟	6
● M.to Rosso Le Grive '10	♟♟	4
● M.to Rosso Le Grive '09	♟♟	4

Gabutti - Franco Boasso

B.TA GABUTTI, 3A
12050 SERRALUNGA D'ALBA [CN]
TEL. 0173613165
www.gabuttiboasso.com

CELLAR SALES
PRE-BOOKED VISITS
ACCOMMODATION
ANNUAL PRODUCTION 30,000 bottles
HECTARES UNDER VINE 6.00

This family-run estate is named after an excellent Gabutti Barolo-producing area and has been owned by the Boasso family since the early 1970s. It possesses 4.5 hectares of plots in the deservedly famous vineyards of Serralunga d'Alba. The wines hail from great crus, carefully tended to ensure top-quality grapes. They are fermented using traditional methods and aged in medium-sized Slavonian oak barrels. A further attraction is represented by the estate's charming agriturismo facility, which is well worth a visit. One of the finest, most renowned Serralunga d'Alba crus lends power and charm to Barolo Margheria 2009, with dark notes of tobacco and liquorice and prominent but well-integrated tannins. Barolo Gabutti 2009 is complex and concentrated, promising long development, and the highly drinkable Barolo Serralunga offers expressive varietal notes.

● Barolo Gabutti '09	♟♟	5
● Barolo Margheria '09	♟♟	5
● Barbera d'Alba '10	♟♟	2*
● Barolo Serralunga '09	♟♟	5
● Dolcetto d'Alba Meriame '12	♟♟	2*
● Langhe Rosso Grappoli '11	♟	3
○ Moscato d'Asti Grappoli '12	♟	2
● Barolo Margheria '05	♟♟♟	5*
● Barolo Gabutti '08	♟♟	5
● Barolo Gabutti '05	♟♟	5
● Barolo Margheria '08	♟♟	5
● Barolo Margheria '06	♟♟	5
● Barolo Serralunga '08	♟♟	5
● Barolo Serralunga '99	♟♟	6
● Dolcetto d'Alba Meriame '11	♟♟	2*

Gaggino

S.DA SANT'EVASIO, 29
15076 OVADA [AL]
TEL. 0143822345
www.gaggino.it

CELLAR SALES
PRE-BOOKED VISITS
ANNUAL PRODUCTION 150,000 bottles
HECTARES UNDER VINE 20.00

Gabriele is one of those vignerons whom it's a pleasure to know: born and raised in the vineyard, at the age of only 40 he has accumulated an experience in the rows and cellar that few can rival in the Ovada area. His anecdotes on the 30 harvests he can personally remember could form the basis for a book on the history of local viticulture. This experience is clear in his wines, whose production he personally follows, from the rows to distribution. He focuses on Dolcetto, Barbera and cortese-based whites, but doesn't disdain international varieties such as cabernet sauvignon, syrah, chardonnay and sauvignon blanc. The Tico has a nose of berry fruit and spice, mirrored on the long, dense palate that is still developing. The Convivio still has vinous nuances on a nose of fresh fruit, while the palate is dominated by alcoholic notes and a very long finish, while the pleasant Charmat-method Courtesia is very good value for money.

● Barbera del M.to Sup. Il Ticco '09	♟♟	3*
● Dolcetto di Ovada Il Convivio '11	♟♟	2*
○ Courteisa Brut	♟	2
○ M.to Bianco La Bionda '12	♟	2
● M.to Rosso La Mora '12	♟	2
● Barbera del M.to La Lazzarina '10	♟♟	2
● Dolcetto di Ovada Il Convivio '10	♟♟	2*
● Dolcetto di Ovada Il Convivio '09	♟♟	2*
● Dolcetto di Ovada Sup. Sant' Evasio '09	♟♟	3*
● Dolcetto di Ovada Sup. Sant' Evasio '08	♟♟	3
● Dolcetto di Ovada Un Rosso '10	♟♟	2*
● M.to Rosso La Mora '11	♟♟	1*

★★★★★Gaja

VIA TORINO, 18
12050 BARBARESCO [CN]
TEL. 0173635158
info@gaja.com

ANNUAL PRODUCTION 350,000 bottles
HECTARES UNDER VINE 92.00

The story of one of the best examples of Italian products in the world is underpinned by a great name and a great family. Angelo, together with his wife Lucia and children Gaia, Rossana and Giovanni, has managed to achieve international renown through his constant commitment to uncompromising quality and his forceful imposition of certain decisions that have characterized the path of winemaking in Langhe over the past few decades. The famous red wines are flanked by a series of excellent whites that are extraordinarily ageworthy, once again demonstrating the absolute versatility of this unique estate. This year a Tre Bicchieri went to the surprising Costa Russi 2010 that, in terms of elegance and structure, currently outclasses the better-known Sorì Tildin and San Lorenzo of the same vintage, which still appeared very young at the time of tasting. The 2009 versions of Sperss and Conteisa are both plush and very elegant.

Filippo Gallino

FRAZ. MADONNA LORETO
VALLE DEL POZZO, 63
12043 CANALE [CN]
TEL. 017398112
www.filippogallino.com

CELLAR SALES
PRE-BOOKED VISITS
ANNUAL PRODUCTION 10,000 bottles
HECTARES UNDER VINE 15.50

The entire Gallino family work on their estate, which was among the first to believe in the potential of the Roero area and strive to produce fine wines. Its vineyards lie on sandy clay soils on the Briccola, Renesio and Mompissano hills in the commune of Canale. They are planted with the typical grape varieties of the region like arneis, barbera and nebbiolo, which yield fruit-rich wines that aim to combine traditional vineyard techniques with a modern approach in the cellar. In the absence of the Roeros, which hadn't been bottled at the time of our tastings, we very much liked the full, complex Barbera d'Alba Superiore 2011, which shows good structure, notes of ripe fruit and spice, and a vibrant, long finish with plenty of character. Roero Arneis 4 Luglio 2011, which focuses on spice and white-fleshed fruit, is interesting but not yet clearly legible due to aggressive unresolved acidity.

● Langhe Nebbiolo Costa Russi '10	♟♟♟ 8
● Barbaresco '10	♟♟ 8
● Langhe Nebbiolo Conteisa '09	♟♟ 8
● Langhe Nebbiolo Sperss '09	♟♟ 8
● Langhe Nebbiolo Sorì S. Lorenzo '10	♟♟ 8
● Langhe Nebbiolo Sorì Tildin '10	♟♟ 8
● Barbaresco '09	♟♟♟ 8
● Barbaresco '08	♟♟♟ 8
● Barbaresco '04	♟♟♟ 8
● Langhe Nebbiolo Costa Russi '08	♟♟♟ 8
● Langhe Nebbiolo Costa Russi '07	♟♟♟ 8
● Langhe Nebbiolo Costa Russi '04	♟♟♟ 8
● Langhe Nebbiolo Costa Russi '03	♟♟♟ 8
● Langhe Nebbiolo Sorì S. Lorenzo '06	♟♟♟ 8
● Langhe Nebbiolo Sorì Tildin '07	♟♟♟ 8
● Langhe Nebbiolo Sorì Tildin '06	♟♟♟ 8

● Barbera d'Alba Sup. '11	♟♟ 4
○ Roero Arneis 4 Luglio '11	♟♟ 2*
● Barbera d'Alba '12	♟ 2
○ Roero Arneis '12	♟ 2
● Barbera d'Alba Sup. '05	♟♟♟ 4*
● Barbera d'Alba Sup. '04	♟♟♟ 4*
● Roero '06	♟♟♟ 4*
● Roero Sup. '03	♟♟♟ 3
● Roero Sup. '01	♟♟♟ 5
● Roero Sup. '99	♟♟♟ 5
● Barbera d'Alba Elaine '09	♟♟ 2*
● Barbera d'Alba Sup. Margherita '08	♟♟ 4
● Roero '09	♟♟ 4
● Roero Sorano Ris. '08	♟♟ 3*

Gancia

c.so Libertà, 66
14053 Canelli [AT]
Tel. 01418301
www.gancia.it

CELLAR SALES
PRE-BOOKED VISITS
ANNUAL PRODUCTION 20,000,000 bottles

Despite changes in the company, with Roustam Tariko's Russian Standard Corporation now holding around 90%, Gancia continues unperturbed in its production of still wines and sparklers. The only other significant news is the sale of some stakes in wineries in other regions of Italy and a consequent repositioning in the Asti territory. Among the many labels produced, the main focus is on metodo classico sparklers and the still wines from Tenute dei Vallarino. The 2010 vintage of Asti Metodo Classico Cuvée 24 has a fresh, concentrated nose of apples and pears and elegant musky notes, combined with a long, zesty finish on the palate. Alta Langa Brut Cuvée 120 2003 is well made, with soft, complex notes of cakes and ripe fruit, as are the succulent Barbera d'Asti Superiore Nizza Bricco Asinari 2010, with cherries and Mediterranean scrubland, and the pleasant, balanced Barbera d'Asti Superiore La Ladra 2010.

○ Alta Langa Brut Cuvée 120 '03	▼▼ 5
○ Asti M. Cl. Cuvée 24 '10	▼▼ 6
● Barbera d'Asti Sup. Nizza Bricco Asinari '10	▼▼ 4
● Barbera d'Asti Sup. La Ladra '10	▼ 3
○ Alta Langa Brut Cuvée 60 Ris. '06	▽▽ 6
○ Alta Langa Cuvée 36 Brut '09	▽▽ 5
○ Alta Langa Cuvée 36 Brut '08	▽▽ 5
○ Alta Langa Cuvée 60 Brut Ris. '05	▽▽ 5
○ Asti M. Cl. Cuvée 24 '09	▽▽ 6
● Barbera d'Asti Sup. La Ladra '09	▽▽ 3

Tenuta Garetto

s.da Asti Mare, 30
14041 Agliano Terme [AT]
Tel. 0141954068
www.garetto.it

CELLAR SALES
PRE-BOOKED VISITS
ANNUAL PRODUCTION 110,000 bottles
HECTARES UNDER VINE 18.00

Barbera reigns supreme on the estate owned by enthusiastic young vigneron Alessandro Garetto, situated in one of the finest areas for this particular grape variety. Indeed, it accounts for 80 per cent of the area under vine, while the remaining 20 per cent is divided between dolcetto, grignolino and chardonnay. Most of the vineyards are between 60 and 70 years old and lie in clay soils of marly-limestone origin. The modern-style wines are fruit rich, with good structure and remarkable aromatic definition. Barbera d'Asti Superiore Nizza Favà 2010 is always among the best of its kind, with a nose of autumn leaves and aromatic herbs on a background of dark berries, and a fresh, full-flavoured palate with good acidity. Barbera d'Asti Superiore In Pectore 2011 is well made, with notes of berry fruit and pencil lead and a rather austere palate, as is the pleasant Barbera d'Asti Tra Neuit e Dì 2012, with typical notes of berries and rain-soaked earth.

● Barbera d'Asti Sup. Nizza Favà '10	▼▼ 4
● Barbera d'Asti Sup. In Pectore '11	▼▼ 8
● Barbera d'Asti Tra Neuit e Dì '12	▼▼ 2*
● Grignolino d'Asti 'l Giget '12	▼ 2
● Barbera d'Asti Sup. Nizza Favà '04	▽▽▽ 4
● Barbera d'Asti Sup. In Pectore '10	▽▽ 8
● Barbera d'Asti Sup. In Pectore '09	▽▽ 3
● Barbera d'Asti Sup. Nizza Favà '09	▽▽ 5
● Barbera d'Asti Sup. Nizza Favà '08	▽▽ 4
● Barbera d'Asti Sup. Nizza Favà '07	▽▽ 4
● Barbera d'Asti Tra Neuit e Dì '10	▽▽ 2*

Ettore Germano

LOC. CERRETA, 1
12050 SERRALUNGA D'ALBA [CN]
TEL. 0173613528
www.germanoettore.com

CELLAR SALES
PRE-BOOKED VISITS
ACCOMMODATION
ANNUAL PRODUCTION 90,000 bottles
HECTARES UNDER VINE 17.50

In many ways, Sergio Germano's estate has
yet to achieve the fame and recognition it
deserves. Few Piedmont wineries can
boast such a high level of quality across
such a full range, in which the labels have
interchangeable roles. They include famous
Barolo crus like Prapò, Cerretta, Lazzarito,
also available in a Riserva, and fabulous
whites, both still and sparkling, produced
on the Aglié estate in Alta Langa. The
headquarters are located at the Serralunga
cellar, where much progress has been
made over the years in terms of delicate
extraction and calibrated ageing in casks of
various sizes and origins. The estate's
wines gave a very good all-round
performance, with Riesling Hérzu reaching
an all-time high with the 2011 vintage.
Varietal and multi-layered, it has a long,
vibrant, zesty palate. The great Barolo
Lazzarito Riserva 2007 is close-focused
and complex, with excellent depth.

○ Langhe Bianco Hérzu '11	♟♟♟	4*
● Barolo Lazzarito Ris. '07	♟♟	8
● Barolo Prapò '09	♟♟	7
○ Alta Langa Brut '10	♟♟	5
● Barbera d'Alba Sup. V. della Madre '11	♟♟	5
● Barolo Cerretta '09	♟♟	7
● Barolo Serralunga '09	♟♟	6
● Dolcetto d'Alba Vign. Lorenzino '12	♟♟	2*
○ Langhe Bianco Binel '11	♟♟	3
○ Langhe Chardonnay '12	♟♟	2*
● Langhe Nebbiolo '11	♟♟	3
○ Langhe Nascetta '11	♟	2
○ Langhe Bianco Hérzu '10	♟♟♟	4*
○ Langhe Bianco Hérzu '09	♟♟♟	5

La Ghibellina

FRAZ. MONTEROTONDO, 61
15066 GAVI [AL]
TEL. 0143686257
www.laghibellina.it

CELLAR SALES
PRE-BOOKED VISITS
CELLAR SALES
ANNUAL PRODUCTION 60,000 bottles
HECTARES UNDER VINE 7.50

Founded in 2000, Alberto and Marina
Ghibillina's modest-sized estate is situated
in the hamlet of Monterotondo di Gavi,
which is home to some of the most
distinctive crus of the DOCG zone. Just
over seven of its total 20 hectares are
planted with typical local grape varieties,
above all cortese, used for the Metodo
Classico, the steel-aged Gavi Manìn and
the Altius selection, which is partly aged in
barriques. Three wines produced from
barbera complete line, used alone in
Chiaretto Sandrino and Monferrato Rosso
Nero del Montone, and blended with merlot
in Monferrato Rosso Pituj. This year saw
the best-ever performance of the estate's
entire range, with Gavi Altius coming within
a hair's breadth of our top accolade. The
combination of powerful structure and racy
acidity make it a highly age worthy white.
The Gavi Mainin and the new Cuvée
Marina, a complex Metodo Classico
sparkler, also did extremely well.

○ Gavi del Comune di Gavi Altius '11	♟♟	3*
○ Gavi del Comune di Gavi M. Cl. Cuvée Marina	♟♟	5
○ Gavi del Comune di Gavi Mainin '12	♟♟	3
● M.to Rosso Nero del Montone '10	♟♟	4
○ Gavi del Comune di Gavi Brut M. Cl.	♟	4
⊙ M.to Chiaretto Sandrino '12	♟	2
● M.to Rosso Pituj '11	♟	3
● M.to Rosso Nero del Montone '08	♟♟	4
● M.to Rosso Pituj '10	♟♟	3
● M.to Rosso Pituj '09	♟♟	3

Attilio Ghisolfi

LOC. BUSSIA, 27
12065 MONFORTE D'ALBA [CN]
TEL. 017378345
www.ghisolfi.com

CELLAR SALES
PRE-BOOKED VISITS
ANNUAL PRODUCTION 45,000 bottles
HECTARES UNDER VINE 6.50

In taking on the challenge of nebbiolo and pinot nero, Gianmarco Ghisolfi has put into practice the dream of scaling the loftiest heights of red grape varieties. This is no exaggeration, for his Barolo selections are flanked by a small production of wine from the famous Burgundy grape, grown in a vineyard in Monforte. Chemical herbicides are banned and great attention is paid to preserving the terroir, in order to produce wines with an authentic, personal flavour, which faithfully reflect the different varietal characteristics. The alluring Barolo Bussia Bricco Visette 2009 has a complex, layered nose of tobacco, spice, liquorice and violet with refreshing balsamic hints, while Barolo Fantini Riserva 2007 is deep and austere, with well-resolved tannins and a long, vibrant palate.

● Barolo Bussia Bricco Visette '09	♥♥♥ 6
● Barolo Fantini Ris. '07	♥♥ 7
● Barbera d'Alba Maggiora '10	♥♥ 2*
● Barolo Bussia '09	♥♥ 5
● Langhe Nebbiolo '11	♥ 3
● Barolo Bricco Visette '05	♀♀♀ 6
● Barolo Bricco Visette '01	♀♀♀ 6
● Barolo Fantini Ris. '01	♀♀♀ 7
● Langhe Rosso Alta Bussia '01	♀♀♀ 5
● Langhe Rosso Alta Bussia '00	♀♀♀ 4
● Langhe Rosso Alta Bussia '99	♀♀♀ 5
● Barolo Bussia Bricco Visette '08	♀♀ 6
● Barolo Bussia Bricco Visette '07	♀♀ 6
● Barolo Fantini Ris. '06	♀♀ 7

★★Bruno Giacosa

VIA XX SETTEMBRE, 52
12057 NEIVE [CN]
TEL. 017367027
www.brunogiacosa.it

ANNUAL PRODUCTION 400,000 bottles
HECTARES UNDER VINE 18.00

Nobody in Italy has managed to embody the figure of the world-class négociant like Bruno Giocosa. His extraordinary knowledge of Langhe vineyards enabled him to make some of the best-ever Barolos and Barbarescos before he founded his Falletto estate, which has given its name to the wines that hail from its vineyards today. He has long been flanked by his daughter Bruna and, albeit with a short break, oenologist Dante Scaglione. However, the style remains the same as ever: classic Nebbiolos through and through, which focus on details rather than body. Although they are wines designed for decades of ageing, the last few vintages have appeared increasingly approachable in terms of fruit. The excellent Barolo Le Rocche del Falletto Riserva 2007 offers notes of berry fruit, rhubarb and leather, close-knit tannins and refreshing acidity. The palate stands out for its unique tanginess and great length. Barolo Le Rocche del Falletto 2009 is good, characterized by sweet tobacco and dried herbs on the nose, followed by a powerful, tannic palate.

● Barolo Le Rocche del Falletto Ris. '07	♥♥♥ 8
● Barbera d'Alba Falletto '11	♥♥ 5
● Barolo Le Rocche del Falletto '09	♥♥ 8
● Nebbiolo d'Alba Valmaggiore '11	♥♥ 5
○ Roero Arneis '12	♥♥ 4
● Barbaresco Asili '05	♀♀♀ 8
● Barbaresco Asili Ris. '07	♀♀♀ 8
● Barbaresco Asili Ris. '04	♀♀♀ 8
● Barbaresco Santo Stefano '01	♀♀♀ 8
● Barolo Falletto '07	♀♀♀ 8
● Barolo Falletto '04	♀♀♀ 8
● Barolo Falletto '01	♀♀♀ 8
● Barolo Le Rocche del Falletto '05	♀♀♀ 8
● Barolo Le Rocche del Falletto '04	♀♀♀ 8
● Barolo Le Rocche del Falletto Ris. '01	♀♀♀ 8

Carlo Giacosa

S.DA OVELLO, 9
12050 BARBARESCO [CN]
TEL. 0173635116
www.carlogiacosa.it

CELLAR SALES
PRE-BOOKED VISITS
ANNUAL PRODUCTION 40,000 bottles
HECTARES UNDER VINE 5.00

It's certainly easier to guarantee excellent wines when you possess vineyards of the calibre of Montefico, Cole, Ovello and Asili. Maria Grazia Giacosa enthusiastically and attentively runs this estate that, year after year, has managed to make a name for itself as one of the soundest in the Barbaresco production zone. Her father Carlo draws on his many years of experience to oversee work in the vineyard, and the resulting wines offer excellent value for money, showing very well made and balanced, aged in medium-sized oak barrels. Barbaresco Narin 2010 is characterized by notes of berry fruit and tobacco with balsamic hints and tannins that do not obstruct the smoothness of the palate. Although Barbaresco Luca Riserva 2008 hints at great potential, it is still a bit closed. Lastly, Nebbiolo Mariagrazia 2012 is extremely drinkable.

● Barbaresco Narin '10	♟♟ 5
● Barbaresco Luca Ris. '08	♟♟ 6
● Barbaresco Montefico '10	♟♟ 5
● Barbera d'Alba Mucin '12	♟♟ 3
● Langhe Nebbiolo Maria Grazia '12	♟♟ 3
● Barbera d'Alba Lina '11	♟ 3
● Dolcetto d'Alba Cuchet '12	♟ 2
● Barbaresco Montefico '08	♟♟♟ 5*
● Barbaresco Luca Ris. '07	♛♛ 6
● Barbaresco Montefico '09	♛♛ 5
● Barbaresco Narin '08	♛♛ 4*
● Barbaresco Narin '07	♛♛ 4
● Barbaresco Narin '06	♛♛ 5*
● Barbera d'Alba Lina '07	♛♛ 3*

F.lli Giacosa

VIA XX SETTEMBRE, 64
12057 NEIVE [CN]
TEL. 017367013
www.giacosa.it

CELLAR SALES
PRE-BOOKED VISITS
ANNUAL PRODUCTION 500,000 bottles
HECTARES UNDER VINE 50.00

In terms of size and history, Fratelli Giacosa commands a position of excellence among Piedmont's major wineries. Its extensive range of labels covers all the main traditional varieties and reflects its variegated vineyard holdings. As for the wines, priority is given to a classic style, without too many special effects. The attention and care given to more sustainable viticulture has also seen the winery committed on various fronts, taking moves such as abandoning the use of pesticides on its estates and installing solar panels to act as heat regulators for the air conditioning system at its premises. Barbera d'Alba Maria Gioana 2010, with well-calibrated notes of lightly charred oak and fresh berry fruit, is particularly juicy and balanced. Barolo Vigna Mandorlo 2008 has a very layered nose, with hints of tobacco, eucalyptus and spice, and a palate that successfully balances vigorous tannins with a well-controlled swathe of acidity.

● Barbera d'Alba Maria Gioana '10	♟♟ 4
● Barolo V. Mandorlo '08	♟♟ 7
● Barbaresco Basarin V. Gianmaté '10	♟♟ 6
● Barolo Bussia '09	♟♟ 6
○ Langhe Chardonnay Rorea '12	♟♟ 3
○ Roero Arneis '12	♟ 3
● Barbaresco Basarin '09	♛♛ 5
● Barbaresco Basarin '06	♛♛ 5
● Barbaresco Basarin V. Gianmaté '09	♛♛ 5
● Barbaresco Basarin V. Gianmaté '07	♛♛ 5
● Barbera d'Alba Maria Gioana '09	♛♛ 3
● Barolo Bussia '08	♛♛ 6
● Barolo Bussia '07	♛♛ 6
● Barolo Bussia '06	♛♛ 5

Giovanni Battista Gillardi

Cascina Corsaletto, 69
12060 Farigliano [CN]
Tel. 017376306
www.gillardi.it

CELLAR SALES
PRE-BOOKED VISITS
ANNUAL PRODUCTION 35,000 bottles
HECTARES UNDER VINE 7.00

Giacolino Gillardi is a skilled vigneron with extensive experience, and his estate reflects his versatile and innovative character. The wines range from Dolcetto in a very classic style to international varietals such as merlot and syrah aged in small French oak casks. While very different, they are all crafted from painstakingly selected grapes, favouring drinkability and a close-focused nose. They display very good body, even when young, but offer excellent sensations after appropriate ageing. The 2011 vintage of Langhe Rosso Harys is particularly good, vaunting a complex, smoky nose of dark berry fruit, leather and quinine, and a long, juicy palate. Dogliani Cursalet 2011 shows typical, fruity and firm with assertive tannins nicely balanced by fresh acidity.

● Dogliani Cursalet '12	▼▼ 3*
● Langhe Rosso Harys '11	▼▼ 6
● Dogliani Maestra '12	▼▼ 2*
● Langhe Fiore di Harys '11	▼ 4
● Dogliani Cursalet '11	▼▼▼ 3*
● Harys '00	▼▼▼ 6
● Harys '99	▼▼▼ 6
● Harys '98	▼▼▼ 6
● Dolcetto di Dogliani Cursalet '10	♀♀ 3
● Dolcetto di Dogliani Cursalet '09	♀♀ 3*
● Dolcetto di Dogliani Cursalet '08	♀♀ 3
● Langhe Harys '10	♀♀ 6
● Langhe Harys '09	♀♀ 6
● Langhe Rosso Harys '07	♀♀ 6

La Giribaldina

reg. San Vito, 39
14042 Calamandrana [AT]
Tel. 0141718043
www.giribaldina.com

CELLAR SALES
PRE-BOOKED VISITS
ACCOMMODATION
ANNUAL PRODUCTION 70,000 bottles
HECTARES UNDER VINE 11.00

Founded in 1995, the Colombo family's winery is housed in the old Giribaldi farm in Calamandrana, in a particularly fine barbera-growing area. Indeed, barbera accounts for 70 per cent of its production, while the remaining 30 per cent is divided between moscato, sauvignon and grignolino. The estate's vineyards are divided between Vaglio Serra, which is home to the fabulous Bricco Castellaro, Calamandrana, and three hectares in the Val Sarmassa nature reserve. Its wines are modern in style, but aim to preserve varietal stamping and a sense of the terroir. Two of the estate's wines made it into our finals this year. Barbera d'Asti Superiore Nizza Cala delle Mandrie 2010 is complex and balanced, with notes of cherry, rain-soaked earth and tobacco, and a dynamic palate with fresh acidity that belies its great structure. Barbera d'Asti Superiore Vigneti della Val Sarmassa 2011 has traditional notes of berries and autumn leaves, good length and superbly dense extraction.

● Barbera d'Asti Sup. Nizza Cala delle Mandrie '10	▼▼ 4
● Barbera d'Asti Sup. Vign. della Val Sarmassa '11	▼▼ 3*
○ Moscato d'Asti '12	▼▼ 2*
● Barbera d'Asti Monte del Mare '12	▼ 2
○ M.to Bianco Ferro di Cavallo '12	▼ 3
● Barbera d'Asti Sup. Vign. della Val Sarmassa '10	♀♀ 3
● Barbera d'Asti Sup. Vign. della Val Sarmassa '09	♀♀ 3
● Grignolino d'Asti Quercino '11	♀♀ 2*
○ M.to Bianco Ferro di Cavallo '11	♀♀ 3

La Gironda

S.DA BRICCO, 12
14049 NIZZA MONFERRATO [AT]
TEL. 0141701013
www.lagironda.com

CELLAR SALES
PRE-BOOKED VISITS
ANNUAL PRODUCTION 40,000 bottles
HECTARES UNDER VINE 8.00

Agostino Galandrino runs his relatively new but extremely interesting estate with the aid of his daughter Susanna and her husband Alberto Adamo. Set in the Bricco Cremosina vineyard, one of the finest crus in the municipality of Nizza Monferrato, its production focuses chiefly on the typical grape varieties of the area: principally barbera, but also moscato, cortese, dolcetto and nebbiolo, flanked by several international cultivars. The resulting wines are pleasant, fresh and very fruity. Barbera d'Asti Superiore Nizza Le Nicchie 2010 has notes of berry fruit, cocoa powder and quinine; nice body with fair texture; good acidity and caressing, well-resolved tannins. Monferrato Rosso Soul '09, from nebbiolo, is long and full, with fine-grained tannins and notes of liquorice and aromatic herbs. We also liked the fresh, balanced Barbera d'Asti La Lippa 2012, with notes of rain-soaked earth, and the fruitier, firm Barbera d'Asti La Gena 2011.

● Barbera d'Asti Sup. Nizza Le Nicchie '10	♟♟ 5
● Barbera d'Asti La Gena '11	♟♟ 3
● Barbera d'Asti La Lippa '12	♟♟ 2*
● M.to Rosso Soul '09	♟♟ 5
○ Moscato d'Asti '12	♟ 2
● Barbera d'Asti La Gena '09	♟♟ 3*
● Barbera d'Asti La Lippa '10	♟♟ 2*
● Barbera d'Asti Sup. Nizza Le Nicchie '09	♟♟ 4
● Barbera d'Asti Sup. Nizza Le Nicchie '08	♟♟ 4
● Barbera d'Asti Sup. Nizza Le Nicchie '07	♟♟ 4
○ Monferrato Bianco L'Aquilone '10	♟♟ 2*

La Giustiniana

FRAZ. ROVERETO, 5
15066 GAVI [AL]
TEL. 0143682132
www.lagiustiniana.it

CELLAR SALES
PRE-BOOKED VISITS
ANNUAL PRODUCTION 200,000 bottles
HECTARES UNDER VINE 39.00

The Lombardini family's magnificent La Giustiniana estate is over 400 years old, located in Rovereto di Gavi, one of the finest growing areas for cortese. Managed with the aid of Enrico Tomalino, its vineyards cover an area of around 40 hectares, at altitudes between 300 and 500 metres, and are tended without the use of chemical herbicides or fungicides. It was one of the first estates in the area to bottle its own crus separately, distinguishing the grey marl of the Lugarara vineyard from the red soil of Montessora, both vinified exclusively in steel. Il Nostro Gavi, the Rovereto vineyard selection, undergoes longer ageing on the fine lees, also in steel. The estate seems to have no trouble in following the path mapped out by its longstanding manager Enrico Tomalino, who recently retired, and once again this year one of its Gavis reached our finals. In this case it was the rather unexpected Lugarara that stood out for the elegant sensations that it offers in the glass. Montessora is still young and clenched, requiring further time.

○ Gavi del Comune di Gavi Lugarara '12	♟♟ 3*
○ Gavi del Comune di Gavi Montessora '12	♟♟ 4
○ Giustiniana Brut M. Cl.	♟♟ 4
● Piemonte Barbera Grangiarossa '11	♟ 2
○ Roveri Frizzante	♟ 4
○ Gavi del Comune di Gavi Il Nostro Gavi '07	♟♟♟ 4
○ Gavi del Comune di Gavi Il Nostro Gavi '06	♟♟ 4
○ Gavi del Comune di Gavi Il Nostro Gavi '04	♟♟ 4
○ Gavi del Comune di Gavi Lugarara '11	♟♟ 3
○ Gavi del Comune di Gavi Montessora '11	♟♟ 4
○ Spumante M. Cl. '07	♟♟ 5

★Elio Grasso

LOC. GINESTRA, 40
12065 MONFORTE D'ALBA [CN]
TEL. 017378491
www.eliograsso.it

PRE-BOOKED VISITS
ANNUAL PRODUCTION 90,000 bottles
HECTARES UNDER VINE 18.00

Elio Grasso, with his wife Marina and son Gianluca, has followed at least two paths to become one of the greatest names in Langhe wine. On the one hand, a history of magnificent bottlings in terms of sheer quality and consistency, on the other a style that has made it impossible to place his Nebbiolos within the tradition-innovation framework, even during the most "ideological" years. The Vigna Casa Matè and Gavarini Vigna Chiniera Barolo crus are aged in 25-hectolitre Slavonian oak casks, and the Runcot Riserva in barriques, but technical details suddenly seem insignificant when faced with the distinctive layered, closely woven texture of these three magnificent Monforte vineyards. The 2009 vintage of Barolo Gavarini Chiniera is a great one, which easily took our top award for its highly convincing overall harmony. The elegant Barolo Ginestra Casa Matè 2009 also gave an excellent performance, while Barolo Runcot Riserva 2007 showed great potential for development.

● Barolo Gavarini Chiniera '09	♟♟♟ 8
● Barolo Ginestra Casa Maté '09	♟♟ 8
● Barolo Rüncot Ris. '07	♟♟ 8
● Barbera d'Alba V. Martina '10	♟♟ 4
● Dolcetto d'Alba dei Grassi '12	♟♟ 3
○ Langhe Chardonnay Educato '12	♟♟ 3
● Langhe Nebbiolo Gavarini '12	♟♟ 3
● Barolo Gavarini V. Chiniera '06	♟♟♟ 8
● Barolo Gavarini V. Chiniera '01	♟♟♟ 7
● Barolo Ginestra Casa Maté '07	♟♟♟ 8
● Barolo Ginestra V. Casa Maté '05	♟♟♟ 8
● Barolo Ginestra V. Casa Maté '04	♟♟♟ 8
● Barolo Ginestra V. Casa Maté '03	♟♟♟ 7
● Barolo Rüncot '01	♟♟♟ 8
● Barolo Rüncot '00	♟♟♟ 8

Silvio Grasso

FRAZ. ANNUNZIATA, 112
12064 LA MORRA [CN]
TEL. 017350322
www.silviograsso.com

CELLAR SALES
PRE-BOOKED VISITS
ANNUAL PRODUCTION 90,000 bottles
HECTARES UNDER VINE 14.00

This winery, with headquarters at Cascina Luciani at La Morra, is currently managed by Federico Grasso, who took over from his father Silvio some years ago, together with his wife Marilena. The winery's identity has its roots in the subzone of Annunziata, and its style is clearly more modern than classic, with short macerations and the use of French barriques, whose influence is however carefully dosed. The latest arrival, the Barolo Turné, instead espouses a more traditional style, with long macerations on the skins and ageing in Slavonian oak barrels. All the labels display excellent reliability and consistent quality. Barolo Bricco Luciani 2009 is characterized by notes of morello cherries, eucalyptus and tobacco that add to its interesting complexity. The sophisticated Barolo Giachini 2009 focuses on berry fruit and tobacco, with silky tannins, while varietal definition and delicious drinkability are the hallmarks of Barolo Turné 2009.

● Barolo Bricco Luciani '09	♟♟ 7
● Barolo Giachini '09	♟♟ 6
● Barolo Turné '09	♟♟ 7
● Barbera d'Alba Fontanile '10	♟♟ 5
● Barolo Annunziata V. Plicotti '09	♟♟ 7
● Barolo Ciabot Manzoni '09	♟♟ 8
● Barolo '09	♟ 5
● Barolo Bricco Luciani '04	♟♟♟ 7
● Barolo Bricco Luciani '01	♟♟♟ 6
● Barolo Bricco Luciani '96	♟♟♟ 6
● Barolo Bricco Luciani '95	♟♟♟ 6
● Barolo Bricco Luciani '90	♟♟♟ 6
● Barolo '08	♟♟ 7
● Barolo Ciabot Manzoni '08	♟♟ 7
● Barolo Turné '08	♟♟ 7

Bruna Grimaldi

VIA RODDINO
12050 SERRALUNGA D'ALBA [CN]
TEL. 0173262094
www.grimaldibruna.it

CELLAR SALES
PRE-BOOKED VISITS
ANNUAL PRODUCTION 80,160 bottles
HECTARES UNDER VINE 11.00

A small family-run estate just waiting to be discovered, offering well-defined great classic wines at reasonable prices: this is how we could sum up the winery run by Bruna Grimaldi and Franco Fiorino. It boasts a fine array of vineyards, and the selections of Barolo are, of course, the jewels of the line, with Bricco Ambrogio from Roddi, Camilla from Grinzane Cavour and Badarina, from the splendid cru in the commune of Serralunga d'Alba. The well-defined style is characterized by a close-focused nose and great drinkability. The excellent Barolo Bricco Ambrogio 2009 is distinguished by nice character, a multi-layered nose and a deep palate, while Barolo Badarina of the same vintage is complex, with a spicy nose of berry fruit and eucalyptus and a well-balanced palate. The juicy Dolcetto d'Alba San Martino deserves a special mention.

● Barolo Badarina '09	♥♥ 6
● Barolo Bricco Ambrogio '09	♥♥ 5
● Dolcetto d'Alba S. Martino '11	♥♥ 2*
● Barolo Camilla '09	♥ 5
● Barolo Badarina '07	♀♀ 6
● Barolo Badarina '06	♀♀ 6
● Barolo Badarina V. Regnola '05	♀♀ 6
● Barolo Badarina V. Regnola '03	♀♀ 6
● Barolo Badarina V. Regnola Ris. '06	♀♀ 6
● Barolo Bricco Ambrogio '08	♀♀ 5
● Barolo Bricco Ambrogio '07	♀♀ 5
● Barolo Camilla '07	♀♀ 5*
● Nebbiolo d'Alba Briccola '10	♀♀ 3
● Nebbiolo d'Alba Briccola '09	♀♀ 3

Giacomo Grimaldi

VIA LUIGI EINAUDI, 8
12060 BAROLO [CN]
TEL. 0173560536
www.giacomogrimaldi.com

CELLAR SALES
PRE-BOOKED VISITS
ANNUAL PRODUCTION 50,000 bottles
HECTARES UNDER VINE 13.00

If it is true that great wine commences in the vineyard, then this estate is well placed for success with its first-rate array of vineyards, which includes plots in the Le Coste cru in Barolo, Sotto Castello in Novello and Valmaggiore in Vezza d'Alba. Although Ferruccio Grimaldi, married to Enrica Scavino and son-in-law of the famous Castiglione Falletto producer, has not been making wine for very long, the results are already showing very interesting and clear-cut intentions. While the cellar is equipped with all of the latest technologies, the wines are characterized by a classic style, nicely balanced by the varietal notes that clearly distinguish each label. Barolo Sotto Castello di Novello 2009 has an alluring nose of currants, strawberries and raspberries that mingle with hints of tobacco and Peruvian bark, while Barolo Le Coste 2009 has darker notes of tar and rhubarb on the nose. The Barolo 2009 is very focused and exceptionally drinkable.

● Barolo Sotto Castello di Novello '09	♥♥ 6
● Barolo '09	♥♥ 5
● Barolo Le Coste '09	♥♥ 6
● Nebbiolo d'Alba Valmaggiore '11	♥♥ 3
● Barolo Sotto Castello di Novello '05	♀♀♀ 6
● Barbera d'Alba Fornaci '07	♀♀ 4
● Barolo '08	♀♀ 5
● Barolo '07	♀♀ 5
● Barolo Le Coste '07	♀♀ 6
● Barolo Le Coste '05	♀♀ 6
● Barolo Le Coste '05	♀♀ 6
● Barolo Sotto Castello di Novello '08	♀♀ 6
● Barolo Sotto Castello di Novello '07	♀♀ 6
● Barolo Sotto Castello di Novello '06	♀♀ 6

Sergio Grimaldi
Ca' du Sindic

loc. San Grato, 7
12058 Santo Stefano Belbo [CN]
Tel. 0141840341
www.cadusindic.it

CELLAR SALES
PRE-BOOKED VISITS
ANNUAL PRODUCTION 110,000 bottles
HECTARES UNDER VINE 14.50

The entire Grimaldi family is involved in Ca' du Sindic, which has been a benchmark for Moscato production for 25 years now. Its vineyards are situated in the district of Santo Stefano Belbo in the hills of San Maurizio, San Grato and Bauda, with vines of up to 60 years old, where moscato keeps company with dolcetto, barbera, cortese, brachetto, favorita, pinot nero and chardonnay. The wines aim to combine complexity and generous fruit with drinkability. This year our favourite version of Moscato d'Asti was the very delicate, concentrated Capsula Argento 2012, with notes of rosemary and lime and a long, fresh, harmonious finish. Capsula Oro 2012 has more aromatic notes of sage and lemon, and nice freshness, but less complexity and depth. Although a little predictable overall, Ventuno Brut Rosé has pleasant notes of berry fruit, while Barbera d'Asti SanGrato 2011 is fruity and balanced.

○ Moscato d'Asti Capsula Argento '12	�♟ 2*
● Barbera d'Asti SanGrato '11	♟♟ 2*
○ Moscato d'Asti Capsula Oro '12	♟♟ 3
⊙ Ventuno Brut Rosé	♟♟ 3
● Barbera d'Asti '11	♟ 2
○ Piemonte Moscato Passito Montaldi '08	♟ 5
● Barbera d'Asti San Grato '10	♟♟ 2*
○ Moscato d'Asti Capsula Oro '11	♟♟ 2*

Clemente Guasti

c.so IV Novembre, 80
14049 Nizza Monferrato [AT]
Tel. 0141721350
www.clementeguasti.it

CELLAR SALES
PRE-BOOKED VISITS
ANNUAL PRODUCTION 120,000 bottles
HECTARES UNDER VINE 27.00

The Guasti family's winery, founded in 1946, successfully continues along its path, which continues to see Barbera in the leading role, accompanied by other important Piedmont wines, from Barolo to Gavi. It has four estates: three in the Nizza area and one at Mombaruzzo. The Boschetto Vecchio vineyard, on clay soils, and Fonda San Nicolao, on sandy terrain, are the crus that yield the Barbera selections of the same names, which vaunt an austere, traditional style designed for ageing. The estate's two main vineyard selections performed well. Barbera d'Asti Superiore Fonda San Nicolao 2009 has a nose of berry fruit, cinnamon and cloves. Although a little short on structure, it's juicy and supple. Barbera d'Asti Superiore Boschetto Vecchio 2009 is balanced with notes of quinine and spice, showing rain-soaked earth and cherries on the finish. The pleasant Moscato d'Asti Santa Teresa 2012 is also well made, showing vibrant acidity.

● Barbera d'Asti Sup. Boschetto Vecchio '09	♟♟ 4
● Barbera d'Asti Sup. Fonda San Nicolao '09	♟♟ 4
○ Moscato d'Asti Santa Teresa '12	♟♟ 3
● Barbera d'Asti Desideria '10	♟ 3
○ Gavi '12	♟ 2
● Barbera d'Asti Desideria '09	♟♟ 2*
● Barbera d'Asti Sup. Boschetto Vecchio '07	♟♟ 4
● Barbera d'Asti Sup. Classica '07	♟♟ 3*
● Barbera d'Asti Sup. Fonda San Nicolao '07	♟♟ 4
● Barbera d'Asti Sup. Nizza Barcarato '07	♟♟ 5

★Hilberg - Pasquero

VIA BRICCO GATTI, 16
12040 PRIOCCA [CN]
TEL. 0173616197
www.hilberg-pasquero.com

CELLAR SALES
PRE-BOOKED VISITS
ANNUAL PRODUCTION 24,000 bottles
HECTARES UNDER VINE 6.50
VITICULTURE METHOD Certified Organic

The Pasquero estate was founded in the
Bricco Gatti vineyard, on one of the hills
overlooking Priocca, at the beginning of the
20th century. For the past 20 years it has
been enthusiastically run by "Miclo"
Pasquero and Annette Hilberg, who devote
great attention to enhancing the terroir. The
vineyards fan out around the cellar on silty,
marly terrains, and are planted exclusively
with the traditional red grape varieties of
Roero: barbera, brachetto and nebbiolo.
The wines of their portfolio are generally
very fruity with a good tannic weave. The
2011 vintage of Nebbiolo d'Alba confirms
its status of flagship wine, showing
complex with oaky notes that still need
time, but very elegant and juicy with solid,
fine-grained tannins and good acidity. The
rest of the range is well made,
commencing with the fresh, powerful,
pulp-rich Barbera d'Alba Superiore 2011,
which proffers spicy notes of plum and
cherry. We also liked the dense,
easy-drinking Vareij, an aromatic blend
from 70% brachetto with barbera.

● Nebbiolo d'Alba '11	♥♥ 5
● Barbera d'Alba '12	♥♥ 3
● Barbera d'Alba Sup. '11	♥♥ 5
● Langhe Nebbiolo '11	♥♥ 4
● Vareij '12	♥♥ 3
● Barbera d'Alba Sup. '09	♀♀♀ 5
● Barbera d'Alba Sup. '98	♀♀♀ 5
● Barbera d'Alba Sup. '97	♀♀♀ 5
● Nebbiolo d'Alba '06	♀♀♀ 5
● Nebbiolo d'Alba '05	♀♀♀ 5
● Nebbiolo d'Alba '04	♀♀♀ 5
● Nebbiolo d'Alba '03	♀♀♀ 5
● Nebbiolo d'Alba '01	♀♀♀ 5
● Nebbiolo d'Alba '00	♀♀♀ 4
● Nebbiolo d'Alba '99	♀♀♀ 4*

Icardi

LOC. SAN LAZZARO
S.DA COMUNALE BALBI, 30
12053 CASTIGLIONE TINELLA [CN]
TEL. 0141855159
www.icardivini.it

CELLAR SALES
PRE-BOOKED VISITS
ANNUAL PRODUCTION 360,000 bottles
HECTARES UNDER VINE 75.00
VITICULTURE METHOD Certified Biodynamic

Established at Castiglione Tinella back in
1914, the Icardi winery, first with Cavalier
Pierino and now under the guidance of his
children Maria Grazia and Claudio, has
grown to its present size of 75 hectares
under vine. Initially limited to the vineyards
next to the winery, these now include plots
in all the wine-growing areas in Monferrato
and Langa. Based on fruity drinkability, the
wines have also acquired structure and
complexity. In recent years, the house style
has shifted towards organic and
biodynamic farming methods. With this in
mind, Icardi have set up Cascina San
Lazzaro, a sort of experimental field for
biodynamic viticulture. Once again this year
the great Langhe reds were the stars of the
estate's wide range. The Barolo 2009 and
Barbaresco 2010 share the same balanced
oak and silky tannins, but differ in
structure. We particularly liked the luscious
aromatic Dadelio Bianco 2012 from
Cascina San Lazzaro.

● Barbaresco Montubert '10	♥♥ 5
● Barolo Parej '09	♥♥ 8
● Barbera d'Asti Nuj Suj '11	♥♥ 5
● Barbera d'Asti Tabaren '12	♥♥ 2*
○ Dadelio Bianco '12	♥♥ 5
● Langhe Rosso Pafoj '10	♥♥ 6
○ M.to Bianco Pafoj '12	♥♥ 4
● Langhe Rosso Dadelio '10	♥ 5
○ Moscato d'Asti La Rosa Selvatica '12	♥ 2
● Barbaresco Montubert '09	♀♀ 7
● Barbera d'Asti Nuj Suj '10	♀♀ 5
● Barolo Parej '08	♀♀ 7
○ Dadelio Bianco '11	♀♀ 5
○ M.to Bianco Pafoj '11	♀♀ 5
○ Moscato d'Asti La Rosa Selvatica '11	♀♀ 3
○ Piemonte Cortese Balera '11	♀♀ 3

Ioppa

FRAZ. MAULETTA
VIA DELLE PALLOTTE, 10
28078 ROMAGNANO SESIA [NO]
TEL. 0163833079
www.viniioppa.it

CELLAR SALES
PRE-BOOKED VISITS
ANNUAL PRODUCTION 95,000 bottles
HECTARES UNDER VINE 16.50

This historic estate belonging to brothers
Giampiero and Giorgio Ioppa, with the
increasing involvement of sons Marco and
Andrea, is enjoying what could be termed a
second lease of life. Their 16 plus hectares
are divided between Romagnano Sesia and
Ghemme and the latter DOC is represented
in three versions: the basic and the two
crus, Bricco Balsina and Santa Fè. Nebbiolo
dominates the range, but we also have
some interesting performances from
erbaluce, uva rara and vespolina, which is
also available in a passito, the Stransì. The
style is decidedly more modern than you
might expect from a cellar that goes back
several centuries. Following the recent
changes, the Ioppa family are making
excellent progress, with two Ghemmes in
our finals and a flawless battery. The
magnificent austere Bricco Balsina gives a
frill-free interpretation of its salty terroir,
while the generic Ghemme appears more
of a crowd pleaser. The mouthfilling
Vespolina 2007 is still young but seems
destined to go far.

Isolabella della Croce

REG. CAFFI, 3
14051 LOAZZOLO [AT]
TEL. 014487166
www.isolabelladellacroce.it

CELLAR SALES
PRE-BOOKED VISITS
ANNUAL PRODUCTION 90,000 bottles
HECTARES UNDER VINE 15.00

Situated about 500 metres above sea level
in Valdiserre, in the Alta Langa hills around
Asti, this young winery was founded by the
Isolabella della Croce family in 2001. It
vaunts vineyards over 50 years old, flanked
by new ones densely planted with up to
11,000 vines per hectare. The estate
produces a fairly wide range of wines, not
only from moscato and barbera but also
from international grape varieties,
particularly pinot nero, which yield
modern-style wines packed with personality
and character. We were particularly taken by
Barbera d'Asti Superiore Serena 2010, with
a nose of citrus peel, medicinal herbs and
berry fruit, combined with a firm, juicy
palate with a long, fresh finish. We also liked
the sagey Loazzolo Vendemmia Tardiva
Solìo 2006, Pinot Nero Monferrato Rosso
Bricco del Falco 2009, with wild berries and
spice, the fresh, gutsy Moscato d'Asti
Valdiserre 2012, and the elegant Barbera
d'Asti Superiore Nizza Augusta 2009.

● Ghemme '07	♟♟ 4	
● Ghemme Bricco Balsina '07	♟♟ 4	
● Colline Novaresi Nebbiolo '09	♟♟ 2*	
● Colline Novaresi Vespolina '07	♟♟ 3	
○ San Grato Bianco	♟♟ 2*	
☉ Colline Novaresi Rusin '12	♟ 2	
● Stransì	♟ 5	
● Colline Novaresi Nebbiolo '08	♟♟ 2*	
● Colline Novaresi Vespolina Coda Rossa '10	♟♟ 2*	
● Ghemme '06	♟♟ 4	
● Ghemme Bricco Balsina '06	♟♟ 5	
● Ghemme Santa Fè '06	♟♟ 6	

● Barbera d'Asti Sup. Serena '10	♟♟ 4	
● Barbera d'Asti Sup. Nizza Augusta '09	♟♟ 4	
○ Loazzolo V. T. Solio '06	♟♟ 5	
● M.to Rosso Bricco del Falco '09	♟♟ 5	
○ Moscato d'Asti Valdiserre '12	♟♟ 3	
● Barbera d'Asti Sup. Nizza Augusta '08	♟♟ 4	
● Barbera d'Asti Sup. Nizza Augusta '07	♟♟ 4	
● M.to Rosso Bricco del Falco '06	♟♟ 5	
● M.to Rosso Superlodo '07	♟♟ 4	
○ Moscato d'Asti Valdiserre '09	♟♟ 2	
○ Piemonte Sauvignon Blanc '11	♟♟ 3	

Iuli

FRAZ. MONTALDO
VIA CENTRALE, 27
15020 CERRINA MONFERRATO [AL]
TEL. 0142946657
www.iuli.it

CELLAR SALES
PRE-BOOKED VISITS
ACCOMMODATION
ANNUAL PRODUCTION 40,000 bottles
HECTARES UNDER VINE 8.50
VITICULTURE METHOD Certified Organic

There's a handful of wineries in the Monferrato Casalese area whose products you could order blindfold, confident you would be impressed, growers who have risked much more than their colleagues in more famous zones of Piedmont, because they have believed in the longevity of Barbera, preferring it to varieties which have the genes of ageing in their DNA. Moreover, they have had the courage – or madness – to leave stocks of Barbera from vintages such as 2004 in the cellar. But when we tasted them, we were awestruck – madness in a glass able to make you feel at peace with the world. The battery opens with a fabulous Barbera Superiore Barabba 2004, presented exclusively in magnums, which displays extraordinary complexity and balance. The Rossore is on top form, with a characterful version that underscores its vegetal nuances, while the Nino has alluring notes of aromatic herbs, developing into berry fruit and black pepper.

Tenuta Langasco

FRAZ. MADONNA DI COMO, 10
12051 ALBA [CN]
TEL. 0173286972
www.tenutalangasco.it

CELLAR SALES
PRE-BOOKED VISITS
ANNUAL PRODUCTION 60,000 bottles
HECTARES UNDER VINE 22.00

This charming, handsome winery is located in the scenic village of Madonna di Como on the hills overlooking Alba. The area has always been renowned for its dolcetto grapes, which possess deep flavour and expressive power, as exemplified by the wines that the estate produces from them. These are flanked by a series of reliable labels of consistently high quality. The range also includes other monovarietals such as Moscato and Brachetto, offering a wide and attractive array of excellent Piedmont wines. The highly drinkable Nebbiolo Sorì Coppa 2011 stands out for its expressive originality, fresh vigour and complex nose of berry fruit, juniper and quinine. Dolcetto Madonna di Como Vigna Miclet 2012 is youthful and vibrant, with a nose of blackberry and plum, accompanied by an edgy, full-flavoured palate.

● Barbera del M.to Sup. Barabba Magnum '04	♈♈ 5
● Barbera del M.to Sup. Rossore '10	♈♈ 3*
● M.to Rosso Nino '11	♈♈ 5
● Barbera del M.to Sup. Barabba '04	♈♈♈ 5
● Barbera del M.to Sup. Barabba '07	♈♈ 5
● Barbera del M.to Sup. Barabba '06	♈♈ 5
● Barbera del M.to Sup. Rossore '09	♈♈ 3*
● Barbera del M.to Sup. Rossore '07	♈♈ 3*
● Barbera del M.to Sup. Umberta '08	♈♈ 2
● M.to Rosso Malidea '09	♈♈ 5
● M.to Rosso Malidea '08	♈♈ 5
● M.to Rosso Malidea '07	♈♈ 5
● M.to Rosso Nino '10	♈♈ 5
● M.to Rosso Nino '09	♈♈ 5
● M.to Rosso Nino '08	♈♈ 5

● Nebbiolo d'Alba Sorì Coppa '11	♈♈ 4
● Barbera d'Alba Madonna di Como '11	♈♈ 2*
● Dolcetto d'Alba Madonna di Como V. Miclet '12	♈♈ 2*
● Alba '11	♈ 4
● Barbera d'Alba Sorì '11	♈ 3
● Barbera d'Alba Madonna di Como '09	♈♈ 3
● Barbera d'Alba Madonna di Como '08	♈♈ 3
● Barbera d'Alba Madonna di Como '07	♈♈ 3
● Barbera d'Alba Sorì '10	♈♈ 3*
● Dolcetto d'Alba Madonna di Como V. Miclet '11	♈♈ 2*
● Dolcetto d'Alba Madonna di Como V. Miclet '10	♈♈ 2*
● Nebbiolo d'Alba Sorì Coppa '10	♈♈ 3
● Nebbiolo d'Alba Sorì Coppa '09	♈♈ 3
● Nebbiolo d'Alba Sorì Coppa '08	♈♈ 3

Ugo Lequio

VIA DEL MOLINO, 10
12057 NEIVE [CN]
TEL. 0173677224
www.ugolequio.it

CELLAR SALES
PRE-BOOKED VISITS
ANNUAL PRODUCTION 30,000 bottles

Quietly, and without posing as a guru, Ugo Lequio has built up a loyal fan base over 30 years that appreciates his cordiality and coherent production. Although he doesn't own any vineyards himself, since the grapes from the Gallina cru are purchased from the Marcorino family, his knowledge of the terroir and his skill in the cellar regularly enable him to make some of the most complex and cellarable Barbarescos of the zone. The style can be considered classic, but not extreme, with ageing mainly in medium French oak barrels. Barbaresco Gallina 2010 is elegant, with well-calibrated notes of liquorice, tobacco and eucalyptus on the nose and a full, caressing attack on the palate, with smooth tannins and a nice long finish. Langhe Arneis 2012 is fresh and typical, with multi-layered floral and appley notes.

Podere Macellio

VIA ROMA, 18
10014 CALUSO [TO]
TEL. 0119833511
www.erbaluce-bianco.it

CELLAR SALES
PRE-BOOKED VISITS
ANNUAL PRODUCTION 20,000 bottles
HECTARES UNDER VINE 2.50

Just a stone's throw from Caluso's main square lies the cellar-house of the Bianco family. They have been producing wine since the latter half of the 18th century and started bottling in the 1960s. Today sees Signor Renato at the helm with his son Daniele. The estate's two and a half hectares are divided into four plots situated in the zone of Macellio on the Caluso hill, on south-facing slopes at an altitude between 310 and 340 metres. Annual production is just 20,000 bottles: a dry still white, a spumante and a passito aged in oak for a minimum of four to five years. The estate uses erbaluce to make the three different wines that have become classics of the Caluso production district. This year we were unable to pick a winner from the Metodo Classico sparkler, the still white and the partially dried dessert wine: all three are very good whites distinguished by their finesse and delicacy.

● Barbaresco Gallina '10	♟♟ 5
○ Langhe Arneis '12	♟♟ 3
● Barbaresco Gallina '09	♟♟ 5
● Barbaresco Gallina '08	♟♟ 5
● Barbaresco Gallina '07	♟♟ 5
● Barbaresco Gallina '06	♟♟ 5
● Barbaresco Gallina '05	♟♟ 5
● Barbaresco Gallina '04	♟♟ 5
● Barbaresco Gallina Ris. '07	♟♟ 6
● Barbera d'Alba Sup. Gallina '10	♟♟ 4
● Barbera d'Alba Sup. Gallina '09	♟♟ 3
● Barbera d'Alba Sup. Gallina '07	♟♟ 3
● Dolcetto d'Alba '09	♟♟ 2
● Langhe Nebbiolo '09	♟♟ 3

○ Caluso Passito '08	♟♟ 5
○ Erbaluce di Caluso '12	♟♟ 2*
○ Erbaluce di Caluso Brut M. Cl.	♟♟ 3*
○ Caluso Passito '07	♟♟ 5
○ Caluso Passito '06	♟♟ 5
○ Caluso Passito '05	♟♟ 5
○ Caluso Passito '04	♟♟ 5
○ Erbaluce di Caluso '11	♟♟ 2*
○ Erbaluce di Caluso '10	♟♟ 2*
○ Erbaluce di Caluso '07	♟♟ 2*

Malabaila di Canale

FRAZ. MADONNA DEI CAVALLI, 19
12043 CANALE [CN]
TEL. 017398381
www.malabaila.com

CELLAR SALES
PRE-BOOKED VISITS
ANNUAL PRODUCTION 100,000 bottles
HECTARES UNDER VINE 22.00

Although this estate was founded just 25 years ago, the Malabaila family have been involved in Roero's viticulture and wine trade since the 16th century. The vineyards lie within a 90-hectare estate on classic sandy-marly Asti soil. The vines are planted on steep slopes that can exceed gradients of 50%. The wines are classic in style and express their terroir mainly in their firm structure and rich fruit. Roero Castelletto Riserva 2009 is excellent, with a nose of dark berries, quinine and tobacco, and plenty of flesh, but is still young and needs time. Barbera d'Alba Mezzavilla 2010 is good too, with fine structure and character; notes of dark berries, juniper and liquorice against a spicy background; and a long, progressive palate sustained by acidity. The lighter, easy-drinking Nebbiolo d'Alba Bric Merli 2011 is well made and the other wines listed are decent.

★Malvirà

LOC. CANOVA
VIA CASE SPARSE, 144
12043 CANALE [CN]
TEL. 0173978145
www.malvira.com

CELLAR SALES
PRE-BOOKED VISITS
ACCOMMODATION AND RESTAURANT SERVICE
ANNUAL PRODUCTION 350,000 bottles
HECTARES UNDER VINE 40.00

Massimo and Roberto Damonte have made Malvirà one of Roero's showcase estates in terms of viticulture and tourist accommodation thanks to their wines and their magnificent relais in the Villa Tiboldi. They obtain their fruit from eight vineyards, most of which are located in the municipality of Canale. These include out-and-out crus like Mombeltramo, Renesio and Trinità, which are home to vines up to 80 years old. The wines on offer are among the most typical and impressive in the entire Roero district. The Roeros have always been among the firmest and most cellarable of the designation, but have appeared less stunning and well made the past couple of years. Roero Renesio Riserva 2009 is an exception: a little oak heavy, but concentrated with floral and fruity notes on a background of peat, and a juicy palate with close-knit tannins and a long finish. The other wines listed are pleasant and well made, particularly the delicate, linear, fruity Roero Arneis Trinità 2012.

● Barbera d'Alba Mezzavilla '10	♟♟ 3*
● Roero Castelletto Ris. '09	♟♟ 4
● Nebbiolo d'Alba Bric Merli '11	♟♟ 3
● Barbera d'Alba Giardino '12	♟ 2
○ Roero Arneis '12	♟ 2
○ Roero Arneis Pradvaj '12	♟ 3
● Barbera d'Alba Mezzavilla '09	♟♟ 3*
○ Roero Arneis '11	♟♟ 2*
○ Roero Arneis '10	♟♟ 2*
○ Roero Arneis Pradvaj '11	♟♟ 3
● Roero Bric Volta '09	♟♟ 2*
● Roero Castelletto Ris. '08	♟♟ 4
● Roero Castelletto Ris. '07	♟♟ 4

● Roero Renesio Ris. '09	♟♟ 5
● Barbera d'Alba S. Michele '10	♟♟ 3
○ Roero Arneis Renesio '12	♟♟ 3
○ Roero Arneis Saglietto '12	♟♟ 3
○ Roero Arneis Trinità '12	♟♟ 3
○ Roero Arneis '12	♟ 2
● Roero Mombeltramo Ris. '09	♟ 5
● Roero Mombeltramo Ris. '05	♟♟♟ 5
● Roero Renesio Ris. '05	♟♟♟ 5
● Roero Sup. Mombeltramo '04	♟♟♟ 5
● Roero Sup. Mombeltramo '00	♟♟♟ 5
● Roero Sup. Trinità '03	♟♟♟ 4
● Roero Sup. Trinità '01	♟♟♟ 5
● Roero Trinità Ris. '07	♟♟♟ 5

Giovanni Manzone

VIA CASTELLETTO, 9
12065 MONFORTE D'ALBA [CN]
TEL. 017378114
www.manzonegiovanni.com

CELLAR SALES
PRE-BOOKED VISITS
ANNUAL PRODUCTION 40,000 bottles
HECTARES UNDER VINE 8.00

It's stories like this that have made Langhe
a leading wine region; estates that seem to
cruise along almost unnoticed, but are
consistently among the very best producers.
Giovanni Manzone, now flanked by his son
Mauro, is a very familiar name to those who
seek an authentic expression of the
Monforte d'Alba terroir and its finest crus
like Gramolere, Bricat and Castelletto. The
estate's Barolos are sometimes edgy and
far from formal, but they're incisive and
forthright in structure, and have nothing to
do with standardized production. Among all
this nebbiolo, we should also spare a word
for the small production of Rosserto, which
is very likely a white biotype of the Ligurian
rossese grape. The complex, multi-layered
Barolo Castelletto 2009 has close-focused
top notes of spice, medicinal herbs, quinine
and tobacco, and a long, deep palate
supported by weighty yet discreet tannins.
Barolo Gramolere 2009 is complex, with a
good balance of elegance and power.

Paolo Manzone

LOC. MERIAME, 1
12050 SERRALUNGA D'ALBA [CN]
TEL. 0173613113
www.barolomeriame.com

CELLAR SALES
PRE-BOOKED VISITS
ACCOMMODATION
ANNUAL PRODUCTION 85,000 bottles
HECTARES UNDER VINE 10.00

The estate vineyards are located in some of
the district's most prestigious winemaking
areas and are the reason why this winery
has been able to build up such a complete,
multifaceted battery of wines over time and
serve as an excellent flagship of the
territory. In the lovely underground cellars
wines are aged in woods of different sizes,
for a better balance of the traits of the
various grape varieties. Paolo Manzone and
his wife Luisella Corino flank their
winemaking with a lovely agritourism
enterprise, located in a memorable nook of
Langa, and the ideal complement for this
tempting winery. Barolo Meriame 2009 has
a complex nose ranging from fresh notes of
berry fruit to darker ones of tar and Peruvian
bark. On the palate it is rich with
well-balanced tannins and acidity. The highly
drinkable Barolo Serralunga 2009 displays a
perfect balance of structure and elegance.

● Barolo Castelletto '09	♔♔♔ 5
● Barolo Bricat '09	♔♔ 6
● Barolo Gramolere '09	♔♔ 6
● Barbera d'Alba Sup. La Serra '10	♔♔ 3
● Barolo Gramolere Ris. '06	♔♔ 7
● Langhe Nebbiolo Il Crutin '11	♔♔ 3
● Barbera d'Alba '11	♔ 3
○ Langhe Bianco Rosserto '11	♔ 3
● Barolo Bricat '05	♕♕♕ 6
● Barolo Gramolere Ris. '05	♕♕♕ 7
● Barolo Le Gramolere '04	♕♕♕ 6
● Barolo Le Gramolere Ris. '01	♕♕♕ 7
● Barolo Le Gramolere Ris. '00	♕♕♕ 7
● Barolo Le Gramolere Ris. '99	♕♕♕ 7

● Barolo Meriame '09	♔♔ 7
● Barolo Serralunga '09	♔♔ 6
○ Dolcetto d'Alba Magna '12	♔♔ 2*
● Langhe Rosso Luvì '11	♔♔ 3
● Barbera d'Alba Fiorenza '11	♔ 3
● Nebbiolo d'Alba Miriné '11	♔ 3
● Barbera d'Alba Fiorenza '10	♕♕ 3
● Barolo Meriame '08	♕♕ 7
● Barolo Meriame '01	♕♕ 6
● Barolo Meriame '00	♕♕ 6
● Barolo Serralunga '08	♕♕ 6
● Barolo Serralunga '05	♕♕ 5
● Langhe Rosso Ardì '11	♕♕ 2*
● Nebbiolo d'Alba Miriné '10	♕♕ 4

Marcalberto

VIA PORTA SOTTANA, 9
12058 SANTO STEFANO BELBO [CN]
TEL. 0141844022
marcalbertopc@libero.it

CELLAR SALES
PRE-BOOKED VISITS
ANNUAL PRODUCTION 30,000 bottles
HECTARES UNDER VINE 5.00

Marco and Alberto Cane's Marcalberto winery is a small-scale operation devoted entirely to the production of Metodo Classico. With the expert supervision of father Piero there have been some quality results that have made Marcalberto one of the most interesting of the new wave of spumante producers. The vineyards are situated in the municipalities of Santo Stefano Belbo and Calosso, planted only to the classic sparkling wine varieties of chardonnay and pinot noir, with a clear predominance of the latter. Two of the estate's wines made it into our finals, underscoring its qualitative growth in recent years. Marcalberto Millesimo Brut 2008 is delicate and complex, with notes ranging from damson to wild berries with hints of crusty bread, and a long, balanced finish, while Marcalberto Nature, produced without added sulphites, does not have the finesse of its vintage counterpart, but displays great character, power and rich body, nicely supported by acidity.

○ Marcalberto Brut M. Cl. '08		🏆🏆 5
○ Marcalberto Nature M. Cl.		🏆🏆 6
○ Marcalberto Brut Rosé M. Cl.		🏆🏆 4
○ Marcalberto Sansannée Brut M. Cl.		🏆🏆 4
○ Marcalberto Brut M. Cl. '07		🏆 5
○ Marcalberto Brut M. Cl. '06		🏆 5
○ Marcalberto Brut M. Cl. '05		🏆 5

Poderi Marcarini

P.ZZA MARTIRI, 2
12064 LA MORRA [CN]
TEL. 017350222
www.marcarini.it

CELLAR SALES
PRE-BOOKED VISITS
ACCOMMODATION
ANNUAL PRODUCTION 125,000 bottles
HECTARES UNDER VINE 18.00

Anna Marcarini Bava, with her daughter Luisa and son-in-law Manuel Marchetti, carries the baton for one of the great names in Langhe wine. Production revolves around the eternal contrast between two of the most famous vineyards in the municipality of La Morra and beyond: Brunate and La Serra. Geographically close but very different in character, the personality of each of these crus is enhanced via a rigorous approach that includes long maceration and patient ageing in 20- and 40-hectolitre oak barrels. The Barolos are extremely classic and age magnificently. They are accompanied by Dolcettos, Barbera, Arneis from Montaldo in Roero, and Moscato from the municipality of Neviglie. Slightly less stunning than in other vintages, the two Barolos presented for this edition are nonetheless faithful to the style that has long characterized the estate's production. Brunate 2009 focuses on estery notes of dried flowers and tobacco, and already vaunts well-integrated tannins, while Barolo La Serra 2009 unfurls with notes of berry fruit and dried flowers with hints of tar.

● Barolo La Serra '09		🏆🏆 6
● Barbera d'Alba Ciabot Camerano '11		🏆🏆 3
● Barolo Brunate '09		🏆🏆 6
● Dolcetto d'Alba Fontanazza '12		🏆 2
○ Roero Arneis '12		🏆 2
● Barolo Brunate '05		🏆🏆🏆 6
● Barolo Brunate '03		🏆🏆🏆 6
● Barolo Brunate '01		🏆🏆🏆 6
● Barolo Brunate '99		🏆🏆🏆 6
● Barolo Brunate '96		🏆🏆🏆 6
● Barolo Brunate Ris. '85		🏆🏆🏆 6
● Dolcetto d'Alba Boschi di Berri '96		🏆🏆🏆 4*
● Barolo La Serra '08		🏆🏆 6
● Langhe Nebbiolo Lasarin '10		🏆🏆 3*

Marchese Luca Spinola

FRAZ. ROVERETO DI GAVI
LOC. CASCINA MASSIMILIANA, 97
15066 GAVI [AL]
TEL. 0143682514
www.marcheselucaspinola.it

CELLAR SALES
PRE-BOOKED VISITS
ANNUAL PRODUCTION 20,000 bottles
HECTARES UNDER VINE 12.00

This profile simply isn't long enough to list all the noble titles associated with Marchese Luca Spinola, the heart and soul of the winery that bears his name and has grown up around the family's old estates. It comprises 12 hectares of vineyards, all planted to cortese, six in the municipality of Tassarolo and six in the classic Gavi production zone. Together, they yield three wines, distinguished by their different terroirs and fermentation techniques. Most of the grapes go to make the Gavi di Gavi, while just 3,000 bottles of the Gavi del Comune di Tassarolo are produced. Production figures aren't much higher for the Tenuta Massimiliana, which is fermented more slowly at lower temperatures. We can confirm the high quality of the wines of this old Ligurian family who have always owned vineyards in and around Tassarolo. Both Gavis from vineyards in the municipality of Gavi itself are very fine, particularly the exceptionally fragrant Tenuta Massimiliana, while the Gavi from Tassarolo is less vibrant.

○ Gavi del Comune di Gavi '12	♔♔ 2*
○ Gavi del Comune di Gavi Tenuta Massimiliana '12	♔♔ 3
○ Gavi del Comune di Tassarolo '12	♔ 2
○ Gavi del Comune di Gavi '11	♕♕ 2*
○ Gavi del Comune di Gavi '10	♕♕ 2
○ Gavi del Comune di Gavi '09	♕♕ 2
○ Gavi del Comune di Gavi Tenuta Massimiliana '10	♕♕ 2
○ Gavi del Comune di Tassarolo '10	♕♕ 2*
○ Gavi del Comune di Tassarolo '09	♕♕ 2*
○ Gavi Tenuta Massimiliana '08	♕♕ 3

Marchesi di Barolo

VIA ROMA, 1
12060 BAROLO [CN]
TEL. 0173564400
www.marchesibarolo.com

CELLAR SALES
PRE-BOOKED VISITS
CELLAR SALES
ANNUAL PRODUCTION 1,500,000 bottles
HECTARES UNDER VINE 47.00

This important estate is one of the best-known Piedmont wineries in Italy and the world, with over 40 hectares of vineyards that include prestigious crus like Cannubi and Sarmassa. The precious work mapped out by Cavalier Felice Abbona was continued with commitment by his successor Commendator Pietro Emilio Abbona, and today by Anna and Ernesto. Marchesi di Barolo offers a very extensive and representative range of wines, whose pillar is naturally Barolo. The wines display different and complementary styles, ranging from modern to traditional, derived partly from the use of both small French oak casks and large Slavonian oak barrels. The entire battery of 2009 Barolos is splendid, headed by a Tre Bicchieri-winning Sarmassa with an elegant, complex nose of tobacco, spice and violets, and a palate underpinned by caressing, close-knit tannins. The Cannubi 2009 is harmonious and balanced, while Barolo Coste di Rose 2009 is delightfully delicate.

● Barolo Sarmassa '09	♔♔♔ 8
● Barolo Cannubi '09	♔♔ 8
● Barolo Coste di Rose '09	♔♔ 6
● Barbaresco '10	♔♔ 5
● Barbaresco Serragrilli '10	♔♔ 6
● Barbera d'Alba Ruvei '11	♔♔ 3
● Barolo del Comune di Barolo '09	♔♔ 7
● Dolcetto d'Alba Buschet '12	♔♔ 4
● Dolcetto d'Alba Madonna di Como '12	♔♔ 3
○ Moscato d'Asti Zagara '12	♔♔ 3
● Barbera d'Alba Peiragal '11	♔ 4
○ Gavi del Comune di Gavi '12	♔ 3
● Nebbiolo d'Alba Michet '11	♔ 4
○ Roero Arneis '12	♔ 3

PIEDMONT

Marchesi Incisa della Rocchetta

VIA ROMA, 66
14030 ROCCHETTA TANARO [AT]
TEL. 0141644647
www.marchesiincisawines.com

CELLAR SALES
PRE-BOOKED VISITS
ACCOMMODATION AND RESTAURANT SERVICE
ANNUAL PRODUCTION 40,000 bottles
HECTARES UNDER VINE 17.00

Situated in Rocchetta Tanaro, in the Monferrato hills, this historic estate has been enthusiastically and competently run by Barbara Incisa della Rocchetta and her son Filiberto Massone since 1986. Its vineyards occupy hillside sites with sandy clay soil and are planted mainly to barbera, with the addition of grignolino, pinot nero, grown here since the late 19th. century, and merlot. The wines that they yield are terroir true and characterized by a modern style that focuses on drinkability, aromatic definition and richness of fruit. Barbera d'Asti Superiore Sant'Emiliano confirms its role as the estate's flagship wine again with the 2010 vintage. The nose of black cherry, aromatic herbs and tobacco is followed by a very expressive palate with a long, elegant finish. Monferrato Rosso Rollone 2012 is a concentrated, gutsy blend of 50% barbera and 50% pinot nero, while Grignolino d'Asti 2012 is succulent and spicy.

Mario Marengo

VIA XX SETTEMBRE, 34
12064 LA MORRA [CN]
TEL. 017350115
marengo1964@libero.it

CELLAR SALES
PRE-BOOKED VISITS
ANNUAL PRODUCTION 28,000 bottles
HECTARES UNDER VINE 6.00

This small estate, now meticulously managed by Marco Marengo, is growing fast in terms of both size and reputation and its star has risen in the Barolo firmament. The only drawback is that its wines remain hard to find in Italy, as the majority are exported to countries that appreciate the well-defined, sober, elegant style that characterizes the entire production. The Brunate cru in particular expresses the incredible potential of this extraordinary terroir and the equally admirable quality of work on the estate. This skilled producer has achieved excellent results, winning our top award with the flawless Barolo Brunate 2009, which vaunts a perfect balance of freshness and depth. Barolo Bricco delle Viole 2009 offers a powerful, juicy palate with a long, full-flavoured finish.

● Barbera d'Asti Sup. Sant'Emiliano '10	♛♛ 4
● Grignolino d'Asti '12	♛♛ 3
● M.to Rosso Rollone '12	♛♛ 3
● Barbera d'Asti Valmorena '12	♛ 3
● Piemonte Pinot Nero Marchese Leopoldo '11	♛ 4
● Barbera d'Asti Sup. Sant'Emiliano '09	♀♀ 4
● Barbera d'Asti Sup. Sant'Emiliano '08	♀♀ 4
● Barbera d'Asti Sup. Sant'Emiliano '07	♀♀ 4
● Barbera d'Asti Valmorena '11	♀♀ 3
● Barbera d'Asti Valmorena '10	♀♀ 3*
● Grignolino d'Asti '11	♀♀ 3
● M.to Rosso Rollone '11	♀♀ 3
● M.to Rosso Rollone '09	♀♀ 3*

● Barolo Brunate '09	♛♛♛ 6
● Barolo Bricco delle Viole '09	♛♛ 5
● Barbera d'Alba Pugnane '11	♛♛ 3
● Barolo '09	♛♛ 5
● Nebbiolo d'Alba Valmaggiore '11	♛♛ 3
● Barolo Brunate '07	♀♀♀ 6
● Barolo Brunate '06	♀♀♀ 6
● Barolo Brunate '05	♀♀♀ 6
● Barolo Brunate '04	♀♀♀ 6
● Barbera d'Alba Pugnane '08	♀♀ 3*
● Barolo '08	♀♀ 5
● Barolo '07	♀♀ 5
● Barolo Bricco Viole '07	♀♀ 5
● Barolo Bricco Viole '06	♀♀ 5
● Barolo Brunate '08	♀♀ 6

Claudio Mariotto

S.DA PER SAREZZANO, 29
15057 TORTONA [AL]
TEL. 0131868500
www.claudiomariotto.it

CELLAR SALES
PRE-BOOKED VISITS
ANNUAL PRODUCTION 100,000 bottles
HECTARES UNDER VINE 32.00

Claudio Mariotto is now a benchmark vigneron as far as the Tortona district is concerned, and his Pitasso is an icon among the wines made from the timorasso variety. What comes as a surprise, however, is the impressive average quality of the wines on offer, especially for their great value for money. Wines like Dolcetto Campo del Gatto, Freisa Braghè, Barbera Territorio il Cortese never disappoint and are pocket friendly. Of course, Claudio achieves his finest results with the selections of Timorasso and the top Barberas. Vhò is one of the very best of these, due to attentive ageing in oak that does not overwhelm the classic freshness of the grape variety, but enhances its varietal characteristics. The three versions of Timorasso are as brilliant as ever, and we found Cavallina particularly excellent this year.

○ Colli Tortonesi Timorasso Cavallina '11	♟♟	4
○ Colli Tortonesi Timorasso Pitasso '11	♟♟	5
● Colli Tortonesi Barbera Vho '11	♟♟	4
● Colli Tortonesi Rosso Territorio '12	♟♟	3
○ Colli Tortonesi Timorasso Derthona '11	♟♟	4
○ Colli Tortonesi Cortese Profilo '12	♟	3
● Colli Tortonesi Freisa Braghè '12	♟	3
○ Colli Tortonesi Bianco Pitasso '06	♟♟♟	5
○ Colli Tortonesi Bianco Pitasso '05	♟♟♟	4
○ Colli Tortonesi Bianco Pitasso '04	♟♟♟	4
○ Colli Tortonesi Timorasso Pitasso '08	♟♟♟	5
○ Colli Tortonesi Timorasso Derthona '10	♟♟	4
○ Colli Tortonesi Timorasso Derthona '09	♟♟	4
○ Colli Tortonesi Timorasso Pitasso '10	♟♟	5

Marsaglia

VIA MADAMA MUSSONE, 2
12050 CASTELLINALDO [CN]
TEL. 0173213048
www.cantinamarsaglia.it

CELLAR SALES
PRE-BOOKED VISITS
ANNUAL PRODUCTION 70,000 bottles
HECTARES UNDER VINE 15.00

Castellinaldo is one of the municipalities with the greatest number of vineyards and wineries in the whole of Roero, and Emilio and Marina Marsaglia's estate is among the most interesting and representative. Boasting vines over 50 years old, all its vineyards lie within the municipal boundaries and are planted with the typical Roero grape varieties – arneis, barbera and brachetto – plus a small amount of syrah for the Langhe Complotto. The entire range, topped by Roero Brich d'America from the vineyard of the same name, is absolutely terroir-true. This year Roero Brich d'America 2009 gave a first-rate performance, showing juicy but rather austere, with nicely prominent tannins and notes of quinine, tobacco and spices. The elegant Barbera d'Alba San Cristoforo 2011 did equally well, focusing more on pleasantness than flesh and rich fruit, without losing any of its gutsy character, and offering a long, supple finish.

● Barbera d'Alba S. Cristoforo '11	♟♟	3*
● Roero Brich d'America '09	♟♟	4
● Barbera d'Alba Castellinaldo '09	♟	4
○ Roero Arneis Serramiana '12	♟	3
● Barbera d'Alba Castellinaldo '07	♟♟	4
● Barbera d'Alba Castellinaldo '06	♟♟	4
● Barbera d'Alba S. Cristoforo '10	♟♟	3
● Nebbiolo d'Alba S. Pietro '08	♟♟	3
● Nebbiolo d'Alba San Pietro '10	♟♟	3
○ Roero Arneis Serramiana '11	♟♟	3
○ Roero Arneis Serramiana '10	♟♟	3
● Roero Brich d'America '08	♟♟	4
● Roero Brich d'America '07	♟♟	4
● Roero Brich d'America '06	♟♟	4

★Franco M. Martinetti

VIA SAN FRANCESCO DA PAOLA, 18
10123 TORINO
TEL. 0118395937
www.francomartinetti.it

PRE-BOOKED VISITS
ANNUAL PRODUCTION 130,000 bottles
HECTARES UNDER VINE 4.00

Franco Martinetti and his winery, which he has carefully crafted to reflect his personality and character, possess the allure of unique and remarkable ventures that are capable of astonishing. A talented grape selector with deep knowledge of the wine world, over the years Franco has built up a range of wines from the main Piedmont grape varieties, imparting to all of them a well-defined classic style. The 2006 vintage of the Brut Quarantatre is very alluring, with fragrant notes of pastry, crusty bread and hints of spice, combined with a vibrant, zesty palate. Barolo Marasco 2009 has balsamic nuances, accompanied by notes of tobacco and quinine and nicely balanced tannins. Don't miss the 2011 Martin, which is the best version ever.

Wine	Rating
● Barolo Marasco '09	♟♟ 7
○ Colli Tortonesi Timorasso Bianco Martin '11	♟♟ 6
○ Quarantatre Brut M. Cl. '06	♟♟ 6
● Barbera d'Asti Bric dei Banditi '12	♟♟ 3
○ Colli Tortonesi Timorasso Biancofranco '11	♟♟ 5
○ Gavi del Comune di Gavi '12	♟♟ 3
● Barbera d'Asti Sup. Montruc '06	♟♟♟ 5
● Barbera d'Asti Sup. Montruc '01	♟♟♟ 5
● Barolo Marasco '01	♟♟♟ 7
● Barolo Marasco '00	♟♟♟ 7
● M.to Rosso Sul Bric '10	♟♟♟ 6
● M.to Rosso Sul Bric '09	♟♟♟ 6
● M.to Rosso Sul Bric '00	♟♟♟ 5
○ Gavi Minaia '11	♟♟ 5

★Bartolo Mascarello

VIA ROMA, 15
12060 BAROLO [CN]
TEL. 017356125

CELLAR SALES
PRE-BOOKED VISITS
ANNUAL PRODUCTION 30,000 bottles
HECTARES UNDER VINE 5.00

Maria Teresa Mascarello faced quite a challenge when she lost her father, Bartolo. An extraordinary character known for his charisma and intellectual prowess, he represented a certain vision of Barolo – and not only Barolo. Maria Teresa has more than achieved the feat with a long series of wines that fully embrace her production and cultural legacy. They display exceptional elegance and clarity within a classic approach featuring lengthy maceration and ageing in large barrels. The Barolo 2009 is impeccably made, in keeping with the classic style of the estate's wines, which are characterized by their freshness. On the nose it is complex, with notes of violet, medicinal herbs, berry fruit and tobacco, while the palate has good flesh, with smooth, discreet tannins.

Wine	Rating
● Barolo '09	♟♟♟ 8
● Barolo '07	♟♟♟ 8
● Barolo '06	♟♟♟ 8
● Barolo '05	♟♟♟ 8
● Barolo '01	♟♟♟ 8
● Barolo '99	♟♟♟ 8
● Barolo '98	♟♟♟ 8
● Barolo '89	♟♟♟ 8
● Barolo '84	♟♟♟ 8
● Barolo '83	♟♟♟ 8
● Barolo '08	♟♟ 8
● Barolo '04	♟♟ 8
● Barolo '03	♟♟ 8
● Barolo '00	♟♟ 8

Giuseppe Mascarello e Figlio

VIA BORGONUOVO, 108
12060 MONCHIERO [CN]
TEL. 0173792126
www.mascarello1881.com

CELLAR SALES
PRE-BOOKED VISITS
ANNUAL PRODUCTION 60,000 bottles
HECTARES UNDER VINE 17.00

Time seems to stand still on the Mascarellos' estate, where Mauro and his son Giuseppe produce wine according to the most rigorous Langhe tradition. Indeed, it is the hallmark of this estate, which was well known as early as the late 1800s. In addition to Barolo, it produces Barbera, Dolcetto and Freisa, using long maceration and lengthy ageing in large barrels. Starting with the colour, the wines appear light and elegant, at times surprisingly aromatic. They cellar extremely well, offering thrilling sensations to those who know how to wait. The alluring, well-orchestrated Barolo Monprivato 2008 walked off with our top accolade. The aristocratic nose offers notes of aniseed accompanied by hints of tobacco and spice, while the palate is balanced, with prominent but controlled tannins. Barolo Villero 2008 has a long, full-flavoured palate.

● Barolo Monprivato '08	♛♛♛ 8
● Barolo Villero '08	♛♛ 8
● Barbera d'Alba Sup. Scudetto '09	♛♛ 5
● Barolo S. Stefano di Perno '08	♛♛ 8
● Langhe Freisa Toetto '09	♛♛ 3
● Langhe Nebbiolo '11	♛♛ 6
● Barolo Monprivato '01	♛♛♛ 8
● Barolo Monprivato '85	♛♛♛ 8
● Barolo S. Stefano di Perno '98	♛♛♛ 8
● Barolo Villero '96	♛♛♛ 8
● Barbera d'Alba Sup. Scudetto '05	♛♛ 5
● Barolo Monprivato '05	♛♛ 8
● Barolo Monprivato Cà d' Morissio Ris. '03	♛♛ 8
● Barolo S. Stefano di Perno '06	♛♛ 8

★Massolino

P.ZZA CAPPELLANO, 8
12050 SERRALUNGA D'ALBA [CN]
TEL. 0173613138
www.massolino.it

CELLAR SALES
PRE-BOOKED VISITS
ANNUAL PRODUCTION 120,000 bottles
HECTARES UNDER VINE 21.00

In Langhe it's not just large barrels that denote a traditionalist cellar. Consider Franco and Roberto Massolino's Barolos dedicated to prestigious crus like Parussi in Castiglione Falletto, which grace the ranks since the 2007 vintage, or the trinity of Serralunga, Parafada, Margheria and Vigna Rionda, which burnish the estate's reputation. All aged in medium and large oak barrels, in many ways the wines offer a transversal interpretation of the nebbiolo cultivated in these hills. Austere, rigorous, even biting in their youth, they also possess power and fruity strength. Their style is continually evolving; ditto the other labels obtained from barbera, dolcetto, chardonnay and moscato. The battery presented for our tastings offered excellent sensations. Barolo Parafada 2009 shows notes of tobacco and berry fruit with hints of tar, while Barolo Margheria 2009 is characterized by freshness and nicely controlled tannins. Barolo Vigna Rionda 2007 needs more time to express its full potential.

● Barolo Margheria '09	♛♛ 7
● Barolo Parafada '09	♛♛ 7
● Barolo Parussi '09	♛♛ 7
● Barolo V. Rionda Ris. '07	♛♛ 8
● Barbera d'Alba '12	♛♛ 3
● Barbera d'Alba Gisep '11	♛♛ 5
● Barolo Serralunga d'Alba '09	♛♛ 7
○ Langhe Chardonnay '12	♛♛ 3
● Langhe Nebbiolo '11	♛♛ 3
● Dolcetto d'Alba '12	♛ 2
○ Moscato d'Asti '12	♛ 2
● Barolo Margheria '05	♛♛♛ 7
● Barolo V. Rionda Ris. '06	♛♛♛ 8
● Barolo Vigna Rionda Ris. '05	♛♛♛ 8
● Barolo Vigna Rionda Ris. '04	♛♛♛ 8

Mazzoni

VIA ROMA, 73
28010 CAVAGLIO D'AGOGNA [NO]
TEL. 0322806612
www.vinimazzoni.it

CELLAR SALES
PRE-BOOKED VISITS
ANNUAL PRODUCTION 15,000 bottles
HECTARES UNDER VINE 4.50

Old documents found in Turin certify the presence of the Mazzoni family in Cavaglio d'Agona as early as the 14th century. A wealth of history and experience that bore fruit in 1999, when Tiziano, Rita and Gilles decided to reopen for business, acquiring new land and refurbishing their vineyards. The family applied a classic approach, with restrained use of large wood, and its wines combine finesse, austerity and aromatic breadth. The flagship Nebbiolo comes in a number of interesting versions, including one from raisined erbaluce. Ghemme dei Mazzoni 2009 is complex and layered, with sound fruit and a taut, austere palate. Nebbiolo Ai Franconi 2011 also offers nicely focused, pure fruit, combined with good body, balance and a succulent, mouthfilling finish. Nebbiolo Monteregio 2011 is more austere, with notes of dried herbs, close-woven tannins and an assertive, full-flavoured finish.

● Ghemme dei Mazzoni '09	♔♔ 5
● Colline Novaresi Nebbiolo Ai Franconi '11	♔♔ 3
● Colline Novaresi Nebbiolo del Monteregio '11	♔♔ 3
● Ghemme Ai Livelli '09	♔♔ 6
○ Passito Le Masche	♔♔ 5
● Colline Novaresi Vespolina Il Ricetto '12	♔ 3
● Ghemme Ai Livelli '08	♔♔ 6
● Ghemme Ai Livelli '07	♔♔ 6
● Ghemme dei Mazzoni '08	♔♔ 5
● Ghemme dei Mazzoni '07	♔♔ 5

Moccagatta

S.DA RABAJÀ, 46
12050 BARBARESCO [CN]
TEL. 0173635228

CELLAR SALES
PRE-BOOKED VISITS
ANNUAL PRODUCTION 65,000 bottles
HECTARES UNDER VINE 12.00

Brothers Sergio and Franco Minuto steadfastly continue along the path of quality and competency that commenced with their first successes in the 1990s and has led them to carve out an important place for themselves, both in Italy and abroad, among the top wineries of the Barbaresco zone. Their style is modern, using small oak casks for the ageing of the various selections. Nebbiolo, the prince of the locally grown grape varieties, accounts for almost half the area under vine, and is accompanied by barbera, dolcetto and chardonnay, which go to make up a consistently good, reliable range. Our favourite of the 2010 Barbarescos is the full-bodied Bric Balin, which manages to offset the sweetness derived from small wood with alluring ripe fruit. The Cole vaunts impressive tannins that are still rather rugged, while the more delicate Basarin is slightly overwhelmed by the spiciness of the oak.

● Barbaresco Bric Balin '10	♔♔ 6
● Barbaresco Basarin '10	♔♔ 6
● Barbaresco Cole '10	♔♔ 6
○ Langhe Chardonnay '12	♔ 2
○ Langhe Chardonnay Buschet '11	♔ 5
● Barbaresco Bric Balin '05	♔♔♔ 6
● Barbaresco Bric Balin '04	♔♔♔ 6
● Barbaresco Bric Balin '01	♔♔♔ 6
● Barbaresco Bric Balin '08	♔♔ 6
● Barbaresco Cole '08	♔♔ 6
○ Langhe Chardonnay '11	♔♔ 2*
○ Langhe Chardonnay Buschet '10	♔♔ 5

Mauro Molino

FRAZ. ANNUNZIATA
B.TA GANCIA, 111
12064 LA MORRA [CN]
TEL. 017350814
www.mauromolino.com

CELLAR SALES
PRE-BOOKED VISITS
ANNUAL PRODUCTION 70,000 bottles
HECTARES UNDER VINE 12.00

This winery vaunts solid family traditions and first-class vineyards. Mauro and his two wine-technician children competently and meticulously oversee work in the vineyard and the cellar, transforming their excellent grapes into sophisticated wines with a well-defined varietal character. Barolo is naturally the estate's pride and joy, and the various versions on offer manage to enhance all the unique traits of a zone characterized by elegance and harmonious flavours. Already very extroverted and accessible while young, the great cellarability and soundness of these wines enables them to surprise pleasantly when aged. Barolo Gallinotto 2009 is very convincing, focusing on expressive notes of berry fruit, autumn leaves and tobacco, accompanied by a well-calibrated palate with discreet tannins. The temptingly drinkable Barolo Vigna Gancia 2009 is elegant and balanced, with notes of dried flowers, quinine and violet.

● Barolo Gallinotto '09	▼▼ 6
● Barolo V. Gancia '09	▼▼ 6
● Barbera d'Alba Sup. Le Gattere '11	▼▼ 5
● Barolo '09	▼▼ 5
● Barolo V. Conca '09	▼▼ 7
● Barbera d'Alba V. Gattere '00	▽▽▽ 5
● Barbera d'Alba V. Gattere '97	▽▽▽ 7
● Barbera d'Alba V. Gattere '96	▽▽▽ 7
● Barolo Gallinotto '03	▽▽▽ 6
● Barolo Gallinotto '01	▽▽▽ 6
● Barolo V. Conca '00	▽▽▽ 7
● Barolo V. Conca '97	▽▽▽ 7
● Barolo V. Conca '96	▽▽▽ 7
● Barolo Gallinotto '08	▽▽ 6
● Barolo V. Conca '08	▽▽ 7

Monchiero Carbone

VIA SANTO STEFANO ROERO, 2
12043 CANALE [CN]
TEL. 017395568
www.monchierocarbone.com

CELLAR SALES
PRE-BOOKED VISITS
ANNUAL PRODUCTION 180,000 bottles
HECTARES UNDER VINE 25.00

The estate owned by the Monchiero family is undoubtedly one of the most dynamic and tenacious in its quest to enhance the wines and land of Roero to the full. The wines it proposes are always produced with an eye to balance and aromatic clarity. Historically, production is centred in Canale and the winery's plots are located in some of the finest Roero crus, including Printi, Monbirone and Renesio. It also owns vineyards in Vezza d'Alba, where white varieties are grown, and in Priocca, which is largely given over to barbera. The extra year of bottle ageing has benefitted Roero Printi Riserva 2009 enormously, earning it a Tre Bicchieri. It is delicate and complex, with attractive notes of raspberry and wild strawberry and hints of spice and autumn leaves. Despite its fresh fruit, it's firm and almost austere, with close-knit tannins on a long, balanced palate. The juicy Barbera d'Alba MonBirone 2011 is also among the best of the designation, with notes of cherry and rain-soaked earth.

● Roero Printi Ris. '09	▼▼▼ 5
● Barbera d'Alba MonBirone '11	▼▼ 5
○ Langhe Bianco Tamardì '12	▼▼ 2*
○ Roero Arneis Cecu d'la Biunda '12	▼▼ 3
○ Roero Arneis Recit '12	▼▼ 2*
● Barbera d'Alba MonBirone '10	▽▽▽ 4*
● Roero Printi '04	▽▽▽ 5
● Roero Printi '00	▽▽▽ 5
● Roero Printi '99	▽▽▽ 6
● Roero Printi Ris. '07	▽▽▽ 5
● Roero Printi Ris. '06	▽▽▽ 5
● Roero Srü '06	▽▽▽ 3

Monfalletto
Cordero di Montezemolo

FRAZ. ANNUNZIATA, 67
12064 LA MORRA [CN]
TEL. 017350344
www.corderodimontezemolo.com

CELLAR SALES
PRE-BOOKED VISITS
ANNUAL PRODUCTION 240,000 bottles
HECTARES UNDER VINE 35.00

Founded over six centuries ago, Tenuta Monfalletto is one of Langhe's oldest wineries. Today it is run by Giovanni Cordero with the increasingly diligent and dynamic support of his children Elena and Alberto. The family channel their commitment and enthusiasm into the ongoing quest for the perfect balance of tradition and innovation in both the vineyard and the cellar, while keeping a careful eye on image and public relations. Their 28 hectares of vineyards are planted with local grape varieties – nebbiolo, dolcetto, barbera and arneis – and tended with natural organic methods. Great attention is also paid to ageing in oak, with small casks used for the elegant Barolo selections. Barolo Monfalletto 2009 is expressive and muscular, with a nose of tobacco, liquorice and spice and a long, full-flavoured palate. The austere Barolo Enrico VI 2009 is still a little closed on the nose, although the palate unfurls smoothly, with discreet tannins and a fresh swathe of acidity.

● Barolo Enrico VI '09		🍷🍷 8
● Barolo Monfalletto '09		🍷🍷 6
● Barbera d'Alba '12		🍷🍷 3
● Barbera d'Alba Sup. Funtanì '10		🍷🍷 5
● Barolo Bricco Gattera '09		🍷🍷 8
○ Langhe Chardonnay Elioro '11		🍷 5
● Barolo Enrico VI '04		🍷🍷🍷 7
● Barolo Enrico VI '03		🍷🍷🍷 7
● Barolo V. Bricco Gattera '99		🍷🍷🍷 8
● Barolo V. Enrico VI '00		🍷🍷🍷 7
● Barolo Enrico VI '08		🍷🍷 8
● Barolo Enrico VI '07		🍷🍷 8
● Barolo Monfalletto '08		🍷🍷 6
● Barolo V. Bricco Gattera '07		🍷🍷 7

Il Mongetto

VIA PIAVE, 2
15049 VIGNALE MONFERRATO [AL]
TEL. 0142933442
www.mongetto.it

CELLAR SALES
PRE-BOOKED VISITS
ANNUAL PRODUCTION 40,000 bottles
HECTARES UNDER VINE 13.00

The Vignale Monferrato winery is fast gaining space and visibility, showing great potential. Production focuses on cellarable wines, including the Grignolino, which acquires the most intriguing nuances after at least a year in the bottle. In addition to classic Monferrato varieties, the estate is planted to merlot and cabernet, used with barbera to blend the Monferrato Rosso Telegro. Two Barberas made it into our finals: Monferrato Superiore Vigneto Mongetto 2010 and Asti Vigneto Guera 2010. The former is concentrated and very fruity, with fine character and complexity derived from ageing in oak, while the latter displays notes of quinine and dark berry fruit. Both are powerful, intense and very lingering on the palate.

● Barbera d'Asti Vign. Guera '10		🍷🍷 4
● Barbera del M.to Sup. Vign. Mongetto '10		🍷🍷 4
● Grignolino del M.to Casalese '12		🍷🍷 3
● M.to Rosso Telegro '10		🍷🍷 3
● Barbera d'Asti V. Guera '09		🍷🍷 4
● Barbera d'Asti V. Guera '08		🍷🍷 4
● Barbera del M.to Sup. V. Mongetto '09		🍷🍷 2*
● Barbera del M.to Sup. V. Mongetto '08		🍷🍷 2
● Casorzo Vign. Rudifrà '11		🍷🍷 2*
● Grignolino del M.to Casalese V. Solin '10		🍷🍷 2

Montalbera

VIA MONTALBERA, 1
14030 CASTAGNOLE MONFERRATO [AT]
TEL. 0119433311
www.montalbera.it

CELLAR SALES
PRE-BOOKED VISITS
ANNUAL PRODUCTION 400,000 bottles
HECTARES UNDER VINE 155.00

The Morando family have expressed their commitment to exploring and developing the ruchó grape in numerous ways. They range from experimentation in the vineyard and the cellar, to the creation of a veritable monograph on the varietal and the Ruché di Castagnole Monferrato designation, and even a series of bottlings reflecting the potential of the grape and the area. The estate owns a single vineyard covering an impressive 100 hectares in Castagnole Lanze, planted mainly to ruché, with small amounts of barbera and grignolino, plus ten hectares of moscato in Castiglione Tinella. Laccento 2012 was our favourite Ruché di Castagnole Monferrato this year, with delicate, complex notes of liquorice, rose and berry fruit, firm structure, and the varietal's characteristic elegance. Other very good wines are the aromatic Grignolino d'Asti Grigné 2012, with soft, caressing, close-knit tannins, the pleasant, fresh Ruché di Castagnole Monferrato La Tradizione 2012, and the balanced, fruity Barbera d'Asti La Ribelle 2012.

● Ruché di Castagnole M.to Laccento '12	♼♼ 3*
● Barbera d'Asti La Ribelle '12	♼♼ 2*
● Grignolino d'Asti Grigné '12	♼♼ 2*
● Ruché di Castagnole M.to La Tradizione '12	♼♼ 3
● Barbera d'Asti Lequilibrio '11	♼ 3
● L'Accento Passito	♼ 4
● Ruché di Castagnole M.to Limpronta '11	♼ 5
● Barbera d'Asti La Ribelle '11	♼♼ 2*
● Barbera d'Asti Lequilibrio '10	♼♼ 3
● Grignolino d'Asti Grigné '11	♼♼ 2*
● Ruché di Castagnole M.to La Tradizione '11	♼♼ 3*
● Ruché di Castagnole M.to Laccento '11	♼♼ 4
● Ruché di Castagnole M.to Limpronta '10	♼♼ 5

Montaribaldi

FRAZ. TRE STELLE
S.DA NICOLINI ALTO, 12
12050 BARBARESCO [CN]
TEL. 0173638220
www.montaribaldi.com

CELLAR SALES
PRE-BOOKED VISITS
ANNUAL PRODUCTION 100,000 bottles
HECTARES UNDER VINE 23.00

Situated in the heart of Barbaresco, this winery has some of the most stunning views in the whole of Langhe. Founded in 1968, today it is competently run by brothers Luciano and Roberto Taliano, backed by the entire family. They are first and foremost Barbaresco producers, offering selections from the Sorì Montaribaldi and Palazzina crus and Ricü, a blend from the Montaribaldi, Rio Sordo and Marcarini vineyards. However they also produce Barolo Borzoni from their vineyards in Grinzane Cavour. The style is modern, with ageing in 225-hectolitre French oak barrels. The leading lights of Montaribaldi's very wide range of Langhe, Roero and Monferrato wines are regularly the Barbarescos, sometimes with a handsome co-star from the less noble grape varieties. This year it was the complex, fruity Barbaresco Ricü 2008 that came closest to the much-coveted award.

● Barbaresco Ricü '08	♼♼ 6
● Barbaresco Palazzina '10	♼♼ 5
● Barbaresco Sorì Montaribaldi '10	♼♼ 5
● Barbera d'Alba dü Gir '10	♼♼ 2*
● Langhe Nebbiolo Gambarin '11	♼♼ 3
● Langhe Nebbiolo Tre Stelle '11	♼♼ 2*
○ Roero Arneis Capural '12	♼♼ 2*
● Barbera d'Alba Frere '11	♼ 2
● Barbera d'Asti La Consolina '11	♼ 2
○ Langhe Chardonnay Stissa d'le Favole '12	♼ 2
● Barbaresco Palazzina '09	♼♼ 4
● Barbaresco Sorì Montaribaldi '09	♼♼ 5
● Barbera d'Alba dü Gir '09	♼♼ 3
● Barolo Borzoni '08	♼♼ 6
○ Langhe Chardonnay Stissa d'le Favole '11	♼♼ 2*
● Langhe Nebbiolo Gambarin '10	♼♼ 3

Tenuta Montemagno

VIA CASCINA VALFOSSATO, 9
14030 MONTEMAGNO [AT]
TEL. 014163624
www.tenutamontemagno.it

CELLAR SALES
PRE-BOOKED VISITS
ACCOMMODATION AND RESTAURANT SERVICE
ANNUAL PRODUCTION 90,000 bottles
HECTARES UNDER VINE 15.00

Tenuta Montemagno's steady wine quality earned it a full profile this year. The estate touches four of the Monferrato municipalities: Montemagno, Viarigi, Altavilla and Casorzo. The winery is located in an 18th-century farmhouse that was already indicated on Napoleonic maps. The complex has been repurposed and now has full wine and general tourism amenities. The brick cellars are still used for ageing wines made from native varieties like barbera, grignolino, freisa, ruché, cortese, timorasso, and malvasia di Casorzo, with international varieties including syrah and sauvignon blanc. The estate presented a wide and very balanced battery of wines. Mysterium displays good character and complexity, while the second Barbera d'Asti, Austerum, is less complex but shows excellent sensory characteristics. Violae is a delicate, concentrated blend of barbera and syrah.

● Barbera d'Asti Austerum '10	♥♥ 2*
● Barbera d'Asti Sup. Mysterium '10	♥♥ 4
● Grignolino d'Asti Ruber '11	♥♥ 2*
○ M.to Bianco Nymphae '11	♥♥ 2*
● M.to Rosso Violae '10	♥♥ 2*
● Malvasia di Casorzo d'Asti Dulcem '12	♥ 2
● Ruchè di Castagnole M.to '12	♥ 3
○ TM Brut M. Cl.	♥ 5
● Barbera d'Asti Austerum '09	♥♥ 2*
● Barbera d'Asti Sup. Mysterium '09	♥♥ 4
○ M.to Bianco Musae '11	♥♥ 3
● Ruchè di Castagnole M.to '10	♥♥ 3

Monti

LOC. SAN SEBASTIANO
FRAZ. CAMIE, 39
12065 MONFORTE D'ALBA [CN]
TEL. 017378391
www.paolomonti.com

CELLAR SALES
PRE-BOOKED VISITS
ANNUAL PRODUCTION 50,000 bottles
HECTARES UNDER VINE 16.00

Almost 20 years have passed since Paolo Monti commenced his winemaking operations. Showing an innovative, experimental spirit, he flanked the classic nebbiolo with other lesser known grape varieties that, over the years, have allowed him to build up a truly extraordinary range of wines for the area. However, the focus naturally remains on the main Langhe varieties and the various labels are always highly convincing, with good overall balance and a clean style. The wines are aged in French oak barrels of varying sizes and the prized Bussia cru is the natural jewel in the estate's crown. The estate's wines have a stylistic continuity that makes them magnificent in very classic vintages, but risks weighing them down in hotter ones, due to the liberal use of new oak. Consequently, a Tre Bicchieri went to the elegant Nebbiolo d'Alba 2010, with a pervasive nose and fresh palate.

● Nebbiolo d'Alba '10	♥♥ 4
● Barolo '09	♥♥ 7
● Barolo Bussia '09	♥♥ 8
● Barbera d'Alba '10	♥ 5
● Barbera d'Alba '09	♥♥ 5
● Barolo '08	♥♥ 7
● Langhe Dossi Rossi '09	♥♥ 5
● Langhe Dossi Rossi '07	♥♥ 5
○ Langhe L'Aura '09	♥♥ 4
● Nebbiolo d'Alba '09	♥♥ 4

Stefanino Morra

VIA CASTAGNITO, 50
12050 CASTELLINALDO [CN]
TEL. 0173213489
www.morravini.it

CELLAR SALES
PRE-BOOKED VISITS
ANNUAL PRODUCTION 65,000 bottles
HECTARES UNDER VINE 10.00

For three generations the Morra family has been at the helm of this estate in Castellinaldo, one of the most important municipalities for Roero wine-making. They also have vineyards on the sandy, clayey terrains of Canale and Vezza d'Alba. The wines are derived from barbera, nebbiolo, arneis and favorita and consistently display structure, power and generous fruit, particularly the most prestigious labels, the Roero Sräi and the Barbera Castellinaldo. This year the spotlight is on Roero Srai Riserva 2009, characterized by tightly-woven, full-bodied tannins and notes of fruit and quinine with hints of Mediterranean scrubland, and Barbera d'Alba Castlè, with ripe dark berry fruit and a very long, elegant palate with alluring acidity. Roero Arneis Metodo Classico Elena 2010 is also interesting and one of Roero's finest sparkling wines, with notes of white-fleshed fruit and crusty bread.

● Barbera d'Alba Castlè '09	♀♀♀ 5
● Roero Srai Ris. '09	♀♀♀ 5
● Roero '10	♀♀♀ 4
○ Roero Arneis M. Cl. Elena '10	♀♀♀ 4
● Barbera d'Alba '10	♀ 3
● Barbera d'Alba '09	♀♀ 3*
● Barbera d'Alba '08	♀♀ 3*
● Barbera d'Alba Castellinaldo '09	♀♀ 4
● Barbera d'Alba Castellinaldo '07	♀♀ 4
● Barbera d'Alba Castlè '07	♀♀ 5
● Roero '09	♀♀ 4
● Roero '07	♀♀ 4
○ Roero Arneis Vign. S. Pietro '09	♀♀ 3
● Roero Srai Ris. '07	♀♀ 5

F.lli Mossio

FRAZ. CASCINA CARAMELLI
VIA MONTÀ, 12
12050 RODELLO [CN]
TEL. 0173617149
www.mossio.com

CELLAR SALES
PRE-BOOKED VISITS
ANNUAL PRODUCTION 50,000 bottles
HECTARES UNDER VINE 10.00

Mossio's Dolcetto selections have long been among the finest in their category. We believe that this is the most important credential for the appreciation of the competency and professionalism that guide the Mossio brothers' production strategies. The estate's vineyards are meticulously tended with a careful eye to preserving their natural assets. Consequently, grass grows between the rows and only essential treatments are undertaken to allow the grapes to express their full authentic potential. The resulting wines, particularly the Dolcettos and Nebbiolos, exhibit taste profiles of rare purity and are reasonably and competitively priced. Among the wines tasted this year, Langhe Nebbiolo 2009 stood out for its trueness to type and temptingly fresh palate. The succulent Dolcetto Piano delli Perdoni 2012 has pleasant notes of plum and blueberry, with a caressing entry and a long, supple finish.

● Dolcetto d'Alba Piano delli Perdoni '12	♀♀ 2*
● Langhe Nebbiolo '09	♀♀ 4
● Dolcetto d'Alba Bricco Caramelli '12	♀♀ 3
● Dolcetto d'Alba Sup. Gamvs '11	♀♀ 4
● Barbera d'Alba '11	♀ 4
● Langhe Rosso '10	♀ 4
● Dolcetto d'Alba Bricco Caramelli '00	♀♀♀ 3*
● Dolcetto d'Alba Bricco Caramelli '11	♀♀ 3*
● Dolcetto d'Alba Bricco Caramelli '10	♀♀ 3*
● Dolcetto d'Alba Bricco Caramelli '09	♀♀ 3*
● Dolcetto d'Alba Bricco Caramelli '07	♀♀ 3
● Dolcetto d'Alba Piano delli Perdoni '11	♀♀ 2*
● Dolcetto d'Alba Piano delli Perdoni '08	♀♀ 2*
● Langhe Nebbiolo '07	♀♀ 4

Mutti

Loc. San Ruffino, 49
15050 Sarezzano [AL]
Tel. 0131884119
aziendagricola.mutti@libero.it

CELLAR SALES
ANNUAL PRODUCTION 55,000 bottles
HECTARES UNDER VINE 3.00

There are people who sometimes get less than they deserve and Andrea Mutti is probably one of these. There are winemakers who, for various reasons, do not earn awards from various guides while being worthy of them. Andrea should be acknowledged for believing in Timorasso some years ago, before it came to the limelight, when his Castagnoli was definitely the best on offer. He has had a couple of poor vintages, when he was overshadowed by other producers, but he has been steadfast in maintaining the style he defined at the start. The estate's Timorassos are characterized by a less powerful but more elegant style, favouring accentuated smoothness over muscular structure. Once again this year the Castagnoli follows this pattern, with a nose of hedgerow and apricot, and a very long mineral palate underscored by almost salty nuances. The steel-aged BoscoBarona, from barbera, is also good.

○ Colli Tortonesi Timorasso Derthona Castagnoli '11	♟♟ 3
● BoscoBarona '12	♟♟ 2*
○ Sull'Aia	♟♟ 2*
○ Colli Tortonesi Bianco Noceto '12	♟ 2
● Colli Tortonesi Rosso BoscoBarona '09	♟♟ 2
● Colli Tortonesi Rosso S. Ruffino '07	♟♟ 4
● Colli Tortonesi Rosso Zerba Soprana '10	♟♟ 2*
○ Colli Tortonesi Timorasso Castagnoli '10	♟♟ 3*
● San Ruffino '09	♟♟ 3*
● San Ruffino '08	♟♟ 4
○ Sull'Aia '10	♟♟ 3*

Ada Nada

Loc. Rombone
via Ausario, 12b
12050 Treiso [CN]
Tel. 0173638127
www.adanada.it

CELLAR SALES
PRE-BOOKED VISITS
ACCOMMODATION AND RESTAURANT SERVICE
ANNUAL PRODUCTION 40,000 bottles
HECTARES UNDER VINE 9.00

We commence with a heartfelt farewell to Giancarlo Nada, who took over the running of this estate in 1989 and commenced his work to shape the cellar and the splendid adjoining guest farm into what they are today. When a fine producer passes away, it's as though the world becomes a little smaller. Turning our attention to the present and the future, we believe that the estate's impressive array of vineyards is its best credential for the continued production of first-rate wines capable of holding their own among the finest of the area, as indeed they have in recent years. The balanced Barbaresco Valeirano 2009 is very convincing, showing notes of spice, eucalyptus and tobacco, followed by vigorous tannins and fresh acidity. Barbaresco Cichin 2009 is characterized by a nose of medicinal herbs and quinine and a pleasant, smooth, confident palate.

● Barbaresco Valeirano '09	♟♟ 5
● Barbaresco Cichin '09	♟♟ 6
● Barbaresco Elisa '09	♟♟ 5
○ Langhe Bianco Neta '12	♟ 2
● Barbaresco Cichin '08	♟♟ 6
● Barbaresco Elisa '08	♟♟ 6
● Barbaresco Elisa '07	♟♟ 6
● Barbaresco Elisa '06	♟♟ 6
● Barbaresco Elisa '04	♟♟ 6
● Barbaresco Valeirano '08	♟♟ 5
● Barbaresco Valeirano '07	♟♟ 5
● Barbaresco Valeirano '06	♟♟ 6
● Barbera d'Alba V. 'd Pierin '09	♟♟ 3
● Barbera d'Alba Vigna 'd Pierin '08	♟♟ 3

★Fiorenzo Nada

LOC. ROMBONE
VIA AUSARIO, 12C
12050 TREISO [CN]
TEL. 0173638254
www.nada.it

CELLAR SALES
PRE-BOOKED VISITS
ANNUAL PRODUCTION 40,000 bottles
HECTARES UNDER VINE 7.00

Fiorenzo Nada is one of Langhe's finest
family-run estates dedicated heart and soul
to the production of excellent wines.
Although Fiorenzo still performs the most
delicate vineyard operations, it is his son
Bruno who enthusiastically and rigorously
manages the small high-quality production
prized by many Italian and foreign
connoisseurs. The character of the wines is
very distinctive, exuberant in youth and
destined to become more elegant and
complex with ageing. Monica and Danilo,
the new generation, contribute to the
venture with their valuable and fruitful work.
Barbaresco Rombone 2009 gave an
excellent performance, showing firm and
assertive, with a rich nose of berry fruit,
rhubarb, eucalyptus and tobacco, supported
by exceptionally full-bodied tannins.
Barbaresco Manzola 2009 is already quite
expressive and will reveal its highly
promising potential with time.

Cantina dei Produttori Nebbiolo di Carema

VIA NAZIONALE, 32
10010 CAREMA [TO]
TEL. 0125811160
www.caremadoc.it

CELLAR SALES
PRE-BOOKED VISITS
CELLAR SALES
ANNUAL PRODUCTION 65,000 bottles

Carema is considered to be one of the very
best terroirs for wine enthusiasts seeking
labels that do not conform to the usual
mild, fruity framework. Much of the credit
for this belongs to producers like Cantina
Produttori Nebbiolo di Carema that
continued to practise a challenging
viticulture in difficult years. Today, the
co-operative numbers 81 member growers
and has around 15 hectares, little parcels
of earth that cling to the mountainside,
planted with pergola-trained vines. The
vintage Carema is distinguished by a black
label and the Riserva by a white one. Both
are aged in large barrels for 24 to 36
months. A careful look at the co-operative's
wines reveals the advantages of
specialization, for they are now impeccable.
The Riserva 2009 earned a Tre Bicchieri for
its complex nose of roots, gentian and
ferrous notes, accompanied by stylish
full-flavoured tannins. The Carema 2010
also came very close.

● Barbaresco Rombone '09	♔♔♔ 7
● Barbaresco Manzola '09	♔♔ 6
● Barbera d'Alba '11	♔♔ 3
● Dolcetto d'Alba '12	♔♔ 2*
● Langhe Rosso Seifile '09	♔♔ 7
● Langhe Nebbiolo '11	♔ 3
● Barbaresco '01	♕♕♕ 6
● Barbaresco Manzola '08	♕♕♕ 6
● Barbaresco Manzola '06	♕♕♕ 6
● Barbaresco Rombone '07	♕♕♕ 7
● Barbaresco Rombone '06	♕♕♕ 7
● Barbaresco Rombone '05	♕♕♕ 7
● Barbaresco Rombone '04	♕♕♕ 7
● Langhe Rosso Seifile '01	♕♕♕ 6

● Carema Et. Bianca Ris. '09	♔♔♔ 3*
● Carema Et. Nera '10	♔♔ 2*
● Carema Et. Bianca '07	♕♕♕ 3*
● Carema Et. Bianca Ris. '08	♕♕♕ 3*
● Carema '05	♕♕ 2
● Carema '04	♕♕ 2
● Carema Barricato '01	♕♕ 4
● Carema Et. Bianca '06	♕♕ 3*
● Carema Et. Bianca '05	♕♕ 3
● Carema Et. Nera '08	♕♕ 2*
● Carema Et. Nera '06	♕♕ 2*
● Carema Ris. '04	♕♕ 3*
● Carema Ris. '02	♕♕ 3
● Carema Ris. '01	♕♕ 3

Lorenzo Negro

FRAZ. SANT'ANNA, 55
12040 MONTEU ROERO [CN]
TEL. 017390645
www.negrolorenzo.com

CELLAR SALES
PRE-BOOKED VISITS
ANNUAL PRODUCTION 30,000 bottles
HECTARES UNDER VINE 8.00

Lorenzo Negro believes wholeheartedly in his work and the quality of his wines, as demonstrated by the time and money he has invested in renovating this historic cellar. Almost all of his vineyards are located in Monteu Roero around the estate's headquarters in the zone of Serra Lupini. They lie at an altitude of around 300 metres and are home to arneis, nebbiolo, barbera, bonarda, dolcetto and a few rows of albarossa. The wines are traditional in style and possess great structure and generous fruit. Barbera d'Alba 2011 made our finals with a nose of forest floor and rain-soaked earth and an appealing, balanced palate with prominent notes of Mediterranean scrubland and cherry. The well-made Roero San Francesco Riserva 2009 is also sound, with balsamic notes and close-knit tannins, as is the freshly acidic Roero Arneis 2012 that is well crafted, albeit a little simple, with a nose of peaches and apricots with vegetal hints.

● Barbera d'Alba '11	♟♟ 2*
○ Roero Arneis '12	♟♟ 2*
● Roero San Francesco Ris. '09	♟♟ 3
● Barbera d'Alba '07	♟♟ 2*
● Barbera d'Alba Sup. La Nanda '07	♟♟ 3
● Barbera d'Alba Sup. La Nanda '06	♟♟ 3
● Langhe Rosso Arbesca '08	♟♟ 3
○ Roero Arneis '11	♟♟ 2*
● Roero San Francesco Ris. '08	♟♟ 3*
● Roero San Francesco Ris. '07	♟♟ 3

Negro Angelo e Figli

FRAZ. SANT'ANNA, 1
12040 MONTEU ROERO [CN]
TEL. 017390252
www.negroangelo.it

CELLAR SALES
PRE-BOOKED VISITS
ANNUAL PRODUCTION 350,000 bottles
HECTARES UNDER VINE 60.00

The Negro family are a leading light in the Roero wine world in terms of both history, presence in the area since the 17th century, and has a series of vineyards in Monteu Roero, Santo Stefano Roero and Canale, plus a property in Neive from which it obtains Barbaresco and Dolcetto d'Alba. The grape varieties grown are the classic local ones, mainly arneis and nebbiolo – that are also the base of the spumante production – alongside barbera, favorita and dolcetto. The wines have a modern slant, yet manage to remain terroir true. Roero Sudisfà Riserva 2010 took a Tre Bicchieri. It is complex and elegant in the finest Roero tradition, with top notes of raspberries on aromatic herbs and a very long, dynamic palate with silky tannins. The whole range is excellent, from the compact, full-flavoured Barbaresco Basarin Riserva 2008 to the spicy, characterful Roero San Bernardo 2010 and the pleasant, juicy Prachiosso 2011.

● Roero Sudisfà Ris. '10	♟♟♟ 6
● Barbaresco Basarin '08	♟♟ 7
● Roero Prachiosso '11	♟♟ 4
● Roero San Bernardo '10	♟♟ 5
● Barbaresco Cascinotta '09	♟♟ 5
● Barbera d'Alba Bertu '11	♟♟ 4
● Barbera d'Alba Nicolon '11	♟♟ 3
○ Roero Arneis Gianat '10	♟♟ 4
○ Roero Arneis Perdaudin '12	♟♟ 3
○ Roero Arneis Serra Lupini '12	♟♟ 2*
● Roero Sudisfà '04	♟♟♟ 5
● Roero Sudisfà '03	♟♟♟ 5
● Roero Sudisfà Ris. '09	♟♟♟ 5
● Roero Sudisfà Ris. '08	♟♟♟ 5
● Barbera d'Alba Nicolon '10	♟♟ 3*
○ Roero Arneis Perdaudin '11	♟♟ 3

Andrea Oberto

B.TA SIMANE, 11
12064 LA MORRA [CN]
TEL. 017350104
www.andreaoberto.com

CELLAR SALES
PRE-BOOKED VISITS
ANNUAL PRODUCTION 100,000 bottles
HECTARES UNDER VINE 16.00

This important La Morra estate offers a range of absolutely top-notch Barolo crus that make it one of the best-known and most reliable names in the area. Andrea Oberto carries out the most crucial work in the vineyards himself, while his son Fabio is responsible for operations in the cellar and the general running of the estate. The wines are very full bodied and exuberant, especially when young, when the outstanding grapes express the full potential of fruit and structure. In addition to the Barolo crus, the range also features the noteworthy Barbera d'Alba Giada, conceived and crafted in a modern style since its first release many years ago. Barolo Vigneto Brunate 2009 is firm and assertive, characterized by a fresh, balsamic nose with soft notes of berry fruit and an enfolding palate with medium length. Although still slightly overwhelmed by oak, Barolo Vigneto Albarella 2009 displays dark notes of quinine and tar.

● Barolo '09	♟♟ 6
● Barolo Vign. Albarella '09	♟♟ 7
● Barolo Vign. Brunate '09	♟♟ 8
● Barolo Vign. Rocche '09	♟ 7
● Barbera d'Alba Giada '00	♟♟♟ 5
● Barbera d'Alba Giada '97	♟♟♟ 5
● Barolo Vign. Albarella '01	♟♟♟ 7
● Barolo Vign. Brunate '05	♟♟♟ 8
● Barolo Vign. Rocche dell'Annunziata '96	♟♟♟ 8
● Barolo Vign. Albarella '06	♟♟ 7
● Barolo Vign. Albarella '05	♟♟ 7
● Barolo Vign. Albarella '04	♟♟ 7
● Barolo Vign. Rocche '08	♟♟ 7
● Barolo Vign. Rocche dell'Annunziata '04	♟♟ 7

Poderi e Cantine Oddero

FRAZ. SANTA MARIA
VIA TETTI, 28
12064 LA MORRA [CN]
TEL. 017350618
www.oddero.com

CELLAR SALES
PRE-BOOKED VISITS
ANNUAL PRODUCTION 150,000 bottles
HECTARES UNDER VINE 35.00
VITICULTURE METHOD Certified Organic

This estate belonging to Mariacristina and Mariavittoria Oddero is one of the most important in Langhe. Just under half of its 35 hectares are planted to nebbiolo destined for Barolo and Barbaresco. But it's not just a question of numbers. The estate's assets also include names such as Villero and Rocche in Castiglione Falletto, Brunate in La Morra, Mondoca di Bussia Soprana in Monforte, Vigna Rionda in Serralunga, and Gallina in Barbaresco,: true grand crus interpreted in an elegant, lean style obtained through the skilled use of large barrels and smaller casks. Completing the line-up we have barbera, dolcetto, some international varieties and moscato from Cascina Fiori in Trezzo Tinella. Barolo Rocche di Castiglione 2009 put up an excellent performance, earning our top award. Its complex nose of tobacco, violet, liquorice and spice is followed by tightly knit tannins and fresh acidity on the palate. Barolo Brunate 2008 is very good, although slightly less expressive on the nose.

● Barolo Rocche di Castiglione '09	♟♟♟ 7
● Barbaresco Gallina '09	♟♟ 6
● Barolo Brunate '08	♟♟ 8
● Barbaresco Gallina '10	♟♟ 6
● Barbera d'Alba Sup. '10	♟♟ 3
● Barbera d'Asti Sup. Vinchio '10	♟♟ 3
● Barolo '09	♟♟ 6
● Barolo Villero '09	♟♟ 7
● Dolcetto d'Alba '12	♟♟ 2*
● Langhe Nebbiolo '10	♟♟ 3
○ Moscato d'Asti Cascina Fiori '12	♟♟ 2*
○ Langhe Chardonnay Collaretto '12	♟ 3
● Barbaresco Gallina '04	♟♟♟ 6
● Barolo Mondoca di Bussia Soprana '04	♟♟♟ 7
● Barolo Vigna Rionda '01	♟♟♟ 8

Vigneti Luigi Oddero

Fraz. S. Maria
b.ta Bettolotti, 95
12604 La Morra [CN]
Tel. 0173500386
www.vignetiluigioddero.it

CELLAR SALES
PRE-BOOKED VISITS
ANNUAL PRODUCTION 100,000 bottles
HECTARES UNDER VINE 35.00

The Oddero family played a crucial role in Piedmontese wine history and the first vinification began in the Morra cellars at the end of the 1800s. Luigi Oddero spent over 50 years running the Oddero winery with his brother Giacomo, before setting up Luigi Oddero & Figli in 20006, with his wife, Lena. He brought with him some iconic La Morra crus, including the Rive-Parà vineyards, the Rocche dei Rivera cru at Castiglione Falletto and Vigna Rionda in Serralunga. The 2009 Barolo has a concentrated, complex nose with fine notes of tobacco and dried flowers, followed by berry fruit and hints of quinine. The palate is fresh and balanced, with good acidity and a long, decidedly multi-layered finish. Barolo Vigna Rionda 2007 is firm, with attractive, bright, focused fruit and a complex, powerful palate with close-knit tannins and perfect length. The pleasant 2010 Nebbiolo is full and focused.

● Barolo '09	▼▼	6
● Barolo Vigna Rionda '07	▼▼	8
● Langhe Nebbiolo '10	▼▼	3
● Barbera d'Alba '10	▼	3
● Barbaresco '08	▽▽	5
● Barolo '08	▽▽	5
● Barolo Rocche Rivera '06	▽▽	6
● Barolo Vigna Rionda '06	▽▽	6
● Langhe Nebbiolo '08	▽▽	3

Tenuta Olim Bauda

via Prata, 50
14045 Incisa Scapaccino [AT]
Tel. 0141702171
www.tenutaolimbauda.it

CELLAR SALES
PRE-BOOKED VISITS
ANNUAL PRODUCTION 180,000 bottles
HECTARES UNDER VINE 30.00

Founded in 1961, this estate has been run by the fourth generation of the Bertolino family, represented by Diana and her brothers Dino and Gianni, since 1998. It vaunts six vineyards, in the municipalities of Nizza Monferrato, Isola d'Asti, Fontanile and Castelnuovo Calcea, at altitudes between 160 and 350 metres, on different soils, ranging from clayey to sandy, and with vines up to 60 years old. Barbera is the mainstay, but moscato, chardonnay, cortese and grignolino are also grown. The wines are well crafted, displaying a style that is both pleasant and drinkable. The Bertolino family's production is of the usual high level. The elegant, dynamic Barbera d'Asti Superiore Nizza 2010 offers succulent fruit and freshness against a backdrop of spice and a long finish, while the rich, juicy Barbera d'Asti Superiore Le Rocchette 2011 shows classic notes of cherry and rain-soaked earth and an impressive vein of acidity. Grignolino d'Asti Isolavilla 2012 is pleasant and well typed.

● Barbera d'Asti Sup. Le Rocchette '11	▼▼	4
● Barbera d'Asti Sup. Nizza '10	▼▼	5
● Grignolino d'Asti Isolavilla '12	▼▼	2*
● Barbera d'Asti La Villa '12	▼	2
○ Moscato d'Asti Centive '12	▼	2
● Barbera d'Asti Sup. Nizza '08	▽▽▽	5
● Barbera d'Asti Sup. Nizza '07	▽▽▽	5
● Barbera d'Asti Sup. Nizza '06	▽▽▽	5
● Barbera d'Asti Sup. Le Rocchette '10	▽▽	4
● Barbera d'Asti Sup. Nizza '09	▽▽	5
○ Gavi del Comune di Gavi '11	▽▽	2*

Orsolani

VIA MICHELE CHIESA, 12
10090 SAN GIORGIO CANAVESE [TO]
TEL. 012432386
www.orsolani.it

CELLAR SALES
PRE-BOOKED VISITS
ANNUAL PRODUCTION 135,000 bottles
HECTARES UNDER VINE 19.00

Gian Francesco Orsolani is recognised as one of the founding fathers of Erbaluce for very good reason. He produced the first spumante version in the 1960s and was the inspiration behind the first crus, Vignot Sant'Antonio and La Rustìa, promoting an aspect of this Canavese variety that is very different from the image of a light, early-drinking white. His son Gian Luigi has long worked alongside him. The estate has expanded to an area of 20 hectares, divided between Caluso, Mazzè and San Giorgio. The lion's share is dedicated to erbaluce and the rest to barbora and neretto, while the grapes of carefully selected growers are used to make Carema Le Tabbie. Hailing from Piedmontese "red" country, the aristocratic Erbaluce di Caluso La Rustìa 2012 is one of Italy's great white wines. Worthy runners-up are the vintages of Cuvée Tradizione: the tauter, more delicate 2009 and the creamier, multi-layered 2007. Erbaluce 2012 is worthy of note, uncomplicated and better than ever, at a very reasonable price.

○ Erbaluce di Caluso La Rustìa '12	♛♛♛ 3*
○ Caluso Brut M. Cl. Cuvée Tradizione '09	♛♛ 4
○ Caluso M. Cl. Cuvée Tradizione 1968 '07	♛♛ 5
○ Erbaluce di Caluso '12	♛♛ 2*
● Canavese Rosso Acini Sparsi '12	♛ 2
○ Caluso Passito Sulé '04	♛♛♛ 5
○ Caluso Passito Sulé '98	♛♛♛ 5
○ Erbaluce di Caluso La Rustìa '11	♛♛♛ 3*
○ Erbaluce di Caluso La Rustìa '10	♛♛♛ 2*
○ Erbaluce di Caluso La Rustìa '09	♛♛♛ 2*
○ Caluso Brut Cuvée Tradizione '07	♛♛ 4
○ Caluso Spumante Cuvée Tradizione Gran Riserva '06	♛♛ 5

I Paglieri - Roagna

LOC. PAJÉ
S.DA PAGLIERI, 7
12050 BARBARESCO [CN]
TEL. 0173635109
www.roagna.com

CELLAR SALES
PRE-BOOKED VISITS
ANNUAL PRODUCTION 50,000 bottles
HECTARES UNDER VINE 15.00

Following a long period in which this estate was remembered only by a few connoisseurs nostalgic for the pure, crystal-clear quality of some of the great wines it produced prior to the 1990s, today it is deservedly back in the limelight. This unique Langhe winery has a fine array of vineyards planted to the noblest grape varieties of the area, with old vines, cover cropping, and absolutely no fertilizers. Its wines exude personality and character, are extremely drinkable, and faithfully reflect the terroir. This extraordinary balancing act of innovative and classic styles is practically unforgettable. The magnificent Barbaresco Crichet Pajè 2004 shows outstanding complexity and assertiveness, with notes of dried flowers, quinine, tobacco and liquorice, accompanied by a long, elegant palate. Barbaresco Asili Vecchie Vigne 2008 is austere and complex, characterized by notes of rhubarb and violet and a vibrant, full-flavoured palate.

● Barbaresco Crichët Pajé '04	♛♛♛ 8
● Barbaresco Asili V. V. '08	♛♛ 8
● Barbaresco Pajè V. V. '08	♛♛ 8
● Barbaresco Montefico V. V. '08	♛♛ 8
● Barbaresco Pajè '08	♛♛ 6
● Barolo La Pira '08	♛♛ 8
● Barolo La Pira V. V. '08	♛♛ 8
● Barbaresco Asili V. V. '07	♛♛♛ 8
● Barbaresco Pajé '01	♛ 6
● Barbaresco Pajè V. V. '07	♛ 8
● Barolo La Pira '07	♛ 8
● Barolo La Pira V. V. '07	♛ 8
● Barolo La Rocca e La Pira '00	♛ 6
● Barolo La Rocca e La Pira '99	♛ 6

Paitin

LOC. BRICCO
VIA SERRA BOELLA, 20
12052 NEIVE [CN]
TEL. 017367343
www.paitin.it

CELLAR SALES
PRE-BOOKED VISITS
ACCOMMODATION
ANNUAL PRODUCTION 80,000 bottles
HECTARES UNDER VINE 17.00

One of the oldest wineries in the Langa area, and one of the first to offer expressions of Barbaresco as early as the late 19thcentury, with the first bottling dated 1893, and when what is now one of the most prestigious names worldwide was just starting to appear on the market. Today the operation is in the hands of Secondo Pasquero Elia and sons Giovanni and Silvano, with 17 hectares under vine. The wines have a modern feel, are rich in structure and well-sustained by cool acidity and feisty tannic weave. The spearhead is the Barbaresco Sorì Paitin, from the older vines. Although the expressive potential of the excellent Barbaresco Sorì Paitin 2010 is still partly hidden by a touch too much oak, it displays attractive tar and liquorice notes on the nose and firm, close-knit tannins. Barbaresco Serra 2010 is fresh and easy drinking.

● Barbaresco Sorì Paitin '10	♟♟ 6
● Barbaresco Serra '10	♟♟ 5
● Dolcetto d'Alba Sorì Paitin '12	♟♟ 3
○ Langhe Arneis Elisa '12	♟♟ 3
● Nebbiolo d'Alba Ca Veja '11	♟♟ 4
● Barbera d'Alba Serra '11	♟ 4
● Barbaresco Sorì Paitin '07	♟♟♟ 5
● Barbaresco Sorì Paitin '04	♟♟♟ 5
● Barbaresco Sorì Paitin '97	♟♟♟ 5
● Barbaresco Sorì Paitin V. V. '04	♟♟♟ 7
● Barbaresco Sorì Paitin V. V. '01	♟♟♟ 7
● Barbaresco Sorì Paitin V. V. '99	♟♟♟ 8
● Barbaresco Serra '09	♟♟ 5
● Langhe Paitin '09	♟♟ 3*

Armando Parusso

LOC. BUSSIA, 55
12065 MONFORTE D'ALBA [CN]
TEL. 017378257
www.parusso.com

CELLAR SALES
PRE-BOOKED VISITS
ANNUAL PRODUCTION 120,000 bottles
HECTARES UNDER VINE 23.00

Marco and Tiziana Parusso enthusiastically and steadfastly run this important and very attractive Langhe estate that vaunts spectacular views, a cutting-edge cellar and first-rate vineyards. It has plots in the Bussia, Le Coste and Mosconi crus in the municipality of Monforte and the Mariondino vineyard in Castiglione Falletto, whose grapes have very distinctive varietal characteristics. The range of wines is extensive and each one is immediately recognizable for the unmistakable and very distinctive house style. They are eminently cellarable and widely available on all the leading international markets. Barolo Le Coste Mosconi 2009 has flavoursome berry fruit with hints of liquorice and tobacco, and a powerful palate, sustained by rather rugged but well-made tannins. Barolo Bussia 2009 vaunts nicely balanced power and elegance, while the now mature Barolo Bussia Riserva Oro 1999 shows complex and velvety.

● Barolo Le Coste Mosconi '09	♟♟ 8
● Barolo '09	♟♟ 6
● Barolo Bussia '09	♟♟ 8
● Barolo Bussia Et. Oro Ris. '99	♟♟ 8
○ Langhe Bianco '12	♟♟ 3
○ Langhe Bianco Bricco Rovella '11	♟♟ 5
● Barbera d'Alba Ornati '12	♟ 3
● Barbera d'Alba Sup. '11	♟ 5
● Dolcetto d'Alba Piani Noci '12	♟ 2
● Barbera d'Alba Sup. '00	♟♟♟ 5
● Barolo Bussia V. Munie '99	♟♟♟ 8
● Barolo Le Coste Mosconi '03	♟♟♟ 7
● Barolo V. V. in Mariondino Ris. '99	♟♟♟ 8
● Barolo Le Coste Mosconi '08	♟♟ 8

Massimo Pastura
Cascina La Ghersa

VIA CHIARINA, 2
14050 MOASCA [AT]
TEL. 0141856012
www.laghersa.it

CELLAR SALES
PRE-BOOKED VISITS
ANNUAL PRODUCTION 160,000 bottles

There are 12 labels for three production lines, eight varieties cultivated in addition to primadonna barbera. This is a snapshot of Cascina La Ghersa today, conceived and transformed by Massimo Pastura. The Vigneti Unici, I Classici and Piagè Pali vineyard selections are all expressions of the barbera grape, from the rosé to the standard label, and flagship products like the Nizza, flanked mainly by moscato, cortese and timorasso. All the wines are stylistically impeccable with good typicity. The estate presented only Barbera d'Asti this year, but an impressive three versions reached our finals. Le Cave 2010 has a nose of ripe berries, with hints of quinine and gentian, and beautifully close-knit tannins on the palate. Vignassa 2010 has an oakier nose, with notes of tobacco, spice and incense, and an austere palate with up-front tannins and alcohol. Camparò 2011 is suppler and fresher, focusing on acidity and rich fruit.

● Barbera d'Asti Sup. Camparò '11	♟♟ 2*
● Barbera d'Asti Sup. Le Cave '10	♟♟ 3*
● Barbera d'Asti Sup.Vignassa '10	♟♟ 5
● Barbera d'Asti Sup. Muaschae '10	♟♟ 6
● Barbera d'Asti Piagé '12	♟ 2
● Barbera d'Asti Sup. Camparò '10	♟♟ 2*
● Barbera d'Asti Sup. Camparò '08	♟♟ 2
● Barbera d'Asti Sup. Muascae '09	♟♟ 6
● Barbera d'Asti Sup.Vignassa '09	♟♟ 5
● Barbera d'Asti Sup.Vignassa '08	♟♟ 3
● Grignolino d'Asti Spineira '10	♟♟ 3*
○ M.to Bianco Sivoy '11	♟♟ 2*

★Pecchenino

B.TA VALDIBERTI, 59
12063 DOGLIANI [CN]
TEL. 017370686
www.pecchenino.com

CELLAR SALES
PRE-BOOKED VISITS
ACCOMMODATION
ANNUAL PRODUCTION 110,000 bottles
HECTARES UNDER VINE 26.00

The excellent performance of this important Langhe winery, skilfully managed by brothers Orlando and Attilio Pecchenino, continues unchecked. In Italy, but particularly abroad, its path has been strewn with many well-deserved accolades. The addition of Barolo to the range is the finishing touch to the profile of a winery that helped write the history of Dolcetto, giving a new image to a grape variety that was wrongly often ignored. The estate's vineyards are meticulously tended, limiting the use of chemicals to the bare minimum. The magnificent 2010 vintage of Bricco Botti demonstrates the full potential of dolcetto, with a nose of plum, cherry, blackberry and leather, followed by silky, close-knit tannins on the palate, blazing a new trail for the most temperamental Alba grape variety. Barolo Le Coste 2009 is very expressive, flaunting layered notes of violet, tobacco and spice.

● Dogliani Sup. Bricco Botti '10	♟♟♟ 4*
● Barolo Le Coste '09	♟♟ 8
● Barbera d'Alba Quass '11	♟♟ 4
● Barolo S. Giuseppe '09	♟♟ 6
● Dogliani S. Luigi '12	♟♟ 3
● Dogliani Sup. Sirì d'Jermu '11	♟♟ 3
○ Langhe Maestro '12	♟ 3
● Barolo Le Coste '05	♟♟♟ 8
● Dogliani Bricco Botti '07	♟♟♟ 4
● Dogliani Sirì d'Jermu '09	♟♟♟ 3*
● Dogliani Sirì d'Jermu '06	♟♟♟ 4
● Dolcetto di Dogliani Sirì d'Jermu '03	♟♟♟ 3
● Dolcetto di Dogliani Sirì d'Jermu '01	♟♟♟ 3*
● Dolcetto di Dogliani Sup. Bricco Botti '04	♟♟♟ 4

Pelissero

VIA FERRERE, 10
12050 TREISO [CN]
TEL. 0173638430
www.pelissero.com

Elio Perrone

S.DA SAN MARTINO, 3BIS
12053 CASTIGLIONE TINELLA [CN]
TEL. 0141855803
www.elioperrone.it

CELLAR SALES
PRE-BOOKED VISITS
ANNUAL PRODUCTION 250,000 bottles
HECTARES UNDER VINE 40.00

CELLAR SALES
PRE-BOOKED VISITS
ANNUAL PRODUCTION 170,000 bottles
HECTARES UNDER VINE 14.00

Over the years Pelissero, now run by the third generation, has carved out an increasingly important place for itself on the international markets. Its 38 hectares, planted with the main local grape varieties, constitute a solid, reliable foundation for production. Giorgio Pelissero runs the estate dynamically and with very clear ideas about the stylistic profile that he seeks to impress on all his wines: cleanliness, drinkability and an elegant palate. The wines are aged in different-sized barrels, with a preference for new oak. Barbaresco Vanotu, from the Basarin cru in Neive, remains the highlight of the very comprehensive range. Barbaresco Vanotu 2010 has lots of personality and character and focuses on dark notes of quinine, liquorice and tar, with vigorous yet discreet tannins. Langhe Long Now 2010 is very convincing, with an excellent balance of backbone and freshness. The juicy Dolcetto d'Alba Augenta 2012 deserves a special mention.

The Perrone family winery has been a Moscato standard-bearer for several years. The vineyards are divided between Castiglione Tinella, where only moscato is grown, in the hills at around 360 metres in altitude, and Isola d'Asti, which is mostly barbera, with some vines reaching 80 years of age. Chardonnay and brachetto are also grown alongside these two varieties. The wines are traditional in design, especially the Moscatos, with a focus on drinkability and pleasurableness The Sourgal 2012 is very convincing, with floral top notes followed by sage and lime on the nose, while the pleasant, fresh palate has just the right degree of sweetness and a long characterful finish. Barbera d'Asti Superiore Mongovone 2011 is even more marked by toasted oak, but has a generous nose of dark berry fruit, quinine and juniper berries, combined with a very concentrated, close-woven palate.

● Barbaresco Vanotu '10	♔♔ 8
● Langhe Rosso Long Now '10	♔♔ 5
● Barbaresco Nubiola '10	♔♔ 5
● Barbaresco Tulin '10	♔♔ 7
● Dolcetto d'Alba Augenta '12	♔♔ 3
● Dolcetto d'Alba Munfrina '12	♔ 2
● Langhe Nebbiolo '12	♔ 3
○ Moscato d'Asti '12	♔ 2
● Barbaresco Vanotu '08	♔♔♔ 8
● Barbaresco Vanotu '07	♔♔♔ 8
● Barbaresco Vanotu '06	♔♔♔ 8
● Barbaresco Vanotu '01	♔♔♔ 7
● Barbaresco Vanotu '99	♔♔♔ 7
● Barbaresco Vanotu '97	♔♔♔ 6
● Barbaresco Vanotu '09	♔♔ 8

○ Moscato d'Asti Sourgal '12	♔♔ 2*
● Barbera d'Asti Sup. Mongovone '11	♔♔ 5
● Barbera d'Asti Tasmorcan '12	♔ 2
● Bigarò '12	♔ 2
○ Gi '12	♔ 3
● Barbera d'Asti Sup. Mongovone '08	♔♔ 5
● Barbera d'Asti Tasmorcan '10	♔♔ 2*
● Barbera d'Asti Tasmorcan '09	♔♔ 2*
○ Moscato d'Asti Clarté '11	♔♔ 3
○ Moscato d'Asti Sourgal '11	♔♔ 2*
○ Moscato d'Asti Sourgal '10	♔♔ 2*

Le Piane

VIA CERRI, 10
28010 BOCA [NO]
TEL. 3483354185
www.bocapiane.com

CELLAR SALES
PRE-BOOKED VISITS
ANNUAL PRODUCTION 48,000 bottles
HECTARES UNDER VINE 8.00

Christoph Künzli can justifiably lay claim to being the creator of present-day Boca, a historic DOC that all but disappeared despite being one of the most densely planted areas in the whole of Piedmont before the war. It's been 15 years since the Swiss wine importer took over the estate in the province of Novara from old viticulturist Antonio Cerri, expanding his role to become a producer. The estate's three and a half hectares are divided into many plots given over to nebbiolo, croatina and vespolina, some of which are trained with the traditional "maggiorina" system. The best-known label is the Boca, which is aged for three years in 25- to 28-hectolitre barrels of Slavonian oak. The 2009 Boca and the croatina-based Colline Novaresi Rosso Le Piane had not been bottled at the time of our tastings, but the estate presented its new Mimmo, destined to become "deuxième vin" to the better-known Boca. The 2010 vintage displays finesse, elegance and complexity, giving it a more aristocratic character than the simpler, more approachable Maggiorina 2012.

● Mimmo '10	▼▼	4
● Maggiorina '12	▼▼	3
● Boca '08	▼▼▼	7
● Boca '06	▼▼▼	6
● Boca '05	▼▼▼	6
● Boca '04	▼▼▼	6
● Boca '03	▼▼▼	6
● Boca '07	▼▼	7
● Colline Novaresi La Maggiorina '09	▼▼	3
● Colline Novaresi Le Piane '09	▼▼	5
● Colline Novaresi Le Piane '08	▼▼	5
● Colline Novaresi Le Piane '07	▼▼	5
● Colline Novaresi Le Piane '06	▼▼	5
● La Maggiorina '11	▼▼	3

Pio Cesare

VIA CESARE BALBO, 6
12051 ALBA [CN]
TEL. 0173440386
www.piocesare.it

PRE-BOOKED VISITS
ANNUAL PRODUCTION 400,000 bottles
HECTARES UNDER VINE 52.00

Founded in 1881 by the great-great grandfather from whom they take their name, Pio Cesare's cellars are the only ones left in Alba's old town and follow the Roman walls. Today they are run by Pio Boffa with his cousin and nephew – the fifth generation of the family – preserving and enhancing the tradition handed down through the centuries. Respect for the terroir and the site climate underpins a production philosophy aimed at reproducing the same style of wines as in the past, despite the use of the latest cellar technologies. Most of the wines hail from the estate's own vineyards, which cover over 50 hectares in some of the finest and most prestigious areas of Barolo and Barbaresco. Barolo Ornato's excellent performance earned the 2009 vintage our highest accolade for its perfectly balanced power and elegance. The highly drinkable 2009 Barolo is also very good, offering attractive notes of tobacco, violet and spice, along with great freshness on the palate.

● Barolo Ornato '09	▼▼▼	8
● Barbaresco Il Bricco '09	▼▼	8
● Barolo '09	▼▼	8
● Barbaresco '09	▼▼	8
● Barbera d'Alba Fides '11	▼▼	5
○ Langhe Chardonnay Piodilei '11	▼▼	6
● Barbera d'Alba '11	▼	4
● Barbaresco Il Bricco '97	▼▼▼	8
● Barolo Ornato '08	▼▼▼	8
● Barolo Ornato '06	▼▼▼	8
● Barolo Ornato '05	▼▼▼	8
● Barolo Ornato '89	▼▼▼	8
● Barolo Ornato '85	▼▼▼	8
○ Langhe Chardonnay Piodilei '10	▼▼	6

Luigi Pira

VIA XX SETTEMBRE, 9
12050 SERRALUNGA D'ALBA [CN]
TEL. 0173613106
pira.luigi@alice.it

CELLAR SALES
PRE-BOOKED VISITS
ANNUAL PRODUCTION 50,000 bottles
HECTARES UNDER VINE 12.00

Gianpaolo and Romolo Pira continue to
expand this estate established by Luigi in
the 1950s, first by selling their grapes and
– around 20 years ago – opting to bottle
their wine under their own brand. Their
nebbiolo vineyards, all located on the slopes
of Serralunga, have always produced
reliable, characterful wines thanks also to
meticulous work in the cellar. The classic
Barolo and the Margheria cru age for
around two years in medium-sized barrels,
while the Marenca and Vigna Rionda
sojourn in barriques and tonneaux for one
year and a further year in 25-hectolitre
barrels. All the wines performed very well,
with Barolo Marenca 2009 reaching lofty
heights. It shows powerful and elegant, with
a spicy balsamic nose, followed by a
caressing, supple palate with exceptional
length. Barolo Vigna Rionda 2009 is
powerful but stylish, with impeccably
balanced structure, depth and freshness.

● Barolo Marenca '09	♥♥♥ 7
● Barolo Margheria '09	♥♥ 6
● Barolo V. Rionda '09	♥♥ 8
● Barbera d'Alba '11	♥♥ 3
● Barolo Serralunga '09	♥♥ 5
● Langhe Nebbiolo '11	♥♥ 3
● Barolo Marenca '08	♀♀♀ 7
● Barolo V. Marenca '01	♀♀♀ 7
● Barolo V. Rionda '06	♀♀♀ 8
● Barolo V. Rionda '04	♀♀♀ 8
● Barolo V. Rionda '00	♀♀♀ 8
● Barolo Margheria '08	♀♀ 6
● Barolo Serralunga '08	♀♀ 5
● Barolo V. Rionda '07	♀♀ 8

E. Pira & Figli
Chiara Boschis

VIA VITTORIO VENETO, 1
12060 BAROLO [CN]
TEL. 017356247
www.pira-chiaraboschis.com

CELLAR SALES
PRE-BOOKED VISITS
ANNUAL PRODUCTION 35,000 bottles
HECTARES UNDER VINE 8.50
VITICULTURE METHOD Certified Organic

Chiara Boschis is the embodiment of
professional fulfilment. She adores her work
and monitors each stage from the vineyard
to the cellar with painstaking attention. Over
the years she has made a name for herself
with the high quality of her wines, whose
distinctive style is derived from the use of
small oak casks. Her array of crus is
first-rate, from the world-famous Cannubi to
the interesting Via Nuova, and Mosconi,
from a large plot in the municipality of
Monforte d'Alba. Pesticides have been
banned in the estate's vineyards, where the
utmost respect for nature is maintained. The
typical aristocratic elegance of this great cru
is the distinguishing characteristic of
Barolo Cannubi 2009, which still displays
very young fruit, combined with nicely
resolved, well-integrated tannins. Barolo
Mosconi 2009 is a little more rugged and
exuberant, promising very interesting
ageing. The highly drinkable, fresh,
well-typed Langhe Nebbiolo 2011 also
deserves a mention.

● Barolo Cannubi '09	♥♥ 8
● Barolo Mosconi '09	♥♥ 8
● Barbera d'Alba Sup. '11	♥♥ 4
● Barolo Via Nuova '09	♥♥ 8
● Langhe Nebbiolo '11	♥♥ 4
● Dolcetto d'Alba '12	♥ 2
● Barolo '94	♀♀♀ 7
● Barolo Cannubi '05	♀♀♀ 8
● Barolo Cannubi '00	♀♀♀ 8
● Barolo Cannubi '97	♀♀♀ 8
● Barolo Cannubi '96	♀♀♀ 8
● Barolo Ris. '90	♀♀♀ 8
● Barolo Cannubi '08	♀♀ 8
● Barolo Cannubi '07	♀♀ 8
● Barolo Via Nuova '06	♀♀ 8
● Langhe Nebbiolo '10	♀♀ 4

143

Poderi Colla

LOC. SAN ROCCO SENO D'ELVIO, 82
12051 ALBA [CN]
TEL. 0173290148
www.podericolla.it

CELLAR SALES
PRE-BOOKED VISITS
ANNUAL PRODUCTION 150,000 bottles
HECTARES UNDER VINE 26.00

The Colla family's vine estate is stunning, with the 12 hectares at Cascina Drago neighbouring on the winery premises, eight hectares in the Roncaglie di Barbaresco cru, and six hectares in Bussia di Monforte d'Alba. This enviable range of wine country allows Tino and Beppe Colla, with the precious input of offspring Federica and Pietro, to offer a battery of wines that interprets the main Langa varieties to the full. The style profile is classic and traditional, very territorial and with few indulgences for wines that arouse intense emotions once aged. The excellent Barolo Bussia Dardi Le Rose 2009 earned our highest award with an extraordinary nose of cherry, blackberry and raspberry with hints of quinine, liquorice and spice. It is flanked by a convincing battery of wines, including the noteworthy Langhe Bricco del Drago 2009.

● Barolo Bussia Dardi Le Rose '09	♟♟♟ 6
● Barbaresco Roncaglie '10	♟♟ 6
● Langhe Bricco del Drago '09	♟♟ 4
● Barbera d'Alba Costa Bruna '11	♟♟ 3
● Dolcetto d'Alba Pian Balbo '12	♟♟ 2*
○ Langhe Riesling '12	♟♟ 3
● Nebbiolo d'Alba '11	♟♟ 3
○ Pietro Colla M. Cl. Extra Brut '10	♟♟ 5
● Langhe Pinot Nero Campo Romano '11	♟ 4
● Barolo Bussia Dardi Le Rose '99	♟♟♟ 6
● Barbaresco Roncaglie '09	♟♟ 6
● Barbera d'Alba Costa Bruna '09	♟♟ 3*
○ Langhe Riesling '11	♟♟ 3*
● Nebbiolo d'Alba '10	♟♟ 3*

Paolo Giuseppe Poggio

VIA ROMA, 67
15050 BRIGNANO FRASCATA [AL]
TEL. 0131784929
www.cantinapoggio.com

CELLAR SALES
PRE-BOOKED VISITS
ANNUAL PRODUCTION 18,000 bottles
HECTARES UNDER VINE 3.50

Although Paolo Poggio's operation is entirely family-run, the experience being fielded certainly comes from way back. Paolo's father was one of the first in the area to bottle his own wine. In recent times the wines have acquired a distinctive style, influenced enormously by the local climate. The nearby Curone torrent channels in very humid, cold air that make Paolo's job arduous in difficult years. The results can then be unpredictable but when the vintage permits, the wines are definitely interesting. It is no coincidence that the finest wines tasted this year are all from the 2011 vintage, commencing with a splendid version of Timorasso Ronchetto and a Barbera Campo la Bà that is one of the estate's best ever.

● Colli Tortonesi Barbera Campo La Bà '11	♟♟ 2*
○ Colli Tortonesi Cortese Campogallo '12	♟♟ 1*
○ Colli Tortonesi Timorasso Ronchetto '11	♟♟ 3
● Colli Tortonesi Barbera Derio '10	♟ 3
● Colli Tortonesi Rosso Prosone '11	♟ 2
● Colli Tortonesi Barbera Campo La Bà '09	♟♟ 2*
● Colli Tortonesi Barbera Campo La Bà '08	♟♟ 2*
● Colli Tortonesi Barbera Derio '09	♟♟ 3
● Colli Tortonesi Croatina Prosone '10	♟♟ 2*
○ Colli Tortonesi Timorasso Ronchetto '10	♟♟ 2*
○ Colli Tortonesi Timorasso Ronchetto '09	♟♟ 2*

Pomodolce

via IV Novembre, 7
15050 Montemarzino [AL]
Tel. 0131878035
www.pomodolce.it

CELLAR SALES
PRE-BOOKED VISITS
CELLAR SALES
ANNUAL PRODUCTION 12,000 bottles
HECTARES UNDER VINE 4.00
VITICULTURE METHOD Certified Organic

Exactly 50 years have gone by since Giuseppe and Camilla opened their Montemarzino restaurant in 1963. Even then they served wines produced by the family vineyards, but it was son Silvio who gave further impetus to the viticulture side when he began producing Pomodolce, applying organic cultivation methods. The experience accumulated in the decades past stood him in good stead and the results were immediately appreciable. The Timorasso Grue went straight on sale in versions that impressed our juries. In recent years the flagship reds seem to have overtaken the whites. Although well made, the two Timorassos did not perform as well as in the past. However, the reds from barbera and croatina are decidedly good. The first, the Marsèn, offers a stunning balance of acidity and power on the palate, enhancing its distinctive features, while the greatest strengths of the second, the Fonanino, are its delicately silky tannins and succulent palate.

● Colli Tortonesi Barbera Marsèn '10	TT 4
● Colli Tortonesi Croatina Fontanino '10	TT 3
○ Colli Tortonesi Timorasso Diletto '11	TT 3
○ Colli Tortonesi Timorasso Grue '11	TT 5
● Colli Tortonesi Rosso Niall '10	T 3
○ Colli Tortonesi Timorasso Derthona Grue '07	YYY 4
● Colli Tortonesi Barbera Marsèn '09	YY 4
● Colli Tortonesi Croatina Fontanino '07	YY 3
○ Colli Tortonesi Timorasso Diletto '10	YY 3*
○ Colli Tortonesi Timorasso Grue '10	YY 5
○ Colli Tortonesi Timorasso Grue '09	YY 5

Marco Porello

c.so Alba, 71
12043 Canale [CN]
Tel. 0173979324
www.porellovini.it

CELLAR SALES
PRE-BOOKED VISITS
ANNUAL PRODUCTION 100,000 bottles
HECTARES UNDER VINE 15.00

Founded in the early 1900s, this estate has been under the management of Marco Porello for almost 20 years now. During this time, it has established itself as one of the best in Roero. The grapes are cultivated in the municipalities of Canale and Vezza d'Alba in essentially sandy terrains. They comprise the classic varieties of the region, namely arneis, nebbiolo, barbera, favorita and brachetto. All the wines are pleasant, harmonious and drinkable, particularly those derived from the various crus of Camestrì, Mommiano and Torretta. Roero Torretta 2010 is among the best of the designation, with a nose of red fruit and vegetal hints, and a tannic palate that's still slightly closed, but has good fruit and a fresh, juicy finish. Both 2012 vintages of Roero Arneis are well made, the basic one zesty and citrussy, and the Camestrì spicy and ready to drink. The two pleasant Barbera d'Albas, Filatura 2011 and Mommiano 2012, are fresh with good fruit.

● Roero Torretta '10	TT 3*
● Barbera d'Alba Filatura '11	TT 3
● Barbera d'Alba Mommiano '12	TT 2*
○ Roero Arneis '12	TT 2*
○ Roero Arneis Camestrì '12	TT 2*
● Nebbiolo d'Alba '11	T 3
● Roero Torretta '06	YYY 3*
● Roero Torretta '04	YYY 3*
● Barbera d'Alba Mommiano '11	YY 2*
● Barbera d'Alba Mommiano '10	YY 2*
● Roero Torretta '09	YY 3*

Guido Porro

VIA ALBA, 1
12050 SERRALUNGA D'ALBA [CN]
TEL. 0173613306
www.guidoporro.com

CELLAR SALES
PRE-BOOKED VISITS
ACCOMMODATION
ANNUAL PRODUCTION 30,000 bottles
HECTARES UNDER VINE 8.00

Guido Porro's star has risen. Definitively. This passionate and sensitive viticulturist based in Serralunga d'Alba has around seven hectares close to his cellar. They straddle Lazzarito, long known as a superior cru particularly well-suited to growing not only nebbiolo, but also barbera and dolcetto. The Lazzairasco and Santa Caterina vineyards are dedicated to two Barolos with very different characters. The first tends to be more intense; the second more delicate. They both demonstrate a very classic approach based on fermentation in stainless steel and cement tanks followed by long ageing in 25-hectolitre barrels of Slavonian oak. Two years after winning its first Tre Bicchieri, Barolo Vigna Lazzairasco has repeated the feat with the 2009 vintage. It has a complex nose, with notes of aniseed, quinine and raspberry, followed by powerful, assertive tannins. Barolo Santa Caterina 2009 is very eloquent and enjoyable.

● Barolo V. Lazzairasco '09	▼▼▼	5
● Barolo Santa Caterina '09	▼▼	5
● Barbera d'Alba V. Santa Caterina '12	▼▼	3
● Dolcetto d'Alba V. l'Pari '12	▼	3
● Barolo V. Lazzairasco '07	♀♀♀	5
● Barbera d'Alba Santa Caterina '11	♀♀	3
● Barolo V. Lazzairasco '08	♀♀	5
● Barolo V. Santa Caterina '08	♀♀	5*
● Barolo V. Santa Caterina '07	♀♀	5
● Lange Nebbiolo '09	♀♀	3*
● Lange Nebbiolo Camilu '11	♀♀	4

Post dal Vin
Terre del Barbera

FRAZ. POSSAVINA
VIA SALIE, 19
14030 ROCCHETTA TANARO [AT]
TEL. 0141644143
www.postdalvin.com

CELLAR SALES
PRE-BOOKED VISITS
ANNUAL PRODUCTION 80,000 bottles
HECTARES UNDER VINE 115.00

For more than 50 years, this co-operative wincry in the municipality of Rocchetta Tanaro consisting of around 100 member growers has served as a point of reference for the territory. The main variety cultivated is, naturally, barbera. It is the basis of all the various typologies produced here, from the fresher, more easy-drinking bottles to more structured offerings. The style is traditional and great care is taken to express the characteristics of the territory. The other grape types featured are the classic cultivars of Monferrato: grignolino, dolcetto, freisa and moscato. The co-operative's wines performed very well overall, headed by the balanced, easy-drinking Barbera d'Asti Superiore BriccoFiore 2011, with fruity, earthy notes and a supple palate. Grignolino d'Asti 2012 has notes of black pepper and a long, gutsy palate, the pleasant Barbera d'Asti Maricca 2012 has a nice vein of acidity, and Barbera d'Asti Superiore Castagnassa 2011 is firm and complex, but with a touch too much alcohol on the finish.

● Barbera d'Asti Sup. BriccoFiore '11	▼▼	2*
● Barbera d'Asti Maricca '12	▼▼	2*
● Barbera d'Asti Sup. Castagnassa '11	▼▼	2*
● Grignolino d'Asti '12	▼▼	1*
● Barbera d'Asti Maricca '11	♀♀	2*
● Barbera d'Asti Maricca '10	♀♀	2*
● Barbera d'Asti Sup. BriccoFiore '09	♀♀	2*
● Barbera d'Asti Sup. BriccoFiore '08	♀♀	2*
● Barbera d'Asti Sup. Castagnassa '10	♀♀	2*
● Barbera d'Asti Sup. Castagnassa '09	♀♀	2
● Grignolino d'Asti '11	♀♀	1*
● Grignolino d'Asti '10	♀♀	1*

Giovanni Prandi

FRAZ. CASCINA COLOMBÈ
VIA FARINETTI, 5
12055 DIANO D'ALBA [CN]
TEL. 017369248
www.prandigiovanni.it

CELLAR SALES
PRE-BOOKED VISITS
ANNUAL PRODUCTION 20,000 bottles
HECTARES UNDER VINE 5.00

The history of the Prandi estate in Diano d'Alba dates back to the 1920s when its founder, Maggiorino Farinetti, started to sell the wine that he and his family consumed at home. The first partial bottlings occurred in the 1950s, and in 1978 the cellar was named Giovanni Prandi. Today, it is Giovanni's son Alessandro who tends the estate vineyards that are scattered between Diano and Alba. Production amounts to 20,000 bottles, king of which are the Dolcetto, Sörì Cristina and Sörì Colombè crus. Great care is also dedicated to the nebbiolo and barbera fermentation, while the whites on offer include the Langhe Arneis and Chardonnay. The battery of wines is dominated by the two versions of Dolcetto di Diano, thanks to their terroir trueness and excellent calibration that shuns over-extraction. Our favourite is Sörì Colombè 2012, which offers irresistible notes of blackcurrants. The 2012 Barbera is also true to this highly drinkable style.

La Prevostura

CASCINA PREVOSTURA, 1
13853 LESSONA [BI]
TEL. 0158853188
www.laprevostura.it

CELLAR SALES
PRE-BOOKED VISITS
CELLAR SALES
ANNUAL PRODUCTION 15,000 bottles
HECTARES UNDER VINE 4.00

Brothers Marco and Davide Bellini in collaboration with Paolo Pulze opted to build their new winery in Lessona. It all started in 2001 with the acquisition of three hectares of land. They planted their first vineyards in 2005 and 2010 with 87% nebbiolo, 10% vespolina and a smattering of croatina, and in 2009 they produced their first few bottles. Along the way, their passion motivated them to rent almost two hectares in Orbello and purchase almost two more in Masserano, giving them a solid foothold in Bramaterra. In 2012, they completed the new cellar where they can use large barrels for ageing the wines in place of the used barriques and 900-litre casks favoured in the early vintages. These first bottles, about 8,000, produced with the aid of oenologists Maurizio Forgia and Cristiano Garella, took our breath away. The Lessona 2009 lets the terroir do the talking, proffering sophisticated tannins and very complex ferrous notes, while the Costa della Sesia 2010 displays richer fruity flesh and attractive oak.

● Dolcetto di Diano Sörì Colombè '12	♀♀ 2*
● Barbera d'Alba Santa Eurosia '12	♀♀ 2*
● Dolcetto di Diano d'Alba Sörì Cristina '12	♀♀ 2*
● Nebbiolo d'Alba Colombè '11	♀ 3
● Dolcetto di Diano Sörì Colombè '11	♀♀ 2*
● Dolcetto di Diano Sörì Colombè '10	♀♀ 2*
● Dolcetto di Diano Sörì Colombè '09	♀♀ 2*
● Dolcetto di Diano Sörì Cristina '10	♀♀ 2*
● Dolcetto di Diano Sörì Cristina '09	♀♀ 2*
● Dolcetto di Diano Sörì Cristina '08	♀♀ 2*
● Nebbiolo d'Alba Colombè '10	♀♀ 3
● Nebbiolo d'Alba Colombè '07	♀♀ 3*

● Lessona '09	♀♀ 4
● Coste della Sesia Muntacc '10	♀♀ 4

Ferdinando Principiano

VIA ALBA, 47
12065 MONFORTE D'ALBA [CN]
TEL. 0173787158
www.ferdinandoprincipiano.it

CELLAR SALES
PRE-BOOKED VISITS
ANNUAL PRODUCTION 80,000 bottles
HECTARES UNDER VINE 16.00

One of the first Langhe vignerons to apply a natural philosophy to his work, Ferdinando Principiano has completely reorganized the family estate, active since the early 1900s. Banishing chemical fertilizers and herbicides from the vineyards and sulphur dioxide and cultured yeasts from the cellar, his Barolos have become veritable beacons for enthusiasts seeking a proudly artisanal personality and can easily be forgiven the odd minor aromatic or phenolic flaw. These are not wines for amateur palates, but the best versions are capable of revealing a side of the Serralunga hills, where most of the nebbiolo is grown, that is new in many respects. The characterful Barolo Ravera 2009 has a nose of dried flowers, liquorice, quinine and tobacco, and a balanced palate sustained by attractive freshness. Barolo Serralunga 2009 focuses on dark notes of tar and rhubarb, with vigorous but discreet tannins, The jury's still out on Barolo Boscareto 2007.

● Barolo Ravera '09	♟♟ 7
● Barbera d'Alba Laura '12	♟♟ 2*
● Barolo Boscareto '07	♟♟ 8
● Barolo Serralunga '09	♟♟ 5
● Dosset	♟ 1
● Langhe Nebbiolo Coste '12	♟ 3
● Nebbiolo d'Alba Montagliato '11	♟ 3
● Barolo Boscareto '93	♟♟♟ 7
● Barbera d'Alba La Romualda '10	♟♟ 6
● Barbera d'Alba La Romualda '06	♟♟ 5
● Barolo Boscareto '06	♟♟ 8
● Barolo Boscareto '05	♟♟ 6
● Barolo Ravera '06	♟♟ 7
● Barolo Serralunga '05	♟♟ 5

★Produttori del Barbaresco

VIA TORINO, 54
12050 BARBARESCO [CN]
TEL. 0173635139
www.produttoridelbarbaresco.com

CELLAR SALES
PRE-BOOKED VISITS
ACCOMMODATION
ANNUAL PRODUCTION 450,000 bottles
HECTARES UNDER VINE 100.00

Founded in 1958, today Produttori del Barbaresco is unquestionably one of the best co-operative wineries in Europe. It is also a benchmark for those who like to balance quality with price. Under the management of Gianni Testa, the 50 plus members cultivate a total of around 100 hectares, which account for just under 20% of the entire area registered under the Barbaresco DOC. The range of wines on offer is obtained exclusively from nebbiolo. It is fiercely traditional in style and enhanced in the best years by the Riserva line that brings together up to nine of the most celebrated crus in the area. The convincing battery presented for tasting included Barbaresco Vigneti in Ovello Riserva 2008, which earned our top award. Its aristocratic profile focuses on dried flowers and quinine, with lingering, well-integrated tannins. Among the other excellent Riservas, we particularly liked the personality of Montefico 2008.

● Barbaresco Vign. in Ovello Ris. '08	♟♟♟ 6
● Barbaresco Vign. in Asili Ris. '08	♟♟ 6
● Barbaresco Vign. in Montefico Ris. '08	♟♟ 6
● Barbaresco Vign. in Montestefano Ris. '08	♟♟ 6
● Barbaresco Vign. in Rio Sordo Ris. '08	♟♟ 6
● Barbaresco '09	♟♟ 5
● Barbaresco Vign. in Mungagota Ris. '08	♟♟ 6
● Barbaresco Vign. in Pajé Ris. '08	♟♟ 6
● Barbaresco Vign. in Pora Ris. '08	♟♟ 6
● Barbaresco Vign. in Rabajà Ris. '08	♟♟ 6
● Langhe Nebbiolo '11	♟ 3
● Barbaresco Vign. in Montefico Ris. '00	♟♟♟ 5*
● Barbaresco Vign. in Pajé Ris. '01	♟♟♟ 5*
● Barbaresco Vign. in Pora Ris. '07	♟♟♟ 6

Cantina Produttori del Gavi

VIA CAVALIERI DI VITTORIO VENETO, 45
15066 GAVI [AL]
TEL. 0143642786
www.cantinaproduttoridelgavi.it

CELLAR SALES
PRE-BOOKED VISITS
ANNUAL PRODUCTION 160,000 bottles
HECTARES UNDER VINE 220.00

Counting over 100 member growers, this is one of the finest co-operatives in the province of Alessandria and beyond. Founded in 1951 and renamed Cantina Produttori del Gavi in 1974, it manages to combine relatively large-scale production with very reasonable prices – without sacrificing personality – in an extremely comprehensive range. Its wines include an impressive eight Gavis, almost all vinified and aged in steel without malolactic fermentation, with the exception of part of the Aureliana selection, which is aged in small oak casks. A single wine with many labels: this is both the strength and the weakness of this co-operative, whose success is underpinned by very high average quality and reasonable prices. Our favourite of the wide range was the GG, a Gavi with good body that focuses wholly on finesse and freshness.

★Prunotto

REG. SAN CASSIANO, 4G
12051 ALBA [CN]
TEL. 0173280017
www.prunotto.it

PRE-BOOKED VISITS
ANNUAL PRODUCTION 600,000 bottles
HECTARES UNDER VINE 50.00

In the minds of many enthusiasts, Prunotto is one of the oldest and most reliable names in quality Piedmont wine. Almost 100 years have passed since Alfredo Prunotto gave his name to the estate that was destined to become an international success. Since 1989 it has been run by the famous Antinori family who, having purchased such a prestigious winery, have been very careful to carry on the excellent work of previous decades. The progressive extension of the estate's vineyards is further proof of its serious commitment to presenting itself as a landmark winery. Once again this year Barolo Bussia delighted us with its elegant nose and sophisticated tannins. Barbaresco Bric Turot '09 is expressive with well-calibrated structure and elegance, and a fresh nose of berry fruit. The Barolo 2009 is very drinkable, with alluring hints of blackberry and cherry, resolved tannins and a positively refreshing swathe of acidity.

○ Gavi del Comune di Gavi GG '12	♈♈ 3*
○ Gavi del Comune di Gavi Et. Nera '12	♈♈ 2*
○ Gavi del Comune di Gavi La Maddalena '12	♈♈ 2*
○ Gavi G '12	♈♈ 3
○ Gavi Primi Grappoli '12	♈♈ 2*
○ Gavi Et. Nera '12	♈ 3
○ Gavi Cascine dell'Aureliana '05	♉♉ 2*
○ Gavi del Comune di Gavi Et. Nera '11	♉♉ 1*
○ Gavi del Comune di Gavi G '11	♉♉ 2*
○ Gavi del Comune di Gavi GG '11	♉♉ 2*
○ Gavi del Comune di Gavi GG '07	♉♉ 2*
○ Gavi G '10	♉♉ 2*
○ Gavi Primi Grappoli '11	♉♉ 1*
○ Gavi Primi Grappoli '10	♉♉ 2

● Barolo Bussia '09	♈♈ 7
● Barbaresco '10	♈♈ 5
● Barbaresco Bric Turot '09	♈♈ 6
● Barbera d'Alba '11	♈♈ 3
● Barolo '09	♈♈ 6
● Dolcetto d'Alba '12	♈♈ 2*
● M.to Bricco Colma '08	♈♈ 5
● Nebbiolo d'Alba Occhetti '10	♈♈ 4
● Barbera d'Alba Pian Romualdo '10	♈ 4
● Barbera d'Asti Fiulòt '12	♈ 3
● M.to Mompertone '10	♈ 3
○ Moscato d'Asti '12	♈ 2
○ Roero Arneis '12	♈ 3
● Barolo Bussia '01	♉♉♉ 8
● Barolo Bussia '99	♉♉♉ 8
● Barolo Bussia '98	♉♉♉ 8

Renato Ratti

FRAZ. ANNUNZIATA, 7
12064 LA MORRA [CN]
TEL. 017350185
www.renatoratti.com

CELLAR SALES
PRE-BOOKED VISITS
ANNUAL PRODUCTION 300,000 bottles
HECTARES UNDER VINE 40.00

Renato Ratti was undoubtedly a man of great culture, an historical figure in the sphere of winegrowing, the author of many books and a fundamental influence on the reclassification of Barolo. His son Pietro, a graduate of the Oenological School in Alba, took over the family winery in 1988 and has industriously continued along Renato's path. The new cellar in Annunziata, where it is also possible to visit the Renato Ratti Museum commemorating the founder, is simply spectacular. The estate's wines are classic in style and aged in both small French oak casks and Slavonian oak barrels. We reserve judgement on the Barolos, currently lacking in harmony and requiring more time before they can be enjoyed. Nebbiolo d'Alba Ochetti 2011 is vivid and true to type, with fresh notes of raspberry, cherry and eucalyptus, and the vibrant, juicy Barbera d'Asti 2011 is exceptionally easy drinking.

Ressia

VIA CANOVA, 28
12052 NEIVE [CN]
TEL. 0173677305
www.ressia.com

CELLAR SALES
PRE-BOOKED VISITS
ANNUAL PRODUCTION 25,000 bottles
HECTARES UNDER VINE 5.50

In the space of about 15 years, this little winery in the Barbaresco district headed by Francesco Ressia, has managed to carve out a respected place for itself among the area's top producers. The Canova vineyard, high in the hills, supplies grapes with a strong personality and unique sensory characteristics. Attentive vineyard management also ensures authentic, terroir-true wines, which sojourn in different-sized barrels, allowing ageing to be calibrated more precisely. Two vintages of Barbaresco Canova were presented for our tastings this year. We slightly preferred the 2010, with a focused nose of raspberry, tobacco and spice, and a firm lively, tannic weave. The Canova 2009 is also eloquent and focused, although its tannins are still slightly rugged.

● Barbera d'Asti '11	▼▼ 3
● Barolo Marcenasco '09	▼▼ 6
● Barolo Rocche '09	▼▼ 8
● M.to Villa Pattono '11	▼▼ 5
● Nebbiolo d'Alba Ochetti '11	▼▼ 4
● Barolo Conca '09	▼ 8
○ M.to Bianco I Cedri '11	▼ 4
● Barolo Rocche '06	▼▼▼ 8
● Barolo Rocche Marcenasco '84	▼▼▼ 6
● Barolo Rocche Marcenasco '83	▼▼▼ 6
● Barolo Conca '07	▼▼ 8
● Barolo Marcenasco '08	▼▼ 6
● Barolo Marcenasco '07	▼▼ 6
● Barolo Rocche '08	▼▼ 8
● Barolo Rocche '05	▼▼ 8

● Barbaresco Canova '10	▼▼ 5
● Barbaresco Canova '09	▼▼ 5
● Barbera d'Alba Sup. Canova '11	▼▼ 3
○ Evien	▼▼ 2*
● Barbera d'Alba Canova '12	▼ 5
● Dolcetto d'Alba Canova '12	▼ 2
● Langhe Nebbiolo Gepù '10	▼ 3
● Barbaresco Canova '06	▼▼▼ 5*
● Barbaresco Canova '08	▼▼ 5*
● Barbaresco Canova '05	▼▼ 5
● Barbaresco Canova '04	▼▼ 5
● Barbera d'Alba Sup. Canova '10	▼▼ 3
● Barbera d'Alba Sup. Canova '07	▼▼ 3*
○ Evien '10	▼▼ 2

F.lli Revello

FRAZ. ANNUNZIATA, 103
12064 LA MORRA [CN]
TEL. 017350276
www.revellofratelli.it

CELLAR SALES
PRE-BOOKED VISITS
ANNUAL PRODUCTION 75,000 bottles
HECTARES UNDER VINE 17.00

We recently had the chance to taste some wines from the late 1990s and can guarantee the soundness and excellent bottle development of the products of brothers Carlo and Enzo Revello. Great care is lavished on the work in both vineyard and cellar, and the style tends to focus on maximum aromatic definition and richness of fruit, ensuring wines that are very pleasantly extroverted and drinkable even when young. The Barolo crus are, of course, the jewel in the estate's crown, but the other wines are consistently well made. A handsome guest farm completes the offerings of this important La Morra winery. Barolo Giachini 2009 shows exemplary precision, with focused notes of berries, tobacco, spice and violet, combined with silky tannins and well-balanced acidity. The Barolo 2009 deserves a special mention, appearing well-typed without any frills and vaunting a fresh, tempting palate with discreet, delicate tannins.

● Barolo '09	♛♛ 5
● Barolo Giachini '09	♛♛ 7
● Barolo V. Conca '09	♛♛ 7
● Barolo Rocche dell'Annunziata '09	♛♛ 8
● Barbera d'Alba Ciabot du Re '05	♛♛♛ 5
● Barbera d'Alba Ciabot du Re '00	♛♛♛ 5
● Barolo '93	♛♛♛ 5
● Barolo Rocche dell'Annunziata '01	♛♛♛ 8
● Barolo Rocche dell'Annunziata '00	♛♛♛ 8
● Barolo Rocche dell'Annunziata '97	♛♛♛ 8
● Barolo V. Conca '99	♛♛♛ 5
● Barolo Rocche dell'Annunziata '08	♛♛ 8
● Barolo V. Conca '08	♛♛ 7
● Barolo V. Gattera '08	♛♛ 6
● Barolo V. Gattera '07	♛♛ 6

Michele Reverdito

FRAZ. RIVALTA
B.TA GARASSINI, 74B
12064 LA MORRA [CN]
TEL. 017350336
www.reverdito.it

CELLAR SALES
PRE-BOOKED VISITS
ANNUAL PRODUCTION 70,000 bottles
HECTARES UNDER VINE 8.00

In the space of just a few years, this little family-run winery has managed to earn itself a place among the top names in Langhe. Michele Reverdito, aided by his wife and parents, produces a range of well-calibrated, expressive wines with a distinctive personality. The top-notch vineyards occupy particularly fine sites and make a decisive contribution to the quality of the estate's production. Its Barolos are, of course, its pride and joy, and are an excellent credential both in Italy and abroad. The intention to release only wines that are ready to drink, initially hailed as a great idea, seems to have produced the opposite effect. We found the older Riservas a little tired, preferring the younger, less woody Barolos that still have good fruit, such as the Moncucco 2008.

● Barolo '09	♛♛ 4
● Barolo Badarina '09	♛♛ 5
● Barolo Moncucco '08	♛♛ 5
● Barbera d'Alba Butti '11	♛ 3
● Barbera d'Alba Delia '10	♛ 4
● Barolo San Giacomo Ris. '05	♛ 7
● Langhe Nascetta '12	♛ 2
● Langhe Nebbiolo Simane '11	♛ 3
● Verduno Pelaverga '12	♛ 2
● Barolo Bricco Cogni '04	♛♛♛ 6
● Barolo Badarina '07	♛♛ 5
● Barolo Bricco Cogni '06	♛♛ 6
● Barolo Moncucco '07	♛♛ 5
● Barolo Riva Rocca Ris. '06	♛♛ 6
● Langhe Nebbiolo Simane '10	♛♛ 3

Giuseppe Rinaldi

via Monforte, 5
12060 Barolo [CN]
Tel. 017356156
rinaldimarta@libero.it

CELLAR SALES
PRE-BOOKED VISITS
ANNUAL PRODUCTION 35,000 bottles
HECTARES UNDER VINE 6.50

A visit to Beppe "Citrico" Rinaldi's estate has become even more interesting and entertaining now that his young daughters Marta and Carlotta are working alongside him. The passing of the baton to the new generation seems to have heightened that magical mix of rigour and fantasy that comes through in the family's crus – witness the Brunate-Le Coste and the Cannubi San Lorenzo-Ravera. Their Barolos are loved intensely by those who disdain technical obsessions and don't mind the odd reductive or acidulous phase, generally balanced by great cellaring potential but above all by a unique expressive naturalness that is classic through and through. Barolo Cannubi San Lorenzo-Ravera 2009 has an estery nose with hints of dried flowers, quinine and tobacco. The austere palate requires further ageing in order to express its potential to the full. Barolo Brunate-Le Coste 2009 has a rather closed nose and a smooth palate sustained by assertive tannins.

● Barolo Brunate-Le Coste '09	ŸŸ 7
● Barolo Cannubi S. Lorenzo-Ravera '09	ŸŸ 7
● Langhe Nebbiolo '11	ŸŸ 4
● Barolo Brunate-Le Coste '07	YYY 7
● Barolo Brunate-Le Coste '06	YYY 7
● Barolo Brunate-Le Coste '01	YYY 6
● Barolo Brunate-Le Coste '00	YYY 6
● Barolo Brunate-Le Coste '97	YYY 6
● Barolo Cannubi S. Lorenzo-Ravera '04	YYY 6
● Barolo Brunate-Le Coste '08	YY 7
● Barolo Cannubi S. Lorenzo-Ravera '08	YY 7
● Barolo Cannubi S. Lorenzo-Ravera '07	YY 7
● Langhe Freisa '08	YY 3
● Langhe Nebbiolo '09	YY 4

Pietro Rinaldi

fraz. Madonna di Como
12051 Alba [CN]
Tel. 0173360090
www.pietrorinaldi.com

CELLAR SALES
PRE-BOOKED VISITS
ACCOMMODATION
ANNUAL PRODUCTION 70,000 bottles
HECTARES UNDER VINE 10.00

The wines produced by Monica Rinaldi and Paolo Tenino impress with the stylistic definition and interpretive clarity of the various varietals used. These characteristics are ideally represented in the Barolo Monvigliero from the municipality of Verduno. The Rinaldis' wine roots go deep; the family started making wine in the early 1900s. The range of wines on offer has expanded over time to achieve its current versatility and includes many of the zone's principal typologies. Production is limited but the quality is high and the prices are reasonable, the perfect combination to carve out a niche in the crowded Langhe wine world. This young estate's wines gave an excellent overall performance. Barolo Monvigliero 2008 is balanced and elegant, with complex notes of tobacco, quinine and tar, accompanied by assertive, close-knit tannins, while the succulent, fruity Dolcetto d'Alba Madonna di Como 2012 is alluringly drinkable.

● Barolo Monvigliero '08	ŸŸ 6
● Barbaresco San Cristoforo '09	ŸŸ 5
● Barbera d'Alba Monpiano '11	ŸŸ 3
● Barbera d'Alba Sup. Bricco Cichetta '11	ŸŸ 3
● Barolo '09	ŸŸ 5
● Dolcetto d'Alba Madonna di Como '12	ŸŸ 2*
○ Langhe Arneis Hortensia '12	Ÿ 2
● Langhe Nebbiolo Argante '10	Ÿ 3
○ Moscato d'Asti d'Ampess '12	Ÿ 3
● Barbaresco San Cristoforo '08	YY 5
● Barbera d'Alba Sup. Bricco Cichetta '10	YY 3
● Barolo '08	YY 5
● Barolo Monvigliero '07	YY 6
● Dolcetto d'Alba Madonna di Como '11	YY 2*

Rizzi

VIA RIZZI, 15
12050 TREISO [CN]
TEL. 0173638161
www.cantinarizzi.it

CELLAR SALES
PRE-BOOKED VISITS
ACCOMMODATION
ANNUAL PRODUCTION 50,000 bottles
HECTARES UNDER VINE 35.00

The Dellapiana family have raised the profile
of their estate step by step, harvest by
harvest. Despite producing wine for almost
50 years, it is only in the last few that the
estate's stylistic and productive potential
has come into its own. Its over 30 hectares
of property are divided between the Rizzi hill
and Pajoré, among some of the most
wine-friendly vineyards in Treiso. The secret
of its success lies in the very reasonable
prices and nebbiolo that always stands out
for its full, balanced almost feminine
character. The various crus are fermented
separately and aged in medium and large
barrels of Slavonian oak. The rest of the
range also performs well, notably the
dolcetto. Barbaresco Pajoré 2010 is very
convincing, with a multi-layered nose of
berry fruit, liquorice and spice, accompanied
by balanced tannins and good acidity.
Barbaresco Nervo Fondetta 2010 is
pleasantly drinkable, showing a nicely
eloquent nose and a full, satisfying palate.

● Barbaresco Pajorè '10	♟♟ 6
● Barbaresco Nervo Fondetta '10	♟♟ 5
○ Extra Brut M. Cl. Rizzi '09	♟♟ 4
○ Moscato d'Asti '12	♟♟ 2*
● Barbera d'Alba '10	♟ 2
● Dolcetto d'Alba '12	♟ 2
● Barbaresco Nervo Fondetta '09	♟♟ 5
● Barbaresco Nervo Fondetta '06	♟♟ 5
● Barbaresco Nervo Fondetta '05	♟♟ 5
● Barbaresco Pajorè '06	♟♟ 5
● Barbaresco Rizzi Boito '08	♟♟ 5
● Barbaresco Rizzi Boito '07	♟♟ 5
● Barbaresco Rizzi Boito '06	♟♟ 5
● Dolcetto d'Alba '11	♟♟ 2*

★Albino Rocca

S.DA RONCHI, 18
12050 BARBARESCO [CN]
TEL. 0173635145
www.roccaalbino.com

CELLAR SALES
PRE-BOOKED VISITS
ANNUAL PRODUCTION 130,000 bottles
HECTARES UNDER VINE 18.00

The untimely death of Angelo Rocca and his
partner Paola is terrible news for all wine
lovers, and many others besides. Those who
knew them are well aware how much
Langhe will miss their affable conviviality –
the same that has always characterized
their Barbarescos, which represent an
almost ideal stylistic bridge between
tradition and modernity. Now it is up to
Paola, Monica and Daniela Rocca, with
Carlo Castellengo, to continue such an
important venture, which today
encompasses over 20 hectares of vineyards
and a formidable range of wines. The
Nebbiolo is aged in 200-hectolitre German
and Austrian oak barrels, while small oak
casks are used for Barbera Gepin and
Cortese La Rocca. Barbaresco Ronchi 2010
took our top award with one of its best ever
vintages. The balsamic nose is
accompanied by notes of berry fruit,
rhubarb and violet, while the palate is firm
and satisfying. Barbaresco Ovello Vigna
Loreto 2010 has a long, fresh palate.

● Barbaresco Ronchi '10	♟♟♟ 6
● Barbera d'Alba Gepin '11	♟♟ 4
● Barbaresco Duemiladieci '10	♟♟ 5
● Barbaresco Ovello V. Loreto '10	♟♟ 6
● Dolcetto d'Alba Vignalunga '12	♟♟ 2*
○ Langhe Chardonnay da Bertü '12	♟♟ 3
○ Moscato d'Asti '12	♟♟ 2*
● Nebbiolo d'Alba '11	♟♟ 3
○ Piemonte Cortese La Rocca '12	♟♟ 4
● Barbera d'Alba '12	♟ 2
● Barbaresco Ovello V. Loreto '09	♟♟♟ 6
● Barbaresco Ovello V. Loreto '07	♟♟♟ 6
● Barbaresco Vign. Brich Ronchi '05	♟♟♟ 6
● Barbaresco Vign. Brich Ronchi Ris. '06	♟♟♟ 8
● Barbaresco Vign. Brich Ronchi Ris. '04	♟♟♟ 8

★Bruno Rocca

VIA RABAJÀ, 60
12050 BARBARESCO [CN]
TEL. 0173635112
www.brunorocca.it

CELLAR SALES
PRE-BOOKED VISITS
ANNUAL PRODUCTION 60,000 bottles
HECTARES UNDER VINE 15.00

The distinctive feather-logo labels are a longstanding icon of Piedmontese and Italian winemaking excellence in many world markets. Bruno, with the precious help of children Luisa and Francesco, runs his famous Barbaresco winery confidently, producing wines of great depth and structure, alluring when young and destined to grow old gracefully. The battery showcases the best varieties in the region. New acquisitions in the Monferrato township of Vaglio Serra contribute to enhancing the range with an interesting Barbera d'Asti. The estate's wines gave an excellent overall performance, topped by Rabaja 2010, one of its best ever vintages. It vaunts a deep, vibrant hue and a balsamic nose with hints of leather and spice, followed by a very long, supple, firm palate. Barbaresco Coparossa 2010 is also very tempting, with tannins that are still slightly rugged but already highly drinkable.

● Barbaresco Rabajà '10	♥♥♥ 8
● Barbaresco Coparossa '10	♥♥ 8
● Barbaresco '10	♥♥ 6
● Barbera d'Alba '11	♥♥ 4
● Barbera d'Asti '11	♥♥ 4
● Dolcetto d'Alba Vigna Trifolè '12	♥♥ 3
● Langhe Rosso Rabajolo '11	♥ 5
● Barbaresco Coparossa '04	♀♀♀ 8
● Barbaresco Maria Adelaide '07	♀♀♀ 8
● Barbaresco Maria Adelaide '04	♀♀♀ 8
● Barbaresco Maria Adelaide '01	♀♀♀ 8
● Barbaresco Rabajà '09	♀♀♀ 8
● Barbaresco Rabajà '01	♀♀♀ 8
● Barbaresco Rabajà '00	♀♀♀ 8
● Barbaresco Rabajà '98	♀♀♀ 8
● Barbaresco Rabajà '88	♀♀♀ 7

Rocche Costamagna

VIA VITTORIO EMANUELE, 8
12064 LA MORRA [CN]
TEL. 0173509225
www.rocchecostamagna.it

CELLAR SALES
PRE-BOOKED VISITS
ACCOMMODATION
ANNUAL PRODUCTION 95,000 bottles
HECTARES UNDER VINE 14.00

It is thanks to Alessandro Locatelli, the son of well-known wine entrepreneur and acclaimed artist Claudia Ferraresi, that this La Morra estate has progressively modified its production style and, in recent years, achieved success not only in Italy but also on many foreign markets. Nebbiolo, barbera and dolcetto are the main grape varieties used. The wines are generally powerful but elegant and caressing, always with an exciting palate, and the vinification style is derived from the skilled use of both small casks and large Slavonian oak barrels. A charming and very picturesque building houses the winery headquarters. Barolo Rocche dell'Annunziata 2009 stands out for its complex nose, with notes of raspberry, tobacco and liquorice, while the palate is sustained by imposing but discreet tannins and refreshing acidity. Bricco Francesco Riserva 2007 is austere and noble, promising interesting development.

● Barolo Rocche dell'Annunziata '09	♥♥ 5
● Barolo Rocche dell'Annunziata Bricco Francesco Ris. '07	♥♥ 6
● Barbera d'Alba Annunziata '11	♥♥ 3
● Barbera d'Alba Sup. Rocche delle Rocche '10	♥♥ 4
● Langhe Nebbiolo Roccardo '11	♥♥ 3
○ Langhe Arneis '12	♥ 2
⊙ Langhe Rosato Osé '12	♥ 2
● Barolo Rocche dell'Annunziata '04	♀♀♀ 5
● Barbera d'Alba Sup. Rocche delle Rocche '07	♀♀ 3
● Barolo Bricco Francesco Rocche dell'Annunziata '06	♀♀ 6
● Barolo Rocche dell'Annunziata '07	♀♀ 5
● Barolo Rocche dell'Annunziata '05	♀♀ 5

★Podere
Rocche dei Manzoni

LOC. MANZONI SOPRANI, 3
12065 MONFORTE D'ALBA [CN]
TEL. 017378421
www.rocchedeimanzoni.it

CELLAR SALES
PRE-BOOKED VISITS
ANNUAL PRODUCTION 250,000 bottles
HECTARES UNDER VINE 50.00

Rocche dei Manzoni was founded in the municipality of Monforte d'Alba, where Valentino Migliorini, Rodolfo's father, purchased an 18th-century farm with excellently aspected adjoining vineyards. Valentino was a great man with talent and vision, an innovator, and one of the first in Langhe to use small French oak casks and produce first-rate Metodo Classicos from chardonnay and pinot nero grapes grown in the Monforte district. The estate's Barolos were originally more classic in style; today they are certainly more modern and less traditional. The battery of wines tasted was very interesting, despite still being marked by oak. Barolo Big 'd Big 2009 is complex and powerful, with a full, enfolding palate, while Barolo Rocche 2008 has attractively nuanced dark notes of quinine and tar, and Valentino Brut Riserva Elena 2008 is as good as ever.

● Barolo Rocche '08	♟♟ 8
● Barolo V. Big 'd Big '09	♟♟ 8
○ Valentino Brut M. Cl. Riserva Elena '08	♟♟ 5
● Barolo V. Cappella di S. Stefano '09	♟♟ 8
● Barolo V. d'la Roul '09	♟♟ 8
○ Langhe Chardonnay L'Angelica '09	♟♟ 7
● Barbera d'Alba Sup. Sorito Mosconi '07	♟ 6
● Langhe Bricco Manzoni '07	♟ 6
● Langhe Quatr Nas '07	♟ 7
● Barolo V. Big 'd Big '99	♟♟♟ 8
● Barolo V. Cappella di S. Stefano '01	♟♟♟ 8
● Barolo V. d'la Roul '07	♟♟♟ 8
● Langhe Rosso Quatr Nas '99	♟♟♟ 6
○ Valentino Brut Zero Ris. '98	♟♟♟ 5

Roccolo di Mezzomerico

CASCINA ROCCOLO BELLINI, 4
28040 MEZZOMERICO [NO]
TEL. 0321920407
www.ilroccolovini.it

CELLAR SALES
PRE-BOOKED VISITS
ANNUAL PRODUCTION 30,000 bottles
HECTARES UNDER VINE 7.00

Margherita and Pietro Gelmini are the owners of this splendid estate in Mezzomerico that possesses five hectares of vineyards and views that alone merit a visit. The varieties cultivated include nebbiolo, vespolina and bonarda, while erbaluce and chardonnay represent the whites. For over 20 years now, they have practised integrated vineyard management, the basis of sustainable viticulture. Production focuses on clear territorial coherence, starting with the two Valentina selections obtained from nebbiolo. Nebbiolo Valentina Vendemmia Tardiva Etichetta Oro 2009 shows an almost inky garnet ruby, with a sophisticated nose of berry fruit and a full, flavoursome palate with plenty of flesh. Siduri Francesca Passito opens with notes of caramel and dried fruit and has a long, dense well-orchestrated palate, while Nebbiolo Valentina 2008 combines notes of berry fruit and sweet spice, and has a slightly drying alcoholic finish.

● Colline Novaresi Nebbiolo Valentina V.T. Et. Oro '09	♟♟ 4
● Colline Novaresi Nebbiolo Valentina '08	♟♟ 3
○ Siduri Francesca Passito	♟♟ 4
○ Il Mataccio V. T.	♟ 2
● Colline Novaresi Nebbiolo La Cascinetta '09	♟♟ 2*
● Colline Novaresi Nebbiolo Valentina '07	♟♟ 3*
● Colline Novaresi Nebbiolo Valentina '06	♟♟ 3*
● Colline Novaresi Nebbiolo Valentina V.T. '07	♟♟ 4

Flavio Roddolo

FRAZ. BRICCO APPIANI
LOC. SANT'ANNA, 5
12065 MONFORTE D'ALBA [CN]
TEL. 017378535

ANNUAL PRODUCTION 22,500 bottles
HECTARES UNDER VINE 6.00

Few Langhe growers have taken the importance of ageing to the full expression of their magnificent wines as seriously as Flavio Roddolo has always done. This is truer than ever now that the expansion of the cellar has given him extra space to lay down his bottles of Barolo (Ravera), Nebbiolo, Barbera, Dolcetto and Cabernet (Bricco Appiani) until he deems them ready for release. His varietal variations always express the personality of this highly distinctive zone of Monforte, thanks in part to their lengthy ageing mostly in small and medium-sized used casks. Barolo Ravera 2008 gave an excellent performance, with a very classic nose of violet, tobacco, tar and berry fruit, and perfectly balanced vigorous fine-grained tannins and refreshing acidity on the palate, earning it a Tre Bicchieri. The deep, complex Nebbiolo d'Alba 2008 is typical and highly drinkable.

● Barolo Ravera '08	♥♥♥ 5
● Dolcetto d'Alba Sup. '10	♥♥ 3*
● Nebbiolo d'Alba '08	♥♥ 4
● Dolcetto d'Alba '11	♥♥ 2*
● Barbera d'Alba Sup. Bricco Appiani '07	♥ 4
● Barolo Ravera '07	♀♀♀ 5
● Barolo Ravera '04	♀♀♀ 5
● Barolo Ravera '01	♀♀♀ 5
● Barolo Ravera '97	♀♀♀ 5
● Bricco Appiani '99	♀♀♀ 5
● Barolo Ravera '06	♀♀ 5
● Dolcetto d'Alba '09	♀♀ 2*
● Dolcetto d'Alba Sup. '09	♀♀ 3*
● Nebbiolo d'Alba '07	♀♀ 4

Ronchi

S.DA RONCHI, 23
12050 BARBARESCO [CN]
TEL. 0173635156
info@aziendaagricolaronchi.it

CELLAR SALES
PRE-BOOKED VISITS
ANNUAL PRODUCTION 30,000 bottles
HECTARES UNDER VINE 7.00

Year after year, the estate run by Giancarlo Rocca with the precious aid of his wife Paola is showing itself to be an excellent interpreter of the local wine. Great attention in the vineyard and cellar is the key to the success achieved with the latest vintages. The grapes are grown in very well-aspected plots in the municipality of Barbaresco, while the style of the wines is an ideal marriage of power and elegance, also due to the skilfully calibrated use of small wooden casks and Slavonian oak barrels. In addition to the selections of Barbaresco, the estate also produces an excellent Barbera and a very juicy Chardonnay. The interesting Barbaresco 2009, distinguished by the red script denoting the Ronchi cru, has a nose dominated by juicy berry fruit and medicinal herbs and a muscular palate with gutsy but discreet tannins. The well-typed and exceptionally focused Dolcetto d'Alba 2012 is juicy and outstandingly drinkable.

● Barbaresco '09	♥♥ 5
● Barbera d'Alba Terlé '11	♥♥ 3
● Dolcetto d'Alba '12	♥♥ 2*
● Langhe Rosso '11	♥♥ 4
● Barbaresco Ronchi '04	♀♀♀ 6
● Barbaresco '07	♀♀ 5
● Barbaresco Et. Blu '08	♀♀ 5
● Barbaresco Et. Rossa '08	♀♀ 5
● Barbaresco Ronchi '07	♀♀ 5*
● Barbaresco Ronchi '06	♀♀ 5*
● Barbaresco Ronchi '05	♀♀ 5
● Barbaresco Ronchi '03	♀♀ 6
○ Langhe Chardonnay '10	♀♀ 3
○ Langhe Chardonnay '09	♀♀ 3

Giovanni Rosso

LOC. BAUDANA, 6
12050 SERRALUNGA D'ALBA [CN]
TEL. 0173613340
www.giovannirosso.com

CELLAR SALES
PRE-BOOKED VISITS
ANNUAL PRODUCTION 55,000 bottles
HECTARES UNDER VINE 10.00

In the space of just a few years, this Langhe estate, now headed by Davide Rosso, has managed to carve out an important place for itself on the Italian and international wine scenes. The wines of its range are characterized by expressive power and well-defined flavours. Exceptionally alluring even when young, they nonetheless offer the finest sensations when aged, as demonstrated by a recent tasting of Barolo Cerretta 2001, which displayed stunningly sound fruit and depth. The Barolo La Serra 2009 shows a complete, complex sensory range revealing notes of aniseed, tobacco, violets and gentian, paving the way for a vibrant, savoury, leisurely palate: Tre Bicchieri. The Barolo Cerretta 2009 is still austere on the nose but promises excellent development in the bottle.

● Barolo La Serra '09	♟♟♟ 7
● Barolo Cerretta '09	♟♟ 7
● Barolo V. Rionda Tommaso Canale '09	♟♟ 8
● Barbera d'Alba Donna Margherita '11	♟♟ 3
● Barolo di Serralunga d'Alba '09	♟♟ 5
● Langhe Nebbiolo '11	♟♟ 4
● Barolo Cerretta '06	♟♟♟ 7
● Barolo La Serra '08	♟♟♟ 7
● Barbera d'Alba Donna Margherita '10	♟♟ 3*
● Barbera d'Alba Donna Margherita '09	♟♟ 3*
● Barolo Cerretta '07	♟♟ 7
● Barolo Cerretta '05	♟♟ 7
● Barolo di Serralunga '08	♟♟ 5
● Barolo V. Rionda Tommaso Canale '08	♟♟ 8

Rovellotti

INTERNO CASTELLO, 22
28074 GHEMME [NO]
TEL. 0163841781
www.rovellotti.it

CELLAR SALES
ANNUAL PRODUCTION 50,000 bottles
HECTARES UNDER VINE 17.00

Situated in the heart of the ancient Ricetto di Ghemme, Antonello and Paolo Rovellotti's winery is one of the most picturesque in Upper Piedmont. Steeped in history and absolute respect for tradition, it is nonetheless a dynamic concern. Nebbiolo, vespolina, uva rara and erbaluce are the focus of the work in the vineyards, but in the past they have also experimented with international varieties such as cabernet, merlot and pinot nero. Despite the challenges of working in confined areas, the reds are released only after prolonged oak-ageing and consistently display a solid, classic approach in terms of extract. The overall performance was below the usual standard, also due to the limited range, but for the first time there was a thoroughly deserved Tre Bicchieri, for the Ghemme Chioso dei Pomi 2007, whose sensations on the palate reflect the generous vintage and the finesse of the terroir. As always, the Nebbiolo Valplazza impressed.

● Ghemme Chioso dei Pomi '07	♟♟♟ 4*
● Colline Novaresi Nebbiolo Valplazza '10	♟♟ 2*
○ Colline Novaresi Bianco Il Criccone '12	♟ 2
○ Colline Novaresi Nebbiolo Valplazza '12	♟ 2
○ Colline Novaresi Bianco Vitigno Innominabile Il Criccone '11	♟♟ 2*
○ Colline Novaresi Bianco Vitigno Innominabile Il Criccone '10	♟♟ 2*
● Colline Novaresi Vespolina Ronco al Maso '11	♟♟ 2*
● Colline Novaresi Vespolina Ronco al Maso '10	♟♟ 2
● Ghemme Chioso dei Pomi '06	♟♟ 5
● Ghemme Costa del Salmino Ris. '05	♟♟ 5

Podere Ruggeri Corsini

LOC. BUSSIA CORSINI, 106
12065 MONFORTE D'ALBA [CN]
TEL. 017378625
www.ruggericorsini.com

CELLAR SALES
PRE-BOOKED VISITS
ANNUAL PRODUCTION 75,000 bottles
HECTARES UNDER VINE 9.80

This family-run winery is very young and dynamic. Founded in 1995 in Monforte d'Alba, it has always been enthusiastically run by agriculture graduates Loredana Addari and Nicola Argamante, who decided to abandon their respective jobs and dedicate themselves to winegrowing by purchasing this little estate. Highly esteemed in Italy and a familiar name on several of the leading international markets, it produces mainly classic Langhe wines: Dolcetto, Barbera and Barolo, alongside international white and Langhe DOC grape varieties. The Barolo Bussia Corsini 2009 offers notes of morello cherry, liquorice and spice, with well-structured tannins and a fresh acid vein. The Barolo San Pietro 2009 is at a difficult age, and while displaying elegance and balance, is still struggling to show its full potential.

● Barbera d'Alba Sup. Armujan '11	♀♀ 3
● Barolo Bussia Corsini '09	♀♀ 5
● Barolo San Pietro '09	♀♀ 5
● Dolcetto d'Alba '12	♀♀ 2*
○ Langhe Bianco '12	♀♀ 2*
● Langhe Rosso Argamakow '11	♀♀ 4
● Langhe Rosso Autenzio '09	♀♀ 4
● Barbera d'Alba '12	♀ 2
● Langhe Rosso Autenzio '10	♀ 4
● Barbera d'Alba Sup. Armujan '09	♀♀ 3
● Barolo Corsini '06	♀♀ 5
● Barolo S. Pietro '05	♀♀ 5
● Barolo San Pietro '08	♀♀ 5
● Langhe Rosso Autenzio '08	♀♀ 3

Josetta Saffirio

LOC. CASTELLETTO, 39
12065 MONFORTE D'ALBA [CN]
TEL. 0173787278
www.josettasaffirio.com

CELLAR SALES
PRE-BOOKED VISITS
ANNUAL PRODUCTION 25,000 bottles
HECTARES UNDER VINE 5.50

We first profiled this estate in the Guide at the end of the 1980s thanks to the extraordinary quality of several unforgettable Barolos. After a long sabbatical, it is back again, several hectares larger and under the management of the young Sara supported by her parents, Josetta and Roberto Vezza. Heir to the winemaking project of her maternal grandfather, Ernesto Saffirio, Sara has decided to give the winery in Castelletto in Monforte d'Alba a good shake-up. In addition to the classic Barolo and a new label, the Barolo Millenovecento48, the year in which Josetta's grandfather planted one of the first nebbiolo vineyards, the estate also produces and sells Barbera d'Alba and Langhe Nebbiolo. The Barolo Persiera 2009 proffers aromas ranging from medicinal herbs to darker, seductive notes of liquorice and quinine, over a palate characterized by taut acidity and incisive tannins. The drinkable Barolo 2009 plays on fresh, balsamic tones and shows good focus. We loved the Barbera d'Alba 2011.

● Barbera d'Alba '11	♀ 3*
● Barolo '09	♀♀ 5
● Barolo Persiera '09	♀♀ 7
● Barolo Millenovecento48 Ris. '07	♀♀ 7
● Langhe Nebbiolo '11	♀♀ 3
● Barolo '89	♀♀♀ 6
● Barolo '88	♀♀♀ 6
● Barolo Francesco Millenovecento48 '07	♀♀ 7
● Barolo Persiera '08	♀♀ 7
● Barolo Persiera '07	♀♀ 7
● Barolo Persiera '06	♀♀ 7
● Barolo Persiera Ris. '04	♀♀ 8
○ Langhe Bianco '09	♀♀ 3*
○ Langhe Bianco '08	♀♀ 3*

San Bartolomeo

LOC. VALLEGGE
CASCINA SAN BARTOLOMEO, 26
15066 GAVI [AL]
TEL. 0143643180
www.sanbartolomeo-gavi.it

CELLAR SALES

At last! An excellent performance sees
Fulvio Bergaglio promoted to a full profile.
The Cascina San Bartolomeo, the site of an
old convent, was acquired way back in
1916 by Fulvio's great-grandfather,
Giuseppe Bergaglio. The family's devotion to
the farm and vineyards has not wavered
over the years, nor has their love of cortese,
which accounts for all of the 20 plus
hectares planted to vine. The secret of their
success remains the same: obsessive care
for the vineyards and a rich ampelography
of great biodiversity thanks to vines of more
than 90 years of age. History, passion and
tradition come together in just two Gavi
labels: Quinto and Pelöia. Our preferences
for the 2012 vintage leaned slightly towards
the Quinto, which proved graceful and
complex, with juicy acidity to liven up the
finish. Trailing behind came the Pelöia,
which lacked that extra gear we appreciated
so much last year.

○ Gavi Quinto '12	♀♀ 2*
○ Gavi del Comune di Gavi Pelöia '12	♀♀ 3
○ Gavi '09	♀♀ 2*
○ Gavi del Comune di Gavi Pelöia '11	♀♀ 3*
○ Gavi del Comune di Gavi Pelöia '09	♀♀ 3
○ Gavi Quinto '11	♀♀ 2*
○ Gavi Quinto '10	♀♀ 2*

Tenuta San Sebastiano

CASCINA SAN SEBASTIANO, 41
15040 LU [AL]
TEL. 0131741353
www.dealessi.it

CELLAR SALES
PRE-BOOKED VISITS
ANNUAL PRODUCTION 70,000 bottles
HECTARES UNDER VINE 9.00

Those who know Roberto De Alessi cannot
help but note the pride and passion with
which he speaks about his estate and his
wines. The same passion has infected his
son, Fabio, who although still young already
has a good grasp of how things work in the
vineyard and cellar. The estate relies largely
on indigenous Piedmont varieties but also
cultivates merlot and cabernet sauvignon
that go to make the Dalera, and pinot nero,
which is used in the Sol-Do, not reviewed
in this edition of the Guide. Mepari was
once again on top form. The 2010 version
shows an impenetrable deep ruby hue, with
a jammy nose and character as well as
good length on the palate. We liked the
2011 version of the Barbera Monferrato,
with its fruity aromas, harmoniously echoed
on the palate. The drinkable Grignolino and
a powerful, intense Dalera, that still needs
to age, are also worthy of note.

● Barbera del M.to '11	♀♀ 2*
● Barbera del M.to Sup. Mepari '10	♀♀ 4
● Piemonte Grignolino '12	♀♀ 2*
● M.to Rosso Dalera '10	♀ 3
● Barbera del M.to '09	♀♀ 2*
● Barbera del M.to Sup. Mepari '09	♀♀ 4
● Barbera del M.to Sup. Mepari '08	♀♀ 4
● Barbera del M.to Sup. Mepari '07	♀♀ 4
● Barbera del M.to Sup. Mepari '06	♀♀ 4
● M.to Rosso Dalera '08	♀♀ 3
● M.to Rosso Sol-Do '09	♀♀ 3
● M.to Rosso Sol-Do '05	♀♀ 3*

★Luciano Sandrone

VIA PUGNANE, 4
12060 BAROLO [CN]
TEL. 0173560023
www.sandroneluciano.com

CELLAR SALES
PRE-BOOKED VISITS
ANNUAL PRODUCTION 95,000 bottles
HECTARES UNDER VINE 25.00

The modernist best loved by the traditionalists one could say, playing on the clichés that are often attached to those who interpret Langhe nebbiolo. Like all the greats, Luciano Sandrone – with the support of his daughter Barbara and brother Luca – manages to express his Barolo crus with a power and a personality that go way beyond mere oenology. Both Cannubi Boschis and Le Vigne age for 24 months in 500-litre barrels after maceration for approximately ten days. The Barbera and Dolcetto are similar in style. Despite no great solos, the overall performance was impressive. The complex, deep Barolo Cannubi Boschis 2009 shows notes of tobacco, quinine, balsam and spice, over a lingering, vibrant palate. The Barolo Le Vigne 2009 is already extremely expressive and beautifully typed, with polished tannins and fresh acidity.

● Barolo Cannubi Boschis '09	♟♟	8
● Barolo Le Vigne '09	♟♟	8
● Barbera d'Alba '11	♟♟	5
● Nebbiolo d'Alba Valmaggiore '11	♟♟	5
● Dolcetto d'Alba '11	♟	3
● Barolo '83	♟♟♟	7
● Barolo Cannubi Boschis '08	♟♟♟	8
● Barolo Cannubi Boschis '07	♟♟♟	8
● Barolo Cannubi Boschis '06	♟♟♟	8
● Barolo Cannubi Boschis '05	♟♟♟	8
● Barolo Cannubi Boschis '04	♟♟♟	8
● Barolo Cannubi Boschis '03	♟♟♟	8
● Barolo Cannubi Boschis '01	♟♟♟	8
● Barolo Cannubi Boschis '00	♟♟♟	8
● Barolo Le Vigne '99	♟♟♟	8

Cantine Sant'Agata

REG. MEZZENA, 19
14030 SCURZOLENGO [AT]
TEL. 0141203186
www.santagata.com

CELLAR SALES
PRE-BOOKED VISITS
CELLAR SALES
ANNUAL PRODUCTION 150,000 bottles
HECTARES UNDER VINE 12.00

Four production lines, three properties and 20 labels, of which eight are dedicated to ruché, are the numbers that describe the estate belonging to brothers Claudio and Franco Cavallero. Their flagship variety is obviously ruché, which they cultivate at Scurzolengo in chalky clayey terrains in vineyards that fan out around the cellar. Their other plots lie in the municipalities of Canelli, which are largely given over to moscato, and Monforte d'Alba, where they grow the nebbiolo that goes to make the two Barolos. Barbera, grignolino, cortese, chardonnay and pinot nero round out the ranks of grape types. The wines of the Cavallero brothers impressed across the board. The Barolo Bussia 2008 shows notes of tobacco and aromatic herbs, and a fleshy, although highly austere palate, due to slightly aggressive tannins, while the Barbaresco La Fenice 2010 is suppler. The Ruché di Castagnole Monferrato Pro Nobis 2011 is fresh and aromatic.

● Barbaresco La Fenice '10	♟♟	4
● Barolo Bussia '08	♟♟	5
● Ruché di Castagnole M.to Pro Nobis '11	♟♟	3
● Barbera d'Asti Baby '11	♟	2
● Barbera d'Asti Sup. Cavalé '10	♟	4
● Ruché di Castagnole M.to 'Na Vota '12	♟	3
● M.to Rosso Monterovere '09	♙♙	4
● Ruché di Castagnole M.to 'Na Vota '11	♙♙	3
● Ruché di Castagnole M.to Genesi '08	♙♙	5
⊙ Suavissimus Rosé Brut '09	♙♙	4

Paolo Saracco

VIA CIRCONVALLAZIONE, 6
12053 CASTIGLIONE TINELLA [CN]
TEL. 0141855113
www.paolosaracco.it

CELLAR SALES
PRE-BOOKED VISITS
ANNUAL PRODUCTION 600,000 bottles
HECTARES UNDER VINE 45.00

Paolo Saracco, the third generation of his family to run this estate, is probably the best-known Moscato producer in the world. In recent years, the quest for the best positions for this variety has led him to acquire a series of plots. Today, he has 14 different vineyards at altitudes that vary between 300 and 460 metres in terrains that are predominantly sandy with elements of silt and limestone. Next to the moscato he cultivates pinot nero, riesling, traminer and chardonnay. The Moscatos favour elegance and aromatic expression over the sweetness of the fruit. This year we particularly liked both the Piemonte Moscato d'Autunno 2012, with its aromas of white-fleshed fruit, lime and medicinal herbs, and full, fresh, leisurely palate, and the less powerful but stylish Moscato d'Asti 2012, fruit-driven and attractively aromatic. The Piemonte Pinot Nero 2010 is graceful, but the tannins are too pushy for the delicately structured palate.

○ Moscato d'Asti '12		♎♎ 3*
○ Piemonte Moscato d'Autunno '12		♎♎ 3*
● Piemonte Pinot Nero '10		♎♎ 5
○ Langhe Chardonnay Prasuè '12		♎ 3
○ Langhe Riesling '12		♎ 3
○ Piemonte Moscato d'Autunno '09		♛♛♛ 3*
● M.to Rosso Pinot Nero '08		♛♛ 5
○ Moscato d'Asti '11		♛♛ 3
○ Piemonte Moscato d'Autunno '11		♛♛ 3*
○ Piemonte Moscato d'Autunno '10		♛♛ 3
● Piemonte Pinot Nero '09		♛♛ 5

Roberto Sarotto

VIA RONCONUOVO, 13
12050 NEVIGLIE [CN]
TEL. 0173630228
www.robertosarotto.com

CELLAR SALES
PRE-BOOKED VISITS
ANNUAL PRODUCTION 700,000 bottles
HECTARES UNDER VINE 84.00

Years ago Sarotto invested in a series of vineyards in the municipalities of Barolo, Barbaresco and Gavi, gradually putting together a truly comprehensive range of the region's leading designations. In addition to selections of the great Langhe wines, production includes the Dolcetto, Barbera, Moscato and small amounts of Cabernet Sauvignon, blended with the Nebbiolo in the Langhe Rosso Enrico I. Today Roberto Sarotto is responsible for both the technical and the business sides of the estate. His wines are fresh, highly drinkable and reasonably priced. The superb Barolo Audace 2009 shows fresh, focused red berry fruit and quinine on the nose, while the Barbaresco Gaia Principe 2010 reveals its character with dark notes of tobacco and tar, over a long, well-focused finish. We also saw a good performance from the attractively mineral, floral Gavi Bric Sassi Manenti 2012.

● Barbaresco Gaia Principe '10		♎♎ 6
● Barolo Audace '09		♎♎ 5
○ Gavi del Comune di Gavi Bric Sassi Manenti '12		♎♎ 2*
● Barbera d'Alba Elena La Luna '11		♎♎ 5
● Barolo Briccobergera '09		♎♎ 5
○ Gavi Aurora '12		♎♎ 2*
○ Langhe Arneis Runcneuv '12		♎♎ 2*
● Langhe Nebbiolo Nativo '11		♎♎ 3
○ Moscato d'Asti Solatìo '12		♎♎ 3
● Barbaresco Currà Ris. '08		♎ 5
● Barbera d'Alba Briccomacchia '12		♎ 2
● Dolcetto d'Alba Angeli '12		♎ 2
○ Langhe Chardonnay Briccomoro '12		♎ 2
○ Piemonte Chardonnay '12		♎ 3
○ Gavi del Comune di Gavi Bric Sassi Tenuta Manenti '11		♛♛ 2*

Scagliola

VIA SAN SIRO, 42
14052 CALOSSO [AT]
TEL. 0141853183
www.scagliola-sansi.com

CELLAR SALES
PRE-BOOKED VISITS
ANNUAL PRODUCTION 150,000 bottles
HECTARES UNDER VINE 37.00

Nestling among the slopes of Calosso, the estate owned by the Scagliola family is one of the most important in Asti. As tradition dictates, the main varieties cultivated here are barbera and moscato, but there are a plethora of others too, including dolcetto, nebbiolo, brachetto, grignolino, cortese, cabernet and chardonnay. The bulk of the barbera vineyards lies around the cellar in Calosso in medium-textured terrains of limestone and clay. The moscato plots are in Canelli, in sandy marly soils. The two versions of Barbera d'Asti Superiore Sansì – the 2011 and the Selezione 2010 – both made our finals. The former is elegant, with fresh red berry fruit, tobacco and quinine, over a long, juicy palate with supporting acidity. The more complex Selezione offers plum jam and cocoa powder and a velvety, caressing palate with great balance and length. The pleasurable Barbera d'Asti Frem 2012 is close-knit and full-flavoured, while the Monferrato Rosso Azörd 2011 offers good complexity.

● Barbera d'Asti Sup. SanSì '11	▼▼ 6
● Barbera d'Asti Sup. SanSì Sel. '10	▼▼ 7
● Barbera d'Asti Frem '12	▼▼ 3
● M.to Rosso Azörd '11	▼▼ 5
○ Moscato d'Asti Primo Bacio '12	▼ 3
● Barbera d'Asti Sup. SanSì Sel. '01	♈♈♈ 6
● Barbera d'Asti Sup. SanSì Sel. '00	♈♈♈ 6
● Barbera d'Asti Sup. SanSì Sel. '99	♈♈♈ 6
● Barbera d'Asti Frem '11	♈♈ 3
● Barbera d'Asti Sup. SanSì '10	♈♈ 6
● Barbera d'Asti Sup. SanSì Sel. '09	♈♈ 7
● M.to Rosso Azörd '10	♈♈ 5

Giorgio Scarzello e Figli

VIA ALBA, 29
12060 BAROLO [CN]
TEL. 017356170
www.barolodibarolo.com

CELLAR SALES
PRE-BOOKED VISITS
ANNUAL PRODUCTION 25,000 bottles
HECTARES UNDER VINE 5.50

The hallmark of this important little Barolo estate is its extremely classic, timeless Langhe wines. Young Federico Scarzello coherently continues to pursue a concept of Nebbiolo and Barbera that fully respects the history of this area and its most venerable traditions. His wines are produced from estate-grown vineyard selections and have alluring personality, elegance and freshness, also due to the use of large oak barrels that give them an extremely austere style. The vineyards occupy prime sites, allowing the production of exceptionally fine grapes. The Barbera d'Alba Superiore 2010 is well typed and complex, playing on fruit notes of blackberry and cherry, with a vigorous palate characterized by taut acidity and juicy stuffing. The Barolo 2008 shows excellent focus on the nose, with dark hints of tar and tobacco, over solid, well-dosed tannins.

● Barbera d'Alba Sup. '10	▼▼ 4
● Barolo del Comune di Barolo '08	▼▼ 5
● Barolo V. Merenda '99	♈♈♈ 5
● Barbera d'Alba Sup. '08	♈♈ 4
● Barbera d'Alba Sup. '07	♈♈ 4
● Barolo '07	♈♈ 5
● Barolo '06	♈♈ 5
● Barolo '05	♈♈ 5
● Barolo Sarmassa V. Merenda '06	♈♈ 6
● Barolo V. Merenda '06	♈♈ 6
● Barolo V. Merenda '05	♈♈ 6
● Barolo V. Merenda '04	♈♈ 6
● Barolo V. Merenda '01	♈♈ 6
● Langhe Nebbiolo '10	♈♈ 3

★★Paolo Scavino

FRAZ. GARBELLETTO
VIA ALBA-BAROLO, 59
12060 CASTIGLIONE FALLETTO [CN]
TEL. 017362850
www.paoloscavino.com

CELLAR SALES
PRE-BOOKED VISITS
ANNUAL PRODUCTION 120,000 bottles
HECTARES UNDER VINE 23.00

This estate's origins reach back to the beginning of the last century and Enrico Scavino, the heart and soul of this important Langhe enterprise, tirelessly lavishes his energy and commitment on ensuring the continued success of his winemaking project. The extensive range well represents the finest wines of the area, with several exceptionally high-quality offerings that star on wine lists throughout the world. The splendid cellar and the vineyards, scattered among the most prestigious crus of the Barolo district, are a guarantee of notable and eminently cellarable wines. We saw outstanding all-round performance from Scavino's wines, headed by the Barolo Bric dël Fiasc 2009. Its complex nose of red berry fruit, mint and violet, paves the way for a gutsy, full-flavoured palate. We also liked the extremely drinkable Barolo Enrico Scavino 2009.

Schiavenza

VIA MAZZINI, 4
12050 SERRALUNGA D'ALBA [CN]
TEL. 0173613115
www.schiavenza.com

CELLAR SALES
PRE-BOOKED VISITS
CELLAR SALES
ANNUAL PRODUCTION 40,000 bottles
HECTARES UNDER VINE 9.00

If we think of the most forbidding and severe character that a Serralunga Barolo can possess, Schiavenza is one of the first names that comes to mind. Prapò, Bricco Cerretta, Broglio and Perno in Monforte: four grand crus interpreted through very lengthy sojourns in medium-sized barrels. These are wines that take time to develop their most lip-smacking, relaxed sensations in full. This style can be disconcerting at first, but not once you have sampled the friendliness of Luciano Pira and the wonderful atmosphere on the terrace of the family-run inn, an absolute must for those who love Piedmont cuisine accompanied by the perfect wines. Elegance and power are the distinctive traits of the Barolo Prapò 2009, with its generous, savoury palate and good length. The Barolo Broglio 2009 boasts dark notes on the nose, ranging from quinine to delicate hints of tar. The classic Barolo Serralunga 2009 was beautifully drinkable.

● Barolo Bric dël Fiasc '09	♔♔♔ 8
● Barolo Enrico Scavino '09	♔♔ 7
● Barolo Monvigliero '09	♔♔ 8
● Barolo Rocche dell'Annunziata Ris. '07	♔♔ 8
● Barbera d'Alba '12	♔♔ 3
● Barbera d'Alba Affinato in Carati '11	♔♔ 5
● Barolo Bricco Ambrogio '09	♔♔ 8
● Barolo Cannubi '09	♔♔ 8
● Barolo Carobric '09	♔♔ 8
○ Langhe Bianco Sorriso '12	♔♔ 3
● Langhe Nebbiolo '11	♔♔ 4
● Dolcetto d'Alba '12	♔ 3
● Barolo Bric dël Fiasc '06	♔♔♔ 8
● Barolo Monvigliero '08	♔♔♔ 8
● Barolo Rocche dell'Annunziata Ris. '05	♔♔♔ 8

● Barolo Bricco Cerretta '09	♔♔ 5
● Barolo Broglio '09	♔♔ 5
● Barolo Prapò '09	♔♔ 6
● Barolo Prapò Ris. '07	♔♔ 7
● Barolo Serralunga '09	♔♔ 5
● Barolo Broglio '05	♔♔♔ 5
● Barolo Broglio '04	♔♔♔ 5
● Barolo Broglio Ris. '04	♔♔♔ 5
● Barolo Prapò '08	♔♔♔ 6
● Barolo Broglio '08	♔♔ 5
● Barolo Broglio '07	♔♔ 5
● Barolo Prapò '07	♔♔ 6
● Barolo Prapò '06	♔♔ 5
● Barolo Serralunga '08	♔♔ 5

Scrimaglio

s.da Alessandria, 67
14049 Nizza Monferrato [AT]
Tel. 0141721385
www.scrimaglio.it

CELLAR SALES
PRE-BOOKED VISITS
ANNUAL PRODUCTION 700,000 bottles
HECTARES UNDER VINE 20.00
VITICULTURE METHOD Certified Organic

Founded in 1920, the estate belonging to
the Scrimaglio family is one of the most
interesting in Monferrato. The wide array of
wines on offer is broken down into several
lines, which feature the most important
Piedmont varieties in addition to several
versions of Barbera. The various labels run
the gamut of the simplest bottles conceived
for everyday drinking to more structured,
ambitious wines. However, they all have the
same common denominator: an approach
that weds respect for the territory's identity
to character, enormous focus and aromatic
precision. The Barbera d'Asti Superiore
Nizza Acsé 2010 was once more one of the
best in its class, and took home a Tre
Bicchieri. Attractive notes of dark berry fruit
and quinine, with hints of tobacco and
spice, lead into a powerful, richly flavoured,
lingering palate. We were also impressed
with the Monferrato Rosso Tantra 2010,
from barbera and 20% cabernet sauvignon,
showing juicy, full fruit and a touch of spice.
The other Barberas presented were as
reliable as ever.

● Barbera d'Asti Sup. Nizza Acsé '10	♥♥♥	5
● M.to Rosso Tantra '10	♥♥	5
● Barbera d'Asti Sup. Fiat '11	♥♥	4
● Barbera d'Asti Sup. Il Sogno '10	♥♥	3
● Barbera d'Asti Sup. RoccaNivo '11	♥♥	2*
● Barbera d'Asti Sup. Nizza Acsé '09	♀♀♀	5
● Barbera d'Asti Sup. Nizza Acsé '08	♀♀♀	5
● Barbera d'Asti Sup. Nizza Acsé '07	♀♀♀	5
● Barbera d'Asti Sup. Crôutin '08	♀♀	5
● Barbera d'Asti Sup. Fiat '10	♀♀	4
● Barbera d'Asti Sup. RoccaNivo '10	♀♀	2*
● M.to Rosso Tantra '09	♀♀	5

Mauro Sebaste

fraz. Gallo
via Garibaldi, 222bis
12051 Alba [CN]
Tel. 0173262148
www.maurosebaste.it

CELLAR SALES
PRE-BOOKED VISITS
ANNUAL PRODUCTION 150,000 bottles
HECTARES UNDER VINE 22.00

Mauro Sebaste, aided by his wife Maria
Teresa, confidently runs this important
cellar that vaunts a comprehensive range
representative of many important Piedmont
wine designations. The estate-owned and
leased vineyards are first-rate and are
crowned by an array of Barolo crus that
have earned the winery an enthusiastic
international following. All the wines, both
Langhe and Roero, have an austere,
elegant style and a perfect balance of
terroir trueness and drinkability. The Barolo
Prapò 2009 boasts a bright ruby hue, with
delicate aromas of gentian, rhubarb and
liquorice, whose close-knit tannins ensure
a long finish. The well-structured Barbera
Superiore Centobricchi 2011 shows juicy
and fruity, and is also wonderfully drinkable
thanks to its fresh acidic vein.

● Barbera d'Alba Sup. Centobricchi '11	♥♥	4
● Barolo Prapò '09	♥♥	7
● Nebbiolo d'Alba Parigi '11	♥♥	4
● Barbera d'Alba S. Rosalia '11	♥	3
○ Langhe Bianco Centobricchi '12	♥	3
○ Roero Arneis '12	♥	3
● Barbera d'Alba Sup. Centobricchi '10	♀♀	4
● Barolo Brunate '03	♀♀	6
● Barolo Brunate '01	♀♀	6
● Barolo Monvigliero '07	♀♀	6
● Barolo Monvigliero '04	♀♀	6
● Barolo Prapò '08	♀♀	7
● Barolo Prapò '05	♀♀	7
● Barolo Prapò '04	♀♀	7

F.lli Seghesio

LOC. CASTELLETTO, 19
12065 MONFORTE D'ALBA [CN]
TEL. 017378108
www.fratelliseghesio.it

Tenute Sella

VIA IV NOVEMBRE, 130
13060 LESSONA [BI]
TEL. 01599455
www.tenutesella.it

CELLAR SALES
PRE-BOOKED VISITS
ANNUAL PRODUCTION 60,000 bottles
HECTARES UNDER VINE 10.00

CELLAR SALES
PRE-BOOKED VISITS
ANNUAL PRODUCTION 95,000 bottles
HECTARES UNDER VINE 21.00

We retasted a Barolo la Villa 2001 and a 2004 vintage on the same evening and can guarantee the soundness and deep complexity of these two superb wines, capable of offering great satisfaction to those who manage to find them in the coming years. This small family-run estate has been steering a steady course for many years, painstakingly tending its fine vineyards and making wines with a well-defined character. Ageing takes place in barrels of different sizes to ensure that the consistently first-rate fruit is never overwhelmed by oak. The Barbera d'Alba Vigneto della Chiesa 2010 stands out for its depth and juiciness, with red berry fruits and autumn leaves underpinning a gutsy, full-flavoured palate. The Barolo La Villa 2009 offers a complex nose of tobacco, sweet liquorice and violets, underpinned by incisive tannins and a well-balanced acidic swathe.

The standing of the Sella family in the production area of Biella – and beyond – is deeply rooted in a tradition that dates back more than three centuries. It is largely thanks to their wines that today we can talk of Lessona's sandy soil and Bramaterra's porphyry not just as oenological rarities, but as remarkable territories that enhance nebbiolo's subtlest characteristics when combined with vespolina and croatina. The barrel cellar houses 25-hectolitre casks of Slavonian oak and partly new barriques, technical variables that have a completely relative bearing on the definition of an authentically classic style, thanks also to the work of Cristiano Garella. Performance across the range was not as brilliant as usual, but only due to the absence of important labels whose release has been delayed. We were however blessed with Sella's pride and joy, the famous Lessona Omaggio a Quintino Sella, whose 2007 version is less focused and elegant than usual, but benefits in terms of unprecedented softness.

● Barbera d'Alba Vign. della Chiesa '10	♀♀ 4
● Barolo La Villa '09	♀♀ 7
● Barbera d'Alba '12	♀♀ 3
● Barbera d'Alba Vign. della Chiesa '00	♀♀♀ 4*
● Barbera d'Alba Vign. della Chiesa '97	♀♀♀ 4*
● Barolo Vign. La Villa '04	♀♀♀ 6
● Barolo Vign. La Villa '99	♀♀♀ 7
● Barolo Vign. La Villa '91	♀♀♀ 4*
● Barbera d'Alba Vign. della Chiesa '06	♀♀ 4
● Barbera d'Alba Vign. della Chiesa '05	♀♀ 4
● Barolo Vign. La Villa '08	♀♀ 6
● Barolo Vign. La Villa '07	♀♀ 6
● Barolo Vign. La Villa '06	♀♀ 6
● Barolo Vign. La Villa '05	♀♀ 6

● Lessona Omaggio a Quintino Sella '07	♀♀ 7
○ Coste della Sesia Bianco Doranda '12	♀♀ 3
● Coste della Sesia Orbello '12	♀♀ 3
● Coste della Sesia Rosso Casteltorto '11	♀♀ 4
⊙ Coste della Sesia Rosato Majoli '12	♀ 3
● Bramaterra I Porfidi '07	♀♀♀ 5
● Bramaterra I Porfidi '05	♀♀♀ 5
● Lessona Omaggio a Quintino Sella '06	♀♀♀ 7
● Lessona Omaggio a Quintino Sella '05	♀♀♀ 6
● Bramaterra '09	♀♀ 5
● Bramaterra I Porfidi '08	♀♀ 5
● Coste della Sesia Orbello '11	♀♀ 3
● Lessona '09	♀♀ 5
● Lessona S. Sebastiano allo Zoppo '07	♀♀ 6

Enrico Serafino

c.so Asti, 5
12043 Canale [CN]
Tel. 0173979485
www.enricoserafino.it

CELLAR SALES
PRE-BOOKED VISITS
ANNUAL PRODUCTION 500,000 bottles
HECTARES UNDER VINE 12.00

Enrico Serafino, owned by the Campari
group, has made a comeback in recent
years and is once again a leading light of
the Roero winemaking world. The estate
makes several product lines, including the
noteworthy Roero Cantina Maestra still
wines and the Alta Langa sparklers. While
the Roero wines hail from estate-owned
vineyards in the municipality of Canale, the
Alta Langa ones are made from the grapes
of 14 growers, whose work in the vineyard
is monitored year-round by Serafino's expert
staff. There is also a series of good wines
from the leading Piedmont winegrowing
regions. Not content with being one of Italy's
best sparklers, this year it took the award
for Sparkler of the Year. The Alta Langa Brut
Zero Cantina Maestra 2007 is intense and
multifaceted, with aromas of spice, cakes
and citrus, over an austere, generous palate
of superb length. The well-executed Roero
Arneis 2012 offers a floral nose with hints
of white-fleshed fruit, followed by good,
dense structure, although a touch too much
alcoholic warmth.

○ Alta Langa Brut Zero	
Cantina Maestra '07	♥♥♥ 6
○ Roero Arneis '12	♥♥ 3
● Barbera d'Alba Bacajé	
Cantina Maestra '12	♥ 3
● Nebbiolo d'Alba Diauleri	
Cantina Maestra '11	♥ 3
○ Roero Arneis Canteiò	
Cantina Maestra '12	♥ 3
○ Alta Langa Brut Zero	
Cantina Maestra '06	♥♥♥ 6
○ Alta Langa Brut Zero	
Cantina Maestra Ris. '05	♥♥♥ 6
○ Alta Langa Brut Zero	
Cantina Maestra Ris. '04	♥♥♥ 4
○ Alta Langa Brut Cantina Maestra '07	♥♥ 4
● Nebbiolo d'Alba Diauleri	
Cantina Maestro '10	♥♥ 3

Aurelio Settimo

fraz. Annunziata, 30
12064 La Morra [CN]
Tel. 017350803
www.aureliosettimo.com

CELLAR SALES
PRE-BOOKED VISITS
ANNUAL PRODUCTION 40,000 bottles
HECTARES UNDER VINE 6.64

Until the 1950s, this estate sold the grapes
from its vineyards to local producers, but in
the mid-1960s it started vinifying a good
proportion of them itself. However, it was
not until 1974 that all the grapes went to
make its own wine. Today it is Aurelio's
daughter Tiziana who manages both the
business side of the venture and operations
in the cellar. The style of the wines is very
classic and restrained, particularly the
Barolo Rocche dell'Annunziata, from the
cru of the same name, which is
magnificently true to its terroir. We saw a
fine overall performance from the range
presented by the Settimo family, and their
interpretation of nebbiolo is perfect. The
approachable Barolo 2009 is brimming
with smooth tannins, in contrast with the
more closed, austere character of the
Rocche dell'Annunziata 2009, that takes
time to open up.

● Barolo '09	♥♥ 5
● Barolo Rocche dell' Annunziata '09	♥♥ 6
● Langhe Nebbiolo '08	♥♥ 3
● Dolcetto d'Alba '11	♥ 2
● Barolo '08	♀♀ 5
● Barolo '07	♀♀ 5
● Barolo Rocche '06	♀♀ 5
● Barolo Rocche '97	♀♀ 5
● Barolo Rocche '96	♀♀ 5
● Barolo Rocche dell' Annunziata '08	♀♀ 6
● Barolo Rocche dell' Annunziata '07	♀♀ 5
● Barolo Rocche Ris. '04	♀♀ 7
● Barolo Rocche Ris. '96	♀♀ 7
● Langhe Nebbiolo '06	♀♀ 3

Giovanni Silva

Cascine Rogge, 1b
10011 Agliè [TO]
Tel. 012433356
www.silvavini.com

CELLAR SALES
PRE-BOOKED VISITS
HECTARES UNDER VINE 8.00

Silva encores its lightening debut in the Guide with an absolutely stellar performance for this edition. The family has always cultivated vines in the municipality of Agliè, south of Ivrea but only started selling their wines in the bottle in 1995. Giovanni manages the estate's eight hectares of vines with the help of his grandson, Stefano. Production obviously centres around Erbaluce in its myriad forms, from spumante to passito, but the estate also has an equally distinguished production of reds that are obtained from Canavese's indigenous varieties, nebbiolo, barbera, freisa, bonarda and neretta. This was a range without any weak points: two wines in the final and another brace just a whisker behind. Top honours went to the artisanally crafted Erbaluce Passito Poetica 2003, a rich, well-balanced wine with outstanding length. Almost as good were the dry whites, especially the Tre Ciochè 2012.

○ Caluso Passito Poetica '03	♀♀ 5
○ Erbaluce di Caluso Tre Ciochè '12	♀♀ 2*
● Canavese Nebbiolo '08	♀♀ 2*
○ Erbaluce di Caluso Dry Silva '12	♀♀ 2*
○ Caluso Passito Poetica '01	♀♀ 5
○ Caluso Passito Poetica '00	♀♀ 5
○ Caluso Passito Poetica '99	♀♀ 5
○ Caluso Passito Poetica '98	♀♀ 5
● Canavese Rosso Tre Ciochè '03	♀♀ 3
● Canavese Rosso Tre Ciochè '01	♀♀ 3
○ Erbaluce di Caluso Tre Ciochè '06	♀♀ 2*

La Smilla

via Garibaldi, 7
15060 Bosio [AL]
Tel. 0143684245
www.lasmilla.it

CELLAR SALES
ANNUAL PRODUCTION 100,000 bottles
HECTARES UNDER VINE 5.00

Danilo Guido's estate is at the southern tip of the Gavi district and the province of Alessandria, in an area that is already culturally and geographically Liguria, and overlaps with the Dolcetto di Ovada production zone. The terroir, particularly its vicinity to the sea, is reflected in a range produced from six hectares of estate-owned vineyards planted with the local grape varieties: barbera, dolcetto and cortese. All the wines are the result of simple vinification and ageing in steel, with the exception of the Gavi I Bergi and Barbera Calicanto, which are both aged in small French oak casks. Although it's hardly a failure, the grid of Smilla's wines is not as eye-catching as usual, with no red glasses. No fewer than three wines were given a two-glass rating, but none of them made the finals this year. The best wines are all still too young, in particular the Gavi I Bergi 2011, with its marked notes of vanilla.

○ Gavi del Comune di Gavi '12	♀♀ 2*
○ Gavi del Comune di Gavi I Bergi '11	♀♀ 3
● M.to Rosso Calicanto '10	♀♀ 3
● Barbera del M.to '11	♀ 2
● Dolcetto di Ovada '11	♀ 2
○ Gavi '12	♀ 2
● Dolcetto di Ovada '10	♀♀ 2*
● Dolcetto di Ovada '09	♀♀ 2*
● Dolcetto di Ovada '08	♀♀ 2*
○ Gavi '11	♀♀ 2*
○ Gavi del Comune di Gavi '11	♀♀ 2*
○ Gavi del Comune di Gavi '10	♀♀ 2*
○ Gavi del Comune di Gavi I Bergi '08	♀♀ 3

Socré

LOC. TRE STELLE
VIA RICCARDO TERZOLO, 7
12050 BARBARESCO [CN]
TEL. 3487121685
www.socre.it

ANNUAL PRODUCTION 20,000 bottles
HECTARES UNDER VINE 5.50

Since its founding in 1871, the Socré farm estate has been tended with passion by generations of the Piacentino family. The vineyards occupy stunning positions, including the magnificent Roncaglie cru. The turning point came in the early 1990s when Marco Piacentino, today joined by sons Giulio and Lorenzo, finished renovating the plots planted to the nebbiolo dedicated to Barbaresco. In 2012, he inaugurated the new cellar and was finally able to vinify on site the grapes grown on the estate. In addition to the Barbaresco and the other classic Langhe wines – Dolcetto, Barbera and Nebbiolo – the estate has hitched its wagon to Croatina and to Cisterna, a small new Asti DOC. In what amounted to a mini vertical tasting, the star was the attractive, fruit-driven Barbaresco Roncaglie 2009, offering complex aromas ranging from raspberry to aniseed. Next came the marvellous, austere Roncaglie 2010. We were also amazed by the class displayed in the 2010 versions.

● Barbaresco Roncaglie '09	♟♟ 7
● Barbaresco '10	♟♟ 5
● Barbaresco '08	♟♟ 5
● Barbaresco Roncaglie '10	♟♟ 7

★Sottimano

LOC. COTTÀ, 21
12052 NEIVE [CN]
TEL. 0173635186
www.sottimano.it

CELLAR SALES
PRE-BOOKED VISITS
ANNUAL PRODUCTION 85,000 bottles
HECTARES UNDER VINE 18.00

It is no coincidence that the Sottimano family's wines have met with acclaim from wine critics and enthusiasts with very different tastes, even during the years in which the debate over the two very different styles of Nebbiolo was at its fiercest. While the use of small oak casks for ageing may place their Barbarescos among the modern interpretations, the long macerations and above all the meticulous tending of prestigious crus such as Currà, Cottà, Fausoni and Pajorè put the Neive winery firmly in the most rigorous Langhe tradition. Exuberant extract and close-woven tannins are nonetheless distinctive traits in these wines when young, and should be borne in mind if opening ahead of time. To set the record straight, last year's prize-winning Barbaresco Currà was in fact from the 2008 vintage. This year, it was the Barbaresco Pajoré 2010 that took home top honours, with outstanding style and impeccable varietal definition. We were very impressed with the whole of the excellent range we tasted.

● Barbaresco Pajoré '10	♟♟♟ 7
● Barbaresco Cottà '10	♟♟ 7
● Barbaresco Currà '09	♟♟ 7
● Barbaresco Ris. '08	♟♟ 8
● Barbaresco Fausoni '10	♟♟ 7
● Barbera d'Alba Pairolero '11	♟♟ 4
● Langhe Nebbiolo '11	♟♟ 3
● Dolcetto d'Alba Bric del Salto '12	♟ 2
● Barbaresco Cottà '05	♟♟♟ 7
● Barbaresco Currà '08	♟♟♟ 7
● Barbaresco Currà '04	♟♟♟ 6
● Barbaresco Pajoré '08	♟♟♟ 7
● Barbaresco Pajorè '01	♟♟♟ 6
● Barbaresco Ris. '05	♟♟♟ 8
● Barbaresco Ris. '04	♟♟♟ 8

Luigi Spertino

VIA LEA, 505
14047 MOMBERCELLI [AT]
TEL. 0141959098
www.luigispertino.it

CELLAR SALES
PRE-BOOKED VISITS
ANNUAL PRODUCTION 40,000 bottles
HECTARES UNDER VINE 9.00

Back in 1978, Luigi Spertino – against the advice of his entire family – decided to bottle the wine that they had produced for two generations. Over the years, his estate has become the standard bearer for Grignolino. Today his son, Mauro, carries on his work with the same passion and dogged determination to follow his convictions in the production of high-quality wines, although he is focusing a bit more of his attention on Barbera. The La Mandorla line is obtained from partially dried grapes and is a prime example of the qualitative consistency and coherence of these wines. The 2010 Barbera d'Asti Superiore La Mandorla from partially dried grapes was back on Tre Bicchieri form. Concentrated and complex, it shows blackberry and plum jam, quinine, tobacco and rain-drenched earth over a close-knit, rounded palate with a long, juicy finish. We also loved the attractive earthy notes of the fresh, dynamic Barbera d'Asti 2011, and the classic, savoury Grignolino d'Asti 2012, which was true to type.

● Barbera d'Asti Sup. La Mandorla '10	♟♟♟ 8
● Barbera d'Asti '11	♟♟ 4
● Grignolino d'Asti '12	♟♟ 3
● Barbera d'Asti Sup. La Mandorla '09	♟♟♟ 8
● Barbera d'Asti Sup. La Mandorla '07	♟♟♟ 7
● M.to Rosso La Mandorla '09	♟♟♟ 7
● M.to Rosso La Mandorla '07	♟♟♟ 5
● Barbera d'Asti '10	♟♟ 4
● Barbera d'Asti '08	♟♟ 3
● Grignolino d'Asti '11	♟♟ 3*
● Grignolino d'Asti '10	♟♟ 3
● Grignolino d'Asti '09	♟♟ 3

★★★La Spinetta

VIA ANNUNZIATA, 17
14054 CASTAGNOLE DELLE LANZE [AT]
TEL. 0141877396
www.la-spinetta.com

CELLAR SALES
PRE-BOOKED VISITS
ANNUAL PRODUCTION 500,000 bottles
HECTARES UNDER VINE 100.00

The story of La Spinetta is one of the greatest in Piedmont winemaking, and is inspired by the entrepreneurism of the Rivetti family and in particular the genius of Giorgio, deus ex machina of this estate. The Rivetti brothers started out in Moscato d'Asti and expanded to Tuscany, where they produce sangiovese-based wines and extra virgin olive oil. The jewels in La Spinetta's crown are the Barolo Campè and the three magnificent Barbaresco crus. The combination of Giorgio's commercial skills and the distinctive production style favouring mature fruit has produced very impressive results in a very short time. Today, the wines are present on all of the most important international markets. Thanks to the inclusion of the Barolo and Barbaresco Riservas produced only in magnums and released 10 years after harvest, we were faced with an extensive range, although two vintages of the Barbaresco Valeirano and the Barolo Campè stood out. The splendid Barbera Bionzo 2011 has also been a benchmark for years.

● Barbaresco Vign. Valeirano '10	♟♟ 8
● Barbaresco Vign. Valeirano Ris. '04	♟♟ 8
● Barbera d'Asti Sup. Bionzo '11	♟♟ 6
● Barolo Campè '09	♟♟ 8
● Barbaresco Vign. Bordini '09	♟♟ 7
● Barbaresco Vign. Gallina '10	♟♟ 8
● Barbaresco Vign. Starderi '10	♟♟ 8
● Barbaresco Vign. Starderi Ris. '04	♟♟ 8
● Barbera d'Alba Vign. Gallina Ris. '04	♟♟ 6
● Barolo Campè Ris. '04	♟♟ 8
● Barolo Garretti '09	♟♟ 7
● M.to Rosso Pin '11	♟♟ 6
○ Moscato d'Asti Bricco Quaglia '12	♟♟ 3
○ Moscato d'Asti Passito Oro '06	♟♟ 6
● Barbera d'Asti Sup. Bionzo '09	♟♟♟ 6
● Barolo Campè '08	♟♟♟ 8

Sylla Sebaste

VIA SAN PIETRO, 4
12060 BAROLO [CN]
TEL. 017356266
www.syllasebaste.com

CELLAR SALES
PRE-BOOKED VISITS
CELLAR SALES
ANNUAL PRODUCTION 120,000 bottles
HECTARES UNDER VINE 10.00

After several ups and downs and almost
15 uninspired years, this historic brand in
Vergne, a district of the municipality of
Barolo, got a new lease of life in 2000
when it was acquired by the Merlo family,
Alba entrepreneurs with a passion for
wine. Since then, the young owner Fabrizio
and his highly skilled staff have made a
tremendous effort to put the estate back
on track. The vineyards have been
replanted and the new, fully equipped
cellar was completed in 2004. Barolo is at
the heart of Sylla Sebaste and it owns six
hectares here, in the Bussia or Monroniolo
di Bussia, San Pietro and Bricco delle Viole
crus planted exclusively to nebbiolo. A
second group of vineyards sits in Canale.
The range is obviously dominated by the
two 2009 Barolos, which share traits of
harmony and finesse. The Bussia, aged in
large and medium-sized barrels and
produced in quantities of almost 20,000
bottles, shows a touch more character
and length. We also liked the drinkable
Barbera 2011.

● Barolo Bussia '09	♟♟ 6
● Barbera d'Alba '11	♟♟ 3
● Barolo '09	♟♟ 6
○ Roero Arneis '12	♟ 3
● Barolo Bussia '85	♟♟♟ 6
● Barolo Bussia Ris. '84	♟♟♟ 6
● Barolo '08	♟♟ 6
● Barolo Bussia '07	♟♟ 7
● Barolo Bussia '06	♟♟ 6
● Nebbiolo d'Alba '09	♟♟ 2*

Luigi Tacchino

VIA MARTIRI DELLA BENEDICTA, 26
15060 CASTELLETTO D'ORBA [AL]
TEL. 0143830115
www.luigitacchino.it

CELLAR SALES
PRE-BOOKED VISITS
ANNUAL PRODUCTION 120,000 bottles
HECTARES UNDER VINE 12.00

We must give credit where credit's due. The
Tacchino family, and in particular the
stubborn Romina, have achieved some very
impressive results with this estate over the
last ten years. We say stubborn because at
a time when bunch thinning was considered
a waste of grapes in Ovada, she also had to
suffer the disapproval of smarter growers
who disapproved of her choices. We
therefore understand why she shed a tear
when the Du Riva earned its first Tre
Bicchieri in last year's edition of the Guide.
This was no emotional reaction to winning a
prize; it was vindication. The range
presented by the Tacchino family was quite
simply outstanding. Du Riva confirms its
place as the best Dolcetto in the Ovada
area: an intense, elegant wine with aromas
of red berry fruit, tobacco and spices,
leading into a marvellous palate of great
finesse and structure. The more modern
Albarola shows toasty oak and spice, but
also masses of fruit, followed by a powerful,
savoury palate with great length.

● Dolcetto di Ovada Sup. Du Riva '10	♟♟♟ 4*
● Barbera del M.to Albarola '11	♟♟ 5
● Barbera del M.to '12	♟♟ 2*
● Dolcetto di Ovada '11	♟♟ 2*
○ Gavi del Comune di Gavi '12	♟♟ 3
● M.to Rosso Di Fatto '10	♟♟ 5
○ Cortese dell'Alto M.to Marsenca '12	♟ 2
● Dolcetto di Ovada Sup. Du Riva '09	♟♟♟ 4*
● Dolcetto di Ovada Sup. Du Riva '08	♟♟♟ 4*
● Barbera del M.to '11	♟♟ 2*
● Barbera del M.to Albarola '09	♟♟ 3*
● Dolcetto di Ovada '10	♟♟ 2*
○ Gavi del Comune di Gavi '11	♟♟ 3
● M.to Rosso Di Fatto '09	♟♟ 5
● M.to Rosso Di Fatto '08	♟♟ 4

Michele Taliano

c.so A. Manzoni, 24
12046 Montà [CN]
Tel. 0173975658
www.talianomichele.com

CELLAR SALES
PRE-BOOKED VISITS
ANNUAL PRODUCTION 60,000 bottles
HECTARES UNDER VINE 12.00

The Taliano family's estate offers a wide range of Roero and Langhe wines. All its Roero vineyards are in the Bossola, Rolandi and Benna districts of the municipality of Montà and are planted with the classic grape varieties of the area, such as arneis, barbera, favorita and nebbiolo, while the Langhe sites, purchased in the 1970s, are situated in San Rocco Seno d'Elvio in the Barbaresco production zone, where nebbiolo, barbera, dolcetto and moscato are grown. The wines are often very solidly built and exceptionally austere, but also show good freshness and staying power. The lion's share goes to the traditional Barbaresco Ad Altiora 2010, vaunting elegant, complex aromas of dried flowers, medicinal herbs and liquorice, with close-knit, austere, yet not drying tannins. The dense, fruit-infused Barbera d'Alba Laboriosa 2010 is well-executed.

● Barbaresco Ad Altiora '10	♥♥ 5
● Barbera d'Alba Laboriosa '10	♥♥ 3
● Barbera d'Alba A Bon Rendre '12	♥ 2
● Nebbiolo d'Alba Blagheur '11	♥ 2
○ Roero Arneis Sernì '12	♥ 2
● Roero Ròche dra Bòssora Ris. '09	♥ 3
● Barbaresco Ad Altiora '09	♥♥ 5
● Barbaresco Ad Altiora '08	♥♥ 5
● Barbaresco Tera Mia Ris. '05	♥♥ 5
● Nebbiolo d'Alba Blagheur '09	♥♥ 3*
● Roero Ròche dra Bòssora Ris. '08	♥♥ 3

Tenuta La Tenaglia

s.da Santuario di Crea, 5c
15020 Serralunga di Crea [AL]
Tel. 0142940252
www.latenaglia.com

CELLAR SALES
PRE-BOOKED VISITS
ACCOMMODATION
ANNUAL PRODUCTION 120,000 bottles
HECTARES UNDER VINE 30.00

The historic La Tenaglia estate in Monferrato Casalese can trace its origins all the way back to the 17th century. The property extends across an area of extraordinary beauty, with woodland and vineyards sitting at an altitude of around 450 metres that have always linked it to viticulture. As for the production, the array of wines offers some splendid interpretations of local varieties barbera and grignolino. The estate also cultivates international grape types that go to make the Monferrato Rossos and the whites. La Tenaglia presented an impressive selection, with the Barbera 1930 and Grignolino both making our finals thanks to extraordinary sensory profiles and varietal character. On their heels is a superb version of the elegant, complex Barbera Emozioni. We also liked the intense power of the Monferrato Rosso Paradiso, which just needs more time to realize its potential.

● Barbera del M.to Sup. 1930 Una Buona Annata '09	♥♥ 5
● Grignolino del M.to Casalese '12	♥♥ 2*
● Barbera d'Asti Bricco Crea '12	♥♥ 2*
● Barbera d'Asti Emozioni '08	♥♥ 5
● M.to Rosso Paradiso '09	♥♥ 5
● Barbera del M.to '12	♥ 2
● Barbera del M.to Cappella 3 del Sacro Monte di Crea '12	♥ 2
⊙ M.to Chiaretto Edenrose '12	♥ 2
○ Piemonte Chardonnay '12	♥ 2
● Barbera d'Asti Giorgio Tenaglia '08	♥♥ 3
● Barbera del M.to '11	♥♥ 2*
● Barbera del M.to Cappella 3 del Sacro Monte di Crea '11	♥♥ 2*
● Grignolino del M.to Casalese '11	♥♥ 2*

Terre da Vino

VIA BERGESIA, 6
12060 BAROLO [CN]
TEL. 0173564611
www.terredavino.it

CELLAR SALES
PRE-BOOKED VISITS
ANNUAL PRODUCTION 1,200,000 bottles
HECTARES UNDER VINE 300.00
VITICULTURE METHOD Certified Organic

Thanks to the efficient staff of agronomist Daniele Eberle and oenologist Bruno Cordero, ever-present in the territory and in constant contact with the selected growers, the Barbera project launched in 1996 by director Piero Quadrumolo is fully underway for all of the estate's wines. The territory's co-operative wineries stepped up to the plate and, in response to the request issued by the main headquarters, they selected zones and growers where they could build a close and loyal relationship. Today, numbering 200 members and almost 300 selected hectares of vineyards, Terre da Vino is capable of offering great wines that encompass all the most prestigious DOCs in the region. In a wide range, it is the Barolo Essenze 2009 that stands out, with focused notes of red berry fruit, tobacco, spices, and close-knit tannins that give elegance to the long finish. The Barolo Essenze Riserva 2001 – bottled only in magnums – is bright and lively, coming from a vintage that, even many years later, shows all its potential.

● Barbera d'Alba Sup. Croere '11	♟♟ 4
● Barbera d'Asti Sup. La Luna e I Falò '11	♟♟ 3*
● Barolo Essenze '09	♟♟ 6
● Barolo Essenze Ris. '01	♟♟ 8
● Barbaresco La Casa in Collina '10	♟♟ 4
● Barolo Paesi Tuoi '09	♟♟ 5
○ Gavi del Comune di Gavi '12	♟♟ 3
● Langhe Nebbiolo La Malora '11	♟♟ 4
○ Piemonte Moscato Passito La Bella Estate '11	♟♟ 5
○ Piemonte Pinot Nero Extra Brut Molinera	♟♟ 3
● Barbera d'Asti San Nicolao '12	♟ 2
● Barolo Poderi Scarrone '08	♟ 7
● Dolcetto d'Alba Roccabella '12	♟ 2
○ Piemonte Chardonnay Vallerenza	♟ 2
○ Piemonte Sauvignon Chardonnay Tra Donne Sole '12	♟ 2

Terre del Barolo

VIA ALBA-BAROLO, 8
12060 CASTIGLIONE FALLETTO [CN]
TEL. 0173262053
www.terredelbarolo.com

CELLAR SALES
PRE-BOOKED VISITS
ANNUAL PRODUCTION 30,000,000 bottles
HECTARES UNDER VINE 650.00

As its name suggests, Terre del Barolo is a large co-operative with many Langhe member growers from different areas, whose vineyards cover a total area of over 600 hectares, ensuring a large production that offers excellent value for money. Founded in far-off 1958, the co-operative has come a long way since then. Today it is headed by Matteo Bosco, who is committed to giving this high-potential winery an increasingly distinctive identity. Some of the finest terroirs of Langhe can be found among the array of crus featured in the range. A brilliant hue and vibrant nose distinguish the Barolo Cannubi 2007, hinging on tones of red berry fruit and tobacco, with close-knit, harmonious tannins and impressive length. We should note the pleasing drinkability of the Barolo 2009, with its fresh fruit and good balance of tannins and acidity.

● Barolo Cannubi '07	♟♟ 7
● Barolo '09	♟♟ 5
● Barolo Monvigliero '07	♟♟ 6
● Barolo Ravera '07	♟♟ 6
● Barolo Rocche di Castiglione Ris. '06	♟♟ 7
● Nebbiolo d'Alba '11	♟♟ 3
● Barbera d'Alba Sup. '11	♟ 2
● Dolcetto d'Alba Castello '12	♟ 2
● Dolcetto di Diano d'Alba '12	♟ 2
● Barolo '06	♟♟ 5
● Barolo Cannubi '04	♟♟ 6
● Barolo Rocche Ris. '04	♟♟ 5*
● Diano d'Alba Cascinotto '11	♟♟ 2*
● Dolcetto d'Alba Castello '11	♟♟ 2*

Torraccia del Piantavigna

VIA ROMAGNANO, 69A
28067 GHEMME [NO]
TEL. 0163840040
www.torracciadelpiantavigna.it

CELLAR SALES
PRE-BOOKED VISITS
ANNUAL PRODUCTION 90,000 bottles
HECTARES UNDER VINE 40.00

The story of how the Francoli brothers
selected the trademark for their Ghemme
estate is a charming one. Torraccia is the
name of the place in Ghemme where the
first nebbiolo vineyard was planted in
1977; Piantavigna was the surname of
their maternal grandfather. The estate's 40
hectares are distributed across six different
zones in the provinces of Novara and
Vercelli. Nebbiolo, vespolina and erbaluce
are the only varieties grown. With the
support of Giuseppe Caviola in the cellar, a
broad and varied range of wines has been
crafted, whose most prestigious labels
require care and patience before they
reveal the immense power behind what can
be a rather oaky first impression. The two
jewels of this winery were on grand form.
These similar expressions of the same
variety come from neighbouring terroirs,
separated by the River Sesia and
administrative borders. The Gattinara
displays a more austere, essential style,
while the Ghemme is more relaxed and
accommodating.

● Gattinara '09	♟♟♟ 5
● Ghemme '09	♟♟ 5
○ Colline Novaresi Bianco Erbavoglio '12	♟ 3
⊙ Colline Novaresi Nebbiolo Rosato Barlàn '12	♟ 3
● Colline Novaresi Vespolina La Mostella '11	♟ 3
● Gattinara '06	♟♟♟ 5
● Gattinara '05	♟♟♟ 5
● Ghemme '07	♟♟♟ 5
● Ghemme Ris. '07	♟♟♟ 5
● Ghemme Ris. '07	♟♟♟ 5
● Colline Novaresi Vespolina La Mostella '10	♟♟ 2*
● Gattinara '08	♟♟ 5
● Gattinara '08	♟♟ 5

Giancarlo Travaglini

VIA DELLE VIGNE, 36
13045 GATTINARA [VC]
TEL. 0163833588
www.travaglinigattinara.it

CELLAR SALES
PRE-BOOKED VISITS
ANNUAL PRODUCTION 250,000 bottles
HECTARES UNDER VINE 45.00

With almost 60 out of a total of around 110
hectares dedicated to Gattinara nebbiolo, it
is no coincidence that this historic estate
run by Cinzia Travaglini and her husband
Massimo Collauto with the support of
Sergio Molino is a point of reference for
this variety. Its distinctive light, lean
personality is formed in the dry, airy climate
and iron-rich acidic soil. The influence of
the nearby Alps does the rest. These
characteristics are present in the basic
version, the Tre Vigne selection and the
Riserva, which differ according to their
vineyard of origin, typology and length of
oak ageing. The estate also produces Il
Sogno from super-ripe nebbiolo grapes.
This year the two most prestigious
Gattinaras from Travaglini just missed top
honours. With a vintage such as 2008, the
recent bottling date definitely contributed to
giving two reds whose quality is undoubted
but which are still young and somewhat
stiff, with austere tannins. We enjoyed
Sogno, made using the same production
technique as Sforzato di Valtellina, also
from nebbiolo.

● Gattinara Ris. '08	♟♟ 6
● Gattinara Tre Vigne '08	♟♟ 5
● Gattinara '09	♟♟ 4
● il Sogno '09	♟♟ 6
● Coste della Sesia Nebbiolo '11	♟ 3
● Gattinara Ris. '06	♟♟♟ 6
● Gattinara Ris. '04	♟♟♟ 5
● Gattinara Tre Vigne '04	♟♟♟ 5
● Coste della Sesia Nebbiolo '10	♟♟ 3
● Coste della Sesia Nebbiolo '09	♟♟ 3*
● Gattinara '08	♟♟ 4
● Gattinara '07	♟♟ 4
● Gattinara Ris. '07	♟♟ 6
● Gattinara Tre Vigne '06	♟♟ 5
● l'altro Sogno '07	♟♟ 5

G. D. Vajra

LOC. VERGNE
VIA DELLE VIOLE, 25
12060 BAROLO [CN]
TEL. 017356257
www.gdvajra.it

CELLAR SALES
PRE-BOOKED VISITS
ANNUAL PRODUCTION 220,000 bottles
HECTARES UNDER VINE 50.00

Vajra has always been a model of devotion to tradition and territory of origin. Over the years, It has become a point of reference for a production style that manages to combine aromatic elegance, significant acidity and extremely lengthy bottle-ageing. The Barolo Bricco delle Viole, named after the Barolo vineyard, is a perfect example of this, although the entire range displays a very distinct character, including the wines derived from riesling renano or freisa. In 2009, the Vajra family acquired the Luigi Baudana estate in Serralunga d'Alba and they have considerably enhanced the offering, notably with the two superb Barolo crus, Baudana and Cerretta. The complex, multifaceted nose of the Barolo Baudana 2009 shows tobacco, violet, red berry fruit and quinine, followed by elegant tannins on the deep, lingering palate, and earned a Tre Bicchieri. Elegance is the keynote in the fresh, lively Dolcetto d'Alba Coste & Fossati 2011, with delicate tannins and rich, fleshy fruit.

● Barolo Baudana Luigi Baudana '09	▼▼▼	6
● Barolo Bricco delle Viole '09	▼▼	8
● Barolo Cerretta Luigi Baudana '09	▼▼	6
● Dolcetto d'Alba Coste & Fossati '11	▼▼	4
● Barbera d'Alba '11	▼▼	3
● Barolo Albe '09	▼▼	6
○ Langhe Bianco Pétracine '12	▼▼	5
● Langhe Freisa Kyè '10	▼▼	5
● Barbera d'Alba Sup. '10	▼	5
● Langhe Nebbiolo '11	▼	3
○ Moscato d'Asti '12	▼	3
● Barolo Bricco delle Viole '05	▼▼▼	8
● Barolo Bricco delle Viole '01	▼▼▼	8
● Barolo Cerretta Luigi Baudana '08	▼▼▼	6

Mauro Veglio

FRAZ. ANNUNZIATA
CASCINA NUOVA, 50
12064 LA MORRA [CN]
TEL. 0173509212
www.mauroveglio.com

CELLAR SALES
PRE-BOOKED VISITS
ANNUAL PRODUCTION 60,000 bottles
HECTARES UNDER VINE 13.00

Mauro Veglio and his wife Daniela Saffirio confidently run their winemaking venture. Year after year, their attentive work and steady progress have contributed to the brand becoming a familiar name on many leading markets. The winery headquarters are located in the same courtyard that is home to Elio Altare, which adds a touch of originality and charm to this picturesque corner of Langhe. All the vineyards are arrayed around the villa, with the exception of Castelletto, in Monforte d'Alba. The style of the wines focuses on clean aromas and well-defined flavours. The lively Barolo Gattera 2009 shows fresh notes of red berry fruit, sweet spice and quinine, with smooth tannins and a long finish. The Barolo Castelletto 2009 displays a variegated nose, playing on notes of tobacco, wild berries and violets, making way for weighty tannins in the mouth, nicely balanced by attractive acidity.

● Barolo Castelletto '09	▼▼	7
● Barolo Gattera '09	▼▼	7
● Barbera d'Alba Cascina Nuova '11	▼▼	5
● Barolo '09	▼▼	5
● Barolo Rocche dell'Annunziata '09	▼▼	8
● Barolo Vign. Arborina '09	▼▼	7
● Langhe Nebbiolo Angelo '11	▼▼	4
● Barbera d'Alba '12	▼	3
● Dolcetto d'Alba '12	▼	2
● Barbera d'Alba Cascina Nuova '99	▼▼▼	5
● Barolo V. Rocche '96	▼▼▼	8
● Barolo Vign. Arborina '01	▼▼▼	6
● Barolo Vign. Arborina '00	▼▼▼	6
● Barolo Vign. Gattera '05	▼▼▼	6

Vicara

Cascina Madonna delle Grazie, 5
15030 Rosignano Monferrato [AL]
Tel. 0142488054
www.vicara.it

Giacomo Vico

via Torino, 80/82
12043 Canale [CN]
Tel. 0173979126
www.giacomovico.it

CELLAR SALES
PRE-BOOKED VISITS
ANNUAL PRODUCTION 200,000 bottles
HECTARES UNDER VINE 51.00
VITICULTURE METHOD Certified Biodynamic

CELLAR SALES
PRE-BOOKED VISITS
ANNUAL PRODUCTION 100,000 bottles
HECTARES UNDER VINE 18.00

Modernity and technology have not changed the principles of the original project known as Vi.Ca.Ra, a compilation of the first two letters of the surnames of the partners, Visconti, Cassinis and Ravizza. It remains intrinsically linked to the territory, and even more so to the characteristics of the terrains that dictated which grapes were selected for planting. Add total respect for the surrounding environment and we have the perfect recipe for producing the antithesis to those technological wines that are created in the cellar. Following selection and bunch thinning, the bought-in grapes arrive in the cellar perfectly ripe and in excellent condition. Process plays second fiddle here. The Grignolino, once again in the finals, this year showed marked varietal traits. It was joined by the Barbera La Rocca, on its début in the Guide, a complex wine with aromas of red berry fruit and notes of tobacco and cocoa powder, boasting a seductive, fleshy palate and incredible length.

For 20 years now, the fourth generation of the Vico family has been rekindling the winegrowing activity that started in the late 1800s and was interrupted in 1954. The vineyards lie mainly in Vezza d'Alba and Canale in the classic loose, sandy Roero terrain. They are home to the classic varieties of the zone, from barbera to nebbiolo, brachetto to arneis and favorita, with a smattering of chardonnay. The wines are modern in style and aim to express the varietal characteristics of the grapes, and more specifically those of the territory, to their fullest. Two wines made the final: the Roero 2010, with classic, elegant aromas of aromatic herbs and tobacco, over a well-balanced, dynamic, long palate, and the Barolo 2008, whose fruit and balsam is swathed in aniseed and wild fennel, followed by a fresh, juicy palate. We also liked the Barbera d'Alba 2011, with focused, fresh black berry fruit and the floral, tangy Roero Arneis 2012.

● Barbera del M.to La Rocca '10	♟♟ 3*
● Grignolino del M.to Casalese '12	♟♟ 3*
● Barbera del M.to Vivace '12	♟ 2
○ M.to Bianco Airales '12	♟ 2
⊙ M.to Chiaretto '12	♟ 2
● Barbera del M.to Sup. Cantico della Crosia '09	♟♟ 4
● Barbera del M.to Sup. Cantico della Crosia '07	♟♟ 4
● Barbera del M.to Sup. Vadmò '09	♟♟ 4
● Barbera del M.to Sup. Vadmò '06	♟♟ 3*
● Barbera del M.to Volpuva '11	♟♟ 2*
● Grignolino del M.to Casalese '11	♟♟ 3*
● Grignolino del M.to Casalese '10	♟♟ 3*
● M.to Rosso Rubello '09	♟♟ 4

● Barolo '08	♟♟ 6
● Roero '10	♟♟ 4
● Barbera d'Alba '11	♟♟ 2*
○ Roero Arneis '12	♟♟ 2*
● Barbera d'Alba '10	♟♟ 2*
● Barbera d'Alba Sup. '10	♟♟ 4
● Langhe Rosso '10	♟♟ 2*
● Nebbiolo d'Alba '08	♟♟ 3
● Roero '09	♟♟ 4
● Roero '08	♟♟ 4

★Vietti

P.ZZA VITTORIO VENETO, 5
12060 CASTIGLIONE FALLETTO [CN]
TEL. 017362825
www.vietti.com

I Vignaioli di Santo Stefano

LOC. MARINI, 26
12058 SANTO STEFANO BELBO [CN]
TEL. 0141840419
www.ceretto.com

CELLAR SALES
PRE-BOOKED VISITS
ANNUAL PRODUCTION 250,000 bottles
HECTARES UNDER VINE 37.00

CELLAR SALES
PRE-BOOKED VISITS
ANNUAL PRODUCTION 335,000 bottles
HECTARES UNDER VINE 35.00

Rocche and Villero in Castiglione Falletto, Brunate in La Morra, Lazzarito in Serralunga d'Alba: it would be hard to imagine a group of more prestigious and varied vineyards than those available to Luca Currado and Mario Cordero. In many ways, their Barolos represent the perfect intersection of modern sensitivity and traditional practices that makes debate over cellar techniques and barrel sizes seem almost irrelevant. But the Vietti brand has not become an absolute must for wine enthusiasts based on nebbiolo alone. The Barberas consistently offer some of the best interpretations in the Alba and Asti areas, and the Moscato, Arneis and Dolcetto are every bit their equals. Long ageing has done nothing to impair the freshness of the Barolo Villero Riserva 2006, but has actually helped emphasize the noble, austere tones of this great wine. The solid, layered Barolo Rocche 2009 reveals notes of tobacco, quinine, aniseed and spices, paving the way for a full-flavoured, lengthy palate.

This estate established in 1976 by the Ceretto, Santi and Scavino families has long been a solid, reliable name in moscato production. The range is limited to just three labels that divide the variety by its various typologies. The lion's share of the vineyards lies in Santo Stefano Belbo, but there are a few small plots in Calosso and Canelli at an altitude of between 320 and 450 metres. The production centre sits on the 18-hectare San Maurizio property on the steep southern slope of Valdivilla. We were without the Passito once again this year, but the range we tasted showed the usual excellent quality. The Moscato d'Asti 2012 boasts a concentrated, layered nose of sage, peach and balsam, while in the mouth sweetness and acidity are perfectly balanced, providing fresh, pleasurable drinkability. The more vegetal, aromatic Asti 2012 is approachable, refreshing and long.

● Barolo Villero Ris. '06	▼▼▼	8
● Barolo Castiglione '09	▼▼	7
● Barolo Lazzarito '09	▼▼	8
● Barolo Rocche '09	▼▼	8
● Barbaresco Masseria '09	▼▼	8
● Barbera d'Alba Scarrone V. Vecchia '11	▼▼	6
● Barbera d'Alba Tre Vigne '11	▼▼	3
● Barbera d'Asti Sup. Nizza La Crena '10	▼▼	5
● Barbera d'Asti Tre Vigne '11	▼▼	3
● Langhe Nebbiolo Perbacco '10	▼▼	3
○ Roero Arneis '12	▼▼	3
● Barbera d'Asti Sup. Nizza La Crena '09	♀♀♀	5
● Barolo Rocche '08	♀♀♀	8
● Barolo Rocche '06	♀♀♀	8
● Barolo Villero Ris. '04	♀♀♀	8

○ Asti '12	▼▼	3
○ Moscato d'Asti '12	▼▼	4
○ Asti '11	♀♀	3
○ Asti '10	♀♀	3
○ Moscato d'Asti '11	♀♀	3
○ Moscato d'Asti '10	♀♀	3
○ Moscato d'Asti '09	♀♀	4
○ Moscato d'Asti '08	♀♀	4
○ Moscato d'Asti '07	♀♀	3

Vigne Regali

VIA VITTORIO VENETO, 76
15019 STREVI [AL]
TEL. 0144362600
www.castellobanfi.it

Vigneti Massa

P.ZZA G. CAPSONI, 10
15059 MONLEALE [AL]
TEL. 013180302
vignetimassa@libero.it

PRE-BOOKED VISITS
ANNUAL PRODUCTION 2,000,000 bottles
HECTARES UNDER VINE 76.00

CELLAR SALES
PRE-BOOKED VISITS
ANNUAL PRODUCTION 80,000 bottles
HECTARES UNDER VINE 19,50

For the province of Alessandria, the numbers associated with Vigne Regali are truly impressive in terms of bottles and range of wines produced. Vigne Regali is part of the Banfi group that operates across several continents and thus the global market. Production focuses on wines obtained from indigenous varieties such as albarossa, dolcetto d'Acqui, cortese di Gavi, moscato d'Asti and brachetto d'Acqui. They also offer a substantial range of extremely well-made sparkling wines, both dry and sweet. The range is led by the metodo classico sparklers Cuvée Aurora, with its bright hue and fine perlage, and Banfi Brut, a complex, intense wine with good structure and length. The Lus, from albarossa, displays a deep ruby hue, with aromas of black berry fruit and quinine coming together on the potent, leisurely palate.

Walter Massa never ceases to surprise us and keep us on our toes. Last year, he released his fourth Timorasso label and any doubts we may have had that it was one too many were instantly shattered when the brand new Montecitorio went home with a resounding Tre Bicchieri. This year we were anxious about the idea of a fifth label, but for the moment our minds are at rest. We do have another newcomer; unlike the Pietra del Gallo that already features in the estate's wine list, the Freisa L'Avvelenata is fermented still. The Moscato Anarchia Costituzionale and the Barbera Sentieri are always very sound. Sterpi and Costa del Vento continue to attract those who prefer the power and opulence typical of the variety, while the Montecitorio also wins over those who like finesse and freshness in their whites. The result is a well-deserved Tre Bicchieri for the latter, for the second year in a row.

○ Alta Langa Cuvée Aurora '07	♟♟ 5
○ Banfi Brut M. Cl.	♟♟ 3
● Dolcetto d'Acqui L'Ardì '12	♟♟ 3
○ Gavi Principessa Gavia '12	♟♟ 3
● Piemonte Albarossa La Lus '10	♟♟ 5
● Brachetto d'Acqui Rosa Regale '12	♟ 4
○ Moscato d'Asti Sciandor '12	♟ 3
○ Tener Brut	♟ 3
○ Alta Langa Brut Cuvée Aurora '06	♟♟ 5
⊙ Alta Langa Brut Cuvée Aurora Rosé '09	♟♟ 5
○ Banfi Brut Talento	♟♟ 3
● Dolcetto d'Acqui L'Ardì '11	♟♟ 2*

○ Montecitorio '11	♟♟♟ 6
○ Derthona '11	♟♟ 5
○ Anarchia Costituzionale '12	♟♟ 3
○ Costa del Vento '11	♟♟ 6
● Pietra del Gallo '12	♟♟ 2*
● Sentieri '12	♟♟ 4
○ Sterpi '11	♟♟ 6
● Freisa L'Avvelenata '10	♟ 4
○ Colli Tortonesi Timorasso Derthona '06	♟♟♟ 5
○ Colli Tortonesi Timorasso Sterpi '08	♟♟♟ 7
○ Colli Tortonesi Timorasso Sterpi '07	♟♟♟ 7
○ Derthona '09	♟♟♟ 5
○ Montecitorio '10	♟♟♟ 6

Villa Giada

REG. CEIROLE, 10
14053 CANELLI [AT]
TEL. 0141831100
www.andreafaccio.it

CELLAR SALES
PRE-BOOKED VISITS
ACCOMMODATION AND RESTAURANT SERVICE
ANNUAL PRODUCTION 190,000 bottles
HECTARES UNDER VINE 25.00

For over 20 years now, Andrea Faccio has been a mover and shaker in terms of promoting the territory of Asti. As is fairly typical in this zone, production focuses on moscato, cultivated mainly in vineyards next to the estate headquarters on the Ceirole hill in Canelli, and barbera, which grows at the Dani cascina and hill in Agliano Terme and at Cascina del Parroco in Calosso. Nebbiolo, dolcetto, merlot, chardonnay, sauvignon, cortese and gamba di pernice complete the range of varieties present. The many labels are all technically well made. The fleshy Barbera d'Asti Superiore Nizza Bricco Dani 2010 shows intense quinine notes and a powerful, close-knit palate, but also somewhat rustic traits, while the attractive, long Barbera d'Asti Superiore Nizza Dedicato a... 2009 plays on its juicy fruit. The concentrated Monferrato Rosso Treponti 2010, from nebbiolo and 10% barbera, is multifaceted, with notes of tobacco and raspberry, but overpowering tannins.

● Barbera d'Asti Sup. Nizza Bricco Dani '10	▼▼ 4
● Barbera d'Asti Sup. Nizza Dedicato a... '09	▼▼ 5
● M.to Rosso Treponti '10	▼▼ 3
● Barbera d'Asti Surì '12	▼ 2
● M.to Rosso Novenove '11	▼ 2
○ Moscato d'Asti '12	▼ 2
● Barbera d'Asti Ajan '10	♀♀ 2*
● Barbera d'Asti Sup. Nizza Bricco Dani '09	♀♀ 4
● Barbera d'Asti Sup. Nizza Dedicato a... '08	♀♀ 5

★Villa Sparina

FRAZ. MONTEROTONDO, 56
15066 GAVI [AL]
TEL. 0143633835
www.villasparina.it

PRE-BOOKED VISITS
ACCOMMODATION AND RESTAURANT SERVICE
ANNUAL PRODUCTION 600,000 bottles
HECTARES UNDER VINE 65.00

We highly recommend a visit to Villa Sparina, an old estate purchased by the Moccagatta family in the 1970s, which is now home to the cellar, but also a splendid resort with adjoining restaurant and spa. The spectacular view does not distract from the hub of activity focused on the over 60 hectares of vineyards, planted mainly to cortese, with sizeable plots also in Cassinelle in the Dolcetto d'Ovada production zone and Rivalta Bormida in Alto Monferrato for barbera. It all converges in a flawless range, which insistently conveys the winery's intent to combine body and grip with expressive fruit and cellarability. Villa Sparina continues to hold a leading place in the DOC zone, combining impressive production figures and an extensive range with inimitable quality. The Monterotondo is one of a small group of wines that has become a benchmark not only here but in Italy as a whole, bringing together power, finesse and complexity. The 2011 version is perfect for long ageing.

○ Gavi del Comune di Gavi Monterotondo '11	▼▼▼ 6
● Barbera del M.to Sup. Rivalta '10	▼▼ 6
● Barbera del M.to Villa Sparina '12	▼▼ 3
○ Villa Sparina Brut M. Cl.	▼▼ 3
○ Gavi del Comune di Gavi Et. Gialla '12	▼ 3
● M.to Rosso Montej '12	▼ 2
○ Gavi del Comune di Gavi Monterotondo '10	♀♀♀ 6
○ Gavi del Comune di Gavi Monterotondo '09	♀♀♀ 6
○ Gavi del Comune di Gavi Monterotondo '08	♀♀♀ 6
○ Gavi del Comune di Gavi Monterotondo '07	♀♀♀ 5
● M.to Rosso Rivalta '04	♀♀♀ 6

Cantina Sociale di Vinchio Vaglio Serra

REG. SAN PANCRAZIO, 1
14040 VINCHIO [AT]
TEL. 0141950903
www.vinchio.com

CELLAR SALES
PRE-BOOKED VISITS
ANNUAL PRODUCTION 1,640,000 bottles
HECTARES UNDER VINE 420.00

This co-operative estate comprising 200 member growers remains one of the most important and substantial in the province of Piedmont. Production naturally centres on Barbera in its various typologies and offers a very extensive array of labels derived from the region's principal varieties, from nebbiolo to cortese, dolcetto to arneis and brachetto to moscato. It's worth mentioning that the vast area of vineyards belonging to the members includes several plots where the vines are over 60 years old. The wines are technically well made, distinctive and typical. The Barbera d'Asti Superiore Sei Vigne Insynthesis 2007 was again one of the best in its class, with complex fruit notes, and hints of spice, coffee and liquorice, over good structure on the long, dynamic palate. We also liked the other Barberas, from the fresh, supple, well-balanced I Tre Vescovi 2011, and the powerful, heady Vigne Vecchie 2009, to the fruit-driven Sorì dei Mori 2012, and the mature Vigne Vecchie 50 2011.

● Barbera d'Asti Sup. Sei Vigne Insynthesis '07	♥♥ 6
● Barbera d'Asti Sorì dei Mori '12	♥♥ 2*
● Barbera d'Asti Sup. I Tre Vescovi '11	♥♥ 2*
● Barbera d'Asti Sup. Vigne Vecchie '09	♥♥ 4
● Barbera d'Asti Vigne Vecchie 50 '11	♥♥ 3
○ Monferrato Bianco Lipiai '12	♥ 2
● Monferrato Rosso Tutti per Uno '09	♥ 3
○ Piemonte Brut Pinot-Chardonnay Castel del Mago '12	♥ 3
● Barbera d'Asti Sup. Sei Vigne Insynthesis '01	♥♥♥ 6
● Barbera d'Asti Sup. Nizza Laudana '09	♥♥ 3*
● Barbera d'Asti Sup. V. V. '08	♥♥ 4
● Barbera d'Asti V. V. 50 '10	♥♥ 3

Virna

VIA ALBA, 73/24
12060 BAROLO [CN]
TEL. 017356120
www.virnabarolo.it

CELLAR SALES
PRE-BOOKED VISITS
ANNUAL PRODUCTION 60,000 bottles
HECTARES UNDER VINE 12.00

Virna Borgogno, after whom this recently founded winery is named, continues to move confidently forward in the world of fine wine, aided by her sister Ivana and her husband Giovanni Abrigo, a producer in the Barbaresco zone. The small Langhe estate surprises with the stylistic definition of all its wines, commencing with a series of Barolos from prestigious crus such as Sarmassa, Preda and Cannubi Boschis, aged in different-sized oak barrels. An array of vineyard selections of this level is undoubtedly the best card for winning the hearts of Italian and foreign wine lovers. We were won over by the multifaceted, complex nose of the Barolo Preda Sarmassa 2009, with notes of raspberry, tobacco and violets, followed by graceful tannins for a smooth finish. The Barolo Cannubi Boschis 2009 is still somewhat edgy, but promises interesting development with further bottle ageing.

● Barolo Preda Sarmassa '09	♥♥ 6
● Barbera d'Alba '11	♥♥ 2*
● Barolo '09	♥♥ 5
● Barolo Cannubi Boschis '09	♥♥ 6
● Nebbiolo d'Alba '10	♥♥ 3
● Barbera d'Alba '10	♥♥ 2*
● Barbera d'Alba San Giovanni '09	♥♥ 3
● Barolo '08	♥♥ 5
● Barolo Cannubi Boschi '04	♥♥ 5
● Barolo Cannubi Boschis '08	♥♥ 6
● Barolo Cannubi Boschis '07	♥♥ 5
● Barolo Cannubi Boschis '04	♥♥ 5
● Barolo Preda Sarmassa '08	♥♥ 6
● Barolo Preda Sarmassa '06	♥♥ 5

179
OTHER WINERIES

F.lli Abrigo

LOC. BERFI
VIA MOGLIA GERLOTTO, 2
12055 DIANO D'ALBA [CN]
TEL. 017369104
www.abrigofratelli.com

CELLAR SALES
PRE-BOOKED VISITS
ANNUAL PRODUCTION 100,000 bottles
HECTARES UNDER VINE 25.00

● Barbera d'Alba La Galùpa '11	♙♙ 3
● Diano d'Alba Sup. V. Pietrin '11	♙♙ 3
● Nebbiolo d'Alba Tardiss '11	♙♙ 3
● Diano d'Alba Rocche dei Berfi '12	♙ 3

Antica Cascina Conti di Roero

LOC. VAL RUBIAGNO, 2
12040 VEZZA D'ALBA [CN]
TEL. 017365459
www.oliveropietro.it

CELLAR SALES
PRE-BOOKED VISITS
ANNUAL PRODUCTION 100,000 bottles
HECTARES UNDER VINE 14.00

● Barbera d'Alba '11	♙♙ 2*
○ Roero Arneis '12	♙♙ 2*
○ Brut M. Cl.	♙ 4
● Nebbiolo d'Alba '11	♙ 2

Odilio Antoniotti

V.LO ANTONIOTTI, 9
13868 SOSTEGNO [BI]
TEL. 0163860309

● Bramaterra '09	♙♙ 3*
● Pramartel	♙♙ 3

Anzivino

C.SO VALSESIA, 162
13045 GATTINARA [VC]
TEL. 0163827172
www.anzivino.it

CELLAR SALES
PRE-BOOKED VISITS
ACCOMMODATION AND RESTAURANT SERVICE
ANNUAL PRODUCTION 60,000 bottles
HECTARES UNDER VINE 11.00

● Coste della Sesia Nebbiolo '08	♙♙ 3*
● Coste della Sesia Faticato '08	♙♙ 5
● Coste della Sesia Il Tarlo '09	♙♙ 2*
● Gattinara '08	♙♙ 4

Antonio Baldizzone Cascina Lana

C.SO ACQUI, 187
14049 NIZZA MONFERRATO [AT]
TEL. 0141726734
www.cascinalanavini.it

CELLAR SALES
ANNUAL PRODUCTION 60,000 bottles
HECTARES UNDER VINE 18.00

● Barbera d'Asti Sup. Nizza '10	♙♙ 5
● Barbera d'Asti La Cirimela '12	♙ 2

Cantina Sociale Barbera dei Sei Castelli

VIA OPESSINA, 41
14040 CASTELNUOVO CALCEA [AT]
TEL. 0141957137
www.barberaseicastelli.it

● Barbera d'Alba 50 Anni di Barbera '11	♙♙ 2*
● Barbera d'Asti '11	♙♙ 2*
● Barbera d'Asti Sup. La Vignole '10	♙ 2

Battaglio

LOC. BORBORE
VIA SALERIO, 15
12040 VEZZA D'ALBA [CN]
TEL. 017365423
www.battaglio.com

CELLAR SALES
PRE-BOOKED VISITS
ANNUAL PRODUCTION 40,000 bottles
HECTARES UNDER VINE 5.00

● Barbaresco '10	♟♟ 6
● Nebbiolo d'Alba Valmaggiore '10	♟♟ 3
● Barbera d'Alba Madunina '10	♟ 3
○ Roero Arneis Piasì '12	♟ 3

Davide Beccaria

VIA GIOVANNI BIANCO, 3
15039 OZZANO MONFERRATO [AL]
TEL. 0142487321
www.beccaria-vini.it

CELLAR SALES
ANNUAL PRODUCTION 30,000 bottles
HECTARES UNDER VINE 10.00

● Grignolino del M.to Casalese Grignò '12	♟♟ 2*
● M.to Freisa Lilàn '12	♟♟ 2*
● Barbera del M.to Evoè '12	♟ 2
○ Monferrato Bianco Garbello '12	♟ 3

Bel Sit

VIA PIANI, 30
14054 CASTAGNOLE DELLE LANZE [AT]
TEL. 0141875162
www.belsitvini.it

CELLAR SALES
PRE-BOOKED VISITS
ANNUAL PRODUCTION 50,000 bottles
HECTARES UNDER VINE 7.00

● Barbera d'Asti La Turna '12	♟♟ 2*
● Barbera d'Asti Sup. Sichivej '10	♟♟ 5
○ Moscato d'Asti '12	♟♟ 2*

Antonio Bellicoso

FRAZ. MOLISSO, 5A
14048 MONTEGROSSO D'ASTI [AT]
TEL. 0141953233
antonio.bellicoso@alice.it

CELLAR SALES
PRE-BOOKED VISITS
ANNUAL PRODUCTION 10,000 bottles
HECTARES UNDER VINE 4.00

● Barbera d'Asti Amormio '12	♟♟ 2*
● Barbera d'Asti Merum '11	♟ 4

Eugenio Bocchino

FRAZ. SANTA MARIA
LOC. SERRA, 96A
12064 LA MORRA [CN]
TEL. 0173500358
www.eugeniobocchino.it

CELLAR SALES
PRE-BOOKED VISITS
ANNUAL PRODUCTION 30,000 bottles
HECTARES UNDER VINE 5.50

● Barbera d'Alba Tom '11	♟♟ 4
● Barolo La Morra '09	♟♟ 5
● Langhe Nebbiolo Roccabella '11	♟♟ 5

Gilberto Boniperti

VIA VITTORIO EMANUELE, 43/45
28010 BARENGO [NO]
TEL. 0321997123
www.bonipertivignaioli.com

● Colline Novaresi Barbera Barblin '10	♟♟ 4
● Colline Novaresi Nebbiolo Bartön '10	♟♟ 4
● Colline Novaresi Nebbiolo Carlin '11	♟♟ 4
⊙ Rosadisera '12	♟ 3

Bussia Soprana

LOC. BUSSIA, 88A
12065 MONFORTE D'ALBA [CN]
TEL. 039305182
www.bussiasoprana.it

CELLAR SALES
PRE-BOOKED VISITS
ANNUAL PRODUCTION 60,000 bottles
HECTARES UNDER VINE 23.00

● Barolo V. Colonnello '09	♟♟ 7
● Barbera d'Alba '10	♟♟ 4
● Langhe Rosso Zenit '09	♟♟ 5

Marco Canato

FRAZ. FONS SALERA
LOC. CA' BALDEA, 18/2
15049 VIGNALE MONFERRATO [AL]
TEL. 0142933653
www.canatovini.it

CELLAR SALES
PRE-BOOKED VISITS
ANNUAL PRODUCTION 30,000 bottles
HECTARES UNDER VINE 11.00

● Grignolino del M.to Casalese Celio '12	♟♟ 2*
● Barbera del M.to Gambaloita '12	♟ 2

Tenuta Carretta

LOC. CARRETTA, 2
12040 PIOBESI D'ALBA [CN]
TEL. 0173619119
www.tenutacarretta.it

CELLAR SALES
PRE-BOOKED VISITS
ACCOMMODATION AND RESTAURANT SERVICE
ANNUAL PRODUCTION 480,000 bottles
HECTARES UNDER VINE 70.00

● Barbera d'Alba Sup. Bric Quercia '11	♟♟ 3
● Barolo Vigneti in Cannubi '09	♟♟ 8
○ Roero Arneis Canorei '12	♟♟ 3
○ Roero Arneis Cayega '12	♟♟ 3

Carussin

REG. MARIANO, 27
14050 SAN MARZANO OLIVETO [AT]
TEL. 0141831358
www.carussin.it

CELLAR SALES
PRE-BOOKED VISITS
RESTAURANT SERVICE
ANNUAL PRODUCTION 90,000 bottles
HECTARES UNDER VINE 22.00

● Barbera d'Asti Lia Vi '12	♟♟ 2*
● Barbera d'Asti Asinoi '12	♟ 2

Cascina Adelaide

VIA AIE SOTTANE, 14
12060 BAROLO [CN]
TEL. 0173560503
www.cascinaadelaide.com

CELLAR SALES
PRE-BOOKED VISITS
ANNUAL PRODUCTION 50,000 bottles
HECTARES UNDER VINE 9.50

● Barolo Cannubi '09	♟♟ 8
● Barolo Fossati '09	♟♟ 8
● Barolo Pernanno '09	♟♟ 8
● Barolo Preda '09	♟♟ 8

Cascina Bertolotto

REG. ROCCHETTA, 1
15018 SPIGNO MONFERRATO [AL]
TEL. 014491551
www.cascinabertolotto.it

CELLAR SALES
PRE-BOOKED VISITS
ACCOMMODATION
ANNUAL PRODUCTION 60,000 bottles
HECTARES UNDER VINE 13.00

● Barbera del M.to I Cheini '10	♟♟ 3
● Dolcetto d'Acqui La Cresta '12	♟♟ 2*
● Dolcetto d'Acqui La Muïette '11	♟♟ 3
● Barbera del M.to La Sbarazzina	♟ 2

Cascina Castlet

S.DA CASTELLETTO, 6
14055 COSTIGLIOLE D'ASTI [AT]
TEL. 0141966651
www.cascinacastlet.com

CELLAR SALES
PRE-BOOKED VISITS
ANNUAL PRODUCTION 240,000 bottles
HECTARES UNDER VINE 23.00

● Barbera d'Asti '12	♟♟ 2*
● Barbera d'Asti Sup. Litina '09	♟♟ 3
● Barbera d'Asti Sup. Passum '09	♟♟ 5
○ Moscato d'Asti '12	♟ 2

Cascina del Monastero

FRAZ. ANNUNZIATA
CASCINA LUCIANI, 112A
12064 LA MORRA [CN]
TEL. 0173509245
www.cascinadelmonastero.it

● Barbera d'Alba Parroco '10	♟♟ 3
● Barolo Bricco Luciani '09	♟♟ 5
● Barolo Perno '09	♟♟ 5
● Barolo Riund Ris. '07	♟♟ 7

Cascina Flino

VIA ABELLONI, 7
12055 DIANO D'ALBA [CN]
TEL. 017369231
silvana.bona@uvetitn.it

CELLAR SALES
PRE-BOOKED VISITS
ACCOMMODATION AND RESTAURANT SERVICE
ANNUAL PRODUCTION 10,000 bottles
HECTARES UNDER VINE 4.00

● Barbera d'Alba Sup. Flin '10	♟♟ 2*
● Barolo San Lorenzo '09	♟♟ 4
● Diano d'Alba V. V. '12	♟♟ 2*
● Nebbiolo d'Alba '11	♟♟ 2*

Cascina Garitina

VIA GIANOLA, 20
14040 CASTEL BOGLIONE [AT]
TEL. 0141762162
www.cascinagaritina.it

CELLAR SALES
PRE-BOOKED VISITS
ANNUAL PRODUCTION 180,000 bottles
HECTARES UNDER VINE 26.00

● Barbera d'Asti Sup. Caranti '10	♟♟ 2*
● Barbera d'Asti Sup. Nizza 900 Neuvsent '10	♟♟ 4
● M.to Rosso Vera '12	♟ 3

Cascina Tavijn

FRAZ. MONTEROVERE, 7
14030 SCURZOLENGO [AT]
TEL. 0141203187
www.cascinatavijn.it

CELLAR SALES
PRE-BOOKED VISITS
ANNUAL PRODUCTION 20,000 bottles
HECTARES UNDER VINE 6.00
VITICULTURE METHOD Certified Organic

● Ruchè di Castagnole Monferrato '12	♟♟ 3*
● Grignolino d'Asti '12	♟♟ 2*

Cascina Zoina

FRAZ. LORETO
VIA RONCHETTO, 5
28047 OLEGGIO [NO]
TEL. 3356350692
www.cascinazoina.it

CELLAR SALES
PRE-BOOKED VISITS
ANNUAL PRODUCTION 20,000 bottles
HECTARES UNDER VINE 6.00

● Colline Novaresi Cordero della Zoina Mot '07	♟♟ 4
● Colline Novaresi Nebbiolo Centoundici '11	♟♟ 2*

Renzo Castella

VIA ALBA, 15
12055 DIANO D'ALBA [CN]
TEL. 017369203
renzocastella@virgilio.it

CELLAR SALES
PRE-BOOKED VISITS
ANNUAL PRODUCTION 25,000 bottles
HECTARES UNDER VINE 10.00

● Dolcetto di Diano d'Alba '12	♥♥ 2*
● Dolcetto di Diano d'Alba Rivolia '12	♥♥ 2*
● Barbera d'Alba Piadvenza '11	♥ 2
● Langhe Nebbiolo Madonnina '11	♥ 2

Castello del Poggio

LOC. POGGIO, 9
14100 PORTACOMARO [AT]
TEL. 0141202543
www.poggio.it

CELLAR SALES
PRE-BOOKED VISITS
ANNUAL PRODUCTION 800,000 bottles
HECTARES UNDER VINE 158.00

● Barbera d'Asti '11	♥♥ 2*
○ Moscato d'Asti '12	♥♥ 2*
○ Asti	♥ 3
● Barbera d'Asti Masaréj '10	♥ 4

Le Cecche

VIA MOGLIA GERLOTTO, 10
12055 DIANO D'ALBA [CN]
TEL. 017369323
www.lececche.com

CELLAR SALES
PRE-BOOKED VISITS
HECTARES UNDER VINE 5.00

● Barbera d'Alba '11	♥♥ 3
● Barolo Sorano '09	♥♥ 5
● Diano d'Alba '12	♥♥ 2*
● Nebbiolo d'Alba '10	♥♥ 3

Cerutti

VIA CANELLI, 205
14050 CASSINASCO [AT]
TEL. 0141851286
www.cascinacerutti.it

PRE-BOOKED VISITS
ANNUAL PRODUCTION 20,000 bottles
HECTARES UNDER VINE 6.00

○ Moscato d'Asti Canelli Sandrinet '12	♥♥ 2*
● Barbera d'Asti '12	♥ 2
● Barbera d'Asti Sup. Foje Russe '09	♥ 3
○ Piemonte Chardonnay Riva Granda '11	♥ 2

Franco Ceste

C.SO ALFIERI, 1
12040 GOVONE [CN]
TEL. 017358635
www.cestevini.com

CELLAR SALES
PRE-BOOKED VISITS
ANNUAL PRODUCTION 180,000 bottles
HECTARES UNDER VINE 20.00

● Barbaresco '09	♥♥ 3
● Barbera d'Alba Sup. '10	♥♥ 3
● Nebbiolo d'Alba La Guardia '10	♥♥ 2*
● Roero Palliano Ris. '09	♥♥ 3

Il Chiosso

VIALE GUGLIELMO MARCONI 45-47A
13045 GATTINARA [VC]
TEL. 0163826739
www.ilchiosso.it

● Colline Novaresi Vespolina '11	♥♥ 3
● Gattinara '08	♥♥ 3
● Ghemme '08	♥ 3

Paride Chiovini

VIA GIUSEPPE GARIBALDI, 20
28070 SIZZANO [NO]
TEL. 3394304954
www.paridechiovini.it

PRE-BOOKED VISITS

● Colline Novaresi Nebbiolo Priamo '10	♙♙ 3
● Colline Novaresi Uva Rara Briseide '11	♙♙ 3
● Colline Novaresi Vespolina Afrodite '11	♙♙ 3
● Sizzano '09	♙♙ 3

Ciabot Berton

VIA SANTA MARIA, 1
12064 LA MORRA [CN]
TEL. 017350217
www.ciabotberton.it

CELLAR SALES
PRE-BOOKED VISITS
ANNUAL PRODUCTION 35,000 bottles
HECTARES UNDER VINE 10.00

● Barolo Rocchettevino '09	♙♙ 5
● Barolo Roggeri '09	♙♙ 6
● Langhe Nebbiolo 3 Utin '11	♙♙ 2*
● Barolo '09	♙ 4

Cantina Clavesana

FRAZ. MADONNA DELLA NEVE, 19
12060 CLAVESANA [CN]
TEL. 0173790451
www.inclavesana.it

CELLAR SALES
PRE-BOOKED VISITS
ANNUAL PRODUCTION 3,400,000 bottles

● Barolo Olo '09	♙♙ 5
● Dogliani Sup. 474 '11	♙♙ 2*
● Dogliani Sup. Il Clou '11	♙♙ 2*
● Dogliani Clavesana '12	♙ 2

Aldo Clerico

LOC. MANZONI, 69
12065 MONFORTE D'ALBA [CN]
TEL. 017378509
www.aldoclerico.com

CELLAR SALES
PRE-BOOKED VISITS
ANNUAL PRODUCTION 30,000 bottles
HECTARES UNDER VINE 6.00

● Barbera d'Alba '11	♙♙ 3
● Barolo '09	♙♙ 6
● Langhe Nebbiolo '11	♙♙ 3
● Dolcetto di Dogliani '12	♙ 2

Collina Serragrilli

VIA SERRAGRILLI, 30
12057 NEIVE [CN]
TEL. 0173677010
www.serragrilli.it

CELLAR SALES
PRE-BOOKED VISITS
ANNUAL PRODUCTION 100,000 bottles
HECTARES UNDER VINE 15.00

● Barbaresco Serragrilli '10	♙♙ 5
● Langhe Grillorosso '09	♙♙ 2*
● Barbera d'Alba '11	♙ 2
○ Langhe Grillobianco '12	♙ 2

Colombo

REG. CAFRA, 172
14051 BUBBIO [AT]
TEL. 0144852807
www.colombovino.it

● Piemonte Pinot Nero Apertura '10	♙♙ 5*
○ Moscato d'Asti Pastù '12	♙ 2

Il Colombo - Barone Riccati

VIA DEI SENT, 2
12084 MONDOVÌ [CN]
TEL. 017441607
www.ilcolombo.com

CELLAR SALES
PRE-BOOKED VISITS
ACCOMMODATION AND RESTAURANT SERVICE
ANNUAL PRODUCTION 12,000 bottles
HECTARES UNDER VINE 3.00
VITICULTURE METHOD Certified Organic

● Dogliani La Chiesetta '12	▼2
● Dogliani Sup. Il Colombo '11	▼2

Giovanni Daglio

VIA MONTALE CELLI, 10
15050 COSTA VESCOVATO [AL]
TEL. 0131838262
www.vignetidaglio.com

CELLAR SALES
ANNUAL PRODUCTION 15,000 bottles
HECTARES UNDER VINE 10.00

● Colli Tortonesi Barbera Basinas '11	▼▼4
● Colli Tortonesi Barbera Plas '12	▼▼2*
○ Colli Tortonesi Timorasso Cantico '11	▼▼4
○ Vigna del Re '12	▼2

Dosio

REG. SERRADENARI, 6
12064 LA MORRA [CN]
TEL. 017350677
www.dosiovigneti.com

CELLAR SALES
PRE-BOOKED VISITS
ANNUAL PRODUCTION 60,000 bottles
HECTARES UNDER VINE 8.00

● Barolo Fossati '09	▼▼5
● Barolo '09	▼▼4
● Dolcetto d'Alba '12	▼▼2*
● Nebbiolo d'Alba '09	▼▼2*

Fabio Fidanza

VIA RODOTIGLIA, 55
14052 CALOSSO [AT]
TEL. 0141826921
castellodicalosso@tin.it

CELLAR SALES
PRE-BOOKED VISITS
ANNUAL PRODUCTION 20,000 bottles
HECTARES UNDER VINE 10.00

● Barbera d'Asti Sup. Sterlino '10	▼▼4
● M.to Rosso Que Duàn '11	▼3

La Fusina

B.GO SANTA LUCIA, 33
12063 DOGLIANI [CN]
TEL. 017370488
www.lafusina.com

CELLAR SALES
PRE-BOOKED VISITS
ANNUAL PRODUCTION 100,000 bottles
HECTARES UNDER VINE 20.00

● Barbera d'Alba '11	▼▼2*
● Barolo '09	▼▼5
● Dogliani Gombe '12	▼▼2*
● Langhe Rosso Pinot Nero '09	▼▼3

Gianni Gagliardo

B.TA SERRA DEI TURCHI, 88
12064 LA MORRA [CN]
TEL. 017350829
www.gagliardo.it

CELLAR SALES
PRE-BOOKED VISITS
RESTAURANT SERVICE
ANNUAL PRODUCTION 180,000 bottles
HECTARES UNDER VINE 30.00

● Barolo Preve '07	▼▼8
● Barolo Serre '09	▼▼8
● Nebbiolo d'Alba San Ponzio '09	▼▼6
● Barolo Gianni Gagliardo '09	▼7

Cantine Garrone

VIA CADUTI DEL LAVORO, 1
28845 DOMODOSSOLA [VB]
TEL. 0324242990
www.cantinegarrone.it

● Valli Ossolane Nebbiolo Sup. Prünent '10	♛♛ 3*
● Cà d'Maté '10	♛♛ 3
● Munaloss	♛♛ 3
● Valli Ossolane Rosso Tarlàp '11	♛♛ 3

Incisiana

VIA SANT'AGATA, 10/12
14045 INCISA SCAPACCINO [AT]
TEL. 0141747113
www.incisiana.com

CELLAR SALES
PRE-BOOKED VISITS
ACCOMMODATION
ANNUAL PRODUCTION 25,000 bottles
HECTARES UNDER VINE 5.00

● Barbera d'Asti '11	♛♛ 3
● M.to Rosso Merlotone '10	♛♛ 5

Marenco

P.ZZA VITTORIO EMANUELE II, 10
15019 STREVI [AL]
TEL. 0144363133
www.marencovini.com

CELLAR SALES
PRE-BOOKED VISITS
ANNUAL PRODUCTION 300,000 bottles
HECTARES UNDER VINE 80.00

● Brachetto d'Acqui Pineto '12	♛♛ 4
○ Moscato d'Asti Scrapona '12	♛♛ 3

Le Marie

VIA SANDEFENDENTE, 6
12032 BARGE [CN]
TEL. 0175345159
www.lemarievini.eu

CELLAR SALES
PRE-BOOKED VISITS
RESTAURANT SERVICE
ANNUAL PRODUCTION 24,000 bottles
HECTARES UNDER VINE 8.00

○ Blanc de Lissart	♛♛ 2
● Pinerolese Debargès '11	♛♛ 3
● Pinerolese Dolcetto '12	♛ 2
○ Sant'Agostino	♛ 3

Tenuta La Meridiana

VIA TANA BASSA, 5
14048 MONTEGROSSO D'ASTI [AT]
TEL. 0141956172
www.tenutalameridiana.com

CELLAR SALES
PRE-BOOKED VISITS
ANNUAL PRODUCTION 90,000 bottles
HECTARES UNDER VINE 10.00
VITICULTURE METHOD Certified Organic

● Barbera d'Asti Le Gagie '11	♛♛ 2*
● Barbera d'Asti Vitis '11	♛♛ 2*
● Barbera d'Asti Sup. Le Quattro Terre '11	♛ 2
○ Sol Passito '07	♛ 5

Negretti

LOC. PESO, 53
FRAZ. SANTA MARIA
12064 LA MORRA [CN]
TEL. 0173509850
www.negrettivini.com

CELLAR SALES
PRE-BOOKED VISITS
ANNUAL PRODUCTION 30,000 bottles
HECTARES UNDER VINE 12.00

● Barbera d'Alba Sup. '10	♛♛ 3
● Barolo '08	♛♛ 6
● Barolo Mirau '08	♛♛ 6
● Barolo Bricco Ambrogio '08	♛ 6

Giuseppe Negro

VIA GALLINA, 22
12052 NEIVE [CN]
TEL. 0173677468
www.negrogiuseppe.com

CELLAR SALES
PRE-BOOKED VISITS
ANNUAL PRODUCTION 50,000 bottles
HECTARES UNDER VINE 8.50

● Barbaresco Gallina '10	♟♟ 5
● Barbaresco Pian Cavallo '10	♟♟ 5
● Barbera d'Alba Pulin '11	♟♟ 3
● Dolcetto d'Alba Pian Cavallo '12	♟♟ 2*

Nervi

C.SO VERCELLI, 117
13045 GATTINARA [VC]
TEL. 0163833228
www.gattinara-nervi.it

CELLAR SALES
PRE-BOOKED VISITS
ANNUAL PRODUCTION 100,000 bottles
HECTARES UNDER VINE 33.00

● Gattinara '06	♟♟ 4
● Gattinara Vign. Molsino '06	♟♟ 5
● Coste della Sesia Nebbiolo Spanna dei Ginepri '10	♟ 4

Pace

FRAZ. MADONNA DI LORETO
CASCINA PACE, 52
12043 CANALE [CN]
TEL. 0173979544
aziendapace@infinito.it

CELLAR SALES
PRE-BOOKED VISITS
ANNUAL PRODUCTION 60,000 bottles
HECTARES UNDER VINE 22.00

● Barbera d'Alba '11	♟♟ 2*
○ Roero Arneis '12	♟ 2
● Roero Ris. '09	♟ 5

Pelassa

B.TA TUCCI, 43
12046 MONTÀ [CN]
TEL. 0173971312
www.pelassa.com

HECTARES UNDER VINE 10.00

● Barbera d'Alba Sup. San Pancrazio '11	♟♟ 3
● Barolo '09	♟♟ 7
● Nebbiolo d'Alba Sot '10	♟♟ 3
● Roero Antaniolo Ris. '09	♟♟ 4

Pasquale Pelissero

CASCINA CROSA, 2
12052 NEIVE [CN]
TEL. 017367376
www.pasqualepelissero.com

CELLAR SALES
PRE-BOOKED VISITS
ANNUAL PRODUCTION 20,000 bottles
HECTARES UNDER VINE 8.00

● Barbaresco Bricco San Giuliano '10	♟♟ 5
● Langhe Nebbiolo Pasqualin '11	♟♟ 2*

Pescaja

VIA SAN MATTEO, 59
14010 CISTERNA D'ASTI [AT]
TEL. 0141979711
www.pescaja.com

PRE-BOOKED VISITS
HECTARES UNDER VINE 19.00

● Barbera d'Asti Soliter '12	♟♟ 2*
○ Roero Arneis '12	♟♟ 2*
○ Terre Alfieri Arneis '12	♟♟ 2*
● Barbera d'Asti Sup. Solneri '10	♟ 4

Pianpolvere Soprano

Loc. Bussia, 32
12065 Monforte d'Alba [CN]
Tel. 017378421
www.pianpolveresoprano.it

PRE-BOOKED VISITS
ANNUAL PRODUCTION 8,000 bottles
HECTARES UNDER VINE 9.00

● Barolo Bussia Ris. '06		♟♟ 8

Pioiero

Cascina Pioiero, 1
12040 Vezza d'Alba [CN]
Tel. 017365492
www.pioiero.com

CELLAR SALES
PRE-BOOKED VISITS
ANNUAL PRODUCTION 35,000 bottles
HECTARES UNDER VINE 6.00

● Barbera d'Alba '11		♟♟ 2*
● Nebbiolo d'Alba '11		♟♟ 3
○ Roero Arneis Cascina Pioiero '12		♟♟ 3
● Roero '11		♟ 3

Platinetti

via Roma, 60
28074 Ghemme [NO]
Tel. 01119567820
platinettiguido@libero.it

CELLAR SALES
PRE-BOOKED VISITS
ANNUAL PRODUCTION 10,000 bottles
HECTARES UNDER VINE 5.00

● Colline Novaresi Barbera Pieleo '10		♟♟ 2*
● Ghemme V. Ronco Maso '08		♟♟ 4

I Pola

via Crosio
15010 Cremolino [AL]
Tel. 3483802465
www.ipola.it

CELLAR SALES
ACCOMMODATION
ANNUAL PRODUCTION 80,000 bottles
HECTARES UNDER VINE 15.00
VITICULTURE METHOD Certified Organic

● Barbera del M.to '11		♟♟ 2*
○ I Pola Brut M. Cl. '09		♟♟ 4
● Dolcetto di Ovada '11		♟ 2

Punset

via Zocco, 2
12052 Neive [CN]
Tel. 017367072
www.punset.com

CELLAR SALES
PRE-BOOKED VISITS
ACCOMMODATION
ANNUAL PRODUCTION 100,000 bottles
HECTARES UNDER VINE 17.00
VITICULTURE METHOD Certified Organic

● Barbaresco Ris. '08		♟♟ 5
● Barbaresco '09		♟♟ 5
● Barbera d'Alba '12		♟ 2

La Querciola

Loc. Piancerreto, 85ter
12060 Farigliano [CN]
Tel. 0713737026
www.laquerciola.com

CELLAR SALES
PRE-BOOKED VISITS
ANNUAL PRODUCTION 100,000 bottles
HECTARES UNDER VINE 23.00

● Barolo Costa di Rose '09		♟♟ 6
● Dogliani Carpeneta '12		♟♟ 2*
● Dogliani Sup. Cornole '11		♟ 3
● Langhe Rosso Chicchivello '12		♟ 2

La Raia

S.DA MONTEROTONDO, 79
15067 NOVI LIGURE [AL]
TEL. 0143743685
www.la-raia.it

CELLAR SALES
PRE-BOOKED VISITS
ANNUAL PRODUCTION 120,000 bottles
HECTARES UNDER VINE 32.00
VITICULTURE METHOD Certified Biodynamic

○ Gavi Pisè '11	♟♟ 3*

F.lli Raineri

VIA TORINO, 2
12060 FARIGLIANO [CN]
TEL. 017376223
www.cantineraineri.it

● Barbera d'Alba Sagrin '11	♟♟ 5
● Dogliani Cornole '12	♟ 3

Rattalino

S.DA GIRO DEL MONDO, 4
12050 BARBARESCO [CN]
TEL. 3492155012
www.massimorattalino.it

ANNUAL PRODUCTION 30,000 bottles
HECTARES UNDER VINE 5.80

● Barolo Trentacinque35 '08	♟♟ 5
● Barbaresco Quarantadue42 '09	♟♟ 5
● Barbaresco Quarantatre43 '09	♟♟ 5
● Barolo Trentaquattro34 '08	♟ 5

Carlo Daniele Ricci

VIA MONTALE CELLI, 9
15050 COSTA VESCOVATO [AL]
TEL. 0131838115
www.aziendaagricolaricci.com

CELLAR SALES
PRE-BOOKED VISITS
ACCOMMODATION AND RESTAURANT SERVICE
ANNUAL PRODUCTION 30,000 bottles
HECTARES UNDER VINE 8.00

○ Colli Tortonesi Terre del Timorasso '11	♟♟ 3
○ Colli Tortonesi San Leto Et. Blu '04	♟ 3
● Colli Tortonesi Elso '06	♟ 2
○ San Leto Et. Verde '09	♟ 3

Francesco Rinaldi & Figli

VIA CROSIA, 30
12051 BAROLO [CN]
TEL. 0173440484
www.rinaldifrancesco.it

CELLAR SALES
PRE-BOOKED VISITS
ANNUAL PRODUCTION 70,000 bottles
HECTARES UNDER VINE 11.00

● Barolo Cannubio '09	♟♟ 6
● Barolo Le Brunata '09	♟♟ 6
● Nebbiolo d'Alba '11	♟♟ 3
● Dolcetto d'Alba Roussot '12	♟ 2

Franco Roero

VIA ZUCCHETTO, 8
14048 MONTEGROSSO D'ASTI [AT]
TEL. 0141956160
franco.roero@gmail.com

CELLAR SALES
PRE-BOOKED VISITS
ANNUAL PRODUCTION 75,000 bottles
HECTARES UNDER VINE 14.00

● Barbera d'Asti Carbunè '12	♟♟ 2*
● Barbera d'Asti Sup. Sichei '11	♟♟ 3
● Barbera d'Asti Cellarino '11	♟ 3

Tenuta Roletto

VIA PORTA PIA, 69
10090 CUCEGLIO [TO]
TEL. 0124492293
www.tenutaroletto.it

CELLAR SALES
PRE-BOOKED VISITS
RESTAURANT SERVICE
ANNUAL PRODUCTION 160,000 bottles
HECTARES UNDER VINE 113.00

○ Erbaluce di Caluso Brut M. Cl. '08	♛♛ 6
○ Erbaluce di Caluso Muliné '11	♛♛ 5
○ Erbaluce di Caluso '12	♛ 3
○ Erbaluce di Caluso Passito '08	♛ 6

Rossi Contini

S.DA SAN LORENZO, 20
15076 OVADA [AL]
TEL. 0143822530
www.rossicontini.com

CELLAR SALES
PRE-BOOKED VISITS
ANNUAL PRODUCTION 20,000 bottles
HECTARES UNDER VINE 5.00

● Barbera del M.to Sup. Cras Tibi '10	♛♛ 3
● Dolcetto di Ovada Vign. Ninan '10	♛♛ 3
○ Cortese dell'Alto M.to Cortesia '12	♛ 2
● Dolcetto di Ovada San Lorenzo '12	♛ 2

Poderi Rosso

P.ZZA ROMA, 1
14041 AGLIANO TERME [AT]
TEL. 0141954006
www.poderirossogiovanni.it

CELLAR SALES
PRE-BOOKED VISITS
ANNUAL PRODUCTION 45,000 bottles
HECTARES UNDER VINE 12.00

● Barbera d'Asti San Bastian '11	♛♛ 2*
● Barbera d'Asti Sup. V. del Carlinet '11	♛♛ 3
● M.to Infine '11	♛♛ 4
● Barbera d'Asti Sup. Cascina Perno '11	♛ 2

Tenuta San Pietro

LOC. SAN PIETRO, 2
15060 TASSAROLO [AL]
TEL. 0143342422
www.tenutasanpietro.it

CELLAR SALES
PRE-BOOKED VISITS
ANNUAL PRODUCTION 150,000 bottles
HECTARES UNDER VINE 30.00
VITICULTURE METHOD Certified Biodynamic

○ Gavi San Pietro '12	♛♛ 3
○ Gavi del Comune di Tassarolo Gorrina '10	♛ 6
○ Gavi del Comune di Tassarolo Il Mandorlo '12	♛ 4

Giacomo Scagliola

REG. SANTA LIBERA, 20
14053 CANELLI [AT]
TEL. 0141831146
www.scagliolagiacomo.it

CELLAR SALES
ANNUAL PRODUCTION 80,000 bottles
HECTARES UNDER VINE 15.00

● Barbera d'Asti Sup. La Faia '11	♛♛ 2*
● M.to Rosso La Virasa Vejia '08	♛♛ 4
○ MejtordcheMoj	♛ 5
○ Moscato d'Asti Sifasol '12	♛ 2

Simone Scaletta

LOC. MANZONI, 61
12065 MONFORTE D'ALBA [CN]
TEL. 3484912733
www.viniscaletta.com

CELLAR SALES
PRE-BOOKED VISITS
ACCOMMODATION
ANNUAL PRODUCTION 20,000 bottles
HECTARES UNDER VINE 4.75

● Barbera d'Alba Sarsera '11	♛♛ 3
● Barolo Chirlet '09	♛♛ 6
● Dolcetto d'Alba Viglioni '12	♛ 2
● Langhe Nebbiolo Autin 'd Madama '11	♛ 3

Poderi Sinaglio

FRAZ. RICCA
VIA SINAGLIO, 5
12055 DIANO D'ALBA [CN]
TEL. 0173612209
www.poderisinaglio.it

CELLAR SALES
PRE-BOOKED VISITS
ACCOMMODATION AND RESTAURANT SERVICE
ANNUAL PRODUCTION 44,000 bottles
HECTARES UNDER VINE 13.00

● Nebbiolo d'Alba Giachét '11	♟♟ 3
● Barbera d'Alba '12	♟ 3
● Dolcetto di Diano d'Alba '12	♟ 2

Sobrero Francesco e Figli

VIA PUGNANE, 3A
12060 CASTIGLIONE FALLETTO [CN]
TEL. 017362864
www.sobrerofrancesco.it

CELLAR SALES
PRE-BOOKED VISITS
ANNUAL PRODUCTION 90,000 bottles
HECTARES UNDER VINE 16.00

● Barolo Ciabot Tanasio '09	♟♟ 5
● Barolo Pernanno Ris. '07	♟♟ 7
● Langhe Nebbiolo '11	♟♟ 3
● Barbera d'Alba La Pichetera '10	♟ 3

La Spinosa Alta

C.NE SPINOSA ALTA, 6
15038 OTTIGLIO [AL]
TEL. 0142921372
www.laspinosaalta.it

CELLAR SALES
PRE-BOOKED VISITS
ACCOMMODATION
ANNUAL PRODUCTION 12,000 bottles
HECTARES UNDER VINE 3.50

● Barbera del M.to Sup. La Punta '09	♟♟ 4
● M.to Rosso Bricco Spinosa '09	♟♟ 3
● Piemonte Barbera '09	♟♟ 4

Giuseppe Stella

S.DA BOSSOLA, 8
14055 COSTIGLIOLE D'ASTI [AT]
TEL. 0141966142
stellavini@libero.it

CELLAR SALES
PRE-BOOKED VISITS
ANNUAL PRODUCTION 45,000 bottles
HECTARES UNDER VINE 12.00

● Barbera d'Asti Stravisan '11	♟♟ 2*
● Barbera d'Asti Sup. Bricco Fubine Il Vino del Maestro '09	♟♟ 3
● Barbera d'Asti Sup. Giaiet '10	♟ 3

Stroppiana

FRAZ. RIVALTA SAN GIACOMO, 6
12064 LA MORRA [CN]
TEL. 0173509419
www.cantinastroppiana.com

CELLAR SALES
PRE-BOOKED VISITS
ANNUAL PRODUCTION 35,000 bottles
HECTARES UNDER VINE 5.50

● Barolo Leonardo '09	♟♟ 5
● Barolo V. S. Giacomo '09	♟♟ 6
● Barolo Gabutti Bussia '09	♟ 6
● Langhe Nebbiolo '11	♟ 3

La Toledana

LOC. SERMOIRA,5
15066 GAVI [AL]
TEL. 0141837287
www.latoledana.it

PRE-BOOKED VISITS
ANNUAL PRODUCTION 145,000 bottles
HECTARES UNDER VINE 28.00

● Barolo Lo Zoccolaio '08	♟♟ 6
● Barolo Ravera Lo Zoccolaio '08	♟♟ 6
○ Gavi del Comune di Gavi La Toledana '12	♟ 4

La Torretta

SP Cavaglio, 10
28074 Ghemme [NO]
Tel. 0163840764
torretta.vini@hotmail.it

HECTARES UNDER VINE 4.00

● Ghemme '07	♟♟ 3*
● Colline Novaresi Rosso Il Tordo '09	♟♟ 3
○ Colline Novaresi Bianco Fogliaretto '10	♟ 3
● Colline Novaresi Vespolina '11	♟ 3

Laura Valditerra

s.da Monterotondo, 75
15067 Novi Ligure [AL]
Tel. 0143321451
laura@valditerra.it

CELLAR SALES
PRE-BOOKED VISITS
ANNUAL PRODUCTION 40,000 bottles
HECTARES UNDER VINE 15.00

○ Gavi '12	♟♟ 2*
○ Gavi Tenuta Merlassino '12	♟♟ 2*

Alessandro Veglio

fraz. Annunziata, 53
12064 La Morra [CN]
Tel. 3385699102
www.risveglioinlanga.it

ANNUAL PRODUCTION 10,000 bottles
HECTARES UNDER VINE 3.00

● Barolo '09	♟♟ 5
● Barolo Gattera '09	♟♟ 7
● Langhe Nebbiolo '11	♟♟ 3
● Barbera d'Alba '12	♟ 2

Vigneti Valle Roncati

via Nazionale, 10a
28072 Briona [NO]
Tel. 3355732548
www.vignetivalleroncati.it

● Colline Novaresi Nebbiolo '09	♟♟ 3
● Fara V. di Sopra '10	♟♟ 3
⊙ Colline Novaresi Nebbiolo Rosato Poderi di Sopra '12	♟ 3

Gianni Voerzio

s.da Loreto, 1
12064 La Morra [CN]
Tel. 0173509194
voerzio.gianni@tiscali.it

CELLAR SALES
PRE-BOOKED VISITS
ANNUAL PRODUCTION 54,000 bottles
HECTARES UNDER VINE 12.00

● Barbera d'Alba Ciabot della Luna '11	♟♟ 4
● Barolo La Serra '09	♟♟ 8
● Langhe Nebbiolo Ciabot della Luna '11	♟♟ 5
● Dolcetto d'Alba Rocchettevino '12	♟ 3

La Zerba

s.da per Francavilla, 1
15060 Tassarolo [AL]
Tel. 0143342259
www.la-zerba.it

CELLAR SALES
PRE-BOOKED VISITS
ANNUAL PRODUCTION 86,000 bottles
HECTARES UNDER VINE 12.00

○ Gavi La Zerba '12	♟♟ 2*
○ Gavi Terrarossa '12	♟♟ 2*
● Piemonte Barbera '11	♟ 2

LIGURIA

In recent years, Liguria has rightly become one of Italy's most interesting winemaking regions. Despite its low production, accounting for just 0.4% of total national amount, the quality, particularly of white wines, is winning over an increasing number of consumers. For many years the region gave the impression of being a self-contained arena, tending to look only to local markets and consumption, lacking presence outside the region, whether on restaurant menus or in wine shops. Now it is able to prove itself with aficionados, attracting the attention of critics. There are many reasons for this but a couple appear significant. The first is the consumer interest seen over recent years for native grape varieties, which is entirely compatible with regional production that has always been devoted to a real promotion of local varieties, from pigato to vermentino, rossese, ormeasco, bosco, albarola, bianchetta Genovese, and lumassina. The second is a new trend in contemporary taste, which is setting aside its preference for sweetness, richness of fruit and structure, and leaning to a greater appreciation of flavour and aromatic complexity, a stylistic profile that sits perfectly with the characteristics we find in most good-quality Liguria whites. This success is affecting virtually all the region's production areas, both niche like the Cinque Terre and rather more extensive with larger-scale productions, like Colli di Luni or Riviera Ligure di Ponente, and that also concerns the only red wine worthy of note, Rossese di Dolceacqua. The other reds produced in the region are still failing to persuade and we are unable to track down one with appreciable overall quality or, as in the case of Ormeasco di Pornassio, with a convincing distinctive identity. This year, despite 2012 turning out to be more complicated than expected, there are seven Tre Bicchieri awards including, and this really is worth mentioning, Edy Bonanini's smashing new Cinque Terre 2012. Other awardees were three Riviera di Ponente Pigatos (a 2012 by Maria Donata Bianchi, a Cycnus 2012 from the Merano family's Poggio dei Gorleri, and Bruna's U Baccan 2011) and two Colli di Luni Vermentinos (Ottaviano Lambruschi's Il Maggiore 2012 and Etichetta Nera 2012 from the Bosoni family's Lunae). Last, but not least, we can speak highly of Rossese Dolceacqua 2012 from Filippo Rondelli's Terre Bianche.

Altavia

LOC. ARCAGNA
18035 DOLCEACQUA [IM]
TEL. 018431539
www.altavia.im.it

CELLAR SALES
PRE-BOOKED VISITS
ACCOMMODATION
ANNUAL PRODUCTION 40,000 bottles
HECTARES UNDER VINE 3.00

This young estate bottled its first wines in 2004 and is one of the most dynamic operations in Val Nervia. Planted in soils of alternating sandy sediment and marl, the vineyards are all bush-trained, high density at 8,500 plants per hectare, and around ten years old, aside from one 40-year old vineyard of rossese. Alongside rossese and vermentino, there are also some rather unusual varieties for this area like carignano, syrah and viognier. Wines made here have a modern style, nice structure and rich fruit. The Rossese di Dolceacqua Superiore 2010 shows clear tones of fresh red berries with shades of spice and Mediterranean scrub, great balance and a long, distinctive finish. An interesting experiment, the Thend 2005, is a monovarietal from touriga nacional, the main variety used in making Port. This wine is intense and fruity, yet not very complex, especially for a wine released to market after eight years.

● Rossese di Dolceacqua Sup. '10	♀♀	3*
● Thend '05	♀♀	4
○ Noname	♀	4
● Dapprimo '10	♀♀	3*
● Dapprimo '08	♀♀	3*
● Grai '07	♀♀	3
● Grai '06	♀♀	3
○ Noname '10	♀♀	3
● Rossese di Dolceacqua Sup. '09	♀♀	3

Laura Aschero

P.ZZA VITTORIO EMANUELE, 7
18027 PONTEDASSIO [IM]
TEL. 3477561709
www.lauraaschero.it

CELLAR SALES
PRE-BOOKED VISITS
ANNUAL PRODUCTION 60,000 bottles
HECTARES UNDER VINE 2.90

This small estate was founded by Laura Aschero in 1981 and is now managed by her son, Mauro Rizzo. Only the native varieties of vermentino, pigato and rossese are grown here, and vineyards are located in two plots, both with a western exposure, and supported by low dry-stone walls. The historic vineyard of around a hectare is in the Monti area, around 150 metres above sea level, on rocky, limestone soils, and the other vineyards are in the Posai region on red earth. These wines show great constancy in their quality, remarkable aromatic clarity, and a clear territorial stamp. The exemplary Riviera Ligure di Ponente Vermentino 2012 is intense and packed with notes of Mediterranean scrub and white-fleshed fruit on the nose. The palate is complex, round and long, with great richness of flavour. The classic Riviera Ligure di Ponente Pigato 2012 has dried herb aromas and a dry, taut palate, almost austere in the finish with slightly acidic tones.

○ Riviera Ligure di Ponente Vermentino '12	♀♀	3*
○ Riviera Ligure di Ponente Pigato '12	♀♀	3
● Riviera Ligure di Ponente Rossese '12	♀	3
○ Riviera Ligure di Ponente Vermentino '10	♀♀♀	3*
○ Riviera Ligure di Ponente Pigato '11	♀♀	3*
○ Riviera Ligure di Ponente Pigato '08	♀♀	3*
○ Riviera Ligure di Ponente Vermentino '11	♀♀	3
○ Riviera Ligure di Ponente Vermentino '09	♀♀	3
○ Riviera Ligure di Ponente Vermentino '08	♀♀	3*
○ Riviera Ligure di Ponente Vermentino '07	♀♀	3

La Baia del Sole

FRAZ. LUNI ANTICA
VIA FORLINO, 3
19034 ORTONOVO [SP]
TEL. 0187661821
www.cantinefederici.com

CELLAR SALES
PRE-BOOKED VISITS
ANNUAL PRODUCTION 150,000 bottles
HECTARES UNDER VINE 24.00

For 25 years now, the Federici family has
been one of the major players on the
winemaking scene in Lunigiana. Vineyards
are planted in the high ground of the
townships of Ortonovo and Castelnuovo
Magra. Although vermentino is clearly the
most important variety on the estate,
planted in real crus like Sarticola, it is also
worth mentioning the presence of albarola
and malvasia for white grapes, and
sangiovese, ciliegiolo, canaiolo, merlot,
syrah and cabernet sauvignon for reds.
Wines produced here are designed with a
preference for rich fruit and drinkability.
This year the Colli di Luni Rosso Eutichiano
from the Federicis is outstanding. The
elegant 2012 version has vegetal tones
accompanied by spicy notes, and is
supple with great length. The successful
range of 2012 Colli di Luni Vermentinos
includes: a floral Solaris with good
structure and freshness; the Sarticola, well
balanced with rosemary aromas; and the
Oro d'Isèe, stylish, long and zesty.

● Colli di Luni Eutichiano '12	♥♥ 3*
○ Colli di Luni Vermentino Oro d'Isèe '12	♥♥ 4
○ Colli di Luni Vermentino Sarticola '12	♥♥ 5
○ Colli di Luni Vermentino Solaris '12	♥♥ 3
○ Colli di Luni Gladius '12	♥ 3
○ Liguria di Levante Bianco Muri Grandi '12	♥ 2
● Colli di Luni Eutichiano '11	♥♥ 3
○ Colli di Luni Gladius '11	♥♥ 3
○ Colli di Luni Gladius '10	♥♥ 2
○ Colli di Luni Vermentino Oro d'Isèe '11	♥♥ 4
○ Colli di Luni Vermentino Oro d'Isèe '10	♥♥ 4
○ Colli di Luni Vermentino Solaris '10	♥♥ 2

Maria Donata Bianchi

LOC. VALCROSA
VIA MEREA
18013 DIANO ARENTINO [IM]
TEL. 0183498233
www.aziendaagricolabianchi.it

CELLAR SALES
PRE-BOOKED VISITS
ACCOMMODATION
ANNUAL PRODUCTION 30,000 bottles
HECTARES UNDER VINE 4.00

This small family operation in Riviera Ligure
di Ponente has produced top quality wines
for more than 30 years. Planted mainly to
vermentino and pigato, most of the vineyards
are located around the estate headquarters
at 350 metres above sea level on clay soils.
Another three small plots with limestone
soils are also planted to vermentino, along
with granaccia and syrah. Estate labels
feature fruity notes and outstanding richness
of flavour. A typical example of this
approach, the intense, multi-faceted Riviera
Ligure di Ponente Pigato 2012, has nice
notes of white-fleshed fruit and resin
shades. The powerful, rich palate is almost
salty and well supported by acidity. Also
interesting, the Antico Sfizio 2012
Vermentino macerated on the skins is
balsamic with clear medicinal herb notes,
powerful and full-bodied but really austere,
with no concessions made to softness or
drinkability.

○ Riviera Ligure di Ponente Pigato '12	♥♥♥ 3*
○ Antico Sfizio '12	♥♥ 4
○ Riviera Ligure di Ponente Vermentino '12	♥ 3
○ Riviera Ligure di Ponente Vermentino '09	♥♥♥ 3
○ Riviera Ligure di Ponente Vermentino '07	♥♥♥ 3*
○ Riviera Ligure di Ponente Pigato '11	♥♥ 4
○ Riviera Ligure di Ponente Pigato '09	♥♥ 3
○ Riviera Ligure di Ponente Vermentino '11	♥♥ 4
○ Riviera Ligure di Ponente Vermentino '10	♥♥ 3
○ Riviera Ligure di Ponente Vermentino '08	♥♥ 4

BioVio

FRAZ. BASTIA
VIA CROCIATA, 24
17031 ALBENGA [SV]
TEL. 018220776
www.biovio.it

CELLAR SALES
PRE-BOOKED VISITS
ANNUAL PRODUCTION 40,000 bottles
HECTARES UNDER VINE 6.00
VITICULTURE METHOD Certified Organic

The entire Vio family is passionately
committed to the growth and development
of this estate, whether this involves
wine-growing, aromatic herbs, or
extra-virgin olive oil. Vineyards are divided
into various plots between Bastia and Ranzo
along the Arroscia valley, planted in soils
that run from clay and limestone to rocky,
with a prevalence of red earth. Varieties are
those of local tradition like vermentino,
pigato, granaccia and rossese, and make
typical wines capable of best expressing the
features of this terroir. Always high quality,
the Riviera Ligure di Ponente Vermentino
Aimone 2012 has iodine and citrus tones
on the nose, and an unusual apricot note on
a rich, well-balanced palate despite the
clear sweet shades. Sound and also well
made, the Riviera Ligure di Ponente Pigato
Ma René 2012 has intense white-fleshed
fruit and rosemary notes, and a complex,
firm palate. The rest of the range is better
than correct.

○ Riviera Ligure di Ponente Vermentino Aimone '12	🍷🍷 2*
○ Riviera Ligure di Ponente Pigato Ma René '12	🍷🍷 2*
● Bacilò '12	🍷 2
● Granaccia Gigò '12	🍷 3
● Riviera Ligure di Ponente Rossese U Bastiò '12	🍷 2
○ Riviera Ligure di Ponente Vermentino Aimone '11	🍷🍷🍷 2*
● Granaccia Gigò '10	🍷🍷 3*
○ Riviera Ligure di Ponente Pigato Bon in da Bon '10	🍷🍷 3*
○ Riviera Ligure di Ponente Pigato MaRenè '11	🍷🍷 2*
○ Riviera Ligure di Ponente Vermentino Aimone '10	🍷🍷 2*

Enoteca Bisson

C.SO GIANELLI, 28
16043 CHIAVARI [GE]
TEL. 0185314462
www.bissonvini.it

CELLAR SALES
PRE-BOOKED VISITS
ANNUAL PRODUCTION 80,000 bottles
HECTARES UNDER VINE 12.00

This estate grows vermentino and pigato,
as well as rare varieties like bianchetta
genovese, and some nearly forgotten like
cimixià, along with ciliegiolo and granaccia,
barbera and dolcetto. Piero Lugano and his
daughter Marta, after making the shift from
just bottling wines to producing grapes on
their estates in Campegli, Trigoso and
Verici, decided to promote Liguria's native
varieties and traditions. Their vineyards are
planted mainly on sandy-clay soils with
pebbly gravel, and go to making wines that
combine pleasantness with an authentic
expression of typicality. The Portofino
Çimixà L'Antico 2012 showed clean and
pleasant fruity notes, though still a bit
simple. However, the Golfo del Tigullio
Bianchetta Genovese Ü Pastine 2012
shows fascinating complexity, with tones of
pine needles and resin, nice structure and
fullness, and is well-balanced with a gutsy
finish. The other wines submitted were
correct and pleasant.

○ Golfo del Tigullio Bianchetta Genovese Ü Pastine '12	🍷🍷 2*
○ Portofino Cimixà L'Antico '12	🍷🍷 4
○ Golfo del Tigullio Vermentino V. Intrigoso '12	🍷 3
● Il Granaccio Passito '09	🍷 5
● Braccorosso '09	🍷🍷 4
○ Golfo del Tigullio Vermentino V. Erta '11	🍷🍷 2*
○ Golfo del Tigullio Vermentino V. Erta '10	🍷🍷 2
○ Golfo del Tigullio Vermentino V . Intrigoso '09	🍷🍷 3
● Il Musaico '09	🍷🍷 3

Samuele Heydi Bonanini

VIA SAN ANTONIO, 72
19017 RIOMAGGIORE [SP]
TEL. 0187920959
www.possa.it

CELLAR SALES
PRE-BOOKED VISITS
ANNUAL PRODUCTION 7,000 bottles
HECTARES UNDER VINE 1.50

Samuele Heydi Bonanini proves one of the most interesting wine-growers in Cinque Terre. His work restoring the surrounding territory, particularly the reconstruction of terraces abandoned for years, reflects the quality of his wines, produced to give greatest expression to the traditions and character of this area. Grapes grown include albarola, vermentino, bosco, piccabun, rossese bianco, and frapelao, along with canaiolo and other native red varieties. The Tre Bicchieri goes to the Cinque Terre 2012 from Edy Bonanini. With light maceration on the skins, this intense, elegant wine has notes of Mediterranean scrub and tobacco, richness and great length. Also quite good, the Sciacchetrà 2012 is perfectly in line with this wine type with tones of orange, hazelnuts and coffee, sweet yet with great richness of flavour, a light, pleasant tannic shade, and a long aromatic herb finish. The Rinascita 2011 and Vin dei Vecci are both interesting and complex.

○ Cinque Terre '12	▼▼▼	5
○ Cinque Terre Sciacchetrà '11	▼▼	8
● Passito La Rinascita '11	▼▼	8
○ Vin dei Vecci	▼▼	2*
● Rosso U Neigru	▼	3
○ Cinque Terre '11	♀♀	5
○ Cinque Terre '10	♀♀	6
○ Cinque Terre '09	♀♀	6
○ Cinque Terre Sciacchetrà '10	♀♀	8
○ Cinque Terre Sciacchetrà '09	♀♀	8
○ Cinque Terre Sciacchetrà '08	♀♀	8
○ Cinque Terre Vetua '11	♀♀	5
● Passito La Rinascita '10	♀♀	8

Cantina Bregante

VIA UNITÀ D'ITALIA, 47
16039 SESTRI LEVANTE [GE]
TEL. 018541388
www.cantinebregante.it

CELLAR SALES
PRE-BOOKED VISITS
ANNUAL PRODUCTION 100,000 bottles
HECTARES UNDER VINE 1.50

Now managed by Sergio Sanguineti, this estate has a winemaking tradition that goes back to the mid-19th century. Around 50 growers work various plots in the areas from the Tigullio Gulf to Val Graveglia. The most important varieties grown are vermentino, bianchetta genovese, ciliegiolo, and moscato, alongside smaller amounts of other native varieties. Increased attention to quality in the last few years has led to wines with remarkable aromatic precision, aimed at expressing the best features from this terroir. Sergio Sanguineti submitted a nice array this year. The Golfo del Tigullio Vermentino Segesta Tigulliorum 2012 is introduced with notes of dried aromatic herbs and ripe white-fleshed fruit. The palate is rich and full-bodied. The typical Golfo del Tigullio Bianchetta Genovese Segesta Tigulliorum 2012 has fresh, pleasant vegetal notes, while the Portofino Moscato 2012 shows peach and melon with shades of Mediterranean scrub.

○ Golfo del Tigullio Bianchetta Genovese Segesta Tigullorium '12	▼▼	2*
○ Golfo del Tigullio Vermentino Segesta Tigullorium '12	▼▼	2*
○ Portofino Moscato '12	▼▼	3
● Golfo del Tigullio Ca' du Diau '12	▼	3
● Golfo del Tigullio Ciliegiolo '12	▼	2
○ Golfo del Tigullio Passito Sole della Costa '10	▼	6
○ Golfo del Tigullio Portofino Bianchetta Genovese Segesta Tigulliorum '11	♀♀	2*
○ Golfo del Tigullio Vermentino '10	♀♀	2
○ Portofino Moscato '11	♀♀	3

Bruna

FRAZ. BORGO
VIA UMBERTO I, 81
18020 RANZO [IM]
TEL. 0183318082
www.brunapigato.it

CELLAR SALES
PRE-BOOKED VISITS
ANNUAL PRODUCTION 38,000 bottles
HECTARES UNDER VINE 7.50

Riccardo Bruna is part of the history of winemaking in Liguria, particularly as regards the development of pigato, the undisputed leading variety grown at this estate. For some years now, his daughter Francesca and son-in-law Roberto have continued along the path blazed by Riccardo, producing wines that combine typicality, finesse and great personality. The five vineyards on the property are all planted in red earth with a pebbly base in the hills between Ranzo and Ortovero. In addition to pigato, we should mention the presence of red varieties like granaccia, barbera, rossese and syrah. The Riviera Ligure di Ponente Pigato U Baccan takes the Tre Bicchieri once more. The 2011 version has complex mineral notes that run toward gunflint. It has great structure yet is fresh and zesty. Also quite nice, the Riviera Ligure di Ponente Pigato Majé 2012 plays more on fruity notes with shades of resin and Mediterranean scrub, and is long and well balanced.

○ Riviera Ligure di Ponente Pigato U Baccan '11	▼▼▼	5
○ Riviera Ligure di Ponente Pigato Majé '12	▼▼	3*
● Rosso Pulin '11	▼▼	4
● Riviera Ligure di Ponente Rossese '12	▼	3
○ Riviera Ligure di Ponente Pigato U Baccan '07	♀♀♀	5
○ Riviera Ligure di Ponente Pigato U Baccan '06	♀♀♀	4
○ Riviera Ligure di Ponente Pigato U Baccan '05	♀♀♀	4

Buranco

VIA BURANCO, 72
19016 MONTEROSSO AL MARE [SP]
TEL. 0187817677
www.burancocinqueterre.it

CELLAR SALES
PRE-BOOKED VISITS
ACCOMMODATION
ANNUAL PRODUCTION 25,400 bottles
HECTARES UNDER VINE 2.00

The Grillo family estate skirts the River Buranco, in the municipality of Monterosso al Mare, and features two hectares of vineyard on one single plot, something rare for this area. Located traditionally on terraces supported by dry stonewalls, the shallow, loose soils rest on shale and are rich in mineral salts. Alongside traditional Cinque Terre varieties of bosco, vermentino and albarola, red varieties are also grown like cabernet sauvignon, syrah and merlot. Wines from Buranco prove some of the best from the zone. The intense Cinque Terre 2012 has a skin-contact timbre, notes of Mediterranean scrub, medicinal herbs and white-fleshed fruit; it is elegant, tangy, fresh and long. Also well made, the sweet, rich Cinque Terre Sciacchetrà 2011 has dried figs followed by slightly salty, iodine tones, and the Syrah-Cabernet Sauvignon 2011 shows pencil lead and ripe red berry fruit on a sweet spice background.

○ Cinque Terre '12	▼▼	4
○ Cinque Terre Sciacchetrà '11	▼▼	8
● Syrah - Cabernet Sauvignon '11	▼▼	2*
○ Cinque Terre Mangioa '12	▼	5
○ Cinque Terre Bianco '09	♀♀	4
○ Cinque Terre Sciacchetrà '10	♀♀	8
○ Cinque Terre Sciacchetrà '09	♀♀	8
○ Cinque Terre Sciacchetrà '07	♀♀	8
○ Mojou '08	♀♀	4

Cascina Nirasca

FRAZ. NIRASCA
VIA ALPI, 3
18026 PIEVE DI TECO [IM]
TEL. 0183368067
www.cascinanirasca.com

CELLAR SALES
PRE-BOOKED VISITS
ANNUAL PRODUCTION 30,000 bottles
HECTARES UNDER VINE 4.00

For ten years, Marco Temesio, in the cellar, and Gabriele Maglio, in the vineyard, have been working to build up this lovely operation in Ponente Ligure. The vineyards have good density, up to 7,000 plants per hectare, are located in the Arroscia valley between 400 and 500 metres above sea level on rocky, limestone soils, and planted almost exclusively to the classic local varieties, first and foremost ormeasco, then pigato and vermentino, and finally syrah and sangiovese. This year we were most convinced by the whites. The excellent Riviera Ligure di Ponente Vermentino 2012 shows classic notes of white-fleshed fruit with mineral shades, great balance between the richness of fruit and acidity, and is long and zesty. The sound Riviera Ligure di Ponente Pigato 2012 has touches of citron and bitter orange, and a citrusy palate with almost austere, bitterish tones. The various Ormeasco di Pornassios are correct, particularly the pleasant, full-flavoured Sciac-trà 2012.

○ Riviera Ligure di Ponente Vermentino '12	♥♥ 3*
○ Riviera Ligure di Ponente Pigato '12	♥♥ 3
● Ormeasco di Pornassio '12	♥ 3
⊙ Ormeasco di Pornassio Sciac-trà '12	♥ 3
● Ormeasco di Pornassio Sup. '11	♥ 3
● Ormeasco di Pornassio '11	♥♥ 3
● Ormeasco di Pornassio '10	♥♥ 3
● Ormeasco di Pornassio Sup. '07	♥♥ 3*
○ Riviera Ligure di Ponente Pigato '11	♥♥ 3
○ Riviera Ligure di Ponente Pigato '10	♥♥ 3
○ Riviera Ligure di Ponente Pigato '09	♥♥ 3
○ Riviera Ligure di Ponente Vermentino '09	♥♥ 3

Cheo

VIA BRIGATE PARTIGIANE, 1
19018 VERNAZZA [SP]
TEL. 0187821189
bartolocheo@gmail.com

CELLAR SALES
PRE-BOOKED VISITS
ANNUAL PRODUCTION 6,600 bottles
HECTARES UNDER VINE 1.70

For the first time Bartolomeo Lercari and Lisc Bertram's young winery has won a large profile in our Guide. On less than two hectares of land in the hills overlooking Vernazza, they grow mainly the typical local varieties of albarola, bosco, piccabun, and vermentino for white grapes, and gambu russu with a few plants of cabernet sauvignon for reds. Wines made here feature the minerality and full flavour typical of this area. Again in our finals, the Cinque Terre Perciò 2012 is lively and intense with lovely aromatic notes, a rich, zesty palate, and a long, taut, harmonious finish. We also like the Riviera di Levante Rosso 2011, with notes of black berry fruit and forest floor, the Cinque Terre Sciacchetrà 2010, with hints of candied orange peel, and the citrusy and expansive Cinque Terre 2012..

○ Cinque Terre Perciò '12	♥♥ 4
○ Cinque Terre '12	♥♥ 4
○ Cinque Terre Sciacchetrà '10	♥♥ 7
● Riviera di Levante '11	♥♥ 4
○ Cinque Terre Cheo '11	♥♥ 3*
○ Cinque Terre Perciò '11	♥♥ 4
○ Cinque Terre Perciò '10	♥♥ 4
○ Cinque Terre Sciacchetrà '09	♥♥ 7
○ Cinque Terre Sciacchetrà '08	♥♥ 7
○ Cinque Terre Sciacchetrà '07	♥♥ 7

LIGURIA

Cantina Cinqueterre

FRAZ. MANAROLA
LOC. GROPPO
19010 RIOMAGGIORE [SP]
TEL. 0187920435
www.cantinacinqueterre.com

PRE-BOOKED VISITS
ANNUAL PRODUCTION 200,000 bottles
HECTARES UNDER VINE 45.00
VITICULTURE METHOD Certified Organic

Founded in 1973 to develop wine-growing in Cinque Terre and at the same time protect its landscapes and ecosystems, today around 250 members contribute to making this co-operative winery an exceptional benchmark for wine production in this district. The land under vine is made up of many small plots, especially between Riomaggiore and Monterosso. The grapes go to making various labels that express the characteristics of this terroir, and even permit the production of selections originating from different zones. Of the three produced, we especially like the Cinque Terre Coste de Sèra 2012, with outstanding mineral notes refreshed by a background of white-fleshed fruit, good body, nice length, and a pleasantly bitterish finish. Also well made, the Cinque Terre Sciacchetrà Riserva 2009 has aromas of candied apricot, dried figs and almonds, and a clear, clean palate that is just a bit simple.

○ Cinque Terre Costa de Sèra '12	🍷🍷 3
○ Cinque Terre Sciacchetrà Ris. '09	🍷🍷 6
○ Cinque Terre Costa da Posa '12	🍷 3
○ Cinque Terre Costa de Campu '12	🍷 3
○ Cinque Terre '10	🍷🍷 2*
○ Cinque Terre Costa da Posa '11	🍷🍷 3
○ Cinque Terre Costa da Posa di Volastra '10	🍷🍷 3
○ Cinque Terre Costa du Campu '10	🍷🍷 3
○ Cinque Terre Sciacchetrà '09	🍷🍷 6
○ Cinqueterre Sciacchetrà Un Paesaggio Un Vino '10	🍷🍷 6

Azienda Agricola Durin

LOC. ORTOVERO
VIA ROMA, 202
17037 ORTOVERO [SV]
TEL. 0182547007
www.durin.it

CELLAR SALES
PRE-BOOKED VISITS
ACCOMMODATION AND RESTAURANT SERVICE
ANNUAL PRODUCTION 130,000 bottles
HECTARES UNDER VINE 15.50

The Basso family's historic estate was founded at the beginning of last century. In the past few years it has added a single plot of over five hectares in the Onzo hills, terraced with dry stone walls, to their vineyards in the Ortovero plain located next to the cellar. Pigato, vermentino, rossese, alicante, granaccia, ormeasco, sangiovese, and barbera go into making the broad range of labels proposed by Durin. The wines show remarkable aromatic richness, and are very typical and recognizable. Of the two 2012 Riviera Ligure di Ponente Pigatos, we like the base version: broad with great complexity, notes running from white-fleshed fruit to Mediterranean scrub, and good balance between fullness and acidity. Characterful but less elegant, the Braie 2012 is dense and almost tannic. The two 2012 Riviera Ligure di Ponente Vermentinos are also well made. The base version is powerful yet full-flavoured, and the intense Lunghèra 2012 has multi-faceted notes of fruit and medicinal herbs.

○ Riviera Ligure di Ponente Pigato '12	🍷🍷 2*
○ Riviera Ligure di Ponente Pigato V. Braie '12	🍷🍷 3
○ Riviera Ligure di Ponente Vermentino '12	🍷🍷 2*
○ Riviera Ligure di Ponente Vermentino Lunghèra '12	🍷🍷 3
● Alicante '10	🍷 3
● Bàsura Riunda Brut M. Cl. '07	🍷 5
● Granaccia '12	🍷 3
● I Matti '10	🍷 3
● Ormeasco di Pornassio Sup. '11	🍷 3
○ Pigato Passito '11	🍷 3
● Riviera Ligure di Ponente Rossese '12	🍷 3
● Granaccia '11	🍷🍷 3
○ Pigato Passito '10	🍷🍷 3

Fontanacota

LOC. PONTI
FRAZ. PORNASSIO
VIA PROVINCIALE
18100 IMPERIA
TEL. 3339807442
www.fontanacota.it

CELLAR SALES
PRE-BOOKED VISITS
ANNUAL PRODUCTION 40,000 bottles
HECTARES UNDER VINE 6.00

Marina and Fabio Berta started their Fontanacota operation in 2001 when Marina restored an existing estate, and is now based on two distinct holdings. The largest is in Val Prino where 70% of the vines are vermentino and the rest pigato and rossese; the smallest is in the high Arroscia valley, located over 500 metres above sea level, and planted exclusively to ormeasco. It is worth noting that both these plots include some 40-years-old vines. This year the Riviera Ligure di Ponente Vermentino 2012 most convinced us. Intense and scented with Mediterranean scrub on a background of white-fleshed fruit, this wine has good body, decent finesse and a long finish. The 2012 version of the Riviera Ligure di Ponente Pigato is pleasant and citrusy with nice tanginess, though less brilliant and gutsy than last year. The Ormeasco di Pornassio Superiore 2011 is balanced with good staying power. The other labels submitted were also sound.

○ Riviera Ligure di Ponente Vermentino '12	♟♟ 3*
● Ormeasco di Pornassio Sup. '11	♟♟ 3
○ Riviera Ligure di Ponente Pigato '12	♟♟ 3
● Ormeasco di Pornassio '12	♟ 2
○ Ormeasco di Pornassio Sciac-Trà '12	♟ 2
● Riviera Ligure di Ponente Rossese '12	♟ 2
○ Riviera Ligure di Ponente Pigato '11	♟♟♟ 3*
● Ormeasco di Pornassio Sup. '10	♟♟ 3
○ Riviera Ligure di Ponente Pigato '10	♟♟ 2*
○ Riviera Ligure di Ponente Pigato '09	♟♟ 2*

Ottaviano Lambruschi

VIA OLMARELLO, 28
19030 CASTELNUOVO MAGRA [SP]
TEL. 0187674261
www.ottavianolambruschi.com

CELLAR SALES
PRE-BOOKED VISITS
ANNUAL PRODUCTION 36,000 bottles
HECTARES UNDER VINE 6.00

With help from his son Fabio, Ottaviano Lambruschi remains the "maestro" of Lunigiana vermentino. Indeed, wines from this estate are a stylistic model for the territory with their ability to bring out the best of the variety's characteristic freshness and tanginess. All the vineyards are planted on hillsides in shale clay soils, with exposures to the south and southeast, and breezes from the sea. Sangiovese, merlot and canaiolo complete the estate range, and go into the only red wine produced. This year the Colli di Luni Vermentino Il Maggiore 2012 won the Tre Bicchieri. With intense aromas of dried medicinal herbs and mineral hints, this wine shows great finesse, taut and tangy yet with remarkable body, and closes on a long, characterful finish. Almost as good, the Colli di Luni Vermentino Costa Marina 2012 shows more fruit and good behaviour, but is less structured and deep. The only estate red, the Maniero 2012 is pleasant.

○ Colli di Luni Vermentino Il Maggiore '12	♟♟♟ 4*
○ Colli di Luni Vermentino Costa Marina '12	♟♟ 4
● Maniero '12	♟♟ 3
○ Colli di Luni Vermentino Costa Marina '11	♟♟♟ 4*
○ Colli di Luni Vermentino Costa Marina '09	♟♟♟ 3
○ Colli di Luni Vermentino Sarticola '08	♟♟♟ 3*
○ Colli di Luni Vermentino Costa Marina '10	♟♟ 3
○ Colli di Luni Vermentino Costa Marina '08	♟♟ 3
○ Colli di Luni Vermentino Il Maggiore '11	♟♟ 4
○ Colli di Luni Vermentino Sarticola '10	♟♟ 3
○ Colli di Luni Vermentino Sarticola '09	♟♟ 3

Cantine Lunae Bosoni

FRAZ. ISOLA DI ORTONOVO
VIA BOZZI, 63
19034 ORTONOVO [SP]
TEL. 0187669222
www.cantinelunae.com

Lupi

VIA MAZZINI, 9
18026 PIEVE DI TECO [IM]
TEL. 018336161
www.casalupi.it

CELLAR SALES
PRE-BOOKED VISITS
ACCOMMODATION
ANNUAL PRODUCTION 450,000 bottles
HECTARES UNDER VINE 65.00

CELLAR SALES
PRE-BOOKED VISITS
ANNUAL PRODUCTION 160,000 bottles
HECTARES UNDER VINE 12.00

Lunae Bosoni is a rare case in Liguria's wine-growing scenario. The 150 growers, the winery's technical staff, and 15 hectares of its own vineyards guarantee Paolo Bosoni's operation can produce a major range both in number of labels and quantity of bottles produced, making this a benchmark in the Colli di Luni DOC zone. The main features of wines here are their clear aromatic exuberance and richness of fruit. The Tre Bicchieri goes to the Colli di Luni Vermentino Etichetta Nera 2012, with aromas of peach and dried aromatic herbs. The palate has remarkable structure, well supported by great freshness, and a long, harmonious finish. Also good, the Colli di Luni Vermentino Cavagino 2012 has outstanding floral, aromatic tones, good complexity, and a classic, gutsy, bitterish finish. The rest of the wines are sound.

Massimo Lupi enthusiastically and skilfully follows the path blazed for more than 50 years by his father, Tommaso. Lupi produces wines from the most important, best-known varieties in Ponente Ligure, from ormeasco to rossese, pigato and vermentino. Vineyards on the property are 80% planted with bush-trained vines, some over 60 years old. Wines, particularly the white selections, are among the few labels from Liguria designed to stand the test of time, and in the past few years have shown they also have the ability. Again this year, Lupi proves his abilities as a great maker of white wines in an area traditionally more suited to reds. Both good wines, the Riviera Ligure di Ponente Vermentino Le Serre 2011 is stylish yet also complex with notes of minerals and Mediterranean scrub, tangy and long, and the Riviera Ligure di Ponente Pigato 2012 is fresh and elegant on notes of white-fleshed fruit and aromatic herbs, and shows great character.

○ Colli di Luni Vermentino Et. Nera '12	♟♟♟	4*
○ Colli di Luni Vermentino Cavagino '12	♟♟	5
○ Colli di Luni Albarola '12	♟♟	4
● Colli di Luni Niccolò V Ris. '06	♟♟	5
● Colli di Luni Niccolò V '09	♟	4
○ Colli di Luni Vermentino Numero Chiuso '09	♟	6
● Horae '11	♟	5
○ Colli di Luni Vermentino Et. Nera '11	♟♟♟	4*
○ Colli di Luni Vermentino Et. Nera '10	♟♟♟	4
○ Colli di Luni Vermentino Lunae Et. Nera '09	♟♟♟	4
○ Colli di Luni Vermentino Lunae Et. Nera '08	♟♟♟	4*
○ Colli di Luni Vermentino Cavagino '11	♟♟	5

○ Riviera Ligure di Ponente Pigato '12	♟♟	3*
○ Riviera Ligure di Ponente Vermentino Le Serre '11	♟♟	3*
○ Riviera Ligure di Ponente Pigato Le Petraie '11	♟♟	3
○ Riviera Ligure di Ponente Vermentino '12	♟♟	3
● Rossese di Dolceacqua '12	♟♟	3
⊙ Ormeasco di Pornassio Sciac-trà '12	♟	3
○ Vignamare '10	♟	4
○ Riviera Ligure di Ponente Vermentino Le Serre '09	♟♟♟	3
○ Riviera Ligure di Ponente Vermentino Le Serre '08	♟♟♟	5
○ Riviera Ligure di Ponente Vermentino Le Serre '07	♟♟♟	5

Maccario Dringenberg

VIA TORRE, 3
18036 SAN BIAGIO DELLA CIMA [IM]
TEL. 0184289947
maccariodringenberg@yahoo.it

CELLAR SALES
PRE-BOOKED VISITS
ANNUAL PRODUCTION 23,000 bottles
HECTARES UNDER VINE 4.00

Little Maccario Dringenberg has been one of the most successful wineries in the past few years with its Rossese di Dolceacqua, which in a short time has gone from a historic DOC with a tarnished image, to a wine particularly prized for its freshness and drinkability. The two most important vineyards, where the estate crus are sourced, Posaù in Val Verbone and Luvaira in Val Nervia, have bush-trained vines that may reach a hundred years of age. Wines produced are elegant with great aromatic precision. A positive debut for the third estate cru, the intense, multi-faceted Rossese di Dolceacqua Brae 2012 has notes of citrus peel and pepper, and is supple, balanced and taut. In the absence of the Posaù and Luvaira, the lion's share goes to the basic Rossese di Dolceacqua 2012, pleasant with red berry and tobacco tones, full flavoured with great acid backbone and nice drinkability, but lacking the complexity of its big brothers.

● Rossese di Dolceacqua '12	♟♟ 3*
● Rossese di Dolceacqua Brae '12	♟♟ 3
☉ Rosacroce '12	♟ 2
● Rossese di Dolceacqua Sup. Vign. Luvaira '07	♟♟♟ 4*
● Rossese di Dolceacqua Sup. Vign. Posaù '10	♟♟♟ 3*
● Rossese di Dolceacqua Sup. Vign. Posaù '08	♟♟♟ 3
● Rossese di Dolceacqua '11	♟♟ 3*
● Rossese di Dolceacqua '10	♟♟ 3
● Rossese di Dolceacqua Sup. Vign. Luvaira '10	♟♟ 4
● Rossese di Dolceacqua Sup. Vign. Luvaira '08	♟♟ 4

Il Monticello

VIA GROPPOLO, 7
19038 SARZANA [SP]
TEL. 0187621432
www.ilmonticello.it

CELLAR SALES
PRE-BOOKED VISITS
ACCOMMODATION
ANNUAL PRODUCTION 68,000 bottles
HECTARES UNDER VINE 10.00

Davide and Alessandro Neri have made their family winery a production leader for the Colli di Luni DOC zone. The vineyards are located in the hills, exposed to breezes from the sea, and planted in clay soils with sandy-silty features for fresh, drinkable wines with outstanding personality and territorial faithfulness. A biodynamic choice was made along with an environmental decision that saved energy with the construction of an integrated photovoltaic plant. Two splendid Vermentinos are at the forefront of the Neri brothers' winery. The fresh, complex Colli di Luni 2012 has notes of pink grapefruit, good body, length and balance. The Poggio Paterno Il Bocciato 2011, so named because it was turned down, or "bocciato", by the commission that assigns the DOC appellation, is intense and rich with lovely notes of medicinal herbs and tropical fruit, gutsy and dynamic. Also well made, the Colli di Luni Rosso Rupestro 2012 is balsamic and structured.

○ Colli di Luni Vermentino '12	♟♟ 3*
○ Poggio Paterno Il Bocciato '11	♟♟ 3*
● Colli di Luni Rosso Rupestro '12	♟♟ 2*
● Colli di Luni Rosso Poggio dei Magni Ris. '10	♟ 3
☉ Serasuolo '12	♟ 2
● Colli di Luni Rosso Poggio dei Magni Ris. '07	♟♟ 3
○ Colli di Luni Vermentino '08	♟♟ 2*
○ Colli di Luni Vermentino Poggio Paterno '10	♟♟ 3*
○ Colli di Luni Vermentino Poggio Paterno '09	♟♟ 3
○ Colli di Luni Vermentino Poggio Paterno '08	♟♟ 3
○ Colli di Luni Vermentino Poggio Paterno '07	♟♟ 3*

Conte Picedi Benettini

VIA MAZZINI, 57
19038 SARZANA [SP]
TEL. 0187625147
www.picedibenettini.it

CELLAR SALES
PRE-BOOKED VISITS
ACCOMMODATION
ANNUAL PRODUCTION 30,000 bottles
HECTARES UNDER VINE 7.00

The wine-growing part of the estate of
Conte Picedi Benettini lies in two holdings,
straddling the Magra valley and Gulf of La
Spezia: Chioso, located in the hills of
Baccano di Arcola, and the Ceserano farm
in Fivizzano. Estate vineyards are planted to
many varieties, almost all of them native,
many nearly extinct, starting with
vermentino, but also including albarola,
trebbiano, malvasia, durella, verdusco and
ruzzese for white grapes, and pollera,
bracciola nera, sangiovese, merlot,
vermentino nero, massaretta, and rossara
for the reds. Really lovely, the well-balanced
Colli di Luni Vermentino 2012 has notes of
almond, peach, lychees and aromatic
herbs, and is dense and zesty with great
body and a long, taut finish. The other
2012 Colli di Luni Vermentinos are also
well crafted. The Chioso is still young with
notes of ripe white-fleshed fruit and
medicinal herbs, and nice tanginess but a
slightly bitter finish. The Stemma is less
precise but has remarkable structure and
rich fruit.

○ Colli di Luni Vermentino '12		♛♛ 2*
○ Colli di Luni Vermentino Il Chioso '12		♛♛ 2*
○ Colli di Luni Vermentino Stemma '12		♛♛ 3
⊙ Ciliegiolo Fattoria di Ceserano '12		♛ 2
⊙ Ciliegiolo '10		♛♛ 2*
○ Colli di Luni Vermentino Il Chioso '11		♛♛ 2*
○ Colli di Luni Vermentino Il Chioso '09		♛♛ 2*
○ Colli di Luni Vermentino Stemma '11		♛♛ 3*
○ Colli di Luni Vermentino Stemma '10		♛♛ 3
○ Colli di Luni Vermentino Stemma '09		♛♛ 2*

Poggio dei Gorleri

FRAZ. GORLERI
VIA SAN LEONARDO
18013 DIANO MARINA [IM]
TEL. 0183495207
www.poggiodeigorleri.com

CELLAR SALES
PRE-BOOKED VISITS
ACCOMMODATION AND RESTAURANT SERVICE
ANNUAL PRODUCTION 69,000 bottles
HECTARES UNDER VINE 6.50

In ten years, the Merano family has made
Poggio dei Gorleri a top wine-growing
estate in Liguria. Over the years this estate
has expanded with the aim of limiting the
purchase of grapes from contributing
growers. The vermentino, pigato, granaccia
and ormeasco varieties are grown, with
respect and attention to nature, between
Diano Marina, Albenga and Pieve di Teco,
in vineyards with excellent expositions,
planted in pebbly, clay soils. The wines
combine territorial typicality with great
character. This year the Tre Bicchieri went
to the stylish and intense Riviera Ligure di
Ponente Pigato Cycnus 2012 featuring
fruity, mineral notes, and a long, tangy
finish. Excellent scores also went to the
Riviera Ligure di Ponente Vermentino Vigna
Sorì 2012 and Riviera Ligure di Ponente
Pigato Albium 2011. The Sorì introduces
white-fleshed fruit and floral notes,
followed by shades of dried aromatic
herbs, and a harmonious, zesty palate. The
Albium has great structure and lovely spicy
notes.

○ Riviera Ligure di Ponente Pigato Cycnus '12		♛♛♛ 3*
○ Riviera Ligure di Ponente Pigato Albium '11		♛♛ 5
○ Riviera Ligure di Ponente Vermentino V. Sorì '12		♛♛ 3*
● Ormeasco di Pornassio Peinetti '12		♛♛ 3
○ Riviera Ligure di Ponente Vermentino '12		♛♛ 2*
● Riviera Ligure di Ponente Granaccia Shalok '11		♛ 3
○ Riviera Ligure di Ponente Pigato Albium '10		♛♛♛ 5
○ Riviera Ligure di Ponente Pigato Cycnus '10		♛♛♛ 3
○ Riviera Ligure di Ponente Pigato Cycnus '09		♛♛♛ 3*

Sancio

VIA LAIOLO, 73
17028 SPOTORNO [SV]
TEL. 019743255
www.cantinasancio.it

CELLAR SALES
PRE-BOOKED VISITS
ANNUAL PRODUCTION 30,000 bottles
HECTARES UNDER VINE 5.00

For decades the Sancio family have been vignerons in the Spotorno wine-growing area. Today Riccardo Sancio manages this lovely estate in the most eastern part of the Riviera Ligure di Ponente DOC zone, planted to the most typical local varieties like lumassina, pigato, rossese and vermentino. In the vineyards and cellar, Riccardo aims for quality as well as respect for the environment, with the use of solar panels and biomass. This year we particularly like the intense, charming Riviera Ligure di Ponente Pigato 2012 with notes of white-fleshed fruit and almonds, and a rich, balanced palate supported by a good acid structure. Also well made, the Riviera Ligure di Ponente Vermentino 2012 features notes of flowers, apricot and dried aromatic herbs, but lacks a bit of grip in the finish. All the other labels submitted were correct.

○ Riviera Ligure di Ponente Pigato '12	🍷🍷 3*
○ Riviera Ligure di Ponente Vermentino '12	🍷🍷 3
○ Lumassina Vivace Lilaria '12	🍷 2
○ Riviera Ligure di Ponente Pigato Cappellania '12	🍷 3
● Riviera Ligure di Ponente Rossese '12	🍷 3
● Rosso dell'Orco	🍷 2
○ Riviera Ligure di Ponente Pigato '11	🍷🍷 3
● Riviera Ligure di Ponente Rossese '11	🍷🍷 3
● Riviera Ligure di Ponente Rossese '10	🍷🍷 3*
● Riviera Ligure di Ponente Rossese '10	🍷🍷 3*
○ Riviera Ligure di Ponente Vermentino '11	🍷🍷 2*
○ Riviera Ligure di Ponente Vermentino '10	🍷🍷 3

Terre Bianche

LOC. ARCAGNA
18035 DOLCEACQUA [IM]
TEL. 018431426
www.terrebianche.com

CELLAR SALES
PRE-BOOKED VISITS
ACCOMMODATION
ANNUAL PRODUCTION 60,000 bottles
HECTARES UNDER VINE 8.50

Filippo Rondelli has now established Terre Bianche as one of the showcase estates in the Dolceacqua area as well as all Liguria, not just for his Rosseses, some of the most characterful and precise in the DOC zone, but also whites from vermentino and pigato, fresh with a pleasant tanginess. Located in Val Nervia, at 350 to 450 metres above sea level, vineyards include: Arcagna planted in sandy soils with hundred-year old rossese vines; Scartozzoni in red clay, planted to white grape varieties; Terre Bianche in white clay soils; and Monte Curto planted in sandy soils with the rossese, pigato and vermentino varieties. We like the Rossese di Dolceacqua Bricco Arcagna 2011, fruity with a nice liveliness, but somewhat veiled by the spice from the oak, and the Riviera Ligure di Ponente Vermentino 2012, vibrant with great freshness and tanginess. But the basic Rossese di Dolceacqua 2012 really wins us over. This juicy, savoury wine has intense, fascinating notes of forest floor and red berries.

● Rossese di Dolceacqua '12	🍷🍷🍷 3*
○ Riviera Ligure di Ponente Vermentino '12	🍷🍷 3*
● Rossese di Dolceacqua Bricco Arcagna '11	🍷🍷 5
○ Riviera Ligure di Ponente Arcana Bianco '10	🍷🍷 4
● Riviera Ligure di Ponente Arcana Rosso '08	🍷🍷 5
○ Riviera Ligure di Ponente Pigato '12	🍷🍷 3
● Rossese di Dolceacqua Bricco Arcagna '09	🍷🍷🍷 4
● Rossese di Dolceacqua Bricco Arcagna '08	🍷🍷🍷 5
○ Riviera Ligure di Ponente Vermentino '11	🍷🍷 3
● Rossese di Dolceacqua Bricco Arcagna '10	🍷🍷 5

Cascina delle Terre Rosse

VIA MANIE, 3
17024 FINALE LIGURE [SV]
TEL. 019698782

CELLAR SALES
PRE-BOOKED VISITS
ANNUAL PRODUCTION 30,000 bottles
HECTARES UNDER VINE 4.50

Vladimiro Galluzzo's estate is located on the high plain of Manie, in the inland area of Savona, and one of the most important operations in Riviera di Ponente. This winery's name means red earth and is a homage to the colour of the local soils, rich in ferrous minerals. Production is centred mainly on white wines, but there is no lack of attention to reds. Vineyards are organically managed, and planted at around 300 metres above sea level. This vintage is in a minor key for the wines submitted. Most of all we like the Riviera Ligure di Ponente Pigato 2012, with classic notes of white-fleshed fruit, almond and saffron. The palate is not enormous but fairly balanced with good length. The Riviera Ligure di Ponente Vermentino 2012 features citrusy tones and decent structure, but the slightly acidic finish lacks some grip. The rest of the wines are correct.

○ Riviera Ligure di Ponente Pigato '12	♈♈ 4
○ Apogeo '12	♈ 4
○ Riviera Ligure di Ponente Vermentino '12	♈ 4
● Solitario '11	♈ 7
○ Riviera Ligure di Ponente Pigato '99	♈♈♈ 3*
○ Apogeo '11	♈♈ 4
○ Apogeo '10	♈♈ 4
○ Apogeo '09	♈♈ 4
○ Le Banche '10	♈♈ 7
○ Riviera Ligure di Ponente Pigato '11	♈♈ 4
○ Riviera Ligure di Ponente Vermentino '09	♈♈ 4

Vis Amoris

LOC. CARAMAGNA
S.DA MOLINO JAVÈ, 23
18100 IMPERIA
TEL. 3483959569
www.visamoris.it

CELLAR SALES
PRE-BOOKED VISITS
ANNUAL PRODUCTION 26,000 bottles
HECTARES UNDER VINE 3.50

Rossana Zappa and Roberto Tozzi's winery has been in operation for ten years now, a decade when the pair have shown their sheer commitment to the success of this lovely wine-growing enterprise in Imperia, focusing completely on the most typical local variety, pigato, which they vinify in six different types, from sparklers to a dried-grape passito. Vineyards grow in clay and limestone-clay soils, enjoy favourable exposures, and are managed with respect for the environment. This is a great vintage year for the Dulcis in Fundo Passito 2011, a fresh yet intense wine with touches of aromatic herbs. We also like the Riviera Ligure di Ponente Pigato Sogno 2011, showing a nice mineral attack with shades of gunflint and good structure. The other labels submitted are pleasant and well made: the Riviera Ligure di Ponente Pigato Verum 2012, Riviera Ligure di Ponente Pigato Domé 2012, and Vis Amoris Brut Metodo Classico 2010.

○ Dulcis in Fundo '11	♈♈ 5
○ Riviera Ligure di Ponente Pigato Sogno '11	♈♈ 4
○ Riviera Ligure di Ponente Pigato V. Domé '12	♈ 3
○ Riviera Ligure di Ponente Pigato Verum '12	♈ 3
○ Vis Amoris Brut M. Cl. '10	♈ 5
○ Dulcis in Fundo '10	♈♈ 5
○ Dulcis in Fundo '09	♈♈ 5
○ Riviera Ligure di Ponente Pigato Sogno '10	♈♈ 4
○ Riviera Ligure di Ponente Pigato Sogno '09	♈♈ 5
○ Riviera Ligure di Ponente Pigato V. Domè '07	♈♈ 3*
○ Riviera Ligure di Ponente Pigato V. Domè '05	♈♈ 3*

Cooperativa Agricoltori della Vallata di Levanto

LOC. GHIARE
VIA SAN MATTEO, 20
19015 LEVANTO [SP]
TEL. 0187800867
www.levanto.com/cooperativa

CELLAR SALES
PRE-BOOKED VISITS
ANNUAL PRODUCTION 100,000 bottles
HECTARES UNDER VINE 3.00

● Colline di Levanto Rosso Canuet '12	♟♟ 2*
○ Colline di Levanto Vermentino '12	♟ 3

Carlo Alessandri

VIA UMBERTO I, 15
18020 RANZO [IM]
TEL. 0183318114
az.alessandricarlo@libero.it

CELLAR SALES
PRE-BOOKED VISITS
ANNUAL PRODUCTION 19,100 bottles
HECTARES UNDER VINE 2.13

● Ormeasco di Pornassio '12	♟♟ 2*
○ Riviera Ligure di Ponente Vermentino '12	♟♟ 2*
○ Riviera Ligure di Ponente Pigato '12	♟ 2

Massimo Alessandri

VIA COSTA PARROCCHIA, 42
18020 RANZO [IM]
TEL. 018253458
www.massimoalessandri.it

CELLAR SALES
PRE-BOOKED VISITS
RESTAURANT SERVICE
ANNUAL PRODUCTION 35,000 bottles
HECTARES UNDER VINE 6.50

○ Riviera Ligure di Ponente Pigato Costa de Vigne '12	♟♟ 3*
○ Riviera Ligure di Ponente Pigato Vigne Vèggie '12	♟♟ 4

Tenuta Anfosso

C.SO VERBONE, 175
18036 SOLDANO [IM]
TEL. 0184289906
www.tenutaanfosso.it

CELLAR SALES
ACCOMMODATION
ANNUAL PRODUCTION 20,000 bottles
HECTARES UNDER VINE 4.00

● Rossese di Dolceacqua Sup. Poggio Pini '11	♟♟ 4
⊙ Antea	♟ 2
● Rossese di Dolceacqua Sup. Luvaira '11	♟ 4

Riccardo Arrigoni

LOC. MIGLIARINI
VIA SARZANA, 224
19126 LA SPEZIA
TEL. 0187504060
www.awf2000.com

CELLAR SALES
PRE-BOOKED VISITS
ACCOMMODATION AND RESTAURANT SERVICE
ANNUAL PRODUCTION 200,000 bottles
HECTARES UNDER VINE 19.00

○ Cinque Terre Sciacchetrà Tramonti '09	♟♟ 8
○ Colli di Luni Vermentino La Cascina Dei Peri '12	♟♟ 2*
○ Colli di Luni Vermentino V. del Prefetto '12	♟ 3

Luigi Bianchi Carenzo

VIA I. LANTERO, 19
18013 DIANO SAN PIETRO [IM]
TEL. 0183429072

CELLAR SALES
PRE-BOOKED VISITS
ANNUAL PRODUCTION 10,000 bottles
HECTARES UNDER VINE 0.70

○ Riviera Ligure di Ponente Vermentino '12	♟♟ 2*
○ Riviera Ligure di Ponente Pigato '12	♟ 2
● Riviera Ligure di Ponente Rossese '12	♟ 2

Cantine Calleri

LOC. SALEA
REG. FRATTI, 2
17031 ALBENGA [SV]
TEL. 018220085
postmaster@cantinecalleri.com

ANNUAL PRODUCTION 55,000 bottles
HECTARES UNDER VINE 6.00

○ Riviera Ligure di Ponente Pigato Albenga '12	♀♀ 3
○ Riviera Ligure di Ponente Vermentino I Müzazzi '12	♀♀ 3

Luigi Calvini

VIA SOLARO, 76-78A
18038 SANREMO [IM]
TEL. 0184660242
www.luigicalvini.com

CELLAR SALES
PRE-BOOKED VISITS
ANNUAL PRODUCTION 50,000 bottles
HECTARES UNDER VINE 3.00

● Riviera Ligure di Ponente Rossese '12	♀♀ 3
○ Le Coste '12	♀ 2
○ Riviera Ligure di Ponente Pigato '12	♀ 3
○ Riviera Ligure di Ponente Vermentino '12	♀ 3

Altare Bonanni De Grazia Campogrande

VIA DI LOCA, 189
19017 RIOMAGGIORE [SP]
TEL. 3384063383
info@5terre-marmar.com

PRE-BOOKED VISITS
ACCOMMODATION
ANNUAL PRODUCTION 6,000 bottles
HECTARES UNDER VINE 2.00

○ Cinque Terre '11	♀♀ 7
● Cinque Terre Telémaco '11	♀♀ 7

Deperi

FRAZ. CANETO, 2
18020 RANZO [IM]
TEL. 0183318143
www.deperi.eu

PRE-BOOKED VISITS
ANNUAL PRODUCTION 50,000 bottles
HECTARES UNDER VINE 5.00

○ Riviera Ligure di Ponente Pigato '12	♀♀ 2*
○ Riviera Ligure di Ponente Vermentino '12	♀♀ 2*
● Ormeasco di Pornassio '11	♀ 3
⊙ Ormeasco di Pornassio Sciac-trà '12	♀ 2

Forlini Cappellini

LOC. MANAROLA
VIA RICCOBALDI, 45
19010 RIOMAGGIORE [SP]
TEL. 0187920496
forlinicappellini@libero.it

PRE-BOOKED VISITS
ANNUAL PRODUCTION 7,500 bottles
HECTARES UNDER VINE 1.10

○ Cinque Terre '12	♀♀ 4

Giacomelli

VIA PALVOTRISIA, 134
19030 CASTELNUOVO MAGRA [SP]
TEL. 0187674155

CELLAR SALES
PRE-BOOKED VISITS
ANNUAL PRODUCTION 50,000 bottles
HECTARES UNDER VINE 8.00

○ Colli di Luni Vermentino Boboli '11	♀♀ 4
● Colli di Luni Rosso Canal di Bocco '11	♀♀ 4
○ Colli di Luni Vermentino Pianacce '12	♀♀ 2*

La Ginestraia

VIA STERIA
18100 CERVO [IM]
TEL. 3272683692
www.laginestraia.com

ANNUAL PRODUCTION 50,000 bottles
HECTARES UNDER VINE 7.00

○ Riviera Ligure di Ponente Pigato Via Maestra '12	♥♥	3
○ Riviera Ligure dl Ponente Pigato '12	♥	3
○ Riviera Ligure di Ponente Vermentino '12	♥	3

Podere Grecale

LOC. BUSSANA
VIA DUCA D'AOSTA, 52E
18038 SANREMO [IM]
TEL. 01841956107
www.poderegrecale.it/

CELLAR SALES
PRE-BOOKED VISITS
ANNUAL PRODUCTION 20,000 bottles
HECTARES UNDER VINE 2.42
VITICULTURE METHOD Certified Organic

○ Riviera Ligure di Ponente Pigato '12	♥♥	3
○ Riviera Ligure di Ponente Vermentino '12	♥	3

Nicola Guglierame

VIA CASTELLO, 10
18024 PORNASSIO [IM]
TEL. 018333037
www.ormeasco-guglierame.it

CELLAR SALES
PRE-BOOKED VISITS
ANNUAL PRODUCTION 20,000 bottles
HECTARES UNDER VINE 2.50

● Ormeasco di Pornassio Sup. '11	♥♥	3
● Ormeasco di Pornassio '11	♥	3
☉ Ormeasco di Pornassio Sciac-trà '11	♥	3

Ka' Manciné

FRAZ. SAN MARTINO
P.ZZA OTTO LUOGHI, 36
18036 SOLDANO [IM]
TEL. 0184289089
www.kamancine.it

CELLAR SALES
PRE-BOOKED VISITS
ANNUAL PRODUCTION 13,000 bottles
HECTARES UNDER VINE 3.00

● Rossese di Dolceacqua Galeae '12	♥♥	3*
● Rossese di Dolceacqua Beragna '12	♥♥	3
☉ Ormeasco di Pornassio Sciac-Trà '12	♥	3

Podere Lavandaro

VIA CASTIGLIONE
54035 FOSDINOVO [MS]
TEL. 018768202
www.poderelavandaro.it

○ Colli di Luni Vermentino '12	♥♥	3
○ Canizzo Passito '09	♥	6
● Colli di Luni Rosso '12	♥	2

Cantine Litan

VIA MATTEOTTI, 32F
19017 RIOMAGGIORE [SP]
TEL. 3407655840
www.litan.it

CELLAR SALES
PRE-BOOKED VISITS
ANNUAL PRODUCTION 4,000 bottles
HECTARES UNDER VINE 2.00

○ Cinque Terre Costa de Sèra '12	♥♥	4

Tenuta Maffone

LOC. ACQUETICO
VIA SAN ROCCO 18
18026 PIEVE DI TECO [IM]
TEL. 3471245271
www.tenutamaffone.it

CELLAR SALES
PRE-BOOKED VISITS
ANNUAL PRODUCTION 12,000 bottles
HECTARES UNDER VINE 2.00

○ Riviera Ligure di Ponente Pigato '12	♟♟ 3
☉ Ormeasco di Pornassio Sciac-trà '12	♟ 3

Podere Terenzuola

VIA VERCALDA, 14
54035 FOSDINOVO [MS]
TEL. 0187670387
www.terenzuola.it

○ Colli di Luni Vermentino Sup.		
Fosso di Corsano '12	♟♟ 3*
● Merla della Miniera '11	♟♟ 3
○ Cinque Terre '12	♟ 3

Poggi dell'Elmo

C.SO VERBONE, 135
18036 SOLDANO [IM]
TEL. 0184289148
www.poggidellelmo.com

CELLAR SALES
PRE-BOOKED VISITS
ACCOMMODATION AND RESTAURANT SERVICE
ANNUAL PRODUCTION 15,000 bottles
HECTARES UNDER VINE 2.00

● Rossese di Dolceacqua Sup.		
Pini Soldano '11	♟♟ 3*
● Rossese di Dolceacqua '11	♟♟ 3

Valdiscalve

LOC. REGGIMONTI
SP 42
19011 BONASSOLA [SP]
TEL. 0187818178
www.vermenting.com

CELLAR SALES
ANNUAL PRODUCTION 5,000 bottles
HECTARES UNDER VINE 1.00

○ Colline di Levanto Bianco		
Costa di Macinara '12	♟♟ 2*
○ Colline di Levanto Bianco		
Terre del Salice '12	♟ 3

La Vecchia Cantina

FRAZ. SALEA
VIA CORTA, 3
17031 ALBENGA [SV]
TEL. 0182559881

CELLAR SALES
PRE-BOOKED VISITS
ANNUAL PRODUCTION 18,000 bottles
HECTARES UNDER VINE 4.00

○ Riviera Ligure di Ponente Pigato '12	♟♟ 2*
○ Colline Savonesi Passito '05	♟ 4
○ Riviera Ligure di Ponente Vermentino '12	♟ 3

Azienda Agricola Zangani

LOC. PONZANO SUPERIORE
VIA GRAMSCI, 46
19037 SANTO STEFANO DI MAGRA [SP]
TEL. 3287665657
www.zangani.it

CELLAR SALES
PRE-BOOKED VISITS
ANNUAL PRODUCTION 25,000 bottles
HECTARES UNDER VINE 3.00

● Colli di Luni Il Montale '12	♟♟ 2*
○ Colli di Luni Il Mortedo '12	♟♟ 2*
○ Marfi '12	♟♟ 2*
○ Colli di Luni Vermentino La Boceda '12	♟ 3

LOMBARDY

Lombardy gave a record-breaking performance in 2014, winning an impressive 23 Tre Bicchieri awards to confirm its status as one of the most important winemaking regions in Italy. The reasons for this success are many, not least the extraordinary ability of Lombard wine entrepreneurs to interpret the economic situation, displaying a business sense sadly lacking in many other regions. However, running a business for a Lombard, whether as a vigneron or as an entrepreneur who loves wine and invests in the vineyards as a hobby, means having a healthy balance sheet and, above all, making quality products. All of this is expressed very effectively in the recent history of Franciacorta, a wine-growing district that was born just 50 years ago but has managed to achieve extraordinary results over the past three decades. Its leading role in the sector of Italian Metodo Classico sparklers is confirmed by 11 Tre Bicchieri awards. Although its undisputedly excellent terroir has been a decisive factor for this achievement, the passion and skill of its wine entrepreneurs, large and small alike, have been equally important in allowing it to scale these dizzy heights. While Ca' del Bosco, Bellavista, Cavalleri, Berlucchi & C., and Ferghettina have long been familiar names to connoisseurs, the repeated successes of Enrico Gatti, Villa, Contadi Castaldi, Barone Pizzini, and Le Marchesine, and the debut of Lo Sparviere, corroborate the solidity of the designation. It is closely followed by Oltrepò Pavese, which confirms itself excellent country for pinot nero reds and sparklers. Monsupello's Brut 2008 is superlative, like the rest of its amazing range, and Fratelli Giorgi's version is also extremely sound. The Pinot Neros from Mazzolino and Frecciarossa were again excellent, and Castello di Cigognola also took a Tre Bicchieri for a delightful interpretation of Barbera. Lugana production in Lombardy is dominated by Ca' dei Frati and Provenza, the latter with two award-winning wines confirming the appeal of this fragrant white. Moving towards the Alps, we find four outstanding wines from Valtellina, an area where vines have been grown for thousands of years. Once again this year the Sforzatos from Rainoldi, Fai and Nino Negri were a concentrate of elegance and power, while Mamete Prevostini's Sassella bowled us over with its terroir trueness and exceptional harmony. All in all, it was a great achievement for the region, which bodes very well for the future.

Marchese Adorno

VIA GALLASSOLO, 30
27050 RETORBIDO [PV]
TEL. 0383374404
www.marcheseadorno-wines.it

CELLAR SALES
PRE-BOOKED VISITS
ANNUAL PRODUCTION 250,000 bottles
HECTARES UNDER VINE 85.00

It has been 16 years since Marchese Marcello Cattaneo Adorno took over the running of this large family estate that follows the traditional farming pattern of cereals and forage on lowland plots and grapes on the hillsides, making it a beacon for Oltrepò wine-growing. Quality has increased noticeably following the building of the new cellar, renovation of the entire courtyard, rationalization of the production chain and appointment of oenologist Francesco Cervetti as manager. Barbera Vigna Del Re 2010 made it into our finals with its remarkable trueness to type, clean-cut nose of berry fruit, firm structure supported by a swathe of acidity, well-calibrated oak and long finish. The very pleasant Poggio Marino is from another vineyard. This doesn't make it a less important Barbera, just different due to the soil type, showing fruitier and earlier drinking. Rile Nero 2010 is a very well-typed Pinot Nero with a nice tannic weave that needs further bottle ageing to reach its best.

● OP Barbera V. del Re '10	♟♟ 4
● OP Barbera Poggio Marino '11	♟♟ 2*
● OP Bonarda Costa del Sole '11	♟♟ 2*
● OP Pinot Nero Rile Nero '10	♟♟ 5
○ OP Riesling Sup. Arcolaio '11	♟♟ 3
○ OP Pinot Grigio Dama D'Oro '12	♟ 2
● OP Pinot Nero Brughero '11	♟ 2
● Cliviano '10	♟♟ 3*
● OP Barbera V. del Re '08	♟♟ 5
● OP Bonarda Vivace Costa del Sole '11	♟♟ 2*
○ OP Pinot Grigio Dama D'Oro '11	♟♟ 2*
● OP Pinot Nero '08	♟♟ 3
● OP Pinot Nero Brughero '09	♟♟ 3
● OP Pinot Nero Rile Nero '09	♟♟ 5
● OP Pinot Nero Rile Nero '08	♟♟ 5

F.lli Agnes

VIA CAMPO DEL MONTE, 1
27040 ROVESCALA [PV]
TEL. 038575206
www.fratelliagnes.it

CELLAR SALES
PRE-BOOKED VISITS
ANNUAL PRODUCTION 120,000 bottles
HECTARES UNDER VINE 21.00

Rovescala, on the eastern edge of Oltrepò Pavese, is the undisputed realm of Bonarda. Over the years, Sergio and Cristiano Agnes's perseverance and enthusiasm have revealed what they are capable of doing with croatina, also due to their excellently aspected vineyards and the variety with small, closely packed bunches known as pignola. The range of wines features all the possible versions of the varietal – still and semi-sparkling, dry and slightly sweet, young and aged – with enviably consistent quality. This year, the Millennium's not yet ready but Poculum 2011, labelled as an IGT wine, is its usual powerful self with aromas of mint and chocolate and sturdy well-woven tannins. The two versions of Bonarda Vivace 2012 – Campo del Monte and Cresta del Ghiffi – are always among the best in Oltrepò. The latter is more fragrant with higher residual sugar, while the former has greater depth on the palate. Vignazzo and Possessione del Console, both still versions without oak, were slightly below par.

● OP Bonarda Campo del Monte '12	♟♟ 2*
● OP Bonarda Cresta del Ghiffi '12	♟♟ 2*
● Poculum '11	♟♟ 4
● Loghetto '12	♟ 3
● Possessione del Console '12	♟ 3
● Vignazzo '11	♟ 3
● OP Bonarda Campo del Monte '11	♟♟ 2*
● OP Bonarda Cresta del Ghiffi '11	♟♟ 2*
● OP Bonarda Millenium '09	♟♟ 4
● OP Bonarda Millenium '08	♟♟ 4
● Poculum '10	♟♟ 3*
● Poculum '09	♟♟ 3
● Poculum '08	♟♟ 3
● Vignazzo '08	♟♟ 2*

Anteo

LOC. CHIESA
27040 ROCCA DE' GIORGI [PV]
TEL. 038599073
www.anteovini.it

CELLAR SALES
PRE-BOOKED VISITS
ANNUAL PRODUCTION 200,000 bottles
HECTARES UNDER VINE 27.00

The aim of Trento Cribellati, father of the current owners Ettore Piero and Antonella, was to create an estate capable of combining quantity and quality in the production of sparkling wines. This intention is borne out by his choice of site, at Rocca de' Giorgi, in the upper part of the Val Versa and Valle Scuropasso, longstanding prime growing areas for pinot nero sparklers, and the construction of the large underground cellar, where riddling is still strictly manual. We reluctantly have to report that this year's results were somewhat disappointing in respect to the recent past and the winery's potential. Let's hope it's just a momentary lapse. Riserva del Poeta 2006, dedicated to Trento Cribellati, is nonetheless very good, with a creamy mousse and a nose of almonds, croissants and medicinal herbs. Nature Écru 2008 tastes of tropical fruit and flowers, but is a little staid. However, we know it will be at its best in years to come, and that this bottle is still too young.

● OP Bonarda Staffolo '12	♈♈ 2*
○ OP Moscato La Volpe e L'Uva '12	♈♈ 2*
○ OP Pinot Nero Brut Riserva del Poeta '06	♈♈ 6
⊙ OP Cruasé	♈ 4
○ OP Pinot Nero Nature Écru '08	♈ 5
○ OP Spumante Brut Tradition '07	♈ 4
○ OP Pinot Nero Brut Cl. Nature Écru '03	♈♈♈ 4
○ OP Pinot Nero Brut Cl.	♈♈ 4*
○ OP Pinot Nero Brut Cl. Nature Écru '05	♈♈ 4
○ OP Pinot Nero Brut Cl. Riserva del Poeta '05	♈♈ 6
⊙ OP Pinot Nero Brut Cl. Rosé '06	♈♈ 4
○ OP Riesling Sup. Quadro di Mezzo '11	♈♈ 2*

Antica Fratta

VIA FONTANA, 11
25040 MONTICELLI BRUSATI [BS]
TEL. 030652068
www.anticafratta.it

CELLAR SALES
PRE-BOOKED VISITS
ANNUAL PRODUCTION 300,000 bottles
HECTARES UNDER VINE 4.00

Antica Fratta is one of Franciacorta's up-and-coming producers. Although it is owned by the Guido Berlucchi winery, the estate in Monticelli Brusati is run independently, under the management of Marcello Bruschetti. Its own grapes are supplemented by purchased fruit from the best-aspected vineyards in the production zone. The winery is housed in a handsome 19th-century villa, perfectly restored by the Ziliani family, that boasts a stunning vaulted cellar laid out in the shape of a cross, known locally as the Cantinon. Extra Brut Riserva Quintessence is the estate's flagship wine, which performed worthily in our finals. It is a Chardonnay cuvée, with 15% Pinot Nero, which is aged for a full 70 months before disgorgement. The 2006 has a complex nose of ripe fruit, vanilla and citrus notes, and a soft, juicy, zesty palate with creamy effervescence and good length. Essence Satèn 2009 is also excellent, with a finish of camomile and aromatic herbs.

○ Franciacorta Quintessence Extra Brut Ris. '06	♈♈ 7
○ Franciacorta Brut	♈♈ 5
⊙ Franciacorta Rosé Essence '09	♈♈ 5
○ Franciacorta Satèn Essence '09	♈♈ 5
○ Franciacorta Brut Essence '06	♈♈ 5
○ Franciacorta Essence Brut '05	♈♈ 5
○ Franciacorta Quintessence Extra Brut '05	♈♈ 7
⊙ Franciacorta Rosé Essence '08	♈♈ 5
⊙ Franciacorta Rosé Essence '07	♈♈ 5
○ Franciacorta Satèn Essence '08	♈♈ 5

Ar.Pe.Pe.

Via del Buon Consiglio, 4
23100 Sondrio
Tel. 0342214120
www.arpepe.com

CELLAR SALES
PRE-BOOKED VISITS
ANNUAL PRODUCTION 50,000 bottles
HECTARES UNDER VINE 12.00

Today the young team formed by Isabella, Emanuele and Guido Pellizzati competently run the estate relaunched in grand style by their father Arturo. Production is characterized by long maceration, the use of large barrels, and slow, patient bottle ageing before release. Some of the selections are only released after ten years, with consequent risk, resulting in a unique, highly recognizable style. Recently the wines appear to have acquired greater aromatic definition, making them fresher and more drinkable without foregoing any of their flinty, savoury identity that has made them so sought-after by connoisseurs. Rocce Rosse 2002 certainly doesn't act its age, displaying a pervasive, complex nose of tobacco and liquorice with ferrous notes and a hint of gentian, accompanied by a complex, plush palate with a very long finish. Sassella Ultimi Raggi 2006 is distinctive, showing spicy with hints of dried herbs, roots and berries. Its full palate displays offers concentrated pulp and fresh acidity.

● Valtellina Sup. Sassella Rocce Rosse Ris. '02	🍷🍷 6
● Valtellina Sup. Sassella Ultimi Raggi '06	🍷🍷 6
● Rosso di Valtellina '11	🍷🍷 3
● Valtellina Sup. Sassella Stella Retica Ris. '06	YYY 4*
● Rosso di Valtellina '10	YY 3
● Valtellina Sup. Grumello Rocca de Piro Ris. '06	YY 4
● Valtellina Sup. Inferno Fiamme Antiche '06	YY 5
● Valtellina Sup. Inferno Fiamme Antiche Ris. '07	YY 5
● Valtellina Sup. Sassella Rocce Rosse Ris. '01	YY 6
● Valtellina Sup. Sassella Rocce Rosse Ris. '99	YY 6
● Valtellina Sup. Sassella Ultimi Raggi '05	YY 6

Ballabio

via San Biagio, 32
27045 Casteggio [PV]
Tel. 0383805728
www.ballabio.net

CELLAR SALES
PRE-BOOKED VISITS
ANNUAL PRODUCTION 100,000 bottles
HECTARES UNDER VINE 60.00

In 1905 Angelo Ballabio founded the winery that bears his name in the spectacular San Biagio hollow above Casteggio, commencing the production of fine wines whose memory still lingers on in Oltrepò. For several years now it has been managed by Filippo Nevelli, who is able to count on a magnificently equipped cellar run by the experienced Francesco Cervetti. Filippo has decided to boost the production of Metodo Classico in particular, in order to make the estate a benchmark for sparkling winemakers in Oltrepò and beyond. The results are encouraging. The elegant, mineral Farfalla, from pinot nero, is the result of long ageing on the lees. It earned a place in our finals this year with its very delicate, complex nose, firm structure, zestiness and lively acidity, which make it the finest expression of the typical characteristics of the terroir and the grape variety.

○ Brut Cl. Farfalla	🍷🍷 4
⊙ OP Pinot Nero Brut Cl. Cruasé	🍷🍷 4
● OP Bonarda V. delle Cento Pertiche '12	🍷 3
● Clastidium di Pinot Nero '08	YY 4
● Narbusto '09	YY 3
● OP Bonarda V. delle Cento Pertiche '11	YY 2*
● OP Bonarda V. delle Cento Pertiche '10	YY 2*
● OP Bonarda Vivace V. delle Cento Pertiche '09	YY 2*
⊙ OP Pinot Nero Cl. Brut Cruasé '07	YY 4

Barbacarlo - Lino Maga

S.DA BRONESE, 3
27043 BRONI [PV]
TEL. 038551212
barbacarlodimaga@libero.it

CELLAR SALES
PRE-BOOKED VISITS
ANNUAL PRODUCTION 20,000 bottles
HECTARES UNDER VINE 12.00

We'd need a whole book to tell the story of Barbacarlo, for the estate is an important piece of Oltrepò history. Its vineyards lie in a unique valley between Broni and the foothills around Canneto Pavese, and are planted with croatina, uva rara and vespolina. The grapes are fermented separately in old oak barrels, followed by second fermentation in bottle. Each year – we could even say each bottle – yields a different wine, of varying sweetness and sparkle. The winery also produces the only semi-sparkling wine capable of ageing 30 years or more. The 2011 vintage is very fruit-rich, with an alcohol content of almost 15%, plus residual sugar. It proffers notes of tobacco and spices, and a unique almondy finish. We recommend a visit to the magical old wine shop in Broni, where time seems to stand still.

● Barbacarlo '11	♈♈ 5
● OP Rosso Montebuono '12	♈ 4
● Barbacarlo '10	♈♈ 5
● Barbacarlo '09	♈♈ 5
● Barbacarlo '08	♈♈ 5
● Barbacarlo '07	♈♈ 5

Barone Pizzini

VIA SAN CARLO, 14
25050 PROVAGLIO D'ISEO [BS]
TEL. 0309848311
www.baronepizzini.it

CELLAR SALES
PRE-BOOKED VISITS
ACCOMMODATION
ANNUAL PRODUCTION 375,000 bottles
HECTARES UNDER VINE 47.00
VITICULTURE METHOD Certified Organic

At the beginning of the 1990s a group of Brescia businessmen bought Barone Pizzini's estate and entrusted it to the capable Silvano Brescianini, who transformed, renovated and expanded it into a world-class winery. All these changes were made with great attention to the natural environment and sustainable development, making the estate a veritable benchmark in the wine sector. This is immediately evident from a visit to the new low-impact cellar, which is extremely modern, and the vineyards, tended with organic and biodynamic techniques. Today the Franciacorta estate is flanked by two others: Ghiaccioforte in Maremma, Tuscany, and Pievalta in Marche, all of which use natural methods. The Brut Nature has once again shown itself to be in a class of its own with the 2009 vintage. It has a very fine bead and a nose with complex, intense top notes of apples and pears, citrus fruit, wholemeal and vanilla, and a very lively, zesty palate that offers crunchy fruit and good length and energy. Franciacorta Extra Brut is elegant and racy with notes of iodine.

○ Franciacorta Brut Nature '09	♈♈♈ 5
○ Curtefranca Polzina Bianco '12	♈♈ 3
○ Franciacorta Brut	♈♈ 5
○ Franciacorta Brut Bagnadore Ris. '06	♈♈ 5
○ Franciacorta Extra Brut	♈♈ 5
⊙ Franciacorta Rosé Brut '09	♈♈ 5
● Curtefranca Rosso '11	♈ 3
○ Franciacorta Satèn '09	♈ 5
○ Franciacorta Brut Nature '08	♈♈♈ 5
⊙ Franciacorta Rosé Brut '08	♈♈ 5
○ Franciacorta Satèn '08	♈♈ 5
○ Franciacorta Satèn '07	♈♈ 5
○ Franciacorta Satèn '07	♈♈ 5

★★Bellavista

VIA BELLAVISTA, 5
25030 ERBUSCO [BS]
TEL. 0307762000
www.bellavistawine.it

F.lli Berlucchi

LOC. BORGONATO
VIA BROLETTO, 2
25040 CORTE FRANCA [BS]
TEL. 030984451
www.fratelliberlucchi.it

PRE-BOOKED VISITS
ANNUAL PRODUCTION 1,300,000 bottles
HECTARES UNDER VINE 184.00

CELLAR SALES
PRE-BOOKED VISITS
ANNUAL PRODUCTION 400,000 bottles
HECTARES UNDER VINE 70.00

Bellavista is an iconic name of the Italian wine world and a landmark estate in Franciacorta. Owned by the Moretti family, it heads the group of estates in Lombardy and Tuscany created by brilliant businessman Vittorio, who now manages it with the aid of his daughter Francesca. Today it boasts over 180 hectares of splendid vineyards and is run by oenologist and general manager Mattia Vezzola. From the prestigious Riservas to the non-vintage Franciacorta, the Bellavista style is an unmistakable blend of elegance and sumptuous complexity. This year, we were captivated by Riserva Vittorio Moretti 2006, with its spicy, creamy intensity, well-defined fruit, and long, caressing finish. The Riserva Moretti Teatro alla Scala 2004 dedicated to Lohengrin and Gran Cuvée Satèn 2008 are also excellent, and indeed the entire range is of extraordinarily high quality.

The Berlucchi family have played a fundamental role the history of Franciacorta and have ancient ties to the area. Their winery, owned by a multitude of brothers and sisters, uses only the grapes from its 70 hectares of vineyards and is enthusiastically headed by Pia Donata, aided by her daughter Tilli Rizzo. The cellars are housed in the family's 16th-century villa in Borgonato. The beautifully orchestrated Franciacorta Casa delle Colonne Zero Riserva 2006 reached our finals with a nose of fresh fruit echoed on the juicy palate, where it's supported by an elegant mineral vein of acidity, and a long, close-focused finish. Franciacorta Brut 2009 and Riserva Casa delle Colonne Brut 2006 are also first-rate, and the rest of the list is excellent.

○ Franciacorta Extra Brut Vittorio Moretti Ris. '06	▼▼▼ 8
○ Franciacorta Extra Brut Vittorio Moretti Lohengrin Ris. '04	▼▼ 8
○ Franciacorta Satèn Gran Cuvée	▼▼ 8
○ Curtefranca Bianco '12	▼▼ 3
○ Curtefranca Convento SS. Annunciata '10	▼▼ 6
○ Curtefranca Uccellanda '10	▼▼ 6
○ Franciacorta Brut Cuvée	▼▼ 5
⊙ Franciacorta Brut Rosé Gran Cuvée '08	▼▼ 7
○ Franciacorta Brut Gran Cuvée '04	▽▽▽ 6
○ Franciacorta Extra Brut Vittorio Moretti '02	▽▽▽ 8
○ Franciacorta Gran Cuvée Pas Operé '06	▽▽▽ 8
○ Franciacorta Gran Cuvée Pas Operé '05	▽▽▽ 7

○ Franciacorta Casa delle Colonne Zero Ris. '06	▼▼ 7
○ Franciacorta Brut '09	▼▼ 5
○ Franciacorta Casa delle Colonne Brut '06	▼▼ 7
○ Franciacorta Pas Dosé '09	▼▼ 5
○ Franciacorta Satèn '09	▼▼ 5
○ Franciacorta Brut 25	▼ 4
⊙ Franciacorta Brut Rosé '09	▼ 5
○ Franciacorta Brut '06	▽▽ 4*
⊙ Franciacorta Brut Rosé '08	▽▽ 5
○ Franciacorta Casa delle Colonne Zero Ris. '05	▽▽ 7
○ Franciacorta Pas Dosé '07	▽▽ 5
○ Franciacorta Satèn '08	▽▽ 5

Guido Berlucchi & C.

LOC. BORGONATO
P.ZZA DURANTI, 4
25040 CORTE FRANCA [BS]
TEL. 030984381
www.berlucchi.it

CELLAR SALES
PRE-BOOKED VISITS
ACCOMMODATION
ANNUAL PRODUCTION 5,000,000 bottles
HECTARES UNDER VINE 650.00

In 1961 Franco Ziliani and his friend Guido Berlucchi had the brilliant idea of making a few thousand bottles of Metodo Classico from the local grapes. It marked the beginning of the glorious history of Franciacorta, which is now internationally renowned for its sparkling wines. Over 50 years later, Guido Berlucchi is one of the best-known wine labels in Italy, with an annual production of around 5 million bottles of Franciacorta. The winery's chairman Franco is flanked by his children Paolo, Cristina and oenologist Arturo. This year, the star of the meticulously crafted wide range is Franciacorta Brut Extrême Palazzo Lana Riserva 2006, which effortlessly took a Tre Bicchieri. It's an elegant, dynamic Blanc de Noirs with great backbone, which displays impressive complexity on both the nose and the palate with sophisticated mineral notes and hints of iodine. The other cuvées are all very sound.

○ Franciacorta Brut Extrême Palazzo Lana Ris. '06	♛♛♛ 6
○ Franciacorta Cuvée Imperiale Vintage '07	♛♛ 5
○ Franciacorta Brut Cuvée 61	♛♛ 5
○ Franciacorta Brut Cuvée Imperiale	♛♛ 5
⊙ Franciacorta Brut Rosé Cuvée 61	♛♛ 5
⊙ Franciacorta Rosé Cuvée Imperiale Max	♛♛ 5
○ Franciacorta Satèn Cuvée 61	♛ 5
○ Franciacorta Brut Cellarius '07	♛♛♛ 5
○ Franciacorta Brut Extrême Palazzo Lana '05	♛♛♛ 6
○ Franciacorta Brut Extrême Palazzo Lana '04	♛♛♛ 6
○ Franciacorta Cellarius Brut '08	♛♛♛ 5

Bersi Serlini

VIA CERETO, 7
25050 PROVAGLIO D'ISEO [BS]
TEL. 0309823338
www.bersiserlini.it

CELLAR SALES
PRE-BOOKED VISITS
ANNUAL PRODUCTION 220,000 bottles
HECTARES UNDER VINE 32.00

In 1886 the Bersi Serlini family purchased this handsome estate on the shores of Lake Iseo that was once the grange of the nearby Benedictine monastery of San Pietro in Lamosa. Attentively restored and extended with a modern new wing and cellars equipped with the latest technology, the winery owns over 30 hectares of vineyards and is enthusiastically and competently run by Maddalena Bersi Serlini and her sister Chiara. Brut Cuvée n. 4 2008 comes from the estate's oldest chardonnay vines. Partly fermented in small oak casks and left to age on the lees for over three and a half years, it displays exemplary balance and finesse, offering alluring notes of ripe white- and yellow-fleshed fruit combined with fresh herbal and citrus hints, followed by nuances of toast and hazelnut. The sumptuous palate is very long. The quality of the rest of the attentively crafted range is excellent.

○ Franciacorta Brut Cuvée n. 4 '08	♛♛ 5
○ Franciacorta Brut Vintage Ris. '06	♛♛ 7
○ Franciacorta Brut	♛♛ 5
○ Franciacorta Satèn	♛♛ 5
⊙ Franciacorta Brut Rosé Rosa Rosae	♛ 6
○ Franciacorta Demi Sec Nuvola	♛ 4
○ Franciacorta Brut Cuvée n. 4 '06	♛♛ 4*
○ Franciacorta Brut Vintage Ris. '04	♛♛ 7
○ Franciacorta Extra Brut '02	♛♛ 5
○ Franciacorta Extra Brut '01	♛♛ 5

Bertagna

LOC. BANDE
VIA MADONNA DELLA PORTA, 14
46040 CAVRIANA [MN]
TEL. 037682211
www.cantinabertagna.it

CELLAR SALES
ANNUAL PRODUCTION 110,000 bottles
HECTARES UNDER VINE 10.00

Gianfranco Bertagna represents the fifth generation of growers who have enthusiastically tended the family winery located a few kilometres from Lake Garda, in the northernmost corner of the province of Mantua. This year its wines – all with Alto Mincio IGP designation – were convincing enough to earn it its first full profile in our Guide. Rosso del Barone 2009 is a well-typed Cabernet that shows a deep ruby, with sound fruit, interesting floral notes, nicely calibrated oak and a well-defined finish. Montevolpe Bianco 2011 is a very well-made Chardonnay with a subtle touch of oak that gives it fullness. Its notes of pineapple and lime are accompanied by an intriguing mineral vein and supported by a good acidic backbone. The elegant Merlot Rosso Del Chino 2010 is also sound and well-typed, with good length, while Montevolpe Rosso 2009 is a little weighed down by super-ripe notes. The Chardonnay 2012 is fresh and pleasantly simple.

○ Montevolpe Bianco '11	♥♥	3
● Rosso del Barone '09	♥♥	3
● Rosso del Chino '10	♥♥	3
○ Chardonnay '12	♥	2
● Montevolpe Rosso '09	♥	3
● Rosso del Chino '09	♀♀	3
● Rosso del Chino '08	♀♀	3

F.lli Bettini

LOC. SAN GIACOMO
VIA NAZIONALE, 4A
23036 TEGLIO [SO]
TEL. 0342786068
bettvini@tin.it

CELLAR SALES
PRE-BOOKED VISITS
ANNUAL PRODUCTION 200,000 bottles
HECTARES UNDER VINE 15.00

The quality of the range of wines presented this year has won the historic estate run by Pietro Bettini its place back among our full profiles. Among the oldest in Valtellina, it is situated in San Giacomo di Teglio, in the heart of Valgella, at an altitude of 900 metres on the slopes of the Rhaetian Alps. Its 15 hectares of vineyards, all planted to nebbiolo, yield increasingly terroir-true characterful wines. They go to make up an intelligent and exceptionally high-quality range, comprising all the subzones of Valtellina Superiore and a Sforzato produced using the traditional technique of part-drying nebbiolo grapes. The elegant Sfursat 2010 is well-made, with a concentrated, spicy nose offering balanced notes of ripe fruit with hints of cloves. On the palate it is full and juicy, with a long, lingering finish. Prodigio 2008 is good, with a deep, complex nose of up-front dried herbs and tobacco, accompanied by a caressing palate with smooth, velvety tannins and a long finish.

● Valtellina Sfursat '10	♥♥	5
● Valtellina Sup. Inferno Prodigio '08	♥♥	3
● Valtellina Sup. Sant'Andrea '09	♥♥	4
● Valtellina Sup. Valgella V. La Cornella '09	♥♥	3
● Valtellina Sfursat '09	♀♀	5
● Valtellina Sfursat '07	♀♀	5
● Valtellina Sup. Inferno Prodigio '07	♀♀	3
● Valtellina Sup. Sant'Andrea '07	♀♀	4
● Valtellina Sup. Sassella Reale '07	♀♀	3
● Valtellina Sup. Sassella Reale '06	♀♀	3
● Valtellina Sup. Valgella V. La Cornella '08	♀♀	3
● Valtellina Sup. Valgella V. La Cornella '07	♀♀	3

Bisi

LOC. CASCINA SAN MICHELE
FRAZ. VILLA MARONE, 70
27040 SAN DAMIANO AL COLLE [PV]
TEL. 038575037
www.aziendagricolabisi.it

CELLAR SALES
PRE-BOOKED VISITS
ANNUAL PRODUCTION 90,000 bottles
HECTARES UNDER VINE 30.00

Claudio Bisi shuns the limelight. He works hard, patiently and painstakingly in both his vineyards and his cellar, with the invaluable aid of his wife Sandra, his right-hand man Angelo, and Professor Leonardo Valenti from the University of Milan. His wines are never boring or predictable, but have a strong personality and always offer new sensations without so much as a nod to passing fashions, as exemplified by a vertical tasting of all the vintages of Barbera Roncolongo recently held at the cellar. Roncolongo 2010 does not appear in this edition of our Guide. Readers will have to wait until next year for it because Claudio has decided that it needs more time in bottle before release. However, there's no shortage of good wines from this estate. They include Senz'Aiuto, a Barbera made – as its name suggests – without the addition of yeast, sulphites or anything else. It displays exemplary colour, fragrance and cleanliness, eloquently recounting its terroir.

○ Bianco Passito Villa Marone '10	♀♀	4
● Barbera Senz'Aiuto '11	♀♀	3
○ Lagrà '12	♀♀	3
● OP Bonarda Vivace La Peccatrice '11	♀♀	2*
● Pramattone '11	♀♀	3
● Ultrapadum '11	♀♀	3
● Calonga '10	♀	5
● Pezzabianca '11	♀	3
○ Bianco Passito Villa Marone '09	♀♀	4
● Calonga '09	♀♀	4
● OP Barbera Roncolongo '08	♀♀	3
● OP Barbera Roncolongo '07	♀♀	3
● OP Barbera Roncolongo '06	♀♀	3
● Primm '09	♀♀	4
● Roncolongo '09	♀♀	4
● Ultrapadum '10	♀♀	3

Tenuta Il Bosco

LOC. IL BOSCO
27049 ZENEVREDO [PV]
TEL. 0385245326
www.ilbosco.com

CELLAR SALES
PRE-BOOKED VISITS
ANNUAL PRODUCTION 1,000,000 bottles
HECTARES UNDER VINE 152.00

During the Middle Ages this handsome Oltrepò estate belonged to the Monastery of Santa Maria Teodote. It was purchased by the Zonin family 26 years ago, with the aim of expanding their holdings outside Veneto under the name Gianni Zonin Vineyards. Since then the area under vine has increased from 30 to 152 hectares, planted mainly with the most widespread locally grown varieties, such as barbera, croatina and pinot nero, from which the oenologist-manager Piernicola Olmo makes a surprisingly ageworthy Metodo Classico. As we await the parent company's decision to embark upon the production of sparkling wines with long ageing on the lees, we're happy to enjoy the freshness of the two Oltrenero Metodo Classicos. The white is floral, with good mineral notes and backbone, while the Cruasé focuses more on wild berries, with a nice fine bead and a slightly almondy finish. We also like the self-assured Poggio Pelato 2011, from pinot nero, which shows true to type with good overall balance.

● OP Bonarda Vivace '12	♀♀	2*
⊙ OP Cruasé Oltrenero	♀♀	5
○ OP Pinot Nero Brut Cl. Oltrenero	♀♀	5
● OP Pinot Nero Poggio Pelato '11	♀♀	3
⊙ Brut Martinotti Phileo Rosé	♀	3
○ OP Malvasia Vivace	♀	2
○ OP Pinot Nero Brut Martinotti Philèo	♀	3
○ Brera '11	♀♀	3
● OP Bonarda Vivace '10	♀♀	2*
● OP Pinot Nero Poggio Pelato '10	♀♀	3
● OP Pinot Nero Poggio Pelato '09	♀♀	3

Bosio

LOC. TIMOLINE
VIA MARIO GATTI
25040 CORTE FRANCA [BS]
TEL. 030984398
www.bosiofranciacorta.it

CELLAR SALES
PRE-BOOKED VISITS
ANNUAL PRODUCTION 100,000 bottles
HECTARES UNDER VINE 30.00

Cesare Bosio and his sister Laura have created one of the most interesting new wineries in Franciacorta. Respected agronomist Cesare acts as a consultant to many local estates, while economics graduate Laura deals with the business side of the venture and the sales network. The brother-and-sister team has a total of 30 hectares of well-aspected vineyards – estate owned and leased – that are scrupulously tended using methods with low environmental impact. The range of wines is very sound and the magnificent modern cellar is worth a visit. Franciacorta Riserva Girolamo Bosio 2006 once again shows itself to be an exceptionally elegant cuvée. It has a very fine bead and a complex nose, with crisp appley top notes and hints of vanilla and wholemeal, which are followed by elegant nuances of tobacco and aromatic herbs. The deep, close-knit palate is lean and edgy. The Rosé 2009 is excellent too, among the best of the DOCG zone.

○ Franciacorta Pas Dosé Girolamo Bosio Ris. '06	♟♟ 5
○ Franciacorta Brut	♟♟ 5
⊙ Franciacorta Brut Rosé '09	♟♟ 5
○ Franciacorta Extra Brut Boschedòr '09	♟♟ 5
● Curtefranca Rosso '10	♟ 4
○ Franciacorta Satèn	♟ 5
⊙ Franciacorta Brut Rosé '08	♑♑ 5
○ Franciacorta Extra Brut Boschedòr '08	♑♑ 5
○ Franciacorta Pas Dosé Girolamo Bosio Ris. '05	♑♑ 5

La Brugherata

FRAZ. ROSCIATE
VIA G. MEDOLAGO, 47
24020 SCANZOROSCIATE [BG]
TEL. 035655202
www.labrugherata.it

CELLAR SALES
PRE-BOOKED VISITS
ANNUAL PRODUCTION 45,000 bottles
HECTARES UNDER VINE 8.00

Our task is to present the estates that we find most interesting in each area, without getting drawn into any local disputes. This is why we continue to acknowledge the quality of the wines of the estate owned by the Bendinelli brothers, even though it doesn't belong to any consortium. Once again this year we found the range presented to be among the most interesting of the Bergamo production zone. Moscato di Scanzo Doge 2010 is always among the best of the DOCG zone, combining spicy notes of pepper and cinnamon with hints of prunes. It vaunts plenty of flesh and a pleasant acid backbone that accompanies it right through to the slightly almondy finish. We also like the pleasant, well-balanced Vescovado del Feudo 2012, a very well-typed Chardonnay with fresh, fragrant tropical notes. Rosso di Alberico 2012 is a Bordeaux blend with no added sulphites, which offers sound fragrant fruit and spicy notes.

● Moscato di Scanzo Doge '10	♟♟ 7
○ Vescovado del Feudo '12	♟♟ 2*
● Moscato Rosso Vermiglio di Roxia '12	♟ 3
● Rosso di Alberico '12	♟ 3
● Vermiglio di Roxia '12	♟ 3
● Moscato di Scanzo Doge '09	♑♑ 7
● Moscato di Scanzo Doge '08	♑♑ 7
● Priore '09	♑♑ 3
○ Valcalepio Bianco Vescovado del Feudo '11	♑♑ 2*
○ Valcalepio Bianco Vescovado del Feudo '09	♑♑ 2*
● Valcalepio Rosso Doglio Ris. '10	♑♑ 4
● Valcalepio Rosso Doglio Ris. '07	♑♑ 3
● Valcalepio Rosso Doglio Ris. '06	♑♑ 3

Tenuta Ca' Boffenisio

FRAZ. BOFFENISIO, 3
27040 BORGO PRIOLO [PV]
TEL. 3392154535
www.caboffenisio.it

ANNUAL PRODUCTION 50,000 bottles
HECTARES UNDER VINE 1,500.00
VITICULTURE METHOD Certified Organic

It would be an understatement to say that Mariele Galanti is dynamic. Full of ideas and resources, this Sicilian woman who arrived in Oltrepò Pavese in 1997 has found in Ca' Boffenisio the ideal environment for expressing her creative flair. The 23-hectare estate is set in the centre of a spectacular natural amphitheatre. Its 15 hectares of vineyards are tended with organic methods and yield wines with a strong personality and character, capable of surprising and delightful development with ageing. This year, the winery presented a wonderfully deep, full Triangolo 2004 laden with spices and wild berries. The elegant, mature croatina, barbera and pinot nero blend is intriguing and dynamic with great verve and a superb finish. Pretesto 2010 is another rather unconventional blend, from sauvignon, chardonnay and riesling. It shows golden yellow, with a nose that is simultaneously mineral, floral and fruity, with hints of bay leaf, and a solid, full-flavoured palate.

○ Pretesto '10	♥♥ 3
● Triangolo '04	♥♥ 4
○ Ghiaia di Monte '05	♀♀ 3
○ Ghiaia di Monte '04	♀♀ 3*
● OP Bonarda '04	♀♀ 3
○ OP Riesling Sup. '10	♀♀ 4
● Tacabrighe '01	♀♀ 4
● Triangolo '01	♀♀ 4

Ca' dei Frati

FRAZ. LUGANA
VIA FRATI, 22
25019 SIRMIONE [BS]
TEL. 030919468
www.cadeifrati.it

CELLAR SALES
PRE-BOOKED VISITS
ACCOMMODATION AND RESTAURANT SERVICE
ANNUAL PRODUCTION 1,800,000 bottles
HECTARES UNDER VINE 150.00

The Dal Cero family have made a decisive contribution to the success of Garda wines with their top-class production capable of enhancing the potential for development of the local whites. Their strength obviously lies in their vineyards, which cover an area of over 150 hectares and are planted mainly to turbiana, and subsequently in the sensitivity displayed in the cellar, where the vineyard and ripeness of the grapes are always taken into account. The wide range of wines is simply excellent and offers something for everyone. Our favourite is Brolettino 2011, a Lugana with perfectly calibrated oak that vaunts a sophisticated nose and a taut, full palate. Frati 2007 has now reached full maturity, its fruit making way for flinty mineral notes and a piquant, racy palate, while the juicy Cuvée dei Frati Brut 2009 proffers citrus notes and fines herbes.

○ Lugana Brolettino '11	♥♥♥ 3*
○ Lugana I Frati Affinato 5 anni in bottiglia '07	♥♥ 4
○ Cuvée dei Frati Brut '09	♥♥ 3
⊙ Cuvée dei Frati Brut M. Cl. Rosé '10	♥♥ 4
○ Lugana Brolettino Affinato 5 anni in bottiglia '07	♥♥ 5
○ Lugana I Frati '12	♥♥ 2*
⊙ Riviera del Garda Bresciano I Frati Chiaretto '12	♥♥ 2*
● Ronchedone '11	♥♥ 3
○ Tre Filer '09	♥♥ 3
○ Pratto '11	♥ 3
○ Lugana Brolettino '10	♀♀♀ 3*
○ Lugana Brolettino '07	♀♀♀ 3*
○ Pratto '96	♀♀♀ 3*

★★★Ca' del Bosco

VIA ALBANO ZANELLA, 13
25030 ERBUSCO [BS]
TEL. 0307766111
www.cadelbosco.it

CELLAR SALES
PRE-BOOKED VISITS
ANNUAL PRODUCTION 1,470,000 bottles
HECTARES UNDER VINE 160.00

Headed by its founder and chairman
Maurizio Zanella, Ca' del Bosco once again
confirms the exceptionally high quality of its
entire production and its place in the
firmament of Italy's top wineries. Each year
it develops sophisticated and increasingly
advanced systems for vineyard
management and work in the cellar, with
the aim of selecting only the highest quality
fruit and enhancing the grapes and the
terroir. The spectacular winery, housing a
collection of contemporary art, is among
the most technologically advanced in the
world and is well worth a visit. This year,
Riserva Annamaria Clementi 2005
effortlessly took our top accolade. It's a very
deep, complex wine, which combines
elegance with wonderful drinkability. The
Vintage Collection makes its debut with the
2008 vintage and features the very good
Brut, Dosage Zéro and Satèn. Annamaria
Clementi Rosé 2005 is similarly excellent.

○ Franciacorta Cuvée Annamaria Clementi Ris. '05	♀♀♀ 8
○ Curtefranca Chardonnay '10	♀♀ 7
○ Franciacorta Brut Vintage Collection '08	♀♀ 6
⊙ Franciacorta Extra Brut Rosé Cuvée Annamaria Clementi '05	♀♀ 8
○ Curtefranca Bianco '12	♀♀ 3
● Curtefranca Rosso '09	♀♀ 3
○ Franciacorta Brut Cuvée Prestige	♀♀ 5
○ Franciacorta Dosage Zéro Vintage Collection '08	♀♀ 8
⊙ Franciacorta Rosé Cuvée Prestige	♀♀ 6
○ Franciacorta Satèn Vintage Collection '08	♀♀ 6
● Maurizio Zanella '07	♀♀ 8
● Pinèro '09	♀♀ 8

Ca' del Gè

FRAZ. CA' DEL GÈ, 3
27040 MONTALTO PAVESE [PV]
TEL. 0383870179
www.cadelge.it

CELLAR SALES
PRE-BOOKED VISITS
ANNUAL PRODUCTION 180,000 bottles
HECTARES UNDER VINE 40.00

The estate that belonged to the late Enzo
Padroggi is now run by his children
Stefania, Sara and Carlo. It vaunts almost
40 hectares of excellently aspected
vineyards on the hills of Montalto Pavese,
dominated by chalky soils ideal for growing
riesling, which is produced in various
versions. Like many family-run Oltrepò
estates, Ca' del Gè has a very wide range
of labels, which generally offer excellent
value for money. Pinot Nero Brut 2007 has
notes of candied peel, lime and croissants,
accompanied by an alluring mineral vein
derived from the terroir, attractive verve and
a beautifully fine bead. Buttafuoco Fajro
2010, from the Montespinato cru in
Cigognola, is a modern interpretation of its
type, with balsamic and vanillaed notes that
go very well with the fruit. The rest of the
range is interesting and includes a very
good, soft, semi-sparkling Bonarda.

● OP Bonarda Vivace '12	♀♀ 2*
● OP Buttafuoco Fajro '10	♀♀ 4
○ OP Pinot Nero Brut '07	♀♀ 3
○ Chardonnay '12	♀ 2
○ OP Moscato Frizzante '11	♀ 3
○ OP Riesling Italico Filagn Long '12	♀ 2
● O. P. Bonarda La Fidela '10	♀♀ 3
○ OP Pinot Nero Brut Cl. '06	♀♀ 3
○ OP Pinot Nero Brut Cl. '05	♀♀ 3
○ OP Pinot Nero Brut Cl. '02	♀♀ 3*
○ OP Riesling Italico Filagn Long '11	♀♀ 2*

Ca' di Frara

VIA CASA FERRARI, 1
27040 MORNICO LOSANA [PV]
TEL. 0383892299
www.cadifrara.com

CELLAR SALES
PRE-BOOKED VISITS
ANNUAL PRODUCTION 400,000 bottles
HECTARES UNDER VINE 46.00

Many years ago the Bellani family, headed
by Luca with the support of his mother
Daniela, father Tullio and brother Matteo,
decided to focus strongly on quality, with
scrupulous selection in the vineyard and
sometimes unusual choices in the cellar. Of
course, there were ups and downs, but
several wines – both whites and reds
– remain fixed in our memory as among
the best produced in the area. A few years
ago an important project for the production
of Metodo Classico was launched. This
year, both the Metodo Classico Rosés
performed well: the copper-coloured
Riserva, with a nose of medicinal herbs,
firm structure supported by a nice acid
backbone, a fine bead and a good finish,
and the more assertive, forthright Nature.
However, our favourite is Riesling Oliva
2009, a splendid interpretation of the
grape, which displays both mineral and
balsamic notes, sound fruit and a
never-ending finish. The young Apogeo
2012 is also sound, as are the two reds,
Frater 2012 and Bonarda La Casetta 2012.

Ca' Lojera

LOC. ROVIZZA
VIA 1886, 19
25019 SIRMIONE [BS]
TEL. 0457551901
www.calojera.com

CELLAR SALES
PRE-BOOKED VISITS
RESTAURANT SERVICE
ANNUAL PRODUCTION 160,000 bottles
HECTARES UNDER VINE 20.00

Ca' Lojera is one of the most interesting
estates in the Garda production district,
with a vineyard covering an area of 20
hectares in the southern region of the lake.
The plot planted to Lugana is on the
lowlands, where the soil is clay based,
while the red wines hail from grapes grown
on the rolling morainic hills surrounding the
lake. Operations in the cellar are kept to a
minimum and the top wines are released
only after long ageing. Riserva del Lupo
2011 is a Lugana with great aromatic
depth, in which apples and pears mingle
with herbs and spices while waiting for the
mineral note to emerge. The palate is rich
but displays excellent grip. The Superiore
2011, on the other hand, is more rustic,
with more prominent vegetable notes and
tannins, which ensure a lively, dynamic
palate.

○ OP Riesling Oliva '09	♥♥ 3*
● OP Bonarda La Casetta '12	♥♥ 3
⊙ OP Brut Pinot Nero Rosé Oltre il Classico Ris. '07	♥♥ 6
⊙ OP Nature Cruasé Oltre il Classico '08	♥♥ 4
○ OP Riesling Renano Apogeo Raccolta Tardiva '12	♥♥ 2*
● OP Rosso Il Frater Ris. '10	♥♥ 6
○ Oltre il Classico Blanc de Blancs	♥ 4
● OP Bonarda La Casetta '10	♀♀ 3
⊙ OP Cruasé Oltre il Classico '09	♀♀ 4
○ OP Oltre il Classico Nature	♀♀ 5
⊙ OP Pinot Nero Brut Oltre il Classico Rosé Ris. '06	♀♀ 5
○ OP Riesling Renano Apogeo Raccolta Tardiva '11	♀♀ 2*
● OP Rosso Il Frater Ris. '07	♀♀ 5

○ Lugana Riserva del Lupo '11	♥♥ 4
○ Lugana Sup. '11	♥♥ 3
● Cabernet Monte della Guardia '11	♥ 2
○ Lugana '12	♥ 2
● Merlot Monte della Guardia '11	♥ 2
⊙ Rosato Monte della Guardia '12	♥ 2
○ Lugana del Lupo '10	♀♀ 4
○ Lugana Sup. '10	♀♀ 3
○ Lugana Sup. '09	♀♀ 3

Ca' Tessitori

VIA MATTEOTTI, 15
27043 BRONI [PV]
TEL. 038551495
www.catessitori.it

CELLAR SALES
PRE-BOOKED VISITS
ANNUAL PRODUCTION 120,000 bottles
HECTARES UNDER VINE 40.00

Last year we decided to award our full profile to the Giorgi family's estate, run by Luigi with the aid of his sons Giovanni and Francesco. It is arranged in the traditional manner, with the cellar – its large concrete vats serving as foundations for the house – in the lowland village of Broni and the vineyards on the hillsides, in Finigeto and Montecalvo Versiggia. The concrete vats have become the focus of the estate's new philosophy, after having gradually abandoned the use of oak. Barbara Marona 2009 is even better this year, following a further 12 months in bottle, while Gnese 2010, from 60% barbera and 40% cabernet sauvignon, has floral notes with a faint grassy hint, fine tannins and sound fruity flesh. The interesting Brut 2008, obtained by particularly long ageing on the lees for 48 months, is intense with evolved aromas, and the two 2012 Bonardas are different but both good.

○ Agolo '12	♟♟	2*
● Gnese '10	♟♟	3
● OP Bonarda Avita '12	♟♟	2*
● OP Bonarda Vivace '12	♟♟	2*
○ OP Pinot Nero Brut '08	♟♟	4
● OP Rosso Borghesa '12	♟♟	2*
● OP Barbera Marona '09	♟♟	4
● OP Barbera Marona '06	♟♟	3
● OP Bonarda Frizzante '10	♟♟	2*
● OP Bonarda Vivace '11	♟♟	2*
☉ OP Cruasé '09	♟♟	3
○ OP Pinot Nero Brut '09	♟♟	4
● OP Rosso Borghesa '10	♟♟	2*
● OP Rosso Borghesa '09	♟♟	2*

Il Calepino

VIA SURRIPE, 1
24060 CASTELLI CALEPIO [BG]
TEL. 035847178
www.ilcalepino.it

CELLAR SALES
PRE-BOOKED VISITS
ANNUAL PRODUCTION 230,000 bottles
HECTARES UNDER VINE 15.00

Year after year the estate owned by the Plebani family confirms itself a benchmark for wine-growing in the province of Bergamo. Its pride and joy are its sparklers, although its closeness to Franciacorta penalizes the visibility of this type of wine, which isn't even contemplated by the Valcalepio appellation. Nonetheless, the estate's Metodo Classico sparklers are well able to hold their own against far more prestigious adversaries. The rest of the range also displays consistently high quality. The beautiful golden Fra' Ambrogio always stands out in our tastings. It's a sparkler that manages to be simultaneously caressing and assertive, and its partial fermentation in oak lends it complexity without weighing it down. We also like the Rosé, which displays good backbone and personality, and the very well-made basic Brut that is full, well-orchestrated and more complex than usual.

○ Brut Cl. Fra' Ambrogio	♟♟	4
○ Brut Cl. Il Calepino	♟♟	3
☉ Brut Cl. Rosé	♟♟	3
● Valcalepio Rosso Surìe Ris. '08	♟	3
○ Brut Cl. Fra' Ambrogio Ris. '06	♟♟	4
● Kalòs '08	♟♟	5
● Kalòs '06	♟♟	5
● Valcalepio Rosso Surìe Ris. '07	♟♟	3

Cantrina

FRAZ. CANTRINA
VIA COLOMBERA, 7
25081 BEDIZZOLE [BS]
TEL. 0306871052
www.cantrina.it

CELLAR SALES
PRE-BOOKED VISITS
ANNUAL PRODUCTION 30,000 bottles
HECTARES UNDER VINE 5.70

The estate run by Cristina Inganni and Diego Lavo is situated in the Lake Garda area, close to Brescia, on soils of alternating glacial and sedimentary origin, the latter formed by the changing course of the riverbed. Over the years chemical treatments have been greatly reduced – initially in the vineyard, which covers an area of less than six hectares, and subsequently also in the cellar – in the quest for the perfect combination of terroir, man and grapes. All the wines, from both international and native grape varieties, display great personality. Cristina's Groppello is among the most convincing in the production zone, characterized by notes of cherries and aromatic herbs and a well-focused, pleasantly subtle profile. The red Zerdi 2009, from rebo grapes, focuses more on balsamic notes and ripe fruit, which assure softness on the palate without detracting from its suppleness, while the dried-grape Sole di Dario, from sauvignon, sémillon and riesling, displays caressing sweetness.

● Garda Cl. Groppello '12	♥♥ 2*
○ Sole di Dario '09	♥♥ 5
● Zerdì '09	♥♥ 3
● Nepomuceno Esercizio 7 '08	♥ 5
○ Rinè '11	♥ 3
⊙ Rosato '12	♥ 2
● Garda Cl. Groppello Libero Esercizio di Stile '11	♀♀ 2*
● Nepomuceno Esercizio 7 '07	♀♀ 5
⊙ Rosanoire '11	♀♀ 2*

CastelFaglia - Monogram

FRAZ. CALINO
LOC. BOSCHI, 3
25046 CAZZAGO SAN MARTINO [BS]
TEL. 0307751042
www.cavicchioli.it

CELLAR SALES
PRE-BOOKED VISITS
ANNUAL PRODUCTION 350,000 bottles
HECTARES UNDER VINE 22.00

Sandro Cavicchioli enthusiastically and competently runs this handsome Franciacorta estate that has made a name for itself over the years with the fresh, clean style of its cuvées. Its vineyards lie at the foot of the Faglia castle in Calino, partly on wide terraces, in an area characterized by its stony soil and wide diurnal temperature range. The well-equipped modern cellar is carved out of the rock to ensure constant temperatures year round. A well-known dynasty of Lambrusco producers from Modena, the Cavicchioli family also own the Bellei estate in Bomporto. This year, the Franciacorta Extra Brut strolled confidently into our finals, revealing itself one of the finest non-vintage wines tasted for this edition of our Guide. It has an elegant nose of cakes, citrus fruit and aromatic herbs – particularly mint – and a full-flavoured, creamy, well-orchestrated palate with good length. The Rosé of the Monogram line is excellent too.

○ Franciacorta Extra Brut	♥♥ 4
○ Franciacorta Brut Blanc de Blancs Monogram	♥♥ 4
○ Franciacorta Brut Monogram '07	♥♥ 5
⊙ Franciacorta Rosé Monogram	♥♥ 5
○ Franciacorta Satèn Monogram '07	♥♥ 5
○ Franciacorta Satèn Monogram	♥♥ 5
○ Curtefranca Bianco '11	♥ 3
● Curtefranca Rosso '11	♥ 3
○ Franciacorta Brut Monogram Cuvée Giunone '07	♀♀ 6
○ Franciacorta Brut Monogram Cuvée Giunone '06	♀♀ 5
○ Franciacorta Satèn Monogram Cuvée Giunone '07	♀♀ 5

Castello Bonomi

VIA SAN PIETRO, 46
25030 COCCAGLIO [BS]
TEL. 0307721015
www.castellobonomi.it

CELLAR SALES
PRE-BOOKED VISITS
ANNUAL PRODUCTION 150,000 bottles
HECTARES UNDER VINE 17.00

The Paladin siblings are an important name in the Veneto wine world, where they own two estates in the Lison-Pramaggiore production zone. Over the years, these have been flanked by Vescine in Chianti Classico, and most recently Castello Bonomi in Franciacorta. Carlo, Roberto and Lucia personally manage the group's estates with great passion. Castello Bonomi's handsome terraced vineyards extend for about 20 hectares around the elegant Art-Nouveau villa in Coccaglio, at the foot of Monte Orfano, and yield excellent grapes for the production of Franciacortas. This year, we were particularly impressed by the performance of the Franciacorta Dosage Zero 2007, which is a beautiful bright yellow with a fine bead. The nose has top notes of apples and pears, vanilla and citrus fruit, while the well-orchestrated palate offers silky texture, creamy effervescence and remarkable aromatic length. Brut CruPerdu and the fragrant Rosé are both excellent.

○ Franciacorta Dosage Zero '07	♟♟ 8
○ Franciacorta Brut CruPerdü	♟♟ 6
⊙ Franciacorta Brut Rosé	♟♟ 7
○ Franciacorta Satèn	♟♟ 7
○ Franciacorta Brut '05	♟♟ 7
○ Franciacorta Extra Brut Lucrezia '04	♟♟ 8

Castello di Cigognola

P.ZZA CASTELLO, 1
27040 CIGOGNOLA [PV]
TEL. 0385284828
www.castellodicigognola.com

CELLAR SALES
PRE-BOOKED VISITS
ANNUAL PRODUCTION 75,000 bottles
HECTARES UNDER VINE 30.00

This splendid castle was founded in 1212 on a site overlooking the Scuropasso Valley, where the mountain stream of the same name runs through vine-covered hills. Owned by Gianmarco and Letizia Moratti, Castello di Cigognola initially focused solely on barbera, traditionally grown in this area, formerly part of Piedmont. However, the estate is devoting increasing attention to the production of Metodo Classicos from pinot nero, now also fermented off the skins. This year, it's the turn of Barbera Dodicidodici 2011 to take a Tre Bicchieri. The full, juicy wine has caressing notes of liquorice and black pepper and hints of alluring dark berry fruit. La Maga 2010 is still very young, Brut 'More 2009 is creamy, and Brut 'More Rosé 2010 has delicious notes of rose and red berries.

● OP Barbera Dodicidodici '11	♟♟♟ 3*
⊙ Brut 'More Rosé '10	♟♟ 4
● OP Barbera La Maga '10	♟♟ 4
○ OP Pinot Nero Brut 'More '09	♟♟ 4
○ La Bianca '12	♟ 2
● OP Barbera Castello di Cigognola '07	♟♟♟ 6
● OP Barbera Castello di Cigognola '06	♟♟♟ 6
● OP Barbera Poggio Della Maga '05	♟♟♟ 7
○ OP Pinot Nero Brut 'More '08	♟♟♟ 4*

★Cavalleri

VIA PROVINCIALE, 96
25030 ERBUSCO [BS]
TEL. 0307760217
www.cavalleri.it

CELLAR SALES
PRE-BOOKED VISITS
ANNUAL PRODUCTION 250,000 bottles
HECTARES UNDER VINE 44.00

Cavalleri is one of the historic names of Franciacorta, and its founder Giovanni Cavalleri was one of the fundamental figures in the history of the DOCG zone. Today his work is continued by his daughter Giulia and her enthusiastic proficient staff. With 45 hectares of the finest vineyards in Erbusco and a series of impeccable wines, the estate is constantly at the forefront of the crowded Franciacorta designation. Once again, the Franciacorta Collezione Esclusiva Giovanni Cavalleri has shown itself to be at the very top of the DOCG, earning a Tre Bicchieri, this time with the 2005 vintage. Refined, mineral and deep on both the nose and the palate, it is truly extraordinary in terms of harmony and elegance. Pas Dosé 2008 is rich, zesty and edgy, and the rest of the list is very good.

Civielle

VIA PERGOLA, 21
25080 MONIGA DEL GARDA [BS]
TEL. 0365502002
www.civielle.com

CELLAR SALES
ANNUAL PRODUCTION 500,000 bottles
HECTARES UNDER VINE 72.00
VITICULTURE METHOD Certified Organic

Civielle is a co-operative winery with just over 70 hectares of vineyards, tended with organic methods, along the western side of Lake Garda, in the Lugana and Valtenesi production zones. This area has very diverse soils, from the morainic hills beyond the lake to the clay of the shore. The winery's production encompasses a wide array of labels, characterized by a style that focuses on simplicity and fragrance. Eusebio 2011, a largely groppello-based blend, has an original aromatic profile that combines fresh, concentrated notes of cherries, basil and aromatic herbs. Its silky tannins and juicy palate make it exceptionally drinkable. Groppello Elianto 2011 is similar, but characterized by clearer, more pronounced notes of berry fruit and spice. Valtenesi Pergola 2011 is another blend based mainly on groppello, with a taut palate nicely delineated by tannins.

○ Franciacorta Brut Collezione Esclusiva Giovanni Cavalleri '05	♔♔♔	8
○ Franciacorta Pas Dosé '08	♔♔	5
○ Franciacorta Blanc de Blancs	♔♔	5
○ Franciacorta Satèn	♔♔	5
○ Curtefranca Bianco '12	♔	3
○ Franciacorta Au Contraire Pas Dosé '01	♔♔♔	7
○ Franciacorta Brut Collezione '05	♔♔♔	6
○ Franciacorta Brut Collezione '99	♔♔♔	5
○ Franciacorta Brut Collezione Esclusiva '99	♔♔♔	7
○ Franciacorta Brut Collezione Esclusiva Giovanni Cavalleri '04	♔♔♔	7
○ Franciacorta Brut Collezione Esclusiva Giovanni Cavalleri '01	♔♔♔	7
○ Franciacorta Pas Dosé '07	♔♔♔	5
○ Franciacorta Pas Dosé R. D. '06	♔♔♔	6

● Garda Cl. Groppello Elianto '11	♔♔	3
● Valtenesi Eusebio '11	♔♔	3
● Valtenesi Pergola '11	♔♔	4
○ Garda Cl. Bianco Zublì '12	♔	3
○ Lugana Biocòra '12	♔	2
○ Lugana Pergola '12	♔	3
⊙ Valtenesi Chiaretto '12	♔	2
● Garda Cl. Groppello Elianto '10	♔♔	3
● Garda Cl. Rosso Sup. Pergola '07	♔♔	4
⊙ Valtenesi Chiaretto Selene '11	♔♔	2*

Contadi Castaldi

LOC. FORNACE BIASCA
VIA COLZANO, 32
25030 ADRO [BS]
TEL. 0307450126
www.contadicastaldi.it

CELLAR SALES
PRE-BOOKED VISITS
ANNUAL PRODUCTION 900,000 bottles
HECTARES UNDER VINE 130.00

Contadi Castaldi, based in Adro, belongs to the Terra Moretti group, which also owns the Bellavista estate. Today the winery, whose striking cellar is housed in Adro's ancient Roman brick kilns, vaunts an impressive array of estate-owned, leased and growers' vineyards, allowing an annual production that is rapidly approaching a million high-quality bottles. It is headed by brilliant oenologist Gian Luca Uccelli, who honed his craft during years spent at the parent company. This year, it is Franciacorta Zero 2009 that preserves the estate's prestige, earning it another Tre Bicchieri with its stunning performance. It's a simple, dynamic wine with clean, sound fruit. The elegant nose offers delicate floral and citrussy notes, while the richly flavoured, lean palate is lively and has an elegant freshly mineral finish.

○ Franciacorta Zero '09	🍷🍷🍷	5
⊙ Franciacorta Brut Rosé '09	🍷🍷	5
⊙ Franciacorta Rosé	🍷🍷	5
⊙ Franciacorta Satèn '09	🍷🍷	5
○ Pinodisé	🍷🍷	5
○ Curtefranca Bianco '12	🍷	3
○ Franciacorta Brut	🍷	4
○ Franciacorta Satèn Soul '05	🍷🍷🍷	6
○ Franciacorta Soul Satèn '06	🍷🍷🍷	6

Conte Vistarino

FRAZ. SCORZOLETTA, 82/84
27040 PIETRA DE' GIORGI [PV]
TEL. 038585117
www.contevistarino.it

CELLAR SALES
PRE-BOOKED VISITS
ANNUAL PRODUCTION 380,000 bottles
HECTARES UNDER VINE 200.00

The history of this noble family is entwined with that of Valle Scuropasso, where Conte Vistarino and Conte Gancia decided to plant French pinot nero clones in the second half of the 19th century, having pinpointed the area as the ideal terroir for the production of Metodo Classico sparklers. Indeed, over the decades millions of bottles of Pinot Spumante were sold throughout the world by the great Piedmont wineries that used these grapes. Today, with Ottavia at the helm, the estate is determined to make a name for itself as an independent producer. Pernice 2010 is one of the most convincing wines presented for our tastings. Although it didn't receive our top accolade like the 2006 version, it offers a distinctive, very earthy soul with autumn leaves and plenty of fruit, spice and depth, which augurs excellent bottle development. The 2006 vintage of Brut Conte Vistarino 1865 is very well-made, showing golden, fruity and juicy, with good backbone. Riesling 7 Giugno 2012, from riesling renano, also made an excellent impression, with tropical fruity notes and minerality that promises good development.

● OP Pinot Nero Pernice '10	🍷🍷	5
○ OP Pinot Nero Brut Conte Vistarino 1865 '06	🍷🍷	4
○ OP Riesling 7 Giugno '12	🍷🍷	3
○ OP Pinot Nero Brut Martinotti Cuvée della Rocca	🍷	3
● OP Sangue di Giuda Costiolo '12	🍷	2
● OP Pinot Nero Pernice '06	🍷🍷🍷	4*
● OP Pinot Nero Pernice '08	🍷🍷	5
● OP Pinot Nero Pernice '07	🍷🍷	5
○ OP Riesling 7 Giugno '09	🍷🍷	3

La Costa

FRAZ. COSTA
VIA CURONE, 15
23888 PEREGO [LC]
TEL. 0395312218
www.la-costa.it

CELLAR SALES
PRE-BOOKED VISITS
ACCOMMODATION AND RESTAURANT SERVICE
ANNUAL PRODUCTION 30,000 bottles
HECTARES UNDER VINE 12.00
VITICULTURE METHOD Certified Organic

Brianza is not exactly among the most renowned wine-growing areas in Italy. However, the Crippa family's gamble to revive what seemed a lost tradition is proving a winning one. La Costa is a veritable sanctuary, set in the Montevecchia and Valle del Curone regional park, which also offers excellent restaurant and accommodation facilities. The talented Claudia Crippa uses biodynamic methods to tend the 12 hectares of vineyards, planted mainly with international grape varieties, whose mineral-rich limestone soils yield truly surprising tangy wines with fresh acidity. The very convincing Solesta 2011, from 100% riesling renano, focuses on freshness and, above all, long ageability. It has a concentrated nose, with petrol notes against a mineral background, and a long, deep, elegant palate. Pinot Nero San Giobbe 2011 is by now a classic, with a well-typed nose of berry fruit and spice. Its complex, well-orchestrated palate has a nicely defined lingering finish.

○ Solesta '11	♥♥ 3*
● San Giobbe '11	♥♥ 4
● Serìz '10	♥♥ 3
○ Brigante Bianco '12	♥ 3
● San Giobbe '10	♀♀ 4
● San Giobbe '09	♀♀ 4
● Serìz '09	♀♀ 3
● Serìz '08	♀♀ 3
● Serìz '07	♀♀ 3
● Serìz '06	♀♀ 3
○ Solesta '10	♀♀ 3*
○ Solesta '09	♀♀ 3
○ Solesta '08	♀♀ 3

Costaripa

VIA COSTA, 1A
25080 MONIGA DEL GARDA [BS]
TEL. 0365502010
www.costaripa.it

CELLAR SALES
PRE-BOOKED VISITS
ANNUAL PRODUCTION 400,000 bottles
HECTARES UNDER VINE 40.00

The Vezzzola family have been producing wine in the excellent growing country of the Valtenesi zone since 1936. Their vineyards cover an area of 40 hectares in the Valtenesi and Lugana production districts. Today the estate is headed by Mattia Vezzola, whose decades of work and success in Franciacorta have earned him universal renown and prestige. Here, in his own winery, Mattia has devoted himself to redefining the style of Chiaretto and investigating the potential of the local grape variety groppello, in addition, of course, to the production of the classic spumante. Our favourite this year is the fragrant, firmly structured Brut, a Blanc de Blancs with plenty of personality, which focuses on soft, rich notes of fruit and vanilla. The pink versions include the Brut Rosé, which is zesty and bursting with berry fruit. Valtenesi Chiaretto Rosamara 2012 is excellent, showing fresh, juicy and supple, and Chiaretto Molmenti 2011 is particularly noteworthy: a charming rosé with riper notes and rich, complex structure.

○ Costaripa Brut	♥♥ 5
⊙ Costaripa Brut Rosé	♥♥ 4
⊙ Garda Cl. Chiaretto Molmenti '11	♥♥ 4
○ Lugana Pievecroce '12	♥♥ 2*
● Valtenesi Campostarne '11	♥♥ 3
⊙ Valtenesi Chiaretto Rosamara '12	♥♥ 2*
⊙ Palmargentina '12	♥ 4
○ Costaripa Brut Ris. '04	♀♀ 4
⊙ Garda Cl. Chiaretto Rosamara '10	♀♀ 2*
● Garda Cl. Groppello Maim '09	♀♀ 4
● Garda Cl. Groppello Maim '08	♀♀ 4
● Garda Cl. Groppello Maim '07	♀♀ 4
● Garda Cl. Rosso Campostarne '09	♀♀ 2*
● Garda Marzemino Mazane '10	♀♀ 2*
⊙ Valtenesi Chiaretto Rosamara '11	♀♀ 2*

Derbusco Cives

VIA PROVINCIALE, 83
25030 ERBUSCO [BS]
TEL. 3929283698
www.derbuscocives.com

CELLAR SALES
PRE-BOOKED VISITS
ANNUAL PRODUCTION 60,000 bottles
HECTARES UNDER VINE 12.00

If Erbusco is the heart of Franciacorta, then its name is certainly worthy of mention on the label of its star product. Consequently, in 2004 a group of five friends – all proud Erbusco citizens – headed by Giuseppe Vezzoli, decided to found a new winery, naming it simply "Citizens of Erbusco". Almost ten years later, the estate has earned itself an impressive reputation and the performance of its Franciacortas have won it a place in our Guide. The grapes for Derbusco's cuvées come from the estate's 12 hectares of vineyards, tended using methods with low environmental impact. This year, our favourite was the Extra Brut 2008, which made it into our finals. It is taut and sinewy, with a fine bead, creamy effervescence, a mineral palate and an alluring long, soft finish, making it one of the most interesting wines tasted for this edition.

○ Franciacorta Extra Brut '08	♥♥	7
○ Franciacorta Brut '07	♥♥	6
○ Franciacorta Brut Doppio Erre Di	♥♥	5
○ Franciacorta Brut Doppio Erre Di '05	♀♀	5
○ Franciacorta Extra Brut '07	♀♀	6

Dirupi

LOC. MADONNA DI CAMPAGNA
VIA GRUMELLO, 1
23020 MONTAGNA IN VALTELLINA [SO]
TEL. 3472909779
www.dirupi.com

CELLAR SALES
PRE-BOOKED VISITS
ANNUAL PRODUCTION 15,000 bottles
HECTARES UNDER VINE 4.50

A generational change is underway in the Valtellina wine world, which is making way for talented youngsters. These include Davide Fasolini and Pierpaolo di Franco, who play a very important role. The name of their winery was inspired by the incredibly steep slopes of their vineyards. They are old plots, tended with a sustainable production philosophy and attentive study of the contribution of the various clones. Vine density is high, coupled with very low yields. The result is taut, crisp, lively wines with great linearity. This year also marks the first release of the promising Sforzato. Riserva Dirupi 2010 is very intriguing, with notes of fresh fruit and autumn leaves, and complex hints of sophisticated spiciness. On the palate, it is rich and full-bodied, with juicy acidity and a long finish. Dirupi 2011 is an exemplary wine, showing concentrated notes of fruit with hints of rain-soaked earth and gentian. The impressive palate has well-behaved tannins supported by fresh acidity.

● Valtellina Sup. Dirupi '11	♥♥	4
● Valtellina Sup. Dirupi Ris. '10	♥♥	6
● Nebbiolo Olè '12	♥♥	3
● Sforzato di Valtellina Dirupi '11	♥♥	6
● Valtellina Sup. Dirupi Ris. '09	♀♀♀	6
● Nebbiolo Olè '11	♀♀	3
● Valtellina Sup. '08	♀♀	4
● Valtellina Sup. Dirupi '10	♀♀	4
● Valtellina Sup. Dirupi '09	♀♀	4
● Valtellina Sup. Ris. '07	♀♀	5

Sandro Fay

LOC. SAN GIACOMO DI TEGLIO
VIA PILA CASELLI, 1
23030 TEGLIO [SO]
TEL. 0342786071
elefay@tin.it

CELLAR SALES
PRE-BOOKED VISITS
ANNUAL PRODUCTION 38,000 bottles
HECTARES UNDER VINE 13.00

The Fay family have long been firm believers in the potential of Valgella, enhancing the terroir by scrupulously preserving old vineyards and making daring investments. Founded by Sandro, today the estate is run by his son Marco whose agronomic research has always paid close attention to the effect of altitude on the quality of the wines. Following years of extensive research, the results in the glass are now very evident, for the wines tasted offered subtle, elegant and very terroir-true sensations. The well-defined Ronco del Picchio 2009 is an excellent personal interpretation of Sforzato. Its very elegant, concentrated nose is balsamic with exemplary notes of dried herbs, red berries and spice. On the palate, it is supple, rhythmic and very well-orchestrated, with a long, clearly defined finish. Costa Bassa 2010 is surprisingly pleasant, showing fresh and fruity, with notes of rain-soaked earth. The firmly structured palate has crisp fruit, well-developed tannins and a distinctive long finish.

● Valtellina Sforzato Ronco del Picchio '09	♟♟♟ 6
● Valtellina Sup. Costa Bassa '10	♟♟ 3*
● La Faya '10	♟♟ 4
● Valtellina Sup. Sassella Il Glicine '10	♟♟ 4
● Valtellina Sforzato Ronco del Picchio '02	♟♟♟ 6
● La Faya '09	♟♟ 4
● Valtellina Sforzato Ronco del Picchio '07	♟♟ 6
● Valtellina Sup. Costa Bassa '09	♟♟ 3
● Valtellina Sup. Sassella Il Glicine '09	♟♟ 4
● Valtellina Sup. Valgella Ca' Morèi '10	♟♟ 4
● Valtellina Sup. Valgella Ca' Morèi '09	♟♟ 4
● Valtellina Sup. Valgella Carterìa '10	♟♟ 4
● Valtellina Sup. Valgella Carterìa '09	♟♟ 4

Ferghettina

VIA SALINE, 11
25030 ADRO [BS]
TEL. 0307451212
www.ferghettina.it

CELLAR SALES
PRE-BOOKED VISITS
ANNUAL PRODUCTION 350,000 bottles
HECTARES UNDER VINE 140.00

Roberto Gatti can be proud of his work: in the space of 20 years he has built one of the most solid wineries in Franciacorta, expanding his venture from a warehouse and a small rented vineyard to 140 hectares of estate-owned plots and a stunning headquarters with a well-equipped cellar just outside Adro. However, the merit for much of this goes to his extraordinary family: his wife Andreina, who has always assisted him, and his oenology graduate children Laura and Matteo, who now play an essential role in production. This year, Gatti's range is crowned by Franciacorta Riserva 33 2006, which earned it another Tre Bicchieri. The Chardonnay cuvée, from the estate's finest vineyards, is aged for over 80 months on the lees before disgorgement. It's a beautiful deep straw yellow, with a very fine, continuous bead. The nose has top notes of white-fleshed fruit and flowers, while the complex palate is full-flavoured, firm and elegant, with a very long finish of vanilla and candied peel.

○ Franciacorta Pas Dosé 33 Ris. '06	♟♟♟ 6
○ Franciacorta Extra Brut '07	♟♟ 5
○ Curtefranca Blanco '12	♟♟ 2*
● Curtefranca Rosso '11	♟♟ 2*
○ Franciacorta Brut Milledì '09	♟♟ 5
⊙ Franciacorta Rosé Milledì '09	♟♟ 5
○ Franciacorta Satèn '09	♟♟ 5
● Merlot Baladello '09	♟♟ 4
○ Franciacorta Brut	♟ 4
○ Franciacorta Extra Brut '06	♟♟♟ 5
○ Franciacorta Extra Brut '05	♟♟♟ 5
○ Franciacorta Extra Brut '04	♟♟♟ 5
○ Franciacorta Extra Brut '02	♟♟♟ 5

Fiamberti

VIA CHIESA, 17
27044 CANNETO PAVESE [PV]
TEL. 038588019
www.fiambertivini.it

CELLAR SALES
PRE-BOOKED VISITS
ANNUAL PRODUCTION 140,000 bottles
HECTARES UNDER VINE 18.00

Each year, step after step, we have the pleasure of seeing that Ambrogio Fiamberti and his son Giulio have not lost sight of their goal to continue to improve the overall quality of their production. The estate's tradition and its fine vineyards allow it to make wines of all types, and it offers the classic wide range of labels typical of Oltrepò producers. Now that the average quality of the wines has risen considerably, it is legitimate to expect the emergence of a few pinnacles of genuine excellence. The estate's traditional wines are always sound and reliable. Bonarda and Sangue di Giuda 2012 are exemplary in terms of colour, nose, cleanliness, restrained tannins and harmony. Buttafuoco Poderi Fiamberti 2009 stands out for its all-round pleasantness, making it an enjoyable red to accompany the entire meal. The sparkling Brut Metodo Classico is also nice, while the Cruasé is not quite as good.

● OP Bonarda Vivace La Briccona '12	♟♟ 2*
● OP Buttafuoco Poderi Fiamberti '09	♟♟ 3
○ OP Pinot Nero Brut Cl. Fiamberti	♟♟ 4
● OP Sangue di Giuda V. Costa Paradiso '12	♟♟ 2*
⊙ OP Cruasé Fiamberti	♟ 4
○ OP Riesling Italico V. Croce Monteveneroso '12	♟ 2
● OP Rosso Monte Acutello '07	♟ 3
● OP Bonarda Vivace Bricco della Sacca '11	♟♟ 2*
● OP Buttafuoco Storico V. Solenga '06	♟♟ 4
● OP Buttafuoco V. Sacca del Prete '07	♟♟ 4
● OP Pinot Nero Nero '10	♟♟ 2*
● OP Sangue di Giuda V. Costa Paradiso '11	♟♟ 2*

Le Fracce

FRAZ. MAIRANO
VIA CASTEL DEL LUPO, 5
27045 CASTEGGIO [PV]
TEL. 038382526
www.lefracce.com

CELLAR SALES
PRE-BOOKED VISITS
ANNUAL PRODUCTION 180,000 bottles
HECTARES UNDER VINE 40.00

This estate, now owned by the Fondazione Bussolera-Branca, is an important part of Oltrepò Pavese history. Its Italian-style gardens and collections of carriages and vintage cars alone are worth a visit. The property lies on the hillsides in Mairano, an upper hamlet of Casteggio, where the white soils ideal for riesling, pinot grigio and pinot nero are flanked by terrain with a higher clay content well suited to croatina and barbera. All the wines bear the elegant hallmark of oenologist Roberto Gerbino. Bohemi 2007 is the flagship red. Initially reluctant, the nose opens to reveal complex notes of berries and autumn leaves with liquorice and spice, and a full, vibrant palate. The good Bonarda La Rubiosa 2012 has a fragrant nose of red berries and violets and a well-behaved palate of just the right softness. Garboso 2011 is a well-typed monovarietal barbera that is forthright, balanced and highly drinkable. Among the whites, we had a slight preference for Pinot Grigio Levriere 2012.

● Garboso '11	♟♟ 3
● OP Bohemi '07	♟♟ 6
● OP Bonarda Vivace La Rubiosa '12	♟♟ 3
○ OP Pinot Grigio Levriere '12	♟♟ 3
● OP Cirgà '07	♟ 5
● OP Pinot Nero '08	♟ 6
○ OP Pinot Nero Extra Brut Cuvée Bussolera '10	♟ 3
○ OP Riesling Landò '12	♟ 3
● Garboso '10	♟♟ 2*
● OP Bonarda Vivace La Rubiosa '11	♟♟ 3
● OP Cirgà '06	♟♟ 3
○ OP Pinot Grigio Levriere '11	♟♟ 3
○ OP Riesling Landò '11	♟♟ 2*
● OP Rosso Bohemi '06	♟♟ 6
● OP Rosso Bohemi '05	♟♟ 6

Frecciarossa

VIA VIGORELLI, 141
27045 CASTEGGIO [PV]
TEL. 0383804465
www.frecciarossa.com

CELLAR SALES
PRE-BOOKED VISITS
ANNUAL PRODUCTION 120,000 bottles
HECTARES UNDER VINE 34.00

This is one of the finest estates in Oltrepò
Pavese, comprising the 19th-century Villa
Odero and its grounds, the farm, the old
cellars and more modern buildings. Here a
team headed by oenologist Gianluca
Scaglione crafts a range of wines that
makes Frecciarossa one of the best Oltrepò
producers, as confirmed by several recent
vertical tastings of old vintages of Riesling
and Pinot Nero no longer available on the
market. The estate recently added Metodo
Classico sparklers to its list. Following a
transitional year, Pinot Pinot Nero Giorgio
Odero 2010 has returned to take our top
accolade. It's simply splendid, with a bright
pale ruby hue and a complex, intriguing
nose of perfectly mingled notes of wild
berries, Mediterranean scrubland and
aromatic herbs. The soft, deep palate is
taut and confident. Riesling Gli Orti 2011
vaunts excellent fruity minerality.

Enrico Gatti

VIA METELLI, 9
25030 ERBUSCO [BS]
TEL. 0307267999
www.enricogatti.it

CELLAR SALES
PRE-BOOKED VISITS
ANNUAL PRODUCTION 120,000 bottles
HECTARES UNDER VINE 17.00

Founded by Enrico Gatti in Erbusco in
1975, the winery that bears his name is
approaching its 40th anniversary, and in
top form too. Enrico's children Lorenzo and
Paola, along with his son-in-law Enzo
Balzarini, have turned it into a little gem, a
veritable boutique winery that uses only the
grapes from its own 17 hectares of
vineyards in Erbusco. More important still,
the Gattis have created their own distinctive
style, focusing on opulence, concentration
and mineral notes, which do not detract
from the freshness and drinkability of their
Franciacortas. Once again this year, a Tre
Bicchieri went to Nature, a chardonnay
cuvée with 15% pinot nero, partly
fermented in used small oak casks. It has a
deep, rich, complex nose of citrussy, fruity
notes and toasty hints of hazelnut and
iodine, and a zesty, lean, racy palate with
impressive structure and a very long, soft
fruity finish. Well done!

● OP Pinot Nero Giorgio Odero '10	▼▼▼ 5
● OP Bonarda Vivace Dardo '12	▼▼ 2*
○ OP Riesling Gli Orti '11	▼▼ 2*
○ OP Pinot Nero Sillery '12	▼ 2
● Uva Rara '12	▼ 2
● OP Pinot Nero Giorgio Odero '08	▽▽▽ 5
● OP Pinot Nero Giorgio Odero '07	▽▽▽ 5
● OP Pinot Nero Giorgio Odero '05	▽▽▽ 5
● Le Praielle '08	▽▽ 3
● OP Bonarda Vivace Dardo '11	▽▽ 2*
○ OP Brut M. Cl. Frecciarossa '08	▽▽ 6
○ OP Pas Dosé Cl. I Moschettieri '10	▽▽ 6
● OP Pinot Nero Giorgio Odero '09	▽▽ 5
○ OP Riesling Gli Orti '10	▽▽ 2*
● Uva Rara '10	▽▽ 2*

○ Franciacorta Nature	▼▼▼ 5
○ Franciacorta Brut	▼▼ 4
⊙ Franciacorta Rosé	▼▼ 5
○ Franciacorta Satèn '09	▼▼ 5
○ Franciacorta Brut '05	▽▽▽ 6
○ Franciacorta Nature '07	▽▽▽ 5
○ Franciacorta Satèn '05	▽▽▽ 5
○ Franciacorta Satèn '03	▽▽▽ 5
○ Franciacorta Satèn '02	▽▽▽ 4
○ Franciacorta Satèn '01	▽▽▽ 4
○ Franciacorta Satèn '00	▽▽▽ 5
○ Franciacorta Brut '06	▽▽ 6
○ Franciacorta Satèn '08	▽▽ 5
○ Franciacorta Satèn '07	▽▽ 5
○ Franciacorta Satèn '04	▽▽ 5

F.lli Giorgi

FRAZ. CAMPONOCE, 39A
27044 CANNETO PAVESE [PV]
TEL. 0385262151
www.giorgi-wines.it

CELLAR SALES
PRE-BOOKED VISITS
ANNUAL PRODUCTION 1,600,000 bottles
HECTARES UNDER VINE 30.00

This long-standing Valle Versa estate has always managed to keep up with the times and reconcile its two different sides: a more commercial one, with consistently high quality, symbolized by the semi-sparkling Pinot, whose production runs to hundreds of thousands of bottles each year, and the top range, produced in limited amounts made from the finest grapes, with the aid of the talented and highly experienced oenologist Alberto Musatti. And that makes five! The 1870 has won its fifth Tre Bicchieri and is rapidly becoming a classic of Oltrepò spumante production. A truly magnificent Metodo Classico, it is fragrant, mineral and full-flavoured, simultaneously discreet and vibrant on the palate, with a caressing fine bead. The Cruasé is also very good, with fresh, fragrant notes of wild berries, and the deep, warm Buttafuoco Storico is excellent, with balsamic notes. Last but not least, is Brut Gianfranco Giorgi 2010, an exemplary expression of the local sparkling wines from pinot nero.

○ OP Pinot Nero Brut Cl. 1870 '09	♟♟♟ 5
⊙ OP Cruasé '10	♟♟ 4
● OP Buttafuoco Storico V. Casa del Corno '09	♟♟ 3
○ OP Pinot Nero Brut Cl. Gianfranco Giorgi '10	♟♟ 5
○ OP Riesling Il Bandito '12	♟♟ 4
● OP Sangue di Giuda '12	♟♟ 3
● OP Bonarda Vivace La Brughera '12	♟ 3
● OP Buttafuoco Clilele '11	♟ 3
○ OP Pinot Nero Brut Cl. 1870 '08	♟♟♟ 5
○ OP Pinot Nero Brut Cl. 1870 '07	♟♟♟ 5
○ OP Pinot Nero Brut Cl. 1870 '06	♟♟♟ 5
○ OP Pinot Nero Brut Cl. 1870 '05	♟♟♟ 5

Isimbarda

FRAZ. CASTELLO
CASCINA ISIMBARDA
27046 SANTA GIULETTA [PV]
TEL. 0383899256
www.tenutaisimbarda.it

CELLAR SALES
PRE-BOOKED VISITS
ANNUAL PRODUCTION 130,000 bottles
HECTARES UNDER VINE 40.00

Isimbarda, owned by Luigi Meroni and run by Daniele Zangelmi, is one of Oltrepò's historic estates, documented on this superb site among the Santa Giulietta hills since the 17th century. The vineyard covers an area of 36 hectares with soils ranging from clay to limestone and marl, which are better suited to white grape varieties and particularly riesling. Several years ago the cellar started flanking the traditional red and white wines with the production of sparklers. Riesling Vigna Martina 2012 is a wine with a double life. The young version has spicy floral notes with hints of apricots and peaches, saffron and aromatic herbs, a good texture and a racy finish. As it ages, it gradually acquires the variety's typical tertiary notes without losing its fundamental fruity character. Rosso Monplò 2010 is good, with wild berries and sturdy supporting acidity.

○ OP Riesling Renano V. Martina '12	♟♟ 2*
● OP Bonarda Vivace V. delle More '12	♟♟ 2*
● OP Pinot Nero V. del Cardinale '11	♟♟ 4
● OP Rosso Monplò '10	♟♟ 3
⊙ OP Cruasé	♟ 4
○ OP Pinot Nero Brut M. Cl.	♟ 2
● OP Bonarda Vivace V. delle More '11	♟♟ 2
○ OP Riesling Renano V. Martina '11	♟♟ 2*
○ OP Riesling Renano V. Martina '10	♟♟ 2*
○ OP Riesling Renano V. Martina '09	♟♟ 2*
○ OP Riesling Renano V. Martina '08	♟♟ 2*
● OP Rosso Montezavo Ris. '08	♟♟ 4
○ Varméi '11	♟♟ 2*
○ Varméi '10	♟♟ 2

Cantina Sociale La Versa

VIA F. CRISPI, 15
27047 SANTA MARIA DELLA VERSA [PV]
TEL. 0385798411
www.laversa.it

CELLAR SALES
PRE-BOOKED VISITS
ANNUAL PRODUCTION 5,000,000 bottles
HECTARES UNDER VINE 1,300.00

Since its foundation by Cesare Gustavo
Faravelli in 1905, little has changed at this
legendary co-operative winery renowned all
over Italy and beyond, particularly for its
Pinot Nero Metodo Classico sparklers. Its
history has seen periods of both difficulty
and glory: the boost given by Duca Antonio
Giuseppe Denari in the 1970s and 1980s, a
renaissance in 2000 under chairman
Giancarlo Vitali, with the management of
Francesco Cervetti and later his successor
Corrado Cavalli, the umpteenth
reorganization of the labels . . . and the wait
for definitive consecration as one of stars of
the Italian wine-growing world. We're
delighted to see clear signs of recovery. The
winery's Cuvée del Duca, dedicated to Duca
Denari, returns as its top-level spumante
with the soft elegance, richness of flavour,
backbone and firm structure typical of the
pinot nero of the upper Valle Versa. The two
Testarossas also performed very well, with
the Cruasé offering a pleasant nose of wild
berries and citrus fruit, echoed on the
palate, and the white with fine development
and notes of croissants.

○ Brut Cl. Cartaoro	🍷🍷 3
○ Brut Cl. Testarossa	🍷🍷 5
○ EIS	🍷🍷 3
● OP Barbera Fermo La Versa '11	🍷🍷 2*
⊙ OP Cruasé Testarossa	🍷🍷 5
○ OP Cuvée del Duca	🍷🍷 4
○ Brut Cl. Cuvée del Duca '04	🏆🍷 4
● OP Barbera '10	🏆🍷 2*
● OP Bonarda Vivace '10	🏆🍷 2
○ OP Pinot Nero Brut Cuvée Testarossa Rosé '04	🏆🍷 5
⊙ OP Pinot Nero Brut Rosé Cuvée Testarossa '05	🏆🍷 5
⊙ OP Pinot Nero Brut Rosé Testarossa '07	🏆🍷 3
○ OP Riesling '11	🏆🍷 2*

Lantieri de Paratico

LOC. COLZANO
VIA VIDETTI
25031 CAPRIOLO [BS]
TEL. 030736151
www.lantierideparatico.it

CELLAR SALES
PRE-BOOKED VISITS
ACCOMMODATION AND RESTAURANT SERVICE
ANNUAL PRODUCTION 150,000 bottles
HECTARES UNDER VINE 18.00

Although the tradition of Franciacorta
commenced just over half a century ago,
the production of fine wines in the area
dates back much further. Indeed, the
Lantieri de Paratico family were already
renowned throughout Europe for the quality
of their wines in the 17th century. After
having abandoned his previous career,
Fabio Lantieri enthusiastically continues the
tradition, crafting a complete range of
wines and Franciacortas from his estate's
20 or so hectares of vineyards at his
historic home in Capriolo, near Lake Iseo.
Arcadia is the estate's top wine: an elegant
cuvée from chardonnay with 30% pinot
nero, aged on the lees for four years before
disgorgement. The 2009 is a bright straw
yellow with a very fine bead, a delicate,
complex nose and a firmly structured,
well-orchestrated palate with elegant,
lingering mineral and citrussy notes. The
entire range is flawless.

○ Franciacorta Brut Arcadia '09	🍷🍷 5
○ Curtefranca Bianco '12	🍷🍷 2*
○ Franciacorta Brut	🍷🍷 4
○ Franciacorta Extra Brut	🍷🍷 4
⊙ Franciacorta Rosé Arcadia	🍷🍷 5
○ Franciacorta Satèn	🍷🍷 5
○ Franciacorta Brut Arcadia '08	🏆🍷 5
○ Franciacorta Brut Arcadia '07	🏆🍷 5
○ Franciacorta Brut Arcadia '06	🏆🍷 5
○ Franciacorta Brut Arcadia '05	🏆🍷 5

Majolini

LOC. VALLE
VIA MANZONI, 3
25050 OME [BS]
TEL. 0306527378
www.majolini.it

CELLAR SALES
PRE-BOOKED VISITS
ANNUAL PRODUCTION 200,000 bottles
HECTARES UNDER VINE 24.00

Majolini is situated in Ome, on the eastern side of Franciacorta, the cradle of this family of Brescian industrialists with a great passion for their agricultural roots. In 1981 they founded this magnificent estate specializing in the production of Franciacorta, entrusting it to the management of Ezio Majolini. Today his work is continued by his highly motivated young nephew Simone. The estate can count on 24 hectares of partly terraced well-aspected vineyards in the Ome district and the expertise of French consultant oenologist Jean-Pierre Valade. The Satèn 2008 is attractively soft and creamy, with caressing effervescence. Its fruity nose offers tropical hints and citrussy floral end notes, while the palate is zesty and mineral, with a long apricot finish. The Extra Brut Riserva Blanc de Blancs 2005 is full and complex, with more evolved notes, while the Brut is floral and harmonious, and the Brut Blanc de Noirs spirited and edgy.

○ Franciacorta Brut	♟♟ 5	
○ Franciacorta Brut Blanc de Blancs Ris. '05	♟♟ 8	
○ Franciacorta Brut Blanc de Noirs	♟♟ 6	
○ Franciacorta Satèn '08	♟♟ 6	
○ Franciacorta Brut Electo '00	♟♟♟ 6	
○ Franciacorta Brut Electo '99	♟♟♟ 5	
○ Franciacorta Brut Electo '97	♟♟♟ 5	
○ Franciacorta Brut Electo '05	♟♟ 8	
○ Franciacorta Pas Dosé Aligi Sassu '06	♟♟ 8	
○ Franciacorta Pas Dosé Aligi Sassu '05	♟♟ 7	
⊙ Franciacorta Rosé Altera	♟♟ 5	
○ Franciacorta Satèn '07	♟♟ 7	
○ Franciacorta Satèn '06	♟♟ 7	

Le Marchesine

VIA VALLOSA, 31
25050 PASSIRANO [BS]
TEL. 030657005
www.lemarchesine.it

CELLAR SALES
PRE-BOOKED VISITS
ANNUAL PRODUCTION 450,000 bottles
HECTARES UNDER VINE 44.00

Although the Biatta family have ancient roots in the Brescian viticultural world, this attractive estate was founded by Giovanni in the mid-1980s. His recent death has spurred his son Loris and his grandchildren Alice and Andrea to do even better, and the family proudly continue the legacy of the winery's founder. The excellent grapes from the estate's 44 hectares of vineyards are transformed into a first-rate array of wines with the aid of consultant oenologist Jean-Pierre Valade. This year, we awarded this estate another Tre Bicchieri for its extraordinary Franciacorta Brut 2009, a deep, elegant Blanc de Noirs with handsome coppery highlights. The sophisticated nose offers black and red berries, cakes and wholemeal, while the palate is full, taut and creamy, with an alluring finish imbued with mineral and iodine notes.

○ Franciacorta Brut Blanc de Noir '09	♟♟♟ 5	
○ Franciacorta Brut Nature Secolo Novo Giovanni Biatta '07	♟♟ 5	
○ Franciacorta Brut	♟♟ 4	
○ Franciacorta Extra Brut	♟♟ 5	
○ Franciacorta Satèn '09	♟♟ 5	
○ Franciacorta Brut '04	♟♟♟ 5	
○ Franciacorta Brut Secolo Novo '05	♟♟♟ 7	
○ Franciacorta Brut Secolo Novo '07	♟♟ 7	
○ Franciacorta Brut Secolo Novo '06	♟♟ 7	
○ Franciacorta Dosage Zero Secolo Novo Ris. '05	♟♟ 7	
○ Franciacorta Satèn '08	♟♟ 5	

Tenuta Mazzolino

via Mazzolino, 26
27050 Corvino San Quirico [PV]
Tel. 0383876122
www.tenuta-mazzolino.com

CELLAR SALES
PRE-BOOKED VISITS
ANNUAL PRODUCTION 130,000 bottles
HECTARES UNDER VINE 22.00

This winery, with its splendid 19th-century villa and grounds overlooking the Po Valley with views of the entire Alpine range on clear days, is definitely worth a visit for the warm welcome of its Burgundian manager Jean-François Coquard and Oltrepò agronomist Claudio Giorgi alone. Enrico and Sandra Braggiotti purchased the estate in 1980 and their intention of producing great wines was gradually achieved with a mingling of France and Italy, using chardonnay and pinot nero together with croatina to craft exceptionally elegant, ageworthy wines. Yet again, the Noir 2010 has emerged as one of Italy's finest Pinot Neros. It style is unmistakable, with notes of blackberries and spicy, balsamic hints, and an exemplary, well-orchestrated palate that is long, lean and very well-typed. We unhesitatingly awarded it a Tre Bicchieri. The Cruasé is fresh and pleasant, with a bright onionskin hue and an intriguing fine mousse.

● OP Pinot Nero Noir '10	♥♥♥ 5
○ OP Chardonnay Blanc '11	♥♥ 3
☉ OP Cruasé Mazzolino	♥♥ 4
○ Pas Dosé Mazzolino Blanc de Blancs	♥♥ 4
○ Brut Cl. Mazzolino Blanc de Blancs	♥ 4
○ Camarà '12	♥ 2
● OP Bonarda Mazzolino '12	♥ 2
○ Terrazze '12	♥ 2
● OP Pinot Nero Noir '09	♥♥♥ 5
● OP Pinot Nero Noir '08	♥♥♥ 5
● OP Pinot Nero Noir '07	♥♥♥ 5
● OP Pinot Nero Noir '06	♥♥♥ 5
○ Mazzolino Brut Blanc de Blancs	♥♥ 3
○ OP Chardonnay Blanc '10	♥♥ 3*
☉ OP Cruasé Mazzolino	♥♥ 3

Mirabella

via Cantarane, 2
25050 Rodengo Saiano [BS]
Tel. 030611197
www.mirabellavini.it

CELLAR SALES
PRE-BOOKED VISITS
ANNUAL PRODUCTION 500,000 bottles
HECTARES UNDER VINE 60.00

In 1979 Teresio Schiavi involved a group of friends – small vineyard owners in Franciacorta – in the creation of a new winery in which they could pool their properties to create a shared brand. Almost 35 years later they have come a long way. The estate boasts a handsome headquarters and a cellar equipped with the latest technology. Mirabella's great success is also due to the commitment of Alessandro Schiavi and his partner and managing director Francesco Bracchi. Production levels are excellent, with almost half a million bottles crafted from the grapes of the estate's 60 hectares of vineyards, denoting particular sensitivity to sustainable development and salubrious products. Two of the estate's wines made it into our finals this year: the stylish, balanced Dosaggio Zero Dom 2004, with aniseed notes, and the new Elite Extra Brut, made with no addition of sulphites. It is an innovative, lip-smacking wine full of aromatic notes of lime blossom and lemon balm and nice structure, which opens up new roads for the estate and the DOCG zone.

○ Franciacorta Dosaggio Zero Dom '04	♥♥ 6
○ Franciacorta Extra Brut Elite	♥♥ 6
○ Franciacorta Brut	♥♥ 4
○ Franciacorta Satèn	♥♥ 4
☉ Franciacorta Rosé Brut	♥ 4
○ Franciacorta Non Dosato '00	♥♥ 4

★Monsupello

VIA SAN LAZZARO, 5
27050 TORRICELLA VERZATE [PV]
TEL. 0383896043
www.monsupello.it

CELLAR SALES
PRE-BOOKED VISITS
ANNUAL PRODUCTION 260,000 bottles
HECTARES UNDER VINE 50.00

The Boatti family's estate once again confirms its ironclad nature. It is difficult to find a family-run operation in the whole of Italy that is capable of producing such consistent and high-quality wines of all types: Metodo Classico, white, red, sweet and semi-sparkling. Although Carlo Boatti passed away three years ago, his wife Carla, children Pierangelo and Laura, and invaluable oenologist Marco Bertelegni proudly continue to honour his memory. As from this year, the vintage Brut no longer bears the "Classese" designation originally apposed by the estate's founder Carletto Boatti, but its exceptionally high quality remains the same. The creaminess, complexity and array of fragrances of the 2008 are extraordinary, putting it in a class of its own, Riserva di Nature 2002 is dedicated to Carlo Boatti himself, and displays astonishing backbone, minerality and depth that make it a true treat for lovers of its kind. After these two champions, the rest of the practically unrivalled range of sparklers risks being overlooked.

○ Brut Cl. '08	♛♛♛	5
○ Brut Cl. Nature	♛♛	4
○ Brut Cl. Nature Carlo Boatti Ris. '02	♛♛	8
☉ Brut Cl. Rosé	♛♛	4
○ Chardonnay Senso '11	♛♛	5
● OP Barbera I Gelsi '09	♛♛	3
● OP Bonarda Vivace Vaiolet '12	♛♛	2*
○ OP Cuvée Ca' Del Tava	♛♛	6
○ OP Pinot Nero Brut Cl.	♛♛	4
○ Pinot Grigio '12	♛♛	2*
● Pinot Nero Junior '12	♛♛	3
○ Riesling Renano '12	♛♛	2*
○ OP Brut Cl. Classese '06	♛♛♛	5
○ OP Brut Cl. Classese '04	♛♛♛	5

Francesco Montagna

VIA CAIROLI, 67
27043 BRONI [PV]
TEL. 038551028
www.cantinemontagna.it

CELLAR SALES
PRE-BOOKED VISITS
RESTAURANT SERVICE
ANNUAL PRODUCTION 800,000 bottles
HECTARES UNDER VINE 18.00

Over the past few years we have monitored the growth of this Broni winery with pleasure. Founded in 1895, it has been owned by the Bertè and Cordini families since 1974. During the 1990s, Natale Bertè decided to select the finest grapes to make top-level wines, and with the advent of his son Matteo, a recent oenology graduate, quality has climbed even higher. Developments include a new cellar and tasting room, separate product lines, and particular attention to Metodo Classicos. We are sure that the future will bring even more interesting surprises. We take our hats off to Matteo, whose passion for Metodo Classico is increasingly evident and his hand ever steadier, so that this year two of his sparklers made it into our finals, both offering excellent value for money. Cuvée della Casa is juicier and more fragrant, while Cuvée Tradizione is fuller flavoured and more mineral. The traditional wines are also good, and the entire range is now very reliable.

○ OP Pinot Nero Brut Cl. Cuvée della Casa Bertè & Cordini	♛♛	5
○ OP Pinot Nero Brut Cl. Cuvée Tradizione Bertè & Cordini	♛♛	5
● OP Bonarda Sabion Bertè & Cordini '12	♛♛	2*
● OP Sangue di Giuda '12	♛♛	2*
○ OP Pinot Nero Brut Cruasé Bertè & Cordini	♛	5
● OP Pinot Nero Nuval Bertè & Cordini '10	♛	3
○ OP Riesling Viti di Luna '12	♛	2
● OP Bonarda Sabion Bertè & Cordini '11	♛♛	2*
☉ OP Cruasé Bertè & Cordini '09	♛♛	3
○ OP Pinot Nero Brut Cl. Cuvée Tradizione '09	♛♛	4
● OP Sangue di Giuda '11	♛♛	2*
○ OP Sauvignon Bertè & Cordini Masaria '11	♛♛	2*

★Monte Rossa

FRAZ. BORNATO
VIA MONTE ROSSA, 1
25040 CAZZAGO SAN MARTINO [BS]
TEL. 030725066
www.monterossa.com

CELLAR SALES
PRE-BOOKED VISITS
ANNUAL PRODUCTION 500,000 bottles
HECTARES UNDER VINE 70.00

One of the most representative wineries of Franciacorta, Monte Rossa was founded by Paolo Rabotti and his wife Paola in the early 1970s, and has stood out ever since for the elegance and stylistic cleanliness of its cuvées. Today it is enthusiastically run by their son Emanuele, who lavishes painstaking attention on the carefully tended vineyards and a range of first-rate wines that have earned all the most prestigious awards over the years. Monte Rossa's style focuses on rich extraction and long ageing that enhances Franciacorta's elegant, mineral character. Brut Cabochon is the most emblematic wine of the estate in Cazzago San Martino and the 2008 vintage is a concentrated, fragrant Franciacorta with a fine soft, tempting character bursting with notes of ripe fruit and vanilla and supported by a lively, mineral tanginess. The alluring Satèn Sansevé has floral notes of lime blossom and Mediterranean herbs.

○ Franciacorta Brut Cabochon '08	♥♥ 7
○ Franciacorta Brut P. R.	♥♥ 5
○ Franciacorta Brut Prima Cuvée	♥♥ 4
⊙ Franciacorta Brut Rosé P. R.	♥♥ 5
○ Franciacorta Satèn Sansevé	♥♥ 5
○ Franciacorta Coupé Non Dosato	♥ 5
○ Franciacorta Brut Cabochon '05	♥♥♥ 6
○ Franciacorta Brut Cabochon '04	♥♥♥ 6
○ Franciacorta Brut Cabochon '03	♥♥♥ 6
○ Franciacorta Brut Cabochon '01	♥♥♥ 6
○ Franciacorta Brut Cabochon '99	♥♥♥ 7
○ Franciacorta Brut Cabochon '98	♥♥♥ 6
○ Franciacorta Brut Cabochon '97	♥♥♥ 6
○ Franciacorta Satèn	♥♥♥ 5

Montenisa

FRAZ. CALINO
VIA PAOLO VI, 62
25046 CAZZAGO SAN MARTINO [BS]
TEL. 0307750838
www.montenisa.it

PRE-BOOKED VISITS
ANNUAL PRODUCTION 300,000 bottles
HECTARES UNDER VINE 60.00

Several years ago the Antinori family made a business agreement with the Maggi family for the management of their estate, and the sisters Albiera, Allegra and Alessia enthusiastically dedicated themselves to modernizing the cellars adjoining the handsome 16th-century villa and renovating the vineyards. The latter cover an area of over 60 hectares in the hamlet of Calino, and yield excellent grapes for the production of a full range of Franciacortas. This year, the Cuvée Speciale – a delicious Blanc de Blancs from chardonnay with a touch of pinot bianco, aged on the lees for over two years before disgorgement – made it into our finals. It is an attractive straw yellow colour, with a complex nose of well-defined fruit, cakes and vanilla with hints of aromatic herbs. On the palate, it is juicy and full-flavoured, with an alluring swathe of acidity and a long finish with nuances of pistachio.

○ Cuvée Speciale	♥♥ 5
○ Franciacorta Brut	♥♥ 5
⊙ Franciacorta Rosé	♥♥ 5
○ Franciacorta Dizero	♥ 5
○ Franciacorta Brut Contessa Camilla Maggi '02	♥♥ 7
○ Franciacorta Brut Contessa Camilla Maggi '01	♥♥ 6
○ Franciacorta Satèn '06	♥♥ 6
○ Franciacorta Satèn '04	♥♥ 6
○ Franciacorta Satèn '03	♥♥ 6

La Montina

VIA BAIANA, 17
25040 MONTICELLI BRUSATI [BS]
TEL. 030653278
www.lamontina.it

CELLAR SALES
PRE-BOOKED VISITS
RESTAURANT SERVICE
ANNUAL PRODUCTION 450,000 bottles
HECTARES UNDER VINE 72.00

The success of the winery owned by the
Bozza brothers is underpinned by the
close-knit technical team formed by
oenologist Cesare Ferrari and agronomists
Alceo Totò and Rocco Marino, with
Michele Bozza, responsible for the
commercial side of the business. Founded
in 1987, it is named after the historic
estate of the Montini family, into which
Pope Paul VI was born . Today the estate
has over 70 hectares of vineyards,
scattered over seven different
municipalities in Franciacorta. Its
headquarters are housed in a beautiful
villa with a large modern underground
cellar and elegant guest accommodation.
The estate's range is as sound as ever,
albeit without reaching dizzy heights this
year, due to the absence of the most
important vintages. Our favourites include
the fragrant, full-flavoured Franciacorta
Extra Brut Rosatum, a rounded
non-vintage Brut with alluring softness,
and the delicately sweet, aromatic Rosé
Demi Sec with a fine nose and tantalizing
notes of wild berries.

○ Franciacorta Brut	♥♥ 4
⊙ Franciacorta Extra Brut Rosé Rosatum	♥♥ 5
⊙ Franciacorta Rosé Demi Sec	♥♥ 4
○ Curtefranca Bianco '12	♥ 2
● Curtefranca dei Dossi '11	♥ 2
○ Franciacorta Extra Brut	♥ 4
○ Franciacorta Satèn Argens	♥ 5
○ Franciacorta Brut '05	♥♥♥ 5
○ Franciacorta Extra Brut Ris. Vintage '04	♥♥♥ 6
○ Franciacorta Extra Brut Vintage Ris. '05	♥♥♥ 6

Monzio Compagnoni

VIA NIGOLINE, 98
25030 ADRO [BS]
TEL. 0307457803
www.monziocompagnoni.com

CELLAR SALES
PRE-BOOKED VISITS
ANNUAL PRODUCTION 250,000 bottles
HECTARES UNDER VINE 30.00

Several years ago longstanding grower
Marcello Monzio Compagnoni founded a
new winery in Franciacorta where he could
express his passion for Metodo Classico,
which now flanks the excellent wines made
on the family estate in nearby Valcalepio. In
his modern cellar in Adro he produces a
meticulously crafted range of Franciacortas
from the estate's 30 hectares of vineyards,
and does the same in Scanzorosciate with
an array of Valcalepio wines. Once again
this year, Franciacorta Extra Brut worthily
represented the estate in our finals. The
2009 vintage has an attractive lean, edgy,
zesty character, with a well-orchestrated
fruity palate of candied peel and delicately
balsamic nuances. Monti della Corte 2007,
a Franciacorta Riserva from 100% pinot
nero, made an interesting debut, offering
appealing fruity and smoky notes.

○ Franciacorta Extra Brut '09	♥♥ 5
○ Curtefranca Bianco Ronco della Seta '12	♥♥ 2*
○ Franciacorta Brut '09	♥♥ 4
○ Franciacorta Brut Rosé '09	♥♥ 5
○ Franciacorta Dosaggio Zero Monti della Corte Ris. '07	♥♥ 6
○ Franciacorta Satèn '09	♥♥ 5
● Moscato di Scanzo Don Quijote '07	♥♥ 5
● Rosso di Nero '09	♥♥ 4
○ Curtefranca Bianco della Seta '11	♥ 2
○ Franciacorta Extra Brut '04	♥♥♥ 5
○ Franciacorta Extra Brut '03	♥♥♥ 5
○ Franciacorta Brut '08	♥♥ 4
○ Franciacorta Extra Brut '08	♥♥ 5
○ Franciacorta Satèn '08	♥♥ 5
● Moscato di Scanzo Don Quijote '06	♥♥ 5

Il Mosnel

LOC. CAMIGNONE
VIA BARBOGLIO, 14
25040 PASSIRANO [BS]
TEL. 030653117
www.ilmosnel.com

CELLAR SALES
PRE-BOOKED VISITS
RESTAURANT SERVICE
ANNUAL PRODUCTION 250,000 bottles
HECTARES UNDER VINE 40.00

Emanuela Barboglio was among the first to sense the oenological potential of Franciacorta. Indeed, as early as the 1960s, she started to convert the large estate purchased by her family in the first half of the 19th century to wine production. Today it vaunts 40 hectares under vine in a single plot in Passirano. At their centre is the 16th-century hamlet where Emanuela's children Lucia and Giulio now welcome visitors, and which is home to the well-equipped modern cellars. Franciacorta Extra Brut EBB 2008 easily reached our finals, where it was appreciated for the fineness of its bead and elegant, concentrated nose of ripe fruit with delicately smoky nuances and hints of iodine. On the palate it is generous and well-behaved, with creamy effervescence and a fresh, lively zesty finish. The rest of the list is also very sound.

Muratori - Villa Crespia

VIA VALLI, 31
25030 ADRO [BS]
TEL. 0307451051
www.arcipelagomuratori.it

CELLAR SALES
PRE-BOOKED VISITS
ANNUAL PRODUCTION 350,000 bottles
HECTARES UNDER VINE 60.00

Villa Crespia is one of the most important estates in Franciacorta, with 60 hectares of vineyards capable of ensuring both quantity and quality in production. The Muratori brothers belong to a family of entrepreneurs with solid agricultural roots. Aided by oenologist Francesco Iacono, they have created a veritable archipelago of estates. In addition to Franciacorta, it includes Rubbia al Colle in Maremma, Tuscany; Oppida Aminea in Sannio; and Giardini Arimei on the island of Ischia. Franciacorta Riserva Francesco Iacono is a "zero-dosage" sparkler from pinot nero that is aged on the lees for at least six years. The 2006 caught our attention for its fine coppery straw hue and complex nose of wild berries, apples and wholemeal. On the palate, it is full-flavoured, deep and creamy, with good backbone and length. Riserva dei Consoli 2005, from 100% chardonnay, is also very interesting.

○ Franciacorta Extra Brut EBB '08	♟♟ 5
● Curtefranca Rosso Fontecolo '10	♟♟ 2*
○ Franciacorta Brut	♟♟ 4
⊙ Franciacorta Brut Rosé	♟♟ 5
⊙ Franciacorta Pas Dosé Parosé '08	♟♟ 5
○ Franciacorta Satèn '09	♟♟ 5
○ Curtefranca Bianco Campolarga '12	♟ 2
○ Franciacorta Pas Dosé	♟ 4
○ Franciacorta Pas Dosé QdE Ris. '04	♟♟♟ 6
○ Franciacorta Satèn '05	♟♟♟ 5
⊙ Franciacorta Pas Dosé Parosé '07	♟♟ 5
○ Franciacorta Pas Dosé QdE Ris. '06	♟♟ 6

○ Franciacorta Dosaggio Zero Francesco Iacono Ris. '06	♟♟ 7
○ Franciacorta Brut Novalia	♟♟ 4
○ Franciacorta Brut Riserva dei Consoli '05	♟♟ 7
○ Franciacorta Brut Simbiotico	♟♟ 5
⊙ Franciacorta Extra Brut Rosé Brolese	♟♟ 5
○ Franciacorta Satèn Cesonato	♟♟ 5
○ Franciacorta Brut Miolo	♟ 5
○ Franciacorta Dosaggio Zero Cisiolo	♟ 5
○ Franciacorta Dosaggio Zero Numerozero	♟ 5
○ Franciacorta Dosaggio Zero Francesco Iacono Ris. '04	♟♟♟ 7
○ Franciacorta Dosaggio Zero Cisiolo '04	♟♟ 5
○ Franciacorta Extra Brut Francesco Iacono Ris. '02	♟♟ 7

★Nino Negri

VIA GHIBELLINI
23030 CHIURO [SO]
TEL. 0342485211
www.ninonegri.it

CELLAR SALES
PRE-BOOKED VISITS
ACCOMMODATION AND RESTAURANT SERVICE
ANNUAL PRODUCTION 800,000 bottles
HECTARES UNDER VINE 36.00

Nino Negri is a legendary name in Italian winemaking and the benchmark for the whole of Valtellina. This dynamic estate was founded over 110 years ago and is now owned by Gruppo Italiano Vini, which has made it a driving force for the group's ceaseless innovation, with projects that focus increasingly on sustainability. Its strengths are many: an estate comprising some of the area's finest vineyards, a network of select growers, and one of the most advanced technical teams in Italy. The style of the wines skilfully combines modern and traditional, enhancing the distinctive features of the individual terroirs with incredibly consistent quality. Sforzato 5 Stelle 2010 unanimously earned a Tre Bicchieri. It's a celebration of elegance, with a concentrated, elegant nose of tobacco and spices, and attractive close-focused fruit with typical partially dried grape aromas. The rich, well-orchestrated palate is very full-bodied, with vibrant tannins and an exceptionally long finish. Nebbiolo L'Inferno C. Negri 2010 has striking notes of liquorice and tobacco, which give way to red berries.

● Valtellina Sfursat 5 Stelle '10	♥♥♥	7
● Valtellina Sup. Inferno C. Negri '10	♥♥	5
● Valtellina Sup. Vign. Fracia '10	♥♥	6
○ Ca' Brione '12	♥♥	5
● Valtellina Sup. Grumello V. Sassorosso '10	♥♥	4
● Valtellina Sup. Sassella Le Tense '10	♥♥	4
● Valtellina Sfursat '05	♥♥♥	8
● Valtellina Sfursat '04	♥♥♥	6
● Valtellina Sfursat 5 Stelle '09	♥♥♥	7
● Valtellina Sfursat 5 Stelle '07	♥♥♥	7
● Valtellina Sfursat 5 Stelle '06	♥♥♥	7
● Valtellina Sup. Vign. Fracia '08	♥♥♥	6
● Valtellina Sfursat '09	♥♥	6
● Valtellina Sup. Sassella Le Tense '09	♥♥	4

Pasini - San Giovanni

FRAZ. RAFFA
VIA VIDELLE, 2
25080 PUEGNAGO SUL GARDA [BS]
TEL. 0365651419
www.pasiniproduttori.it

CELLAR SALES
PRE-BOOKED VISITS
RESTAURANT SERVICE
ANNUAL PRODUCTION 300,000 bottles
HECTARES UNDER VINE 36.00

Luca, Sara and Paolo Pasini have been running the family estate for over 20 years. It covers an area of over 30 hectares along the western shore of Lake Garda, allowing them to focus on the wines of both the Lugana and the Valtenesi production zones. Great care has been paid to the environmental impact of all the stages of production – first in the vineyard and then in the cellar – with the installation of a large photovoltaic system on the roof, and the adoption of other less conspicuous but nonetheless significant choices, such as the use of lighter bottles. Ceppo 326 Rosé, a chardonnay and groppello sparkler, gave an excellent performance, with a concentrated nose of wild berries, biscuits and aromatic herbs accompanied by a vibrant, invigorating palate with caressing effervescence. The white spumante Centopercento, from 100% groppello, is creamier, soft and citrussy, while the two Valtenesi reds display a nose of red berries and spices and a sophisticated, lean palate.

○ Brut M. Cl. Centopercento	♥♥	4
○ Brut M. Cl. Lugana	♥♥	3
● Brut M. Cl. Rosé Ceppo 326	♥♥	4
● Valtenesi Il Valtenesi '12	♥♥	2*
● Valtènesi Picedo '12	♥♥	2*
○ Brut M. Cl. Ceppo 326	♥	5
● Garda Cl. Groppello Vign. Arzane '10	♥	3
○ Lugana Il Lugana '12	♥	2
● San Gioan Rosso I Carati '09	♥	4
☉ Valtenesi Il Chiaretto Il Vino di una Notte '12	♥	3
● Garda Cl. Groppello Vign. Arzane Ris. '09	♥♥	5
● Garda Rosso Cl. Sup. Ca' del Priù '09	♥♥	5
● Valtenesi Il Chiaretto Il Vino di una Notte '11	♥♥	3
● Valtenesi Picedo '11	♥♥	4

Perla del Garda

LOC. LONATO DEL GARDA
VIA FENIL VECCHIO, 9
25017 LONATO [BS]
TEL. 0309103109
www.perladelgarda.it

CELLAR SALES
PRE-BOOKED VISITS
ANNUAL PRODUCTION 120,000 bottles
HECTARES UNDER VINE 30.00

Although Perla del Garda is one of the wineries recently founded on the Brescian shore of Lake Garda, the area that it occupies – around 30 hectares – was formerly under vine and was replanted by the Prandini family. Trebbiano di Lugana, or turbiana, obviously accounts for the lion's share, but the estate also grows also other grape varieties, both red and white, which yield over 100,000 good-quality bottles per year. The still wines are flanked by an interesting Metodo Classico. The excellent white Lugana Madreperla 2011 undergoes long ageing in steel and offers an elegant, generous nose that is nicely reflected on the rich, full-flavoured palate with nice grip. Settimo Cielo, on the other hand, is a Brut with appealing spicy notes of peaches and apricots, and a full, juicy palate with an intriguing citrussy finish. Lugana Perla 2012 is huskier and more approachable, while the Vendemmia Tardiva focuses on alluring sweetness.

○ Garda Cl. Brut Settimo Cielo	♟♟	6
● Leonatus '09	♟♟	4
○ Lugana Madreperla '11	♟♟	4
○ Lugana V. T. '11	♟♟	4
○ Lugana Perla '12	♟	3
○ Lugana Sup. Madonna della Scoperta '10	♟	4
⊙ Rose delle Siepi '12	♟	3
○ Drajibo Passito '09	♟♟	5
○ Lugana Perla '11	♟♟	3
○ Lugana Sup. Madreperla '10	♟♟	5

Andrea Picchioni

FRAZ. CAMPONOCE, 8
27044 CANNETO PAVESE [PV]
TEL. 0385262139
www.picchioniandrea.it

CELLAR SALES
PRE-BOOKED VISITS
ANNUAL PRODUCTION 70,000 bottles
HECTARES UNDER VINE 10.00

Several years have passed since the determined and single-minded Andrea Picchioni managed to bring the labels of his small estate and his production philosophy to the attention of the wine world. The beautiful and inaccessible ridges of Val Solinga, where most of the estate's vineyards are situated, produce croatina, barbera and ughetta di Canneto, ideal for wines destined for long ageing, which reach their best after many years. Recently the range has been extended to encompass other types, including Metodo Classico. This year, the two Buttafuocos performed very well again. The aged version, Riva Bianca 2009, is as austere as ever, but displays attractive juicy fruit with a series of very pleasant spicy aromas and an excellent tannic weave. It is certain to improve further with ageing. The very enjoyable easy-drinking Luogo della Cerasa 2012 is fresher, crisper and more fragrant, while Rosso D'Asia 2009 is still very closed, but its great potential is evident.

● OP Bonarda Vivace Luogo dei Ronchi '12	♟♟	2*
● OP Buttafuoco Bricco Riva Bianca '09	♟♟	4
● OP Buttafuoco Luogo della Cerasa '12	♟♟	2*
● Rosso d'Asia '09	♟♟	4
● OP Sangue di Giuda Fior del Vento '12	♟	2
● Pinot Nero Arfena '11	♟	4
● Monnalisa '08	♟♟	4
● OP Bonarda Vivace Luogo dei Ronchi '11	♟♟	3
● OP Buttafuoco Bricco Riva Bianca '08	♟♟	4
● OP Pinot Nero Arfena '10	♟♟	3
● Rosso d'Asia '08	♟♟	3

Plozza

VIA SAN GIACOMO, 22
23037 TIRANO [SO]
TEL. 0342701297
www.plozza.com

CELLAR SALES
PRE-BOOKED VISITS
ANNUAL PRODUCTION 450,000 bottles
HECTARES UNDER VINE 28.00

Andrea Zanoli's winery, founded in 1919, has always been at the forefront in terms of production technologies, marketing strategies and foreign sales. Its cellars are located in Tirano and in Brusio, in Switzerland, while its vineyards are scattered over the main subzones of Valtellina. Long very active on the Swiss and German markets, today the winery seems increasingly oriented towards a return to a style more closely associated with its area of origin, more austere and elegant than in the past. Sforzato Vin da Ca' 2009 vaunts an appealing classic style. The partial drying of the grapes is perfect, with fruity notes of cherries, plums and cocoa powder. On the palate, it's powerful, with good flesh and length. Inferno Riserva 2009 is attractive, with a reassuring nose of spice and prunes, and a firm, solid palate with pleasant fruity pulp and a satisfying well-typed finish.

● Valtellina Sforzato Vin da Ca' '09	♀♀ 5
● Passione Barrique '09	♀♀ 6
● Valtellina Numero Uno '10	♀♀ 7
● Valtellina Sup. Inferno Ris. '09	♀♀ 3
● Valtellina Sup. Sassella La Scala Ris. '09	♀♀ 3
● Valtellina Numero Uno '01	♀♀♀ 7
● Passione Barrique '07	♀♀ 6
● Valtellina Numero Uno '09	♀♀ 7
● Valtellina Numero Uno '07	♀♀ 7
● Valtellina Sforzato Vin da Ca' '08	♀♀ 5
● Valtellina Sforzato Vin da Ca' '07	♀♀ 5
● Valtellina Sup. Inferno Ris. '08	♀♀ 3
● Valtellina Sup. Sassella La Scala Ris. '08	♀♀ 3

Mamete Prevostini

VIA LUCCHINETTI, 63
23020 MESE [SO]
TEL. 034341522
www.mameteprevostini.com

CELLAR SALES
PRE-BOOKED VISITS
RESTAURANT SERVICE
ANNUAL PRODUCTION 160,000 bottles
HECTARES UNDER VINE 18.00

The winery inaugurated by Mamete Prevostini, head of the Valtellina wine consortium, has taken a further step in the direction of total environmental sustainability. It has been granted certification not only for its energy consumption, but also for its sociocultural quality, low-impact transport and packaging, and transparency of financial management. Although the cellar has been modernized, the style of the wines remains unaltered, offering a perfect blend of rich aromatics, power and finesse. Several labels, derived from attentive zoning, offer memorable interpretations of mountain Nebbiolos. Technical precision merges perfectly with elegance and terroir in Sassella San Lorenzo 2010. The nose has close-focused notes of red berries, with hints of spice and pencil lead. It is powerful without being monumental, with rich texture and a very good acid background that gives it finesse and excellent all-round harmony. The interesting austere Sassella Sommarovina 2011 has a nose of tobacco, spice and roots, and a caressing palate with velvety tannins and a long, enfolding finish.

● Valtellina Sup. Sassella San Lorenzo '10	♀♀♀ 5
● Valtellina Corte di Cama '11	♀♀ 5
● Valtellina Sforzato Albareda '11	♀♀ 6
● Valtellina Sup. Sassella Sommarovina '11	♀♀ 4
● Valtellina Sup. Grumello '11	♀♀ 3
● Valtellina Sup. Ris. '10	♀♀ 5
● Valtellina Sup. Sassella '11	♀♀ 3
○ Vertemate '11	♀♀ 6
⊙ Rosato '12	♀ 3
● Valtellina Santarita '12	♀ 2
● Valtellina Sforzato Albareda '09	♀♀♀ 6
● Valtellina Sforzato Albareda '08	♀♀♀ 6
● Valtellina Sforzato Albareda '06	♀♀♀ 6
● Valtellina Sup. Ris. '09	♀♀♀ 5
● Valtellina Corte di Cama '10	♀♀ 5
● Valtellina Sforzato Albareda '10	♀♀ 6

Provenza - Cà Maiol

VIA DEI COLLI STORICI
25015 DESENZANO DEL GARDA [BS]
TEL. 0309910006
www.provenzacantine.it

CELLAR SALES
PRE-BOOKED VISITS
ANNUAL PRODUCTION 1,500,000 bottles
HECTARES UNDER VINE 155.00

Fabio Contato has given a great boost to this family estate that, in the space of a few short years, has increased its area under vine, the quality of its wines and its annual production figure. The wines, on the other hand, have remained more or less unchanged, headed by the Lugana, which maintains the estate's reputation. The vineyards cover an area of over 100 hectares, concentrated mainly in the southern area of Lake Garda, which is the undisputed realm of turbiana, while the reds hail from the nearby Valtenesi area. Lugana Molin 2012, derived from strict grape selection and ageing in steel, has made a qualitative leap to become one of the most interesting wines in the entire production zone. Its elegant nose of flowers and white-fleshed fruit is accompanied by a taut, lean palate with a very long finish. Fabio Contato 2011, on the other hand, is the usual masterly combination of fruit and oak that yields a sophisticated enfolding palate. Turning to the reds now, we were most impressed by Negresco 2009.

○ Lugana Molin '12	▼▼▼ 3*
○ Lugana Sup. Sel. Fabio Contato '11	▼▼▼ 5
⊙ Garda Cl. Chiaretto Tenuta Maiolo '12	▼▼▼ 3
● Garda Cl. Negresco '09	▼▼ 4
○ Lugana Brut M. Cl. '08	▼▼ 4
○ Lugana Dosage Zero Sel. Fabio Contato '07	▼▼ 7
○ Lugana Prestige '12	▼▼ 3
⊙ Garda Cl. Chiaretto '12	▼ 3
● Garda Cl. Groppello Joel '11	▼ 3
● Garda Rosso Cl. Sel. Fabio Contato '09	▼ 5
○ Lugana Sel. Fabio Contato '07	▼▼▼ 5
○ Lugana Sup. Sel. Fabio Contato '10	▼▼▼ 5
○ Lugana Sup. Sel. Fabio Contato '09	▼▼▼ 5
○ Lugana Sup. Sel. Fabio Contato '06	▼▼▼ 5

Francesco Quaquarini

LOC. MONTEVENEROSO
VIA CASA ZAMBIANCHI, 26
27044 CANNETO PAVESE [PV]
TEL. 038560152
www.quaquarinifrancesco.it

CELLAR SALES
PRE-BOOKED VISITS
ANNUAL PRODUCTION 650,000 bottles
HECTARES UNDER VINE 60.00
VITICULTURE METHOD Certified Organic

Our apologies to Francesco Quacquarini for having mistakenly declared him dead last year: he jokingly commented that we had extended his life. In the meantime, with the precious aid of his oenologist son Umberto and his daughter Maria Teresa, the family estate successfully continues to combine quantity with quality, focusing chiefly on the most characteristic Oltrepò wines, which always fare extremely well in blind tastings. This year, Buttafuoco Storico Vigna Pregana 2007 is the best in its class: characteristically full-bodied and beefy, but not heavy, with prominent supporting acidity and silky tannins. It offers laudably crisp fruit and all-round balance. The reliable Bonarda and Sangue di Giuda – both the basic version and the Vigna Acqua Calda selection – are always perfect, showing fragrant and balanced.

● OP Barbera Poggio Anna '10	▼▼ 3
● OP Bonarda Vivace '12	▼▼ 2*
● OP Buttafuoco V. Pregana '07	▼▼ 5
● OP Sangue di Giuda '12	▼▼ 2*
● OP Sangue di Giuda V. Acqua Calda '12	▼▼ 3
● OP Barbera Poggio Anna '09	▽▽ 2*
● OP Bonarda Vivace '11	▽▽ 2*
⊙ OP Cruasé '09	▽▽ 5
● OP Pinot Nero Blau '09	▽▽ 3
● OP Pinot Nero Blau '07	▽▽ 3
● OP Pinot Nero Blau '05	▽▽ 2*
○ OP Pinot Nero Brut Classese '06	▽▽ 2*
● OP Sangue di Giuda '11	▽▽ 2*
● OP Sangue di Giuda V. Acqua Calda '11	▽▽ 3

LOMBARDY

Aldo Rainoldi

Loc. Casacce di Chiuro
via Stelvio, 128
23030 Chiuro [SO]
Tel. 0342482225
www.rainoldi.com

CELLAR SALES
PRE-BOOKED VISITS
ANNUAL PRODUCTION 200,000 bottles
HECTARES UNDER VINE 9.60

Aldo Rainoldi is playing an increasingly important role in this winery founded by his grandfather in 1925. He is involved in both its promotion on international markets and meticulous agronomical research in the estate-owned vineyards, redefining the relationship that has long bound the winery to its selected growers. In addition to the classic Sassella, Grumello and Inferno, aged in Slavonian oak barrels, the range also features a Riserva version of each, held in the cellars for three years before release. It is topped by the extremely solid, firmly structured Sfursat Fruttaio Ca' Rizzieri, which spends 15 months in barriques and is eminently ageworthy. The 2009 vintage has a slow-opening nose of fruit in alcohol, with hints of ginger, Peruvian bark and tobacco. Its rich palate has sturdy tannins that harmoniously accompany the rich fruit, and a never-ending finish. Inferno Riserva 2009 is excellent, with very delicate notes of tobacco on a background of plums and rain-soaked earth. The palate is linear, its acidity balanced by vigorous fruit, with a long, very classic finish.

Wine	Rating
● Valtellina Sfursat Fruttaio Ca' Rizzieri '09	▼▼▼ 6
● Valtellina Sfursat '09	▼▼ 5
⊙ Rosé Nature Cuvée Maria Vitto	▼▼ 6
● Valtellina Sup. Inferno Ris. '09	▼▼ 5
● Valtellina Sup. Prugnolo '09	▼▼ 3
● Valtellina Sup. Sassella '09	▼▼ 5
⊙ Brut Rosé '09	▼ 4
● Valtellina Sfursat '08	♈♈♈ 5
● Valtellina Sfursat Fruttaio Ca' Rizzieri '06	♈♈♈ 6
● Valtellina Sfursat Fruttaio Ca' Rizzieri '02	♈♈♈ 6
● Valtellina Sfursat Fruttaio Ca' Rizzieri '00	♈♈♈ 6
● Valtellina Sfursat Fruttaio Ca' Rizzieri '98	♈♈♈ 6

Ricci Curbastro

via Adro, 37
25031 Capriolo [BS]
Tel. 030736094
www.riccicurbastro.it

CELLAR SALES
PRE-BOOKED VISITS
ACCOMMODATION
ANNUAL PRODUCTION 240,000 bottles
HECTARES UNDER VINE 25.50

The recent death of Gualberto Ricci Cubastro, who was among the promoters of the foundation of the Franciacorta designation in 1967, follows a lifetime of commitment in the growing sector. Since the late 1970s he was flanked by Riccardo, one of his four sons, who has now been at the helm of the estate for years, enthusiastically continuing his father's work. Formerly the chairman of the Franciacorta Consortium, agronomist and oenologist Riccardo currently chairs the European Federation of Origin Wines and its Italian counterpart the FederDoc. His estate produces a comprehensive range of Franciacortas and local wines. Two cuvées reached our finals this year. The exceptionally harmonious Franciacorta Satèn 2009 successfully balances ripe fruit notes with a fresh, creamy swathe of acidity to underpin it, while the Extra Brut 2009 has an attractive floral nose with balsamic notes and an elegant, zesty palate with a lingering finish.

Wine	Rating
○ Franciacorta Extra Brut '09	▼▼ 5
○ Franciacorta Satèn Brut '09	▼▼ 5
⊙ Franciacorta Brut	▼▼ 4
⊙ Franciacorta Brut Rosé	▼▼ 5
○ Franciacorta Extra Brut M.R. '05	▼▼ 5
○ Pinot Bianco Sebino '12	▼▼ 2*
○ Curtefranca Bianco '12	▼ 2
○ Franciacorta Demi Sec	▼ 4
○ Franciacorta Satèn	▼ 4
○ Franciacorta Dosaggio Zero Gualberto '06	♈♈♈ 6
○ Franciacorta Extra Brut '07	♈♈♈ 5
○ Franciacorta Extra Brut '08	♈♈ 5
○ TdF Curtefranca V. Bosco Alto '09	♈♈ 3

Ronco Calino

loc. Quattro Camini
fraz. Torbiato
via Fenice, 45
25030 Adro [BS]
Tel. 0307451073
www.roncocalino.it

CELLAR SALES
PRE-BOOKED VISITS
ANNUAL PRODUCTION 70,000 bottles
HECTARES UNDER VINE 10.00

Several years ago textile entrepreneur Paolo Radici decided to purchase the magnificent villa in Torbiato di Adro that once belonged to famed pianist Arturo Benedetti Michelangeli. The villa is surrounded by ten hectares of beautiful vineyards in a spectacular morainic amphitheatre, and the modern new cellar produces a carefully crafted range of local wines and Franciacortas with the aid of consulting oenologist Leonardo Valenti. Today Paolo is aided in the management of the estate by his his daughter Lara Imberti Radici. This year, it was the Brut 2008 that stood out among the estate's wines and made it into our finals. It is firm and elegant, with a complex floral nose of chamomile and aromatic herbs, and a creamy palate with a long finish of soft damson and apricot notes. The non-vintage Franciacorta Brut is also convincing, with citrussy notes and a fresh, supple plate with excellent depth. The rest of the list is also good.

○ Franciacorta Brut '08	🍷🍷 5
○ Curtefranca Bianco Lèant '11	🍷🍷 3
● Curtefranca Rosso Ponènt '09	🍷🍷 4
○ Franciacorta Brut	🍷🍷 4
○ Franciacorta Satèn	🍷🍷 5
⊙ Franciacorta Brut Rosé Radijan	🍷 5
○ Curtefranca Bianco '10	🍸🍸 3
○ Franciacorta Nature '08	🍸🍸 5
○ Franciacorta Nature '07	🍸🍸 5

San Cristoforo

via Villanuova, 2
25030 Erbusco [BS]
Tel. 0307760482
www.sancristoforo.eu

CELLAR SALES
PRE-BOOKED VISITS
ANNUAL PRODUCTION 80,000 bottles
HECTARES UNDER VINE 10.00

Bruno Dotti and Claudia Cavalleri tend their ten hectares of vineyards in Erbusco with the passion of true vignerons, using their grapes to produce a complete range of clean, elegant Franciacortas. They personally attend to work in the vineyard and the cellar, and have made enormous progress since their first harvests 20 years ago, as reflected in the consistently high quality of their wines. Today production focuses on Franciacorta, a chardonnay-based Blanc de Blancs, with the exception of the Rosé, made entirely from pinot nero. San Cristoforo does not produce Satèn. This year, the excellent Pas Dosé 2009 reached our finals. It is a bright greenish straw hue, with a very fresh nose of apples and pears featuring hints of aromatic herbs and mint. On the palate, it is remarkably long and elegant, showing edgy, fresh and zesty. The Franciacorta Brut is citrussy, tangy and supple.

○ Franciacorta Pas Dosé '09	🍷🍷 6
○ Franciacorta Brut '09	🍷🍷 6
○ Franciacorta Brut	🍷🍷 5
⊙ Franciacorta Rosé	🍷 5
○ Franciacorta Brut '08	🍸🍸 6
○ Franciacorta Brut '06	🍸🍸 4
○ Franciacorta Pas Dosé '08	🍸🍸 6
● San Cristoforo Uno '07	🍸🍸 4

Lo Sparviere

VIA COSTA, 2
25040 MONTICELLI BRUSATI [BS]
TEL. 030652382
www.losparviere.com

CELLAR SALES
PRE-BOOKED VISITS
ANNUAL PRODUCTION 120,000 bottles
HECTARES UNDER VINE 30.00

Ugo Gussalli Beretta descends from one of the oldest industrial dynasties in the world. His passion for wine has led him to form the Agricole Gussalli Beretta group, which also includes Castello di Radda in Chianti Classico, Orlandi Contucci Ponno in Abruzzo and Cascina Pressenda in Castelletto di Monforte d'Alba. The beautiful 150-hectare Franciacorta estate has 30 hectares of vineyards, which surround a perfectly restored 16th-century villa with outbuildings. Franciacorta Extra Brut 2007, an elegant cuvée from chardonnay with 10% pinot nero, did very well in our finals, earning the estate its first Tre Bicchieri. Aged for five years on the lees, it shows a bright straw yellow with a very fine bead. The nose opens with complex, rich notes of fruit, honey and spice, and is accompanied by a deep, full-flavoured, invigorating palate with hints of hazelnut, citrus fruit and vanilla on the fresh, elegant finish.

○ Franciacorta Extra Brut '07	▼▼▼	5
○ Franciacorta Brut	▼▼	5
○ Franciacorta Dosaggio Zero Ris. '06	▼▼	8
⊙ Franciacorta Rosé Monique	▼	5
○ Franciacorta Brut '08	♀♀	5
○ Franciacorta Brut '06	♀♀	4
○ Franciacorta Extra Brut '05	♀♀	5

Pietro Torti

FRAZ. CASTELROTTO, 9
27047 MONTECALVO VERSIGGIA [PV]
TEL. 038599763
www.pietrotorti.it

CELLAR SALES
PRE-BOOKED VISITS
ANNUAL PRODUCTION 30,000 bottles
HECTARES UNDER VINE 10.00

The Torti family have been growers in Montecalvo Versiggia for generations. Many years have passed since Pietro handed over the reins of the estate to his son Sandro, who does practically everything singlehanded, in both the vineyard and the cellar. This year we have rewarded his convincing range of wines and his determined work as a small grower in a difficult area with our full profile. The Brut 2009 is undoubtedly the finest produced so far. It's a deep straw yellow, with notes of saffron, citrus and tropical fruit and an oxidized style with a very interesting mineral finish. The attractive coppery hued Cruasé 2010 is very well-made, displaying the typical notes of pinot nero, wild berries, autumn leaves and aromatic herbs, with floral hints. Bonarda Vivace 2012 remains one of the best of its kind, showing fragrant and harmonious, soft and alluring with notes of wild berries and Parma violets.

○ OP Pinot Nero Brut M. Cl. Torti '09	▼▼	3*
● OP Bonarda Vivace '12	▼▼	2*
⊙ OP Cruasé '10	▼▼	2*
○ Fagù '12	▼	2
● OP Bonarda Verzello '12	▼	2
● OP Pinot Nero Otto '10	▼	3
○ OP Riesling Italico Moglialunga '12	▼	2
● Castelrotto '09	♀♀	5
○ Fagù '11	♀♀	2*
● OP Bonarda Vivace '11	♀♀	2*

★Uberti

LOC. SALEM
VIA E. FERMI, 2
25030 ERBUSCO [BS]
TEL. 0307267476
www.ubertivini.it

PRE-BOOKED VISITS
ANNUAL PRODUCTION 180,000 bottles
HECTARES UNDER VINE 24.00

Agostino Uberti and his wife Eleonora have made some of the most alluring cuvées in the history of Franciacorta, contributing to the area's extraordinary reputation, acquired in the space of just 50 years. Their vineyards, often veritable grand crus, such as Comarì del Salem in Erbusco, assure exceptional grapes on which they work their magic in the cellar. Over the past few years the estate has also benefitted from the arrival of the next generation of Ubertis: oenologist Silvia and Francesca, who manages hospitality. Satèn Magnificentia worthily represented the Erbusco winery in our finals, displaying creamy consistency, chewy fruit, alluring vanilla notes and fresh poise. The complex, full-flavoured Quinque Brut, with iodine notes, is a blend of five vintages from 2002 to 2006.

○ Franciacorta Satèn Magnificentia	♀♀	6
○ Franciacorta Extra Brut Francesco I	♀♀	5
○ Franciacorta Extra Brut Quinque	♀♀	8
⊙ Franciacorta Rosé Francesco I	♀♀	5
○ Franciacorta Brut Francesco I	♀	5
○ Franciacorta Brut Comarì del Salem '00	♀♀♀	6
○ Franciacorta Brut Comarì del Salem '93	♀♀♀	6
○ Franciacorta Extra Brut Comarì del Salem '03	♀♀♀	6
○ Franciacorta Extra Brut Comarì del Salem '02	♀♀♀	6
○ Franciacorta Extra Brut Comarì del Salem '01	♀♀♀	6
○ Franciacorta Extra Brut Comarì del Salem '98	♀♀♀	6
○ Franciacorta Extra Brut Comarì del Salem '95	♀♀♀	6

Vanzini

FRAZ. BARBALEONE, 7
27040 SAN DAMIANO AL COLLE [PV]
TEL. 038575019
www.vanzini-wine.com

CELLAR SALES
PRE-BOOKED VISITS
ANNUAL PRODUCTION 600,000 bottles
HECTARES UNDER VINE 27.00

The Vanzini brothers have been combining tradition and toil for years in order to offer enthusiasts of the most genuine, typical semi-sparkling Oltrepò wines a product range that is excellent value for money. Quality is assured when it comes to second fermentation in pressure tanks, for both the semi-sparkling wines and the Charmat-method spumantes, the latter made exclusively from estate-grown pinot nero. We can only hope that sooner or later Antonio, Michela and Pierpaolo will decide to add a Metodo Classico to the range. Both Bonarda Vivace and Sangue di Giuda 2012 are always among the best of the production zone, showing fresh and fragrant with notes of red berries and violets. Aedo joins the long Martinotti-Charmat Method sparklers, sporting a shorter, wider bottle and a sweeter flavour, but our favourite remains the Rosé, which is alluring in every respect, commencing with its colour.

● OP Bonarda Vivace '12	♀♀	2*
● OP Sangue di Giuda '12	♀♀	3
⊙ Pinot Nero Spumante Extra Dry Martinotti Rosé	♀♀	3
● OP Barbera '12	♀	2
● OP Pinot Nero '12	♀	3
○ Pinot Nero Spumante Extra Dry Martinotti	♀	3
○ Pinot Nero Spumante Extra Dry Martinotti Aedo	♀	3
○ Moscato Spumante '11	♀♀	3
● OP Barbera '10	♀♀	2
● OP Bonarda Vivace '11	♀♀	2*
● OP Bonarda Vivace '10	♀♀	2*
● OP Sangue di Giuda '11	♀♀	3
● OP Sangue di Giuda '10	♀♀	2*

Bruno Verdi

VIA VERGOMBERRA, 5
27044 CANNETO PAVESE [PV]
TEL. 038588023
www.brunoverdi.it

CELLAR SALES
PRE-BOOKED VISITS
ANNUAL PRODUCTION 100,000 bottles
HECTARES UNDER VINE 10.00

Paolo Verdi is in practice a one-man band who also pays meticulous attention to the wines that it would be wrong to dismiss as "minor". Determined, dynamic and enthusiastic, he took over the family estate at the age of 20 and has made it one of the most reliable wineries in the whole of Oltrepò Pavese. The average level of his wines is very high and continues to rise, year after year, with pinnacles of excellence that never fail to emerge during our tastings. Paolo Verdi never lets us down. It's true that the big reds appear less explosive than usual this year: the Cavariola not making it into the finals is newsworthy after all these years, but its sound fruit and balsamic notes are there and it just requires time. However, we awarded a Tre Bicchieri to the finest Cruasé we've ever tasted, with a complex nose of wild berries and aromatic herbs, and an alluring mineral vein.

⊙ OP Cruasé	♟♟ 4
● OP Barbera Campo del Marrone '10	♟♟ 3
● OP Bonarda Vivace Possessione di Vergombera '12	♟♟ 2*
○ OP Moscato Volpara '12	♟♟ 2*
○ OP Riesling Renano V. Costa '11	♟♟ 2*
● OP Rosso Cavariola Ris. '09	♟♟ 5
● OP Sangue di Giuda Dolce Paradiso '12	♟♟ 2*
● OP Vergomberra Brut Nature '08	♟♟ 4
○ OP Pinot Grigio '12	♟ 2
● OP Rosso Cavariola Ris. '07	♟♟♟ 4
● OP Barbera Campo del Marrone '09	♟♟ 3*
● OP Bonarda Vivace Possessione di Vergombera '11	♟♟ 2*
● OP Buttafuoco '11	♟♟ 2*
● OP Rosso Cavariola Ris. '08	♟♟ 5

Giuseppe Vezzoli

VIA COSTA SOPRA, 22
25030 ERBUSCO [BS]
TEL. 0307267579
www.vezzolivini.it

CELLAR SALES
PRE-BOOKED VISITS
ANNUAL PRODUCTION 130,000 bottles
HECTARES UNDER VINE 60.00

Giuseppe Vezzoli's winery is one of the most interesting in Franciacorta. Since taking over the management of the estate about 15 years ago, Giuseppe has upgraded the original family vineyards in Erbusco in terms of both quantity and quality. Today he vaunts an impressive annual production of 130,000 bottles, made from the grapes of around 60 hectares of vineyards, both estate-owned and leased. The winery's Franciacortas are characterized by their clean style and full body. The Nefertiti, in the Brut and Extra Brut Dizeta versions, is Vezzoli's most representative label. This year, we particularly liked the Extra Brut Dizeta 2007, from 100% chardonnay, fermented in small wood, which is aged for more than 40 months before disgorgement. Its elegant nose of liquorice and white-fleshed fruit is accompanied by a delicate, well-orchestrated palate with good length.

○ Franciacorta Extra Brut Nefertiti Dizeta '07	♟♟ 6
○ Franciacorta Brut '09	♟♟ 5
○ Franciacorta Brut	♟♟ 4
⊙ Franciacorta Rosé Brut	♟♟ 5
○ Franciacorta Satèn	♟ 5
○ Franciacorta Brut '08	♟♟ 5
○ Franciacorta Brut '07	♟♟ 5
○ Franciacorta Brut '06	♟♟ 5
○ Franciacorta Brut Nefertiti '05	♟♟ 6
○ Franciacorta Brut Nefertiti '04	♟♟ 6
○ Franciacorta Extra Brut Nefertiti Dizeta '06	♟♟ 6
○ Franciacorta Extra Brut Nefertiti Dizeta '05	♟♟ 6
○ Franciacorta Extra Brut Nefertiti Dizeta '04	♟♟ 6

Villa

VIA VILLA, 12
25040 MONTICELLI BRUSATI [BS]
TEL. 030652329
www.villafranciacorta.it

PRE-BOOKED VISITS
ACCOMMODATION AND RESTAURANT SERVICE
ANNUAL PRODUCTION 300,000 bottles
HECTARES UNDER VINE 37.00

The 16th-century hamlet of Villa in
Monticelli Brusati is the pride and joy of
Alessandro Bianchi, the successful
businessman who purchased it in the
1960s and painstakingly restored the
historic home and its beautiful adjoining
farm. The estate covers an area of over
100 hectares, with around 40 hectares of
vineyards, many set on the terraces at the
foot of Monte della Rosa. Managed by
Paolo Pizziol, it produces a range of
Franciacortas whose elegance and stylistic
austerity is practically unrivalled.
Franciacorta Brut Emozione 2009 perfectly
expresses the house style, combining
delicate, creamy effervescence with a
remarkably elegant, complex nose of
apples and pears, vanilla and aromatic
herbs with hints of star anise. On the palate
it is alluringly juicy, with a long floral and
citrussy finish: Tre Bicchieri!

Chiara Ziliani

VIA FRANCIACORTA, 7
25050 PROVAGLIO D'ISEO [BS]
TEL. 030981661
www.cantinazilianichiara.it

PRE-BOOKED VISITS
ANNUAL PRODUCTION 230,000 bottles
HECTARES UNDER VINE 17.00

Chiara Ziliani is a brilliant young wine
entrepreneur who perfectly represents the
new generations of keen growers that have
emerged in Franciacorta in recent years.
Her modern, well-equipped cellar is located
in Provaglio d'Iseo, amidst 17 hectares of
densely planted vines – over 7,000 per
hectare – that are tended using methods
with low environmental impact. The ideal
location of the vineyards, at an altitude of
250 metres on south- and south-east-
facing-hillsides, and the care lavished in
the cellar have ensured that the estate's
wide range, based on three lines has
earned an excellent reputation. The many
wines tasted this year include the
noteworthy, plush, succulent Satèn Ziliani
C, with complex mineral nuances, and the
very good Non Dosato 2008 from the same
line, which is creamy with hints of cakes.
The non-vintage Brut Ziliani C is also very
sound, but the quality of the entire range is
outstanding.

○ Franciacorta Brut Emozione '09	♀♀♀ 5
○ Franciacorta Satèn '09	♀♀ 5
○ Campèi '11	♀♀ 2*
○ Curtefranca Pian della Villa '09	♀♀ 3
● Curtefranca Rosso Gradoni '08	♀♀ 4
⊙ Franciacorta Brut Rosé '09	♀♀ 5
○ Franciacorta Extra Brut Solomille '07	♀♀ 6
○ Franciacorta Pas Dosé Diamant '06	♀♀ 5
⊙ Franciacorta Demi Sec Rosé	♀ 5
○ Franciacorta Extra Brut '98	♀♀♀ 4*
○ Franciacorta Brut Emozione '08	♀♀ 5
○ Franciacorta Extra Blu '07	♀♀ 5

○ Franciacorta Brut Conte di Provaglio	♀♀ 3
○ Franciacorta Brut Ziliani C	♀♀ 3
○ Franciacorta Extra Brut Ziliani C '08	♀♀ 4
○ Franciacorta Non Dosato Ziliani C '08	♀♀ 4
⊙ Franciacorta Rosé Conte di Provaglio	♀♀ 3
⊙ Franciacorta Rosé Ziliani C	♀♀ 4
○ Franciacorta Satèn Conte di Provaglio	♀♀ 3
○ Franciacorta Satèn Ziliani C '08	♀♀ 4
● Curtefranca Rosso Conte di Provaglio '11	♀ 2
○ Franciacorta Brut Duca d'Iseo	♀ 3
○ Franciacorta Satèn Duca d'Iseo	♀ 3
○ Franciacorta Satèn Ziliani C	♀ 3
○ Franciacorta Satèn Ziliani C '07	♀♀ 4

Elisabetta Abrami

S.DA VICINALE DELLE FOSCHE
25050 PROVAGLIO D'ISEO [BS]
TEL. 0306857185
www.vinielisabettaabrami.it

○ Franciacorta Brut	♟♟ 5
○ Franciacorta Brut Ris. '06	♟♟ 5
○ Franciacorta Satèn	♟♟ 5
⊙ Franciacorta Brut Rosé	♟ 5

Al Rocol

VIA PROVINCIALE, 79
25050 OME [BS]
TEL. 0306852542
www.alrocol.com

CELLAR SALES
PRE-BOOKED VISITS
ACCOMMODATION AND RESTAURANT SERVICE
ANNUAL PRODUCTION 60,000 bottles
HECTARES UNDER VINE 13.00

○ Franciacorta Brut Ca' del Luf	♟♟ 3
⊙ Franciacorta Brut Rosé Le Rive '09	♟♟ 5
○ Franciacorta Dosaggio Zero Castellini '09	♟♟ 5
○ Franciacorta Satèn Martignac	♟ 4

Riccardo Albani

LOC. CASONA
S.DA SAN BIAGIO, 46
27045 CASTEGGIO [PV]
TEL. 038383622
www.vinialbani.it

CELLAR SALES
PRE-BOOKED VISITS
ANNUAL PRODUCTION 55,000 bottles
HECTARES UNDER VINE 28.00
VITICULTURE METHOD Certified Organic

● OP Bonarda Vivace '12	♟♟ 3

Alziati Annibale
Tenuta San Francesco

LOC. FRAZ. SCAZZOLINO
VIA SCAZZOLINO, 55
27040 ROVESCALA [PV]
TEL. 038575261
www.alziati.it

CELLAR SALES
PRE-BOOKED VISITS
ANNUAL PRODUCTION 100,000 bottles
HECTARES UNDER VINE 15.00

● OP Bonarda Gaggiarone '07	♟♟ 4
● OP Bonarda Gaggiarone Vitigni Giovani '10	♟♟ 3
● OP Bonarda Gaggiarone Vitigni Giovani '11	♟ 3
● OP Bonarda Gaggiarone Vitigni Giovani '11	♟ 3

Tenuta degli Angeli

FRAZ. SANTO STEFANO
VIA FARA, 2
24060 CAROBBIO DEGLI ANGELI [BG]
TEL. 035687130
www.tenutadegliangeli.it

CELLAR SALES
PRE-BOOKED VISITS
ANNUAL PRODUCTION 12,000 bottles
HECTARES UNDER VINE 2.00

○ Spumante Extra Brut M. Cl. degli Angeli	♟♟ 5
○ Valcalepio Bianco Triplok '12	♟♟ 4
● Valcalepio Moscato Passito '08	♟♟ 6

Antica Tesa

LOC. MATTINA
VIA MERANO, 28
25080 BOTTICINO [BS]
TEL. 0302691500

CELLAR SALES
PRE-BOOKED VISITS
ANNUAL PRODUCTION 40,000 bottles
HECTARES UNDER VINE 10.00

● Botticino Pià della Tesa '09	♟♟ 3
● Botticino V. del Gobbio '09	♟♟ 5
● Botticino Colle degli Ulivi '09	♟ 2

Avanzi

VIA TREVISAGO, 19
25080 MANERBA DEL GARDA [BS]
TEL. 0365551013
www.avanzi.net

CELLAR SALES
PRE-BOOKED VISITS
ANNUAL PRODUCTION 500,000 bottles
HECTARES UNDER VINE 77.00

● Garda Cl. Groppello Giovanni Avanzi '12	♈♈ 2*
☉ Garda Cl. Chiaretto Il Vino di una Notte '12	♈ 2
○ Lugana Brut	♈ 3
○ Lugana Sirmione '12	♈ 2

Barboglio De Gaioncelli

FRAZ. COLOMBARO
VIA NAZARIO SAURO
25040 CORTE FRANCA [BS]
TEL. 0309826831
www.barbogliodegaioncelli.it

CELLAR SALES
PRE-BOOKED VISITS
RESTAURANT SERVICE
ANNUAL PRODUCTION 90,000 bottles
HECTARES UNDER VINE 60.00

○ Franciacorta Brut	♈♈ 5
○ Franciacorta Salèn	♈♈ 5
☉ Franciacorta Brut Rosé	♈ 5

La Basia

LOC. LA BASIA
VIA PREDEFITTE, 31
25080 PUEGNAGO SUL GARDA [BS]
TEL. 0365555958
www.labasia.it

CELLAR SALES
PRE-BOOKED VISITS
ANNUAL PRODUCTION 17,000 bottles
HECTARES UNDER VINE 4.00

● Garda Cl. Groppello La Botte Piena '11	♈♈ 2*
● Garda Marzemino Le Morene '12	♈♈ 2*
● Valtenesi Chiaretto '12	♈ 2

Cantina Sociale Bergamasca

VIA BERGAMO, 10
24060 SAN PAOLO D'ARGON [BG]
TEL. 035951098
www.cantinabergamasca.it

CELLAR SALES
PRE-BOOKED VISITS
ANNUAL PRODUCTION 650,000 bottles
HECTARES UNDER VINE 90.00

○ Terre del Colleoni Incrocio Manzoni 6013 '12	♈♈ 5
● Valcalepio Moscato Passito Perseo '08	♈♈ 4
○ Terre del Colleoni Pinot Grigio '12	♈ 5

Biava

FRAZ. SCANZO
VIA MONTE BASTIA, 7
24020 SCANZOROSCIATE [BG]
TEL. 035655581
www.aziendabiava.it

ANNUAL PRODUCTION 6,000 bottles
HECTARES UNDER VINE 2.00

● Moscato di Scanzo '10	♈♈ 7
○ Exenthia	♈♈ 6
● Ghibellino '09	♈♈ 5
● Guelfo '09	♈ 5

Podere Bignolino

LOC. BIGNOLINO
SP 44
27040 BRONI [PV]
TEL. 0383870160
www.poderebignolino.it

ANNUAL PRODUCTION 80,000 bottles
HECTARES UNDER VINE 40.00

● OP Barbera Costa Bercé '11	♈♈ 2*
○ OP Chardonnay '12	♈♈ 2*
○ OP Pinot Grigio Dama D'Oro '12	♈♈ 2*

Bonaldi - Cascina del Bosco

LOC. PETOSINO
VIA GASPAROTTO, 96
24010 SORISOLE [BG]
TEL. 035571701
www.cascinadelbosco.it

CELLAR SALES
PRE-BOOKED VISITS
ANNUAL PRODUCTION 25,000 bottles
HECTARES UNDER VINE 4.00

● Valcalepio Rosso Cantoalto Ris. '10	♟♟	3
○ Brut M. Cl. Bonaldi '10	♟	3
○ Valcalepio Bianco '12	♟	2

Borgo La Gallinaccia

VIA IV NOVEMBRE, 15
25050 RODENGO SAIANO [BS]
TEL. 030611314
www.borgolagallinaccia.it

CELLAR SALES
PRE-BOOKED VISITS
ANNUAL PRODUCTION 16,000 bottles
HECTARES UNDER VINE 3.40

● Colmo dei Colmi '08	♟♟	4
⊙ Franciacorta Brut Rosé	♟♟	4
○ Franciacorta Brut	♟	4
○ Franciacorta Satèn	♟	4

La Boscaiola

VIA RICCAFANA, 19
25033 COLOGNE [BS]
TEL. 0307156386
www.laboscaiola.com

CELLAR SALES
PRE-BOOKED VISITS
ANNUAL PRODUCTION 50,000 bottles
HECTARES UNDER VINE 7.00

○ Franciacorta Brut La Capinera	♟♟	3
○ Franciacorta Dosaggio Zero Zero	♟♟	3
○ Franciacorta Extra Brut Nelson Cenci	♟	6

Alessio Brandolini

FRAZ. BOFFALORA, 68
27040 SAN DAMIANO AL COLLE [PV]
TEL. 038575232
www.alessiobrandolini.com

ANNUAL PRODUCTION 50,000 bottles
HECTARES UNDER VINE 9.00

○ Bardughino '12	♟♟	2*
● OP Bonarda Il Soffio '11	♟♟	2*
● OP Bonarda Vivace Il Cassino '12	♟♟	2*
● Beneficio '10	♟	2

Luciano Brega

FRAZ. BERGAMASCO, 7
27040 MONTÙ BECCARIA [PV]
TEL. 038560237
www.lucianobrega.it

CELLAR SALES
PRE-BOOKED VISITS
ANNUAL PRODUCTION 150,000 bottles
HECTARES UNDER VINE 70.00

● OP Bonarda Vivace '12	♟♟	2*
⊙ Brut M. Cl. Gran Montù '10	♟	4
● OP Bonarda Casapaia '11	♟	2

Bulgarini

LOC. VAIBÒ, 1
25010 POZZOLENGO [BS]
TEL. 030918224
www.vini-bulgarini.com

CELLAR SALES

○ Lugana 010 '12	♟♟	3
○ Lugana '12	♟	2

Ca' del Santo

loc. Campolungo, 4
27040 Montalto Pavese [PV]
Tel. 0383870545
www.cadelsanto.it

CELLAR SALES
PRE-BOOKED VISITS
ANNUAL PRODUCTION 25,000 bottles
HECTARES UNDER VINE 6.00

- ● OP Bonarda Vivace Grand Cuvée '12 🍷🍷 2*
- ○ OP Pinot Nero Brut Cl. Nature '09 🍷🍷 4
- ○ OP Riesling Rivalunga '12 🍷 2

Calatroni

fraz. 27040
loc. Casa Grande
27040 Montecalvo Versiggia [PV]
Tel. 038599013
www.calatronivini.it

CELLAR SALES
RESTAURANT SERVICE
ANNUAL PRODUCTION 80,000 bottles
HECTARES UNDER VINE 15.00

- ○ OP Riesling '10 🍷🍷 2*
- ● OP Bonarda Vivace Unico '12 🍷 2
- ⊙ OP Cruasé 🍷 3

Calvi

fraz. Vigalone, 13
27044 Canneto Pavese [PV]
Tel. 038560034
www.andreacalvi.it

CELLAR SALES
PRE-BOOKED VISITS
ANNUAL PRODUCTION 80,000 bottles
HECTARES UNDER VINE 35.00

- ○ Brut Rosé M. Cl. 🍷🍷 4
- ● OP Bonarda Vivace '12 🍷🍷 2*

Caminella

Dante Alighieri, 13
24069 Cenate Sotto [BG]
Tel. 035941828
www.caminella.it

CELLAR SALES
PRE-BOOKED VISITS
ANNUAL PRODUCTION 50,000 bottles
HECTARES UNDER VINE 5.50

- ● Luna Rossa '09 🍷🍷 4
- ○ Brut Ripa di Luna '10 🍷 3
- ● Goccio di Sole '10 🍷 5
- ● Valcalepio Rosso Ripa di Luna '10 🍷 2

Camossi

via Metelli, 5
25030 Erbusco [BS]
Tel. 0307268022
www.camossi.it

CELLAR SALES
ANNUAL PRODUCTION 60,000 bottles
HECTARES UNDER VINE 30.00

- ○ Franciacorta Extra Brut 🍷🍷 5
- ○ Franciacorta Satèn 🍷🍷 5
- ⊙ Franciacorta Brut Rosé 🍷 5

Le Cantorìe

fraz. Casaglio
via Castello di Casaglio, 24/25
25064 Gussago [BS]
Tel. 0302523723
www.lecantorie.it

ANNUAL PRODUCTION 75,000 bottles
HECTARES UNDER VINE 12.00

- ○ Franciacorta Satèn 🍷🍷 5
- ○ Franciacorta Brut 🍷 4
- ○ Franciacorta Dosaggio Zero Ris. '06 🍷 5

Cascina Belmonte

FRAZ. MONIGA DEL BOSCO
LOC. TOPPE
25080 MUSCOLINE [BS]
TEL. 3335051606
www.cascinabelmonte.it

PRE-BOOKED VISITS
ANNUAL PRODUCTION 15,000 bottles
HECTARES UNDER VINE 6.00

● Fuochi nella Notte di San Giovanni '11	♔♔ 3
● Stramonia '11	♔♔ 3
● Rebo Singia '11	♔ 3
○ Serése '12	♔ 3

Cascina la Pertica

LOC. PICEDO
VIA ROSARIO, 44
25080 POLPENAZZE DEL GARDA [BS]
TEL. 0365651471
www.cascinalapertica.it

CELLAR SALES
PRE-BOOKED VISITS
ANNUAL PRODUCTION 40,000 bottles
HECTARES UNDER VINE 11.00
VITICULTURE METHOD Certified Biodynamic

⊙ Garda Cl. Chiaretto Le Sincette '12	♔♔ 3
○ Garda Chardonnay Le Sincette '12	♔ 3
● Garda Cl. Groppello Le Sincette '12	♔ 3
● Garda Marzemino '12	♔ 3

Castello di Gussago

VIA MANICA, 9
25064 GUSSAGO [BS]
TEL. 0302525267
www.castellodigussago.it

CELLAR SALES
PRE-BOOKED VISITS
ANNUAL PRODUCTION 120,000 bottles
HECTARES UNDER VINE 15.00

○ Franciacorta Brut	♔♔ 4
⊙ Franciacorta Brut Rosé	♔ 5
○ Franciacorta Satèn	♔ 5

Castello di Luzzano

LOC. LUZZANO, 5
27040 ROVESCALA [PV]
TEL. 0523863277
www.castelloluzzano.it

CELLAR SALES
PRE-BOOKED VISITS
ACCOMMODATION AND RESTAURANT SERVICE
ANNUAL PRODUCTION 100,000 bottles
HECTARES UNDER VINE 70.00

● OP Bonarda Vivace Sommossa '12	♔♔ 2*
● OP Bonarda Carlino '11	♔ 2
○ OP Pinot Nero Brut Martinotti Magòt	♔ 2

Castelveder

VIA BELVEDERE, 4
25040 MONTICELLI BRUSATI [BS]
TEL. 030652308
www.castelveder.it

CELLAR SALES
PRE-BOOKED VISITS
ANNUAL PRODUCTION 90,000 bottles
HECTARES UNDER VINE 11.00

⊙ Franciacorta Brut Rosé	♔♔ 5
○ Franciacorta Dosaggio Zero	♔♔ 5
○ Franciacorta Extra Brut	♔♔ 4
○ Franciacorta Satèn	♔ 5

Le Chiusure

FRAZ. PORTESE
VIA BOSCHETTE, 2
25010 SAN FELICE DEL BENACO [BS]
TEL. 0365626243
www.lechiusure.net

CELLAR SALES
PRE-BOOKED VISITS
ACCOMMODATION
ANNUAL PRODUCTION 22,000 bottles
HECTARES UNDER VINE 4.00

● Campei '10	♔♔ 3
● Valtènesi '11	♔♔ 2*
● Benaco Bresciano Rosso Malborghetto '09	♔ 5
⊙ Valtenesi Chiaretto '12	♔ 3

Il Cipresso

FRAZ. TRIBULINA
VIA CERRI, 2
24020 SCANZOROSCIATE [BG]
TEL. 0354597005
www.ilcipresso.info

CELLAR SALES
PRE-BOOKED VISITS
ANNUAL PRODUCTION 20,000 bottles
HECTARES UNDER VINE 4.00

● Moscato di Scanzo Serafino '10	🍷🍷 6
○ Valcalepio Bianco Melardo '12	🍷 2
● Valcalepio Rosso Dionisio '11	🍷 2

Citari

FRAZ. SAN MARTINO DELLA BATTAGLIA
LOC. CITARI, 2
25015 DESENZANO DEL GARDA [BS]
TEL. 0309910310
www.citari.it

CELLAR SALES
PRE-BOOKED VISITS
ANNUAL PRODUCTION 150,000 bottles
HECTARES UNDER VINE 22.00

● Garda Rosso Cl. '08	🍷🍷 3
○ Lugana Vign. La Conchiglia '12	🍷 3
○ Lugana Vign. La Sorgente '12	🍷 2

Battista Cola

VIA INDIPENDENZA, 3
25030 ADRO [BS]
TEL. 0307356195
www.colabattista.it

CELLAR SALES
PRE-BOOKED VISITS
ANNUAL PRODUCTION 60,000 bottles
HECTARES UNDER VINE 10.00

○ Franciacorta Brut	🍷🍷 4
○ Franciacorta Brut Ris. '07	🍷🍷 5
○ Franciacorta Dosage Zero	🍷 5
○ Franciacorta Extra Brut	🍷 4

Corte Aura

VIA COLZANO, 13
25030 ADRO [BS]
TEL. 030 7357281
www.corteaura.com

ANNUAL PRODUCTION 75,000 bottles
HECTARES UNDER VINE 5.00

○ Franciacorta Satèn	🍷🍷 4
○ Franciacorta Demi Sec	🍷🍷 4
○ Franciacorta Brut	🍷 4

Tenuta La Costaiola

VIA COSTAIOLA, 25
27054 MONTEBELLO DELLA BATTAGLIA [PV]
TEL. 038383169
www.lacostaiola.it

CELLAR SALES
PRE-BOOKED VISITS
ANNUAL PRODUCTION 180,000 bottles
HECTARES UNDER VINE 17.00

○ Brut M. Cl. Nové	🍷🍷 3
● OP Barbera Giada '12	🍷🍷 2*
○ OP Pinot Nero Brut M. Cl. Rossetti & Scrivani	🍷🍷 3

Delai

VIA MORO, 1
25080 PUEGNAGO SUL GARDA [BS]
TEL. 0365555527

ANNUAL PRODUCTION 80,000 bottles
HECTARES UNDER VINE 8.00

● Fronsaga '10	🍷🍷 2*
⊙ Garda Bresciano Chiaretto '12	🍷 2
● Garda Bresciano Groppello Mogrì '11	🍷 2
⊙ Rosé Brut	🍷 3

Lorenzo Faccoli & Figli

VIA CAVA, 7
25030 COCCAGLIO [BS]
TEL. 0307722761
az.faccoli@libero.it

CELLAR SALES
PRE-BOOKED VISITS
ANNUAL PRODUCTION 50,000 bottles
HECTARES UNDER VINE 6.50

○ Franciacorta Brut	♛♛ 3
○ Franciacorta Extra Brut	♛♛ 4
⊙ Franciacorta Brut Rosé	♛ 3
○ Franciacorta Dosage Zero '08	♛ 5

Finigeto

LOC. CELLA
27040 MONTALTO PAVESE [PV]
TEL. 328 7095347
www.finigeto.com

ANNUAL PRODUCTION 50,000 bottles
HECTARES UNDER VINE 32.00

● OP Barbera Il Ribaldo '12	♛♛ 2*
○ OP Riesling Lo Spavaldo '12	♛♛ 2*
● OP Bonarda '12	♛ 2

La Fiòca

FRAZ. NIGOLINE
VIA VILLA, 13B
25040 CORTE FRANCA [BS]
TEL. 0309826313
www.lafioca.com

CELLAR SALES
PRE-BOOKED VISITS
ACCOMMODATION
ANNUAL PRODUCTION 40,000 bottles
HECTARES UNDER VINE 4.00

○ Franciacorta Brut	♛♛ 4
⊙ Franciacorta Brut Rosé	♛♛ 4
● TdF Rosso del Diavolo Allegro '08	♛♛ 2*
○ Franciacorta Satèn Ris. '05	♛ 6

La Fiorita

VIA MAGLIO, 14
25020 OME [BS]
TEL. 030652279
www.lafiorita.bs.it

CELLAR SALES
PRE-BOOKED VISITS
ANNUAL PRODUCTION 60,000 bottles
HECTARES UNDER VINE 7.00

⊙ Franciacorta Brut Rosé '09	♛♛ 4
○ Franciacorta Dosaggio Zero	♛♛ 4
○ Franciacorta Extra Brut Ris. '06	♛♛ 4
○ Franciacorta Brut	♛ 4

Franca Contea

VIA VALLI, 130
25030 ADRO [BS]
TEL. 0307451217
www.francacontea.it

CELLAR SALES
PRE-BOOKED VISITS
ANNUAL PRODUCTION 70,000 bottles
HECTARES UNDER VINE 15.00

○ Franciacorta Brut '09	♛♛ 3
○ Franciacorta Satèn '09	♛ 5

I Gessi - Fabbio De Filippi

FRAZ. FOSSA, 8
27050 OLIVA GESSI [PV]
TEL. 0383896606
www.cantinagessi.it

CELLAR SALES
PRE-BOOKED VISITS
ACCOMMODATION
ANNUAL PRODUCTION 120,000 bottles
HECTARES UNDER VINE 30.00
VITICULTURE METHOD Certified Organic

○ OP Pinot Nero Brut M. Cl. Maria Cristina	♛♛ 3
○ OP Riesling I Gessi '12	♛♛ 1*
⊙ OP Pinot Nero Brut Rosé M. Cl. Maria Cristina	♛ 3

Giorgio Gianatti

VIA DEI PORTICI, 82
23020 MONTAGNA IN VALTELLINA [SO]
TEL. 0342380033
gianatti.giorgio@alice.it

CELLAR SALES
PRE-BOOKED VISITS
ANNUAL PRODUCTION 8,000 bottles
HECTARES UNDER VINE 2.00

● Valtellina Sup. Grumello '08	♟♟ 4
● Valtellina Sup. Grumello San Martino '10	♟♟ 4

Cantina Sociale di Gonzaga

VIA STAZIONE, 39
46023 GONZAGA [MN]
TEL. 037658051
www.cantinagonzaga.it

CELLAR SALES
ANNUAL PRODUCTION 1,000,000 bottles
HECTARES UNDER VINE 170.00

● Lambrusco Mantovano Rosso della Signoria '12	♟♟ 3
● Lambrusco Mantovano Rosso Mantè '12	♟♟ 2*

F.lli Guerci

FRAZ. CROTESI, 20
27045 CASTEGGIO [PV]
TEL. 038382725
guerci_flli@libero.it

○ OP Pinot Nero Brut M. Cl. 222 a.C.	♟♟ 3
○ OP Riesling Fior Fiore '12	♟♟ 2*
● OP Barbera Vignole '08	♟ 3
⊙ OP Cruasé 222 a.C.	♟ 3

La Valle

VIA SANT'ANTONIO, 4
25050 RODENGO SAIANO [BS]
TEL. 0307722045
www.vinilavalle.it

CELLAR SALES
PRE-BOOKED VISITS
ANNUAL PRODUCTION 50,000 bottles
HECTARES UNDER VINE 6.00

○ Franciacorta Brut Regium '06	♟♟ 5
○ Franciacorta Extra Brut Naturalis '06	♟♟ 5
○ Franciacorta Satèn	♟♟ 5
⊙ Franciacorta Brut Rosé	♟ 5

Leali di Monteacuto

FRAZ. MONTEACUTO
VIA DOSSO, 5
25080 PUEGNAGO SUL GARDA [BS]
TEL. 0365651291
antonio.leali@genie.it

CELLAR SALES
PRE-BOOKED VISITS
ANNUAL PRODUCTION 40,000 bottles
HECTARES UNDER VINE 3.00

● Rebo Montagü '11	♟♟ 4
● Simut '11	♟♟ 5
⊙ Garda Bresciano Chiaretto '12	♟ 3
○ Garda Riesling '12	♟ 2

Cantina Lovera

VIA LOVERA, 14A
25030 ERBUSCO [BS]
TEL. 0307760491
www.cantinalovera.it

PRE-BOOKED VISITS
ANNUAL PRODUCTION 200,000 bottles
HECTARES UNDER VINE 19.00

○ Franciacorta Brut '08	♟♟ 4
○ Franciacorta Dosaggio Zero	♟♟ 3
○ Franciacorta Brut Adamantis	♟ 5
○ Franciacorta Brut Merum	♟ 5

Lurani Cernuschi

VIA CONVENTO, 3
24031 ALMENNO SAN SALVATORE [BG]
TEL. 035642576
www.luranicernuschi.it

CELLAR SALES
PRE-BOOKED VISITS
RESTAURANT SERVICE
ANNUAL PRODUCTION 80,000 bottles
HECTARES UNDER VINE 13.00

● Valcalepio Rosso Tornago '09	♥♥ 4
○ Opis '12	♥ 2
○ Valcalepio Bianco Armisa '12	♥ 3

Marangona

LOC. MARANGONA 1
25010 POZZOLENGO [BS]
TEL. 030919379
www.marangona.com

CELLAR SALES
PRE-BOOKED VISITS
ANNUAL PRODUCTION 30,000 bottles
HECTARES UNDER VINE 27.00

○ Lugana Tre Campane '12	♥♥ 2*
○ Lugana '12	♥ 2

Martilde

FRAZ. CROCE, 4A/1
27040 ROVESCALA [PV]
TEL. 0385756280
www.martilde.it

CELLAR SALES
PRE-BOOKED VISITS
ANNUAL PRODUCTION 30,000 bottles
HECTARES UNDER VINE 15.00

○ Malvasia Piume '12	♥♥ 2*
● OP Bonarda '12	♥♥ 2*
● OP Bonarda Ghiro Rosso d'Inverno '07	♥ 4

Marzaghe

VIA CONSOLARE, 19
25030 ERBUSCO [BS]
TEL. 0307267245
www.marzaghefranciacorta.it

ANNUAL PRODUCTION 40,000 bottles
HECTARES UNDER VINE 6.00

○ Franciacorta Satèn Premier	♥♥ 5
○ Franciacorta Brut Treha	♥ 5

Medolago Albani

VIA REDONA, 12
24069 TRESCORE BALNEARIO [BG]
TEL. 035942022
www.medolagoalbani.it

CELLAR SALES
PRE-BOOKED VISITS
ANNUAL PRODUCTION 200,000 bottles
HECTARES UNDER VINE 23.00

● Valcalepio Rosso '11	♥♥ 4
○ Valcalepio Bianco '12	♥ 2
● Valcalepio I Due Lauri Ris. '08	♥ 4

Marchesi di Montalto

LOC. COSTA GALLOTTI, 5
27040 MONTALTO PAVESE [PV]
TEL. 0383870358
www.marchesidimontalto.it

CELLAR SALES
PRE-BOOKED VISITS
ANNUAL PRODUCTION 50,000 bottles
HECTARES UNDER VINE 100.00

○ OP Riesling Monsaltus '12	♥♥ 3

Monte Cicogna

VIA DELLE VIGNE, 6
25080 MONIGA DEL GARDA [BS]
TEL. 0365503200
www.montecicogna.it

CELLAR SALES
PRE-BOOKED VISITS
ANNUAL PRODUCTION 150,000 bottles
HECTARES UNDER VINE 24.50

● Garda Cl. Rosso Cardinale '11	♥♥ 2*
○ Lugana S.Caterina '12	♥♥ 3
◉ Garda Cl. Chiaretto Siclì '12	♥ 2
● Garda Cl. Rosso Groppello Beana '11	♥ 2

Tenuta Monte Delma

VIA VALENZANO, 23
25050 PASSIRANO [BS]
TEL. 0306546161
www.montedelma.it

CELLAR SALES
PRE-BOOKED VISITS
ANNUAL PRODUCTION 100,000 bottles
HECTARES UNDER VINE 20.00

○ Franciacorta Satèn	♥♥ 5
○ Franciacorta Brut	♥ 4
◉ Franciacorta Brut Rosé	♥ 5

Montelio

VIA D. MAZZA, 1
27050 CODEVILLA [PV]
TEL. 0383373090
montelio.gio@alice.it

CELLAR SALES
PRE-BOOKED VISITS
ACCOMMODATION AND RESTAURANT SERVICE
ANNUAL PRODUCTION 130,000 bottles
HECTARES UNDER VINE 27.00

● OP Bonarda '12	♥♥ 2*
○ Brut Martinotti La Stroppa	♥ 3
● Comprino Mirosa '07	♥ 4
● OP Rosso Solarolo Ris. '09	♥ 4

Nettare dei Santi

VIA CAPRA, 17
20078 SAN COLOMBANO AL LAMBRO [MI]
TEL. 0371200523
www.nettaredeisanti.it

CELLAR SALES
PRE-BOOKED VISITS
ANNUAL PRODUCTION 600,000 bottles
HECTARES UNDER VINE 40.00

○ Brut M. Cl. Domm '09	♥♥ 3

Olivini

LOC. DEMESSE VECCHIE, 2
25015 DESENZANO DEL GARDA [BS]
TEL. 0309910268
www.famigliaolivini.com

CELLAR SALES
PRE-BOOKED VISITS
ANNUAL PRODUCTION 180,000 bottles
HECTARES UNDER VINE 26.00

○ Lugana '12	♥♥ 3
○ Lugana Brut M. Cl. '09	♥ 5
○ Lugana Demesse Vecchie '10	♥ 4
○ Lugana Pas Dosé M. Cl. '07	♥ 8

Panigada - Banino

VIA DELLA VITTORIA, 13
20078 SAN COLOMBANO AL LAMBRO [MI]
TEL. 037189103
www.banino.it

CELLAR SALES
PRE-BOOKED VISITS
ANNUAL PRODUCTION 30,000 bottles
HECTARES UNDER VINE 5.00

● San Colombano Banino V. La Merla Ris. '08	♥♥ 4
● San Colombano Banino Rosso '12	♥ 3

Angelo Pecis

VIA SAN PIETRO DELLE PASSERE, 12
24060 SAN PAOLO D'ARGON [BG]
TEL. 035959104
www.pecis.it

CELLAR SALES
PRE-BOOKED VISITS
ANNUAL PRODUCTION 25,000 bottles
HECTARES UNDER VINE 5.00

● Valcalepio Rosso della Pezia Ris. '07	♥♥ 4
○ Valcalepio Bianco San Pietro delle Passere '12	♥ 2

Pian Del Maggio

VIA VALLI
25030 ADRO [BS]
TEL. 0307254451
www.piandelmaggio.it

PRE-BOOKED VISITS
ANNUAL PRODUCTION 25,000 bottles
HECTARES UNDER VINE 5.86

○ Franciacorta Brut Nature Furente '06	♥♥ 5
○ Franciacorta Brut Proemio	♥♥ 4

Piccolo Bacco dei Quaroni

FRAZ. COSTAMONTEFEDELE
27040 MONTÙ BECCARIA [PV]
TEL. 038560521
www.piccolobaccodeiquaroni.it

CELLAR SALES
PRE-BOOKED VISITS
ANNUAL PRODUCTION 35,000 bottles
HECTARES UNDER VINE 11.50

☉ OP Cruasé PBQ '10	♥♥ 3

Pilandro

FRAZ. SAN MARTINO DELLA BATTAGLIA
LOC. PILANDRO, 1
25010 DESENZANO DEL GARDA [BS]
TEL. 0309910363
www.pilandro.it

CELLAR SALES
PRE-BOOKED VISITS
ANNUAL PRODUCTION 200,000 bottles
HECTARES UNDER VINE 20.00

○ Lugana Arilica '11	♥♥ 2*
○ Lugana Terecrea '12	♥♥ 2*
○ Lugana '12	♥ 2

Plozza di Ome

VIA LIZZANA, 13
25050 OME [BS]
TEL. 0306527775
www.plozzaome.it

CELLAR SALES
PRE-BOOKED VISITS
ANNUAL PRODUCTION 40,000 bottles
HECTARES UNDER VINE 4.00

○ Franciacorta Brut	♥♥ 5
○ Franciacorta Satèn	♥♥ 5

Quadra

VIA SANT'EUSEBIO, 1
25033 COLOGNE [BS]
TEL. 0307157314
www.quadrafranciacorta.it

CELLAR SALES
PRE-BOOKED VISITS
RESTAURANT SERVICE
ANNUAL PRODUCTION 180,000 bottles
HECTARES UNDER VINE 30.00

○ Franciacorta Brut QBlack	♥♥ 4
○ Franciacorta Brut '08	♥ 4

Le Quattro Terre

VIA RISORGIMENTO, 11
25040 CORTE FRANCA [BS]
TEL. 030984312
www.quattroterre.it

CELLAR SALES
ACCOMMODATION AND RESTAURANT SERVICE
ANNUAL PRODUCTION 40,000 bottles

○ Franciacorta Brut	♥♥	5
○ Franciacorta Dosaggio Zero '09	♥♥	6
○ Franciacorta Dosaggio Zero '08	♥♥	6
○ Franciacorta Satèn	♥	5

Cantina Sociale Cooperativa di Quistello

VIA ROMA, 46
46026 QUISTELLO [MN]
TEL. 0376618118
www.cantinasocialequistello.it

CELLAR SALES
PRE-BOOKED VISITS
ANNUAL PRODUCTION 1,000,000 bottles
HECTARES UNDER VINE 330.00

● Gran Rosso del Vicariato di Quistello '12	♥♥	1*
● Lambrusco Mantovano Rossissimo '12	♥♥	2*

Redaelli de Zinis

VIA N.H. UGO DE ZINIS, 10
25080 CALVAGESE DELLA RIVIERA [BS]
TEL. 030601001
www.dezinis.it

CELLAR SALES
ANNUAL PRODUCTION 200,000 bottles
HECTARES UNDER VINE 52.70

● Garda Cl. Groppello Poggio dei Sassi Ris. '08	♥♥	3
⊙ Garda Rosé Brut	♥	2
● Valtenesi '11	♥	2

Riccafana - Fratus

VIA FACCHETTI, 91
25033 COLOGNE [BS]
TEL. 0307156797
www.riccafana.com

CELLAR SALES
ANNUAL PRODUCTION 10,000 bottles
HECTARES UNDER VINE 15.00
VITICULTURE METHOD Certified Organic

○ Franciacorta Brut '09	♥♥	4
○ Franciacorta Satèn	♥♥	5
○ Franciacorta Brut	♥	4

Ricchi

FRAZ. RICCHI
VIA FESTONI, 13D
46040 MONZAMBANO [MN]
TEL. 0376800238
www.cantinaricchi.it

CELLAR SALES
PRE-BOOKED VISITS
ANNUAL PRODUCTION 300,000 bottles
HECTARES UNDER VINE 40.00

○ Spumante Pas Dosé Essenza 0	♥♥	4
○ Le Cime	♥	3
○ Spumante Brut Espressione 8	♥	4

Riva di Franciacorta

LOC. FANTECOLO
VIA CARLO ALBERTO, 19
25050 PROVAGLIO D'ISEO [BS]
TEL. 0309823701
www.rivadifranciacorta.it

CELLAR SALES
PRE-BOOKED VISITS
ANNUAL PRODUCTION 200,000 bottles
HECTARES UNDER VINE 31.00

○ Franciacorta Brut	♥	5
⊙ Franciacorta Brut Rosé	♥	5
○ Franciacorta Satèn	♥	5

San Michele

via Parrocchia, 57
25020 Capriano del Colle [BS]
Tel. 0309444091
www.sanmichelevini.it

CELLAR SALES
PRE-BOOKED VISITS
ANNUAL PRODUCTION 80,000 bottles
HECTARES UNDER VINE 16.00

○ Corso	♥♥ 2*
● M	♥♥ 5
○ Capriano del Colle Bianco Netto '12	♥ 2

Poderi di San Pietro

via Steffenini 2/6
20078 San Colombano al Lambro [MI]
Tel. 0371208054
www.poderidisanpietro.it

CELLAR SALES
PRE-BOOKED VISITS
ANNUAL PRODUCTION 300,000 bottles
HECTARES UNDER VINE 80.00

○ Bianco della Torre '09	♥♥ 4
● San Colombano Rosso di Valbissera '11	♥♥ 3
● San Colombano Collada '12	♥ 2

Cantine Selva Capuzza

fraz. San Martino della Battaglia
loc. Selva Capuzza
25010 Desenzano del Garda [BS]
Tel. 0309910381
www.selvacapuzza.it

CELLAR SALES
PRE-BOOKED VISITS
ACCOMMODATION AND RESTAURANT SERVICE
ANNUAL PRODUCTION 300,000 bottles
HECTARES UNDER VINE 25.00

○ Lugana Selva '12	♥♥ 3
○ Lume	♥♥ 4
⊙ Garda Brut Rosé Hirundo	♥ 3
○ Lugana San Vigilio '12	♥ 2

Le Sincette

loc. Picedo di Polpenazze del Garda
via Rosario, 44
25080 Polpenazze del Garda [BS]
Tel. 0365651471
www.lesincette.it

ANNUAL PRODUCTION 30,000 bottles
HECTARES UNDER VINE 11.00

⊙ Valtenesi Chiaretto '12	♥♥ 2*
○ Garda Chardonnay '12	♥ 2
● Garda Cl. Groppello '12	♥ 2
● Garda Marzemino '12	♥ 2

Solive

via Bellavista
25030 Erbusco [BS]
Tel. 0307450138
www.solive.it

CELLAR SALES
PRE-BOOKED VISITS
ANNUAL PRODUCTION 100,000 bottles
HECTARES UNDER VINE 34.00

⊙ Franciacorta Brut Rosé	♥♥ 5
○ Franciacorta Dosaggio Zero	♥♥ 5
○ Franciacorta Brut	♥ 5
○ Franciacorta Satèn	♥ 5

Vincenzo Tallarini

via Fontanile, 7/9
24060 Gandosso [BG]
Tel. 035834003
www.tallarini.com

CELLAR SALES
PRE-BOOKED VISITS
ACCOMMODATION AND RESTAURANT SERVICE
ANNUAL PRODUCTION 240,000 bottles
HECTARES UNDER VINE 24.00

● Moscato di Scanzo '08	♥♥ 6
● Serafo '07	♥ 5

Terrazzi Alti

VIA DEL VECCHIO MACELLO, 4D
23100 SONDRIO
TEL. 3315207109
www.terrazzialti.com

CELLAR SALES
PRE-BOOKED VISITS
ANNUAL PRODUCTION 3,000 bottles
HECTARES UNDER VINE 1.00

● Valtellina Sup. Sassella '10	♥♥ 4
● Valtellina Sup. Sassella '09	♀♀ 5

Terre d'Oltrepò

VIA TORINO, 96
27045 CASTEGGIO [PV]
TEL. 038551505
www.bronis.it

CELLAR SALES
PRE-BOOKED VISITS
ANNUAL PRODUCTION 4,000,000 bottles
HECTARES UNDER VINE 4,500.00

● OP Bonarda Bronis '12	♥♥ 2*
⊙ OP Cruasé	♥♥ 2*

Torrevilla

VIA EMILIA, 4
27050 TORRAZZA COSTE [PV]
TEL. 038377003
www.torrevilla.it

CELLAR SALES
PRE-BOOKED VISITS
ANNUAL PRODUCTION 3,000,000 bottles
HECTARES UNDER VINE 650.00

● OP Bonarda La Genisia '12	♥♥ 3
⊙ OP Cruasé La Genisia '10	♥♥ 4
○ Brut M. Cl. La Genisia '08	♥ 4

Travaglino

LOC. TRAVAGLINO, 6A
27040 CALVIGNANO [PV]
TEL. 0383872222
www.travaglino.it

CELLAR SALES
PRE-BOOKED VISITS
ANNUAL PRODUCTION 220,000 bottles
HECTARES UNDER VINE 80.00

○ OP Riesling Campo della Fojada '12	♥♥ 3

Cooperativa Agricola Triasso e Sassella

FRAZ. TRIASSO, 25
23100 SONDRIO
TEL. 034221710
www.cooptriasso.it

ANNUAL PRODUCTION 8,600 bottles
HECTARES UNDER VINE 2.00

● Valtellina Sup. Sassella Sassi Solivi '10	♥♥ 4

F.lli Turina

VIA PERGOLA, 68
25080 MONIGA DEL GARDA [BS]
TEL. 0365502103
www.turinavini.it

○ Lugana V. Fenil Boi '12	♥♥ 2*
○ Lugana '12	♥ 2

Vercesi del Castellazzo

VIA AURELIANO, 36
27040 MONTÙ BECCARIA [PV]
TEL. 0385262098
www.vercesidelcastellazzo.it

CELLAR SALES
PRE-BOOKED VISITS
ANNUAL PRODUCTION 80,000 bottles
HECTARES UNDER VINE 13.00

○ OP Pinot Nero in Bianco Gugiarolo '12	♟♟ 2*
● OP Bonarda Vivace Luogo della Milla '12	♟ 2
● Pezzalunga '12	♟ 2

Tenuta La Vigna

CASCINA LA VIGNA
25020 CAPRIANO DEL COLLE [BS]
TEL. 0309748061
lavignavini@libero.it

CELLAR SALES
PRE-BOOKED VISITS
ANNUAL PRODUCTION 47,000 bottles
HECTARES UNDER VINE 7.00

○ Brut M. Cl. Botti	♟♟ 4
● Capriano del Colle Marzemino '12	♟ 3

Vigna Dorata

FRAZ. CALINO
VIA SALA, 80
25046 CAZZAGO SAN MARTINO [BS]
TEL. 0307254275
www.vignadorata.it

CELLAR SALES
PRE-BOOKED VISITS
ANNUAL PRODUCTION 70,000 bottles
HECTARES UNDER VINE 6.00

○ Franciacorta Brut	♟♟ 4
○ Franciacorta Satèn '08	♟♟ 6
○ Franciacorta Satèn	♟♟ 5
○ Franciacorta Extra Brut	♟ 5

Vignenote

FRAZ. TIMOLINE
VIA BRESCIA, 3A
25040 CORTE FRANCA [BS]
TEL. 0309826807
www.vignenote.it

ANNUAL PRODUCTION 91,000 bottles
HECTARES UNDER VINE 12.00

○ Franciacorta Satèn '09	♟♟ 5
○ Franciacorta Brut	♟ 5
⊙ Franciacorta Brut Rosé	♟ 5

Visconti

VIA C. BATTISTI, 139
25015 DESENZANO DEL GARDA [BS]
TEL. 0309120681
www.luganavisconti.it

CELLAR SALES
PRE-BOOKED VISITS
ANNUAL PRODUCTION 250,000 bottles
HECTARES UNDER VINE 20.00

○ Lugana Collo Lungo '12	♟♟ 2*
⊙ Garda Cl. Chiaretto '12	♟ 3
○ Lugana Et. Nera '12	♟ 3
○ Lugana Franco Visconti '12	♟ 3

Zamichele

VIA ROVEGLIA PALAZZINA, 2
25010 POZZOLENGO [BS]
TEL. 030918631
cantinazamichele@libero.it

CELLAR SALES
PRE-BOOKED VISITS
ANNUAL PRODUCTION 45,000 bottles
HECTARES UNDER VINE 8.00

○ Lugana '12	♟♟ 2*

TRENTINO

Trentino is making very good progress, with Metodo Classico in the lead thanks to the very worthy Trento designation. The project has been embraced by 39 wineries, which have mapped its course with an annual production of seven million bottles. New cuvées have been born while the classic labels perfect style and identity. The best-known name in the Dolomites is Ferrari, remaining firmly at the top with Perlé Nero, at its fourth consecutive award, even in Giulio's absence. The top of the ladder is also occupied by Letrari, headed by Nello Letrari, patriarch of Trentino sparklers, with almost 70 harvests under his belt, and daughter Lucia, with their Trento that acts as a real benchmark for the category in terms of elegance and balance. Cavit's Riserva Graal Altemasi is equally fine, as is Abate Nero's brand-new Nero, the latest Blanc de Noirs from a tiny winery owned by veteran duo Luciano Lunelli and Eugenio de Castel Terlago. Last but not least, the jury was impressed by the debut of Flavio, a Riserva produced by the Mezzacorona co-operative. The region's still wines are also on the up, offering something new with Trentino's first Müller Thurgau to win a Tre Bicchieri. This one comes from Valle di Cembra, produced by the La Vis group and a perfect embodiment of the Dolomite vision and style of freshness, finesse and tension. The other newcomer is from Marchesi Guerrieri Gonzaga, which decided to continue ageing its gem San Leonardo and present Carmenere 2007, available in magnums only, which has infinite flavour and length. The teroldego-based wines also performed exceedingly well and the 2011 vintage yielded very enjoyable, succulent, decent wines. The entire range from Elisabetta Foradori, the queen of Teroldego, put up a stunning performance. Her Granato 2010, made using strictly biodynamic growing methods, is once again marvellous, with truly astonishing energy and vitality. Continuing the overview with the red wines, Erika Pedrini confirms her talent, with Fratagranda winning its third award, and allowing three former students of the San Michele all'Adige wine academy to celebrate the 40th anniversary of their diploma with a Tre Bicchieri each. They are Erika's father Domenico Pedrini, his classmate Roberto Zeni, who won with an exceptional Teroldego Pini, and Mario Pojer, another dynamic grower and experimenter who graduated in 1954, whose fabulous Pinot Nero earned him our top award, the first of its kind in the region to manage this feat.

Abate Nero

FRAZ. GARDOLO
SPONDA TRENTINA, 45
38014 TRENTO
TEL. 0461246566
www.abatenero.it

CELLAR SALES
PRE-BOOKED VISITS
ANNUAL PRODUCTION 68,000 bottles
HECTARES UNDER VINE 65.00

Luciano Lunelli displays the patience of the truly wise and the unfailing hand of a veteran winemaker. He and his staff are stubbornly painstaking in making their sparkling wines, with intense quality checks of the grapes that long-trusted growers cultivate in the high hills of Trento, Lavis, and the Cembra valley. The reserve dedicated to the renowned monastic father of sparkling wines is the object of even more far-sighted commitment, while the traditional Trentodoc versions are rigorously crafted, and display a bright maturity. The all-pinot nero Domini Nero, the new Trentodoc, has emerged with commendable graduality. Soundly made, it boasts a solid, complex structure and smooth, gentle aromatics, with an ultra-lengthy progression and vibrant flavours. While waiting for the other traditional vintage sparklers to finish evolving in the cellar, we liked the always-fine Brut, a pleasant Extra Brut and a tasty Rosé.

○ Trento Brut Domini Nero '08	♟♟♟	5
○ Trento Brut Abate Nero '10	♟♟	4
○ Trento Extra Brut Abate Nero '10	♟♟	4
⊙ Trento Brut Rosé Abate Nero '10	♟	5
○ Trento Brut Cuvée dell'Abate Ris. '04	♟♟♟	6
○ Trento Brut Cuvée dell'Abate Ris. '03	♟♟♟	5
○ Trento Brut Cuvée dell'Abate Ris. '02	♟♟♟	5
○ Trento Brut Cuvée dell'Abate Ris. '01	♟♟♟	5
○ Trento Brut Domini '07	♟♟♟	5
○ Trento Brut Domini '05	♟♟♟	5
○ Trento Brut Domini '08	♟♟	5

Nicola Balter

VIA VALLUNGA II, 24
38068 ROVERETO [TN]
TEL. 0464430101
www.balter.it

CELLAR SALES
PRE-BOOKED VISITS
ANNUAL PRODUCTION 80,000 bottles
HECTARES UNDER VINE 12.00

The traditional and the contemporary meld together in Balter, where classic method sparklers reign supreme, thanks to the children of Nicola Balter, a grower increasingly committed to Trentodoc. Giacomo, still involved in his crop sciences studies, and Clementina, who has been working at the winery for a couple of seasons now, today lead this magnificent winery in the Rovereto Alta woods in a new direction. They carefully tend a dozen or so hectares, and the wines are equally impressive and appealing. The Trentodocs here are benchmarks for the category, reflecting their vintage, the harvest conditions and the vigneron's expertise. Together with the other two versions of the Balter sparklers, Trentodoc Riserva 2008 is one of the finest, all but a sector leader. The forceful, firm Cabernet Sauvignon is a fine, cellarable bottling, and equally good are the simpler wines styled for immediate enjoyment, such as Lagrein-Merlot 2012 and the fragrant Sauvignon 2012.

● Cabernet Sauvignon '10	♟♟	3*
○ Trento Brut Ris. '08	♟♟	5
○ Trento Brut Balter	♟♟	4
⊙ Trento Brut Rosé Balter	♟♟	5
● Lagrein-Merlot '12	♟	3
○ Sauvignon '12	♟	3
○ Barbanico '97	♟♟♟	4*
○ Trento Balter Ris. '06	♟♟♟	5
○ Trento Balter Ris. '05	♟♟♟	5
○ Trento Balter Ris. '04	♟♟♟	5
○ Trento Balter Ris. '01	♟♟♟	5

Barone de Cles

VIA G. MAZZINI, 18
38017 MEZZOLOMBARDO [TN]
TEL. 0461601081
www.baronedecles.it

CELLAR SALES
PRE-BOOKED VISITS
ANNUAL PRODUCTION 80,000 bottles
HECTARES UNDER VINE 39.00

The noble Cles family were among the forerunners of Trentino autonomy. Cardinal Bernardo Cesio was one of the proponents of the Council of Trent, and a figure who contributed to making the Castello di Buonconsiglio the symbol of the city. In addition, the dynasty was always associated with the vast expanses of Campo Rotaliano vineyards, in Mezzolombardo, with centuries of history and harvests that contributed to the appreciation of Teroldego. After studying classics and crop sciences, young Giorgio de Cles, with a vigneron's dedication, is striving to re burnish the renown of the dynasty. Teroldego, and only Teroldego. While waiting for the recovery of the vineyards next to Castel Cles, in the Val di Non, we tasted three versions of this grape. The most impressive is dedicated to family ancestor Cardinal de Cesio, an elegant, well-typed Riserva 2009 showing an inky hue and vaunting seductive fruit tones over weighty tannins. The more straightforward Maso Scari 2011 needs more time, while Primo 2012 is uncomplicated and approachable.

● Teroldego Rotaliano Maso Scari '11	♀♀	3
● Teroldego Rotaliano Sup. Riserva del Cardinale '09	♀♀	5
● Teroldego Rotaliano Primo '12	♀	2
● Rosso del Cardinale '99	♀♀	4
● Teroldego Rotaliano Maso Scari '04	♀♀	3
● Teroldego Rotaliano Maso Scari '01	♀♀	3*

Bellaveder

LOC. MASO BELVEDERE
38010 FAEDO [TN]
TEL. 0461650171
www.bellaveder.it

CELLAR SALES
PRE-BOOKED VISITS
ANNUAL PRODUCTION 50,000 bottles
HECTARES UNDER VINE 8.00
VITICULTURE METHOD Certified Organic

The underground cellar lies in perhaps the most-photographed alluvial area of all Trentino, with its gorgeous panorama of evenly-spaced vine rows, and the hill that links San Michele all'Adige with Faedo was perhaps divinely ordained for viticulture. In just a few years Tranquillo Lucchetta has transformed the steep-sloped farm into one of the most fascinating vineyards in the Dolomites. His portfolio boasts a careful selection of full-charactered wines, Trentodoc in first place, all in utter harmony with their terroir and vineyards. Impressive varietal fidelity is obvious in all the wines, starting with, surprisingly enough, the decisively austere and masterful Mansum 2010, a Riserva di Lagrein. No less fine are the all-teroldego Mas Picol 2011 and the white wines, Faedi, from sauvignon blanc, and San Lorenz, from müller thurgau; both are nicely varietal, well crafted and delicious, as is the traditional Traminer. Likewise the Trentos, another winery icon. Finally absolutely textbook are the spumantes, particularly the Riserva, utterly intriguing and ultra flavourful.

● Trentino Lagrein Dunkel Mansum Ris. '10	♀♀	4
○ Trento Brut Ris. '08	♀♀	5
○ Sauvignon Faedi '12	♀♀	4
● Teroldego Mas Picol '11	♀♀	3
○ Trentino Müller Thurgau San Lorenz '12	♀♀	2*
○ Trento Brut Nature '08	♀♀	5
○ Trentino Traminer '12	♀	3
● Trentino Lagrein Mansum '09	♀♀	4
● Trentino Lagrein Mansum '08	♀♀	4
○ Trentino Müller Thurgau '11	♀♀	2*
○ Trento Brut Ris. '07	♀♀	5

Borgo dei Posseri

LOC. POZZO BASSO, 1
38061 ALA [TN]
TEL. 0464671899
www.borgodeiposseri.com

CELLAR SALES
PRE-BOOKED VISITS
ANNUAL PRODUCTION 60,000 bottles
HECTARES UNDER VINE 21.00
VITICULTURE METHOD Certified Organic

Not far ahead, the mountain is fit only for pasture, so it is no wonder that only a fiercely enthusiastic couple such as Martin Mainenti and wife Margherita de Pilati would confront the challenge of grape-growing in this steep, and in some ways impossible, area among the Piccole Dolomiti. They have struggled tirelessly to rebuild this long-abandoned rural hamlet, helped in their winemaking project by business friends. The fruits are admirable, producing wines of character with unusual elegance, yet undeniably wines of the mountain. Dedication in the rows and commitment to every aspect of management are reaping their rewards. We saw a spectacular performance from the new arrivals, especially a traditional sparkler, the full-flavoured, gutsy Tananai 2008, a delicious Brut with real mountain character, in which pinot nero holds sway over ripe chardonnay. The other vineyard selections are equally impressive, with the Paradis 2011, from pinot nero, standing out for class, elegance, and typical mountain style. The other whites also convinced, starting with the Quaron 2012, from müller thurgau.

○ Müller Thurgau Quaron '12	♍♍ 3
● Pinot Nero Paradis '11	♍♍ 3
○ Tananai Brut '08	♍♍ 5
○ Gewürztraminer Arliz '12	♍ 3
○ Sauvignon Furiel '12	♍ 3
● Merlot Rocol '09	♍♍ 3
● Merlot Rocol '05	♍♍ 3*
○ Müller Thurgau Quaron '11	♍♍ 3
● Pinot Nero Paradis '06	♍♍ 3

Cantina Sociale di Trento

VIA DEI VITICOLTORI, 2
38123 VOLANO [TN]
TEL. 0461920186
www.cantinasocialetrento.it

CELLAR SALES
PRE-BOOKED VISITS
ANNUAL PRODUCTION 250,000 bottles
HECTARES UNDER VINE 50.00

This has been the city winery since 1956, processing grapes that grower-members bring from the nearby hills. The striking vineyards, which literally define the landscape enclosed by the three hills that give Trento Tridentum its name, are ideal for Dolomites viticulture. The state-of-the-art co-operative is skilled in vinifying the grapes brought in, respecting the origins of each type to produce a series of individual cru wines, all markedly Trentino in character. Zell, for example, is a Trentodoc from grapes grown in the hamlet of the same name, a Trento vineyard documented as early as the 1400s. This co-operative winery is well on the road to recovery. We just need to wait, especially for the reds. Meanwhile, we have two fine whites, the Pinot Grigio 2012 and a traditional Chardonnay 2012, heading the Heredia line of wines, from plots tended as if they were vegetable gardens. These two well-made wines show judiciously dosed minerality, masses of flavour and superb sinew.

○ Trentino Pinot Grigio Heredia '12	♍♍ 2*
○ Trento Brut Zell	♍♍ 3
○ Trentino Chardonnay Heredia '12	♍ 2
● Trentino Lagrein Heredia '11	♍ 2
● Trentino Marzemino Sup. dei Ziresi Heredia '11	♍ 2
○ Trentino Traminer 1339 '12	♍ 2

★Cavit

VIA DEL PONTE, 31
38040 TRENTO
TEL. 0461381711
www.cavit.it

CELLAR SALES
PRE-BOOKED VISITS
ANNUAL PRODUCTION 62,000,000 bottles
HECTARES UNDER VINE 5,500.00

Cavit's reputation remains untarnished as it continues to enjoy its firmly-anchored status, not only in Trentino, achieves increasing market presence while keeping high the quality of its wines. The involvement of over 6,000 member-growers, some 15 associated winemaking co-operatives, and the sum of so much vigneron expertise is the truest expression of Trentino, yielding sound wines and splendid sparklers, all destined to an ever-growing global market, one that no longer forgives the banal. The Trento Altemasi Riserva Graal has become a benchmark for artisanal sparklers, and the 2006 lived up to its reputation with another Tre Bicchieri. The qualities of this marvellous spumante can be seen in every aromatic nuance, the long effervescence, and highly pleasurable palate. But Cavit's skill and winemaking style emerge in all the dozen or so wines presented for our selections.

Cesarini Sforza

FRAZ. RAVINA
VIA STELLA, 9
38123 TRENTO
TEL. 0461382200
www.cesarinisforza.com

CELLAR SALES
PRE-BOOKED VISITS
ANNUAL PRODUCTION 1,300,000 bottles
HECTARES UNDER VINE 800.00

For 40 years, Cesarini Sforza, founded with the goal of proving that Trento could be the capital of artisanal spumante, has been one of Trentino's benchmark sparkling wine houses. Now in the La Vis group, it has firmly pursued a course of stepping up both production and marketing resources. Starting from the indisputable quality of its Trentodocs, all of its wines are in the top ranks, with power joined to elegance, symbolized by the winery's iconic eagle. The Aquila Reale 2006 proves to be a thoroughbred Trento: mature, drinkable and satisfying. All the other sparklers from this increasingly important operation performed equally well, from the fresh, inviting, approachable Tridentum Dosaggio Zero 2009, to the Riserva Extra Brut 2007, whose acidity charms from the first sip, as it unleashes the quintessential aromas and flavours of Trentino.

○ Trento Brut Altemasi Graal Ris. '06	♔♔♔	6
○ Trentino Chardonnay Sup. Maso Toresella '11	♔♔	4
○ Maso Toresella Cuvée '11	♔♔	4
● Teroldego Rotaliano Maso Cervara '10	♔♔	4
● Trentino Pinot Nero I Masi Trentini '10	♔♔	5
○ Trentino Sup. Müller Thurgau Zeveri '12	♔♔	3
● Trentino Sup. Quattro Vicariati '09	♔♔	4
○ Trento Brut Altemasi '09	♔♔	4
● Teroldego Rotaliano Maso Cervara '07	♔♔♔	4
○ Trento Altemasi Graal Brut '01	♔♔♔	5
○ Trento Altemasi Graal Brut Ris. '03	♔♔♔	6
○ Trento Altemasi Graal Brut Ris. '02	♔♔♔	6
○ Trento Altemasi Graal Brut Ris. '00	♔♔♔	5
○ Trento Brut Altemasi Graal Ris. '05	♔♔♔	7
○ Trento Brut Altemasi Graal Ris. '04	♔♔♔	7

○ Trento Aquila Reale Ris. '06	♔♔	7
⊙ Trento Brut Rosé '07	♔♔	4
○ Trento Extra Brut Tridentum Ris. '07	♔♔	5
○ Trento Pinot Nero Dosaggio Zero Tridentum '09	♔♔	5
○ Trento Tridentum	♔♔	4
○ Trento Aquila Reale Ris. '05	♔♔♔	7
○ Trento Aquila Reale Ris. '02	♔♔♔	7
○ Trento Pinot Nero Dosaggio Zero Tridentum '08	♔♔	5
⊙ Trento Tridentum Rosé	♔♔	4

Corbelli

FRAZ. SORNI
LOC. MASO DI SOPRA, 22
38015 LAVIS [TN]
TEL. 3495259503
www.cobelli.it

CELLAR SALES
PRE-BOOKED VISITS
ANNUAL PRODUCTION 90,000 bottles
HECTARES UNDER VINE 6.00

We dedicated our first profile to the Corbellis in 2010, impressed by the fragrance of each wine, so varietal and diverse, part and parcel of an impeccable winemaking style. Young brothers Denis and Tiziano Corbelli inherited a few microscopic vineyards on the hillsides of Pressano, towards Faedo and the Val di Cembra. Taking advantage of various terroirs, they planted traminer in an abandoned chalk quarry, teroldego on less-steep slopes, and nosiola and chardonnay closer to Faedo. Watch for sparkling wines in the near future. The new arrival from this small winery, ready to join the top league of Trentino growers, is the Chardonnay Arlevo 2011. This deeply hued wine belies its variety, with chestnut honey and dried apricots on the nose, followed by apple and citrus fruits in the mouth. The Traminer Gess 2011 also displays a focused nose, with tropical aromas of lychees and mango, over a lean, racy palate. The Teroldego Grill 2010 has a gutsy vein, tamed by mouthfilling, impeccable structure.

○ Chardonnay Arlevo '11	♥♥	4
● Teroldego Grill '10	♥♥	5
○ Traminer Gess '11	♥♥	5

Cantina d'Isera

VIA AL PONTE, 1
38060 ISERA [TN]
TEL. 0464433795
www.cantinaisera.it

CELLAR SALES
PRE-BOOKED VISITS
ANNUAL PRODUCTION 500,000 bottles
HECTARES UNDER VINE 246.00
VITICULTURE METHOD Certified Organic

Cinema comes to Isera and Marzemino becomes the motif of "Vinodentro", a film whose star, Giovanna Mezzogiorno, becomes involved in an oeno-erotic-sentimental affair. A film noir not to be missed and which may be the impetus to re-launch Isera's Marzemino, a wine this co-operative produces in appropriate versions, easy quaffers at terrific prices. The variety is a good stepping stone to the operation's diversified portfolio of aromatic whites and, of course, the increasingly impressive Trentodoc. The winery offers no fewer than six different versions of the same wine, and since this is Isera, that means six Marzeminos, from an everyday drinker to exclusive selections, one from organic grapes. This is Marzemino heaven, basically. The fine Vignetti 2010, velvety and caressing on the palate, is more complex than usual. The other two vineyard selections, the Corè and the Sanzel, are both 2011s and both graceful, as the reputation of this traditional Lagarina wine demands.

● Trentino Marzemino d'Isera Sup. Corè '11	♥♥	4
● Trentino Marzemino d'Isera Sup. Vignetti '10	♥♥	4
○ Trento Brut 907	♥♥	4
○ Trento Brut Ris. '08	♥♥	5
○ Trentino Gewürztraminer '12	♥	2
● Trentino Marzemino Bio '12	♥	3
● Trentino Marzemino d'Isera Sup. Sanzel '11	♥	4
○ Trentino Müller Thurgau '12	♥	2
○ Trentino Chardonnay '11	♥♥	2*
● Trentino Marzemino d'Isera Sup. Sanzel '10	♥♥	4
● Trentino Marzemino d'Isera Sup. Vignetti '09	♥♥	4

De Vescovi Ulzbach

P.zza Garibaldi, 12
38016 Mezzocorona [TN]
Tel. 0461605648
www.devescoviulzbach.it

CELLAR SALES
PRE-BOOKED VISITS
ANNUAL PRODUCTION 20,000 bottles
HECTARES UNDER VINE 3.50

Giulio de Vescovi, a young talent in the
world of Trentino wines, has quickly shown
his skill in the vineyards of his family the
Ulzbachs, whose roots go deep into local
winemaking history. He reduced yields,
dusted off the values of local traditions and,
above all, modernized vinification. The result
was that his wines, particularly his
Teroldegos, in a short span of time assumed
the status of cult wines, and not only locally.
They show forceful but graceful, with
distinctive personalities, and surely with
bright futures. For now, just Teroldego,
although joint projects with oenologist
friends for even more interesting wines are
in the pipeline. Giulio de Vescovi has made
it his mission to amaze us with focused yet
drinkable labels, in which simplicity meets
elegance. A perfect example is the
Teroldego Rotaliano 2011, the epitome of a
Trentino wine, from vineyards in Campo
Rotaliano. The Vigilius 2011 is more
complex and rounded.

● Teroldego Rotaliano Vigilius Ris. '11	🍷🍷 5
● Teroldego Rotaliano '11	🍷🍷 3
● Teroldego Rotaliano '10	🍷🍷 3
● Teroldego Rotaliano '07	🍷🍷 3
● Teroldego Rotaliano '05	🍷🍷 3
● Teroldego Rotaliano '04	🍷🍷 3
● Teroldego Rotaliano Vigilius Ris. '09	🍷🍷 5
● Teroldego Rotaliano Vigilius Ris. '04	🍷🍷 5
● Teroldego Rotaliano Vigilius Ris. '03	🍷🍷 5

I Dolomitici

via Damiano Chiesa, 1
38017 Mezzolombardo [TN]
Tel. 0461601046
www.idolomitici.com

I Dolomitici are ten mountain growers on a
mission to preserve the environment and
promote diversity through a sound,
ethically-sustainable viticulture, and
low-impact practices. Consorzio President is
Elisabetta Foradori, and the others are
Eugenio Rosi, Marco Zani of Castel Noarna,
and Lorenzo Cesconi, in leading positions,
plus Alessandro Fanti, Alessandro Poli, Gigi
Spagnolli of Vilar, Elisabetta Dalzocchio,
Giuseppe Pedrotti and Marco Zanoni of Maso
Furli. Together they produce Ciso, made from
the lambrusco a foglia frastagliata variety
grown in an Avio vineyard over 100 years old.
Not everyone presented their latest wines,
apart from Foradori and Poli, but they can be
found in well-stocked wine merchants. We
found both tradition and curiosities, with
Rosi's rosé Cabernet in a crown-capped
bottle rubbing shoulders with the country
elegance of jewels from Fanti, Pedrotti, Poli
and Spagnolli. Cesconi's Olivar 2010
showed good structure, and we also loved
their excellent spumante. Equally good were
perfect sparklers from Marco Zani, and
Dalzocchio's Dolomite-style Pinot Nero.

○ Castel Noarna Blanc de Blancs	🍷🍷 5
○ Manzoni Bianco Fanti '10	🍷🍷 4
● Marzemino Vilar/Spagnolli '12	🍷🍷 2*
○ Olivar Cesconi '10	🍷🍷 5
● Pinot Nero Dalzocchio '09	🍷🍷 5
● Riflesso Rosi Eugenio Rosi '12	🍷🍷 3
○ Sauvignon Maso Furli '11	🍷🍷 3
● Schiava Nera Pedrotti '12	🍷🍷 2*
○ Castel Noarna Blanc de Blancs	🍷🍷 5
○ Incrocio Manzoni Maso Furli '09	🍷🍷 5
○ Isidor Fanti '09	🍷🍷 5
○ Olivar Cesconi '09	🍷🍷 5
● Schiava Nera Pedrotti '11	🍷🍷 4

Marco Donati

VIA CESARE BATTISTI, 41
38016 MEZZOCORONA [TN]
TEL. 0461604141
donatimarcovini@libero.it

CELLAR SALES
PRE-BOOKED VISITS
ANNUAL PRODUCTION 90,000 bottles
HECTARES UNDER VINE 20.00

Marco Donati displays the self-confident authority of a great grower, expertise gained right in Rotaliano, in the vineyards that the family has been tending since 1863. The plantings privilege teroldego, classic to Rotaliano, and the cellar housed in the 15th-century residence once produced wines that supplied the imperial court of Austria. In recent years, the Donatis have widened their horizon to add other wines to their portfolio, cultivating vineyards in other prestigious growing areas, even rather far from the motherhouse. This estate's honesty is tangible, and the wines have the merit of being enjoyable now while also responding well to ageing, especially the two versions of Teroldego – including the outstanding Sangue di Drago 2011, and the Lagrein – in addition to an unusual vinification of marzemino grapes. These are drinkable wines, forthright on the palate, that aim to be approachable rather than exclusive.

● Teroldego Rotaliano Marco Donati '12	♟♟	3
● Teroldego Rotaliano Sangue del Drago '11	♟♟	5
● Trentino Lagrein Rubino Fratte Alte '12	♟♟	3
○ Trentino Gewürztraminer Tramonti '12	♟	3
○ Trentino Müller Thurgau Albeggio '12	♟	3
○ Trentino Sauvignon Luna Nuova '12	♟	3
○ Teroldego Rotaliano Bagolari '10	♟♟	3
● Teroldego Rotaliano Sangue del Drago '10	♟♟	5
● Teroldego Rotaliano Sangue del Drago '09	♟♟	5
○ Trentino Müller Thurgau Albeggio '11	♟♟	3
○ Trentino Riesling Stellato '10	♟♟	3*
● Vino del Maso Rosso '09	♟♟	3

F.lli Dorigati

VIA DANTE, 5
38016 MEZZOCORONA [TN]
TEL. 0461605313
www.dorigati.it

CELLAR SALES
PRE-BOOKED VISITS
ANNUAL PRODUCTION 100,000 bottles
HECTARES UNDER VINE 13.00

The vivaciousness of a Metodo Classico married to the forcefulness of a Teroldego conveys the balance on which the Dorigatis base their house style. This winemaking dynasty has poured its passion into viticultural research for over 150 years, coaxing the finest qualities from the area of Campo Rotaliano. They concentrated on local varieties, with grapes from long-trusted growers but also harvested by young family members Paolo and Michele, now with degrees and totally involved in the winery. The performances of the wines are increasingly impressive. Although just missing out on top honours, the Methius 2007 remains one of Trento's best wines. This is a spumante of substance, with its complex nose and firm backbone, set off by an unmistakable resinous timbre that makes it one of a kind. It should evolve nicely over the next few years. The mellow, mouthfilling Chardonnay Majerla 2011 impressed as always, vaunting acidulous tones superbly balanced by full flavour and overall length.

○ Trentino Chardonnay Majerla Ris. '11	♟♟	3*
○ Trento Brut Methius Ris. '07	♟♟	6
● Teroldego Rotaliano '11	♟♟	3
● Teroldego Rotaliano Diedri Ris. '10	♟♟	5
● Trentino Rebo '11	♟♟	3
● Trentino Cabernet '11	♟	3
○ Trentino Pinot Grigio '12	♟	3
○ Trento Brut Methius Ris. '06	♟♟♟	6
○ Trento Brut Methius Ris. '05	♟♟♟	6
○ Trento Brut Methius Ris. '04	♟♟♟	6
○ Trento Brut Methius Ris. '03	♟♟♟	6
○ Trento Brut Methius Ris. '02	♟♟♟	6
○ Trento Brut Methius Ris. '00	♟♟♟	6
● Teroldego Rotaliano Diedri Ris. '09	♟♟	5
○ Trentino Chardonnay Majerla Ris. '09	♟♟	3*

Endrizzi

LOC. MASETTO, 2
38010 SAN MICHELE ALL'ADIGE [TN]
TEL. 0461650129
www.endrizzi.it

CELLAR SALES
PRE-BOOKED VISITS
ANNUAL PRODUCTION 600,000 bottles
HECTARES UNDER VINE 55.00

Touch the past and savour its traditions, but taste the future too. The Endici family run Endrizzi, the name a play in dialect on their own name, and boast a multi-century history, but they are always ready for tomorrow's challenges. Their magnificent winery lies on the alluvial fan leading to Faedo and Monreale, in a truly striking country house, with the estate managed with a main eye to nature. The wines represent the evolution of Trentino itself, with a style fixed on the future. They make wines with passion, involving their children, growing the winery's prestige, establishing joint initiatives with local museums, and investing in Teroldego, with versions ranging from the sweet to the austere, not to mention a rosé. The mouthfilling Gran Masetto is a richly concentrated sipping wine, in a class of its own. No less impressive is the more approachable and internationally-styled traditional version.

● Gran Masetto '09	♟♟	7
○ Masetto Bianco '11	♟	3
● Teroldego Rotaliano Tradizione '11	♟♟	2ᴬ
● Trentino Pinot Nero Pian di Castello '10	♟♟	3
○ Trento Brut Pian di Castello '08	♟♟	4
☉ Trento Brut Rosé Pian di Castello '07	♟♟	4
● Masetto Nero '10	♟	3
● Trentino Cabernet Sauvignon '11	♟	2
○ Trentino Gewürztraminer '12	♟	3
● Gran Masetto '08	♕♕	6
● Gran Masetto '07	♕♕	6
● Teroldego Rotaliano Sup. '09	♕♕	3
● Teroldego Rotaliano Tradizione '10	♕♕	2*
○ Trentino Gewürztraminer '09	♕♕	3

★★Ferrari

VIA PONTE DI RAVINA, 15
38123 TRENTO
TEL. 0461972311
www.cantineferrari.it

CELLAR SALES
PRE-BOOKED VISITS
RESTAURANT SERVICE
ANNUAL PRODUCTION 4,500,000 bottles
HECTARES UNDER VINE 120.00

Lunelli is the prestigious name of a strong family that knows how to exploit its own resources, diversifying responsibility and playing solo without abandoning the choir. They are now strengthening brand reputation, having enlarged their holdings and planted vineyards at even higher elevations to increase their already celebrated line, produced in a state-of-the-art cellar, directed by Ruben Larentis. These are strategies that the new Lunellis, Alessandro, Camilla, Marcello and Matteo, plan to develop quickly, giving new force to a legend in the sparkling wine sector, and not only in Italy. The Riserva Giulio Ferrari and the classic Perlé were given a "year off", in line with the winery's pursuit of excellence. This means, not for the first time, that the task of defending family honour went to the Perlé Nero. The 2007 is on terrific form, cosseting yet austere, with a bouquet of rare finesse and real weight. Similar harmony can be found in the Riserva Lunelli 2006 and the vast range of Trento wines.

○ Trento Extra Brut Perlé Nero '07	♟♟♟	8
○ Trento Extra Brut Lunelli Ris. '06	♟♟	7
○ Trentino Bianco Villa Margon '11	♟♟	3
○ Trento Brut	♟♟	5
○ Trento Brut Maximum	♟♟	5
☉ Trento Brut Perlé Rosé '08	♟♟	7
○ Trento Démi Sec Maximum	♟♟	5
● Trentino Pinot Nero Maso Montalto '10	♟	5
○ Trento Brut Giulio Ferrari Riserva del Fondatore '01	♕♕♕	8
○ Trento Brut Giulio Ferrari Riserva del Fondatore '00	♕♕♕	8
○ Trento Brut Perlé '02	♕♕♕	5
○ Trento Extra Brut Perlé Nero '06	♕♕♕	8
○ Trento Extra Brut Perlé Nero '05	♕♕♕	8

★Foradori

VIA DAMIANO CHIESA, 1
38017 MEZZOLOMBARDO [TN]
TEL. 0461601046
www.elisabettaforadori.com

CELLAR SALES
PRE-BOOKED VISITS
ANNUAL PRODUCTION 160,000 bottles
HECTARES UNDER VINE 23.00
VITICULTURE METHOD Certified Biodynamic

Elisabetta Foradori is a doyenne of Trentino, or rather, Dolomite vigneron, exquisite interpreter of Campo Rotaliano, nursery of her wines. She painstakingly oversees every step, observing faithfully the rhythms and methods of biodynamic farming, a philosophy perfectly attuned to her way of life; with stubborn expertise, she has patiently studied and experimented, working out vineyard and winemaking practices in which nature holds the upper hand, with rackings into amphorae, and lush vineyards where the vine flourishes almost of its own accord. The wines exhibit nonpareil quality and shine on the international stage. The Granato, a rich, yet never pompous wine, with polished tannins and a sober, gentle acidic vein to counterpoint its alcoholic warmth, was beautifully satisfying, and romped off with a Tre Bicchieri. The other wines, some matured in amphorae, are hard on its heels, such as the Teroldego Sgarzon and the meaty Morei, both 2011s.

● Granato '10	▼▼▼ 7
○ Manzoni Bianco Fontanasanta '11	▼▼ 4
● Teroldego Rotaliano Morei '11	▼▼ 5
○ Nosiola Fontanasanta '11	▼▼ 4
● Teroldego Rotaliano Foradori '11	▼▼ 4
● Teroldego Rotaliano Sgarzon '11	▼▼ 5
● Granato '07	♀♀♀ 7
● Granato '04	♀♀♀ 6
● Granato '03	♀♀♀ 6
● Granato '02	♀♀♀ 6
● Granato '01	♀♀♀ 6
● Granato '00	♀♀♀ 6
● Granato '99	♀♀♀ 6

Gaierhof

VIA IV NOVEMBRE, 51
38030 ROVERÉ DELLA LUNA [TN]
TEL. 0461658514
www.gaierhof.com

CELLAR SALES
PRE-BOOKED VISITS
ANNUAL PRODUCTION 500,000 bottles
HECTARES UNDER VINE 130.00

Gaierhof, a flourishing operation on the border between Trentino and Alto Adige, has functioned as an outstanding reflection of the evolution of Trentino wines for over half a century. The owners practice the most exacting selections of the area's grapes, but they are accomplished winegrowers on their own hillside estate in Sorni, above Lapis, where their technologically-advanced cellar vinifies the grapes of Maso Poli, for a modest but impressive and quite appealing line of wines, all as elegant as they are fragrant, including a seductive Trentodoc. The full-flavoured Sauvignon 2012, as varietal as it is elegant, superbly executed and imbued with the character of the Dolomites, stands a head above the other attractive wines from the Togn family. Teroldego and other whites display a distinctive aromatic verve, especially the Traminer and the Nosiola, while Siris, their Trento, as light-hued as it is characterful on the palate, gets better every year.

● Teroldego Rotaliano Sup. '10	▼▼ 3
● Trentino Moscato Rosa '12	▼▼ 5
○ Trentino Müller Thurgau dei Settecento '12	▼▼ 3
○ Trentino Nosiola '12	▼▼ 2*
○ Trentino Sauvignon '12	▼▼ 3
● Trentino Sorni Rosso Marmoran '09	▼▼ 3
○ Trento Siris	▼▼ 4
● Trentino Marzemino '12	▼ 2
○ Trentino Traminer Aromatico '12	▼ 3
● Trentino Moscato Rosa '11	♀♀ 5
● Trentino Moscato Rosa '09	♀♀ 5
○ Trentino Müller Thurgau dei Settecento '11	♀♀ 3
● Trentino Teroldego Rotaliano '11	♀♀ 2*
○ Trento Siris '07	♀♀ 4

Grigoletti

VIA GARIBALDI, 12
38060 NOMI [TN]
TEL. 0464834215
www.grigoletti.com

CELLAR SALES
PRE-BOOKED VISITS
ANNUAL PRODUCTION 60,000 bottles
HECTARES UNDER VINE 7.00

The Grigoletti family are marked by
viticultural determination and passion for
winemaking, as well as uncontained
enthusiasm. They are an engaging family,
and to understand this one has only to
enter their cellar, excavated beneath the
vineyards, with its small rooms transformed
through attention and unusual furnishings
into a kind of temple to wine. They make
everything themselves, from aromatic
whites to classic spumantes; Merlot,
however, remains their favourite child, a
grape that has always been particularly
cherished here in Nomi, on the right bank
of the Adige. The wines from this dynasty of
uncompromising growers combine
authenticity with the charm that only quality
can bring. The attractive Merlot, a cuvée of
three vintages, is dedicated to the winery's
30th anniversary, and combines country
elegance with good typing. It should age
well. The whites were also well above
average – the Retiko 2011, from a blend
dominated by incrocio Manzoni, and
L'Opera 2012, from chardonnay.

○ Retiko '11	♟♟	3
● Speciale 30° '09	♟♟	6
○ Trentino Chardonnay L'Opera '12	♟♟	3
● Trentino Marzemino '12	♟♟	2*
● Gonzalier '10	♟	5
○ San Martim V.T. '11	♟	3
● Gonzalier '09	♟♟	5
○ Retiko '10	♟♟	3
○ Retiko '09	♟♟	3
○ Retiko '08	♟♟	3
○ Trentino Chardonnay L'Opera '11	♟♟	3
● Trentino Merlot Antica Vigna di Nomi '09	♟♟	4
● Trentino Merlot Antica Vigna di Nomi '05	♟♟	4

La Vis/Valle di Cembra

VIA CARMINE, 7
38034 LAVIS [TN]
TEL. 0461440111
www.la-vis.com

CELLAR SALES
PRE-BOOKED VISITS
ACCOMMODATION AND RESTAURANT SERVICE
ANNUAL PRODUCTION 1,000,000 bottles
HECTARES UNDER VINE 1,400.00
VITICULTURE METHOD Certified Organic

With the storm over financial
mismanagement behind it, the La Vis group
can now put forward its undeniably high
quality, thanks to a highly motivated
executive staff determined to reinforce the
prestige of the wines made by this historic
and powerful co-operative winery. Every
department has been totally examined and
reorganized, and the focus is back on the
diverse collection of vineyards, all expertly
tended by a legion of member-growers,
and harvests of uniformly high quality. The
wines are made at Lavis and at Cembra,
rightly called a mountain cellar. Confirmation
in fact comes from the mountains, with a
Tre Bicchieri for the iconic wine of Val di
Cembra, the Müller Thurgau. Gracefulness
and simplicity join great character in an
impeccable oenological interpretation that
will hopefully bring prestige to an area often
unfairly left off the map, and recognition to
all those who bravely continue to farm here.
The rest of the range shows reliability
across the board.

○ Trentino Müller Thurgau Vigna delle Forche '12	♟♟♟	3*
○ Trentino Pinot Grigio Ritratti '12	♟♟	3
● Trentino Pinot Nero V. di Saosent '11	♟♟	4
○ Trentino Riesling Simboli '12	♟♟	2*
○ Trentino Sauvignon Valtini Valle di Cembra '12	♟♟	3
● Trentino Schiava Piaggi '12	♟♟	3
● Teroldego Rover '11	♟	3
○ Trentino Gewürztraminer Ai Padri '12	♟	3
● Trentino Lagrein Greggi '11	♟	3
○ Trentino Nosiola Sette Fontane '12	♟	3
○ Trentino Pinot Grigio Arcadia '12	♟	3
○ Ritratto Bianco '07	♟♟♟	4
● Ritratto Rosso '03	♟♟♟	4
● Maso Franch L'Altro Manzoni '10	♟♟	3*
● Teroldego Rover '10	♟♟	2*

Letrari

VIA MONTE BALDO, 13/15
38068 ROVERETO [TN]
TEL. 0464480200
www.letrari.it

CELLAR SALES
PRE-BOOKED VISITS
ANNUAL PRODUCTION 160,000 bottles
HECTARES UNDER VINE 23.00

Recognized patriarch of Trentino wines, Leonello Nello Letrari has nearly 70 vintages as a winemaker behind him, and he is still on the front line, even if the winery has been in the hands of his children for some years now. Lucia tends the wines and Paolo looks after sales. Resolute by nature, Leonello patiently accepts new ideas too, considering future directions for the wines. His children inherited his love for the vineyards and the world in which he lives, but in particular for producing Trentodoc, the familiy's always-iconic sparkler. The Letrari style hinges on fragrance, with wines offering an almost unbeatable aromatic range, whose citrus notes, toasted hazelnut and bay leaves are set in beautifully woven structure that will stand the test of time. A Tre Bicchieri deservedly went to the Trento Riserva 2008, a floral symphony backed up by focused fresh notes and minerality to match. They are not confined to sparklers, as shown by the Bordeaux blend Ballistarius 2008, with more graceful power than usual.

○ Trento Brut Letrari Ris. '08	♈♈♈	5
○ Trento Riserva del Fondatore '03	♈♈	8
● Ballistarius '08	♈♈	5
● Trentino Cabernet Franc '08	♈♈	5
● Trentino Marzemino Sel. '12	♈♈	5
○ Trento Brut Letrari '10	♈♈	5
○ Trento Dosaggio Zero '10	♈♈	5
☉ Fossa Bandita '12	♈	3
☉ Trento Brut Rosé '10	♈	5
○ Trento Brut Letrari Ris. '07	♈♈♈	5
○ Trento Brut Letrari Ris. '05	♈♈♈	5
○ Trento Brut Ris. '06	♈♈♈	5
● Ballistarius '07	♈♈	5
○ Trento Dosaggio Zero '07	♈♈	4
○ Trento Dosaggio Zero Ris. '07	♈♈	5
○ Trento Riserva del Fondatore 976 '01	♈♈	8

MezzaCorona

VIA DEL TEROLDEGO, 1
38016 MEZZOCORONA [TN]
TEL. 0461616399
www.mezzacorona.it

CELLAR SALES
PRE-BOOKED VISITS
ANNUAL PRODUCTION 30,000,000 bottles
HECTARES UNDER VINE 2,800.00

Power and grace are the hallmarks of Mezzacorona, a highly-respected colossus and not only in Italy. It boasts cutting-edge facilities in almost every sector, from management and monitoring of the vineyards of almost 1,500 Trentino growers, to production diversification, with winemaking outposts as far away as Sicily. The wines are reliable and reflect their terroirs. High annual production, as well as equally sound wines, allows them to maintain a decisive presence in the most selective markets, with wine types ranging from Pinot Grigio to Trentodoc, without ever neglecting Teroldego. The Trento Rotari Flavio 2006 was the Mezzacorona wine that most appealed to and impressed our Tre Bicchieri tasting panels. This thoroughbred Trento comes exclusively from chardonnay, and enjoys a long period resting on the lees. Its intense hue is matched by unique apricot aromas, over extremely fine texture on the palate, bursting with flavour, and finishing long. The versions of Teroldego also impressed, as did a series of typical Trentino wines.

○ Trento Rotari Flavio Ris. '06	♈♈♈	5
● Teroldego Rotaliano Ris. '10	♈♈	4
○ Trentino Chardonnay Castel Firmian '12	♈♈	3
● Trentino Lagrein Castel Firmian '11	♈♈	4
○ Trentino Traminer Castel Firmian '12	♈♈	3
○ Trento Extra Brut AlpeRegis '07	♈♈	5
● Teroldego Rotaliano Castel Firmian '11	♈	3
● Trentino Marzemino Castel Firmian '12	♈	3
○ Trentino Nosiola Castel Firmian '12	♈	3
○ Trentino Pinot Grigio Castel Firmian '12	♈	3
● Trentino Pinot Nero Castel Firmian '11	♈	3
○ Trento Rotari Cuvée 28°	♈	4
☉ Trento Rotari Rosé	♈	4
● Teroldego Rotaliano Nos Ris. '04	♈♈♈	5
● Teroldego Rotaliano Nos '07	♈♈	5

Casata Monfort
Maso Cantanghel

VIA CARLO SETTE, 21
38015 LAVIS [TN]
TEL. 0461246353
www.cantinemonfort.it

CELLAR SALES
PRE-BOOKED VISITS
ANNUAL PRODUCTION 150,000 bottles
HECTARES UNDER VINE 40.00

The heart of Monfort-Maso Cantanghel is at
Lavis, but its many vineyards stud the
hillsides dominating the Val d'Adige between
Trento and the Valsugana, particularly along
the Strada dei Forti, the ancient high-altitude
pass where the Simonis have transformed
into a winery the formidable military
fortifications in Cantanghel built by the
Habsburgs in World War I. Their most
ambitious wines are made here, Pinot Nero
above all, although they also pay great
attention to traditional wines and to
old-fashioned varieties like wanderbara, san
laurent, veltriner rosato, and vernaza. The
operation's two brands produce a dozen
wines of great variety and a marked sense
of place. One is a Trento spumante brimming
with floral notes and ripe, fleshy, intact fruit,
produced at Lavis; another is the graceful
Pinot Nero Maso Cantanghel 2010, whose
deep hue is matched by a crisp palate.
Sotsaa Cuvée 2011 is a well-managed
blend of chardonnay and sauvignon, with
citrus and lemon tea on the nose followed by
charming balance on the palate.

○ Sauvignon V. Piccola Maso Cantanghel '12	♟♟	3
○ Sotsas Cuvée '11	♟♟	3
○ Trentino Gewürztraminer Casata Monfort '12	♟♟	3
○ Trentino Müller Thurgau Casata Monfort '12	♟♟	2*
● Trentino Pinot Nero Maso Cantanghel '10	♟♟	3
○ Trento Brut Monfort '10	♟♟	4
○ Blanc de Sers '11	♟	3
⊙ Trento Monfort Rosé '09	♟	4
○ Blanc de Sers '10	♟♟	2*
○ Moscato Giallo '10	♟♟	3
○ Sotsas Cuvée '11	♟♟	3
● Trentino Lagrein '09	♟♟	3
● Trentino Pinot Nero '09	♟♟	3

Opera Vitivinicola
in ValdiCembra

FRAZ. VERLA
VIA TRE NOVEMBRE, 8
38030 GIOVO [TN]
TEL. 0461684302
www.operavaldicembra.it

CELLAR SALES
PRE-BOOKED VISITS
ANNUAL PRODUCTION 60,000 bottles
HECTARES UNDER VINE 15.00

Steel, wood, glass and particularly porphyry
go to compose a cellar looking out over the
Cembra valley, on the promontory
above the hillside vineyards with their
traditional dry-wall terraces and dizzying
slopes. A welcome development for
Trentodoc, this all-spumante operation was
founded in 2006 by two enthusiastic local
businessmen and quickly won a name for
itself, thanks to the character of its Metodo
Classico, made with valley-grown grapes.
The extreme care shown in every phase of
vinification, selection of the grapes and
precise sparkling winemaking techniques
have given convincing results. Three
versions of Trento, all showing authentic
mountain character, embody the hallmark
Opera style, especially the Rosé, a
monovarietal pinot nero. This well-
orchestrated Blanc de Noirs boasts a
seemingly undying mousse, and offers red
berry fruit and candyfloss on the nose over
a caressing palate with a zesty finish.

⊙ Trento Brut Rosé Noir '09	♟♟	5
⊙ Trento Brut Rosé	♟♟	5
○ Trento Nature '08	♟♟	4

Pojer & Sandri

LOC. MOLINI, 4
38010 FAEDO [TN]
TEL. 0461650342
www.pojeresandri.it

CELLAR SALES
PRE-BOOKED VISITS
ACCOMMODATION
ANNUAL PRODUCTION 250,000 bottles
HECTARES UNDER VINE 26.00
VITICULTURE METHOD Certified Organic

Mario Pojer's showman-like expertise and
Fiorentino Sandri's agronomic wisdom
constitute a vinous duet that is still
instructive after 40 years, a paradigm of
grape-growing innovation, masterful
winemaking and careful winery
management. They have shown no
hesitation in confronting challenges, first
with Müller Thurgau, then with fortified
wines, even at lower alcohol levels; next out
the gate will be zero-impact wines. Their
ultra-diverse portfolio reflects a desire to try
whatever vinification makes possible, from
vinegars to experimental fruit juices to
Classic Methods. Pinot nero is the most
difficult variety to tame, which is why Mario
Pojer, the winemaking soul of this renowned
winery, has always dedicated such passion
to it. His commitment has been rewarded by
a Tre Bicchieri for the 2009 vintage, a wine
of rare elegance with masses of acidity
perfectly counterpointed by cosseting
softness, but none of the variety's typical
grassiness.

● Pinot Nero Rodel Pianezzi '09	�♥♥ 5
○ Bianco Faye '10	♥♥ 5
● Rosso Faye '10	♥♥ 6
○ Palai '12	♥♥ 3
⊙ Pojer & Sandri Rosé	♥♥ 6
○ Besler Biank '08	♥ 3
○ Filii	♥ 2
● Pinot Nero '12	♥ 4
○ Sauvignon '12	♥ 4
○ Bianco Faye '08	♥♥♥ 5
○ Bianco Faye '01	♥♥♥ 5
● Rosso Faye '05	♥♥♥ 5
● Rosso Faye '00	♥♥♥ 5
○ Besler Biank '07	♥♥ 4
○ Bianco Faye '09	♥♥ 5
● Rosso Faye '09	♥♥ 5

Pravis

LOC. LE BIOLCHE, 1
38076 LASINO [TN]
TEL. 0461564305
www.pravis.it

CELLAR SALES
PRE-BOOKED VISITS
ANNUAL PRODUCTION 200,000 bottles
HECTARES UNDER VINE 32.00

Erika and Giulia Pedrini, Alessio Chistè and
Alice Zambarda, are the children of three
friends and founders of this now 40-year-old
operation. The first two, both oenologists, are
fully involved in the management of the
winery, while agronomist Alessio follows the
vines and biologist Alice the harvests; all
show competence, fraternal spirit and
commitment. The vineyards lie at various
elevations between the lakes near Garda
and a valley that opens in the direction of the
Brenta-area Dolomites, which still preserves
sound country values. Fratagranda 2010
takes a Tre Bicchieri for the third year
running. This forthright wine with a sense of
place shows a youthful nose of red berry
fruit, paving the way for a juicy palate with
harmoniously balanced tannins and acidity,
and no useless frills. The unusual,
full-flavoured Stravino di Stravino 2010
comes from partially overripe grapes and is
matured in acacia wood.

● Fratagranda '10	♥♥♥ 4*
○ Stravino di Stravino '10	♥♥ 4
○ L'Ora '10	♥♥ 4
○ Nosiola Le Frate '12	♥♥ 2*
● Syrae '09	♥♥ 4
○ Kerner '12	♥ 2
● Naran Cortis '12	♥ 3
○ Sauvignon Teramara '12	♥ 3
● Fratagranda '09	♥♥♥ 4*
● Fratagranda '07	♥♥♥ 4
○ Stravino di Stravino '99	♥♥♥ 4*
○ L'Ora '05	♥♥ 4
● Pinot nero Madruzzo '08	♥♥ 4
○ Soliva '06	♥♥ 5
○ Stravino di Stravino '09	♥♥ 4
○ Stravino di Stravino '07	♥♥ 4

Cantina Rotaliana

VIA TRENTO, 65B
38017 MEZZOLOMBARDO [TN]
TEL. 0461601010
www.cantinarotaliana.it

CELLAR SALES
PRE-BOOKED VISITS
ANNUAL PRODUCTION 1,000,000 bottles
HECTARES UNDER VINE 330.00

Teroldego calls this home and what a slogan that could be for a co-operative that has ranked so high for so long, both in quality and quantity of producers of Campo Rotaliano's iconic wine. A hefty team of member-growers work the hillside vineyards, some of which are fairly distant from Mezzolombardo, planted to the white grapes used in the operation's newest challenge, a Trentodoc sparkler. The current line is quite diverse, with wines prized for their self-confidence, typicity and their reasonable price tags. Leonardo Pilati, the manager of this dynamic co-operative winery, presented a wide range of wines, from the Trento Redor to various Teroldegos. The best of the bunch is the Clesurae, produced only in the best vintages, when Teroldego can guarantee quality and offer interesting ageing potential. We found good value for money in the Etichetta Rossa and a whole series of whites.

● Teroldego Rotaliano Clesurae '10	♟♟ 6
○ Trentino Pinot Bianco '12	♟♟ 2*
○ Trento Brut Redor Ris. '07	♟♟ 5
● Teroldego Rotaliano Et. Rossa '12	♟ 2
○ Trentino Chardonnay '12	♟ 2
○ Trentino Gewürztraminer '12	♟ 3
● Trentino Lagrein '12	♟ 2
○ Trentino Pinot Grigio '12	♟ 2
● Teroldego Rotaliano Clesurae '06	♟♟♟ 5
● Teroldego Rotaliano Clesurae '02	♟♟♟ 5
● Teroldego Rotaliano Ris. '04	♟♟♟ 3
● Teroldego Rotaliano Clesurae '09	♟♟ 5
● Teroldego Rotaliano Clesurae '07	♟♟ 5
○ Thamè Bianco '11	♟♟ 3
○ Trento Brut Redor Ris. '06	♟♟ 5

★Tenuta San Leonardo

FRAZ. BORGHETTO ALL'ADIGE
LOC. SAN LEONARDO
38060 AVIO [TN]
TEL. 0464689004
www.sanleonardo.it

CELLAR SALES
PRE-BOOKED VISITS
ANNUAL PRODUCTION 180,000 bottles
HECTARES UNDER VINE 25.00

Fascination, elegance and undeniable quality are the hallmarks of this wine estate, managed by the entire family of Marchese Carlo Guerrieri Gonzaga. Their first goal is to respect and protect the beauty of their local area, Campi Sarni, where wine was being made even before the year 1000, and the absolute quality of their wines, particularly San Leonardo. His son Anselmo is part of the operation, along with a staff that is uniformly professional and committed to their work of producing wines that enhance life. The San Leonardo 2008 needs more time in the bottle, so it was up to an exclusive Carmenère 2007 to show off the charm and outstanding quality of this attractive operation. Only a few thousand bottles, all magnums, were produced, and will be on sale from late 2013. Its deep, inky red hue accompanies spice on the nose along with hints of pencil lead and berry fruit, followed by a seemingly endless finish. We also loved the Villa Gresti 2008.

● Carmenère '07	♟♟♟ 8
● Terre di San Leonardo '10	♟♟ 3
○ Vette di San Leonardo '12	♟♟ 3
● Villa Gresti '08	♟♟ 5
● San Leonardo '07	♟♟♟ 7
● San Leonardo '06	♟♟♟ 7
● San Leonardo '05	♟♟♟ 7
● San Leonardo '04	♟♟♟ 7
● San Leonardo '03	♟♟♟ 7
● San Leonardo '01	♟♟♟ 7
● San Leonardo '00	♟♟♟ 7
● San Leonardo '99	♟♟♟ 7
● San Leonardo '97	♟♟♟ 7
● Villa Gresti '03	♟♟♟ 6
● Terre di San Leonardo '09	♟♟ 3
● Villa Gresti '07	♟♟ 5

Istituto Agrario Provinciale San Michele all'Adige

via Edmondo Mach, 1
38010 San Michele all'Adige [TN]
Tel. 0461615252
www.ismaa.it

CELLAR SALES
PRE-BOOKED VISITS
ANNUAL PRODUCTION 250,000 bottles
HECTARES UNDER VINE 60.00
VITICULTURE METHOD Certified Organic

The Istituto continues to be as dynamic as it is traditional, researching viticulture and winemaking without pause, only natural in a school with more than a century of activity. It has trained a legion of oenologists, vineyard experts, and winegrowers, through a wide range of courses, and still attracts increasing numbers of students. It is now a kind of wine university, with offerings in biotechnology and biodynamic practices, fully capable of training a legion of expert researchers ready to apply their knowledge and present exemplary wines. The Trento dedicated to the school's founder, Edmund Mach, is itself a textbook performance, thanks to Enrico Paternoster, the winery manager, who respects the wine's inherent nature. The multifaceted 2008 is perhaps still evolving, but will be perfect with time. The still wines, both whites and reds, were very well executed.

● Trentino Pinot Nero Monastero '10	▼▼	6
○ Trento Mach Riserva del Fondatore '08	▼▼	5
● Trentino Cabernet Franc Monastero '10	▼▼	3
○ Trentino Müller Thurgau '12	▼▼	3
○ Trentino Sauvignon '12	▼▼	3
○ Trentino Manzoni Bianco '12	▼	3
○ Trentino Traminer Aromatico '12	▼	3
○ Trento Mach Riserva del Fondatore '07	▽▽▽	5
○ Trento Mach Riserva del Fondatore '04	▽▽▽	5
○ Trentino Müller Thurgau Monastero '10	▽▽	3
○ Trentino Pinot Bianco '09	▽▽	2*
● Trentino Pinot Nero '09	▽▽	6
○ Trentino Riesling Monastero '11	▽▽	5
○ Trentino Sauvignon Monastero '10	▽▽	3

Armando Simoncelli

via Navicello, 7
38068 Rovereto [TN]
Tel. 0464432373
www.simoncelli.it

CELLAR SALES
PRE-BOOKED VISITS
ANNUAL PRODUCTION 90,000 bottles
HECTARES UNDER VINE 10.50

The vineyards are planted on an alluvial terrace alongside the Adige river, in a spot where the port of Rovereto was active up to the mid-1700s. Armando Simoncelli, legendary Vallagarina vigneron, personally tends the vines, assisted for a few years now by his children. The area is most celebrated for its red grapes, particularly cabernet sauvignon and marzemino, but attention is fully paid to other Trentino treasures too, such as pinot bianco. The country style of the wines has consciously been maintained, above all to respect the identity of Marzemino and Schiava, while energies have also focused on the Bordeaux blend Navesèl, whose character hinges on its full, exuberantly ripe fruit. The Marzemino is a must, as always. The immensely enjoyable Schiava was one of the best we tasted in the region.

● Trentino Marzemino '12	▼▼	2*
● Trentino Rosso Navesèl '10	▼▼	3
○ Trento Brut '10	▼▼	4
● Vallagarina Schiava '12	▼▼	2*
● Trentino Cabernet Franc '11	▼	3
○ Trentino Pinot Bianco '12	▼	3
● Trentino Marzemino '11	▽▽	2*
○ Trentino Pinot Bianco '11	▽▽	3
● Trentino Rosso Navesèl '08	▽▽	3
● Trentino Rosso Navesèl '07	▽▽	3
● Trentino Rosso Navesèl '06	▽▽	3
○ Trento Brut '09	▽▽	4

Vallarom

FRAZ. MASI, 21
38063 AVIO [TN]
TEL. 0464684297
www.vallarom.it

CELLAR SALES
PRE-BOOKED VISITS
ANNUAL PRODUCTION 45,000 bottles
HECTARES UNDER VINE 7.00
VITICULTURE METHOD Certified Organic

Barbara and Filippo Scienza work hard but are happy to stop and talk about the future of wine, which they see as a sustainable product that is a tribute from the earth to the grower's hard work. They have carefully chosen this life, demonstrated by the attention they devote to their operation, with garden-like vineyards tended with practices respectful of nature, recovery of indigenous varieties and preservation of vineyards with near-centenarian vines. The open, self-confident, joyous, wines reflect the values of these two sterling vignerons. The impeccable wines showed clear growth in terms of quality, as seen in the characterful Pinot Nero 2010, the result of painstaking care in the rows and dedication in the cellar, and the Bordeaux blend Campi Sarni 2010, full of character and steeped in history, with records of viticulture here dating back to the 11th century. The Cabernet 2010 impressed, with its grassy, elegant fullness, as did the Trentatrè 2012, a blend of white moscato varieties.

● Cabernet Sauvignon '10	♟♟ 3
● Campi Sarni Rosso '10	♟♟ 4
● Pinot Nero '10	♟♟ 4
● Trentino Marzemino '12	♟♟ 3
○ Vo' Dosaggio Zero '10	♟♟ 4
○ Trentatrè '12	♟ 3
○ Vo' Rosé Dosaggio Zero '10	♟ 4
● Cabernet Sauvignon '09	♟♟ 3
● Campi Sarni Rosso '05	♟♟ 4
○ Chardonnay Vign. Casetta '06	♟♟ 3
○ Enantio '11	♟♟ 3
● Lambrusco a Foglia Frastagliata Enantio '11	♟♟ 3
● Pinot Nero '09	♟♟ 4
● Syrah '10	♟♟ 5
● Trentino Marzemino '12	♟♟ 3

Roberto Zeni

FRAZ. GRUMO
VIA STRETTA, 2
38010 SAN MICHELE ALL'ADIGE [TN]
TEL. 0461650456
www.zeni.tn.it

CELLAR SALES
PRE-BOOKED VISITS
ANNUAL PRODUCTION 190,000 bottles
HECTARES UNDER VINE 20.00

The young Zenis soon forged ahead and in just a few vintages have almost equalled the respected expertise of their fathers, Andrea and Roberto Zeni, two of modern Trentino winemaking's most influential figures. Now, with 40 harvests to their credit, they are happy to step back for their offspring. One of the top projects, brainchild of siblings and cousins Rudy, Mattia, Veronica and Massimo, is Schwarzhof, an ultra-steep vineyard in the hills overlooking Lavis, which will be planted to an unusual mix of varietics to produce some decidedly upscale wines. The Teroldego Pini 2009 fends off all comers in its category, even getting one over on the winery's other star, the excellent Teroldego Ternet 2011, tended in person by Rudy, the young son of Roberto Zeni, in the Maso Schwarzhof. So, Pini beats Ternet, albeit by a whisker, perhaps because it better exploits the growing year and the vinification of super-ripe grapes, to give an unmistakable wine that is concentrated but not cloying.

● Teroldego Rotaliano Pini '09	♟♟♟ 6
● Ternet Schwarzhof '11	♟♟ 5
● Teroldego Rotaliano Le Albere '11	♟♟ 3*
○ Trentino Chardonnay Vign. Zaraosti '10	♟♟ 2*
○ Trentino Nosiola Palustella '12	♟♟ 3
● Trentino Pinot Nero Spiazol '10	♟♟ 4
○ Trento Maso Nero Dosaggio Zero '10	♟♟ 5
☉ Trento Maso Nero Rosé '08	♟♟ 5
○ Trentino Moscato Rosa '11	♟ 4
○ Trentino Müller Thurgau '12	♟ 2
○ Trentino Pinot Bianco Sei Pergole '12	♟ 2
○ Trentino Sauvignon Piazzole '12	♟ 3
● Ternet Schwarzhof '10	♟♟♟ 5
● Teroldego Rotaliano Pini '08	♟♟ 6
● Trentino Pinot Nero Spiazol '09	♟♟ 4
○ Trento Maso Nero '05	♟♟ 5

Acino d'Oro

FRAZ. BORGHETTO ALL'ADIGE
LOC. SAN LEONARDO, 3
38060 AVIO [TN]
TEL. 0464689004

ANNUAL PRODUCTION 180,000 bottles
HECTARES UNDER VINE 25.00

● Villa Imperiale '10	♀♀ 2*

Cantina Aldeno

VIA ROMA, 76
38060 ALDENO [TN]
TEL. 0461842511
www.cantina-aldeno.it

CELLAR SALES
PRE-BOOKED VISITS
ANNUAL PRODUCTION 240,000 bottles
HECTARES UNDER VINE 339.00

○ Trento Brut Altinum	♀♀ 4
● Trentino Lagrein Atesim Flumen '11	♀ 3
● Trentino Merlot Althesin Flumen '11	♀ 2
● Trentino Pinot Nero '11	♀ 3

Bolognani

VIA STAZIONE, 19
38015 LAVIS [TN]
TEL. 0461246354
www.bolognani.com

CELLAR SALES
PRE-BOOKED VISITS
ANNUAL PRODUCTION 60,000 bottles
HECTARES UNDER VINE 4.40

● Teroldego Armilo '11	♀♀ 3
○ Trentino Traminer Aromatico Sanròc '11	♀♀ 3
○ Moscato Giallo '12	♀ 3
○ Pinot Grigio '12	♀ 2

Conti Bossi Fedrigotti

VIA UNIONE, 43
38068 ROVERETO [TN]
TEL. 0456832511
www.fedrigotti.it

CELLAR SALES
PRE-BOOKED VISITS
ANNUAL PRODUCTION 160,000 bottles
HECTARES UNDER VINE 40.00

● Fojaneghe Rosso '10	♀♀ 5
● Mas'est '11	♀ 3

De Tarczal

FRAZ. MARANO D'ISERA
VIA G. B. MIORI, 4
38060 ISERA [TN]
TEL. 0464409134
www.detarczal.com

CELLAR SALES
PRE-BOOKED VISITS
RESTAURANT SERVICE
ANNUAL PRODUCTION 120,000 bottles
HECTARES UNDER VINE 17.00

● Trentino Marzemino d'Isera Sup. '10	♀♀ 3
● Trentino Cabernet Franc '08	♀ 3

Donatoni

LOC. MASI, 6
38063 AVIO [TN]
TEL. 3316320238
www.donatoniwines.i

HECTARES UNDER VINE 10.00

● Terra dei Forti Coletto Ris. '08	♀♀ 4
● Massenà '11	♀♀ 3
● Terra dei Forti Guglia '09	♀♀ 4

Cipriano Fedrizzi

VIA 4 NOVEMBRE, 1
38017 MEZZOLOMBARDO [TN]
TEL. 0461602328
fedrizzicipriano@alice.it

CELLAR SALES
PRE-BOOKED VISITS
ANNUAL PRODUCTION 32,000 bottles
HECTARES UNDER VINE 6.50

● Teroldego Rotaliano Teroldigo '11	🍷🍷 3
● Teroldego Rotaliano Due Vigneti '11	🍷 5

Francesco Moser

FRAZ. MEANO
VIA CASTEL DI GARDOLO, 5
38121 TRENTO
TEL. 0461990786
www.cantinemoser.com

CELLAR SALES
PRE-BOOKED VISITS
ACCOMMODATION
ANNUAL PRODUCTION 100,000 bottles
HECTARES UNDER VINE 10.00

○ 51,151 '10	🍷🍷 5
○ Riesling '12	🍷🍷 3
○ Gewürztraminer '12	🍷 3
● Lagrein Dea Mater '11	🍷 3

Grigolli

VIA SAN BERNARDINO, 10
38065 MORI [TN]
TEL. 3471608619
www.grigollibruno.it

ANNUAL PRODUCTION 11,000 bottles
HECTARES UNDER VINE 5.00

● Trentino Rosso Trilogia '07	🍷🍷 5
● Trentino Rosso Germano '07	🍷🍷 4

Maso Martis

LOC. MARTIGNANO
VIA DELL'ALBERA, 52
38121 TRENTO
TEL. 0461821057
www.masomartis.it

CELLAR SALES
PRE-BOOKED VISITS
ANNUAL PRODUCTION 65,000 bottles
HECTARES UNDER VINE 12.00
VITICULTURE METHOD Certified Organic

○ Trento Brut Ris. '07	🍷🍷 5
○ Trento Dosaggio Zero '10	🍷🍷 5
○ Trentino Chardonnay L'Incanto '09	🍷 3
⊙ Trento Brut Rosé	🍷 5

Pisoni

LOC. SARCHE
FRAZ. PERGOLESE DI LASINO
VIA SAN SIRO, 7A
38076 LASINO [TN]
TEL. 0461564106
www.plsoni.net

CELLAR SALES
PRE-BOOKED VISITS
ANNUAL PRODUCTION 23,500 bottles
HECTARES UNDER VINE 16.00

○ Trento Brut '09	🍷🍷 4
⊙ Trento Brut Rosé '10	🍷🍷 5
○ Trento Extra Brut Ris. '07	🍷🍷 5

Francesco Poli

LOC. SANTA MASSENZA
VIA DEL LAGO, 13
38070 VEZZANO [TN]
TEL. 0461340090
www.franccscopoli.it

CELLAR SALES
ANNUAL PRODUCTION 28,000 bottles
HECTARES UNDER VINE 6.50
VITICULTURE METHOD Certified Organic

● Trentino Lagrein V. Le Vallette '10	🍷🍷 3
○ Trentino Nosiola V. Sottovi '12	🍷 2

Revì

VIA FLORIDA, 10
38060 ALDENO [TN]
TEL. 0461842557
www.revispumanti.com

CELLAR SALES
PRE-BOOKED VISITS
ANNUAL PRODUCTION 13,000 bottles
HECTARES UNDER VINE 1.70

○ Trento Extra Brut Bio Revì Paladino '09	♀♀ 7
○ Trento Brut Revì '09	♀♀ 4
○ Trento Dosaggio Zero Revì '09	♀♀ 5
○ Trento Rosé Revì '09	♀♀ 5

Arcangelo Sandri

VIA VANEGGE, 4A
38010 FAEDO [TN]
TEL. 0461650935
www.arcangelosandri.it

CELLAR SALES
PRE-BOOKED VISITS
ANNUAL PRODUCTION 20,000 bottles
HECTARES UNDER VINE 3.00

○ Trentino Chardonnay I Canopi '12	♀♀ 2*
● Trentino Lagrein Capòr Ris. '10	♀ 3
○ Trentino Müller Thurgau Cosler '12	♀ 2
○ Trentino Traminer Razer '12	♀ 2

Alessandro Secchi

FRAZ. SERRAVALLE ALL'ADIGE
LOC. COLLERI, 10
38061 ALA [TN]
TEL. 0464696647
www.secchivini.it

CELLAR SALES
PRE-BOOKED VISITS
ANNUAL PRODUCTION 40,000 bottles
HECTARES UNDER VINE 12.00

● Trentino Cabernet Sauvignon '11	♀♀ 4
● Trentino Lagrein Cinabro '10	♀ 3
● Trentino Marzemino '12	♀ 4
● Trentino Merlot '10	♀ 4

Toblino

FRAZ. SARCHE
VIA LONGA, 1
38070 CALAVINO [TN]
TEL. 0461564168
www.toblino.it

CELLAR SALES
PRE-BOOKED VISITS
RESTAURANT SERVICE
ANNUAL PRODUCTION 400,000 bottles
HECTARES UNDER VINE 700.00

● Elimarò '09	♀♀ 3
○ Trento Brut Antàres '09	♀♀ 3
○ L'Ora '10	♀ 3
○ Manzoni Bianco '12	♀ 2

Villa Corniole

FRAZ. VERLA
VIA AL GREC', 23
38030 GIOVO [TN]
TEL. 0461695067
www.villacorniole.com

CELLAR SALES
PRE-BOOKED VISITS
ANNUAL PRODUCTION 60,000 bottles
HECTARES UNDER VINE 4.00

○ Salisa '09	♀♀ 5
● Trentino Lagrein Petramontis '11	♀♀ 3
● Trentino Cabernet Sauvignon Gregiòti '09	♀ 5
○ Trentino Müller Thurgau Petramontis '12	♀ 3

Zanotelli

V.LE 4 NOVEMBRE, 52
38034 CEMBRA [TN]
TEL. 0461683131
www.zanotelliwines.com

CELLAR SALES
PRE-BOOKED VISITS
ANNUAL PRODUCTION 40,000 bottles
HECTARES UNDER VINE 11.00

● Trentino Pinot Nero Le Strope '10	♀♀ 3
○ Trentino Riesling Le Strope '12	♀♀ 3
○ Trento Brut Forneri	♀♀ 4
○ Trentino Müller Thurgau '12	♀ 2

ALTO ADIGE

Here and now this successful region is very much invested in territorial specialization, while it prepares for the future with a quality leap in the interpretation of its range of terroirs shaped by the mountains. Pinot bianco, reaping more Tre Bicchieri in this edition of the Guide than ever before, is now considered native in all respects for its level of adaptation and precision in reflecting the different habitats. As already mentioned in the last edition, it is a grape variety that displays precise identities: smoky in Val Venosta, peaty in the Appiano area, and subtle and long-lived in Terlano. We might say the same for gewürztraminer, of excellent quality and typicity in the Termeno area, and riesling for the surprising results it offers in Val Venosta and elsewhere. Eisacktal also has a style of its own, producing razor-sharp wines with knife-edged palates. Alto Adige might become a benchmark for the whole peninsula, demonstrating how important it is to age wines and enhance complexity as they develop. This region can also offer its contribution in another respect, perhaps due to its closeness to German culture, which has been using wine bottle caps in materials other than cork for quite a while now. Wineries with years of testing behind them are now guaranteeing some persuasive and reliable results. Alto Adige reds are equally important in regional production and on that front there are two important considerations to be made. The first concerns the awareness of the value of schiava, now rightly deemed a great wine whose production is aimed at ensuring optimum quality, starting in the vineyard. The second is a reflection on international grape varieties, first and foremost cabernet sauvignon, which offer increasingly deep, stylish wines with an incredible ability to evolve in bottle. The technique is underpinned by increasingly responsible use of small casks for ageing, now less intrusive and marked. To close, a few words on a variety that is very common but undervalued: pinot grigio. Year after year we are seeing more well-defined, persuasive interpretations for surprisingly elegant, well-typed wines.

★Abbazia di Novacella

FRAZ. NOVACELLA
VIA DELL'ABBAZIA, 1
39040 VARNA/VAHRN [BZ]
TEL. 0472836189
www.abbazianovacella.it

CELLAR SALES
PRE-BOOKED VISITS
RESTAURANT SERVICE
ANNUAL PRODUCTION 650,000 bottles
HECTARES UNDER VINE 20.00

The imposing Abbazia di Novacella, built in 1142, is now an icon, boasting a thousand years of history, fascinating architecture and artistic merits. It is also linked to wine and for centuries was an important part of the Augustinian abbey. Urban von Klebelsberg, the winery's dynamic director, and Celestino Lucin, its capable, easy-going oenologist, are aware both of what is expected of them and the future possibilities open to them. They are behind the runaway success of the Abbazia wines, mainly the Valle Isarco whites like Sylvaner, Kerner, Riesling and Veltliner, and the reds from the estate-owned vineyards at Bolzano and Cornaiano. The Praepositus line is as good as ever. Sylvaner 2012 is a Tre Bicchieri winner, with aromas of melon, aniseed and flowers in a freshly supple, flavoursome palate. Riesling 2012 is minerally, Pinot Nero Riserva 2010 austere and succulent, and Veltliner 2012 rich and crispy dry.

Baron Widmann

ENDERGASSE, 3
39040 CORTACCIA/KURTATSCH [BZ]
TEL. 0471880092
www.baron-widmann.it

CELLAR SALES
PRE-BOOKED VISITS
ANNUAL PRODUCTION 35,000 bottles
HECTARES UNDER VINE 15.00

Andreas Widmann is an engaging baron farmer, inheriting the long traditions of his family in the romantic mediaeval hamlet of Cortaccia. This splendid operation with its esteemed cellars and perfectly tended vineyards, under the direction of a discreet, supremely courteous man, assures production of great quality. The wines fully reflect the estate's utter confidence in its cultivation and winemaking choices. The Pinot Bianco, Gewürztraminer, Sauvignon, Weiss, Rot, and Schiava are always outstanding for their understated elegance, as well as for their assertive character. Once again, a wine is in the finals and this time it is the full, solidly built Weiss 2012, opening elegantly to offer a lingering minerality and zest. Sauvignon 2012 offers notes of elderflower on the nose and a crisp sapidity in a lean, leisurely mouth. The soft, fruity Schiava 2012 is very typical and easy-drinking.

○ A. A. Valle Isarco Sylvaner Praepositus '12	♥♥♥ 4*
● A. A. Pinot Nero Praepositus Ris. '10	♥♥ 4
○ A. A. Valle Isarco Riesling Praepositus '12	♥♥ 4
● A. A. Lagrein Praepositus Ris. '10	♥♥ 5
○ A. A. Valle Isarco Kerner Praepositus '12	♥♥ 4
○ A. A. Valle Isarco Sylvaner '12	♥♥ 3
○ A. A. Valle Isarco Veltliner '12	♥♥ 3
○ A. A. Valle Isarco Veltliner Praepositus '12	♥♥ 3
○ A. A. Valle Isarco Müller Thurgau '12	♥ 3
○ A. A. Valle Isarco Pinot Grigio '12	♥ 3
○ A. A. Valle Isarco Riesling Praepositus '09	♀♀♀ 5
○ A. A. Valle Isarco Riesling Praepositus '08	♀♀♀ 5

○ Vigneto delle Dolomiti Bianco Weiss '12	♥♥ 5
○ A. A. Sauvignon '12	♥♥ 3
● A. A. Schiava '12	♥♥ 3
● Vigneto delle Dolomiti Rosso Rot '11	♥ 4
A. A. Cabernet-Merlot Auhof '97	♀♀♀ 4*
○ Vigneto delle Dolomiti Bianco Weiss '11	♀♀♀ 5
○ A. A. Sauvignon '10	♀♀ 3*
● A. A. Schiava '11	♀♀ 2*
● A. A. Schiava '10	♀♀ 2*
○ Vigneto delle Dolomiti Bianco Weiss '10	♀♀ 5
● Vigneto delle Dolomiti Rosso Rot '10	♀♀ 4
● Vigneto delle Dolomiti Rosso Rot '09	♀♀ 3

Bessererhof - Otmar Mair

LOC. NOVALE DI PRESULE, 10
39050 FIÈ ALLO SCILIAR/VÖLS AM SCHLERN [BZ]
TEL. 0471601011
www.bessererhof.it

CELLAR SALES
PRE-BOOKED VISITS
ANNUAL PRODUCTION 35,000 bottles
HECTARES UNDER VINE 1.50

The Besserer winery, owned by Otmar and Rosmarie Mair, is in the extreme south of the Valle Isarco at Novale di Presule, at the foot of the towering Sciliar Massif. The secret of these special wines lies in the warm days of nearby Bolzano and cool Val d'Isarco nights. The estate has been bottling natural wines produced from the steep, well-aspected vineyards since 1998, mainly classic whites like Pinot Bianco, Chardonnay, Gewürztraminer, and Moscato Giallo, and two reds, Schiava and Zweigelt Roan. These fragrant, close-focused wines are full of lip-smacking minerality, like the superb Chardonnay, fermented and aged in wood, classed annually as one of the best in the region. This year, Kerner 2012 is superb, with a flowery-herby nose, a fresh, sapid elegance on the palate and finishing with hints of bitter herbs. The well-crafted, slightly oaky Chardonnay Riserva 2010 offers notes of tropical fruit and grapefruit, then expanding with a full creamy elegance.

○ A. A. Chardonnay Ris. '10	♥♥ 3
○ A. A. Valle Isarco Eisacktal Kerner '12	♥♥ 4
○ A. A. Moscato Giallo '12	♥ 4
○ A. A. Pinot Bianco '12	♥ 3
○ A. A. Chardonnay Ris. '09	♀♀ 3
○ A. A. Chardonnay Ris. '08	♀♀ 3
○ A. A. Chardonnay Ris. '07	♀♀ 3
○ A. A. Chardonnay Fellis '04	♀♀ 8
○ A. A. Moscato Giallo '10	♀♀ 3
○ A. A. Pinot Bianco '11	♀♀ 3*
○ A. A. Pinot Bianco '10	♀♀ 2

★Cantina Bolzano

VIA BRENNERO, 15
39100 BOLZANO/BOZEN
TEL. 0471270909
www.cantinabolzano.com

CELLAR SALES
PRE-BOOKED VISITS
ANNUAL PRODUCTION 1,100,000 bottles
HECTARES UNDER VINE 320.00

Cantina Bolzano was set up in 2001 when two iconic wineries merged. Gries, founded in 1908, and Santa Maddalena, founded in 1930, are now a leading operation in the Alto Adige wine production scenario. The 200 or so members supply grapes from 320 hectares located at altitudes of 240 to 800 metres, from some of the region's best vineyards. This is thanks at least in part to the professional skill of oenologist Stephan Filippi. The winery focuses mainly on Santa Maddalena and Lagrein, with Lagrein Taber and Santa Maddalena Huck am Bach at the top of the range, although the others are also very worthy. Lagrein Riserva Taber is a permanent member of the Tre Bicchieri club. In the 2011 version, it is again a standard-bearer for the native grape, spicy and fruity on the nose with soft, sweet tannins and a rounded elegance on the palate. The Santa Maddalena Classico Huck Am Bach 2012 is outstanding.

● A. A. Lagrein Taber Ris. '11	♥♥♥ 6
○ A. A. Pinot Bianco Dellago '12	♥♥ 4
● A. A. Santa Maddalena Cl. Huck am Bach '12	♥♥ 2*
● A. A. Lagrein Grieser Prestige Line Ris. '11	♥♥ 4
○ A. A. Moscato Giallo Passito Vinalia '11	♥♥ 3
⊙ A. A. Moscato Rosa Rosis '12	♥♥ 3
○ A. A. Sauvignon Mock '12	♥♥ 4
● A. A. Cabernet Mumelter Ris. '11	♥ 6
○ A. A. Chardonnay Kleinstein '12	♥ 4
○ A. A. Gewürztraminer Kleinstein '12	♥ 5
● A. A. Pinot Nero Ris. '11	♥ 5
● A. A. Lagrein Scuro Taber Ris. '07	♀♀♀ 6
● A. A. Lagrein Scuro Taber Ris. '05	♀♀♀ 5
● A. A. Lagrein Taber Ris. '10	♀♀♀ 6
● A. A. Lagrein Taber Ris. '09	♀♀♀ 6

Josef Brigl

LOC. SAN MICHELE
VIA MADONNA DEL RIPOSO, 3
39057 APPIANO/EPPAN [BZ]
TEL. 0471662419
www.brigl.com

CELLAR SALES
PRE-BOOKED VISITS
RESTAURANT SERVICE
ANNUAL PRODUCTION 1,200,000 bottles
HECTARES UNDER VINE 50.00

Brigl is one of the region's leading wineries, with vineyards in the best-aspected terroirs. The cellars dates back to the 15th century and this long tradition and history are now entrusted to Ignaz Brigl and his son Josef, who have taken on a hugely important task. This massive operation, with a production of over one million bottles a year covering the entire vast range of Alto Adige wines, works to meet market demand. The downside is that they do not always achieve their true potential in terms of quality. This year, Lagrein Riserva Briglhof 2010 is in the finals. It has notes of chocolate and cherries and is generously tangy with velvety tannins and a crisp finish. The Santa Maddalena Rielerhof 2012 expresses its family well, with great grip and deliciously austere flavours. Gewürztraminer Windegg 2012 is very typical.

● A. A. Lagrein Briglhof Ris. '10	♟♟ 5
○ A. A. Gewürztraminer Windegg '12	♟♟ 3
● A. A. Lagrein Anno 1309 Ris. '10	♟♟ 3
● A. A. Santa Maddalena Rielerhof '12	♟♟ 2*
● A. A. Merlot Windegg Ris. '10	♟ 3
○ A. A. Müller Thurgau '12	♟ 2
○ A. A. Pinot Grigio Windegg '12	♟ 3
● A. A. Schiava Grigia Kaltenburg '12	♟ 2
○ A. A. Pinot Grigio Windegg '11	♟♟♟ 3*
● A. A. Lago di Caldaro Cl. Sup. Kaltenburg '11	♟♟ 2*
● A. A. Lago di Caldaro Scelto Cl. Sup. Windegg '09	♟♟ 2*
○ A. A. Pinot Bianco Haselhof '11	♟♟ 2*
● A. A. Schiava Grigia Kaltenburg '11	♟♟ 2*
○ A. A. Terlano Drei König Hof '11	♟♟ 2*
○ A. A. Terlano Drei König Hof '10	♟♟ 2*

★Cantina di Caldaro

VIA CANTINE, 12
39052 CALDARO/KALTERN [BZ]
TEL. 0471963149
www.kellereikaltern.com

CELLAR SALES
PRE-BOOKED VISITS
ANNUAL PRODUCTION 2,000,000 bottles
HECTARES UNDER VINE 300.00
VITICULTURE METHOD Certified Biodynamic

Caldaro, Lago di Caldaro, Cantina di Caldaro and Kellerei Kaltern are now virtually synonymous. The dynamic team, under the professional management of director Tobias Zingerle and oenologist Andreas Prast, has turned this co-operative winery into one of the best operations in South Tyrol. The typical Lago di Caldaro, in all its variations from the most basic to the famous Pfarrhof, remains the focus of the cellar, attracting increasing interest from customers. Each year the Pinot Nero and Cabernet are also excellent products. As for the whites, we must mention the Pinot Bianco, Sauvignon and Gewürztraminer, as well as the raisined Serenade, for years one of Italy's great sweet whites. The Moscato Giallo Passito Serenade pulls off a tenth Tre Bicchieri. The 2010 version has its familiarly complex nose, with fresh apricot, dried fruit and petals, followed by a delicate saltiness and a full well-balanced length. Cabernet Sauvignon Riserva Pfarrhof 2010 is among the best in the region.

○ A. A. Moscato Giallo Passito Serenade '10	♟♟♟ 6
● A. A. Cabernet Sauvignon Pfarrhof Ris. '10	♟♟ 5
○ A. A. Pinot Bianco Solos Biodinamico Demeter '12	♟♟ 4
○ A. A. Pinot Bianco Vial '12	♟♟ 3*
○ A. A. Gewürztraminer Campaner '12	♟♟ 3
● A. A. Lago di Caldaro Scelto Cl. Sup. Pfarrhof '12	♟♟ 2*
● A. A. Lagrein Spigel '11	♟♟ 3
○ A. A. Sauvignon Castel Giovanelli '11	♟♟ 5
○ A. A. Sauvignon Premstaler '12	♟♟ 3
○ A. A. Pinot Grigio Söll '11	♟ 3
● A. A. Pinot Nero Pfarrhof Ris. '10	♟ 6
○ A. A. Moscato Giallo Passito Serenade '09	♟♟♟ 6

Castel Sallegg

v.lo di Sotto, 15
39052 Caldaro/Kaltern [BZ]
Tel. 0471963132
www.castelsallegg.it

CELLAR SALES
PRE-BOOKED VISITS
ANNUAL PRODUCTION 120,000 bottles
HECTARES UNDER VINE 30.00

The story of how moscato rosa was
brought to Alto Adige from Sicily by the von
Kuenberg family is the perfect illustration of
a territory that has always absorbed culture
from Italy and South Tyrol and, more
broadly, from Austria. Georg von Kuenberg
is the fiercely enthusiastic guardian of his
family's traditions, and recently brought in a
young cellarmaster, Matthias Hauser, to
infuse new energy into a project that risked
being weighed down by a wonderful yet
burdensome tradition. The results are
positive, reflected in the growing quality of
the wines. Merlot 2009 is crisp and
compact, with a hint of hot spices. The
palate is close-knit and dry, with a fine
flavoursome finish. The classical Moscato
Rosa 2010 is very traditional in its
approach, where complexity is sustained by
a lovely acidity. The exceedingly fresh Pinot
Bianco 2012 has a linear, subtle elegance.

Castelfeder

via Portici, 11
39040 Egna/Neumarkt [BZ]
Tel. 0471820420
www.castelfeder.it

CELLAR SALES
PRE-BOOKED VISITS
ANNUAL PRODUCTION 400,000 bottles
HECTARES UNDER VINE 20.00

Castelfeder, one of the Lower Adige Valley's
emerging wineries, is a family business
established a few decades ago at Cortina
all'Adige, on the South Tyrol and Trentino
border. This is a classic zone for white
grapes like chardonnay, pinot grigio,
sauvignon, and gewürztraminer. Günther
Giovanett now works with his children, Ivan
and Ines, who are both oenologists. It would
seem that Castelfeder is benefitting from
these injections of youthfulness and new
ideas, bringing the promise of great things.
As always, Pinot Bianco Tecum 2011 is a
great wine, with a fruity crispness and a
polished structure. We like the two top
reds. The spicy, rich Cabernet Riserva
Burgum Novum 2009 has lovely flavours
and a full texture and the fruity Lagrein
Riserva Burgum Novum 2010 reveals
overtones of cherry on the nose, soft
tannins and a rich, full length.

● A. A. Merlot '09	▼▼	2*
☉ A. A. Moscato Rosa Passito '10	▼▼	6
● A. A. Lago di Caldaro Cl. Bischofsleiten '12	▼▼	3
○ A. A. Pinot Bianco '12	▼▼	3
● A. A. Merlot Ris. '10	▼	4
○ A. A. Pinot Grigio '12	▼	3
○ A. A. Sauvignon '12	▼	3
● A. A. Lago di Caldaro Scelto Bischofsleiten '11	♀♀	3*
● A. A. Lago di Caldaro Scelto Bischofsleiten '10	♀♀	2*
● A. A. Lago di Caldaro Scelto Bischofsleiten '09	♀♀	2*
○ A. A. Pinot Bianco '07	♀♀	2*
○ A. A. Pinot Grigio '10	♀♀	2*
○ A. A. Pinot Grigio '09	♀♀	2*

● A. A. Cabernet Burgum Novum Ris. '09	▼▼	4
○ A. A. Pinot Bianco Tecum '11	▼▼	3*
○ A. A. Gewürztraminer Passito Endidae	▼▼	3
● A. A. Lagrein Burgum Novum Ris. '10	▼▼	4
○ A. A. Pinot Grigio 15 '12	▼▼	2*
● A. A. Pinot Nero Burgum Novum Ris. '10	▼▼	5
● A. A. Schiava Breitbacher '12	▼▼	2*
● A. A. Pinot Nero Glener '11	▼	3
○ Sauvignon Raif '12	▼	3
○ A. A. Pinot Bianco Tecum '10	♀♀♀	3*
● A. A. Cabernet Burgum Novum '09	♀♀	4
○ A. A. Gewürztraminer Passito '09	♀♀	3*
○ A. A. Gewürztraminer Vom Lehm '11	♀♀	3*
● A. A. Pinot Nero Burgum Novum '09	♀♀	5

★Cantina Produttori Colterenzio

LOC. CORNAIANO/GIRLAN
S.DA DEL VINO, 8
39057 APPIANO/EPPAN [BZ]
TEL. 0471664246
www.colterenzio.it

CELLAR SALES
PRE-BOOKED VISITS
ANNUAL PRODUCTION 1,400,000 bottles
HECTARES UNDER VINE 300.00

If Alto Adige is today a leader in the Italian wine world, this is also thanks to Cantina Colterenzio. Luis Raifer, who founded the winery in 1960 and was its president for many years, has always concentrated on achieving top quality. Today, his son Wolfgang has taken over as managing director, working with oenologist Martin Lemayr. Wines like Cabernet Sauvignon Lafòa and Sauvignon Lafòa are in a class of their own, enjoyed across the world. All the other wines in the range have an excellent reputation. Cabernet Sauvignon Lafòa 2010 richly deserves a Tre Bicchieri. Its personality is defined by spices, pepper and brambles and full juicy flavours. The elegant Sauvignon Lafòa 2011 is an impeccable wine with well-integrated oak. Gewürztraminer Atisis 2011 has amazing aromas of roses, pear and damson, with typical fullness on the palate, sound flavours and a lovely fresh finish.

Cantina Produttori Cortaccia

S.DA DEL VINO, 23
39040 CORTACCIA/KURTATSCH [BZ]
TEL. 0471880115
www.cantina-cortaccia.it

CELLAR SALES
PRE-BOOKED VISITS
ANNUAL PRODUCTION 1,100,000 bottles
HECTARES UNDER VINE 175.00

The Cantina Produttori Cortaccia is just getting its breath back, once again producing wines of persuasive quality thanks to the 250 members and 180 hectares of vineyard underpinning the operation. Some zones are true crus, known for great reds and whites, while the Cortaccia estate has always been acclaimed for its superb Cabernets and Merlots. Cabernet Freienfeld is certainly one of the region's best reds, along with Merlot Brenntal, although there are also excellent whites like Pinot Bianco, Sauvignon, Gewürztraminer, and Müller Thurgau, from the higher zones in the village. Our vote goes to Sauvignon Kofl 2012, with notes of hedgerow and flint on the nose and an elegant, stylish saltiness in the mouth. Pinot Bianco Hofstatt 2012 is fruity with notes of crunchy apples, and a lovely acidity and grip, while the crisp, lively Pinot Grigio Penòner 2012 has aromas of citrus fruit and grapefruit.

● A. A. Cabernet Sauvignon Lafòa '10	▾▾▾ 7
○ A. A. Gewürztraminer Atisis '11	▾▾ 5
○ A. A. Sauvignon Lafòa '11	▾▾ 5
○ A. A. Chardonnay Cornell Formigar '11	▾▾ 5
○ A. A. Pinot Bianco Weisshaus '12	▾▾ 3
● A. A. Pinot Nero St. Daniel '10	▾▾ 4
● A. A. Pinot Nero Villa Nigra Cornell '10	▾▾ 5
○ A. A. Sauvignon Prail '12	▾▾ 3
● A. A. Schiava Mentzenhof '12	▾▾ 3
○ A. A. Chardonnay Altkirch '12	▾ 2
○ A. A. Pinot Grigio Puiten '12	▾ 3
● A. A. Cabernet Sauvignon Lafòa '09	♈♈♈ 7
● A. A. Cabernet Sauvignon Lafòa '04	♈♈♈ 6
● A. A. Cabernet Sauvignon Lafòa '03	♈♈♈ 7
○ A. A. Pinot Bianco Thurner '11	♈♈ 2*
○ A. A. Sauvignon Prail Praedium '11	♈♈ 3*

○ A. A. Sauvignon Kofl '12	▾▾ 3*
○ A. A. Chardonnay Pichl '12	▾▾ 3
○ A. A. Gewürztraminer Brenntal Ris. '10	▾▾ 5
● A. A. Lagrein Frauriegl '11	▾▾ 5
○ A. A. Pinot Bianco Hoftatt '12	▾▾ 3
○ A. A. Pinot Grigio Penòner '12	▾▾ 3
● A. A. Merlot Brenntal '10	▾ 5
○ A. A. Müller Thurgau Graun '12	▾ 3
● A. A. Schiava Grigia Sonntaler '12	▾ 2
○ Bianco Aruna V.T. '11	▾ 6
○ A. A. Chardonnay Pichl '11	♈♈ 3
● A. A. Lagrein Frauriegl '09	♈♈ 5
● A. A. Merlot Brenntal '09	♈♈ 5
● A. A. Schiava Grigia Sonntaler '11	♈♈ 2*
○ Aruna Passito '10	♈♈ 6

Hartmann Donà

VIA RAFFEIN, 8
39010 CERMES/TSCHERMS [BZ]
TEL. 3292610628
hartmann.dona@rolmail.net

ANNUAL PRODUCTION 35,000 bottles
HECTARES UNDER VINE 4.65

Hartmann Donà studied oenology at the German University of Geisenheim, working at Cantina di Terlano as its oenologist from 1994 to 2002. In 2000, he started making wine independently and today produces between 30,000 and 35,000 bottles a year. He is an expert who fills his bottles with the wonderful potential of his vineyards with their mineral-rich soils. The wines reflect their terroir and show great promise. The elegant, typical aromas of the first impact are followed by delightful drinkability. Donà Blanc is a blend of 60% Pinot Blanc and 40% Chardonnay, Donà Rouge is 85% Schiava, 10% Pinot Noir and 5% Lagrein, and Donà Noir is a pure Pinot Noir. This year, the best wines are Pinot Nero Donà Noir 2009, open and relaxed with varietal aromas and a bitterish, dry palate full of acidity, and the austerely mineral Donà Rouge 2008, with well-balanced crispness and a dry suppleness on the palate.

● A.A. Pinot Nero Donà Noir '09	♟♟	3*
● Donà Rouge '08	♟♟	3*
○ A.A. Pinot Bianco '11	♟♟	3
○ Chardonnay '11	♟	3
○ Donà Blanc '09	♟	3
○ Gewürtztraminer '11	♟	3
○ Chardonnay '10	♟♟	3
○ Donà Blanc '08	♟♟	3
● Donà Noir '08	♟♟	3*
● Donà Rouge '07	♟♟	3*
○ Pinot Bianco '10	♟♟	3
○ Sauvignon Blanc '10	♟♟	3

Egger-Ramer

VIA GUNCINA, 5
39100 BOLZANO/BOZEN
TEL. 0471280541
www.egger-ramer.com

CELLAR SALES
PRE-BOOKED VISITS
ANNUAL PRODUCTION 120,000 bottles
HECTARES UNDER VINE 14.00

Egger-Ramer is a long-standing winery in the heart of Bolzano. Today, smart, young Peter Egger runs an operation of 14 hectares and 100,000 bottles a year, which is no mean feat for a family-run winery. Over the years, the Egger-Ramers have been able to tap into quality and a correct pricing policy to build up their image in the Alto Adige viticulture world. The typical, native wines of Bolzano, above all Santa Maddalena and Lagrein, represent the apex of their production, revealing elegance and a distinctive personality. Our favourites are the two Lagreins. The fruity, spicy Gries Tenuta Kristan Riserva 2010 is full of character and the genuine Lagrein Gries 2012 offers a lovely fruitiness, austere aromas and a palate of earthy softness. Lagrein Rosato Kretzer 2012 is bursting with crisp fruit and Santa Maddalena Classico Reisegger 2012 is elegant with a crunchy finish. All the other wines presented are very well made.

● A. A. Lagrein Gries Tenuta Kristan Ris. '10	♟♟	5
● A. A. Lagrein Gries '12	♟♟	2*
⊙ A. A. Lagrein Kretzer Gries '12	♟♟	2*
⊙ A. A. Santa Maddalena Cl. Reisegger '12	♟♟	2*
○ A. A. Gewürztraminer '12	♟	3
● A. A. Lagrein Gries Tenuta Kristan '11	♟	3
○ A. A. Pinot Bianco '12	♟	2
● A. A. Santa Maddalena Cl. '12	♟	2
○ A. A. Valle Isarco Müller Thurgau '12	♟	2
○ A. A. Valle Isarco Müller Thurgau Sabbiolino '12	♟	2
● A. A. Lagrein Gries Tenuta Kristan '10	♟♟	3
● A. A. Lagrein Gries Tenuta Kristan Ris. '09	♟♟	5
● A. A. Lagrein Kristan '09	♟♟	3*
● A. A. Santa Maddalena Cl. '11	♟♟	2*
● A. A. Santa Maddalena Cl. Reisegger '10	♟♟	2*

Erbhof Unterganzner Josephus Mayr

FRAZ. CARDANO
VIA CAMPIGLIO, 15
39053 BOLZANO/BOZEN
TEL. 0471365582
www.tirolensisarsvini.it

CELLAR SALES
PRE-BOOKED VISITS
ANNUAL PRODUCTION 65,000 bottles
HECTARES UNDER VINE 9.00

Josephus Mayr owns the renowned Erbhof Unterganzner farm in the far east of the Bolzano basin. The enterprise has a lengthy history and Josephus is an extraordinary figure in the Alto Adige wine world. Besides being the first to produce South Tyrol extra-virgin olive oil, every year he crafts very distinctive wines with great passion and skill. His Lagrein is possibly one of the best expressions of this native grape, and his Lamarein from raisined lagrein is a pure class act. The Santa Maddalenas are full of character, while the Cabernets are solidly built and assertive. Cabernet Riserva Kampill 2010 is superb this year: fruits and spices join pepper and pencil lead and the profile is deep yet fully open. The compact but supple Composition Reif 2010 is equally great. Notes of leather and cocoa blend with fine spices leading to a full finish. They are two truly great reds, as is the legendary Lamarein 2011, with its extraordinary Amarone-style interpretation of an Alto Adige Lagrein.

● A. A. Cabernet Kampill Ris. '10	♛♛ 5
● Composition Reif '10	♛♛ 6
● A. A. Lagrein Scuro Ris. '10	♛♛ 4
● A. A. Santa Maddalena Cl. '12	♛♛ 3
● Lamarein '11	♛♛ 6
⊙ A. A. Lagrein Rosato V. T. '12	♛ 3
○ A. A. Sauvignon Platt & Pignat '12	♛ 3
● A. A. Lagrein Scuro Ris. '05	♛♛♛ 4
● A. A. Lagrein Scuro Ris. '01	♛♛♛ 4
● Lamarein '05	♛♛♛ 5
● A. A. Cabernet Kampill Ris. '09	♛♛ 5
● A. A. Lagrein Scuro Ris. '09	♛♛ 4
● A. A. Santa Maddalena Cl. '10	♛♛ 3
● Lamarein '10	♛♛ 6

Erste+Neue

VIA DELLE CANTINE, 5/10
39052 CALDARO/KALTERN [BZ]
TEL. 0471963122
www.erste-neue.it

CELLAR SALES
PRE-BOOKED VISITS
ANNUAL PRODUCTION 1,400,000 bottles
HECTARES UNDER VINE 260.00

Caldaro-based Erste + Neue or First + New winery has 500 members and 320 hectares under vine, producing a million bottles a year. It is one of the outstanding co-operative wineries of the enchanting Alto Adige town of Caldaro and the most active in winemaking terms. The Puntay range is the jewel in their crown, with Sauvignon, Gewürztraminer, Chardonnay, Lagrein, Cabernet, Merlot, and Lago di Caldaro in the amazing selection of wonderfully well-structured wines. The Tre Bicchieri goes to Lago di Caldaro Classico Superiore Leuchtenburg 2012 this year. It portrays its type well, with typical fresh fruity aromas of cherry and violets, soft flavoursome tannins and a delightful dry thrust. Pinot Grigio Grauer 2012 is excellent, fine-tuning the white-fleshed fruit and spring flowers fully reflected in an expansive palate bursting with vitality.

● A. A. Lago di Caldaro Cl. Sup. Leuchtenburg '12	♛♛♛ 2*
○ A. A. Pinot Grigio Grauer '12	♛♛ 3*
● A. A. Pinot Nero Mezzan '11	♛♛ 3*
● A. A. Cabernet Puntay Ris. '11	♛♛ 5
● A. A. Lago di Caldaro Cl. Sup. Puntay '12	♛♛ 3
○ A. A. Pinot Bianco Prunar '12	♛♛ 3
○ A. A. Anthos Bianco Passito '09	♛ 5
● A. A. Lagrein Puntay Ris. '10	♛ 5
○ A. A. Sauvignon Stern '12	♛ 3
● A. A. Lago di Caldaro Cl. Sup. Puntay '10	♛♛♛ 3*
○ A. A. Sauvignon Puntay '06	♛♛♛ 4
○ A. A. Chardonnay Puntay '10	♛♛ 3
● A. A. Lago di Caldaro Leuchtenburg '11	♛♛ 2*
○ A. A. Pinot Bianco Prunar '11	♛♛ 3*
● A. A. Santa Maddalena Gröbnerhof '11	♛♛ 2*

★Falkenstein Franz Pratzner

VIA CASTELLO, 15
39025 NATURNO/NATURNS [BZ]
TEL. 0473666054
www.falkenstein.bz

CELLAR SALES
PRE-BOOKED VISITS
ANNUAL PRODUCTION 45,000 bottles
HECTARES UNDER VINE 7.00

Val Venosta is not like the rest of South Tyrol. Its particular setting and rich culture make this valley the ideal destination for a tour to a place where viticulture has always found the best nooks and tiny plots for great wines. Reflecting this reality, there are few producers but they are larger-than-life figures. Franz Pratzner, from the Falkenstein estate above Naturno, is one such figure, a true grower and a man of few words. His exceptional wines need time to open but overflow with their own distinctive personalities, and the various Pinot Biancos, Rieslings, Sauvignons, Gewürztraminers, and Pinot Neros are one better than the last. This Riesling 2012 can rekindle ardour. Delicate notes of citrus fruit and white pepper blend on a salty palate in a distinctive marine key, while an assertive, elegant progression leads leisurely to a finish that holds together well. Pinot Bianco 2012 is austere and yet to open on the nose, although the classical smoky notes of Valle Venosta still surface.

○ A. A. Val Venosta Riesling '12	♥♥♥	5
○ A. A. Val Venosta Pinot Bianco '12	♥♥	4
○ A. A. Val Venosta Sauvignon '12	♥♥	4
○ A. A. Val Venosta Gewürztraminer '12	♥♥	4
● A. A. Val Venosta Pinot Nero '10	♥	5
○ A. A. Val Venosta Pinot Bianco '07	♥♥♥	4
○ A. A. Val Venosta Riesling '11	♥♥♥	5
○ A. A. Val Venosta Riesling '10	♥♥♥	5
○ A. A. Val Venosta Riesling '09	♥♥♥	5
○ A. A. Val Venosta Riesling '08	♥♥♥	5
○ A. A. Val Venosta Riesling '07	♥♥♥	5
○ A. A. Val Venosta Riesling '06	♥♥♥	5
○ A. A. Val Venosta Riesling '05	♥♥♥	5
○ A. A. Val Venosta Riesling '00	♥♥♥	3

Cantina Girlan

LOC. CORNAIANO/GIRLAN
VIA SAN MARTINO, 24
39050 APPIANO/EPPAN [BZ]
TEL. 0471662403
www.girlan.it

CELLAR SALES
PRE-BOOKED VISITS
ANNUAL PRODUCTION 1,000,000 bottles
HECTARES UNDER VINE 230.00

Gerhard Kofler, oenologist, and Oscar Lorandi, commercial director, are a winning pair. Since they took over its management, Cantina Girlan in Cornaiano has become something else entirely, and much of it has been substantially overhauled in the last few years. The one-time Cinderella is now a princess. Their wines are classy and full of depth, reflecting their territory with a wonderful energy and, furthermore, sold at a very fair quality-price ratio. Just look of the cellar's top line Flora or its two famous Schiavas, Fass N° 9 and Gschleier. Girlan also looks after the historic cellar Lun in Egna, which has a couple of very interesting wines. The area of Cornaiano-Appiano is emerging as the wine country for Pinot Nero as well as being the classical zone of great whites. Pinot Nero Trattmann Riserva 2010 gains the Tre Bicchieri due to its complex nose with strawberries and brambles to the fore and delightful drinkability.

● A. A. Pinot Nero Trattmann Ris. '10	♥♥♥	5
○ A. A. Gewürztraminer Flora '12	♥♥	5
○ A. A. Pinot Bianco Plattenriegl '12	♥♥	3*
● A. A. Schiava Gschleier '11	♥♥	4
● A. A. Cabernet Sauvignon Merlot Ris. '10	♥♥	5
○ A. A. Chardonnay Flora '11	♥♥	5
○ A. A. Pinot Grigio '12	♥	3
● A. A. Pinot Nero Patricia '11	♥	4
○ A. A. Sauvignon Flora '12	♥	4
○ A. A. Sauvignon Indra '12	♥	4
● A. A. Schiava Faß N° 9 '12	♥	3
○ A. A. Gewürztraminer Flora '11	♥♥♥	5
○ A. A. Sauvignon Flora '10	♥♥♥	5
○ A. A. Sauvignon Sel. Flora '09	♥♥♥	4

Glögglhof - Franz Gojer

FRAZ. SANTA MADDALENA
VIA RIVELLONE, 1
39100 BOLZANO/BOZEN
TEL. 0471978775
www.gojer.it

CELLAR SALES
PRE-BOOKED VISITS
ANNUAL PRODUCTION 50,000 bottles
HECTARES UNDER VINE 7.40

Franz Gojer's cellar is a true fortress ensconced on the Santa Maddalena hill north of Bolzano. He runs the long-standing Glögglhof farm together with his son Florian, who is mainly involved in their new venture at Carnedo, where they have 2.7 hectares planted to sauvignon, kerner and pinot bianco, rounding off their range of traditional reds. Up until now, Glögglhof has been linked to Santa Maddalena and Lagrein, since here Franz is a true master and his wines are always among the best in their type. They love their Port and, for some years now, they have been producing a wine with similar features, Pipa, based on lagrein. Lagrein Riserva 2010 is a true oenological high for the Gojers. With an intense personality, where fruity spices mix with attractive toastiness, this earthy, compact wine is full of flavours but never cumbersome. Santa Maddalena wines include the solidly built, intensely mouthfilling Rondell 2012 and the freshly elegant Classico 2012.

● A. A. Lagrein Ris. '10	♜♜ 4
● A. A. Santa Maddalena Cl. Rondell '12	♜♜ 3*
● A. A. Santa Maddalena Cl. '12	♜♜ 2*
● A. A. Vernatsch Alte Reben '12	♜♜ 2*
○ A. A. Sauvignon Karneid '12	♜ 3
● A. A. Lagrein '09	♙♙ 3*
● A. A. Lagrein Furggl '11	♙♙ 3*
● A. A. Lagrein Ris. '09	♙♙ 4
● A. A. Santa Maddalena Cl. '11	♙♙ 2*
● A. A. Santa Maddalena Rondell '11	♙♙ 3*
● A. A. Santa Maddalena Rondell '09	♙♙ 2*
● A. A. Schiava Karneid '11	♙♙ 2*

Gottardi

LOC. MAZZON
VIA DEGLI ALPINI, 17
39044 EGNA/NEUMARKT [BZ]
TEL. 0471812773
www.gottardi-mazzon.com

ANNUAL PRODUCTION 45,000 bottles
HECTARES UNDER VINE 9.00

The Gottardi family relied on their vast experience in selling wine in Innsbruck to acquire, in 1986, 6.5 hectares of vineyard in the hills of Mazzon, at the heart of the classical area consecrated to the great Pinot Neros of Alto Adige. The first Pinot Nero Gottardi made its appearance in 1995 and was immediately crowned as one of the very best Blauburgunders of the region. Today, the very French style of the wine, its elegance and typicity still distinguish it from all the others in the area. Alexander Gottardi, working initially with his father and now alone, personally takes care of the vineyard and cellar, producing a very distinctive Gewürztraminer alongside two types of Pinot Nero. Gottardi's Pinot Nero Mazzon 2011 is certainly among Alto Adige's best. Fruity and varietal on the nose, with red berry fruit, cherries and strawberries, it is then fragrantly dry on the palate with soft tannins and an elegant profile. This approachable, delightful wine earns its first Tre Bicchieri.

● A. A. Pinot Nero Mazzon '11	♜♜♜ 5
● A. A. Pinot Nero '06	♙♙ 4
● A. A. Pinot Nero '05	♙♙ 5
● A. A. Pinot Nero Mazzon '10	♙♙ 5
● A. A. Pinot Nero Mazzon '09	♙♙ 5
● A. A. Pinot Nero Mazzon '07	♙♙ 5

Griesbauerhof
Georg Mumelter

VIA RENCIO, 66
39100 BOLZANO/BOZEN
TEL. 0471973090
www.griesbauerhof.it

CELLAR SALES
PRE-BOOKED VISITS
ANNUAL PRODUCTION 30,000 bottles
HECTARES UNDER VINE 3.80

The Griesbauerhof farm has been in the
Mumelter family since 1785 and is located
north of Bolzano at the foot of the Santa
Maddalena and the Santa Giustina hills. Set
close to the hotel belonging to the
Rentschnerhof family and managed by
Georg Mumelter's two sisters, the historical
farmhouse is surrounded by 3.5 hectares
of vineyard perfect for growing the native
schiava and lagrein varieties, as well as the
pinot grigio used to make a very
concentrated wine. Merlot grapes come
from the Spitz vineyard between the Adige
and Isarco rivers, and the leased vines at
San Maurizio on the other side of Bolzano.
Lagrein Riserva 2010 presents austerely
juicy fruit, with extremely elegant tannins
and a soft sapid freshness and long finish.
Lagrein 2011 is very typical, with garden
vegetables on the nose and soft velvety
tannins on the palate.

● A. A. Lagrein Ris. '10	♥♥ 5
● A. A. Lagrein '11	♥♥ 3
● A. A. Merlot Spitz '11	♥♥ 3
● A. A. Santa Maddalena Cl. '12	♥ 3
● A. A. Lagrein Ris. '09	♥♥♥ 5
● A. A. Lagrein Scuro Ris. '99	♥♥♥ 5
● A. A. Cabernet Sauvignon Ris. '05	♥♥ 3
● A. A. Lagrein '09	♥♥ 2
● A. A. Lagrein '07	♥♥ 2*
● A. A. Lagrein Ris. '08	♥♥ 4
● A. A. Merlot Spitz '09	♥♥ 4
● A. A. Santa Maddalena Cl. '11	♥♥ 3
● A. A. Santa Maddalena Cl. '10	♥♥ 2*

Gummerhof - Malojer

VIA WEGGESTEIN, 36
39100 BOLZANO/BOZEN
TEL. 0471972885
www.malojer.it

CELLAR SALES
PRE-BOOKED VISITS
ANNUAL PRODUCTION 100,000 bottles
HECTARES UNDER VINE 18.00

The first documented reference to the
Gummer estate dates back to 1480,
although the most interesting part of its
history is more recent and associated with
the Majoler family. In 1940, Rudolf Malojer
recommended winemaking and today the
whole family - Alfred, his son Urban and
wife Elisabeth - are engaged in the
estate's small production. Their specialities
are Gur zu Sand and Loamerhof Santa
Maddalena wines, and Lagrein, sourced
from vineyards ideal for these grapes,
although the whites are interesting too.
The entire range is very fairly priced.
Sauvignon Gur zu Sand 2012 is protected
by reductive vinification, expanding once
open to release a fragrant fresh fruit. An
elegant wine full of guts and energy, it
kicks off in the finish, leaving a trail of
spring flowers and flavours. The fruit,
although ripe, remains fresh and fragrant.

○ A. A. Sauvignon Gur zur Sand '12	♥♥ 3*
● A. A. Cabernet Ris. '10	♥♥ 4
● A. A. Cabernet-Lagrein	
Bautzanum Cuvée Ris. '10	♥♥ 4
● A. A. Lagrein Ris. '10	♥♥ 4
○ A. A. Pinot Bianco '12	♥♥ 3
○ A. A. Pinot Grigio Gur zu Sand '12	♥♥ 3
● A. A. Pinot Nero Gstrein '11	♥♥ 3
○ A. A. Chardonnay Justina '12	♥ 3
● A. A. Lagrein Gummerhof Gries '12	♥ 2
● A. A. Pinot Nero Ris. '10	♥ 4
● A. A. Santa Maddalena Cl. '12	♥ 2
● A. A. Lagrein Gries '09	♥♥♥ 2*
● A. A. Cabernet Ris. '09	♥♥ 4

Gumphof - Markus Prackwieser

LOC. NOVALE DI PRESULE, 8
39050 FIÈ ALLO SCILIAR/VÖLS AM SCHLERN [BZ]
TEL. 0471601190
www.gumphof.it

CELLAR SALES
PRE-BOOKED VISITS
ANNUAL PRODUCTION 45,000 bottles
HECTARES UNDER VINE 5.00

The first documented reference to the Gummer estate dates back to 1480, although the most interesting part of its history is more recent and associated with the Majoler family. In 1940, Rudolf Malojer recommended winemaking and today the whole family, Alfred, son Urban and wife Elisabeth, are engaged in the estate's small production. Their specialities are Schiava Santa Maddalenas Gur zu Sand and Loamerhof, and Lagrein, sourced from the wine country for these grapes. The whites are interesting too and the entire range is very fairly priced. Pinot Bianco Praesulis 2012 is jam-packed with grip, upholding a busy, richly caressing palate. The style aims at sweetness, helped along by hints of white-fleshed fruit. Pinot Bianco 2012 is a wine with a delightfully fresh rustic feel, brimming with Alpine grass and damson. Schiava 2012 has a pleasant tannic weave and fruit, part wild strawberry, part cherry.

○ A. A. Pinot Bianco '12	♟♟	3*
○ A. A. Pinot Bianco Praesulis '12	♟♟	3*
● A. A. Pinot Nero '11	♟	4
● A. A. Schiava '12	♟	2
○ A. A. Pinot Bianco Praesulis '06	♟♟♟	3*
○ A. A. Sauvignon Praesulis '09	♟♟♟	3
○ A. A. Sauvignon Praesulis '07	♟♟♟	3*
○ A. A. Sauvignon Praesulis '04	♟♟♟	3*
○ A. A. Pinot Bianco '11	♟♟	3*
○ A. A. Pinot Bianco Praesulis '11	♟♟	3*
○ A. A. Pinot Bianco Praesulis '10	♟♟	3*
○ A. A. Pinot Bianco Praesulis '09	♟♟	3*
● A. A. Pinot Nero Gumphof '09	♟♟	4
○ A. A. Sauvignon Praesulis '10	♟♟	3

Franz Haas

VIA VILLA, 6
39040 MONTAGNA/MONTAN [BZ]
TEL. 0471812280
www.franz-haas.it

CELLAR SALES
PRE-BOOKED VISITS
ANNUAL PRODUCTION 300,000 bottles
HECTARES UNDER VINE 50.00

Franz Haas is a formidable experimenter, always ready to reason, and open to new ideas and challenges. He seeks to improve farm management in new ways, whether by introducing organic methods or by trying less technical winemaking practices in the cellar. Luisa Manna has the task of telling this to the outside world. She is the commercial force and a great communicator, and has a network of relationships criss-crossing Italy built up over many years. Moscato Rosa 2011 is graceful and delicate with a complex nose of roses, coffee beans, zabaglione, cherries, candied orange and citron peel, to followed by generous extension on the palate. Schweizer 2010 is a linear dry wine, with great energy and flavour. Multi-faceted and classy, it shows impressive expansion.

● A. A. Moscato Rosa '11	♟♟♟	5
● A. A. Pinot Nero Schweizer '10	♟♟	6
○ A. A. Pinot Grigio '12	♟♟	3
● A. A. Pinot Nero '11	♟♟	5
○ Manna '11	♟♟	4
○ Moscato Giallo '12	♟	5
● A. A. Moscato Rosa Schweizer '00	♟♟♟	4
● A. A. Pinot Nero Schweizer '02	♟♟♟	5
● A. A. Pinot Nero Schweizer '01	♟♟♟	5
○ Manna '07	♟♟♟	4
○ Manna '05	♟♟♟	4
○ Manna '04	♟♟♟	4

Haderburg

FRAZ. BUCHOLZ
LOC. POCHI, 30
39040 SALORNO/SALURN [BZ]
TEL. 0471889097
www.haderburg.it

CELLAR SALES
PRE-BOOKED VISITS
ANNUAL PRODUCTION 100,000 bottles
HECTARES UNDER VINE 12.00
VITICULTURE METHOD Certified Biodynamic

Alois Ochsenreiter and his wife Christine are veterans in sparkling wine production, having converted their estate to specialize in the type in the 1970s. They were the first to make this choice and the Alto Adige wine world has always acknowledged their courage and farsightedness. About ten years ago, the family purchased the Obermairlhof holding in the Chiusa area of Valle Isarco, with three hectares of vineyards planted to the traditional white-skinned grape varieties of the area. The very elegant, multi-layered Metodo Classico Hausmannhof Brut Riserva 2004 is sapid in the mouth, unbending delicately to offer deep, complex flavours that span herbs, hazelnut and honey. The austere Pinot Nero Hausmannhof Riserva 2010 has a vibrant mineral-washed palate. Powerful yet delicate, it is a subtle wine full of energy and with a delightful dry finish.

● A. A. Pinot Nero Hausmannhof Ris. '10	TT 6
○ A. A. Spumante Hausmannhof Ris. '04	TT 5
○ A. A. Gewürztraminer '12	TT 3
● A. A. Merlot - Cabernet Sauvignon Erah '09	TT 5
● A. A. Pinot Nero Hausmannhof '11	TT 5
○ A. A. Spumante Pas Dosé '09	TT 5
○ A. A. Chardonnay '12	T 3
⊙ A. A. Haderburg Brut Rosé	T 5
○ A. A. Haderburg M. Cl. Brut.	T 5
○ A. A. Spumante Hausmannhof Ris. '97	YYY 6
○ A. A. Valle Isarco Sylvaner Obermairlhof '05	YYY 3*
○ A. A. Spumante Hausmannhof Ris. '02	YY 5
○ A. A. Spumante Hausmannhof Ris. '00	YY 5
○ A. A. Valle Isarco Sylvaner Obermairl '09	YY 3

Hoandlhof Manfred Nössing

FRAZ. KRANEBIH
VIA DEI VIGNETI, 66
39042 BRESSANONE/BRIXEN [BZ]
TEL. 0472832672
www.manni-noessing.com

PRE-BOOKED VISITS
ANNUAL PRODUCTION 17,000 bottles
HECTARES UNDER VINE 4.30

The thread linking vineyard to cellar, and grape to bottle, often involves precise, conscious fusion work that Manfred Nössing, with his great talent, carries out without hesitation. The result is wonderfully clear, focused whites, showing razor-sharp precision, among the best of the Isarco Valley. The four hectares under vine are set on loose soil in positions where fluctuations in temperature are the prerequisite to conferring minerality and retaining aromas in the grapes. The challenge today is to produce wines that are less alcoholic and more essential in style without losing any of their complexity. With its fresh fragrance and grip, Sylvaner 2012 offers a direct link to its grape and is a supple, dry wine of pure elegance. Veltliner 2012 reveals a fruity tanginess and a rich razor-sharp mouth with well-sustained grip and an exceedingly stylish finish. An assertive wine, it offers a totally focused, linear progression.

○ A. A. Valle Isarco Sylvaner '12	TT 3*
○ A. A. Valle Isarco Veltliner '12	TT 3*
○ A. A. Valle Isarco Kerner '12	TT 3
○ A. A. Valle Isarco Müller Thurgau Sass Rigais '12	TT 3
○ A. A. Valle Isarco Kerner '10	YYY 3*
○ A. A. Valle Isarco Kerner '06	YYY 3*
○ A. A. Valle Isarco Kerner '05	YYY 3*
○ A. A. Valle Isarco Kerner '03	YYY 3*
○ A. A. Valle Isarco Kerner '02	YYY 3
○ A. A. Valle Isarco Sylvaner '08	YYY 3*
○ A. A. Valle Isarco Sylvaner '04	YYY 3*
○ A. A. Valle Isarco Veltliner '09	YYY 3*
○ A. A. Valle Isarco Veltliner '07	YYY 3

Hof Gandberg
Rudolf Niedermayr

S.DA CASTEL PALÚ, 1
39057 APPIANO/EPPAN [BZ]
TEL. 0471664152

Kettmeir

VIA DELLE CANTINE, 4
39052 CALDARO/KALTERN [BZ]
TEL. 0471963135
www.kettmeir.com

CELLAR SALES
PRE-BOOKED VISITS
ANNUAL PRODUCTION 10,000 bottles
HECTARES UNDER VINE 1.50
VITICULTURE METHOD Certified Organic

CELLAR SALES
PRE-BOOKED VISITS
ACCOMMODATION
ANNUAL PRODUCTION 330,000 bottles
HECTARES UNDER VINE 36.00

The lovely winery is managed with organic methods and has been tended for generations by the Niedermayer family. There are only three and a half hectares of estate and part is covered by orchards. Just over one hectare, in the higher part, is planted to vine, facing south east on basic soils, ideal for producing the best Pinot Biancos. There are five labels in all, from typical varieties that include bronner, nova, sonnrain and berrl, the latter a red grape. Mitterberg 2011 reached the national finals. Delicious wood resin aromas mix with delicate notes of spices and just-sliced melon, followed by a palate in keeping, decidedly austere and full of flavour, while finishing on a slightly bitter note. Pinot Bianco Mitterberg 2012 is one step down, with damson, apples and pears on the nose and a tangy mouth with a lingering, crunchy-fresh finish.

Founded in 1919 by Giuseppe Kettmeir, this old Alto Adige estate has played a leading role among the region's wineries and seen production rise to impressive numbers. In 1986, the winery was taken over by the Santa Margherita Group, which proceeded to restyle its image while still recognizing the brand's historic value. Consequently, production was reduced with a view to building a high-quality wine project, in which an important role was given to sparklers, based on the intuition that the great acidity of Alto Adige whites will make a crucial difference. The complex, elegant Müller Thurgau Athesis 2012 expresses a modern, austere language, changing key suddenly from fruitiness to a peaty note. The Pinot Neroinot Nero Maso Reiner 2010 conveys a thoroughly relaxed freshness. Fragrant fruit with strawberries to the fore is joined by a lovely acidity and a mature, silky tannic weave.

○ Nova Mitterberg '11	♥♥ 4
○ Bronner Mitterberg '12	♥♥ 3
○ Pinot Bianco Mitterberg '12	♥♥ 4
○ Sonnrain '12	♥ 5
○ A. A. Pinot Bianco '11	♀♀ 3
○ A. A. Pinot Bianco '10	♀♀ 3*
● Beerl '10	♀♀ 5
○ Bronner '11	♀♀ 3
○ Sonnrain '11	♀♀ 3

○ A. A. Müller Thurgau Athesis '12	♥♥ 3*
● A. A. Moscato Rosa Athesis '10	♥♥ 5
○ A. A. Pinot Bianco '12	♥♥ 2*
● A. A. Pinot Nero Maso Reiner '10	♥♥ 3
○ A. A. Pinot Bianco Athesis '12	♥ 3
⊙ A. A. Spumante Brut Athesis M. Cl. '10	♥ 3
⊙ A. A. Spumante Rosé Brut Athesis	♥ 3
○ A. A. Chardonnay '11	♀♀ 2*
○ A. A. Chardonnay Maso Reiner '10	♀♀ 3
○ A. A. Chardonnay Reinerhof '08	♀♀ 3
● A. A. Moscato Rosa Athesis '09	♀♀ 5
○ A. A. Müller Thurgau Athesis '11	♀♀ 3
○ A. A. Müller Thurgau Athesis '10	♀♀ 3
○ A. A. Pinot Bianco '09	♀♀ 2*

Tenuta Klosterhof
Oskar Andergassen

Loc. Clavenz, 40
39052 Caldaro/Kaltern [BZ]
Tel. 0471961046
www.garni-klosterhof.com

CELLAR SALES
PRE-BOOKED VISITS
ACCOMMODATION AND RESTAURANT SERVICE
ANNUAL PRODUCTION 20,000 bottles
HECTARES UNDER VINE 3.50

Oskar Andergassen and his son Hannes look after all the phases from vineyard to cellar themselves. The vineyards extend for some three and a half hectares across various zones, each right for a particular grape. The south-east facing Trifall, behind the winery in the direction of Pianizza di Sopra, contains pinot bianco, moscato giallo and merlot, Plantaditsch, nearer to the Lake of Caldaro, is the realm of the schiava grape, while Panigl, south of Caldaro and also facing south-east, is planted with pinot nero. In the cellar, wood is used for the red grape varieties, while white wines age in stainless steel to ensure that all the freshness and characteristics of the grape are kept intact. There were two wines in the finals. Lago di Caldaro Plantaditsch R 2012 has lovely fruity aromas and a rich, harmonious mouth; it drinks well and has character. Pinot Nero Panigl 2010 has oaky aromas with pleasant tobacco and red berry notes. A powerfully compact and firm palate offers a certain pleasant acidity.

● A. A. Lago di Caldaro Cl. Sup. Plantaditsch R '12	♈♈ 3*	
● A. A. Pinot Nero Panigl '10	♈♈ 5	
● A. A. Lago di Caldaro Cl. Sup. Plantaditsch '12	♈♈ 2*	
○ Oskar Gewürztraminer Passito Mitterberg '12	♈♈ 4	
● A. A. Merlot Ris. '10	♈ 4	
○ A. A. Pinot Bianco Trifall '12	♈ 3	
● A. A. Lago di Caldaro Cl. Sup. Plantaditsch '10	♈♈ 2*	
○ A. A. Pinot Bianco Trifall '11	♈♈ 3	
○ A. A. Pinot Bianco Trifall '10	♈♈ 3	
● A. A. Pinot Nero Panigl '09	♈♈ 5	

Köfererhof
Günther Kershbaumer

Fraz. Novacella
via Pusteria, 3
39040 Varna/Vahrn [BZ]
Tel. 3474778009
www.koefererhof.it

CELLAR SALES
PRE-BOOKED VISITS
RESTAURANT SERVICE
ANNUAL PRODUCTION 80,000 bottles
HECTARES UNDER VINE 10.00

Five hectares set high in the Upper Isarco Valley are at the heart of a particularly impressive long-term quality-based project. Günther Kershbaumer is universally considered as an outstanding producer of sapid, mineral-rich whites, the offspring of a territory marked by breathtaking differences in temperature. The style of the wines is sharp, clearly expressed and full of great depth. Günther makes wines that are not easy to understand when young but, after a few months, reveal a character that few can rival in Italy. The Pinot Grigio remains extraordinary. In the 2012 vintage, the nose is rather stiff and the familiar Alpine grasses struggle to emerge but the mouth brims with acid grip and rocky tanginess. The Riesling 2012 matches it with minerals and benzene, finishing as sharp as the wind.

○ A. A. Valle Isarco Pinot Grigio '12	♈♈♈ 3*
○ A. A. Valle Isarco Sylvaner '12	♈♈ 3*
○ A. A. Valle Isarco Kerner '12	♈♈ 3
○ A. A. Valle Isarco Gewürztraminer '12	♈ 4
○ A. A. Valle Isarco Müller Thurgau '12	♈ 3
○ A. A. Valle Isarco Pinot Grigio '11	♈♈♈ 3*
○ A. A. Valle Isarco Pinot Grigio '09	♈♈♈ 3*
○ A. A. Valle Isarco Riesling '10	♈♈♈ 4
○ A. A. Valle Isarco Sylvaner R '09	♈♈♈ 4
○ A. A. Valle Isarco Sylvaner R '08	♈♈♈ 4
○ A. A. Valle Isarco Sylvaner R '07	♈♈♈ 4
○ A. A. Valle Isarco Sylvaner R '06	♈♈♈ 4

Tenuta Kornell

FRAZ. SETTEQUERCE
VIA BOLZANO, 23
39018 TERLANO/TERLAN [BZ]
TEL. 0471917507
www.kornell.it

CELLAR SALES
PRE-BOOKED VISITS
ANNUAL PRODUCTION 100,000 bottles
HECTARES UNDER VINE 15.00

Tenuta Kornell vaunts a long tradition, first documented as early as 1210. The Brigl family also has a long history as winemakers. They have been here since 1927 and began bottling wines under the estate name in 2001. Florian Brigi, the current owner, is extremely passionate about his work and his 15 hectares under vine - 12 estate-owned - with their loose clay, sand and porphyry soils and a warm site climate that protects them from temperature extremes. These wines are generous, precise and reliable across the range. Merlot Staves Riserva 2010 is an open wine that lingers and changes register, acquiring complexity to add to its array of fruity spiciness. The fragrantly dry, lip-smacking palate unbends over fresh fruit, with cherry to the fore, also reflected in the finish. Marith 2011's strength lies in a well-paced palate full of juicy acidity.

● A. A. Merlot Staves Ris. '10	♟♟ 5
● A. A. Pinot Nero Marith '11	♟♟ 6
● A. A. Lagrein Staves Ris. '10	♟♟ 3
○ A. A. Sauvignon Oberberg '11	♟♟ 3
● Zeder '11	♟♟ 3
○ A. A. Pinot Bianco Eich '12	♟ 3
○ A. A. Sauvignon Cosmas '12	♟ 3
● A. A. Lagrein Greif '05	♟♟ 3*
○ A. A. Pinot Bianco Pinus '09	♟♟ 3
○ A. A. Sauvignon Cosmas '10	♟♟ 3
○ A. A. Sauvignon Cosmas '09	♟♟ 3
○ A. A. Sauvignon Cosmas '08	♟♟ 3
○ A. A. Sauvignon Cosmas '07	♟♟ 3*
● A. A. Zeder '05	♟♟ 3*

Tenuta Kränzlhof
Graf Franz Pfeil

VIA PALADE, 1
39010 CERMES/TSCHERMS [BZ]
TEL. 0473564549
www.labyrinth.bz

CELLAR SALES
PRE-BOOKED VISITS
ANNUAL PRODUCTION 35,000 bottles
HECTARES UNDER VINE 6.00

At Kränzlhof, wine is just one element of many in a project to achieve quality. The result of this complex process involves the atmosphere and the ideology of the people working here with their multiple human aspects. At the basis of it all is their capacity to share a tiny utopia where their true direction is sought through harmony between man and nature. The place that reflects this best is probably the garden. Here, the labyrinths, half fun and half art, symbolize the innate knowledge that Franz Pfeil prefers not to reveal, convinced as he is that all knowledge is at hand, as readily accessible as in an open book. Meranese Baslan 2012 has a wealth of woodland aromas and fruits. Complex and austere, it is brimming with a dry earthy minerality. The elegant Pinot Bianco 2012 is close-focused and razor-sharp in the mouth, with fine hints of damson and grapefruit.

● A. A. Meranese Baslan '12	♟♟ 3*
○ Pinot Bianco Mitterberg '12	♟♟ 4
○ Mitterberg Sauvignon '12	♟ 5
● Pinot Nero '10	♟ 6
● A. A. Cabernet Lagrein Sagittarius '09	♟♟ 5
● A. A. Meranese Hügel Baslan Ris. '05	♟♟ 3*
○ A. A. Pinot Bianco Helios '08	♟♟ 4
○ Farnatzer '00	♟♟ 8
○ Pinot Bianco Helios '10	♟♟ 4
○ Pinot Bianco Helios '07	♟♟ 4
● Sagittarius '05	♟♟ 5
● Schiava Baslan '10	♟♟ 3*
● Schiava Baslan '09	♟♟ 3*
● Schiava Baslan '07	♟♟ 3*

★Kuenhof - Peter Pliger

Loc. Mara, 110
39042 Bressanone/Brixen [BZ]
Tel. 0472850546
pliger.kuenhof@rolmail.net

CELLAR SALES
PRE-BOOKED VISITS
ANNUAL PRODUCTION 27,000 bottles
HECTARES UNDER VINE 6.00

The vineyards owned by Peter Pliger, who runs his winery with his wife Brigitte, are at 800 metres plus above sea level, delicately balanced on steep slopes and exposed to the much sought-after differences in temperature that impart aromas, character and acidity. Peter lends a hand to strengthen this purity, working on both complexity and expression, to deliver his truly genuine wines. Clean, pure and bursting with personality, they play on the exchange between the deep aromas of the territory and the many aspects that allow them to express themselves more intensely. Clear understanding of this unique territory and infallible instinct in the cellar combine towards achieving this outcome. Flint and hedgerow are Kaiton 2012's two faces, with minerality offsetting sweet, perfectly ripe, austere fruit, for a razor-sharp, elegant yet fragrant wine. Veltliner 2012 is generous, full, overwhelming, and expansive. Its aromas vary in scope and depth, from wax, glycerine and damson to minerals, earth and iodine.

Alois Lageder

Loc. Tôr Löwengang
v.lo dei Conti, 9
39040 Magrè/Margreid [BZ]
Tel. 0471809500
www.aloislageder.eu

CELLAR SALES
PRE-BOOKED VISITS
RESTAURANT SERVICE
ANNUAL PRODUCTION 1,500,000 bottles
HECTARES UNDER VINE 50.00
VITICULTURE METHOD Certified Biodynamic

This estate is divided into two parts: Alois Lageder vinifies fruit from grapes from growers selected and overseen by the winery; and Tenutae Lageder ferments grapes from the estate's own 50 hectares of vineyards, managed with biodynamic methods since the 1990s. The latter yield the products that have earned this estate its reputation: Löwengang, Krafuss and Cor Römigberg. With an annual production just shy of 300,000 bottles, these wines are elegant and innovative yet terroir true. There were three wines in the finals. Lago di Caldaro 2012, with intense peppery and berry notes on the nose, has a well-balanced harmonious palate with a tiny dip in the finish. Pinot Grigio Porer 2012 has overtones of fruit skins and russet pear, and the mouth is richly compact while still in crisp harmony.

○ A. A. Valle Isarco Riesling Kaiton '12	♔♔♔ 4*
○ A. A. Valle Isarco Veltliner '12	♔♔ 3*
○ A. A. Valle Isarco Sylvaner '12	♔♔ 3
○ A. A. Valle Isarco Gewürztraminer '12	♔ 3
○ A. A. Valle Isarco Riesling Kaiton '11	♔♔♔ 4*
○ A. A. Valle Isarco Riesling Kaiton '10	♔♔♔ 4
○ A. A. Valle Isarco Riesling Kaiton '07	♔♔♔ 3*
○ A. A. Valle Isarco Riesling Kaiton '05	♔♔♔ 3*
○ A. A. Valle Isarco Sylvaner '08	♔♔♔ 3
○ A. A. Valle Isarco Sylvaner '06	♔♔♔ 3*
○ A. A. Valle Isarco Sylvaner '03	♔♔♔ 3*
○ A. A. Valle Isarco Sylvaner '02	♔♔♔ 3*
○ A. A. Valle Isarco Sylvaner V.T. '04	♔♔♔ 3*
○ A. A. Valle Isarco Veltliner '09	♔♔♔ 3*

○ A. A. Chardonnay Löwengang '10	♔♔ 6
● A. A. Lago di Caldaro Cl. Romigberg '12	♔♔ 3*
● A. A. Pinot Grigio Porer '12	♔♔ 4
● A. A. Cabernet Löwengang '09	♔ 7
● A. A. Lagrein Lindenburg '09	♔ 5
● A. A. Cabernet Sauvignon Cor Römigberg '08	♔♔♔ 7
● A. A. Cabernet Löwengang '08	♔♔ 6
○ A. A. Chardonnay Löwengang '08	♔♔ 6
○ A. A. Chardonnay Löwengang '07	♔♔ 6
● A. A. Lagrein Lindenburg '07	♔♔ 6
○ A. A. Pinot Bianco Haberle '09	♔♔ 4
○ A. A. Pinot Grigio Porer '11	♔♔ 4
● A. A. Pinot Nero Krafuss '09	♔♔ 6
● A. A. Pinot Nero Krafuss '08	♔♔ 6

Laimburg

LOC. LAIMBURG, 6
39040 VADENA/PFATTEN [BZ]
TEL. 0471969700
www.laimburg.bz.it

CELLAR SALES
PRE-BOOKED VISITS
ANNUAL PRODUCTION 160,000 bottles
HECTARES UNDER VINE 42.00

The Laimburg estate is part of the Bolzano provincial authority's agricultural experimental centre, founded in the 1970s to carry out research to promote innovation in agriculture. Wines here are made from grapes sourced from approximately 50 hectares of vineyards, divided into numerous plots scattered across the province of Bolzano, often in prime positions. The range features two separate lines: the current-vintage Vini del Podere and the more ambitious Selezione Maniero with wines generally aged in oak. Riesling 2012 embraces a land of mouthfilling yellow-fleshed fruit. It unbends in the mouth, threaded by notes of cereal grains and dried grass, leading to a savoury finish. With its dense tannic weave, Cabernet Sass Roà 2010 is fresh and razor-sharp. On first impact, Ölleiten 2012 imparts an acid thrust, it then veers towards a typical country soul and finishes austerely.

○ A. A. Riesling '12	🏆 3*
● A. A. Cabernet Sauvignon Sass Roà Ris. '10	🏆 5
● A. A. Lago di Caldaro Scelto Olleiten '12	🏆 3
● A. A. Lagrein Barbagòl Ris. '10	🏆 5
● A. A. Pinot Nero Ris. '11	🏆 3
○ A. A. Pinot Bianco '12	🏆 3
○ A. A. Pinot Grigio '12	🏆 3
● A. A. Lagrein Scuro Barbagòl Ris. '00	🏆🏆🏆 5
● A. A. Lago di Caldaro Scelto Olleitenhof '11	🏆🏆 3
● A. A. Lagrein Barbagòl Ris. '09	🏆🏆 5
● A. A. Lagrein Barbagòl Ris. '07	🏆🏆 5
○ A. A. Pinot Bianco '11	🏆🏆 3*
○ A. A. Riesling '10	🏆🏆 3

Loacker Schwarhof

LOC. SANTA JIUSTINA, 3
39100 BOLZANO/BOZEN
TEL. 0471365125
www.loacker.net

CELLAR SALES
PRE-BOOKED VISITS
ANNUAL PRODUCTION 60,000 bottles
HECTARES UNDER VINE 7.00
VITICULTURE METHOD Certified Biodynamic

Hayo and Franz Josef Loacker's work is a strong and courageous way of life, engaging them in a special relationship with nature. Biodynamic techniques and homeopathic treatments are employed in the vineyards and an all-natural philosophy is followed in the cellar. The setting is the 14th century Schwarhof estate at Santa Maddalena, bought by their father Rainer in 1978, with a history based on the long-term and an acceptance of associated risks. Today the estate has reached maturity, as testified by these extremely interesting, expressive and original wines. The intriguing Cabernet Sauvignon Lagrein 2010, with mineral-gamey tones and full of well-paced energy, has very elegant tannins and a savoury finish. The chalky, refined Merlot 2011 has classic Bordeaux overtones. Its style proves itself in the mouth. Lagrein 2011 has oodles of fruit, spices and cocoa on a dense, tangy palate.

● Cabernet Sauvignon - Lagrein '10	🏆🏆 4
● Merlot '11	🏆🏆 4
● A. A. Lagrein Ris. '10	🏆🏆 4
○ Gewürztraminer '12	🏆🏆 4
● Lagrein '11	🏆🏆 4
● A. A. Santa Maddalena Cl. '12	🏆 3
○ Chardonnay '11	🏆 4
○ Sauvignon '12	🏆 4
● A. A. Merlot Ywain '04	🏆🏆🏆 4*
● A. A. Lagrein Gran Lareyn Ris. '10	🏆🏆 4
● A. A. Santa Maddalena Morit '11	🏆🏆 3
○ Gewürztraminer Atagis '11	🏆🏆 5
● Kastlet '09	🏆🏆 5
● Lagrein Gran Lareyn '10	🏆🏆 5

Manincor

LOC. SAN GIUSEPPE AL LAGO, 4
39052 CALDARO/KALTERN [BZ]
TEL. 0471960230
www.manincor.com

CELLAR SALES
PRE-BOOKED VISITS
ANNUAL PRODUCTION 300,000 bottles
HECTARES UNDER VINE 50.00
VITICULTURE METHOD Certified Biodynamic

In the 1990s, Michael Goëss-Enzenberg began an ambitious long-term venture to further develop his long-established vineyards, starting from a magnificent collection in great wine areas. Today Manincor ferments its own grapes in the cellar inaugurated in 2004 and is gaining renown as one of the most interesting wineries in all Alto Adige. All the vineyards are conducted using biodynamic methods, without taking the approach to extremes and with the simple aim of producing good quality wines. Since 2008, Manincor has been managed by the charismatic Helmut Zozin, a leading figure in the wine world and a man with a big personality. The expressive and unusual Eichhorn 2012 is at once exotic, with passion fruit, mango and melon, and Mediterranean, with citron peel, herbs and wild thyme, and a touch of peat to give it depth. Elegantly expansive on the palate, it finishes dry and full of flavour. Réserve della Contessa 2012 lingers over yellow flowers and springs assertively on the palate.

○ A. A. Terlano Pinot Bianco Eichhorn '12	♛♛♛ 5
○ A. A. Terlano Réserve della Contessa '12	♛♛ 3*
○ Le Petit '11	♛♛ 5
● A. A. Pinot Nero Mason di Mason '11	♛♛ 7
○ A. A. Terlano Chardonnay Sophie '12	♛♛ 5
○ A. A. Moscato Giallo '12	♛ 3
● A. A. Pinot Nero Mason '11	♛ 5
○ A. A. Terlano Sauvignon Tannenberg '12	♛ 5
● A. A. Cabernet Sauvignon Cassiano '97	♛♛♛ 5
○ A. A. Terlano Pinot Bianco Eichhorn '10	♛♛♛ 4
○ A. A. Terlano Pinot Bianco Eichhorn '09	♛♛♛ 4
○ A. A. Terlano Sauvignon '08	♛♛♛ 4
○ A. A. Terlano Chardonnay Sophie '11	♛♛ 4
○ A. A. Terlano Réserve della Contessa '11	♛♛ 3*

K. Martini & Sohn

LOC. CORNAIANO
VIA LAMM, 28
39057 APPIANO/EPPAN [BZ]
TEL. 0471663156
www.martini-sohn.it

CELLAR SALES
PRE-BOOKED VISITS
ANNUAL PRODUCTION 230,000 bottles
HECTARES UNDER VINE 28.00

Founded in 1979 by Karl Martini and his son Gabriel, the operation today also employs his grandchildren Maren and Lukas. The latter has contributed to defining the style of the wines in the cellar and brought new energy to a business priding itself on its family-management approach and classical, reliable wines. The grapes vinified by the Martinis are sourced from selected growers supplemented by a small amount from the estate's own vineyards. The leading product lines from this estate are Palladium and Maturum. Pinot Bianco Palladium 2012 offers ripe fruit and the sweet flesh of late damson, then blossom, broom and acacia, and lasltly yellow-fleshed fruit, overlaid by peach. On the palate, it has a linear, fresh expansion. Lago di Caldaro Felton 2012 is typical and direct, with a country fragrance. Chardonnay Maturum 2011 lingers over citrus fruit and flowers, then the acidity kicks off, elegant, tidy and direct.

○ A. A. Pinot Bianco Palladium '12	♛♛ 3*
○ A. A. Chardonnay Maturum '11	♛♛ 4
○ A. A. Chardonnay Palladium '12	♛♛ 3
● A. A. Lago di Caldaro Cl. Felton '12	♛♛ 2*
● A. A. Lagrein Rueslhof '12	♛♛ 3
● A. A. Pinot Nero Gurnzan '11	♛♛ 3
○ A. A. Kerner '12	♛ 2
○ A. A. Sauvignon '12	♛ 3
○ A. A. Sauvignon Palladium '12	♛ 3
● A. A. Schiava Palladium '12	♛ 2
● A. A. Lagrein Maturum '09	♛♛ 5
● A. A. Lagrein Scuro Maturum '07	♛♛ 4
● A. A. Sauvignon Palladium '11	♛♛ 4

Cantina Meran Burggräfler

VIA CANTINA, 9
39020 MARLENGO/MARLING [BZ]
TEL. 0473447137
www.cantinamerano.it

CELLAR SALES
PRE-BOOKED VISITS
ANNUAL PRODUCTION 1,000,000 bottles
HECTARES UNDER VINE 250.00

This major co-operative operation came from the merger between Cantina Produttori Burggräfler and Cantina di Merano, giving life to a new brand and leading to the reorganization of the winery's entire range. Today, the joint operation is run by chairman Kaspar Platzer, manager Zeno Staffler and the long-serving cellarmaster Stefan Kapfinger, who has at his disposal an extraordinary array of vineyards extending from Lana to Val Venosta. An army of 380 grower members lovingly tends this mosaic of territories and identities. In an outstanding range, there is a Tre Bicchieri for the Pinot Bianco Sonnenberg 2012. It has fresh, ripe aromas of pear and damson, with hints of almond, and a wide, firm mouth leading to a lengthy finish. Meranese 2012 made the finals, with its crisp, captivating aromas reflected on the palate.

○ A. A. Val Venosta Pinot Bianco Sonnenberg '12	▼▼▼ 3*
● A. A. Meranese Schickenburg Graf von Meran '12	▼▼ 3*
○ A. A. Pinot Bianco Graf Von Meran '12	▼▼ 3
○ A. A. Pinot Grigio Festival '12	▼▼ 2*
● A. A. Pinot Nero Zeno '11	▼▼ 5
○ A. A. Riesling Graf von Meran '12	▼▼ 4
● A. A. Merlot Freiherr '11	▼ 5
○ A. A. Sauvignon Graf Von Meran '12	▼ 4
● A. A. Meranese Schickenburg Graf von Meran '11	♀♀♀ 3*
○ A. A. Moscato Giallo Passito Sissi Graf von Meran '08	♀♀♀ 5
○ A. A. Val Venosta Pinot Bianco Sonnenberg '08	♀♀♀ 2*

★Cantina Convento Muri-Gries

FRAZ. GRIES
P.ZZA GRIES, 21
39100 BOLZANO/BOZEN
TEL. 0471282287
www.muri-gries.com

CELLAR SALES
PRE-BOOKED VISITS
ANNUAL PRODUCTION 650,000 bottles
HECTARES UNDER VINE 55.00

Muri Gries was founded in 1845, when the Benedictine monks, expelled from the Muri monastery in Switzerland, received as a donation in 1027, took up residence in the monastery in Gries. In the early 20th century, monks here began making unbottled wine that immediately earned an excellent reputation. The estate is located on the Greis floodplain, in the heart of great lagrein terroir. Not surprisingly, the cellar's finest product is Lagrein, crafted since the 1980s by Christian Werth, an exceptionally enthusiastic and talented yet modest cellarmaster. The cellar's output has now achieved excellent overall reliability. Lagrein Abtei Muri 2010's quality and ageing potential are rooted in an unmatched experience. It is spicy, austere and has the mineral tones of pencil lead. On the palate, the fruit is juicy and generous, unbending with dense tannins. The elegant Pinot Grigio 2012 is spicy, with original hints of tangerine peel.

● A. A. Lagrein Abtei Muri Ris. '10	▼▼▼ 5
○ A. A. Pinot Grigio '12	▼▼ 2*
○ A. A. Bianco Abtei Muri '11	▼▼ 3
● A. A. Schiava Grigia '12	▼▼ 2*
○ A. A. Terlano Pinot Bianco '12	▼▼ 3
● A. A. Lagrein '12	▼ 3
⊙ A. A. Lagrein Rosato '12	▼ 2
● A. A. Moscato Rosa v.t. Abtei Muri '11	▼ 5
● A. A. Pinot Nero '12	▼ 3
● A. A. Pinot Nero Abtei Muri Ris. '10	♀♀♀ 5
● A. A. Lagrein Abtei Ris. '07	♀♀♀ 5
● A. A. Lagrein Abtei Ris. '06	♀♀♀ 4
● A. A. Lagrein Abtei Ris. '05	♀♀♀ 4

Cantina Nals Margreid

VIA HEILIGENBERG, 2
39010 NALLES/NALS [BZ]
TEL. 0471678626
www.kellerei.it

CELLAR SALES
PRE-BOOKED VISITS
ANNUAL PRODUCTION 950,000 bottles
HECTARES UNDER VINE 150.00

This exciting co-operative cellar came out of the union, in 1985, between two well-established operations, Cantine Nalles, founded in 1932, and Magrè-Niclara, founded in 1954. The result is a group of 140 members who cultivate a total of 150 hectares. Nals Margreid is still undergoing impressive changes with energy radiating from the new cellar designed by architect Markus Scherer. Every year, the winery style is acquiring better definition and territorial character, thanks to the skill and painstaking efforts of cellarmaster Harald Schraffl. No shortcuts here: progress is based on hard work and respect. Pinot Bianco Sirmian 2012 has a smoky finesse, and flowers follow white-fleshed fruit. It runs ahead and expands in the mouth, and then apples appear with a surprising mass of plum blossom. A lovely bitter touch, both delicate and original, hints at Alpine grasses. For these reasons, it is the white of the year. The dryly mineral Schiava Galea 2012 has strength and ripe tannins.

Josef Niedermayr

LOC. CORNAIANO/GIRLAN
VIA CASA DI GESÙ, 15/23
39057 APPIANO/EPPAN [BZ]
TEL. 0471662451
www.niedermayr.it

CELLAR SALES
PRE-BOOKED VISITS
ANNUAL PRODUCTION 250,000 bottles
HECTARES UNDER VINE 35.00

Josef Niedermayr has inherited a family tradition that dates back to the 19th century. Over the years, he has changed the nature of his winery, beginning in 2002 with work on his cellar and then reducing production, only making wine from grapes sourced in the estate's own vineyards - Tenuta Hof zu Pramol, Tenuta Ascherhof, Vigneto Naun, Vigneto Doss and Kaiserau - a total of 30 hectares spread across different territories and positions. His new ethos focuses on quality and a truly family-based approach to his work. The subtle, elegant Pinot Bianco 2012 is stylish in all phases. Herbs and celery leaves offer their vegetable aromas, while the fruity tones are given by white melon and damson. The mouth has a lively acidity, followed by a dry, full-flavoured finish. Classical in style, this wine is traditional in the very best sense.

○ A. A. Pinot Bianco Sirmian '12	♆♆♆ 4*
○ A. A. Moscato Giallo Passito Baronesse '10	♆♆ 6
○ A. A. Pinot Grigio Punggl '12	♆♆ 4
● A. A. Schiava Galea '12	♆♆ 3*
○ A. A. Chardonnay Magré '12	♆♆ 4
○ A. A. Sauvignon Mantele '12	♆♆ 4
○ A. A. Chardonnay Baron Salvadori '11	♆ 5
● A. A. Lagrein Gries Ris. '10	♆ 4
○ A. A. Pinot Bianco Penon '12	♆ 3
○ A. A. Pinot Bianco Sirmian '11	♆♆♆ 3*
○ A. A. Pinot Bianco Sirmian '10	♆♆♆ 3*
○ A. A. Pinot Bianco Sirmian '09	♆♆♆ 3*
○ A. A. Pinot Bianco Sirmian '08	♆♆♆ 3*
○ A. A. Pinot Bianco Sirmian '07	♆♆♆ 3*

○ A. A. Terlano Hof zu Pramol '11	♆♆ 3
○ A. A. Terlano Pinot Bianco '12	♆♆ 2*
⊙ A. A. Lagrein Gries Rosé '12	♆ 2
● A. A. Pinot Nero Precios '10	♆ 4
○ A. A. Aureus '99	♆♆♆ 6
○ A. A. Aureus '00	♆♆♆ 6
○ A. A. Aureus '95	♆♆♆ 6
○ A. A. Aureus '07	♆♆ 6
○ A. A. Aureus '06	♆♆ 6
● A. A. Lagrein Gries Ris. '10	♆♆ 5
● A. A. Lagrein Gries Ris. '09	♆♆ 5
● A. A. Lagrein Gries Ris. '08	♆♆ 5
○ A. A. Sauvignon Naun '10	♆♆ 3
● A. A. Schiava Ascherhof '11	♆♆ 2*

Ignaz Niedrist

LOC. CORNAIANO/GIRLAN
VIA RONCO, 5
39050 APPIANO/EPPAN [BZ]
TEL. 0471664494
ignazniedrist@rolmail.net

CELLAR SALES
PRE-BOOKED VISITS
ANNUAL PRODUCTION 40,000 bottles
HECTARES UNDER VINE 8.50

In a class of his own, Ignaz Niedrist is a genuine grower and countryman who can put into play his technical and intellectual know-how as an outstanding producer of classical zone Alto Adige wines. The vineyards are mostly at Cornaiano, between 400 and 500 metres above sea level, with several plots in other areas, some being further north in Greis, others to the south in Caldaro. Every year, he crafts ever purer and more compelling wines, refined in their language and expressed with a mature awareness of territory. Pinot Bianco 2012 is essential, with rigorous precision. Opening slowly and showing that less is more, it reveals an austerity that hides a kaleidoscope of fruit, with apple and pear, grapefruit peel, and a salty note finish. Initially conveying reductive sensations, Berg 2012 is superbly elegant and tidy. Alpine grass and aniseed mix with earthy tones and the finish is tangy. Pinot Nero 2011 is taut and dry, with dense, ripe tannins.

○ A. A. Terlano Pinot Bianco '12	♟♟♟ 3*
● A. A. Pinot Nero '11	♟♟ 5
○ A. A. Riesling Berg '12	♟♟ 4
● A. A. Lagrein Berger Gei '11	♟♟ 4
○ A. A. Terlano Sauvignon '12	♟♟ 4
○ Trias '12	♟♟ 4
○ A. A. Riesling Berg '11	♟♟♟ 4*
○ A. A. Terlano Sauvignon '10	♟♟♟ 3
○ A. A. Terlano Sauvignon '00	♟♟♟ 3*
● A. A. Pinot Nero '09	♟♟ 4
○ A. A. Riesling Berg '10	♟♟ 3
○ A. A. Terlano Pinot Bianco '11	♟♟ 3*
○ A. A. Terlano Pinot Bianco '10	♟♟ 3*
○ Trias '11	♟♟ 4

Niklaserhof - Josef Sölva

LOC. SAN NICOLÒ
VIA DELLE FONTANE, 31A
39052 CALDARO/KALTERN [BZ]
TEL. 0471963434
www.niklaserhof.it

CELLAR SALES
PRE-BOOKED VISITS
ANNUAL PRODUCTION 50,000 bottles
HECTARES UNDER VINE 6.00

Josef Sölva and his son Dieter are craftsmen and growers who interpret their tradition superbly. These knowledgeable countrymen with their vineyard wisdom run their small agriturismo with exquisite hospitality. They approach their five hectares under vine in a very precise way, keeping intervention to the minimum and obtaining the perfect grapes they send to the cellar. Josef is an inspired white wine specialist always thoroughly committed to Pinot Bianco even when its success was not that it enjoys today. His wines are refined, stressing the grapes' delicately fruity essence. With its hints of white-fleshed fruit and spring flowers, Pinot Bianco 2012 is vibrant and very elegant. The finish is racy, with lingering flavours and a mineral trail. The fresh and tasty Kerner Mondevinum Riserva 2010 has the sweetness of ripe fruit, glycerine and no added sugar. Klaser 2010 opens to mountain grasses, sage and delicate fruit.

○ A. A. Kerner Mondevinum Ris. '10	♟♟ 4
○ A. A. Pinot Bianco '12	♟♟ 2*
○ A. A. Bianco Mondevinum Ris. '10	♟♟ 4
○ A. A. Kerner '12	♟♟ 2*
○ A. A. Pinot Bianco Klaser '10	♟♟ 3
○ A. A. Sauvignon '12	♟♟ 3
● A. A. Lago di Caldaro Scelto Cl. '12	♟ 2
● A. A. Lagrein Mondevinum Ris. '10	♟ 4
● A. A. Lagrein-Cabernet Klaser Ris. '10	♟ 4
○ A. A. Bianco Mondevinum '05	♟♟ 4
○ A. A. Kerner '05	♟♟ 2*
○ A. A. Pinot Bianco Klaser '07	♟♟ 3
○ A. A. Pinot Bianco Klaser '00	♟♟ 3
○ A. A. Pinot Bianco Klaser R '05	♟♟ 3*

Obermoser
H. & T. Rottensteiner

FRAZ. RENCIO
VIA SANTA MADDALENA, 35
39100 BOLZANO/BOZEN
TEL. 0471973549
www.obermoser.it

CELLAR SALES
PRE-BOOKED VISITS
ANNUAL PRODUCTION 30,000 bottles
HECTARES UNDER VINE 3.80

The Rottensteiner family has been tending
these vineyards on the Santa Maddalena
hill since 1890, when Christian purchased
the first plots. Their estate has been
producing Lagrein and Santa Maddalena
ever since and, with such deeply rooted
family tradition, the style could not fail to be
impeccably classical and true to type.
Today, Heinrich and his son Thomas are in
charge of the winery. Production is very
reliable and the Lagrein Grafenleiten is one
of the most interesting examples of its type.
Obermoser's performance this year was not
up to its usual standard. The challenging
Lagrein Grafenleiten Riserva 2011 reached
the final, with intense aromas and a lovely
fresh fruitiness. Powerful in the mouth yet
harmonious, the finish is succulent but
lacks finesse. The Lagrein 2012 is tannic
and dense, while the Sauvignon 2012 is a
touch immature.

Pacherhof - Andreas Huber

FRAZ. NOVACELLA
V.LO PACHER, 1
39040 VARNA/VAHRN [BZ]
TEL. 0472835717
www.pacherhof.com

CELLAR SALES
PRE-BOOKED VISITS
ACCOMMODATION AND RESTAURANT SERVICE
ANNUAL PRODUCTION 30,000 bottles
HECTARES UNDER VINE 8.00

Wine-making in Valle Isarco is entwined
with the history of this family and that of
the Pacherof estate. Andreas Huber and his
father Josef were among the first
viticulturists in the valley, pioneers by
tradition and by vocation. They own eight
hectares under vine near Bressanone,
above the Abbey of Novacella at about 600
metres over sea level, planted with mature
vines that are on average 20 years old.
Wines are interesting, with a fresh
elegance and crafted in a classical style. All
the wines presented are good. We like
Veltliner 2012 best, with its brilliance of
colour and multi-faceted nose, where
pepper and spices overlay close-focused
fruit. A nearly tannic entry is followed by the
severe austerity typical of the grape and a
lingering finish. The complex, layered
Pinot Grigio 2012 is just a step below.

● A. A. Lagrein Grafenleiten Ris. '11	♔♔ 5
● A. A. Lagrein '12	♔ 3
○ A. A. Sauvignon '12	♔ 3
● A. A. Lagrein Grafenleiten Ris. '09	♔♔♔ 4
● A. A. Cabernet Sauvignon Putz Ris. '09	♔♔ 5
● A. A. Lagrein '11	♔♔ 3
● A. A. Lagrein Grafenleiten Ris. '10	♔♔ 5
● A. A. Lagrein Scuro Grafenleiten Ris. '07	♔♔ 4
● A. A. Santa Maddalena Cl. '11	♔♔ 3

○ A. A. Valle Isarco Veltliner '12	♔♔ 4
○ A. A. Valle Isarco Pinot Grigio '12	♔♔ 4
○ A. A. Valle Isarco Sylvaner '12	♔♔ 3
○ A. A. Valle Isarco Riesling '04	♔♔♔ 3
○ A. A. Valle Isarco Sylvaner Alte Reben '05	♔♔♔ 4
○ A. A. Valle Isarco Kerner '10	♔♔ 3
○ A. A. Valle Isarco Pinot Grigio '11	♔♔ 4
○ A. A. Valle Isarco Riesling '11	♔♔ 4
○ A. A. Valle Isarco Sylvaner '10	♔♔ 3
○ A. A. Valle Isarco Sylvaner Alte Reben '10	♔♔ 5
○ A. A. Valle Isarco Sylvaner Alte Reben '09	♔♔ 5

Pfannenstielhof Johannes Pfeifer

VIA PFANNESTIEL, 9
39100 BOLZANO/BOZEN
TEL. 0471970884
www.pfannenstielhof.it

CELLAR SALES
PRE-BOOKED VISITS
ANNUAL PRODUCTION 40,000 bottles
HECTARES UNDER VINE 4.00

Johannes Pfeifer is a scrupulous grower who, together with his wife Margareth, cultivates four hectares of vineyards, where plants of the right age grow over the sunny slopes of the Renon, on loose soils that are ideal for schiava and lagrein. If you're looking for classic wines in a traditional style, this is the estate for you. The consistency here makes it a benchmark for both Sciava and Lagrein. The signature wine is Santa Maddalena, which always presents elegant and full of the characteristic energy of the type. Although the range was not as convincing as usual, we loved the Pinot Nero 2010, with its fresh berry fruit but just a tad too much alcoholic warmth. The moderately firm mouth has a back palate defined by freshness and pleasant tannins, and the long finish shows personality. Lagrein 2012 has rather stiff tannins and the Riserva 2010 has full, harmonious flavours.

Tenuta Ritterhof

S.DA DEL VINO, 1
39052 CALDARO/KALTERN [BZ]
TEL. 0471963298
www.ritterhof.it

CELLAR SALES
PRE-BOOKED VISITS
RESTAURANT SERVICE
ANNUAL PRODUCTION 297,000 bottles
HECTARES UNDER VINE 7.50

In brief, the wines offered by Tenuta Ritterhof are reliable, classical and well-priced. The cellar is run by the Roner family, who has a long-standing family tradition acquired over many years. The winery is located between Caldaro and Termeno, where the family owns seven hectares, and they also select grapes grown by 40 or so trusted growers under the watchful eye of cellarmaster Bernhard Hannes. Visitors to Ritterhof can enjoy a very pleasant meal at the restaurant, and the Roner family also owns the distillery - www.roner.con - producing grappas and fruit spirits. Gewürztraminer Crescendo 2012 offers multi-faceted, crisp flavours of roses, geranium, dried grass and camomile in a focused style with a slightly salty, lingering finish. The varietal Sonus 2010 is typical, with original hints of sage and saffron and a taut, fresh palate.

● A. A. Pinot Nero '10	♥♥ 4
● A. A. Lagrein Ris. '10	♥ 5
● A. A. Lagrein vom Boden '12	♥ 3
● A. A. Santa Maddalena Cl. '12	♥ 3
● A. A. Santa Maddalena Cl. '09	♥♥♥ 2*
● A. A. Lagrein Ris. '09	♥♥ 5
● A. A. Lagrein Ris. '07	♥♥ 4
● A. A. Lagrein vom Boden '10	♥♥ 3*
● A. A. Pinot Nero '07	♥♥ 3*
● A. A. Santa Maddalena Cl. '10	♥♥ 3*

○ A. A. Gewürztraminer Crescendo Aureus '12	♥♥♥ 4*
○ A. A. Gewürztraminer Sonus '10	♥♥ 5
○ A. A. Pinot Bianco Varius '12	♥♥ 3
○ A. A. Pinot Grigio Crescendo '11	♥♥ 4
● A. A. Pinot Nero Crescendo '09	♥♥ 5
● A. A. Lago di Caldaro Cl. Sup. Novis '12	♥ 3
● A. A. Lagrein Crescendo '10	♥ 4
● A. A. Lagrein Manus '09	♥ 4
○ A. A. Müller Thurgau '12	♥ 2
○ A. A. Pinot Grigio '12	♥ 2
● A. A. Santa Maddalena '12	♥ 3
● A. A. Lago di Caldaro Cl. Ritterhof '10	♥♥ 2*
○ A. A. Pinot Bianco Ritterhof '10	♥♥ 2*
○ A. A. Pinot Grigio Ritterhof '11	♥♥ 2*

Röckhof - Konrad Augschöll

VIA SAN VALENTINO, 22
39040 VILLANDRO/VILLANDERS [BZ]
TEL. 0472847130
roeck@rolmail.net

CELLAR SALES
PRE-BOOKED VISITS
RESTAURANT SERVICE
ANNUAL PRODUCTION 18,000 bottles
HECTARES UNDER VINE 3.50

Konrad Augschöll is a fully rounded craftsman, creating classical, reliable wines and other traditional products of the territory. He is at the head of this 15th century estate set on the road leading up to Villandro from Chiusa, on the right bank of the river Isarco. The three hectares under vine, at altitudes between 600 and 700 metres, are nearly all cultivated to white grape varieties. They have a small production of red-skinned grapes, pinot nero and zweigelt, from which they make the wines consumed in the agriturismo, especially during the Törggelen autumn festival. These are genuine wines bursting with character and never boring, to be followed patiently, waiting for them to age. While rich, Veltliner Gail Fuass 2012 is supple, with a peppery entry bursting with acidity and flavours upon flavours. In the finish, mineral tones emerge, blending with saltiness. It speaks a lovely language, with delicate phases despite its weight. Caruess 2012 has a crisp palate and offers tones of citrus fruit with the warmth of a sunny day.

○ A. A. Valle Isarco Veltliner Gail Fuass '12	♟♟	3*
○ Caruess '12	♟♟	3*
○ A. A. Valle Isarco Riesling Viel Anders '12	♟	3
○ A. A. Valle Isarco Riesling Viel Anders '08	♟♟♟	3*
○ A. A. Valle Isarco Veltliner '11	♟♟♟	3*
○ A. A. Valle Isarco Riesling Viel Anders '10	♟♟	3*
○ Caruess '11	♟♟	3*

Hans Rottensteiner

FRAZ. GRIES
VIA SARENTINO, 1A
39100 BOLZANO/BOZEN
TEL. 0471282015
www.rottensteiner-weine.com

CELLAR SALES
PRE-BOOKED VISITS
ANNUAL PRODUCTION 450,000 bottles
HECTARES UNDER VINE 95.00

Heirs to a long family tradition, Toni and Hanes Rottensteiner are true schiava specialists, growing the grapes in vineyards containing red porphyry, the basis of ideal schiava terrain. Set north of Bolzano, at the mouth of Val Sarentino, the provenance of the grapes indicate their special relationship with long-established suppliers, for example with the Vogels of Maso Premstallerhof or with the Kristplonerhof. Lagrein Select 2010 has peppery spices and fresh sound fruit, joined by pleasant notes of embers and earth, and a mineral austerity. The typical, classical Cancenai 2012 has a wealth of apple-like fruit, flowers and herbs. The palate is brimming with flavour and saltiness, and shows a certain elegance. Pinot Bianco Carnol 2012 has a refined language of subtle elegance. Exotic fruit blend on the nose, mixing passion fruit, citrus peel and melon, with grip on the palate.

○ A. A. Gewürztraminer Cancenai '12	♟♟	3*
● A. A. Lagrein Grieser Select Ris. '10	♟♟	4
● A. A. Cabernet Select Ris. '10	♟♟	4
● A. A. Pinot Bianco Carnol '12	♟♟	3
● A. A. Santa Maddalena Cl. Premstallerhof '12	♟♟	2*
☉ A. A. Lagrein Rosato '12	♟	2
○ A. A. Müller Thurgau '12	♟	2
● A. A. Pinot Nero Select Ris. '10	♟	4
○ A. A. Sauvignon '12	♟	3
● A. A. Lagrein Ris. '02	♟♟♟	2*
○ A. A. Gewürztraminer Passito Cresta '08	♟♟	5
● A. A. Lagrein Grieser Select Ris. '07	♟♟	4
● A. A. Lagrein Grieser Select Ris. '05	♟♟	4
● A. A. Santa Maddalena Cl. Premstallerhof '09	♟♟	2*

★★Cantina Produttori San Michele Appiano

VIA CIRCONVALLAZIONE, 17/19
39057 APPIANO/EPPAN [BZ]
TEL. 0471664466
www.stmichael.it

CELLAR SALES
PRE-BOOKED VISITS
ANNUAL PRODUCTION 200,000 bottles
HECTARES UNDER VINE 380.00

The recent story of this prime co-operative winery is linked to its manager, Hans Terzer, who is so much more than a simple cellarmaster. He is the true heart of this operation, tenaciously moulding it over the years with his farsightedness and great skill. Production covers a series of basic wines and the legendary Sanct Valentin range, which, over time, has fashioned a distinctive personality and impressively long-living wines. The stylistic benchmark is always their Sauvignon, a citrussy, alluring wine with great ageing potential. Pinot Bianco Sanct Valentin 2011 treads the most classical path in the line. Oak is handled with masterly skill and the palate combines richness with freshness. With the dual complexity of wood and fruit, a changing, multi-layered expression and great acidity, it is easy to forecast its potential and longevity. In the Schulthauser 2012, the many undertones of saffron, damson, lemon peel and hedgerow pack a relaxed mouth.

Cantina Produttori San Paolo

LOC. SAN PAOLO
VIA CASTEL GUARDIA, 21
39050 APPIANO/EPPAN [BZ]
TEL. 0471662183
www.kellereistpauls.com

CELLAR SALES
PRE-BOOKED VISITS
ANNUAL PRODUCTION 1,200,000 bottles
HECTARES UNDER VINE 175.00

When this long-established winery in the territory of Appaino took on the challenge of young Wolfgang Tratter, a passionate oenologist with the capacity of making wines that are totally true to the territory, it was expressing its energy and desire to emerge. The exceptional quality of the winery's great Riservas reveals their potential and, in line with their longevity, wines in the Passion range are placed on the market only after lengthy bottle ageing. Under Alessandro Righi's courageous tenacity, this operation is back among the top players in its territory. Pinot Bianco Passion 2011 opens on a wonderful smoky note, with hints ranging from camomile to a fruit basket of damson, melon and grapes. The palate is alluringly full and generous, bursting with flavour. Schiava Passion 2011 shows a rich kaleidoscopic nose, thrust and soft tannins on the palate, finding austerity in the finish.

○ A. A. Pinot Bianco St. Valentin '11	♟♟♟	5
○ A. A. Chardonnay Merol '12	♟♟	3*
○ A. A. Pinot Bianco Schulthauser '12	♟♟	3*
○ A. A. Sauvignon St. Valentin '12	♟♟	5
○ A. A. Chardonnay St. Valentin '11	♟♟	5
○ A. A. Pinot Grigio Anger '12	♟♟	3
○ A. A. Pinot Grigio St. Valentin '11	♟♟	5
● A. A. Pinot Nero Ris. '10	♟♟	4
○ A. A. Riesling Montiggl '12	♟♟	3
○ A. A. Pinot Grigio Anger '11	♟♟♟	3*
○ A. A. Sauvignon St. Valentin '10	♟♟♟	5
○ A. A. Sauvignon St. Valentin '09	♟♟♟	5
○ A. A. Sauvignon St. Valentin '08	♟♟♟	5
○ A. A. Sauvignon St. Valentin '07	♟♟♟	5

○ A. A. Pinot Bianco Passion Ris. '11	♟♟♟	4*
● A. A. Pinot Nero Passion Ris. '10	♟♟	5
● A. A. Schiava Passion '11	♟♟	3*
○ A. A. Chardonnay Kössler '12	♟♟	3
● A. A. Lagrein Passion Ris. '11	♟♟	5
● A. A. Santa Maddalena Kössler '12	♟♟	2*
● A. A. Schiava Missianer '12	♟♟	2*
○ A. A. Pinot Bianco Kössler '12	♟	2
○ A. A. Pinot Bianco Plotzner '12	♟	2
○ A. A. Pinot Grigio '12	♟	2
○ A. A. Pinot Grigio Kössler '12	♟	2
● A. A. Pinot Nero Kössler '11	♟	2
○ A. A. Sauvignon Kössler '12	♟	2
○ A. A. Sauvignon Passion '11	♟	4
○ A. A. Pinot Bianco Passion '09	♟♟♟	4

Peter Sölva & Söhne

VIA DELL'ORO, 33
39052 CALDARO/KALTERN [BZ]
TEL. 0471964650
www.soelva.com

CELLAR SALES
PRE-BOOKED VISITS
ANNUAL PRODUCTION 75,000 bottles
HECTARES UNDER VINE 6.00

The Sölva family's long tradition of producing wine was documented as early as the late 18th century, placing them among the most important families of Caldaro and a benchmark for the area. The winery is managed by Stephen Sölva, who is helped in the cellar by the young, passionate oenologist Christian Belutti. Production is split between two lines, De Silva and Amistar. The whites are the main players, where well-balanced wines bursting with energy are crafted in an elegantly fresh style. The reds are full and rich although they sometimes bear the brunt of ageing in wood by a slight loss of finesse and freshness. Exotic in its overtones, Pinot Bianco 2012 has a well-balanced, subtle palate of lively acidity, leading to a savoury, citrus, lip-smacking finish. Lago di Caldaro 2012 is an exceptionally fine wine that develops freshly and finishes on a mineral tone.

○ A. A. Pinot Bianco DeSilva '12	♟♟ 4
● A. A. Lago di Caldaro Cl. Sup. '12	♟♟ 2*
● A. A. Lagrein Ris. '11	♟♟ 3
● A. A. Pinot Nero '11	♟♟ 4
○ A. A. Sauvignon DeSilva '12	♟ 4
○ A. A. Terlano Pinot Bianco DeSilva '10	♟♟♟ 3
○ A. A. Terlano Pinot Bianco DeSilva '09	♟♟♟ 3
● A. A. Lago di Caldaro Scelto Cl. Sup. DeSilva Peterleiten '11	♟♟ 2*
● A. A. Lagrein DeSilva '08	♟♟ 3
○ A. A. Sauvignon Blanc DeSilva '11	♟♟ 4
○ A. A. Terlano Pinot Bianco DeSilva '11	♟♟ 3*

Stachlburg
Baron von Kripp

VIA MITTERHOFER, 2
39020 PARCINES/PARTSCHINS [BZ]
TEL. 0473968014
www.stachlburg.com

CELLAR SALES
PRE-BOOKED VISITS
ANNUAL PRODUCTION 30,000 bottles
HECTARES UNDER VINE 7.00
VITICULTURE METHOD Certified Organic

The family has owned the castle of Stachlburg since 1540 but it was Sigmund von Krippof who instilled energy and strength into the estate's fine traditions. He was responsible for the recent planting of the first vines, back in the 1990s. Since then, the estate has grown, becoming one of the surprises of Alto Adige, with wines of impressive quality, personality and style. Young Dominic Würth, who divides his time between vineyard and cellar, brings out all Val Venosta's elegance and minerality, nuancing the sensations with a slightly smoky tone. Pinot Grigio 2011 is a wine that lingers on many fragrances while remaining austerely tidy. The flavoursome palate displays good grip, ensuring leisurely finish. Pinot Bianco 2012 reveals a delicate fruit and superb firmness. The dry, elegant palate shows linear, leisurely progression.

○ A. A. Pinot Grigio '11	♟♟ 3*
○ A. A. Valle Venosta Chardonnay '12	♟♟ 3
○ A. A. Valle Venosta Pinot Bianco '12	♟♟ 3
○ Praesepium Bianco '11	♟♟ 2*
○ A. A. Valle Venosta Gewürztraminer '11	♟ 3
● A. A. Valle Venosta Pinot Nero '10	♟ 3
○ A. A. Valle Venosta Pinot Bianco '10	♟♟♟ 3*
○ A. A. Pinot Grigio '09	♟♟ 3*
○ A. A. Valle Venosta Chardonnay '11	♟♟ 3*
○ A. A. Valle Venosta Gewürztraminer '10	♟♟ 3*
● A. A. Valle Venosta Pinot Nero '09	♟♟ 3
○ A. A.Terlano Sauvignon '11	♟♟ 3*

Strasserhof
Hannes Baumgartner

FRAZ. NOVACELLA
LOC. UNTERRAIN, 8
39040 VARNA/VAHRN [BZ]
TEL. 0472830804
www.strasserhof.info

CELLAR SALES
PRE-BOOKED VISITS
ACCOMMODATION
ANNUAL PRODUCTION 45,000 bottles
HECTARES UNDER VINE 5.00

Strasserhof, which also serves simple food in a traditional setting, is one of the oldest Valle Isarco estates and its vineyards are among the most northerly in the valley. This is reflected in the linear, mineral sensory profile that Hannes Baumgartner uses to good effect to make pure, sharp wines. This estate's rapid rise on the Alto Adige wine scene is the result of Hannes's skill at interpreting varieties and producing original, exciting wines with distinctive personalities. Though the first bottles only date from 2003, the elegant, sophisticated style is already clearly defined. The fine Riesling 2012 opens slowly, with energetic force on the palate, followed by beautifully expansive, rhythmic progression, with myriad floral notes and flavours. In its expression, the deeply austere Sylvaner 2012 darts between glycerine and acidity, and white melon and grape.

Stroblhof

LOC. SAN MICHELE
VIA PIGANÒ, 25
39057 APPIANO/EPPAN [BZ]
TEL. 0471662250
www.stroblhof.it

CELLAR SALES
PRE-BOOKED VISITS
ANNUAL PRODUCTION 39,000 bottles
HECTARES UNDER VINE 5.20

Andreas Nicolussi-Leck runs this estate with his wife Rosi Hanny, which includes a hospitality project, making Stroblhof a true emissary of its territory. Located at the heart of one of the best white wine areas in Alto Adige, the estate is increasingly moving towards sustainable management where the territorial facet can take on a purer form, with its delicate nuances and wines that, while difficult to decipher when young, have great ageing potential. Pinot Nero Riserva 2010 is a tidy, crisp wine with pleasantly clear varietal tones, exploding juicily in the mouth. A well-paced rhythm is underpinned by acidity. Strahler 2012 opens on the hardness that forms its character, to relax elegantly with very clear fruity notes, mainly damson. It finishes with a lingering, flavoursome tautness. Pigeno 2011 shows hints of wild berries and an austere freshness.

○ A. A. Valle Isarco Riesling '12	♀♀♀	3*
○ A. A. Valle Isarco Sylvaner '12	♀♀	3*
○ A. A. Valle Isarco Veltliner '12	♀♀	3
○ A. A. Valle Isarco Gewürztraminer '12	♀	3
○ A. A. Valle Isarco Kerner '12	♀	3
○ A. A. Valle Isarco Müller Thurgau '12	♀	3
○ A. A. Valle Isarco Riesling '11	♀♀♀	3*
○ A. A. Valle Isarco Veltliner '10	♀♀♀	3*
○ A. A. Valle Isarco Veltliner '09	♀♀♀	3*
○ A. A. Valle Isarco Kerner '11	♀♀	3*
○ A. A. Valle Isarco Riesling '10	♀♀	3
○ A. A. Valle Isarco Sylvaner '11	♀♀	3*
○ A. A. Valle Isarco Sylvaner '10	♀♀	3*

○ A. A. Chardonnay Schwarzhaus '12	♀♀	3
○ A. A. Pinot Bianco Strahler '12	♀♀	3
● A. A. Pinot Nero Ris. '10	♀♀	6
● A. A. Pinot Nero Pigeno '11	♀	5
○ A. A. Sauvignon Nico '12	♀	4
○ A. A. Pinot Bianco Strahler '09	♀♀♀	3*
● A. A. Pinot Nero Ris. '05	♀♀♀	5
○ A. A. Chardonnay Schwarzhaus '11	♀♀	3*
○ A. A. Pinot Bianco Strahler '11	♀♀	3*
○ A. A. Pinot Bianco Strahler '10	♀♀	3*
○ A. A. Pinot Bianco Strahler '08	♀♀	3*
● A. A. Pinot Nero Pigeno '09	♀♀	4
● A. A. Pinot Nero Ris. '09	♀♀	5
○ A. A. Sauvignon Nico '10	♀♀	3

Taschlerhof - Peter Wachtler

LOC. MARA, 107
39042 BRESSANONE/BRIXEN [BZ]
TEL. 0472851091
www.taschlerhof.com

CELLAR SALES
PRE-BOOKED VISITS
ANNUAL PRODUCTION 28,500 bottles
HECTARES UNDER VINE 4.00

Since 1990, Peter Wachter has been cultivating the vineyards of the small farmstead in Valle Isarco that he inherited from his father. The position is perfect for white varieties, in keeping with the local tradition. The south-east facing vineyards are set at over 500 metres above sea level on lean, shale soils that impart a distinctive minerality to the wines, deftly retained by Peter and his masterly craftsmanship. The labels are very few but express the typicity of these native grapes superbly. Kerner 2012 handles its texture and body well, with an explosion of acidity in the mouth then slowly finding tangy flavours and a leisurely finish. The austere, razor-sharp Sylvaner 2012 has aromas of citrus fruit and many nuances. Its refined expression flows in the mouth. Lahner 2012 offers an intensely close-knit, sea-washed palate.

★Cantina Terlano

VIA SILBERLEITEN, 7
39018 TERLANO/TERLAN [BZ]
TEL. 0471257135
www.cantina-terlano.com

CELLAR SALES
PRE-BOOKED VISITS
ANNUAL PRODUCTION 1,000,000 bottles
HECTARES UNDER VINE 165.00

The meticulous work to upgrade the vineyards belonging to their members is a reflection of the close bond between this co-operative winery and its territory. The secret of this long and stable success is based upon these dynamic, eminently ageworthy mineral-rich wines that nonchalantly defy the passage of time. Old vintages, set aside since Sebastian Stocker's days, testify to an exceptional ability to read and interpret the different territories. In 2008, the winery merged with Andiano, one of Alto Adige's oldest co-operatives but still maintains its own brand, while the wines are all crafted by Rudi Kofler. Vorberg 2010 offers a skilled interpretation of its great year, with a stylish, dynamic profile awash with many tones and complex aromas that reflect the grape. The palate, initially alluring then bursting with acidity, discovers exotic sensations of passion fruit and grapefruit and is packed with flavour in the finish.

○ A. A. Valle Isarco Kerner '12	♚♚ 3*
○ A. A. Valle Isarco Sylvaner '12	♚♚ 3
○ A. A. Valle Isarco Sylvaner Lahner '12	♚♚ 4
○ A. A. Valle Isarco Gewürztraminer '12	♚ 4
○ A. A. Valle Isarco Riesling '12	♚ 4
○ A. A. Valle Isarco Gewürztraminer '10	♔♔ 4
○ A. A. Valle Isarco Kerner '11	♔♔ 3
○ A. A. Valle Isarco Kerner '10	♔♔ 3
○ A. A. Valle Isarco Riesling '11	♔♔ 4
○ A. A. Valle Isarco Riesling '10	♔♔ 4
○ A. A. Valle Isarco Sylvaner '11	♔♔ 3
○ A. A. Valle Isarco Sylvaner Lahner '11	♔♔ 4
○ A. A. Valle Isarco Sylvaner Lahner '10	♔♔ 4

○ A. A. Terlano Pinot Bianco Vorberg Ris. '10	♚♚♚ 4*
○ A. A. Sauvignon Andrius Andriano '11	♚♚♚ 3*
○ A. A. Sauvignon Floreado '12	♚♚ 3*
○ A. A. Terlano Chardonnay Rarità '00	♚♚ 8
○ A. A. Terlano Nova Domus Ris. '10	♚♚ 6
○ A. A. Chardonnay '12	♚♚ 3
● A. A. Lagrein Riserva Andriano Tor di Lupo '10	♚♚ 4
● A. A. Lagrein Rubeno Andriano '12	♚♚ 3
● A. A. Schiava Bocado Andriano '12	♚♚ 2*
○ A. A. Terlano Cl. '12	♚♚ 2*
○ A. A. Terlano Pinot Bianco Cl. '12	♚♚ 2*
○ A. A. Terlano Sauvignon Quarz '11	♚♚ 6
○ A. A. Terlano Sauvignon Winkl '12	♚♚ 3
○ A. A. Pinot Bianco Vorberg Ris. '09	♔♔♔ 3*

Tiefenbrunner

FRAZ. NICLARA
VIA CASTELLO, 4
39040 CORTACCIA/KURTATSCH [BZ]
TEL. 0471880122
www.tiefenbrunner.com

CELLAR SALES
PRE-BOOKED VISITS
RESTAURANT SERVICE
ANNUAL PRODUCTION 800,000 bottles
HECTARES UNDER VINE 25.00

Tiefenbrunner's solid family tradition is now in the hands of Christoph, although the wealth of experience accrued by his father Herbert, who ran and developed this winery since the 1970s, will always be there as a challenge and inspiration. Winemaking at Turmhof Castle began in the 19th century but it was Herbert who focused the estate on quality. The wines are divided into several product lines, the simpler ones being obtained from grapes supplied by selected growers. The estate's own grapes are used for the more ambitious labels, commencing with Feldmarschall von Fenner from a vineyard located at 1,000 metres above sea level. The creamy, flavoursome Feldmarschall 2011 reveals its classical notes of saffron, with complex, unusual late-harvest tones. The Lagrein Riserva Linticlarus 2010 has a dense palate with ripe, tasty tannins and delicious notes of cocoa and red berries.

★★Cantina Tramin

S.DA DEL VINO, 144
39040 TERMENO/TRAMIN [BZ]
TEL. 0471096633
www.cantinatramin.it

CELLAR SALES
PRE-BOOKED VISITS
ANNUAL PRODUCTION 1,500,000 bottles
HECTARES UNDER VINE 250.00
VITICULTURE METHOD Certified Biodynamic

Willi Stürz and his staff at this outstanding co-operative winery have looked at the big picture when designing and building the new cellar, and above all they looked towards the future. This ensures a solid structure to an operation that every year turns out an extensive and impressive range of wines where even the simplest labels are always reliable. The co-operative's flagship wine is the Gewürztraminer, always beautifully interpreted in what is the heart of the variety's oldest and finest growing zone. Top of the line is the Nussbaumer, a quality benchmark and an excitingly ageworthy wine. The 2012 version is again flawless. It has complex aromas of damson, rose, hawthorn, apricot, black tea and a hint of peat. With a fine sapidity, the spirited, weighty palate is backed by acidity, giving it style. Lagrein Urban 2011 is austerely earthy yet relaxed and juicy, with fine, close-knit tannins and lots of taste.

○ A. A. Müller Thurgau Feldmarschall von Fenner zu Fennberg '11	♀♀♀ 5
● A. A. Cabernet Sauvignon Linticlarus '09	♀♀ 6
● A. A. Lagrein Linticlarus Ris. '10	♀♀ 5
● A. A. Cabernet - Merlot Linticlarus '10	♀♀ 6
○ A. A. Chardonnay Linticlarus '10	♀♀ 5
○ A. A. Chardonnay Turmhof '12	♀♀ 3
○ A. A. Pinot Bianco Anna Turmhof '12	♀♀ 3
○ A. A. Sauvignon Kirchleiten '12	♀♀ 4
○ A. A. Gewürztraminer Turmhof '12	♀ 5
○ A. A. Pinot Grigio Turmhof '12	♀ 3
● A. A. Pinot Nero Linticlarus Ris. '10	♀ 5
● A. A. Lagrein Linticlarus Ris. '07	♀♀♀ 5
○ A. A. Pinot Bianco Anna Turmhof '11	♀♀♀ 3*
○ Feldmarschall von Fenner zu Fennberg '08	♀♀♀ 5

○ A. A. Gewürztraminer Nussbaumer '12	♀♀♀ 5
○ A. A. Gewürztraminer Passito Terminum V. T. '11	♀♀ 7
● A. A. Lagrein Urban '11	♀♀ 5
○ A. A. Pinot Bianco Moriz '12	♀♀ 3*
○ A. A. Sauvignon Montan '12	♀♀ 4
● A. A. Cabernet Merlot Loam '11	♀♀ 5
○ A. A. Pinot Grigio Unterebner '12	♀♀ 4
● A. A. Pinot Nero Maglen '11	♀♀ 5
○ A. A. Sauvignon '12	♀♀ 3
○ A. A. Gewürztraminer '12	♀ 3
● A. A. Schiava Freisinger '12	♀ 3
○ A. A. Stoan '12	♀ 4
○ A. A. Gewürztraminer Nussbaumer '11	♀♀♀ 5
○ A. A. Gewürztraminer Terminum V. T. '07	♀♀♀ 5

Untermoserhof
Georg Ramoser

VIA SANTA MADDALENA, 36
39100 BOLZANO/BOZEN
TEL. 0471975481
untermoserhof@rolmail.net

CELLAR SALES
PRE-BOOKED VISITS
ACCOMMODATION
ANNUAL PRODUCTION 35,000 bottles
HECTARES UNDER VINE 4.50

The Ramoser family has been making wine for three generations from the most traditional grapes of their territory, lagrein and schiava. Located at the heart of Santa Maddalena, their vineyards, some very old, are tended passionately by Georg Ramoser, whose increasing discernment has led to their current conversion to organic management. Georg is an enthusiastic grower, establishing in his small production a good balance between the more rustic typicity of the Santa Maddalena and Lagrein and a more innovative idea of wine. Lagrein Riserva Untermoserhof 2010 is a fresh, country-feel wine, expressive yet reserved and austere. Both mouth and progression are fresh, with notes of dried fruit and a rigorously clean finish of tidy dryness. Santa Maddalena 2012 is a crisp, fruity wine.

★Tenuta Unterortl
Castel Juval

LOC. JUVAL, 1B
39020 CASTELBELLO CIARDES/KASTELBELL TSCHARS [BZ]
TEL. 0473667580
www.unterortl.it

CELLAR SALES
PRE-BOOKED VISITS
ANNUAL PRODUCTION 33,000 bottles
HECTARES UNDER VINE 4.00

Val Venosta is a new territory for Alto Adige wines, establishing itself over very few years as a top player. This is due above all to the Rieslings but closely also to its incredible bent for sharp, deep wines. In an area of outstanding beauty, Martin and Gisela Aurich have understood the potential of their vineyards set at altitudes between 600 and 900 metres above sea level, on steep soils that are difficult to cultivate, yet which can express their qualities with continuity and at the highest level. Pinot Bianco 2012 offers a refined expression of chiaroscuro elegance. An initial smoky note is followed by damson and then sea breezes. The palate offers taut subtlety and a delicious acidity contrasts a perfectly balanced glycerine sweetness. Windbichel 2011 reveals crisp varietal notes and has mouthfilling fine flavours.

● A. A. Lagrein Untermoserhof Ris. '10	♟♟ 4
● A. A. Santa Maddalena Cl. '12	♟♟ 3
● A. A. Lagrein '12	♟ 3
● A. A. Lagrein Scuro Ris. '03	♟♟♟ 4*
● A. A. Lagrein '11	♟♟ 3
● A. A. Lagrein '10	♟♟ 3
● A. A. Lagrein Ris. '09	♟♟ 4
● A. A. Lagrein Ris. '08	♟♟ 4
● A. A. Lagrein Scuro '09	♟♟ 3*
● A. A. Lagrein Scuro Ris. '07	♟♟ 4
● A. A. Lagrein Scuro Ris. '06	♟♟ 4
● A. A. Santa Maddalena Cl. '11	♟♟ 3
● A. A. Santa Maddalena Cl. '09	♟♟ 2*

○ A. A. Val Venosta Pinot Bianco Castel Juval '12	♟♟♟ 3*
○ A. A. Val Venosta Riesling Castel Juval '12	♟♟ 4
○ A. A. Val Venosta Riesling Windbichel '11	♟♟ 5
● Juval Gneis '12	♟♟ 3
○ A. A. Val Venosta Müller Thurgau Castel Juval '12	♟ 3
● A. A. Val Venosta Pinot Nero Castel Juval '11	♟ 5
○ A. A. Val Venosta Pinot Bianco '07	♟♟♟ 2*
○ A. A. Val Venosta Riesling '10	♟♟♟ 4
○ A. A. Val Venosta Riesling '09	♟♟♟ 4
○ A. A. Val Venosta Riesling '08	♟♟♟ 4
○ A. A. Val Venosta Riesling '07	♟♟♟ 3*
○ A. A. Val Venosta Riesling Castel Juval '11	♟♟♟ 4*

Cantina Produttori Valle Isarco

VIA COSTE, 50
39043 CHIUSA/KLAUSEN [BZ]
TEL. 0472847553
www.cantinavalleisarco.it

CELLAR SALES
PRE-BOOKED VISITS
ANNUAL PRODUCTION 750,000 bottles
HECTARES UNDER VINE 140.00

Located at the entry to Valle Isarco, slightly north of Bolzano, this cellar gathers and vinifies grapes sourced from 130 hectares cultivated by members in vineyards scattered across 11 different municipal areas. Production is in the hands of cellarmaster Thomas Dorfmann, following in the footsteps of a father who for many years crafted the cellar's wines. Alongside their entry-level wines, they produce the Aristos line, which brings together the winery's top labels. The winery also vinifies the grapes of the Sabiona monastery or the Kloster Säben, built on a high cliff overhanging the small town of Chiusa. The refined Sylvaner Aristos 2012 is austerely tangy with a lively acidity. A wealth of aromas span Alpine grasses to white pepper and there is a fragrant, clear reference to its grape. Veltiner Aristos 2012 is taut and salty, with ice-cool aromas and a sea of flavours. Sylvaner Sabiona 2011 has a pinch of aniseed and a long, generous mouth. It is an ample wine with a certain grace.

○ A. A. Valle Isarco Sylvaner Aristos '12	♟♟ 3*
○ A. A. Valle Isarco Veltliner Aristos '12	♟♟ 3*
○ A. A. Sauvignon Aristos '12	♟♟ 3
○ A. A. Valle Isarco Pinot Grigio Aristos '12	♟♟ 3
○ A. A. Valle Isarco Riesling Aristos '12	♟♟ 4
○ A. A. Valle Isarco Sylvaner Sabiona '11	♟♟ 5
○ A. A. Valle Isarco Gewürztraminer Aristos '12	♟ 4
○ A. A. Valle Isarco Gewürztraminer Passito Nectaris '11	♟ 6
○ A. A. Valle Isarco Kerner Passito Nectaris '11	♟ 6
○ A. A. Valle Isarco Kerner Aristos '05	♟♟♟ 3*
○ A. A. Valle Isarco Veltliner Aristos '03	♟♟♟ 3*
○ A. A. Valle Isarco Kerner Passito Nectaris '10	♟♟ 6
○ A. A. Valle Isarco Riesling Aristos '11	♟♟ 4

Vivaldi - Arunda

VIA JOSEF-SCHWARZ, 18
39010 MELTINA/MÖLTEN [BZ]
TEL. 0471668033
www.arundavivaldi.it

CELLAR SALES
PRE-BOOKED VISITS
ANNUAL PRODUCTION 90,000 bottles

Since the 1970s, when he decided to focus on Metodo Classico sparkling wines, Joseph Reiterer has been carefully selecting the base wines - Chardonnay, Pinot Bianco and Pinot Nero - that go into producing the various house blends. The different batches of grapes are sent by a collection of trusty growers from various territories in Alto Adige, giving the winery a certain freedom in blending them, with production covering about half the total regional output of sparkling wines. The wines remain at length on the lees, at least for 24 months. This very simple wine has absolutely amazing qualities. Arunda Brut presents a sweet, spicy complexity, with hints of acacia and broom, honey and hazelnut. The palate is edgy, with a good acidity and drinkability, and a dry finish. Arunda Rosé is elegantly racy, with complex tertiary notes and a dry back palate bursting with flavour.

○ A. A. Spumante Brut Arunda	♟♟ 5
○ A. A. Spumante Arunda Cuvée Marianna	♟♟ 5
○ A. A. Spumante Arunda Ris. '08	♟♟ 5
⊙ A. A. Spumante Arunda Rosé	♟♟ 5
○ A. A. Spumante Blanc de Blancs Arunda	♟ 5
○ A. A. Spumante Extra Brut Arunda	♟ 5
○ A. A. Spumante Brut Vivaldi '99	♟♟ 3
○ A. A. Spumante Extra Brut Arunda Ris. '05	♟♟ 5
○ A. A. Spumante Extra Brut Arunda Ris. '04	♟♟ 5
○ A. A. Spumante Extra Brut Arunda Ris. '98	♟♟ 5
○ A. A. Spumante Vivaldi Ris. '97	♟♟ 4

★Elena Walch

VIA A. HOFER, 1
39040 TERMENO/TRAMIN [BZ]
TEL. 0471860172
www.elenawalch.com

CELLAR SALES
PRE-BOOKED VISITS
RESTAURANT SERVICE
ANNUAL PRODUCTION 500,000 bottles
HECTARES UNDER VINE 33.00

Elena Walch reaps the benefits of a
victorious challenge to show that wine
needs a human touch and culture over and
above technology. She has been running
her winery for 20 years, uplifting her
husband Werner's long-established family
tradition to levels most likely never attained
in the past. The best vineyards are at Castel
Ringberg and Kastelaz, the latter a true
gewürztraminer grand cru producing
exceptionally elegant top quality wines. The
2012 version is complex, revealing smoky
notes, hawthorn, rose, pear, camomile and
even aniseed, followed by an extended,
subtle palate full of elegant flavour. Merlot
Kastelaz 2009 is spicy and lip-smacking,
with fruit hinting at wild strawberries and
plum. Pinot Bianco Kastelaz 2012 shows
lovely rigour, hints of damson and passion
fruit and a taut, austere palate.

Tenuta Waldgries

LOC. SANTA GIUSTINA, 2
39100 BOLZANO/BOZEN
TEL. 0471323603
www.waldgries.it

CELLAR SALES
PRE-BOOKED VISITS
ANNUAL PRODUCTION 70,000 bottles
HECTARES UNDER VINE 8.40

Tenuta Walgries is set at the foot of the
Santa Maddalena hill, managed
passionately by Christian Plattner, a highly
skilled schiava and lagrein specialist. Vines
are at the heart of his project and he tends
them with infinite time and energy,
recovering, for example, old clones of
schiava, plausibly the queen of the
winery's output, growing at the heart of the
Santa Maddalena hills. The results,
following a continuous improvement in
recent years, are reliable, with wines
always true to the territory and soundly
wedded to tradition. Antheos 2012 is a
well-balanced wine and a racy delight in
the mouth, it is full of energy and the fruit
is never overpowering. The finish is dry
and sapid. The fruity Lagrein Riserva 2011
offers fresh elegant flavours, with a
delightful hint of cocoa in a well-paced
mouth. Moscato Rosa Passito 2010
expresses a very traditional style.

○ A. A. Gewürztraminer Kastelaz '12	♥♥♥ 5
● A. A. Merlot Kastelaz Ris. '09	♥♥ 6
○ A. A. Bianco Beyond the Clouds '11	♥♥ 6
● A. A. Lagrein Castel Ringberg Ris. '09	♥♥ 5
○ A. A. Pinot Bianco Kastelaz '12	♥♥ 4
○ A. A. Pinot Grigio Castel Ringberg '12	♥♥ 4
● Kermesse '09	♥♥ 6
○ A. A. Chardonnay Cardellino '12	♥ 3
○ A. A. Chardonnay Castel Ringberg Ris. '11	♥ 5
○ A. A. Gewürztraminer Passito Cashmere '11	♥ 3
○ A. A. Sauvignon Castel Ringberg '12	♥ 4
○ A. A. Gewürztraminer Kastelaz '11	♀♀♀ 5
○ A. A. Gewürztraminer Kastelaz '10	♀♀♀ 3*
○ A. A. Gewürztraminer Kastelaz '09	♀♀♀ 5

● A. A. Santa Maddalena Cl. Antheos '12	♥♥♥ 4*
● A. A. Lagrein Ris. '11	♥♥ 5
● A. A. Moscato Rosa Passito '10	♥♥ 5
● A. A. Santa Maddalena Cl. '12	♥ 3
○ A. A. Sauvignon '12	♥♥ 4
● A. A. Cabernet Sauvignon Laurenz '11	♥ 5
● A. A. Lagrein Mirell '11	♥ 6
● A. A. Cabernet Sauvignon '99	♀♀♀ 5
● A. A. Lagrein Mirell '09	♀♀♀ 6
● A. A. Lagrein Scuro Mirell '08	♀♀♀ 6
● A. A. Lagrein Scuro Mirell '07	♀♀♀ 6
● A. A. Lagrein Scuro Mirell '01	♀♀♀ 6
● A. A. Santa Maddalena Cl. Antheos '11	♀♀♀ 4*
● A. A. Lagrein Mirell '10	♀♀ 6

Josef Weger

LOC. CORNAIANO
VIA CASA DEL GESÙ, 17
39050 APPIANO/EPPAN [BZ]
TEL. 0471662416
www.wegerhof.it

CELLAR SALES
PRE-BOOKED VISITS
ACCOMMODATION AND RESTAURANT SERVICE
ANNUAL PRODUCTION 80,000 bottles
HECTARES UNDER VINE 8.00

Josef Weger started his family winery back in 1820. Six generations have handed down their combined experience, nowadays brought into to play to manage the estate-owned vineyards and purchase the grapes selected by the family. The estate's production is divided into two lines, Tenuta Josef Weger and the more highly valued Maso delle Rose, made from a selection of grapes sourced from the three-odd hectare property they own at Cornaiano and normally aged in wood. The wines presented this year are not a happy bunch. Many were tired, oxidization abounded and there was a general lack of energy. Pinot Bianco Maso delle Rose 2012 has two souls. One is is a wealth of fresh citrus aromas; the other has a complexity born of some tertiary elements.

Peter Zemmer

S.DA DEL VINO, 24
39040 CORTINA SULLA STRADA DEL VINO/KURTINIG [BZ]
TEL. 0471817143
www.peterzemmer.com

CELLAR SALES
PRE-BOOKED VISITS
ANNUAL PRODUCTION 500,000 bottles
HECTARES UNDER VINE 65.00

The winery is at Cortina, a place where viticulture has always played an important role within the social fabric. Here, the combination of a harsh climate and a very particular land formation creates the ideal conditions for a superb wine production. The soil is composed of calcareous and dolomitic debris with boulder clay, with consistent water reserves accumulated over the long snowy winters. Summers are defined by great swings in temperature between night and day, allowing the grapes to keep all their aromas intact. They produce a very wide range of wines. The best wines are the Pinot Grigio 2012, with marked sensations of pear and apricot, and a rich, firm palate with a generous, lively finish; the Pinot Bianco Punggl 2012, with clear, refined fruit and notes of fresh herbs and minerals and a long, harmonious, nearly salty palate; and the Lagrein Reserve 2011, with ripe fruit and assertive tannins.

○ A. A. Pinot Bianco Maso delle Rose '12	♥♥ 4
○ A. A. Müller Thurgau Pursgla '12	♥ 3
⊙ A. A. Lagrein Rosé '12	♥ 3
● A. A. Schiava '12	♥ 2
○ A. A. Gewürztraminer Maso delle Rose '11	♀♀3
● A. A. Lagrein '09	♀♀ 3
○ A. A. Pinot Bianco Maso delle Rose '10	♀♀ 4
○ A. A. Pinot Bianco Maso delle Rose '09	♀♀ 4
● Joanni Maso delle Rose '06	♀♀ 4

○ A. A. Pinot Grigio Peter Zemmer '12	♥♥ 3*
● A. A. Lagrein Reserve '11	♥♥ 4
○ A. A. Pinot Bianco Punggl '12	♥♥ 3
● A. A. Pinot Nero Rollhütt '11	♥♥ 4
○ A. A. Chardonnay '12	♥ 2
○ A. A. Chardonnay Reserve '11	♥ 4
○ Cortinie Bianco '12	♥ 3
● A. A. Lagrein Reserve '10	♀♀ 4
● A. A. Lagrein Reserve '07	♀♀ 4
○ A. A. Pinot Bianco '11	♀♀ 3
○ A. A. Pinot Grigio '11	♀♀ 3*
● A. A. Pinot Nero '07	♀♀ 3*

VENETO

We have no major changes to report in terms of rankings, but there are profound changes to their geography, especially in Valpolicella. The trend in recent years was to focus efforts to make a crisper, more austere Amarone and this has led to a production that sometimes sacrificed harmony for more clenched tannins, which is certainly more versatile at the table but also more challenging for the palate. On top form, however, we found Valpolicella Superiore, which is slowly finding its feet, with wild berries, fines herbes and spices coming together in a taut palate with an original profile that does not blindly mimic Amarone. So, while we see the confirmation of Amarones from the most renowned wineries like Allegrini, Tenuta Sant'Antonio or Bertani on one hand, we witness the assertion of the Valpolicellas from the Mazzis, Tedeschis and Castellanis on the other, flanked by Marion and Monte dall'Ora. For the whites, we are seeing Soaves and Custozas once again leading the troops and using traditional grapes for a wine that is not only up-to-the-minute but also tied fast to traditions and terroirs. Lake Garda offers the aromatic richness of Ottella's Luganas and the finesse of the Custozas from Cavalchina and Monte del Fra, while Soave is now proclaiming a style that restores richness after years of pared-down styling, with the wines from Vicentini and Francesco Tessari leading the sprint. In Valdobbiadene the Adamis took home a Tre Bicchieri with their Col Credas, a refined, spirited Brut that since arriving on the scene has been a complement to the veterans Merotto, Ruggeri and Villa Sandi. Also interesting is the excitement brewing around the Bordeaux grape varieties, perfectly expressed in summery Colli Euganei wines, where Vignalta and Il Mottolo fly the flag, while Serafini & Vidotto lay claim to the role of these grapes in an area advocating prosecco-based sparklers. The Colli Berici district sends forth a fantastic Carmenere from Inama, echoed by the completely contrasting Brol Grande proposed by Matilde Poggi, tasked with adding lustre to the Bardolino zone with a wine that is slowly recovering its rightful place. Finally, Quintarelli presents a Recioto of rare finesse and complexity, an icon of a type to be protected.

Stefano Accordini

FRAZ. CAVALO
LOC. CAMPAROL, 10
37022 FUMANE [VR]
TEL. 0457760138
www.accordinistefano.it

Adami

FRAZ. COLBERTALDO
VIA ROVEDE, 27
31020 VIDOR [TV]
TEL. 0423982110
www.adamispumanti.it

CELLAR SALES
PRE-BOOKED VISITS
ANNUAL PRODUCTION 120,000 bottles
HECTARES UNDER VINE 13.00

CELLAR SALES
PRE-BOOKED VISITS
ANNUAL PRODUCTION 700,000 bottles
HECTARES UNDER VINE 12.00

Focus on the estate's vineyards and on the environment, re-evaluation of high hillside vineyards, promotion of traditional grape varieties partly discarded by the DOC: all these aspects summarize the working philosophy of Tiziano Accordini, one of the most dedicated and meticulous exponents of Valpolicella and Amarone, assisted by his family. The new Mazzurega cellar is fully equipped and environmentally friendly, with ample space for all the processes required for products characterized by healthy fruit and good firm flavour. The Amarone Il Fornetto 2006 is emblematic of this style. Produced exclusively in the best years, its aromas of super-ripe red fruit, spices and aromatic herbs combine with a solid, powerful palate and smooth tannin. The Recioto Acinatico 2010 is much livelier and more approachable, with intensely fruity aromas and well-calibrated sweetness perfectly countered by acidity and tannins.

The Prosecco sector has undergone some profound and revolutionary changes in recent years. Expansion of the DOC zone has flooded the market with large quantities of sparkling wines, resulting in upheaval of prices and quality that is not always up to traditional standards. Great credit goes to estates like Armando and Franco Adami's for staying firmly on course in their pursuit of finesse and elegance, the real trademark of this classic Treviso winery and its products, as this year's tastings also demonstrated. The Col Credas makes an excellent debut as a very assertive Brut made from grapes grown at the Torri di Credazzo: a dry, edgy sparkler with a firm palate and almost electric finish. Armando and Franco present their customary high quality in the classic products too, especially the Dry Vigneto Giardino.

● Amarone della Valpolicella Cl. Vign. Il Fornetto '06	♈♈ 8	
● Recioto della Valpolicella Cl. Acinatico '10	♈♈ 5	
● Amarone della Valpolicella Cl. Acinatico '09	♈♈ 7	
● Valpolicella Cl. '12	♈♈ 2*	
● Valpolicella Cl. Sup. Ripasso Acinatico '11	♈♈ 3	
● Paxxo '11	♈ 4	
● Amarone della Valpolicella Cl. Acinatico '95	♈♈♈ 5	
● Amarone della Valpolicella Cl. Vign. Il Fornetto '95	♈♈♈ 5	
● Amarone della Valpolicella Cl. Vign. Il Fornetto '93	♈♈♈ 5	
● Recioto della Valpolicella Cl. Acinatico '04	♈♈♈ 6	

○ Valdobbiadene Rive di Farra di Soligo Brut Col Credas '12	♈♈♈ 4*	
○ Valdobbiadene Rive di Colbertaldo Dry Vign. Giardino '12	♈♈ 4	
○ Cartizze	♈♈ 5	
○ Valdobbiadene Brut Bosco di Gica	♈♈ 3	
○ Valdobbiadene Extra Dry Dei Casel	♈♈ 3	
○ Prosecco di Treviso Brut Garbèl	♈ 2	
○ Valdobbiadene P. Frizzante Sul Lievito	♈ 3	
○ Valdobbiadene Rive di Colbertaldo Dry Vign. Giardino '11	♈♈ 3*	
○ Valdobbiadene Rive di Colbertaldo Dry Vign. Giardino '10	♈♈ 3	
○ Valdobbiadene Rive di Colbertaldo Dry Vign. Giardino '09	♈♈ 3*	

Ida Agnoletti

LOC. SELVA DEL MONTELLO
VIA SACCARDO, 55
31040 VOLPAGO DEL MONTELLO [TV]
TEL. 0423621555
www.agnoletti.com

★★Allegrini

VIA GIARE, 5
37022 FUMANE [VR]
TEL. 0456832011
www.allegrini.it

CELLAR SALES
PRE-BOOKED VISITS
ANNUAL PRODUCTION 50,000 bottles
HECTARES UNDER VINE 7.00

CELLAR SALES
PRE-BOOKED VISITS
RESTAURANT SERVICE
ANNUAL PRODUCTION 900,000 bottles
HECTARES UNDER VINE 100.00

Ida Agnoletti's winery is situated on high ground on the southern slope of Montello, in the northern part of the province of Treviso. This is a particularly unspoilt environment with little urban development. With less than ten hectares, Ida focuses on products of an excellent standard, subdivided into a wide range of labels which speak of the producer's desire to experiment and challenge herself. The lion's share goes to black Bordeaux grape varieties, leaving Prosecco a secondary role, which goes against the usual grain. The most impressive wine from Agnoletti this year is in fact a Merlot. The 2011 displays vibrant fruity aromas echoed by discreet vegetal hints, nicely mirrored on the refreshing palate. Its dry, extremely fresh flavour is guided by nicely smooth tannins and tangy acidity. The rest of the range is dependably good.

This estate has without question done more than any other to make Amarone known around the world, offering a combination of high-quality wines at fair prices and widespread presence on the market. This is undoubtedly due to considerable skill in the cellar, not to mention more than 100 hectares of vineyards which have gradually been converted to high profile winegrowing methods to enhance the climate and soil differences between plots. While the more recently planted vineyards use the vertical-trellised training system, the older vines are still pergola-trained. Once again, the most impressive wine chez Allegrini is the Amarone 2009 which succeeds in the difficult task of combining traditional richness with a fresh, sound palate, which is powerful and full-flavoured yet racy. The La Poja 2009, a monovarietal Corvina, is on top form with a suppler, more linear structure than in previous years.

● Montello e Colli Asolani Merlot '11	▼▼ 2*
● Recantina '12	▼▼ 2*
○ Manzoni Bianco '12	▼ 2
● Montello e Colli Asolani Cabernet Sauvignon '11	▼ 2
● Montello e Colli Asolani Merlot La Ida '11	▼ 2
○ Prosecco di Treviso Frizzante Selva n. 55	▼ 2
○ Prosecco di Treviso Il Tranquillo '12	▼ 2
○ Verdiso '12	▼ 2
● Ludwy '09	♀♀ 3
● Montello e Colli Asolani Cabernet Sauvignon '10	♀♀ 2*
● Montello e Colli Asolani Merlot '10	♀♀ 2*
● Montello e Colli Asolani Merlot La Ida '09	♀♀ 2
● Seneca '09	♀♀ 3

● Amarone della Valpolicella Cl. '09	▼▼▼ 8
● La Poja '09	▼▼ 8
● Recioto della Valpolicella Cl. Giovanni Allegrini '10	▼▼ 6
● La Grola '10	▼▼ 5
● Palazzo della Torre '10	▼▼ 4
○ Soave '12	▼▼ 2*
● Valpolicella Cl. '12	▼▼ 3
● Amarone della Valpolicella Cl. '08	♀♀♀ 8
● Amarone della Valpolicella Cl. '07	♀♀♀ 8
● Amarone della Valpolicella Cl. '06	♀♀♀ 8
● Amarone della Valpolicella Cl. '05	♀♀♀ 7
● Amarone della Valpolicella Cl. '04	♀♀♀ 7
● La Poja '01	♀♀♀ 7
● La Poja '97	♀♀♀ 8
● Recioto della Valpolicella Cl. Giovanni Allegrini '00	♀♀♀ 5

★Roberto Anselmi

VIA SAN CARLO, 46
37032 MONTEFORTE D'ALPONE [VR]
TEL. 0457611488
www.anselmi.eu

CELLAR SALES
PRE-BOOKED VISITS
RESTAURANT SERVICE
ANNUAL PRODUCTION 700,000 bottles
HECTARES UNDER VINE 70.00

Roberto Anselmi is the soul of this large Monteforte d'Alpone estate. It was the first to bring fine quality Veronese white wine to the world's attention and is still a benchmark for the whole area today, despite leaving the DOC. Roberto's children Lisa and Tommaso work alongside him with the same passion and increasing skill. The cellar is one of the best-equipped in the area, faithfully reflecting the meticulous approach, leaving nothing to chance, that Roberto has always pursued. Despite significant production quantities, the winery has always focused on classic traditional labels. Anselmi offers three absolutely top-quality whites, led by the Capitel Croce 2011 that is aged in oak to enhance its deep, harmonious character rather than to enrich its aroma, thus gaining in charm and finesse. The Capitel Foscarino and San Vincenzo, both 2012, are more aromatic and tropical, with an approachable, juicy palate.

○ Capitel Croce '11	♀♀ 3*
○ Capitel Foscarino '12	♀♀ 3
○ San Vincenzo '12	♀♀ 2*
○ Capitel Croce '09	♀♀♀ 3*
○ Capitel Croce '06	♀♀♀ 3
○ Capitel Croce '05	♀♀♀ 3
○ Capitel Croce '04	♀♀♀ 3
○ Capitel Croce '03	♀♀♀ 3
○ Capitel Croce '02	♀♀♀ 3*
○ Capitel Croce '01	♀♀♀ 3
○ Capitel Croce '00	♀♀♀ 3
○ Capitel Croce '99	♀♀♀ 3*
○ Recioto dei Capitelli '87	♀♀♀ 8
○ Recioto dei Capitelli '86	♀♀♀ 8
○ Recioto dei Capitelli '85	♀♀♀ 8
○ Recioto di Soave I Capitelli '96	♀♀♀ 5

Antolini

VIA PROGNOL, 22
37020 MARANO DI VALPOLICELLA [VR]
TEL. 0457755351
www.antolinivini.it

CELLAR SALES
PRE-BOOKED VISITS
ANNUAL PRODUCTION 60,000 bottles
HECTARES UNDER VINE 8.00

Pierpaolo and Stefano Antolini brought their estate to life a few years ago and quickly hit the headlines thanks to products that are firmly linked to tradition. Withering is never simply muscle-flexing for the grapes, but a history-rooted practice which endows the wines with noble and authentic qualities. The estate's modest number of hectares is located mainly in the Marano valley, with a few in the Negrar valley, and produces a reliable and solidly rustic range of wines. The Negrar vineyard, a couple of hectares planted in 2000, yields the most impressive wine, Amarone Ca' Coato 2009. Evident raisining on the nose is enhanced by hints of spice and crushed flowers, while a change of gear on the palate highlights a rich palate guided by confident, taut acidity and tannins. The Ripasso also gave an excellent performance with a firm, juicy palate.

● Amarone della Valpolicella Cl. Ca' Coato '09	♀♀ 6
● Amarone della Valpolicella Cl. Moròpio '09	♀♀ 6
● Valpolicella Cl. Sup. Ripasso '11	♀♀ 3
● Theobroma '10	♀ 4
● Amarone della Valpolicella Cl. Ca' Coato '08	♀♀ 6
● Amarone della Valpolicella Cl. Ca' Coato '07	♀♀ 6
● Amarone della Valpolicella Cl. Ca' Coato '06	♀♀ 6
● Amarone della Valpolicella Cl. Moròpio '06	♀♀ 5
● Valpolicella Cl. Sup. '10	♀♀ 3
● Valpolicella Cl. Sup. Ripasso '10	♀♀ 3
● Valpolicella Cl. Sup. Ripasso '09	♀♀ 3*
● Valpolicella Cl. Sup. Ripasso '08	♀♀ 3

Balestri Valda

VIA MONTI, 44
37038 SOAVE [VR]
TEL. 0457675393
www.vinibalestrivalda.com

Barollo

VIA RIO SERVA, 4B
35123 PREGANZIOL [TV]
TEL. 0422633014
www.barollo.com

CELLAR SALES
PRE-BOOKED VISITS
ANNUAL PRODUCTION 60,000 bottles
HECTARES UNDER VINE 13.00

CELLAR SALES
PRE-BOOKED VISITS
ANNUAL PRODUCTION 57,000 bottles
HECTARES UNDER VINE 45.00

Travelling from Soave towards Castelcerino, the winery owned by Guido Rizzotto and his daughter Laura is surrounded by woods and vineyards facing southwards to capture the warmth of the sun. The 20-odd hectares yield a small amount of high profile wines, with the Soave Sengialta aged in large casks and left to mature for a further year in the cool cellar. Rizzotto wines are based on garganega and trebbiano di Soave and all fall into the traditional Soave categories. The Rizzotto style favours elegance and grip on the palate over aromatic features, so expect a tangy, taut, mouth-watering flavour rather than special effects on the nose. A textbook performance from the Soave Classico: subtle, floral aromas are confidently and harmoniously mirrored on the palate. A richer, mature nose and palate for the Lunalonga, a blend of Garganega and Trebbiano di Soave, aged respectively in steel and oak.

The Barollo family winery is situated between Venice and Treviso, behind the historical Via Terraglio that connects the two cities. Close to 30 hectares of vineyards are mainly planted with black Bordeaux varieties but there is also space for the native glera and Manzoni bianco varieties which create dependably good quality wines. Since the winery was established Nicola and Marco Barollo have chosen to use the sector's leading professionals to guarantee the estate's swift yet high-profile development. Once again the most impressive wine is the Frank!, a Cabernet Franc that blends spicy freshness with red berries, resulting in a particularly elegant, full, succulent palate. A good debut for the Sauvignon, from a recently planted vineyard, with tropical, vegetal aromas reflected on a racy, harmonious palate.

○ Soave Cl. '12	♟♟ 2*
○ Soave Cl. Lunalonga '11	♟♟ 3
○ Recioto di Soave Cl. '09	♟ 5
○ Recioto di Soave Spumante '11	♟ 3
○ Recioto di Soave Cl. '08	♟♟ 5
○ Soave Cl. '11	♟♟ 2*
○ Soave Cl. '09	♟♟ 2
○ Soave Cl. '06	♟♟ 2
○ Soave Cl. Lunalonga '08	♟♟ 3*
○ Soave Cl. Sengialta '11	♟♟ 2*
○ Soave Cl. Sengialta '10	♟♟ 2*
○ Soave Cl. Sengialta '09	♟♟ 2*
○ Soave Cl. Sengialta '08	♟♟ 2*
○ Soave Cl. Sengialta '07	♟♟ 2

● Frank! '11	♟♟ 4
○ Manzoni Bianco '12	♟♟ 3
○ Sauvignon '12	♟♟ 3
○ Piave Chardonnay Frater '12	♟ 3
● Piave Merlot Frater '12	♟ 3
○ Pinot Bianco '12	♟ 3
○ Prosecco di Treviso Extra Dry	♟ 2
● Frank '09	♟♟ 3
● Frank '08	♟♟ 3*
● Frank! '10	♟♟ 3*
○ Manzoni Bianco '11	♟♟ 2*
○ Pinot Bianco '11	♟♟ 2*
○ Pinot Bianco '09	♟♟ 2*
○ Pinot Grigio '09	♟♟ 2*

Beato Bartolomeo da Breganze

VIA ROMA, 100
36042 BREGANZE [VI]
TEL. 0445873112
www.cantinabreganze.it

CELLAR SALES
ANNUAL PRODUCTION 3,500,000 bottles
HECTARES UNDER VINE 700.00

The Breganze DOC zone extends along the foothills between Bassano and Thiene, a long strip of land with a variety of different weather and soil conditions. The Cantina Beato Bartolomeo da Breganze co-operative is the largest winery in the area and has always prioritized values of tradition and everyday wine consumption. The range naturally covers different levels: the Savardo line represents the top quality products and Bosco Grande the flagship wines. The Breganze products are rather below par this year: the pursuit of extract has cost the wines a little of their elegance and grip. The Cabernet Bosco Grande 2010 is the best of the bunch thanks to nicely blended aromas of fruit and oak and a firm palate guided by prominent tannin. The Torcolato 2010 of the same line is complex and exuberantly sweet.

● Breganze Cabernet Bosco Grande '10	♟♟ 3
○ Breganze Torcolato Bosco Grande Ris. '10	♟♟ 4
● Breganze Cabernet Kilò Ris. '10	♟ 4
● Breganze Cabernet Sup. Savardo '11	♟ 2
○ Breganze Chardonnay Bosco Grande '11	♟ 3
● Breganze Merlot Bosco Grande '10	♟ 3
● Breganze Merlot Sup. Savardo '11	♟ 2
● Breganze Pinot Nero Sup. Savardo '11	♟ 2
○ Breganze Torcolato '10	♟ 4
○ Breganze Vespaiolo Extra Dry	♟ 2
○ Breganze Vespaiolo Sulla Rotta del Bacalà '12	♟ 2
○ Breganze Vespaiolo Sup. Savardo '12	♟ 2
○ Breganze Torcolato '06	♟♟ 5
○ Breganze Torcolato Bosco Grande '09	♟♟ 4

★Lorenzo Begali

VIA CENGIA, 10
37020 SAN PIETRO IN CARIANO [VR]
TEL. 0457725148
www.begaliwine.it

CELLAR SALES
PRE-BOOKED VISITS
ANNUAL PRODUCTION 60,000 bottles
HECTARES UNDER VINE 9.50

In the last 20 years, the Valpolicella area has undergone considerable development and increased its renown, leading to the appearance of countless new wineries often attracted by the opportunity for swift development. Lorenzo Begali has maintained a steady pace, growing wisely and continually, bringing to life one of the area's most representative wineries today. The estate's ten or so hectares of vineyards are situated partly on the plain and partly on the hillside. The winery pays close attention to partial drying of the grapes used in these wines, which are typically meticulously put-together with grip on the palate. Another great performance from the Amarone Monte Ca' Bianca 2008, which is generous and powerful while maintaining a profile so dry and taut it almost appears light. The Amarone Classico 2009 is fresher and more approachable, while the Recioto 2010 displays vibrant fruit and cocoa aromas and a charming, racy flavour. Lastly, the excellent non-vintage Valpolicella is fragrant and well-typed.

● Amarone della Valpolicella Cl. Vign. Monte Ca' Bianca '08	♟♟♟ 8
● Amarone della Valpolicella Cl. '09	♟♟ 6
● Recioto della Valpolicella Cl. '10	♟♟ 6
● Tigiolo '09	♟♟ 5
● Valpolicella Cl. '12	♟♟ 2*
● Valpolicella Cl. Sup. Ripasso Vign. La Cengia '11	♟♟ 3
● Amarone della Valpolicella Cl. Vign. Monte Ca' Bianca '07	♔♔♔ 8
● Amarone della Valpolicella Cl. Vign. Monte Ca' Bianca '06	♔♔♔ 8
● Amarone della Valpolicella Cl. Vign. Monte Ca' Bianca '05	♔♔♔ 8
● Amarone della Valpolicella Cl. Vign. Monte Ca' Bianca '04	♔♔♔ 8

Cecilia Beretta - Pasqua

loc. San Felice Extra
s.da della Giara, 135
37131 Verona
Tel. 0458432111
www.ceciliaberetta.it

PRE-BOOKED VISITS
ANNUAL PRODUCTION
350,000+14,000,000 bottles
HECTARES UNDER VINE 89.00+1,000.00

The Pasqua family's large estate comprises two distinct businesses: Pasqua, which uses grapes and wines from all over Italy, and family winery Cecilia Beretta which focuses entirely on Veronese products. Here, the production process is closely followed in all its phases, from the almost 100 hectares of vineyards to the winery at San Felice, opened a few years ago. The winery deals with all stages of production, allowing the technical staff plenty of calm and space to work. The Amarone Terre di Cariano 2009 gave its usual thoroughbred performance, with vibrant dried fruit, spice and crushed flowers on the nose, and a mouth-watering, firm palate with smooth tannin and a long finish. The excellent Valpolicella Superiore 2011 of the same line displays polished aromas and a racy yet deep palate, making it one of the best in its category. Meanwhile all the Pasqua wines are beautifully drinkable.

★Cav. G. B. Bertani

via Asiago, 1
37023 Grezzana [VR]
Tel. 0458658444
www.bertani.net

CELLAR SALES
PRE-BOOKED VISITS
ANNUAL PRODUCTION 1,800,000 bottles
HECTARES UNDER VINE 200.00

Bertani, which recently joined the Angelini family group, is an emblematic estate for Valpolicella tradition, able to undergo innovations and modernizations without losing sight of the area's distinctive characteristic features and customs. The wine which probably best represents this style is the Secco Bertani, a Valpolicella made using the Ripasso technique to create generous, rather than raisiny, aromas and deep rather than powerful flavour in a synthesis between modern wine and the wine Giovan Battista Bertani created over a hundred years ago. Bertani's Amarone 2006 has it all: deep aromas, finesse, full body and grip, tradition and texture. This classic DOC wine never fails to show off its high rank. The Secco Bertani 2011 continues to improve despite its large production and is more impressive each year for its typicality and finesse. Among the whites, we have singled out the excellent Soave Sereole 2012.

● Amarone della Valpolicella Cl. Terre di Cariano Cecilia Beretta '09	🍷🍷 8
● Amarone della Valpolicella Cecilia Beretta '09	🍷🍷 6
● Amarone della Valpolicella Cl. Villa Borghetti Pasqua '09	🍷🍷 6
● Valpolicella Cl. Sup. Terre di Cariano Cecilia Beretta '11	🍷🍷 3
● Valpolicella Sup. Ripasso Cecilia Beretta '11	🍷🍷 3
○ Soave Cl. Brognoligo Cecilia Beretta '12	🍷 3
● Soraie Cecilia Beretta '10	🍷 5
● Valpolicella Cl. Villa Borghetti Pasqua '12	🍷 3
● Valpolicella Sup. Mizzole Cecilia Beretta '10	🍷 3
● Valpolicella Sup. Ripasso Villa Borghetti Pasqua '11	🍷 3

● Amarone della Valpolicella Cl. '06	🍷🍷🍷 8
● Valpolicella Cl. Sup. Ognisanti '11	🍷🍷 4
● Valpolicella Valpantena Secco Bertani '11	🍷🍷 3*
● Amarone della Valpolicella Valpantena Villa Arvedi '10	🍷🍷 6
○ Le Lave '11	🍷🍷 3
● Secco Bertani Vintage Edition '10	🍷🍷 4
○ Soave Sereole '12	🍷🍷 2*
⊙ Bertarose Chiaretto '12	🍷 2
● Amarone della Valpolicella Cl. '05	🍷🍷🍷 8
● Amarone della Valpolicella Cl. '04	🍷🍷🍷 8
● Amarone della Valpolicella Cl. '03	🍷🍷🍷 8
● Amarone della Valpolicella Cl. '01	🍷🍷🍷 8
● Amarone della Valpolicella Cl. '00	🍷🍷🍷 8
● Valpolicella Cl. Sup. Vign. Ognisanti '06	🍷🍷🍷 2*

La Biancara

FRAZ. SORIO
C.DA BIANCARA, 14
36053 GAMBELLARA [VI]
TEL. 0444444244
www.biancaravini.it

CELLAR SALES
PRE-BOOKED VISITS
ANNUAL PRODUCTION 65,000 bottles
HECTARES UNDER VINE 13.00

Celebrations this year for 25 years in business at the winery owned by Angiolino Maule, groundbreaking spearhead of the movement to reiterate meticulous care for the environment and healthier products. Today his sons Francesco and Alessandro work alongside him with Giacomo and Tommaso hot on their heels. Production mostly takes place within the Gambellara zone, with a small but prestigious component in the nearby Colli Berici. Spontaneous fermentation and the banishment of chemicals from the cellar are fundamental to the production of high quality, authentic wines. We only tasted garganega-based wines from Maule this year, including one of the best-ever versions of Pico, obtained through spontaneous fermentation of grapes from hillside vineyards, aged in casks for a year. The aromas are strikingly vibrant and broad: peaches and apricots, Mediterranean scrubland and fines herbes, which follow through on the tangy, dry and very lingering palate.

○ Pico '11	♥♥ 4
○ Masieri Bianco '12	♥♥ 2*
○ Sassaia '12	♥♥ 3
○ Pico '02	♥♥♥ 4*
○ Recioto di Gambellara '07	♥♥♥ 5
○ Pico '10	♀♀ 4
○ Pico '09	♀♀ 4
○ Pico '08	♀♀ 4
○ Pico '07	♀♀ 4
○ Recioto di Gambellara '08	♀♀ 5
○ Recioto di Gambellara '02	♀♀ 5
○ Sassaia '10	♀♀ 3*
○ Sassaia '09	♀♀ 2*

BiancaVigna

LOC. SAN PIETRO DI FELETTO
VIA CREVADA, 9/1
31010 SOLIGO
TEL. 0438801098
www.biancavigna.it

PRE-BOOKED VISITS
ACCOMMODATION
ANNUAL PRODUCTION 400,000 bottles
HECTARES UNDER VINE 18.00

BiancaVigna, owned by Elena and Enrico Moschetta, covers 18 hectares in the eastern part of the designation, where the grapes are able to obtain greater richness and structure. The hillsides of Soligo, San Pietro di Feletto and Conegliano provide the bases for the top wines while the entry-level ones hail from the vineyards at the bottom of these hills. Enrico monitors all the production phases in the cellar at Crevada, pursuing wines with great finesse and grip, before the business moves to the Ogliano building now under construction. The Conegliano Valdobbiadene Brut 2012 displays lime blossom and appley fruit on the nose, while the tangy palate is invigorated and lengthened by the fizz and acidity. The more approachable and exuberant Extra Dry 2012 is fruitier on the nose with perfectly balanced sugar on the succulent palate. The other wines are leaner and more approachable.

○ Conegliano Valdobbiadene Brut '12	♥♥ 3
○ Conegliano Valdobbiadene Extra Dry '12	♥♥ 3
○ Prosecco Brut	♥ 2
○ Prosecco Extra Dry	♥ 2
○ Conegliano Valdobbiadene Brut '11	♀♀ 3*
○ Conegliano Valdobbiadene Brut '09	♀♀ 2

Desiderio Bisol & Figli

FRAZ. SANTO STEFANO
VIA FOLLO, 33
31049 VALDOBBIADENE [TV]
TEL. 0423900138
www.bisol.it

CELLAR SALES
PRE-BOOKED VISITS
ANNUAL PRODUCTION 1,800,000 bottles
HECTARES UNDER VINE 126.00

The Bisol family own one of the most typical estates in the world of Prosecco, with a lengthy history of sparkling wine production and prestigious vineyards. In addition to all this, Gianluca Bisol displays great skill in the role of ambassador for his winery and similarly for the denomination itself. The entire range is dedicated to Treviso fizz, subdivided into different lines to provide the most suitable type for each market sector. Of the few wines we tasted from the wide range, the Vigneti del Fol 2012 stood out for its classy performance. An Extra Dry made from grapes grown in one of the designation's best zones, its fresh notes, ranging from apples and pears to flowers, develop into a crisp, succulent palate with subtle sweetness to counter the acidity. We were impressed by the excellent Relio 2009 Metodo Classico made from glera, which came close to a Due Bicchieri.

F.lli Bolla

FRAZ. PEDEMONTE
VIA ALBERTO BOLLA, 3
37029 SAN PIETRO IN CARIANO [VR]
TEL. 0456836555
www.bolla.it

CELLAR SALES
PRE-BOOKED VISITS
ANNUAL PRODUCTION 12,000,000 bottles
HECTARES UNDER VINE 350.00

The Gruppo Italiano Vini heads this large Verona winery which has set forth on a virtuoso path to excellent production standards, as a faithful exponent of tradition without clinging to ideological models. Despite the dizzying numbers, the leading wines are among the best in the DOC zone thanks also to the direction of Cristian Scrinzi, who has succeeded in giving the winery a boost while maintaining its strongly Veronese character. The Amarone Le Origini 2008 is on top form as an exemplary traditional wine without excessive roundness or ageing: instead, it shows fresh, rich and complex on the nose, and vigorous and full-bodied on the harmonious palate. We also liked the Ripasso Le Poiane 2011 with its impressively mature, balsamic aromas developing into a taut, beautifully fresh flavour. The simpler wines all show an approach that fully respects the grape variety.

○ Cartizze '12	♟♟ 5
○ Valdobbiadene Brut Crede '12	♟♟ 4
○ Valdobbiadene Extra Dry Vigneti del Fol '12	♟♟ 4
○ Relio Extra Brut M. Cl. '09	♟ 6
○ Valdobbiadene Extra Dry Colmei Jeio	♟ 2
○ Cartizze '11	♟♟ 5
○ Cartizze '09	♟♟ 5
○ P. di Valdobbiadene Extra Dry Vigneti del Fol '06	♟♟ 3
○ Valdobbiadene Brut Crede '11	♟♟ 4
○ Valdobbiadene Brut Garnei '10	♟♟ 3
○ Valdobbiadene Extra Dry Vigneti del Fol '11	♟♟ 4

● Amarone della Valpolicella Cl. Le Origini '08	♟♟ 7
● Creso '10	♟♟ 4
● Valpolicella Cl. Sup. Ripasso '11	♟♟ 2*
● Valpolicella Cl. Sup. Ripasso Le Poiane '11	♟♟ 3
⊙ Bardolino Chiaretto '12	♟ 2
● Bardolino Cl. '12	♟ 2
● Bolla Rosso '11	♟ 2
○ Custoza '12	♟ 2
○ Soave Cl. '12	♟ 3
○ Soave Cl. Retrò '12	♟ 2
○ Soave Cl. Sup. Tufaie '12	♟ 3
● Valpolicella Cl. '12	♟ 3

...ech

[VE]
Tel. 0...29
www.borg...tajnbech.com

Borgoluce

Loc. Musile, 2
31058 Susegana [TV]
Tel. 0438435287
www.borgoluce.it

CELLAR SALES
PRE-BOOKED VISITS
ANNUAL PRODUCTION 70,000 bottles
HECTARES UNDER VINE 14.00

CELLAR SALES
PRE-BOOKED VISITS
ACCOMMODATION AND RESTAURANT SERVICE
ANNUAL PRODUCTION 250,000 bottles
HECTARES UNDER VINE 70.00

This Pramaggiore estate is one of the most interesting in the Riviera zone. The 14-odd hectares of vineyards are planted on clayey soil along the coastal area overlooking the Adriatic, mainly with international grapes to produce wines of reliable quality whose essential features are crystal clear fruit and recognizable varieties. Traditional local cultivars tai and refosco are also grown for wines that display strong links between the grape and the terroir. The Lison 150 2012 is, in fact, the most impressive Valent wine, thanks to its nose of white peaches and almonds and the usual buttery palate, freshened up with tangy, succulent acidity. The Stajnbech Bianco 2011 is a very good Chardonnay aged in oak, flaunting ripe, sweet fruit aromas with creamy, oaky notes completing the full, caressing palate.

Borgoluce was established a few years ago although Lodovico Giustiniani has been involved in the wine sector for decades, and Borgoluce is just his latest venture. The farm covers over 1000 hectares used for livestock, grazing, woodlands and crops, with vineyards obviously the jewel in the estate's crown. Production focuses mainly on Prosecco, although other grapes are also grown, and all the work is done in the winery which is a stone's throw from Susegana. The sparkling Rive di Collalto 2012 put up an excellent performance. Its strength lies in expressive and highly typical aromas of apples, pears and wisteria. These follow through on the palate, where the prominent sweetness is held in check by tangy acidity. The Brut is lighter and fresher while the Extra Dry reveals clear-cut fruity aromas and a crisp, harmonious palate.

○ Lison-Pramaggiore Chardonnay Stajnbech Bianco '11	♟♟ 3
○ Lison-Pramaggiore Cl. 150 '12	♟♟ 3
● Rosso '09	♟♟ 3
● Lison-Pramaggiore Refosco P.R. '11	♟ 2
○ Lison-Pramaggiore Sauvignon Bosco della Donna '12	♟ 3
● Malbech '11	♟ 2
● Venezia Cabernet Franc '11	♟ 2
○ Venezia Pinot Grigio '12	♟ 2
○ Lison-Pramaggiore Chardonnay Stajnbech Bianco '10	♟♟ 4
○ Lison-Pramaggiore Cl. 150 '11	♟♟ 2*
○ Lison-Pramaggiore Cl. 150 '10	♟♟ 2*
● Lison-Pramaggiore Stajnbech Rosso '07	♟♟ 3
● Rosso '08	♟♟ 5

○ Valdobbiadene Extra Dry	♟♟ 3
○ Valdobbiadene Rive di Collalto Extra Dry Mill. '12	♟♟ 2*
○ Valdobbiadene Brut	♟ 3
○ Valdobbiadene Frizzante Gaiante	♟ 3
○ Prosecco di Valdobbiadene Extra Dry Mill. '09	♟♟ 3
○ Prosecco di Valdobbiadene Extra Dry Mill. '08	♟♟ 2*
○ Valdobbiadene Dry Mill. '10	♟♟ 3
○ Valdobbiadene Rive di Collalto Extra Dry Mill. '11	♟♟ 2*

Borin Vini & Vigne

FRAZ. MONTICELLI
VIA DEI COLLI, 5
35043 MONSELICE [PD]
TEL. 042974384
www.viniborin.it

CELLAR SALES
PRE-BOOKED VISITS
ANNUAL PRODUCTION 105,000 bottles
HECTARES UNDER VINE 28.00

The Euganean area has undergone a leap in quality in the last ten years, with the development of traditional estates and the appearance of many new wineries. Gianni Borin, helped by his wife Teresa and children Francesco and Giampaolo, runs the family business with passionate devotion and has developed a balanced range of products which share a distinctive generosity and recognizability of the grape variety. This year we sensed that the leading wines have upped their game, aiming for greater finesse and elegance and losing the overripe hints of the past. An emblematic tasting was provided by the Zuan 2011, which is now in the designation, showing a fresh, crisp nose of red berries and herbs, combined with a racy, mouth-watering, very lingering palate. Fiore di Gaia 2012 and Corte Borin 2011, from fior d'arancio and Manzoni bianco respectively, enhance their varietal features with a rounded, satisfying palate.

● Colli Euganei Rosso Zuan '11	♙♙ 3*
○ Colli Euganei Fior d'Arancio '12	♙♙ 2*
○ Colli Euganei Fior d'Arancio Fiore di Gaia '12	♙♙ 2*
○ Colli Euganei Manzoni Bianco Corte Borin '11	♙♙ 3
● Colli Euganei Merlot Rocca Chiara Ris. '10	♙♙ 4
● Coldivalle '10	♙ 3
● Colli Euganei Cabernet Sauvignon V. Costa '11	♙ 3
○ Colli Euganei Chardonnay V. Bianca '11	♙ 3
● Colli Euganei Merlot V. del Foscolo '11	♙ 2
○ Colli Euganei Pinot Bianco Monte Archino '12	♙ 2
○ Colli Euganei Serprino '12	♙ 2

Bortolomiol

VIA GARIBALDI, 142
31049 VALDOBBIADENE [TV]
TEL. 04239749
www.bortolomiol.com

CELLAR SALES
PRE-BOOKED VISITS
RESTAURANT SERVICE
ANNUAL PRODUCTION 1,800,000 bottles
HECTARES UNDER VINE 5.00

The Bortolomiol estate has made one of the greatest contributions to the promotion and diffusion of Prosecco worldwide, first with Giuliano at the helm and today with his daughters Maria Elena, Elvira, Luisa and Giuliana following in his footsteps. Today, as in the past, they farm their own few hectares of vineyards while relying on a well-stocked network of growers, monitored at each stage of production throughout the year, to provide the grapes for their large-scale production. The sheer volume has made it necessary to create different lines, interpreting the glera variety with accuracy and finesse. We witnessed an excellent performance from the Ius Naturae 2012, an organic Brut with well-defined apple and pear aromas and a relaxed, pleasing flavour. The Banda Rossa 2012 is probably the winery's standard-bearer, with subtle aromas of flowers and appley fruit on the nose and a lean, mouth-watering palate combining sweetness and fresh acidity. The Dry Maior is full-bodied, sunny and mouthfilling.

○ Valdobbiadene Brut Ius Naturae '12	♙♙ 4
○ Valdobbiadene Brut Rive San Pietro di Barbozza Motus Vitae '11	♙♙ 4
○ Valdobbiadene Dry Maior	♙♙ 2
○ Valdobbiadene Extra Dry Banda Rossa '12	♙♙ 3
○ Cartizze '12	♙ 5
○ Filanda Rosé Brut	♙ 3
● Piave Cabernet Sauvignon Mormorò '11	♙ 3
○ Riserva del Governatore Extra Brut '11	♙ 3
○ Valdobbiadene Brut Prior	♙ 2
○ Valdobbiadene Demi Sec Suavis	♙ 3
○ Valdobbiadene Extra Dry Senior	♙ 3
○ Valdobbiadene Frizzante Il Ponteggio	♙ 3
○ Valdobbiadene Tranquillo Canto Fermo '12	♙ 3
○ Ris. del Governatore Extra Brut '07	♙♙ 3
○ Valdobbiadene Extra Dry Banda Rossa '11	♙♙ 3

Carlo Boscaini

VIA SENGIA, 15
37010 SANT'AMBROGIO DI VALPOLICELLA [VR]
TEL. 0457731412
www.boscainicarlo.it

CELLAR SALES
PRE-BOOKED VISITS
ACCOMMODATION
ANNUAL PRODUCTION 70,000 bottles
HECTARES UNDER VINE 14.00

Carlo and Mario Boscaini's winery extends over the hills of Sant'Ambrogio di Valpolicella, the westernmost part of the DOC that reaches as far as the Valdadige. The estate began making wine over 60 years ago but was given a boost in the 1990s aimed at giving the winery a facelift, first renewing the vineyards and then a series of improvements in the cellar where the production process concerns only estate-grown traditional grapes. The winery approach aims for wines of weighty texture with supple, taut palates. The exemplary Amarone San Giorgio 2009 has dried fruit, black pepper and medicinal herbs on the nose following through into a generous, juicy palate offset by tangy acidity. The Valpolicella di Ripasso Zane 2009 shows a similar but less weighty profile, like the La Preosa 2010, upholding a very traditional, super-ripe style.

Bosco del Merlo

VIA POSTUMIA, 14
30020 ANNONE VENETO [VE]
TEL. 0422768167
www.boscodelmerlo.it

CELLAR SALES
PRE-BOOKED VISITS
ANNUAL PRODUCTION 240,000 bottles
HECTARES UNDER VINE 84.00

The Paladin family are among the most meticulous producers in the Venice area, with over 100 hectares of vineyards in the Lison-Pramaggiore denomination. The proximity to the Adriatic Sea, a clay-rich soil and the marked respect for the environment apparent in the vineyard management allow Lucia, Carlo and Roberto to produce wines which combine recognizable grape variety with the area's natural expressiveness. The Sauvignon Turranio 2012 is one of the most interesting whites in Veneto, showing vibrant tropical fruit and medicinal herbs on the nose, finishing off with a typical vegetal hint to denote the grape. The palate is full-bodied and especially tangy with succulent acidity and a long finish. We also liked the Roggio dei Roveri 2010 Refosco for its polished aromas and firm, harmonious palate. The Soandre 2010 passito shows complex aromas and well-controlled sweetness.

● Amarone della Valpolicella Cl. San Giorgio '09	♟♟ 5
● Valpolicella Cl. Sup. Ripasso Zane '09	♟♟ 3
● Valpolicella Cl. Sup. La Preosa '10	♟ 3
● Amarone della Valpolicella Cl. San Giorgio '08	♟♟ 5
● Amarone della Valpolicella Cl. San Giorgio '07	♟♟ 4
● Amarone della Valpolicella Cl. San Giorgio '04	♟♟ 4
● Amarone della Valpolicella Cl. San Giorgio '03	♟♟ 4
● Valpolicella Cl. Sup. La Preosa '09	♟♟ 5
● Valpolicella Cl. Sup. Ripasso Zane '08	♟♟ 3
● Valpolicella Cl. Sup. Ripasso Zane '06	♟♟ 3
● Valpolicella Cl. Sup. Ripasso Zane '04	♟♟ 3

● Lison-Pramaggiore Refosco P. R. Roggio dei Roveri '10	♟♟ 5
○ Lison-Pramaggiore Sauvignon Turranio '12	♟♟ 4
● 360 Ruber Capitae '10	♟♟ 5
○ Lison-Pramaggiore Lison Cl. Juti '12	♟♟ 4
○ Lison-Pramaggiore Verduzzo Soandre '10	♟♟ 5
○ Prosecco Brut Mill. '12	♟ 4
○ Venezia Chardonnay Nicopeja '12	♟ 3
○ Venezia Pinot Grigio Tudaio '12	♟ 3
● 360 Ruber Capitae '08	♟♟ 5
● 360 Ruber Capitae '07	♟♟ 5
● Lison-Pramaggiore Refosco P. R. Roggio dei Roveri '07	♟♟ 5
● Lison-Pramaggiore Rosso Vineargenti Ris. '08	♟♟ 6

Brigaldara

FRAZ. SAN FLORIANO
VIA BRIGALDARA, 20
37020 SAN PIETRO IN CARIANO [VR]
TEL. 0457701055
www.brigaldara.it

CELLAR SALES
PRE-BOOKED VISITS
ANNUAL PRODUCTION 250,000 bottles
HECTARES UNDER VINE 50.00

Riding on the wave of a golden age for
Amarone, Stefano Cesari has developed his
estate and now manages 50 hectares of
vineyards partly in the classic area and
partly to the east. Apart from Soave, his
wines are firmly rooted in Valpolicella with a
restricted range that combines traditional
and modern features. The Amarone Riserva
2007 makes an impressive debut
performance, originating from a strict
selection of the best grapes in both the
classic and the eastern growing zones.
Dried fruit, cocoa powder and spice on the
nose are followed by a powerful yet fresh
palate and smooth tannins. The
Amarone Classico 2009 has fresher
aromas and a leaner, more elegant palate
that favours sophistication over strength.
We liked the Soave 2012 and the fruity
Ripasso Il Vegro 2010 with its mouthwatering flavour.

● Amarone della Valpolicella Ris. '07	♟♟♟ 8
● Amarone della Valpolicella Cl. '09	♟♟ 7
○ Soave '12	♟♟ 3
● Valpolicella Cl. Sup. Ripasso Il Vegro '10	♟♟ 4
● Valpolicella Cl. '12	♟ 3
● Amarone della Valpolicella Case Vecie '07	♟♟♟ 7
● Amarone della Valpolicella Case Vecie '03	♟♟♟ 7
● Amarone della Valpolicella Case Vecie '00	♟♟♟ 6
● Amarone della Valpolicella Cl. '06	♟♟♟ 6
● Amarone della Valpolicella Cl. '05	♟♟♟ 6
● Amarone della Valpolicella Cl. '99	♟♟♟ 6
● Amarone della Valpolicella Cl. '98	♟♟♟ 6
● Amarone della Valpolicella Cl. '97	♟♟♟ 6

Sorelle Bronca

FRAZ. COLBERTALDO
VIA MARTIRI, 20
31020 VIDOR [TV]
TEL. 0423987201
www.sorellebronca.com

CELLAR SALES
PRE-BOOKED VISITS
ANNUAL PRODUCTION 250,000 bottles
HECTARES UNDER VINE 20.00
VITICULTURE METHOD Certified Organic

Despite the huge success that the Prosecco
sector is currently experiencing, the Bronca
sisters have not lost their way and helped
by Piero Balcon they keep a steady hand on
the helm of the family winery. Although
sparkling wine is naturally at the heart of
the estate's production, the still wines do
not necessarily play a secondary role but
express a strong link between the land and
traditions of Felettano. The 20-odd
hectares, passionately and meticulously
managed with respect for the
environment , are the estate's best
calling-card. Particella 68 2012 is one of
the best sparklers in Veneto, with notes of
appley fruit and flowers on the nose and a
very long, zesty, dry palate The equally
good Ser Bele 2010 is a Bordeaux blend
with a pinch of marzemino, generous and
fruity on the nose and developing into a
firm-bodied palate with smooth, close-knit
tannins. The Brut and Extra Dry are both
very good, while the Delico 2012 has
strikingly polished aromas.

● Colli di Conegliano Rosso Ser Bele '10	♟♟ 5
○ Valdobbiadene Brut Particella 68 '12	♟♟ 4
○ Colli di Conegliano Bianco Delico '12	♟♟ 3
○ Valdobbiadene Brut	♟♟ 3
○ Valdobbiadene Extra Dry	♟♟ 3
○ Valdobbiadene Prosecco Frizzante Difetto Perfetto	♟ 3
● Colli di Conegliano Rosso Ser Bele '09	♟♟♟ 5
● Colli di Conegliano Rosso Ser Bele '05	♟♟♟ 5
● Colli di Conegliano Rosso Ser Bele '08	♟♟ 5
● Colli di Conegliano Rosso Ser Bele '07	♟♟ 5
○ Valdobbiadene Brut Particella 68 '11	♟♟ 4
○ Valdobbiadene Brut Particella 68 '10	♟♟ 3
○ Valdobbiadene Extra Dry Particella 68 '09	♟♟ 3

Luigi Brunelli

VIA CARIANO, 10
37029 SAN PIETRO IN CARIANO [VR]
TEL. 0457701118
www.brunelliwine.com

CELLAR SALES
PRE-BOOKED VISITS
ACCOMMODATION
ANNUAL PRODUCTION 100,000 bottles
HECTARES UNDER VINE 12.00

At the Brunelli family winery, situated on the plains of the Valpolicella Classica zone, Alberto has become increasingly present alongside his father Luigi, carrying forward the promotion of the wines and the winery that began over 20 years ago. The dozen-odd hectares of vineyards produce mainly Valpolicella wines with a smaller number of secondary products. An excellent performance from the two 2008 Amarone Riservas. The Campo del Titari displays vibrant dried red fruit enhanced with chocolate and spice on the nose, opening smoothly on the palate with tight-knit tannins on the finish. The degli Inferi seems softer and more approachable, closing on a juicy hint of cherry jam. The Recioto 2011 is vibrantly fragrant and alluringly sweet, while the excellent non-vintage Valpolicella shows typical fruit and spice aromas with a dynamic, racy palate.

● Amarone della Valpolicella Cl. Campo del Titari Ris. '08	♥♥ 8
● Amarone della Valpolicella Cl. Campo Inferi Ris. '08	♥♥ 8
● Recioto della Valpolicella Cl. '11	♥♥ 5
● Valpolicella Cl. '12	♥♥ 2*
● Amarone della Valpolicella Cl. '10	♥ 6
● Corte Cariano Rosso '11	♥ 2
● Valpolicella Cl. Sup. Campo Praesel '11	♥ 3
● Valpolicella Cl. Sup. Ripasso Pa' Riondo '11	♥ 3
● Amarone della Valpolicella Cl. '09	♡♡ 6
● Amarone della Valpolicella Cl. Campo del Titari Ris. '06	♡♡ 8
● Valpolicella Cl. '10	♡♡ 2*
● Valpolicella Cl. Sup. Campo Praesel '10	♡♡ 3*

Tommaso Bussola

LOC. SAN PERETTO
VIA MOLINO TURRI, 30
37024 NEGRAR [VR]
TEL. 0457501740
www.bussolavini.com

CELLAR SALES
PRE-BOOKED VISITS
ANNUAL PRODUCTION 70,000 bottles
HECTARES UNDER VINE 15.00

Tommaso Bussola's estate has benefited from the years of success enjoyed by Amarone, with an increase in vineyards and renovations in the cellar. Today there are about 15 hectares, partly located on slopes surrounding the cellar and partly on higher hillsides, producing just under 100,000 bottles per year. The winery's style always favoured strength but has now acquired greater finesse and tauter flavour. Of the three Amarone selections we preferred the simpler version for its outstandingly fresh aromas with hints of red berries, spices and medicinal herbs. The generous texture flaunted on the palate is precisely guided by the acidity and tannins, closing with a long, full-flavoured finish. We also liked the Vigneto Alto 2007 with its more complex nose and even more generous palate with prominent tannins. The Valpolicella TB 2008 is very good, showing evolved aromas and harmonious flavour.

● Amarone della Valpolicella Cl. '07	♥♥ 8
● Amarone della Valpolicella Cl. TB '08	♥♥ 8
● Amarone della Valpolicella Cl. TB Vign. Alto '07	♥♥ 8
● Valpolicella Cl. Sup. TB '08	♥♥ 5
● Recioto della Valpolicella Cl. '04	♡♡♡ 6
● Recioto della Valpolicella Cl. BG '03	♡♡♡ 5
● Recioto della Valpolicella Cl. TB '04	♡♡♡ 8
● Recioto della Valpolicella Cl. TB '99	♡♡♡ 8
● Recioto della Valpolicella Cl. TB '98	♡♡♡ 8
● Recioto della Valpolicella Cl. TB '97	♡♡♡ 8
● Recioto della Valpolicella Cl. TB '95	♡♡♡ 8
● Amarone della Valpolicella Cl. TB '06	♡♡ 8
● Recioto della Valpolicella Cl. '08	♡♡ 7
● Recioto della Valpolicella Cl. '05	♡♡ 6

Ca' Ferri

via Ca' Ferri, 9
35020 Casalserugo [PD]
Tel. 049655518
www.vinicaferri.com

CELLAR SALES
PRE-BOOKED VISITS
ANNUAL PRODUCTION 400,000 bottles
HECTARES UNDER VINE 8.00

Gian Paolo Prandstraller established Ca' Ferri about ten years ago, planting a few hectares of black Bordeaux grapes on the slopes of Monte Rua, and later around Torreglia in the heart of the Colli Euganei area. Here production pursues high quality wines, while the vineyards planted subsequently on the plains around Casalserugo produce lighter, more accessible wines. The cellar benefits from the skill of Guido Busatto, whose deep knowledge of the local area informs his ability to highlight its different expressive aspects. The Taurilio 2011 is the winery's leading product, a merlot-heavy Bordeaux blend from the Colli Euganei vineyards. Strikingly clear-cut fruit on the nose is echoed by spicy and vegetal hints, and the lovely full-bodied palate is guided by smooth tannins and nice acidity, reflecting the sunny terroir. Outstanding in the Ser Ugo line, from Casalserugo, is the taut, harmonious Cabernet 2011.

● Colli Euganei Rosso Taurilio '11	♟♟	3
● Corti Benedettine Cabernet Ser Ugo '11	♟♟	3
● Corti Benedettine Merlot Ser Ugo '11	♟	2
● Raboso Ser Ugo '12	♟	3

Ca' La Bionda

fraz. Valgatara
via Bionda, 4
37020 Marano di Valpolicella [VR]
Tel. 0456801198
www.calabionda.it

CELLAR SALES
PRE-BOOKED VISITS
ANNUAL PRODUCTION 150,000 bottles
HECTARES UNDER VINE 29.00
VITICULTURE METHOD Certified Organic

Nicola and Alessandro Castellani were among the first to embrace the notion of organic winegrowing in Valpolicella, and today this Marano estate is a benchmark for the whole denomination. About 30 hectares of hillside vineyards are the estate's best visiting-card, especially given the age of the vines, and are still managed with the help of their father Pietro. The style pursues a balance between taut flavour and generosity from the partially dried grapes. The great version of Valpolicella Casal Vegri 2011, obtained exclusively from fresh grapes, faithfully displays varietal features: vibrant aromas blending fruit and spice, and a palate whose strength lies in tangy, acidic grip. This great wine paves the way for Valpolicella's long overdue emancipation from Amarone. The very interesting Corvina 2008 pursues a similar dimension to Pinot Nero, but holds on to its original character.

● Valpolicella Cl. Sup. Campo Casal Vegri '11	♟♟♟	5
● Amarone della Valpolicella Cl. Vign. di Ravazzol '09	♟♟	8
● Amarone della Valpolicella Cl. '09	♟♟	6
● Corvina '08	♟♟	7
● Amarone della Valpolicella Cl. Vign. di Ravazzol '07	♛♛♛	6
● Amarone della Valpolicella Cl. '08	♛♟	6
● Amarone della Valpolicella Cl. '07	♛♟	6
● Amarone della Valpolicella Cl. Vign. di Ravazzol '08	♛♟	7
● Amarone della Valpolicella Cl. Vign. di Ravazzol '06	♛♟	6
● Amarone della Valpolicella Cl. Vign. di Ravazzol '03	♛♟	6

Ca' Lustra

LOC. FAEDO
VIA SAN PIETRO, 50
35030 CINTO EUGANEO [PD]
TEL. 042994128
www.calustra.it

CELLAR SALES
PRE-BOOKED VISITS
ANNUAL PRODUCTION 170,000 bottles
HECTARES UNDER VINE 25.50
VITICULTURE METHOD Certified Organic

Franco Zanovello is one of the most
meticulous and scrupulous exponents of
the Paduan DOC, with over 20 hectares of
organically farmed vineyards. The vines
benefit from different altitudes and aspects
which enhance the varietal features and
create a wide but balanced range of high
quality products in a style that emphasizes
fullness in the basic products, while the
Riservas favour expressivity over strength.
The top selections were absent this year
due to the wise winery decision to let them
mature further in the cellar. However our
tasting included good wines like the
mouthfilling Chardonnay Roverello 2011,
aged in oak, the richly textured Marzemino
Belvedere 2010,and the Merlot 2010
which shows mature aromas and a
generous flavour even at entry level.

○ Colli Euganei Chardonnay Roverello '11	♀♀ 2*
○ Colli Euganei Fior d'Arancio '12	♀♀ 3
● Colli Euganei Merlot '10	♀♀ 2*
● Marzemino Belvedere '10	♀♀ 2*
● Marzemino Passito '09	♀♀ 2*
⊙ Aganoor Rosato '12	♀ 2
● Colli Euganei Cabernet '10	♀ 2
○ Colli Euganei Manzoni Bianco Pedevenda '11	♀ 3
○ Colli Euganei Moscato Secco 'A Cengia '11	♀ 2
● Colli Euganei Cabernet Girapoggio '05	♀♀♀ 3
○ Colli Euganei Fior d'Arancio Passito '07	♀♀♀ 4
● Colli Euganei Merlot Sassonero Villa Alessi '05	♀♀♀ 3
● Colli Euganei Cabernet Girapoggio '08	♀♀ 3*

Ca' Orologio

VIA CA' OROLOGIO, 7A
35030 BAONE [PD]
TEL. 042950099
www.caorologio.com

CELLAR SALES
PRE-BOOKED VISITS
ACCOMMODATION
ANNUAL PRODUCTION 24,000 bottles
HECTARES UNDER VINE 12.00
VITICULTURE METHOD Certified Organic

The Baone area in the extreme south of the
Colli Euganei zone has a warm,
Mediterranean climate which translates into
generously fruity, alluringly drinkable wines.
All this is apparent in the products of
Mariagioia Rosellini, who has swiftly made
her name with a small but solid range.
About a dozen hectares of organically
farmed vineyards provide the grapes, with
Bordeaux varieties at the heart of
production. Ca'Orologio wines may have
suffered recent bottling but they still amply
impressed our panels. Locally, 2011 was a
particularly hot year, endowing the Calaóne
with vibrantly fruity aromas supported by
tangy, well-blended acidity on the palate,
making it one of the best in its category.
The Relógio, made from carmenère with a
pinch of cabernet sauvignon, has a sunny,
open character while the Barbera Lunisóle
demonstrates fruity, juicy fullness.

● Colli Euganei Rosso Calaóne '11	♀♀ 4
● Relógio '11	♀♀ 5
● Lunisóle '11	♀♀ 4
○ Salaróla '12	♀♀ 3
● Colli Euganei Rosso Calaóne '05	♀♀♀ 3*
● Relógio '09	♀♀♀ 4*
● Relógio '07	♀♀♀ 4
● Relógio '06	♀♀♀ 4
● Relógio '04	♀♀♀ 4*
● Colli Euganei Rosso Calaóne '10	♀♀ 4
● Colli Euganei Rosso Calaóne '09	♀♀ 4
● Relógio '10	♀♀ 5
● Relógio '08	♀♀ 4

★Ca' Rugate

VIA PERGOLA, 36
37030 MONTECCHIA DI CROSARA [VR]
TEL. 0456176328
www.carugate.it

CELLAR SALES
PRE-BOOKED VISITS
ANNUAL PRODUCTION 550,000 bottles
HECTARES UNDER VINE 58.00

Within the Soave DOC the Tessari family winery has undoubtedly responded best to the challenge of the global market, with high-profile products that successfully express traditional features with a clearly defined style and great precision. All this is due to the efforts of Michele and his father Amedeo who moved over for him, as well as farsighted choices like investing primarily in the land. Today the estate consists of 60-odd hectares divided between Soave and Valpolicella. Soave Monte Fiorentine and Monte Alto are definitely two of the designation's benchmark wines. The former displays a more confident, edgy character while the Monte Alto expresses greater maturity and deeper flavour as a white wine that has found its calling in oak maturation. While the Amarone 2009 and Recioto 2010 reaffirm their characteristic qualities, we recommend the newest entry in the line-up: a Pas Dosé 2008 with very fresh aromas and a tangy, vigorous, almost biting flavour.

○ Soave Cl. Monte Alto '11	♟♟♟	3*
● Amarone della Valpolicella '09	♟♟	7
○ Recioto di Soave La Perlara '10	♟♟	5
○ Soave Cl. Monte Fiorentine '12	♟♟♟	3*
○ Studio '11	♟♟	4
○ Lessini Durello Pas Dosé Amedeo M. Cl. '08	♟♟	5
○ Soave Cl. San Michele '12	♟♟	2*
● Valpolicella Rio Albo '12	♟♟	2*
● Valpolicella Sup. Campo Lavei '11	♟♟	4
● Valpolicella Sup. Ripasso '11	♟♟	3
○ Soave Cl. Monte Alto '10	♟♟♟	3*
○ Soave Cl. Monte Fiorentine '09	♟♟♟	3*
○ Studio '10	♟♟♟	4*
○ Studio '09	♟♟♟	4

Giuseppe Campagnola

FRAZ. VALGATARA
VIA AGNELLA, 9
37020 MARANO DI VALPOLICELLA [VR]
TEL. 0457703900
www.campagnola.com

CELLAR SALES
PRE-BOOKED VISITS
ANNUAL PRODUCTION 4,800,000 bottles
HECTARES UNDER VINE 130.00

Giuseppe Campagnola has succeeded in developing the estate established by his grandfather in the early 1900s, extending the estate's own vineyards and varying the range so that high-profile wines are presented alongside more basic, accessible products. The most ambitious range is dedicated to Caterina Zardini, the founder's wife, and consists of one Amarone and one Valpolicella Superiore. The rest of the range focuses on classic Veronese wines. The Valpolicella Superiore Caterina Zardini 2011 is, in fact, the most impressive wine this year. The nose is unexpectedly fruity and spicy, and the palate shows strikingly successful handling of the powerful flavour with ease and grip. The Amarone of the same line is still resting in the cellar, but the more basic version was one of the most interesting in the designation, with a racy profile and remarkable finesse. The Ripasso 2011 is uncomplicated and very good.

● Valpolicella Cl. Sup. Caterina Zardini '11	♟♟	3*
● Amarone della Valpolicella Cl. '09	♟♟	6
● Recioto della Valpolicella Cl. Casotto del Merlo '11	♟♟	5
● Valpolicella Cl. Sup. Ripasso '11	♟♟	3
⊙ Bardolino Cl. Chiaretto Roccolo del Lago '12	♟	2
● Bardolino Cl. Roccolo del Lago '12	♟	2
○ Soave Cl. Monte Foscarino Le Bine '12	♟	2
● Valpolicella Cl. Le Bine '12	♟	2
● Amarone della Valpolicella Cl. Caterina Zardini '04	♟♟♟	6
● Amarone della Valpolicella Cl. Caterina Zardini '01	♟♟♟	6
● Amarone della Valpolicella Cl. Caterina Zardini '99	♟♟♟	6

I Campi

LOC. ALLODOLA
FRAZ. CELLORE D'ILLASI
VIA DELLE PEZZOLE, 3
37032 ILLASI [VR]
TEL. 0456175915
www.icampi.it

CELLAR SALES
PRE-BOOKED VISITS
ANNUAL PRODUCTION 60,000 bottles
HECTARES UNDER VINE 14.00

Every year, Flavio Prà's estate develops a more clearly defined distinction between its two different souls. On one hand white wine, focusing on the racy profile of Soave, and red wine on the other, characterized by the fruity strength of Valpolicella. The vineyards have been carefully selected over the years to make the most of the different altitudes, soils and aspects enabling each variety to find its fullest expression blending fragrance and grip, fruit and freshness, strength and elegance. Once again the Soave Campo Vulcano 2012 was our favourite, thanks to the avoidance of easily accessible aromatic features and the pursuit of the very essence of the garganega grape: appley fruit, vegetal hints and gradually released minerality. The palate is firm, tangy and very gutsy. The Campo Ciotoli 2011 Ripasso focuses on the spiciness of traditional grapes and a racy, but not overly complex, flavour.

Cantina del Castello

CORTE PITTORA, 5
37038 SOAVE [VR]
TEL. 0457680093
www.cantinacastello.it

CELLAR SALES
PRE-BOOKED VISITS
ANNUAL PRODUCTION 130,000 bottles
HECTARES UNDER VINE 12.00

Cantina di Castello is located in the heart of the old town of Soave, where Arturo Stocchetti works with grapes grown on the dozen hectares he owns in the Soave Classico zone. The vineyards, partly renovated in the past, are guyot-trained although one section remains faithful to the traditional pergola system. Production has settled at over 100,000 bottles per year, gradually reducing the more ambitious wines to make room for simpler products. Stocchetti is not the place to seek full-bodied, powerful wines since all the products are based on uncomplicated features and accessible flavour. The flagship wine is a Soave Castello with enjoyably approachable aromas of clear-cut apple and pear fruit and flowers, followed by a light-bodied palate and soft-centred flavour. The Recioto Corte Pittora 2007 shows tropical features and prominent sweetness.

○ Soave Cl. Campo Vulcano '12	♀♀♀ 3*
● Valpolicella Sup. Ripasso Campo Ciotoli '11	♀♀ 3*
● Amarone della Valpolicella Campo Marna 500 '07	♀♀ 8
● Campo Prognare '08	♀♀ 8
○ Soave Campo Base '12	♀♀ 2*
● Valpolicella Campo Base '12	♀♀ 3
○ Soave Cl. Campo Vulcano '11	♀♀♀ 5
○ Soave Cl. Campo Vulcano '10	♀♀♀ 3*
○ Soave Cl. Campo Vulcano '09	♀♀♀ 3*
○ Soave Cl. Campo Vulcano '08	♀♀♀ 3*
● Valpolicella Sup. Ripasso Campo Ciotoli '10	♀♀ 6
● Valpolicella Sup. Ripasso Campo Ciotoli '09	♀♀ 4

○ Soave Cl. Castello '12	♀♀ 2*
○ Recioto di Soave Cl. Corte Pittora '07	♀ 5
○ Soave Cl. Sup. Monte Pressoni '01	♀♀♀ 3
○ Soave Cl. Carniga '04	♀♀ 3*
○ Soave Cl. Pressoni '08	♀♀ 3*
○ Soave Cl. Pressoni '07	♀♀ 3
○ Soave Cl. Pressoni '06	♀♀ 3*
○ Soave Cl. Pressoni '05	♀♀ 3*
○ Soave Cl. Pressoni '04	♀♀ 3*

La Cappuccina

FRAZ. COSTALUNGA
VIA SAN BRIZIO, 125
37032 MONTEFORTE D'ALPONE [VR]
TEL. 0456175036
www.lacappuccina.it

CELLAR SALES
PRE-BOOKED VISITS
ACCOMMODATION
ANNUAL PRODUCTION 300,000 bottles
HECTARES UNDER VINE 40.00
VITICULTURE METHOD Certified Organic

Elena, Pietro and Sisto Tessari run the family winery at Costalunga, a small village at the foot of the volcanic Soave hills. Their vineyards were among the first to convert from Veronese pergola to vertical-trellised training systems, and to be organically farmed. The estate's 40 hectares produce a range of products focusing on Soave, although there are also other fruity, accessible designer wines. The Recioto Arzìmo 2010 is a dried-grape wine with ripe peach, liquorice, citrus and dried flower aromas, perfectly mirrored on the palate where the exuberant sweetness culminates in a caramel sensation. We also liked the Soave Fontégo 2012: appley fruit aromas entwined with fresher vegetal hints and a zesty, racy flavour. San Brizio 2011 enjoys greater depth and fuller flavour thanks to a period of oak-ageing.

Carpenè Malvolti

VIA ANTONIO CARPENÈ, 1
31015 CONEGLIANO [TV]
TEL. 0438364611
www.carpene-malvolti.com

CELLAR SALES
PRE-BOOKED VISITS
ANNUAL PRODUCTION 5,300,000 bottles
HECTARES UNDER VINE 26.00

Prosecco is one of the best-known and enjoyed Italian wines in the world today and the decisive contribution made by the Carpenè family to this success deserves to be recognized. The family have been linked to sparkling Treviso wine for 150 years, and today Carpenè Malvolti is one of the biggest Prosecco Superiore producers in the whole area. The winery has an enduring connection with many growers who have entrusted their grapes to this Conegliano Veneto winery for generations. The style of Carpenè wines gently enhances the fragrance of the grape variety, avoiding excessive or untypical aromas. The Extra Dry displays fresh fruit salad on the nose, nicely mirrored on the palate, with creamy fizz and beautifully balanced sweetness and acidity. The Brut is subtler on the nose and edgier on the palate, showing a markedly tangy flavour. Lastly, the Dry shows skilful handling of the sweetness expected in this type.

○ Recioto di Soave Arzìmo '10	♥♥ 4
○ Soave Fontégo '12	♥♥ 2*
○ Soave San Brizio '11	♥♥ 3
● Madégo '12	♥ 2
○ Sauvignon Basaltik '12	♥ 2
○ Soave '12	♥ 2
● Campo Buri '09	♀♀ 4
● Campo Buri '08	♀♀ 4
● Madégo '10	♀♀ 2*
○ Recioto di Soave Arzìmo '09	♀♀ 4
○ Recioto di Soave Arzìmo '08	♀♀ 4
○ Soave '11	♀♀ 2*
○ Soave Fontégo '10	♀♀ 2*
○ Soave San Brizio '10	♀♀ 3
○ Soave San Brizio '09	♀♀ 3

○ Conegliano Valdobbiadene Brut 1868	♥♥ 3
○ Conegliano Valdobbiadene Dry 1868	♥♥ 3
○ Conegliano Valdobbiadene Extra Dry 1868	♥♥ 3
○ Cartizze 1868	♥ 5
○ Conegliano Valdobbiadene Dry Cuvée Oro	♀♀ 3*

Casa Cecchin

VIA AGUGLIANA, 11
36054 MONTEBELLO VICENTINO [VI]
TEL. 0444649610
www.casacecchin.it

CELLAR SALES
PRE-BOOKED VISITS
ANNUAL PRODUCTION 25,000 bottles
HECTARES UNDER VINE 6.00

The fact that the world is beginning to take an interest in Durello Spumante is due to wineries like the Cecchin family's, which has always been committed to promoting the traditional Lessinia variety. The limited number of wines makes use of an ampelographic heritage focusing on garganega and durella, the former as a still wine and the latter both still and Classic Method. The most immediately striking feature of Durello is its thrusting acidity, which is perfectly expressed in the Brut Riserva 2008: subtle on the nose, it unleashes firm but dry texture on the palate and almost electric acidic pressure. The still version follows the same pattern and is by far the most interesting in the designation: a supple, racy, edgy palate with subtle aromas of fresh flowers, apples and pears. The dried-grape version displays well-judged sweetness.

○ Lessini Durello Brut M. Cl. Ris. '08	▾▾ 3
○ Lessini Durello Passito Il Duello '09	▾▾ 5
○ Lessini Il Durello '12	▾▾ 2*
○ Lessini Durello Pietralava '11	▾ 2
○ Lessini Durello Vivace Mandégolo '12	▾ 2
○ Recioto Cl. Gambellara Le Ginestre '09	▾ 5
○ Gambellara Cl. San Nicolò '11	♀♀ 2*
○ Lessini Il Durello '11	♀♀ 2*
○ Lessini Durello Passito Il Montebello '08	♀♀ 4
○ Lessini Durello Sup. '10	♀♀ 2*
○ Lessini Durello Sup. '09	♀♀ 2*
○ Recioto Cl. Gambellara Le Ginestre '08	♀♀ 4

Casa Roma

VIA ORMELLE, 19
31020 SAN POLO DI PIAVE [TV]
TEL. 0422855339
www.casaroma.com

CELLAR SALES
PRE-BOOKED VISITS
ANNUAL PRODUCTION 250,000 bottles
HECTARES UNDER VINE 17.00

Gigi Peruzzetto is the life and soul of this lovely estate in the Piave area, with about 30 hectares of vineyards planted on land which combines clay and gravel from the river. Typically for this denomination, production centres on monovarietal wines and the winery's distinctive style emphasizes fresh aromas and approachable flavour. Every year the Nesio shows a more clearly defined profile. Made from raboso grapes that undergo rosé fermentation, it remains on the yeasts for 30 months before dégorgement. Today it presents vibrant fruit and dried flowers, nicely reflected on the firm-bodied, dry, very lingering palate. We also liked the Malanotte 2009, which hovers between aromas of dried fruit and fresher aromatic herbs, while the weighty palate is offset by refreshing acidity.

⊙ Nesio Brut M. Cl. '09	▾▾ 5
● Piave Malanotte '09	▾▾ 6
○ Piave Manzoni Bianco '12	▾▾ 2*
○ Marzemina Bianca '12	▾ 3
● Piave Carmenère '12	▾ 2
● Venezia Cabernet Sauvignon '12	▾ 2
○ Venezia Chardonnay '12	▾ 2
● Venezia Merlot '12	▾ 2
○ Venezia Pinot Grigio '12	▾ 2
● Piave Merlot '11	♀♀ 2*
● Piave Raboso '08	♀♀ 4
● Piave Raboso '06	♀♀ 4
● Piave Raboso '02	♀♀ 4
● Raboso Passito Callarghe '07	♀♀ 5

Case Paolin

VIA MADONNA MERCEDE, 53
31040 VOLPAGO DEL MONTELLO [TV]
TEL. 0423871433
www.casepaolin.it

CELLAR SALES
PRE-BOOKED VISITS
ANNUAL PRODUCTION 66,000 bottles
HECTARES UNDER VINE 10.00
VITICULTURE METHOD Certified Organic

Adelino, Diego and Mirco Pozzobon run the family winery in Volpago where the Treviso plain meets the lower Montello foothills. According to local tradition the focus is on Bordeaux grapes while glera, used for the Asolo Prosecco denomination, has always played a secondary role. This is still the case at Case Paolin, where mainly still wines are produced in a generous and nicely taut style. The merlot- and cabernet-based reds are on top form, as we traditionally expect from this corner of Veneto. Made from grapes grown on the slopes of Montello in the San Carlo district, the San Carlo displays aromas ranging from red berries to aromatic herbs and opens with sensual fullness on the palate to reveal a full-bodied, mouthwatering flavour. The merlot-heavy Bordeaux blend Rosso del Milio 2010 shows fresher aromas and a more supple, racy development. The very interesting Manzoni Santi Angeli 2011 has harmonious, tangy flavour.

Michele Castellani

FRAZ. VALGATARA
VIA GRANDA, 1
37020 MARANO DI VALPOLICELLA [VR]
TEL. 0457701253
www.castellanimichele.it

CELLAR SALES
PRE-BOOKED VISITS
ANNUAL PRODUCTION 350,000 bottles
HECTARES UNDER VINE 45.00

The Castellani family winery has been operative for decades in the Valgatara zone, in the heart of Valpolicella Classica. Here, Sergio is joined by his children Michele, Martina and Mara in farming about 40 hectares of vineyards almost exclusively planted with traditional Valpolicella varieties. The wines pursue a style whose distinctive features are strength and richness, and are divided into two lines: Ca' del Pipa, which is clearly modern in style, and I Castei, reflecting the more traditional profile of local wines. The excellent aromas displayed by the Recioto Monte Fasenara 2010 include cherries and spices, with oak very much in the background. The marked sweetness on the palate is nicely countered by acidity and tannins. The Amarone Cinquestelle 2009 focuses on rich extract, developing oaky and fruity aromas on a solidly-built palate with tight-knit tannins. The Ripasso Costamaran 2011 is well-made, ripe and soft.

○ Manzoni Bianco Santi Angeli '11	🍷🍷 2*
● Montello e Colli Asolani Rosso del Milio '10	🍷🍷 3
● Montello e Colli Asolani Sup. San Carlo '09	🍷🍷 4
○ Asolo Brut	🍷 2
● Cabernet '12	🍷 2
○ Prosecco di Treviso Frizzante	🍷 2
○ Asolo Brut '09	🍷🍷 2*
○ Manzoni Bianco Santi Angeli '10	🍷🍷 2*
● Montello e Colli Asolani Rosso del Milio '09	🍷🍷 3*
● Montello e Colli Asolani Sup. San Carlo '08	🍷🍷 4
● Montello e Colli Asolani Sup. San Carlo '07	🍷🍷 4
○ Soér Passito '09	🍷🍷 4

● Recioto della Valpolicella Cl. Monte Fasenara I Castei '10	🍷🍷 5
● Amarone della Valpolicella Cl. Cinquestelle Collezione Ca' del Pipa '09	🍷🍷 7
● Recioto della Valpolicella Cl. Il Casale Ca' del Pipa '10	🍷🍷 6
● Valpolicella Cl. Sup. Ripasso Costamaran I Castei '11	🍷🍷 3
● Amarone della Valpolicella Cl. Campo Casalin I Castei '09	🍷 6
● Valpolicella Cl. Campo del Biotto I Castei '12	🍷 2
● Amarone della Valpolicella Cl. Campo Casalin I Castei '07	🍷🍷 6
● Recioto della Valpolicella Cl. Il Casale Ca' del Pipa '09	🍷🍷 6

Cavalchina

LOC. CAVALCHINA
FRAZ. CUSTOZA
VIA SOMMACAMPAGNA, 7
37066 SOMMACAMPAGNA [VR]
TEL. 045516002
www.cavalchina.com

CELLAR SALES
PRE-BOOKED VISITS
ANNUAL PRODUCTION 450,000 bottles
HECTARES UNDER VINE 30.00

The Piona brothers, Luciano and Franco run the family winery which works in three directions: Custoza, Mozambano and Valpolicella, with different interpretations according to each area. The zone south of Lake Garda produces fresh, taut wines while those grown in the Mantova area, using international grape varieties, are full-bodied and vigorous and Valpolicella yields generous, powerful wines. This is all achieved with an eye on value for money, making this one of the most interesting estates in the Verona area. Once again the Amedeo is the best wine chez Piona: a Custoza 2011 with subtle oaky aromas blending with flowers and crisp fruit, revealing a slender body and tangy, well-balanced flavour on the palate. Where Valpolicella is concerned, pursuit of rich extract is the name of the game as we experienced in our tasting of the Amarone Torre d'Orti 2009. The Garganega Paroni and Sauvignon Valbruna, both 2011, give a vibrant, precise expression of the varietal features of their grapes.

○ Custoza Sup. Amedeo '11	♟♟♟	3*
● Amarone della Valpolicella Torre d'Orti '09	♟♟	6
● Bardolino Sup. S. Lucia '11	♟♟	3
● Garda Cabernet Sauvignon Vign. Il Falcone La Prendina '10	♟♟	5
○ Garda Garganega Paroni La Prendina '11	♟♟	4
● Garda Merlot Faial La Prendina '10	♟♟	3
○ Garda Sauvignon Valbruna La Prendina '11	♟♟	3
● Bardolino '12	♟	2
☉ Bardolino Chiaretto '12	♟	2
○ Custoza '12	♟	2
● Garda Merlot La Prendina '12	♟	3
○ Garda Pinot Bianco La Prendina '12	♟	3
○ Pinot Grigio La Prendina '12	♟	3

Domenico Cavazza & F.lli

C.DA SELVA, 22
36054 MONTEBELLO VICENTINO [VI]
TEL. 0444649166
www.cavazzawine.com

CELLAR SALES
PRE-BOOKED VISITS
ANNUAL PRODUCTION 890,000 bottles
HECTARES UNDER VINE 140.00

The Cavazza family began work in the Thirties in the Gambellara zone and rapidly rose to a leading position. In the post-War period they turned their attention to the nearby Colli Berici, creating two distinct estates, managed with the same passion and skill. The original winery works almost exclusively with garganega grapes, while international varieties are planted on the warm Colli Berici hills. And indeed, Cavazza's most interesting wine comes from the Colli Berici. The Syrah 2011, from the Cicogna estate, has vibrant red berry and black pepper aromas, and a firm-bodied palate with smooth tannins. The estate's other reds are still maturing in the cellar, making room for the uncomplicated, fresh-tasting Cabernet Costiera 2010. Turning to Gambellara, the Creari 2010, wrongly reviewed last year, is very good, while the La Bocara 2012 is strikingly well-balanced and light.

○ Gambellara Cl. Creari '10	♟♟	3
○ Gambellara Cl. La Bocara '12	♟♟	2*
● Syrah Cicogna '11	♟♟	4
● Colli Berici Cabernet Costiera '10	♟	3
● Colli Berici Tai Rosso '12	♟	3
● Cicogna Syrhae '09	♟♟	4
● Colli Berici Merlot Cicogna '10	♟♟	4
● Colli Berici Merlot Cicogna '09	♟♟	4
○ Gambellara Cl. Creari '09	♟♟	3
○ Gambellara Cl. Creari Capitel S. Libera '06	♟♟	3*
○ Recioto di Gambellara Cl. Capitel S. Libera '08	♟♟	4
● Syrah Cicogna '10	♟♟	4
○ Vin Santo di Gambellara Cl. Selva '04	♟♟	5

Giorgio Cecchetto

FRAZ. TEZZE DI PIAVE
VIA PIAVE, 67
31028 VAZZOLA [TV]
TEL. 043828598
www.rabosopiave.com

CELLAR SALES
PRE-BOOKED VISITS
ANNUAL PRODUCTION 200,000 bottles
HECTARES UNDER VINE 73.00

Giorgio Cecchetti and his wife Cristina are at the heart of this Piave winery, one of the most influential benchmark exponents for the whole denomination. The vineyards are planted on the plain, on clay-rich land, and production alternates between international varieties and classic local grapes like raboso and Manzoni bianco. Many of the wines in the range are drinkable everyday products, with Riservas concentrating on raboso, Malanotte and merlot. Rosa Bruna is a Brut Metodo Classico made exclusively from raboso grapes. Red berries and breadcrust aromas on the nose but the wine performs best on the dry, edgy, very lingering palate. The Sante Rosso 2010, a monovarietal Merlot, is also very good: aromas of plums and thyme and a hint of oak in the background, while the palate reveals a good full body and well-balanced flavour.

Gerardo Cesari

LOC. SORSEI, 3
37010 CAVAION VERONESE [VR]
TEL. 0456260928
www.cesariverona.it

CELLAR SALES
PRE-BOOKED VISITS
ANNUAL PRODUCTION 1,600,000 bottles
HECTARES UNDER VINE 109.00

The Cesari family estate was established between the Wars and has been continuously operative in the Valpolicella DOC zone ever since. The grapes are both estate-grown and bought from growers who are monitored throughout the year. There are two production centres: San Floriano for the Valpolicella reds, and the cellar at Cavaion for the other Veronese wines. The estate aims to produce full-bodied, supple wines. Cesari's Amarones are only released after a long maturation period, as shown by our tasting of the 2005 vintage Bosan. The nose is complex and mature while the palate shows smooth tannins and mouthwatering flavour. The Bosco 2007 displays sounder, fresher aromas followed by a dry, very harmonious palate. Among the Valpolicellas the Mara 2011 was strikingly aromatic and fresh, racy and succulent.

● Merlot Sante Rosso '10	♥♥ 3
⊙ Rosa Bruna Cuvée 21 Brut M.Cl. '10	♥♥ 3
○ Manzoni Bianco '12	♥ 2
● Piave Raboso '09	♥ 3
● Raboso Passito RP	♥ 4
● Venezia Cabernet Sauvignon '12	♥ 2
● Gelsaia '07	♥♥ 3
● Malanotte Gelsaia '09	♥♥ 5
● Merlot Sante Rosso '09	♥♥ 3*
● Piave Merlot Sante '08	♥♥ 3
● Piave Merlot Sante '07	♥♥ 3
● Piave Raboso '06	♥♥ 3

● Amarone della Valpolicella Bosan '05	♥♥ 8
● Amarone della Valpolicella Cl. Il Bosco '07	♥♥ 7
● Jèma Corvina Veronese '09	♥ 5
○ Lugana Cento Filari '12	♥ 2
● Valpolicella Sup. Ripasso Bosan '10	♥ 5
● Valpolicella Sup. Ripasso Mara '11	♥ 3
● Amarone della Valpolicella Bosan '04	♥♥ 8
● Amarone della Valpolicella Bosan '03	♥♥ 8
● Amarone della Valpolicella Cl. '07	♥♥ 5
● Amarone della Valpolicella Cl. Il Bosco '05	♥♥ 7
● Valpolicella Sup. Ripasso Mara '10	♥♥ 3

Italo Cescon

FRAZ. RONCADELLE
P.ZZA DEI CADUTI, 3
31024 ORMELLE [TV]
TEL. 0422851033
www.cesconitalo.it

CELLAR SALES
PRE-BOOKED VISITS
ANNUAL PRODUCTION 800,000 bottles
HECTARES UNDER VINE 115.00

The Cescon brothers' winery is at Roncadelle but the 100-plus hectares of vineyards extend over different zones. Most of the estate is in the Piave area, but there are plots in Friuli and in the Valdobbiadene DOC zone, which all provide the grapes for a large range divided into two lines. The winery style pursues clear-cut expression of the grape variety with fresh aromas and a supple palate, in both the simpler and the more ambitious wines. A good deal of attention is focused on Manzoni Bianco, which appears in two different versions. The Svejo 2012 enhances the grape's typical aromatic features, with uncomplicated, mouthwatering flavour. On the other hand, the Non Filtrato 2011 matures for a year longer to explore the potential of a very interesting grape variety. The aromas revealed range from tropical fruit to spice, with mineral hints playing a leading role, and a strikingly zesty and taut palate.

Coffele

VIA ROMA, 5
37038 SOAVE [VR]
TEL. 0457680007
www.coffele.it

CELLAR SALES
PRE-BOOKED VISITS
ANNUAL PRODUCTION 120,000 bottles
HECTARES UNDER VINE 25.00

In an area like Soave which is extremely divided into plots, it is very rare indeed to find an estate with almost 30 hectares of vineyards in a single plot. Alberto and Chiara Coffele have demonstrated skill in subdividing production according to the propensity of each individual vineyard, and selecting the most suitable growing zones for each wine. The vineyards are in excess of the winery's requirements, which makes it possible to use only the best plots for the estate's own wines. The grapes for the Coffele champion Ca' Visco, are grown in the highest vineyards around the recently renovated old farmhouse. The wine's aromas range from spring flowers to peaches and close with an original tropical note. The 2012 vintage produced a weightier version than in the past, full-bodied and firm. The Alzari is aged in oak, endowing it with more mature aromas and a creamily alluring palate with a lingering finish.

● Chieto '10	♟♟ 3
○ Manzoni Bianco Non Filtrato '11	♟♟ 3
○ Manzoni Bianco Svejo '12	♟ 2
● Piave Raboso Rabià '08	♟ 3
○ Sauvignon Mejo '12	♟ 3
● Chieto '09	♟♟ 3
● Chieto '08	♟♟ 3
● Chieto '07	♟♟ 3
○ Manzoni Bianco '10	♟♟ 2*
○ Manzoni Bianco '09	♟♟ 2*
○ Manzoni Bianco '08	♟♟ 2*
○ Manzoni Bianco Svejo '11	♟♟ 2*
○ Manzoni Bianco Svejo '10	♟♟ 2*
● Piave Merlot La Cesura Ris. '05	♟♟ 3
● Piave Raboso Rabià Ris. '03	♟♟ 3

○ Soave Cl. Alzari '11	♟♟ 3*
○ Soave Cl. Ca' Visco '12	♟♟ 3*
○ Recioto di Soave Cl. Le Sponde '11	♟♟ 5
○ Soave Cl. '12	♟ 2
○ Recioto di Soave Cl. Le Sponde '09	♟♟♟ 5
○ Soave Cl. Ca' Visco '05	♟♟♟ 3*
○ Soave Cl. Ca' Visco '04	♟♟♟ 2
○ Soave Cl. Ca' Visco '03	♟♟♟ 2
○ Recioto di Soave Cl. Le Sponde '10	♟♟ 5
○ Soave Cl. Alzari '10	♟♟ 3*
○ Soave Cl. Alzari '09	♟♟ 3
○ Soave Cl. Ca' Visco '10	♟♟ 3*
○ Terra Crea Passito '06	♟♟ 8

Col Vetoraz

FRAZ. SANTO STEFANO
S.DA DELLE TRESIESE, 1
31040 VALDOBBIADENE [TV]
TEL. 0423975291
www.colvetoraz.it

CELLAR SALES
PRE-BOOKED VISITS
ANNUAL PRODUCTION 800,000 bottles
HECTARES UNDER VINE 12.00

The history of Prosecco has undergone two distinct stages: the first linked to a few brands which represented most of the denomination, and the second to a large number of good quality estates making Treviso sparkling wines famous around the world. The estate owned by Francesco Miotto, Paolo De Bortoli and Loris Dall'Acqua falls into the latter category, and has created a true style for this type. The estate relies on a network of growers who bring their grapes to the winery. The Millesimato Dry has a strikingly broad range of aromas, including a vibrant sensation of tropical fruit alongside the hints of fresh-cut flowers, beautifully mirrored on the palate which opens out into well-balanced sweetness and acidity. The Cartizze is subtler and slower to reveal its aromas but explodes on the palate with tangy flavour and full body, in a beautiful contrast with the acidity. Lastly, the Brut displays a dry, gutsy profile.

○ Valdobbiadene Dry Mill. '12	♙♙ 3
○ Cartizze	♙♙ 4
○ Valdobbiadene Brut	♙♙ 3
○ Valdobbiadene Extra Dry	♙ 3

Conte Collalto

VIA 24 MAGGIO, 1
31058 SUSEGANA [TV]
TEL. 0438738241
www.cantine-collalto.it

CELLAR SALES
PRE-BOOKED VISITS
ANNUAL PRODUCTION 850,000 bottles
HECTARES UNDER VINE 141.00

The history of the Conti Collalto is deeply connected to that of the province of Treviso, especially the northern zone, where the plains gradually give way to the Alpine foothills. The estate's cellars are located at Susegana, the very last strip of plains land, while the vineyards extend over 150 hectares on the surrounding hills. Glera takes the lion's share, followed by the Bordeaux grape varieties and, last but not least, incrocio Manzoni and wildbacher. A very good Dry version of the Conegliano Valdobbiadene: aromas of apple and pear fruit, and roses, with strikingly skilled handling of sweetness and acidity on a balanced, lingering palate. The Incrocio Manzoni 2.15 2010 is fruitier and more vibrant with hints of plums and aromatic herbs mirrored on the palate which displays tautness and tangy flavour. Good quality and faithful interpretation of the grapes from the rest of the range too.

○ Conegliano Valdobbiadene Dry Mill. '12	♙♙ 3
● Incrocio Manzoni 2.15 '10	♙ 2*
○ Colli di Conegliano Bianco Schenella I '11	♙ 2
○ Conegliano Valdobbiadene Brut	♙ 2
○ Conegliano Valdobbiadene Extra Dry	♙ 2
○ Manzoni Bianco '12	♙ 2
⊙ Rosabianco '12	♙ 3
⊙ Rosé Extra Dry	♙ 2
○ Verdiso '12	♙ 2
● Wildbacher '10	♙ 2
● Colli di Conegliano Rosso Vinciguerra '06	♟♟ 4
○ Conegliano Valdobbiadene Dry Mill. '11	♟♟ 3
● Piave Cabernet Torrai Ris. '07	♟♟ 5

Le Colture

FRAZ. SANTO STEFANO
VIA FOLLO, 5
31049 VALDOBBIADENE [TV]
TEL. 0423900192
www.lecolture.it

CELLAR SALES
PRE-BOOKED VISITS
ACCOMMODATION
ANNUAL PRODUCTION 700,000 bottles
HECTARES UNDER VINE 40.00

The Ruggeri family winery develops over two distinct plots: the traditional plot in the Conegliano Valdobbiadene DOC zone and more recently purchased vineyards in the Montello area. The total of about 40 hectares guarantees fine quality grapes for use in most of the products. The remainder are made using grapes from longstanding professional cooperations with growers, who are supervised in all the stages of the production process. The designation's most famous vineyard, Cartizze, shows its pedigree at Le Colture with a class performance. The nose displays hints of pears, jasmine and chamomile flowers, while a tangy, mouthwatering flavour is released on the palate with a lingering, clean finish. We also liked the Cruner, a refreshing Dry with apple and citrus aromas, and excellent balance between sweetness and acidity with well-sustained fizz.

○ Cartizze	♚♚ 3
○ Valdobbiadene Dry Cruner	♚♚ 2
⊙ Roseé Brut	♚ 3
○ Valdobbiadene Brut Fagher	♚ 3
○ Valdobbiadene Extra Dry Pianer	♚ 2
○ Valdobbiadene Prosecco Frizzante Mas	♚ 2

Contrà Soarda

LOC. CONTRÀ SOARDA, 26
36061 BASSANO DEL GRAPPA [VI]
TEL. 0424505562
www.contrasoarda.it

CELLAR SALES
PRE-BOOKED VISITS
RESTAURANT SERVICE
ANNUAL PRODUCTION 80,000 bottles
HECTARES UNDER VINE 20.00

About ten years ago, Mirco Gottardi and his wife Gloria created Contrà Soarda, a small winery in the hills around Bassano del Grappa. Having tidied up an old vineyard and restored it to productivity, with the help of Marco Bernabei they developed the other plots to make a total of about a dozen hectares. The proximity of the estate to Valsugana and its cool breezes make it possible to grow pinot nero, interestingly. The Contrà Soarda Rosso 2009, made exclusively from native grape varieties grown in Breganze, reveals red berries and forest floor on the nose and a firm-bodied, succulent palate with good prominent tannin. Maintaining its high standard, the Vigna Correjo 2010 is a Pinot Nero with complex aromas ranging from wild berries to fines herbes with smoky hints. A mouthwatering, lingering flavour and excellent balance on the palate.

● Breganze Rosso Terre di Lava Ris. '05	♚♚ 5
● Contrà Soarda '09	♚♚ 3
● Vigna Correjo '10	♚♚ 7
○ Breganze Torcolato Sarson '10	♚ 5
○ Breganze Vespaiolo Soarda '12	♚ 2
○ Breganze Vespaiolo Vignasilan '10	♚ 4
○ Il Pendio '11	♚ 3
● Marzemino Nero Gaggion '10	♚ 3
● Breganze Rosso Terre di Lava Ris. '09	♚♚ 4
○ Il Pendio '10	♚♚ 3
● Il Saggio '08	♚♚ 4
● Marzemino Gaggion '08	♚♚ 3
● Vigna Correjo '09	♚♚ 7

Corte Gardoni

LOC. GARDONI, 5
37067 VALEGGIO SUL MINCIO [VR]
TEL. 0457950382
www.cortegardoni.it

CELLAR SALES
PRE-BOOKED VISITS
ANNUAL PRODUCTION 200,000 bottles
HECTARES UNDER VINE 25.00

The Piccoli family estate is one of the most interesting in the Garda denominations, with 25 hectares of vineyards and an enhanced awareness thanks to countless trips to the other side of the Alps. Apart from a handful of wines dedicated to international grape varieties, the traditional grapes for Bardolino and Custoza wines characterize the estate's products in a style that pursues a taut, elegant ideal evident throughout the range. An impressive performance from the Pradicà 2011, which succeeds in appearing deep, complex and well-structured without losing the light, drinkability typical of Garda Bardolinos. A classic for this designation, the Custoza Mael benefits from the 2012 vintage with a fruity and floral nose, while the palate is slender-bodied with tangy flavour. The spicy, smoky Becco Rosso 2011 is made from corvina grapes while the Bardolino Le Fontane 2012 is generous and juicy.

● Bardolino Sup. Pradicà '11	♥♥	3*
○ Custoza Mael '12	♥♥	3*
● Bardolino Le Fontane '12	♥♥	2*
● Becco Rosso '11	♥♥	3
⊙ Bardolino Chiaretto '12	♥	2
○ Custoza '12	♥	2
○ Bianco di Custoza Mael '09	♥♥♥	2*
○ Bianco di Custoza Mael '08	♥♥♥	2*
○ Custoza Mael '11	♥♥♥	3*
● Bardolino Sup. '06	♀♀	2
● Bardolino Sup. Pradicà '10	♀♀	3*
● Bardolino Sup. Pradicà '09	♀♀	4
● Becco Rosso '09	♀♀	3*

Tenuta Corte Giacobbe

VIA MOSCHINA, 11
37030 RONCÀ [VR]
TEL. 0457460110
www.vinidalcero.com

CELLAR SALES
PRE-BOOKED VISITS
ANNUAL PRODUCTION 60,000 bottles
HECTARES UNDER VINE 20.00

Corte Giacobbe is certainly one of the most significant new estates to appear in the Soave area in the last ten years. The Dal Cero family divides its time between Roncà in Veneto and Cortona in Tuscany, with unquestionably valid results. The 15 hectares of vineyards on the volcanic hills around Roncà yield a range of products focusing on meticulous and well-typed interpretations of Soave. An excellent performance from the Soave Superiore Runcata 2011 from the vineyard of the same name, found between two extinct volcanoes, Calvarina and Crocetta. Maturation in large casks lets this white express vibrant aromas in which appley fruit makes room for mineral sensations and hints of dried flowers. The generous texture is nicely countered by acidity and tangy flavour on the dynamic palate. The interesting Brut, a monovarietal chardonnay, has straightforward, approachable aromas and creamily structured fizz.

○ Soave Sup. Runcata '11	♥♥	2*
○ Brut M. Cl.	♥♥	2
○ Pinot Grigio '12	♥	2
○ Pinot Grigio Blush '12	♥	2
○ Soave Corte Giacobbe '12	♥	2
○ Soave Corte Giacobbe '11	♀♀	2*
○ Soave Runcata '10	♀♀	2*
○ Soave Runcata '09	♀♀	2*

Corte Moschina

VIA MOSCHINA, 1
37030 RONCÀ [VR]
TEL. 0457460788
www.cortemoschina.it

CELLAR SALES
PRE-BOOKED VISITS
ANNUAL PRODUCTION 70,000 bottles
HECTARES UNDER VINE 28.00

Patrizia Niero is the heart and soul of the
Corte Moschina estate, established a few
years ago but testimony to the family's
longstanding involvement in the world of
Soave. Today her husband Silvano works
alongside her and sons Alessandro and
Giacomo play an increasingly important role.
The vineyards are situated in the extreme
eastern area of the designation, a position
which brings them into both the Soave and
the Lessinia zones. The wines produced are
principally Soave and Durello, the latter
always in the sparkling version. We were
impressed by our tasting of the Recioto di
Soave Incanto 2008, a raisined wine with
dried flowers and citrus fruit on the nose,
and well-judged sweetness on the palate
creating a balanced and polished flavour.
Late-harvested grapes are used for the
Tarai, a Soave with vibrant, mature aromas
of peach fruit and spice. The palate is nicely
supple with a slightly aromatic finish. The
Durello Brut 2012 is a dry, gutsy sparkler.

○ Recioto di Soave Incanto '08	♟♟ 4
○ Soave I Tarai '11	♟♟ 3
● Colle Alto '10	♟ 3
○ Lessini Durello Brut '12	♟ 2
○ Lessini Durello Brut M. Cl. Ris. '07	♟ 5
○ Lessini Durello M. Cl. '09	♟ 4
○ Soave Roncathe '12	♟ 2
○ Soave I Tarai '10	♟♟ 3*
○ Soave I Tarai '09	♟♟ 3
○ Soave Roncathe '10	♟♟ 2*

Corte Rugolin

FRAZ. VALGATARA
LOC. RUGOLIN, 1
37020 MARANO DI VALPOLICELLA [VR]
TEL. 0457702153
www.corterugolin.it

CELLAR SALES
PRE-BOOKED VISITS
ANNUAL PRODUCTION 80,000 bottles
HECTARES UNDER VINE 12.00

In Valpolicella, some estates have taken
advantage of the favourable period to
develop their business exponentially, with
extensions to the cellar and purchases of
new vineyards. But Elena and Federico
Coati have chosen to take things one step
at a time, without losing sight of principles
like tradition and personal supervision of all
the production phases. Today the estate
produces just over 100,000 bottles per
year, all from Valpolicella in the various
types. The grapes for the house champion,
Amarone Monte Danieli, are grown on the
hillside leading to Castelrotto. The aromas
range from dried red berries to medicinal
herbs, spices and cocoa powder, and
develop on the full-bodied, juicy palate
which displays soft alcohol and sugar
contrasting nicely with the tannin. The
Valpolicella Superiore Ripasso 2010
features generous fruit on the nose and a
well-rounded, vigorous flavour.

● Amarone della Valpolicella Cl. Monte Danieli '08	♟♟ 6
● Valpolicella Cl. Sup. Ripasso '10	♟♟ 4
● Amarone della Valpolicella Cl. Crosara de le Strie '08	♟ 5
● Valpolicella Cl. '12	♟ 2
● Amarone della Valpolicella Cl. Crosara de le Strie '07	♟♟ 6
● Amarone della Valpolicella Cl. Monte Danieli '07	♟♟ 7
● Amarone della Valpolicella Cl. Monte Danieli '05	♟♟ 7
● Amarone della Valpolicella Cl. Monte Danieli '03	♟♟ 6
● Valpolicella Cl. Sup. Ripasso '09	♟♟ 3
● Valpolicella Cl. Sup. Ripasso '04	♟♟ 3
● Valpolicella Cl. Sup. Ripasso '03	♟♟ 3

Corte Sant'Alda

Loc. Fioi
via Capovilla, 28
37030 Mezzane di Sotto [VR]
Tel. 0458880006
www.cortesantalda.it

CELLAR SALES
PRE-BOOKED VISITS
ACCOMMODATION
ANNUAL PRODUCTION 80,000 bottles
HECTARES UNDER VINE 19.00
VITICULTURE METHOD Certified Biodynamic

"Only personal dedication to the search for the best possible balance between things". This sums up Marinella Camerani's philosophy, as shown on her website, in support of a 20-year journey including an in-depth overhauling of the estate, especially in terms of sustainability and respect for the environment. The 20-odd hectares are biodynamically farmed with minimal procedures in the cellar on the Valpolicella-centric ranges of authentic, characterful wines. The Valpolicella Campi Magri is produced using the Ripasso technique but unusually for the area it steps away from the Amarone model and pursues a style of its own with elegant aromas and a taut flavour. The Amarone 2009 is naturally more mature and alluring on the nose, with well-controlled sweetness and rigorous tannin on the palate. The Soave and Valpolicella Ca' Fiui, both 2012, are uncomplicated but characterful.

● Amarone della Valpolicella '09	▼▼	8
● Valpolicella Sup. Ripasso Campi Magri '10	▼▼	4
○ Soave V. di Mezzane '12	▼▼	3
● Valpolicella Ca' Fiui '12	▼▼	3
● Recioto della Valpolicella '11	▼	6
● Amarone della Valpolicella '06	▼▼▼	7
● Amarone della Valpolicella '00	▼▼▼	7
● Amarone della Valpolicella '98	▼▼▼	7
● Amarone della Valpolicella '95	▼▼▼	7
● Amarone della Valpolicella '90	▼▼▼	7
● Amarone della Valpolicella Mithas '95	▼▼▼	7
● Valpolicella Sup. '03	▼▼▼	3*
● Valpolicella Sup. Mithas '04	▼▼▼	6

Casa Coste Piane

fraz. Santo Stefano
via Coste Piane, 2
31040 Valdobbiadene [TV]
Tel. 0423900219
casacostepiane@libero.it

CELLAR SALES
PRE-BOOKED VISITS
ANNUAL PRODUCTION 50,000 bottles
HECTARES UNDER VINE 6.00

Today Loris Follador seems like an innovative figure in the world of Prosecco, yet he is perhaps the most faithful custodian of local tradition, inextricably linked to simple, light, satisfying wines which are nonetheless never commonplace. The few hectares in the Santo Stefano area almost reluctantly produce a paltry number of bottles of spumante. But the estate's best grapes are destined for the wines produced through natural bottle fermentation, with little pressure and a cloudy aspect. Production is now exclusively focused on sparkling wines, following the realization that only this traditional path will lead to really unpretentious, authentic wines that truly represent the variety and terroir. Another prestigious result this year: the wine shows slightly hazy colour but releases ripe peach fruit and wild flowers on the nose, and a very refreshing and tangy flavour.

○ Valdobbiadene Naturalmente Frizzante	▼▼	7

...gino Dal Maso

C.DA SELVA, 62
36054 MONTEBELLO VICENTINO [VI]
TEL. 0444649104
www.dalmasovini.com

CELLAR SALES
PRE-BOOKED VISITS
ANNUAL PRODUCTION 450,000 bottles
HECTARES UNDER VINE 30.00

The estate established by Luigino Dal Maso is run with skill and perspicacity by his children Nicola, Anna and Silvia, who have transformed a winery making ordinary products into a benchmark for the Gambellara and Colli Berici areas. The northern part of the estate is entirely dedicated to garganega and its wines, while south of Vicenza international grape varieties alternate with the classic tai rosso. In the Berici hills the grenache grape goes by the name of tai rosso, and it is used in one of the area's most interesting wines. Colpizzarda has vibrant aromas ranging from wild berries to aromatic herbs, reflected on a solid – but not bulky – lingering palate with smooth tannins. The Recioto Riva dei Perari is also very good, with an explosion of dried fruit and citrus on the nose, exuberant sweetness and a dry finish.

● Colli Berici Tai Rosso Colpizzarda '11	⚑⚑ 3*
○ Recioto di Gambellara Cl. Riva dei Perari '11	⚑⚑ 5
● Colli Berici Cabernet Casara Roveri '11	⚑⚑ 3
● Colli Berici Cabernet Montebelvedere '11	⚑⚑ 2*
● Colli Berici Merlot Casara Roveri '10	⚑⚑ 4
○ Gambellara Cl. Ca' Fischele '12	⚑⚑ 2*
● Terra dei Rovi Rosso '11	⚑⚑ 5
○ Gambellara Cl. Riva del Molino '12	⚑ 3
○ Serafino '12	⚑ 2
○ Gambellara Cl. Riva del Molino '07	⚑⚑⚑ 2*
● Colli Berici Tai Rosso Colpizzarda '10	⚑⚑ 3*
○ Gambellara Cl. Riva del Molino '11	⚑⚑ 3*

De Stefani

VIA CADORNA, 92
30020 FOSSALTA DI PIAVE [VE]
TEL. 042167502
www.de-stefani.it

CELLAR SALES
PRE-BOOKED VISITS
ANNUAL PRODUCTION 300,000 bottles
HECTARES UNDER VINE 40.00

This winery owned by the De Stefani family was established in the heart of the Treviso hills 50 years ago, but the production nerve centre has now been moved along the river Piave where Alessandro and his father Tiziano continue their work as growers. The 50 hectares of vineyards are situated in three separate areas: Monastier, Fossalta di Piave and, of course, Refrontolo. In the latter zone the inevitable glera grape grows alongside marzemino, which is given plenty of attention and interpreted in a style that favours strength and high alcohol content. A great deal of care goes into production of the Stefen, a Marzemino made from dried grapes and aged at length in oak casks. Six years after the harvest, this wine now shows vibrant aromas of super-ripe red fruit, spices and cocoa powder, all mirrored on the palate with weighty structure and prominent alcohol and tannins. In a softer and more approachable style, the Vitalys 2012 is a fruity Chardonnay with a soft flavour.

● Soler '11	⚑⚑ 5
● Stefen 1624 '08	⚑⚑ 8
○ Vitalys '12	⚑⚑ 3
● Cabernet Sauvignon '11	⚑ 3
● Colli di Conegliano Refrontolo Passito '07	⚑ 6
○ Conegliano Valdobbiadene Brut	⚑ 3
● Piave Raboso '09	⚑ 8
○ Pinot Grigio '12	⚑ 4
○ Prosecco di Treviso Extra Dry Zero	⚑ 2
● Terre Nobili '10	⚑ 6
○ Tombola di Pin Brut M. Cl. Ris. '07	⚑ 5
○ Venis '12	⚑ 4
● Kreda '09	⚑⚑ 5
○ Olmera '11	⚑⚑ 5

Giovanni Fattori

FRAZ. TERROSSA
VIA OLMO, 6
37030 RONCÀ [VR]
TEL. 0457460041
www.fattorigiovanni.it

CELLAR SALES
PRE-BOOKED VISITS
ANNUAL PRODUCTION 200,000 bottles
HECTARES UNDER VINE 57.00

Antonio Fattori has succeeded in developing the family business, combining wines sold to other bottlers with an increasingly large quantity of bottled wines. He has achieved this by obtaining vineyards planted with grapes for both garganega and Valpolicella for a total of almost 60 hectares. The products are ever more impressive, the typical features of the winery style consisting of nicely defined aromas and outstandingly drinkable flavour. Apparently uncomplicated, the Recioto Motto Piane 2011 looks to be one of the most interesting wines in the designation thanks to tropical and candied fruit aromas, well-judged sweetness and a tangy, racy palate. The Amarone 2008 is also very good with an approachably fruity nose and soft succulent flavour. Our favourite of the Soaves presented was the Runcaris 2012 with subtle, delicate aromas and a stylish, nicely taut palate. The Sauvignon Vecchie Scuole 2012 is vibrant, tropical and fresh.

● Amarone della Valpolicella '08	♟♟ 8
○ Recioto di Soave Motto Piane '11	♟♟ 4
○ Soave Cl. Runcaris '12	♟♟ 2*
○ Vecchie Scuole Sauvignon '12	♟♟ 3
○ Lessini Durello Brut I Singhe	♟ 3
○ Pinot Grigio Valparadiso '12	♟ 3
○ Soave Cl. Danieli '12	♟ 2
● Valpolicella Ripasso Col de la Bastia '10	♟ 5
○ Vino Senza Nome '12	♟ 3
○ Recioto di Soave Motto Piane '10	♟♟ 4
○ Recioto di Soave Motto Piane '09	♟♟ 4
○ Soave Motto Piane '11	♟♟ 3
● Valpolicella Ripasso Col de la Bastia '09	♟♟ 4

Il Filò delle Vigne

VIA TERRALBA, 14
35030 BAONE [PD]
TEL. 042956243
www.ilfilodellevigne.it

CELLAR SALES
PRE-BOOKED VISITS
ANNUAL PRODUCTION 50,000 bottles
HECTARES UNDER VINE 17.00

Filò delle Vigne is situated in the extreme south of the Colli Euganei zone along the southern slopes of Monte Cecilia, one of the warmest areas in Veneto. Hereabouts cabernet sauvignon ripens perfectly every year, losing any vegetal tones in favour of densely fruity, spicy and minerally expression. The vineyards cover about 20 hectares and are mostly planted with black varieties, producing 50,000 bottles per year in a generous, rigorous style. The estate's most interesting wine has to be the Borgo delle Casette Riserva 2009: a red with vibrant aromas of red berries and spices, gradually making room for a deep, minerally sensation. The generous nose is mirrored on the palate, which is rounded and powerful yet supple and lingering. The Cecilia di Baone Riserva 2010, matured in concrete vats, seems more approachable and accessible with evident fruitiness and a mouthwatering, relaxed flavour.

● Colli Euganei Cabernet Borgo delle Casette Ris. '09	♟♟ 5
● Colli Euganei Cabernet V. Cecilia di Baone Ris. '10	♟♟ 3
○ Colli Euganei Fior d'Arancio '12	♟♟ 3
○ Il Calto delle Fate '10	♟ 4
● Colli Euganei Cabernet Borgo delle Casette Ris. '06	♟♟♟ 5
● Colli Euganei Cabernet Borgo delle Casette Ris. '08	♟♟ 5
● Colli Euganei Cabernet Borgo delle Casette Ris. '07	♟♟ 5
● Colli Euganei Cabernet Borgo delle Casette Ris. '05	♟♟ 5
○ Colli Euganei Fior d'Arancio Luna del Parco '04	♟♟ 5

Silvano Follador

LOC. FOLLO
FRAZ. SANTO STEFANO
VIA CALLONGA, 11
31040 VALDOBBIADENE [TV]
TEL. 0423900295
www.silvanofollador.it

CELLAR SALES
PRE-BOOKED VISITS
ANNUAL PRODUCTION 30,000 bottles
HECTARES UNDER VINE 3.50

Valdobbiadene is scattered with very small farms, sometimes less than one hectare, growing grapes for bottling wineries so that they have large quantities of grapes available. Alberta and Silvano Follador are following a different path, and their farm is run with the utmost respect for the environment. They only use their estate-grown grapes for their products, just three wines and all made without additional use of sugars. No classic method this year but the Cartizze and Valdobbiadene Brut amply made up for it. The first has subtle aromas of appley fruit and flowers, and displays firm body and gutsy flavour on the palate. The Valdobbiadene is even more impressive: uncomplicated, subtle floral and fresh fruit aromas with vegetal hints balanced by the weighty, confident, linear palate, highlighting the heart and soul of this type.

○ Cartizze Nature '12	♥♥	4
○ Valdobbiadene Brut Nature '12	♥♥	3*
○ Cartizze Brut '08	♀♀♀	4
○ Cartizze Brut '10	♀♀	4
○ Cartizze Brut '09	♀♀	4
○ Cartizze Brut Nature '11	♀♀	4
○ Dosaggio Zero '09	♀♀	4
○ Valdobbiadene Brut Dosaggio Zero M. Cl. '10	♀♀	3
○ Valdobbiadene Brut Nature '11	♀♀	3*

Fongaro

VIA MOTTO PIANE, 12
37030 RONCÀ [VR]
TEL. 0457460240
www.fongarospumanti.it

CELLAR SALES
PRE-BOOKED VISITS
ANNUAL PRODUCTION 68,000 bottles
HECTARES UNDER VINE 7.00
VITICULTURE METHOD Certified Organic

In a region where sparkling wines are nearly always produced using the Charmat method, it is rare to find a winery that exclusively uses the Metodo Classico. The Fongaro family has embraced this direction since the estate was established in the Seventies, aiming to use the austerity of the durella grape to enhance their taut, vigorous sparkling wines. The few hectares of vineyards are organically farmed and surrounded by woodlands. The wines are dependable in quality and nicely severe. When the tastings were conducted only the Brut Etichetta Viola was available, while the others awaited dégorgement. The 2009 displays aromas dominated by minerally, bready sensations, leaving the fruit in the background, while the palate shows good solid structure, nicely backed up by acidity and fizz. A wine that expresses the more gutsy and pleasantly husky nature of Lessinia-grown grapes.

○ Lessini Durello Brut M. Cl. Et. Viola '09	♥♥	5
○ Brut M. Cl. '08	♀♀	5
○ Lessini Durello Brut M. Cl. Et. Viola '08	♀♀	5*
○ Lessini Durello Pas Dosé M. Cl. Ris. '06	♀♀	4

Le Fraghe

LOC. COLOMBARA, 3
37010 CAVAION VERONESE [VR]
TEL. 0457236832
www.fraghe.it

CELLAR SALES
PRE-BOOKED VISITS
ACCOMMODATION
ANNUAL PRODUCTION 120,000 bottles
HECTARES UNDER VINE 28.00
VITICULTURE METHOD Certified Organic

The northern part of the Bardolino DOC zone has a decidedly cooler, breezier climate than the classic zone, guaranteeing healthy grapes with plenty of finesse on one hand but also causing smaller yields and sometimes a slighter profile. Matilde Poggi focuses entirely on Bardolino, which is the winery's flagship wine, in a meticulous interpretation that aims to enhance the elegance and tautness that are its best qualities. Making its debut this year the Brol Grande, a 2011 Bardolino, steps away from the role of the light, quaffable wine to reveal depth on the nose and a firm, spicy flavour, while maintaining the customary free-and-easy nature of this type. We also liked the Bardolino 2012, which follows the same approach but is fresher and edgier – one of the best in the designation. The Quaiare 2011, a blend of cabernet sauvignon and franc only produced in the best years, is on excellent form.

● Bardolino Cl. Brol Grande '11	▼▼▼	3*
● Bardolino '12	▼▼	2*
○ Garganega Camporengo '12	▼▼	2*
● Quaiare '11	▼▼	4
⊙ Bardolino Chiaretto Ròdon '12	▼	2
● Bardolino '11	♀♀	2*
● Bardolino '10	♀♀	2*
● Bardolino '09	♀♀	2*
● Bardolino '08	♀♀	2*
○ Garganega Camporengo '11	♀♀	2*
○ Garganega Camporengo '09	♀♀	2*
○ Garganega Camporengo '08	♀♀	2*

Marchesi Fumanelli

FRAZ. SAN FLORIANO
VIA SQUARANO, 1
37029 SAN PIETRO IN CARIANO [VR]
TEL. 0457704875
www.squarano.com

CELLAR SALES
PRE-BOOKED VISITS
RESTAURANT SERVICE
ANNUAL PRODUCTION 50,000 bottles
HECTARES UNDER VINE 23.00

This San Pietro in Cariano estate is one of the most beautiful in Valpolicella, with vineyards surrounding the villa positioned on a hillock in the centre of the valley. The vineyards extend over many hectares and only some of the grapes, obviously those from the best growing plots, are destined for the estate's own wines. The cellar occupies the recently restored underground space and work aims to enhance the features of the traditional grape varieties and the terroir of origin. The most interesting wine this year is the Amarone 2007, which displays vibrant aromas of fruit and aromatic herbs, while on the palate the natural exuberance is held in check by the acidity and tannin, avoiding excessive complexity. The result is a full-bodied, tangy, beautifully supple flavour. The Valpolicella Superiore 2009, in a version aiming for firm texture as well as lightness, is fresher on both nose and palate.

● Amarone della Valpolicella Cl. '07	▼▼	5
● Valpolicella Cl. Sup. '09	▼▼	3
○ Terso Bianco '08	▼	3
● Valpolicella Cl. '12	▼	2
● Amarone della Valpolicella Cl. '06	♀♀	5
● Amarone della Valpolicella Cl. Octavius Ris. '05	♀♀	8
○ Terso '06	♀♀	5
● Valpolicella Cl. Sup. '05	♀♀	2*
● Valpolicella Cl. Sup. Squarano '06	♀♀	3

★Gini

VIA MATTEOTTI, 42
37032 MONTEFORTE D'ALPONE [VR]
TEL. 0457611908
www.ginivini.com

CELLAR SALES
PRE-BOOKED VISITS
ANNUAL PRODUCTION 200,000 bottles
HECTARES UNDER VINE 56.00

Sandro and Claudio Gini's estate is undoubtedly one of those to have played a decisive role in the success of fine quality Soave around the world. Following in the footsteps of their father Olinto, they developed a well-organized farm able to translate sound country judgment into high profile wines. Some of the credit goes to the vineyards, which are planted in a few of the most prestigious parts of the zone, carefully managed to maintain a history that in some cases is almost a century old. Gini presented many impressive wines this year, starting with the Salvarenza 2011: a Soave aged in oak which reveals generous, mature aromas and a zesty, full-bodied, balanced flavour. The La Froscà 2012 is fresher on the nose with appley fruit and floral aromas mirrored on the succulent, supple palate. Turning to the sweet wines, we particularly liked the Renobilis 2008 with complex aromas and exuberant sweetness on the palate.

○ Soave Cl. Contrada Salvarenza V. V. '11	♥♥	5
○ Soave Cl. La Froscà '12	♥♥	4
● Campo alle More '09	♥♥	5
○ Gran Cuveé Brut M. Cl. '08	♥♥	4
○ Recioto di Soave Cl. Col Foscarin '08	♥♥	4
○ Recioto di Soave Renobilis '08	♥♥	4
○ Soave Cl. '12	♥♥	3
○ Soave Cl. Contrada Salvarenza V. V. '09	♡♡♡	5
○ Soave Cl. Contrada Salvarenza V. V. '08	♡♡♡	5
○ Soave Cl. Contrada Salvarenza V. V. '07	♡♡♡	5
○ Soave Cl. La Froscà '11	♡♡♡	4*
○ Soave Cl. La Froscà '06	♡♡♡	4*

Gregoletto

FRAZ. PREMAOR
VIA SAN MARTINO, 83
31050 MIANE [TV]
TEL. 0438970463
www.gregoletto.com

CELLAR SALES
PRE-BOOKED VISITS
ANNUAL PRODUCTION 200,000 bottles
HECTARES UNDER VINE 18.00

The small village of Premaor is situated halfway between Valdobbiadene and Conegliano, where vineyards alternate with woods as far as the eye can see and the hills seem to raise the Treviso plains up towards the Alpine foothills. Here the Gregoletto family has cultivated vines for centuries, although credit goes to Luigi for making the estate what it is today. The 15 hectares are not entirely dedicated to Prosecco, indeed the winery also offers an interesting range of still wines. The still wines achieved the most satisfactory results, starting with the intriguing Cabernet 2011: seemingly uncomplicated, it displays a multifaceted set of aromas and a basic, flavoursome palate. The Prosecco Tranquillo 2012 is possibly the estate's flagship wine: fragrant and dry with a tangy, drinkable flavour. Turning to the sparklers, the Extra Dry gave a good performance while the sparkling sur lies version of the Prosecco is refreshing and well-balanced.

● Cabernet '11	♥♥	3
○ Colli di Conegliano Bianco Albio '12	♥♥	3
○ Conegliano Valdobbiadene Extra Dry	♥♥	3
○ Conegliano Valdobbiadene Prosecco Tranquillo '12	♥♥	2*
○ Manzoni Bianco '12	♥♥	3
○ P. di Treviso Frizzante sui Lieviti '12	♥♥	4
○ Chardonnay '12	♥	3
○ Conegliano Valdobbiadene Extra Dry Monte Corbino	♥	2
○ Pinot Bianco '12	♥	3
○ Verdiso Frizzante Sui Lieviti '12	♥	3
● Cabernet '10	♡♡	3*
○ Chardonnay '11	♡♡	3
○ Colli di Conegliano Bianco Albio '11	♡♡	3
○ Manzoni Bianco '11	♡♡	3*
○ Manzoni Bianco '10	♡♡	3*

Guerrieri Rizzardi

S.DA CAMPAZZI, 2
37011 BARDOLINO [VR]
TEL. 0457210028
www.guerrieri-rizzardi.it

CELLAR SALES
PRE-BOOKED VISITS
ANNUAL PRODUCTION 700,000 bottles
HECTARES UNDER VINE 100.00

There are not many estates that can be considered symbolic for Veneto wine but Guerrieri Rizzardi is one of them. The estate's property is spread over most of the Verona area, from Soave to Valdadige, Bardolino and Valpolicella, with 100 hectares of meticulously farmed vineyards focusing on traditional varieties. In the new Bardolino cellar, the Garda wines are processed while Negrar is still the production centre for Valpolicella. The Valpolicella reds are on top form again, with a memorable version of the Calcarole, red wine of the year, closely followed by the classic Villa Rizzardi – both 2009. The Calcarole displays deep aromas ranging from cut flowers to spices, with red berries very much in the foreground, and a full-bodied, well-balanced flavour. The Villa Rizzardi seems fresher and more approachable, with a racy, more accessibly drinkable flavour. Lastly, an excellent performance from the Ripasso Pojega 2011.

Inama

LOC. BIACCHE, 50
37047 SAN BONIFACIO [VR]
TEL. 0456104343
www.inamaaziendaagricola.it

CELLAR SALES
PRE-BOOKED VISITS
ANNUAL PRODUCTION 450,000 bottles
HECTARES UNDER VINE 62.00
VITICULTURE METHOD Certified Organic

Although traditionally a white wine-producing estate, Stefano Inama's winery continues to develop the project linked to Colli Berici, an area with huge and still unexplored potential for red wines. While the winery's central hub for the Soave zone is situated on Monte Foscarino, the estate has three different plots on the Colli Berici: Lonigo, planted mainly with cabernet sauvignon; Oratorio di San Lorenzo for carmenère, and lastly the whole San Germano property. Welcoming in the new Colli Berici designation is the Oratorio San Lorenzo 2009, vibrant with fruit and spice and showing its trademark firm palate and polished tannins. Bradisismo 2009, a sunny, ripe Bordeaux blend, shows its usual good texture, while turning to the white, the Soave Du Lot 2011 is once again the best of the bunch: expressive peach fruit, wildflowers and flint aromas nicely masking the oak, and with a generous, taut palate.

● Amarone della Valpolicella Cl. Calcarole '09	♟♟♟ 8
● Amarone della Valpolicella Cl. Villa Rizzardi '09	♟♟ 7
● Bardolino Cl. Sup. Munus '11	♟♟ 3
● Castello Guerrieri Rosso '09	♟♟ 4
○ Soave Cl. Costeggiola '12	♟♟ 2*
● Valpolicella Cl. Sup. Ripasso Pojega '11	♟♟ 3
⊙ Bardolino Chiaretto Cl. '12	♟ 2
● Bardolino Cl. '12	♟ 2
⊙ Rosa Rosae '12	♟ 2
○ Soave Cl. '12	♟ 2
● Valpolicella Cl. '12	♟ 2
● Amarone della Valpolicella Cl. Calcarole '06	♟♟♟ 8
● Amarone della Valpolicella Cl. Villa Rizzardi '08	♟♟♟ 7

● Colli Berici Carmenère Oratorio di San Lorenzo Ris. '09	♟♟♟ 6
● Bradisismo '09	♟♟ 5
○ Soave Cl. Vign. Du Lot '11	♟♟ 4
● Cabernet Sauvignon Sel. '09	♟♟ 6
● Carmenère Più '10	♟♟ 3
○ Soave Cl. Vign. di Foscarino '11	♟♟ 4
○ Soave Cl. Vin Soave '12	♟♟ 3
○ Vulcaia Sauvignon '12	♟♟ 3
○ Chardonnay '12	♟ 3
○ Vulcaia Fumé '11	♟ 5
● Bradisismo '08	♟♟♟ 5
○ Soave Cl. Vign. di Foscarino '08	♟♟♟ 4
○ Soave Cl. Vign. Du Lot '05	♟♟♟ 4
○ Soave Cl. Vign. Du Lot '01	♟♟♟ 4

Lenotti

VIA SANTA CRISTINA, 1
37011 BARDOLINO [VR]
TEL. 0457210484
www.lenotti.com

CELLAR SALES
PRE-BOOKED VISITS
ANNUAL PRODUCTION 1,400,000 bottles
HECTARES UNDER VINE 105.00

The Lenotti family farm over 100 hectares of vineyards in some of Verona's leading designations, from Lake Garda to Soave and Valpolicella. Production figures are close to a million and a half bottles per year and the typical style favours recognizable grapes and a stylish palate. This is particularly evident in the Riviera DOC zones where Claudio and his father Giancarlo carry on the work commenced over a century ago. The wide range of wines is of a high standard. The Bardolino Superiore Le Olle 2011 is one of the most interesting versions of this type with generous ripe red berry aromas and a tangy, firm palate maintaining the proverbial lightness of the lakeside reds. An interesting performance from the Amarone 2009 which does not pursue strength for the sake of it chez Lenotti but offers a taut and supple interpretation. The Capomastro 2011 is an original blend of corvina and rebo, with fresh aromas and a bright flavour.

● Amarone della Valpolicella Cl. '09	▼▼ 6
● Bardolino Cl. Sup. Le Olle '11	▼▼ 3
● Capomastro '11	▼▼ 2*
● Valpolicella Cl. Sup. Ripasso Le Crosare '10	▼▼ 4
⊙ Bardolino Chiaretto Cl. '12	▼ 2
● Bardolino Cl. '12	▼ 2
○ Colle dei Tigli '12	▼ 2
● Massimo '10	▼ 4
○ Soave Capocolle '12	▼ 2
● Valsorda '11	▼ 2
● Amarone della Valpolicella Cl. Di Carlo '07	♈♈ 8
● Capomastro '10	♈♈ 2*

Conte Loredan Gasparini

FRAZ. VENEGAZZÙ
VIA MARTIGNAGO ALTO, 23
31040 VOLPAGO DEL MONTELLO [TV]
TEL. 0438870024
www.loredangasparini.it

CELLAR SALES
PRE-BOOKED VISITS
ACCOMMODATION
ANNUAL PRODUCTION 400,000 bottles
HECTARES UNDER VINE 80.00

The winery at Venegazzù, a small town nestling on the southern slop of Montello, was taken over by the Palla family in the Seventies. The estate now covers about 100 hectares, 80 of which are planted with vines. Black Bordeaux varieties are mainly grown round the winery buildings and in the Nervesa estate while the whole Giavera vineyard is used for Prosecco. In recent years there has been a reduction in the use of small barrels to give more space to larger casks. The classic Bordeaux blend from Venegazzù Capo di Stato 2008 gives an impressive performance in a version with vibrant red berries and spice on the nose, as well as a subtle hint of coffee in the background. Generous, firm body on the palate is guided by close-knit tannins which suggest longevity. The Rosso della Casa 2008 is a fruitier, more succulent glassful while the Manzoni Bianco 2012 and Cabernet Sauvignon 2011 have refreshing flavour.

● Capo di Stato '08	▼▼ 6
● Venegazzù Rosso della Casa '08	▼▼ 4
○ Manzoni Bianco '12	▼ 2
● Montello e Colli Asolani Cabernet Sauvignon '11	▼ 2
● Capo di Stato '07	♈♈ 6
● Capo di Stato '06	♈♈ 6
● Capo di Stato '05	♈♈ 6
● Capo di Stato '04	♈♈ 5
● Capo di Stato '02	♈♈ 5
● Falconera Merlot '08	♈♈ 3
● Falconera Rosso '09	♈♈ 4
● Montello e Colli Asolani Cabernet Sauvignon '09	♈♈ 2*

★Maculan

VIA CASTELLETTO, 3
36042 BREGANZE [VI]
TEL. 0445873733
www.maculan.net

CELLAR SALES
PRE-BOOKED VISITS
ANNUAL PRODUCTION 750,000 bottles
HECTARES UNDER VINE 50.00

The Maculan family estate at Breganze is protected from cool winds by the hills leading to the Sette Comuni plateau which guarantee a mild, airy climate. The vineyards, both owned and rented, cover about 40 hectares and provide grapes for the most ambitious wines, while the simpler products are made using grapes bought from local winegrowers. All the wines are full-bodied and sound. An excellent performance from the Fratta 2010, Maculan's traditional Bordeaux blend. This wine has lost a little fullness in recent years but gained in elegance and grip, displaying fresh fruit aromas and nicely blended oak, with a long, lingering finish. The Palazzotto 2010 follows a similar route but is fresher and suppler, and while the Torcolato 2009 still has marked oakiness, it is able to reveal alluring dried apricot and dried flower aromas.

Manara

FRAZ. SAN FLORIANO
VIA DON CESARE BIASI, 53
37029 SAN PIETRO IN CARIANO [VR]
TEL. 0457701086
www.manaravini.it

CELLAR SALES
PRE-BOOKED VISITS
ANNUAL PRODUCTION 120,000 bottles
HECTARES UNDER VINE 11.00

Giovanni, Fabio and Lorenzo Manara run this winery established by their father in the 1950s. Today, about ten hectares of vineyards in the classic zone, trained using the traditional pergoletta system, provide the grapes for all the estate's wines. The wines display a good combination of traditional style with the generosity of more modern products. The lively, racy Amarone Corta Manara 2009 shows exemplary workmanship with traditional dried red berries, crushed flowers and medicinal herbs on the nose, and a dynamic, taut palate. The Postera 2008, on the other hand, expresses sweeter, riper sensations on both nose and palate, with a soft, mouthfilling flavour. The supple and edgy Valpolicella Vecio Belo and soft, accessible Le Morete follow the same pattern.

● Fratta '10	♟8
● Breganze Cabernet Sauvignon Palazzotto '10	♟♟4
○ Breganze Torcolato '09	♟♟6
● Brentino '11	♟♟3
● Crosara '10	♟♟8
● Marzemino Cornorotto '11	♟♟3
○ Bidibì '12	♟2
● Breganze Pinot Nero '11	♟3
○ Breganze Vespaiolo '12	♟2
● Cabernet '11	♟2
⊙ Costadolio '12	♟2
○ Dindarello '12	♟4
○ Ferrata Chardonnay '11	♟4
● Madoro '11	♟3
○ Pino & Toi '12	♟2
● Salgarone '12	♟2

● Amarone della Valpolicella Cl. Corte Manara '09	♟♟5
● Amarone della Valpolicella Cl. Postera '08	♟♟6
● Recioto della Valpolicella Cl. El Rocolo '10	♟♟5
● Valpolicella Cl. Sup. Vecio Belo '10	♟♟2*
● Guido Manara '08	♟6
● Valpolicella Cl. Sup. Le Morete Ripasso '10	♟3
● Amarone della Valpolicella Cl. '00	♟♟♟5
● Amarone della Valpolicella Cl. '05	♟♟5*
● Amarone della Valpolicella Cl. '01	♟♟5*
● Guido Manara '07	♟♟6
● Valpolicella Cl. Sup. Le Morete Ripasso '08	♟♟3
● Valpolicella Cl. Sup. Vecio Belo '09	♟♟2*

Marcato

VIA PRANDI, 10
37030 RONCÀ [VR]
TEL. 0457460070
www.marcatovini.it

CELLAR SALES
PRE-BOOKED VISITS
ANNUAL PRODUCTION 400,000 bottles
HECTARES UNDER VINE 40.00

The Marcato family have worked for decades in this area between the provinces of Vicenza and Verona, processing grapes from over 80 hectares of vineyards. Alongside Lino and Giovanni, Enrico and Andrea have taken up the reins of this estate which is boosting its production of Classic Method sparkling wines in Lessinia and reds in the nearby Colli Berici. The former display a clearly identifiable style, generous and solidly defined, while the latter type alternates between simpler wines and those with a weightier structure. Thanks to the lively acidity of the durella grape, the estate's interesting interpretations of sparkling wines are increasingly impressive. The A.R. 2004 is a late-disgorged Brut which reveals hazelnut and biscuit aromas opening out into a firm, gutsy palate. The 2007, on the other hand, has a vibrantly fruity noise and a rounded, juicy flavour refreshed by acidity. Turning to the reds, we were impressed by the Merlot Baraldo 2009.

● Barattaro Pinot Nero '10	♟♟ 4
● Colli Berici Cabernet Franc La Giareta '11	♟♟ 2*
● Colli Berici Merlot Baraldo La Giareta '09	♟♟ 4
○ Lessini Durello Brut M. Cl. '07	♟♟ 2*
○ Lessini Durello Brut M. Cl. A.R. '04	♟♟ 5
● Colli Berici Merlot Asinara La Giareta '10	♟ 2
● Colli Berici Pianalto Ris. '09	♟ 5
⊙ Cuvée Maffea Rosè Brut M. Cl.	♟ 4
○ Lessini Durello Brut M. Cl. 36 Mesi	♟ 4
○ Soave I Prandi '12	♟ 2
● Colli Berici Cabernet Pianalto La Giareta Ris. '08	♟♟ 6
○ Lessini Durello Brut M. Cl. '06	♟♟ 2*

Marion

FRAZ. MARCELLISE
VIA BORGO MARCELLISE, 2
37036 SAN MARTINO BUON ALBERGO [VR]
TEL. 0458740021
www.marionvini.it

PRE-BOOKED VISITS
ANNUAL PRODUCTION 40,000 bottles
HECTARES UNDER VINE 14.00

The Marcellise area north-east of Verona is one of the most interesting and least-known zones of Valpolicella. The estate run here by Stefano Capedelli and his wife Nicoletta has about 15 hectares of vineyards planted with classic local varieties as well as imported grapes. The wines are typically generous and sound with excellent ageing potential. Marion's Valpolicella Superiore 2009 is always a benchmark for the type, made from perfectly ripe grapes which undergo a slow maturation process in the cellar. The nose reveals intriguing spicy, minerally hints alongside the fruit, following through on the generous yet tangy and taut palate. The Amarone 2008 follows a more open, raisiny aroma profile, but recovers freshness on the palate. An excellent performance from the fresh, racy Valpolicella Borgomarcellise 2011.

● Valpolicella Sup. '09	♟♟♟ 4*
● Amarone della Valpolicella '08	♟♟ 7
● Calto '08	♟♟ 4
● Teroldego '09	♟♟ 5
● Valpolicella Borgomarcellise '11	♟♟ 3
● Amarone della Valpolicella '06	♟♟♟ 7
● Amarone della Valpolicella '03	♟♟♟ 7
● Amarone della Valpolicella '01	♟♟♟ 7
● Valpolicella Sup. '06	♟♟♟ 4
● Valpolicella Sup. '05	♟♟♟ 4
● Amarone della Valpolicella '07	♟♟ 7
● Valpolicella Sup. '08	♟♟ 4

Masari

LOC. MAGLIO DI SOPRA
VIA BEVILACQUA, 2A
36078 VALDAGNO [VI]
TEL. 0445410780
www.masari.it

CELLAR SALES
PRE-BOOKED VISITS
ANNUAL PRODUCTION 30,000 bottles
HECTARES UNDER VINE 4.00

Masari is an acronym formed from the names Massimo and Arianna, the young viticulturists who put their previous experience to good use and started this project to develop an estate covering a handful of hectares in the upper Agno valley north of Vicenza. Here the gradual abandoning of farming in the twentieth century allowed Massimo Dal Lago and Arianna Tessari to embark on a journey of rediscovery and revaluation of the area, producing typically generous and sound wines. There are no weak links in the winery's chain of products, even with an original oxidized raisined wine like the Antico Pasquale. The amber colour anticipates aromas of walnuts, dried figs and lavender, progressing into a palate rich in sweetness, backed up by sparky acidity that adds tautness and length to the flavour. The San Martino 2010 is a blend of equal parts cabernet and merlot, with fresh aromas and a stylish flavour.

○ Antico Pasquale Passito Bianco '06	♲♲	8
● Vicenza Rosso San Martino '10	♲♲	3*
○ Doro Passito Bianco '10	♲♲	5
○ Leon Durello Brut M. Cl.	♲♲	4
○ Doro Passito Bianco '08	♲♲	5
○ Doro Passito Bianco '07	♲♲	5
○ Doro Passito Bianco '06	♲♲	5
○ Doro Passito Bianco '05	♲♲	4
○ Doro Passito Bianco '04	♲♲	4
● Masari '09	♲♲	5
● Masari '05	♲♲	5
● Masari '04	♲♲	5

★Masi

FRAZ. GARGAGNAGO
VIA MONTELEONE, 26
37015 SANT'AMBROGIO DI VALPOLICELLA [VR]
TEL. 0456832511
www.masi.it

CELLAR SALES
PRE-BOOKED VISITS
ACCOMMODATION
ANNUAL PRODUCTION 4,200,000 bottles
HECTARES UNDER VINE 640.00

Sandro Boscaini is one of the best known Italian wine producers worldwide thanks to the widespread presence of his large range of wines, emblematic of Veronese traditions and products. The estate's vineyards extend across many areas of Valpolicella, producing over three million bottles. Despite these significant quantities, Masi preserves its indissoluble links with the local area and devotes the greatest care and passion to the production of Amarone and Valpolicella, wines interpreted in a generous, richly extracted style. And naturally the Amarones are Masi's most impressive wines, with Campolongo di Torbe 2007 and Costasera Riserva 2008 as our pick of the bunch. The former has lost the decadent feel that characterized recent versions, and reveals vibrantly fruity, generous sensations on the palate. Since its debut the Costasera Riserva has always displayed considerable strength, and this vintage is no exception, while the Costasera 2009 shows textbook excellence in its style.

● Amarone della Valpolicella Cl. Campolongo di Torbe '07	♲♲♲	8
● Amarone della Valpolicella Cl. Costasera Ris. '08	♲♲	8
● Amarone della Valpolicella Cl. Costasera '09	♲♲	G
● Brolo di Campofiorin '10	♲♲	4
○ Possessioni Bianco '12	♲	3
● Valpolicella Cl. Sup. Monte Piazzo 650° Anniversario '10	♲	3
● Amarone della Valpolicella Cl. Campolongo di Torbe '04	♲♲♲	8
● Amarone della Valpolicella Cl. Mazzano '06	♲♲♲	8
● Amarone della Valpolicella Cl. Vaio Armaron Serègo Alighieri '06	♲♲♲	8

Masottina

LOC. CASTELLO ROGANZUOLO
VIA BRADOLINI, 54
31020 SAN FIOR [TV]
TEL. 0438400775
www.masottina.it

CELLAR SALES
PRE-BOOKED VISITS
ANNUAL PRODUCTION 1,000,000 bottles
HECTARES UNDER VINE 57.00

Castello di Roganzuolo is a small village
north-east of Conegliano, in the land of
Prosecco and fizz. Here the Dal Bianco
family established a large, reliable estate
after the Second World War, facing the
challenges involved year after year. The
estate has 50 hectares of vineyards but
also purchases grapes from many trusted
local winegrowers for use in all its wines.
The Treviso sparklers are on top form, and
our favourite is the Extra Dry Rive di
Ogliano 2012 with typical apple, pear and
wisteria aromas followed by a beautifully
balanced and drinkable palate. The Brut
and the Extra Dry are also very good: the
former shows appley aromas and a
dynamic, racy flavour, while the Extra Dry
has a more tropical sensation, with silky
fizz and a dry finish. Among the reds the
Cabernet Sauvignon 2009 gives a good
performance.

○ Conegliano Valdobbiadene Brut	♔♔ 5
○ Conegliano Valdobbiadene Extra Dry	♔♔ 5
○ Conegliano Valdobbiadene Extra Dry Rive di Ogliano '12	♔♔ 5
● Piave Cabernet Sauvignon Vign. ai Palazzi Ris. '09	♔♔ 4
○ Colli di Conegliano Bianco Rizzardo '10	♔ 7
○ Manzoni Bianco '12	♔ 2
● Piave Merlot Vign. Ai Palazzi Ris. '09	♔ 6
● Colli di Conegliano Rosso Montesco '07	♕♕ 5
● Piave Cabernet Sauvignon Vign. ai Palazzi Ris. '07	♕♕ 4
● Piave Merlot Vign. Ai Palazzi Ris. '08	♕♕ 6
● Piave Merlot Vign. ai Palazzi Ris. '07	♕♕ 3

Massimago

VIA GIARE, 21
37030 MEZZANE DI SOTTO [VR]
TEL. 0458880143
www.massimago.com

ANNUAL PRODUCTION 45,000 bottles
HECTARES UNDER VINE 12.00

In 2003 Camilla Rossi Chauvenet
transformed the family farm into a fully
operative estate, stopped selling on the
grapes to the co-operative winery and
brought Massimago to life. Today only
estate-grown grapes from the Mezzane
valley are processed in the winery, and
almost exclusively concern the Valpolicella
types. The early choice to proceed in small
stages is starting to yield results, and the
wines are gaining in prestige and
personality every year, making them some
of the most interesting newcomers. An
exemplary performance from the Tempo
Per Creare, a Valpolicella 2012 in which the
fresh, spicy, wild berry aromas of the
traditional grapes are enhanced on both
the nose and the slim-bodied, succulent
palate. The Superiore 2011 shows mature
aromas and more texture on the palate.
Lastly, the Amarone 2009 reveals a
generously fruity nose following through
onto a rounded, dynamic and mouthfillingly
smooth flavour.

● Amarone della Valpolicella '09	♔♔ 8
● Valpolicella Sup. Profasio '11	♔♔ 5
● Valpolicella Tempo per Creare '12	♔♔ 5
● Amarone della Valpolicella '08	♕♕ 8
● Valpolicella Cl. Sup. '10	♕♕ 6

Roberto Mazzi

LOC. SAN PERETTO
VIA CROSETTA, 8
37024 NEGRAR [VR]
TEL. 0457502072
www.robertomazzi.it

CELLAR SALES
PRE-BOOKED VISITS
ACCOMMODATION AND RESTAURANT SERVICE
ANNUAL PRODUCTION 45,000 bottles
HECTARES UNDER VINE 8.00

Stefano and Antonio Mazzi have continued and improved the business set up by their father Roberto in the Sixties, extending the cellar and reorganizing the vineyards to focus more closely on quality. They have achieved this without taking things too quickly, aware that in the wine sector, time and traditions are values that must not be overlooked. The products are all typical Valpolicella wines, interpreted through the pursuit of clean fruit and strength alongside elegance. The Amarone Punta di Villa has been maturing for longer every year, enabling it to reveal a more expressive range of aromas today with dried fruit embracing minerally hints and aromatic herbs. The palate is silky and very lingering with an excellent balance between sweetness and tannins. Great freshness and integrity from the Valpolicella Sanperetto 2011 which favours the spicy, floral expressive features of the local traditional grapes over the pursuit of strength.

● Valpolicella Cl. Sup. Sanperetto '11	▼▼▼ 3*
● Amarone della Valpolicella Cl. Punta di Villa '08	▼▼ 7
● Valpolicella Cl. '12	▼▼ 2*
● Valpolicella Cl. Sup. Vign. Poiega '10	▼▼ 4
● Amarone della Valpolicella Cl. Castel '05	▽▽ 7
● Amarone della Valpolicella Cl. Punta di Villa '05	▽▽ 7
● Recioto della Valpolicella Cl. Le Calcarole '09	▽▽ 5
● Recioto della Valpolicella Cl. Le Calcarole '07	▽▽ 5
● Valpolicella Cl. Sup. Sanperetto '10	▽▽ 3*
● Valpolicella Cl. Sup. Vign. Poiega '08	▽▽ 4
● Valpolicella Cl. Sup. Vign. Poiega '07	▽▽ 4
● Valpolicella Cl. Sup. Vign. Poiega '06	▽▽ 4

Merotto

LOC. COL SAN MARTINO
VIA SCANDOLERA, 21
31010 FARRA DI SOLIGO [TV]
TEL. 0438989000
www.merotto.it

CELLAR SALES
PRE-BOOKED VISITS
ACCOMMODATION AND RESTAURANT SERVICE
ANNUAL PRODUCTION 550,000 bottles
HECTARES UNDER VINE 21.00

If one winery in the Valdobbiadene area has made a huge leap in quality in recent years, it is undoubtedly Merotto. While in the past there were no lack of prestigious wines, the estate has more recently succeeded in creating continuity throughout the whole range and established itself as a benchmark for the whole denomination. Alongside the more sought-after wines the simpler products are also growing in quantity and quality, and are always based on glera, which takes the leading role in wines that are dynamic and never commonplace. Once again this year the Brut Graziano Merotto 2012 is one of the best of its type with vibrant aromas of fresh flowers, pears and almonds and a dry, gutsy palate with tangy acidity and creamy fizz. The Cartizze is also very good, with a sunnier, more approachable nose and beautifully balanced sweetness and acidity. The Brut Bareta is firm in texture, dry and confident. Good performances also from the Extra Brut Le Fare and La Primavera di Barbara 2012.

○ Valdobbiadene Brut Rive di Col San Martino Cuvée del Fondatore Graziano Merotto '12	▼▼▼ 4*
○ Cartizze	▼▼ 5
○ Le Fare Glera Extra Brut	▼▼ 2
● Rosso Dogato '10	▼▼ 4
○ Valdobbiadene Brut Bareta	▼▼ 2
○ Valdobbiadene Dry Rive di Col San Martino La Primavera di Barbara '12	▼▼ 3
○ Valdobbiadene Extra Dry Colbelo	▼▼ 2
⊙ Grani Rosa di Nero Brut	▼ 3
○ Prosecco di Treviso Dry Colmolina Mill. '12	▼ 3
○ Valdobbiadene Brut Rive di Col San Martino Cuvée del Fondatore Graziano Merotto '11	▽▽▽ 4*

Ornella Molon Traverso

FRAZ. CAMPO DI PIETRA
VIA RISORGIMENTO, 40
31040 SALGAREDA [TV]
TEL. 042280480
www.ornellamolon.it

CELLAR SALES
PRE-BOOKED VISITS
RESTAURANT SERVICE
ANNUAL PRODUCTION 350,000 bottles
HECTARES UNDER VINE 42.00

Molon is undoubtedly the classic flagship estate of the Piave zone, the first to grasp how the future of Veneto wines would need to experience a significant improvement in quality. Today, 30 years after those choices were made, Ornella Molon and Giancarlo Traverso have not changed their philosophy: their wines remain a paradigm for the whole DOC zone as faithful exponents of the grape and the terroir. The products are subdivided into a line of younger wines and a more ambitious line named Ornella. The Rosso di Villa is a monovarietal Merlot with lovely deep, ripe aromas including hints of plum and aromatic herbs, with perceptible smoky and minerally sensations in the firm palate texture. The Bianco di Ornella 2009 gave a very impressive performance: a dried-grape wine made from verduzzo, sauvignon and traminer, it has intoxicating tropical aromas and a sweet, racy palate. Turning to the dry whites, we liked the freshly aromatic character of the Sauvignon 2012.

○ Bianco di Ornella '09	♀♀	4
● Piave Merlot Rosso di Villa '09	♀♀	5
● Piave Raboso Ornella '09	♀♀	5
○ Sauvignon Ornella '12	♀♀	3
● Vite Rossa Ornella '09	♀♀	4
● Piave Cabernet Ornella '09	♀	3
● Piave Merlot Ornella '09	♀	3
○ Piave Tai Ornella '12	♀	2
○ Traminer Ornella '12	♀	3
○ Vite Bianca Ornella '10	♀	3
○ Piave Tai Ornella '11	♀♀	2*
● Vite Rossa Ornella '08	♀♀	4

Monte dall'Ora

LOC. CASTELROTTO
VIA MONTE DALL'ORA, 5
37029 SAN PIETRO IN CARIANO [VR]
TEL. 0457704462
www.montedallora.com

CELLAR SALES
PRE-BOOKED VISITS
ANNUAL PRODUCTION 35,000 bottles
HECTARES UNDER VINE 6.00
VITICULTURE METHOD Certified Organic

Monte Dall'Ora was established just a few years ago at the behest of Carlo Venturini and, possibly to a greater degree, that of his wife Alessandra, with their cellar and home set on the hill along the way to Castelrotto. The winery's few hectares of vineyard are located around the cellar, with the vines being all pergola-trained to give the bunches the right amount of shade, and are adorned with all the wild, aromatic plants that attract insects and micro-organisms. Production concentrates on traditional Valpolicella wines, including making excellent use of old local grape varieties. The Camporenzo represents a very interesting interpretation of Valpolicella Superiore, pursuing a path away from Amarone with a broad range of spicy aromas and a generous flavour, free from hints of raisining. The Recioto Sant'Ulderico 2009, on the other hand, appears more quintessentially traditional with exuberant aromas of wild fruit jam nicely developed in the sweetness on the palate.

● Valpolicella Cl. Sup. Camporenzo '10	♀♀♀	4*
● Recioto della Valpolicella Cl. Sant' Ulderico '09	♀♀	6
● Amarone della Valpolicella Cl. Stropa '06	♀♀	8
● Valpolicella Cl. Saseti '12	♀♀	2*
● Valpolicella Cl. Sup. Ripasso Saustò '09	♀♀	5
● Valpolicella Cl. Sup. Ripasso Saustò '07	♀♀♀	5
● Amarone della Valpolicella Cl. '08	♀♀	6
● Amarone della Valpolicella Cl. '07	♀♀	6
● Amarone della Valpolicella Cl. '06	♀♀	6
● Recioto della Valpolicella Cl. Sant' Ulderico '07	♀♀	6
● Recioto della Valpolicella Cl. Sant' Ulderico '06	♀♀	6
● Valpolicella Cl. Sup. Camporenzo '09	♀♀	4

Monte del Frà

S.DA PER CUSTOZA, 35
37066 SOMMACAMPAGNA [VR]
TEL. 045510490
www.montedelfra.it

CELLAR SALES
PRE-BOOKED VISITS
ANNUAL PRODUCTION 1,000,000 bottles
HECTARES UNDER VINE 172.00

The winery owned by Eligio and Claudio Bonomo has been operational since the late 1950s, and with the arrival of the second generation, the bar has been raised in terms of quality. Marica, Silvia and Massimo have energetically spurred on this cellar, which is now a leading light for the entire designation. Today, they cultivate over 150 hectares, mainly in the area at the southern end of Lake Garda, with the exquisite Lena di Mezzo estate representing the Valpolicella designation. The aim of Monte del Fra is to produce elegant wines full of tautness. The Ca' del Magro 2011 is a classy white with a wide range of aromas in which flowers, peach and spice blend sumptuously together and open out into a very rounded, taut palate. The Colombara 2011 is an overripe Garganega which pursues complex aromas and deep flavour rather than rich texture, with dry, edgy results. Lastly, raisiny effects are very much in the background in the Scarnocchio, an Amarone 2008.

○ Custoza Sup. Ca' del Magro '11	♟♟♟ 2*
● Amarone della Valpolicella Cl. Scarnocchio Tenuta Lena di Mezzo '08	♟♟ 7
○ Garda Garganega Vign. Colombara '11	♟♟ 3*
● Amarone della Valpolicella Cl. Tenuta Lena di Mezzo '09	♟♟ 7
● Bardolino '12	♟♟ 2*
○ Custoza '12	♟♟ 2*
● Valpolicella Cl. Sup. Ripasso Tenuta Lena di Mezzo '11	♟♟ 3
● Valpolicella Cl. Sup. Tenuta Lena di Mezzo '11	♟♟ 4
⊙ Bardolino Chiaretto '12	♟ 3
● Valpolicella Cl. Tenuta Lena di Mezzo '12	♟ 2
○ Custoza Sup. Ca' del Magro '10	♟♟♟ 2*
○ Custoza Sup. Ca' del Magro '09	♟♟♟ 2*

La Montecchia
Conte Emo Capodilista

VIA MONTECCHIA, 16
35030 SELVAZZANO DENTRO [PD]
TEL. 049637294
www.lamontecchia.it

CELLAR SALES
PRE-BOOKED VISITS
ACCOMMODATION
ANNUAL PRODUCTION 130,000 bottles
HECTARES UNDER VINE 20.00

Over the years, Giordano Emo Capodilista has bonded into a single operation his two long-established family wineries, La Montecchia, in the northern part of Colli Euganei, and Conte Emo Capodilista, which has its operational centre at the extreme south of the Colli. Of the two estates, the former produces wines that are particularly fine and elegant, while the latter makes use of the strong Mediterranean sun of the area to yield wines that are rich, full and powerful. All the products are on top form, starting with the Ireneo 2010, a Cabernet Sauvignon produced on Monte Castello which displays vibrant, ripe aromas of red berries and spice with perfectly blended oak and a firm, tangy flavour. The Baon 2010, a cabernet sauvignon-heavy Bordeaux blend, is equally good and more approachable on the nose, with a smooth, alluring profile. Lastly, the Villa Capodilista 2010 displays the freshest aromas and the raciest palate.

● Baon '10	♟♟ 5
● Colli Euganei Cabernet Sauvignon Ireneo Capodilista '10	♟♟ 4
● Colli Euganei Rosso Villa Capodilista '10	♟♟ 5
○ Colli Euganei Fior d'Arancio Passito Donna Daria '11	♟♟ 5
○ Colli Euganei Fior d'Arancio Spumante '12	♟♟ 2*
● Colli Euganei Merlot '10	♟♟ 3
● Colli Euganei Rosso Ca' Emo '11	♟♟ 2*
● Godimondo Cabernet Franc '12	♟♟ 2*
● Turca	♟♟ 2
○ Acinidoro '11	♟ 5
○ Colli Euganei Pinot Bianco '12	♟ 2
● Forzaté Raboso '11	♟ 2
○ Piùchebello '12	♟ 2

Monteforche

LOC. ZOVON
VIA ROVAROLLA, 2005
35030 VO [PD]
TEL. 3332376035
soranzo1968@gmail.com

CELLAR SALES
PRE-BOOKED VISITS
ANNUAL PRODUCTION 19,000 bottles
HECTARES UNDER VINE 4.50

The Colli Eugeni regional park has protected this splendid hilly area deep within the Po Valley from industrial and urban development. Here Alfonso Soranzo has gathered up the reins of his family's vineyards, blowing life into one of the most interesting operations in Veneto. Viticulture is carried out with respect for the environment, following organic practices with an eye to biodynamic methods, and their wines are defined by their richness and grip. Alfonso Soranzo's reds are all absent from this year's tastings, since they are still maturing in the cellar. To make up for it we tasted an excellent range of whites, with an outstanding coppery Pinot Grigio 2011 displaying a fruity nose and palate, with a rounded, juicy flavour. The Vigneto Carantina 2011 is a monovarietal Garganega with aromas of Mediterranean scrubland, liquorice and iodine, and a pleasingly husky, characterful flavour.

Cantina Sociale di Monteforte d'Alpone

VIA XX SETTEMBRE, 24
37032 MONTEFORTE D'ALPONE [VR]
TEL. 0457610110
www.cantinadimonteforte.it

CELLAR SALES
PRE-BOOKED VISITS
ANNUAL PRODUCTION 2,000,000 bottles
HECTARES UNDER VINE 1,300.00

The Soave area is at the centre of a packed network of co-operative wineries that control a large chunk of the area under vine within the designation. Among these, the Cantina di Monteforte is the cellar providing the greatest depth in terms of quality, with its combination of vineyards extending for over 1,000 hectares and the skill of Gaetano Tobin, who is capable of managing the different parcels of grapes, assigning each to the most appropriate type of wine. Much of the wine is often passed on to other bottlers and only the best is bottled under their own label. An interim year for Cantina di Monteforte, lacking the necessary high note to repeat last year's excellent results. The most impressive wine is from outside the DOC zone: the Valpolicella Ripasso 2011, characterized by its overripe fruit and spices on the nose and tangy, nicely taut flavour. Turning to the Soaves, the Vigneto di Castellaro 2011 came close to a Due Bicchieri. Aged in oak, it displays a lovely rounded, mature profile.

○ Pinot Grigio '11	♟♟ 3
○ Vigneto Carantina '11	♟♟ 4
○ Cassiara '11	♟ 4
● Cabernet Franc '10	♟♟ 5
● Cabernet Franc '09	♟♟ 5
● Cabernet Franc '08	♟♟ 5
○ Cassiara '10	♟♟ 4
○ Cassiara '09	♟♟ 4
● Vigna del Vento '09	♟♟ 6
● Vigna del Vento '08	♟♟ 4
● Vigna del Vento '07	♟♟ 4
○ Vigneto Carantina '09	♟♟ 4

● Valpolicella Ripasso '11	♟♟ 2*
● Amarone della Valpolicella Re Teodorico '10	♟ 5
○ Lessini Durello Brut	♟ 2
○ Lessini Durello Brut M. Cl.	♟ 3
○ Soave Cl. Clivus '12	♟ 1*
○ Soave Cl. Il Vicario '12	♟ 2
○ Soave Cl. Sup. Vign. di Castellaro '11	♟ 2
● Amarone della Valpolicella Re Teodorico '09	♟♟ 5
○ Soave Cl. Clivus '11	♟♟ 1*
○ Soave Cl. Clivus '10	♟♟ 2
○ Soave Cl. Sup. Vign. di Castellaro '10	♟♟ 2*
○ Soave Cl. Sup. Vign. di Castellaro '09	♟♟ 2*
○ Soave Cl. Terre di Monteforte '10	♟♟ 2*
○ Soave Passo Avanti '10	♟♟ 1*

Montegrande

VIA TORRE, 2
35030 ROVOLON [PD]
TEL. 0495226276
www.vinimontegrande.it

CELLAR SALES
PRE-BOOKED VISITS
ANNUAL PRODUCTION 250,000 bottles
HECTARES UNDER VINE 30.00

Over the past ten years, Raffaele
Cristofanon has radically revived his
family's winery, improving the management
of the vineyards and channelling the best
grapes to the production of new wines.
Their deliberate care in using wine to
complement food and not simply as
specimens for tasting purposes has
inevitably led to a style where wines are not
powerful just for the sake of it but have
elegance and ease of drinking, something
reflected throughout the range. An
excellent standard in the more ambitious
wines, Vigna delle Roche and Sereo, both
2010. The former is a merlot-heavy
Bordeaux blend with an interesting array of
fruity, peppery aromas and a dry, racy
texture on the palate. The Sereo focuses
more on strength, with minerally, spicy
aromas contrasting with a generous, juicy
palate. Among the more basic wines we
liked the nonchalant assurance of the Colli
Euganei Rosso 2012.

● Colli Euganei Cabernet Sereo '10	♥♥ 3
● Colli Euganei Rosso '12	♥♥ 2*
● Colli Euganei Rosso V. delle Roche '10	♥♥ 3
○ Castearo '12	♥ 2
○ Colli Euganei Bianco '12	♥ 2
● Colli Euganei Cabernet '12	♥ 3
○ Colli Euganei Chardonnay S. Giorgio '11	♥ 2
○ Colli Euganei Fior d'Arancio Passito '10	♥ 3
● Colli Euganei Merlot '12	♥ 2
○ Colli Euganei Pinot Bianco '12	♥ 2
● Colli Euganei Cabernet Sereo '09	♥♥ 3*
● Colli Euganei Rosso V. delle Roche '09	♥♥ 3

Montetondo

LOC. MONTE TONDO
VIA SAN LORENZO, 89
37038 SOAVE [VR]
TEL. 0457680347
www.montetondo.it

CELLAR SALES
PRE-BOOKED VISITS
ACCOMMODATION
ANNUAL PRODUCTION 200,000 bottles
HECTARES UNDER VINE 32.00

The Magnabosco family winery is the
missing link between a rural past and a
modern farming enterprise. It may seem a
platitude but the atmosphere in the cellar
smells both of the land, where Gino has the
dominant role, and also of more modern
practices and a care for how wine is
produced and marketed, prompted by his
children. The vineyards stretch out over the
Soave area, although in recent years they
have extended into the neighbouring
Valpolicella, where the family has bought
new vineyards. The Soave area produces
the most interesting products, starting with
the Foscarin Slavinus 2011, a white aged
in oak displaying ripe peach fruit and dried
flowers on the nose, enhanced with subtle
minerally hints, and a generous, succulent
palate. The Monte Tondo 2012 is fresher
and racier, with a floral, appley nose and
light, tangy palate. On the other hand, the
Casette Foscarin 2011 has more prominent
oaky aromas with a generous, juicy profile.

○ Soave Cl. Sup. Foscarin Slavinus '11	♥♥ 4
○ Soave Cl. Casette Foscarin '11	♥♥ 3
○ Soave Cl. Monte Tondo '12	♥♥ 2*
● Valpolicella Ripasso Campo Grande '10	♥ 4
● Valpolicella San Pietro '11	♥ 2
○ Soave Cl. Monte Tondo '06	♥♥♥ 0*
○ Soave Cl. Casette Foscarin '08	♥♥ 3*
○ Soave Cl. Monte Tondo '11	♥♥ 2*
○ Soave Cl. Sup. Foscarin Slavinus '10	♥♥ 4
○ Soave Cl. Sup. Foscarin Slavinus '09	♥♥ 4
○ Soave Cl. Sup. Foscarin Slavinus '08	♥♥ 3
○ Soave Cl. Sup. Foscarin Slavinus '07	♥♥ 3

Monteversa

via Monte Versa, 1024
35030 Vò [PD]
Tel. 0499941092
www.monteversa.it

CELLAR SALES
PRE-BOOKED VISITS
ANNUAL PRODUCTION 23,000 bottles
HECTARES UNDER VINE 17.00
VITICULTURE METHOD Certified Organic

A few years ago the Voltazza family purchased this estate, situated in one of the most interesting areas of the Colli Euganei and began a process of enhancement with the help of Guido Busatto. The estate's vineyards, on the western slopes, are home to biancone and scaglia rossa planted with two different aspects: one overlooking Cinto Euganeo, destined for the production of red wines, and the other, cooler location facing Vò, for white wines. However the estate's best grapes end up in the Animaversa, whose debut greatly impressed our tasting panel. The fruity rich texture of merlot blends with rigorous cabernet sauvignon to create a dynamic, very harmoniously balanced flavour that will surely improve over the coming years. The very interesting Versavò 2011 is a fragrant, slender-bodied white, while the Versacinto 2011 is generous, fruity and very drinkable.

Giacomo Montresor

via Ca' di Cozzi, 16
37124 Verona
Tel. 045913399
www.vinimontresor.it

PRE-BOOKED VISITS
ANNUAL PRODUCTION 2,500,000 bottles
HECTARES UNDER VINE 150.00

Montresor is one of Verona's classic names and although it is now operative in many different Italian DOCs, the winery's heart is still in Verona itself, where the Montresor family farm 150 hectares of vineyards in all the leading growing zones. The range includes DOC wines alongside more original products, using both native and international grapes. What never varies though is the care poured into the wines, which are meticulous and well-defined, independent of their origin. We have an exemplary, almost textbook interpretation of the Amarone Capitel della Crosara 2009, with fragrant dried fruit and medicinal herbs on the nose, and a firm-bodied, juicy palate backed up by acidity, closing in a lovely finish. The Castelliere delle Guaite 2007 is more modern in style and seems slightly affected by oak, while the very interesting Campo Madonna 2010 is a Cabernet Sauvignon with vibrant aromas and a taut, racy palate.

● Colli Euganei Animaversa Rosso '10	♟♟ 4
○ Colli Euganei Bianco Versavò '11	♟♟ 2*
● Colli Euganei Rosso Versacinto '11	♟♟ 2*
○ Animaversa Bianco '11	♟♟ 4
○ Colli Euganei Chardonnay Animaversa '10	♟♟ 4
○ Colli Euganei Fior d'Arancio '10	♟♟ 4
● Colli Euganei Rosso Versacinto '10	♟♟ 4

● Amarone della Valpolicella Cl. Capitel della Crosara '09	♟♟ 8
● Amarone della Valpolicella Cl. Castelliere delle Guaite '07	♟♟ 8
● Cabernet Sauvignon Vign. Campo Madonna '10	♟♟ 3
○ Soave Cl. Capitel Alto '12	♟ 3
● Valpolicella Cl. Sup. Castelliere delle Guaite '10	♟ 5
● Amarone della Valpolicella Cl. Capitel della Crosara '08	♟♟ 8
● Amarone della Valpolicella Il Fondatore '08	♟♟ 6
● Cabernet Sauvignon Vign. Campo Madonna '09	♟♟ 3
● Valpolicella Cl. Ripasso Castelliere delle Guaite '08	♟♟ 5

Mosole

LOC. CORBOLONE
VIA ANNONE VENETO, 60
30029 SANTO STINO DI LIVENZA [VE]
TEL. 0421310404
www.mosole.com

CELLAR SALES
PRE-BOOKED VISITS
ANNUAL PRODUCTION 220,000 bottles
HECTARES UNDER VINE 30.00

Lucio Mosole is a grower who, for years, has been working at promoting the wines from the Venetian plain, and is now producing increasingly impressive wines. Here the intensely clayey soil and the effect of the nearby Adriatic Sea allow the grapes to acquire an indisputably superb character while ripening, at its best in the house reserve wines. His collaboration with Gianni Menotti has brought about a further hike in quality, with a style that does not impose power or freshness at any cost, but seeks rather to create a fusion between grape, soil and human hand. Lucio is delighted with their work on the tai grape, resulting in an excellent Eleo Bianco 2012, where aromas of yellow-fleshed fruit and almond lead to a rich but not cumbersome palate and a sapid, refined drinkability. Hora Sexta 2011 is also very good, a blend of carmenère and cabernet franc with strikingly intense spices, followed on the palate by a lean crunchiness. The style of Merlot Ad Nonam 2010 offers exceedingly rich fruit and a fleshy mouth.

● Lison-Pramaggiore Cabernet Hora Sexta '11	♟♟ 3*
○ Lison-Pramaggiore Lison Eleo Bianco '12	♟♟ 2*
○ Ad Nonam Passito '11	♟♟ 4
● Lison-Pramaggiore Merlot Ad Nonam '10	♟♟ 4
○ Tai '12	♟♟ 2*
● Venezia Cabernet Franc '12	♟♟ 2*
● Lison-Pramaggiore Refosco P.R. '12	♟ 2
○ Pinot Grigio '12	♟ 2
○ Sauvignon '12	♟ 2
● Venezia Chardonnay '12	♟ 2
● Lison-Pramaggiore Cabernet Hora Sexta '10	♟♟ 3
● Lison-Pramaggiore Merlot Ad Nonam '09	♟♟ 4
○ Tai Eleo Bianco '11	♟♟ 3*

Il Mottolo

LOC. LE CONTARINE
VIA COMEZZARE
35030 BAONE [PD]
TEL. 3479456155
www.ilmottolo.it

CELLAR SALES
PRE-BOOKED VISITS
ANNUAL PRODUCTION 18,000 bottles
HECTARES UNDER VINE 6.00

The area of the Colli Euganei is certainly one of the most interesting In Veneto, especially at its southernmost point where the climate takes on a decidedly more Mediterranean feel. According to Sergio Fortin, however, a wine's power must always defer to its tension and elegance, and therefore his house wines are never specimens of concentration but are polished wines with a great potential for ageing. The vineyards are scattered around the cellar, and are mainly planted with Bordeaux varieties. Vignànima and Serro compete for the flagship role. The first is a Cabernet Franc with intense fruity and spicy aromas, and a rich, solid taste profile that retains crispness and vigour. Serro is a predominately merlot Bordeaux blend, hinging mainly on complexity and elegance, and one of the most convincing reds in the region. We found the raisined wine very good, while the Merlot and Cabernet base wines are defined by their energetic and succulent mouthfeel.

● Colli Euganei Rosso Serro '10	♟♟♟ 3*
● Vingnànima '10	♟♟ 3*
● Colli Euganei Cabernet V. Marè '11	♟♟ 2*
○ Colli Euganei Fior d'Arancio Passito V. del Pozzo '11	♟♟ 3
● Colli Euganei Merlot Comezzara '11	♟♟ 2*
○ Le Contarine '12	♟♟ 2*
● Colli Euganei Rosso Serro '09	♟♟♟ 3*
○ Colli Euganei Fior d'Arancio Passito V. del Pozzo '11	♟♟ 3*
● Colli Euganei Rosso Serro '08	♟♟ 3
● Colli Euganei Rosso Serro '07	♟♟ 3*
● Colli Euganei Rosso Serro '06	♟♟ 3*
● Vingnànima '08	♟♟ 3*

Musella

LOC. FERRAZZE
VIA FERRAZZETTE, 2
37036 SAN MARTINO BUON ALBERGO [VR]
TEL. 045973385
www.musella.it

CELLAR SALES
PRE-BOOKED VISITS
ACCOMMODATION
ANNUAL PRODUCTION 200,000 bottles
HECTARES UNDER VINE 40.00
VITICULTURE METHOD Certified Biodynamic

The winery is set within the ancient Musella estate, which is in effect an island with woods and vineyards and olive groves a stone's throw from Verona. Maddalena Pasqua has been running this operation since it was founded, less than 20 years ago, with the support of her cousin Enrico Raber, initially involved in the process of planting the vineyards and now directing the winery's conversion to biodynamic farming. In the cellar, the intervention is minimal, allowing the wine to find its own way without contrivances, as a true expression of this blissful land. Musella wines had a clear run this year, with all of them good if not excellent. Amarone, offspring of the 2009 harvest, displays aromas of partially dried fruit and aromatic herbs, gifting the palate with pressure and an unexpected lightness. The more complex Riserva version has greater depth of flavours, with spices to the fore and a solid, crispy drinkability. We found the Ripasso 2010 to be excellent.

● Amarone della Valpolicella '09	♟♟ 6
● Amarone della Valpolicella Ris. '09	♟♟ 6
○ Bianco del Drago '12	♟♟ 2*
● Monte del Drago '09	♟♟ 5
● Valpolicella Sup. '11	♟♟ 2*
● Valpolicella Sup. Ripasso '10	♟♟ 3
● Amarone della Valpolicella Ris. '07	♟♟♟ 6
● Amarone della Valpolicella Ris. '08	♟♟ 7
● Amarone della Valpolicella Ris. '06	♟♟ 6
● Amarone della Valpolicella Ris. '05	♟♟ 6
● Amarone della Valpolicella Ris. '04	♟♟ 6
● Recioto della Valpolicella '06	♟♟ 5
● Valpolicella Sup. Ripasso '07	♟♟ 3*

Daniele Nardello

VIA IV NOVEMBRE, 56
37032 MONTEFORTE D'ALPONE [VR]
TEL. 0457612116
www.nardellovini.it

CELLAR SALES
PRE-BOOKED VISITS
ANNUAL PRODUCTION 30,000 bottles
HECTARES UNDER VINE 15.00

Daniele Nardello and his sister Federica run their family-owned winery, which extends over approximately 15 hectares at the southern extremity of the classic area. Here the soil is particularly deep and rich in clay and volcanic deposits, which confer to the grapes a richness and particularly Mediterranean quality that translates into wines produced in a caressingly full style. The simple cellar is located just outside the town centre, close to the hill, with the pale volcanic soil typical of this area. Soave Monte Zoppega 2011 has a perfectly expressed style. Partially aged in oak, it releases intensely fruity aromas, with a dusting of spices in the background that does not mask the mineral tones. In the mouth, it is rich and succulent. Vigna Turbian 2012, due to some intriguing trebbiano di Soave in the blend, offers greater freshness and a thrust of acidity. Soave Meridies 2012 came up trumps. This crisp, approachable white with a rewarding drinkability, has a winning card in its simplicity.

○ Soave Cl. Monte Zoppega '11	♟♟ 3*
○ Soave Cl. Meridies '12	♟♟ 2*
○ Soave Cl. V. Turbian '12	♟♟ 2*
○ Blanc De Fe '12	♟ 2
○ Recioto di Soave Suavissimus '10	♟ 4
○ Recioto di Soave Suavissimus '09	♟♟ 4
○ Recioto di Soave Suavissimus '08	♟♟ 4
○ Recioto di Soave Suavissimus '07	♟♟ 4
○ Soave Cl. Meridies '11	♟♟ 2*
○ Soave Cl. Monte Zoppega '10	♟♟ 3*
○ Soave Cl. Monte Zoppega '09	♟♟ 3*
○ Soave Cl. V. Turbian '11	♟♟ 2*
○ Soave Cl. V. Turbian '10	♟♟ 2*

Angelo Nicolis e Figli

VIA VILLA GIRARDI, 29
37029 SAN PIETRO IN CARIANO [VR]
TEL. 0457701261
www.vininicolis.com

CELLAR SALES
PRE-BOOKED VISITS
ANNUAL PRODUCTION 220,000 bottles
HECTARES UNDER VINE 42.00

Founded half a century ago, the winery
owned by the Nicolis family has known how
to expand without haste, retaining tight-knit
links to land and traditions, even during the
years when the scene was set in Veneto for
a massive commercial growth throughout
the industry. The credit for this rests with
Angela and the passion she passed on to
her sons Giancarlo and Giuseppe, who look
after vineyards and cellar, respectively. The
vineyards are set in both the classic and the
eastern zones, and they are all planted with
the traditional grapes of Valpolicella. The
house superstar is Amarone Ambrosan
2007, defined by overripe red fruit and an
unusually spicy note in the background that
contrasts with the oakiness. The mouth is
very concentrated but also able to unbend
with a supple energy. Amarone Classico
2007 is decidedly less rich on the palate,
while Recioto 2009 is crisply succulent.
Among the Valpolicellas, we prefer the
harmonious, sound Superiore 2010.

● Amarone della Valpolicella Cl. Ambrosan '07		🍷🍷 7
● Amarone della Valpolicella Cl. '07		🍷🍷 6
● Recioto della Valpolicella Cl. '09		🍷🍷 5
● Valpolicella Cl. Sup. '10		🍷🍷 3
● Valpolicella Cl. Sup. Ripasso Seccal '10		🍷🍷 3
● Testal '08		🍷 4
● Valpolicella Cl. '12		🍷 2
● Amarone della Valpolicella Cl. Ambrosan '06		🍷🍷🍷 7
● Amarone della Valpolicella Cl. Ambrosan '98		🍷🍷🍷 7
● Amarone della Valpolicella Cl. Ambrosan '93		🍷🍷🍷 6
● Amarone della Valpolicella Cl. '05		🍷🍷 6
● Amarone della Valpolicella Cl. Ambrosan '05		🍷🍷 7

Nino Franco

VIA GARIBALDI, 147
31049 VALDOBBIADENE [TV]
TEL. 0423972051
www.ninofranco.it

CELLAR SALES
PRE-BOOKED VISITS
ACCOMMODATION AND RESTAURANT SERVICE
ANNUAL PRODUCTION 1,100,000 bottles
HECTARES UNDER VINE 2.50

The winery belonging to the Franco family
is rapidly reaching its first century although,
to give Primo his due, it is through his
efforts that this cellar is among the most
respected and successful in Italy today. In
the 1970s, he had the perception to
produce nothing but Prosecco, becoming
an ambassador for this sparkling wine in
Italy and around the world. Today
production can count on a dense network
of growers who are monitored all year
round, over and above the small
estate-owned property that they manage
directly and use for their top labels. The
Franco winery's flagship, Grave di Stecca,
is still ageing in the cellar, proof of the
unstinting care they lavish on their wines.
With a line-up including Riva di San
Floriano 2012, it was not missed. This
Brut stands out for its ample fruity aromas,
where pear, apple and almond are
reflected in a solid, crunchy mouth. The
Cartizze 2012 is particularly well-made,
while Primo Franco 2012 is the familiar
caressingly rich sparkler.

○ Valdobbiadene Brut V. della Riva di S. Floriano '12		🍷🍷 3*
○ Cartizze '12		🍷🍷 5
○ Prosecco di Treviso Brut Rustico		🍷🍷 2*
○ Valdobbiadene Brut		🍷🍷 3
○ Valdobbiadene Dry Primo Franco '12		🍷🍷 3
⊙ Rosé Brut Faive		🍷 3
○ Brut Grave di Stecca '09		🍷🍷🍷 5
○ Valdobbiadene Brut Grave di Stecca '08		🍷🍷🍷 5
○ Valdobbiadene Brut V. della Riva di S. Floriano '11		🍷🍷🍷 3*
○ Brut Grave di Stecca '10		🍷🍷 5
○ P. di Valdobbiadene Dry Primo Franco '07		🍷🍷 3
○ P. di Valdobbiadene Dry Primo Franco '05		🍷🍷 3*

Novaia

VIA NOVAIA, 1
37020 MARANO DI VALPOLICELLA [VR]
TEL. 0457755129
www.novaia.it

CELLAR SALES
PRE-BOOKED VISITS
ANNUAL PRODUCTION 40,000 bottles
HECTARES UNDER VINE 7.00
VITICULTURE METHOD Certified Organic

The great success achieved by Valpolicella over the past 20 years produced the rapid creation and growth of many wineries that are known all over the world today. Giampaolo Vaona and his son Marcello decided instead to follow a virtuous path, first setting up a new installation in the upper Marano valley, then converting to organic farming and finally renovating their cellar. Production may be limited in terms of quantity but the level of quality is excellent. Amarone Corte Vaona 2009 acquitted itself well, with its aromas of dried red fruits, liquorice and dried flowers, it develops richly in the mouth while keeping the acidity under check, offering a taut succulence. Ripasso 2010 is also convincing: very flowery on the nose, it slowly releases spices and wild berries, presenting a slim, racy palate, and is a faithful expression of Valpolicella tradition and grapes. This year's Valpolicella is a whisker from being awarded a Due Bicchieri.

● Amarone della Valpolicella Cl. Corte Vaona '09	♈♈ 5
● Valpolicella Cl. Sup. Ripasso '10	♈♈ 3
● Recioto della Valpolicella Cl. Le Novaje '11	♈ 4
● Valpolicella Cl. '12	♈ 2
● Valpolicella Cl. Sup. I Cantoni '10	♈ 3
● Amarone della Valpolicella Cl. '08	♈♈ 5
● Amarone della Valpolicella Cl. Le Balze '01	♈♈ 6
● Recioto della Valpolicella Cl. Le Novaje '09	♈♈ 4
● Valpolicella Cl. Sup. I Cantoni '09	♈♈ 3
● Valpolicella Cl. Sup. I Cantoni '07	♈♈ 3
● Valpolicella Cl. Sup. Ripasso '10	♈♈ 3*
● Valpolicella Cl. Sup. Ripasso '09	♈♈ 3*

Ottella

FRAZ. SAN BENEDETTO DI LUGANA
LOC. OTTELLA
37019 PESCHIERA DEL GARDA [VR]
TEL. 0457551950
www.ottella.it

CELLAR SALES
PRE-BOOKED VISITS
ANNUAL PRODUCTION 350,000 bottles
HECTARES UNDER VINE 40.00

The Montresor family is among the most highly regarded producers for the Garda designation, capable of bringing developments to the operation founded by Ludovico and of establishing themselves as a winery of reference. The estate makes use of two different sites: the first is located on the intensely clayey soil that surrounds Lake Garda and is entirely made over to the grapes for Lugana, and the second is on the hills of Ponti sul Mincio, where they grow red grape varieties. The entire production is defined by its freshness, tautness and racy drinkability. The winery's flagship wine is Molceo, which often claims a Tre Bicchieri, and Le Creete 2012 has also upped its quality. A Lugana aged in stainless steel, it has fresh aromas of apple-like fruit and white flowers, and a palate that, while solid, is lean and succulent. The oak-aged Molceo is more solar and open, nearly exotic, revealing a harmonious mouth of great sapidity. Prima Luce 2010 is exotic and minerally, with sweetness and acidity in elegant balance.

○ Lugana Sup. Molceo '11	♈♈♈ 4*
○ Lugana Le Creete '12	♈♈ 3*
● Campo Sireso '11	♈♈ 4
○ Prima Luce Passito '10	♈♈ 5
● Gemei Rosso '12	♈ 2
⊙ Roses Roses '12	♈ 2
○ Lugana Sup. Molceo '10	♈♈♈ 4*
○ Lugana Sup. Molceo '09	♈♈♈ 4
○ Lugana Sup. Molceo '08	♈♈♈ 4
○ Lugana Sup. Molceo '07	♈♈♈ 4
○ Prima Luce Passito '09	♈♈ 5
○ Prima Luce Passito '08	♈♈ 5
○ Prima Luce Passito '07	♈♈ 5

★★Leonildo Pieropan

VIA CAMUZZONI, 3
37038 SOAVE [VR]
TEL. 0456190171
www.pieropan.it

CELLAR SALES
PRE-BOOKED VISITS
ANNUAL PRODUCTION 400,000 bottles
HECTARES UNDER VINE 45.00
VITICULTURE METHOD Certified Organic

While the Pieropan family winery is not in any sense becoming an operation identified with Valpolicella, they are certainly making considerable inroads with their reds. At Trenago, production is based on only two wines, a Valpolicella Superiore and an Amarone, as if to underline the winery's special relationship with Soave, a wine they produce under four labels. The style is however unique, defined by a pronounced aromatic freshness and a taut, elegant drinkability. Ruberpan 2010 proposes a perfect style in its best-ever version, with fine aromas on the nose and great grip on the palate. Among the whites, there is no lack of choice. Calvarino is crisp with perfectly balanced white-flesh fruit, a whisper of minerality, and a lean-edged, solid mouthfeel. La Rocca 2011 is sun-drenched and open, where almost exotic yellow-fleshed fruit imparts a velvety richness and grip to the palate. Soave Classico 2012 is fresh, flowery and linear.

Albino Piona

FRAZ. CUSTOZA
VIA BELLAVISTA, 48
37060 SOMMACAMPAGNA [VR]
TEL. 045516055
www.albinopiona.it

CELLAR SALES
PRE-BOOKED VISITS
ANNUAL PRODUCTION 400,000 bottles
HECTARES UNDER VINE 77.00

Do not be misled by the new cellar at Villafranca, as the winery belonging to the Piona family has ancient roots and is one of the most emblematic of the zone to the south of Lake Garda. Here they cultivate 70 hectares nearly all with the traditional varieties that form the framework of the Custoza and Bardolino designations. Today, Silvio, Monica, Alessandro and Massimo have taken over the reins from their father Albino, setting out on a ethical path to bring a greater depth to the entire production range. The hard work of recent years is now paying off, with two wines reaching our finals. Custoza SP 2012 is distinguished by its flowery, minerally aromatic profile, and lean, linear, mouth underpinned by a spirited acidity. Bardolino 2011 spotlights the intense spiciness of the historical varieties of Lake Bardolino, presenting a palate of zesty, racy elegance. Custoza 2012 is one of the best in its designation, offering generous aromas and a harmonious mouth.

○ Soave Cl. La Rocca '11	▼▼▼ 5
○ Soave Cl. Calvarino '11	▼▼ 4
○ Soave Cl. '12	▼▼ 3
● Valpolicella Sup. Ruberpan '10	▼▼ 3
○ Soave Cl. Calvarino '09	♔♔♔ 4*
○ Soave Cl. Calvarino '08	♔♔♔ 4
○ Soave Cl. Calvarino '07	♔♔♔ 4
○ Soave Cl. Calvarino '06	♔♔♔ 4
○ Soave Cl. Calvarino '05	♔♔♔ 3
○ Soave Cl. Calvarino '04	♔♔♔ 3
○ Soave Cl. Calvarino '03	♔♔♔ 3
○ Soave Cl. Calvarino '02	♔♔♔ 3
○ Soave Cl. La Rocca '10	♔♔♔ 5
○ Soave Cl. La Rocca '02	♔♔♔ 5

● Bardolino SP '11	▼▼ 2*
○ Custoza SP '12	▼▼ 2*
● Bardolino '12	▼▼ 2*
○ Custoza '12	▼▼ 2*
⊙ Bardolino Chiaretto '12	▼ 2
⊙ Estro di Pinna Rosé Brut	▼ 4
○ Gran Cuvée Brut M. Cl.	▼ 4
○ Verde Piona	▼ 2
● Azobé '08	♔♔ 4
● Bardolino '10	♔♔ 2*
○ Bianco di Custoza '10	♔♔ 2*
○ Bianco di Custoza Passito La Rabitta '08	♔♔ 5
● Campo Massimo Corvina Veronese '09	♔♔ 2*
○ Custoza SP '11	♔♔ 2*
○ Custoza SP '10	♔♔ 2*

Piovene Porto Godi

FRAZ. TOARA
VIA VILLA, 14
36020 VILLAGA [VI]
TEL. 0444885142
www.piovene.com

CELLAR SALES
PRE-BOOKED VISITS
ANNUAL PRODUCTION 100,000 bottles
HECTARES UNDER VINE 36.00

Tommaso Piovene's cellar is located at
Toara, at the southernmost point of the Colli
Berici. Here, the climate takes on a
Mediterranean flavour that translates into
wines whose distinguishing factor is a rich
fruitiness and full palate. Tommaso decided
not to fight against the forces of nature but
to accede to its inclinations, simply trying to
rein in any excesses and direct his
production towards an optimum tautness.
The vineyards are located both on the level
area in front of the cellar and on the slopes
overshadowing it. The grapes for the better
reds are sourced from the slopes above the
winery. Among them, the richly fruity Merlot
Fra i Broli 2011 has intense overtones of
medicinal herbs alongside plum. In the
mouth, richness become rounded and
fleshy, refreshed by the acidity. Slightly
more edgy in the mouth but equally sunny
and ripe is Cabernet Pozzare 2011, while
Tai Rosso 2012 is the perfect example of a
simple, fragrant and very drinkable red.

★Graziano Prà

VIA DELLA FONTANA, 31
37032 MONTEFORTE D'ALPONE [VR]
TEL. 0457612125
www.vinipra.it

CELLAR SALES
PRE-BOOKED VISITS
ACCOMMODATION
ANNUAL PRODUCTION 300,000 bottles
HECTARES UNDER VINE 33.00

The two-faced image projected by
Graziano Prà's winery is becoming more
pronounced. One side reflects the Soave
traditions they have been following for 30
years, the other, the operation at
Morandina, an estate in the upper valley of
Mezzane where they grow grapes for their
Valpolicella wines. Vineyard management
is increasingly geared towards viticulture
sustainability and the choices that come
with it, striving to obtain a wine that is
recognizably good and produced in a
healthy environment, away from man's
aggressive influence. Graziano Prà
regularly makes some of the best Soaves
in the designation, confirmed once again
with the Staforte, a white that goes
through lengthy ageing in stainless steel
before bottling. Its aromas range from fruit
to white flowers, highlighting a tangy,
harmonious mouth. Monte Grande 2012
benefits from a pass in oak that imparts
greater softness and elegance, both on the
nose and in the mouth.

● Colli Berici Merlot Fra i Broli '11	♟♟ 4
● Colli Berici Cabernet Vign. Pozzare '11	♟♟ 4
● Colli Berici Tai Rosso Vign. Riveselle '12	♟♟ 2*
● Polveriera Rosso '12	♟♟ 2*
○ Thovara Passito '11	♟♟ 5
○ Colli Berici Garganega Vign. Riveselle '12	♟ 2
○ Colli Berici Sauvignon Vign. Fostine '12	♟ 2
● Colli Berici Cabernet Vign. Pozzare '07	♟♟♟ 3
● Colli Berici Cabernet Vign. Pozzare '08	♟♟ 3
● Colli Berici Merlot Fra i Broli '09	♟♟ 5
● Colli Berici Merlot Fra i Broli '08	♟♟ 5
● Colli Berici Tai Rosso Thovara '09	♟♟ 5

○ Soave Cl. Staforte '11	♟♟♟ 4*
○ Soave Cl. Monte Grande '12	♟♟ 4
● Amarone della Valpolicella '08	♟♟ 6
○ Soave Cl. Colle S. Antonio '09	♟♟ 4
○ Soave Cl. Otto '12	♟♟ 2*
● Valpolicella Morandina '12	♟♟ 2*
● Valpolicella Sup. Rip. Morandina '11	♟♟ 4
○ Soave Cl. Monte Grande '11	♟♟♟ 4*
○ Soave Cl. Monte Grande '08	♟♟♟ 4
○ Soave Cl. Monte Grande '06	♟♟♟ 4
○ Soave Cl. Staforte '08	♟♟♟ 4
○ Soave Cl. Staforte '06	♟♟♟ 4*

★Giuseppe Quintarelli

VIA CERÈ, 1
37024 NEGRAR [VR]
TEL. 0457500016
giuseppe.quintarelli@tin.it

CELLAR SALES
PRE-BOOKED VISITS
ANNUAL PRODUCTION 60,000 bottles
HECTARES UNDER VINE 10.00

Today, Fiorenza Quintarelli, helped by her son Francesco, is at the helm of the long-established winery founded by her father, one of the ambassadors who made Amarone known across the world. The winery's vineyard wealth consists of a few dozen hectares scattered over several plots and cellar work consists of simply transforming the grapes and allowing the wines to age over a long period, which can be more than ten years for the most important bottles. We waited several years for a release of the Recioto, as it is only produced in exceptional years. The 2001 version keeps its promise, unveiling itself as a sweet wine of rare harmony and complexity. The long time spent in the cellar confers depth to the aromas, which sweep from dried fruit to sweet spices, and finishes on a balsamic, medicinal note. In the mouth, the sweetness is restrained, the tannins mellow, and the palate full and juicy. Valpolicella Superiore 2004 offers a great energetic succulence.

● Recioto della Valpolicella Cl. '01	♥♥♥ 8
● Valpolicella Cl. Sup. '04	♥♥ 7
● Amarone della Valpolicella Cl. '03	♀♀♀ 8
● Amarone della Valpolicella Cl. '00	♀♀♀ 8
● Amarone della Valpolicella Cl. '98	♀♀♀ 8
● Amarone della Valpolicella Cl. '97	♀♀♀ 8
● Amarone della Valpolicella Cl. Sup. Monte Cà Paletta '00	♀♀♀ 8
● Amarone della Valpolicella Cl. Sup. Monte Cà Paletta '93	♀♀♀ 8
● Amarone della Valpolicella Cl. Sup. Ris. '85	♀♀♀ 8
● Recioto della Valpolicella Cl. '95	♀♀♀ 5
● Recioto della Valpolicella Cl. Monte Ca' Paletta '97	♀♀♀ 8
● Rosso del Bepi '96	♀♀♀ 8
● Valpolicella Cl. Sup. '99	♀♀♀ 7

Le Ragose

FRAZ. ARBIZZANO
VIA LE RAGOSE, 1
37024 NEGRAR [VR]
TEL. 0457513241
www.leragose.com

CELLAR SALES
PRE-BOOKED VISITS
ANNUAL PRODUCTION 150,000 bottles
HECTARES UNDER VINE 18.00

The story of Le Ragose started a long time ago, at the tail end of the 1960s, when the Gallo family decided to acquire a derelict hillside estate which today covers an operational area of around 20 hectares. Paolo and Marco are following in the path set out by their parents, upholding their strong ties with tradition and whose ideal is a particularly elegant wine, highlighting the freshness that the hilly location can impart to the grapes. In the vineyards, they make nearly exclusive use of the pergoletta overhead training method to ensure that the bunches are correctly shaded. Valpolicella Ripasso 2009 reveals a generous aromatic expression composed of wild berries, mint and peppery hints, reflected perfectly on the palate, where the wine offers a solid, exceptionally agile body. In the Amarone Marta Galli 2006, a register based on dried grapes and flowers is prominent on both the nose and the palate, revealing a rich, fleshy wine. The unusual Recioto 2009, with aromas of red fruit preserve, reveals notes of olives and wild thyme in a full, juicy mouth.

● Valpolicella Cl. Ripasso '09	♥♥ 3*
● Amarone della Valpolicella Cl. Marta Galli '06	♥♥ 7
● Recioto della Valpolicella Cl. '09	♥♥ 5
● Valpolicella Cl. '12	♥♥ 2*
● Valpolicella Cl. Sup. Le Sassine '00	♥♥ 3
● Cabernet Sauvignon '08	♥ 3
● Amarone della Valpolicella Cl. Marta Galli '05	♀♀♀ 8
● Amarone della Valpolicella Marta Galli '01	♀♀ 7
● Valpolicella Cl. Sup. Le Sassine '05	♀♀ 3
● Valpolicella Cl. Sup. Ripasso Le Sassine '07	♀♀ 3

F.lli Recchia

LOC. JAGO
VIA CA' BERTOLDI, 30
37024 NEGRAR [VR]
TEL. 0457500584
www.recchiavini.it

CELLAR SALES
PRE-BOOKED VISITS
ANNUAL PRODUCTION 100,000 bottles
HECTARES UNDER VINE 100.00

Despite having cultivated vines for over a century, it is only in the last ten years or so that the Recchia family has made a significant leap in quality, investing increasing care in producing and bottling the finest parcels of grapes that reach the cellar. The estate covers many hectares in the heart of the Valpolicella Classica zone, but only a small part of the production leaves under the Recchia brand. The style follows the classic concept of wines from the areas around Verona, where complex aromas combine with an elegant drink. Amarone and Recioto, the wines from partially dried grapes, are magnificent. Amarone Ca' Bertoldi 2006, released after a long maturation in the cellar, proposes very mature aromas of fruit and cocoa, while the oak makes its presence felt. The palate is rich and centred around power. While expressing dried grapes along traditional lines, the style proposed by Amarone Masua di Jago 2010 still has weight. The juicy, racy Recioto La Guardia 2009 is intriguing.

● Amarone della Valpolicella Cl. Ca' Bertoldi '06	♥♥ 5
● Amarone della Valpolicella Cl. Masua di Jago '10	♥♥ 5
● Recioto della Valpolicella Cl. La Guardia '09	♥♥ 4
● Korvilot '11	♥ 5
● Recioto della Valpolicella Cl. Masua di Jago '11	♥ 4
● Valpolicella Cl. Masua di Jago '12	♥ 2
● Valpolicella Cl. Sup. Le Muraie Ripasso '10	♥ 3
● Valpolicella Cl. Sup. Masua di Jago '11	♥ 2
● Valpolicella Cl. Sup. Masua di Jago Ripasso '11	♥ 2
● Amarone della Valpolicella Cl. Masua di Jago '08	♥♥ 6

Roccolo Grassi

VIA SAN GIOVANNI DI DIO, 19
37030 MEZZANE DI SOTTO [VR]
TEL. 0458880089
www.roccolograssi.it

PRE-BOOKED VISITS
ANNUAL PRODUCTION 47,000 bottles
HECTARES UNDER VINE 14.00

Marco and Francesca Sartori have transformed a family-owned winery that focused on producing ready-to-drink wines into one of the most interesting operations of Valpolicella, with a limited range of wines centred entirely on applying a traditional approach. The estate owns 14 hectares, farmed using environmentally friendly methods with extreme care for the quality of the grapes. They obtain the grapes for Soave from the vines set on calcareous soil, while the grapes to be used in Valpolicella reds come from the basaltic area of volcanic origins. Over the years, the Sartori siblings have worked on a style to solve the difficult task of keeping power under control with grace and suppleness. The tasting of Amarone 2009 was exemplary. With its notes of sound fruit, spices and a delicate mineral edge reflected perfectly on the palate, the wine unbends with precision and strength. The same interpretation, with greater crispness, is repeated in the Valpolicella Superiore 2010.

● Amarone della Valpolicella '09	♥♥ 8
● Valpolicella Sup. '10	♥♥ 5
● Amarone della Valpolicella Roccolo Grassi '07	♥♥♥ 8
● Amarone della Valpolicella Roccolo Grassi '00	♥♥♥ 7
● Amarone della Valpolicella Roccolo Grassi '99	♥♥♥ 7
● Valpolicella Sup. Roccolo Grassi '09	♥♥♥ 5
● Valpolicella Sup. Roccolo Grassi '07	♥♥♥ 5
● Valpolicella Sup. Roccolo Grassi '04	♥♥♥ 5
● Amarone della Valpolicella Roccolo Grassi '08	♥♥ 8
● Recioto della Valpolicella Roccolo Grassi '08	♥♥ 5
● Valpolicella Sup. Roccolo Grassi '08	♥♥ 5

Roeno

VIA MAMA, 5
37020 BRENTINO BELLUNO [VR]
TEL. 0457230110
www.cantinaroeno.com

CELLAR SALES
PRE-BOOKED VISITS
ACCOMMODATION AND RESTAURANT SERVICE
ANNUAL PRODUCTION 190,000 bottles
HECTARES UNDER VINE 20.00

Roberta, Cristina and Giuseppe Fugatti took up their father Rolando's legacy, expanding the winery he founded and turning it into a leading light for Valdadige, a narrow tongue of land that extends from the area surrounding Verona to the north, up to the province of Bolzano. The vineyards belonging to the Fugatti family are located on the slopes confining the course of the river Adige, and along the valley bottom, where the texture of the soil, which contains a significant amount of sand, allows ungrafted 100-year old vines to thrive. This year, Cristina 2010 puts class over power. A late-harvested wine from chardonnay, sauvignon, pinot grigio and traminer, it offers aromas from citrus fruit to spices, reflected in the mouth where it expands sweetly and harmoniously. Enantio Riserva 2009's origins are in a century-old vineyard on the banks of the River Adige. This approachable wine with spices and dark berries offers a palate where richness is joined by polished tannins and an essential acidity.

○ Cristina V. T. '10	♥♥	5
● Enantio Terra dei Forti '09	♥♥	4
● Enantio Terra dei Forti Ris. '09	♥♥	4
○ Praecipuus '11	♥♥	4
● Rosso Roeno '08	♥♥	4
○ Valdadige Pinot Grigio Tera Alta '12	♥♥	2*
○ Dardollno Chiaretto Brut Mati Rosé	♥	3
○ Valdadige Chardonnay Le Fratte '12	♥	2
○ Cristina V. T. '08	♥♥♥	5
○ Cristina V. T. '09	♥♥	5
○ Cristina V. T. '07	♥♥	5
○ Cristina V. T. '06	♥♥	5
● Valdadige Terra dei Forti Enantio Ris. '08	♥♥	4

Ruggeri & C.

VIA PRÀ FONTANA, 4
31049 VALDOBBIADENE [TV]
TEL. 04239092
www.ruggeri.it

PRE-BOOKED VISITS
ANNUAL PRODUCTION 1,000,000 bottles
HECTARES UNDER VINE 17.00

Ruggeri is certainly one of the best known and highly regarded operations in the world, with its Valdobbiadene-based activity spanning 60 years. Today, Giustino and Isabella Bisol work alongside their father Paolo in running a winery that produces over 1,000,000 bottles a year and is a reference for the entire designation. Their strength, alongside perfect cellar management, lies in their tightly consolidated ties with more than 100 growers, who supply the grapes for the entire production, under the winery's direction. Giustino B probably embodies the spirit of extra dry wines above any other label, with its aromas of fresh fruit and flowers while, in the mouth, it masks sweetness under fresh acidity and sapidity, showing a harmonious length. Vecchie Viti 2012 highlights the gutsy, dry core that is typical of the variety, offering an energetic, lively progression. We must applaud Giall'Oro, Ruggeri's best selling wine, which is always reliable and juicy.

○ Valdobbiadene Extra Dry Giustino B. '12	♥♥♥	3*
○ Valdobbiadene Brut Vecchie Viti '12	♥♥	3*
○ Cartizze	♥♥	4
○ L'Extra Brut '12	♥♥	3
○ Valdobbiadene Dry S. Stefano	♥♥	3
○ Valdobbiadene Extra Dry Altevigne	♥♥	4
○ Valdobbiadene Extra Dry Giall'Oro	♥♥	3
○ Valdobbiadene Brut Quartese	♥	3
○ Valdobbiadene Extra Dry Giustino B. '11	♥♥♥	3*
○ Valdobbiadene Extra Dry Giustino B. '10	♥♥♥	3
○ Valdobbiadene Extra Dry Giustino B. '09	♥♥♥	3

Le Salette

via Pio Brugnoli, 11c
37022 Fumane [VR]
Tel. 0457701027
www.lesalette.it

CELLAR SALES
PRE-BOOKED VISITS
ACCOMMODATION
ANNUAL PRODUCTION 130,000 bottles
HECTARES UNDER VINE 20.00

Franco Scamperle is the soul and driving force behind Le Salette, a cellar that takes its name from a Sanctuary erected at the end of the 19th century on the hills above Fumane. The vineyards are all in the classic area, largely in Fumane itself and the rest on the Conca d'Oro at Sant'Ambrogio and on the slopes of the Masua at San Floriano. Here they only grow the traditional varieties of Valpolicella, producing wines that sit mid-way between tradition and a modern style. Nimble fingers make a good Amarone in the Scamperle family, as we found with La Marega 2009, a wine so simple and elementary on the nose yet of great tension and elegance in the mouth. With a richer theme, the Amarone Pergole Vece 2009 has aromas of dried fruit and oak that develop in a softly alcoholic and mouthfilling palate. Valpolicella Ripasso I Progni 2010 hinges on mature aromas with a soft taste.

● Amarone della Valpolicella Cl. La Marega '09	♟♟ 6
● Valpolicella Cl. Sup. Ripasso I Progni '10	♟♟ 3
● Ca' Carnocchio '10	♟ 5
● Recioto della Valpolicella Cl. Pergole Vece '10	♟ 6
● Valpolicella Cl. '12	♟ 2
● Amarone della Valpolicella Cl. Pergole Vece '05	♟♟♟ 8
● Amarone della Valpolicella Cl. Pergole Vece '95	♟♟♟ 8
● Amarone della Valpolicella Cl. Pergole Vece '07	♟♟ 8
● Amarone della Valpolicella Cl. Pergole Vece '06	♟♟ 8
● Recioto della Valpolicella Cl. Pergole Vece '09	♟♟ 6

San Rustico

fraz. Valgatara di Valpolicella
via Pozzo, 2
37020 Marano di Valpolicella [VR]
Tel. 0457703348
www.sanrustico.it

CELLAR SALES
PRE-BOOKED VISITS
ANNUAL PRODUCTION 170,000 bottles
HECTARES UNDER VINE 22.00

Marco and Enrico Campagnola hold the reins of the family-owned winery and are directly involved in all the phases, with Enrico looking after the vineyards and Marco the cellar, turning out a limited production of nearly 200,000 bottles. The vineyards are in the heart of the Valpolicella Classica zone, mainly in the valley of Marano, with a smaller part in the valley of Fumane, all cultivated using the traditional pergola training system. The best vineyard, Gaso, produces the grapes for the Valpolicella, Amarone and Recioto wines with the Gaso name. Gaso produced an outstanding Amarone 2007, an emblem of tradition in its aromas of dried flowers, aromatic herbs and spices, offering a succulently soft palate that highlights smooth tannins and a great drinkability. Amarone Classico 2008 has a pleasant country style, while Ripasso Gaso 2010 has generous deep aromas, evolving fully on the palate.

● Amarone della Valpolicella Cl. Gaso '07	♟♟ 6
● Amarone della Valpolicella Cl. '08	♟♟ 5
● Valpolicella Cl. Sup. Ripasso Gaso '10	♟♟ 3
● Recioto della Valpolicella Cl. '11	♟ 5
● Valpolicella Cl. '12	♟ 2
● Valpolicella Cl. Sup. Ripasso '11	♟ 2
● Amarone della Valpolicella Cl. '07	♟♟ 5
● Amarone della Valpolicella Cl. '06	♟♟ 6
● Amarone della Valpolicella Cl. Gaso '05	♟♟ 6
● Recioto della Valpolicella Cl. '09	♟♟ 5
● Valpolicella Cl. Sup. '09	♟♟ 2*

La Sansonina

LOC. SANSONINA
37019 PESCHIERA DEL GARDA [VR]
TEL. 0457551905
www.sansonina.it

CELLAR SALES
ANNUAL PRODUCTION 21,000 bottles
HECTARES UNDER VINE 12.00

Sansonina was established 15 years ago, almost for fun, at the behest of Carla Prospero who had decided to restore an almost abandoned old vineyard near Lake Garda to its original splendour. The expansion of the vineyard was mirrored by the reconstruction of the old Sansonina farmstead, where tradition and modernity were deeply entwined, as immediately evident from the exterior of the cellar. In the last couple of years Merlot has been joined by Lugana, the classic local wine, both produced in a style whose distinctive features include clear definition and plenty of texture. Aromatic limpidity is perfectly expressed in Lugana 2012, a white Garda with fragrant spring flowers and white-fleshed fruit, unbending on the palate to reveal the richness and fresh acidity typical of the grape. The Merlot hinges on ripe fruit, seemingly immersed in coffee and spices. During tastings, the wine confirmed the richness suggested by the nose to reveal a juicy roundness and delightful harmony.

○ Lugana Sansonina '12	♥♥ 3
● Sansonina '10	♥♥ 6
○ Lugana Sansonina '09	♥♥ 3*
● Sansonina '07	♥♥ 6
● Sansonina '06	♥♥ 6
● Sansonina '05	♥♥ 6
● Sansonina '04	♥♥ 6
● Sansonina '03	♥♥ 6
● Sansonina '01	♥♥ 6
● Sansonina '00	♥♥ 6

★Tenuta Sant'Antonio

LOC. SAN ZENO
VIA CERIANI, 23
37030 COLOGNOLA AI COLLI [VR]
TEL. 0457650383
www.tenutasantantonio.it

CELLAR SALES
PRE-BOOKED VISITS
ANNUAL PRODUCTION 700,000 bottles
HECTARES UNDER VINE 100.00

The Castagnedi brothers have been able to develop their cellar incredibly rapidly while still combining respect for the environment with market requirements and traditions. After a decade under the banner of very full, fruity wines, they have now taken a new direction, settling on an increasingly clear idea of elegance that makes use of the wealth of aromas and acidity of the traditional varieties to produce wines based upon tautness and depth. The most interesting wines come from Alto Adige, with a Pinot Grigio Impronta del Fondatore 2012 of substance, where fine aromas of pear and meadow flowers confer a firm elegance to the mouth. Looking at the Proseccos, Rive di Refrontolo Brut is one the best in the district, featuring fragrant close-focused aromas and, while simple on the palate, it is dry through and through. The reds from the area of Lison are very good.

● Amarone della Valpolicella Campo dei Gigli '08	♥♥♥ 8
● Recioto della Valpolicella Argille Bianche '06	♥♥ 5
● Amarone della Valpolicella Sel. Antonio Castagnedi '10	♥♥ 6
○ Soave Monte Ceriani '11	♥♥ 3
○ Soave Monte Ceriani Vecchie Vigne '11	♥♥ 3
● Valpolicella Sup. La Bandina '09	♥♥ 5
● Valpolicella Sup. Rip. Monti Garbi '11	♥♥ 3
● Amarone della Valpolicella Campo dei Gigli '07	♥♥♥ 8
● Amarone della Valpolicella Campo dei Gigli '06	♥♥♥ 8
● Amarone della Valpolicella Campo dei Gigli '05	♥♥♥ 8
● Amarone della Valpolicella Campo dei Gigli '04	♥♥♥ 8

Santa Margherita

VIA ITA MARZOTTO, 8
30025 FOSSALTA DI PORTOGRUARO [VE]
TEL. 0421246111
www.santamargherita.com

CELLAR SALES
PRE-BOOKED VISITS
ANNUAL PRODUCTION 12,500,000 bottles

Challenges are won though focused actions that can solve the problems thrown up by the modern market. The Marzotto winery has undertaken an expansion of the estate-owned area under vine, the building of a new cellar and the strengthening of its ties with the production world that connects with Santa Margherita, particularly in the Alto Adige district, where the winery can rely on major collaborations for the production of its flagship wine, Pinot Grigio. Today, the challenge features the world of Prosecco, where results are increasingly promising. Amarone Campo dei Gigli 2008 reveals rich fruits on the nose, gradually replaced by spices and minerality. In the mouth, the wine is striking for its ability to control power with elegance and energy. Recioto Argille Bianche 2006, finally released after the proper ageing time, is complex on the nose and caressing on the palate, with smooth tannins and a generous mouthfeel. The Valpolicellas are offspring of the new direction and have more verve than in the past.

Santi

VIA UNGHERIA, 33
37031 ILLASI [VR]
TEL. 0456269600
www.carlosanti.it

CELLAR SALES
PRE-BOOKED VISITS
ANNUAL PRODUCTION 2,000,000 bottles
HECTARES UNDER VINE 70.00

Santi is certainly one of the most typical wineries belonging to the Gruppo Italiano Vini. With their strong roots in the Valpolicella territory, they can rely on the grapes that make them a torchbearer for the entire designation. Under the technical direction of Christian Scrinzi, they have come up with a style that observes tradition without losing precision or freshness, as is clearly perceived when tasting either their most important or their simplest wines. The range mainly covers the wine types of the areas around Verona. With Amarone Proemio, the Santi winery's flagship, still spending time ageing in the cellar, we focused on Solane, for years one of the most credible Ripasso wines of the designation. Sensations of dried grapes come through in its aromas, while the picture emerges of a more complex wine, setting it apart from the Amarone, and offering a full-flavoured, taut mouth. Bardolino Ca' Bordenis 2012 is fully convincing.

○ A. A. Pinot Grigio Impronta del Fondatore '12		♟♟ 2*
○ A. A. Pinot Grigio M. Cl. '10		♟♟ 3
○ Cartizze		♟♟ 4
● Lison-Pramaggiore Malbech Impronta del Fondatore '11		♟♟ 2*
● Lison-Pramaggiore Refosco P.R. Impronta del Fondatore '11		♟♟ 2*
○ Valdobbiadene Brut Rive di Refrontolo 52		♟♟ 3
○ Valdobbiadene Extra Dry 52		♟♟ 2
○ Luna dei Feldi '12		♟ 3
⊙ Spumante Extra Dry 52 Rosé		♟ 3
○ Valdadige Pinot Grigio '12		♟ 2
○ Valdobbiadene Brut		♟ 2
○ Valdobbiadene Extra Dry		♟ 2

● Valpolicella Cl. Sup. Ripasso Solane '11		♟♟ 4
● Bardolino Cl. Vign. Ca' Bordenis '12		♟♟ 2*
● Valpolicella Cl. Le Caleselle '12		♟♟ 2*
⊙ Bardolino Chiaretto L'Infinito '12		♟ 2
○ Custoza I Frari '12		♟ 2
● Amarone della Valpolicella Proemio '05		♟♟♟ 6
● Amarone della Valpolicella Proemio '03		♟♟♟ 6
● Amarone della Valpolicella Proemio '00		♟♟♟ 5
● Valpolicella Cl. Sup. Ripasso Solane '09		♟♟♟ 3*
● Amarone della Valpolicella Proemio '08		♟♟ 7
● Amarone della Valpolicella Proemio '07		♟♟ 6
● Valpolicella Cl. Sup. Solane Ripasso '08		♟♟ 3*

Casa Vinicola Sartori

FRAZ. SANTA MARIA
VIA CASETTE, 4
37024 NEGRAR [VR]
TEL. 0456028011
www.sartorinet.com

PRE-BOOKED VISITS
ANNUAL PRODUCTION 15,000,000 bottles
HECTARES UNDER VINE 120.00

The winery owned by the Sartori family now turns out a large production without betraying its links to the Valpolicella area and its traditions, expanding its offers through tight collaborations with other wine-making operations of the area. Today, the most prestigious labels gravitate around the designations of the area near Verona, interpreted carefully and precisely, so that the ease of drinking required by the market is coupled with the power traditionally attributed to these wines. To round it off, the prices are absolutely spot on. The Sartori winery has an ample selection of four thoroughly satisfactory Amarone labels. Our preference goes to Amarone I Saltari 2008, produced in the small family estate in the eastern part of Valpolicella. Deeply intense aromas sweeping from dried grapes to fines herbes offer a generously silky palate. Recioto Rerum 2011 has crisp, approachable aromas where fruit enfolds spices, leading to a sweet, juicy finish.

● Amarone della Valpolicella Cl. Arena '09	♛♛ 5
● Amarone della Valpolicella Cl. Corte Brà '08	♛♛ 7
● Amarone della Valpolicella Cl. Reius '08	♛♛ 7
● Amarone della Valpolicella I Saltari '08	♛♛ 8
● Recioto della Valpolicella Cl. Rerum '11	♛♛ 6
○ Marani '11	♛ 3
○ Recioto di Soave Vernus '11	♛ 5
○ Soave Cl. Sella '12	♛ 2
● Valpolicella Cl. Sup. Vign. di Montegradella '10	♛ 3
● Amarone della Valpolicella Cl. Reius '07	♛♛ 7
● Amarone della Valpolicella I Saltari '07	♛♛ 8
● Amarone della Valpolicella I Saltari '06	♛♛ 8
● Amarone della Valpolicella Le Vigne di Turano I Saltari '04	♛♛ 8

Secondo Marco

V.LE CAMPOLONGO, 9
37022 FUMANE [VR]
TEL. 0456800954
www.secondomarco.it

PRE-BOOKED VISITS
ANNUAL PRODUCTION 40,000 bottles
HECTARES UNDER VINE 15.00

After only a few years of activity, Marco Speri has gone all out and is now able to offer a range of well-balanced wines that accurately reflect their traditions. His strength lies obviously in his vineyards, but he also has a profound knowledge of the land and of his grapes, and how they can best express themselves, backed by the extensive experience he has acquired over the years and the continuous, skilled input of his father, Benedetto. The style of his wines tends towards tautness and drinkability, eschewing any easy sugary softness and highlighting the aromatics of the traditional grapes of the area. Instead of following the Amarone model, Marco Speri's Ripasso breaks free in its search for a union between the complex aromas of dried grapes and an altogether more rigorous, leaner mouth, where power comes from the tannins and acidity, and the palate is long and succulent. The Amarone toys with its power, proposing a rich, juicy mouth to echo a sweet super-ripe profile. The Valpolicella Classico 2011, aged for one year, is very interesting.

● Valpolicella Cl. Sup. Ripasso '10	♛♛ 4
● Amarone della Valpolicella Cl. '08	♛♛ 7
● Recioto della Valpolicella Cl. '10	♛♛ 6
● Valpolicella Cl. '11	♛♛ 3
● Amarone della Valpolicella Cl. '07	♛♛ 7
● Amarone della Valpolicella Cl. '06	♛♛ 7
● Recioto della Valpolicella Cl. '09	♛♛ 6
● Recioto della Valpolicella Cl. '08	♛♛ 6
● Valpolicella Cl. Ripasso Sup. '08	♛♛ 6
● Valpolicella Cl. Sup. Ripasso '09	♛♛ 4

★Serafini & Vidotto

VIA CARRER, 8/12
31040 NERVESA DELLA BATTAGLIA [TV]
TEL. 0422773281
www.serafinividotto.it

CELLAR SALES
PRE-BOOKED VISITS
ANNUAL PRODUCTION 180,000 bottles
HECTARES UNDER VINE 21.00

In less than 30 years, the cellar owned by Francesco Serafini and Antonello Vidotto has managed to impose itself as a standard bearer for Bordeaux blend wines in Italy. Today, the challenge is all about the vineyards, which are managed according to systems where the quality of the grapes is of utmost importance, while limiting as far as possible any impact on the environment, encouraging the vines to develop a natural protection against external aggression, without any chemical help. On the productive front, there is a new, more positive attention for sparkling wines. Rosso dell'Abazia is delicious and, under a stricter selection of the grapes, unleashes a memorable performance, criss-crossed by deep aromas of wild berries, spices and medicinal herbs, released generously on the palate and joined by smooth tannins and a lively acidity. Oltre il Rosso 2010 follows on closely, produced in a style that places power at its centre. Recantina 2012 is generous, fragrant and an exceptionally.

● Montello e Colli Asolani		
Il Rosso dell'Abazia '10	▼▼▼ 5	
○ Asolo Extra Dry Bollicine di Prosecco	▼▼ 2	
○ Il Bianco '12	▼▼ 3	
○ Montello e Colli Asolani		
Manzoni Bianco '12	▼▼ 2*	
● Montello e Colli Asolani Phigaia '10	▼▼ 3	
● Oltre Il Rosso '10	▼▼ 4	
● Pinot Nero '10	▼▼ 5	
● Recantina '12	▼▼ 3	
⊙ Bollicine Rosé Brut	▼ 3	
○ Prosecco di Treviso		
Bollicine di Prosecco	▼ 3	
● Montello e Colli Asolani		
Il Rosso dell'Abazia '08	♈♈♈ 5	
● Montello e Colli Asolani		
Il Rosso dell'Abazia '07	♈♈♈ 5	

★Viticoltori Speri

LOC. PEDEMONTE
VIA FONTANA, 14
37020 SAN PIETRO IN CARIANO [VR]
TEL. 0457701154
www.speri.com

CELLAR SALES
PRE-BOOKED VISITS
ANNUAL PRODUCTION 350,000 bottles
HECTARES UNDER VINE 50.00

There are wineries that, in order to face the trials of the modern market, will overhaul themselves rapidly and pursue models set out by the market itself. In the Speri household, thinking like this has never worked. Their strength lies in the territory and traditions that are able to be renewed slowly without betraying their origins, breathing life into a style defined by solidity, power and aromatic breadth. Around 50 hectares, totally made over to the traditional varieties, supply the grapes for a production totally centred on Valpolicella wines. We found the darkly-hued Amarone Vigneto Monte Sant'Urbano 2009 excellent, slowly releasing its aromas, first fruit, then spices and finally overtones of aromatic herbs. On tasting it, we were impressed by its power and the precision of its craftsmanship. Recioto La Roggia 2010 hinges on exuberant fruit in a sweet palate, while Valpolicella Monte Sant'Urbano 2010 vaunts a wide array of aromatics and a harmoniously rich taste profile.

● Amarone della Valpolicella Cl.		
Vign. Monte Sant'Urbano '09	▼▼▼ 7	
● Recioto della Valpolicella Cl.		
La Roggia '10	▼▼ 6	
● Valpolicella Cl. Sup.		
Monte Sant'Urbano '10	▼▼ 4	
● Valpolicella Cl. Sup. Ripasso '11	▼▼ 4	
● Valpolicella Cl. '12	▼ 2	
● Amarone della Valpolicella Cl.		
Vign. Monte Sant'Urbano '08	♈♈♈ 7	
● Amarone della Valpolicella Cl.		
Vign. Monte Sant'Urbano '07	♈♈♈ 7	
● Amarone della Valpolicella Cl.		
Vign. Monte Sant'Urbano '06	♈♈♈ 7	
● Amarone della Valpolicella Cl.		
Vign. Monte Sant'Urbano '04	♈♈♈ 7	
● Amarone della Valpolicella Cl.		
Vign. Monte Sant'Urbano '01	♈♈♈ 6	

I Stefanini

VIA CROSARA, 21
37032 MONTEFORTE D'ALPONE [VR]
TEL. 0456175249
www.istefanini.it

CELLAR SALES
PRE-BOOKED VISITS
ANNUAL PRODUCTION 100,000 bottles
HECTARES UNDER VINE 17.00

Francesco Tessari is one of the producers who, in recent years, launched the concept of a Soave of high quality capable of offering a rich fleshiness without losing its drinkability or fragrance. The credit for this should be evenly split between Francesco's capacity for interpretation and the territory, especially the area of Monte Tenda, containing the winery's finest vineyards. He controls yields in the vineyard, even for the simplest wines, which is coupled with a rather spasmodic search for maturity, so that the most ambitious labels are only produced in excellent years. The grapes are sourced from neighbouring vineyards, but Monte de Toni 2012 and Monte di Fice 2012 are in a very different mould. Aromatically they seem similar, both offering a fruity, dried flowery richness, but the pace changes on the palate. Fice hinges on elegance and a lush mouth, while the super-gutsy Toni also reveals a touch of sulphur, leading to an almost tannic finish. The fresh Selese 2012 is approachable and juicy.

○ Soave Cl. Monte de Toni '12	♀♀♀	2*
○ Soave Cl. Sup. Monte di Fice '12	♀♀	3*
○ Soave Il Selese '12	♀♀	1*
○ Soave Cl. Sup. Monte di Fice '07	♀♀♀	2*
○ Soave Cl. Monte de Toni '11	♀♀	2*
○ Soave Cl. Monte de Toni '08	♀♀	2*
○ Soave Cl. Monte de Toni '07	♀♀	2*
○ Soave Cl. Monte de Toni '06	♀♀	2*
○ Soave Cl. Monte di Fice '10	♀♀	2*
○ Soave Cl. Sup. Monte di Fice '08	♀♀	2*
○ Soave Cl. Sup. Monte di Fice '06	♀♀	2*
○ Soave Il Selese '11	♀♀	1*

David Sterza

VIA CASTERNA, 37
37022 FUMANE [VR]
TEL. 0457704201
www.davidsterza.it

CELLAR SALES
PRE-BOOKED VISITS
ANNUAL PRODUCTION 30,000 bottles
HECTARES UNDER VINE 4.50

David Sterza and his cousin Paolo Mascanzoni have been running their family-owned winery for only 15 years yet, given its results, it is one of the operations that has successfully exploited a particularly good moment in the market and concentrated on producing wines in a limited quantity but of high quality and with strong links to tradition. This tradition regularly pops up in their chosen varieties, while in terms of style they decided to abandon the typical redundancy of the past and offer a fresh glass of crisply sound wine that perfectly respects the grape type. The Amarone improves year after year, offering close-focused aromas of juicy, sound, red fruit, while spices and oaky tones remain in the background. On tasting, the wine reveals its full body with smooth tannins, confirming it is among the finest in the designation. The first-rate harvest-year Valpolicella expresses the typical aromas of its variety, joined by wild berries, cherry and pepper, exploding on the palate in a delicious crunchiness backed by acidity.

● Amarone della Valpolicella Cl. '09	♀♀	6
● Valpolicella Cl. '12	♀♀	2*
● Valpolicella Cl. Sup. Ripasso '11	♀♀	3
● Corvina Veronese '10	♀	4
● Amarone della Valpolicella Cl. '08	♀♀	6
♀ Amarone della Valpolicella Cl. '07	♀♀	0

★Suavia

FRAZ. FITTA DI SOAVE
VIA CENTRO, 14
37038 SOAVE [VR]
TEL. 0457675089
www.suavia.it

CELLAR SALES
PRE-BOOKED VISITS
ANNUAL PRODUCTION 100,000 bottles
HECTARES UNDER VINE 12.00

Meri, Valentina and Alessandra run their family-owned winery located in the small town of Fitta, intrepidly set between the vines and the sky in the heart of the Soave zone, where the black soil immediately betrays its volcanic origins. The vineyards extend for around a dozen hectares in the high hills, where the warmth of the daytime gives way to breezes once the sun goes down. Old vines, no acceptance of international varieties and a great respect for grapes in the cellar are the ingredients for one of the most amazing formulas in the designation. With the harvest of 2011, Soave Monte Carbonare loses a touch of its normally distinctive edginess, gaining in elegance and harmony. On the nose, flowers and yellow-fleshed fruit rise up over the mineral tones, in a rich, supple mouth. Massifitti 2010, a Trebbiano di Soave aged entirely in stainless steel, is very good, with generous, delicate aromas revealing golden apple and a smoky minerality. In the mouth, the wine has harmonious zest.

○ Soave Cl. Monte Carbonare '11	♟♟♟	3*
○ Massifitti '10	♟♟	3*
○ Soave Cl. '12	♟♟	2*
○ Opera Semplice Dosaggio Zero M. Cl.	♟	4
○ Soave Cl. Le Rive '02	♟♟♟	4
○ Soave Cl. Monte Carbonare '10	♟♟♟	3*
○ Soave Cl. Monte Carbonare '09	♟♟♟	3*
○ Soave Cl. Monte Carbonare '08	♟♟♟	3*
○ Soave Cl. Monte Carbonare '07	♟♟♟	3*
○ Soave Cl. Monte Carbonare '06	♟♟♟	3*
○ Soave Cl. Monte Carbonare '05	♟♟♟	3*
○ Soave Cl. Monte Carbonare '04	♟♟♟	3

Sutto

LOC. CAMPO DI PIETRA
VIA ARZERI, 34/1
31040 SALGAREDA [TV]
TEL. 0422744063
www.sutto.it

CELLAR SALES
PRE-BOOKED VISITS
RESTAURANT SERVICE
ANNUAL PRODUCTION 150,000 bottles
HECTARES UNDER VINE 75.00

Stefano and Luigi Sutto have been able to impose a turning point in terms of quality to the winery founded by their father Ferruccio. Today they manage a vineyard that extends for over 70 hectares in the surroundings of Campo di Pietra, one of the best known zones in the Piave designation. Production focuses on two lines: the first aims at early-drinking wines, distinguished by their strong ties to the grape and produced with great respect for aromas and their readiness as regards drinking; the second includes Riserva wines that explore the richer, more elegant features of the zone, with increasingly impressive results. Improvements can be seen in the quality of the best house reds, Dogma Rosso 2011 and Campo Sella 2011. The former is a mainly cabernet Bordeaux blend, with delightfully fine aromas, while black berry fruit, aromatic herbs and spices expand purposefully in a rigorous, crispy mouth. The latter is an open, sunny wine, expressing the fruity generosity of merlot in an elegantly taut style. The juicy, supple Ultimo 2011, a raisined Manzoni Bianco, is also very good.

● Campo Sella '11	♟♟	5
● Dogma Rosso '11	♟♟	4
○ Manzoni Bianco '12	♟♟	2*
○ Ultimo '11	♟♟	3
● Cabernet '12	♟	2
○ Chardonnay '12	♟	2
● Merlot '12	♟	2
● Pinot Grigio '12	♟	2
● Campo Sella '10	♟♟	5
● Dogma Rosso '10	♟♟	4
○ Manzoni Bianco '11	♟♟	2*
○ Ultimo '10	♟♟	3
○ Ultimo '09	♟♟	3

T.E.S.S.A.R.I.

LOC. BROGNOLIGO
VIA FONTANA NUOVA, 86
37032 MONTEFORTE D'ALPONE [VR]
TEL. 0456176041
www.cantinatessari.com

CELLAR SALES
PRE-BOOKED VISITS
ANNUAL PRODUCTION 35,000 bottles
HECTARES UNDER VINE 13.00

The Tessari family's estate is now 20 years old, although their relationship with Soave vineyards began half a century earlier, and it is now one of the most interesting emerging wineries in the area. The vineyards cover about a dozen hectares and are entirely planted with garganega, which is used for various interpretations of terroirs and wines. The vineyards faithfully employ the pergola training system, updated with reduction of the more vigorous shoots thus considerably limiting production. Soave Le Bine Longhe di Costalta 2011 tasted excellent, impressing us with its intense aromas, where ripe approachable yellow-fleshed fruit is joined by saffron and dried flowers. The mouth is full and pulpy, tapering elegantly to a crisp finish. Soave Grisela 2012 is themed on simplicity, with aromas of apples and pears, and a lean drinkability backed by a pinch of sweetness. Recioto Tre Colli 2011 offers a citrussy, well-gauged sweetness.

○ Soave Cl. Grisela '12	♥♥ 2*
○ Soave Cl. Le Bine Longhe di Costalta '11	♥♥ 3
○ Garganega Brut	♥ 3
○ Recioto di Soave Tre Colli '11	♥ 5
○ Soave Cl. Grisela '11	♥♥ 2*
○ Soave Cl. Grisela '08	♥♥ 2*
○ Soave Cl. Grisela '07	♥♥ 2*
○ Soave Cl. Le Bine Longhe '10	♥♥ 5*

Tamellini

FRAZ. COSTEGGIOLA
VIA TAMELLINI, 4
37038 SOAVE [VR]
TEL. 0457675328
piofrancesco.tamellini@tin.it

CELLAR SALES
PRE-BOOKED VISITS
ANNUAL PRODUCTION 250,000 bottles
HECTARES UNDER VINE 25.00

Established in the late 1990s, the winery belonging to Gaetano and Piofrancesco Tamellini has rapidly climbed the listings for top wines in the Veronese designations, with its wealth of old vineyards extending across very prestigious areas. Here, at the westernmost end of the classic zone, on soil where tufa and limestone have gradually eroded the basalt, garganega is the most widespread and calming presence in the landscape. Limited yields and fully completed ageing are the green light for rich wines of a sapid drinkability. Soave Le Bine de Costiola 2011 rolls out a superb performance, where well-developed aromas sweep from exotic to candied fruit, leaving behind a subtle mineral trace. The mouth confirms the rich sensations on the nose, in total harmony. The approachable, racy Soave Classico 2012 is very good, while the Extra Brut 2009, disgorged after three years, offers flowers aromas and a gutsy, lean mouth.

○ Soave Cl. Le Bine de Costiola '11	♥♥♥ 3*
○ Extra Brut M. Cl. 36 mesi '09	♥♥ 4
○ Soave Cl. '12	♥♥ 2*
○ Soave Cl. Le Bine '04	♥♥♥ 3*
○ Soave Cl. Le Bine de Costiola '06	♥♥♥ 3*
○ Soave Cl. Le Bine de Costiola '05	♥♥♥ 3*
○ Recioto di Soave V. Marogne '02	♥♥ 5
○ Soave Cl. Le Bine de Costiola '09	♥♥ 3*
○ Soave Cl. Le Bine de Costiola '08	♥♥ 3*
○ Soave Cl. Le Bine de Costiola '07	♥♥ 3*

Tanorè

FRAZ. SAN PIETRO DI BARBOZZA
VIA MONT DI CARTIZZE, 3
31040 VALDOBBIADENE [TV]
TEL. 0423975770
www.tanore.it

CELLAR SALES
PRE-BOOKED VISITS
ANNUAL PRODUCTION 90,000 bottles
HECTARES UNDER VINE 10.00

In the Valdobbiadene wine world estates almost always have agreements with local growers for the supply of the necessary quantities of grapes for their wine production. However Tanorè, owned by brothers Sergio and Renato Follador, belongs to the small circle of wineries choosing to use exclusively estate-grown grapes, limiting production quantities and focusing on quality. All the more so since the brothers' estate is situated on the Cartizze hillside, the DOC's best-known subzone. The Folladors' finest wine, Cartizze, originates from the vineyards surrounding the winery, and is threaded with aromas expressing apple and wisteria flowers overlaying a delicately vegetal note. In the mouth, its sweetness is regulated by a piquantly juicy acidity. The Brut is made along a very different line, revealing an edgy, dry spirit in keeping with the type and imparting to the nose very fresh aromas of white-fleshed and citrus fruits.

○ Cartizze	🍷🍷 4
○ Valdobbiadene Brut	🍷🍷 3
○ Valdobbiadene Dry Il Tanorè '12	🍷 3
○ Valdobbiadene Extra Dry	🍷 2
○ Cartizze	🍷🍷 4
○ Valdobbiadene Dry Il Tanorè '11	🍷🍷 3
○ Valdobbiadene Dry Il Tanorè '10	🍷🍷 3
○ Valdobbiadene Dry Il Tanorè '09	🍷🍷 3

Giovanna Tantini

LOC. I MISCHI
37014 CASTELNUOVO DEL GARDA [VR]
TEL. 0457575070
www.giovannatantini.it

CELLAR SALES
PRE-BOOKED VISITS
ACCOMMODATION
ANNUAL PRODUCTION 25,000 bottles
HECTARES UNDER VINE 11.50

Giovanna Tantini's winery is in Castelnuovo del Garda, where the vineyards produce wines for both the Custoza and the Bardolino designations. Since her very first harvest in 2002, Giovanna has concentrated more on the latter, and is one of the finest producers of this wine today. With the collaboration of Federico Curtaz, Attilio Pagli and Laura Zuddas, she has reinterpreted the Garda reds, trying to combine their typical lightness and drinkability with longevity, aromatic depth and elegance. A further year's ageing in the cellar has imparted aromatic depth and harmony to the Bardolino 2011 and spices and medicinal herbs now blend on the taut palate, expanding stylishly in a long, smoky finish. Ettore 2009 is a blend of corvina, cabernet sauvignon and merlot left to over-ripen on the vines. The aromas are intensely fruity and spicy while, in the mouth, the wine reveals tanginess and a dry, racy drinkability.

● Bardolino '11	🍷🍷 2*
● Ettore '09	🍷🍷 4
⊙ Bardolino Chiaretto '12	🍷 2
● Bardolino '10	🍷🍷 2*
● Bardolino '09	🍷🍷 2*
● Bardolino '08	🍷🍷 2*
● Bardolino '07	🍷🍷 2*
● Ettore '08	🍷🍷 4
● Ettore '07	🍷🍷 4
● Ettore '06	🍷🍷 4
● Greta '09	🍷🍷 5
● Greta '08	🍷🍷 5

F.lli Tedeschi

FRAZ. PEDEMONTE
VIA G. VERDI, 4
37029 SAN PIETRO IN CARIANO [VR]
TEL. 0457701487
www.tedeschiwines.com

CELLAR SALES
PRE-BOOKED VISITS
ANNUAL PRODUCTION 500,000 bottles
HECTARES UNDER VINE 45.00

The massive effort put into developing the Maternigo estate is finally bearing fruit, revealing a potential that up until now only Antonietta, Sabrina and Riccardo had fully appreciated. Set at altitudes of between 200 and 450 metres above the sea, the estate has recently been able to bank on about 30 hectares under vine, all made over to traditional varieties. Simultaneously, the first wine produced by this new-look operation has seen the light of day: the Valpolicella Superiore Maternigo, a wine of great class, in a pure style. Its aromas are intensely fruity and the mouth powerful yet well-crafted with a taut precision. The complex Amarone La Fabriseria 2007 releases its aromas slowly, with dried fruit embracing overtones of minerality and medicinal herbs, offering a full, gutsy, yet slightly severe, drinkability. Capitel Monte Olmi 2008 offers a more expressive fruitiness, displaying a full body leading to a finish with curious underlying olive notes.

● Valpolicella Sup. Maternigo '11	♟♟♟	4*
● Amarone della Valpolicella Cl. Capitel Monte Olmi '08	♟♟	8
● Amarone della Valpolicella Cl. La Fabriseria '07	♟♟	8
● Amarone della Valpolicella Cl. '09	♟♟	6
● Recioto della Valpolicella Cl. Capitel Monte Fontana '07	♟♟	6
● Valpolicella Cl. Sup. La Fabriseria '10	♟♟	5
● Amarone della Valpolicella Cl. Capitel Monte Olmi '07	♟♟♟	8
● Amarone della Valpolicella Cl. Capitel Monte Olmi '01	♟♟♟	7
● Amarone della Valpolicella Cl. Capitel Monte Olmi '99	♟♟♟	7
● Amarone della Valpolicella Cl. Capitel Monte Olmi '97	♟♟♟	8

Viticoltori Tommasi

LOC. PEDEMONTE
VIA RONCHETTO, 2
37020 SAN PIETRO IN CARIANO [VR]
TEL. 0457701266
www.tommasiwine.it

CELLAR SALES
PRE-BOOKED VISITS
ANNUAL PRODUCTION 1,000,000 bottles
HECTARES UNDER VINE 162.00

This is one of the great families of Verona wines. The Tommasi started their activity in the mid-19th century and today they own vineyards extending over 150 hectares, mainly in Valpolicella, and their wines are loved throughout the world. Dario, who belongs to the generation that spurred on the development, is now flanked by a packed contingent of siblings and cousins all busily involved in every aspect of the operation, some in the vineyards, others in the cellar, not to mention those looking after administration and sales. The wines remain true to tradition and a style reflecting a taut drinkability. An explosive debut for Amarone Ca' Florian Riserva 2007, with a nose expressing aromas of overripe fruit and coffee, spices and medicinal herbs. It changes pace on the palate, revealing a firm body and a lean, nearly severe profile. Amarone Classico 2009 is themed on the freshness of ripe, juicy fruit, leading logically to a generous, succulent palate. The Valpolicella Superiore Rafael 2011, defined by a racy drinkability, is interesting.

● Amarone della Valpolicella Cl. Ca' Florian Ris. '07	♟♟	7
● Amarone della Valpolicella Cl. '09	♟♟	7
● Crearo della Conca d'Oro '11	♟♟	4
● Valpolicella Cl. Sup. Rafael '11	♟♟	3
● Valpolicella Cl. Sup. Ripasso '11	♟♟	4
● Arele '11	♟	3
○ Lugana Vign. San Martino Il Sestante '12	♟	2
● Amarone della Valpolicella Cl. '07	♟♟	6
● Amarone della Valpolicella Cl. '06	♟♟	6
● Crearo della Conca d'Oro '07	♟♟	4*
● Crearo della Conca d'Oro '06	♟♟	4
● Valpolicella Cl. Sup. Vign. Rafael '08	♟♟	4

Trabucchi d'Illasi

LOC. MONTE TENDA
37031 ILLASI [VR]
TEL. 0457833233
www.trabucchidillasi.it

CELLAR SALES
PRE-BOOKED VISITS
ANNUAL PRODUCTION 120,000 bottles
HECTARES UNDER VINE 25.00
VITICULTURE METHOD Certified Organic

The Trabucchis' family-owned winery
extends over a total of about 30 hectares
astride the designations of Soave and
Valpolicella, along the ridges of Monte
Tenda, at an altitude of between 140 and
300 metres above sea level. Here the vines
are partly cultivated using the Guyot system
and partly pergola-trained, all farmed
organically and yielding grapes of a superb
quality which, on reaching the cellar, are
gently escorted along the path from grape
to wine, with minimum intervention. The
Amarone 2007 performed well, slowly
releasing aromas of dried fruit and aromatic
herbs, which slowly give way to minerally,
spicy tones. The winery's trademark sound
palate leads to a taut, rigorous progression.
Valpolicella Terra del Cereolo 2007 only
emerges after lengthy ageing and highlights
complex, layered aromas closing on a dry,
sapid yet lively palate. The spicy, succulent
Valpolicella Un Anno 2012 is very good.

● Amarone della Valpolicella '07	▼▼	8
● Valpolicella Sup. Terre del Cereolo '07	▼▼	5
● Valpolicella Un Anno '12	▼▼	2*
○ Margherita '12	▼	2
● Amarone della Valpolicella '06	▼▼▼	8
● Amarone della Valpolicella '04	▼▼▼	8
● Recioto della Valpolicella Cereolo '05	▼▼▼	8
● Valpolicella Sup. Terre di S. Colombano '03	▼▼▼	4*
● Amarone della Valpolicella Cent'Anni Ris. '04	▼▼	8
● Recioto della Valpolicella '06	▼▼	7
● Valpolicella Sup. Terre del Cereolo '06	▼▼	5
● Valpolicella Sup. Terre di S. Colombano '07	▼▼	3*

Spumanti Valdo

VIA FORO BOARIO, 20
31049 VALDOBBIADENE [TV]
TEL. 04239090
www.valdo.com

CELLAR SALES
PRE-BOOKED VISITS
ANNUAL PRODUCTION 9,000,000 bottles
HECTARES UNDER VINE 155.00

Valdo is one of the classic names in the
Conegliano Valdobbiadene DOC zone, with a
strong historical background, rooted in the
post-WW1 period. The Bolla family has
owned the estate since the 1940s and it is
managed today by Pierluigi. Production
quantities are high but the heart of the
operation remains strongly linked to the
DOCG type, of which Bolla is one of the
leading producers. The necessary grapes
are provided by an extensive network of
growers every year. Another good year for
many of the Valdo sparkling wines, with
Cuvée di Boj, a zesty, gutsy Brut, standing
out for its aromatic clarity and grip. Extra
Dry 1926 expresses a greater fruitiness of
aromas and a fuller mouth, while Cartizze
Cuvée Viviana offers a convincing aromatic
breadth and harmonious palate, perfectly
underpinned by acidity and a dense, creamy
array of bubbles.

○ Cartizze Cuvée Viviana	▼▼	5
○ Valdobbiadene Brut Cuvée di Boj	▼▼	2
○ Valdobbiadene Extra Dry Cuvée 1926	▼▼	2*
○ Numero 10 Brut M. Cl. '09	▼	4
○ Prosecco di Treviso Extra Dry	▼	2
○ Valdobbiadene Cuvée del Fondatore '11	▼	3

Cantina Valpolicella Negrar

VIA CA' SALGARI, 2
37024 NEGRAR [VR]
TEL. 0456014300
www.cantinanegrar.it

Odino Vaona

LOC. VALGATARA
VIA PAVERNO, 41
37020 MARANO DI VALPOLICELLA [VR]
TEL. 0457703710
www.vaona.it

CELLAR SALES
PRE-BOOKED VISITS
RESTAURANT SERVICE
ANNUAL PRODUCTION 7,000,000 bottles
HECTARES UNDER VINE 600.00
VITICULTURE METHOD Certified Organic

Several co-operative wineries operate in the territory of Valpolicella, including the one managed by Daniele Accordini, which has proved able to fully understand the changes that have turned this territory on its head over the last few decades. Obviously, there are wines of all levels, with Domini Veneti representing the absolute pinnacle in terms of quality. This wine is the result of the work carried out by the most assiduous members, who follow a process that focuses on the vineyards, chosen and cultivated so as to maximize the traits of the soil, the grapes and the altitude. Their best wines offer great concentration and power, as revealed in the Amarone Vigneti di Jago 2007, from vineyards set on the eastern slope of the Negrar Valley. Aromas are dominated by dried red berries and chocolate, deftly replicated in the mouth, where the wine highlights power and tannicity. In the Recioto Vigneti di Moron 2010, fruit explodes in a full, juicy and decidedly sweet mouth. Among the many Valpolicellas, Torbe 2011 is particularly successful.

CELLAR SALES
PRE-BOOKED VISITS
ANNUAL PRODUCTION 60,000 bottles
HECTARES UNDER VINE 10.00

Alberto Vaona runs his family-owned winery located in the valley of Marano, the only area in the classic zone with volcanic residue in the soil. Here, the estate-owned vineyards are set at an altitude of nearly 250 metres. The oldest plots are cultivated using the traditional Veronese pergola overhead training system, while the most recent are Guyot-trained, following a logic centred on the vineyard. Production, still limited in terms of quantity, offers many sparks of quality, starting from the Amarone, interpreted with a light elegance. The tasting of Amarone Pegrandi 2009 was exemplary. With its crunchy fruit and aromatic herbs, it offers a rich, juicy palate, crafted in a delightfully light style. Riserva 2007 focuses more on concentrated dried fruity-flowery sensations, while relinquishing neither tension nor drinkability. Amarone Paverno 2010 is simple and succulent while, among the Valpolicellas, we like the aromatic freshness and zest of Ripasso Pegrandi 2011.

- Amarone della Valpolicella Cl.
  Vigneti di Jago Domini Veneti '07   ♔♔ 6
- Recioto della Valpolicella Cl.
  Vign. di Moron Domini Veneti '10   ♔♔ 4
- Valpolicella Cl. Sup. Ripasso
  La Casetta Domini Veneti '10   ♔♔ 4
- Valpolicella Cl. Sup. Ripasso
  Vign. di Torbe Domini Veneti '11   ♔♔ 3
- Valpolicella Cl. Sup. Verjago
  Domini Veneti '08   ♔♔ 4
- Valpolicella Cl. Biologico
  Domini Veneti '12   ♔ 2
- Valpolicella Cl. Sup. Domini Veneti '11   ♔ 2
- Amarone della Valpolicella Cl.
  Villa Domini Veneti '05   ♔♔♔ 8
- Recioto della Valpolicella Cl.
  Vigneti di Moron Domini Veneti '01   ♔♔♔ 5

- Amarone della Valpolicella Cl.
  Pegrandi '09   ♔♔♔ 5
- Amarone della Valpolicella Cl.
  Pegrandi Ris. '07   ♔♔ 8
- Amarone della Valpolicella Cl.
  Paverno '10   ♔♔ 5
- Recioto della Valpolicella Le Peagnà '11   ♔♔ 4
- Valpolicella Cl. Sup. Ripasso
  Pegrandi '11   ♔♔ 3
- Castaroto '10   ♔ 4
- Valpolicella Cl. '12   ♔ 2
- Valpolicella Sup. '11   ♔ 2
- Amarone della Valpolicella Cl.
  Pegrandi '08   ♔♔♔ 5
- Amarone della Valpolicella Cl.
  Paverno '09   ♔♔ 5
- Recioto Cl. Le Peagnè '09   ♔♔ 4

Massimino Venturini

FRAZ. SAN FLORIANO
VIA SEMONTE, 20
37020 SAN PIETRO IN CARIANO [VR]
TEL. 0457701331
www.viniventurini.com

CELLAR SALES
PRE-BOOKED VISITS
ANNUAL PRODUCTION 100,000 bottles
HECTARES UNDER VINE 12.00

The Venturini house production has finally moved from its historical location in Via Semonte to its new cellar at the foot of Monte Olmi, where Daniele and Mirco can carry out all the necessary operations in peace and order. In the vineyards, on the other hand, work continues at the usual pace, slowly and patiently, waiting for the grapes to become a wine that excites, that talks about its territory and traditions. About a dozen hectares and less than 100,000 bottles speak volumes, expressing the concept of quality better than any words. At the Venturini winery, they have particularly nimble fingers in crafting Amarone, proposing two very different wines. Classico 2009 has aromas of late-harvest fruit and spices, followed by a dry, racy palate. Campo Masua 2008 hits the notes of dried fruit, highlighting a full, powerful body, with a precisely crafted tautness. Recioto 2010 is particularly enjoyable, where a sweet, crispy cherry is expressed exuberantly, conferring pronounced sweetness and a lovely acidic thrust to the mouth.

● Amarone della Valpolicella Cl. '09	▼▼ 5
● Amarone della Valpolicella Cl. Campo Masua '08	▼▼ 6
● Recioto della Valpolicella Cl. '10	▼▼ 5
● Valpolicella Cl. Sup. Ripasso Semonte Alto '09	▼▼ 3
● Massimino '09	▼ 4
● Valpolicella Cl. '12	▼ 2
● Amarone della Valpolicella Cl. Campo Masua '07	♀♀♀ 6
● Amarone della Valpolicella Cl. Campo Masua '05	♀♀♀ 6
● Recioto della Valpolicella Cl. Le Brugnine '97	♀♀♀ 5
● Amarone della Valpolicella Cl. '08	♀♀ 5

Agostino Vicentini

FRAZ. SAN ZENO
VIA C. BATTISTI, 62c
37030 COLOGNOLA AI COLLI [VR]
TEL. 0457650539
www.vinivicentini.com

CELLAR SALES
PRE-BOOKED VISITS
ANNUAL PRODUCTION 100,000 bottles
HECTARES UNDER VINE 20.00

There is certainly no doubt that the winery of Via Battisti is a focal point for lovers of Soave. What is less known is that it also produces some Valpolicella and over the years these wines have captured greater elegance and depth, re-proposing the idea of a red that can be appreciated for qualities that are not based solely on power. Credit is undoubtedly due to the meticulous grower Agostino, and to the skilled cellar-work of his son Manuele, whose sister Francesca looks after the commercial side together with their mother, Teresa. Casale is a Soave produced in the eastern part of the designation from garganega grapes only. Yields are very limited and ripening is followed carefully, allowing the wine to express richness on the nose and firmness in the mouth, keeping a tight grip on a palate of harmonious sapidity. Terre Lunghe 2012 is lean and racy. As for the reds, we like Idea Bacco 2010 for its ability to pace its power on the palate.

○ Soave Sup. Il Casale '12	▼▼▼ 3*
○ Soave Vign. Terre Lunghe '12	▼▼ 2*
● Valpolicella Sup. '10	▼▼ 3
● Valpolicella Sup. Idea Bacco '10	▼▼ 5
○ Soave Sup. Il Casale '09	♀♀♀ 3*
○ Soave Sup. Il Casale '08	♀♀♀ 3*
○ Soave Sup. Il Casale '07	♀♀♀ 3*
○ Soave Il Casale '10	♀♀ 3*
○ Soave Sup. Il Casale '11	♀♀ 3*
○ Soave Vign. Terre Lunghe '11	♀♀ 2*
○ Soave Vign. Terre Lunghe '10	♀♀ 2*
○ Soave Vign. Terre Lunghe '09	♀♀ 2*

Vigna Roda

LOC. CORTELÀ
VIA MONTE VERSA, 1569
35030 Vo [PD]
TEL. 0499940228
www.vignaroda.com

CELLAR SALES
PRE-BOOKED VISITS
ANNUAL PRODUCTION 52,000 bottles
HECTARES UNDER VINE 17.00

Set on the western slopes of the Colli
Euganei, the winery owned by Gianni
Strazzacapa and his wife Elena, is one of
the most interesting of the designation.
Founded at the end of the 1990s, the
family vineyards were gradually converted
to achieve greater quality in the grapes,
reflected in wines of greater richness and
harmony. Production is mainly concentrated
on Merlot and Cabernet, varieties that have
been present in this corner of Veneto for
nearly 200 years. As for the whites, the
jewel in their crown is the Fior d'Arancio.
The best wine from the Strazzacappa
winery is once again Scarlatto, a
prevalently merlot Bordeaux blend
expressing intense fruity notes with hints of
spices and garden vegetables that remain
in the background. It has a generous,
crunchy mouth, defined by a succulent
drinkability and lively tannins. Espero 2012
is a Cabernet that hinges on very
approachable aromas of plum and delicate
grassy notes that confer freshness.

● Colli Euganei Cabernet Espero '12	♟♟ 2*
● Colli Euganei Rosso '12	♟♟ 2*
● Colli Euganei Rosso Scarlatto '10	♟♟ 3
○ Colli Euganei Fior d'Arancio	♟ 4
● Colli Euganei Merlot Il Damerino '12	♟ 4
○ Colli Euganei Serprino Frizzante '12	♟ 2
● Colli Euganei Cabernet Espero '11	♟♟ 2*
○ Colli Euganei Fior d'Arancio Passito	
Petali d'Ambra '09	♟♟ 4
● Colli Euganei Merlot Il Damerino '10	♟♟ 4
● Colli Euganei Rosso '11	♟♟ 2*
● Colli Euganei Rosso Scarlatto '09	♟♟ 3
● Colli Euganei Rosso Scarlatto '08	♟♟ 3*

Vignale di Cecilia

LOC. FORNACI
VIA CROCI, 14
35030 BAONE [PD]
TEL. 042951420
www.vignaledicecilia.it

PRE-BOOKED VISITS
ANNUAL PRODUCTION 20,000 bottles
HECTARES UNDER VINE 8.00
VITICULTURE METHOD Certified Organic

Paolo Brunello created Vignale di Cecilia, a
small estate extending over the
south-western crest of Monte Cecilia,
which is one of the last hills in the Euganei
DOC zone before the area reverts to
lowlands. While the amphitheatre of
vineyards surrounding the winery is mainly
planted with Bordeaux varieties, the rented
vineyards include garganega and tai. These
lesser-known varieties are interpreted with
care and originality by Paolo. The weighty
wines highlight the sunny character of the
terroir. Passacaglia is a mainly merlot
Bordeaux mix with a convincing breadth of
aromas, a ripe, pulpy fruit inlaid with spices
and medicinal herbs. In the mouth, richness
is carefully kept in place by tannins and
acidity, providing a long succulence. Cocài
is a Tai with summery expressions and
fruity drinkability, while El Moro 2010,
based on carmenère, reveals itself very
slowly, with the best reserved for a savoury,
minerally palate.

○ Cocài '11	♟♟ 3
● Colli Euganei Rosso Covolo '10	♟♟ 3
● Colli Euganei Rosso Passacaglia '09	♟♟ 4
● El Moro '10	♟♟ 3
○ Benavides '11	♟♟ 2*
○ Benavides '10	♟♟ 2*
○ Benavides '09	♟♟ 2
○ Cocài '10	♟♟ 3
○ Cocài '09	♟♟ 3
● Colli Euganei Rosso Passacaglia '08	♟♟ 4
● Colli Euganei Rosso Passacaglia '07	♟♟ 4
● El Moro '08	♟♟ 3*

★Vignalta

VIA SCALETTE, 23
35032 ARQUÀ PETRARCA [PD]
TEL. 0429777305
www.vignalta.it

CELLAR SALES
PRE-BOOKED VISITS
ANNUAL PRODUCTION 280,000 bottles
HECTARES UNDER VINE 50.00

Vignalta is certainly the winery that has contributed more than any other towards bringing the name of Colli Euganei into the limelight. This winery, whose vineyards extend for more than 50 hectares in the southern part of the designation, is under the management of Lucio Gomiero who relies on the collaboration of Filippo Scortegagna, in the vineyards, and Michele Montecchio, in the cellar. The knowledge he has of the territory, acquired over 30 years of activity, means that they can allocate the best suited vineyards to each label, highlighting their characteristics through non-invasive vinification techniques. The winery's flagship is certainly Gemola, a blend of merlot and cabernet franc, which is the designation's benchmark year after year. Its aromas, joined by red fruits, express a lovely symphony of spices and aromatic herbs, replicated perfectly in a crisp, firm and very long palate. We like Alpianae 2009, included in the Guide by mistake last year, for its rich aromas of citrus and candied fruit, and sweet exuberance in the mouth.

● Colli Euganei Rosso Gemola '09	♟♟♟ 5
○ Colli Euganei Fior d'Arancio Passito Alpianae '09	♟♟ 4
○ Brut Nature M. Cl.	♟♟ 5
○ Colli Euganei Pinot Bianco '12	♟♟ 3
● Colli Euganei Rosso Ris. '09	♟♟ 3
● Marrano '08	♟♟ 5
○ Colli Euganei Chardonnay '11	♟ 4
○ Colli Euganei Fior d'Arancio Passito Alpianae '08	♟♟♟ 4
● Colli Euganei Rosso Arquà '04	♟♟♟ 6
● Colli Euganei Rosso Gemola '07	♟♟♟ 5
● Colli Euganei Rosso Gemola '01	♟♟♟ 5
● Colli Euganei Rosso Gemola '00	♟♟♟ 6

Le Vigne di San Pietro

VIA SAN PIETRO, 23
37066 SOMMACAMPAGNA [VR]
TEL. 045510016
www.levignedisanpietro.it

CELLAR SALES
PRE-BOOKED VISITS
ANNUAL PRODUCTION 70,000 bottles
HECTARES UNDER VINE 10.00

The Le Vigne di San Pietro estate was founded at the start of the 1980s, and today covers an area of about 20 hectares around Sommacampagna, where the Custoza and Bardolino designations compete for the best aspects. Carlo Nerozzi, backed by his wife Regina and with the precious collaboration of Federico Giotto, is constantly searching for a contact point between the lightness that belongs to wines from the Garda designations and the richness and depth demanded by the market. His aim is to produce fragrant wines that can always captivate with their personality and elegance. These qualities duly emerge in the Bardolino 2012, a red with aromas of wild berries, spices and fines herbes that come together splendidly in the mouth, highlighting a wine of good intensity with no loss of tautness or lightness. Custoza 2012 takes a similar path, with a more exuberant fruit, while the Amarone 2009 is crafted by Carlo's deft hands. It expresses cherry and pepper, with a full-flavoured, harmonious expansion on the palate.

● Bardolino '12	♟♟ 2*
○ Custoza '12	♟♟ 2*
● Amarone della Valpolicella Cl. '09	♟♟ 7
⊙ CorDeRosa '12	♟ 2
● Bardolino '11	♟♟♟ 2*
● Refolà Cabernet Sauvignon '04	♟♟♟ 6
○ Sud '95	♟♟♟ 6
● Bardolino '10	♟♟ 2*
○ Custoza '11	♟♟ 2*
○ Custoza '10	♟♟ 2*
● Refolà '09	♟♟ 6
● Refolà Cabernet Sauvignon '05	♟♟ 6

Vigneto Due Santi

V.LE ASIAGO, 174
36061 BASSANO DEL GRAPPA [VI]
TEL. 0424502074
www.vignetoduesanti.it

CELLAR SALES
PRE-BOOKED VISITS
ANNUAL PRODUCTION 100,000 bottles
HECTARES UNDER VINE 19.00

Adriano and Stefano Zonta are the architects of the success of Vigneto Due Santi, a family-owned winery that extends over about 20 hectares at Bassano del Grappa, where the hills with their perfect southern aspect bask in the fresh breezes from the nearby Valsugana valley. Their production focuses mainly on Bordeaux varieties, with both the simpler versions and their flagship labels expressing a particularly rich, clear-cut fruit. They have, instead, been aiming for greater freshness and grip in their whites, in recent years. The winery's star, Cabernet Due Santi, is still ageing in the cellar, underlining the care they take during this important phase. Merlot and Cabernet, both 2010, convinced us with their aromatic wealth where fruit is just one key performer, and is joined by spices, aromatic herbs and oak, each offering a different, subtle input. The former has a full, sunny mouth with a good thrust of acidity; the latter is crispy with a succulent drinkability.

● Breganze Cabernet '10	🍷🍷 2*
● Breganze Merlot '10	🍷🍷 2*
○ Breganze Sauvignon '12	🍷🍷 3
○ Malvasia Campo di Fiori '12	🍷🍷 2*
○ Breganze Bianco Rivana '12	🍷 2
○ Breganze Torcolato '08	🍷 5
○ Prosecco Extra Dry	🍷 2
● Breganze Cabernet Vign. Due Santi '08	🍷🍷🍷 4*
● Breganze Cabernet Vign. Due Santi '07	🍷🍷🍷 4
● Breganze Cabernet Vign. Due Santi '05	🍷🍷🍷 4
● Breganze Cabernet Vign. Due Santi '04	🍷🍷🍷 4
● Breganze Cabernet Vign. Due Santi '03	🍷🍷🍷 4*

Villa Bellini

LOC. CASTELROTTO DI NEGARINE
VIA DEI FRACCAROLI, 6
37020 SAN PIETRO IN CARIANO [VR]
TEL. 0457725630
www.villabellini.com

CELLAR SALES
PRE-BOOKED VISITS
ANNUAL PRODUCTION 10,000 bottles
HECTARES UNDER VINE 3.50
VITICULTURE METHOD Certified Organic

Resting on the eastern slopes of the hill of Castelrotto, Cecila Trucchi's winery is a standard for lovers of Valpolicella and for people wanting more from Veronese designation reds than simply power, seeking dynamism and aromatic depth instead. The pathway was not straightforward and involved replanting the vineyards, using organic farming methods and stopping the production of Amarone, so that the finest grapes can go into the Taso. Today, following the restoration of their cellar, they can carry out increasingly more focused and minimalistic procedures. Sotto le Fresche Frasche, a Valpolicella conceived to set off a fresh aromaticity and grip, remains among the best of its type. Taso follows an arduous path searching for a rich depth without losing its mouthfeel, successfully accomplished with the 2010 harvest. On the nose, the wine has aromas of wild berries and spices, with balsamic notes emerging in a dry, lean palate of incredible length.

● Valpolicella Cl. Sup. Il Taso '10	🍷🍷 5
● Valpolicella Cl. Sotto le Fresche Frasche '12	🍷🍷 3
● Recioto della Valpolicella Cl. Uva Passa '06	🍷🍷 6
● Recioto della Valpolicella Cl. Uva Passa '04	🍷🍷 6
● Valpolicella Cl. Sup. Il Taso '09	🍷🍷 5
● Valpolicella Cl. Sup. Il Taso '08	🍷🍷 5
● Valpolicella Cl. Sup. Il Taso '07	🍷🍷 5
● Valpolicella Cl. Sup. Il Taso '06	🍷🍷 5
● Valpolicella Cl. Sup. Il Taso '05	🍷🍷 5
● Valpolicella Cl. Sup. Il Taso '04	🍷🍷 5
● Valpolicella Cl. Sup. Il Taso '03	🍷🍷 5

Villa Sandi

VIA ERIZZO, 112
31035 CROCETTA DEL MONTELLO [TV]
TEL. 0423665033
www.villasandi.it

CELLAR SALES
PRE-BOOKED VISITS
ACCOMMODATION AND RESTAURANT SERVICE
ANNUAL PRODUCTION 4,000,000 bottles
HECTARES UNDER VINE 340.00

A small plain lies between the Montello and the Venetian Prealps, which is where the Moretti's family winery is located, at Crocetta. The vineyards, extending for numerous hectares over the northern slopes of the Montello hill, are mainly cultivated with Bordeaux varieties, while the plots providing the grapes for the Prosecco are in the district of Valdobbiadene, where the resplendent Rivetta vineyard at the heart of Cartizze was snatched from oblivion. The range on offer is vast and contains a good production of Metodo Classico sparkling wines. Corpore has given a shine to the selection of reds with its perfect marriage of merlot and cabernet, exalting the fruitiness of the former and revealing its harmony. Cartizze La Rivetta has given its customary classy performance, presenting subtle aromas conveying pear and lime blossom that develop in a dry, savoury and exquisitely fine progression. Among the Metodo Classico wines, we like Opere Trevigiane Riserva 2008 best.

○ Cartizze V. La Rivetta	▼▼▼	6
● Còrpore '10	▼▼	5
○ Marinali Bianco Manzoni '12	▼▼	4
○ Opere Trevigiane Brut Ris. '08	▼▼	5
○ Valdobbiadene Brut Mill. '12	▼▼	3
● Filio Corpore '11	▼	4
● Marinali Rosso Raboso '09	▼	3
○ Opere Trevigiane Brut	▼	4
○ Prosecco di Treviso Il Fresco	▼	2
○ Valdobbiadene Dry Cuvée Oris	▼	3
● Venezia Cabernet Sauvignon '12	▼	2
○ Cartizze Brut V. La Rivetta '09	▽▽▽	4
○ Cartizze V. La Rivetta '11	▽▽▽	4*
○ Cartizze V. La Rivetta '10	▽▽▽	4
● Corpore '09	▽▽	5

Villa Spinosa

LOC. JAGO DALL'ORA
VIA COLLE MASUA, 12
37024 NEGRAR [VR]
TEL. 0457500093
www.villaspinosa.it

CELLAR SALES
PRE-BOOKED VISITS
ACCOMMODATION
ANNUAL PRODUCTION 45,000 bottles
HECTARES UNDER VINE 20.00

Over the past decades the valley of Negrar has been affected by urban development, which has undermined its beauty and reduced its production area, as houses stand where there were once vineyards. However, on the climb up to the locality of Jago, nature and viticulture reclaim the ownership of the landscape, providing the setting for the cellar belonging to Enrico Cascella. The property extends for about 20 hectares, here and along the easternmost slopes of the hill, cultivating only the traditional Valpolicella grapes, and production is directed towards great rigour and respect for the traditional varieties. The Casella's Amarone toys with an explosive dried fruit and spices that develop completely in a full, succulent palate of great impact. Jago, a Ripasso from the Jago area, reveals an aromatic wealth of overripe fruit, aromatic herbs and a delicate mineral note. On tasting, it thrills with its firmness on the palate, where richness is kept at bay by a dense tannic weave.

● Amarone della Valpolicella Cl. Anteprima '08	▼▼	6
● Valpolicella Cl. Sup. Ripasso Jago '10	▼▼	3
● Amarone della Valpolicella Cl. '04	▽▽	7
● Amarone della Valpolicella Cl. Anteprima '06	▽▽	5
● Amarone della Valpolicella Cl. Guglielmi di Jago '01	▽▽	7
● Recioto della Valpolicella Cl. Francesca Finato Spinosa '08	▽▽	5
● Valpolicella Cl. '07	▽▽	2*
● Valpolicella Cl. Sup. Figari '08	▽▽	3*
● Valpolicella Cl. Sup. Figari '07	▽▽	2*
● Valpolicella Cl. Sup. Figari '06	▽▽	2*
● Valpolicella Cl. Sup. Ripasso Jago '08	▽▽	3
● Valpolicella Cl. Sup. Ripasso Jago '06	▽▽	3

Vigneti Villabella

FRAZ. CALMASINO
LOC. CANOVA, 2
37011 BARDOLINO [VR]
TEL. 0457236448
www.vignetivillabella.com

CELLAR SALES
PRE-BOOKED VISITS
ACCOMMODATION AND RESTAURANT SERVICE
ANNUAL PRODUCTION 500,000 bottles
HECTARES UNDER VINE 220.00
VITICULTURE METHOD Certified Organic

The Delibori and Cristoforetti families'
organically farmed estate extends along the
banks of Lake Garda. The 200-plus
hectares cover most of the Riviera DOC
zones and only a small part of the wine
made from their grapes produce is bottled.
Alongside Bardolino and Custoza are, of
course, the Valpolicella reds, and a series
of original blends of international and
traditional grape varieties. The Bardolino
Morlongo 2012 gives a grandstand display
where classic aromas of wild berries and
spices, flank delicate hints of earth and
aromatic herbs, replicated perfectly in the
mouth, resulting in a red that is effortlessly
rich yet light and taut. Il Fiordilej 2010 is a
raisined wine whose sweetness is kept in
check by a tangy, racy acidity, while
Amarone Fracastoro 2005 offers a rounded
pulpiness with pleasantly grainy tannins.

● Amarone della Valpolicella Cl. Fracastoro '05	♥♥ 6
● Bardolino Cl. V. Morlongo '12	♥♥ 2*
○ Fiordilej Passito '10	♥♥ 3
⊙ Bardolino Chiaretto '12	♥ 2
⊙ Bardolino Chiaretto Brut	♥ 2
● Bardolino Cl. Sup. Terre di Cavagion '11	♥ 3
○ Custoza '12	♥ 2
○ Pinot Grigio V. di Pesina '12	♥ 2
○ Rebianco Brut	♥ 2
● Valpolicella Cl. I Roccoli '12	♥ 2
● Valpolicella Cl. Sup. Ripasso '10	♥ 3
● Villa Cordevigo Rosso '07	♥ 5
○ Fiordilej Passito '09	♥♥ 3

★Viviani

VIA MAZZANO, 8
37020 NEGRAR [VR]
TEL. 0457500286
www.cantinaviviani.com

CELLAR SALES
PRE-BOOKED VISITS
ANNUAL PRODUCTION 80,000 bottles
HECTARES UNDER VINE 10.00

From the heights of Mazzano, Claudio
Viviani has known how to exploit the
moment of great expansion for
Valpolicella wines to give his cellar a cast
that is simultaneously modern and
traditional. In the past, he has expanded
the area under vine abandoning the
traditional pergola overhead training
method in favour of the Guyot system and,
more recently, he has been revamping his
wines to give them their own identity,
where the rich, partially dried grapes are
used to produce wines whose main
strengths are aromatic depth, elegance
and tautness. Amarone Classico 2009 is
the perfect example of a wine that retains
its raisined profile yet flows across the
palate with a taut elegance, revealing a
finesse not expressed before. While Casa
dei Bepi 2008 is naturally rich and
caressing on the nose, the mouth hints at a
more taut and edgy progression than in the
past. Campo Morar 2010 is themed on a
round fruit and juicy progression,
expressing a supple length.

● Amarone della Valpolicella Cl. Casa dei Bepi '08	♥♥ 8
● Valpolicella Cl. Sup. Campo Morar '10	♥♥ 5
● Amarone della Valpolicella Cl. '09	♥♥ 6
● Valpolicella Cl. '12	♥♥ 2*
● Amarone della Valpolicella Cl. Casa dei Bepi '05	♥♥♥ 8
● Amarone della Valpolicella Cl. Casa dei Bepi '04	♥♥♥ 8
● Amarone della Valpolicella Cl. Casa dei Bepi '01	♥♥♥ 8
● Amarone della Valpolicella Cl. Casa dei Bepi '00	♥♥♥ 8
● Valpolicella Cl. Sup. Campo Morar '09	♥♥♥ 5
● Valpolicella Cl. Sup. Campo Morar '05	♥♥♥ 5
● Valpolicella Cl. Sup. Campo Morar '01	♥♥♥ 5

★Zenato

FRAZ. SAN BENEDETTO DI LUGANA
VIA SAN BENEDETTO, 8
37019 PESCHIERA DEL GARDA [VR]
TEL. 0457550300
www.zenato.it

CELLAR SALES
PRE-BOOKED VISITS
ANNUAL PRODUCTION 2,000,000 bottles
HECTARES UNDER VINE 75.00

The soul of the winery founded by Sergio Zenato, and run today by his children Nadia and Alberto, has always been split between the most prestigious territories of Verona, Valpolicella to the west and Lugana to the east. To this day this is the philosophy of the cellar, strengthened by a renewed viticultural effort that has resulted in the development of important vineyards, especially in Valpolicella, where the winery is a standard bearer. Production has become more consistent over the years, and its fighting strength lies in particularly close-focused fruit and powerful drinkability. Amarone Sergio Zenato Riserva 2007 is the standard-bearer of its type. With a nose of dried red fruit and spices, it develops into a delightful sapid palate, where the tannins keep its power under control. Lugana 2010 seems to be changing direction, relinquishing the explosive richness of the last ten years to gain in aromatic elegance and suppleness of mouth. The excellent Lugana San Benedetto 2012 is a very reliable wine produced in large quantities.

● Amarone della Valpolicella Cl. Sergio Zenato Ris. '07	♟♟ 8
○ Lugana Sergio Zenato '10	♟♟ 5
● Amarone della Valpolicella Cl. '09	♟♟ 6
○ Lugana S. Benedetto '12	♟♟ 2*
● Valpolicella Cl. Sup. '10	♟♟ 3
● Valpolicella Cl. Sup. Rip. Ripassa '10	♟♟ 4
○ Lugana Brut M. Cl. '10	♟ 4
○ Lugana Vign. Massoni Santa Cristina '12	♟ 3
● Amarone della Valpolicella Cl. '05	♟♟♟ 6
● Amarone della Valpolicella Cl. Sergio Zenato '05	♟♟♟ 6
● Amarone della Valpolicella Cl. Sergio Zenato '03	♟♟♟ 6
○ Lugana Sergio Zenato '08	♟♟♟ 4

F.lli Zeni

VIA COSTABELLA, 9
37011 BARDOLINO [VR]
TEL. 0457210022
www.zeni.it

CELLAR SALES
PRE-BOOKED VISITS
ANNUAL PRODUCTION 1,000,000 bottles
HECTARES UNDER VINE 25.00

Fausto, Elena and Federica run the family estate that extends largely along the Verona shore of Lake Garda. The family work with many local growers who supply the necessary quantities of grapes for production. The estate's own vineyards, about 25 hectares, grow the grapes for the more ambitious wines which are always a respectful interpretation of both the variety and the terroir without ever foregoing drinkability, which is the true strength of the entire range. The Zeni winery gave some great results this year, with many wines making a leap in quality. Among the Valpolicellas, Amarone Vigne Alte 2009 shows a good aromatic breadth, and is dry and pleasantly supple on drinking. The Ripasso Marogne 2011 is harmoniously deep and full of flavours. Along the lakeside, the best results come from Bardolino Classico Superiore 2011 and Lugana Vigne Alte 2012. The first is firm and racy, the latter full and juicy.

● Amarone della Valpolicella Cl. Barrique '08	♟♟ 6
● Amarone della Valpolicella Cl. Vigne Alte '09	♟♟ 6
● Bardolino Cl. Filari del Nino '12	♟♟ 5
● Bardolino Cl. Sup. '11	♟♟ 3
● Costalago Rosso '11	♟♟ 3
○ Lugana Vigne Alte '12	♟♟ 2*
○ Soave Cl. Marogne '11	♟♟ 3
● Valpolicella Cl. Sup. Ripasso Marogne '11	♟♟ 3
⊙ Bardolino Chiaretto Brut	♟ 2
⊙ Bardolino Chiaretto Cl. Vigne Alte '12	♟ 2
● Bardolino Cl. Vigne Alte '12	♟ 2
● Corvar '10	♟ 5
○ Lugana Marogne '12	♟ 2
● Recioto della Valpolicella Cl. '11	♟ 4
● Valpolicella Cl. Vigne Alte '12	♟ 2

Zonin

VIA BORGOLECCO, 9
36053 GAMBELLARA [VI]
TEL. 0444640111
www.zonin.it

CELLAR SALES
PRE-BOOKED VISITS
ANNUAL PRODUCTION 38,000,000 bottles
HECTARES UNDER VINE 2,000.00

The Zonin family is one of the largest groups in the Italian wine world. They own vineyards located in the most famous production areas in Italy and abroad, but their heart remains soundly bonded to their territory of origin, Gambellara. Production here has remained faithful to tradition, offering wines with distinguishing traits linked to freshness, sapidity and lightness, which make them approachable and immensely enjoyable. Alongside their wines from the area around Vincenza, they are increasingly making space for the production of Prosecco. The best wines come from the nearby Valpolicella, with an Amarone 2010 succeeding in the difficult task of offering mature, caressing tones alongside the winery's style based on drinkability. Ripasso 2011 has a finer nose and leaner palate. In terms of the Proseccos, Brut Cuvée 1821, a sparkling wine with flowery-fruity aromas in a light, tangy mouth sustained by bubbles, is a hair's breadth from a Due Bicchieri.

● Amarone della Valpolicella '10	♥♥ 6
● Valpolicella Sup. Ripasso '11	♥♥ 3
○ Gambellara Cl. Podere Il Giangio '12	♥ 2
○ Müller Thurgau Brut	♥ 2
○ Prosecco Brut	♥ 2
○ Prosecco Brut Cuvée 1821	♥ 3
○ Recioto di Gambellara Spumante	♥ 3
● Amarone della Valpolicella '09	♥♥ 6
● Amarone della Valpolicella '06	♥♥ 6
● Amarone della Valpolicella '05	♥♥ 6
● Amarone della Valpolicella '04	♥♥ 5
● Berengario '09	♥♥ 4
● Berengario '08	♥♥ 4
● Berengario '06	♥♥ 4
○ Recioto di Gambellara Cl. Il Giangio '04	♥♥ 4
● Valpolicella Sup. Ripasso '07	♥♥ 3

Zymè

VIA CA' DEL PIPA, 1
37029 SAN PIETRO IN CARIANO [VR]
TEL. 0457701108
www.zyme.it

CELLAR SALES
PRE-BOOKED VISITS
ANNUAL PRODUCTION 80,000 bottles
HECTARES UNDER VINE 30.00

Celestino Gaspari has begun work on his new cellar at San Pietro in Cariano, set around an old sandstone quarry in which he already ages his wines. What is not visible, however, is the major effort that the winery has undertaken to develop the area under vine, centred on the traditional Valpolicella grapes, while still finding room for interesting diversions, such as working with unusual varieties or exploring new territories, like the nearby Colli Berici. Based on a sound 20 years of experience, his production methods bring out the most distinctive individual traits of his wines. The Amarone from the 2006 harvest has passed a long time in the cellar ageing and now we can reap the benefits. On the nose, the aromas surface slowly, and the over-ripe fruit gradually gives way to spices and mineral tones. In the mouth, smooth tannins joined with acidity firmly keep the wine's richness under control. Valpolicella Superiore 2009 follows the same path, offering less richness and the same class.

● Amarone della Valpolicella Cl. '06	♥♥♥ 8
● Valpolicella Cl. Sup. '09	♥♥ 6
○ Il Bianco From Black to White '12	♥♥ 3
● Kairos '07	♥♥ 7
● Valpolicella Revirie '12	♥♥ 2*
● Amarone della Valpolicella Cl. La Mattonara Ris. '01	♥♥♥ 8
● Amarone della Valpolicella Cl. '04	♥♥ 8
● Amarone della Valpolicella Cl. '03	♥♥ 8
● Amarone della Valpolicella Cl. '01	♥♥ 8
● Harlequin '06	♥♥ 8
● Harlequin '01	♥♥ 8
● Kairos '05	♥♥ 7

Andreola

LOC. COL SAN MARTINO
VIA CAL LONGA, 52
31010 FARRA DI SOLIGO [TV]
TEL. 0438989379
www.andreola.eu

CELLAR SALES
PRE-BOOKED VISITS
ANNUAL PRODUCTION 700,000 bottles
HECTARES UNDER VINE 35.00

○ Valdobbiadene Brut Dirupo	♼♼ 3
○ Valdobbiadene Brut Vign. Dirupo Extra Dry '12	♼♼ 2*
○ Cartizze	♼ 4

Luciano Arduini

LOC. CORRUBBIO
VIA BELVEDERE, 3
37029 SAN PIETRO IN CARIANO [VR]
TEL. 0457725880
www.arduinivini.it

CELLAR SALES
PRE-BOOKED VISITS
ANNUAL PRODUCTION 45,000 bottles
HECTARES UNDER VINE 8.00

● Valpolicella Cl. Sup. Ripasso '11	♼♼ 3
● Amarone della Valpolicella Cl. '09	♼ 5
● Valpolicella Cl. Fontana del Fongo '12	♼ 2

Astoria Vini

VIA CREVADA, 44
31020 REFRONTOLO [TV]
TEL. 04236699
www.astoria.it

CELLAR SALES
PRE-BOOKED VISITS
ANNUAL PRODUCTION 15.000,000 bottles
HECTARES UNDER VINE 40.00

○ Cartizze	♼♼ 4
○ Valdobbiadene Brut Casa di Vittorino	♼♼ 3
● Colli di Conegliano Rosso Croder '10	♼ 3
○ Valdobbiadene Extra Dry '12	♼ 3

Bellenda

FRAZ. CARPESICA
VIA GIARDINO, 90
31029 VITTORIO VENETO [TV]
TEL. 0438920025
www.bellenda.it

CELLAR SALES
PRE-BOOKED VISITS
ACCOMMODATION
ANNUAL PRODUCTION 1,000,000 bottles
HECTARES UNDER VINE 38.00

○ Conegliano Valdobbiadene Brut S.C. 1931 M. Cl.	♼♼ 3
○ Conegliano Valdobbiadene Sup. Brut San Fermo '12	♼♼ 3

Antonio Bigai

FRAZ. LISON
VIA CADUTI PER LA PATRIA, 29
30026 PORTOGRUARO [VE]
TEL. 336592660
www.amimanera.com

CELLAR SALES
ANNUAL PRODUCTION 35,000 bottles
HECTARES UNDER VINE 5.00

○ A Mi Manera Bianco '12	♼♼ 2*
○ Malvasia d'Istria '12	♼♼ 2*
○ Chardonnay A Mi Manera '12	♼ 2
○ Tai '12	♼ 2

Bonotto delle Tezze

FRAZ. TEZZE DI PIAVE
VIA DUCA D'AOSTA, 16
31020 VAZZOLA [TV]
TEL. 0438488323
www.bonottodelletezze.it

CELLAR SALES
PRE-BOOKED VISITS
ANNUAL PRODUCTION 120,000 bottles
HECTARES UNDER VINE 44.00

○ Manzoni Bianco Novalis '12	♼♼ 2*
● Piave Malanotte '09	♼♼ 6
○ Chardonnay Oseada '12	♼ 2
● Piave Raboso Potestà '09	♼ 3

F.lli Bortolin

FRAZ. SANTO STEFANO
VIA MENEGAZZI, 5
31049 VALDOBBIADENE [TV]
TEL. 0423900135
www.bortolin.com

CELLAR SALES
PRE-BOOKED VISITS
ANNUAL PRODUCTION 300,000 bottles
HECTARES UNDER VINE 20.00

○ Valdobbiadene Extra Dry Rù '12	♟♟ 3
○ Cartizze	♟ 4
○ Valdobbiadene Brut	♟ 2
○ Valdobbiadene Extra Dry	♟ 2

Canevel Spumanti

LOC. SACCOL
VIA ROCCAT E FERRARI, 17
31049 VALDOBBIADENE [TV]
TEL. 0423975940
www.canevel.it

PRE-BOOKED VISITS
ANNUAL PRODUCTION 700,000 bottles
HECTARES UNDER VINE 12.00
VITICULTURE METHOD Certified Organic

○ Valdobbiadene Extra Dry '12	♟♟ 4
○ Valdobbiadene Brut	♟ 3
○ Valdobbiadene Extra Dry	♟ 2
○ Valdobbiadene Extra Dry Vign. del Faè '12	♟ 4

Le Carline

VIA CARLINE, 24
30020 PRAMAGGIORE [VE]
TEL. 0421799741
www.lecarline.com

CELLAR SALES
PRE-BOOKED VISITS
ANNUAL PRODUCTION 400,000 bottles
HECTARES UNDER VINE 18.00
VITICULTURE METHOD Certified Organic

● Carline Rosso '10	♟♟ 3
○ Lison-Pramaggiore Cl. '12	♟♟ 2*
○ Dogale Passito	♟ 3
● Lison-Pramaggiore Refosco P.R. '12	♟ 2

Casa Geretto

VIA VANONI, 3
30029 SANTO STINO DI LIVENZA [VE]
TEL. 0421460253
www.geretto.it

CELLAR SALES
PRE-BOOKED VISITS
ANNUAL PRODUCTION 700,000 bottles
HECTARES UNDER VINE 39.00

● Friuli Aquileia Refosco P.R. V. V. Merk '11	♟♟ 3
● Friuli Aquileia Rosso Treuve Merk '11	♟♟ 3
● Lison-Pramaggiore Merlot Brumaio Merk '12	♟ 2

Castello di Lispida

VIA IV NOVEMBRE, 4
35043 MONSELICE [PD]
TEL. 0429780530
www.lispida.com

CELLAR SALES
PRE-BOOKED VISITS
ANNUAL PRODUCTION 18,000 bottles
HECTARES UNDER VINE 8.00

○ Amphora '11	♟♟ 6
● Terraforte '09	♟♟ 5
○ Terralba '12	♟♟ 5
● Montelispida '09	♟ 5

Col Sandago - Case Bianche

VIA BARRIERA, 41
31058 SUSEGANA [TV]
TEL. 043864468
www.colsandago.com

CELLAR SALES
PRE-BOOKED VISITS
ANNUAL PRODUCTION 400,000 bottles
HECTARES UNDER VINE 20.00

○ Conegliano Valdobbiadene Brut Vigna del Cuc	♟♟ 2*
○ Conegliano Valdobbiadene Extra Dry	♟♟ 2*

Corte Adami

VIA CIRCONVALLAZIONE ALDO MORO, 32
37038 SOAVE [VR]
TEL. 0457680423
www.corteadami.it

CELLAR SALES
ANNUAL PRODUCTION 50,000 bottles
HECTARES UNDER VINE 36.00

○ Soave V. della Corte '11	♟♟ 3
● Amarone della Valpolicella '09	♟ 6
○ Soave '12	♟ 2
● Valpolicella Sup. Ripasso '11	♟ 3

Corteforte

LOC. FUMANE
VIA OSAN, 45
37022 FUMANE [VR]
TEL. 0456839104
www.corteforte.com

CELLAR SALES
PRE-BOOKED VISITS
ACCOMMODATION AND RESTAURANT SERVICE
ANNUAL PRODUCTION 22,000 bottles
HECTARES UNDER VINE 2.90

● Amarone della Valpolicella Cl. Vign. di Osan '05	♟♟ 7
● Valpolicella Cl. Sup. Ripasso Podere Bertarole '10	♟♟ 4

Alla Costiera

VIA NINA, 900
35030 VÒ [PD]
TEL. 0499940492
www.allacostiera.it

ANNUAL PRODUCTION 30,000 bottles
HECTARES UNDER VINE 7.00

● Colli Euganei Cabernet Franc '11	♟♟ 3
● Colli Euganei Cabernet Sauvignon '11	♟ 3
○ Colli Euganei Fior d'Arancio Secco Agnese '12	♟ 3

Valentina Cubi

VIA CASTERNA, 60
37022 FUMANE [VR]
TEL. 0457701806
www.valentinacubi.it

CELLAR SALES
PRE-BOOKED VISITS
ANNUAL PRODUCTION 35,000 bottles
HECTARES UNDER VINE 10.00
VITICULTURE METHOD Certified Organic

● Amarone della Valpolicella Cl. Morar '08	♟♟ 7
● Valpolicella Cl. Iperico '12	♟♟ 2*
● Valpolicella Cl. Sup. Il Tabarro '10	♟ 3

Giulietta Dal Bosco

VIA CAPOVILLA, 10A
37030 MEZZANE DI SOTTO [VR]
TEL. 045 8880396
www.sisure.it

ANNUAL PRODUCTION 6,000 bottles
HECTARES UNDER VINE 2.00

● Amarone della Valpolicella '06	♟♟ 5
● Valpolicella Sup. '07	♟♟ 5
● Valpolicella Sup. Ripasso '07	♟ 5

F.lli Farina

LOC. PEDEMONTE
VIA BOLLA, 11
37029 SAN PIETRO IN CARIANO [VR]
TEL. 0457701349
www.farinawines.com

CELLAR SALES
PRE-BOOKED VISITS
ANNUAL PRODUCTION 600,000 bottles
HECTARES UNDER VINE 10.00

● Amarone della Valpolicella Cl. Montefante Ris. '07	♟♟ 8
● Valpolicella Cl. Sup. Ripasso Montecorna '11	♟ 3

La Ghidina

LOC. DOSSOBUONO
VIA CADELLORA, 10
37062 VILLAFRANCA DI VERONA [VR]
TEL. 0458008721
www.ancillalugana.it

○ Lugana La Ghidina '09	♥♥	3
○ Lugana 1909 '12	♥	3
○ Lugana Ancilla '11	♥	3
○ Lugana Ella '12	♥	3

Le Morette

V.LE INDIPENDENZA
37019 PESCHIERA DEL GARDA [VR]
TEL. 0457552724
www.lemorette.it

CELLAR SALES
ANNUAL PRODUCTION 120,000 bottles
HECTARES UNDER VINE 24.00

○ Lugana Benedictus '11	♥♥	3
○ Lugana V. La Mandolara '12	♥	2

Malibràn

VIA BARCA II, 63
31058 SUSEGANA [TV]
TEL. 0438781410
www.malibranvini.it

CELLAR SALES
PRE-BOOKED VISITS
ANNUAL PRODUCTION 80,000 bottles
HECTARES UNDER VINE 7.00

○ Valdobbiadene Brut 5 Grammi	♥♥	2*
○ Valdobbiadene Dry	♥♥	3
○ Valdobbiadene Brut Ruio	♥	2
○ Valdobbiadene Extra Dry	♥	2

Le Mandolare

LOC. BROGNOLIGO
VIA SAMBUCO, 180
37032 MONTEFORTE D'ALPONE [VR]
TEL. 0456175083
www.cantinalemandolare.com

CELLAR SALES
PRE-BOOKED VISITS
ANNUAL PRODUCTION 65,000 bottles
HECTARES UNDER VINE 20.00

○ Soave Cl. Monte Sella '11	♥♥	3
○ Il Vignale Passito '10	♥	4
○ Soave Cl. Corte Menini '12	♥	2
○ Soave Cl. Il Roccolo '12	♥	2

Monte Santoccio

LOC. SANTOCCIO, 6
37022 FUMANE [VR]
TEL. 3496461223
www.montesantoccio.it

ANNUAL PRODUCTION 14,000 bottles
HECTARES UNDER VINE 3.00

● Amarone della Valpolicella Cl. '09	♥♥	7
● Valpolicella Cl. Sup. Rip. '10	♥♥	4
● Valpolicella Cl. Sup. '10	♥	4

Monte Zovo

LOC. ZOVO, 23A
37013 CAPRINO VERONESE [VR]
TEL. 0457281301
www.montezovo.com

CELLAR SALES
PRE-BOOKED VISITS
ACCOMMODATION AND RESTAURANT SERVICE
ANNUAL PRODUCTION 1,000,000 bottles
HECTARES UNDER VINE 100.00

● Amarone della Valpolicella '07	♥♥	8
● Valpolicella Sup. Ripasso '11	♥♥	4
○ Sauvignon Bianco del Veneto '12	♥	4
● Valpolicella '12	♥	2

Marco Mosconi

VIA PARADISO, 5
37031 ILLASI [VR]
TEL. 0456529109
www.marcomosconi.it

CELLAR SALES
PRE-BOOKED VISITS
ANNUAL PRODUCTION 25,000 bottles
HECTARES UNDER VINE 10.00

● Amarone della Valpolicella '09	♟♟ 8
● Recioto della Valpolicella '07	♟♟ 6
○ Soave Corte Paradiso '12	♟ 2
● Valpolicella Sup. '09	♟ 5

Walter Nardin

LOC. RONCADELLE
VIA FONTANE, 5
31024 ORMELLE [TV]
TEL. 0422851622
www.vinwalternardin.it

PRE-BOOKED VISITS
ANNUAL PRODUCTION 350,000 bottles
HECTARES UNDER VINE 30.00

● Rosso della Ghiaia La Zerbaia '09	♟♟ 3
● Refosco P. R. La Zerbaia '09	♟ 3
● Venezia Cabernet Franc '12	♟ 2
● Venezia Merlot '12	♟ 2

Orto di Venezia

LOC. ISOLA DI SANT'ERASMO
VIA DELLE MOTTE, 1
30141 VENEZIA
TEL. 0415237410
www.ortodivenezia.com

○ Orto '10	♟♟ 5

Paladin

VIA POSTUMIA, 12
30020 ANNONE VENETO [VE]
TEL. 0422768167
www.paladin.it

CELLAR SALES
PRE-BOOKED VISITS
ACCOMMODATION
ANNUAL PRODUCTION 950,000 bottles
HECTARES UNDER VINE 90.00

● Malbech Gli Aceri '10	♟♟ 6
● Lison-Pramaggiore Refosco P.R. '12	♟ 3
○ Prosecco Extra Dry Mill. '12	♟ 3
● Raboso Fiore Frizzante '12	♟ 3

Umberto Portinari

LOC. BROGNOLIGO
VIA SANTO STEFANO, 2
37032 MONTEFORTE D'ALPONE [VR]
TEL. 0456175087
portinarivini@libero.it

CELLAR SALES
PRE-BOOKED VISITS
ANNUAL PRODUCTION 30,000 bottles
HECTARES UNDER VINE 4.00

○ Soave Albare '11	♟♟ 2*
○ Soave Cl. Ronchetto '12	♟♟ 2*
○ Recioto di Soave Oro '10	♟ 5

Raval

VIA RAVAL, 1
37011 BARDOLINO [VR]
TEL. 045 7236569

ANNUAL PRODUCTION 95,000 bottles
HECTARES UNDER VINE 12.00

● Bardolino Cl. Sup. '11	♟♟ 2*
⊙ Bardolino Chiaretto Brut	♟ 3
⊙ Bardolino Chiaretto Cl. '12	♟ 2
● Bardolino Cl. '12	♟ 1*

Urbano Salvan

LOC. PIGOZZO
VIA MINCANA, 143
35020 DUE CARRARE [PD]
TEL. 049525841
www.salvan.it

CELLAR SALES
PRE-BOOKED VISITS
ANNUAL PRODUCTION 30,000 bottles
HECTARES UNDER VINE 20.00

● Colli Euganei Cabernet Sauvignon San Marco '09	♟♟ 3

Marco Sambin

LOC. VALNOGAREDO
VIA, FATTORELLE 20A
35030 CINTO EUGANEO [PD]
TEL. 3493625965
www.vinimarcus.com

CELLAR SALES
PRE-BOOKED VISITS
ANNUAL PRODUCTION 7.600 bottles
HECTARES UNDER VINE 3.00

● Marcus '10	♟♟ 5
● Micael '11	♟♟ 5
● Francisca '09	♟ 5
● Johannes '11	♟ 5

Sanfeletto

VIA BORGO ANTIGA, 39
31020 SAN PIETRO DI FELETTO [TV]
TEL. 0438486832
www.sanfeletto.it

CELLAR SALES
PRE-BOOKED VISITS
ANNUAL PRODUCTION 150,000 bottles
HECTARES UNDER VINE 4.00

○ Conegliano Valdobbiadene Brut Bosco di Fratta	♟♟ 2*
○ Conegliano Valdobbiadene Extra Dry	♟♟ 2*
○ Conegliano Valdobbiadene Brut	♟ 2

Tenuta Sant'Anna

LOC. LONCON
VIA MONSIGNOR P. L. ZOVATTO, 71
30020 ANNONE VENETO [VE]
TEL. 0422864511
www.tenutasantanna.it

CELLAR SALES
PRE-BOOKED VISITS
ANNUAL PRODUCTION 2,500,000 bottles
HECTARES UNDER VINE 140.00

● Lison-Pramaggiore Cabernet Sauvignon P 47 '09	♟♟ 3
○ Lison-Pramaggiore Chardonnay Goccia '12	♟ 2

Santa Sofia

FRAZ. PEDEMONTE
VIA CA' DEDÉ, 61
37020 SAN PIETRO IN CARIANO [VR]
TEL. 0457701074
www.santasofia.com

CELLAR SALES
PRE-BOOKED VISITS
ANNUAL PRODUCTION 550,000 bottles
HECTARES UNDER VINE 38.00

○ Lugana '12	♟♟ 2*
● Valpolicella Sup. Ripasso '10	♟♟ 3
● Predaia '06	♟ 4
● Recioto della Valpolicella Cl. '09	♟ 5

Le Tende

FRAZ. COLÀ DI LAZISE
VIA TENDE, 35
37017 LAZISE [VR]
TEL. 0457590748
www.letende.it

CELLAR SALES
PRE-BOOKED VISITS
ANNUAL PRODUCTION 80,000 bottles
HECTARES UNDER VINE 10.00

● Bardolino Cl. Sup. '11	♟♟ 2*
○ Bianco di Custoza Lucillini '12	♟♟ 2*
● Bardolino Cl. '12	♟ 2
○ Bianco di Custoza '12	♟ 2

Cantina Sociale della Valpantena

Fraz. Quinto
Via Colonia Orfani di Guerra, 5b
37034 Verona
Tel. 045550032
www.cantinavalpantena.it

CELLAR SALES
PRE-BOOKED VISITS
ANNUAL PRODUCTION 8,000,000 bottles
HECTARES UNDER VINE 718.00

● Valpolicella Sup. Ripasso Torre del Falasco '11	❦❦ 3
● Valpolicella Sup. Torre del Falasco '11	❦ 2

Villa Erbice

Via Villa, 22
37030 Mezzane di Sotto [VR]
Tel. 0458880086
agricolavillaerbice@virgilio.it

CELLAR SALES
PRE-BOOKED VISITS
ANNUAL PRODUCTION 90,000 bottles
HECTARES UNDER VINE 15.00

● Amarone della Valpolicella Vign. Tremenel '07	❦❦ 6
● Recioto della Valpolicella Terrazzine '11	❦❦ 5
● Valpolicella Sup. Ripasso '09	❦ 3

Villa Monteleone

Fraz. Gargagnago
Via Monteleone, 12
37020 Sant'Ambrogio di Valpolicella [VR]
Tel. 0457704974
www.villamonteleone.com

CELLAR SALES
PRE-BOOKED VISITS
ACCOMMODATION
ANNUAL PRODUCTION 40,000 bottles
HECTARES UNDER VINE 6.00

● Amarone della Valpolicella Cl. '09	❦❦ 7
● Valpolicella Cl. Campo S. Lena '12	❦❦ 2*
● Valpolicella Cl. Sup. Campo S. Vito '11	❦ 4

Villa Angarano

Via Corte, 15
36061 Bassano del Grappa [VI]
Tel. 0424503086
www.villaangarano.com

CELLAR SALES
PRE-BOOKED VISITS
ANNUAL PRODUCTION 40,000 bottles
HECTARES UNDER VINE 8.00

○ Ca' Michiel '10	❦❦ 4
● Quare di Angarano '09	❦❦ 3
● Breganze Rosso Angarano '10	❦ 3
● Breganze Torcolato San Biagio Ris. '10	❦ 2

Villa Medici

Via Campagnol, 11
37066 Sommacampagna [VR]
Tel. 045515147
www.cantinavillamedici.it

ANNUAL PRODUCTION 220,000 bottles
HECTARES UNDER VINE 32.00

○ Custoza '12	❦❦ 2*
● Bardolino '12	❦ 2
● Bardolino Sup. '10	❦ 3
○ Custoza Sup. '11	❦ 2

Zardetto Spumanti

Via Martiri delle Foibe, 18
31015 Conegliano [TV]
Tel. 0438394969
www.zardettoprosecco.com

CELLAR SALES
PRE-BOOKED VISITS
ANNUAL PRODUCTION 1,900,000 bottles
HECTARES UNDER VINE 25.00

○ Conegliano Valdobbiadene Sup. Cartizze '12	❦❦ 5
○ Conegliano Valdobbiadene Sup. Brut Refosso '12	❦❦ 3

FRIULI VENEZIA GIULIA

The wines of Friuli Venezia Giulia reap their just rewards yet again. In this year's Guide we gave accolades to 24 wines, 22 of which are white. No other region in Italy vaunts a landscape so lavish and extensive that it can notch up so many Tre Bicchieri awards for white wines. Meanwhile, we might mention the two prizewinning reds, which were the excellent Sacrisassi Rosso 2011 de Le Due Terre by winemakers Silvana and Flavio Basilicata, and Le Vigne di Zamò's Merlot Vigne Cinquant'anni 2009, a winner for its fullness and complexity. Among the whites, we find five newcomers to the Tre Bicchieri club, starting with Collio-based Draga's excellent Malvasia 2010 and the stunning Collio 2012 from Ronco Blanchis. Colli Orientali proffered the fantastic Bianco Eclisse 2012 from La Roncaia; an elegant, spirited Friulano Vigna delle Robinie 2011 from Ronc Soreli; finally, we tasted Torre Rosazza's sumptuous Pinot Grigio 2012. This year we can confirm an excellent result from another Colli Orientali winery, Volpe Pasini, which took two awards, one for its classic Sauvignon Zuc di Volpe 2012 and another for the amazing Pinot Bianco 2012 in the same line. The two other great Colli wines are Meroi's rich, fruity Friulano 2011 and Livio Felluga's ultra-classic Rosazzo Terre Alte 2011. After many years of silence, a Grave white takes home an award, with a Pinot Blanc 2012 from Le Monde, a fast-growing cellar. For the record, we should also say that in terms of the many "authentic" wines we tasted, those from Friuli were some of the most genuine and convincing performers of natural winemaking. Alongside a striking Breg Amphora 2006 from the undisputed master, Josko Gravner, we have two excellent versions of Skerk's Ograde 2011 and Podversic's Malvasia 2009. The Collios, even those that are not DOC certified, offer us two great blends. One is Jermann's Vintage Tunina 2010, with its usual clean elegance and a screw cap. Some food for thought, there! The other is Livon's fleshy, fruity Braide Alte 2011. The 2012 vintage Collio DOCs showed a real trend of confident Malvasias like Princic, Raccaro and Ronco dei Tassi, all sending three beautiful interpretations, without forgetting the Toròs Friulano and a stalwart, delicious Sauvignon from Venica & Venica. Isonzo's two flagship producers are Vie di Romans and Lis Neris, and neither let the side down this year: the Friulano Dolée 2011 from the former, and the latter's Pinot Grigio Gris 2011, are some of the most fascinating whites we tasted in Friuli this year.

Tenuta di Angoris

LOC. ANGORIS, 7
34071 CORMÒNS [GO]
TEL. 048160923
www.angoris.com

CELLAR SALES
PRE-BOOKED VISITS
ANNUAL PRODUCTION 750,000 bottles
HECTARES UNDER VINE 110.00

Angoris has named its line of Classic Method sparklers 1648, a homage to the founding year of a winery that vaunts over three centuries of history and many owners. Eminent businesswoman Claudia Locatelli currently directs the operation. The estate's 630 hectares extend over the hills and countryside of Cormòns, with a full 130 of those under vine. Many of the vineyards surround the estate villa in the Friuli Isonzo DOC, while others lie in the Collio and Colli Orientali del Friuli DOCs. Marco Simonit and Alessandro Dal Zovo oversee, respectively, the vineyards and the cellars, ensuring Angoris enjoys increasing quality. Just as last year, we were most convinced by the Pignolo 2007 from the Angoris line, with its excellent balsamic shades, fruity flavour and delicate hint of liquorice. The fragrant, varietal Friulano 2012 also showed excellent quality, and the Bianco Spiule 2010 and Rosso Ravòst 2010 both had great character.

Antonutti

FRAZ. COLLOREDO DI PRATO
VIA D'ANTONI, 21
33037 PASIAN DI PRATO [UD]
TEL. 0432662001
www.antonuttivini.it

CELLAR SALES
PRE-BOOKED VISITS
ANNUAL PRODUCTION 700,000 bottles
HECTARES UNDER VINE 46.00

Together with their respective children, Caterina and Nicola, life partners Adriana and Lino run their wine properties in Colloredo di Prato, near Udine, and Barbeano, in the municipality of Spilimbergo. The vineyards of both extend out over the vast Grave del Friuli plain, a rocky, challenging environment. It's no surprise, then, that this family operation is deeply rooted in the area and its winemaking traditions, with over a century of experience here. But they display a pronounced sensitivity to innovation too, as exhibited in their Vis Terrae line. It eloquently expresses the quality potential of this terroir, with wines that are self-confident and aromatically distinctive. The broad range of wines tasted confirmed their perfectly decent quality, especially considering the price. This year we slightly preferred the Pinot Grigio 2012, with hay and ripe apple aromas, and the Pinot Nero 2011, an intriguing wine, supple and caressing on the palate.

○ COF Friulano '12	♟♟ 3
● COF Pignolo '07	♟♟ 5
● COF Ravòst '10	♟♟ 3
○ COF Spiule '10	♟♟ 4
○ Friuli Isonzo Friulano Villa Locatelli '12	♟♟ 2*
○ Friuli Isonzo Pinot Grigio Villa Locatelli '12	♟♟ 3
○ Friuli Isonzo Pinot Bianco Villa Locatelli '12	♟ 2
○ Friuli Isonzo Sauvignon Villa Locatelli '12	♟ 3
○ Modolet Bianco Brut	♟ 2
○ 1648 Brut '08	♟♟ 5
☉ 1648 Rosé '07	♟♟ 5
○ COF Bianco Spiule '09	♟♟ 4
○ COF Friulano '11	♟♟ 3*
○ COF Friulano Vôs da Vigne '10	♟♟ 3
● COF Pignolo '06	♟♟ 5
○ COF Sauvignon Vôs da Vigne '10	♟♟ 3

○ Friuli Grave Pinot Grigio '12	♟♟ 2*
● Friuli Grave Pinot Nero '11	♟♟ 2*
○ Brut M. Cl. Ant '09	♟ 5
● Friuli Grave Merlot '11	♟ 2
● Friuli Grave Merlot Vis Terrae '08	♟ 3
○ Friuli Grave Pinot Grigio Vis Terrae '11	♟ 3
○ Friuli Grave Traminer Aromatico '11	♟ 2
● Friuli Grave Cabernet '10	♟♟ 2*
○ Friuli Grave Pinot Grigio '10	♟♟ 3
○ Friuli Grave Traminer Aromatico Vis Terrae '09	♟♟ 5
○ Lindul '10	♟♟ 6
○ Lindul '08	♟♟ 8

Aquila del Torre

FRAZ. SAVORGNANO DEL TORRE
VIA ATTIMIS, 25
33040 POVOLETTO [UD]
TEL. 0432666428
www.aquiladeltorre.it

CELLAR SALES
PRE-BOOKED VISITS
ACCOMMODATION
ANNUAL PRODUCTION 50,000 bottles
HECTARES UNDER VINE 18.00
VITICULTURE METHOD Certified Organic

Aquila del Torre, whose activities go back to the early 20th century, was purchased in 1996 by the Ciani family. They immediately launched an ambitious programme of vineyard restructuring with the objective of preserving the priceless indigenous biotypes. Claudio Ciani laid the foundations, and son Michele, with a degree in agrarian sciences and professional experience in Alsace, now oversees production. In the multi-level cellar set amidst the surrounding woods, they separately vinify grapes from 16 vineyard parcels subdivided according to the pedoclimate of the Savorgnano del Torre slopes. Coming close to our highest award, this excellent Friulano Ronc di Miez 2011 shows great texture and personality, aromas of spring flowers and beeswax, and an intense, pleasant flavour. Also outstanding, the Sauvignon Vit dai Maz 2011 recalls bergamot, and the Oasi 2011 is dry vinified from picolit.

● COF Friulano Ronc di Miez '11	♟♟ 5	
○ COF At Friulano '12	♟♟ 3	
● COF At Refosco P. R. '10	♟♟ 3	
○ COF At Sauvignon Blanc '12	♟♟ 3	
○ COF Picolit '10	♟♟ 6	
☺ OOr Cauvignon Vit dai Maz '11	♟♟ 6	
○ Oasi '11	♟♟ 6	
○ COF Riesling '11	♟ 3	
○ COF At Friulano '11	♟♟ 3	
● COF At Refosco P. R. '09	♟♟ 3	
○ COF At Sauvignon Blanc '11	♟♟ 3	
○ COF At Sauvignon Blanc '10	♟♟ 3*	
○ COF Picolit '09	♟♟ 6	
● COF Solsire '09	♟♟ 5	
○ Oasi '10	♟♟ 6	

Bastianich

LOC. GAGLIANO
VIA DARNAZZACCO, 44/2
33043 CIVIDALE DEL FRIULI [UD]
TEL. 0432700943
www.bastianich.com

CELLAR SALES
PRE-BOOKED VISITS
ACCOMMODATION AND RESTAURANT SERVICE
ANNUAL PRODUCTION 180,000 bottles
HECTARES UNDER VINE 33.00

It seems like nearly everyone knows Joe and Lidia Bastianich, owners of a string of restaurants in the U.S. known for their fine Italian foods and wines. In 1997, Joe decided to launch a winery in Friuli, in Gagliano, near Cividale, which he visits frequently and directs personally to this day. A smoothly operating, expert team takes care of production, with Claudio Rizzi as general manager, Wayne Young in marketing and public relations, and Denis Lepore in sales. The lengthy winemaking experience of Emilio Del Medico and consulting services of Maurizio Castelli ensure that quality remains high. Three wines landed in our finals. The Vespa Bianco 2011 is a particularly complex and multi-layered wine from equal parts of chardonnay and sauvignon with a magical touch of picolit. This wine shows aromas of dried flowers, honey and russet pears, and is creamy and flavourful.

○ Plus '09	♟♟ 6	
○ Vespa Bianco '11	♟♟ 5	
● Vespa Rosso '10	♟♟ 5	
● Calabrone '09	♟♟ 8	
○ COF Friulano Vigne Orsone '12	♟♟ 3	
○ COF Sauvignon Vigne Orsone '12	♟♟ 3	
○ COF Tocai Friulano Plus '02	♟♟♟ 3*	
○ Vespa Bianco '04	♟♟♟ 4	
○ Vespa Bianco '03	♟♟♟ 4	
○ Vespa Bianco '01	♟♟♟ 4	
○ Vespa Bianco '00	♟♟♟ 3	
○ Vespa Bianco '99	♟♟♟ 3*	
○ Malvasia Istriana '07	♟♟ 4	
○ Vespa Bianco '09	♟♟ 5	
○ Vespa Bianco '08	♟♟ 5	
○ Vespa Bianco '07	♟♟ 5	

Benincasa

LOC. SPESSA DI CIVIDALE
S.DA RONCHI SAN GIUSEPPE, 5
33043 CIVIDALE DEL FRIULI [UD]
TEL. 0432716419
vinibenincasa@libero.it

ANNUAL PRODUCTION 25,000 bottles
HECTARES UNDER VINE 10.00

In the early 1990s, Franco Benincasa had the chance to purchase a land holding that included a cottage surrounded by vineyards. With skilful remodelling, he transformed that cottage into a comfortable residence with an attached cellar, in perfect harmony with surrounding nature. He entrusted management to his two daughters, Anna and Francesca, who assumed responsibility for estate development and vinification, assisted in planning the vineyard by Rainer Zierok, a renowned professor from San Michele all'Adige. They chose to produce just a few, high-quality wines, entrusted care of the vineyards to Carlo Petrussi, and availed themselves of valuable oenological consulting from Donato Lanati. This is the first year wines from this estate have been tasted, and they have received considerable scores. First place goes to the stylistically perfect, varietal Sauvignon 2010 that reached the finals because of its excellent aroma, and pleasant, persistent palate.

○ COF Sauvignon '10	♟♟ 4
○ COF Chardonnay '11	♟♟ 4
● COF Pignolo '09	♟♟ 7
○ COF Pinot Grigio '11	♟♟ 4
○ COF Valderada '08	♟♟ 5

Borgo del Tiglio

FRAZ. BRAZZANO
VIA SAN GIORGIO, 71
34070 CORMÒNS [GO]
TEL. 048162166

CELLAR SALES
PRE-BOOKED VISITS
ANNUAL PRODUCTION 35,000 bottles
HECTARES UNDER VINE 8.50

Wines from Nicola Manferrari, owner of Borgo del Tiglio, reflect his determined, precise character. His past as a pharmacist led him to seek a natural balance between the soul of an alchemist and that of an apothecary, accustomed to measuring himself against the precision of the balances. His wines are the result of strict vineyard selections and low grape yields per plant. He aims for wines that stand up to time and are complex, elegant and structured, with great class and personality, a benchmark for many fans of Friuli wines, even at international level. It may take a few years to appreciate them fully, but they are well worth it. We could only taste two wines from the 2010 vintage and both deservedly landed in our finals. They stood out in elegance, structure and personality, and proved themselves leading players and ambassadors for the potential of the unique Collio terroir.

○ Collio Bianco '10	♟♟ 5
○ Collio Malvasia '10	♟♟ 6
○ Collio Bianco Ronco della Chiesa '06	♟♟♟ 6
○ Collio Bianco Ronco della Chiesa '02	♟♟♟ 6
○ Collio Bianco Ronco della Chiesa '01	♟♟♟ 6
○ Collio Bianco Ronco della Chiesa '09	♟♟ 6
○ Collio Malvasia '09	♟♟ 6
● Collio Rosso della Centa '06	♟♟ 8
○ Collio Sauvignon '09	♟♟ 4

Borgo delle Oche

via Borgo Alpi, 5,
33098 Valvasone [PN]
Tel. 0434840640
www.borgodelleoche.it

CELLAR SALES
PRE-BOOKED VISITS
ANNUAL PRODUCTION 40,000 bottles
HECTARES UNDER VINE 7.00

Borgo delle Oche is a newly-minted operation, launched officially in 2004. It takes its name from the splendid hamlet where it is located, which in turn lies in the medieval area of Valvasone, in the province of Pordenone. It was founded by Luisa Menini and Nicola Pittini, united in both life and work, she with a degree in food technology, he in agronomy and oenology. Luisa, who has always nourished a passion for the outdoors, lavishes on the vines all the attention they need to produce perfect fruit, which then goes to Nicola for transformation. The results are wines that are the highest expression of the quality potential of the Grave area. Intriguing and amusing, this sweet Traminer Alba 2011, from part-dried traminer aromatico grapes, has a bouquet of propolis, dried apricots and dates, and a caressing, indelible palate. The other wines were excellent, linear and fragrant, with special praise for the sparkling Spumante Terra & Cielo Brut.

○ Traminer Aromatico Alba '11	🍷🍷 5
● Merlot '10	🍷🍷 2*
○ Pinot Grigio '12	🍷🍷 2*
● Rosso Svual '09	🍷🍷 3
○ Terra & Cielo Brut	🍷🍷 3
○ Traminer Aromatico '12	🍷🍷 2*
● Refosco P. R. '10	🍷 2
○ Bianco Alba '09	YY 3*
○ Bianco Alba '08	YY 3*
○ Bianco Alba '07	YY 4
○ Bianco Lupi Terrae '07	YY 3*
○ Pinot Grigio '07	YY 2

Borgo Judrio

via Aquileia, 79
33040 Corno di Rosazzo [UD]
Tel. 0432755896
www.viniborgojudrio.it

CELLAR SALES
PRE-BOOKED VISITS
ANNUAL PRODUCTION 20,000 bottles
HECTARES UNDER VINE 12.00

The Gigante family and their Corno di Rosazzo-based winery of the same name have been for some time now synonymous with high quality wines. Brothers Alberto and Ariedo Gigante decided in 2007 to go down the path of independence and started their own operation, naming it after the Judrio river, which separates the region's two finest viticultural zones, Collio and Colli Orientali del Friuli. Passionate about their land and their vineyards, the Gigante brothers, following their tried and true policy of providing consistent quality at very reasonable prices, have crafted a line of wines that won immediate admiration for their no-nonsense self-confidence and easy drinkability. An excellent performance comes from these fresh, fragrant and convincing vintage white wines. The refined, varietal Sauvignon 2012 won us over with a white peach aroma and satisfying palate. The Friulano and Ribolla Gialla, both from 2012, displayed delicious, citrussy notes, and rich flavour and minerality.

○ COF Friulano '12	🍷🍷 2*
○ COF Ribolla Gialla '12	🍷🍷 2*
○ COF Sauvignon '12	🍷🍷 2*
○ Brut 3 Uve	🍷 2
● COF Cabernet Franc '11	🍷 2
● COF Merlot '11	🍷 2
● COF Refosco P. R. '10	🍷 2
● COF Cabernet Sauvignon '10	YY 2*
○ COF Chardonnay '10	YY 2*
○ COF Friulano '11	YY 2*
○ COF Friulano '09	YY 2*
● COF Refosco P. R. '09	YY 2*
● COF Refosco P. R. '06	YY 2*
○ COF Sauvignon '11	YY 2*
○ COF Sauvignon '08	YY 2*
○ COF Verduzzo Friulano '10	YY 2*

★Borgo San Daniele

VIA SAN DANIELE, 16
34071 CORMÒNS [GO]
TEL. 048160552
www.borgosandaniele.it

Borgo Savaian

VIA SAVAIAN, 36
34071 CORMÒNS [GO]
TEL. 048160725
stefanobastiani@libero.it

CELLAR SALES
PRE-BOOKED VISITS
ACCOMMODATION
ANNUAL PRODUCTION 56,000 bottles
HECTARES UNDER VINE 18.75

CELLAR SALES
PRE-BOOKED VISITS
ANNUAL PRODUCTION 100,000 bottles
HECTARES UNDER VINE 18.00

Borgo San Daniele is the story of a brother and sister, Mauro and Alessandra, both courageous and perhaps a tad foolhardy, who decided to change the course of their life and dedicate themselves totally to the vineyard left to them by their grandfather. In a remarkably short period of time, Mauro's viticultural talents bore superb fruit. Only four of their wines bear the name Borgo San Daniele, two monovarietals and two blends, in addition to Gortmarin, produced only in exceptional vintages. They gave the name Arbis, or "weeds", to the blends, for the grasses that are allowed to sprout up in the vineyards to dampen the vines' vigour and mitigate the effects of a grape growing monoculture. A new item this year, the Malvasia 2011 went straight to the finals because of its complex, pleasant bouquet that recalls bay leaf, as well as wafer and white chocolate, and its well-balanced palate. The Pinot Grigio 2011 is also stunning and elegant, with hints of aloe and yellow plum.

Borgo Savaian traces its beginnings to 2001, when Stefano and Rosanna Bastiani, who inherited the family operation from their father Mario, gave it the name of the small hamlet in Cormòns where it is located, at the foot of Monte Quarin. The cellar has been recently restructured and substantially enlarged, so Stefano is able to work more efficiently and apply the precious lessons from his family traditions and oenology studies. Reasonable prices and consistent quality are the distinctive hallmarks of their wines, which have won appreciation for their faithful transmission of varietal characteristics. The last vintage produced three outstanding white wines: the Sauvignon 2012, refined, fresh and fragrant on the nose, refreshing and citrussy on the palate; the Malvasia 2012, soft and fruity on the palate; and the Pinot Bianco 2012 with a curious caramel note, nicely tangy on the palate.

○ Friuli Isonzo Malvasia '11	♀♀ 4	
○ Friuli Isonzo Pinot Grigio '11	♀♀ 4	
● Arbis Ros '07	♀♀ 5	
○ Friuli Isonzo Friulano '11	♀♀ 4	
○ Arbis Blanc '11	♀ 4	
○ Arbis Blanc '10	♀♀♀ 4*	
○ Arbis Blanc '09	♀♀♀ 4	
○ Arbis Blanc '05	♀♀♀ 4	
○ Friuli Isonzo Friulano '08	♀♀♀ 4*	
○ Friuli Isonzo Friulano '07	♀♀♀ 4*	
● Gortmarin '03	♀♀♀ 5	
○ Friuli Isonzo Friulano '09	♀♀ 4	
● Gortmarin '06	♀♀ 7	

○ Collio Pinot Bianco '12	♀♀ 3	
○ Collio Sauvignon '12	♀♀ 3	
○ Friuli Isonzo Malvasia '12	♀♀ 3	
○ Collio Friulano '12	♀ 3	
● Friuli Isonzo Cabernet Franc '12	♀ 3	
○ Friuli Isonzo Traminer Aromatico '12	♀ 3	
● Collio Merlot Tolrem '08	♀♀ 4	
● Collio Merlot Tolrem '07	♀♀ 3	
○ Collio Pinot Bianco '05	♀♀ 2*	
○ Collio Pinot Grigio '05	♀♀ 2	
○ Collio Sauvignon '08	♀♀ 3*	
● Friuli Isonzo Cabernet Franc '07	♀♀ 3*	
○ Friuli Isonzo Traminer Aromatico '11	♀♀ 3	

Cav. Emiro Bortolusso

VIA OLTREGORGO, 10
33050 CARLINO [UD]
TEL. 043167596
www.bortolusso.it

CELLAR SALES
PRE-BOOKED VISITS
ACCOMMODATION
ANNUAL PRODUCTION 120,000 bottles
HECTARES UNDER VINE 40.00

Sergio and Clara continue developing the quality potential of the local growing area, following in the footsteps of their father Emiro, who was one of the foremost promoters of the Annia DOC. This ever-growing and constantly improving operation lies on the Adriatic Riviera, just back from the Marano Lagunare nature oasis, among fishing ponds and endless rows of vines in a truly striking and unusual landscape. The Bortolussos vinify only their estate-grown grapes, which benefit from the favourable influence of the sea, displaying a crisp tanginess as their primary sensory hallmark. The competitive price-tags of the wines, which certainly increase their attractiveness, should not go unremarked. The Malvasia 2012 always achieves greatest consensus with its citrussy bouquet and a palate that shows flavour, fullness and minerality. The Sauvignon 2012 is outstandingly supple and drinkable. The Friulano 2012 has rosemary and dried sage aromas, and adds a pleasant iodine note to the varietal quality.

○ Friuli Annia Friulano '12		♟♟ 2*
○ Friuli Annia Malvasia '12		♟♟ 2*
○ Friuli Annia Sauvignon '12		♟♟ 2*
● Friuli Annia Cabernet Franc '12		♟ 2
● Friuli Annia Refosco P. R. '11		♟ 3
○ Friuli Annia Traminer Aromatico '12		♟ 2
○ Friuli Annia Malvasia '11		♟♟ 2*
○ Friuli Annia Malvasia '10		♟♟ 2*
○ Friuli Annia Malvasia '09		♟♟ 2*
○ Friuli Annia Malvasia '08		♟♟ 2*
○ Friuli Annia Traminer Aromatico '10		♟♟ 2*

Branko

LOC. ZEGLA, 20
34071 CORMÒNS [GO]
TEL. 0481639826
info@brankowines.com

CELLAR SALES
PRE-BOOKED VISITS
ANNUAL PRODUCTION 45,000 bottles
HECTARES UNDER VINE 9.00

Igor Erzetic's wine operation bears the name of his father Branko, who in 1950 legally formalized a family wine-growing tradition that stretched back many generations. First Branko and later Igor planted the rows of vine that surround the winery in Zegla near Cormòns and gently descend the surrounding slopes of Plessiva and Novali, both highly-respected crus in the Gorizia area. The modest size of the operation and the restricted number of bottlings allow Igor to focus all his energies tightly on production to obtain the highest possible level of quality from the grapes that he himself cultivates, tends and selects. Again this year, two wines merited a place in our finals. The Pinot Grigio 2012 is embellished with refined, persuasive notes on the nose, and a fragrant, electric palate. The Sauvignon 2012 brings out the notoriously vegetal, varietal characteristics, with exotic hints echoed on the palate.

○ Collio Pinot Grigio '12		♟♟ 4
○ Collio Sauvignon '12		♟♟ 4
○ Collio Chardonnay '12		♟♟ 4
○ Collio Friulano '12		♟♟ 4
○ Collio Pinot Grigio '08		♟♟♟ 3*
○ Collio Pinot Grigio '07		♟♟♟ 3
○ Collio Pinot Grigio '06		♟♟♟ 3
○ Collio Chardonnay '11		♟♟ 3*
○ Collio Chardonnay '08		♟♟ 3
○ Collio Friulano '11		♟♟ 3*
○ Collio Friulano '08		♟♟ 3
○ Collio Pinot Grigio '09		♟♟ 3

FRIULI VENEZIA GIULIA

Livio e Claudio Buiatti

VIA LIPPE, 25
33042 BUTTRIO [UD]
TEL. 0432674317
www.buiattivini.it

CELLAR SALES
PRE-BOOKED VISITS
ANNUAL PRODUCTION 35,000 bottles
HECTARES UNDER VINE 8.00

Claudio Buiatti, assisted by his wife Viviana, directs this modest family operation inherited from his father Livio. The cellar is right in Buttrio, while their eight hectares of vines cover the gentle, sun-kissed slopes that extend from the town towards Premariacco, planted in the panoramic beauty of the hamlet of In Mont e Poanis. Generations of Buiattis have cleaved to local traditions but have always been open to innovation as well and from them Claudio has inherited the love he lavishes on his vines, all of which have made this winery one of the finest and most well-known in the area. The Sauvignon 2012 offers notes of grapefruit, sage and rosemary, and the supple palate has great acid backbone. The Merlot 2011 has a complex, intense bouquet with notes of leather, cocoa powder and red fruit jam; the caressing palate is rich in flavour. The Picolit 2011 is also delicious.

○ COF Friulano '12		�� 3
○ COF Malvasia '12		♥♥ 3
● COF Merlot '11		♥♥ 3
● COF Momon Ros Ris. '09		♥♥ 4
○ COF Picolit '11		♥♥ 6
○ COF Sauvignon '12		♥♥ 3
● COF Cabernet Franc '11		♥ 3
● COF Refosco P. R. '10		♥ 3
○ COF Friulano '11		♀♀ 3
○ COF Malvasia '11		♀♀ 3
● COF Merlot '10		♀♀ 3
● COF Rosso Momon Ros Ris. '05		♀♀ 4
○ COF Sauvignon '11		♀♀ 3*

Valentino Butussi

VIA PRÀ DI CORTE, 1
33040 CORNO DI ROSAZZO [UD]
TEL. 0432759194
www.butussi.it

CELLAR SALES
PRE-BOOKED VISITS
ACCOMMODATION
ANNUAL PRODUCTION 100,000 bottles
HECTARES UNDER VINE 18.00
VITICULTURE METHOD Certified Organic

The history of Butussi wines is a mosaic of many generations of long experience, expertise, and little secrets, all rooted in the sandstone soils of Prà di Corte in Corno di Rosazzo, in the Colli Orientali del Friuli DOC. Valentino Butussi founded the operation early in the last century, but Angelo has given it its current prominence, ably assisted by his wife Pierina and now by their four children, Tobia, Filippo, Mattia, and Erika. It's a remarkably effective team, based on a close-knit family and a well thought-out division of responsibilities. The result is the very high quality level of an impressive number of wines at reasonable, honest prices. The vintage whites achieved unanimous consensus for their elegant aromas and fragrance on tasting. The Friulano 2012 reflects the varietal stamp on both the nose and palate, and closes on a pleasant, slightly bitterish note. The other wines boast a delicate nose, and flavourful, balanced, powerful palate.

○ COF Chardonnay '12		♥♥ 2*
○ COF Friulano '12		♥♥ 2*
○ COF Sauvignon '12		♥♥ 2*
● COF Cabernet Franc '11		♥ 3
○ COF Pinot Grigio '12		♥ 2
○ COF Ribolla Gialla '12		♥ 2
○ COF Chardonnay '11		♀♀ 2*
○ COF Friulano '09		♀♀ 2*
○ COF Picolit '08		♀♀ 6
○ COF Sauvignon '11		♀♀ 2*
○ COF Sauvignon '09		♀♀ 2*
○ COF Verduzzo Friulano '10		♀♀ 2*

Maurizio Buzzinelli

Loc. Pradis, 20
34071 Cormòns [GO]
Tel. 048160902
www.buzzinelli.com

CELLAR SALES
PRE-BOOKED VISITS
ACCOMMODATION AND RESTAURANT SERVICE
ANNUAL PRODUCTION 100,000 bottles
HECTARES UNDER VINE 26.00

Maurizio Buzzinelli, together with his wife
Marzia, decided to follow in the footsteps of
his grandfather Luigi, who in 1937 founded
this winery in the village of Pradis, near
Cormòns. The property, in the heart of the
Collio DOC zone, extends over a series of
sunny slopes overlooking the Friulan
countryside and the Adriatic. They also have
a few hectares of vineyards, mostly red
varieties, planted in the equally respected
zone of Friuli Isonzo. Maurizio remains true
to the precious expertise built up by three
generations of wine-growers, personally
tending the vineyards and making the wine.
Today's fine results augur well for an even
better future. One wine landed in the finals
again this year. The Friulano 2012 won our
favours for the elegance and typicality of the
aroma, but mostly for the pleasant palate.
The excellent Malvasia is harmonious and
well balanced, and deserves the same
praise as previous vintages.

○ Collio Friulano '12	♥♥	3*
○ Collio Chardonnay '12	♥♥	3
○ Collio Malvasia '12	♥♥	3
○ Collio Pinot Grigio '12	♥♥	3
○ Collio Sauvignon '12	♥	2
○ Collio Friulano '11	♥♥	3
○ Collio Malvasia '11	♀♀	2*
○ Collio Malvasia '10	♀♀	2*
○ Collio Malvasia Ronc dal Luis '08	♀♀	3*
○ Collio Pinot Grigio '11	♀♀	3*
○ Collio Ribolla Gialla '09	♀♀	2*
● Collio Rosso Frututis '09	♀♀	2*
○ Collio Sauvignon '09	♀♀	2*

Ca' Bolani

via Ca' Bolani, 2
33052 Cervignano del Friuli [UD]
Tel. 043132670
www.cabolani.it

CELLAR SALES
PRE-BOOKED VISITS
ANNUAL PRODUCTION 2,700,000 bottles
HECTARES UNDER VINE 550.00

Tenuta Cà Bolani extends over three
separate properties, Ca' Bolani, Molin del
Ponte, and Ca' Vescovo, all in the heart of
the Friuli Aquileia DOC. After acquiring the
winery in 1970, the Zonin family restored it
to its former splendour, restructuring the
main winemaking facility and building a
new cellar with state-of-the-art technology.
Of the estate's total 800 hectares, 550 are
under vine, making it the largest vineyard
holding in northern Italy. In addition to the
standard line are special selections that
bear the Gianni Zonin Vineyards name.
Oenologist Marco Rabino directs the team,
assisted by Roberto Marcolini and Gabriele
Carboni who oversee the cellar and the
vineyards respectively. Refosco dal
peduncolo rosso is the most common
native red grape variety in the region and
the Aquileia plain is its cradle. It is not for
nothing that the wine that deserved our
finals this year is the fruity, balsamic
Alturio 2009. The Refosco dal Peduncolo
Rosso 2011 also deserves mention for its
pleasant taste.

● Friuli Aquileia Refosco P. R. Alturio '09	♥♥	4
○ Friuli Aquileia Friulano '12	♥♥	3
● Friuli Aquileia Refosco P. R. '11	♥♥	3
● Friuli Aquileia Cabernet Franc '11	♥	3
● Friuli Aquileia Merlot '11	♥	3
○ Friuli Aquileia Pinot Bianco '12	♥	3
○ Friuli Aquileia Pinot Grigio '12	♥	3
○ Friuli Aquileia Sauvignon '12	♥	3
○ Prosecco Brut	♥	3
○ Friuli Aquileia Pinot Bianco '09	♀♀♀	2*
● Friuli Aquileia Merlot '10	♀♀	2*
● Friuli Aquileia Refosco P. R. '08	♀♀	2*
○ Friuli Aquileia Sauvignon Aquilis '11	♀♀	2*
○ Friuli Aquileia Sauvignon Aquilis '10	♀♀	2*

Ca' Tullio & Sdricca di Manzano

VIA BELIGNA, 41
33051 AQUILEIA [UD]
TEL. 0431919700
www.catullio.it

CELLAR SALES
PRE-BOOKED VISITS
ANNUAL PRODUCTION 300,000 bottles
HECTARES UNDER VINE 78.00

Ca' Tullio is headquartered in Aquileia, in a majestic structure dating from the early 20th century once used to dry tobacco. Today, it serves as a rare example of industrial archaeology. In 1994 it was meticulously restored to its former beauty and exhibits its pristine architectural features. Here the grapes grown in the vineyards of the Friuli Aquileia DOC are vinified, as well as those obtained from Sdricca di Manzano in the Colli Orientali del Friuli. Owner Paolo Calligaris has long relied on the winemaking talents of Francesco Visintin, who is responsible for both lines. This year we noted the clear superiority of the Sdricca di Manzano line over the Ca' Tullio. In particular our favour was won by the Schioppettino Sdricca 2011 and Pignolo Sdricca 2010, both still vibrant and rich in vitality but already well balanced and ready to drink.

● COF Pignolo Sdricca '10	♟♟ 3	
○ COF Sauvignon Sdricca '12	♟♟ 3	
● COF Schioppettino Sdricca '11	♟♟ 3	
○ COF Friulano Sdricca '12	♟ 3	
○ COF Ribolla Gialla Sdricca '12	♟ 3	
○ Friuli Aquileia Friulano '12	♟ 2	
○ Friuli Aquileia Pinot Grigio '12	♟ 2	
● Friuli Aquileia Refosco P. R. '11	♟ 2	
○ COF Friulano Sdricca '09	♟♟ 3*	
● COF Pignolo Sdricca '06	♟♟ 3	
○ Friuli Aquileia Friulano '11	♟♟ 2*	
○ Friuli Aquileia Traminer Viola '08	♟♟ 2*	

Cadibon

VIA CASALI GALLO, 1
33040 CORNO DI ROSAZZO [UD]
TEL. 0432759316
www.cadibon.com

CELLAR SALES
PRE-BOOKED VISITS
RESTAURANT SERVICE
ANNUAL PRODUCTION 55,000 bottles
HECTARES UNDER VINE 14.00

Founded in 1977 by Gianni Bon, Cadibon is now enthusiastically managed with indisputable skill by his two children, Luca and Francesca. For some years now we have noticed a constant growth in quality that has launched this estate into the exclusive realm of excellent wines. Since last spring, these two have worked at the new cellar in Corno di Rosazzo, equipped with the latest technology, and ample spaces reserved for hospitality and events. The recent restyling of the bottles and labels for the entire line of whites shows the desire to be seen on the market with an elegant, refined new image that expresses the freshness and fragrance of the wines inside. In the local dialect, "Bon taj" means a good glass of wine, and the Friulano Bontaj 2012 proves its excellent calibre, typically fragrant and rustic, with great freshness and a pleasant drinkability. The Schioppettino 2011 and Ronco del Nonno 2012 also return for an encore of last year's performance.

○ COF Friulano Bontaj '12	♟♟ 3	
● COF Schioppettino '11	♟♟ 3	
○ Friuli Grave Sauvignon '12	♟♟ 3	
○ Ronco del Nonno '12	♟♟ 3	
● COF Cabernet Franc '11	♟ 3	
● COF Refosco P. R. '11	♟ 3	
○ COF Ribolla Gialla '12	♟ 3	
○ COF Friulano Bontaj '11	♟♟ 2*	
○ COF Friulano Bontaj '10	♟♟ 2*	
○ COF Ribolla Gialla '11	♟♟ 3	
● COF Schioppettino '10	♟♟ 3	
○ Friuli Grave Sauvignon '09	♟♟ 3*	
○ Ronco del Nonno '11	♟♟ 3*	

Canus

LOC. CASALI GALLO
VIA GRAMOGLIANO, 21
33040 CORNO DI ROSAZZO [UD]
TEL. 0432759427
www.canus.it

CELLAR SALES
PRE-BOOKED VISITS
ANNUAL PRODUCTION 45,000 bottles
HECTARES UNDER VINE 9.00

In 2004, Pordenone businessman Ugo Rossetto purchased a flourishing winery that he named Canus in Gramogliano, in the municipality of Corno di Rosazzo, near the Judrio river, which in that area divides the Colli Orientali del Friuli and Collio DOCs. Canus is now run by his two forward-looking children, Dario and Lara, who have given the operation that qualitative push necessary to maintain their role on the regional wine stage. The main line is Canus, from organic grapes, but a second line, Ronco del Gris, was added a while back which offers crisper wines with a tad less alcohol. All these wines are distinguished by their clear varietal stamp, pleasantness and balance. But our greatest consensus went to the Friulano 2012, rich in colour and aroma, zesty and caressing. Also excellent, the Bianco Jasmine 2011 is a blend of chardonnay, sauvignon and pinot grigio.

○ COF Friulano '12	♟♟ 3*
○ COF Bianco Jasmine '11	♟♟ 3
○ Pinot Grigio Ronco del Gris '12	♟♟ 2*
○ Sauvignon Ronco del Gris '12	♟♟ 2*
○ Bianco Flor di Cuar '12	♟ 2
○ Chardonnay Ronco del Gris '12	♟ 2
○ COF Ribolla Gialla '12	♟ 3
○ Ribolla Gialla Ronco del Gris '12	♟ 2
○ COF Bianco Jasmine '07	♟♟ 3
○ COF Malvasia Ronco del Gris '11	♟♟ 2*
● COF Pignolo '08	♟♟ 4
● COF Refosco P. R. '06	♟♟ 4

Carlo di Pradis

LOC. PRADIS, 22B
34071 CORMÒNS [GO]
TEL. 048162272
www.carlodipradis.it

CELLAR SALES
PRE-BOOKED VISITS
ANNUAL PRODUCTION 70,000 bottles
HECTARES UNDER VINE 15.00

Quite a few of the region's top-notch wineries are headquartered in Pradis, a lively, hill town near Cormòns that enjoys a splendid, strategic location, as well as exceptional soils and weather. Carlo Buzzinelli, a life-long resident, transferred the reins of his operation to his sons Boris and David in 1992. The two have worked together in perfect synergy for some time now. Their spacious, impressively-equipped cellar is perched on a hill, modern in style but perfectly integrated into the landscape. About half of their estate vineyards surround the cellar, and thus lie in the Collio DOC, while others are planted down on the plain in Friuli Isonzo. Beyond the excellent performance of all these wines, the Sauvignon 2012 del Collio shows a complex, intriguing, intense bouquet with notes of white peach and orange flower, and a caressing, fragrant and pleasing palate. The other wines are fragrant, supple and coherent, with good nose-palate consistency.

○ Collio Sauvignon '12	♟♟ 3*
○ Collio Friulano '12	♟♟ 3
○ Collio Pinot Grigio '12	♟♟ 3
○ Friuli Isonzo Chardonnay '12	♟♟ 3
○ Friuli Isonzo Sauvignon '12	♟♟ 2*
○ Friuli Isonzo Friulano '12	♟ 2
○ Friuli Isonzo Pinot Grigio '12	♟ 2
○ Collio Friulano '11	♟♟ 3
○ Collio Friulano '08	♟♟ 3*
○ Collio Friulano Scusse '08	♟♟ 3*
○ Collio Friulano Scusse '07	♟♟ 3*
○ Collio Sauvignon '11	♟♟ 3
● Friuli Isonzo Merlot '10	♟♟ 3
○ Friuli Isonzo Pinot Grigio '11	♟♟ 2*

Il Carpino

LOC. SOVENZA, 14A
34070 SAN FLORIANO DEL COLLIO [GO]
TEL. 0481884097
www.ilcarpino.com

CELLAR SALES
PRE-BOOKED VISITS
ANNUAL PRODUCTION 70,000 bottles
HECTARES UNDER VINE 16.00

As is often the case, this winery is named after its location. Borgo del Carpino is in the town of Sovenza, on the road that connects Oslavia to San Floriano del Collio. Here Anna and Franco Sosol set up their winery in 1987, and they are now helped by their children Naike and Manuel. Being a family operation, they can personally supervise every step of production – vineyards, winemaking, maturation, and marketing. Their philosophy favours traditional methods, a good example being the enlargement of the cellar, which houses Slavonian oak casks of 15-20 hectolitres. All these wines received top scores again this year, and the Malvasia proved the best in the range in the stainless steel version as well as the one macerated in wood. The Malvasia Vigna Runc 2012 is fresh and fragrant. The Malvasia 2010 is refined and creamy.

Casa Zuliani

VIA GRADISCA, 23
34072 FARRA D'ISONZO [GO]
TEL. 0481888506
www.casazuliani.com

CELLAR SALES
PRE-BOOKED VISITS
ANNUAL PRODUCTION 130,000 bottles
HECTARES UNDER VINE 17.00

Founded 90 years ago by Zuliano Zuliani, Casa Zuliani is now owned and directed by Riccardo Monfardino, who, with his business acumen, has given it a forward-looking thrust that has kept it in the now-crowded group of top regional producers. The majestic estate villa and the cellar are in Farra d'Isonzo, while the vineyards are cultivated in the Collio and Friuli Isonzo DOCs. Exceptionally talented winemaker Omar Caffar, assisted by Gianni Menotti, has kept all of the wines at a very high level indeed, although the best fruit goes to the Winter line, the winery's standard-bearer. The Winter Rosso 5/95 2009, from cabernet sauvignon with added merlot, won a place in our finals because of its development, complex aromas and robust palate. The Winter Rosso 95/5 2009, from merlot with a bit of cabernet sauvignon, is excellent but still somewhat dominated by oak.

○ Bianco Runc '12	♟♟ 3*
○ Collio Malvasia V. Runc '12	♟♟ 3*
○ Malvasia '10	♟♟ 5
○ Chardonnay '10	♟♟ 5
○ Collio Pinot Grigio V. Runc '12	♟♟ 3
○ Ribolla Gialla '10	♟♟ 4
○ Vis Uvae '10	♟♟ 5
○ Collio Bianco V. Runc '10	♟♟♟ 2*
○ Collio Malvasia V. Runc '11	♟♟♟ 3*
● Rubrum '99	♟♟♟ 3*
○ Bianco Carpino '09	♟♟ 4
○ Bianco Runc '11	♟♟ 3*
○ Exordium '09	♟♟ 5
○ Malvasia '09	♟♟ 5

● Winter Rosso 5/95 '09	♟♟ 5
○ Collio Friulano '12	♟♟ 3
○ Collio Malvasia '12	♟♟ 3
○ Collio Pinot Grigio '12	♟♟ 3
○ Collio Sauvignon '12	♟♟ 3
○ Winter Chardonnay '10	♟♟ 5
● Winter Rosso 95/5 '09	♟♟ 5
○ Collio Chardonnay '12	♟ 3
○ Collio Ribolla Gialla '12	♟ 3
● Winter Rosso '04	♟♟♟ 4
○ Collio Pinot Grigio '11	♟♟ 3
● Winter Rosso 5/95 '08	♟♟ 5
● Winter Rosso 95/5 '08	♟♟ 5

La Castellada

FRAZ. OSLAVIA, 1
34170 GORIZIA
TEL. 048133670
nicolobensa@virgilio.it

CELLAR SALES
PRE-BOOKED VISITS
ANNUAL PRODUCTION 23,000 bottles
HECTARES UNDER VINE 9.00

Wines from La Castellada are powerful, austere, and loaded with colour and intriguing, original aromas. They develop slowly, first resting in barrels and then ageing in bottles, and see light only after many years. All the grapes, even the white, undergo long macerations and thanks to must contact with skins, fermentation starts spontaneously and tannins are extracted. These natural anti-oxidants mean very small quantities of sulphites are used. Giorgio and Nicolò Bensa began bottling their wines in 1978 and are now aided in the vineyard and cellar by the energy and enthusiasm of Nicolò's sons, Stefano and Matteo. We tasted the Collio Bianco, in the finals, and the Ribolla Gialla from the 2008 vintage. Both these wines show great complexity, an intriguing nose and a powerful, finely structured palate. Also in the finals, the Rosso della Castellada 2001 is spicy and balsamic on the nose, and rich and gratifying to the taste

○ Collio Bianco della Castellada '08	♔♔ 5
● Collio Rosso della Castellada '01	♔♔ 8
○ Collio Ribolla Gialla '08	♔♔ 5
○ Collio Bianco della Castellada '99	♔♔♔ 5
● Collio Rosso della Castellada '99	♔♔♔ 7
○ Collio Tocai Friulano '03	♔♔♔ 5
○ Collio Bianco della Castellada '07	♔♔ 5
○ Collio Friulano '07	♔♔ 5
○ Collio Pinot Grigio '07	♔♔ 5
○ Collio Ribolla Gialla '07	♔♔ 5
○ Collio Ribolla Gialla '05	♔♔ 5
● Collio Rosso della Castellada '04	♔♔ 7

Castello di Buttrio

VIA MORPURGO, 9
33042 BUTTRIO [UD]
TEL. 0432673015
www.castellodibuttrio.it

CELLAR SALES
PRE-BOOKED VISITS
ACCOMMODATION AND RESTAURANT SERVICE
ANNUAL PRODUCTION 50,000 bottles
HECTARES UNDER VINE 27.00

Marco Felluga is considered, and quite rightly, one of the pioneers of quality winemaking in Friuli Venezia Giulia. His intuitions have always proved well-justified, as was his acquisition, in 1994, of the Castello di Buttrio estate. His daughter Alessandra has been directing it for some years now, and her patient efforts have restored its ancient walls to their historic splendour. The recent purchase of a neighbouring winery with its fine vineyards has given broader scope to the outstanding talents of winemaker Andrea Pittana, under the watchful eye of Alessandra. For the second consecutive year, the Friulano 2012 deservedly landed in our final selections, and is distinguished by a generosity of aromas and flavour. The Sauvignon 2012 is also excellent, and the other wines are all becoming more and more convincing in both the latest vintage as well as the Riservas.

○ COF Friulano '12	♔♔ 3*
○ COF Bianco Mon Blanc '12	♔♔ 3
○ COF Dolce Mille e una Botte '10	♔♔ 5
○ COF Sauvignon '12	♔♔ 3
○ COF Torre Butria Chardonnay Ris. '09	♔♔ 5
● COF Uve Carate Merlot Rls. '09	♔♔ 3
● COF Refosco '11	♔ 3
○ COF Ribolla Gialla '12	♔ 3
○ COF Friulano '11	♔♔ 3*
○ COF Bianco Mon Blanc '11	♔♔ 3*
○ COF Chardonnay '11	♔♔ 3
○ COF Friulano '10	♔♔ 3
● COF Merlot '09	♔♔ 3*
○ COF Sauvignon '11	♔♔ 3

Castello di Spessa

VIA SPESSA, 1
34070 CAPRIVA DEL FRIULI [GO]
TEL. 048160445
www.paliwines.com

CELLAR SALES
PRE-BOOKED VISITS
ACCOMMODATION AND RESTAURANT SERVICE
ANNUAL PRODUCTION 300,000 bottles
HECTARES UNDER VINE 80.00

After purchasing Castello di Spessa in
1987 along with its surrounding vineyards,
Loretto Pali infused it with new life, making
it the heart of an extensive complex that
includes the winery, a comfortable resort,
an 18-hole golf course, and a restaurant.
In World War II, occupying troops used a
bunker that was built in 1939 to connect
the castle and the cellar. Today, its natural
and constant humidity and temperature
are a boon for wines ageing there.
Long-time consultant Gianni Menotti
ensures high-level quality and assists the
work of expert winemaker Domenico Lovat.
Again this year, two wines achieved entry
to our finals. The Pinot Bianco 2012 won
us over with its elegant bouquet and
refined palate. The Sauvignon Segrè 2012
is quite citrussy and fragrant. Special
mention also goes to the promising, fruity
and flavourful Pinot Nero Casanova 2009.

○ Collio Pinot Bianco '12	♟♟ 3*
○ Collio Sauvignon Segrè '12	♟ 5
○ Collio Friulano '12	♟♟ 3
○ Collio Pinot Grigio '12	♟♟ 3
● Collio Pinot Nero Casanova '09	♟♟ 5
○ Collio Sauvignon '12	♟♟ 3
○ Collio Ribolla Gialla '12	♟ 3
○ Friuli Isonzo Chardonnay '12	♟ 3
○ Isonzo Sauvignon '12	♟ 3
○ Collio Pinot Bianco '11	♟♟♟ 3*
○ Collio Pinot Bianco '06	♟♟♟ 3*
○ Collio Tocai Friulano '05	♟♟♟ 3*
● Collio Merlot V. Rosaris '09	♟♟ 5

Castello Sant'Anna

LOC. SPESSA
VIA SANT'ANNA, 9
33043 CIVIDALE DEL FRIULI [UD]
TEL. 0432716289
centasantanna@libero.it

CELLAR SALES
PRE-BOOKED VISITS
ANNUAL PRODUCTION 25,000 bottles
HECTARES UNDER VINE 7.00

Two round towers, a dozen or so metres
high, restored in the 17th century, but with
foundations going back to the 13th and
14th centuries, define the borders of the
rectangular walls of Castello Sant'Anna,
surrounding buildings from the 18th
century. Once the summer residence of
noble families from Cividale and surrounded
by vineyards, this estate was purchased in
1966 by Giuseppe Giaiotti, who left his
industrial career to return to the countryside
where he felt more connected. Things are
now run by Andrea, the third generation of
the family, who has completed restoring the
old vineyards and is now building a new
underground cellar that maintains
constant temperatures. An excellent Pinot
Grigio 2011 won over our palates with
refined, fragrant aromas, and most
especially the opulent, pleasing flavour. Also
excellent, the Friulano 2011 is rich on the
nose and palate, and the Merlot 2009 is
elegant, complex, full and enveloping.

○ COF Pinot Grigio '11	♟♟ 3*
○ COF Friulano '11	♟♟ 3
● COF Merlot '09	♟♟ 4
● COF Pinot Nero '09	♟ 4
● COF Merlot Ris. '08	♟♟ 4
● COF Pignolo '07	♟♟ 4
● COF Pinot Nero '07	♟♟ 4
○ COF Sauvignon '10	♟♟ 3
○ COF Sauvignon '09	♟♟ 3*
● COF Schioppettino '08	♟♟ 5

Castelvecchio

VIA CASTELNUOVO, 2
34078 SAGRADO [GO]
TEL. 048199742
www.castelvecchio.com

CELLAR SALES
PRE-BOOKED VISITS
ANNUAL PRODUCTION 180,000 bottles
HECTARES UNDER VINE 35.00

Over the years, the Carso Goriziano area has witnessed both splendour and ruin. Still today, amidst corners of pristine, fascinating natural beauty, it offers the challenge of a difficult growing area, arid and rocky, but one that forms unexpected partnerships with those who respect it. Here, just above Sagrado, lies the Castelvecchio estate that is managed with passionate commitment, tenacity, and professionalism by the Terraneo family. The seasoned Saverio Di Giacomo has been overseeing winemaking operations for some time now, supported in decisions by the respected expertise of Gianni Menotti. They are both intent on raising the quality bar as high as it will go. This year a splendid Sauvignon 2012 came close to excellence, distinguished by an intriguing bouquet of orange flowers and elderflower, and a full, caressing palate. Also excellent, the Malvasia Dileo 2012 is rich in balsamic and floral notes. All the other wines are good, flavourful and appealing.

○ Carso Sauvignon '12	♟♟ 3*
● Carso Cabernet Franc '10	♟♟ 4
● Carso Cabernet Sauvignon '10	♟♟ 4
○ Carso Malvasia Dileo '12	♟♟ 5
○ Carso Malvasia Istriana '12	♟♟ 3
● Carso Merlot '07	♟♟ 5
● Carso Refosco P. R. '10	♟♟ 4
○ Terrano Rosé Brut	♟♟ 4
○ Brut Masia	♟ 4
● Carso Terrano '12	♟ 3
● Carso Cabernet Sauvignon '09	♟♟ 4
● Carso Merlot '06	♟♟ 5
○ Carso Sauvignon '11	♟♟ 3
● Sagrado Rosso '05	♟♟ 5

Marco Cecchini

LOC. CASALI DE LUCA
VIA COLOMBANI
33040 FAEDIS [UD]
TEL. 0432720563
www.cecchinimarco.com

CELLAR SALES
PRE-BOOKED VISITS
ACCOMMODATION
ANNUAL PRODUCTION 35,000 bottles
HECTARES UNDER VINE 7.00

Marco Cecchini's winery was founded almost as a pastime in 1998 on one hectare of vineyard inherited from his grandfather in Faedis in the Colli Orientali del Friuli. A free spirit who left behind the world of economics, Cecchini took the first steps here that irreversibly bonded him to nature. He now cultivates some ten hectares of vineyard, half of which boast vines that average 40 years of age. Cecchini considers himself an artisan in winemaking but an artist in interpreting his terroir, as he coaxes the best from the local soil and climate to produce wines that are straightforward yet elegant, brimming with personality. The Pinot Grigio 2012 and Friulano 2011 are both excellent, though greatest consensus went to the Verduzzo Friulano Verlit 2008 that landed in the finals. The bouquet shows honey and candied citrus, and the delicious palate has endless sweetness.

○ COF Verduzzo Friulano Verlit '08	♟♟ 3*
○ COF Friulano '11	♟♟ 3
○ Pinot Grigio '12	♟♟ 3
○ Riesling '10	♟ 5
○ COF Bianco Tovè '10	♟♟ 3*
○ COF Bianco Tovè '09	♟♟ 0*
○ COF Bianco Tovè '08	♟♟ 3*
● COF Refosco P. R. '09	♟♟ 3
○ COF Refosco P. R. '08	♟♟ 3*
○ Picolit '07	♟♟ 5
○ Pinot Grigio '11	♟♟ 3
○ Pinot Grigio Vigneto Bellagioia '08	♟♟ 2*
○ Riesling '08	♟♟ 2*

Eugenio Collavini

LOC. GRAMOGLIANO
VIA FORUM JULII, 2
33040 CORNO DI ROSAZZO [UD]
TEL. 0432753222
www.collavini.it

CELLAR SALES
PRE-BOOKED VISITS
ANNUAL PRODUCTION 1,500,000 bottles
HECTARES UNDER VINE 173.00

The winery founded by Eugenio Collavini in 1896 is located in Corno di Rosazzo, in a villa owned by the Conti Zucco di Cuccanea that was a fortified village back in the 16th century. Today, Manlio Collavini directs the estate flanked by sons Luigi and Giovanni. Collavini enlarged operations in the 1970s, and in 1996 he brought in up-to-date equipment and secured the loyalty of his independent grape growers under the management of a winery agronomist. This is one of the few Friulan wineries to offer such an extensive production without ever having dropped its quality standards, thanks to the outstanding winemaking expertise of Walter Bergnach. First in line as usual is the Bianco Broy 2012, a blend of friulano, chardonnay and sauvignon del Collio we have had the pleasure of tasting in our finals for many editions now. Also excellent, the Forresco 2006 is made from varieties of refosco and pignolo.

● COF Rosso Forresco '06	♟♟ 5
○ Collio Bianco Broy '12	♟♟ 5*
○ COF Ribolla Gialla Turian '12	♟♟ 4*
○ Collio Pinot Grigio '12	♟♟ 2*
○ Collio Sauvignon Blanc Fumât '12	♟♟ 3*
○ Verdàc '09	♟♟ 8
○ Collio Bianco Broy '11	♟♟♟ 4*
○ Collio Bianco Broy '10	♟♟♟ 4
○ Collio Bianco Broy '09	♟♟♟ 4*
○ Collio Bianco Broy '08	♟♟♟ 4*
○ Collio Bianco Broy '07	♟♟♟ 4
○ Collio Bianco Broy '06	♟♟♟ 4
○ Collio Bianco Broy '04	♟♟♟ 4*
○ Collio Bianco Broy '03	♟♟♟ 4
● COF Rosso Forresco '05	♟♟ 5
● Collio Merlot dal Pic '06	♟♟ 5

Colle Duga

LOC. ZEGLA, 10
34071 CORMÒNS [GO]
TEL. 048161177
www.colleduga.com

CELLAR SALES
PRE-BOOKED VISITS
ANNUAL PRODUCTION 50,000 bottles
HECTARES UNDER VINE 9.00

Maps of local place names identify Colle Duga as the hill across which the vineyards of Damian Princic lie. This is the heart of the Collio, within touching distance of the Goriska Brda hills in Slovenia. Here, the Princic family have dedicated themselves to wine-growing for generations. In 1991, the very young Damian took over the reins of the family winery. His philosophy is based on maximizing sensory expression in the wine, with a balance between structure, personality, and typicity, all in harmony with the specific character of the terroir. All these wines gave another excellent performance and three come close to perfection. The fragrant, alluring Friulano 2012 is perfectly in line with previous vintages. The Sauvignon and Collio Bianco, both from 2012, show agreeable citrussy notes and above all a satisfying palate.

○ Collio Bianco '12	♟♟ 4
○ Collio Friulano '12	♟♟ 3*
○ Collio Sauvignon '12	♟♟ 3*
○ Collio Chardonnay '12	♟♟ 3
● Collio Merlot '11	♟♟ 4
○ Collio Pinot Grigio '12	♟♟ 3
○ Collio Bianco '11	♟♟♟ 4*
○ Collio Bianco '08	♟♟♟ 3*
○ Collio Bianco '07	♟♟♟ 3
○ Collio Friulano '09	♟♟♟ 3*
○ Collio Bianco '10	♟♟ 3
○ Collio Friulano '11	♟♟ 3*
○ Collio Pinot Grigio '11	♟♟ 3*
○ Collio Sauvignon '11	♟♟ 3*

Colmello di Grotta

Loc. GROTTA
VIA GORIZIA, 133
34072 FARRA D'ISONZO [GO]
TEL. 0481888445
www.colmello.it

CELLAR SALES
PRE-BOOKED VISITS
ANNUAL PRODUCTION 85,000 bottles
HECTARES UNDER VINE 15.00

Luciana Bennati launched Colmello di Grotta in 1965. She restructured an old, decrepit hamlet and transformed it into a vibrant, well-equipped wine estate in a project that was highly sensitive to tradition. Her daughter Francesca Bortolotto Possati now holds the reins, and her business acumen and passionate commitment have catapulted Colmello di Grotta into the front ranks of the region's producers. The vineyards extend along both the bank of the Isonzo river and the slopes of the Collio Goriziano DOC. These two terroirs are strikingly different, but Fabio Coser, who knows this territory inside out, has been successful in coaxing out the best qualities of each. Collio wines show something more than Isonzo wines. They are much more fruity, fragrant and finely structured. The Chardonnay 2012 has peach and jasmine aromas, and a great finish on the palate. The broad, full-flavoured Collio Bianco Sanfilip 2011, from chardonnay, sauvignon and friulano, is also excellent.

○ Collio Bianco Sanfilip '11	♥♥ 3
○ Collio Chardonnay '12	♥♥ 3
○ Collio Friulano '12	♥♥ 3
○ Collio Pinot Grigio '12	♥♥ 3
○ Collio Sauvignon '12	♥♥ 3
○ Collio Ribolla Gialla '12	♥ 3
● Friuli Isonzo Cabernet Franc '11	♥ 3
● Friuli Isonzo Merlot '10	♥ 3
○ Friuli Isonzo Sauvignon '12	♥ 3
○ Collio Friulano '11	♥♥ 3*
○ Collio Ribolla Gialla '10	♥♥ 3*
○ Collio Sauvignon '11	♥♥ 3*
○ Friuli Isonzo Chardonnay '11	♥♥ 2*
● Friuli Isonzo Merlot '04	♥♥ 3
○ Friuli Isonzo Sauvignon '11	♥♥ 2*

Giorgio Colutta - Bandut

VIA ORSARIA, 32
33044 MANZANO [UD]
TEL. 0432740315
www.colutta.it

CELLAR SALES
PRE-BOOKED VISITS
ACCOMMODATION
ANNUAL PRODUCTION 140,000 bottles
HECTARES UNDER VINE 21.00

Giorgio Colutta, who possesses a degree in medicine and a deep love for the earth, is the owner of this winery that is also known as Bandut, the old local name for an estate. An old 18th-century estate villa, purchased by Antonio Colutta in the early 1900s, houses the cellar and lodgings for customers and wine tourists. The vineyards, planted in the prestigious Wine and Vine Park of the Colli Orientali del Friuli, are under the supervision of viticulturalist Antonio Maggio. The traditional line has always featured wines of exemplary soundness and self-confidence. Now there are interesting sparkling wines and, in the better growing years, some very impressive crus. The continuous increase in wine quality has led the Pignolo 2007 to compete with wines in the finals. This wine is emotional and complex on the nose, and appealing on the palate. Strongly varietal and fragrant, these vintage wines also show notes of high quality.

● COF Pignolo '07	♥♥ 7
○ COF Friulano '12	♥♥ 3
○ COF Pinot Grigio '12	♥♥ 3
● COF Refosco P. R. '11	♥♥ 3
○ COF Ribolla Gialla '12	♥♥ 4
○ COF Sauvignon '12	♥♥ 3
○ COF Friulano '11	♥♥ 3
○ COF Friulano '10	♥♥ 3*
● COF Pignolo '06	♥♥ 7
● COF Refosco P. R. '08	♥♥ 3
○ COF Ribolla Gialla '11	♥♥ 4
○ COF Sauvignon '11	♥♥ 3
○ Picolit '07	♥♥ 7

Paolino Comelli

CASE COLLOREDO, 8
33040 FAEDIS [UD]
TEL. 0432711226
www.comelli.it

CELLAR SALES
PRE-BOOKED VISITS
ACCOMMODATION AND RESTAURANT SERVICE
ANNUAL PRODUCTION 60,000 bottles
HECTARES UNDER VINE 12.50

In 1946, Paolino Comelli purchased an abandoned old village of dilapidated farmhouses in the hills of Colloredo di Soffumbergo, in the municipality of Faedis. With amazing far-sightedness, he transformed it into a thriving agricultural estate. It is directed today by Pierluigi Comelli, Pigi to his friends, assisted by his wife Daniela and their sons Nicola and Filippo. Consultant Emilio Del Medico's considerable talents, in concert with the technical team, have always kept quality consistently high, producing pleasurable, varietally faithful wines with distinctive personalities. The Bianco Soffumbergo 2011 shows great fragrance and personality, expressing the varietal characteristics of friulano enriched with aromatic notes from malvasia, chardonnay and a touch of picolit. The Friulano 2012 and Rosso Soffumbergo 2010 confirmed the praises from previous vintages.

○ Bianco Soffumbergo '11	♟♟ 4
○ COF Friulano '12	♟♟ 3
○ COF Sauvignon '12	♟♟ 3
● Rosso Soffumbergo '10	♟♟ 4
● COF Pignolo '09	♟ 5
○ COF Pinot Grigio Amplius '12	♟ 3
○ COF Friulano '11	♟♟ 3
● COF Pignolo '08	♟♟ 5
● COF Pignolo '07	♟♟ 5
○ COF Pinot Grigio Amplius '11	♟♟ 3
○ COF Sauvignon '09	♟♟ 3*
● Rosso Soffumbergo '09	♟♟ 4
● Rosso Soffumbergo '08	♟♟ 4
● Rosso Soffumbergo '07	♟♟ 4

Dario Coos

VIA RAMANDOLO, 5
33045 NIMIS [UD]
TEL. 0432790320
www.dariocoos.it

CELLAR SALES
PRE-BOOKED VISITS
ANNUAL PRODUCTION 50,000 bottles
HECTARES UNDER VINE 10.00

The Coos family have been making wine on the steep hills of the northernmost reaches of the Colli Orientali del Friuli since the early 1800s. Dario, who founded this winery in 1986, represents the fifth generation of these knowledgeable wine-growers. He was one of the founders of the region's first DOC, Ramandolo, named for a village in the municipality of Nimis where production focuses on the verduzzo giallo grape, whose small clusters and thick skins make it ideal for natural drying. Dario still oversees all of the cellar operations, but his efficient team also enjoys the exceptional services and long experience of consultant Andrea Pittana. Friulano, ribolla gialla and sauvignon go into the Vindos 2011, distinguished by a fragrant bouquet and caressing palate. Showing excellent texture, the fruity Pignolo 2009 is still young, but quite promising. Also excellent, the Schioppettino 2011 is extremely typical, lively and inviting.

● COF Pignolo '09	♟♟ 4
● Schioppettino '11	♟♟ 4
○ Vindos '11	♟♟ 3
○ COF Friulano '12	♟ 3
○ COF Malvasia '12	♟ 3
○ Ramandolo '09	♟ 4
● Refosco P.R. '10	♟ 2
○ Ribolla Gialla '12	♟ 3
○ Sauvignon '12	♟ 3
○ COF Picolit '06	♟♟ 6
○ Picolit '10	♟♟ 6
● Pignolo '08	♟♟ 4
● Pignolo '07	♟♟ 4
○ Ramandolo V. T. '04	♟♟ 4

Cantina Produttori di Cormòns

VIA VINO DELLA PACE, 31
34071 CORMÒNS [GO]
TEL. 048162471
www.cormons.com

CELLAR SALES
PRE-BOOKED VISITS
ACCOMMODATION AND RESTAURANT SERVICE
ANNUAL PRODUCTION 2,250,000 bottles
HECTARES UNDER VINE 470.00
VITICULTURE METHOD Certified Organic

In the late1960s, a group of Cremona growers realized that success in the wine industry lay not in following passing wine trends, but in tenaciously developing their local territory. Joining forces, they drew up a founding agreement, supported by an extremely detailed production code obligatory for all members. Luigi Soini, at that time cellarmaster and today director of the now-flourishing operation, utilizes qualified agronomists to supervise the vineyards of the more than 200 grower members and the proven expertise of consultant Rodolfo Rizzi, a sine qua non for managing such a large number of labels. Again this year a wine from this major winery won entry to our final selection. This is the Pinot Bianco 2012 del Collio, distinguished by cleanliness and pleasant aromas but above all smoothness on the palate. Always intriguing, the Vino della Pace 2008 is a messenger of world peace.

○ Collio Friuliano '12	▼▼ 3
○ Collio Pinot Bianco '12	▼▼ 3*
○ Friuli Isonzo Malvasia Istriana '12	▼▼ 3
○ Vino della Pace '08	▼▼ 5
○ Collio Pinot Grigio '12	▼ 3
○ Collio Friuliano '11	▽▽ 2*
○ Collio Friuliano '10	▽▽ 2*
○ Collio Pinot Grigio '11	▽▽ 3
○ Collio Sauvignon '10	▽▽ 2*
○ Friuli Isonzo Friuliano '09	▽▽ 2*
○ Vino della Pace '06	▽▽ 5

Crastin

LOC. RUTTARS, 33
34070 DOLEGNA DEL COLLIO [GO]
TEL. 0481630310
www.vinicrastin.it

CELLAR SALES
PRE-BOOKED VISITS
ANNUAL PRODUCTION 35,000 bottles
HECTARES UNDER VINE 6.00

In the early 1950s, Olivo and Cornelia Collarig, as tenants, founded an estate dedicated to mixed farming. In 1980, management was taken over by their son Sergio who sensed the potential and focused most attention on the two and a half hectares planted to vines. He began to make clearly top-quality wines and served them to visitors at the agriturismo in the Ruttars hills, which he had opened in the meantime with his sister Vilma. Planting new vineyards led to the current six hectares under vine, with a clear prevalence of white grape varieties, producing completely pleasant, fragrant wines from Collio Goriziano. In a repeat of last year's exploits, the Friulano 2012 deservedly won a place in our finals. The complexity and elegance of the bouquet is followed by a pleasant taste with the right amount of freshness, softness and minerality. All the other wines are good, especially in relation to price.

○ Collio Friulano '12	▼▼ 2*
● Collio Merlot '11	▼▼ 2*
○ Collio Pinot Grigio '12	▼▼ 3
○ Collio Ribolla Gialla '12	▼▼ 2*
○ Collio Sauvignon '12	▼▼ 3
○ Collio Friulano '11	▽▽ 2*
● Collio Merlot '10	▽▽ 2*
○ Collio Pinot Grigio '11	▽▽ 3*
○ Collio Ribolla Gialla '09	▽▽ 2*
○ Collio Sauvignon '11	▽▽ 3

Conte D'Attimis-Maniago

VIA SOTTOMONTE, 21
33042 BUTTRIO [UD]
TEL. 0432674027
www.contedattimismaniago.it

CELLAR SALES
PRE-BOOKED VISITS
ANNUAL PRODUCTION 400,000 bottles
HECTARES UNDER VINE 85.00

The 17th-century palace of the Attimis-Maniago family and its stable annex, now a hotel and restaurant, are in Maniago, in the Pordenone area. The wine estate, run by Conte Alberto d'Attimis-Maniago Marchiò, extends over the sunny hills of Buttrio, where the vineyards enjoy the sea breezes off the nearby Adriatic. Dating back to 1585, Conte d'Attimis-Maniago is one of Friuli's historic producers. It has always been territorial in style, preferring local grapes to imported varieties. This gives the estate the advantage of perfectly acclimated vines and enables it to produce truly classic wines of consistent quality. Expert Francesco Spitaleri has long overseen the winemaking. From almost equal parts of friulano and pinot bianco, the Bianco Ronco Broilo 2009 offers a nose with intriguing touches of dried flowers and roasted peanuts. The palate is mouthfilling and rich in flavour. The other wines are also remarkable and confirm the top quality achieved and maintained.

○ COF Ronco Broilo '09	♟♟ 5
○ COF Malvasia '11	♟♟ 3
○ COF Picolit '11	♟♟ 8
● COF Tazzelenghe '08	♟♟ 6
○ COF Chardonnay '07	♟♟ 3
○ COF Friulano '09	♟♟ 3*
○ COF Malvasia '06	♟♟ 3*
● COF Pignolo '07	♟♟ 7
○ COF Sauvignon '11	♟♟ 3*
○ COF Sauvignon '10	♟♟ 3*
○ COF Sauvignon '09	♟♟ 3*
● COF Tazzelenghe '07	♟♟ 6
● COF Tazzelenghe '04	♟♟ 5
○ COF Verduzzo Friulano Tore delle Signore '11	♟♟ 3

di Lenardo

FRAZ. ONTAGNANO
P.ZZA BATTISTI, 1
33050 GONARS [UD]
TEL. 0432928633
www.dilenardo.it

CELLAR SALES
PRE-BOOKED VISITS
ANNUAL PRODUCTION 600,000 bottles
HECTARES UNDER VINE 45.00

The vines of di Lenardo Vineyards extend over several areas, and the winery has chosen to designate all of its wines IGT. The winery itself lies in the village of Ontagnano, on the Friulan plain a few kilometres from the famous battlements of Palmanova, the city in the shape of a nine-pointed star. The operation is actually two centuries old, but Massimo di Lenardo has given it a contemporary push. He has also been directing the winemaking for some time now, flanked by Giuliano Cattinelli. Di Lenardo has successfully made the most of his plains environment and marketing overseas, in particular in the U.S., cleverly calibrating his production to local demands. The Chardonnay Father's Eyes 2012 recalls exotic fruit, custard and dried fruit, and has a soft, creamy palate. The Sauvignon Blanc 2012 shows a fragrant bouquet of yellow peach and tangerine, and is varietal and very flavourful. The Merlot Just Me 2010 has a texture in a class of its own, but suffers a bit from its youth.

○ Chardonnay '12	♟♟ 2*
○ Father's Eyes '12	♟♟ 2*
○ Friuli Grave Friulano Toh! '12	♟♟ 2*
● Just Me '10	♟♟ 4
○ Sarà Brut	♟♟ 3
○ Sauvignon Blanc '12	♟♟ 2*
● Cabernet '12	♟ 2
○ Gossip '12	♟ 2
○ Pass the Cookies '12	♟ 3
○ Pinot Grigio '12	♟ 2
○ Chardonnay '11	♟♟ 2*
○ Chardonnay '10	♟♟ 2*
○ Come mi vuoi '11	♟♟ 2*
○ Friuli Grave Friulano Toh! '11	♟♟ 2*
○ Sauvignon Blanc '11	♟♟ 2*

★★Dorigo

LOC. BELLAZOIA
VIA SUBIDA, 16
33040 POVOLETTO [UD]
TEL. 0432634161
www.dorigowines.com

CELLAR SALES
PRE-BOOKED VISITS
ANNUAL PRODUCTION 120,000 bottles
HECTARES UNDER VINE 20.00

"Dorigo. A brand, excitement, and a mission projected into the future". This is the slogan that Alessio Dorigo introduced last year, announcing the generational change in a family winery that under Girolamo Dorigo has seen 40 years of winemaking history in Friuli. In place of its historic headquarters in Buttrio, there is a new cellar in Bellazoia, near Povoletto. A number of vineyards are also here, in addition to the family's heritage of eight hectares; the 10,000 vines per hectare make them the most densely planted in the region. Alessio has significantly upped production of classic-method sparklers and focused attention on developing local indigenous grape varieties. The wine we liked most this year is the Chardonnay 2011, winning on the nose with lightly smoky, exotic hints, and satisfying on the palate with soft, creamy touches. Also top quality, the Montsclapade 2010 shows cocoa powder, liquorice and coffee. The excellent Blanc de Noir Brut is from pinot nero.

○ COF Chardonnay '11	♀♀ 5
○ Blanc de Noir Brut	♀♀ 5
○ COF Friulano '12	♀♀ 3
○ COF Ribolla Gialla '12	♀♀ 3
● COF Rosso Montsclapade '10	♀♀ 6
○ COF Sauvignon Ronc di Juri '11	♀♀ 5
○ COF Sauvignon '12	♀ 3
○ COF Traminer '11	♀ 3
○ Dorigo Brut	♀ 4
● COF Pignolo di Buttrio '03	♀♀♀ 8
● COF Pignolo di Buttrio '02	♀♀♀ 8
● COF Pignolo di Buttrio '01	♀♀♀ 8
● COF Rosso Montsclapade '06	♀♀♀ 6
● COF Rosso Montsclapade '04	♀♀♀ 6
● COF Rosso Montsclapade '01	♀♀♀ 6
● COF Rosso Montsclapade '98	♀♀♀ 6

Draga

LOC. SCEDINA, 8
34070 SAN FLORIANO DEL COLLIO [GO]
TEL. 0481884182
www.draga.it

CELLAR SALES
PRE-BOOKED VISITS
ANNUAL PRODUCTION 35,000 bottles
HECTARES UNDER VINE 15.00

For three generations now, the Miklus family has passionately lavished attention on the estate vineyards at San Floriano del Collio, where the steep slopes require work by hand. Milan Miklus is in charge, supported by his wife Anna and children Denis and Mitja. In 1982, Milan restructured the vineyards subdivided into two parcels, Draga and Breg, and ten years later he started bottling his wines to immediate and wide plaudits. The standard line, Draga, bears the same name as the winery. A new line, Miklus, highlights the family endeavour and offers emphatic wines of significant personality and distinction. Milan wins its first Tre Bicchieri award with the Malvasia Miklus 2010. Maceration of the grapes gives this wine an amber colour and aromas of fruit in syrup, dried figs, custard and hazelnut cream puffs. The palate is dense, powerful and well orchestrated. The Sauvignon Miklus 2010 also deservedly made it to the finals.

○ Collio Malvasia Miklus '10	♀♀♀ 7
○ Sauvignon Miklus '10	♀♀ 5
○ Collio Negro di Collina '10	♀♀ 4
○ Collio Sauvignon Draga '12	♀♀ 3
● Collio Cabernet Sauvignon '10	♀ 4
○ Collio Friulano '12	♀ 3
○ Collio Pinot Grigio '12	♀ 3
○ Collio Ribolla Gialla Draga '12	♀ 3
○ Collio Malvasia Draga '10	♀♀ 3*
○ Collio Malvasia Miklus '08	♀♀ 3
● Collio Merlot Miklus '09	♀♀ 5
● Collio Merlot Miklus '08	♀♀ 3*
○ Collio Ribolla Gialla Miklus '07	♀♀ 5

Mauro Drius

VIA FILANDA, 100
34071 CORMÒNS [GO]
TEL. 048160998
www.driusmauro.it

CELLAR SALES
PRE-BOOKED VISITS
ANNUAL PRODUCTION 50,000 bottles
HECTARES UNDER VINE 15.00

Wine-grower Mauro Drius concentrates on coaxing the finest qualities out of his terroir and above all from his priceless vineyards, which stretch out over the high plateau of the Isonzo river and the slopes of Monte Quarin in the heart of the Collio. The family history goes far back across generation after generation of farmers in Cormòns. The unity of the family is an additional advantage that has allowed Drius to unfold his own talents to the fullest. His father Sergio still lends a hand in the vineyard and, while his children Denis, Erika, and Valentina are growing up, his wife Nadia assists in managing the operation. The entire line of wines is first class. The differences between these scores are minimal and the results are hard to classify. We preferred the Friulano 2012 del Collio because of its remarkable fragrance and marked typicality. The Malvasia 2012 shows excellent hints of aroma, and the Bianco Vignis di Siris 2011 maintains its usual impeccable balance.

○ Collio Friulano '12	♥♥ 3*
○ Collio Sauvignon '12	♥♥ 3
○ Friuli Isonzo Malvasia '12	♥♥ 3
○ Friuli Isonzo Pinot Grigio '12	♥♥ 3
○ Friuli Isonzo Vignis di Siris '11	♥♥ 4
○ Friuli Isonzo Chardonnay '12	♥ 3
○ Friuli Isonzo Pinot Bianco '12	♥ 3
○ Collio Tocai Friulano '05	♥♥♥ 3*
○ Collio Tocai Friulano '02	♥♥♥ 2*
○ Friuli Isonzo Bianco Vignis di Siris '02	♥♥♥ 3*
○ Friuli Isonzo Friulano '07	♥♥♥ 3
○ Friuli Isonzo Malvasia '08	♥♥♥ 3*
○ Friuli Isonzo Pinot Bianco '09	♥♥♥ 3*
○ Collio Sauvignon '11	♥♥ 3*
○ Friuli Isonzo Malvasia '10	♥♥ 3*

★Le Due Terre

VIA ROMA, 68B
33040 PREPOTTO [UD]
TEL. 0432713189

CELLAR SALES
PRE-BOOKED VISITS
ANNUAL PRODUCTION 20,000 bottles
HECTARES UNDER VINE 5.00

Flavio Basilicata and Silvana Forte own this modest operation of barely five hectares of vineyard atop a small hill, where their house serves as both residence and cellar. During the excavations for construction of the cellar, they found stones that could have been part of an ancient church, hence the name Sacrisassi for some of the wines. Meanwhile, the mixed limestone and clay composition of the soil inspired the name of the winery. Its small size and limited production allow Flavio to practise the kind of winemaking in which he has always believed: ambient yeasts, spontaneous fermentations, lengthy sojourns in barriques and no rackings. The Sacrisassi Rosso becomes more interesting every year, and the 2001 easily wins our Tre Bicchieri, proving its absolute excellence. This wine is made from schioppettino and refosco dal peduncolo rosso, the native red grape varieties most common in the region, masterfully measured and blended.

● COF Rosso Sacrisassi '11	♥♥♥ 5
○ COF Bianco Sacrisassi '11	♥♥ 5
● COF Merlot '11	♥♥ 5
● COF Pinot Nero '11	♥♥ 5
○ COF Bianco Sacrisassi '05	♥♥♥ 5
● COF Merlot '03	♥♥♥ 5
● COF Merlot '02	♥♥♥ 5
● COF Merlot '00	♥♥♥ 5
● COF Rosso Sacrisassi '10	♥♥♥ 5
● COF Rosso Sacrisassi '09	♥♥♥ 5
● COF Rosso Sacrisassi '08	♥♥♥ 5
● COF Rosso Sacrisassi '07	♥♥♥ 5
● COF Rosso Sacrisassi '98	♥♥♥ 5
● COF Rosso Sacrisassi '97	♥♥♥ 5
○ COF Bianco Sacrisassi '10	♥♥ 5
● COF Merlot '10	♥♥ 5

Ermacora

FRAZ. IPPLIS
VIA SOLZAREDO, 9
33040 PREMARIACCO [UD]
TEL. 0432716250
www.ermacora.com

CELLAR SALES
PRE-BOOKED VISITS
ANNUAL PRODUCTION 175,000 bottles
HECTARES UNDER VINE 47.00

It is well known that the nutrient-poor but mineral-rich marly arenaceous soils of the Colli Orientali del Friuli, made up of Eocene limestone and clay, make for exceptional quality viticulture. The Ermacora family understood this as early as 1922, when they planted their vineyards on the Ipplis hill, thus laying the foundation for wines of noble character. Dario and Luciano now run this well-respected avant-garde operation guided by a simple philosophy that respects nature's rhythms and avoids over-manipulation even while making use of innovative technology. The results are sound, clean wines with distinctive personalities and varietal fidelity. At the top of the list are four native wines, excellently crafted from different vintages: the Friulano 2012 with a typical wild flower aroma; the soft and spicy Schioppettino 2011; the pleasantly sweet and caramelly Picolit 2011; and the powerful, muscular Pignolo 2008.

○ COF Friulano '12	♼♼ 3
○ COF Picolit '11	♼♼ 6
● COF Pignolo '08	♼♼ 5
○ COF Pinot Bianco '12	♼♼ 3
○ COF Pinot Grigio '12	♼♼ 3
● COF Schioppettino '11	♼♼ 3
○ COF Ribolla Gialla '12	♼ 3
○ COF Sauvignon '12	♼ 3
○ COF Friulano '11	♼♼ 3
○ COF Friulano '10	♼♼ 3*
○ COF Picolit '09	♼♼ 6
○ COF Picolit '07	♼♼ 6
● COF Pignolo '05	♼♼ 5
● COF Pignolo '04	♼♼ 5

Fantinel

FRAZ. TAURIANO
VIA TESIS, 8
33097 SPILIMBERGO [PN]
TEL. 0427591511
www.fantinel.com

CELLAR SALES
PRE-BOOKED VISITS
RESTAURANT SERVICE
ANNUAL PRODUCTION 4,000,000 bottles
HECTARES UNDER VINE 300.00

Fantinel boasts a collection of wines that stand out despite their number. Its history goes back to 1969, when Carnia hotelier-restaurateur Mario Fantinel purchased his first vineyards. Successive generations have followed his example, growing the family inheritance so that the winery now possesses 300 hectares of vineyards in three separate areas: the Sant'Helena property at Vencò in the Collio, La Roncaia in Nimis in the Colli Orientali, and Borgo Tesis in Tauriano di Spilimbergo in Grave del Friuli. The last is an elegant complex surrounded by vineyards, whose offices and cellar are run by winemakers Gianni Campo Dall'Orto and Alberto Zanello. White grapes with powerful ties to the terroir were selected to make the Collio Bianco Frontiere San'Helena 2011. The delicious nose has hints of exotic and candied fruits, and the palate is full and caressing. Special mention also goes to the fresh and lively sparkling Ribolla Gialla.

○ Collio Bianco Frontiere Vigneti Sant'Helena '11	♼♼ 3*
○ Collio Friulano Vigneti Sant'Helena '12	♼♼ 3
● Collio Rosso Venko Vigneti Sant'Helena '07	♼♼ 3
○ Collio Sauvignon V igneti Sant'Helena '12	♼♼ 3
○ Ribolla Gialla Brut	♼♼ 3
○ Prosecco	♼ 3
○ Collio Bianco Sant'Helena '10	♼♼ 3
○ Collio Chardonnay Sant'Helena '11	♼♼ 3*
○ Collio Ribolla Gialla Vigneti Sant'Helena '10	♼♼ 3
○ Collio Sauvignon Sant'Helena '11	♼♼ 3
● Friuli Grave Refosco P. R. Sant'Helena '06	♼♼ 3
○ Ribolla Gialla Vigneti Sant'Helena '11	♼♼ 3

★★Livio Felluga

FRAZ. BRAZZANO
VIA RISORGIMENTO, 1
34071 CORMÒNS [GO]
TEL. 048160203
www.liviofelluga.it

CELLAR SALES
PRE-BOOKED VISITS
ANNUAL PRODUCTION 800,000 bottles
HECTARES UNDER VINE 145.00

The Felluga family boast pages of history first under the Austro-Hungarian Empire and later in the young Kingdom of Italy. They started out on the rocky coast of the Istrian peninsula, moved to Grado in the Venetian lagoon, and finally ended up in the Friuli hills. Livio Felluga, born in Isola d'Istria in 1914 – and therefore about to celebrate his century – is rightfully known in the region as 'the patriarch' of Friulan wine. To his four children he has passed an immense legacy of tradition, love for the earth, and overcoming of daily challenges to keep undimmed the prestige of this famous label that bears the map of his own local hills designed by Livio himself in 1956. The new Friuli DOC zone, recently awarded to the Rosazzo Bianco, gives greater lustre to the Terre Alte 2011 that, after a year in the background, has again won our Tre Bicchieri. The delicious nose has notes of roasted hazelnuts and lemon yogurt, and the dancing palate is refined, energetic and velvety.

○ Rosazzo Bianco Terre Alte '11	♼♼♼ 7
○ COF Bianco Illivio '11	♼♼ 5
○ COF Friulano '12	♼♼ 4
○ COF Pinot Grigio '12	♼♼ 4
● COF Refosco P. R. '09	♼♼ 5
● COF Rosazzo Sossò Ris. '09	♼♼ 7
○ COF Bianco Illivio '10	♼♼♼ 5
○ COF Rosazzo Bianco Terre Alte '09	♼♼♼ 7
○ COF Rosazzo Bianco Terre Alte '08	♼♼♼ 7
○ COF Rosazzo Bianco Terre Alte '07	♼♼♼ 7
○ COF Rosazzo Bianco Terre Alte '06	♼♼♼ 6
○ COF Rosazzo Bianco Terre Alte '04	♼♼♼ 6
○ COF Rosazzo Bianco Terre Alte '02	♼♼♼ 7
● COF Rosazzo Sossò Ris. '01	♼♼♼ 6

Marco Felluga

VIA GORIZIA, 121
34070 GRADISCA D'ISONZO [GO]
TEL. 048199164
www.marcofelluga.it

CELLAR SALES
PRE-BOOKED VISITS
ANNUAL PRODUCTION 600,000 bottles
HECTARES UNDER VINE 100.00

Directing this winery is Roberto Felluga, the fifth generation of a dynasty of wine-growers whose roots go back to Istria in the latter part of the 1800s. Fortune brought them to Grado, then Friuli after World War I. The two are separated by only a few kilometres, but the differences are substantial, and so was the change for the family fortunes. Marco settled in the Collio Goriziano area and in 1956 founded the winery that bears his name. He dedicated himself to developing and promoting the terroir that today, with its great success, owes him a debt of honour. Marco Felluga wines can be relied upon for high quality, tradition, and distinctive personalities. The Pinot Grigio Mongris Riserva 2010 has aromas of citron and lemon yogurt, and flaunts bold fragrance and zesty minerality. The Sauvignon 2012 is varietal and citrussy with a crisp, continuous palate. The Friulano 2012 has aromas of Mediterranean scrub on a balsamic background.

○ Collio Pinot Grigio Mongris Ris. '10	♼♼ 6
○ Collio Chardonnay '12	♼♼ 5
○ Collio Friulano '12	♼♼ 5
○ Collio Pinot Grigio '12	♼♼ 5
○ Collio Sauvignon '12	♼♼ 5
● Collio Carantan '09	♼ 7
○ Collio Ribolla Gialla '12	♼ 5
○ Collio Friulano '11	♼♼ 3
● Collio Merlot Varneri '06	♼♼ 3*
○ Collio Pinot Grigio Mongris '11	♼♼ 3
○ Collio Pinot Grigio Mongris Ris. '09	♼♼ 4
○ Collio Pinot Grigio Mongris Ris. '08	♼♼ 4
○ Collio Pinot Grigio Mongris Ris. '07	♼♼ 4
● Refosco P.R. Ronco dei Moreri '10	♼♼ 3

Fiegl

FRAZ. OSLAVIA
LOC. LENZUOLO BIANCO, 1
34070 GORIZIA
TEL. 0481547103
www.fieglvini.com

CELLAR SALES
PRE-BOOKED VISITS
ANNUAL PRODUCTION 150,000 bottles
HECTARES UNDER VINE 30.00

A deed dated 1782 attests to Valentino Fiegl's purchase of a vineyard in the village of Oslavia not far from Slovenia, in northern Collio, an area boasting many prestigious wineries today. Many generations of winegrowers followed, of a family that has always been a model of closeness. Brothers Alessio, Giuseppe, and Rinaldo direct it today, but they can already count on the participation of the new generation, comprising Martin, Robert, and Matej. The various responsibilities are shared in perfect synergy, contributing to that consistent quality trajectory that has propelled Fiegl into the regional group of top-ranked producers. The Merlot Leopold 2007 repeats last year's success and landed in our finals. Initial notes of crushed red fruit are followed by spicy, balsamic aromas, and a satisfying palate with good development. All the other wines in this range show perfectly decent quality.

● Collio Merlot Leopold '07	♟♟ 4
○ Collio Friulano '12	♟♟ 3
○ Collio Malvasia '12	♟♟ 3
○ Collio Sauvignon '12	♟♟ 3
☉ Fiegl Brut Rosé	♟♟ 4
○ Mcja '01 '09	♟♟ 5
○ Collio Cuvée Blanc Leopold '10	♟ 4
○ Collio Pinot Grigio '12	♟ 3
○ Collio Ribolla Gialla '12	♟ 3
○ Collio Pinot Grigio '04	♟♟♟ 2*
○ Collio Malvasia '07	♟♟ 3
○ Collio Malvasia '06	♟♟ 3
● Collio Merlot Leopold '06	♟♟ 4
● Collio Merlot Leopold '04	♟♟ 4
○ Collio Sauvignon '07	♟♟ 3

Flaibani

VIA CASALI COSTA, 7
33043 CIVIDALE DEL FRIULI [UD]
TEL. 0432730943
www.flaibani.it

CELLAR SALES
PRE-BOOKED VISITS
ANNUAL PRODUCTION 15,000 bottles
HECTARES UNDER VINE 3.50
VITICULTURE METHOD Certified Organic

Pino Flaibani's operation runs totally counter to the other wineries in the region, which are well known for privileging white over red wines. His contrary direction may have been suggested by the pre-existing vineyards, which Flaibani purchased along with the house and small cellar. His history has a connection with the terrible events surrounding the 1976 Friuli earthquake: born in Udine, he returned to his area to help his fellows. There he got the idea of returning permanently as soon as he reached retirement age, to dedicate himself full time to winegrowing. The reds here win our greatest appreciation. The Merlot Seduzione Riserva 2009 introduces opulent notes of cocoa powder, crushed black berries and forest floor. The palate is caressing and leaves a long memory. The Cabernet Sauvignon 2011 is fruity, fragrant and continuous.

● COF Cabernet Sauvignon '11	♟♟ 3
● COF Merlot '11	♟♟ 3
● COF Merlot Seduzione Ris. '09	♟♟ 5
● COF Schioppettino '10	♟♟ 5
○ COF Pinot Grigio '12	♟ 3
● Refosco P.R. '11	♟ 3
● COF Cabernet Franc '09	♟♟ 3
● COF Cabernet Sauvignon Ris. '09	♟♟ 4
● COF Cabernet Sauvignon Ris. '06	♟♟ 4
● COF Merlot '09	♟♟ 4
○ COF Pinot Grigio '11	♟♟ 3
● COF Tentazione '10	♟♟ 3
○ Pinot Grigio '10	♟♟ 3
● Refosco P.R. '10	♟♟ 3

FRIULI VENEZIA GIULIA

Adriano Gigante

VIA ROCCA BERNARDA, 3
33040 CORNO DI ROSAZZO [UD]
TEL. 0432755835
www.adrianogigante.it

CELLAR SALES
PRE-BOOKED VISITS
ANNUAL PRODUCTION 60,000 bottles
HECTARES UNDER VINE 25.00

Many of the region's finest producers are located in the Rocca Bernarda hills; Adriano Gigante's winery, lying on the slope facing Corno di Rosazzo, is a long-established cellar that expresses well the distinctive characteristics of the Colli Orientali del Friuli. Most know the story of his grandfather Ferruccio, who in 1957 left behind his long-exercised career as miller to dedicate himself to cultivating a vineyard of tocai friulano, whose potential he recognised; the vineyard, named Historic, still exists. Assisted by his wine Giuliana in managing the winery and by his cousin Ariedo in the cellar and vineyard, Gigante continues the family traditions with a line of wines of the highest quality. The Friulano Vigneto Storico made the top of our list, specifically the wine from the 2011 vintage, fragrant on the nose and crisp on the palate. Also excellent, the version from the following vintage is fresher, both in aromas and on the palate. The other wines are also notable.

○ COF Friulano Vign. Storico '11	♟♟ 4
○ COF Chardonnay '12	♟♟ 3
○ COF Friulano '12	♟♟ 3
○ COF Friulano Vign. Storico '12	♟♟ 4
○ COF Pinot Grigio '12	♟♟ 3
○ COF Sauvignon '12	♟♟ 3
○ COF Verduzzo Friulano '09	♟♟ 3
● COF Cabernet Franc '11	♟ 3
○ COF Ribolla Gialla '12	♟ 3
⊘ Prima Gialla Brut Rosé	♟ 3
⊘ Prima Nera Brut Rosé	♟ 3
○ COF Tocai Friulano Vign. Storico '06	♟♟♟ 4
○ COF Tocai Friulano Vign. Storico '05	♟♟♟ 4
○ COF Tocai Friulano Vign. Storico '03	♟♟♟ 4
○ COF Friulano '11	♟♟ 3*
○ COF Verduzzo Friulano '08	♟♟ 3*

Gradis'ciutta

LOC. GIASBANA, 10
34070 SAN FLORIANO DEL COLLIO [GO]
TEL. 0481390237
robigradis@libero.it

CELLAR SALES
PRE-BOOKED VISITS
ANNUAL PRODUCTION 60,000 bottles
HECTARES UNDER VINE 17.00

When Robert Princic founded Gradis'ciutta, he named it for a small hamlet at Giasbana, near San Floriano del Collio, known ages ago as Monvinoso, which speaks volumes about the ancient winegrowing traditions in these hills. They fit in with family tradition, since the Princic family had been producing wines in Kosana, in nearby Slovenia, since 1780. Despite his youth, Princic manages the operation with competence and a firm hand, fully knowledgeable about the qualities of the area. The distribution of the vineyards at different elevations makes it possible to find sites appropriate to all the varieties, both indigenous and international. This year the Friulano 2012 topped this range of ever more pleasing and convincing wines. With its fruity tones of golden apple and white peach, this wine shows a creamy, velvety palate. The always excellent, fragrant Bianco Bratinis 2011 is made from chardonnay, sauvignon and ribolla gialla.

○ Collio Friulano '12	♟♟ 2*
○ Collio Bianco Bratinis '11	♟♟ 3
○ Collio Chardonnay '12	♟♟ 2*
○ Collio Malvasia '12	♟♟ 2*
○ Collio Ribolla Gialla '12	♟♟ 2*
○ Collio Pinot Grigio '12	♟ 3
○ Collio Bianco Bratinis '10	♟♟ 3*
○ Collio Bianco Bratinis '07	♟♟ 3*
○ Collio Bianco del Tüzz '05	♟♟ 3*
○ Collio Friulano '10	♟♟ 2*
● Collio Merlot '07	♟♟ 3*
○ Collio Pinot Grigio '08	♟♟ 2*
○ Collio Ribolla Gialla '07	♟♟ 2*

★★Gravner

FRAZ. OSLAVIA
LOC. LENZUOLO BIANCO, 9
34070 GORIZIA
TEL. 048130882
www.gravner.it

CELLAR SALES
PRE-BOOKED VISITS
ANNUAL PRODUCTION 30,000 bottles
HECTARES UNDER VINE 18.00

Josko Gravner's wines are always striking and thought-provoking. Over the years, whatever vinification process he has chosen, the wines have always been exciting, the fruit of a philosophy that has remained uncompromising. Gravner is a great winegrower and passionate researcher, trying out the most avant-garde practices, only to trace back on his steps, just as his father predicted. Today, he no longer uses either steel or barriques, only terracotta amphorae from the Caucasus, in which the grapes-even the white grapes-macerate for over six months, then large oak barrels where the wine spends many years. The result is golden-hued, amber wines, the fruit of exceptionally sound grapes and ancestral practices. A Tre Bicchieri award goes to the Breg Anfora 2006, with intriguing aromas of aromatic herbs, sour cherries and stewed pear juice, and a long, flavourful palate. The same goes for the Ribolla Anfora 2006, with great texture and personality. In its first release, the Breg Rosso is from pignolo harvested in 2003.

○ Breg Anfora '06	♥♥♥ 7
○ Ribolla Anfora '06	♥♥ 5
● Rosso Breg '03	♥♥ 7
○ Breg '00	♥♥♥ 8
○ Breg Anfora '03	♥♥♥ 7
○ Breg Anfora '02	♥♥♥ 7
○ Chardonnay '87	♥♥♥ 7
○ Chardonnay '83	♥♥♥ 7
○ Ribolla Anfora '05	♥♥♥ 7
○ Ribolla Anfora '04	♥♥♥ 7
○ Ribolla Anfora '02	♥♥♥ 7
○ Ribolla Anfora '01	♥♥♥ 7
● Rosso Gravner '04	♥♥♥ 7

Jacùss

FRAZ. MONTINA
V.LE KENNEDY, 35A
33040 TORREANO [UD]
TEL. 0432715147
www.jacuss.com

CELLAR SALES
PRE-BOOKED VISITS
ANNUAL PRODUCTION 50,000 bottles
HECTARES UNDER VINE 10.00

Brothers Sandro and Andrea Iacuzzi operate this winery in perfect synch with each other. In 1990, after years of mixed agriculture, they decided to transform the property into a wine estate and called it Jacùss, the local dialect version of their last name. Together they manage their estate vineyards, which extend over the hills of Montina, a small village in the commune of Torreano di Cividale, and make the wine. Their outstanding results have propelled them to constant improvements, and the wines, sound, self-confident, and varietally faithful, have conquered many palates. Preferences in the vintage wines ran to the Pinot Bianco 2012 with a bouquet of ripe, white-fleshed fruit and pencil lead; the creamy palate closes on a vanilla note. The Merlot and Cabernet Sauvignon, both from 2009, are rich in spicy, balsamic hints that accompany the taste.

● COF Cabernet Sauvignon '09	♥♥ 3
● COF Merlot '09	♥♥ 3
○ COF Picolit '08	♥♥ 6
○ COF Pinot Bianco '12	♥♥ 3
○ COF Friulano '12	♥ 3
● COF Refosco P.R. '09	♥ 3
○ COF Sauvignon '12	♥ 3
● COF Tazzelenghe '09	♥ 3
○ COF Verduzzo Friulano '08	♥ 3
○ COF Pinot Bianco '04	♥♥ 2*
○ COF Sauvignon '02	♥♥ 3
● COF Schioppettino Fucs e Flamis '10	♥♥ 3*
● COF Tazzelenghe '08	♥♥ 3
○ COF Verduzzo Friulano '07	♥♥ 3

★★Jermann

FRAZ. RUTTARS
VIA MONTE FORTINO, 21
34072 FARRA D'ISONZO [GO]
TEL. 0481888080
www.jermann.it

PRE-BOOKED VISITS
ANNUAL PRODUCTION 900,000 bottles
HECTARES UNDER VINE 150.00

In 1881, founder Anton Jermann left the Austrian winegrowing region of Burgerland and sent his roots deep into Friuli-Venezia Giulia. Silvio Jermann added an epochal milestone to this century-plus history in the 1970s, when his genius and imagination propelled the winery into the very top ranks of Italian, and then international, producers. The historical cellar in Villanova di Farra is still in operation, but the iconic wines that have made the winery so famous are produced in the splendid new cellar in Ruttars, custom-designed for such wines. This year the legendary Vintage Tunina 2011 once again won the Tre Bicchieri award. This fascinating wine with great structure displays fresh, fragrant, rich aromas and flavours from the magical mix of sauvignon and chardonnay, topped off with ribolla gialla, malvasia istriana and picolit.

○ Vintage Tunina '11	♟♟♟ 6
○ W.... Dreams.... '11	♟♟ 8
○ Pinot Bianco '12	♟♟ 4
○ Pinot Grigio '12	♟♟ 4
○ Ribolla Gialla Vinnae '12	♟♟ 4
○ Riesling Afix '12	♟♟ 4
○ Capo Martino '10	♟♟♟ 8
○ Capo Martino '05	♟♟♟ 8
● Pignacolusse '00	♟♟♟ 5
○ Vintage Tunina '08	♟♟♟ 7
○ Vintage Tunina '07	♟♟♟ 7
○ Vintage Tunina '01	♟♟♟ 7
○ Vintage Tunina '00	♟♟♟ 7
○ W.... Dreams... .... '09	♟♟♟ 6
○ W.... Dreams... .... '06	♟♟♟ 6

Kante

FRAZ. SAN PELAGIO
LOC. PREPOTTO, 1A
34011 DUINO AURISINA [TS]
TEL. 040200255
www.kante.it

ANNUAL PRODUCTION 45,000 bottles
HECTARES UNDER VINE 13.00

Edi Kante is a volcano of ideas, a poet, a painter, a sensitive soul, and an obstinate, ever-curious person. In the Carso area around Trieste everyone considers him the founder, the trail-blazer, the one who compelled universal attention for winemaking in an area where all thought it difficult, if not impossible, to plant vines and make wine. His jaw-dropping cellar, a true monument to oenology, consists of three levels completely carved from hard rock. The wines, which need some time to find their best expression, are the fruit of a long process, of a challenge to rock, cold winds, and searing heat. Straightforward and authentic, they are eloquent expressions of their terroir. The Malvasia and Sauvignon from the 2010 vintage, along with the Chardonnay La Bora di Kante 2005, earned a place in our final tastings. These energetic wines have great fragrance and complexity, and present the palate with flavourful, lingering mineral notes, at times citrussy or iodine.

○ Carso Chardonnay La Bora di Kante '05	♟♟ 6
○ Malvasia '10	♟♟ 4
○ Sauvignon '10	♟♟ 4
○ Brut KK	♟♟ 4
⊙ Brut KK Rosé	♟♟ 4
○ Chardonnay '10	♟ 4
○ Vitovska '10	♟ 4
○ Carso Malvasia '07	♟♟♟ 5
○ Carso Malvasia '06	♟♟♟ 5
○ Carso Malvasia '05	♟♟♟ 5
○ Carso Chardonnay la Bora di Kante '01	♟♟ 5
○ Carso Malvasia '09	♟♟ 5
○ Carso Sauvignon '07	♟♟ 5
○ Carso Vitovska Sel. '04	♟♟ 5
○ Sauvignon '08	♟♟ 5

★Edi Keber

Loc. Zegla, 17
34071 Cormòns [GO]
Tel. 048161184
www.edikeber.it

CELLAR SALES
PRE-BOOKED VISITS
ACCOMMODATION
ANNUAL PRODUCTION 50,000 bottles
HECTARES UNDER VINE 12.00

The Keber name is connected to those
living in Zegla and Medana, a border area
over which have flown various national
flags, thanks at times to chance, at others
to human intervention; those living here
found themselves sometimes in Austria,
then in Italy, then in Slovenia, then once
more in Italy, all without moving an inch.
Edi Keber produces a single wine, Collio, a
choice that might seem either a tad risky or
perhaps presumptuous, but it is the fruit of
careful, applied research and years of
experimentation, ensuring that all energies
are focused on its success, from growing
the grapes to the vinification, and on the
daily monitoring of that wine's progress.
Tocai friulano, malvasia istriana and ribolla
gialla are their varieties that traditionally go
into the Collio white wine, the object of
attention and appreciation again this year
in the 2012 version. This electric wine is
scented and fragrant, and expresses the
features of a unique terroir.

○ Collio '12	♥♥	3*
○ Collio Bianco '10	♥♥♥	3*
○ Collio Bianco '09	♥♥♥	3
○ Collio Bianco '08	♥♥♥	3*
○ Collio Bianco '04	♥♥♥	3*
○ Collio Bianco '02	♥♥♥	3
○ Collio Tocai Friulano '07	♥♥♥	3
○ Collio Tocai Friulano '06	♥♥♥	3
○ Collio Tocai Friulano '05	♥♥♥	3
○ Collio Tocai Friulano '03	♥♥♥	3*
○ Collio Tocai Friulano '01	♥♥♥	3
○ Collio Tocai Friulano '99	♥♥♥	3*
○ Collio Tocai Friulano '97	♥♥♥	3*
○ Collio Tocai Friulano '95	♥♥♥	3*

Renato Keber

Loc. Zegla, 15
34071 Cormòns [GO]
Tel. 0481639844
www.renatokeber.com

CELLAR SALES
PRE-BOOKED VISITS
ACCOMMODATION
ANNUAL PRODUCTION 60,000 bottles
HECTARES UNDER VINE 15.00

Renato Keber has become a benchmark
among the region's winegrowers. The
Keber family settled in the village of Zegla
in the latter half of the 1800s, in a border
land ravaged by wars that separated
regions and peoples. But the Kebers
persisted, and Renato, when he finished his
oenology studies, took over the winery in
the 1980s. He immediately imparted to the
wines a definite character, in a kind of
symbiosis with the growing area. He makes
wine in the most natural manner possible,
without exaggerating, never in a hurry, and
always respecting varietal character.
Before release, his wines spend years in
the winding tunnels of his cellar. Coming
close to greatness, the Friulano Zegla
Riserva 2009 is rich in aroma and flavour,
well structured and enveloping. Also
excellent, the Collio Bianco Beli Grici 2010
is balsamic and gutsy.

○ Collio Friulano Zegla Ris. '09	♥♥	5
○ Collio Bianco Beli Grici '10	♥♥	4
○ Collio Friulano Zegla '05	♥♥♥	5
○ Collio Friulano Zegla Ris. '08	♥♥♥	5
○ Collio Friulano Zegla '07	♥♥	5
○ Collio Bianco Beli Grici '05	♥♥	6
○ Collio Chardonnay Grici '06	♥♥	5
○ Collio Chardonnay Grici '01	♥♥	5
○ Collio Friulano Ris. '08	♥♥	3
○ Collio Friulano Zio Romi Ris. '09	♥♥	5
● Collio Merlot Grici Ris. '06	♥♥	5
○ Collio Pinot Grigio '06	♥♥	3
○ Collio Ribolla Gialla Extreme '06	♥♥	4
○ Collio Sauvignon Grici '05	♥♥	5

Thomas Kitzmüller

fraz. Brazzano
via XXIV Maggio, 56
34071 Cormòns [GO]
Tel. 048163936
www.kitzmuller.it

CELLAR SALES
PRE-BOOKED VISITS
ACCOMMODATION
ANNUAL PRODUCTION 30,000 bottles
HECTARES UNDER VINE 6.00

In 1987, Thomas Kitzmüller decided to work the family vineyards, which are equally distributed between the Collio and Friuli Isonzo zones. The modest but attractive cellar lies in the heart of Brazzano, in the municipality of Cormòns. A venerable 18th-century farmhouse, inhabited some one hundred years ago by an old aunt nicknamed Mummel, now houses the winemaking operation, small but well-organised, as well as an agriturismo, named of course Mummelhaus, that exudes old-world charm. The winery's modest size allows Kitzmüller to lavish attention on the vines, which yield healthy fruit for straightforward wines, full-bodied and delicious. The Malvasia Juliae 2012 from the Friuli Isonzo DOC zone shows a typical lemon balm, bay and lemon leaf bouquet, and full-flavoured, continuous palate. A classic example of typicality, the Friulano 2012 del Collio has a fragrant nose and supple palate. The other wines are good, flavourful and fragrant.

○ Collio Friulano '12	🍷🍷 3
○ Friuli Isonzo Malvasia Juliae '12	🍷🍷 2*
● Cabernet Franc Corte Marie '12	🍷 2
○ Collio Ribolla Gialla '12	🍷 3
○ Friuli Isonzo Friulano Corte Marie '12	🍷 2
○ Collio Friulano '11	YYY 3*
○ Collio Friulano '09	YYY 2*
○ Collio Friulano '10	YY 2*
○ Collio Ribolla Gialla '08	YY 2*
○ Collio Sauvignon '09	YY 2*
○ Collio Traminer Aromatico '11	YY 3
○ Collio Traminer Aromatico '08	YY 2*
○ Friuli Isonzo Friulano Corte Marie '10	YY 2*

Albino Kurtin

loc. Novali, 9
34071 Cormòns [GO]
Tel. 048160685
www.winekurtin.it

CELLAR SALES
PRE-BOOKED VISITS
ANNUAL PRODUCTION 60,000 bottles
HECTARES UNDER VINE 11.00

Albino Kurtin inherited his winegrowing expertise from his ancestors. The wine estate, founded in 1906 and located in Novali, near Cormòns, an area long famed for quality wine production, now boasts three generations of winegrowers. Relying on a new cellar with innovative equipment, Kurtin also has the help of his son Alessio, who brings to the operation the experience of his oenological studies as well as successive work in various Italian wineries. They are successfully walking the fine line between respect for tradition and sensitivity to the demands of the market. Once again this year, the Opera Prima Bianco 2012, a blend of pinot bianco, ribolla gialla and chardonnay, proved itself the pride of Kurtin. The nose offers an opulent, complex bouquet of melon and ripe exotic fruit that echoes on the palate and leaves an enduring memory.

○ Collio Friulano '12	🍷🍷 3
○ Collio Sauvignon '12	🍷🍷 3
○ Opera Prima Bianco '12	🍷🍷 3
○ Collio Ribolla Gialla '12	🍷 3
● Collio Rosso '10	🍷 4
○ Collio Friulano '11	YY 3
○ Collio Malvasia '11	YY 3
○ Collio Malvasia '08	YY 3*
● Collio Rosso '08	YY 4
○ Collio Sauvignon '11	YY 3
○ Opera Prima Bianco '11	YY 3*
○ Opera Prima Bianco '10	YY 3

Vigneti Le Monde

LOC. LE MONDE
VIA GARIBALDI, 2
33080 PRATA DI PORDENONE [PN]
TEL. 0434622087
www.vignetilemonde.eu

CELLAR SALES
PRE-BOOKED VISITS
ANNUAL PRODUCTION 200,000 bottles
HECTARES UNDER VINE 49.00

Le Monde, located between the banks of the Livenza and Meduna rivers, is considered a true cru winery, with ultra-low yields per hectare and average vine ages considerably beyond 30 years. The vineyards, planted in clay-calcareous soils, are quite different from others in the Friuli Grave denomination, which are usually in gravel. Alex Maccan, the young, well-trained owner, purchased Vigneti Le Monde in 2008 and gave it a modern home and state-of-the-art winemaking facility. He immediately availed himself of the services of the equally young and dynamic winemaker, Matteo Bernabei, an apple fallen not far from the paternal tree. The commitment of this estate has meant increasing quality that this year has led to a Tre Bicchieri award for the Pinot Bianco 2012. This honour also went to the same label back in 2001. This exemplary wine is fruity, fragrant and soft, satisfying on the nose and caressing on the palate.

○ Friuli Grave Pinot Bianco '12	🍷🍷🍷	2*
○ Friuli Grave Pinot Grigio '12	🍷🍷	2*
● Friuli Grave Refosco P. R. '11	🍷🍷	2*
○ Friuli Grave Sauvignon '12	🍷🍷	2*
● Friuli Grave Cabernet Franc '11	🍷	2
● Friuli Grave Cabernet Sauvignon '11	🍷	2
○ Friuli Grave Friulano '12	🍷	2
○ Ribolla Gialla '12	🍷	2
○ Friuli Grave Pinot Bianco '01	YYY	2
○ Friuli Grave Chardonnay '10	YY	2*
○ Friuli Grave Pinot Bianco '10	YY	2*
● Friuli Grave Refosco P. R. '10	YY	2*
● Friuli Grave Refosco P. R. Inaco Ris. '08	YY	4
○ Friuli Grave Sauvignon '10	YY	2*

★Lis Neris

VIA GAVINANA, 5
34070 SAN LORENZO ISONTINO [GO]
TEL. 048180105
www.lisneris.it

CELLAR SALES
PRE-BOOKED VISITS
ACCOMMODATION
ANNUAL PRODUCTION 400,000 bottles
HECTARES UNDER VINE 70.00

Lis Neris, directed by Alvaro Pecorari, lies in the town of San Lorenzo Isontino, just a stone's throw from their vineyards, which stretch out over a small plateau resting on deep gravel transported by the waters of the melting glaciers of the eastern Alps, in an area between the Slovene border and the right bank of the Isonzo river. Pecorari represents the fourth generation of a family that settled in the area in 1879. 1981 was a crucial year for the winery, when it successfully launched its unmistakable style, which one could call the Pecorari style, characterized by smoothness, fragrance, and complexity. The Pinot Grigio Gris 2011 proves worthy of its fame as one of the best white wines in Italy, and once again wins our Tre Bicchieri award. This wine has a splendid nose and captivating palate. The Sauvignon Picòl 2011 and Tal Lùc 2010 also made it to the finals, and praise goes to all the other wines.

○ Friuli Isonzo Pinot Grigio Gris '11	🍷🍷🍷	4*
○ Friuli Isonzo Sauvignon Picòl '11	🍷🍷	4
○ Tal Lùc '10	🍷🍷	8
○ Confini '10	🍷🍷	5
○ Friuli Isonzo Chardonnay Jurosa '11	🍷🍷	4
○ Friuli Isonzo Friulano La Vila '11	🍷🍷	4
○ Friuli Isonzo Pinot Grigio '12	🍷🍷	3
○ Lis '09	🍷🍷	5
○ Fiore di Campo '06	YYY	3
○ Friuli Isonzo Pinot Grigio Gris '10	YYY	4*
○ Friuli Isonzo Pinot Grigio Gris '09	YYY	4*
○ Lis '03	YYY	5
○ Pinot Grigio Gris '08	YYY	4*
○ Pinot Grigio Gris '04	YYY	4*
○ Sauvignon Picòl '06	YYY	3*
○ Tal Lùc '02	YYY	8

★Livon

FRAZ. DOLEGNANO
VIA MONTAREZZA, 33
33048 SAN GIOVANNI AL NATISONE [UD]
TEL. 0432757173
www.livon.it

CELLAR SALES
PRE-BOOKED VISITS
ACCOMMODATION
ANNUAL PRODUCTION 950,000 bottles
HECTARES UNDER VINE 180.00

In 1964, Dorino Livon founded this winery, passing it on later to sons Valneo and Tonino. In just a few years, they achieved remarkable growth, so that now Livon can boast a total of five wine brands, two of which out of the region. The historic headquarters are in Dolegnano, part of San Giovanni al Natisone. The RoncAlto label is reserved for an extraordinary vineyard in the Collio Goriziano, while Villa Chiopris takes in 110 hectares on the Friulan plain. Outside Friuli, Borgo Salcetino in Radda in Chianti and Colsanto in Umbria complete the roster. Legendary winemaster Rinaldo Stocco oversees all of the estates. The diverse and multi-faceted Livon portfolio encompasses a remarkable number of bottlings. The Braide Alte 2011, an original blend of chardonnay, sauvignon, moscato giallo and picolit, proved a major wine and won our Three Glass award. The TiareBlù 2010, from merlot and cabernet sauvignon, and the Collio Bianco Solarco 2012 from friulano and ribolla gialla, also made it to the finals.

Tenuta Luisa

FRAZ. CORONA
VIA CAMPO SPORTIVO , 13
34070 MARIANO DEL FRIULI [GO]
TEL. 048169680
www.viniluisa.com

CELLAR SALES
PRE-BOOKED VISITS
ANNUAL PRODUCTION 300,000 bottles
HECTARES UNDER VINE 79.00

Eddi Luisa and his wife Nella, together with their sons Michele and Davide, operate this striking cellar in Corona a Mariano del Friuli, in the Friuli Isonzo denomination. Two generations in dialogue sapiently marry tradition to ceaseless research, innovation, enthusiasm, courage, and far-sightedness, achieving significant growth over the years. The attention that the family has given to the cellar and its surroundings testifies to their passionate commitment to their art. The extensive number of wines has made it necessary to differentiate the I Ferretti line from the standard wines. All these wines are excellently made and feature a noticeable estate imprint. The Friulano Selezione I Ferretti 2011 is rich in colour and aroma, and broad and fragrant on the palate. The Desiderium Selezione I Ferretti 2011, from chardonnay, friulano and sauvignon, is rich in exotic shades that return on the palate.

○ Braide Alte '11	♀♀♀ 5
○ Collio Bianco Solarco '12	♀♀ 3*
● TiareBlù '10	♀♀ 4
○ Malvasia Soluna '12	♀♀ 3
● Picotis '10	♀♀ 4
○ Collio Ribolla Gialla RoncAlto '12	♀ 3
○ Braide Alte '09	♀♀♀ 5
○ Braide Alte '07	♀♀♀ 5
○ Braide Alte '00	♀♀♀ 5
○ Braide Alte '98	♀♀♀ 5
○ Braide Alte '97	♀♀♀ 5
● COF Refosco P. R. Riul '02	♀♀♀ 3
○ COF Verduzzo Friulano Casali Godia '94	♀♀♀ 4
○ Collio Braide Alte '08	♀♀♀ 3
○ Collio Friulano Manditocai '10	♀♀♀ 5
● TiareBlù '00	♀♀♀ 5

○ Desiderium Sel. I Ferretti '11	♀♀ 4
○ Friuli Isonzo Friulano I Ferretti '11	♀♀ 3
○ Friuli Isonzo Chardonnay '12	♀ 3
○ Friuli Isonzo Friulano '12	♀ 3
○ Friuli Isonzo Pinot Bianco '12	♀ 3
○ Friuli Isonzo Pinot Grigio '12	♀ 3
● Friuli Isonzo Refosco P. R. '11	♀ 3
○ Friuli Isonzo Sauvignon '12	♀ 3
○ Ribolla Gialla '12	♀ 3
○ Desiderium Sel. I Ferretti '09	♀♀♀ 4*
○ Desiderium Sel. I Ferretti '10	♀♀ 4
○ Friuli Isonzo Chardonnay '10	♀♀ 3
○ Friuli Isonzo Friulano '11	♀♀ 3
○ Friuli Isonzo Friulano '10	♀♀ 3*
○ Friuli Isonzo Pinot Bianco '10	♀♀ 3*
○ Friuli Isonzo Sauvignon '11	♀♀ 3

Magnàs

LOC. BOATINA
VIA CORONA, 47
34071 CORMÒNS [GO]
TEL. 048160991
www.magnas.it

CELLAR SALES
PRE-BOOKED VISITS
ACCOMMODATION AND RESTAURANT SERVICE
ANNUAL PRODUCTION 25,000 bottles
HECTARES UNDER VINE 10.00

In the early 1970s, Luciano Visintin, relying on the centuries-old expertise of a family deeply rooted in agriculture, decided to give a highly personal imprint to a brand-new wine venture and founded Magnàs. Valiantly assisted by his wife Sonia, who devotes most of her attention now to managing their charming agriturismo, Visintin has for some time handed over winemaking to their son Andrea. The cellar lies in the village of Boatina, in the Cormòns area, while the vineyards extend over the sunny plains of the Friuli Isonzo denomination, whose famously rocky, nutrient-poor, dry soils proved themselves ideal for the cultivation of the vine. Again this year, we enjoyed Andrea's wines not only for their coherency and fragrance, but also their varietal correspondence. The Malvasia 2012 is rich in notes of citrus and resin; the palate is fresh and crisp. The Friulano and Sauvignon, both 2012, are also well balanced and pleasant.

○ Friuli Isonzo Friulano '12	▼▼ 3
○ Friuli Isonzo Sauvignon '12	▼▼ 3
○ Malvasia '12	▼▼ 3
○ Friuli Isonzo Chardonnay '12	▼ 3
○ Friuli Isonzo Pinot Grigio '12	▼ 3
○ Friuli Isonzo Chardonnay '11	▽▽ 3
○ Friuli Isonzo Chardonnay '09	▽▽ 3
○ Friuli Isonzo Friulano '11	▽▽ 3
○ Friuli Isonzo Friulano '10	▽▽ 3
○ Friuli Isonzo Friulano '09	▽▽ 3*
○ Friuli Isonzo Malvasia '09	▽▽ 3
○ Friuli Isonzo Pinot Grigio '11	▽▽ 3
○ Friuli Isonzo Sauvignon '11	▽▽ 3
○ Friuli Isonzo Sauvignon '10	▽▽ 3
○ Malvasia '11	▽▽ 3
○ Malvasia '10	▽▽ 3

Valerio Marinig

VIA BROLO, 41
33040 PREPOTTO [UD]
TEL. 0432713012
www.marinig.it

CELLAR SALES
PRE-BOOKED VISITS
ANNUAL PRODUCTION 30,000 bottles
HECTARES UNDER VINE 8.00

Fourth-generation Valerio Marinig directs the family's wine operation, now enjoying almost a century of activity, since in 1921 his great-grandfather Luigi, owner of a small farm, bought a second and poured into it all of his viticultural expertise. Today, Marinig, with the help in the vineyard of his father Sergio and relying on ancestral experience, manages the estate with the commitment and professionalism classic to the family, personally overseeing both vineyard and winemaking operations. The vineyards extend over the Prepotto hills, with their well-known climate that creates the conditions for a truly high-quality viticulture, reflected in these terroir-rich wines. Again this year, wines from Valerio expressed excellent quality with good varietal correspondence, coherence, and no frills. The Sauvignon 2012 is citrussy on the nose and forthright on the palate; the Schioppettino di Prepotto 2010 is complex and spicy on the nose, and supple and soft on the palate.

○ COF Friulano '12	▼▼ 2*
○ COF Pinot Bianco '12	▼▼ 2*
○ COF Sauvignon '12	▼▼ 3
● COF Schioppettino di Prepotto '10	▼▼ 4
● COF Cabernet Franc '11	▼ 2
● COF Refosco P. R. '11	▼ 3
○ COF Verduzzo Friulano '12	▼ 3
● Biel Cûr Rosso '09	▽▽ 3
○ COF Friulano '11	▽▽ 2*
○ COF Friulano '08	▽▽ 2*
● COF Pignolo '08	▽▽ 4
○ COF Sauvignon '11	▽▽ 2*
○ COF Sauvignon '09	▽▽ 2*
○ COF Sauvignon '06	▽▽ 2

Piera Martellozzo

VIA PORDENONE, 33
33080 SAN QUIRINO [PN]
TEL. 0434963100
www.martellozzo.com

CELLAR SALES
PRE-BOOKED VISITS
ANNUAL PRODUCTION 5,000,000 bottles

Veneto-born Piera Martellozzo found a second home in Friuli. Having inherited from her family the art of selecting grapes and wines, she surrounded herself with a professional staff that performs efficiently and quickly all of the winemaking and marketing functions. Love and respect for the land are an essential part of the winery philosophy, which focuses on wines made from indigenous grapes, which faithfully reflect their local terroir of Grave del Friuli. Both still and sparkling, they easily satisfy a wide range of consumer palates. This year we mostly tasted wines from the Terre Magre line that includes the dry, rocky terroir of Grave del Friuli. These wines are coherent, easy drinking, and supple. The Perle di Piera line of lively, fragrant sparklers is instead more interesting and pleasant.

○ Ribolla Gialla Yellow Pearl	♔♔ 3
● Friuli Grave Cabernet Franc Terre Magre '12	♔ 2
○ Friuli Grave Chardonnay Terre Magre '12	♔ 2*
○ Friuli Grave Pinot Grigio Terre Magre '12	♔ 3
● Friuli Grave Rosso Tabbor '11	♔ 3
○ Friuli Grave Traminer Aromatico Terre Magre '12	♔ 3
○ Malvasia Terre Magre '12	♔ 3
○ Prosecco Blue Pearl	♔ 3
○ Friuli Grave Bianco Milo '09	♔♔ 2*
● Friuli Grave Rosso Tabbor '10	♔♔ 4
○ Ribolla Gialla Brut 075 Carati	♔♔ 2*

Masùt da Rive

VIA MANZONI, 82
34070 MARIANO DEL FRIULI [GO]
TEL. 048169200
www.masutdarive.com

CELLAR SALES
PRE-BOOKED VISITS
ANNUAL PRODUCTION 80,000 bottles
HECTARES UNDER VINE 20.00

Masùt da Rive is the nickname of a branch of the Gallo family, which has been deeply rooted in Mariano del Friuli since the early 1900s. It became the name of the winery too upon its entrance into the international markets, and the North American market in particular, to ward off legal challenges from the colossal Gallo family of California's Central Valley. Silvano Gallo put out his first bottles in 1979; his sons Fabrizio and Marco have been running the operation for some time now, but still with a hand from Silvano, especially in the vineyard. The vineyards stretch across the Isonzo-sculpted flatlands, in iron-rich gravel perfect for production of both red and white wines. The Rosso Semidis 2009 is produced only in the best vintages from a careful selection of merlot grapes. This wine is rich in colour and opulent on the nose with notes of tobacco, wood tar, and dark spices, and is structured, soft, and caressing.

○ Friuli Isonzo Chardonnay Rive Alte '12	♔♔ 3
○ Friuli Isonzo Pinot Grigio Rive Alte '12	♔♔ 3
● Friuli Isonzo Rosso Semidis '09	♔♔ 5
○ Friuli Isonzo Friulano '12	♔ 3
● Friuli Isonzo Merlot '11	♔ 4
● Friuli Isonzo Refosco P. R. '11	♔ 4
○ Friuli Isonzo Sauvignon '12	♔ 3
○ Friuli Isonzo Tocai Friulano '04	♔♔♔ 3*
○ Friuli Isonzo Pinot Bianco '09	♔♔ 3*
○ Friuli Isonzo Pinot Bianco '07	♔♔ 3
○ Friuli Isonzo Pinot Bianco '06	♔♔ 3
○ Friuli Isonzo Pinot Grigio '08	♔♔ 3*
● Friuli Isonzo Refosco P. R. '06	♔♔ 3
○ Friuli Isonzo Sauvignon '07	♔♔ 3*
○ Friuli Isonzo Sauvignon '06	♔♔ 3

Davino Meroi

VIA STRETTA, 7B
33042 BUTTRIO [UD]
TEL. 0432673369
www.meroidavino.it

★Miani

VIA PERUZZI, 10
33042 BUTTRIO [UD]
TEL. 0432674327
aletulissi@libero.it

CELLAR SALES
PRE-BOOKED VISITS
ANNUAL PRODUCTION 30,000 bottles
HECTARES UNDER VINE 13.00

CELLAR SALES
PRE-BOOKED VISITS
ANNUAL PRODUCTION 8,000 bottles
HECTARES UNDER VINE 16.00

Paolo Meroi manages the wine operation of his father Davino, who inculcated in him the priceless knowledge he gained in the vineyards planted by grandfather Domenico on the gently-rolling slopes of Buttrio, just where the hills of the Colli Orientali del Friuli begin. Vines in excess of 30 years old yield rich, sound, concentrated grapes that made possible the forging of a very personal style, the fruit of sapient vinification and cask ageing. Meroi grew up with Enzo Pontoni of Miani winery; Meroi shared with him his winemaking expertise, against the current at that time but now followed by quite a few other producers. Young oenologist Mirko Degan assists him in both the cellar and vineyard. Great wines win the Tre Bicchieri. Truly great wines win this more than once. This happened to the Friulano 2011 with an encore of last year's success thanks to its characteristic extraordinary grip. The Chardonnay and Verduzzo Friulano, both from 2011, came close to this award.

Enzo Pontoni, a serious and committed winegrower, has been for some time now the model of the Italian "garagistes". He only produces a few thousand bottles of each label, so they are often impossible to track down, and his wines have become real cult objects for wine lovers and collectors. His tiny cellar is located in Buttrio, in the Colli Orientali del Friuli, along with the 16-hectare vineyard, to which this true vineyard maestro devotes maniacal attention from dawn to dark. The mild-mannered and understated Pontoni is generous with his invaluable advice, and like any maestro he has many disciples, to the clear advantage of the region's winemaking. The small number of bottles produced means that, if you miss the chance, Miani wines frequently cannot be found. This year we were able to taste the Friulano 2011 in the two versions, Buri and Filip, named after their different vineyards, and both deservedly in our finals.

○ COF Friulano '11	♉♉♉ 5
○ COF Chardonnay '11	♉♉ 5
○ COF Verduzzo Friulano '11	♉♉ 5
● COF Merlot V. Dominin '10	♉♉ 8
● COF Refosco P. R. Dominim '10	♉♉ 8
● COF Rosso Ros di Buri '10	♉♉ 6
○ COF Sauvignon '11	♉♉ 4
○ COF Friulano '10	♉♉♉ 5
○ COF Verduzzo Friulano '08	♉♉♉ 5
○ COF Chardonnay '10	♉♉ 5
○ COF Chardonnay '09	♉♉ 5
○ COF Picolit '10	♉♉ 6
○ COF Picolit '09	♉♉ 6
○ COF Verduzzo Friulano '10	♉♉ 5

○ COF Friulano Buri '11	♉♉ 5
○ COF Friulano Filip '11	♉♉ 6
● Calvari '02	♉♉♉ 8
● COF Merlot '02	♉♉♉ 8
● COF Merlot '99	♉♉♉ 8
● COF Merlot '00	♉♉♉ 8
● COF Merlot '94	♉♉♉ 8
● COF Merlot Filip '06	♉♉♉ 8
● COF Merlot Filip '04	♉♉♉ 8
● COF Rosso '97	♉♉♉ 8
○ COF Sauvignon '96	♉♉♉ 6
○ COF Tocai Friulano '00	♉♉♉ 6
○ COF Tocai Friulano '98	♉♉♉ 6
○ COF Tocai Friulano '96	♉♉♉ 6

Moschioni

LOC. GAGLIANO
VIA DORIA, 30
33043 CIVIDALE DEL FRIULI [UD]
TEL. 0432730210
www.michelemoschioni.it

PRE-BOOKED VISITS
ANNUAL PRODUCTION 40,000 bottles
HECTARES UNDER VINE 14.00

Michele Moschioni, marching in the
opposite direction to his regional
counterparts, produces a portfolio of highly
respected reds of superb body and
personality. In processing the grapes, he
utilises a dehydration step, which he
prefers to call "asciugatura", or drying-out,
which concentrates the primary aromas.
The alcohol is often a tad high but in
perfect balance with the other components,
so it actually contributes to the wine's
overall harmony. He operates in Gagliano,
part of Cividale del Friuli, in the Colli
Orientali zone. He now enjoys the help of
his children Alessia and Valentino, who are
fresh from professional experiences in
Argentina and Australia, respectively. To
allow wines further bottle aging, Michele,
as he did some years ago, decided to
postpone release to market for another
year. We fully agree with his choice since
we found that those from last year had
greatly improved on re-tasting.

● COF Rosso Celtico '04	♀♀♀	5
● COF Schioppettino '06	♀♀♀	6
● COF Pignolo '07	♀♀	6
● COF Refosco P. R. '07	♀♀	4
● COF Refosco P. R. '07	♀♀	4
● COF Refosco P. R. '06	♀♀	4
● COF Rosso Celtico '07	♀♀	5
● COF Rosso Celtico '06	♀♀	5
● COF Rosso Reâl '08	♀♀	5
● COF Rosso Reâl '06	♀♀	5
● COF Schioppettino '08	♀♀	6
● Rosso Pit Franc '08	♀♀	6

Mulino delle Tolle

FRAZ. SEVEGLIANO
VIA MULINO DELLE TOLLE, 15
33050 BAGNARIA ARSA [UD]
TEL. 0432924723
www.mulinodelletolle.it

CELLAR SALES
PRE-BOOKED VISITS
ACCOMMODATION AND RESTAURANT SERVICE
ANNUAL PRODUCTION 100,000 bottles
HECTARES UNDER VINE 22.00

Eminent winegrower Giorgio Bertossi
worked together with his cousin Eliseo to
restore to its ancient splendour the Casa
Bianca, a farmhouse that served as a
leprosarium in the 1600s and later as a
customs house under the Habsburgs. The
magnificent restructuring has given him a
new cellar, set in the flourishing vineyards
in the Aquileia denomination. Mulino delle
Tolle made wine for many generations, but
started bottling it only in 1988. Aquileia's
soil often yields archaeological remains
that testify to the area's millennial vocation
for the production of fine wine. The Bianco
Palmade 2012, a blend of chardonnay,
sauvignon, friulano and malvasia istriana,
is introduced on the nose with dried herbs
and Mediterranean scrub. The palate is
soft and well balanced. Also quite good,
the Rosso Sabellius 2011 is made from
refosco dal peduncolo rosso, merlot, and
cabernet sauvignon.

○ Friuli Aquileia Bianco Palmade '12	♀♀	3
○ Friuli Aquileia Malvasia '12	♀♀	3
● Friuli Aquileia Rosso Sabellius '11	♀♀	3
● Friuli Aquileia Refosco P. R. '12	♀	2
○ Friuli Aquileia Traminer Aromatico '12	♀	2
○ Friuli Aquileia Bianco Palmade '08	♀♀	2*
○ Friuli Aquileia Friulano '09	♀♀	2*
○ Friuli Aquileia Friulano '08	♀♀	2*
○ Friuli Aquileia Malvasia '10	♀♀	2*
● Friuli Aquileia Refosco P. R. '10	♀♀	2*
○ Friuli Aquileia Sauvignon '09	♀♀	2*
○ Friuli Aquileia Traminer Aromatico '11	♀♀	2*

Muzic

LOC. BIVIO, 4
34070 SAN FLORIANO DEL COLLIO [GO]
TEL. 0481884201
www.cantinamuzic.it

CELLAR SALES
PRE-BOOKED VISITS
ANNUAL PRODUCTION 90,000 bottles
HECTARES UNDER VINE 20.00

Muzic, located in San Floriano del Collio, was founded in 1963 by the parents of current owner Giovanni Muzic, when they purchased the five hectares of vines they had worked as sharecroppers. Giovanni, better known for some reason as Ivan, is a true artisan of wine who loves tending his vines and working in the open air. Helping him are his wife Orieta and young children Elija and Fabijan, while oenology consultant Giorgio Bertossi lends a hand from time to time in the cellar. Another picture-perfect year for Muzic. The Friulano and Pinot Grigio both competed in the final round and both receive the same laurels as last year. The former, the Vigna Valeris 2012, marries aromatic elegance to a crisp grip, while a smooth, supple palate follows the clean-edged bouquet of the Pinot Grigio 2012.

○ Collio Friulano V. Valeris '12	❦❦ 3*
○ Collio Pinot Grigio '12	❦❦ 3*
○ Collio Bianco '12	❦❦ 3
○ Collio Chardonnay '12	❦❦ 3
○ Collio Malvasia '12	❦❦ 3
○ Collio Ribolla Gialla '12	❦❦ 3
○ Collio Sauvignon V. Pàjze '12	❦❦ 3
● Collio Cabernet Sauvignon '11	❦ 3
○ Collio Bianco Bric '11	♈♈ 3*
○ Collio Friulano V. Valeris '11	♈♈ 3*
○ Collio Malvasia '11	♈♈ 3
○ Collio Malvasia '09	♈♈ 3*
○ Collio Pinot Grigio '11	♈♈ 3*
○ Collio Ribolla Gialla '11	♈♈ 3
○ Collio Sauvignon V. Pàjze '11	♈♈ 3

Evangelos Paraschos

LOC. BUCUJE, 13A
34070 SAN FLORIANO DEL COLLIO [GO]
TEL. 0481884154
www.paraschos.it

CELLAR SALES
PRE-BOOKED VISITS
ANNUAL PRODUCTION 14,000 bottles
HECTARES UNDER VINE 6.50

The name leaves no doubt about the Greek origins of Evangelos Paraschos, who has lived and worked at San Floriano del Collio since 1979. Enthusiastically absorbing the local winemaking traditions, he founded this estate in 1998 and began using biodynamic growing methods right from the start. The grapes, even the white ones, undergo maceration on the skins in open Slavonian oak vats or terracotta amphorae. No sulphur dioxide is ever added to either the musts or wines. No stabilization, clarification or filtration is used, and bottling is done only after at least two years. These wines are rich in colour, occasionally undefined, but still intriguing and captivating. The taut, ultra-fruity Bianco Amphoreus 2009 conjures up fresh-mown wheat and wild herbs, while the Malvasia Amphoreus 2010, lengthy and dry on the palate, boasts crisp laurel notes on the nose. Humus and roasted espresso bean usher in the Merlot Ros di Lune 2009, which continues crisp, supple, and just a tad tannic.

○ Amphoreus Bianco '09	❦❦ 5
○ Amphoreus Malvasia '10	❦❦ 6
● Ros di Lune '09	❦❦ 5
○ Chardonnay '09	♈♈ 3
○ Kaj '09	♈♈ 5
● Merlot '09	♈♈ 4
○ Ponka '09	♈♈ 5
○ Ribolla Gialla '09	♈♈ 5
○ Ribolla Gialla '08	♈♈ 5
● Skala '07	♈♈ 5

Alessandro Pascolo

LOC. RUTTARS, 1
34070 DOLEGNA DEL COLLIO [GO]
TEL. 048161144
www.vinipascolo.com

CELLAR SALES
PRE-BOOKED VISITS
ANNUAL PRODUCTION 25,000 bottles
HECTARES UNDER VINE 7.00

In the 1970s, his grandfather Angelo had the foresight to invest in plots in the countryside, and today young Alessandro Pascolo manages those valuable seven hectares under vine scattered across the sunny slopes of the hill of Ruttàrs in the scenic area around Dolegna del Collio. Nothing better could have happened to Alessandro who is an agronomist, oenologist, and sommelier as well as a great lover of nature and the open air. He immediately put to good use the knowledge acquired from his studies, interpreting this terroir and successfully giving the highest expression to its great potential. The varietal imprint he manages to give his wines shows off all his winemaking skills. Once again, Alessandro's wines are at the top of the quality chart, each just as good as the other. The 2010 Merlot Selection, ever harmonious and reliable, continues on its upward trajectory, while the Pinot Bianco 2012 showcases fine acidic grip and lovely hedgerow fragrances.

○ Bolla Gialla Brut	🍷🍷 3	
○ Collio Bianco '12	🍷🍷 3	
○ Collio Friulano '12	🍷🍷 3	
○ Collio Malvasia '12	🍷🍷 3	
● Collio Merlot Sel. '10	🍷🍷 4	
○ Collio Pinot Bianco '12	🍷🍷 3	
● Collio Rosso Pascal '10	🍷🍷 3	
○ Collio Bianco Agnul '10	🍷🍷 3	
○ Collio Bianco Agnul '09	🍷🍷 3	
○ Collio Friulano '11	🍷🍷 3*	
● Collio Merlot Sel. '09	🍷🍷 4	
● Collio Merlot Sel. '08	🍷🍷 4	
○ Collio Pinot Grigio '11	🍷🍷 3*	
● Collio Rosso Pascal '09	🍷🍷 3	

Pierpaolo Pecorari

VIA TOMMASEO, 56
34070 SAN LORENZO ISONTINO [GO]
TEL. 0481808775
www.pierpaolopecorari.it

CELLAR SALES
PRE-BOOKED VISITS
ANNUAL PRODUCTION 150,000 bottles
HECTARES UNDER VINE 30.00

The estate of Pierpaolo Pecorari, for some time now assisted in management by his son Alessandro, is headquartered in San Lorenzo Isontino, while the vineyards are spread across the triangle formed by Cormòns, Gorizia and Gradisca. It is now well known that this estate prefers not to display the DOC designation on the label, but instead distributes all its wines under the IGT Venezia Giulia appellation. Production is divided into three lines: one is assigned to wines produced in oak that take their names from the Olivers, Kolaus and Soris vineyards; a second line named Altis includes wines aged on the lees in stainless steel; and a third line is reserved for young wines. This year saw the two Sauvignon Blancs, Kolaus and Altis, both 2011, climb into the final round. Both are varietally faithful, but the former is better structured, laying out a broad array of tropical nuances, while the latter is crisper, sporting hawthorn blossom and pungent tomato leaf.

○ Sauvignon Blanc Altis '11	🍷🍷 4	
○ Sauvignon Kolaus '11	🍷🍷 5*	
○ Chardonnay Soris '11	🍷🍷 5	
○ Pinot Grigio Olivers '11	🍷🍷 5	
○ Malvasia '12	🍷 3	
○ Sauvignon Kolàus '96	🍷🍷🍷 3*	
○ Friuli Isonzo Friulano '11	🍷🍷 3*	
○ Pinot Bianco Altis '10	🍷🍷 4	
○ Pinot Grigio Olivers '09	🍷🍷 4	
○ Sauvignon Blanc '10	🍷🍷 3	
○ Sauvignon Kolaus '09	🍷🍷 5	

Perusini

LOC. GRAMOGLIANO
VIA TORRIONE, 13
33040 CORNO DI ROSAZZO [UD]
TEL. 0432675018
www.perusini.com

CELLAR SALES
PRE-BOOKED VISITS
ACCOMMODATION AND RESTAURANT SERVICE
ANNUAL PRODUCTION 70,000 bottles
HECTARES UNDER VINE 13.00

Giacomo Perusini, grandfather of the
current owner, was responsible for
preserving and promoting picolit, a fine
variety closely linked in name with this
estate. Teresa Perusini, an enthusiastic
grower, now manages the estate with skill
and dedication, aided by her husband
Giacomo de Pace. Passionate about art
history, she had a cellar tower built where
frequent art shows are organized. The new
generation of Carlo, Tommaso and Michele
will be entrusted with managing the
valuable vineyards spread across the sunny
hills of Gramogliano, Rosazzo and Rocca
Bernarda, in the area around Colli Orientali.
The merlot-cabernet sauvignon Rosso del
Postiglione 2009 offers up elegant scents
of cinchona, spice, and rhubarb, which
glide onto a supple, appealing palate. The
palate impresses on the Refosco dal
Peduncolo Rosso 2009 too, redolent of
tobacco leaf and pungent underbrush,
while the Pinot Grigio 2012 displays a
citrussy crispness.

○ COF Pinot Grigio '12	🏆🏆 3	
● COF Refosco P.R. '09	🏆🏆 3	
● COF Rosso del Postiglione '09	🏆🏆 3	
● COF Cabernet Franc '10	🏆 3	
○ COF Picolit '10	🏆 8	
○ COF Ribolla Gialla '12	🏆 3	
○ COF Sauvignon '12	🏆 3	
○ Perusini Brut	🏆 3	
● COF Cabernet Franc '09	🏆🏆 3	
● COF Cabernet Sauvignon '09	🏆🏆 3	
● COF Merlot '09	🏆🏆 3	
○ COF Ribolla Gialla '11	🏆🏆 3	
● COF Rosso del Postiglione '08	🏆🏆 3	
○ COF Sauvignon '11	🏆🏆 3	

Petrucco

VIA MORPURGO, 12
33042 BUTTRIO [UD]
TEL. 0432674387
www.vinipetrucco.it

CELLAR SALES
PRE-BOOKED VISITS
ANNUAL PRODUCTION 80,000 bottles
HECTARES UNDER VINE 20.00

In 1981 Paolo Petrucco and his wife Lina
took over this estate in the hills of Buttrio.
This place already had a rich history
because of the work of Italo Balbo who
planted most of the vineyards, though they
say he was never able to taste his wines
since his plane was shot down over Libya
in 1940. Careful selection of the best
grapes from those old vineyards now helps
to produce the Riserva Ronco del Balbo,
pride and joy of the Petruccos. These wines
are aged in oak and destined to age well
over time. The assistance of Gianni Menotti
alongside the valuable estate oenologist,
Flavio Cabas, has given new energy to the
winery. The Ronco del Balbo wines were
the ones that excited us most, with the
Merlot Ronco del Balbo 2010 strutting
stunning aromatics of morello cherry and
black liquorice in our final round, then a
real stand-out of a palate, smooth,
delightful and appealing.

● COF Merlot Ronco del Balbo '10	🏆🏆 3*	
○ COF Friulano '12	🏆🏆 3	
● COF Pignolo Ronco del Balbo '09	🏆🏆 5	
● COF Refosco P. R. '11	🏆🏆 3	
● COF Refosco P. R. Ronco del Balbo '10	🏆🏆 4	
○ COF Sauvignon '12	🏆🏆 3	
○ COF Chardonnay '12	🏆 3	
○ COF Pinot Bianco '12	🏆 3	
○ COF Pinot Grigio '12	🏆 3	
○ COF Ribolla Gialla '12	🏆 3	
● COF Merlot Ronco del Balbo '09	🏆🏆 3	
● COF Pignolo Ronco del Balbo '08	🏆🏆 5	
● COF Refosco P. R. '10	🏆🏆 3*	
● COF Refosco P. R. Ronco del Balbo '09	🏆🏆 4	
○ COF Ribolla Gialla '11	🏆🏆 3*	

Petrussa

VIA ALBANA, 49
33040 PREPOTTO [UD]
TEL. 0432713192
www.petrussa.it

CELLAR SALES
PRE-BOOKED VISITS
ANNUAL PRODUCTION 40,000 bottles
HECTARES UNDER VINE 10.00

In 1986, when Gianni and Paolo Petrussa decided to quit their secure jobs with guaranteed salaries and dedicate themselves to the family estate, their parents were somewhat dismayed, aware as they were that this choice would mean an economically uncertain and difficult future. Certain of the potential of the terroir at Prepotto and driven by the iron will to bring out all the local features, they put to use their forefathers' knowledge of farming culture and endowed their wines with personality and sincerity. The whites as well as the reds are the results of simple, essential winemaking, inviting to the taste and satisfying on the palate. The Pinot Bianco 2012 is stunning for the elegance of its bouquet and its silk-smooth palate, while the Chardonnay Sant'Elena 2011 lays out a creamy, tactile richness. The Friulano and Sauvignon Blanc, both 2012, exhibit terrific aromatics on the nose and crunchy fruit in the mouth.

○ COF Pinot Bianco '12	♥♥	3*
○ COF Chardonnay S. Elena '11	♥♥	4
○ COF Friulano '12	♥♥	3
● COF Rosso Petrussa '10	♥♥	5
○ COF Sauvignon '12	♥♥	3
● COF Merlot '11	♥	3
○ COF Pensiero '10	♥	5
○ COF Chardonnay S. Elena '10	♀♀	4
○ COF Friulano '11	♀♀	3*
○ COF Pinot Bianco '11	♀♀	3*
○ COF Sauvignon '11	♀♀	3*
● COF Schioppettino di Prepotto '09	♀♀	5

Roberto Picéch

LOC. PRADIS, 11
34071 CORMÒNS [GO]
TEL. 048160347
www.picech.it

CELLAR SALES
PRE-BOOKED VISITS
ACCOMMODATION
ANNUAL PRODUCTION 25,000 bottles
HECTARES UNDER VINE 7.00

Roberto Picéch is an undisputed star among top winemakers on the regional stage. In 1963, his father, Egidio, called locally "il Ribel", purchased the vineyards where he already worked. Roberto inherited the vineyards from him as well as a stubborn, no-nonsense character, which helps him give his wines a personal, characteristic stamp. Always open to innovation and constantly searching for new inspiration, he allows his grapes long maceration, lasting several days even for the whites, creating succulent, complex wines. The traditional local ribolla gialla, tocai friulano and malvasia istriana go to make up Collio Bianco Jelka 2011, a long-established blend redolent of Golden Delicious apple foregrounding dried wild herbs and sun-dried hay and with a tangy mineral palate.

○ Collio Bianco Jelka '11	♥♥	4
○ Collio Bianco Athena Magnum '10	♥♥	7
○ Collio Friulano '12	♥♥	3
○ Collio Malvasia '12	♥♥	3
● Collio Rosso '11	♥♥	3
○ Collio Pinot Bianco '12	♥	3
○ Collio Bianco Athena '05	♀♀♀	7
○ Collio Bianco Jelka '99	♀♀♀	7
○ Collio Pinot Bianco '11	♀♀	3*

Vigneti Pittaro

VIA UDINE, 67
33033 CODROIPO [UD]
TEL. 0432904726
www.vignetipittaro.com

CELLAR SALES
PRE-BOOKED VISITS
ACCOMMODATION
ANNUAL PRODUCTION 400,000 bottles
HECTARES UNDER VINE 90.00

Piero Pittaro is an outstanding character on the winemaking landscape. Over his long career, he has played many institutional roles internationally. He comes from a family of winemakers with a history of over 450 years, always working to bring out the greatest potential from these arid, pebbly plots in Grave del Friuli, renowned for grape-growing. Most of the vineyards surround the historic headquarters at Codroipo, but the estate also includes five hectares under vine in the beautiful hills of Ramandolo. The cellar director, Stefano Trinco, has tried and true experience in producing the classic method sparkler that is the estate's showcase wine. The sparklers are the team leaders for points this year, and as expected the laurels again go to the Pittaro Brut Etichetta Oro 2005, which easily stands out for the richness and elegance of its bouquet, the sheer impetuosity and length of its bead, and its wealth of fragrances and unashamed minerality.

○ Pittaro Brut Et. Oro '05	♟♟ 4
○ COF Friulano Ronco Vieri '12	♟♟ 3
○ Pittaro Brut Et. Argento	♟♟ 4
☉ Pittaro Brut Pink	♟♟ 5
○ Ramandolo Ronco Vieri '10	♟♟ 3
○ Friuli Grave Chardonnay Mousqué '12	♟ 3
● Moscato Rosa Valzer in Rosa '12	♟ 3
○ COF Friulano Ronco Vieri '10	♟♟ 3
○ Pittaro Brut Et. Oro '04	♟♟ 4
○ Pittaro Brut Et. Oro '03	♟♟ 6
○ Ramandolo Ronco Vieri '09	♟♟ 3

Denis Pizzulin

VIA BROLO, 43
33040 PREPOTTO [UD]
TEL. 0432713425
www.pizzulin.com

CELLAR SALES
PRE-BOOKED VISITS
ANNUAL PRODUCTION 25,000 bottles
HECTARES UNDER VINE 11.00

Denis Pizzulin is a young winemaker who personally manages the vineyards on his estate, spread across the hills of Prepotto on plots where viticulture boasts a thousand years of history. These soils are a mix of sandstone and marl, ideal for growing vines, which stretch across a sunny valley, protected from the cold northern winds, between Slovenia and Collio Goriziano. There are only 11 hectares here, divided into various plots, allowing him to operate carefully and meticulously in producing healthy, juicy grapes. With few equals on the regional winemaking scene, Denis immediately met with well-deserved appreciation. Once again, the entire portfolio achieved truly impressive levels of quality. The standard wines did very well indeed. The score-leader, though, was the Refosco dal Peduncolo Rosso Riserva 2009, ennobled by the sheer elegance of its bouquet, shot through with spice, and by its well-rounded palate.

○ COF Bianco Rarisolchi '12	♟♟ 3
● COF Merlot '12	♟♟ 3
○ COF Pinot Bianco '12	♟♟ 3
● COF Refosco P. R. Ris. '09	♟♟ 4
● COF Schioppettino di Prepotto '10	♟♟ 3
○ COF Friulano '12	♟ 3
○ COF Sauvignon '12	♟ 3
○ COF Friulano '11	♟♟ 2*
○ COF Pinot Bianco '11	♟♟ 2*
○ COF Pinot Bianco '10	♟♟ 2
● COF Refosco P. R. Ris. '08	♟♟ 3
● COF Schioppettino di Prepotto '09	♟♟ 3

Damijan Podversic

VIA BRIGATA PAVIA, 61
34170 GORIZIA
TEL. 048178217
www.damijanpodversic.com

CELLAR SALES
PRE-BOOKED VISITS
ANNUAL PRODUCTION 22,600 bottles
HECTARES UNDER VINE 10.00
VITICULTURE METHOD Certified Organic

Damijan Podversic owns this small estate in Collio. His vineyards stretch across the lovely slopes of Monte Calvario, a hill west of Gorizia, on the right bank of the River Isonzo. In his philosophy of life, being a farmer means working with nature, respecting seasons and accepting hardships. Grape yields per hectare are quite low. No fertilizers, no pesticides, no nothing! Damijan accepts no compromises in vinification either: fermentation on the skins for 90 days, long macerations in oak with no added yeasts, and no clarification or filtration, leading to complex, intriguing and unusual wines. Damijan's reliability was rewarded this year, with a full three wines vaulting into the final round and the Malvasia 2009 taking home a Tre Bicchieri. Pungent balsam is the background to sun-dried hay, thyme, basil and hazelnut, and the palate, though showing alcoholic warmth, is dry, smooth and compelling.

○ Malvasia '09	♟♟♟	6
○ Kaplja '09	♟♟	6
○ Ribolla Gialla '09	♟♟	6
○ Nekaj '09	♟♟	6
○ Pinot Grigio '10	♟♟	6
● Rosso Prelit '09	♟♟	6
○ Kaplja '08	♟♟♟	6
○ Kaplja '07	♟♟	6
○ Kaplja '06	♟♟	5
○ Ribolla Gialla '07	♟♟	5
○ Ribolla Gialla '05	♟♟	5
● Rosso Prelit '06	♟♟	5

Aldo Polencic

LOC. PLESSIVA, 13
34071 CORMÒNS [GO]
TEL. 048161027
aldopolencic@virgilio.it

CELLAR SALES
PRE-BOOKED VISITS
ANNUAL PRODUCTION 20,000 bottles
HECTARES UNDER VINE 6.00

Aldo Polencic's tiny estate is a real pearl in the crowded ranks of family-run producers in Collio. It is located in Plessiva, in the muncipality of Cormòns, a place renowned for ideal and special features for growing vines. Aldo is a real wine artisan or, rather, artist. The small size allows him to give extra-special care to his vineyards, with help from his father Ferdinando. The recently expanded cellar displays well-ordered, 900-litre tonneaux, indispensable tools for his vinification techniques, which include long ageing in oak, even for the whites. These wines require calm waiting. The aromatic opulence and complexity of these wines raise expectations that invite closer examination on the palate. And it is that consistency between nose and palate that is determining. Yes, the oak is still obvious, but the wines are fragrant, well-structured, forceful, smooth, well-balanced and exceptionally full flavoured.

○ Collio Friulano Bianco degli Ulivi '11	♟♟	5
● Collio Merlot Rosso degli Ulivi '09	♟♟	5
○ Collio Pinot Bianco Bianco degli Ulivi '11	♟♟	5
○ Collio Pinot Grigio '11	♟♟	4
○ Collio Tocai Friulano '00	♟♟♟	4*
○ Collio Friulano Bianco degli Ulivi '10	♟♟	5
○ Collio Friulano Bianco degli Ulivi '08	♟♟	5
● Collio Merlot Rosso degli Ulivi '08	♟♟	5
● Collio Merlot Rosso degli Ulivi '06	♟♟	5
○ Collio Pinot Bianco Bianco degli Ulivi '10	♟♟	5
○ Collio Pinot Bianco Bianco degli Ulivi '08	♟♟	5

Isidoro Polencic

LOC. PLESSIVA, 12
34071 CORMÒNS [GO]
TEL. 048160655
www.polencic.com

CELLAR SALES
PRE-BOOKED VISITS
ACCOMMODATION
ANNUAL PRODUCTION 120,000 bottles
HECTARES UNDER VINE 25.00

Historic documents show the Polencics
have lived and worked in the hills of
Plessiva since the second half of the 19th
century. In 1968, Isidoro Polencic decided
to bottle the wines he had always
produced, and founded the winery now
managed by his three children, Elisabetta,
Michele and Alex, who, after the premature
passing of their father, were forced to
speed things up. In short, they divided their
tasks and now run this estate with skill and
perseverance, displaying a rare
determination for their young ages. They
have known how to make the most of the
soil and climate of their plots, distributed in
various locations, creating forthright,
enjoyable wines that are above all varietal.
Once again, the Friulano Fisc 2011 finishes
ahead of its team-mates, thanks to
intriguing notes of mixed nuts, raisins and
saffron, but above all to a stunning palate.
The base wines, though, are admirable for
their greater fragrance, ease of drinking
and pronounced minerality.

○ Collio Friulano Fisc '11	▼▼	4
○ Collio Chardonnay '12	▼▼	3
○ Collio Friulano '12	▼▼	3
○ Collio Pinot Bianco '12	▼▼	3
○ Collio Pinot Grigio '12	▼	3
○ Collio Friulano Fisc '07	▼▼▼	?*
○ Collio Pinot Bianco '07	▼▼▼	3
○ Collio Tocai Friulano '04	▼▼▼	3*
○ Collio Chardonnay '11	▼▼	3
○ Collio Friulano '11	▼▼	3*
○ Collio Pinot Bianco '11	▼▼	3
○ Collio Pinot Grigio '11	▼▼	3

La Ponca

LOC. SCRIÒ, 3
34070 DOLEGNA DEL COLLIO [GO]
TEL. 0422800026
www.laponca.it

CELLAR SALES
PRE-BOOKED VISITS
ANNUAL PRODUCTION 24,000 bottles
HECTARES UNDER VINE 16.00

Collio soils are made up of Eocene stratified
marls and sandstone, known locally as
"ponca," which were brought to the surface
in remote times by the upheaval of the
Adriatic seabed, as one can see from
abundant marine fossils. Collio's felicitous
topography, protected on the north by the
Julian Alps and open on the south to the
beneficent influences of the Adriatic,
creates an outstanding, temperate climate.
La Ponca's vineyards lie precisely here, in
the village of Scriò, near Dolegna del Collio.
Paolo Mason and Luigi Schiochet founded
the winery in 2005, and entrusted the
winemaking to the very experienced Andrea
Pittana. The Collio Friulano 2012 compels
attention for its classic character and
clean-edged aromas, but even more for its
suppleness and drive in the mouth, which
make for sheer delight. The Collio
Sauvignon 2012, though a tad rustic,
preserves good varietal fidelity, while the
Schioppettino 2011 exhibits delicious spice.

○ Collio Friulano '12	▼▼	3
○ Collio Sauvignon '12	▼▼	3
○ Collio Ribolla Gialla '12	▼	3
● Schioppettino '11	▼	3
○ Collio Friulano '10	▼▼	3
○ Collio Ribolla Gialla '10	▼▼	3

Primosic

FRAZ. OSLAVIA
LOC. MADONNINA DI OSLAVIA, 3
34070 GORIZIA
TEL. 0481535153
www.primosic.com

CELLAR SALES
PRE-BOOKED VISITS
ANNUAL PRODUCTION 200,000 bottles
HECTARES UNDER VINE 30.00

Marko and Boris Primosic now manage this estate founded in 1956 by their father, Silvestro, one of the first to believe in the importance of creating a Consortium for protecting wines from Collio, and they proudly display bottle "number one". The vineyards spread across the hills of Oslavia, bulwark of Collio on the border with Slovenia, a location that enjoys a unique site climate in terms of ventilation, exposure and temperature range. A zoning process, aimed at recognizing various crus, has helped identify the best-suited areas for each variety, and wine names are frequently accompanied by the place name of the vineyard where the grapes originate. The Collio Bianco Klin Riserva 2009, a blend of sauvignon blanc, chardonnay, ribolla gialla and friulano, boasts a classy nose and a velvety palate. Likewise outstanding are the Merlot Murno 2008, Malvasia Istrana 2012 and, drum roll, please, the Friulano Belvedere 2012.

○ Collio Friulano Belvedere '12	♟♟ 3*	
○ Collio Bianco Klin Ris. '09	♟♟ 5	
● Collio Merlot Murno '08	♟♟ 3	
○ Malvasia Istriana '12	♟♟ 3	
○ Ribolla Gialla '12	♟ 3	
○ Collio Bianco Klin Ris. '08	♟♟ 5	
○ Collio Chardonnay Gmajne '10	♟♟ 4	
○ Collio Friulano Belvedere '11	♟♟ 3*	
● Collio Merlot '08	♟♟ 3	
○ Collio Pinot Grigio Murno '10	♟♟ 3	
○ Collio Sauvignon Gmajne '10	♟♟ 4	
○ Malvasia Istriana '11	♟♟ 3	

★Doro Princic

LOC. PRADIS, 5
34071 CORMÒNS [GO]
TEL. 048160723
doroprincic@virgilio.it

CELLAR SALES
PRE-BOOKED VISITS
ANNUAL PRODUCTION 60,000 bottles
HECTARES UNDER VINE 10.00

Everyone in Collio Goriziano remembers Doro Princic as a man who was a symbol, a charismatic figure, and a reference point during difficult times. Now the estate he founded in Pradis in 1950 is managed by his son, Sandro, and his son's wife, Grazia, a wonderful couple working with fantastic synergy at this now historic estate, which they have improved even further, in part with the help of young Carlo, who works alongside Sandro in both the vineyards and cellar. They put into practice the winemaking skills inherited from Doro, producing wines that show outstanding respect for the features of each variety, with no manipulations, forcing or blending. That the Tre Bicchieri award goes to Malvasia 2002 raises not an eyebrow, seeing that this is the fifth year in a row that it is so honoured. Sandro Princic has made this indigenous grape his own, and its unmistakable, distinctive aromatics are a priceless gift to the wine lover's nose and palate alike.

○ Collio Malvasia '12	♟♟♟ 5	
○ Collio Pinot Bianco '12	♟♟ 5	
○ Collio Friulano '12	♟♟ 5	
○ Collio Pinot Grigio '12	♟ 5	
○ Collio Ribolla Gialla '12	♟ 5	
○ Collio Malvasia '11	♟♟♟ 5	
○ Collio Malvasia '10	♟♟♟ 4	
○ Collio Malvasia '09	♟♟♟ 4*	
○ Collio Malvasia '08	♟♟♟ 4	
○ Collio Pinot Bianco '07	♟♟♟ 3	

★Dario Raccaro

FRAZ. RÒLAT
VIA SAN GIOVANNI, 87
34071 CORMÒNS [GO]
TEL. 048161425
az.agr.raccaro@alice.it

CELLAR SALES
PRE-BOOKED VISITS
ANNUAL PRODUCTION 30,000 bottles
HECTARES UNDER VINE 6.00

The Raccaros have almost a hundred years of history in Cormòns. It was in 1928 that Giuseppe Raccaro decided to abandon the dry, unrewarding valleys of Natisone and relocate to the old farmhouse at the foot of Monte Quarin. Here he found fertile terrain for farming. Dario now proudly pursues this career. In the 1980s he decided to work mainly in wine and grape production, and has managed to expand the estate property with an old, leased vineyard planted to tocai friulano that has made him famous: the Vigna del Rolàt. His rather tiny cellar shows how a winery can become and remain a major player with just a few labels and great consistency. The Malvasia 2012 brings home a Tre Bicchieri, repeating its exploit of last year. Its self-confident, multi-layered nose impresses with dried herbs, laurel and Mediterranean scrub, while the palate is seduction itself, with fragrances that run throughout the length of the progression.

○ Collio Malvasia '12	♥♥♥ 5
○ Collio Bianco '12	♥♥ 4
○ Collio Friulano V. del Rolat '12	♥♥ 4
● Collio Merlot '11	♥♥ 5
○ Collio Bianco '03	♀♀♀ 3
○ Collio Bianco '02	♀♀♀ 3
○ Collio Friulano V. del Rolat '09	♀♀♀ 4
○ Collio Friulano V. del Rolat '08	♀♀♀ 4
○ Collio Friulano V. del Rolat '07	♀♀♀ 4
○ Collio Malvasia '11	♀♀♀ 4*
○ Collio Tocai Friulano '05	♀♀♀ 4
○ Collio Tocai Friulano '04	♀♀♀ 3
○ Collio Tocai Friulano '01	♀♀♀ 3*
○ Collio Tocai Friulano '00	♀♀♀ 3
○ Collio Tocai Friulano V. del Rolat '06	♀♀♀ 4

La Rajade

LOC. PETRUS, 2
34070 DOLEGNA DEL COLLIO [GO]
TEL. 0481639273
www.larajade.it

CELLAR SALES
PRE-BOOKED VISITS
ANNUAL PRODUCTION 40,000 bottles
HECTARES UNDER VINE 6.50

The La Rajade estate, whose name means "sunbeam" in the Friuli dialect, is located in the northernmost section of Collio, in the valley of the Judrio river. The owner, Sergio Campeotto, has entrusted management to Diego Zanin who, despite his young age, already boasts major winemaking experience and is also supported by the choices of Andrea Romano Rossi. The vineyards run down to the valley from Ronco Petrus following the topological profile of the hills. The special site climate enjoyed by this valley and the shape of the hills allow excellent exposure to the sun's rays, and create the requirements for a good temperature range, perfect for producing the characteristic aromas of these wines. Both the white base wines and the red Riservas scored more than well, attesting to very high overall quality indeed and to consistency of performance. Pinot Grigio 2012 shows juicy and crisp, while the almost-electric Ribolla Gialla 2012 is fragrant, ultra-crisp and yet creamy smooth.

○ Collio Bianco '12	♥♥ 3
● Collio Cabernet Sauvignon Ris. '10	♥♥ 4
● Collio Merlot Ris. '10	♥♥ 4
○ Collio Pinot Grigio '12	♥♥ 3
○ Collio Ribolla Gialla '12	♥♥ 3
○ Collio Sauvignon '12	♥ 3
○ Collio Bianco '11	♀♀ 3
● Collio Cabernet Sauvignon Ris. '09	♀♀ 4
○ Collio Friulano '11	♀♀ 3
○ Collio Malvasia '10	♀♀ 3
● Collio Merlot Ris. '09	♀♀ 4
○ Collio Sauvignon '11	♀♀ 3

Rocca Bernarda

FRAZ. IPPLIS
VIA ROCCA BERNARDA, 27
33040 PREMARIACCO [UD]
TEL. 0432716914
www.roccabernarda.com

CELLAR SALES
PRE-BOOKED VISITS
ANNUAL PRODUCTION 200,000 bottles
HECTARES UNDER VINE 43.00

A magnificent complex dominates Rocca Bernarda, with four cylindrical towers at its corners, once the noble country residence of the Conti Valsason Maniago in 1567. A stone inscription states that the cellars predated the villa, and a winemaking tradition was maintained there over the centuries, thanks to the Conti Perusini. In 1977 they passed on the property to the Sovereign Military Order of Malta, but since 2006 it has been directed by the Società Agricola Vitivinicola Italiana, who entrusted wine production to Maurilio Chioccia. His objective has been to raise the quality standards while preserving the wines' varietal fidelity and traditional characteristics. The fragrant Sauvignon 2012 shows fine citrus aromas and is crisp and well-balanced in the mouth. The Pignolo Novecento 1113-2013, which is a 2007 vintage, memorializes the foundation of the Order of Malta in 1113; spice and tobacco leaf precede a delicious palate with noticeable yet already tamed tannins.

○ COF Friulano '12	♟♟ 3
● COF Pignolo Novecento 1113-2013 '07	♟♟ 5
○ COF Sauvignon '12	♟♟ 3
○ COF Chardonnay '12	♟ 3
○ COF Ribolla Gialla '12	♟ 3
● COF Merlot Centis '99	♟♟♟ 7
○ COF Picolit '03	♟♟♟ 7
○ COF Picolit '98	♟♟♟ 7
○ COF Friulano '11	♟♟ 3
○ COF Sauvignon '11	♟♟ 3

Paolo Rodaro

LOC. SPESSA
VIA CORMONS, 60
33040 CIVIDALE DEL FRIULI [UD]
TEL. 0432716066
www.rodaropaolo.it

CELLAR SALES
PRE-BOOKED VISITS
ANNUAL PRODUCTION 250,000 bottles
HECTARES UNDER VINE 50.00

The Rodaros have been making wine since 1846. Paolo Rodaro now manages this estate and carries the same name as the founder. With purchase of the Conte Romano farm, he has overseen the expansion of the estate, but must also give great credit to his father Luigi and uncle Edo who, in the 1960s and 1970s, transformed this small growing operation into one of the most important and respected winemaking estates in Colli Orientali del Friuli. Wines from the Romain line are made from grapes left to rest in crates for around a month after harvest. Laurel and cinnamon infuse the Malvasia 2012, while the Picolit 2010 releases dates, dried apricots and crunchy almonds. The Friulano 2012 shows fine typicity, straightforward and a tad citrussy. Both the Merlot Romain 2008 and Pignolo Romain 2007 display intense bouquets and equally fine palates, the latter with forceful balsam.

○ COF Friulano '12	♟♟ 2*
○ COF Malvasia '12	♟♟ 2*
● COF Merlot Romain '08	♟♟ 4
○ COF Picolit '10	♟♟ 5
● COF Pignolo Romain '07	♟♟ 5
○ COF Ribolla Gialla '12	♟♟ 2*
○ COF Sauvignon '12	♟♟ 2*
○ COF Chardonnay '12	♟ 2
● COF Refosco P. R. Romain '03	♟♟♟ 6
○ COF Sauvignon Bosc Romain '96	♟♟♟ 4*
○ Ronc '00	♟♟♟ 3
● COF Merlot Romain '09	♟♟ 5

Ronc di Vico

FRAZ. BELLAZOIA
VIA CENTRALE, 5
33040 POVOLETTO [UD]
TEL. 3208822002
roncdivicobellazoia@libero.it

CELLAR SALES
PRE-BOOKED VISITS
ANNUAL PRODUCTION 10,500 bottles
HECTARES UNDER VINE 7.00

In 2004, Gianni Del Fabbro, aware of the potential of the vineyards inherited from his father Lodovico, decided to create this winery. Knowing he could count on help from his young son, named after his grandfather, and supported by invaluable advice from a producer friend, he began tending seven hectares of vineyards, half owned and half leased, distributed across the hills of Faedis. On plots treated exclusively with organic products, the old vines awaited reconversion by expert hands and were not long in producing grapes that created excellent wines, shooting straight to the top in regional excellence. The merlot Vicorosso 2010 offers a mosaic of dried herbs, dark berry fruit and liquorice, followed by more aromatics on an attractive, fine-structured palate. The Friulano 2012 is still a bit callow, but it already displays the multi-starred qualities of previous vintages. The Picolit 2011 is likewise excellent.

○ COF Il Friulano '12	TT	4
○ COF Picolit '11	TT	7
● COF Vicorosso '10	TT	4
○ COF Il Friulano '09	YYY	4
○ COF Il Friulano '08	YYY	4*
○ COF Il Friulano '11	YY	4
○ COF Il Friulano '10	YY	4
○ COF Picolit '09	YY	6
○ COF Sauvignon '11	YY	4
● COF Titut Ros '09	YY	5
● COF Vicorosso '09	YY	4

Ronc Soreli

LOC. NOVACUZZO, 46
33040 PREPOTTO [UD]
TEL. 0432713005
www.roncsoreli.com

CELLAR SALES
ANNUAL PRODUCTION 100,000 bottles
HECTARES UNDER VINE 42.00

Though only recently established, the Ronc Soreli estate, assisted by the winemaking know-how of Emilio Del Medico, is already among the best regional production operations. At the turn of this century, Flavio Schiratti restored and re-launched this winery, located in the old village of Borgo di Novacuzzo. The name was inspired by the shape of the hills where the vineyards are distributed, which allows constant exposure to the rays of the sun. This ambitious project also envisages restoring the landowner's villa to its former splendour, as well as expanding the cellar and refitting it with current technologies. These ripe, sunny wines are only released to market after at least two years. Ronc Soreli's wines are attracting considerable attention, climbing in quality so rapidly that we are extremely pleased to award the Tre Bicchieri to the Friulano Vigna delle Robinie 2011. With its spot-on varietal fidelity, this wine is a true stand-out among the region's best bottlings of indigenous grapes.

○ COF Friulano V. delle Robinie '11	TTT	3*
○ COF Picolit '08	TT	5
○ COF Bianco Uis Blanc '11	TT	3
○ COF Friulano Otto Lustri '10	TT	5
○ COF Pinot Grigio V. dei Melograni '11	TT	3
○ COF Sauvignon V. dei Peschi '11	TT	3
● COF Schioppettino V. delle Marasche '11	TT	3
○ COF Friulano '09	YY	3*
○ COF Friulano Otto Lustri '09	YY	3*
○ COF Friulano V. delle Robinie '10	YY	3
○ COF Pinot Grigio V. dei Melograni '10	YY	3
○ COF Sauvignon V. dei Peschi '10	YY	3
● COF Schioppettino di Prepotto Ris. '08	YY	5

La Roncaia

FRAZ. CERGNEU
VIA VERDI, 26
33045 NIMIS [UD]
TEL. 0432790280
www.fantinel.com

CELLAR SALES
PRE-BOOKED VISITS
ANNUAL PRODUCTION 50,000 bottles
HECTARES UNDER VINE 22.00

In 1998, the Fantinel group, growers for three generations, decided to purchase an estate in Cergneu, near Nimis, in the extreme north of Colli Orientali del Friuli, the cradle of Ramandolo, and so founded La Roncaia, alongside its other properties: Tenuta Sant'Helena at Vencò in Collio, and Borgo Tesis at Tauriano di Spilimbergo in Grave del Friuli. La Roncaia has rapidly become established as the feather in the cap of this group, benefitting from collaboration with the expert winemaker, Marco Pecchiari. Expansion across this area reinforces the estate objective aimed at expressing the best winemaking traditions of Friuli, creating typical and original high quality wines. The Ploe di Stelis 2011, an equal blend of riesling, chardonnay and sauvignon blanc, releases rich apricot, russet pear and cakes, and is delicious and compelling in the mouth. The other whites display exemplary crispness and aromatics, while the 2010 reds are well-balanced and ready.

○ Eclisse '12	♟♟♟ 4*	
○ Ramandolo '10	♟♟ 5	
○ COF Friulano '11	♟♟ 4	
● COF Merlot '10	♟♟ 4	
○ COF Picolit '10	♟♟ 5	
● COF Refosco P.R. '10	♟ 5	
○ Eclisse '10	♟♟ 4	
○ Eclisse '09	♟♟ 4	
● COF Cabernet Sauvignon '09	♟♟ 3	
○ COF Friulano '10	♟♟ 3*	
● COF Merlot '09	♟♟ 3	
● COF Merlot '07	♟♟ 3	
● COF Refosco P.R. '07	♟♟ 5	

Il Roncal

VIA FORNALIS, 148
33043 CIVIDALE DEL FRIULI [UD]
TEL. 0432730138
www.ilroncal.it

CELLAR SALES
PRE-BOOKED VISITS
ACCOMMODATION AND RESTAURANT SERVICE
ANNUAL PRODUCTION 120,000 bottles
HECTARES UNDER VINE 20.00

The current owner, Martina Moreale, a woman gifted with a strong will and indisputable business skills, has been successful in her attempt to complete the project begun by Roberto Zorzettig in 1986 to create a model estate where tradition and technology could co-exist. He designed the new cellar himself, overseeing the smallest details, and began the construction work. Later he decided to replant and improve the vineyards on the hill of Montebello, in the heart of Colli Orientali del Friuli. The sadness at the premature loss of Roberto was overcome by realizing his dream, producing wines that immediately established themselves in terms of personality, typicity and forthrightness. The Ploe di Stelis 2011, an equal blend of riesling, chardonnay and sauvignon blanc, releases rich apricot, russet pear and cakes, and is delicious and compelling in the mouth. The other whites display exemplary crispness and aromatics, while the 2010 reds are well-balanced and ready.

○ COF Bianco Ploe di Stelis '11	♟♟ 4	
● COF Cabernet Franc '10	♟♟ 4	
● COF Merlot '10	♟♟ 3	
○ COF Pinot Grigio '12	♟♟ 3	
● COF Refosco P.R. '10	♟♟ 4	
○ COF Sauvignon '12	♟♟ 3	
● COF Schioppettino '10	♟♟ 4	
○ COF Friulano '12	♟ 3	
● COF Pignolo '07	♟ 5	
○ COF Ribolla Gialla '12	♟ 3	
○ COF Verduzzo Friulano '11	♟ 4	
● COF Merlot '09	♟♟ 3	
○ COF Pinot Grigio '11	♟♟ 3	
○ COF Ploe di Stelis '10	♟♟ 3	
○ COF Ribolla Gialla '11	♟♟ 3	

Ronchi di Cialla

FRAZ. CIALLA
VIA CIALLA, 47
33040 PREPOTTO [UD]
TEL. 0432731679
www.ronchidicialla.it

CELLAR SALES
PRE-BOOKED VISITS
ANNUAL PRODUCTION 100,000 bottles
HECTARES UNDER VINE 26.00

In 1970, Dina and Paolo Rapuzzi decided to abandon their previous activities and renovate a farmhouse in Cialla, a small valley surrounded by forests of chestnut, oak and wild cherry, officially known as a prestigious subzone for growing only native grape varieties from Friuli. Ronchi di Cialla was born, now also managed by their sons, Pierpaolo and Ivan, who follow in their parents' footsteps with new enthusiasm. The Rapuzzis deserve credit for having saved Schioppettino from extinction, a wine that later became the estate's flagship, fermented and aged for years in oak and only released to market at least five years after harvest. The Schioppettino di Cialla 2009 reprises the varietal qualities of previous vintages. Pale in colour, seductive and supple in the mouth, it is still youthful, but with rich personality and mouthfeel. The Refosco dal Peduncolo Rosso di Cialla 2009 is redolent of cherry over a foundation of mint and pungent balsam.

● COF Refosco P.R. di Cialla '09	♟♟	6
● COF Schioppettino di Cialla '09	♟♟	6
○ COF Cialla Bianco '11	♟	5
● COF Schioppettino di Cialla '05	♟♟♟	6
○ COF Cialla Bianco '09	♟♟	4
○ COF Picolit di Cialla '07	♟♟	6
● COF Refosco P.R. di Cialla '08	♟♟	6
● COF Schioppettino di Cialla '08	♟♟	6
● COF Schioppettino di Cialla '07	♟♟	6

Ronchi di Manzano

VIA ORSARIA, 42
33044 MANZANO [UD]
TEL. 0432740718
www.ronchidimanzano.com

CELLAR SALES
PRE-BOOKED VISITS
ANNUAL PRODUCTION 264,800 bottles
HECTARES UNDER VINE 55.00

A hard-working woman in winemaking, Roberta Borghese manages this estate purchased by her family in 1984. Ronchi di Manzano stretches across 55 hectares in Colli Orientali del Friuli, divided into several production zones: Ronc di Scossai and Ronc di Subule surround the beautiful winery, which sits on two underground levels built into the earth; another major plot is part of the hills of Rosazzo, renowned for its special subsoil, as well as the features of its soil and climate. Roberta was captivated by the atmosphere and natural rhythms of this place. She oversees the entire production cycle, from vineyard to cellar, aided by her skilled partners. The Rosazzo Bianco Ellègri 2012, team leader here, is a near-encore of last year's award-winner. Friulano, sauvignon blanc and chardonnay release creamy impressions of ripe tropical fruit, which continue onto the palate. The rest of the line is similarly outstanding, in line with its long-established reputation.

○ COF Verduzzo Friulano '10	♟♟	2*
○ Rosazzo Bianco Ellègri '12	♟♟	3*
○ COF Chardonnay '12	♟♟	3
○ COF Friulano '12	♟♟	3
● COF Merlot Ronc di Subule '09	♟♟	4
○ COF Pinot Grigio '12	♟♟	3
○ COF Sauvignon '12	♟♟	3
● COF Cabernet Sauvignon '11	♟	3
○ COF Friulano '10	♟♟♟	3
○ COF Friulano '09	♟♟♟	3*
● COF Merlot Ronc di Subule '99	♟♟♟	3*
○ COF Rosazzo Bianco Ellègri '11	♟♟♟	3*

Ronchi San Giuseppe

VIA STRADA DI SPESSA, 8
33043 CIVIDALE DEL FRIULI [UD]
TEL. 0432716172
www.ronchisangiuseppe.com

PRE-BOOKED VISITS
ANNUAL PRODUCTION 300,000 bottles
HECTARES UNDER VINE 64.00

The town of Spessa, in the Colli Orientali del Friuli, has always been known for the quality of its wine, and in particular that made by Zorzettig family. Pietro founded the operation, and his sons have started up their own wineries in the area over the years, but Franco and his son Fulvio have remained at the mother house, renaming it after the church of San Giuseppe, built on its hill in 1522. The pair has dedicated careful attention to cultivating indigenous varieties that were once little known and enjoyed only by locals, raising the quality of the wines and thus promoting priceless traditions. This is the first year that this winery sent its wines for tasting, and the performances were very good indeed. Indeed, the Friulano 2012 went right into our final tasting round, thanks to the richness of its aromatics and its delicious palate.

○ COF Friulano '12	♟♟ 2*
○ COF Chardonnay '12	♟♟ 2*
○ COF Pinot Grigio '12	♟♟ 2*
○ COF Ribolla Gialla '12	♟♟ 2*
○ COF Sauvignon '12	♟♟ 2*
○ COF Verduzzo Friulano '12	♟ 2

Ronco Blanchis

VIA BLANCHIS, 70
34070 MOSSA [GO]
TEL. 048180519
www.roncoblanchis.it

PRE-BOOKED VISITS
ANNUAL PRODUCTION 40,000 bottles
HECTARES UNDER VINE 12.00

Fantastic exposure made the hill of Blanchis, one of the tallest in Collio Goriziano, famous for the production of top-quality wines. Historic documents certify that a couple of centuries ago it belonged to the noble Austrian Catterini de Herzberg family and subsequently to Don Silverio de Baguer, minister to the King of Spain. The current owner is Giancarlo Palla who, with his sons Alberto and Lorenzo, relies on valuable winemaking advice from Gianni Menotti. Ronco Blanchis only makes four wines, all white, and the best grapes, those from the oldest vineyards, go into blending one single wine, the Collio, the highest expression of this terroir. Both nose and palate of the Collio 2012, a cuvée of friulano, chardonnay and sauvignon blanc, display such generous floral and citrus notes that it captured a Tre Bicchieri. The Sauvignon 2012 is likewise terrific, with multi-layered aromatics infusing every stage of the wine's presentation.

○ Collio '12	♟♟♟ 3*
○ Collio Sauvignon '12	♟♟ 3*
○ Collio Pinot Grigio '12	♟♟ 3
○ Collio Friulano '12	♟ 3
○ Collio '10	♟♟ 3
○ Collio Chardonnay '09	♟♟ 3*
○ Collio Friulano '11	♟♟ 3*
○ Collio Friulano '09	♟♟ 3
○ Collio Friulano Blanchis '11	♟♟ 3
○ Collio Pinot Bianco '08	♟♟ 3
○ Collio Pinot Grigio '11	♟♟ 3*
○ Collio Pinot Grigio '10	♟♟ 3
○ Collio Pinot Grigio '09	♟♟ 3*
○ Collio Pinot Grigio '08	♟♟ 3*
○ Collio Sauvignon '11	♟♟ 3

★Ronco dei Tassi

LOC. MONTONA, 19
34071 CORMÒNS [GO]
TEL. 048160155
www.roncodeitassi.it

CELLAR SALES
PRE-BOOKED VISITS
ANNUAL PRODUCTION 110,000 bottles
HECTARES UNDER VINE 18.00

Ronco dei Tassi was founded in 1989 by Fabio Coser who, after various experiences at other winemaking operations, decided to purchase an estate on the border of the beautiful natural park in Cormòns near Montona, on the side of Mount Quarin facing Slovenia. He immediately set about rebuilding the rural homestead and moved his family there. Fabio is also the owner of Vigna del Lauro and, as one of the best-qualified regional winemakers, oversees many other production operations too. For some time now his sons, Matteo and Enrico, have also worked at the estate, contributing to the unanimously recognized success of all its labels. The Malvasia 2012 dei Coser repeats its Tre Bicchieri performance of last year; the palate perfectly fulfils the promise encountered on the nose, with a thrilling, aromatic progression. The deliciously sweet Picolit 2009 too merits enthusiastic applause.

○ Collio Malvasia '12	ΨΨΨ	3*
○ Picolit '09	ΨΨ	6
○ Collio Friulano '12	ΨΨ	3
○ Collio Pinot Grigio '12	ΨΨ	3
● Collio Rosso Cjarandon Ris. '09	ΨΨ	5
○ Collio Sauvignon '12	ΨΨ	3
○ Collio Ribolla Gialla '12	Ψ	3
○ Collio Bianco Fosarin '10	ΨΨΨ	3
○ Collio Bianco Fosarin '09	ΨΨΨ	3*
○ Collio Bianco Fosarin '08	ΨΨΨ	3*
○ Collio Bianco Fosarin '07	ΨΨΨ	3
○ Collio Bianco Fosarin '06	ΨΨΨ	3
○ Collio Bianco Fosarin '04	ΨΨΨ	3*
○ Collio Malvasia '11	ΨΨΨ	3*
○ Collio Sauvignon '05	ΨΨΨ	3*

★Ronco del Gelso

VIA ISONZO, 117
34071 CORMÒNS [GO]
TEL. 048161310
www.roncodelgelso.com

CELLAR SALES
PRE-BOOKED VISITS
ANNUAL PRODUCTION 150,000 bottles
HECTARES UNDER VINE 25.00

In 1987 Giorgio Badin, fresh from his studies, acquired two hectares of poor, pebbly, dry level terrain, ideal for growing vines, located near Cormòns. These few hectares were enough for a start, and the next year he founded Ronco del Gelso. With devotion and determination, growth has progressed to the current 25 hectares under vine. With increased production, other spaces had to be expanded and so a new modern and functional cellar was built, equipped with a photovoltaic plant and boiler fuelled by pruning waste to guarantee self-sufficiency in energy. This year too, Giorgio's wines are resplendent for their crisp liveliness, appealing bouquet and inviting palate. The Sauvignon Sottomonte 2012 shows outstanding varietal fidelity and almost electric energy in the mouth, while the Pinot Grigio Sot lis Rivis 2012 is a textbook example of smoothness and balance.

○ Friuli Isonzo Bianco Latimis '12	ΨΨ	3
○ Friuli Isonzo Friulano Rive Alte Toc Bas '11	ΨΨ	3
○ Friuli Isonzo Pinot Bianco '12	ΨΨ	3
○ Friuli Isonzo Pinot Grigio Sot lis Rivis '12	ΨΨ	3
○ Friuli Isonzo Sauvignon Rive Alte Sottomonte '12	ΨΨ	4
○ Friuli Isonzo Malvasia '10	ΨΨΨ	3*
● Friuli Isonzo Merlot '01	ΨΨΨ	4
○ Friuli Isonzo Sauvignon '00	ΨΨΨ	2
○ Friuli Isonzo Tocai Friulano '06	ΨΨΨ	3*
○ Friuli Isonzo Tocai Friulano '05	ΨΨΨ	3
○ Friuli Isonzo Tocai Friulano '04	ΨΨΨ	3*
○ Friuli Isonzo Tocai Friulano '03	ΨΨΨ	3*
○ Friuli Isonzo Tocai Friulano '01	ΨΨΨ	2
○ Friuli Isonzo Tocai Friulano '97	ΨΨΨ	2

Ronco delle Betulle

LOC. ROSAZZO
VIA ABATE COLONNA, 24
33044 MANZANO [UD]
TEL. 0432740547
www.roncodellebetulle.it

CELLAR SALES
PRE-BOOKED VISITS
ANNUAL PRODUCTION 70,000 bottles
HECTARES UNDER VINE 14.00

Ronco delle Betulle is the brand from this estate managed since 1990 by Ivana Adami, a strong-willed and enterprising woman, daughter of the founder, Giovanbattista, who in 1967 had the wise premonition to focus on the potential of the hills of Rosazzo, though the special features of this place were unknown at the time. Not much was needed. In no time at all, this place took on such importance it was recognized with its own subzone appellation. Ivana, now aided by her son Simone, with tried and true skill and precision, oversees the vinification of her grapes at first hand, respecting the original character and maintaining the powerful typicity of these wines. The Rosazzo Bianco Vanessa 2010, mostly pinot bianco with a spot of friulano and ribolla gialla, offers rich flavours and notes of vanilla, mixed nuts and cakes, while the Friulano 2012, crisp and smooth on the palate, is redolent of bergamot. No less outstanding is the Pinot Grigio 2012.

○ COF Friulano '12	♼♼	3
○ COF Pinot Grigio '12	♼♼	3
● COF Refosco P. R. '10	♼♼	3
○ COF Rosazzo Bianco Vanessa '10	♼♼	3
○ COF Sauvignon '12	♼♼	3
○ COF Ribolla Gialla '12	♼	3
● Franconia '10	♼	3
○ COF Friulano '10	♼♼	3*
○ COF Friulano V. Bocois '11	♼♼	3
○ COF Pinot Grigio '11	♼♼	3
● COF Rosazzo Pignolo '07	♼♼	6
● COF Rosazzo Rosso Narciso '07	♼♼	5
● Franconia '09	♼♼	3

Ronco Severo

VIA RONCHI, 93
33040 PREPOTTO [UD]
TEL. 04337133440
info@roncosevero.it

CELLAR SALES
PRE-BOOKED VISITS
ANNUAL PRODUCTION 22,000 bottles
HECTARES UNDER VINE 8.00
VITICULTURE METHOD Certified Organic

Stefano Novello manages this estate which was founded by his father, Severo, in 1968. The few hectares available allow him to use old winemaking practices perfected through his experience gained in California and New Mexico. Stefano leaves his musts, even those from white grapes, in contact with the skins for several weeks, sometimes months, to allow the extraction of those substances that will help them last over time. This natural vinification sees no use of chemical products, cultured yeasts, enzymes or sulphur dioxide. These genuine wines are bottled while the moon is waning, with no filtration or clarification. The fierce competition among the skin-macerated whites brought not one but two wines into the final round, and the Friulano 2011 came second only by a hair. Perfectly balanced, it releases fascinating impressions of cakes and dried flowers.

○ COF Friulano '11	♼♼	3*
○ COF Pinot Grigio '11	♼♼	4
● COF Merlot Artiûl Ris. '10	♼♼	5
○ Severo Bianco '11	♼♼	4
○ COF Friulano Osteria '11	♼	3
○ COF Friulano Ris. '10	♼♼	4
○ COF Friulano Ris. '09	♼♼	3
● COF Merlot Artiûl '08	♼♼	5
● COF Merlot Artiûl '07	♼♼	5
● COF Merlot Artiûl '05	♼♼	4
● COF Merlot Artiûl Ris. '09	♼♼	5
○ COF Pinot Grigio '10	♼♼	4
○ COF Severo Bianco '07	♼♼	3*
○ Severo Bianco '09	♼♼	3*

Roncùs

via Mazzini, 26
34076 Capriva del Friuli [GO]
Tel. 0481809349
www.roncus.it

CELLAR SALES
PRE-BOOKED VISITS
ACCOMMODATION
ANNUAL PRODUCTION 40,000 bottles
HECTARES UNDER VINE 10.00

Roncùs was founded in 1985, when Marco Perco decided to transform the family estate, which had always been planted to mixed crops, into one focused exclusively on grape and wine production. These vineyards consist of several small plots scattered around the terraced hillsides of Capriva del Friuli, in the heart of Collio. Many of these are over 50 years old. Aware of the potential of this area, his aim has always been to interpret the features of each individual variety through vinification, inspired by the great wines of Alsace. These wines are always rich, complex, concentrated and long-lived. We had to wait an extra year to taste the Collio Bianco Vecchie Vigne 2009, and we have to admit that Marco was right. It is now a totally complete wine, bright and compelling, with rich fruit over summer hay, utterly beguiling flavours and a near-endless finish.

○ Collio Bianco V. V. '09	♀♀	5
○ Collio Friulano '11	♀♀	4
● Collio Merlot '11	♀♀	3
○ Pinot Bianco '11	♀♀	4
● Val di Miez '09	♀♀	5
○ Roncùs Bianco V. V. '01	♀♀♀	5
○ Collio Bianco '11	♀♀	3
○ Collio Bianco V. V. '08	♀♀	5
○ Collio Friulano '10	♀♀	4
○ Pinot Bianco '10	♀♀	4
○ Sauvignon '10	♀♀	4

★Russiz Superiore

via Russiz, 7
34070 Capriva del Friuli [GO]
Tel. 048180328
www.marcofelluga.it

CELLAR SALES
PRE-BOOKED VISITS
ACCOMMODATION
ANNUAL PRODUCTION 200,000 bottles
HECTARES UNDER VINE 50.00

In the hills of Capriva del Friuli, in the heart of Collio, the village of Russiz Superiore lent its name to this estate founded in 1966 by Marco Felluga, considered by everyone a pioneer on the regional winemaking scene. An innovator par excellence and man of innate farsightedness, he knew how best to draw out the potential of this terroir, creating a brand that guarantees absolute quality across the entire range. His son Roberto now does an excellent job of managing this estate, setting ever greater goals, and supporting the project aimed at promoting consumer appreciation of white wines for laying down. We tasted wines mostly of the 2012 vintage, and the Pinot Grigio 2012 once again stood out, releasing fragrant fruit, particularly nectarine, followed by a crisp tanginess in the mouth. The full-flavoured, very varietal Sauvignon 2012 was likewise a finalist, at the same time supple and dynamic.

○ Collio Pinot Grigio '12	♀♀	4*
○ Collio Sauvignon '12	♀♀	4*
○ Collio Bianco Col Disôre '10	♀♀	5
○ Collio Friulano '12	♀♀	4
○ Collio Pinot Bianco '12	♀♀	4
○ Collio Bianco Russiz Disôre '01	♀♀♀	5
○ Collio Bianco Russiz Disôre '00	♀♀♀	4
○ Collio Pinot Bianco '07	♀♀♀	4
○ Collio Pinot Grigio '11	♀♀♀	4*
● Collio Rosso Riserva degli Orzoni '94	♀♀♀	5
● Collio Rosso Riserva degli Orzoni '93	♀♀♀	5
○ Collio Sauvignon '05	♀♀♀	3
○ Collio Sauvignon '04	♀♀♀	5
○ Collio Sauvignon '98	♀♀♀	5
○ Collio Tocai Friulano '99	♀♀♀	4

Sant'Elena

VIA GASPARINI, 1
34072 GRADISCA D'ISONZO [GO]
TEL. 048192388
www.sant-elena.com

CELLAR SALES
PRE-BOOKED VISITS
ANNUAL PRODUCTION 130,000 bottles
HECTARES UNDER VINE 30.00

The Sant'Elena estate, founded in the 19th century by the Klodic family, was purchased in 1997 by Dominic Nocerino, renowned importer of Italian wines to the United States, with the aim of bringing out the highest potential of this area in the Isonzo DOC appellation. As is well-known, these vineyards are planted on the plain, but the soil, formed by a superficial layer of iron-rich red earth of alluvial origin that rests on top of decalcified soils poor in organic material, produces top-quality grapes, rich in aromas and minerality, endowing these wines with unique, incomparable features. This year saw the release not only of the base wines, but of the 2009 reds as well, which grab attention for their verve and personality. Chief among them is the Merlot Ròs di Rôl, with aromatic complexity and drive in the mouth. No less fine is the rhubarb and tobacco-infused Pignolo Quantum, high-powered throughout.

● Merlot Ròs di Rôl '09	♟♟	6
● Friuli Isonzo Pignolo Quantum '09	♟♟	7
● Merlot '09	♟♟	3
○ Sauvignon '12	♟♟	3
● Tato '09	♟♟	5
● Cabernet Franc '09	♟	3
○ Pinot Grigio '12	♟	3
● Cabernet Sauvignon '08	♟♟	3*
● Merlot '08	♟♟	3
● Merlot Ròs di Rôl '08	♟♟	6
○ Mil Rosis '10	♟♟	4
○ Sauvignon '10	♟♟	3

Sara & Sara

LOC. SAVORGNANO DEL TORRE
VIA DEI MONTI, 5
33040 POVOLETTO [UD]
TEL. 04323859042
www.saraesara.com

CELLAR SALES
PRE-BOOKED VISITS
ANNUAL PRODUCTION 24,000 bottles
HECTARES UNDER VINE 7.00

Young Alessandro Sara is becoming established as one of those artisans who use old techniques to produce enjoyable wines that have great impact. This estate, founded in 1954 by his father, Giuliano, is located in Savorgnano del Torre, in the heart of Colli Orientali del Friuli, an area rich in waterways, forests and hills formed of marl and sand with a clayey texture. The special mesoclimate in this zone encourages the natural formation of botrytis cinerea (noble rot) on grape bunches that contributes to the elegance and special aromatic qualities of the part-dried verduzzo and piccolit grapes. These wines are unfiltered in order to safeguard their integrity. The modest size of this estate allows Alessandro artisan-scale work in the vineyards and winemaking. He has won recognition above all for his jewel, the scrumptiously sweet Verduzzo Friulano Crei, of which the 2011 boasts dried figs and candied orange zest.

○ COF Verduzzo Friulano Crei '11	♟♟	5
○ COF Picolit '09	♟♟	5
● Refosco P. R. '11	♟	2
○ COF Verduzzo Friulano Crei '10	♟♟♟	5
○ COF Friulano '10	♟♟	3
○ COF Picolit '07	♟♟	5
● COF Refosco P. R. '10	♟♟	3
● COF Rosso Il Rio Falcone '08	♟♟	3
○ COF Verduzzo Friulano Crei '09	♟♟	5

★Schiopetto

VIA PALAZZO ARCIVESCOVILE, 1
34070 CAPRIVA DEL FRIULI [GO]
TEL. 048180332
www.schiopetto.it

CELLAR SALES
PRE-BOOKED VISITS
ANNUAL PRODUCTION 180,000 bottles
HECTARES UNDER VINE 30.00

Maria Angela, Carlo and Giorgio Schiopetto manage this estate founded in 1965 by the great Mario, with the same passion he himself inherited from his father, Giorgio, a much loved innkeeper in Udine at the beginning of the 20th century. A keen innovator with an enquiring mind, Mario Schiopetto manages to put to good use his many experiences from his frequent trips abroad, successfully adapting the refined vision of the French and technology of the Germans to the territory of Collio. He was the first to introduce to Friuli the concept of the garden-vineyard, entrusting the care of his vineyards to Sirch and Simonit, creators of the Grape Preparers group. Schiopetto's wines come out at least two years after the harvest, so this year it is the turn of the Friulano 2011, with fragrant tropical fruit and hazelnut followed by a full-volumed, seductive palate. Close behind is the forceful Podere dei Blumeri Rosso 2009, succulent and a real sensory feast.

La Sclusa

LOC. SPESSA
VIA STRADA DI SANT'ANNA, 7/2
33043 CIVIDALE DEL FRIULI [UD]
TEL. 0432716259
www.lasclusa.it

CELLAR SALES
PRE-BOOKED VISITS
ACCOMMODATION
ANNUAL PRODUCTION 160,000 bottles
HECTARES UNDER VINE 30.00

The trunk of the Zorzettig family tree bears the name Giobatta, founder of a family of growers who since 1963 have worked in Spessa di Cividale, in the heart of Colli Orientali del Friuli. Each branch later created its own identity, and one of the most important is Gino, who managed his estate for over 40 years before passing it on to his sons, Germano, Maurizio and Luciano. This new generation also subscribes to the estate philosophy of genuine wines with no excesses or forcing. The name of this estate is inspired by a section of the Corno river that runs through the vineyards and is called La Sclusa. High marks this year simply confirm the overall consistent quality here. The Chardonnay 2012 displays fine breeding from first to last, while the convincingly varietal Friulano 2012 is quite emphatic and flavour-rich.

○ Collio Friulano '11	♥♥ 4
● Podere dei Blumeri Rosso '09	♥♥ 5
○ Blanc des Rosis '11	♥♥ 4
○ Collio Pinot Bianco '12	♥♥ 4
○ Collio Pinot Grigio '12	♥♥ 4
○ Collio Sauvignon '11	♥♥ 4
● Rivarossa '10	♥♥ 4
○ Blanc des Rosis '07	♥♥♥ 4
○ Blanc des Rosis '06	♥♥♥ 4
○ Collio Pinot Bianco '00	♥♥♥ 4
○ Collio Tocai Friulano '00	♥♥♥ 4
○ Mario Schiopetto Bianco '08	♥♥♥ 5
○ Mario Schiopetto Bianco '07	♥♥♥ 5
○ Mario Schiopetto Bianco '03	♥♥♥ 5
○ Mario Schiopetto Bianco '02	♥♥♥ 5

○ COF Chardonnay '12	♥♥ 3
○ COF Friulano '12	♥♥ 2*
○ COF Ribolla Gialla '12	♥♥ 3
○ COF Sauvignon '12	♥♥ 3
○ COF Pinot Grigio '12	♥ 2
● COF Refosco P. R. '11	♥ U
● COF Cabernet Franc '11	♥♥ 3
○ COF Friulano '11	♥♥ 2*
○ COF Pinot Grigio '11	♥♥ 2*
○ COF Pinot Grigio '10	♥♥ 2
○ COF Ribolla Gialla '11	♥♥ 3
○ COF Sauvignon '10	♥♥ 3

Roberto Scubla

FRAZ. IPPLIS
VIA ROCCA BERNARDA, 22
33040 PREMARIACCO [UD]
TEL. 0432716258
www.scubla.com

CELLAR SALES
PRE-BOOKED VISITS
ANNUAL PRODUCTION 60,000 bottles
HECTARES UNDER VINE 12.00

More than once we have had the chance to mention the great foresight that led Roberto Scubla in 1991 to leave his job as a banker and purchase several vineyards and a decaying farmhouse on the slopes of Rocca Bernarda. That rustic dwelling has been transformed into a villa of great architectural beauty, with welcoming rooms and surrounded by a pastoral atmosphere. The limited production means painstaking care can be taken of the vineyards, and the friendship between Roberto and Gianni Menotti is clearly a great help in running the cellar. We like to recall that the Bianco Pomèdes bears the name of the Alpine retreat where the two men, stranded in a storm, first came up with the idea for this wine. The Verduzzo Friulano Cràtis 2010 turned in a fine performance this year again, with dandelion honey as the dominant motif overall. Joining it in the final round was the Pomèdes 2011, an interesting trio of elegant pinot bianco, smooth friulano, and aromatic riesling.

○ COF Bianco Pomèdes '11	ΨΨ 5
○ COF Verduzzo Friulano Cràtis '10	ΨΨ 5
○ COF Bianco Speziale '12	ΨΨ 3
● COF Cabernet Sauvignon '11	ΨΨ 3
○ COF Friulano '12	ΨΨ 3
● COF Merlot '11	ΨΨ 3
● COF Cabernet Franc '11	Ψ 3
○ COF Pinot Bianco '12	Ψ 3
○ COF Bianco Pomèdes '04	ΥΥΥ 4
○ COF Bianco Pomèdes '99	ΥΥΥ 4*
○ COF Bianco Pomèdes '98	ΥΥΥ 4*
○ COF Verduzzo Friulano Cràtis '09	ΥΥΥ 5
○ COF Verduzzo Friulano Cràtis '06	ΥΥΥ 5
○ COF Verduzzo Friulano Cràtis '04	ΥΥΥ 5
○ COF Verduzzo Friulano Graticcio '99	ΥΥΥ 5

Renzo Sgubin

VIA FAET, 15
34071 CORMÒNS [GO]
TEL. 3385601209
www.renzosgubin.it

CELLAR SALES
PRE-BOOKED VISITS
ANNUAL PRODUCTION 28,000 bottles
HECTARES UNDER VINE 12.00

The labels on Renzo Sgubin's wines feature the unmistakable image of Monte Quarin (the hill behind Cormòns), a tribute to his roots. Both his parents were born here at the foot of the castle, settled in the heart of the village, and later moved to Pradis, which straddles the Collio and Friuli Isonzo DOC zones, where they worked as tenant farmers and later purchased their first vineyards in the 1970s. A man of few words and many deeds, Renzo likes to call himself a farmer. Supported by his wife Michela, he decided to found this estate in 1997 and began bottling the first wines in 2003. There has been constant, continuous improvement ever since. The exceptional Merlot 2010 del Collio earned a place in the final round for the richness and appeal of its bouquet but in particular the breadth and sheer seduction of its palate. The remainder of the wines, both the base whites and the blends, were outstanding examples of varietal fidelity.

● Collio Merlot '10	ΨΨ 3*
○ 3, 4, 3 '11	ΨΨ 3
○ Friuli Isonzo Friulano '12	ΨΨ 3
○ Friuli Isonzo Sauvignon '12	ΨΨ 3
● Plagnis '08	ΨΨ 3
○ Friuli Isonzo Chardonnay '12	Ψ 3
○ Friuli Isonzo Malvasia '12	Ψ 3
○ Friuli Isonzo Pinot Grigio '12	Ψ 3
● Collio Merlot '09	ΥΥ 3*
● Collio Merlot '08	ΥΥ 3*
○ Friuli Isonzo Friulano '11	ΥΥ 3
○ Friuli Isonzo Malvasia '11	ΥΥ 3
○ Friuli Isonzo Sauvignon '11	ΥΥ 3
● Plagnis '06	ΥΥ 3

Sirch

VIA FORNALIS, 277/1
33043 CIVIDALE DEL FRIULI [UD]
TEL. 0432709835
www.sirchwine.com

CELLAR SALES
PRE-BOOKED VISITS
ANNUAL PRODUCTION 150,000 bottles
HECTARES UNDER VINE 20.00

Sirch has always produced its wines in
Cividale del Friuli, in the Colli Orientali, but
they are currently distributed solely by Feudi
San Gregorio. Luca Sirch is committed to
making classic monovarietal wines, turning
out clean, modern bottlings while paying no
attention to fad or fashion. His are wines are
self-confident, straightforward, and crisp,
with price-tags that are more than
reasonable. In 2000, he introduced the
Cru:Chale line with the goal of promoting
wine made from small vineyards that are
distinctive for their age, aspect, and
elevation, and imprint valuable
characteristics on the fruit. This high-quality
line grew in 2011 with the addition of
Chardonnay and Sauvignon Blanc. The
whites of the current vintage received top
marks, thanks to expressive bouquets and
exemplary varietal character. The Friulano
2012 in particular demonstrates magnificent
typicity: fragrant, supple and full-flavoured.
The other wines are no less sound.

○ COF Chardonnay '12	♀♀	3
○ COF Friulano '12	♀♀	3*
○ COF Malvasia '12	♀♀	3
○ COF Pinot Grigio '12	♀♀	3
○ COF Ribolla Gialla '12	♀♀	3
● COF Cabernet '11	♀	3
● COF Merlot '11	♀	3
● COF Refosco P.R. '11	♀	3
○ COF Sauvignon '12	♀	3
● COF Schioppettino '11	♀	3
○ COF Friulano '07	♀♀♀	2*
○ COF Malvasia '11	♀♀	3
○ COF Sauvignon '11	♀♀	3

Skerk

FRAZ. SAN PELAGIO
LOC. PREPOTTO, 20
34011 DUINO AURISINA [TS]
TEL. 040200156
www.skerk.com

CELLAR SALES
PRE-BOOKED VISITS
RESTAURANT SERVICE
ANNUAL PRODUCTION 22,000 bottles
HECTARES UNDER VINE 6.00
VITICULTURE METHOD Certified Organic

Sandi Skerk has proved to be one of the
best interpreters of grapes from Carso, a
place where the conflict between man and
rock is part of daily life. Everything is done
by hand; space is limited. The red earth is
poor, dry, barren and rocky, yet rich in
limestone and iron. Here and there,
vineyards tended like gardens can be seen
in sunny spots that overlook the sea. Sandi
knows how to exploit these peculiarities: he
treats his grapes with natural growing
methods and, in the lovely cellar literally
ripped from the karstic rock, makes wine
with long maceration, no clarification or
filtration, and bottles them only during the
first days of the waning moon. The
Ograde 2001 is not only an assemblage of
vitovska, malvasia and sauvignon blanc
whose roseate hue also bespeaks a tad of
pinot grigio, but it is a Tre Bicchieri
champion as well for the third year in a
row, which makes it truly legendary. Also
superb is the fragrant Malvasia 2011.

○ Ograde '11	♀♀♀	4*
○ Malvasia '11	♀♀	5
● Terrano '11	♀♀	5
○ Vitovska '11	♀♀	5
○ Carso Malvasia '08	♀♀♀	4
○ Ograde '10	♀♀♀	4
○ Ograde '09	♀♀♀	4*
○ Malvasia '10	♀♀	5
● Terrano '10	♀♀	5
○ Vitovska '10	♀♀	5

Edi Skok

LOC. GIASBANA, 15
34070 SAN FLORIANO DEL COLLIO [GO]
TEL. 0481390280
www.skok.it

CELLAR SALES
PRE-BOOKED VISITS
ANNUAL PRODUCTION 38,000 bottles
HECTARES UNDER VINE 11.00

Since 1991 Edi and Orietta Skok have managed this estate founded in 1968 by their father, Giuseppe, along with his brother, Armando, in San Floriano del Collio, near the border with Slovenia. A hospitable tasting hall is located in the old landowner's villa built by the Counts of Salzburg in the 16th century. The Skoks have a long farming tradition, deeply tied to tradition, but they are also very open to innovation. The cellar is equipped with a modern photovoltaic plant that produces enough energy for processing the grapes, running the refrigeration unit, and maintaining the proper temperature for the production environment. For the second year in a row, the Friulano Zabura 2012 competed in our final tasting round, thanks to its appealing peach, citron, dried flowers and honey on the nose, and no less superb palate and lengthy finish. The Collio Pinot Grigio 2012 sports pear and elderflower and magisterial balance overall.

○ Collio Friulano Zabura '12	♥♥	3*
○ Collio Bianco Pe Ar '11	♥♥	3
○ Collio Chardonnay '12	♥♥	2*
○ Collio Pinot Grigio '12	♥♥	3
● Collio Merlot '11	♥	3
○ Collio Sauvignon '12	♥	3
○ Collio Bianco Pe Ar '09	♀♀	3
○ Collio Friulano Zabura '11	♀♀	3*
● Collio Merlot Villa Jasbinae '07	♀♀	3
○ Collio Pinot Grigio '11	♀♀	3

Leonardo Specogna

VIA ROCCA BERNARDA, 4
33040 CORNO DI ROSAZZO [UD]
TEL. 0432755840
www.specogna.it

CELLAR SALES
PRE-BOOKED VISITS
ANNUAL PRODUCTION 110,000 bottles
HECTARES UNDER VINE 18.00

Begun in 1963 by their grandfather, Leonardo, the Specogna estate is now run by young Michele and Cristian, both with oenology degrees, who still rely on active collaboration from their father, Graziano, and uncle, Gianni, who took on the project of expanding the vineyards and passing this superb operation on to the next generation. The vineyards stretch across the sunny slopes of Rocca Bernarda and enjoy an ideal site climate, protected by the Alps and exposed to breezes from the nearby Adriatic. In perfect synergy, Michele and Cristian have shared the duties and production responsibilities, and always produce well-managed wines that are consistent with market expectations. The Sauvignon Duality 2009 and Rosso Oltre 2009, both new bottlings, are the fruit of rigorous quality selection of fruit, and both performed so well that they figured in the tasting finals. The former is exuberant on the nose and near-endless on the palate, while the latter, a blend of refosco, pignolo and schioppettino, is redolent of spice and tobacco leaf, then seductively silky in the mouth.

● Rosso Oltre '09	♥♥	5
○ Sauvignon Duality '09	♥♥	3*
○ COF Friulano '12	♥♥	3
● COF Pignolo '09	♥♥	6
○ COF Pinot Grigio '12	♥♥	3
○ COF Sauvignon '12	♥♥	3
● COF Refosco P. R. '11	♥	3
○ COF Ribolla Gialla '12	♥	3
○ COF Friulano '11	♀♀	3
● COF Merlot Oltre '08	♀♀	6
● COF Pignolo '08	♀♀	5
○ COF Pinot Grigio '11	♀♀	3
○ COF Sauvignon '11	♀♀	3

Oscar Sturm

LOC. ZEGLA, 1
34071 CORMÒNS [GO]
TEL. 048160720
www.sturm.it

CELLAR SALES
PRE-BOOKED VISITS
ANNUAL PRODUCTION 80,000 bottles
HECTARES UNDER VINE 10.00

The current owner, Oscar Sturm, comes from a family originally from the village of Andritz, Austria, which in 1850 settled around Cormòns, in Zegla, where a series of slopes runs down from Collio Goriziano to nearby Slovenia. A true man of the vine and a real artisan, he has successfully passed on his passion to his children. The youngest son, Patrick, has already taken on the responsibility of running the cellar and, determined, quickly achieved excellent results; Denis, making use of his degree in economics, concentrates on publicity and marketing, aiming constantly toward new goals. The complexity and scented appeal of the Collio Bianco Andritz 2012, friulano, sauvignon blanc and pinot grigio, propelled it into the final tasting round, while the Collio Rosso Andritz 2009, composed of merlot, cabernet sauvignon and refosco dal peduncolo rosso, retains its splendid fruit and exhibits a compelling warmth and attractiveness in the mouth.

○ Collio Bianco Andritz '12	♀♀	5
○ Collio Friulano '12	♀♀	3
○ Collio Pinot Grigio '12	♀♀	3
● Collio Rosso Andritz '09	♀♀	7
○ Collio Ribolla Gialla '12	♀	3
○ Collio Sauvignon '12	♀	3
○ Collio Sauvignon '06	♀♀♀	3
○ Collio Tocai Friulano '05	♀♀♀	3*
○ Collio Friulano '11	♀♀	3*
○ Collio Pinot Grigio '11	♀♀	3*
○ Collio Sauvignon '11	♀♀	3*

Subida di Monte

LOC. SUBIDA
VIA SUBIDA, 6
34071 CORMÒNS [GO]
TEL. 048161011
www.subidadimonte.it

CELLAR SALES
PRE-BOOKED VISITS
ACCOMMODATION
ANNUAL PRODUCTION 45,000 bottles
HECTARES UNDER VINE 9.00

The lovely winery of Subida di Monte dominates a steep slope in Collio Goriziano that runs between Isonzo and Judrio, where sun-drenched vineyards are cradled by the Alps and enjoy salty breezes from the Adriatic. Here, in 1972, Luigi Antonutti brought to life his dream of becoming a grower. A far-sighted man open to innovation, he blazed the trail now enthusiastically followed by his sons, Cristian and Andrea. With respect for the characteristics of the terroir, which show Collio as an area well suited to top quality production, they produce real textbook wines with well-focused varietal aromas and great drinkability. The Malvasia 2012 won a place in the final tastings for its exemplary varietal fidelity, refined bouquet and near-endless length. Cherry and raspberry grace the Merlot 2011, with a no less impressive palate, while the Friulano 2012 is straightforward and full-flavoured.

○ Collio Malvasia '12	♀♀	3*
○ Collio Friulano '12	♀♀	3
● Collio Merlot '11	♀♀	3
● Collio Cabernet Franc '11	♀	3
○ Collio Pinot Grigio '12	♀	3
○ Colllio Sauvignon '12	♀	3
○ Collio Friulano '11	♀♀	3*
○ Collio Malvasia '11	♀♀	3*
○ Collio Pinot Grigio '11	♀♀	3*
○ Collio Sauvignon '11	♀♀	3*
○ Collio Sauvignon '10	♀♀	2*

Matijaz Tercic

LOC. BUCUIE, 4
34070 SAN FLORIANO DEL COLLIO [GO]
TEL. 0481884920
www.tercic.com

CELLAR SALES
PRE-BOOKED VISITS
ANNUAL PRODUCTION 30,000 bottles
HECTARES UNDER VINE 11.00

In 1990 young Matijaz Tercic began a career that has since brought him honours for his forthright, fragrant wines, winning over the most demanding markets and consumers. He comes from a family that has been dedicated to vineyards and winemaking for many generations, but the real leap in quality came in 1994, the year of the first bottling. The cellar faces the lovely valley dominated by the village of San Floriano del Collio on the border with Slovenia. This site enjoys ideal ventilation that fixes the aromas and dries the grapes. In constant growth, the estate has reached the top of regional excellence. Matijaz is spot on once again this year, with an elegant, stylish Sauvignon 2011 that releases tropical fruit and vanilla and a palate that is all suppleness and satisfaction. The Pinot Grigio 2011 beguiles with elderflower and russet pear, and fine grip complemented by a mouthfilling smoothness.

○ Collio Pinot Grigio '11	🍷🍷 3*
○ Collio Sauvignon '11	🍷🍷 3*
○ Collio Chardonnay '11	🍷🍷 3
● Collio Merlot '10	🍷🍷 4
○ Friuli Isonzo Friulano '11	🍷🍷 3
○ Vino degli Orti '11	🍷🍷 3
○ Collio Ribolla Gialla '11	🍷 3
○ Collio Pinot Grigio '07	🍷🍷🍷 3*
○ Collio Pinot Grigio '10	🍷🍷 3*
○ Collio Sauvignon '10	🍷🍷 3
○ Collio Sauvignon Scemen '09	🍷🍷 4

Tiare - Roberto Snidarcig

LOC. SANT'ELENA, 3A
34070 DOLEGNA DEL COLLIO [GO]
TEL. 048162491
www.tiaredoc.com

CELLAR SALES
PRE-BOOKED VISITS
RESTAURANT SERVICE
ANNUAL PRODUCTION 100,000 bottles
HECTARES UNDER VINE 10.00

Tiare means earth in the local dialect, and the estate by that name was founded by Roberto Snidarcig in 1985 on the slopes of Mount Quarin in Cormòns with little more than a hectare of vineyard. Supported by his wife, Sandra, he transferred the estate headquarters in 1991 to Dolegna del Collio, built a new cellar and greatly increased the number of hectares under vine. What in the beginning could only be considered a small, amateur operation is now an impressive estate that is highly thought of and has become established on the winemaking landscape, giving further distinction to the region. This year's fine cadre of wines is led by the Sauvignon Empire 2011, seducing with intriguing tropical impressions that morph in the mouth into aromatic nuances truly refined and memorable. Friulano 2012, redolent of wildflowers, dried herbs and coconut, is beautifully balanced, smooth and bursting with flavours.

○ Collio Friulano '12	🍷🍷 3*
○ Collio Sauvignon Empire '11	🍷🍷 3*
○ Collio Bianco Rosemblanc '11	🍷🍷 5
○ Collio Malvasia '12	🍷🍷 3
○ Collio Pinot Grigio '12	🍷🍷 3
○ Collio Sauvignon '12	🍷🍷 3
● Collio Schioppettino '11	🍷🍷 2*
● Friuli Isonzo Merlot Ronco del Merlo '09	🍷🍷 4
○ Collio Chardonnay '12	🍷 3
○ Collio Chardonnay '11	🍷🍷 3
○ Collio Malvasia '11	🍷🍷 3*
○ Collio Pinot Grigio '11	🍷🍷 3
○ Collio Rosemblanc '10	🍷🍷 5
○ Collio Sauvignon '11	🍷🍷 3*

★Franco Toros

LOC. NOVALI, 12
34071 CORMÒNS [GO]
TEL. 048161327
www.vinitoros.com

CELLAR SALES
PRE-BOOKED VISITS
ANNUAL PRODUCTION 50,000 bottles
HECTARES UNDER VINE 10.00

Like all the greats, Franco Toros gives the greatest credit for his quality wines to mother nature, even though we all know the results would not be the same without the right interpreter. He comes from a farming family that in the early 1900s settled near Cormòns, in the area of Novali, where it was easy to see these plots were perfect for vineyards, and quickly became skilled winemakers. These wines stand out for their clean, uncompromising qualities, great respect for varietal characteristics, and above all an easy drinkability despite their individual complexity. The Friulano 2012 continues to capture the Tre Bicchieri. The nose is marked by delicate nuances of spring flowers, medicinal herbs and star anise, while abundant fruit and depth in the mouth precede a lengthy, taut finale.

○ Collio Friulano '12	♔♔♔ 4*
○ Collio Pinot Bianco '12	♔♔ 4
○ Collio Sauvignon '12	♔♔ 4
○ Collio Chardonnay '12	♔♔ 4
○ Collio Pinot Grigio '12	♔♔ 4
○ Collio Friulano '11	♔♔♔ 4*
○ Collio Friulano '10	♔♔♔ 4
○ Collio Friulano '09	♔♔♔ 4*
○ Collio Friulano '08	♔♔♔ 4*
○ Collio Pinot Bianco '08	♔♔♔ 4*
○ Collio Pinot Bianco '07	♔♔♔ 4
○ Collio Pinot Bianco '05	♔♔♔ 4
○ Collio Pinot Bianco '03	♔♔♔ 3
○ Collio Tocai Friulano '06	♔♔♔ 4
○ Collio Tocai Friulano '04	♔♔♔ 4
○ Collio Tocai Friulano '03	♔♔♔ 3

Torre Rosazza

FRAZ. OLEIS
LOC. POGGIOBELLO, 12
33044 MANZANO [UD]
TEL. 0422864511
www.torrerosazza.com

CELLAR SALES
PRE-BOOKED VISITS
ANNUAL PRODUCTION 300,000 bottles
HECTARES UNDER VINE 95.00

Genagricola's holdings in Friuli include Poggiobello, Borgo Magredo and Tenuta Sant'Anna. In 1974 they also purchased Torre Rosazza, a flourishing estate positioned on the summit of a hill in the commune of Manzano, which quickly became the jewel of the group. The vineyards form two splendid, naturally-terraced amphitheatres which are permanently sunny and surround the 18th-century Palazzo De Marchi where both the offices and cellars are still located. Enrico Raddi acts as director and the talented estate technicians are assisted in their wine-growing and wine-making choices by the undisputed skill of the internationally famous winemaker, Donato Lanati. Constant quality growth of the wines here has brought the first Tre Bicchieri award to the superb Pinot Grigio 2012, resplendent with tropical fruit, mixed nuts and honey, which enrich its already-delicious varietal qualities. Superb as well is the Ribolla Gialla 2012, citrussy, crisp and yet velvet-smooth.

○ COF Pinot Grigio '12	♔♔♔ 3*
○ COF Ribolla Gialla '12	♔♔ 3*
○ COF Friulano '12	♔♔ 3
● COF Merlot '11	♔♔ 3
● COF Merlot L'Altromerlot '09	♔♔ 5
● COF Pignolo '09	♔♔ 6
● COF Rosso Bandaròs '09	♔♔ 5
● COF Sauvignon '12	♔♔ 3
○ COF Bianco Ronco del Masiero '10	♔♔ 3*
○ COF Bianco Ronco del Masiero '09	♔♔ 3*
○ COF Friulano '11	♔♔ 3
● COF Merlot L'Altromerlot '08	♔♔ 5
● COF Pignolo '08	♔♔ 5
● COF Pignolo '07	♔♔ 3*
○ COF Pinot Grigio '11	♔♔ 3
● COF Sauvignon '11	♔♔ 3*

La Tunella

FRAZ. IPPLIS
VIA DEL COLLIO, 14
33040 PREMARIACCO [UD]
TEL. 0432716030
www.latunella.it

CELLAR SALES
PRE-BOOKED VISITS
ANNUAL PRODUCTION 390,000 bottles
HECTARES UNDER VINE 70.00

Tunella is a modern and functional model estate, producing significant quantities and managed by Massimo and Mauro Zorzettig, two young brothers aided for some years now by the expert oenologist, Luigino Zamparo. Supported by a dynamic team in a cellar at the cutting edge of architectural design as well as advanced technology, with ample space for oak casks and drying rooms equipped with controlled refrigeration and ventilation. Putting the experience inherited from three generations of producers and their training to god use , they have conquered the international markets with wines with approachability on both the nose and palate. The release of the BiancoSesto and some of the big reds has been put off a year, but we are amply consoled by three new wines, all fine quality selections. The Friulano Col Livius 2011 and Bianco La Linda 2011 were both finalists, each opulent, fragrant and crisp at every stage of their presentation.

○ COF Bianco La Linda '11	♟♟	5
○ COF Friulano Col Livius '11	♟♟	4
○ COF Ribolla Gialla Col de Bliss '11	♟♟	4
○ COF Friulano '12	♟♟	3
○ COF Malvasia Valmasia '12	♟♟	3
○ COF Ribolla Gialla Rjgialla '12	♟♟	3
○ COF Sauvignon '12	♟♟	3
○ COF Sauvignon Col Matiss '11	♟♟	4
● COF Refosco P.R. '11	♟	3
○ COF BiancoSesto '11	♟♟♟	4*
○ COF BiancoSesto '07	♟♟♟	3
○ COF BiancoSesto '06	♟♟♟	3*
○ COF Noans '10	♟♟	5
● COF Pignolo '07	♟♟	5
○ COF Ribolla Gialla Rjgialla '11	♟♟	3

Valchiarò

FRAZ. TOGLIANO
VIA DEI LAGHI, 4C
33040 TORREANO [UD]
TEL. 0432715502
www.valchiaro.it

CELLAR SALES
PRE-BOOKED VISITS
ANNUAL PRODUCTION 40,000 bottles
HECTARES UNDER VINE 12.00

The municipality of Torreano di Cividale is located among the foothills and the Julian Prealps, in eastern Friuli and is traversed from north to south by the Chiarò river. This valley inspired the name of this estate, founded in 1991 when six partners decided to join forces into a single operation. A history of passion and friendship led Armando, Doris, Galliano, Lauro, Luigi and Stefano to create an association, making use of valuable oenological consultancy from Gianni Menotti and immediately going for quality. So what seemed a venture sparked by a bit of recklessness has instead been revealed as the right choice given the goals achieved. The majestic Verduzzo Friulano 2009, a top scorer that went into the final round, pours out barley sugar, yellow peach and dried apricot, then coats the palate with an almost irremovable, luscious sweetness. Likewise enjoyable is the fascinating and very tasty Friulano Nexus 2012.

○ COF Verduzzo Friulano '09	♟♟	4*
○ COF Friulano Nexus '12	♟♟	3
● COF Rosso Torre Qual Ris. '08	♟♟	3
○ COF Sauvignon '12	♟♟	3*
○ COF Friulano '12	♟	3
○ COF Pinot Grigio '12	♟	3
○ COF Friulano Nexus '11	♟♟	3
● COF Merlot Ris. '08	♟♟	4
● COF Merlot Ris. '07	♟♟	4
● COF Refosco P. R. '07	♟♟	3
○ COF Sauvignon '11	♟♟	2*

Valpanera

VIA TRIESTE, 5A
33059 VILLA VICENTINA [UD]
TEL. 0431970395
www.valpanera.it

PRE-BOOKED VISITS
ANNUAL PRODUCTION 450,000 bottles
HECTARES UNDER VINE 55.00

This was a brave but winning choice by Giampietro Dal Vecchio, owner of Valpanera, together with his son, Giovanni. The sign "Casa del Refosco" towers over the entrance to the winery, a clear message that sums up the estate philosophy based on improving the most common native red grape in the region. In the larger world of refosco, the refosco dal peduncolo rosso variety finds an ideal habitat here in the sand and clay soils of the Aquileia DOC zone, where breezes from the nearby Adriatic sea help to ripen healthy grapes, full of flavour. A few hectares planted to other varieties make up the remainder and extend the range of wines on offer. Tre Bicchieri again go to the Refosco dal Peduncolo Rosso Riserva 2008 for its rich, pleasurable bouquet, still fruity with a hint of spice; both the palate and finish are magnificent. Wild dark berry fruit and eucalyptus animate the Refosco dal Peduncolo Rosso Superiore 2009.

● Friuli Aquileia Refosco P. R. Sup. '09	♀♀	3*
● Friuli Aquileia Refosco P. R. Ris. '08	♀♀	5
● Friuli Aquileia Refosco P. R. '11	♀	2
● Friuli Aquileia Rosso Alma '07	♀	5
● Rosso di Valpanera '11	♀	2
○ Bianco di Valpanera '11	♀♀	2*
● Friuli Aquileia Refosco P. R. Ris. '07	♀♀	5
● Friuli Aquileia Refosco P. R. Sup. '08	♀♀	3*
● Friuli Aquileia Rosso Alma '06	♀♀	3*
● Rosso di Valpanera '10	♀♀	2*

★Venica & Venica

LOC. CERÒ, 8
34070 DOLEGNA DEL COLLIO [GO]
TEL. 048161264
www.venica.it

CELLAR SALES
PRE-BOOKED VISITS
ACCOMMODATION
ANNUAL PRODUCTION 257,000 bottles
HECTARES UNDER VINE 37.00

Gianni and Giorgio Venica, with the cohesive spirit of a farming family and undisputed skill as both artisans and businessmen, have led this estate into the top ranks of regional excellence. They are a benchmark, an example to be imitated, and have even become major players internationally. The dynamic quality of Ornella and energy of Giampaolo are the added value at this wonderful operation that has successfully brought out the potential of their vineyards purchased over 80 years ago on the hill of Cerò by their grandfather Daniele. The large number of labels has no negative effect on the average quality level, definitely high right across the product range. The Sauvignon Ronco delle Mele 2012 has led the race for many years now, and once again wins the Tre Bicchieri. An absolutely iconic Sauvignon Blanc, it embodies the hallmarks of the Collio terroir and represents both a benchmark and a goal for local producers of this variety.

○ Collio Sauvignon Ronco delle Mele '12	♀♀♀	6
○ Collio Friulano Ronco delle Cime '12	♀♀	4
○ Collio Malvasia Pètris '12	♀♀	4
○ Collio Pinot Bianco '12	♀♀	4
○ Collio Sauvignon Ronco del Cerò '12	♀♀	4
○ Collio Traminer Aromatico '12	♀♀	4
○ Collio Sauvignon Ronco delle Mele '11	♀♀♀	6
○ Collio Sauvignon Ronco delle Mele '10	♀♀♀	5
○ Collio Sauvignon Ronco delle Mele '09	♀♀♀	5
○ Collio Sauvignon Ronco delle Mele '08	♀♀♀	5
○ Collio Sauvignon Ronco delle Mele '07	♀♀♀	5
○ Collio Sauvignon Ronco delle Mele '05	♀♀♀	5
○ Collio Tocai Friulano Ronco delle Cime '06	♀♀♀	4
○ Collio Tocai Friulano Ronco delle Cime '02	♀♀♀	5

La Viarte

VIA NOVACUZZO, 51
33040 PREPOTTO [UD]
TEL. 0432759458
www.laviarte.it

★★Vie di Romans

LOC. VIE DI ROMANS, 1
34070 MARIANO DEL FRIULI [GO]
TEL. 048169600
www.viediromans.it

CELLAR SALES
PRE-BOOKED VISITS
ACCOMMODATION
ANNUAL PRODUCTION 100,000 bottles
HECTARES UNDER VINE 26.30

CELLAR SALES
PRE-BOOKED VISITS
ANNUAL PRODUCTION 280,000 bottles
HECTARES UNDER VINE 53.00

La Viarte was recently acquired by Alberto Piovan. But this change of hands has had no effect on the organization of the estate, and instead aims at realizing as yet untapped potential. The estate was founded in 1973 by Giuseppe and Carla Ceschin, in the lovely hills that run from Corno di Rosazzo to Prepotto, and called La Viarte, meaning springtime in the local dialect, beginning a journey that over 40 years has written many of the best pages in the story of regional wines. Since 2003, their son Giulio has been in charge with a motivated and highly professional staff that will continue to work with the new owner. The Friulano 2002 releases fragrant spring flowers and citrus, while the palate is so crisp and fluid as to actually seem thirst-quenching. The Pinot Bianco 2012 shows classy on both nose and palate, while the merlot and cabernet sauvignon Rosso Roi Riserva 2009 is rich, mouthfilling and vibrant.

Vie di Romans is a real jewel in the regional crown of winemaking estates. Founded in 1978 by Gianfranco Gallo, the headquarters are located in the impressive yet functional cellar in Mariano del Friuli. In the underground halls, countless masterfully managed barriques contain the wines, mostly whites, destined for release to market at least two years after harvest. The tale of the Gallo family in the world of vineyards and wine already covers a century of history, but the best chapters are clearly those now being written by Gianfranco. His complex, fragrant wines bring out all the special quality of the Isonzo DOC zone, protected by mountains and lapped by the sea. The quality of the wines here is so high that they take turns winning the Tre Bicchieri. This year, the Friulano Dolée 2011 turns in the definitive performance thanks to its simultaneous elegance and thrust, and the Sauvignon Vieris 2011 eclipses the multi-award-winning Sauvignon Pierre.

○ COF Bianco Incò '12	¶¶ 3
○ COF Friulano '12	¶¶ 3
○ COF Pinot Bianco '12	¶¶ 3
● COF Rosso Roi Ris. '09	¶¶ 5
○ COF Pinot Grigio '12	¶ 3
○ COF Ribolla Gialla '12	¶ 3
○ COF Sauvignon '12	¶ 3
○ COF Friulano '11	¶¶ 3
● COF Merlot '09	¶¶ 4
● COF Refosco P.R. '09	¶¶ 4
○ COF Sauvignon '11	¶¶ 3
● COF Schioppettino di Prepotto '09	¶¶ 4
● COF Tazzelenghe '08	¶¶ 5
○ Siùm '07	¶¶ 5

○ Friuli Isonzo Friulano Dolée '11	¶¶¶ 4*
○ Friuli Isonzo Bianco Flors di Uis '11	¶¶ 4
○ Friuli Isonzo Sauvignon Vieris '11	¶¶ 5
○ Dut'Un '10	¶¶ 6
○ Friuli Isonzo Chardonnay Ciampagnis Vieris '11	¶¶ 4
○ Friuli Isonzo Chardonnay Vie di Romans '11	¶¶ 5
○ Friuli Isonzo Malvasia Dis Cumieris '11	¶¶ 4
○ Friuli Isonzo Pinot Grigio Dessimis '11	¶¶ 5
○ Friuli Isonzo Sauvignon Pierre '11	¶¶ 5
○ Friuli Isonzo Bianco Flors di Uis '09	¶¶¶ 4*
○ Friuli Isonzo Rive Alte Sauvignon Pierre '07	¶¶¶ 4*
○ Friuli Isonzo Sauvignon Pierre '10	¶¶¶ 4*
○ Friuli Isonzo Sauvignon Pierre '08	¶¶¶ 4*

Vigna del Lauro

LOC. MONTONA, 19
34071 CORMÒNS [GO]
TEL. 0481629549
www.vignadellauro.it

CELLAR SALES
PRE-BOOKED VISITS
ANNUAL PRODUCTION 60,000 bottles
HECTARES UNDER VINE 10.00

In 1994 Fabio Coser, renowned winemaker and already owner of the Ronco dei Tassi estate, began a project driven by the need to differentiate production to satisfy the German market that wanted simple, easy-drinking wines that respected type, but were not too expensive. For this purpose, he found a vineyard surrounded by old bay trees that gave the estate its name. Other plots were added, some owned and some rented, which now total around ten hectares in the area near Cormòns, divided between the Collio and Isonzo DOC zones. Friulano, Sauvignon and Pinot Grigio del Collio, all of the 2012 vintage, are ultra-fragrant and of exemplary typicity. They each continuously pour out their individual varietal aromas and are easy-drinking to a fare-thee-well. Likewise outstanding is the Merlot 2011, from the Friuli Isonzo DOC.

○ Collio Friulano '12	♥♥ 3*	
○ Collio Pinot Grigio '12	♥♥ 3	
○ Collio Sauvignon '12	♥♥ 3	
● Friuli Isonzo Merlot '11	♥♥ 2*	
○ Collio Ribolla Gialla '12	♥ 3	
○ Friuli Isonzo Chardonnay '12	♥ 2	
○ Friuli Isonzo Traminer Aromatico '12	♥ 2	
● Collio Sauvignon '99	♥♥♥ 2*	
○ Collio Friulano '11	♥♥ 2*	
○ Collio Pinot Grigio '11	♥♥ 3*	
○ Collio Sauvignon '11	♥♥ 3*	
○ Friuli Isonzo Traminer Aromatico '11	♥♥ 2*	

Vigna Petrussa

VIA ÀLBANA, 47
33040 PREPOTTO [UD]
TEL. 0432713021
www.vignapetrussa.it

CELLAR SALES
PRE-BOOKED VISITS
ANNUAL PRODUCTION 28,000 bottles
HECTARES UNDER VINE 6.50

This estate was founded back in 1890 and flourished in the early part of the 20th century, but later fell into a state of abandonment, only to then find new life in 1995 when Hilde Petrussa decided to return home to Albana, near Prepotto, and take charge of the family estate. In converting the vine stock, she aimed for native varieties, giving priority to ribolla nera, the variety used to make Schioppettino, a wine forever tied to the Prepotto valley, where the Judrio river follows the border between Collio and Colli Orientali del Friuli. With a large group of other local winemakers, she fought for years till finally obtaining a DOC designation for the Schioppettino di Prepotto subzone. This year, the base white wines turned in the best performances. The Friulano 2012 impresses with graceful fruit then crowns a full-flavoured palate with that classic bitter-almond finish. The Sauvignon 2012 offers up wonderful summer flowers, tropical fruit and medicinal herbs.

● COF Cabernet Franc '10	♥♥ 3	
○ COF Friulano '12	♥♥ 3	
○ COF Sauvignon '12	♥♥ 3	
● COF Refosco P. R. '11	♥ 4	
○ COF Bianco Richenza '10	♥♥ 4	
○ COF Friulano '11	♥♥ 3	
● COF Refosco P. R. '10	♥♥ 4	
○ COF Sauvignon '11	♥♥ 3	
● COF Schioppettino di Prepotto '09	♥♥ 4	

Vigna Traverso

VIA RONCHI, 73
33040 PREPOTTO [UD]
TEL. 0422804807
www.vignatraverso.it

CELLAR SALES
PRE-BOOKED VISITS
RESTAURANT SERVICE
ANNUAL PRODUCTION 80,000 bottles
HECTARES UNDER VINE 22.00

Vigna Traverso, once known as Ronco di Castagneto, was purchased in 1998 by the Molon Traverso family, owner of the famous Veneto-based wine operation, and re-baptised. Directing it now is the young Stefano, a degreed oenologist with long experience in the industry to his credit. He immediately set out to recover older vineyards, in close collaboration with viticultural expert Stefano Zaninotti. For some years now he has enjoyed the advantage of the most up-to-date technology in the cellar in Prepotto, where he has re-introduced the use of concrete vats, a classic example of innovation and respect for tradition. The Friulano 2012 stands out from a very extensive portfolio thanks to its utterly classic aromas of hay and wild flowers and to a palate that is both supple and attractively rustic. The Pinot Grigio 2012 excels for its lovely bouquet and absolutely delicious flavours. The Sottocastello blends are excellent.

○ COF Bianco Sottocastello '10	▼▼	4
● COF Cabernet Franc '10	▼▼	3
○ COF Friulano '12	▼▼	3
● COF Merlot '10	▼▼	3
○ COF Pinot Grigio '12	▼▼	3
● COF Rosso Sottocastello '09	▼▼	5
● COF Schioppettino '10	▼▼	3
● COF Refosco P. R. '10	▼	3
○ COF Ribolla Gialla '12	▼	3
● COF Rosso Troj '10	▼	3
● COF Cabernet Franc '09	♈♈	3*
○ COF Friulano '11	♈♈	3
● COF Merlot '09	♈♈	3
● COF Rosso Sottocastello '08	♈♈	5
○ COF Sauvignon '11	♈♈	3

★Le Vigne di Zamò

LOC. ROSAZZO
VIA ABATE CORRADO, 4
33044 MANZANO [UD]
TEL. 0432759693
www.levignedizamo.com

CELLAR SALES
PRE-BOOKED VISITS
ANNUAL PRODUCTION 280,000 bottles
HECTARES UNDER VINE 67.00

Tullio Zamò, legendary pioneer in quality Friuli wines, founded Vigne dal Leon in 1978 on the slopes of Rocca Bernarda, and several years later created the Abbazia di Rosazzo label. He started Le Vigne di Zamò with his sons, Pierluigi and Silvano in 1996 after purchasing another 15 hectares under vine in the area of Rosazzo, directly in front of the Abbey. Now the paths of the Zamò family have merged with those of the Farinetti group, creator of Eataly, which purchased half of the operation. This joining of forces has enabled them to consolidate their properties and guarantee major international visibility for wines that continue to benefit from the consultancy of Franco Bernabei. That older vines produce the best grapes is neither a mystery nor all that unusual, and so it is little surprise that the Tre Bicchieri go to the Merlot Vigne Cinquant'Anni 2009. It vaunts multi-layered aromas of red rose petals, morello cherry, chocolate, roast espresso bean and clove, followed by a well-rounded, impressive palate.

● COF Merlot V. Cinquant'Anni '09	▼▼▼	5
○ COF Friulano V. Cinquant'Anni '11	▼▼	5
○ COF Dolce Vola... Vola...	▼▼	5
○ COF Friulano '12	▼▼	3
○ COF Pinot Bianco Tullio Zamò '09	▼▼	5
○ COF Rosazzo Bianco Ronco delle Acacie '10	▼▼	5
○ COF Sauvignon '12	▼▼	3
○ COF Malvasia '11	▼	4
○ COF Friulano V. Cinquant'Anni '09	♈♈♈	5
○ COF Friulano V. Cinquant'Anni '08	♈♈♈	5
● COF Merlot V. Cinquant'Anni '06	♈♈♈	5
○ COF Rosazzo Bianco Ronco delle Acacie '01	♈♈♈	4
● COF Rosazzo Pignolo '01	♈♈♈	6
○ COF Tocai Friulano V. Cinquant'Anni '06	♈♈♈	5

Villa de Puppi

VIA ROMA, 5
33040 MOIMACCO [UD]
TEL. 0432722461
www.depuppi.it

★★Villa Russiz

VIA RUSSIZ, 6
34070 CAPRIVA DEL FRIULI [GO]
TEL. 048180047
www.villarussiz.it

CELLAR SALES
PRE-BOOKED VISITS
ANNUAL PRODUCTION 50,000 bottles
HECTARES UNDER VINE 25.00

CELLAR SALES
PRE-BOOKED VISITS
ANNUAL PRODUCTION 220,000 bottles
HECTARES UNDER VINE 40.00

Founded in 1991, Luigi de Puppi's estate is managed by his children, Caterina and Valfredo, and headquartered in the country villa at Moimacco, surrounded by estate vineyards. Another 10 hectares stretch across the beautiful hills of Rosazzo in Colli Orientali del Friuli. Originally from Tuscany, the De Puppi family descended from the famous Conti Guidi in Casentino, landowners and mercenary soldiers who settled in Cividale del Friuli in the 13th century. This family has given Friuli a number of major figures in politics, law and the church hierarchy. Caterina never shirks work in the vineyards, but entrusts the winemaking to the skills of Marco Pecchiari. Villa de Puppi and Rosa Bosco are almost the same winery, with a base line of wines that are simple but show fine typicity and linearity. The Sauvignon Rosa Bosco 2010 and Chardonnay Cate 2008, however, are opulent bottlings, with generous vanilla and hazelnut, and beguiling palates.

For many years synonymous with great wines, this estate is known worldwide for consistent top level production, rewarding the efforts of the Villa Russiz Foundation, now presided over by Silvano Stefanutti, established with an endowment from the French Count Teodoro de La Tour. After settling in the hills of Capriva in 1867 with his Austrian wife, Elvine Ritter, he imported new varieties and winemaking techniques from France that were unknown locally at the time, thereby contributing significantly to recognition of the winemaking potential of Collio. Having no heirs, the couple left their fortune to needy children and some of the best wines now carry the names of the benefactor couple. We couldn't taste the Riservas since they are still ageing, but the line nevertheless won high marks. The whites are marked by generous, varietal bouquets and crispness on the palate, while the reds are well-structured, smooth, and utterly delicious.

○ Blanc de Blancs	
Rosa Bosco Brut M. Cl. '08	♥♥ 4
○ Chardonnay Cate '08	♥♥ 5
● Refosco P.R. Cate '09	♥♥ 4
○ Sauvignon Rosa Bosco '10	♥♥ 4
● Cabernet '10	♥ 2
● Merlot '10	♥ 2
● Refosco P. R. '10	♥ 3
○ Ribolla Gialla Extra Dry	♥ 3
● Cabernet '09	♀♀ 2
● Merlot '09	♀♀ 2
○ Pinot Grigio '11	♀♀ 3
○ Sauvignon '11	♀♀ 3
○ Taj Blanc '11	♀♀ 2
○ Taj Blanc '10	♀♀ 2*

● Collio Cabernet Sauvignon '11	♥♥ 4
○ Collio Friulano '12	♥♥ 4
○ Collio Malvasia '12	♥♥ 4
● Collio Merlot '11	♥♥ 4
○ Collio Pinot Bianco '12	♥♥ 4
○ Colllo Pinot Grigio '12	♥♥ 4
○ Collio Sauvignon '12	♥♥ 4
○ Collio Sauvignon de La Tour '12	♥♥ 5
○ Collio Chardonnay	
Gräfin de La Tour '02	♀♀♀ 5
● Collio Merlot Graf de La Tour '02	♀♀♀ 6
○ Collio Pinot Bianco '07	♀♀♀ 3
○ Collio Sauvignon de La Tour '05	♀♀♀ 5
○ Collio Sauvignon de La Tour '02	♀♀♀ 5
○ Collio Tocai Friulano '04	♀♀♀ 3

Tenuta Villanova

LOC. VILLANOVA
VIA CONTESSA BERETTA, 29
34072 FARRA D'ISONZO [GO]
TEL. 0481889311
www.tenutavillanova.com

CELLAR SALES
PRE-BOOKED VISITS
ANNUAL PRODUCTION 600,000 bottles
HECTARES UNDER VINE 105.00

Giuseppina Grossi Bennati still tenaciously manages the estate purchased in 1932 by her husband and farsighted entrepreneur, Arnaldo. Founded in 1499, Tenuta Villanova holds more than five centuries of history behind its walls. Meadowlands and thick woods on the property surround the 105 hectares under vine spread across the hills of Collio and along the less well-suited Isonzo plain. Giuseppina's nephew, Alberto Grossi, acts as general manager and relies on a fully-trained, energetic staff of technicians and qualified collaborators. This is the only estate in Friuli equipped with an on-site distillery where all the grape skins are collected to make excellent grappa. With their hillside terroirs, the Collio wines turned in the best performances. The Pinot Grigio Ronco Cucco 2012 shows quite youthful in its crisp fruit and easy drinkability, while the opulent Chardonnay Ronco Cucco 2011 fills the mouth with impressions of mixed nuts and cakes.

○ Collio Chardonnay Ronco Cucco '11	♟♟ 4
○ Collio Friulano Ronco Cucco '11	♟♟ 4
○ Collio Pinot Grigio Ronco Cucco '12	♟♟ 3
○ Friuli Isonzo Chardonnay '12	♟ 2
○ Friuli Isonzo Malvasia '12	♟ 2
● Friuli Isonzo Merlot '10	♟ 2
○ Friuli Isonzo Pinot Grigio '12	♟ 2
● Friuli Isonzo Refosco P. R. '10	♟ 2
○ Friuli Isonzo Sauvignon '12	♟ 2
○ Friuli Isonzo Traminer Aromatico Villanova '12	♟ 2
○ Collio Chardonnay Monte Cucco '97	♟♟♟ 3*
● Fraja '07	♟♟ 5
○ Friuli Isonzo Malvasia Saccoline '11	♟♟ 2*
○ Friuli Isonzo Pinot Grigio Mansi di Villanova '11	♟♟ 2*

Andrea Visintini

VIA GRAMOGLIANO, 27
33040 CORNO DI ROSAZZO [UD]
TEL. 0432755813
www.vinivisintini.com

CELLAR SALES
PRE-BOOKED VISITS
ANNUAL PRODUCTION 150,000 bottles
HECTARES UNDER VINE 28.00
VITICULTURE METHOD Certified Biodynamic

The Visintini estate is headquartered in a rustic farmhouse annexed to an impressive 16th-century watchtower, all that remains of the ancient feudal castle of Gramogliano that stretched for hundreds of metres all around, with its towers and keep. Expert restoration, overseen by the Arts Ministry, and remodelling of the underground areas of the cellar, now allow Oliviero, Cinzia and Palmira to operate in a prestigious yet functional estate headquarters. Old vineyards and young energy are the ingredients in this winning cocktail. Oliviero practises respectful viticulture, limiting treatments to only what is strictly necessary, and reducing the amounts of fertilizers and thus nitrates in the soil. This year, all the wines, and particularly the while base bottlings, scored very high, testifying to the high quality of the entire line. Fine tropical fruit marks the Sauvignon 2012, and the other wines stand out for their complexity and fragrances on both nose and palate.

○ COF Bianco '12	♟♟ 2*
○ COF Friulano '12	♟♟ 2*
○ COF Pinot Bianco '12	♟♟ 2*
○ COF Pinot Grigio '12	♟♟ 2*
○ COF Ribolla Gialla '12	♟♟ 2*
○ COF Sauvignon '12	♟♟ 2*
● COF Merlot '11	♟ 2
● COF Refosco P. R. '11	♟ 2
○ COF Bianco '11	♟♟ 2*
○ COF Friulano '11	♟♟ 2*
○ COF Pinot Grigio '11	♟♟ 2
○ COF Sauvignon '11	♟♟ 2*

Vistorta

VIA VISTORTA, 82
33077 SACILE [PN]
TEL. 0434782490
www.vistorta.it

CELLAR SALES
PRE-BOOKED VISITS
ANNUAL PRODUCTION 250,000 bottles
HECTARES UNDER VINE 36.00
VITICULTURE METHOD Certified Organic

Back in 1800, Guido Brandolini, with astonishing foresight, transformed the small hamlet of Vistorta, surrounded by an agricultural holding owned by his family in the heart of Friuli Occidentale, into a modern, efficient winemaking estate. Since 1980 this has been managed by Brandino Brandolini d'Adda who, after his first winemaking experience at the other family estate of Chateau Greysac in Bordeaux, remodelled Vistorta on the basis of the French model, planting new varieties of vines and integrating them into the existing stock, while still focusing attention on production of one single great red wine. Merlot was chosen since it gave and continues to give the greatest satisfaction. The Merlot Vistorta 2010 offers beguiling aromas of smooth spice, cocoa powder, liqueur plums and pipe tobacco, then a youthful energy on a palate whose rich tannic mass is a guarantee for future growth. The Sauvignon 2012 evidences a slight toastiness on the nose, and a solid, driving progression.

● Friuli Grave Merlot Vistorta '10	♟♟ 4
○ Friuli Grave Sauvignon '12	♟♟ 2*
○ Friuli Grave Chardonnay '12	♟ 2
○ Friuli Grave Friulano '12	♟ 2
○ Friuli Grave Pinot Grigio '12	♟ 2
○ Friuli Grave Traminer Aromatico '12	♟ 2
● Friuli Grave Merlot Vistorta '07	♟♟♟ 4
● Friuli Grave Merlot Vistorta '06	♟♟♟ 4
● Friuli Grave Merlot Vistorta '05	♟♟♟ 4
○ Friuli Grave Chardonnay '09	♟♟ 2*
○ Friuli Grave Friulano '08	♟♟ 2*
● Friuli Grave Merlot Vistorta '08	♟♟ 4
○ Friuli Grave Sauvignon '08	♟♟ 2*
○ Friuli Grave Sauvignon '07	♟♟ 2*

★Volpe Pasini

FRAZ. TOGLIANO
VIA CIVIDALE, 16
33040 TORREANO [UD]
TEL. 0432715151
www.volpepasini.net

CELLAR SALES
PRE-BOOKED VISITS
ACCOMMODATION
ANNUAL PRODUCTION 400,000 bottles
HECTARES UNDER VINE 52.00

Volpe Pasini is a major historic estate in Friuli Venezia Giulia, and currently managed with tireless effort by Emilio Rotolo and his son, Francesco. The excellent quality immediately achieved and maintained over time with enviable consistency is also due to consultancy from Lorenzo Landi, internationally famous agronomist and oenologist. The model cellar, vineyards with excellent exposure, and Villa Rosa, a lovely 17th-century villa splendidly restored by Emilio and dedicated to his wife, Rosa Tommaselli, are all the pride of this estate. In this excellent range of wines, the elegance and personality of the whites is outstanding, while the reds show good structure and a nice sense of place. The Sauvignon and Pinot Bianco of the Zuc di Volpe line are this winery's iconic bottlings; every year they compete for top billing, but this year, as in 2010, they both brought home the Tre Bicchieri. The Sauvignon is fragrant and minty, the Pinot Bianco tropical and creamy.

○ COF Pinot Bianco Zuc di Volpe '12	♟♟♟ 4*
○ COF Sauvignon Zuc di Volpe '12	♟♟♟ 4*
● COF Merlot Togliano Volpe Pasini '10	♟♟ 2*
○ COF Sauvignon Volpe Pasini '12	♟♟ 2*
○ Crypto Zuc di Volpe Cuvée Brut	♟♟ 4
● COF Cabernet Volpe Pasini '10	♟♟ 2*
○ COF Friulano Volpe Pasini '12	♟♟ 2*
○ COF Pinot Grigio Grivò Volpe Pasini '12	♟♟ 2*
○ COF Pinot Grigio Zuc di Volpe '12	♟♟ 3
○ COF Pinot Bianco Zuc di Volpe '10	♟♟♟ 4
○ COF Pinot Bianco Zuc di Volpe '08	♟♟♟ 4
○ COF Pinot Bianco Zuc di Volpe '07	♟♟♟ 3
○ COF Sauvignon Zuc di Volpe '11	♟♟♟ 4*
○ COF Sauvignon Zuc di Volpe '10	♟♟♟ 3*
○ COF Sauvignon Zuc di Volpe '09	♟♟♟ 3*
○ COF Tocai Friulano Zuc di Volpe '06	♟♟♟ 3

Francesco Vosca

FRAZ. BRAZZANO
VIA SOTTOMONTE, 19
34070 CORMÒNS [GO]
TEL. 048162135
www.voscavini.it

CELLAR SALES
PRE-BOOKED VISITS
ANNUAL PRODUCTION 50,000 bottles
HECTARES UNDER VINE 10.00

Francesco Vosca's small estate boasts proud farming roots and is located in Brazzano, a village near Cormòns, in the middle of the Collio DOC zone. A place now associated with great wines, flourishing nature and widespread well being, but where there once was much misery, even during the 1960s. Many were forced to emigrate, and as a child Francesco went into the fields to till the soil. Even today the location of the vineyards, scattered on the hills of Collio as well as the Isonzo plain, requires constant manual intervention. His wife Anita makes valuable contributions in the vineyard while his son, Gabriele, helps out in cellar operations. This year saw the Friulano 2012 compete in the final round, thanks to a splendid nose and drink-me-now palate. Redolent of acacia blossom and elderflower, it also offers clean notes of medlar and banana with hints of summer hay. A supple attack leads to an aroma-laden, impressive expansion in the mouth.

○ Collio Friulano '12	🍷🍷 3*
○ Collio Malvasia '12	🍷🍷 3
○ Friuli Isonzo Pinot Grigio '12	🍷🍷 3
○ Collio Ribolla Gialla '12	🍷 3
○ Friuli Isonzo Chardonnay '12	🍷 3
○ Friuli Isonzo Sauvignon '12	🍷 3
○ Collio Friulano '11	ΥΥ 3
○ Collio Malvasia '11	ΥΥ 3*
○ Collio Malvasia '10	ΥΥ 2
○ Collio Malvasia '09	ΥΥ 2*
○ Collio Pinot Grigio '11	ΥΥ 3
○ Friuli Isonzo Chardonnay '11	ΥΥ 3

Zidarich

LOC. PREPOTTO, 23
34011 DUINO AURISINA [TS]
TEL. 040201223
www.zidarich.it

CELLAR SALES
PRE-BOOKED VISITS
ANNUAL PRODUCTION 18,000 bottles
HECTARES UNDER VINE 8.00

With little land but an innovative spirit and enviable determination, Beniamino Zidarich established his estate in 1988 in the Trieste section of the Karst plateau, at Prepotto in the township of Duino Aurisina. Set among the vines and typical Karst vegetation, this estate enjoys remarkable exposure over the Gulf of Trieste. The cellar was carved entirely from the rock, as only people from here know how. Rocks from this excavation were later reused to build tunnels that carefully protect the wooden casks. Though particular climate conditions limit the choice of grape varieties, the vitovska and terrano varieties are always here, guaranteeing harvests even in the most difficult vintage years. The Malvasia 2011 is stunning, while the Prulke 2011 grabs immediate attention for its uncommon bouquet but particularly for the energy it unleashes in the mouth. A blend of vitovska, malvasia istriana and sauvignon, it releases impressions of aloe, raspberry, dried flowers, mixed nuts and yellow peach preserves.

○ Malvasia '11	🍷🍷 5
○ Prulke '11	🍷🍷 5
● Carso Terrano '11	🍷🍷 5
● Ruje '07	🍷🍷 5
○ Vitovska '11	🍷🍷 5
○ Carso Malvasia '09	ΥΥΥ 5
○ Carso Malvasia '06	ΥΥΥ 5
○ Prulke '10	ΥΥΥ 5
○ Prulke '08	ΥΥΥ 5
○ Carso Malvasia '10	ΥΥ 5
○ Carso Vitovska '10	ΥΥ 5
○ Carso Vitovska Collection '06	ΥΥ 5
○ Prulke '09	ΥΥ 5
○ Prulke '06	ΥΥ 5
● Ruje '04	ΥΥ 5
● Ruje '03	ΥΥ 5

Zorzettig

FRAZ. SPESSA
S.DA SANT'ANNA, 37
33043 CIVIDALE DEL FRIULI [UD]
TEL. 0432716156
www.zorzettigvini.it

CELLAR SALES
PRE-BOOKED VISITS
ACCOMMODATION AND RESTAURANT SERVICE
ANNUAL PRODUCTION 800,000 bottles
HECTARES UNDER VINE 110.00

Zorzettig is a well-known name on the regional winemaking scene, tied to a family that has been making wine for many generations at Spessa di Cividale, in the heart of Colli Orientali del Friuli. Different estates derive from the same branch, and are generally renamed so as not to be confused. But the cellar founded in 1986 by Cavalier Giuseppe Zorzettig has managed to keep its original identify. The search for new inspiration and a desire to stand out have led Annalisa, who now manages the estate alongside her brother Alessandro, to choose the best grapes and create a new production line called Myò. This ambitious project is entrusted to the oenological skills of Fabio Coser. The wines of the Myò line were top-notch, but the base line also did very well indeed. Well-ripened apple and pear characterize the Friulano Myò 2012, followed by a velvety, smooth palate, while the elegant, flavour-rich Sauvignon Myò 2012 shows more verve and energy.

○ COF Chardonnay '11	♥♥	3
○ COF Friulano '12	♥♥	3
○ COF Friulano Myò '12	♥♥	4
○ COF Malvasia Myò '12	♥♥	4
○ COF Pinot Bianco Myò '12	♥♥	4
○ COF Sauvignon Myò '12	♥♥	4
○ COF Ribolla Gialla '12	♥	4
○ COF Ribolla Gialla Myò '12	♥	4
○ Optimum Brut	♥	3
○ COF Friulano Myò '11	♀♀	4
○ COF Malvasia Myò '11	♀♀	4
● COF Pignolo Myò '09	♀♀	6
○ COF Pinot Bianco Myò '11	♀♀	4

Zuani

LOC. GIASBANA, 12
34070 SAN FLORIANO DEL COLLIO [GO]
TEL. 0481391432
www.zuanivini.it

CELLAR SALES
PRE-BOOKED VISITS
ACCOMMODATION
ANNUAL PRODUCTION 70,000 bottles
HECTARES UNDER VINE 12.00

This jewel of an estate was established by Patrizia Felluga in the area of Giasbana on the lovely slopes of San Floriano del Collio. Zuani is the expression of a philosophy accumulated over years of experience in the vineyard and cellar, supported by the knowledge acquired from competent entrepreneurial abilities. Entering the market with a single wine is definitely an act of courage, a quality never lacking in Patrizia. In 2001, with her two children, Antonio and Caterina, she started a project that envisaged one wine, the Collio, as the authentic expression of a terroir. The wine is made in two versions, one in stainless steel and the other in oak. In the intriguing rivalry between the two wines that compete with each other for top honours, the prize last year went to the opulent, more complex cask-conditioned version; this year, the steel-aged version comes out on top, offering crisp mint and tropical nuances and a panoply of flavours on the palate.

○ Collio Bianco Zuani Vigne '12	♥♥	3*
○ Collio Bianco Zuani Ris. '10	♥♥	5
○ Collio Bianco Zuani Vigne '10	♀♀♀	3
○ Collio Bianco Zuani Vigne '07	♀♀♀	3
○ Collio Bianco Zuani '08	♀♀	5
○ Collio Bianco Zuani Ris. '09	♀♀	5
○ Collio Bianco Zuani Vigne '11	♀♀	3
○ Collio Bianco Zuani Vigne '09	♀♀	3
○ Collio Bianco Zuani Vigne '08	♀♀	3*

Giuseppe e Luigi Anselmi

VIA BASSI, 16
33050 POCENIA [UD]
TEL. 0432779157
www.vinianselmi.it

CELLAR SALES
PRE-BOOKED VISITS
ANNUAL PRODUCTION 1,000,000 bottles
HECTARES UNDER VINE 160.00

● Collio Cabernet Sauvignon La Reguta '11	♟♟	3
○ Collio Sauvignon La Reguta '12	♟♟	3
○ Collio Friulano La Reguta '12	♟	3
○ Collio Pinot Grigio La Reguta '12	♟	3

Anzelin

VIA PLESSIVA, 4
34071 CORMÒNS [GO]
TEL. 0481639821
www.anzelin.it

CELLAR SALES
PRE-BOOKED VISITS
ANNUAL PRODUCTION 20,000 bottles
HECTARES UNDER VINE 9.00

○ Collio Friulano '12	♟♟	3
○ Collio Pinot Bianco '12	♟♟	3
○ Collio Pinot Grigio '12	♟♟	3
○ Collio Sauvignon '12	♟♟	3

Maurizio Arzenton

FRAZ. SPESSA
VIA CORMONS, 221
33043 CIVIDALE DEL FRIULI [UD]
TEL. 0432716139
www.arzentonvini.it

CELLAR SALES
PRE-BOOKED VISITS
ANNUAL PRODUCTION 40,000 bottles
HECTARES UNDER VINE 10.00

○ COF Pinot Grigio '12	♟♟	2*
○ COF Sauvignon '12	♟♟	2*
○ COF Chardonnay '12	♟	2
○ COF Pinot Bianco '12	♟	2

Bajta

VIA SALES, 108
34010 SGONICO [TS]
TEL. 0402296090
www.bajta.it

ANNUAL PRODUCTION 18,000 bottles
HECTARES UNDER VINE 4.00

○ Vitovska '12	♟♟	3
○ Malvasia '12	♟	3

La Bellanotte

S.DA DELLA BELLANOTTE, 3
34072 FARRA D'ISONZO [GO]
TEL. 0481888020
www.labellanotte.it

CELLAR SALES
PRE-BOOKED VISITS
ANNUAL PRODUCTION 100,000 bottles
HECTARES UNDER VINE 12.00

● Friuli Isonzo Merlot Roja de Isonzo '10	♟♟	4
○ Armonico '12	♟	2
○ Collio Friulano '12	♟	3
○ Friuli Isonzo Malvasia Istriana '12	♟	3

Tenuta Beltrame

FRAZ. PRIVANO
LOC. ANTONINI, 4
33050 BAGNARIA ARSA [UD]
TEL. 0432923670
www.tenutabeltrame.it

CELLAR SALES
PRE-BOOKED VISITS
ANNUAL PRODUCTION 80,000 bottles
HECTARES UNDER VINE 25.00

● Friuli Aquileia Merlot Ris. '09	♟♟	3*
● Cabernet Sauvignon '09	♟	3
● Friuli Aquileia Refosco P. R. '11	♟	2
○ Pinot Grigio '12	♟	2

Anna Berra

VIA RAMANDOLO, 29
33045 NIMIS [UD]
TEL. 0432790296
www.annaberra.it

CELLAR SALES
PRE-BOOKED VISITS
ANNUAL PRODUCTION 23,000 bottles
HECTARES UNDER VINE 6.00

○ Ramandolo Sel. Anna Berra '08	♥♥ 4
● COF Merlot Sel. Anna Berra Ris. '07	♥ 5
○ COF Ribolla Gialla La Bernadia '12	♥ 2

Blason

VIA ROMA, 32
34072 GRADISCA D'ISONZO [GO]
TEL. 048192414
www.blasonwines.com

CELLAR SALES
PRE-BOOKED VISITS
ANNUAL PRODUCTION 60,000 bottles
HECTARES UNDER VINE 16.00

○ Friuli Isonzo Bruma Bianco '10	♥♥ 4
○ Friuli Isonzo Pinot Grigio '12	♥♥ 2*
○ Malvasia '12	♥♥ 3*
● Friuli Isonzo Bruma Rosso '09	♥ 4

Blazic

LOC. ZEGLA, 16
34071 CORMÒNS [GO]
TEL. 048161720
www.blazic.it

CELLAR SALES
PRE-BOOKED VISITS
ANNUAL PRODUCTION 15,000 bottles
HECTARES UNDER VINE 6.50

○ Collio Friulano '12	♥♥ 3*
○ Collio Bianco '12	♥♥ 3
○ Collio Malvasia '12	♥♥ 3
○ Collio Ribolla Gialla '12	♥♥ 3

Borgo Magredo

LOC. TAURIANO
VIA BASALDELLA, 5
33090 SPILIMBERGO [PN]
TEL. 0422864511
www.borgomagredo.it

CELLAR SALES
PRE-BOOKED VISITS
ANNUAL PRODUCTION 710,000 bottles
HECTARES UNDER VINE 87.00

○ Friuli Grave Friulano '12	♥ 2
○ Friuli Grave Pinot Grigio '12	♥ 2
● Friuli Grave Refosco P. R. '12	♥ 2
○ Friuli Grave Sauvignon '12	♥ 2

La Buse dal Lôf

VIA RONCHI, 90
33040 PREPOTTO [UD]
TEL. 0432701523
www.labusedallof.com

CELLAR SALES
PRE-BOOKED VISITS
ANNUAL PRODUCTION 100,000 bottles
HECTARES UNDER VINE 25.00

○ COF Chardonnay '12	♥♥ 3
○ COF Friulano '12	♥♥ 3
○ COF Pinot Bianco In Bocca al Lupo '12	♥♥ 3
● COF Schioppettino di Prepotto '09	♥♥ 4

Ca' Ronesca

LOC. LONZANO, 27
34070 DOLEGNA DEL COLLIO [GO]
TEL. 048160034
www.caronesca.it

CELLAR SALES
PRE-BOOKED VISITS
ANNUAL PRODUCTION 200,000 bottles
HECTARES UNDER VINE 52.00

○ Collio Friulano '12	♥♥ 3
○ Collio Pinot Grigio '12	♥♥ 3
○ Collio Sauvignon '12	♥♥ 3
○ Collio Sauvignon Podere di Ipplis '11	♥♥ 3

Fernanda Cappello

S.DA DI SEQUALS, 15
33090 SEQUALS [PN]
TEL. 042793291
www.fernandacappello.it

CELLAR SALES
PRE-BOOKED VISITS
ANNUAL PRODUCTION 60,000 bottles
HECTARES UNDER VINE 130.00

○ Friuli Grave Chardonnay '12	♥♥ 2*
● Friuli Grave Merlot '11	♥♥ 2*
○ Friuli Grave Sauvignon '12	♥♥ 2*
○ Friuli Grave Pinot Grigio '12	♥ 2

Lino Casella

VIA ALBANA, 55
33040 PREPOTTO [UD]
TEL. 0432713429
lino.casella@libero.it

ANNUAL PRODUCTION 16,000 bottles
HECTARES UNDER VINE 3.50

○ COF Friulano '11	♥♥ 3
● COF Tazzelenghe '10	♥♥ 3*
● Franconia '10	♥♥ 3*
● COF Schioppettino di Prepotto '10	♥ 5

Cencig - Borgo dei Sapori

S.DA DI PLANEZ, 60
33043 CIVIDALE DEL FRIULI [UD]
TEL. 0432732477
www.borgodeisapori.net

PRE-BOOKED VISITS
ANNUAL PRODUCTION 27,000 bottles
HECTARES UNDER VINE 10.50

○ COF Sauvignon '12	♥♥ 2*
○ COF Friulano '12	♥ 2

Colli di Poianis

VIA POIANIS, 34A
33040 PREPOTTO [UD]
TEL. 0432713185
www.collidipoianis.com

ACCOMMODATION
ANNUAL PRODUCTION 40,000 bottles
HECTARES UNDER VINE 11.00

○ COF Chardonnay '12	♥♥ 3
● COF Rosso Ronco della Poiana '10	♥♥ 4
○ COF Sauvignon '12	♥ 3
● COF Schioppettino di Prepotto '10	♥ 5

Gianpaolo Colutta

VIA ORSARIA, 32A
33044 MANZANO [UD]
TEL. 0432510654
www.coluttagianpaolo.it

CELLAR SALES
PRE-BOOKED VISITS
ANNUAL PRODUCTION 150,000 bottles
HECTARES UNDER VINE 30.00

○ COF Bianco Prarion '12	♥♥ 4
● COF Merlot '09	♥♥ 3
● COF Tazzelenghe '07	♥♥ 6
○ COF Friulano '12	♥ 3

Conti Formentini

VIA OSLAVIA, 5
34070 SAN FLORIANO DEL COLLIO [GO]
TEL. 0481884131
www.contiformentini.it

CELLAR SALES
PRE-BOOKED VISITS
ANNUAL PRODUCTION 400,000 bottles
HECTARES UNDER VINE 85.00

○ Collio Pinot Grigio '12	♥♥ 5
○ Collio Ribolla Gialla Raiade '12	♥♥ 5
○ Collio Chardonnay '12	♥ 5
○ Collio Friulano Furlanà '12	♥ 5

Le Due Torri

LOC. VICINALE DEL JUDRIO
VIA SAN MARTINO, 19
33040 CORNO DI ROSAZZO [UD]
TEL. 0432759150
www.le2torri.com

CELLAR SALES
PRE-BOOKED VISITS
ANNUAL PRODUCTION 36,000 bottles
HECTARES UNDER VINE 7.60

○ Malvasia '12	♥♥ 2*
○ Friuli Grave Friulano '12	♥ 2
○ Friuli Grave Sauvignon '12	♥ 2
○ Ribolla Gialla '12	♥ 2

Le Favole

LOC. TERRA ROSSA
VIA DIETRO CASTELLO, 7
33077 CANEVA [PN]
TEL. 0434735604
www.lefavole.com

CELLAR SALES
PRE-BOOKED VISITS
ACCOMMODATION
ANNUAL PRODUCTION 55,000 bottles
HECTARES UNDER VINE 18.00 .

○ Friuli Annia Pinot Grigio '12	♥♥ 2*
● Friuli Annia Cabernet Franc '11	♥ 2
○ Friuli Annia Friulano '12	♥ 2
○ Friuli Annia Traminer Aromatico '12	♥ 2

Forchir

FRAZ. FELETTIS
VIA CODROIPO, 18
33050 BICINICCO [UD]
TEL. 042796037
www.forchir.it

CELLAR SALES
PRE-BOOKED VISITS
ANNUAL PRODUCTION 1,200,000 bottles
HECTARES UNDER VINE 226.00
VITICULTURE METHOD Certified Organic

● Refoscone '09	♥♥ 3
○ Friuli Grave Pinot Grigio Lamis '12	♥ 2
● Friuli Grave Refosco P. R. Manin '11	♥ 2
○ Friuli Grave Traminer Aromatico Glere '12	♥ 2

Fantin Nodar

LOC. ORSARIA
VIA CASALI OTTELIO, 4
33040 PREMARIACCO [UD]
TEL. 043428735
www.fantinnodar.it

CELLAR SALES
PRE-BOOKED VISITS
ANNUAL PRODUCTION 40,000 bottles
HECTARES UNDER VINE 22.00

○ COF Bianco Carato '11	♥♥ 3
○ COF Friulano '11	♥♥ 2*
○ COF Verduzzo Friulano '11	♥♥ 3
● COF Merlot '11	♥ 2

I Feudi di Romans

LOC. PIERIS
VIA CÀ DEL BOSCO, 16
34075 SAN CANZIAN D'ISONZO [GO]
TEL. 048176445
www.ifeudi.it

CELLAR SALES
PRE-BOOKED VISITS
ANNUAL PRODUCTION 500,000 bottles
HECTARES UNDER VINE 120.00

○ Malvasia Istriana '12	♥♥ 2*
● Friuli Isonzo Cabernet Franc '11	♥ 2
○ Friuli Isonzo Pinot Bianco '12	♥ 2
○ Friuli Isonzo Sauvignon '12	♥ 2

Marcello e Marino Humar

LOC. VALERISCE, 2
34070 SAN FLORIANO DEL COLLIO [GO]
TEL. 0481884094
www.humar.it

CELLAR SALES
PRE-BOOKED VISITS
ANNUAL PRODUCTION 100,000 bottles
HECTARES UNDER VINE 30.00

○ Collio Friulano '12	♥♥ 3
○ Collio Pinot Grigio '12	♥ 2
○ Collio Ribolla Gialla '12	♥ 2
○ Collio Sauvignon '12	♥ 2

Rado Kocjancic

FRAZ. DOLINA
VIA CROGOLE, 11
34018 SAN DORLIGO DELLA VALLE [TS]
TEL. 3483063298
www.radokocjancic.eu

CELLAR SALES
PRE-BOOKED VISITS
ANNUAL PRODUCTION 15,000 bottles
HECTARES UNDER VINE 5.00

○ Brejanka '09	🍷🍷 5
○ Carso Malvasia Dolina '11	🍷🍷 2*
● Carso Refosco P. R. '07	🍷🍷 5
● Carso Rosso '11	🍷🍷 3

Lupinc

FRAZ. PREPOTTO, 11B
34011 DUINO AURISINA [TS]
TEL. 040200848

CELLAR SALES
PRE-BOOKED VISITS
ANNUAL PRODUCTION 15,000 bottles
HECTARES UNDER VINE 3.00

○ Carso Malvasia '11	🍷🍷 3
○ Carso Vitovska '11	🍷🍷 3
○ Stara Brajda '11	🍷🍷 3*
○ Dulcis in Fundo '11	🍷 3

Obiz

B.GO GORTANI, 2
33052 CERVIGNANO DEL FRIULI [UD]
TEL. 043131900
www.obiz.it

CELLAR SALES
ANNUAL PRODUCTION 100,000 bottles
HECTARES UNDER VINE 25.00

● Friuli Aquileia Merlot Popone '11	🍷🍷 2*
○ Friuli Aquileia Friulano '12	🍷 2
● Friuli Aquileia Refosco P.R. Teodoro '11	🍷 2
○ Friuli Aquileia Traminer Aromatico '12	🍷 2

Norina Pez

VIA ZORUTTI, 4
34070 DOLEGNA DEL COLLIO [GO]
TEL. 0481639951
www.norinapez.it

CELLAR SALES
PRE-BOOKED VISITS
ANNUAL PRODUCTION 40,000 bottles
HECTARES UNDER VINE 7.00

○ Collio Friulano '12	🍷🍷 2*
○ Collio Pinot Grigio '12	🍷🍷 2*
● Collio Rosso El Neri di Norina '08	🍷🍷 5
○ Collio Sauvignon '12	🍷🍷 2*

Piè di Mont

LOC. PIEDIMONTE DEL CALVARIO
VIA MONTE CALVARIO, 30
34170 GORIZIA
TEL. 0481391338
www.piedimont.it

CELLAR SALES
PRE-BOOKED VISITS
ANNUAL PRODUCTION 10,000 bottles
HECTARES UNDER VINE 1.20

○ Brut Cuvée Mill. '09	🍷🍷 6

Pighin

FRAZ. RISANO
V.LE GRADO, 1
33050 PAVIA DI UDINE [UD]
TEL. 0432675444
www.pighin.com

CELLAR SALES
PRE-BOOKED VISITS
ANNUAL PRODUCTION 1,000,000 bottles
HECTARES UNDER VINE 180.00

● Collio Merlot '10	🍷🍷 3
○ Collio Chardonnay '12	🍷 3
○ Collio Pinot Grigio '12	🍷 3
● Friuli Grave Rosso Ris. '09	🍷 3

Tenuta Pinni

VIA SANT'OSVALDO, 3
33098 SAN MARTINO AL TAGLIAMENTO [PN]
TEL. 0434899464
www.tenutapinni.com

CELLAR SALES
PRE-BOOKED VISITS
ANNUAL PRODUCTION 35,000 bottles
HECTARES UNDER VINE 20.70

○ Chardonnay '12	♟♟ 2*
○ Pinot Grigio '12	♟♟ 2*
● Refosco P.R. '11	♟ 2
○ Sauvignon '12	♟ 2

Pitars

VIA TONELLO, 10
33098 SAN MARTINO AL TAGLIAMENTO [PN]
TEL. 043488078
www.pitars.it

CELLAR SALES
PRE-BOOKED VISITS
ANNUAL PRODUCTION 250,000 bottles
HECTARES UNDER VINE 125.00

○ Friuli Grave Bianco Sèris '11	♟ 3
○ Friuli Grave Pinot Grigio '12	♟ 2
○ Friuli Grave Ribolla Gialla '12	♟ 2
○ Tureis '10	♟ 3

Polje

LOC. NOVALI, 11
34071 CORMÒNS [GO]
TEL. 047160660
www.polje.com

CELLAR SALES
PRE-BOOKED VISITS
ANNUAL PRODUCTION 22,400 bottles
HECTARES UNDER VINE 12.00

○ Collio Friulano '12	♟♟ 3
○ Malvasia '12	♟♟ 3
○ Collio Ribolla Gialla '12	♟ 3
○ Collio Sauvignon '12	♟ 3

Flavio Pontoni

VIA PERUZZI, 8
33042 BUTTRIO [UD]
TEL. 0432674352
www.pontoni.it

CELLAR SALES
PRE-BOOKED VISITS
ACCOMMODATION
ANNUAL PRODUCTION 30,000 bottles
HECTARES UNDER VINE 4.50

○ COF Chardonnay '12	♟♟ 2*
○ COF Friulano '12	♟♟ 2*
○ COF Pinot Grigio '12	♟♟ 2*
● Refosco P. R. '11	♟ 2

Principi di Porcia e Brughera

VIA CASTELLO, 12
33080 PORCIA [PN]
TEL. 0434631001
www.porcia.com

CELLAR SALES
PRE-BOOKED VISITS
ANNUAL PRODUCTION 450,000 bottles
HECTARES UNDER VINE 140.00

○ Principe Serafino '09	♟♟ 2*
○ Friuli Grave Pinot Grigio '12	♟ 1*
● Friuli Grave Refosco P. R. Conte di Porcia '08	♟ 3

Pradio

LOC. FELETTIS
VIA UDINE, 17
33050 BICINICCO [UD]
TEL. 0432990123
www.pradio.it

CELLAR SALES
PRE-BOOKED VISITS
ANNUAL PRODUCTION 300,000 bottles
HECTARES UNDER VINE 33.00

○ Friuli Grave Chardonnay Teraje '12	♟♟ 2*
○ Friuli Grave Pinot Grigio Priara '12	♟♟ 2*
● Friuli Grave Cabernet Sauvignon Crearo '11	♟ 2

Puiatti - Tenimenti Angelini

LOC. ZUCCOLE, 4
34076 ROMANS D'ISONZO [GO]
TEL. 0481804101
www.puiatti.com

PRE-BOOKED VISITS
ANNUAL PRODUCTION 500,000 bottles
HECTARES UNDER VINE 50.00

○ Blanc de Blancs Extra Brut	♟♟ 3
○ Oltre il Metodo Extra Brut '06	♟♟ 5
○ Chardonnay Emozioni '12	♟ 3
● Pinot Nero Pur '12	♟ 3

Il Roncat - Giovanni Dri

LOC. RAMANDOLO
VIA PESCIA, 7
33045 NIMIS [UD]
TEL. 0432790260
www.drironcat.com

CELLAR SALES
PRE-BOOKED VISITS
ANNUAL PRODUCTION 50,000 bottles
HECTARES UNDER VINE 10.00

● COF Pignolo Monte dei Carpini '08	♟♟ 5
● COF Rosso Il Roncat '06	♟♟ 4
● COF Refosco P.R. '09	♟ 3
○ Ramandolo '10	♟ 5

Ronco dei Folo

VIA DI NOZZOLE, 12
33020 PREPOTTO [UD]
TEL. 055859811
www.tenutefolonari.com

PRE-BOOKED VISITS
ANNUAL PRODUCTION 50,000 bottles
HECTARES UNDER VINE 25.00

○ Collio Friulano '12	♟♟ 2*
○ Collio Sauvignon '12	♟♟ 2*
○ Collio Pinot Grigio '12	♟ 3
○ Collio Ribolla Gialla '12	♟ 3

Ronco Margherita

VIA UDINE, 40
33044 MANZANO [UD]
TEL. 0427949809
www.roncomargherita.it

CELLAR SALES
PRE-BOOKED VISITS
ANNUAL PRODUCTION 100,000 bottles
HECTARES UNDER VINE 40.00

○ COF Chardonnay '12	♟♟ 3
● COF Merlot '11	♟♟ 3
● COF Rosso Ovalis '09	♟♟ 4
○ Ribolla Gialla Brut '12	♟♟ 3

San Simone

LOC. RONDOVER
VIA PRATA, 30
33080 PORCIA [PN]
TEL. 0434578633
www.sansimone.it

CELLAR SALES
PRE-BOOKED VISITS
ANNUAL PRODUCTION 900,000 bottles
HECTARES UNDER VINE 85.00

○ Friuli Grave Pinot Grigio Case Sugan '12	♟♟ 2*
○ Friuli Grave Friulano Case Sugan '12	♟ 2
○ Friuli Grave Pinot Grigio '12	♟ 2
● Friuli Grave Refosco P. R. Re Sugano '11	♟ 2

Scarbolo

FRAZ. LAUZACCO
V.LE GRADO, 4
33050 PAVIA DI UDINE [UD]
TEL. 0432675612
www.scarbolo.com

CELLAR SALES
PRE-BOOKED VISITS
RESTAURANT SERVICE
ANNUAL PRODUCTION 160,000 bottles
HECTARES UNDER VINE 30.00

○ Friuli Grave Bianco My Time '10	♟♟ 4
● Friuli Grave Refosco P. R. '09	♟♟ 4
● Friuli Grave Merlot '11	♟ 3
○ Friuli Grave Sauvignon '12	♟ 2

Skerlj

VIA SALES, 44
34010 SGONICO [TS]
TEL. 040229253
www.agriturismoskerlj.com

CELLAR SALES
PRE-BOOKED VISITS
ACCOMMODATION AND RESTAURANT SERVICE
ANNUAL PRODUCTION 2,600 bottles
HECTARES UNDER VINE 2.30
VITICULTURE METHOD Certified Organic

○ Vitovska '10	▼▼ 5
○ Malvasia '10	▼▼ 5
● Terrano '10	▼ 5

F.lli Stanig

VIA ALBANA, 44
33040 PREPOTTO [UD]
TEL. 0432713234
www.stanig.it

CELLAR SALES
PRE-BOOKED VISITS
ACCOMMODATION AND RESTAURANT SERVICE
ANNUAL PRODUCTION 45,000 bottles
HECTARES UNDER VINE 9.00

○ COF Sauvignon '12	▼▼ 2*
○ COF Friulano '12	▼▼ 2*
○ COF Malvasia '12	▼▼ 2*
● COF Cabernet '12	▼ 2

Stocco

VIA CASALI STOCCO, 12
33050 BICINICCO [UD]
TEL. 0432934906
www.vinistocco.it

CELLAR SALES
PRE-BOOKED VISITS
RESTAURANT SERVICE
ANNUAL PRODUCTION 150,000 bottles
HECTARES UNDER VINE 39.00

○ Pinot Grigio '12	▼▼ 2*
○ Ribolla Gialla '12	▼▼ 2*
○ Sauvignon '12	▼ 2
○ Sericus '11	▼ 3

Talis

VIA PALMARINA, 113/4
33048 SAN GIOVANNI AL NATISONE [UD]
TEL. 3355393920
www.taliswine.it

ANNUAL PRODUCTION 20,000 bottles
HECTARES UNDER VINE 40.00

● COF Cabernet '12	▼▼ 3
● COF Refosco P. R. '09	▼▼ 3
○ Friuli Grave Friulano '12	▼ 3
○ Sauvignon '12	▼ 3

Terre del Faet

V.LE ROMA, 82
34071 CORMÒNS [GO]
TEL. 3470103325
andreadrius.vino@hotmail.it

PRE-BOOKED VISITS
ANNUAL PRODUCTION 6,000 bottles
HECTARES UNDER VINE 2.00

○ Collio Friulano '12	▼▼ 3
○ Collio Malvasia '12	▼▼ 3
○ Collio Pinot Bianco '12	▼ 3

Terre di Ger

FRAZ. FRATTINA
S.DA DELLA MEDUNA, 17
33076 PRAVISDOMINI [PN]
TEL. 0434644452
www.terrediger.it

CELLAR SALES
PRE-BOOKED VISITS
ANNUAL PRODUCTION 100,000 bottles
HECTARES UNDER VINE 50.00

● Friuli Grave Merlot '11	▼▼ 2*
● Arcioni Rosso '11	▼▼ 3
○ Friuli Grave Chardonnay '12	▼ 2
○ Sauvignon Blanc '12	▼ 2

Tenuta Valdomini

B.GO PICCOLI
33045 ATTIMIS [UD]
TEL. 0432789889
www.valdomini.com

CELLAR SALES
PRE-BOOKED VISITS
ANNUAL PRODUCTION 20,000 bottles
HECTARES UNDER VINE 7.50

○ COF Friulano '12	♟♟ 2*
● COF Refosco P. R. '09	♟♟ 2*
○ COF Ribolla Gialla '12	♟♟ 2*
○ COF Soffio Bianco '12	♟♟ 3

Paolo Venturini

VIA ISONZO, 135
34071 CORMÒNS [GO]
TEL. 048160446
www.venturinivini.it

CELLAR SALES
PRE-BOOKED VISITS
ANNUAL PRODUCTION 70,000 bottles
HECTARES UNDER VINE 17.00

● Collio Merlot '11	♟♟ 3
○ Collio Pinot Bianco '12	♟♟ 3
○ Collio Sauvignon '12	♟♟ 3
○ Collio Chardonnay '12	♟ 3

Vidussi

VIA SPESSA, 18
34071 CAPRIVA DEL FRIULI [GO]
TEL. 048180072
www.vinimontresor.it

CELLAR SALES
PRE-BOOKED VISITS
ANNUAL PRODUCTION 500,000 bottles
HECTARES UNDER VINE 30.00

○ Collio Friulano '12	♟♟ 2*
○ Collio Ribolla Gialla '12	♟♟ 2*
● Collio Rosso Are di Miute '09	♟♟ 4
● Ribolla Nera o Schioppettino '12	♟♟ 3*

Vigne del Malina

FRAZ. ORZANO
VIA PASINI VIANELLI, 9
33047 REMANZACCO [UD]
TEL. 0432649258
www.vignedelmalina.com

CELLAR SALES
PRE-BOOKED VISITS
ANNUAL PRODUCTION 45,000 bottles
HECTARES UNDER VINE 10.00

○ Pinot Grigio '10	♟♟ 3
○ Chardonnay '10	♟ 3
○ Chardonnay Aur '09	♟ 4
○ Sauvignon '10	♟ 3

Le Vigne del Nord Est

VIA DEL DONATORE, 13
33040 CORNO DI ROSAZZO [UD]
TEL. 3405327418
www.lune.it

CELLAR SALES
PRE-BOOKED VISITS
ANNUAL PRODUCTION 60,000 bottles

○ COF Friulano '11	♟♟ 2*
○ COF Sauvignon '11	♟♟ 2*
○ COF Malvasia '11	♟ 2
○ COF Pinot Grigio '11	♟ 2

Zof

FRAZ. SANT'ANDRAT DEL JUDRIO
VIA GIOVANNI XXIII, 32A
33040 CORNO DI ROSAZZO [UD]
TEL. 0432759673
www.zof.it

CELLAR SALES
PRE-BOOKED VISITS
ACCOMMODATION
ANNUAL PRODUCTION 90,000 bottles
HECTARES UNDER VINE 15.00

○ COF Bianco San Michele '12	♟♟ 2*
○ COF Bianco Sonata '11	♟♟ 4
○ COF Friulano '12	♟♟ 3*
○ COF Ribolla Gialla '12	♟ 3

EMILIA ROMAGNA

The region has developed increasingly strong territorial specialization and is now able to flank the quantity of its production with discernibly higher quality. The credit for this is largely attributable to the co-operatives with their energy and commitment in addressing the challenge of producing increasingly good wines with a more identifiable territorial stamp. We can say this of Emilia, with its Lambrusco, but also of Romagna. The popular appeal of the product is safeguarded but positive export and domestic market data are clearly counter-cyclical, elevating the region to the status of a true supply-chain model. Romagna continues to roll with its production of Sangiovese and while years ago the best expressions of this variety were all Riservas, today the leaders include several Superiores: a clear sign of how this type may mark the region's future. These are fresh, stylish wines with well-defined fruit that are becoming progressively more cellarable. The credit for this lies in the courage required to let the variety express itself to the full, daring to use longer macerations and investing more hours in the vineyard. Lambrusco has achieved unprecedented success and now has to cope with being a grown-up, firstly by simply acknowledging the burden and the honour of the vintage shown on the label. There are still too many quality wines failing to declare their date of birth on the label and this is not acceptable for products with any kind of aspirations. Secondly, Sorbara apart, they need to dare longer maceration to acquire a deeper, more interesting tannic weave. Thirdly, work should focus more than ever on exploring second fermentation without disgorgement, a far more appropriate approach here than the traditional method. If the provinces of Modena and Reggio are the homeland of Lambrusco, with an historical role attributed to the former, Parma can be declared the territory of sparkling Barbera. Piacenza, and this is good news, now has a new generation of small producers of gutsy, interesting wines. We have reviewed the best of them because we believe that the future of the Piacenza hills lies here. To close, a few words on the Colli Bolognesi, today a massive testing ground devoted to pignoletto, which is a challenge, but results are on the horizon.

Ancarani

via San Biagio Antico, 14
48018 Faenza [RA]
Tel. 0546642162
www.viniancarani.it

CELLAR SALES
PRE-BOOKED VISITS
RESTAURANT SERVICE
ANNUAL PRODUCTION 30,000 bottles
HECTARES UNDER VINE 14.00

Ancarani is a sound operation that over the years has gained market share in the region with wines that are attractively countryish but express local traditions with a modern panache, reflecting forgotten varieties, harsh winters and torrid summers refreshed with the "Albana of yore". Claudio Ancarani inherited his passion for wine from his grandfather, and in his work he has never faltered in holding to the magic he experienced as a child. His Albana Santa Lusa, always a standout, is one of the classic interpretations of this challenging white grape, displaying a distinctive harmony of acidity and tannin, power and delicacy all at once. Santa Lusa 2011 is classic Albana, elegantly rustic and countryish, and conveying the soul of the variety, one side tannic, the other unexpectedly delicate, both married to a lovely acidity. The stylistically gorgeous Biagio Antico 2011 is taut and minerally, lifted by a lively volatile acidity.

○ Albana di Romagna Santa Lusa '11	♟♟	3
● Sangiovese di Romagna Oriolo '11	♟♟	2
● Sangiovese di Romagna Sup. Biagio Antico '11	♟♟	2*
● Uvappesa '09	♟♟	4
● Sâvignon Rosso '11	♟	3
○ Signore Famoso '12	♟	2
○ Albana di Romagna Santa Lusa '10	♟♟	3
○ Albana di Romagna Santa Lusa '09	♟♟	3
○ Albana di Romagna Santa Lusa '08	♟♟	3
○ Albana di Romagna Santa Lusa '07	♟♟	3
● Sangiovese di Romagna Sup. Biagio Antico '10	♟♟	2*
● Sangiovese di Romagna Sup. Biagio Antico '09	♟♟	2
● Sâvignon Rosso '10	♟♟	3
● Sâvignon Rosso '09	♟♟	3

Balìa di Zola

via Casale, 11
47015 Modigliana [FC]
Tel. 0546940577
www.baliadizola.com

CELLAR SALES
PRE-BOOKED VISITS
ANNUAL PRODUCTION 50,000 bottles
HECTARES UNDER VINE 5.00

The area of Modigliana has developed at a stunning pace in recent years, demonstrating a capability for quality wine production that makes it one of Romagna's hottest tickets, above all where the soils are loose marls and sandstone. Balìa di Zola is deservedly one of the icons of this phenomenon, making elegant wines with plenty of grip, character, and cellarability. Veruska Eluci and her husband Claudio Fiore, having purchased this winery in 2003, restructured all of the vineyards and crafted a terroir-focused style, with crisp wines that express the minerality classic to the area and preserve their fragrances even with a few years in the bottle. A lacklustre Redinoce 2010 betrays the effects of a poor growing year, suffering under the weight of an excessively sweet oak. Balitore 2011, with ripe fruit, lacks terroir character as well as its usual suppleness.

● Sangiovese di Romagna Redinoce Ris. '10	♟♟	4
● Sangiovese di Romagna Balitore '11	♟	2
● Sangiovese di Romagna Redinoce Ris. '09	♟♟♟	4*
● Sangiovese di Romagna Redinoce Ris. '08	♟♟♟	4*
● Redinoce '07	♟♟	4
● Redinoce '06	♟♟	4
● Redinoce '05	♟♟	4
● Redinoce '04	♟♟	4
● Sangiovese di Romagna Balitore '10	♟♟	2*
● Sangiovese di Romagna Balitore '09	♟♟	2
● Sangiovese di Romagna Balitore '08	♟♟	2

Le Barbaterre

LOC. BERGONZANO
VIA CAVOUR, 2A
42020 QUATTRO CASTELLA [RE]
TEL. 3358053454
www.barbaterre.com

CELLAR SALES
ANNUAL PRODUCTION 10,000 bottles
HECTARES UNDER VINE 9.00
VITICULTURE METHOD Certified Organic

The energy of Massimo Bedogni will be missed, even though Erika Tagliavini displays plenty of enthusiasm and her accustomed joie de vivre. Le Barbaterre is quite a distinctive operation, exemplary of the new wind blowing through Emilia, evidenced by growing interest in hillslope viticulture and bottle-refermented wines. The nine hectares of estate vineyards lie in loose soils of silt, clay, and marl at 350 metres' elevation in the first hills rising from Quattro Castella, almost in the Val d'Enza; historically, this is in the heart of the area that Matilda of Tuscany defended by means of a series of castles: Pianello, Rossena, Canossa, Sarzano, and Carpineti. The ultra-elegant Besmein 2012, re-fermented in the bottle without disgorgement, is delicious, delicately hinting of nutmeg and tangerine. The nicely austere Brut Sauvignon 2010 exhibits nuances of blossoms and smoke, alongside full-fruited notes of plum, plus hints of salty sea breezes.

⊙ Besmein Capoleg	
Marzemino Frizzante Rosé '12	🍷🍷 2*
● Lambrusco dell'Emilia '12	🍷🍷 2*
● Sauvignon Brut M. Cl. '10	🍷🍷 3
⊙ Besmein Capoleg	
Marzemino Frizzante Rosé '11	🍷🍷 2*
● Besmein Capoleg	
Marzemino Rifermentato in Bottiglia '10	🍷🍷 2*
○ Colli di Scandiano e Canossa	
Sauvignon '08	🍷🍷 3
○ Colli di Scandiano e Canossa	
Sauvignon '07	🍷🍷 2*
⊙ L'Angelica Rosé M. Cl. '10	🍷🍷 3
○ Lambruscante Brut Nature '10	🍷🍷 3
● Lambrusco dell'Emilia '11	🍷🍷 2*
● Lambrusco dell'Emilia '09	🍷🍷 2*
● Lambrusco dell'Emilia	
Rifermentato in Bottiglia '10	🍷🍷 3

Francesco Bellei

FRAZ. CRISTO DI SORBARA
VIA NAZIONALE, 132
41030 BOMPORTO [MO]
TEL. 059812449
www.francescobellei.it

CELLAR SALES
ANNUAL PRODUCTION 60,000 bottles
HECTARES UNDER VINE 5.00

A lengthy history, a superb reputation and invaluable expertise with metodo classico are the highlights of an operation begun in 1926 and passed on through three generations, up to the current owners, the Cavicchioli family. Sandro Cavicchioli has been making the Bellei wines since 2003, and his sapient hand has ensured its reputation and quality, producing with remarkable sensitivity "ancestral fermentation" wines, in-bottle fermentations with no disgorging that belong to the most classic local repertoire. L'Ancestrale, In particular, has become the stuff of legends, a must-visit on any journey through the world of Sorbara. Lambrusco Rifermentazione Ancestrale 2012, displaying admirable forcefulness and energy, is elegant, supple and knife-edged, its finish laden with sea spray, flowers and spice, plus a touch of citrus. Speciale Cuvée 2005 sports rich saffron, honey, sage and hazelnut on the nose and crispness in the mouth.

● Lambrusco di Modena	
Rifermentazione Ancestrale '12	🍷🍷 2*
○ Cuvée Blanc de Noir Brut M. Cl. '05	🍷🍷 5
○ Speciale Cuvée Brut M. Cl. '05	🍷🍷 5
○ Extra Cuvée Brut	🍷 3
● Modena Pignoletto	
Rifermentazione Ancestrale '12	🍷 2
● Extra Cuvée Brut Rosso '08	🍷🍷 3
● Lambrusco di Modena	
Rifermentazione Ancestrale '11	🍷🍷 2*
● Lambrusco di Modena	
Rifermentazione Ancestrale '10	🍷🍷 2*
● Lambrusco	
Rifermentazione Ancestrale '07	🍷🍷 2*
● Modena Pignoletto	
Rifermentazione Ancestrale '11	🍷🍷 2*
● Modena Pignoletto	
Rifermentazione Ancestrale '10	🍷🍷 2*

La Berta

VIA BERTA, 13
48013 BRISIGHELLA [RA]
TEL. 054684998
www.labera.it

CELLAR SALES
PRE-BOOKED VISITS
ANNUAL PRODUCTION 55,000 bottles
HECTARES UNDER VINE 20.00

Giovanni Poggiali and his siblings purchased this small operation in 2008, pouring into it all their experience gained from the other family-run winery, Fattoria Felsina in Chianti Classico, particularly their ability to look at viticulture and winemaking with long-term vision. They have committed enormous efforts to the vineyards, lavishing attention on them as well as careful study of the soils. The best results will take some time to appear, of course, but the winery has already achieved the quality position in the area that it historically enjoyed. Overall, Olmatello 2010 is dry and well put-together, elegant and crisp; these classic qualities enable it to handle easily some slight excesses: oak a tad too high, a touch of sweetness and a whiff of florality. The full-bodied yet sometimes hesitant Solano 2011 displays good overall proportions.

● Sangiovese di Romagna Solano '11		▼▼ 3
● Sangiovese di Romagna Sup. Olmatello Ris. '10		▼▼ 4
○ Trebbiano di Romagna Floresco '12		▼▼ 2*
● Sangiovese di Romagna '10		� 2
● Sangiovese di Romagna Olmatello Ris. '09		♀♀ 2*
● Sangiovese di Romagna Olmatello Ris. '08		♀♀ 2*
● Sangiovese di Romagna Olmatello Ris. '03		♀♀ 2*

Tenuta Bonzara

VIA SAN CHIERLO, 37A
40050 MONTE SAN PIETRO [BO]
TEL. 0516768324
www.bonzara.it

CELLAR SALES
PRE-BOOKED VISITS
ACCOMMODATION AND RESTAURANT SERVICE
ANNUAL PRODUCTION 70,000 bottles
HECTARES UNDER VINE 15.00

Francesco Lambertini's father Angelo purchased this wine estate of almost 100 hectares in the Colli Bolognesi in 1963, and Francesco follows his family tradition by continuing to lavish attention on it. The high-elevation vineyards in San Chierlo di Monte San Pietro are capable of yielding wonderful crispness in the grapes, particularly those for white wines, where winemaker Lorenzo Landi has always shown a rare talent. All of the wines exhibit fine quality, but the Pignoletto is a true benchmark for the area. Pignoletto Vigna Antica 2012 receives oxygen-free vinification to protect its varietal grassiness; additional notes of grapefruit zest contribute to an impressive sapidity. The monovarietal Borgo di Qua 2012 is sea salt, sage and citron zest, while Bonzarone 2010, elegant, vegetal and peppery and a touch of pencil lead, will gain over the years.

● C. B. Cabernet Sauvignon Bonzarone '10	▼▼ 5
○ C. B. Pignoletto Cl. V. Antica '12	▼▼ 2*
○ C.B. Pignoletto Cl. Borgo di Qua '12	▼▼ 1*
● C. B. Bologna Rosso '12	▼ 2
● C. B. Cabernet Sauvignon Bonzarone '05	♀♀♀ 5
● C. B. Cabernet Sauvignon Bonzarone '97	♀♀♀ 3*
● C. B. Cabernet Sauvignon Bonzarone '96	♀♀♀ 5
● C. B. Merlot Rocca di Bonacciara '95	♀♀♀ 3*
● C. B. Cabernet Sauvignon Bonzarone '09	♀♀ 5
● C. B. Cabernet Sauvignon Bonzarone '04	♀♀ 4
● C. B. Cabernet Sauvignon Bonzarone '03	♀♀ 4
● C. B. Cabernet Sauvignon Bonzarone '01	♀♀ 4
● C. B. Merlot Rocca di Bonacciara '09	♀♀ 3
● C. B. Merlot Rocca di Bonacciara '05	♀♀ 5
● C. B. Merlot Rocca di Bonacciara '03	♀♀ 4
● C. B. Merlot Rocca di Bonacciara '01	♀♀ 4

Ca' di Sopra

LOC. MARZENO
VIA FELIGARA, 15
48013 BRISIGHELLA [RA]
TEL. 0544521209
www.cadisopra.com

CELLAR SALES
PRE-BOOKED VISITS
ANNUAL PRODUCTION 19,000 bottles
HECTARES UNDER VINE 28.00

The intimate knowledge that Camillo and Giacomo Montanari show of their 28 hectares of vineyard goes back in time, honed through the years when all they did was sell their grapes. Gradually they developed a plan for vinifying the grapes from their best parcels, and their work in the vineyards, carried out personally by Giacomo, then became ever more maniacal. The vineyards, in the Marzeno valley, are planted in clay at around 250 metres' elevation; they face northeast, but those at the hilltop are in full sun. Quality has increased in recent years, and is increasingly consistent. Despite obvious oak, Crepe 2011, sourced from the winery's highest vineyard, is crisp and distinctive, with an elegantly crisp palate. Cadisopra 2010 is well proportioned, dry and well balanced, apart from overly-warm fruit. Uait 2012, of chardonnay assisted with albana, is refreshing, multifaceted and vibrant.

● Remel '10	♟♟ 3
● Roncodipacì '10	♟♟ 5
● Sangiovese di Romagna Crepe '11	♟♟ 2*
● Sangiovese di Romagna Sup. Cadisopra Ris. '10	♟♟ 4
○ Uait '12	♟♟ 2*
● Cadisopra '09	♟♟ 4
● Cadisopra '08	♟♟ 2
● Crepe '08	♟♟ 2*
● Remel '09	♟♟ 3
● Remel '07	♟♟ 3*
● Roncodipacì '09	♟♟ 4

Ca' Montanari

FRAZ. LEVIZZANO RANGONE
VIA MEDUSIA, 32
41014 CASTELVETRO DI MODENA [MO]
TEL. 059741019
www.opera02.it

CELLAR SALES
PRE-BOOKED VISITS
ACCOMMODATION AND RESTAURANT SERVICE
ANNUAL PRODUCTION 80,000 bottles
HECTARES UNDER VINE 21.00
VITICULTURE METHOD Certified Organic

Ca' Montanari has a two-fold operation. On the one hand is their production of Lambrusco, largely grasparossa; on the other is the establishment of a hospitality centre that would serve as ambassador for the entire area, starting with their vinegar cellar that produces an Aceto Tradizionale di Modena, guest lodgings and an agritourism that showcases local cooking and produce. Although the winery was founded in 2002, the first vineyards were planted in 2004 and are now in full production; the 21 hectares are in clay soils, facing south and southeast. Working them now is young Mattia. The pleasantly rustic Opera 02 2012, made of grasparossa with a tot of salamino, displays generous cherry and plum fruit along with impressions of earth and woods, and is thus a classic pairing with Emilian cuisine. The near-electric Opera Rosa 2012 is slender and nicely citrussy.

● Lambrusco di Modena Opera 02 '12	♟♟ 2*
☉ Lambrusco di Modena Rosato Brut Opera Rosa '12	♟♟ 4
● Opera 02 Lambrusco di Modena Amabile '12	♟♟ 3
● Lambrusco Grasparossa di Castelvetro Opera Pura '12	♟ 3
● Lambrusco di Modena Opera 02 '11	♟♟ 2*
● Lambrusco di Modena Opera 02 '10	♟♟ 2*
● Lambrusco di Modena Opera 02 '09	♟♟ 2*
● Lambrusco di Modena Opera 02 '08	♟♟ 2*
● Lambrusco Grasparossa di Castelvetro Opera Pura '10	♟♟ 3*
● Lambrusco Grasparossa di Castelvetro Opera Pura '09	♟♟ 3
● Opera Pura Lambrusco di Modena '08	♟♟ 3

Calonga

LOC. CASTIGLIONE
VIA CASTEL LEONE, 8
47100 FORLÌ
TEL. 0543753044
www.calonga.it

CELLAR SALES
PRE-BOOKED VISITS
ANNUAL PRODUCTION 30,000 bottles
HECTARES UNDER VINE 8.00

Maurizio Baravelli, with his son Matteo
sharing responsibilities, is a dyed-in-the-
wool wine-grower, and his Michelangiolo
has lately become one of the hottest wines
in Romagna. The style here is powerful,
broad-shouldered wines, part products of
an uncommon terroir of molasse sands that
poke up in the vineyards and even
predominate in the soils, and part the result
of a palate that has always leant towards
very full body and burnished textures.
These are soundly made, always reliable
artisanal wines that faithfully mirror the
growing year. Michelangiolo was not
produced in 2010. Ordelaffo 2011,
sangiovese with some cabernet sauvignon,
is dry and taut, a vibrant wine from first to
last, with lean fruit and a delicious finale.
The Castellione 2010, all Cabernet
Sauvignon, shows fine body marred by oak
that dries the palate and impacts the nose.

Cantina della Volta

VIA PER MODENA, 82
41030 BOMPORTO [MO]
TEL. 0597473312
www.cantinadellavolta.com

CELLAR SALES
PRE-BOOKED VISITS
ANNUAL PRODUCTION 100,000 bottles
HECTARES UNDER VINE 9.00

Cantina della Volta has shown
unprecedented speed in becoming, in the
space of just a few harvests, one of the
benchmark cellars in the Modena area,
thanks to the synergistic partnership
between Christian Bellei's extraordinary
fund of family experience on the one hand
and, on the other, a group of partners who
have made a powerful investment of energy
and resources in the winery and in an
admirably ambitious marketing programme.
In the old Bellei cellar, now completely
restructured, the winemaking focuses on
sorbara, without neglecting the pinot noir,
pinot meunier, and chardonnay growing in
the historic hillside vineyards at Riccò di
Serramazzoni in the province of Modena.
The graceful yet forceful Rimosso 2012
offers a delicate, citrus-lifted florality with a
hint of wild strawberry, a wine of lifting
linearity with a fine minerally sapidity. La
Svolta 2010 has a piercing acidity and a
rhythmic progression, a bouquet including
hawthorn, rose and tangerine, and peat and
spice on the finish.

● Ordelaffo '11	♟♟ 2*
● Castellione '10	♟ 4
● Sangiovese di Romagna Sup. Michelangiolo Ris. '07	♟♟♟ 4*
● Sangiovese di Romagna Sup. Michelangiolo Ris. '06	♟♟♟ 4
● Sangiovese di Romagna Sup. Michelangiolo Ris. '05	♟♟♟ 4*
● Sangiovese di Romagna Sup. Michelangiolo Ris. '04	♟♟♟ 4*
● Sangiovese di Romagna Sup. Michelangiolo Ris. '03	♟♟♟ 4
● Sangiovese di Romagna Sup. Michelangiolo Ris. '09	♟♟ 4
● Sangiovese di Romagna Sup. Michelangiolo Ris. '08	♟♟ 4

● Lambrusco di Sorbara Rimosso '12	♟♟♟ 3*
⊙ Brut M. Cl. La Svolta Rosato '10	♟♟ 7
○ Il Mattaglio Brut D.Z. '10	♟♟ 5
○ Il Mattaglio Brut	♟♟ 5
○ Il Mattaglio Brut '09	♟♟ 5
⊙ Lambrusco di Modena Brut Rosé Spumante '10	♟♟ 5
● Lambrusco di Modena Brut Spumante '10	♟♟ 4
● Lambrusco di Modena Spumante '09	♟♟ 2
● Lambrusco di Sorbara Rimosso '10	♟♟ 3*
● Lambrusco di Sorbara Rimosso '09	♟♟ 3

Cardinali

POD. MONTEPASCOLO
29014 CASTELL'ARQUATO [PC]
TEL. 0523803502
www.cardinalidoc.it

CELLAR SALES
PRE-BOOKED VISITS
ANNUAL PRODUCTION 30,000 bottles
HECTARES UNDER VINE 5.50

The history of this small operation just a few steps from the hamlet of Castell'Arquato has been bound up with that of the Cardinali family since the 1970s. Alberto and Laura Cardinali may have begun as city dwellers, but over time they became true wine-growers, dedicated to the care of their seven hectares of vines and committed to a philosophy increasingly bonded to nature. As a result, their wines also genuinely express their local terroir, and make this winery ever more impressive, with its carefully-chosen, consistent direction. The terroir-rich Gutturnios di Cardinali display generous mineral and earth, which showcases their gamey, austere qualities. The bonarda and barbera Nicchio 2011 is kaleidoscopic, with mineral, sulphur, and game, then a fine acidity in the mouth. The austerely elegant Gutturnio Superiore 2012 shows supple breadth.

Casetto dei Mandorli

LOC. PREDAPPIO ALTA
VIA UMBERTO I, 21
47010 PREDAPPIO [FC]
TEL. 0543922361
www.vini-nicolucci.it

CELLAR SALES
PRE-BOOKED VISITS
ANNUAL PRODUCTION 60,000 bottles
HECTARES UNDER VINE 12.00

Alessandro Nicolucci, heir of a lengthy family tradition, personifies the admirable figure of the wine artisan uninterested in trends or ideological stances, focusing rather on making classic, reliable wines. His Vigna del Generale is the perfect example, exhibiting a cellarability and elegance that few Sangioveses achieve, a wine distinctive for its minerality, fruit of an unusual terroir that intersperses sulphur outcroppings among its vineyards. Predappio Alta is emblematic of Romagna viticulture, since even in the 1800s head-trained vines at 7,000 per hectare were common here, planted to a classic sangiovese cultivar, with elliptic-shaped berries that yielded a widely respected wine. Overcoming a difficult year, Vigna del Generale 2010 shows classic and elegant, its fine performance the fruit of earthy nuances and a distinctive, refined impression of sulphur-lifted fresh vegetable, a hallmark of the unusual Predappio area vineyards. The Tre Rocche 2012, elegant, crisp and austere, shows good typicity.

● C. P. Gutturnio Cl. Nicchio '11	♔♔ 3
● C. P. Gutturnio Frizzante Tomà '12	♔♔ 2*
● C. P. Gutturnio Sup. '12	♔♔ 3
○ C. P. Monterosso Val d'Arda Solata '11	♔♔ 2*
○ Moscato V. T. '11	♔♔ 3
● C. P. Cabernet Sauvignon Ronchello '01	♔♔ 3
● C. P. Gutturnio Cl. Nicchio '09	♔♔ 3
● C. P. Gutturnio Cl. Nicchio '07	♔♔ 3*
● C. P. Gutturnio Cl. Nicchio '06	♔♔ 3*
● C. P. Gutturnio Cl. Nicchio '03	♔♔ 3*
● C. P. Gutturnio Cl. Torquato Ris. '05	♔♔ 4
● C. P. Gutturnio Cl. Torquato Ris. '04	♔♔ 4
● C. P. Gutturnio Frizzante Tomà '10	♔♔ 2*
○ C. P. Monterosso Val d'Arda Solata '10	♔♔ 2*
○ C. P. Monterosso Val d'Arda Solata '07	♔♔ 2*
○ Moscato V. T. '09	♔♔ 3

● Sangiovese di Romagna Sup. del Generale Ris. '10	♔♔♔ 5
● Nero di Predappio '11	♔♔ 5
● Sangiovese di Romagna Sup. Tre Rocche '12	♔♔ 3
● Sangiovese di Romagna Sup. V. del Generale Ris. '08	♔♔♔ 5
● Sangiovese di Romagna V. del Generale Ris. '09	♔♔♔ 5
● Sangiovese di Romagna V. del Generale Ris. '05	♔♔♔ 4
● Sangiovese di Romagna Sup. Tre Rocche '09	♔♔ 3
● Sangiovese di Romagna Sup. Tre Rocche '07	♔♔ 3*
● Sangiovese di Romagna V. del Generale Ris. '07	♔♔ 3*

Castelluccio

LOC. POGGIOLO DI SOTTO
VIA TRAMONTO, 15
47015 MODIGLIANA [FC]
TEL. 0546942486
www.ronchidicastelluccio.it

CELLAR SALES
PRE-BOOKED VISITS
ACCOMMODATION
ANNUAL PRODUCTION 100,000 bottles
HECTARES UNDER VINE 16.00

Castelluccio was among the first Romagna producers to share the conviction that this region too was capable of making great wines, and its fabled Ronco bottlings are in fact just that: subtle and elegant, tranquilly unafraid of years in the cellar, cherished and sought after by their fans even today. Founded in the late 1970s by the Baldi family, the winery has been directed since 1999 by owner Vittorio Fiore, who has been making the wines since the winery's first harvest. The Ronco wines, genuine crus, are the product of sandstone marl soils, quite distinctive for the elegance and character of the wines that spring from them. The dynamic Ronco delle Ginestre 2008 is impressively elegant and full-flavoured, with well-crafted, ripe tannins. The lush Le More 2012 boasts clean-edged fruit and a supple, dry palate, while the sangiovese and cabernet sauvignon Massicone 2009 is lean and straightforward. The heavy Ronco dei Ciliegi 2008 lacks terroir character.

Cavicchioli U. & Figli

VIA CANALETTO, 52
41030 SAN PROSPERO [MO]
TEL. 059812411
www.cavicchioli.it

CELLAR SALES
PRE-BOOKED VISITS
ANNUAL PRODUCTION 10,000,000 bottles
HECTARES UNDER VINE 100.00

The Gruppo Italiano Vini, which purchased Cavicchioli in 2010, has tried to preserve the heritage represented by the family's long experience, keeping brothers Sandro and Claudio in the leadership position. This smooth-running collaboration has boosted wine quality, and consistency has benefited as well. Cavicchioli is one of the benchmark producers for classic Lambruscos, and for Sorbara in particular; the winery has been an intimate part of that wine's history and growth over the last 30 years. A great growing year for sorbara helps Vigna del Cristo 2012 unleash its best showing ever, with a wondrous acidity and salty tang fuelling the progression, along with fragrant pink grapefruit, citron zest and mineral, followed by gunflint and roses. A well-contoured wine, all rhythm and drive. The richly-faceted Rosé del Cristo 2010 lays out blossoms, apple, pear and iodine, with a lovely briny finale.

● Massicone '09	♥♥ 3
● Ronco delle Ginestre '08	♥♥ 4
● Sangiovese di Romagna Le More '12	♥♥ 2*
● Ronco dei Ciliegi '08	♥ 3
● Massicone '01	♥♥♥ 5
● Ronco dei Ciliegi '02	♥♥♥ 5
● Ronco dei Ciliegi '00	♥♥♥ 5
● Ronco delle Ginestre '90	♥♥♥ 5
● Massicone '06	♥♥ 4
● Massicone '03	♥♥ 5
● Massicone '02	♥♥ 5
● Massicone '00	♥♥ 5
● Ronco dei Ciliegi '03	♥♥ 5
● Ronco dei Ciliegi '01	♥♥ 5
● Ronco delle Ginestre '02	♥♥ 5
● Ronco delle Ginestre '00	♥♥ 5

● Lambrusco di Sorbara V. del Cristo '12	♥♥♥ 2*
⊙ Rosé del Cristo Brut Rosé '10	♥♥ 5
● Lambrusco di Modena 1928 '12	♥♥ 2*
● Lambrusco di Sorbara Secco Marchio Storico '12	♥♥ 2*
● Lambrusco di Sorbara V. del Cristo '11	♥♥♥ 2*
● Lambrusco di Sorbara Rifermentazione Ancestrale Francesco Bellei '09	♥♥ 4
● Lambrusco di Sorbara Rifermentazione Ancestrale Francesco Bellei '08	♥♥ 4
● Lambrusco di Sorbara Secco Marchio Storico '11	♥♥ 2*
● Lambrusco di Sorbara V. del Cristo '10	♥♥ 3*
● Lambrusco di Sorbara V. del Cristo '08	♥♥ 2*
● Lambrusco di Sorbara V. del Cristo '07	♥♥ 2*

Celli

VIA CARDUCCI, 5
47032 BERTINORO [FC]
TEL. 0543445183
www.celli-vini.com

CELLAR SALES
PRE-BOOKED VISITS
ANNUAL PRODUCTION 270,000 bottles
HECTARES UNDER VINE 29.00

The Sirri and Casadei families manage this historic cellar that has always turned out wines whose price tags are an amazing bargain given their high quality, all of them solidly traditional, even the lowest tier bottlings. The 30 hectares of vineyards, some estate owned, others leased, are all in the Bertinoro area, planted in the local calcareous soils rich with seabed tuff. As a result of the wines' reliability and their classic local traits, the winery boasts long-term relationships with its customers. Mauro Sirri, who has always been the winery's public face, is focused on several projects directed at further developing the local area, an objective fundamental to the winery's philosophy. Secco I Croppi 2012 is a classic, traditional Albana, with perfectly-crafted tannins and a varietally-faithful acidity complementing its dry, aromatic palate. Le Grillaie 2012, an austerely classic Sangiovese, gradually reveals its ultra-crisp fruit and rolls out an elegant, full-volumed conclusion.

○ Albana di Romagna Dolce Le Querce '12	▼▼	2*
○ Albana di Romagna Passito Solara '11	▼▼	4
○ Albana di Romagna Secco I Croppi '12	▼▼	2*
● Sangiovese di Romagna Sup. Le Grillaie '12	▼▼	2*
○ Albana di Romagna Passito Solara '08	▽▽	3
○ Albana di Romagna Secco I Croppi '10	▽▽	2*
○ Albana di Romagna Secco I Croppi '09	▽▽	2*
○ Albana di Romagna Secco I Croppi '08	▽▽	2*
○ Albana di Romagna Secco I Croppi '07	▽▽	2*
○ Albana di Romagna Secco I Croppi '05	▽▽	2*
● Sangiovese di Romagna Sup. Le Grillaie '09	▽▽	2*
● Sangiovese di Romagna Sup. Le Grillaie Ris. '08	▽▽	2

Umberto Cesari

VIA STANZANO, 1120
40024 CASTEL SAN PIETRO TERME [BO]
TEL. 051941896
www.umbertocesari.it

CELLAR SALES
PRE-BOOKED VISITS
ANNUAL PRODUCTION 3,000,000 bottles
HECTARES UNDER VINE 280.00
VITICULTURE METHOD Certified Organic

For many foreign markets, Umberto Cesari is the go-to producer in Romagna, an effective ambassador with almost omnipresent representation of the region, the fruit of years of investments and travel, and of a long-time focus on its local cultural area. This producer learned many years ago that to be a successful farmer one must also be a good businessman. The wines, therefore, tell Romagna's story across the globe as well, marrying the soul of local traditions to the taste of international markets; hence they show rich and spicy, with generous depth, without the traditional burr of the most classic local expressions. The wines presented this year are marked by good volume and body, dense tannins and emphatic oak, all signs of a philosophy quite successful in the global market but one that does few favours for terroir and typicity. Laurento 2010 is all about warmth, with dried herbs and ripe red berry, and rich, fleshy fruit in the mouth.

● Sangiovese di Romagna Laurento Ris. '10	▼▼	3
○ Liano '10	▼	4
● Sangiovese di Romagna Sup. Ca' Grande '12	▼	2
● Tauleto '07	▼	6
● Liano '09	▽▽	5
● Liano '05	▽▽	4
● Moma Rosso '04	▽▽	2*
● Polvere di Stelle '01	▽▽	8
● Sangiovese di Romagna Laurento Ris. '09	▽▽	3
● Sangiovese di Romagna Ris. '06	▽▽	3*
● Tauleto Sangiovese '05	▽▽	6
● Tauleto Sangiovese '04	▽▽	5
● Tauleto Sangiovese '04	▽▽	5
● Tauleto Sangiovese '01	▽▽	5

Chiarli 1860

VIA DANIELE MANIN, 15
41100 MODENA
TEL. 0593163311
www.chiarli.it

CELLAR SALES
ANNUAL PRODUCTION 900,000 bottles
HECTARES UNDER VINE 100.00

The activities of the Chiarli family go as far back as the 1800s, and the precise date, 1860, underscores a history with few peers in Italy. It also demonstrates the family's strong bond with their local area, for example the construction by Anselmo and Mauro Chiarli of a new cellar exclusively dedicated to production from their estate vineyards, this in addition to their traditional production in Modena, amounting to 25 million bottles yearly. The new operation, Cleto Chiarli Tenute Agricole, has revolutionized in just a few years the concept of quality in the Lambrusco world. Fondatore 2012 is a Lambrusco di Sorbara with a restrained, very delicate nose but loads of personality, body and flavour in the mouth, offering surprising impressions of bitter orange and earthiness, fruit of its bottle refermentation. Villa Cialdini 2012 is archetypal Grasparossa, vaunting plenty of tannins, game and earth, a wine with decisive character, fine-contoured fruit and minerality, dry and generously flavoured.

● Lambrusco di Sorbara del Fondatore '12	🍷🍷🍷 3*
● Lambrusco Grasparossa di Castelvetro Villa Cialdini '12	🍷🍷 2*
● Lambrusco di Sorbara Vecchia Modena Premium '12	🍷🍷 2*
● Lambrusco Grasparossa di Castelvetro Centenario '12	🍷🍷 2*
● Lambrusco Grasparossa di Castelvetro Vign. Enrico Cialdini '12	🍷🍷 2*
● Lambrusco di Sorbara Centenario 1860-1960 '12	🍷 2
● Lambrusco di Sorbara del Fondatore '11	🍷🍷🍷 2*
● Lambrusco di Sorbara del Fondatore '09	🍷🍷🍷 2*
● Lambrusco di Sorbara Vecchia Modena Premium '10	🍷🍷🍷 2*
● Lambrusco di Sorbara Vecchia Modena Premium '08	🍷🍷🍷 2*

La Collina

VIA PAGLIA, 19
48013 BRISIGHELLA [RA]
TEL. 054683110
www.lacollina-vinicola.com

CELLAR SALES
ANNUAL PRODUCTION 17,000 bottles
HECTARES UNDER VINE 4.00

In 2002, André Eggli left Switzerland to follow his dream of making wine. Not only did he settle in Romagna, but he accepted the challenge of an unusual and difficult terroir, the loose soils that separate the clays of the first band of hills from nutrient-poor sandstone marls. At his side right from the start was Francesco Bordini, who took the time necessary to forge an impressive style, with expressive yet restrained wines that display crisp, finely delineated fruit. La Collina also makes a very high-quality extravirgin olive oil from Brisighella that is quite extraordinary. The monovarietal sangiovese Sangiovita 2011 is emphatic and taut, with a dry, full-flavoured palate, admirable typicity and an unusual touch of citrus zest on the finish. Cupola 2010 displays nicely-spiced fruit, then well-calibrated tannins, along with good volume and acidity; it closes with tasty mineral. No less attractive is a very classy hint of gaminess.

● Cupola '10	🍷🍷 4
● Sangiovita '11	🍷🍷 3
● Colli di Faenza Sangiovese Cupola '06	🍷🍷 5
● Colli di Faenza Sangiovese Cupola '05	🍷🍷 5
● Colli di Faenza Sangiovese Cupola '04	🍷🍷 5
● Cupola '09	🍷🍷 4
● Cupola '08	🍷🍷 4
● Cupola '07	🍷🍷 5
● Sangiovese di Romagna Sup. Cupola '03	🍷🍷 3
● Sangiovita '10	🍷🍷 3
● Sangiovita '09	🍷🍷 3

Condè

VIA LUCCHINA, 27
47016 PREDAPPIO [FC]
TEL. 0543940860
www.conde.it

CELLAR SALES
RESTAURANT SERVICE
ANNUAL PRODUCTION 250,000 bottles
HECTARES UNDER VINE 77.00

Francesco Condello, now with his daughter Chiara by his side, has carried out one of the most impressive projects in Romagna, collecting into one estate some 100 hectares of vineyards purchased from more than 20 different owners. Assisted by consultant Federico Curtaz, Condello planted 80 hectares of sangiovese, all in full production. He is now building an unusual subterranean cellar, which to the eye looks like a classic Romagna hamlet. The long-term consistency of his initiative has begun to yield very intriguing results. With the most straightforward Sangiovese no longer being produced, only Superiore and Riserva remain, and the latter will spend another year ageing before release. Superiore 2011, which is always the most impressive and crisp, shows lean and elegant; though not the most impressive vintage, it is nonetheless excellent.

● Sangiovese di Romagna Sup. '11	🍷🍷 2*
● Sangiovese di Romagna '09	🍷🍷 2
● Sangiovese di Romagna Capsula Nera '10	🍷🍷 2*
● Sangiovese di Romagna Sup. '09	🍷🍷 2*
● Sangiovese di Romagna Sup. Condè Capsula Blu Ris. '09	🍷🍷 5
● Sangiovese di Romagna Sup. Condè Capsula Rossa '10	🍷🍷 3
● Sangiovese di Romagna Sup. Ris. '08	🍷🍷 2*

Leone Conti

LOC. SANTA LUCIA
VIA POZZO, 1
48018 FAENZA [RA]
TEL. 0546642149
www.leoneconti.it

CELLAR SALES
PRE-BOOKED VISITS
ANNUAL PRODUCTION 80,000 bottles
HECTARES UNDER VINE 17.00

Leone Conti's vineyards are planted in the cool, rich soils of the foothills, ideal for albana and for white grapes in general, which are precisely the iconic wines of Conti and his nephew who helps in this operation. But albana occupies pride of place, with a mature style that is the fruit of a lengthy process of experimentation with styles and processes carried out by the sensitive Conti. His line today displays an admirable reliability and consolidated style. Current research is centred on other minor grape varieties, and the results should be of vivid interest to the entire area. Energy, depth and suppleness mark the lean Contiriserva 2009, which also shows a nice earthiness and sweetish oak. The distinctive Progetto 1 2012 is full-volumed, with the expected tannins. The admirably varietal Never Walk Alone 2012 is crisp, direct and fruity, while the albana and sauvignon blanc Oro et Laboro is all figs and apricots.

● Sangiovese di Romagna Sup. Contiriserva Ris. '09	🍷🍷 4
○ Albana di Romagna Secco Progetto 1 '12	🍷🍷 3
○ Anghingò '11	🍷🍷 3
○ Oro et Laboro	🍷🍷 5
● Sangiovese di Romagna Sup. Never Walk Alone '12	🍷🍷 2*
○ LeOne '11	🍷 3
○ Albana di Romagna Passito Nontiscordardime '07	🍷🍷🍷 6
○ Albana di Romagna Progetto 1 '08	🍷🍷 2*
○ Albana di Romagna Secco Progetto 1 '10	🍷🍷 2*
○ Albana di Romagna Secco Progetto 1 '09	🍷🍷 2*
● Arcolaio '03	🍷🍷 4
● Colli di Faenza Rosso Le Ghiande '03	🍷🍷 3*
● Sangiovese di Romagna '09	🍷🍷 2*
● Sangiovese di Romagna Sup. Contiriserva Ris. '06	🍷🍷 4

Cantine Cooperative Riunite

VIA G. BRODOLINI, 24
42040 CAMPEGINE [RE]
TEL. 0522905711
www.riunite.it

ANNUAL PRODUCTION 65,000,000 bottles
HECTARES UNDER VINE 3,700.00

The enormous Riunite cooperative, owned by the Gruppo Italiano Vini, comprises 2,600 grower-members and their 3,500 hectares of vineyard, with the fruit processed in nine facilities in the Reggio Emilia and Modena areas, making it Italy's largest producer in sales and volume. Despite its bulk, however, its soul and values remain those of a local farmer, as well as its spirit of solidarity; this guiding philosophy is the fruit too of the personal histories of Riunite's managers, starting with President Corrado Casoli. Its bond with the growing area and its growers has led Riunite to invest in the small Albinea Canali cooperative and make it a true laboratory for high quality. Riunite wines are reliable, with incredibly reasonable price-tags for the quality. With a clean, refined bouquet, the elegant monovarietal sorbara Metodo Ancestrale 2012 is minerally, floral, and as tasty as they come. Foglie Rosse 2012 is austere, but fruit-rich, broad, and very well balanced.

- Lambrusco Emilia Metodo Ancestrale
  Albinea Canali '12 ▼▼ 3*
- Lambrusco Chiaro della Falconaia
  Albinea Canali '12 ▼▼ 2*
- Colli di Scandiano e di Canossa
  Albore Gasparossa Codarossa
  Albinea Canali '12 ▼▼ 2*
- Ottocento Nero Lambrusco
  Albinea Canali '12 ▼▼ 2*
- Reggiano Foglie Rosse Albinea Canali '12 ▼▼ 2*
- Reggiano Lambrusco Secco dell'Olma '12 ▼▼ 2*
- Lambrusco Grasparossa di Castelvetro
  Il Fojonco '12 ▼ 2
- ⊙ Reggiano Lambrusco Cuvée 1950 '12 ▼ 2
- ⊙ Reggiano Lambrusco Rosato Secco '12 ▼ 2
- Lambrusco Emilia Vivante '11 ♈ 2*

Corte Manzini

LOC. CÀ DI SOLA DI CASTELVETRO
VIA PER MODENA, 131/3
41014 CASTELVETRO DI MODENA [MO]
TEL. 059702658
www.cortemanzini.it

CELLAR SALES
PRE-BOOKED VISITS
ACCOMMODATION AND RESTAURANT SERVICE
ANNUAL PRODUCTION 85,000 bottles
HECTARES UNDER VINE 20.00

The Manzinis have always exemplified the viticultural family, of which Emilia has legion, but with the added trait, this time rare, of vinifying their estate grapes and selling their own bottled wine. Their 12 hectares of beautifully tended vineyards are in the first band of Modena's hills, prime growing land for grasparossa, and their house style has gradually moved closer to the area's historical style, now harder and harder to find, a Grasparossa with perceptible tannins, a fresh, elegant wine. Immediately evident to the eye is the animal soul of Bolla Rossa 2012, deep and fruit-rich, in the mouth countryish, lean and appropriately dry. Secco 2012 releases violets and petunias, black tea and bitter orange peel, followed by a vibrant tautness in the mouth. The sober Fior di Lambrusco 2012 is crisp and citrussy, with sea tang on the finish.

- Lambrusco
  Grasparossa di Castelvetro Secco '12 ▼▼ 2*
- Lambrusco
  Grasparossa di Castelvetro Secco
  Bolla Rossa '12 ▼▼ 2*
- ⊙ Lambrusco
  Grasparossa di Castelvetro Secco
  Fior di Lambrusco '12 ▼▼ 2*
- Lambrusco
  Grasparossa di Castelvetro
  Amabile '11 ♈ 2*
- ⊙ Lambrusco
  Grasparossa di Castelvetro
  Fior di Lambrusco '11 ♈ 2*
- Lambrusco
  Grasparossa di Castelvetro Secco
  Bolla Rossa '11 ♈ 2*

Costa Archi

LOC. SERRA
VIA RINFOSCO, 1690
48014 CASTEL BOLOGNESE [RA]
TEL. 3384818346
costaarchi.wordpress.com

CELLAR SALES
PRE-BOOKED VISITS
ANNUAL PRODUCTION 15,000 bottles
HECTARES UNDER VINE 13.00

Gabriele Succi's 13 hectares of vines are divided into two separate vineyards on the first row of hillslopes of Castel Bolognese: Podere Beneficio at an elevation of some 80 metres, and Podere Monte Brullo higher up. Both vineyards are planted in evolved reddish calcareous clays with silt and sand intrusions. Despite a certain tendency to produce forceful, dense wines, Succi is evolving a style that privileges the crispness characteristic of sangiovese to express some elegance and to give the palate a sustained progression. Monte Brullo 2009 is quite expressive of its terroir, exhibiting the forcefulness of the clay soils of the first band of hills in northern Romagna. Dry and lean, even hard in spots, with minerally pencil lead and fine fruit, its supple palate flows evenly, creating fine character and thrust.

Denavolo

LOC. GATTAVERA
FRAZ. DENAVOLO
29020 TRAVO [PC]
TEL. 3356480766
denavolo@gmail.com

CELLAR SALES
ANNUAL PRODUCTION 15,000 bottles
HECTARES UNDER VINE 3.00

Denavolo, located in the upper Val Trebbia, boasts a historical heritage of white varieties: ortrugo, malvasia di Candia aromatica, trebbiano romagnolo, and marsanne. Giulio Armani interprets these in his own way, using lengthy macerations, which he manages with masterful ability. The results are complex, multifaceted wines with kaleidoscopic bouquets and crisp, vibrant, dry palates. The harmony of components in these whites is remarkable, creating ultra sheer easy drinking without loss of character and interest. Catavela 2012, with fragrant spring flowers, grapefruit and plum, lays out a self-confident acidity and ultra-tasty flavours. Dinavolo 2009 presents kaleidoscopic aromas of yellow peach, black tea, wild herbs and curry plant, with an entry displaying tannins from its lengthy maceration; its acidity powers a crisp finish.

● Sangiovese di Romagna Sup. Monte Brullo Ris. '09	♟♟ 2*
● Sangiovese di Romagna Sup. Assiolo '11	♟♟ 2*
● Colli di Faenza Prima Luce '09	♟♟ 2*
● Colli di Faenza Prima Luce '07	♟♟ 2*
● Il Beneficio '08	♟♟ 2*
● Prima Luce '05	♟♟ 2*
● Sangiovese di Romagna Sup. Assiolo '10	♟♟ 2*
● Sangiovese di Romagna Sup. Assiolo '07	♟♟ 2*
● Sangiovese di Romagna Sup. Il Beneficio '05	♟♟ 2*
● Sangiovese di Romagna Sup. Monte Brullo Ris. '08	♟♟ 2*

○ Catavela '12	♟♟ 2*
○ Dinavolo '09	♟♟ 4
○ Catavela '11	♟♟ 2*
○ Dinavolino '10	♟♟ 2*
○ Dinavolino '09	♟♟ 2*
○ Dinavolo '10	♟♟ 4
○ Dinavolo '08	♟♟ 4
○ Dinavolo '07	♟♟ 4
○ Dinavolo '06	♟♟ 5
○ Dinavolo '05	♟♟ 5

Camillo Donati

LOC. AROLA, 32
43013 LANGHIRANO [PR]
TEL. 0521637204
camillo@camillodonati.it

CELLAR SALES
PRE-BOOKED VISITS
ANNUAL PRODUCTION 70,000 bottles
HECTARES UNDER VINE 11.00
VITICULTURE METHOD Certified Organic

Camillo Donati's passionate commitment to his land and his work are the central tenets of a philosophy that never trivializes the idea of terroir but rather nourishes it with humanity, culture, and the age-old belief that wine is sharing and a sense of community. Add to that his pleasure in talking with those who make the climb up to his cellar to buy his wines; his passion for hunting, which is nothing less than love for nature and its cycles; and his readiness to accept the growing year and whatever nature brings. He manages his 11 hectares of vineyard together with his niece Minia, and his wines, all made by bottle refermentation with no disgorgement, are among the region's most exciting. La Mia Barbera 2012 truly enthuses, a wine that is meaty, well-fruited, bright and multifaceted, with blossoms scattered here and there; there's lovely minerality, and an acidity that drives it forever. Il Mio Lambrusco 2012, dry and well cadenced, alternates delicate fresh vegetable with clean-contoured fruit.

● Il Mio Lambrusco '12	♟♟ 2*
● La Mia Barbera '12	♟♟ 2*
○ Il Mio Malvasia '11	♟♟ 2*
☉ Il Mio Malvasia Rosa '12	♟♟ 2*
○ Il Mio Sauvignon '12	♟♟ 2*
○ Il Mio Trebbiano '12	♟♟ 2*
● Il Mio Lambrusco '10	♟♟ 2*
○ Il Mio Malvasia '10	♟♟ 2*
○ Il Mio Malvasia '09	♟♟ 2*
☉ Il Mio Malvasia Rosa '10	♟♟ 2
○ Il Mio Sauvignon '09	♟♟ 2*
○ Il Mio Sauvignon '08	♟♟ 2*
○ Il Mio Sauvignon '07	♟♟ 2*
○ Il Mio Trebbiano '09	♟♟ 2*
● La Mia Barbera '10	♟♟ 2*
● La Mia Barbera '08	♟♟ 2*

Drei Donà Tenuta La Palazza

LOC. MASSA DI VECCHIAZZANO
VIA DEL TESORO, 23
47100 FORLÌ
TEL. 0543769371
www.dreidona.it

CELLAR SALES
PRE-BOOKED VISITS
ANNUAL PRODUCTION 130,000 bottles
HECTARES UNDER VINE 27.00

The Drei Donà family enjoys a historic relationship with Romagna, even if the modern stage of this experience only began in 1981, with Claudio's decision to invest in a high quality project with the family vineyards in Vecchiazzano. Apart from its obvious success, what bears underscoring is the stylistic consistency that the wines exhibit, always offering austerity and depth, with rich, ripe tannins, wines that always figure among the top-ranked in the region. Pruno 2010 rests solidly in the furrow of tradition, warm and rich on the nose, followed by a gorgeous acidity plus dense tannins that show a hint of dryness from a tad too much oak, but overall nicely balanced. The elegant yet austere Cuvée Palazza 2010, dry and vibrant, hints of toast and mint.

● Sangiovese di Romagna Sup. Pruno Ris. '10	♟♟ 5
● Le Vigne Nuove '12	♟♟ 2*
● Sangiovese di Romagna Sup. Cuvée Palazza Ris. '10	♟♟ 5
○ Il Tornese '11	♟ 3
● Notturno '11	♟ 3
○ Il Tornese Chardonnay '95	♟♟♟ 3*
● Magnificat Cabernet Sauvignon '94	♟♟♟ 3*
● Sangiovese di Romagna Sup. Pruno Ris. '08	♟♟♟ 5
● Sangiovese di Romagna Sup. Pruno Ris. '07	♟♟♟ 5
● Sangiovese di Romagna Sup. Pruno Ris. '06	♟♟♟ 5
● Sangiovese di Romagna Sup. Pruno Ris. '01	♟♟♟ 4*

Stefano Ferrucci

VIA CASOLANA, 3045/2
48014 CASTEL BOLOGNESE [RA]
TEL. 0546651068
www.stefanoferrucci.it

CELLAR SALES
PRE-BOOKED VISITS
ANNUAL PRODUCTION 95,000 bottles
HECTARES UNDER VINE 15.00

Ferrucci has 16 hectares of vineyards in the Serra subzone, planted in mid-slope clay soils at elevations of 200-250 metres, in an area historically respected for its Albanas. Sangiovese, however, is the winery standard-bearer, and Domus Caia admirers in Romagna are legion. Ilaria and Serena Ferrucci, together with Federico Giotto and Andrea Ruggeri, re-styled this historic wine made from slightly-dried sangiovese, preferring it a tad crisper and more elegant, but keeping loyally to the basic style set by their father Stefano. A complex bouquet marks Domus Caia 2010, with tanned leather, spices and dried plum, complemented by a sapid, elegant palate marrying notes of semi-dried grapes to classic Sangiovese verve. The full, taut Domus Aurea 2011 hints at dried figs and apricot; it has a rich earthiness and closes on lovely candied lemon.

Paolo Francesconi

LOC. SARNA
VIA TULIERO, 154
48018 FAENZA [RA]
TEL. 054643213
www.francesconipaolo.it

CELLAR SALES
PRE-BOOKED VISITS
RESTAURANT SERVICE
ANNUAL PRODUCTION 20,000 bottles
HECTARES UNDER VINE 16.00
VITICULTURE METHOD Certified Organic

Wine-grower Paolo Francesconi cultivates 16 hectares of vineyards in evolved red clay soils in the very first band of hills of Faenza, vinifying only a part of the grapes he grows. He farms biodynamically and follows a rigorously artisanal philosophy in his winemaking, using no additives of any kind. Francesconi long ago perfected his expertise with sangiovese, and he has now begun to work on albana, Romagna's other main player; he utilizes lengthy macerations on the skins, with intriguing results. Limbecca 2011 is an archetypal Romagna Sangiovese grown in the clays of the first band of hills. Generous, fruit-full and chewy, it displays good energy from the union of acidity and a concluding touch of mineral. Maceration on the skins gives a special quality to Arcaica, a dry, crisp and elegant Albana, with summer flowers and herbs forming a nice complexity.

○ Albana di Romagna Passito Domus Aurea '11	♙♙ 5
● Sangiovese di Romagna Sup. Domus Caia Ris. '10	♙♙ 5
○ Colli di Faenza Bianco Chiaro della Serra '12	♙ 2
● Sangiovese di Romagna Auriga '12	♙ 2
● Sangiovese di Romagna Sup. Centurione '12	♙ 2
○ Trebbiano di Romagna Mattinale '12	♙ 1*
○ Albana di Romagna Passito Domus Aurea '10	♟♟ 5
○ Albana di Romagna Passito Domus Aurea '09	♟♟ 5
● Sangiovese di Romagna Auriga '11	♟♟ 2*
● Sangiovese di Romagna Sup. Domus Caia Ris. '09	♟♟ 5

● Sangiovese di Romagna Sup. Limbecca '11	♙♙♙ 3*
○ Arcaica '12	♙♙ 3
● D'Incanto Centesimo Passito '12	♙♙ 4
● Vite in Fiore '11	♙♙ 3
● Sangiovese di Romagna Sup. Limbecca '10	♟♟♟ 3*
● D'Incanto '11	♟♟ 5
● D'Incanto '09	♟♟ 4
● Impavido '09	♟♟ 5
● Impavido '08	♟♟ 5
● Sangiovese di Romagna Sup. Le Iadi Ris. '08	♟♟ 5
● Sangiovese di Romagna Sup. Limbecca '09	♟♟ 3*
● Sangiovese di Romagna Sup. Limbecca '08	♟♟ 2*

Maria Galassi

LOC. PADERNO DI CESENA
VIA CASETTE, 688
47023 CESENA [FC]
TEL. 054721177
www.galassimaria.it

CELLAR SALES
PRE-BOOKED VISITS
ANNUAL PRODUCTION 18,000 bottles
HECTARES UNDER VINE 18.00
VITICULTURE METHOD Certified Organic

Maria Galassi has been managing her 20 hectares of vineyards for 20 years now with the deepest respect, making them an invaluable asset for all of Romagna. Located in the valley of the Savio river and Bertinoro, they are planted in classic Bertinoro soils, with abundant active limestone and seabed tuff. Winemaker Francesco Bordini vinifies and bottles a selection of the grapes, following a production philosophy that is now mature and consistent: vibrant, mineral-edged wines, always showing elegance and clean contours. NatoRe 2010 is elegantly terroir faithful and aged in large casks. Delicate white peach, violets, woods and earth delight the nose, while a forceful character propels its lengthy progression, aided by dense, ripe tannins. Paternus 2011 is open, broad and full-flavoured.

Gallegati

VIA LUGO, 182
48018 FAENZA [RA]
TEL. 0546621149
www.aziendaagricolagallegati.it

CELLAR SALES
PRE-BOOKED VISITS
ACCOMMODATION
ANNUAL PRODUCTION 15,000 bottles
HECTARES UNDER VINE 6.00

The thoroughly artisanal commitment of Cesare and Antonio Gallegati is the stylistic hallmark of this operation, long one of the most interesting in the Faenza area. High quality vineyard management and an increasingly self-confident, classic approach in the cellar make Corallo Nero one of the most impressive interpreters of the Romagna clay soils, with a style magically balanced between the terroir's forcefulness and an admirably lean austerity well supported by crisp acidities. The Gallegati Sangioveses display great depth and an extraordinary longevity. Albana Regina di Cuori 2010 showcases the tannins classic to the variety, infusing them indeed with tangy capers and eucalyptus; the expected fig, apricot and honey are in evidence as well, enhancing its full, supple structure. The austere, dry Corallo Nero 2010 shows fruit that segues into mineral.

● Sangiovese di Romagna Sup. NatoRe '10	♟♟♟ 2*
● Sangiovese di Romagna Sup. Paternus '11	♟♟ 2*
● Sangiovese di Romagna NatoRe Ris. '07	♟♟ 5
● Sangiovese di Romagna Paternus '07	♟♟ 2*
● Sangiovese di Romagna Sup. NatoRe '07	♟♟ 2
● Sangiovese di Romagna Sup. NatoRe Ris. '09	♟♟ 2*
● Sangiovese di Romagna Sup. NatoRe Ris. '08	♟♟ 2*
● Sangiovese di Romagna Sup. Paternus '10	♟♟ 2*
● Sangiovese di Romagna Sup. Paternus '09	♟♟ 2*

○ Albana di Romagna Passito Regina di Cuori Ris. '10	♟♟♟ 4*
● Sangiovese di Romagna Sup. Corallo Nero Ris. '10	♟♟ 4
● Colli di Faenza Rosso Corallo Blu Ris. '10	♟♟ 4
○ Albana di Romagna Passito Regina di Cuori Ris. '09	♟♟♟ 4*
● Sangiovese di Romagna Sup. Corallo Nero Ris. '06	♟♟♟ 3
● Colli di Faenza Rosso Corallo Blu Ris. '06	♟♟ 4
● Sangiovese di Romagna Sup. Corallo Nero Ris. '09	♟♟ 4
● Sangiovese di Romagna Sup. Corallo Nero Ris. '08	♟♟ 4
● Sangiovese di Romagna Sup. Corallo Nero Ris. '07	♟♟ 4

Gruppo Cevico

VIA FIUMAZZO, 72
48022 LUGO [RA]
TEL. 0545284711
www.gruppocevico.com

CELLAR SALES
PRE-BOOKED VISITS
ANNUAL PRODUCTION 20,000,000 bottles
HECTARES UNDER VINE 6,700.00
VITICULTURE METHOD Certified Organic

Cevico, one of the region's largest cooperatives, exhibits an attachment to its local area that has given it a major role in the renaissance of the region's traditional wines. Its home-field advantage is its ability to produce terroir-driven wines with excellent quality-price ratios and to self-confidently assume ambassadorship of an often undervalued area. Cevico's 4,500 grower-members tend 6,700 hectares of vineyard, which yield 2.5% of Italy's wine production. The main brands are Terre Cevico, Vigneti Galassi, Tenuta Masselina, Sancrispino, Ronco, Romandiola, Bernardi, and Rocche Malatestiane. Cevico's bottlings put out very good performances, testifying to an overall reliability which over the last few years has literally become the house style. Terre Cevico Superiore 2011 shows superb typicity, chewy, crisp and fragrant on the palate, dry and with impressive tannins.

Lini 910

LOC. CANOLO DI CORREGGIO
VIA VECCHIA CANOLO, 7
42015 CORREGGIO [RE]
TEL. 0522690162
www.lini910.it

CELLAR SALES
PRE-BOOKED VISITS
ANNUAL PRODUCTION 400,000 bottles
HECTARES UNDER VINE 25.00
VITICULTURE METHOD Certified Organic

The priceless expertise that Fabio and Massimo Lini gained as consultants to various local wineries gave this small family operation the opportunity to select truly fine base wines for the production of their classic method wines, for which they enjoy one of Italy's most historic reputations. Now the winery is experiencing a thrust of new energy thanks to their children, cousins Alicia and Alberto, who are today communicating that history and marketing their prestigious wines. One hundred years of history and ceaseless striving for quality have forged a line of classic, reliable wines. The complex La Gran Cuvée, a monovarietal salamino of the 2009 and 2010 vintages, offers an array of bitterish citrus zest, black tea and earth tones developed over its 36 months on lees. It is dry, richly-flavoured and spicy, with superb depth. The clean and rigorous Rosé 2012 is full-volumed, with an energy-laden, sea-salt finale.

● Sangiovese di Romagna Sup. Terre Cevico '11	⚆⚆ 3
○ Albana di Romagna Secco Romandiola '12	⚆⚆ 3
○ Colli di Rimini Biancame Le Rocche Malatestiane San Gregorio '12	⚆⚆ 2*
● Colli di Rimini Rosso Le Rocche Malatestiane '12	⚆⚆ 2
● Sangiovese di Romagna Sup. Vign. Galassi '12	⚆⚆ 2*
● Sangiovese di Romagna Terre Cevico '12	⚆⚆ 2*
● Sangiovese di Romagna Vign. Galassi '12	⚆⚆ 2*
● Sangiovese di Romagna Il Malatesta Sup. Romandiola '10	⚇⚇ 2*
● Sangiovese di Romagna Sup. Vign. Galassi '10	⚇⚇ 2*
● Sangiovese di Romagna Vign. Galassi '11	⚇⚇ 2*

○ In Correggio Brut M. Cl. Bianco '09	⚆⚆ 4
● In Correggio Brut M. Cl. Gran Cuvée	⚆⚆ 4
○ In Correggio Lambrusco Rosato '12	⚆⚆ 2*
○ In Correggio Moscato Spumante '12	⚆⚆ 2*
● In Correggio Lambrusco Scuro '12	⚆ 2
○ In Correggio Brut M. Cl. '07	⚇⚇ 4
○ In Correggio Brut M. Cl. '06	⚇⚇ 4
○ In Correggio Brut M. Cl. '04	⚇⚇ 4
● In Correggio Brut Rosso M. Cl. '08	⚇⚇ 4
● In Correggio Brut Rosso M. Cl. '05	⚇⚇ 3*
● In Correggio Brut Rosso M. Cl. '03	⚇⚇ 3*
⊙ In Correggio Lambrusco Rosato '11	⚇⚇ 2*
⊙ In Correggio Lambrusco Rosato '10	⚇⚇ 2*
● In Correggio Lambrusco Scuro '10	⚇⚇ 2*
⊙ In Correggio Moscato Spumante '11	⚇⚇ 2*
○ In Correggio Moscato Spumante '09	⚇⚇ 2*

Luretta

CASTELLO DI MOMELIANO
29010 GAZZOLA [PC]
TEL. 0523971070
www.luretta.com

CELLAR SALES
PRE-BOOKED VISITS
ANNUAL PRODUCTION 300,000 bottles
HECTARES UNDER VINE 50.00
VITICULTURE METHOD Certified Organic

Felice Salamini and his son Lucio display adroit creativity and personality in running this operation, founded in 1992. Their 50 hectares of vineyards are distributed in various areas of the Colli Piacentini. White wines are in the spotlight here, with regard to both quantity and philosophy, reflecting Salamini's passion not only for such wines but for classic methods as well, which he focused on right from the earliest years here. So it's no wonder that his most popular wine is a classic method, Principessa, with On Attend Les Invités close behind, which enjoys a cadre of loyal aficionados. On Attend Les Invités 2011, brimming with surprises, starts out broad and kaleidoscopic then develops a fine rhythm, finally closing, full-volumed and dry, on hazelnut and sea-salt. Selin dl'Armari 2011 is a well-made, crisp cask-aged white, with a silver-like timbre of gunflint and white-fleshed fruit

Lusenti

LOC. CASE PICCIONI, 57
29010 ZIANO PIACENTINO [PC]
TEL. 0523868479
www.lusentivini.it

CELLAR SALES
PRE-BOOKED VISITS
ANNUAL PRODUCTION 120,000 bottles
HECTARES UNDER VINE 17.00

Ludovica Lusenti tends 17 hectares in the high part of Val Tidone, near the regional border. At around 300 metres above sea level, this area shows great potential for wines with freshness and elegance. For some years now, Ludovica has aimed toward a philosophy of respect in the vineyard and cellar, and the winery has undergone a real transformation, moving closer to the world of natural wine and the more traditional spirit of the area. For example, two products are made with the technique of bottle refermentation with no disgorgement: the Malvasia Frizzante Emiliana and Gutturnio Frizzante Tournesol. The deep Cresta al Sole 2009 is earthy, minerally and dry, even showing a touch of gaminess, with tight tannins but an acidity-driven breadth. Emiliana 2012, bottle refermented without disgorgement, shows citrussy and zesty, with lovely bitter notes and a consistent drive of fine acidity.

⊙ C. P. Brut Rosé On Attend les Invités '11	♀♀ 4
○ C. P. Chardonnay Selin dl'Armari '11	♀♀ 4
○ C. P. Malvasia Dolce Le Rane '10	♀♀ 6
○ Principessa Pas Dosé Brut M. Cl. '09	♀♀ 4
○ C. P. Malvasia Boccadirosa '12	♀ 3
○ C. P. Sauvignon I Nani e Le Ballerine '12	♀ 3
● C. P. Cabernet Sauvignon Corbeau '00	♀♀♀ 4*
● C. P. Barbera Carabas '03	♀♀ 4
● C. P. Cabernet Sauvignon Corbeau '03	♀♀ 4
● C. P. Cabernet Sauvignon Corbeau '01	♀♀ 4
○ C. P. Malvasia Boccadirosa '11	♀♀ 2*
○ C. P. Malvasia Boccadirosa '10	♀♀ 2*
○ C. P. Malvasia Boccadirosa '07	♀♀ 3*
○ C. P. Malvasia Dolce Le Rane '08	♀♀ 2*
○ C. P. Sauvignon I Nani e Le Ballerine '11	♀♀ 3
○ C.P. Sauvignon Cardass '07	♀♀ 3*

● C. P. Gutturnio Sup. Cresta al Sole '09	♀♀ 3*
● C. P. Gutturnio Frizzante Tournesol '11	♀♀ 2*
○ C. P. Malvasia Frizzante Emiliana '12	♀♀ 2*
○ C. P. Malvasia Passito Il Piriolo '10	♀♀ 5
● C. P. Bonarda La Picciona '02	♀♀ 3
● C. P. Cabernet Sauvignon Villante '00	♀♀ 4
● C. P. Gutturnio Frizzante '10	♀♀ 2*
● C. P. Gutturnio Frizzante Tournesol '10	♀♀ 2*
● C. P. Gutturnio Sup. Cresta al Sole '08	♀♀ 3
● C. P. Gutturnio Sup. Cresta al Sole '07	♀♀ 3
○ C. P. Malvasia Bianca Regina '08	♀♀ 3
○ C. P. Malvasia Bianca Regina '07	♀♀ 3
○ C. P. Malvasia Frizzante Emiliana '11	♀♀ 2*
○ C. P. Malvasia Passito Il Piriolo '09	♀♀ 5
○ C. P. Malvasia Passito Il Piriolo '08	♀♀ 5
● Vigna Martin IV '08	♀♀ 3

Alberto Lusignani

LOC. VIGOLENO
VIA CASE ORSI, 9
29010 VERNASCA [PC]
TEL. 0523895178
lusignani@agonet.it

CELLAR SALES
PRE-BOOKED VISITS
ANNUAL PRODUCTION 3,000 bottles
HECTARES UNDER VINE 10.00

Vigoleno is a strikingly beautiful, perfectly intact, fortified village, like travelling back in time to over a thousand years ago. Here, a small core of producers proudly carries on the ancient tradition for Vin Santo from Vigoleno. This wine is made from rare native grapes like melara and santa maria, as well as berverdino, trebbiano, and marsanne, the latter a variety grown here historically and known locally as champagne. These grapes are harvested, rather early, part dried, allowed long fermentation and aged for a few years with no topping up. Lusignani is the principal producer in this tradition, mostly carried on in a family operation. Vin Santo 2003 is produced in over 1,000 bottles, a rarity at family-run Vigoleno, where "production" is on a small scale. A complex nose boasts espresso, zabaglione and hints of sea salt, plus capers and laurel. Candied citrus and black liquorice lace the palate, while the finish lays out richly fragrant flavours.

○ C. P. Vin Santo di Vigoleno '03	♥♥ 8
○ C. P. Vin Santo di Vigoleno '02	♀♀ 6
○ C. P. Vin Santo di Vigoleno '01	♀♀ 6
○ C. P. Vin Santo di Vigoleno '99	♀♀ 7
○ C. P. Vin Santo di Vigoleno '98	♀♀ 6
○ C. P. Vin Santo di Vigoleno '97	♀♀ 6
○ C. P. Vin Santo di Vigoleno '96	♀♀ 6
○ C. P. Vin Santo di Vigoleno '94	♀♀ 6
● Cabernet Sauvignon '03	♀♀ 2*
● Cabernet Sauvignon '02	♀♀ 2*
○ Colli Piacentini Vin Santo di Vigoleno '91	♀♀ 6

Giovanna Madonia

LOC. VILLA MADONIA
VIA DE' CAPPUCCINI, 130
47032 BERTINORO [FC]
TEL. 0543444361
www.giovannamadonia.it

CELLAR SALES
PRE-BOOKED VISITS
RESTAURANT SERVICE
ANNUAL PRODUCTION 55,000 bottles
HECTARES UNDER VINE 12.00

The Bertinoro soils are unique to Romagna, with a high proportion of active limestone and the presence of spungone seabed tuff that is widespread and visible in the vineyards. Giovanna Madonia's operation adds a third characteristic, the terroir of Monte Maggio, which is cooler than that facing the Adriatic, and consequently with a ripening period up to 20 days slower, a contributing factor to the considerable ageing time her wines need in the bottle. Somewhat rough but always authentic, classic even, these are fascinating, multifaceted wines. Even the labels are remarkable, based on the drawings of famous political cartoonist Altan, a family friend. The sangiovese Ombroso 2009 needs time to display its qualities, even in the glass; lean and minerally, it is a wild thing, resistant in its evanescence. Very linear, yet broad and earthy, this is an ultra-elegant wine that over the years has maintained a great stylistic consistency.

● Sangiovese di Romagna Sup. Ombroso Ris. '09	♥♥ 5
● Colli Romanga Centrale Barlume Ris. '11	♥♥ 4
○ Albana di Romagna Secco Neblina '12	♥ 2
● Sangiovese di Romagna Sup. Ombroso Ris. '06	♀♀♀ 5
● Sangiovese di Romagna Sup. Ombroso Ris. '01	♀♀♀ 5
● Colli Romanga Centrale Barlume Ris. '09	♀♀ 4
● Sangiovese di Romagna Sup. Fermavento '10	♀♀ 3
● Sangiovese di Romagna Sup. Fermavento '09	♀♀ 3
● Sangiovese di Romagna Sup. Ombroso Ris. '08	♀♀ 5
● Sangiovese di Romagna Sup. Ombroso Ris. '07	♀♀ 5

Ermete Medici & Figli

LOC. GAIDA
VIA NEWTON, 13A
42040 REGGIO EMILIA
TEL. 0522942135
www.medici.it

CELLAR SALES
PRE-BOOKED VISITS
ANNUAL PRODUCTION 800,000 bottles
HECTARES UNDER VINE 75.00

Alberto Medici has been one of the most formidable ambassadors of Lambrusco in Italy and around the world, and his winery has become a recognized and much appreciated brand. Many harvests ago, the Medici family expanded their long-standing family operation with an agricultural project that gave them complete control over the production chain and improved product quality. The most important wines are produced with grapes from estate-owned plots and a philosophy that lends elegance, continuity and above all longevity. Medici also produces an excellent traditional balsamic vinegar of Reggio Emilia. Concerto has always exhibited impressive consistency; this year it conquers its fifth consecutive Tre Bicchieri, completely unprecedented for a Lambrusco. Austere, deep, with clean-edged fruit, and even smoky at some moments, it lays out a beautiful mosaic of white peach, black tea and violets.

● Reggiano Lambrusco Concerto '12	♛♛♛	2*
● Reggiano Assolo '12	♛♛	2*
● Reggiano I Quercioli '12	♛♛	1*
○ Colli di Scandiano e di Canossa Malvasia Frizzante Secco Daphne '12	♛	3
○ Nebbie d'Autunno Frizzante '12	♛	2
● Reggiano Concerto '10	♛♛♛	2*
● Reggiano Lambrusco Concerto '11	♛♛♛	2*
● Reggiano Lambrusco Concerto '09	♛♛♛	2*
● Reggiano Lambrusco Concerto '08	♛♛♛	2*
● Reggiano Assolo '09	♛♛	2
● Reggiano Assolo '08	♛♛	2*
● Reggiano Assolo '07	♛♛	2*
● Reggiano Assolo '06	♛♛	1*
● Reggiano Lambrusco Assolo '11	♛♛	2*

Monte delle Vigne

LOC. OZZANO TARO
VIA MONTICELLO, 13
43046 COLLECCHIO [PR]
TEL. 0521309704
www.montedellevigne.it

CELLAR SALES
PRE-BOOKED VISITS
ACCOMMODATION
ANNUAL PRODUCTION 350,000 bottles
HECTARES UNDER VINE 60.00

With the new cellar finished and many hectares of vineyards planted, Andrea Ferrari and Paolo Pizzarotti have put a lot of resources into play with their project, one that shows remarkable potential in the area around Parma. Production is aimed mostly at still wines, original and unusual for an operation in Emilia, and they have also invested heavily in terms of experimentation. The international style always shows a quality that is the product of good grapes and well-managed vineyards. The wines evidence at times a tad too much technique and wood over terroir quality. The acidity of Malvasia Callas 2012 drives a fine, fruit-laden progression, with a touch of grapefruit and citron, and even, unusually, tropical fruit. Malvasia Frizzante Dolce 2012 gives the variety a most balanced and elegant development, with superb overall proportion in the mouth.

○ Callas Malvasia '12	♛♛	2
● Colli di Parma Malvasia Poem '12	♛♛	2*
○ Malvasia Frizzante Dolce '12	♛♛	2*
● Colli di Parma Lambrusco I Calanchi '12	♛	5
● Lambrusco Emilia '12	♛	2
● Nabucco '11	♛	4
● Argille Malvasia '08	♛♛	5
○ Callas Malvasia '11	♛♛	4
○ Callas Malvasia '07	♛♛	3
● Colli di Parma Malvasia Poem '11	♛♛	2*
● Colli di Parma Rosso Frizzante '10	♛♛	2*
● Lambrusco '08	♛♛	2*
● Lambrusco '07	♛♛	2*
● Lambrusco Emilia '10	♛♛	2*
● Nabucco '06	♛♛	4
● Nabucco '03	♛♛	4

Fattoria Monticino Rosso

VIA MONTECATONE, 7
40026 IMOLA [BO]
TEL. 054240577
www.fattoriadelmonticinorosso.it

CELLAR SALES
PRE-BOOKED VISITS
ANNUAL PRODUCTION 70,000 bottles
HECTARES UNDER VINE 18.00

The partnership of Gianni and Luciano Zeoli, and Giancarlo Soverchia always gives Romagna some interesting wines, especially whites, produced with a philosophy of constant research, patience, and waiting times respectful of development. With the reds, Giancarlo's research, at times quite creative and poetic, produces dreamy, original wines, although occasionally not exactly within the reach of everyone, but he achieves his most successful results with the albana variety. The Codronchio, a dry wine made from botrytized albana grapes, has become the showcase wine for this estate and philosophy. A Special Edition 2011, produced only in magnum, displays a delicate, stylish nose of great richness, with toastiness, melon, plum, spring flowers and mountain herbs, then a vibrant, zesty palate and a richly-flavoured, minerally finish. Codronchio 2011 is rich and briny, with a long-driving acidity.

○ Albana di Romagna Secco A Special Edition '11	▼▼ 3*
○ Albana di Romagna Secco A '12	▼▼ 2*
○ Albana di Romagna Secco Codronchio '11	▼▼ 3
○ Albana di Romagna Secco Codronchio Special Edition '10	▼▼ 3
● Sangiovese di Romagna Sup. Le Morine '09	▼▼ 3
● Sangiovese di Romagna Sup. Le Morine Ris. '08	▼▼ 4
● Sangiovese di Romagna Sup. S '11	▼▼ 2*
○ Albana di Romagna Secco Codronchio '08	♀♀♀ 3*
○ Albana di Romagna Secco Codronchio '10	♀♀ 3*
○ Albana di Romagna Secco Codronchio '09	♀♀ 3*

Fattoria Moretto

VIA TIBERIA, 13B
41014 CASTELVETRO DI MODENA [MO]
TEL. 059790183
www.fattoriamoretto.it

CELLAR SALES
PRE-BOOKED VISITS
ANNUAL PRODUCTION 60,000 bottles
HECTARES UNDER VINE 6.40
VITICULTURE METHOD Certified Organic

With small steps but great focus, this small operation is making a name for itself as one of the top producers of Grasparossa, a classic, country-style Lambrusco that is extremely difficult to calibrate. Fausto and Fabio Altariva tend vineyards at 200 metres above sea level, all with southern or south-eastern exposures and planted in clay soils, where the site climate is ideal for organic management. Vinification includes long maceration and respect for the proper waiting periods, resulting in classic wines with personality, organized by plot, following a concept of interpreting the terroir that is rare for this type. The refined language of the Canova 2012 is a balancing act of well-represented country traditions and features that overcome the difficulties of this complex variety. This wine shows black tea, cherry, orange peel, and a deep, full-flavoured minerality.

● Lambrusco Grasparossa di Castelvetro Secco Canova '12	▼▼ 3*
● Lambrusco Grasparossa di Castelvetro Secco Monovitigno '12	▼▼ 2
● Lambrusco Grasparossa di Castelvetro Secco Tasso '12	▼ 2
● Lambrusco Grasparossa di Castelvetro Secco Canova '11	♀♀ 3
● Lambrusco Grasparossa di Castelvetro Secco Monovitigno '11	♀♀ 3*
● Lambrusco Grasparossa di Castelvetro Secco Tasso '11	♀♀ 2*

Poderi Morini

LOC. ORIOLO DEI FICHI
VIA GESUITA
48018 FAENZA [RA]
TEL. 0546634257
info@poderimorini.com

ANNUAL PRODUCTION 100,000 bottles
HECTARES UNDER VINE 40.00

Alessandro Morini has established a
powerful relationship with this territory,
thanks in part to his extraordinary work
with native varieties from around Faenza
and in part to his constant, clear presence
in the world of wines from Romagna. His
40 hectares under vine are all in the
foothills of Faenza, near the Torre di Oriolo
dei Fichi, a structure that has become the
symbol of this subzone and is even used in
the name. In 2010, Maurizio Castelli joined
the estate, and winery production made a
clear leap in quality. Despite the difficult
vintage, the Sangiovese Nonno Rico 2010
is expansive and well gauged. The nose
has clear fruit, and the palate shows a
precise, supple tannic weave. Unfortunately,
a vegetal note runs right to the finish.
Despite being so eager to please, the Torre
di Oriolo 2011 has great drinkability and
proper overall balance.

● Sangiovese di Romagna Sup. Nonno Rico Ris. '10	♛♛ 2*
● Sangiovese di Romagna Sup. Torre di Oriolo '11	♛ 3
○ Albana di Romagna Secco Sette Note '11	♛ 2
● Sangiovese di Romagna Sup. Morale '10	♛♛ 3
● Sangiovese di Romagna Sup. Nonno Rico Ris. '09	♛♛ 2*
● Sangiovese di Romagna Sup. Nonno Rico Ris. '04	♛♛ 3
● Sangiovese di Romagna Sup. Torre di Oriolo '10	♛♛ 3
● Savignone '11	♛♛ 2*
● Savignone '06	♛♛ 2*
● Traicolli '10	♛♛ 2*

Moro - Rinaldini

FRAZ. CALERNO
VIA ANDREA RIVASI, 27
42049 SANT'ILARIO D'ENZA [RE]
TEL. 0522679190
www.rinaldinivini.it

CELLAR SALES
PRE-BOOKED VISITS
ANNUAL PRODUCTION 100,000 bottles
HECTARES UNDER VINE 15.50

The history of Moro is bound up with the
Rinaldini family, and it is Paola who directs
the operation today, assisted by her
husband Marco Melegari and by their son
Luca on the agricultural side. It was in the
early 1960s when Paola's father, Rinaldo,
began to see that in order to maintain the
quality of the wines, charcuterie and raw
ingredients used in the family restaurant,
he would have to have better control of the
supply chain. Thus the idea of a farm,
which later became the family's main
focus. It lies in the first stretch of hills
between Reggio Emilia and Parma, where
the alluvial soils give the vines good
balance and the wines a lovely minerality.
From a classic concept of Lambrusco, the
well-crafted Pjcol Ross 2012 is dry and
austere, and made from an old native
variety the Rinaldini family has always
promoted and protected. The Rosé 2012 is
a zesty, supple wine.

● Lambrusco Reggiano Pjcol Ross '12	♛♛ 2*
⊙ Rosé Lambrusco Secco '12	♛♛ 2*
● Lambrusco Reggiano '12	♛ 2
● Colli di Scandiano e di Canossa Cabernet Sauvignon Ris. '04	♛♛ 3
● Moro del Moro '04	♛♛ 5
● Moro del Moro '01	♛♛ 5
● Moro del Moro '00	♛♛ 5
● Vigna del Picchio '02	♛♛ 3

Orsi - San Vito

FRAZ. OLIVETO
VIA MONTE RODANO, 8
40050 MONTEVEGLIO [BO]
TEL. 051964521
www.vignetosanvito.it

CELLAR SALES
ANNUAL PRODUCTION 20,000 bottles
HECTARES UNDER VINE 10.00
VITICULTURE METHOD Certified Biodynamic

Having become a full-time winemaker and expert, Federico Orsi is ever more committed to this wonderful family operation. The Orsi family venture began in 2005 when the land was purchased. Federico took charge and immediately began rethinking the entire estate philosophy, aiming for long-term choices that would give precedence to the vines and an agriculture style closer to nature. With great consistency, he also directed cellar operations along the same lines and the results took off in just a few years. Interesting in their language, these wines express the specific character of the various vintages and are fresher and more precise every year. The Vigna del Grotto 2011 is multifaceted, full of details and perspectives. The nose is marine and citrussy, and the palate vibrates on a lovely acidity. The Sui Lieviti 2011 shows expansive, refined tangy notes, and recalls grapefruit, herbs and sage.

Gianfranco Paltrinieri

FRAZ. SORBARA
VIA CRISTO, 49
41030 BOMPORTO [MO]
TEL. 059902047
www.cantinapaltrinieri.it

CELLAR SALES
PRE-BOOKED VISITS
ANNUAL PRODUCTION 90,000 bottles
HECTARES UNDER VINE 15.00

Paltrinieri wines have a country spirit but a refined expression, and are among the great wines from the sorbara grape: fine, sharp, delicate, and full of energy, the pampered offspring of a process that begins in the earth on the estate's 15 hectares, and ends in the small cellar alongside the old family villa where generations of Paltrinieris have lived. The atmosphere is marked by fog and the banks of this spit of land between the Secchia and Panaro rivers, with loose soils unique in the vast Po Valley plain, a place Alberto has interpreted in keeping with the idea of a cru. Despite the non-typical nose, the Leclisse 2012 is sharp and properly lean, with a mineral finish. The Radice 2012 has exotic pineapple and banana nose notes, not of this terroir, but restores full flavour and citrus on the palate, with acidity from this lovely year for Sorbara. The Piria 2012 is elegant and iridescent.

○ C. B. Pignoletto Cl. V. del Grotto '11	♟♟ 3*
○ C. B. Pignoletto Frizzante Sui Lieviti '11	♟♟ 3
● C. B. Rosso Bologna Pro.Vino '10	♟♟ 4
○ C. B. Pignoletto Cl. V. del Grotto '09	♟♟♟ 3*
● C. B. Barbera Pro.Vino '09	♟♟ 2*
● O. D. Cabernet Sauvignon '00	♟♟ £
● C. B. Cabernet Sauvignon Monte Rodano '08	♟♟ 2*
● C. B. Cabernet Sauvignon Monte Rodano '06	♟♟ 2*
○ C. B. Pignoletto Cl. V. del Grotto '10	♟♟ 3*
○ C. B. Pignoletto Cl. V. del Grotto '07	♟♟ 3*
○ C. B. Pignoletto Frizzante '10	♟♟ 2*
○ C. B. Pignoletto Frizzante Sui Lieviti '10	♟♟ 2*
○ C. B. Pignoletto Sup. '09	♟♟ 3
○ C. B. Pignoletto Sup. '05	♟♟ 3
○ C. B. Pignoletto Sup. Monte Rodano '07	♟♟ £

● Lambrusco di Sorbara La Piria '12	♟♟ 2*
● Lambrusco di Sorbara Leclisse '12	♟♟ 2*
● Lambrusco di Sorbara Radice '12	♟♟ 2*
● Lambrusco di Modena Greto '12	♟ 2
● Lambrusco di Sorbara Sant'Agata '12	♟ 2
● Lambrusco di Sorbara Leclisse '10	♟♟♟ 3*
○ Bianco Frizzante Secco '11	♟♟ 2*
● Lambrusco di Sorbara Leclisse '08	♟♟ 2*
● Lambrusco di Sorbara Fermentazione in Bottiglia '09	♟♟ 2
● Lambrusco di Sorbara La Piria '08	♟♟ 1*
● Lambrusco di Sorbara Leclisse '11	♟♟ 3*
● Lambrusco di Sorbara Radice '11	♟♟ 3*
● Lambrusco di Sorbara Radice '10	♟♟ 2*
● Lambrusco di Sorbara Sant'Agata '11	♟♟ 2*
● Lambrusco di Sorbara Sant'Agata '10	♟♟ 2*
● Lambrusco di Sorbara Sant'Agata '08	♟♟ 2*

Fattoria Paradiso

LOC. CAPOCOLLE
VIA PALMEGGIANA, 285
47032 BERTINORO [FC]
TEL. 0543445044
www.fattoriaparadiso.com

CELLAR SALES
PRE-BOOKED VISITS
ANNUAL PRODUCTION 500,000 bottles
HECTARES UNDER VINE 100.00

The history of wine in Romagna runs through here, where for the first time a Riserva version of Sangiovese di Romagna was invented and where Veronelli induced Mario Pezzi to consider the revolutionary idea of a cru in this area back in the early 1970s. Today Graziella Pezzi enthusiastically manages the estate with her family's typical love for the land. She works alongside her son Jacopo Lupo, and together they have helped Fattoria Paradiso play its well-deserved leading role. A cru from the historic Vigna delle Lepri, the Rina Pezzi 2010 has a classic design, especially on the dry, taut palate. There is some sweetness on the nose, but overall it has good balance. A Bordeaux blend produced only in the best vintage years, the Mito 2010 is a fairly technical wine with an interesting vegetal profile, richness and good architecture.

● Mito '10	♥♥ 6
● Sangiovese di Romagna Cuvée Rina Pezzi Ris. '10	♥♥ 3
○ La Vendemmia Tardiva '12	♥ 2
● Sangiovese di Romagna Sup. Cuvée Paradiso '12	♥ 3
● Barbarossa '08	♀♀ 4
● Barbarossa '06	♀♀ 4
● Barbarossa Mario Pezzi Cuvée '09	♀♀ 4
○ Frutto Proibito '08	♀♀ 6
○ Gradisca '10	♀♀ 3
● Mito '05	♀♀ 6
● Sangiovese di Romagna Sup. V. delle Lepri Ris. '08	♀♀ 3
● Sangiovese di Romagna V. Lepri Rina Pezzi Ris. '09	♀♀ 3

Tenuta Pertinello

S.DA ARPINETO PERTINELLO, 2
47010 GALEATA [FC]
TEL. 0543983156
www.tenutapertinello.it

CELLAR SALES
ANNUAL PRODUCTION 50,000 bottles
HECTARES UNDER VINE 12.00

Moreno Mancini chose to aim his production towards elegant, classic Sangioveses, and the work he continues with Fabrizio Moltard, oenologist here since the 2008 harvest, and Luigi Martini, hand and heart of the estate, focuses directly on this objective with the ever-stronger desire to become free from any form of compromise. The sandy, marly soils of the nine hectares under vine in the high part of the Bidente valley, in plots at around 350 metres above sea level, with some reaching 430 metres, are ideal and give these wines freshness, longevity, and a lot of character. The Sasso 2009 expresses the energy of top Sangioveses through tension and power, always in movement. The nose is a world of aromas that escape and return. The palate is a sharp blade that leaves earthy, minerally traces. The upfront oak is a shame, because this wine could aspire to great results. The Bosco 2012 is territorial and austere with clear, juicy fruit.

● Colli Romagna Centrale Sangiovese Il Sasso Ris. '09	♥♥ 5
● Colli della Romagna Centrale Sangiovese Il Bosco '12	♥♥ 2*
● Colli della Romagna Centrale Sangiovese Pertinello '10	♥♥ 3
● Colli Romagna Centrale Sangiovese Pertinello '08	♀♀♀ 3
● Colli della Romagna Centrale Sangiovese Il Bosco '11	♀♀ 2*
● Colli della Romagna Centrale Sangiovese Il Bosco '10	♀♀ 2
● Colli della Romagna Centrale Sangiovese Pertinello '09	♀♀ 3*
● Colli Romagna Centrale Sangiovese Il Sasso Ris. '08	♀♀ 3*
● Sangiovese di Romagna Il Bosco '09	♀♀ 2
● Sangiovese di Romagna Il Bosco '08	♀♀ 2

Poderi dal Nespoli

LOC. NESPOLI
VILLA ROSSI, 50
47012 CIVITELLA DI ROMAGNA [FC]
TEL. 0543989911
www.poderidalnespoli.com

CELLAR SALES
PRE-BOOKED VISITS
ANNUAL PRODUCTION 700,000 bottles
HECTARES UNDER VINE 150.00

The success of this estate is the result of a successful combination of close ties with the area, boasting almost 100 years of history, and an entrepreneurial vision that guarantees resources and farsightedness. This result is possible thanks to the smooth-running association between the Martini family, and Fabio and Celita Ravaioli. The production is the result of an extraordinary knowledge of this land. Grapes from the 30 estate-owned hectares are added to grapes expertly purchased mainly from the same growers in the Bidente valley year after year, guaranteeing quality and consistency. The Nespoli 2010 is a wonderful version of a great classic from Romagna. It is elegant and shows a refined vegetal note and austerity. The palate is close knit, yet always fresh and supple. The tannins are dry, but never rough. This is a deep, expansive wine with good ageing potential.

● Sangiovese di Romagna Sup.	
Il Nespoli Ris. '10	▼▼ 4
● Borgo dei Guidi '11	▼▼ 5
● Sangiovese di Romagna Sup.	
Il Prugneto '12	▼▼ 2*
● Sangiovese di Romagna Sup.	
Il Nespoli Ris. '07	♀♀♀ 4*
● Sangiovese di Romagna Sup.	
Il Nespoli Ris. '06	♀♀♀ 4*
● Sangiovese di Romagna Prugneto '10	♀♀ 2*
● Sangiovese di Romagna Sup.	
Il Nespoli Ris. '09	♀♀ 4
● Sangiovese di Romagna Sup.	
Il Nespoli Ris. '08	♀♀ 4
● Sangiovese di Romagna Sup.	
Il Prugneto '11	♀♀ 2*

Il Pratello

VIA MORANA, 14
47015 MODIGLIANA [FC]
TEL. 0546942038
www.ilpratello.net

CELLAR SALES
PRE-BOOKED VISITS
ANNUAL PRODUCTION 20,000 bottles
HECTARES UNDER VINE 5.50
VITICULTURE METHOD Certified Organic

Instinct has always guided Emilio Placci through the narrow, difficult passages along his visionary and persistent career path, a journey travelled with consistency and great humanity. The challenge began in 1991 with vineyards at 600 metres above sea level seemingly foolish at the time. Today he continues protecting the pure expression and character of his wines, respecting the long periods in their search for balance, and finding the meeting point between the subtle, mineral register of a more natural language and the desire for power and depth. Wine is the child of man, and artisans like Emilio have understood this well. The Mantignano Vecchie Vigne 2009 missed roll call since it has been left to age another year in bottle. The deep, compact Badia 2008 shows earthy, mineral notes, and is powerful and taut on lovely acidity. Woodland motifs and a nice gamey note run alongside austere dark fruit.

● Badia Raustignolo '08	▼▼ 5
● Colli di Faenza Sangiovese	
Mantignano Vecchie Vigne Ris. '04	♀♀♀ 3*
● Mantignano Vecchie Vigne '08	♀♀♀ 3*
● Colli di Faenza Sangiovese	
Badia Raustignolo Ris. '03	♀♀ 5
● Colli di Faenza Sangiovese	
Mantignano Ris. '04	♀♀ 3*
● Colli di Faenza Sangiovese	
Mantignano Ris. '03	♀♀ 3*
● Mantignano Vecchie Vigne '07	♀♀ 2*
● Sangiovese di Romagna Morana '10	♀♀ 2*
● Sangiovese di Romagna Morana '09	♀♀ 2*
● Sangiovese di Romagna Morana '08	♀♀ 2
● Sangiovese di Romagna Morana '06	♀♀ 2*

Tenimenti San Martino in Monte

VIA SAN MARTINO IN MONTE
47015 MODIGLIANA [FC]
TEL. 3292984507
www.sanmartinoinmonte.com

ANNUAL PRODUCTION 4,000 bottles
HECTARES UNDER VINE 5.60

Maurizio Costa has strengthened his family roots in Romagna and become ever more committed over the years to his project here in Modigliana, at 350 metres above sea level, on sandy plots that produce elegant, long-lived wines. Today this estate is going through a period of change that will shift the operation in an ever more territorial direction, with the aim of producing Sangiovese as well as major white wines, exploiting the temperature ranges at this altitude. This estate also has the oldest vine in Romagna, planted in 1922. This bush-trained plant has been patiently revived by the estate oenologist and agronomist, Francesco Bordini. The Vigna 1922 shows best in the coolest vintage years when it assumes grace and an original quality, with a subtle palate and glycerine sweetness that echoes the Mediterranean. This is the case with this dry, elegant 2010 that combines minerality with aromas that range from thyme to pine needles and even pepper.

● Sangiovese di Romagna Sup. V. 1922 Ris. '10	♟♟ 6
○ Colli di Faenza Torre '12	♟♟ 2*
● Sangiovese di Romagna Sup. Gemme '11	♟♟ 6
○ Colli di Faenza V. della Signora '12	♟ 2
● Sangiovese di Romagna Sup. V. 1922 Ris. '07	♟♟ 6
● Sangiovese di Romagna Sup. V. 1922 Ris. '06	♟♟ 6
● Sangiovese di Romagna V. 1922 '08	♟♟ 6
● Sangiovese di Romagna V. 1922 '05	♟♟ 6
● Sangiovese di Romagna V. 1922 '04	♟♟ 6
● Sangiovese di Romagna V. 1922 '03	♟♟ 6
● Vigna alle Querce '08	♟♟ 5
● Vigna alle Querce '07	♟♟ 5
● Vigna alle Querce '06	♟♟ 5
● Vigna alle Querce '05	♟♟ 5

★San Patrignano

VIA SAN PATRIGNANO, 53
47853 CORIANO [RN]
TEL. 0541362111
www.sanpatrignano.org

PRE-BOOKED VISITS
RESTAURANT SERVICE
ANNUAL PRODUCTION 500,000 bottles
HECTARES UNDER VINE 110.00
VITICULTURE METHOD Certified Organic

The community of San Patrignano has always been closely tied to its vineyards, which have become a symbol for top quality production. Since the first harvest, Riccardo Cotarella has managed this winemaking operation. With 110 hectares under vine, this is one of the most important operations in Romagna. Here in the foothills of Rimini, a climate mitigated by the closeness of the sea marks these wines with expressive fruit and smooth tannins even in the Sangiovese, generally an austere and edgy wine. The vineyards are now in their productive maturity, and organized by quality and characteristics, providing a valuable map to help manage production choices starting in the fields. The Ora 2012 comes from an interesting project that exploits the ripeness of the hectares of sangiovese in the community to produce a top quality vintage wine. In its second release, it once again wins the Tre Bicchieri. This wine expands across a lovely freshness, and is dry, savoury and overall well balanced.

● Sangiovese di Romagna Sup. Ora '12	♟♟♟ 3*
● Sangiovese di Romagna Sup. Avi Ris. '09	♟♟ 5
○ Vie '12	♟♟ 3
○ Aulente Bianco '12	♟ 2
● Aulente Rosso '12	♟ 2
● Colli di Rimini Cabernet Montepirolo '06	♟♟♟ 5
● Colli di Rimini Cabernet Montepirolo '04	♟♟♟ 5
● Colli di Rimini Rosso Noi '04	♟♟♟ 4
● Sangiovese di Romagna Sup. Avi Ris. '08	♟♟♟ 5
● Sangiovese di Romagna Sup. Avi Ris. '07	♟♟♟ 5
● Sangiovese di Romagna Sup. Avi Ris. '06	♟♟♟ 5
● Sangiovese di Romagna Sup. Avi Ris. '05	♟♟♟ 5
● Sangiovese di Romagna Sup. Ora '11	♟♟♟ 3*

San Valentino

FRAZ. SAN MARTINO IN VENTI
VIA TOMASETTA, 13
47900 RIMINI
TEL. 0541752231
www.vinisanvalentino.com

CELLAR SALES
PRE-BOOKED VISITS
ACCOMMODATION
ANNUAL PRODUCTION 120,000 bottles
HECTARES UNDER VINE 20.00
VITICULTURE METHOD Certified Biodynamic

Roberto Mascarin, today accompanied at
the estate by his wife, Valeria, had the
acumen and character to close a period at
the estate featuring soft, rich wines, and
much recognition, and begin a new phase
that started by introducing biodynamic
methods to produce fresh, well-balanced
wines. French agronomist Michel Barbaud
and the original and interesting Belgian
consultant Benoit De Coster work alongside
him in this new estate project. The change
will require years to be up and running, but
early results are quite interesting and show
much hope for the future. From mostly
sangiovese with some syrah and
montepulciano, the Vivian 2011 has an
interesting language and ability to express
the idea of a warm territory in an original
way, combining a Mediterranean soul and a
deep, elegant, gamey quality. The finish is
dry and taut. The Scabi 2011 is racy,
supple, balsamic, expansive and fresh.

Cantina Sociale Santa Croce

SS 468 DI CORREGGIO, 35
41012 CARPI [MO]
TEL. 059664007
www.cantinasantacroce.it

CELLAR SALES
PRE-BOOKED VISITS
ANNUAL PRODUCTION 400,000 bottles
HECTARES UNDER VINE 500.00

This historical operation, dating to 1907, is
located in Santa Croce, near Carpi, in the
heart of the zone that gives its name to
Lambrusco Salamino. Its 250 member-
growers farm more than 500 hectares of
vineyard in the plains south of Modena.
Some members are in the province of
Reggio Emilia, just north of the loose-
textured soils ideal for growing sorbara, at
Limidi and Sozzigalli, on the left bank of the
Secchia. These richer, clayey terrains are
perfect for salamino. The original cellar still
serves as the centre of production, where
the expert Villiam Friggeri reigns over the
winemaking and puts his name on the
denomination's finest Salaminos. The fresh,
expansive Salamino Tradizione 2012 is
creamy and direct in its austerely expressed
fruity notes. The Salamino Enoteca 2012 is
dense and meaty, dry and minerally, floral
and elegant. The Sorbara Secco 2012
shows great typicity, and is especially
convincing on the subtle, supple palate.

● Sangiovese di Romagna Sup. Scabi '11	♟♟ 2*
● Vivian '11	♟♟ 3
● Sangiovese di Romagna Sup. Terra di Covignano Ris. '10	♟ 5
● Sangiovese di Romagna Sup. Terra di Covignano Ris. '05	♟♟♟ 5
● Sangiovese di Romagna Sup. Terra di Covignano Ris. '03	♟♟♟ 4
● Sangiovese di Romagna Sup. Terra di Covignano Ris. '02	♟♟♟ 4
● Luna Nuova '04	♟♟ 5
● Sangiovese di Romagna Sup. Scabi '10	♟♟ 2*
● Sangiovese di Romagna Sup. Scabi Capsula Rossa '09	♟♟ 2*
● Vivian '10	♟♟ 3

● Lambrusco di Sorbara Secco '12	♟♟ 2*
● Lambrusco Grasparossa di Castelvetro Linea DOC '12	♟♟ 2*
● Lambrusco Salamino di S. Croce Enoteca '12	♟♟ 1*
● Lambrusco Salamino di S. Croce Tradizione '12	♟♟ 1*
● Il Castello Lambrusco Emilia '12	♟ 1
⊙ Il Castello Lambrusco di Modena Rosato '11	♟♟ 1*
● Lambrusco di Sorbara Secco '11	♟♟ 2*
● Lambrusco Salamino di S. Croce Enoteca '11	♟♟ 1*
● Lambrusco Salamino di S. Croce Enoteca '10	♟♟ 1*
● Reggiano Rosso '11	♟♟ 2*
● Santa Croce Lambrusco Emilia '11	♟♟ 1*

Cantina di Sorbara

VIA RAVARINO-CARPI, 116
41030 BOMPORTO [MO]
TEL. 059909103
www.cantinasorbara.it

CELLAR SALES
PRE-BOOKED VISITS
ANNUAL PRODUCTION 1,400,000 bottles
HECTARES UNDER VINE 600.00

This major operation was born out of the recent merger between the co-operative wineries of Carpi, founded in 1903, and Sorbara, founded in 1923. These dates highlight the powerful roots of co-operative wineries in the culture around Modena, with a tradition starting in the early 20th century, promoted by that great personality, Gino Friedman. Only a small part of production is bottled, and this with the Sorbara winery trademark, allowing precise selection of the parcels of wine destined for bottling. The quality of production has risen over the past few years, and these wines are clearly varietal and speak an interesting language. The Sorbara Terre della Verdeta 2012 has an interesting minerality and great richness of flavour on the palate. This wine has a certain rustic quality and an acidity that gives it energy. The Salamino Le Bolle 2012 has character, personality, gutsy tannins, elegance and overall balance.

● Lambrusco di Modena Rosato Secco Cantina di Carpi 1903 '12	▼▼ 2*
● Lambrusco di Sorbara Secco Omaggio a Gino Friedmann '12	▼▼ 3
● Lambrusco di Sorbara Secco Terre della Verdeta '12	▼▼ 2*
● Lambrusco Salamino di Santa Croce Secco Le Bolle '12	▼▼ 2*
● Lambrusco Salamino di Santa Croce Secco Terre della Verdeta '12	▼▼ 2*
● Lambrusco di Sorbara Secco '12	▼ 2
● Lambrusco di Sorbara Secco '11	♀♀ 2*
● Lambrusco di Sorbara Secco Terre della Verdeta '11	♀♀ 2*
● Lambrusco di Sorbara Secco Villa Badia '11	♀♀ 2*

La Stoppa

LOC. ANCARANO
29029 RIVERGARO [PC]
TEL. 0523958159
www.lastoppa.it

CELLAR SALES
PRE-BOOKED VISITS
RESTAURANT SERVICE
ANNUAL PRODUCTION 160,000 bottles
HECTARES UNDER VINE 32.00
VITICULTURE METHOD Certified Organic

Elena Pantaleoni and Giulio Armani are artisans who classically and reliably interpret their local terroir. Wines from this estate, boasting 100 years of history, are the result of a process that starts in the poor, warm, red clay soils on this narrow spit of land between Val Trebbia and Val Nure, and arrives at cellarwork that is respectful of the waiting periods required by the wine and the expression of the land, with no hypocrisies or invasive procedures. The result is pure, multifaceted wines that are incredibly deep, austere and extraordinarily long-lived. The top wines from this estate are missing: the Macchiona was not produced in 2008, and the 2009 vintage of the Ageno is still ageing. The Trebbiolo 2011, from barbera and bonarda, is clear and direct, balanced between barely hinted earthy notes and fruit. The palate is sharp, juicy and deep. The savoury, taut Vigna del Volta 2009 is multifaceted with notes of dried figs, apricot, black tea and water mint.

● Trebbiolo '11	▼▼ 2*
○ Vigna del Volta '09	▼▼ 5
● C. P. Cabernet Sauvignon Stoppa '96	♀♀♀ 5
○ C. P. Malvasia Passito V. del Volta '06	♀♀♀ 5
○ C. P. Malvasia Passito V. del Volta '04	♀♀♀ 5
○ C. P. Malvasia Passito V. del Volta '03	♀♀♀ 4
○ C. P. Malvasia Passito V. del Volta '97	♀♀♀ 4*
● Macchiona '06	♀♀♀ 4*
● Macchiona '05	♀♀♀ 4
○ Vigna del Volta '08	♀♀♀ 5
○ Ageno '06	♀♀ 4
● Barbera della Stoppa '07	♀♀ 4
● C. P. Barbera della Stoppa '06	♀♀ 4
● C. P. Cabernet Sauvignon Stoppa '02	♀♀ 4
● Macchiona '07	♀♀ 4
● Macchiona '02	♀♀ 5

Terre della Pieve

FRAZ. DIEGARO
VIA EMILIA PONENTE, 2412
47023 CESENA [FC]
TEL. 0547611535
www.terredellepieve.com

PRE-BOOKED VISITS
ANNUAL PRODUCTION 25,000 bottles
HECTARES UNDER VINE 5.00

Sergio Lucchi's five hectares under vine are near Bertinoro, at around 300 metres above sea level, set precisely alongside the Pieve di Polenta featured in the estate name. Soils on estate plots are in every way the classic soils from Bertinoro: clay with a high percentage of active lime and "spungone", a sort of marine tufa typical of this area. The resulting wines are long lived, characterful, minerally, and earthy with a deep, close-knit tannic weave. Lucchi is a timid but tireless winemaker who in the past few years has taken no short cuts to make wines that have become more and more territorial and convincing. The Nobis 2010 is a typical, terroir-based wine with some power on the palate, and dry like the most classic wines from Romagna. A monovarietal from albana grapes left long to dry, the Stil Novo 2009 finds complexity in the oxidative notes of zabaglione, figs, dates and coffee beans, and a dense, rich palate.

● Sangiovese di Romagna Sup. Nobis Ris. '10	♟♟ 3
○ Stil Novo '09	♟♟ 4
● Sangiovese di Romagna Sup. A Virgilio '11	♟ 2
● Sangiovese di Romagna Sup. A Virgilio '10	♟♟ 2*
● Sangiovese di Romagna Sup. A Virgilio '06	♟♟ 2*
● Sangiovese di Romagna Sup. Nobis '04	♟♟ 3
● Sangiovese di Romagna Sup. Nobis Ris. '09	♟♟ 3*

La Tosa

LOC. LA TOSA
29020 VIGOLZONE [PC]
TEL. 0523870727
www.latosa.it

CELLAR SALES
PRE-BOOKED VISITS
ANNUAL PRODUCTION 120,000 bottles
HECTARES UNDER VINE 19.00

Val Nure is known in Piacenza as one of the best-suited areas for producing quality wines. These estate vineyards in particular are planted on quite an interesting stretch of poor red clay, and when we also consider that Stefano Pizzamiglio is a meticulous and sensitive winemaker, we can clearly understand how La Tosa always has perfect, ripe grapes. The process in the cellar tends toward precise, fruity wines, carefully crafted in the smallest detail, soft in expression, and impeccable from a formal standpoint. These wines are the children of this man, and are aimed at mediating some of the most difficult and intractable features of this land. The TerredellaTosa 2012, the Gutturnio from the youngest vineyards, is full of energy expressed through a mineral note, clear, meaty fruit with cherry upfront, and an expansive, full-flavoured body. The Sorriso di Cielo 2012 rediscovers the freshness of the earliest vintages and shows a close-knit texture that expands thanks to lovely acidity. The nose is less interesting, all elderflower.

● C. P. Gutturnio Sup. TerredellaTosa '12	♟♟ 2*
○ C. P. Malvasia Sorriso di Cielo '12	♟♟ 3
● C. P. Cabernet Sauvignon Luna Selvatica '11	♟ 5
● C. P. Gutturnio Sup. Vignamorello '12	♟ 4
○ L'Ora Felice '12	♟ 2
● C. P. Cabernet Sauvignon Luna Selvatica '06	♟♟♟ 5
● C. P. Cabernet Sauvignon Luna Selvatica '04	♟♟♟ 5
● C. P. Cabernet Sauvignon Luna Selvatica '97	♟♟♟ 5
● C. P. Gutturnio Vignamorello '09	♟♟ 4
● C. P. Gutturnio Vignamorello '05	♟♟ 4
● C. P. Gutturnio Vignamorello '03	♟♟ 4*
○ C. P. Malvasia Sorriso di Cielo '07	♟♟ 3*
○ C. P. Sauvignon '07	♟♟ 3*

Tre Monti

LOC. BERGULLO
VIA LOLA, 3
40026 IMOLA [BO]
TEL. 0542657116
www.tremonti.it

CELLAR SALES
PRE-BOOKED VISITS
ANNUAL PRODUCTION 180,000 bottles
HECTARES UNDER VINE 55.00

This estate is divided into two holdings: one in Serra, in the hills of Colli Imolesi, and one in Petrignone, in the foothills of Colli Forlivesi. Soils in the former are mostly white clay with some areas of silt while at Petrignone the clay is more evolved, containing some sand and a river terrace of pebbles that emerges like a leopard's spots. The 55 hectares under vine and years of great experience allow Vittorio Navacchia to choose the best-suited grapes every time for the various estate projects. His authority and skill in managing the vineyards and cellar are proof of the maturity of this major Romagna operation. The Petrignone 2010 is a classic Sangiovese: dry, vibrant, energetic, supple in development and mineral in the finish. The Albana Vigna Rocca 2012 has a refreshing volatile note, and is dry and linear, typical in the elegant tannic touch.

○ Albana di Romagna Secco V. della Rocca '12	🍷🍷 2*
● Colli d'Imola Rosso Boldo '11	🍷🍷 3
● Sangiovese di Romagna Sup. Petrignone Ris. '10	🍷🍷 3
● Sangiovese di Romagna Sup. Campo di Mezzo '12	🍷 2
● Colli di Imola Boldo '97	🍸🍸🍸 3*
● Sangiovese di Romagna Sup. Petrignone Ris. '08	🍸🍸🍸 3*
● Sangiovese di Romagna Sup. Petrignone Ris. '07	🍸🍸🍸 4
● Sangiovese di Romagna Sup. Petrignone Ris. '06	🍸🍸🍸 3
● Sangiovese di Romagna Sup. Petrignone Ris. '05	🍸🍸 3*
● Sangiovese di Romagna Sup. Thea Ris. '07	🍸🍸 4

Vallona

FRAZ. FAGNANO
VIA SANT'ANDREA, 203
40050 CASTELLO DI SERRAVALLE [BO]
TEL. 0516703333
www.fattorievallona.it

CELLAR SALES
PRE-BOOKED VISITS
ANNUAL PRODUCTION 90,000 bottles
HECTARES UNDER VINE 29.00

With his close ties to the area, Maurizio Vallona faithfully interprets the Colli Bolognesi zone. The centre of activity here is work in the vineyards, conducted with precision and rare dedication. In the cellar, his very personal taste gives these wines precision, clarity, and a softness tied to significant residual sugars. Although his choices may be divisive and at times bring debate, they are justified and express a style never betrayed, leading to deep, complex wines that bear witness to the quality of these grapes. From mostly cabernet, the Bologna Rosso 2011 has a mineral, elegant, vegetal character that opens slowly on clear fruit, a palate with decisive flavour and a savoury finish. The Bologna Bianco 2012 opens on spring flowers then leans toward a nice acidity. This masterfully exploits the bitterish aspects of the Pignoletto in all its herb and mineral qualities.

○ C. B. Bologna Bianco '12	🍷🍷 2*
● C. B. Bologna Rosso '11	🍷🍷 2*
○ Primedizione Cuvée 13	🍷🍷 2*
○ C. B. Pignoletto Cl. '12	🍷 4
● C. B. Cabernet Sauvignon Sel. '99	🍸🍸🍸 4*
● C. B. Cabernet Sauvignon Sel. '97	🍸🍸🍸 4*
● C. B. Merlot Affederico '01	🍸🍸🍸 4
● Diggioanni Cabernet Sauvignon '04	🍸🍸🍸 4
● Affederico Merlot '05	🍸🍸 4
● Affederico Merlot '04	🍸🍸 4
● Affederico Merlot '03	🍸🍸 4
○ C. B. Pignoletto '05	🍸🍸 2*
● Diggioanni Cabernet Sauvignon '05	🍸🍸 4
● Diggioanni Cabernet Sauvignon '03	🍸🍸 4

Cantina Valtidone

VIA MORETTA, 58
29011 BORGONOVO VAL TIDONE [PC]
TEL. 0523846832
www.cantinavaltidone.it

CELLAR SALES
PRE-BOOKED VISITS
ANNUAL PRODUCTION 4,500,000 bottles
HECTARES UNDER VINE 1,200.00

Founded in 1966, this co-operative numbers 300 members spread over the ten municipalities of Borgonovo, Castel San Giovanni, Ziano, Pianello, Nibbiano, Caminata, Piozzano, Agazzano, Gazzola and Pecorara, farming 1,200 hectares of hillside vineyards. President Vito Pezzati has succeeded in growing the operation along the lines of new initiatives. In addition to its own brand, it produces the Castelli del Duca line, in collaboration with Ermete Medici. The most satisfaction comes from the Castelli del Duca wines, now managed by the oenologist Beppe Caviola. Reds from this line stand apart from other wines from this cellar in quality and personality. A wine with character, the Ottavio 2011 is fruity, spicy and deep, balanced on the palate thanks to good freshness and a perfectly calibrated tannic weave. The Ranuccio 2011 is mellow and focused, expansive in acidity, and austere in the notes of cherry.

○ Brut M.Cl. Perlage	♟♟ 6
● C. P. Barbera Castelli del Duca Ranuccio '11	♟♟ 2*
● C. P. Bonarda Castelli del Duca Ottavio '11	♟♟ 2*
● C. P. Gutturnio Ris. Castelli del Duca Duca Alessandro '10	♟♟ 2
○ C. P. Malvasia Frizzante Aurora '12	♟ 2
○ C. P. Ortrugo Armonia Frizzante '12	♟ 2
● C. P. Gutturnio Cl. Caesar Augustus '08	♟♟ 2*
● C. P. Gutturnio Cl. Julius '06	♟♟ 2*
● C. P. Gutturnio Sup. Borgo del Conte Flerido '04	♟♟ 2*

Francesco Vezzelli

FRAZ. SAN MATTEO
VIA CANALETTO NORD, 878A
41122 MODENA
TEL. 059318695
aavezzelli@gmail.com

CELLAR SALES
PRE-BOOKED VISITS
ANNUAL PRODUCTION 120,000 bottles
HECTARES UNDER VINE 15.00

Vezzelli is a small family operation founded in 1958, with the third generation now on board. Francesco directs the vineyards and winemaking, while his son Roberto oversees sales. The cellar is located in San Matteo, close to Modena, while the vineyards are in Sozzigalli, in the floodplains between in lowest river levees and the main levee, at the Secchia. These loose, nutrient-poor soils do extraordinary favours for lambrusco sorbara, bringing out lovely floral and mineral qualities. The Grasparossas are vinified here with grapes bought in from Levizzano Rangone. The Selezione 2012 brings out the characteristics of a good year for Sorbara, expressed on a salty, minerally palate that is spirited and elegant. Also made in an interesting, non-filtered version, the MoRosa 2012 is citrussy, sharp, multifaceted, full-flavoured, and always taut.

● Lambrusco di Sorbara Il Selezione '12	♟♟ 2*
⊙ Lambrusco di Sorbara Rosé MoRosa '12	♟♟ 2*
● Lambrusco Grasparossa di Castelvetro Rive dei Ciliegi '12	♟ 2
● Lambrusco Il Bricco di Checco '12	♟ 2
● Lambrusco di Sorbara '09	♟♟ 2
● Lambrusco di Sorbara Il Selezione '11	♟♟ 2*
● Lambrusco di Sorbara Il Selezione '10	♟♟ 2*
⊙ Lambrusco di Sorbara Rosé MoRosa '11	♟♟ 2*
● Lambrusco Grasparossa di Castelvetro Rive dei Ciliegi '11	♟♟ 2*
● Lambrusco Grasparossa di Castelvetro Rive dei Ciliegi '10	♟♟ 2*
● Lambrusco Grasparossa di Castelvetro Rive dei Ciliegi '09	♟♟ 2
● Lambrusco Il Bricco di Checco '11	♟♟ 2*
● Lambrusco Il Bricco di Checco '09	♟♟ 2

EMILIA ROMAGNA

Vigne dei Boschi

LOC. VALPIANA
VIA TURA, 7A
48013 BRISIGHELLA [RA]
TEL. 054651648
www.vignedeiboschi.it

CELLAR SALES
PRE-BOOKED VISITS
ANNUAL PRODUCTION 15,000 bottles
HECTARES UNDER VINE 6.50
VITICULTURE METHOD Certified Biodynamic

Paolo Babini's sensitivity has helped him bring focus to wines in a style made of complex light and dark shades, never boring in their language, and the result of years of patience, experimentation, perseverance, and intuition. The vineyards are located in the Lamone river valley, with marly sandstone soils at the edge of the woods, a major presence in this high part of the valley. The most interesting estate project is the Sangiovese Poggio Tura, made from a vine produced by collecting grafts from hundred-year-old plants in the valley. This open, multifaceted wine is minerally, subtle, and full of energy and flavour. The Poggio Tura 2009 expresses its high territory with earthy tones competing with a fruit that is juicy, deep, austere and mineral. The salty, vibrant palate is full of energy, all grip and elegance. The Monteré 2011, Albana from a 30-year old vine, is linear and dry.

Villa di Corlo

LOC. BAGGIOVARA
S.DA CAVEZZO, 200
41126 MODENA
TEL. 059510736
www.villadicorlo.com

CELLAR SALES
PRE-BOOKED VISITS
ANNUAL PRODUCTION 80,000 bottles
HECTARES UNDER VINE 25.00

Maria Antonietta Munari directs Villa di Corlo with passionate verve, producing not only wine but also Aceto Balsamico Tradizionale di Modena in her recently-restored "acetaia". The winery has two separate properties. The lambrusco vineyards are in Villa di Corlo, in the Modena area, while the international varieties are planted at Cà del Vento, in the Reggio Emilia hills. Each is profoundly different, with the Modena wines more classic and traditional, and Cà del Vento more adventuresome, where its handful of vineyards lie at 500 metres, surrounded by hundreds of hectares of woods. The Grasparossa 2012 is a wine with a country spirit, upfront tannins and a fruit that contrasts with the earthy aspects of the variety. The expansive palate has energy. The Primevo 2012 is mineral, elegant, savoury, subtle, and dry in a flavourful closing. From chardonnay sourced from Cà del Vento, the delicate, fresh Fraeli 2010 has a lovely note of summer flowers, broom in particular.

● Poggio Tura '09	♟♟ 4
○ Monteré '11	♟♟ 6
○ Sedici Anime '11	♟♟ 3
● Poggio Tura '05	♟♟♟ 5
○ Borgo Casale '05	♟♟ 4
○ Monteré '06	♟♟ 6
● Nero Selva '06	♟♟ 3
● Poggio Tura '08	♟♟ 4
● Poggio Tura '07	♟♟ 4
● Rosso per Te '06	♟♟ 3
○ Sedici Anime '10	♟♟ 3
○ Sedici Anime '09	♟♟ 3
○ Sedici Anime '08	♟♟ 3
○ Sedici Anime '07	♟♟ 3
● Sette Pievi '03	♟♟ 4
● Sette Pievi '01	♟♟ 4*

○ Fraeli Brut Blanc de Blancs '10	♟♟ 3
● Lambrusco di Sorbara Primevo '12	♟♟ 2*
● Lambrusco Grasparossa di Castelvetro '12	♟♟ 2*
● Lambrusco di Sorbara '12	♟ 2
● Lambrusco Grasparossa di Castelvetro Corleto '12	♟ 2
● Corleto Lambrusco '08	♟♟ 2*
● Lambrusco Grasparossa di Castelvetro '10	♟♟ 2*
● Lambrusco Grasparossa di Castelvetro '08	♟♟ 2*
● Lambrusco Grasparossa di Castelvetro Amabile '10	♟♟ 2*
● Lambrusco Grasparossa di Castelvetro Corleto '10	♟♟ 2*
● Rosso Estella Lambrusco '09	♟♟ 2*

Villa Liverzano

FRAZ. RONTANA
VIA VALLONI, 47
48013 BRISIGHELLA [RA]
TEL. 054680461
www.liverzano.it

CELLAR SALES
PRE-BOOKED VISITS
ACCOMMODATION
ANNUAL PRODUCTION 15,000 bottles
HECTARES UNDER VINE 3.20
VITICULTURE METHOD Certified Organic

Marco Montanari has wagered on Romagna, transforming Villa Liverzano into a beautiful retreat. This complex project brings together the wonders of this place with a refined idea of hospitality in order to promote an unknown area full of opportunity. Wines play a major role in all this and Marco, together with the oenologist, Francesco Bordini, has a long relationship with the original soils of his vineyards, abundant in chalk from the Romagnola Vein, and has discovered over time a language that communicates freshness, fruit, spice, and minerality, with constantly greater results. From cabernet franc and carmenere, the Don 2010 is an elegant, spicy wine where the typical vegetal note from these varieties shows refined expression thanks to the altitude and soils. The fruity motif is lovely, austere and fresh. From sangiovese and merlot, the Rebello 2010 is juicy and vibrant.

Villa Papiano

VIA IBOLA, 24
47015 MODIGLIANA [FC]
TEL. 0546941790
www.villapapiano.it

CELLAR SALES
PRE-BOOKED VISITS
ANNUAL PRODUCTION 50,000 bottles
HECTARES UNDER VINE 10.00

Villa Papiano is one of the emerging estates in Romagna, a success built with the tenacity and reliability of the Bordini family, who have patiently waited during the long periods needed for their vineyards. Soils in this corner of Romagna, along the southern slope of Mount Chioda at 500 metres above sea level, in an extreme location, are marly sandstone, a difficult situation for these spirited and long-lived wines. Now a mature professional, Francesco Bordini has aimed his vinification toward a classic, territorial tone, achieving results with a pure, clear mineral expression. The Probi 2010 is peppery, mineral, earthy and elegant, and expands on lovely acidity. The tannins are precise and ripe. The Le Papesse 2011 shows a refined language, subtle and quite fresh. The zesty sauvignon Le Tresche 2012 has original notes of orange peel, elderflower and mountain herbs.

● Don '10	▼▼ 6
● Donna '09	▼▼▼ 7
● Rebello '10	▼▼ 5
● Trecento '12	▼▼ 4
● Don '09	♀♀ 6
● Don '08	♀♀ 6
● Don '07	♀♀ 5
● Don '06	♀♀ 5
● Don '04	♀♀ 5
● Rebello '08	♀♀ 5
● Rebello '07	♀♀ 5
● Rebello '05	♀♀ 5
● Rebello '04	♀♀ 5
● Rebello '03	♀♀ 4
● Trecento '11	♀♀ 4
● Trecento '10	♀♀ 4

● Sangiovese di Romagna I Probi di Papiano Ris. '10	▼▼▼ 3*
○ Le Tresche di Papiano '12	▼▼ 3
● Sangiovese di Romagna Sup. Le Papesse di Papiano '11	▼▼ 2*
○ Tregenda Albana Passita '11	▼▼ 3
● Papiano di Papiano '04	♀♀♀ 4
● Sangiovese di Romagna I Probi di Papiano Ris. '09	♀♀♀ 3*
○ Albana di Romagna Passito Tregenda Ris. '10	♀♀ 5
● Sangiovese di Romagna Le Papesse di Papiano '10	♀♀ 2*
● Sangiovese di Romagna Le Papesse di Papiano '09	♀♀ 2*
○ Tregenda '10	♀♀ 3

Tenuta Villa Trentola

LOC. CAPOCOLLE DI BERTINORO
VIA MOLINO BRATTI, 1305
47032 BERTINORO [FC]
TEL. 0543741389
www.villatrentola.it

CELLAR SALES
PRE-BOOKED VISITS
ANNUAL PRODUCTION 50,000 bottles
HECTARES UNDER VINE 20.00

Enrico Prugnoli and his daughter Federica, together with the oenologist, Fabrizio Moltard, have brought into focus one of the clearest and most convincing expressions of the Bertinoro area, interpreting the tannic power of this terroir with courage and precision. The estate only vinifies a selection of grapes from the estate and the full productive maturity of the vineyards today means top-quality results. Villa Trentola is the result of combining three different estates: Valle, Colombaia, and Molino, all property of this family since 1890. This estate's top wine is missing. The Moro was not produced in the difficult 2010 growing season. This choice proves the seriousness of this winery, which over the past few years has made quality wines with great continuity. The Prugnolo 2011 finds its best expression on the palate, and is fresh with a precise, clear tannic weave.

● Sangiovese di Romagna Sup. Il Prugnolo '11	♟♟ 3
● Sangiovese di Romagna Sup. Il Moro Ris. '09	♟♟♟ 4*
● Sangiovese di Romagna Sup. Il Moro Ris. '08	♟♟♟ 4
● Sangiovese di Romagna Sup. Il Moro di Villa Trentola Ris. '07	♟♟ 4
● Sangiovese di Romagna Sup. Il Prugnolo '08	♟♟ 3
● Sangiovese di Romagna Sup. Il Prugnolo di Villa Trentola '07	♟♟ 3
● Sangiovese di Romagna Sup. Il Prugnolo di Villa Trentola '06	♟♟ 3*
● Sangiovese di Romagna Sup. Ultimo Atto '08	♟♟ 5
● Ultimo Atto '10	♟♟ 2*

Villa Venti

LOC. VILLAVENTI DI RONCOFREDDO
VIA DOCCIA, 1442
47020 FORLÌ
TEL. 0541949532
www.villaventi.it

CELLAR SALES
PRE-BOOKED VISITS
ACCOMMODATION
ANNUAL PRODUCTION 27,500 bottles
HECTARES UNDER VINE 7.00
VITICULTURE METHOD Certified Organic

The Villa Venti estate has now reached full maturity with the release of an interesting Riserva 2009. The seven hectares under vine are planted on a mosaic of soils, alternating between sand, evolved red clay and sandy yellow clay, and energetically managed by Mauro Giardini and Davide Castellucci, sensitive and meticulous winemakers. Their perseverance, along with the ability to see that respect for the environment is one of the cardinal elements in modern agricultural production, have made them valuable interpreters of wine from Romagna particularly in the area of Cesenate. These classic, reliable wines are handcrafted in the most positive sense of the word. The Primo Segno 2011 has flavour, rhythm and language. Starting from a perfectly calibrated weight, it finds depth and minerality, and manages to accurately express the entire, delicate suite of aromas offered by the sangiovese variety. The Maggese 2010 is austere and earthy; the Riserva 2010 was not produced.

● Sangiovese di Romagna Longiano Primo Segno '11	♟♟♟ 3*
● Sangiovese di Romagna Sup. Maggese '10	♟♟ 3*
○ Felis Leo '09	♟♟ 3
○ Serenaro Famoso '12	♟♟ 3
● Sangiovese di Romagna Sup. Primo Segno '09	♟♟♟ 3*
● Sangiovese di Romagna Sup. Primo Segno '08	♟♟♟ 3*
● Felis Leo '08	♟♟ 3
● Felis Leo '07	♟♟ 3
● Sangiovese di Romagna Sup. Primo Segno '10	♟♟ 3*
● Sangiovese di Romagna Sup. Primo Segno '07	♟♟ 3
● Sangiovese di Romagna Sup. Ris. '09	♟♟ 4

Tenuta La Viola

VIA COLOMBARONE, 888
47032 BERTINORO [FC]
TEL. 0543445496
www.tenutalaviola.it

CELLAR SALES
PRE-BOOKED VISITS
ANNUAL PRODUCTION 40,000 bottles
HECTARES UNDER VINE 7.00
VITICULTURE METHOD Certified Organic

Since 1998, Stefano Gabellini has tirelessly worked his seven hectares under vine on the side of Bertinoro facing the sea. After a few years of increasing quality, Stefano is now dealing with the most difficult aspect of wine – the expressive language. So although these wines possess a quality that comes from impeccable care in the vineyards and meticulous management in the cellar, there are still a few details missing that would make theme wines authoritative interpreters of their territory, in other words, a pinch of austerity and tension. The Petra Honorii 2010 is a wine unable to express a terroir, and despite a certain quality, never manages to develop the classic motifs of Romagna Sangioveses. It develops without the suppleness and depth we expect from Bertinoro, with a weight that hides the world of details and shades that make up the key stylistic feature of this variety.

● Particella 25 '10	♙♙ 5
● Sangiovese di Romagna Sup. Il Colombarone '11	♙ 3
● Sangiovese di Romagna Sup. Petra Honorii Ris. '10	♙ 4
● Particella 25 '08	♗♗ 2*
● Particella 25 '07	♗♗ 2*
● Sangiovese di Romagna Sup. Il Colombarone '06	♗♗ 3*
● Sangiovese di Romagna Sup. Il Colombarone '05	♗♗ 3*
● Sangiovese di Romagna Sup. Petra Honorii Ris. '09	♗♗ 4
● Sangiovese di Romagna Sup. Petra Honorii Ris. '08	♗♗ 4
● Sangiovese di Romagna Sup. Petra Honorii Ris. '07	♗♗ 4

★Fattoria Zerbina

FRAZ. MARZENO
VIA VICCHIO, 11
48018 FAENZA [RA]
TEL. 054640022
www.zerbina.com

CELLAR SALES
PRE-BOOKED VISITS
ANNUAL PRODUCTION 220,000 bottles
HECTARES UNDER VINE 33.00

The Fattoria Zerbina operation is so important in Romagna that the local wine consortium, Consorzio Vini di Romagna, has practically dedicated the Marzeno subzone to them. This is only proper recognition for all the successes of Cristina Geminiani, head and heart of this project. Thanks to 30 hectares under vine in full productive maturity and precise work in both vineyards and cellar, wines from this estate are consistently among the best in top-quality production from Romagna. Stylistic choices and the well-suited features of this terroir make these wines powerful and austere, we could say mouthfilling, and always supported by a nice freshness. The Pietramora 2009 expresses power and remains supple thanks to a lovely acidity. The nose has dried herbs and austere fruit, white peach and cherry, and the palate shows a mineral pencil lead note. It is dense with tannins that unfortunately are too drying in the mouth. The Scacco Matto 2009 is fresh and elegant.

○ Albana di Romagna Passito Scacco Matto '09	♙♙ 3*
● Sangiovese di Romagna Sup. Pietramora Ris. '09	♙♙ 6
○ Albana di Romagna Secco Ceperano '12	♙♙ 2*
● Sangiovese di Romagna Sup. Ceregio '12	♙♙ 2*
○ Tergeno 10 anni dopo '03	♙♙ 3
○ Trebbiano di Romagna Dalbiere '12	♙ 2
○ Albana di Romagna Passito AR Ris. '06	♗♗♗ 8
● Marzieno '08	♗♗♗ 4*
● Marzieno '04	♗♗♗ 5
● Sangiovese di Romagna Sup. Pietramora Ris. '08	♗♗♗ 6
● Sangiovese di Romagna Sup. Pietramora Ris. '06	♗♗♗ 6
● Sangiovese di Romagna Sup. Pietramora Ris. '04	♗♗♗ 6

Ariola Vigne e Vini

LOC. CALICELLA DI PILASTRO
FRAZ. PILASTRO
S.DA DELLA BUCA, 5A
43010 LANGHIRANO [PR]
TEL. 0521637678
www.viniariola.it

CELLAR SALES
PRE-BOOKED VISITS
RESTAURANT SERVICE
ANNUAL PRODUCTION 1,000,000 bottles
HECTARES UNDER VINE 70.00

● Lambrusco Emilia Marcello '12		♟♟ 2*
○ Forte Rigoni Malvasia Frizzante '12		♟ 2

Raffaella Alessandra Bissoni

LOC. CASTICCIANO
VIA COLECCHIO, 280
47032 BERTINORO [FC]
TEL. 0543460382
www.vinibissoni.com

CELLAR SALES
PRE-BOOKED VISITS
ANNUAL PRODUCTION 25,000 bottles
HECTARES UNDER VINE 5.00

● Sangiovese di Romagna Sup. '11		♟♟ 2*
○ Albana di Romagna Passito '09		♟ 4

Braschi

VIA ROMA, 37
47025 MERCATO SARACENO [FC]
TEL. 054791061
www.cantinabraschi.com

ANNUAL PRODUCTION 180,000 bottles
HECTARES UNDER VINE 10.00

○ Albana di Romagna '12		♟♟ 2*
● Sangiovese di Romagna Sup. Il Costone '11		♟♟ 3

La Casetta dei Frati

VIA DEI FRATI, 8
47015 MODIGLIANA [FC]
TEL. 0546940628
www.casettadeifrati.com

CELLAR SALES
PRE-BOOKED VISITS
ACCOMMODATION AND RESTAURANT SERVICE
ANNUAL PRODUCTION 12,000 bottles
HECTARES UNDER VINE 8.00

○ Fravento '10		♟♟ 2*
● Sangiovese di Romagna Modigliana Fratémpo Ris. '11		♟♟ 3

Cavim - Cantina Viticoltori Imolesi

FRAZ. SASSO MORELLI
VIA CORRECCHIO, 54
40026 IMOLA [BO]
TEL. 054255003
www.cavimimola.it

CELLAR SALES
PRE-BOOKED VISITS
ANNUAL PRODUCTION 400,000 bottles
HECTARES UNDER VINE 1,300.00

○ Colli d'Imola Pignoletto '12		♟♟ 2*
● Sangiovese di Romagna Sup. '12		♟♟ 2*
● Sangiovese di Romagna Sup. Moro di Serrafelina Ris. '09		♟♟ 2*

Caviro

VIA CONVERTITE, 12
48018 FAENZA [RA]
TEL. 0546629111
www.caviro.it

CELLAR SALES
ANNUAL PRODUCTION 25.000,000 bottles
HECTARES UNDER VINE 44.00

● Sangiovese di Romagna Brumale '12		♟♟ 2*
● Sangiovese di Romagna Terre Forti '12		♟♟ 2*

Crocizia

S.DA PER CROCIZIA, 7
43010 LANGHIRANO [PR]
TEL. 0521854450
www.crocizia.com

CELLAR SALES
ANNUAL PRODUCTION 10,000 bottles
HECTARES UNDER VINE 5.00
VITICULTURE METHOD Certified Organic

● Marc'Aurelio '11	♥♥ 2*
○ Znèstra '12	♥♥ 2*

Donelli

VIA CARLO SIGONIO, 54
41100 MODENA
TEL. 0522908715
www.donellivini.it

ANNUAL PRODUCTION 25,000,000 bottles
HECTARES UNDER VINE 120.00

● Lambrusco di Sorbara Secco Sergio Scaglietti '12	♥♥ 2*
● Lambrusco Reggiano Secco Sergio Scaglietti '12	♥♥ 2*

Fiorini

LOC. GANACETO
VIA NAZIONALE PER CARPI, 1534
41010 MODENA
TEL. 059386028
www.fiorini1919.com

CELLAR SALES
PRE-BOOKED VISITS
ANNUAL PRODUCTION 100,000 bottles
HECTARES UNDER VINE 9.00

● Lambrusco di Sorbara Corte degli Attimi '12	♥♥ 2*
● Lambrusco V. del Caso '11	♥♥ 2*

Gualdora

LOC. CASE GUALDORA, 196
29010 ZIANO PIACENTINO [PC]
TEL. 3923902160
www.gualdora.it

ANNUAL PRODUCTION 10,000 bottles
HECTARES UNDER VINE 3.00

● C.P. Gutturnio Sup. Otto '11	♥♥ 2*
○ C.P. Malvasia Secco Frizzante Blanca '12	♥♥ 1*

Cantine Intesa

VIA PROVINCIALE FAENTINA, 46
47015 MODIGLIANA [FC]
TEL. 0546941195
www.cantineintesa.it

CELLAR SALES
PRE-BOOKED VISITS
ANNUAL PRODUCTION 100,000 bottles
HECTARES UNDER VINE 70.00

○ Albana di Romagna Poderi delle Rose '12	♥♥ 2*
● Sangiovese di Romagna Poderi delle Rose '12	♥♥ 2*

Lamoretti

LOC. CASATICO
S.DA DELLA NAVE, 6
43013 LANGHIRANO [PR]
TEL. 0521863590
www.lamorettivini.com

CELLAR SALES
PRE-BOOKED VISITS
ANNUAL PRODUCTION 100,000 bottles
HECTARES UNDER VINE 25.00

○ Colli di Parma Malvasia Frizzante '12	♥♥ 2*
● Colli di Parma Rosso Montefiore '11	♥ 2

La Piana

VIA OSSI, 4B
41014 CASTELVETRO DI MODENA [MO]
TEL. 059790303
www.lambruscolapiana.it

ANNUAL PRODUCTION 40,000 bottles
HECTARES UNDER VINE 8.00

● Lambrusco	
Grasparossa di Castelvetro Secco	
Lacrime di Bosco '12	♥♥ 1*

Quarticello

VIA MATILDE DI CANOSSA 1A
42027 MONTECCHIO EMILIA [RE]
TEL. 0522866220
www.quarticello.it

ANNUAL PRODUCTION 25,000 bottles
HECTARES UNDER VINE 5.00

○ Despina '12	♥♥ 2*
⊙ Ferrando '11	♥♥ 2*
⊙ Ferrando '11	♀♀ 2*

San Biagio Vecchio

VIA SALITA DI ORIOLO, 13
48018 FAENZA [RA]
TEL. 3393523168
www.cantinasanbiagiovecchio.com

CELLAR SALES
PRE-BOOKED VISITS
ANNUAL PRODUCTION 8,000 bottles
HECTARES UNDER VINE 5.50

○ Sabbiagialla '12	♥♥ 2*
● Sangiovese di Romagna Sup.	
Serraglio '09	♥♥ 2*

Vigne di San Lorenzo

VIA CAMPIUME, 6
48013 BRISIGHELLA [RA]
TEL. 3391137070
www.vignedisanlorenzo.it

CELLAR SALES
PRE-BOOKED VISITS
ACCOMMODATION AND RESTAURANT SERVICE
ANNUAL PRODUCTION 10,000 bottles
HECTARES UNDER VINE 3.00
VITICULTURE METHOD Certified Organic

● Campiume '09	♥♥ 4
● San Lorenzo '09	♥♥ 4
● Sangiovese Campaglione '11	♥♥ 2*

Tenuta Santini

FRAZ. PASSANO
VIA CAMPO, 33
47853 CORIANO [RN]
TEL. 0541656527
www.tenutasantini.com

CELLAR SALES
PRE-BOOKED VISITS
ANNUAL PRODUCTION 40,000 bottles
HECTARES UNDER VINE 22.00

● Sangiovese di Romagna Sup.	
Cornelianum Ris. '10	♥♥ 4
● Sangiovese di Romagna Sup.	
Beato Enrico '12	♥ 2

Cantina Sociale Settecani

VIA MODENA, 184
41014 CASTELVETRO DI MODENA [MO]
TEL. 059702505
www.cantinasettecani.it

CELLAR SALES
ANNUAL PRODUCTION 1,000,000 bottles
HECTARES UNDER VINE 530.00

● Lambrusco	
Grasparossa di Castelvetro Amabile '12	♥♥ 1*
● Lambrusco	
Grasparossa di Castelvetro Secco '12	♥♥ 1*

TUSCANY

With even more Tre Bicchieri awards in Tuscany, the region is confirmed as the benchmark for Italy's top wine production. There are countless prestigious areas and all with names of international renown, but this year's leader was Chianti Classico, vaunting no less than 24 DOCs and IGTs. The district is certainly extensive, but that is not enough to explain the results, which are actually driven by the prevalent quality encountered and a significant return to a more defined style, true to tradition. Sangiovese is back in its starring role too, both as a component of blends and because it is now enjoying a correct interpretation. We hope this widespread quality reaps the just rewards on the market and that such wonderful, authentic wine country is given its due recognition in terms of sales and pricing. The 2008 Brunello di Montalcino and the 2007 Riserva were a little under par this year but there is no way to control a vintage, which is why the area has serried ranks to offset this tricky growing year, with a focus on increasingly refined, elegant product profiles. Even Bolgheri is let down by the less-than-memorable vintage. The 2010 wines certainly show finesse and elegance, but risk being lightweight. Without doubt there are plenty of leading lights that confirm their calibre, but designation results are less compact than last year. Then there are the many other zones, smaller in size, but certainly no less significant, mainly because they play a part in creating the viticultural variety that makes this region unique in its ability to speak very different languages depending on latitude and tradition. One such area is Maremma, now awaking from a period of silence to set aside its redundant interpretation of the territory and get on with styling some fragrant easy-drinkers. Then there are Montepulciano, Lucca , Arezzo ... In conclusion, we should point out that in this region, as is the case in the whole of Italy, small family cellars co-exist alongside some enormous wineries, despite the profound differences that characterize them, and this co-existence affords the different scales of enterprise the opportunity for debate and reflection, which can only benefit the entire sector. *Gambassi - San Ginign.*

Siena (Montalcino San Quirico Montepulciano San Radicofani

Abbadia Ardenga

FRAZ. TORRENIERI
VIA ROMANA, 139
53028 MONTALCINO [SI]
TEL. 0577834150
www.abbadiardengapoggio.it

CELLAR SALES
PRE-BOOKED VISITS
ANNUAL PRODUCTION 35,000 bottles
HECTARES UNDER VINE 10.00

Before becoming the headquarters of Abbadia Ardenga, the Castello della Torre Nera was one of Montalcino's most active and well-known outposts dating back to medieval times. It now belongs to the Società di Esecutori di Pie Disposizioni di Siena and offers refreshment and lodging. The sangiovese grosso grapes obtained from around ten hectares in the marly terrains of the north-east quadrant are vinified here in the old cellar. The style of the Brunellos, both the basic and the Vigna Piaggia cru, is perforce traditional, based on macerations lasting around three weeks and ageing in Slavonian oak for about 36 months. Once again the ranking in the winery seems to be reversed, with the Brunello 2008 revealing its meaty, Mediterranean character, not to mention well-balanced tannins. While the Vigna Piaggia seems to be a vintage, the body profile is offset by a hint of aroma that is just a little too open and tertiary in texture.

● Brunello di Montalcino '08	▼▼ 5
● Brunello di Montalcino V. Piaggia '08	▼▼ 5
● Rosso di Montalcino '11	▼ 3
● Brunello di Montalcino '07	♀♀ 5
● Brunello di Montalcino '06	♀♀ 5
● Brunello di Montalcino '05	♀♀ 5
● Brunello di Montalcino '03	♀♀ 5
● Brunello di Montalcino '01	♀♀ 5
● Brunello di Montalcino '00	♀♀ 5
● Brunello di Montalcino V. Piaggia '07	♀♀ 5
● Brunello di Montalcino V. Piaggia '04	♀♀ 5
● Brunello di Montalcino V. Piaggia '03	♀♀ 5
● Rosso di Montalcino '10	♀♀ 3

Acquabona

LOC. ACQUABONA
57037 PORTOFERRAIO [LI]
TEL. 0565933013
www.acquabonaelba.it

CELLAR SALES
PRE-BOOKED VISITS
ANNUAL PRODUCTION 90,000 bottles
HECTARES UNDER VINE 18.00

This estate was first recorded in the 18th century. It takes its name from a fresh water spring, a vital source for the inhabitants of an island. Initially, the estate practised viticulture alongside the cultivation of grain and pasture, but at the end of the 1950s it began to focus more on wine-growing and eventually created specialized vineyards. In the mid-1908s, three agronomists, two Lombards, Ugo and Marcello, and a Tuscan, Luciano, acquired and relaunched the property. They continue to apply their rigorous and consistent philosophy of respect for the environment and the terroir. The Aleatico 2011 has penetrating spicy aromas of bramble jelly and currants, full and delicious in the long, lingering mouth. The pure merlot Benvenuto 2011 is pleasant, generous in aromas, and soft in flavour; the Voltraio 2009 is a delicious merlot and syrah blend, spicy, tempting, and with good follow through.

● Aleatico dell'Elba '11	▼▼ 5
● Benvenuto '11	▼▼ 2*
● Voltraio '09	▼▼ 4
○ Elba Ansonica '12	▼ 3
○ Elba Bianco '12	▼ 2
○ Elba Bianco Tradizione '12	▼ 3
⊙ Elba Rosato '12	▼ 2
● Elba Rosso Camillo Bianchi Ris. '09	▼ 4
○ Elba Vermentino '12	▼ 3
● Benvenuto '09	♀♀ 3
● Elba Rosso '09	♀♀ 2*

Agricola Alberese

FRAZ. ALBERESE
LOC. SPERGOLAIA
58010 GROSSETO
TEL. 0564407180
www.alberese.com

CELLAR SALES
PRE-BOOKED VISITS
ACCOMMODATION
ANNUAL PRODUCTION 95,000 bottles
HECTARES UNDER VINE 53.00
VITICULTURE METHOD Certified Organic

This estate belonging to the Region of
Tuscany is one of the biggest farm holdings
in Italy. Much of the property is pine groves
and forest, but many hectares are arable
and grow, e.g., barley, huge tracts are
planted with olive trees, and a good area is
under vines whose grapes go to make
several different labels of Morellino.
Free-range cattle graze on the natural
pastures and the estate still practises one of
the oldest professions in the territory:
cowboy or cattle herder. There is also an
agriturismo and you can buy all the
products direct. The two Morellinos
definitely passed muster: the Serrata dei
Cavalleggeri 2011 has intense fruit aromas,
tempered by notes of spice, firm structure,
good length and tasty finish. The Villa
Fattoria Granducale 2011 stands out for its
vegetal notes of Mediterranean scrub, lovely
consistency and long finish.

● Morellino di Scansano Barbicato '10		♀♀ 5
● Morellino di Scansano Serrata dei Cavalleggeri '11		♀♀ 2*
● Morellino di Scansano Villa Fattoria Granducale '11		♀♀ 2*
● Morellino di Scansano Pellegrone '11		♀ 3
● Morellino di Scansano Barbicato '07		♀♀ 5
● Morellino di Scansano Pellegrone '08		♀♀ 3
● Morellino di Scansano Pellegrone '06		♀♀ 3*
● Morellino di Scansano Serrata dei Cavalleggeri '10		♀♀ 2*
● Morellino di Scansano Serrata dei Cavalleggeri '07		♀♀ 2*
● Morellino di Scansano Villa Fattoria Granducale '09		♀♀ 2

Agricoltori del Chianti Geografico

LOC. MULINACCIO, 10
53013 GAIOLE IN CHIANTI [SI]
TEL. 0577749489
www.chiantigeografico.it

CELLAR SALES
PRE-BOOKED VISITS
ACCOMMODATION
ANNUAL PRODUCTION 1,900,000 bottles
HECTARES UNDER VINE 580.00

With substantial output in terms of
numbers of bottles, this co-operative
winery based in Gaiole has now reached a
solid and reassuring level of sustained
quality, decisively disproving the cliché that
quantity cannot mean quality. This, in a
nutshell, is the hallmark of this winery that
in recent years has reached dizzying
heights. In style, the wines display a
modern approach, austere in character with
no unnecessary gimmicks. The result,
therefore, is never ordinary in the glass,
expressing original character and matching
the territory well. The impeccable Chianti
Classico Montegiachi Riserva 2010 has a
boisterous, well-sustained progression. The
sangiovese and cabernet sauvignon
Ferraiolo 2010 has clean aromas. The soft
Pulleraia 2010 from merlot grapes, is quite
refined. The Chianti Classico Contessa di
Radda 2011 is a fresh, easy drinker.

● Chianti Cl. Montegiachi Ris. '10		♀♀ 4
● Ferraiolo '10		♀♀ 5
● Chianti Cl. Contessa di Radda '11		♀♀ 3
● Pulleraia '10		♀♀ 5
● Brunello di Montalcino Castello Tricerchi '08		♀ 7
● Chianti Cl. '11		♀ 3
● Rosso di Montalcino Castello Tricerchi '10		♀ 3
● Chianti Cl. Montegiachi Ris. '09		♀♀♀ 4*
● Chianti Cl. Montegiachi Ris. '07		♀♀♀ 4
● Chianti Cl. Montegiachi Ris. '05		♀♀♀ 4
● Brunello di Montalcino Castello Tricerchi '07		♀♀ 7
● Brunello di Montalcino Castello Tricerchi '05		♀♀ 7
● Chianti Cl. Contessa di Radda '09		♀♀ 3

Podere Albiano

LOC. PETROIO
S.DA DI PODERE ALBIANO
53020 TREQUANDA [SI]
TEL. 05776653
www.poderealbiano.it

CELLAR SALES
PRE-BOOKED VISITS
ANNUAL PRODUCTION 15,000 bottles
HECTARES UNDER VINE 4.00

This property, nestling in an extraordinarily beautiful landscape belongs to Ada Becheri. She runs it jointly with Alberto Turri, the two united by their passion for wine and for the territory. Ada takes care of the sales and PR side, while Alberto devotes his energies to the vineyards and cellar. The estate was established in 2002, with work commencing on the land and the planting of the vineyards, then moving on to renovation of the buildings. The cellar was completed in 2009. The three wines are offered are all well made. The pure sangiovese Tribolo 2009 has pencil lead and leather, in a fruity framework with firm body and tasty finish. The Ciriè 2009, a sangiovese and merlot blend, has spice and aromatic herbs on a cherry base, with soft structure and elegant, subtle tannins. The tempting Petro 2009 cabernet sauvignon and merlot with a touch of petit verdot, is dynamic and juicy, revealing fresh notes with balsam, vegetal hints of capsicum, and a lovely tasty finish.

● Ciriè '09	♙♙ 3
● Petro '09	♙♙ 4
● Tribolo '09	♙♙ 4

Fattoria Ambra

VIA LOMBARDA, 85
59015 CARMIGNANO [PO]
TEL. 3358282552
www.fattoriaambra.it

CELLAR SALES
PRE-BOOKED VISITS
ANNUAL PRODUCTION 80,000 bottles
HECTARES UNDER VINE 20.00

The Romei Rigoli family have owned the estate since the mid-20th century. The vineyards are planted in four areas, including the best crus of the Carmignano zone, which was renowned back in the 13th century for the quality of its wines: Collina di Montalbiolo, Elzana, Santa Cristina in Pilli and Montefortini. The estate's driving force is the focus on expression of the terroir, which led to specific choices in training and processing, and in the wines produced by the owner, expert agronomist and oenologist Beppe Rigoli. The winery also makes a Rosé, a Barco Reale and a Vin Santo. The Vin Santo 2006 stood out in tastings with its enchanting aromas of dried fruits and spice, sweet, well-orchestrated body and good length. The rest of the range is characterized by prominent tannins but reveals a complex and powerful structure.

● Carmignano S. Cristina in Pilli '11	♙♙ 3
● Carmignano V. di Montefortini '11	♙♙ 3
○ Vin Santo di Carmignano '06	♙♙ 5
● Barco Reale '12	♙ 2
⊙ Rosato di Carmignano Vin Ruspo '12	♙ 2
○ Trebbiano '12	♙ 2
● Barco Reale '11	♟♟ 2*
● Carmignano Elzana Ris. '09	♟♟ 4
● Carmignano Elzana Ris. '05	♟♟ 4
● Carmignano Le Vigne Alte di Montalbiolo Ris. '09	♟♟ 4
● Carmignano Le Vigne Alte di Montalbiolo Ris. '04	♟♟ 4

Stefano Amerighi

FRAZ. FARNETA
VIA DI POGGIOBELLO
52044 CORTONA [AR]
TEL. 0575648340
www.stefanoamerighi.it

ANNUAL PRODUCTION 5,000 bottles
HECTARES UNDER VINE 13,50

Located in the countryside surrounding
Cortona, owner Stefano Amerighi built up
his estate from a desire to make fine
quality Syrahs, respecting the rules of
country tradition while applying knowledge
of biodynamic farming. Great care was
invested in the project from the very start,
from the choice of the land destined for
planting vineyards, and it has grown in size
and significance ensuring that the estate
would become a kind of sustainable
agriculture workshop where certain
techniques would be applied to all sectors
of farming. In just a few years, what
seemed like vague visionary ideas have
become a firmly grounded reality. It is Tre
Bicchieri time again for the only wine
presented, the Syrah 2010, with elegant,
varied aromas and spicy fragrances of
pepper, red berry fruits like crisp cherry
and fresh herbs like mint. The well-
measured palate is caressing, with
balanced tannins and a fresh acid note for
the discreet, relaxing finish.

● Cortona Syrah '10	♈♈♈	5
● Cortona Syrah '09	♈♈♈	5
● Cortona Syrah '08	♈♈	5
● Cortona Syrah '07	♈♈	5
● Cortona Syrah Apice '09	♈♈	5

Amiata

LOC. MONTEGIOVI
58033 CASTEL DEL PIANO [GR]
TEL. 0564974864
www.amiatavini.it

CELLAR SALES
PRE-BOOKED VISITS
ANNUAL PRODUCTION 6,000 bottles
HECTARES UNDER VINE 3.00

The idea that fine quality wines can only be
produced in a context of great and
long-standing winemaking tradition does
not always hold water: Amiata is a young
estate but already rich in family values.
Here on the slopes of the old extinct
volcano, Mount Amiata, the clayey land
furrowed with streams is mainly planted
with vines and olives. This is where young
entrepreneurs Simone Toninelli and
Stefania Colombini combined their passion
for wine-growing and business acumen,
launching into the wine sector with
promising results. In the Montecucco area
sangiovese has proved it can yield
excellent results, planted near the Montalcino
DOC zone. The Montecucco Sangiovese
Lavico 2009 makes its first finals , with
complex ripe fruit aromas of cherries and
blackberries combined with clean minerally
notes. On the palate the impact is rich, with
close-knit, in no way oppressive tannins, and
long, pleasing flavour. The rest of the
production is enjoyable.

● Montecucco Sangiovese Lavico '09	♈♈	3*
● Montecucco Sangiovese Cenere Ris. '08	♈♈	3
● Lapillo '10	♈	3
● Lapillo '09	♈♈	3
● Montecucco Sangiovese Cenere Ris. '07	♈♈	3
● Montecucco Sangiovese Lavico '08	♈♈	3*

Ampeleia

FRAZ. ROCCATEDERIGHI
LOC. MELETA
58028 ROCCASTRADA [GR]
TEL. 0564567155
www.ampeleia.it

CELLAR SALES
PRE-BOOKED VISITS
ANNUAL PRODUCTION 100,000 bottles
HECTARES UNDER VINE 40.00

The Ampeleia project is the result of the combined efforts of three friends with a shared love of the land and vineyards. The estate's plots are situated at three different altitudes and the land varies in features, requiring continually evolving care and attention. The result is extremely dynamic wine-growing techniques, like the seven grape varieties planted on the estate according to the morphological features of the land: these terroirs, situated at a considerable distance from one another, create a single and unique expression which translates into characterful and extremely drinkable wines. The grenache, mourvèdre and carignano Kepos 2011 is fresh and stylish on the nose, with soft body, fresh taste, silky tannins and fruity after-aroma. Also very drinkable, the mainly cabernet franc Ampeleia 2010 has fruit notes and medium structure. The enjoyable Unilitro 2012 is a blend of seven grape types grown on site.

★★Marchesi Antinori

P.ZZA DEGLI ANTINORI, 3
50123 FIRENZE
TEL. 05523595
www.antinori.it

PRE-BOOKED VISITS
ACCOMMODATION AND RESTAURANT SERVICE
ANNUAL PRODUCTION 2,000,000 bottles
HECTARES UNDER VINE 2,350.00

The "universe" represented by Antinori's Tuscan estates is truly all-inclusive, ranging as it does from those in Tignanello, Badia a Passignano and Peppoli in Chianti, to Le Mortelle and Fattoria Aldobranesca in the Maremma, from the Florentine estate of Monteloro, to Santa Cristina in Cortona and La Braccesca at Montepulciano, as well as the Pian delle Vigne estate at Montalcino. These major areas are part of perhaps the best-known Italian wine brand in the world. With a centuries-old history dating back to the middle ages, this company produces absolutely excellent, genuine wines that are always well focused in terms of type. The intriguing aromas of the Chianti Classico Marchese Antinori Riserva 2009 lead to a soft palate attack and stylish, smooth evolution. The aromas in the Tignanello 2010 are hard to define, but it has powerful development and close-knit, pleasantly spirited tannins. The Solaia 2010 is sweet, with a little oak still to digest.

● Kepos '11	♟♟ 3*
● Ampeleia '10	♟♟ 5
● Unlitro '12	♟♟ 2*
● Kepos '06	♟♟♟ 3*
● Ampeleia '09	♟♟ 5
● Ampeleia '08	♟♟ 5
● Ampeleia '07	♟♟ 5
● Ampeleia '06	♟♟ 5
● Empatia '07	♟♟ 4
● Kepos '10	♟♟ 3*
● Kepos '09	♟♟ 3
● Kepos '08	♟♟ 3

● Chianti Cl. Marchese Antinori Ris. '09	♟♟ 5
● Tignanello '10	♟♟ 8
● Brunello di Montalcino Domus Vitae Pian delle Vigne '08	♟♟ 7
● Brunello di Montalcino Pian delle Vigne '08	♟♟ 7
● Brunello di Montalcino Vignaferrovia Pian delle Vigne Ris. '07	♟♟ 7
● Chianti Cl. Pèppoli '11	♟♟ 3
● Poggio alle Nane Tenuta Le Mortelle '10	♟♟ 7
● Solaia '10	♟♟ 8
● Solaia '07	♟♟♟ 8
● Solaia '06	♟♟♟ 8
● Tignanello '09	♟♟♟ 8
● Tignanello '08	♟♟♟ 8
● Tignanello '05	♟♟♟ 8
● Tignanello '04	♟♟♟ 8

Tenuta di Arceno - Arcanum

LOC. ARCENO
FRAZ. SAN GUSMÉ
53010 CASTELNUOVO BERARDENGA [SI]
TEL. 0577359346
www.tenutadiarceno.com

CELLAR SALES
PRE-BOOKED VISITS
ANNUAL PRODUCTION 250,000 bottles
HECTARES UNDER VINE 92.00

The historic Arceno estate and its 90 hectares of vineyards were acquired in 1994 by Jess Jackson and Barbara Banke, owners of the famous Kendall-Jackson winery in California. Today their daughter Julia is in charge. This is southern Chianti Classico, near Castelnuovo Berardenga, where the clayey terrain is rich in granite and basalt. Over the years, famed oenologist Pierre Seillan has divided the property into 63 plots in ten different climatic conditions. The secret of the estate's flagship line, Arcanum, lies in the separate vinifications of vineyard and cru. Cabernet franc, cabernet sauvignon and merlot go to make wines of an international stamp. The Arcanum, mainly cabernet franc, is deep ruby, with a clear aroma of dark berry fruit and spices; in the mouth it is concentrated, solid, rich in fruit, but also very fresh and balanced. The Valadrona is dry and very expansive. We liked the Fauno di Arcanum, a Bordeaux blend mainly of merlot with a touch of sangiovese, juicy and rounded, with a long finish.

● Arcanum '08	♟♟ 8
● Il Fauno '08	♟♟ 4
● Chianti Classico '11	♟♟ 3
● Valadorna '08	♟♟ 7
● Arcanum I '07	♟♟ 8
● Arcanum I '04	♟♟ 7
● Arcanum I '03	♟♟ 7
● Arcanum I '02	♟♟ 8
● Arcanum II '04	♟♟ 8
● Arcanum II '02	♟♟ 8

Tenuta Argentiera

LOC. DONORATICO
VIA AURELIA, 412A
57022 CASTAGNETO CARDUCCI [LI]
TEL. 0565773176
www.argentiera.eu

CELLAR SALES
PRE-BOOKED VISITS
ANNUAL PRODUCTION 450,000 bottles
HECTARES UNDER VINE 75.00

Once the property of the Florentine Serristori family and part of the old Donoratico estate, today this winery is a real point of reference for the Bolgheri territory. It belongs to brothers Corrado and Marcello Fratini and boasts an expanse of vineyards that few can rival in some of the district's beautiful plots where the clayey soil is fairly stony. Of the 500 total hectares, 75 are planted to vine. They cultivate the classic varieties of the zone: cabernet, sauvignon and franc, merlot, syrah. The wines are the product of this viticultural wealth and increasingly precise techniques in the cellar. A splendid return for the Bolgheri Superiore Argentiera, despite the challenges it faced in 2010. We were taken with this sound, well-balanced red with its brisk, precise vertical aromatics and palate, a hint of pulp lending flavour and maturity, making it one of the best this year. The Bolgheri Villa Donoratico 2010 is less convincing, let down by the nose; the simple Poggio ai Ginepri 2012 is pleasant.

● Bolgheri Sup. Argentiera '10	♟♟♟ 7
● Bolgheri Poggio ai Ginepri '12	♟ 3
● Bolgheri Villa Donoratico '10	♟ 4
● Bolgheri Sup. Argentiera '06	♟♟♟ 7
● Bolgheri Sup. Argentiera '05	♟♟♟ 7
● Bolgheri Sup. Argentiera '04	♟♟♟ 7
● Bolgheri Poggio ai Ginepri '05	♟♟ 2*
● Bolgheri Rosso Poggio ai Ginepri '09	♟♟ 3
● Bolgheri Sup. Argentiera '09	♟♟ 7
● Bolgheri Sup. Argentiera '07	♟♟ 7
● Bolgheri Sup. Argentiera '03	♟♟ 7
● Bolgheri Villa Donoratico '07	♟♟ 4
● Bolgheri Villa Donoratico '05	♟♟ 4
● Bolgheri Villa Donoratico '04	♟♟ 4

Argiano

FRAZ. SANT'ANGELO IN COLLE
53024 MONTALCINO [SI]
TEL. 0577844037
www.argiano.net

PRE-BOOKED VISITS
ACCOMMODATION
ANNUAL PRODUCTION 350,000 bottles
HECTARES UNDER VINE 51.00

The acquisition of the Argiano estate by a group of wealthy Brazilian investors has been one of the most significant developments of the last year in Montalcino. Giorgio Gabelli has been appointed the new managing director in charge of this splendid property of over 100 hectares, half of which are under vine, in the far south-west corner of the DOC. We wish him well and are curious to see if and how he will change the ampelographic base, currently consisting of sangiovese, merlot, cabernet, syrah and petit verdot, and the style, previously distinctive for its generous, horizontal stamp. The IGTs, from international grape varieties, have once again made the biggest impact in this round of tastings. The elegantly herbaceous leader is the Non Confunditur 2011, full of dark fruit and with solid, close-knit palate progression free of any extractive or bitterish notes. The Suolo 2010 is more spicy and meaty, but also crisper.

● Non Confunditur '11	♟♟ 3
● Suolo '10	♟♟ 8
● Rosso di Montalcino '11	♟ 3
● Brunello di Montalcino Ris. '88	♟♟♟ 7
● Brunello di Montalcino Ris. '85	♟♟♟ 7
● Solengo '97	♟♟♟ 6
● Solengo '95	♟♟♟ 6
● Brunello di Montalcino '04	♟♟ 6
● Brunello di Montalcino '02	♟♟ 7
● Rosso di Montalcino '07	♟♟ 3
● Solengo '08	♟♟ 8
● Solengo '07	♟♟ 8
● Suolo '08	♟♟ 8
● Suolo '07	♟♟ 8

Artimino

FRAZ. ARTIMINO
V.LE PAPA GIOVANNI XXIII, 1
59015 CARMIGNANO [PO]
TEL. 0558751423
www.artimino.com

CELLAR SALES
PRE-BOOKED VISITS
ACCOMMODATION AND RESTAURANT SERVICE
ANNUAL PRODUCTION 420,000 bottles
HECTARES UNDER VINE 88.00

Artimino signifies tradition – of men, land and wine, of noble varieties typical of a historic territory. Its large area of vineyards, unusual for this territory, and expanse of olive groves add to the landscape. The estate also offers a restaurant, wine shop, hotel and an agriturismo comprising 50 or so apartments. La Ferdinanda, the Medici villa designed by Buontalenti, is one of the most popular conference and banquet centres in Tuscany. The wine activity is very interesting, based on south-facing vineyards that are home to the varieties traditional to the territory. The excellent Grumarello Riserva 2009 tasted well, with a full, varied aromatic profile expressing hints of cloves and ripe fruit, and some balsam. On the palate it displays power, generosity, good structure and a long, complex finish. The Carmignano 2010 is fresh and relaxed; the Riserva Villa Artimino 2009 is austere, with well-defined aromas.

● Carmignano V. Grumarello Ris. '09	♟♟ 4
● Carmignano '10	♟♟ 3
● Carmignano Villa Artimino Ris. '09	♟♟ 2*
● Barco Reale '12	♟ 2
⊙ Vin Ruspo '12	♟ 2
○ Vin Santo di Carmignano Occhio di Pernice '08	♟ 5
● Carmignano '09	♟♟ 3
● Carmignano V. Grumarello Ris. '08	♟♟ 4
● Carmignano V. Grumarello Ris. '07	♟♟ 4
● Carmignano Villa Medicea Ris. '08	♟♟ 3
○ Vin Santo di Carmignano Occhio di Pernice '06	♟♟ 5

Assolati

FRAZ. MONTENERO
POD. ASSOLATI, 47
58040 CASTEL DEL PIANO [GR]
TEL. 0564954146
www.assolati.it

CELLAR SALES
PRE-BOOKED VISITS
ACCOMMODATION
ANNUAL PRODUCTION 13,000 bottles
HECTARES UNDER VINE 3.00

Loriano Giannetti owns this estate founded
by his grandparents and carried on by his
parents, who transformed a harsh territory
adapted to Mediterranean scrub into a
fertile terrain that can support vines and
olive trees. Loriano has turned what was a
simple agricultural wine production into a
quality product. He also produces
extra-virgin olive oil, runs an agriturismo,
and has a particular passion for cooking
local dishes. All Montecucco wines are
interesting and of excellent quality. The
Rosso 2011 has fruit-led aromatics, with
notes of spice and a light, smooth body. The
aromas of the Sangiovese 2009 express
more mineral and vegetal notes, the body is
firm, the tannins elegant and the finish tasty.
The Sangiovese Riserva 2009 has a
well-balanced, layered structure and
remarkable length.

Fattoria di Bacchereto

LOC. BACCHERETO
VIA FONTEMORANA, 179
59015 CARMIGNANO [PO]
TEL. 0558717191
terreamano@gmail.com

CELLAR SALES
PRE-BOOKED VISITS
ACCOMMODATION
ANNUAL PRODUCTION 15,000 bottles
HECTARES UNDER VINE 8.00

This farm on the slopes of the Montalbano
zone has belonged to the Bencini Tesi
family since 1925. The property is home to
woodland, chestnut trees, olive groves and
vineyards, some of which are being
replanted. In 2001, it opted to produced
wine naturally according to biodynamic
methods thanks to the will and dedication
of Rossella, who instinctively yet stubbornly
change the destiny of the estate
completely. Today, each plant produces no
more than a kilogramme of grapes; cover
cropping is practised and invasive grass is
cut by hand. The yeasts used in the cellar
are those present on the skins. The solid,
firm Carmignano 2010 is lovely, with
intense vegetal, Mediterranean scrub, plum
and cherry notes, well-embedded tannins,
and a zesty acid with a tasty finish. The
macerated-style trebbiano and malvasia
Sassocarlo 2011 has oxidative aromas and
well-orchestrated structure.

● Montecucco Rosso '11	♥♥ 2*
● Montecucco Sangiovese '09	♥♥ 3
● Montecucco Sangiovese Ris. '09	♥♥ 4
○ Dionysos '12	♥ 2
● Montecucco Rosso '10	♀♀ 2*
● Montecucco Rosso '08	♀♀ 2*
● Montecucco Sangiovese Ris. '07	♀♀ 4

● Carmignano Terre a Mano '10	♥♥ 5
○ Sassocarlo '11	♥♥ 4
○ Vin Santo di Carmignano '03	♥♥ 6
● Carmignano Terre a Mano '09	♀♀ 5
● Carmignano Terre a Mano '05	♀♀ 5
● Carmignano Terre a Mano '03	♀♀ 4
● Carmignano Terre a Mano '02	♀♀ 5
○ Sassocarlo '10	♀♀ 4

Badia a Coltibuono

LOC. BADIA A COLTIBUONO
53013 GAIOLE IN CHIANTI [SI]
TEL. 0577746110
www.coltibuono.com

CELLAR SALES
PRE-BOOKED VISITS
ACCOMMODATION AND RESTAURANT SERVICE
ANNUAL PRODUCTION 350,000 bottles
HECTARES UNDER VINE 58.00
VITICULTURE METHOD Certified Organic

The major goal of every winery is successfully interpreting the true spirit of a territory when making wine. Badia a Coltibuono has also proven its ability to repeat this achievement consistently over time. This puts products from this estate in Gaiole in Chianti in that exclusive circle of wines that must not be missed. Though this winery already shows high quality standards, these have been raised further by the style of the whole production, capable of displaying extraordinary refinement and personality. While still lagging in the approach on the nose, the Chianti Classico Riserva 2009 reveals its character fully on the palate, showing elegance, verve and a deep finish with citrus hints. Almost as good, the Sangioveto 2009 pure sangiovese, is tasty and subtle. The Chianti Classico 2011 is good, if a little rustic at times.

Badia di Morrona

VIA DEL CHIANTI, 6
56030 TERRICCIOLA [PI]
TEL. 0587658505
www.badiadimorrona.it

CELLAR SALES
PRE-BOOKED VISITS
ACCOMMODATION
ANNUAL PRODUCTION 260,000 bottles
HECTARES UNDER VINE 91.00

The abbey is a magnificent building that houses many treasures assembled through the real passion of the owners. It is the symbol of this estate, which also shares its name. The property lies in the municipality of Terricciola, in the upper Val d'Era, halfway between Pisa and Volterra. It possesses around 600 hectares in total, 91 of which are planted to vine and 40 to olive trees. The grapes speak the language of the sangiovese of these lands, with an inflection of cabernet and merlot. White varieties chardonnay and viognier are cultivated alongside the local vermentino and colombara. The wines have good personality and can excel in the zone. The N'Antia 2010 is mainly from sauvignon, with top-ups of cabernet franc and merlot, expressing distinct grassy notes, packed with dark forest fruits, and toasty notes from ageing in small French wood. The Sangiovese Vigna Alta 2009 is also good; the I Sodi del Paretaio 2012 is juicy.

● Chianti Cl. Ris. '09	▼▼▼ 5
● Chianti Cl. '11	▼▼ 3
● Sangioveto '09	▼▼ 6
● Chianti Cl. '06	♈♈♈ 3*
● Chianti Cl. Cultus Boni '09	♈♈♈ 4*
● Chianti Cl. Ris. '07	♈♈♈ 5
● Chianti Cl. Ris. '04	♈♈♈ 5
● Sangioveto '95	♈♈♈ 6
● Chianti Cl. '10	♈♈ 3*
● Chianti Cl. '09	♈♈ 3
● Chianti Cl. Ris. '08	♈♈ 5

● N'Antia '10	▼▼ 5
● Vigna Alta '09	▼▼ 5
● Chianti I Sodi del Paretaio '12	▼ 2
○ Felciaio '12	▼ 2
○ Bianco Pisano di San Torpè Vin Santo '05	♈♈ 4
● Chianti I Sodi del Paretaio '07	♈♈ 2*
● N'Antia '09	♈♈ 4
● N'Antia '07	♈♈ 4
● N'Antia '06	♈♈ 4
● N'Antia '05	♈♈ 4
● N'Antia '01	♈♈ 5
● Taneto '08	♈♈ 3*
● Taneto '06	♈♈ 3*
● Vigna Alta '04	♈♈ 5
● Vigna Alta '01	♈♈ 5
● Vign Alta '07	♈♈ 5

Fattoria di Bagnolo

LOC. BAGNOLO-CANTAGALLO
VIA IMPRUNETANA PER TAVARNUZZE, 48
50023 IMPRUNETA [FI]
TEL. 0552313403
www.bartolinibaldelli.it

CELLAR SALES
PRE-BOOKED VISITS
ANNUAL PRODUCTION 27,000 bottles
HECTARES UNDER VINE 10.00

Marco Bartolini Baldelli is the owner of
Fattoria di Bagnolo, situated in the locality
of the same name in the Chianti Colli
Fiorentini production zone. He also owns
other farm estates in Tuscany: 20 hectares
of vineyards at San Miniato in the province
of Pisa, and Castello di Montozzo in the
province of Arezzo which primarily
produces extra-virgin olive oil. The buildings
have recently been restored, respecting the
historical features, without neglecting
production quality: a modern vinification
cellar stands alongside the barrique cellar
in the beautiful 16th-century building.
Another sound year is confirmed thanks to
the Capro Rosso 2010, a sangiovese,
colorino and cabernet sauvignon blend that
soared with pleasant minty aromas, a soft,
juicy body, and lovely finish on fruity
after-aromas. The Riserva 2009 is good
too, with mainly fruity notes, a nice tannin
imprint and tasty finish.

● Capro Rosso '10	♥♥ 5
● Chianti Colli Fiorentini Ris. '10	♥♥ 4
● Chianti Colli Fiorentini '11	♥ 2
● Capro Rosso '09	♀♀ 5
● Capro Rosso '08	♀♀ 5
● Capro Rosso '07	♀♀ 4
● Capro Rosso '04	♀♀ 4
● Chianti Colli Fiorentini '08	♀♀ 2
● Chianti Colli Fiorentini Ris. '08	♀♀ 3
○ Vin Santo del Chianti Ris. '01	♀♀ 5

I Balzini

LOC. PASTINE, 19
50021 BARBERINO VAL D'ELSA [FI]
TEL. 0558075503
www.ibalzini.it

PRE-BOOKED VISITS
ANNUAL PRODUCTION 50,000 bottles
HECTARES UNDER VINE 8,40

Vincenzo d'Isanto, an accountant with a
passion for the country, founded this estate
in 1980 spurred by his desire to produce
quality wine. His wife, Antonella, joined him
in the business in 2006 and threw herself
wholeheartedly into the adventure, leaving
her job as labour consultant. The property
fans out around the old farmhouse and
takes the name Balzini from the small
ridges or terraces on which the vineyards
are planted. Sitting amidst a stunning
panorama, the cellar was built partially
underground so as to blend in to its
surroundings. The wine production has
gradually expanded yet retains its original
style. The Black Label 2010 blend of
cabernet sauvignon and merlot made a
good impression, with ripe cherry jam
aromas and spice notes, a firm, lusty body,
and well-embedded tannins. The soft,
well-balanced Red Label 2011 is a similar
blend with a touch of sangiovese; the
fresh-tasting Green Label 2012 is from
sangiovese and mammolo.

● I Balzini Black Label '10	♥♥ 6
● I Balzini Green Label '12	♥♥ 2*
● I Balzini Red Label '11	♥♥ 3
⊙ I Balzini Pink Label '12	♥ 2
● I Balzini White Label '10	♥ 5
● I Balzini Black Label '09	♀♀ 6
● I Balzini Black Label '08	♀♀ 5
● I Balzini Black Label '07	♀♀ 5
● I Balzini Green Label '11	♀♀ 2*
● I Balzini White Label '08	♀♀ 5
● I Balzini White Label '07	♀♀ 5
● I Balzini White Label '05	♀♀ 5

Bandini - Villa Pomona

LOC. POMONA
S.DA CHIANTIGIANA, 222
53011 CASTELLINA IN CHIANTI [SI]
TEL. 0577740930
www.fattoriapomona.it

CELLAR SALES
PRE-BOOKED VISITS
ACCOMMODATION
ANNUAL PRODUCTION 15,000 bottles
HECTARES UNDER VINE 4.60
VITICULTURE METHOD Certified Organic

The winery at Castellina in Chianti can be seen as a fine example of artisanal Italian winemaking that marks our production tradition. What sets the wines of Villa Pomona apart is their classic style, which starts from ageing in large barrels, with no easy shortcuts in the cellar, and relies above all on work in the vineyard, managed with organic methods. The resulting wines are austere and sometimes hard to gauge at first, but always original and show outstanding character and a connection to one of the most solid territories currently in production in Chianti. The Chianti Classico Riserva 2010 really is one of the best of its type, with its clean, well-defined aromatic profile, alternating notes of ripe cherry and mulberry blossom, with a long silky palate. The Chianti Classico 2011 is also good, perhaps a little grassy, its strength lying in its aromas.

● Chianti Cl. Ris. '10	♟♟ 4
● Chianti Cl. '11	♟♟ 3
● Chianti Cl. '10	♀♀ 3
● Chianti Cl. '09	♀♀ 3
● Chianti Cl. Ris. '09	♀♀ 4
● Chianti Cl. Ris. '08	♀♀ 4
● Chianti Cl. Ris. '07	♀♀ 4

Riccardo Baracchi

LOC. SAN MARTINO
VIA CEGLIOLO, 21
52042 CORTONA [AR]
TEL. 0575612679
www.baracchiwinery.com

CELLAR SALES
PRE-BOOKED VISITS
ACCOMMODATION AND RESTAURANT SERVICE
ANNUAL PRODUCTION 95,000 bottles
HECTARES UNDER VINE 25.00

Riccardo Baracchi owns this traditional family estate, immersed in an area of rare beauty, which has produced wine since 1860. However he takes the credit for modernization of the production system, building the cellar, experimentation, like making sparkling wines from trebbiano and sangiovese, and building a hotel which has become a favourite destination for food connoisseurs thanks to his wife Silvia's management of the kitchen. Their son Benedetto is Riccardo's right-hand man. The vineyards are distributed over three locations, including San Martino where the winery is also situated. The choice of grape varieties was based on the features of each terroir. The Ardito 2010, from syrah and cabernet sauvignon, has intense notes of cloves and berry fruits, a velvety, well-balanced body, and nice long finish. The Smeriglio range is also good, from sangiovese, merlot and syrah grapes, for rounded, balanced wines.

● Ardito '10	♟♟ 6
● Cortona Smeriglio Merlot '11	♟♟ 4
● Cortona Smeriglio Sangiovese '11	♟♟ 4
● Cortona Smeriglio Syrah '11	♟♟ 4
● Brut Sangiovese '11	♟ 5
○ Brut Trebbiano '10	♟ 3
● Ardito '09	♀♀ 6
● Ardito '08	♀♀ 6
● Ardito '06	♀♀ 6
● Cortona Smeriglio Merlot '10	♀♀ 4
● Cortona Smeriglio Sangiovese '10	♀♀ 4

Fattoria dei Barbi

LOC. PODERNOVI, 170
53024 MONTALCINO [SI]
TEL. 0577841111
www.fattoriadeibarbi.it

Baricci

LOC. COLOMBAIO DI MONTOSOLI, 13
53024 MONTALCINO [SI]
TEL. 0577848109
www.baricci1955.com

CELLAR SALES
PRE-BOOKED VISITS
ACCOMMODATION AND RESTAURANT SERVICE
ANNUAL PRODUCTION 600,000 bottles
HECTARES UNDER VINE 67.00

CELLAR SALES
PRE-BOOKED VISITS
ANNUAL PRODUCTION 30,000 bottles
HECTARES UNDER VINE 4.00

Owning agricultural properties in Montalcino since the mid-14th century and Fattoria dei Barbi since 1790, the Cinelli Colombini family is constantly mentioned in the history of Brunello. This winery has a glorious past coupled with an interesting present. Now the passion and commitment of Stefano Cinelli Colombini and his team go into managing around a hundred hectares almost totally planted to sangiovese grosso. Tradition and classic style in this case are not merely rhetorical terms but rather what determine the style of the estate's three Brunellos: the Vigna del Fiore cru and Riserva as well as the vintage version. The Brunello di Barbi missed another top award by a whisker. This is thanks to a Riserva 2007 with a proudly retro feel, revealing notes of tobacco and roots, reined in only by an insistent reductive saltiness and severe tannins not entirely offset by the medium weight of the structure.

The successful combination of historic memory and modern sensibility make Baricci wines an absolute must for fans of Montalcino Sangiovese. As proprietors since 1955 of the Colombaio estate in the northern part of Montosoli, the family was involved in the pioneering years of Brunello and the early days of the Consortium, but is also and especially linked with wines unanimously recognized as paradigms of character and a sense of terroir, as well as being astonishing value for money. With long maceration in steel and ageing in 20 and 25-litre Slavonian oak barrels, these wines prove reliable, yet able to immediately express their racy, succulent structure. The Rosso di Montalcino 2011 is a perfect example, certainly one of the best interpretations of the vintage. Fresh berry fruits, pepper and incense compose a complete wine in terms of flavour and extract. The Brunello 2008, on the other hand, is straggling more than usual, but has its usual hints of chalk and new-mown grass.

● Brunello di Montalcino Ris. '07	▼▼ 7
● Brunello di Montalcino '08	▼▼ 5
● Morellino di Scansano '11	▼▼ 3
● Rosso di Montalcino '11	▼ 3
● Brunello di Montalcino '07	♀♀ 5
● Brunello di Montalcino '06	♀♀ 5
● Brunello di Montalcino '04	♀♀ 5
● Brunello di Montalcino Ris. '04	♀♀ 7
● Brunello di Montalcino V. del Fiore '07	♀♀ 7
● Brunello di Montalcino V. del Fiore '06	♀♀ 7
● Brunello di Montalcino V. del Fiore '05	♀♀ 7
● Brunello di Montalcino V. del Fiore '04	♀♀ 7
● Brusco dei Barbi '08	♀♀ 2*
● Morellino di Scansano Sole '07	♀♀ 4

● Rosso di Montalcino '11	▼▼ 3*
● Brunello di Montalcino '08	▼▼ 5
● Brunello di Montalcino '07	♀♀♀ 5
● Brunello di Montalcino '83	♀♀♀ 5
● Rosso di Montalcino '10	♀♀ 3

★Barone Ricasoli

LOC. CASTELLO DI BROLIO
53013 GAIOLE IN CHIANTI [SI]
TEL. 05777301
www.ricasoli.it

CELLAR SALES
PRE-BOOKED VISITS
RESTAURANT SERVICE
ANNUAL PRODUCTION 2,000,000 bottles
HECTARES UNDER VINE 230.00

Barone Ricasoli is one of the most important wineries in the Chianti Classico DOC zone, not only because of its thousand-year history, but the quality of its products, now comfortably reliable. Just a few years ago these wines were characterized mainly by their intense aromatic complexity, powerful structure and decisive oak. This has clearly undergone change in recent years, primarily by using less intrusive oak and seeking a more refined and polished style. This change is the result of a major commitment in the vineyard and cellar that only happens in wineries of this calibre. Intense smoky notes mark the Chianti Classico Brolio Riserva 2010, which on the palate reveals a complete wine with no lack of character. The progression of the Chianti Classico Rocca Guicciarda Riserva 2010 is nicely contrasted. The most persuasive label is the decisive, elegant Colledilà 2010.

● Chianti Cl. Colledilà '10	♟♟♟ 7
● Chianti Cl. Brolio Ris. '10	♟♟ 6
● Chianti Cl. Castello di Brolio '10	♟♟ 8
● Casalferro '10	♟♟ 7
● Chianti Cl. Brolio '11	♟♟ 5
● Chianti Cl. Rocca Guicciarda Ris. '10	♟♟ 5
● Casalferro '08	♟♟♟ 8
● Casalferro '05	♟♟♟ 8
● Casalferro '03	♟♟♟ 5
● Chianti Cl. Castello di Brolio '07	♟♟♟ 8
● Chianti Cl. Castello di Brolio '06	♟♟♟ 8
● Chianti Cl. Castello di Brolio '04	♟♟♟ 7
● Chianti Cl. Castello di Brolio '03	♟♟♟ 5
● Chianti Cl. Castello di Brolio '01	♟♟♟ 6
● Chianti Cl. Castello di Brolio '00	♟♟♟ 6

Fattoria di Basciano

V.LE DUCA DELLA VITTORIA, 159
50068 RUFINA [FI]
TEL. 0558397034
www.renzomasibasciano.it

CELLAR SALES
PRE-BOOKED VISITS
ANNUAL PRODUCTION 200,000 bottles
HECTARES UNDER VINE 35.00

The Masi family have run Fattoria di Basciano, in the heart of Chianti Rufina, since the early 20th century. However when Paolo Masi, winemaker and son of the estate's founder, took over in the late 1980s he effected a profound renewal of the vineyards, with enlargements and general investment in improving the quality of the wines. Although trading is the estate's basic activity, the vineyards in the productive areas are meticulously managed. The wines follow a style that aims to please international palates, typically reflected in their colour, multilayered and spicy aromas, and pursuit of softer flavour. The top wine this year is the Pini 2011, a blend of cabernet sauvignon, sangiovese and syrah, with spice and pepper dominating the nose and some stellar cherry and raspberry fruit notes. The soft palate is nicely weighty and the tannins are well integrated with the alcohol. The Vin Santo del Chianti Rufina Riserva 2006 is sweet and aromatic.

● Chianti Rufina Ris. '10	♟♟ 3
● I Pini '11	♟♟ 4
○ Vin Santo Chianti Rufina Ris. '06	♟♟ 3
● Chianti Ris. '10	♟ 2
● Chianti Rufina '11	♟ 2
● Erta e China '11	♟ 2
● Il Corto '11	♟ 3
⊙ Rosato '12	♟ 1*
● Chianti Rufina '09	♟♟ 2*
● Erta e China '10	♟♟ 2*
● Erta e China '09	♟♟ 2*
● Il Corto '10	♟♟ 3
○ Vin Santo Rufina '06	♟♟ 3
○ Vin Santo Rufina '05	♟♟ 3

Begnardi

LOC. MONTEANTICO
POD. CAMPOROSSO, 34
58030 CIVITELLA PAGANICO [GR]
TEL. 0564991030
www.begnardi.com

CELLAR SALES
PRE-BOOKED VISITS
ACCOMMODATION AND RESTAURANT SERVICE
ANNUAL PRODUCTION 20,000 bottles
HECTARES UNDER VINE 5.00

Luca and Michele Begnardi are the owners of this estate located in the heart of the DOC. Their dedication and passion for agriculture are evident in the various activities on the property, from an agriturismo to a restaurant. They are also kept busy full-time on the land by their production of extra-virgin olive oil. The wines are decidedly territorial and are the fruit of a linear and effective philosophy that weds quality with an accurate simplicity. Two Montecuccos stood out in tastings: the Riserva Pigna Rossa 2010 has intense notes of fruit, tertiary hints of leather and tobacco, and a firm body with an engaging long finish. The Sangiovese Ceneo 2011 has mineral notes with vegetal hints of herbs and dark fruit, a tasty, well-structured palate, well-integrated tannins and a pleasant, juicy finish.

● Montecucco Sangiovese Ceneo '11	♟♟ 3
● Montecucco Sangiovese Pigna Rossa Ris. '10	♟♟ 5
⊙ Maremma Toscana 34 '12	♟ 2
● Montecucco Rosso '11	♟ 3
● Montecucco Sangiovese Ceneo '09	♟♟ 3
● Montecucco Sangiovese Pigna Rossa Ris. '09	♟♟ 5
● Montecucco Sangiovese Pigna Rossa Ris. '08	♟♟ 5
● Montecucco Sangiovese Pigna Rossa Ris. '07	♟♟ 5

Podere Le Berne

LOC. CERVOGNANO
VIA POGGIO GOLO, 7
53040 MONTEPULCIANO [SI]
TEL. 0578767328
www.leberne.it

CELLAR SALES
ANNUAL PRODUCTION 25,000 bottles
HECTARES UNDER VINE 6.00

This name of this estate derives from the Etruscan "verna" or "verena", meaning hill where one hibernates. Le Berne started producing in the 1960s, when the owner, Egisto Natalini, decided to make wine from the grapes in his vineyards. Since then his passion has enveloped the family and today his son Andrea, president of the Consorzio Vino Nobile di Montepulciano, is at the helm. He is cultivates his vineyards with great enthusiasm using modern techniques to obtain the best quality and perfect his production processes. The Nobile Riserva 2009, with mature notes of jam, good structure, decisive tannins and a supple, meaty palate stood out. L'Affronto 2011, mainly colorino with mammolo, has fresh acidity and herbal aromas. The Vin Santo 2006 is enchanting, with hints of dates and figs, a soft, creamy and stylish body, with a long satisfying finish.

● L'Affronto '11	♟♟ 2*
● Nobile di Montepulciano Ris. '09	♟♟ 5
○ Vin Santo di Montepulciano Ada '06	♟♟ 5
● Nobile di Montepulciano '10	♟ 3
● Rosso di Montepulciano '12	♟ 2
● Nobile di Montepulciano '06	♟♟♟ 3
● Nobile di Montepulciano '09	♟♟ 3
● Nobile di Montepulciano '08	♟♟ 3
● Nobile di Montepulciano '07	♟♟ 3
● Nobile di Montepulciano Ris. '08	♟♟ 5
● Nobile di Montepulciano Ris. '07	♟♟ 5
● Rosso di Montepulciano '11	♟♟ 2*

Tenuta di Bibbiano

VIA BIBBIANO, 76
53011 CASTELLINA IN CHIANTI [SI]
TEL. 0577743065
www.tenutadibibbiano.com

CELLAR SALES
PRE-BOOKED VISITS
ACCOMMODATION
ANNUAL PRODUCTION 100,000 bottles
HECTARES UNDER VINE 25.00
VITICULTURE METHOD Certified Organic

This estate in Castellina in Chianti sold its first bottles in 1969 and since then has barely altered a style that offers very coherent expressions of the DOC. The vineyards are managed using organic methods and in the cellar the oenological interventions are cut to the absolute minimum, relying completely on the quality of the grapes. The result is labels with great character and personality that consistently display expressive clarity and links to the territory. Ageing takes place in stainless steel, and large and small barrels. The Chianti Classico 2011 is very typical, with aromas of flowers and earth, and a delicate, lively flavour. A hint of reduction attenuates aromas in the Chianti Classico Montornello 2011 and its forte is the well-paced, spirited finish. The Chianti Classico Vigna del Capannino Riserva 2010 is rich and mouth filling.

● Chianti Cl. '11	♟♟ 3
● Chianti Cl. Montornello '11	♟♟ 3
● Chianti Cl. V. del Capannino Ris. '10	♟♟ 5
● Chianti Cl. '10	♟♟ 3
● Chianti Cl. '07	♟♟ 3*
● Chianti Cl. '06	♟♟ 2*
● Chianti Cl. Montornello '10	♟♟ 3
● Chianti Cl. Montornello '09	♟♟ 3
● Chianti Cl. Montornello '08	♟♟ 3
● Chianti Cl. Montornello '06	♟♟ 2*
● Chianti Cl. V. del Capannino Ris. '06	♟♟ 5
● Chianti Cl. V. del Capannino Ris. '05	♟♟ 4

Bindella

FRAZ. ACQUAVIVA
VIA DELLE TRE BERTE, 10A
53045 MONTEPULCIANO [SI]
TEL. 0578767777
www.bindella.it

CELLAR SALES
ANNUAL PRODUCTION 130,000 bottles
HECTARES UNDER VINE 30.00

The Bindella family have cultivated vines for over a century. Around 30 years ago, Rudy Bindella, a Swiss entrepreneur in the food service sector, chose Montepulciano and Vino Nobile production as the ideal place in which to practise his profession of vigneron, after the family had started wine growing in Switzerland. The vineyards cover part of the property that is divided between woods, arable land and olive groves. The philosophy of earth, vine, life that drives this estate is emblazoned on every bottle, expressing a passion for the land and joie de vivre. The Occhio di Pernice 2004 Vin Santo reveals a persuasive bouquet of forest fruits, various spices and aromatic herbs, a creamy, enveloping body, and a long tasty palate. The Nobile I Quadri 2010 has fresh, fruity nose notes, a full, balanced body, and compelling finish. The Nobile 2010 is a fresh and lively for a stylish tipple.

○ Vin Santo Occhio di Pernice Dolce Sinfonia '04	♟♟ 6
● Nobile di Montepulciano '10	♟♟ 3
● Nobile di Montepulciano I Quadri '10	♟♟ 5
○ Vin Santo di Montepulciano Dolce Sinfonia '06	♟♟ 5
● Antenata '10	♟ 3
○ Gemella '12	♟ 3
● Rosso di Montepulciano '12	♟ 2
● Nobile di Montepulciano I Quadri '09	♟♟ 5
● Nobile di Montepulciano I Quadri '08	♟♟ 4
● Nobile di Montepulciano I Quadri '07	♟♟ 4
● Nobile di Montepulciano Ris. '06	♟♟ 4
● Rosso di Montepulciano Fosso Lupaio '11	♟♟ 2*
○ Vin Santo Dolce Sinfonia '06	♟♟ 5

★Biondi Santi
Tenuta Il Greppo

LOC. VILLA GREPPO, 183
53024 MONTALCINO [SI]
TEL. 0577848087
www.biondisanti.it

CELLAR SALES
PRE-BOOKED VISITS
ACCOMMODATION
ANNUAL PRODUCTION 80,000 bottles
HECTARES UNDER VINE 25.00

More than just one of the most important figures of all time in the history of wine in Montalcino, Italy, and the world, Franco Biondi Santi was above all a remarkable gentleman. His fans will always remember him walking along the avenue towards the Tenuta Il Greppo or using a map and a light to explain the complexities of the Montalcino territory, its zones, exposures and site climates. His passing leaves a human void impossible to fill, but one that will be made lighter by the dozens of bottles of Brunello Riserva that are his legacy, bottles as immortal as his spirit. The Brunello Riserva 2007 from Il Greppo may not be as long-lived as other versions, but it easily wins the Tre Bicchieri with its usual striking freshness and youth, still needing time for full definition, especially of its aromatic framework. The 2008 is not far behind, subtle as may be expected from the vintage.

● Brunello di Montalcino Ris. '07	♟♟♟	8
● Brunello di Montalcino '08	♟♟	8
● Brunello di Montalcino '06	♟♟♟	7
● Brunello di Montalcino '04	♟♟♟	8
● Brunello di Montalcino '03	♟♟♟	8
● Brunello di Montalcino '01	♟♟♟	8
● Brunello di Montalcino '83	♟♟♟	8
● Brunello di Montalcino Ris. '06	♟♟♟	8
● Brunello di Montalcino Ris. '04	♟♟♟	8
● Brunello di Montalcino Ris. '01	♟♟♟	8
● Brunello di Montalcino Ris. '99	♟♟♟	8
● Brunello di Montalcino Ris. '95	♟♟♟	8
● Brunello di Montalcino '07	♟♟	8

Tenuta di Biserno

LOC. PALAZZO GARDINI
P.ZZA GRAMSCI, 9
57020 BIBBONA [LI]
TEL. 0586671099
www.biserno.it

ANNUAL PRODUCTION 160,000 bottles
HECTARES UNDER VINE 99.00

Founded by brothers Lodovico and Piero Antinori with Umberto Mannoni, the Tenuta was born of an intuition and a gamble: invest in the wine-growing potential of the district of Bibbona. As a result of this venture, this magnificent land swathed in Mediterranean scrub was transformed in a short time into a sanctuary for vines planted in the Bordeaux style, once the best sites had been identified. Aged in small barrels, the wines are the oenological product of the land and the technicians and reflect a style based on extraction, concentration and roundness. Another Tre Bicchieri for this winery goes to its Biserno 2010, a classic Bordeaux blend mainly of merlot and cabernet sauvignon. The intense, fragrant nose expresses forest fruits ennobled by hints of spice and green bell pepper. The flavoursome palate is spacious, very rich and dense, with a long, satisfyingly complex finish.

● Biserno '10	♟♟♟	8
● Il Pino di Biserno '10	♟♟	6
● Insoglio del Cinghiale Campo del Sasso '11	♟♟	4
● Biserno '08	♟♟♟	6
● Il Pino di Biserno '09	♟♟♟	6
● Biserno '09	♟♟	3
● Il Pino di Biserno '08	♟♟	6
● Insoglio del Cinghiale '09	♟♟	4*

Borgo Salcetino

Loc. Lucarelli
53017 Radda in Chianti [SI]
Tel. 0577733541
www.livon.it

CELLAR SALES
PRE-BOOKED VISITS
ANNUAL PRODUCTION 66,000 bottles
HECTARES UNDER VINE 20.00

Livon, the famous Friulia wine family known for their white production, diversified its production when it took over two red-based estates, Col Santo in Umbria and Borgo Salcetino in Tuscany. The latter is located in the area fringing the Chianti in Radda in Chianti and was acquired in the mid-1990s. It is producing some really prestigious bottles, although not always consistently. The style is very faithful to the traditional rules of the Chianti Classico, starting with ageing in big barrels. The wines are elegant and dynamic on the palate. The Chianti Classico 2011 is quite simply a delicious wine. The aromas are clean and airy; the palate shows grip and contrast, revealing a fluent, assertive palate. In the Chianti Classico Lucarello Riserva 2010 the nose is smoky, the palate fresh with good complexity, weighed down slightly by some lingering oak.

● Chianti Cl. '11	♟♟♟ 3*
● Chianti Cl. Lucarello Ris. '10	♟♟ 4
● Chianti Cl. '10	♟♟ 3
● Chianti Cl. '09	♟♟ 3
● Chianti Cl. '08	♟♟ 3
● Chianti Cl. '07	♟♟ 3*
● Chianti Cl. '03	♟♟ 3
● Chianti Cl. '01	♟♟ 3
● Chianti Cl. Lucarello Ris. '07	♟♟ 4
● Chianti Cl. Lucarello Ris. '06	♟♟ 4
● Chianti Cl. Lucarello Ris. '99	♟♟ 4
● Rossole '08	♟♟ 3
● Rossole '06	♟♟ 3
● Rossole '04	♟♟ 3
● Rossole '02	♟♟ 3
● Rossole '00	♟♟ 3

Poderi Boscarelli ✓

Fraz. Cervognano
via di Montenero, 28
53045 Montepulciano [SI]
Tel. 0578767277
www.poderiboscarelli.com

CELLAR SALES
PRE-BOOKED VISITS
ANNUAL PRODUCTION 100,000 bottles
HECTARES UNDER VINE 14.00

Podere Boscarelli lies at an altitude of 300 metres between Montepulciano and the Valdichiana. It is run by Nicoló and Luca De Ferrari, grandsons of Egidio Corradi, who are so enthusiastic about wine and this territory that they decided to invest launching a high-quality production in 1962. The work is neatly divided: Nicolò looks after the vineyards and cellar while Luca deals with sales and PR. The cellar is under continuous modernization to keep pace with new requirements. Grapes and ambient yeasts, knowledge and great passion characterize this estate that has many fans among the great lovers of Tuscan wines. The Nobile Riserva 2008 is austere on the nose with aromas of sage and rosemary, hints of jam and tobacco, a firm body and balance, leading to a fluid finish. A Tre Bicchieri goes to the Nocio dei Boscarelli 2009, with clean notes of fruit, cherry and plum, a balanced body, just the right amount of tannins, and good drinkability.

● Nobile di Montepulciano Nocio dei Boscarelli '09	♟♟♟ 8
● Nobile di Montepulciano Ris. '08	♟♟ 6
● De Ferrari '12	♟ 3
● Nobile di Montepulciano '10	♟ 5
● Rosso di Montepulciano Prugnolo '11	♟ 3
● Nobile di Montepulciano Nocio dei Boscarelli '08	♟♟♟ 8
● Nobile di Montepulciano Nocio dei Boscarelli '07	♟♟♟ 8
● Nobile di Montepulciano Nocio dei Boscarelli '04	♟♟♟ 6
● Nobile di Montepulciano Nocio dei Boscarelli '01	♟♟♟ 6
● Nobile di Montepulciano Ris. '06	♟♟♟ 5

★Brancaia

LOC. POPPI, 42
53017 RADDA IN CHIANTI [SI]
TEL. 0577742007
www.brancaia.com

CELLAR SALES
PRE-BOOKED VISITS
ACCOMMODATION
ANNUAL PRODUCTION 475,000 bottles
HECTARES UNDER VINE 66.00

With vineyards scattered between Castellina and Radda in Chianti, and a guesthouse in the Maremma, the Brancaia winery has, over its thirty-year history, reached a position at the top of Tuscan winemaking. This success is due mainly to the consistently solid quality of its wines, modern in style, and distinguished by aromatic intensity and powerful structure, yet never lacking refinement. This style is still convincing and represents one of the best compromises between wines with immediate appeal and more complex wines more closely linked to their area of provenance. Once again we tasted a truly great Chianti Classico Riserva 2010, this one with a discreet nose profile hinting at bay leaf that enhances freshness, opening into a terrific, vertical, almost hard palate, but equally deep and juicy. Il Blu 2009 is a sangiovese, merlot and cabernet sauvignon blend offering fragrant, relaxed drinking despite its big structure.

● Chianti Cl. Ris. '10	♟♟♟	4*
● Brancaia Il Blu '10	♟♟	7
○ Bianco '12	♟	3
● Brancaia Tre '11	♟	3
● Ilatraia '11	♟	6
● Brancaia '99	♟♟♟	6
● Brancaia '98	♟♟♟	6
● Brancaia Il Blu '08	♟♟♟	8
● Brancaia Il Blu '07	♟♟♟	7
● Brancaia Il Blu '06	♟♟♟	6
● Brancaia Il Blu '05	♟♟♟	6
● Brancaia Il Blu '04	♟♟♟	6
● Brancaia Il Blu '03	♟♟♟	6
● Brancaia Il Blu '01	♟♟♟	6
● Brancaia Il Blu '00	♟♟♟	6
● Chianti Cl. Ris. '09	♟♟♟	7

Brunelli - Le Chiuse di Sotto ✎

LOC. PODERNOVONE, 154
53024 MONTALCINO [SI]
TEL. 0577849337
www.giannibrunelli.it

CELLAR SALES
PRE-BOOKED VISITS
ACCOMMODATION AND RESTAURANT SERVICE
ANNUAL PRODUCTION 30,000 bottles
HECTARES UNDER VINE 6.50

Superfluous rhetoric aside, it is impossible not to recall the figure of Gianni Brunelli every time the tale of Le Chiuse di Sotto is told. His wife Laura has completely absorbed the legacy, more moral than winemaking, of this character who had a profound impact on the Montalcino district and beyond. This is also because of these great wines, which continue to reflect the almost complementary features of the two main wine-growing areas: one north-east of the village in the Canalicchio area, and one to the south in Podernovone. The two areas are quite different, yet they share the same traditional sensibility, which means attention and patience for the house Brunellos. We can really recommend the Brunello Riserva 2007, a concentrate of contradictions, the evolving features set against an edgy, clenched palate. The Brunello 2008 is more easy-going, very classic in its hints of resin and steak tartare, but it fails to change gear through to the finish.

● Brunello di Montalcino '08	♟♟	6
● Brunello di Montalcino Ris. '07	♟♟	8
● Rosso di Montalcino '11	♟	4
● Amor Costante '05	♟♟♟	5
● Brunello di Montalcino '07	♟♟	6
● Brunello di Montalcino '06	♟♟	6
● Brunello di Montalcino Ris. '06	♟♟	8

Bulichella

LOC. BULICHELLA, 131
57028 SUVERETO [LI]
TEL. 0565829892
www.bulichella.it

CELLAR SALES
PRE-BOOKED VISITS
ACCOMMODATION AND RESTAURANT SERVICE
ANNUAL PRODUCTION 60,000 bottles
HECTARES UNDER VINE 17.00
VITICULTURE METHOD Certified Organic

This estate was founded in 1983 when four families from different areas of Italy decided to up sticks and move to a pristine area where they could farm. All the crops, both vegetables and grapes for wine production, were set up using organic methods. In 1999 the family headed by Mijakawa Hideyuki and his wife Maria Luisa Bassano became the sole proprietor. They have invested in the property, creating a new cellar, new vineyards, and an agriturismo. All the wines we received were good. The Hide 2010, a monovarietal syrah, has gamey notes on the nose, delicate, spicy notes of pepper, and concentrated fruit. In the mouth it is juicy, with well-embedded, lively tannins and a long, tasty finish. The new viognier-based raisiny Tesoro 2012 is intriguing on the nose and pleasantly creamy in taste.

● Hide '10	▼▼ 5
● Aleatico Sfiziale '12	▼▼ 4
○ Passito Tesoro '12	▼▼ 3
● Val di Cornia Col di Pietre Rosse '10	▼▼ 5
● Val di Cornia Merlot Maria Shizuko '10	▼▼ 6
● Val di Cornia Suvereto Tuscanio '10	▼▼ 5
○ Val di Cornia Vermentino Tuscanio '12	▼ 3
● Aleatico Sfiziale '11	♀♀ 4
● Hide '09	♀♀ 5
● Val di Cornia Rosso Tuscanio '08	♀♀ 5
● Val di Cornia Suvereto Tuscanio '09	♀♀ 5

Tenuta del Buonamico

LOC. CERCATOIA
VIA PROVINCIALE DI MONTECARLO, 43
55015 MONTECARLO [LU]
TEL. 058322038
www.buonamico.it

CELLAR SALES
PRE-BOOKED VISITS
ACCOMMODATION
ANNUAL PRODUCTION 140,000 bottles
HECTARES UNDER VINE 33.00

Now the property of the Fontana family, the Tenuta del Buonamico is a historic estate in the territory of Montecarlo. It is located in the zone of Cercatoia that has always been known for its wine growing and therefore quite famous. The terrains are largely made up of sand and clay and are home to mainly international varieties that have grown here since the second half of the 1800s: sauvignon, semillon, roussanne, pinot bianco and grigio, merlot, cabernet sauvignon and franc, syrah imported directly from France, and locals trebbiano and sangiovese. The convincing Cercatoja Rosso 2010, from sangiovese, syrah and cabernet sauvignon, reveals its fragrance right from the nose, with aromas of berry fruits, notes of balsam and mountain herbs. The palate does not disappoint. The acidity orchestrates the palate, underpinned by good fragrant tannins, with a clean, long finish. The Fortino Syrah 2010 is also good, peppery and caressing on the nose, with an appealing palate.

● Cercatoja Rosso '10	▼▼ 5
● Il Fortino Syrah '10	▼▼ 6
● Montecarlo Rosso '11	▼▼ 3
○ Montecarlo Bianco '12	▼ 2
○ Montecarlo Vermentino '12	▼ 3
● Cercatoja Rosso '09	♀♀ 5
● Cercatoja Rosso '08	♀♀ 4
● Il Fortino Syrah '09	♀♀ 6

Ca' Marcanda

LOC. SANTA TERESA, 272
57022 CASTAGNETO CARDUCCI [LI]
TEL. 0565763809
info@camarcanda.com

ANNUAL PRODUCTION 450,000 bottles
HECTARES UNDER VINE 100.00

Angelo Gaja's beautiful Bolgheri estate has an impressive expanse of vineyards totalling 100 hectares and a large, futuristic cellar that allows him the space he needs to manage his grapes to best advantage. The style of the wines is modern as dictates the young Bolgheri tradition. Full, enveloping fruit and precise use of oak create wines that live up to all expectations. The varieties cultivated are the international cabernet sauvignon and franc, merlot, and a little syrah, whose percentages vary by label. 2010 was a difficult year for the zone, yet the Camarcanda is as full and fruity as ever, with its strawberry and cherry jam, barley sugar, and balsam on the nose, and compact palate, only slightly curbed by mouth-drying tannin. The hotter summer was beneficial for the structure and concentration of both the 2011 second-label wines, Magari and Promis. The Rennina 2008 from the Montalcino Pieve di Santa Restituta is also good.

● Bolgheri Camarcanda '10	▼▼ 8
● Brunello di Montalcino Rennina Pieve di Santa Restituta '08	▼▼ 7
● Magari '11	▼▼ 8
● Promis '11	▼▼ 7
● Brunello di Montalcino Sugarille Pieve di Santa Restituta '08	▼ 7
● Bolgheri Camarcanda '07	▽▽▽ 8
● Bolgheri Camarcanda '01	▽▽▽ 8
● Magari '03	▽▽▽ 6
● Bolgheri Camarcanda '09	▽▽ 8
● Brunello di Montalcino Rennina Pieve di Santa Restituta '07	▽▽ 7
● Brunello di Montalcino Sugarille Pieve di Santa Restituta '07	▽▽ 7
● Magari '10	▽▽ 8
● Promis '10	▽▽ 7

Tenuta Le Calcinaie

LOC. SANTA LUCIA, 36
53037 SAN GIMIGNANO [SI]
TEL. 0577943007
www.tenutalecalcinaie.it

CELLAR SALES
PRE-BOOKED VISITS
ANNUAL PRODUCTION 60,000 bottles
HECTARES UNDER VINE 9.50
VITICULTURE METHOD Certified Organic

Simone Santini and his personal microcosm are in tune with nature. With the ideas of a true original, apparently carefree but actually extraordinarily painstaking, he shows a genuine, almost obsessive attention to his vines and the wines he creates. Started up in 1986, Le Calcinaie boasts vineyards and a winery in the Santa Lucia area, where there is no lack of variation at least in terms of plot characteristics. The organic methods begun in 1995, a difficult and somewhat pioneering period, never sacrifice but instead enhance this careful, clean style with great precision and flavour. The Riserva Vigna ai Sassi 2009 reached the finals, making an altogether superb impression. The white is anything but modest or on the wane, and it is possibly at its peak, displaying the most elegant hazelnut fragrance on a charming base with lively green notes. Certainly an intense, big impact wine, that is only a tad lacking in the finish.

○ Vernaccia di S. Gimignano V. ai Sassi Ris. '09	▼▼ 3*
○ Vernaccia di S. Gimignano '12	▼▼ 2*
● Ingeredienti: Uva	▼ 3
● Gabriele '07	▽▽ 4
● Teodoro '07	▽▽ 4
● Teodoro '06	▽▽ 4
○ Vernaccia di S. Gimignano '10	▽▽ 2*
○ Vernaccia di S. Gimignano '09	▽▽ 2
○ Vernaccia di S. Gimignano '08	▽▽ 2*
○ Vernaccia di S. Gimignano '07	▽▽ 2*
○ Vernaccia di S. Gimignano Ris. '08	▽▽ 2*
○ Vernaccia di S. Gimignano V. ai Sassi '07	▽▽ 3
○ Vernaccia di S. Gimignano V. ai Sassi '06	▽▽ 3

Camigliano

LOC. CAMIGLIANO
VIA D'INGRESSO, 2
53024 MONTALCINO [SI]
TEL. 0577816061
www.camigliano.it

CELLAR SALES
PRE-BOOKED VISITS
ACCOMMODATION AND RESTAURANT SERVICE
ANNUAL PRODUCTION 300,000 bottles
HECTARES UNDER VINE 92.00

Ancient in its history and located on the western border of the territory of Montalcino, the village of Camigliano is an absolutely stunning place. It sits amidst the scrub in a pristine landscape with a splendid view over the Alta Maremma and the Colline Metallifere. The Ghezzi family acquired it in the late 1950s and gave it a new lease of life as the heart of a wine business centred around 100 or so hectares of vineyards, mostly planted to sangiovese. The new underground cellar has the double attraction of wider spaces for the eye to roam over, and capacity for a highly functional production. We are still waiting for a change in personality and territorial stamp from the Brunello di Camigliano, but the 2008 is well made, combining attractive oak with a fresh balsamic streak. The Gualto Riserva 2007 is lighter and more flowery but also a little hasty in the finish.

Camporignano

FRAZ. MONTEGUIDI
53031 CASOLE D'ELSA [SI]
TEL. 0577963915
www.camporignano.com

CELLAR SALES
ANNUAL PRODUCTION 30,000 bottles
HECTARES UNDER VINE 10.00

Camporignano wines, produced by Renzo and Lucia Rustici, express a synergy between the grapes and the land here in a protected area of Etruscan historical value alongside the Berignone forest, between Val d'Elsa and Val di Cecina. The grapes planted here are all international varieties that adapt well to the features of the land. The winery structure has an advanced CO_2 extraction system which creates ideal environmental conditions. Of great interest is the space dedicated to a well-organized calendar of exhibitions, which combine art and wine. The entire production is good. The Mattaione 2010 has its classic aromatic profile of cherry jam and vegetal hints, with a well-structured solid body, and serious progression. The Cerronero 2010 merlot and cabernet sauvignon blend, has mineral notes on the nose, fresh hints of balsam, firm but rounded body, and long, juicy finish.

● Brunello di Montalcino '08	▼▼ 6
● Brunello di Montalcino Gualto Ris. '07	▼▼ 7
● Rosso di Montalcino '11	▼ 3
● Brunello di Montalcino '08	♀♀ 6
● Brunello di Montalcino '06	♀♀ 6
● Brunello di Montalcino '05	♀♀ 5
● Brunello di Montalcino '04	♀♀ 5
● Brunello di Montalcino Gualto Ris. '06	♀♀ 7
● Brunello di Montalcino Gualto Ris. '05	♀♀ 7
● Brunello di Montalcino Gualto Ris. '04	♀♀ 7
○ Moscadello di Montalcino L'Aura '10	♀♀ 5
● Poderuccio '07	♀♀ 2*
● Rosso di Montalcino '08	♀♀ 3
● Sant'Antimo Cabernet Sauvignon Campo ai Mori '08	♀♀ 4
● Sant'Antimo Cabernet Sauvignon Campo ai Mori '06	♀♀ 4

● Terre di Casole Mattaione '10	▼▼ 3
● Cerronero '10	▼▼ 5
● Camporignano '08	♀♀ 2
● Cerronero '09	♀♀ 5
● Cerronero '07	♀♀ 5
● Cerronero '06	♀♀ 5
● Mattaione '09	♀♀ 3

Canalicchio Franco Pacenti

LOC. CANALICCHIO DI SOPRA, 6
53024 MONTALCINO [SI]
TEL. 0577849277
www.canalicchiofrancopacenti.it

CELLAR SALES
PRE-BOOKED VISITS
RESTAURANT SERVICE
ANNUAL PRODUCTION 40,000 bottles
HECTARES UNDER VINE 10.00

Situated around 300 metres above sea level on medium-bodied soil, with more clay than stones, Franco Pacenti's small winery takes its name from the Canalicchi area and is one of the most respected and consistent voices in the northern quadrant of Montalcino. The ten hectares of this estate are planted exclusively to Sangiovese, which here expresses nebbiolo-type characteristics. The wines are austere and tannic. Tough when young, they enjoy good aeration in the glass and are especially suitable for ageing in bottle. This is a no-frills Brunello produced with traditional fermentation and long maceration in large barrels. The Brunello 2008 is a copybook wine, with medicinal, iron and root notes, but is a little short on density and reach, as might be expected from a year that was poor from the start. There are some over-evolved traits in the Riserva 2007, with its pared-down dry pace.

● Brunello di Montalcino '08	♥♥ 5
● Brunello di Montalcino Ris. '07	♥♥ 7
● Rosso di Montalcino '11	♥ 3
● Brunello di Montalcino '04	♀♀♀ 5
● Brunello di Montalcino '07	♀♀ 5
● Brunello di Montalcino '06	♀♀ 5
● Rosso di Montalcino '10	♀♀ 3

Canalicchio di Sopra

LOC. CASACCIA, 73
53024 MONTALCINO [SI]
TEL. 0577848316
www.canalicchiodisopra.com

CELLAR SALES
PRE-BOOKED VISITS
ACCOMMODATION
ANNUAL PRODUCTION 55,000 bottles
HECTARES UNDER VINE 15.00

Between the slopes of the Canalicchi and Le Gode di Montosoli lie 15 hectares managed by Simonetta, Marco and Francesco Ripaccioli, third generation at the winery founded in 1961 by their grandfather Primo Pacenti and led for a long time by their father Pier Luigi. We are on the side of Montalcino facing Buonconvento, to the north of the town. In this highly characteristic area, they constantly aim for a style with energy and deep rich flavour, using long maceration and ageing in 30-hectolitre Slavonian oak barrels. 2007 was a year to remember at the Ripaccioli winery and the Tre Bicchieri taken last year by the vintage Brunello can be added those of the Riserva. The hot summer is revealed by the more open nose, which finds character and fullness in hints of spice and sea air, dried herbs and black olives. The tannin is challenging but the piquant, fruity texture is the measure of its true worth.

● Brunello di Montalcino Ris. '07	♥♥♥ 8
● Brunello di Montalcino '08	♥♥ 6
● Rosso di Montalcino '11	♥♥ 3
● Brunello di Montalcino '07	♀♀♀ 6
● Brunello di Montalcino '06	♀♀♀ 6
● Brunello di Montalcino '04	♀♀♀ 6
● Brunello di Montalcino Ris. '04	♀♀♀ 7
● Brunello di Montalcino Ris. '01	♀♀♀ 7
● Brunello di Montalcino '05	♀♀ 5
● Brunello di Montalcino Ris. '06	♀♀ 8
● Rosso di Montalcino '09	♀♀ 3
● Rosso di Montalcino '08	♀♀ 3*
● Rosso di Montalcino '06	♀♀ 3

Canneto

VIA DEI CANNETI, 14
53045 MONTEPULCIANO [SI]
TEL. 0578757737
www.canneto.com

CELLAR SALES
PRE-BOOKED VISITS
ACCOMMODATION
ANNUAL PRODUCTION 100,000 bottles
HECTARES UNDER VINE 29.00

In 1987, a group of friends living near
Zurich with a passion for Nobile di
Montepulciano, decided to move from
consuming to producing it. They bought a
farm in the territory that produced their
beloved wine and started their own cellar.
The task was all-consuming; first they
restored the old buildings, then built a
cellar and acquired all the equipment
required to process the grapes, all this
while running the farm too. It was a good
tasting for the Nobile Riserva 2009, with
notes of spice on the nose, nuanced with
clove and cinnamon, on a focused base of
woodland berries. The soft, meaty palate
reveals elegant, subtle tannins and a long,
dynamic finish. The Vendemmia Tardiva
2010 is a pleasant blend that includes
Istrian and Tuscan malvasia, petit manseng,
traminer, and riesling, with delicate flowery
aromas, a creamy, velvety body and a
restrained sweet finish.

● Nobile di Montepulciano Ris. '09	♟♟ 4
○ Vendemmia Tardiva '10	♟♟ 4
○ Calamus '12	♟ 2
● Nobile di Montepulciano '10	♟ 3
● Rosso di Montepulciano '12	♟ 2
● Nobile di Montepulciano '09	♟♟ 3*
● Nobile di Montepulciano '08	♟♟ 3
● Nobile di Montepulciano '07	♟♟ 3
● Nobile di Montepulciano Ris. '07	♟♟ 4
○ Vendemmia Tardiva '09	♟♟ 3

Capanna

LOC. CAPANNA, 333
53024 MONTALCINO [SI]
TEL. 0577848298
www.capannamontalcino.com

CELLAR SALES
PRE-BOOKED VISITS
ANNUAL PRODUCTION 70,000 bottles
HECTARES UNDER VINE 19.50

Patrizio Cencioni has no need to pontificate
when explaining his ideas about Montalcino
Sangiovese. He only need talk about his
Brunellos, which, especially in the Riserva
versions, embody that rare sense of pride,
rigour, and the simple tension expected
from Montosoli vineyards and long
maceration in large barrels. We should
mention, therefore, some youthful shyness
in aroma and taste, but a little patience is
rewarded with classic eloquence in the
finest sense of the word. The range is
completed by a Sant'Antimo Rosso, mostly
merlot, and the Rosso del Cerro, pure
sangiovese. As so often happens with a
good harvest, this is another fabulous
version of the Brunello Riserva 2007 from
Capanna. Dark, plump fruit, with topsoil
and incense give depth, finding aromatic
persistence and piquant grip in a palate
that is more horizontal than usual, just a
little dry in the finish. The Brunello 2008 is
excellent.

● Brunello di Montalcino Ris. '07	♟♟ 7
● Brunello di Montalcino '08	♟♟ 6
● Rosso di Montalcino '11	♟♟ 3
● Rosso del Cerro '11	♟ 2
● Brunello di Montalcino Ris. '06	♟♟♟ 7
● Brunello di Montalcino Ris. '04	♟♟♟ 7
● Brunello di Montalcino Ris. '90	♟♟♟ 6
● Brunello di Montalcino '07	♟♟ 5
● Brunello di Montalcino '06	♟♟ 5
● Brunello di Montalcino '05	♟♟ 5
● Brunello di Montalcino '04	♟♟ 5
● Brunello di Montalcino Ris. '01	♟♟ 7
● Rosso del Cerro '10	♟♟ 2*
● Rosso di Montalcino '08	♟♟ 3

Tenuta Caparzo

LOC. CAPARZO
SP DEL BRUNELLO
53024 MONTALCINO [SI]
TEL. 0577848390
www.caparzo.com

CELLAR SALES
PRE-BOOKED VISITS
ACCOMMODATION
ANNUAL PRODUCTION 455,000 bottles
HECTARES UNDER VINE 90.00

A historic label in the Montalcino area, Elisabetta Gnudi's winery spreads over around 90 hectares of vineyards, located in various areas of the DOC zone. Sangiovese is naturally the leading variety in a large group that also includes chardonnay, sauvignon, traminer, cabernet, syrah, colorino, merlot and petit verdot. The house style is well known, due particularly to the best versions of La Casa, a Brunello selection that shows the characteristics of the northern quadrant with a hint of modernity, and is gradually undergoing some adjustments. In this year's tastings the 2007s fared best: in the Riserva the aromatics are a little predictable, with ripe fruit, liquorice and some oaky notes, but it is still fluent and proficient. La Casa is more conflicting, with notes of jam leading into a stronger taste than usual. The modern, confident style is also seen in the Rosso La Caduta 2010.

● Brunello di Montalcino La Casa '07	♥♥	8
● Brunello di Montalcino Ris. '07	♥♥	7
● Morellino di Scansano		
Doga delle Clavure '11	♥♥	3
● Rosso di Montalcino La Caduta '10	♥♥	4
● Brunello di Montalcino '08	♥	6
● Rosso di Montalcino '11	♥	3
● Brunello di Montalcino La Casa '93	♥♥♥	6
● Brunello di Montalcino La Casa '88	♥♥♥	6
● Brunello di Montalcino '07	♥♥	6
● Ca' del Pazzo '07	♥♥	5
○ Moscadello di Montalcino V. T. '06	♥♥	5

Tenuta di Capezzana

LOC. SEANO
VIA CAPEZZANA, 100
59015 CARMIGNANO [PO]
TEL. 0558706005
www.capezzana.it

CELLAR SALES
PRE-BOOKED VISITS
ACCOMMODATION AND RESTAURANT SERVICE
ANNUAL PRODUCTION 450,000 bottles
HECTARES UNDER VINE 80.00

Belonging to a terroir which guarantees the production of excellent wines makes it possible to uphold the tradition of wine-growing and hand it down to generation after generation. Oil and wine were produced at Capezzana 1200 years ago, so this is the background of the estate situated to the north of Carmignano which produces oil and Vin Santo as well as wines. The Contini Bonacossi patriarch recently passed away, leaving his mark on the winery now managed by his children. Great care is taken over respecting traditional characteristics as well as renewal, and this well-balanced combination produces wines in an extremely modern style. The Trebbiano 2011 made the finals, with subtle, layered aromatic complexity, solid body, freshness and tanginess, and a deep, tantalising finish. The 804, made on one occasion from syrah grapes also made the finals with its intense aromas of mixed spices, combined with leather and ripe dark fruit. It is juicy, full and generous on the palate, with lovely length.

● Capezzana 804 '04	♥♥	8
○ Trebbiano '11	♥♥	4
● Carmignano Villa di Capezzana '09	♥♥	4
● Barco Reale '11	♥	2
⊙ Carmignano Vin Ruspo '12	♥	2
● Carmignano Villa di Capezzana '07	♥♥♥	4
● Carmignano Villa di Capezzana '05	♥♥♥	4
● Ghiaie della Furba '01	♥♥♥	5
○ Vin Santo di Carmignano Ris. '05	♥♥♥	5
● Barco Reale '10	♥♥	2*
● Carmignano Villa di Capezzana '08	♥♥	4
● Ghiaie della Furba '08	♥♥	5
● Sessanta '07	♥♥	2*

Caprili

FRAZ. TAVERNELLE
POD. CAPRILI, 268
53024 MONTALCINO [SI]
TEL. 0577848566
www.caprili.it

CELLAR SALES
PRE-BOOKED VISITS
ANNUAL PRODUCTION 75,000 bottles
HECTARES UNDER VINE 18.00

The Bartolommei family bought Caprili in the mid-1960s from the Signori Castelli-Martinozzi, owners of the Villa Santa Restituta. 1978 was the first vintage of Brunello bottled and from the outset it showed a very traditional slant with lengthy ageing in big barrels of Slavonian oak. The various plots are vinified separately then blended: Ceppo Nero, dell'Esse, Testucchiaia, Quadrucci, del Pino and del Palazzetto come together in the standard-label Brunello; Vigna Madre is dedicated to the Riserva; Vigna della Fornacina provides the trebbiano and malvasia for the Sant'Antimo Bianco and the Moscadello. The wonderful performance of recent years was lacking this time, but the Brunello 2008 is a very faithful interpretation of Montalcino Sangiovese in the Caprili style. With dried flowers, yellow peach and light glutamate, the clear development of tertiary aromas is confirmed by a gentle, welcoming palate on entry, then warm and edgy in the second part.

● Brunello di Montalcino '08	♀♀ 5
● Brunello di Montalcino '06	♀♀♀ 5
● Brunello di Montalcino Ris. '06	♀♀♀ 5
● Brunello di Montalcino Ris. '04	♀♀♀ 5
● Brunello di Montalcino '07	♀♀ 5
● Brunello di Montalcino '05	♀♀ 5

Podere II Carnasciale

LOC. PODERE IL CARNASCIALE
52020 MERCATALE VALDARNO [AR]
TEL. 0559911142
bettina.rogosky@gmail.com

ANNUAL PRODUCTION 3,000 bottles

The story of Podere II Carnasciale and the birth of the Caberlot has all the makings of a fairytale, a love story featuring Bettina Schnabel and Wolf Rogosky who met in Berlin in 1963. In 1972 they decided to buy some land in Tuscany and create a welcoming home in which to stay between their trips to New York and Paris. In 1986 they started making wine from an unknown variety. The early vintages were satisfactory and in 1991 the Caberlot became an independent reality that Bettina continues to produce with on-going success following the death of Wolf in 1996. The Caberlot 2010, produced only as a magnum, takes another Tre Bicchieri with a unique, easily recognizable floral aroma of geranium mingling with aromatic marjoram and mint on a fruity base of currants and cherry. The mouth is sturdy, rich, with balanced acidity, richness of flavour, subtle tannins and exhilarating length of taste.

● Caberlot '10	♀♀♀ 8
● Caberlot '08	♀♀♀ 8
● Caberlot '05	♀♀♀ 8
● Caberlot '04	♀♀♀ 8
● Caberlot '00	♀♀♀ 8
● Caberlot '09	♀♀ 8

Fattoria Carpineta Fontalpino

FRAZ. MONTAPERTI
LOC. CARPINETA
53019 CASTELNUOVO BERARDENGA [SI]
TEL. 0577369219
www.carpinetafontalpino.it

CELLAR SALES
PRE-BOOKED VISITS
ACCOMMODATION
ANNUAL PRODUCTION 100,000 bottles
HECTARES UNDER VINE 23.00
VITICULTURE METHOD Certified Organic

The recent leap in quality witnessed by this estate in Monteaperti is no longer news, but rather the hallmark of a winery that is consistently among the best in the DOC zone. The wines produced at Carpineta Fontalpino are generous and impeccably made, with ample personality. With judicious use of small barrels for ageing, the modern-style profile shows good colour extraction and big structure, but plenty of decisive acidity and spirited, well-articulated tannins. This nicely balanced mix offers convincing wines that never understate their link to the territory. The Chianti Classico 2011 is truly expressive for its clean, complex aromas that alternate with notes of fruit and mild spice, and a wonderful deep, mature, taut palate. Firm and austere, the Dofana 2010 has a multifaceted bouquet and flavoursome palate.

● Dofana '10	♟♟♟	7
● Chianti Cl. Fontalpino '11	♟♟	3*
● Chianti Cl. Fontalpino Ris. '10	♟♟	5
● Do ut des '10	♟♟♟	5
● Do ut des '09	♟♟♟	5
● Do ut des '07	♟♟♟	5
● Dofana '07	♟♟♟	8
● Chianti Cl. Ris. '06	♟♟	5
● Do ut des '08	♟♟	5
● Do ut des '06	♟♟	5
● Do ut des '05	♟♟	5
● Do ut des '04	♟♟	5
● Do ut des '03	♟♟	5
● Do ut des '02	♟♟	5
● Dofana '06	♟♟	8
● Dofana '04	♟♟	8

Casa alle Vacche

FRAZ. PANCOLE
LOC. LUCIGNANO, 73A
53037 SAN GIMIGNANO [SI]
TEL. 0577955103
www.casaallevacche.it

CELLAR SALES
PRE-BOOKED VISITS
ACCOMMODATION AND RESTAURANT SERVICE
ANNUAL PRODUCTION 115,000 bottles
HECTARES UNDER VINE 28.00

This lovely estate covers around 30 hectares in all, 20 of these planted in vineyards. The Ciappi family have opted for a mix of local varieties like sangiovese, canaiolo, vernaccia and malvasia del Chianti, with some well-known international grapes like cabernet sauvignon, merlot and chardonnay. The estate's name is based on the former use of Lucignano, the subzone of this winery, as an area for sheltering livestock. In line with the terroir and respectful of its characteristics, these wines are wonderfully expressive and full of vigour and flavour. The best tasting of the year was without a doubt the San Gimignano Riserva Crocus 2010. The mature bouquet, brimming with peachy fruit aromas, is well balanced with iodine and slightly minty notes. The palate is equally full in attack, underpinned by a vein of freshness and enough acidity to make it pleasant and never too heavy.

○ Vernaccia di S. Gimignano Crocus Ris. '10	♟♟	2*
● Chianti Colli Senesi Cinabro Ris. '10	♟	3
⊙ Rosato '12	♟	2
○ Vernaccia di S. Gimignano '12	♟	2
○ Vernaccia di S. Gimignano I Macchioni '12	♟	2
● Aglieno '08	♟♟	2*
○ Vernaccia di S. Gimignano '11	♟♟	2*
○ Vernaccia di S. Gimignano Crocus Ris. '09	♟♟	3
○ Vernaccia di S. Gimignano Crocus Ris. '08	♟♟	2*
○ Vernaccia di S. Gimignano I Macchioni '11	♟♟	2*
○ Vernaccia di S. Gimignano I Macchioni '10	♟♟	2*
○ Vernaccia di S. Gimignano I Macchioni '09	♟♟	2*

Casa Emma

LOC. CORTINE
SP DI CASTELLINA IN CHIANTI, 3
50021 BARBERINO VAL D'ELSA [FI]
TEL. 0558072239
www.casaemma.com

CELLAR SALES
PRE-BOOKED VISITS
ANNUAL PRODUCTION 85,000 bottles
HECTARES UNDER VINE 23.00

For years the property of the Bucalossi
family, who bought it from Florentine
noblewoman Emma Bizzarri and kept a
trace of its history in the name, Casa Emma
is in the heart of the Chianti Classico DOCG
between Barberino Val d'Elsa in the
province of Florence and Castellina in
Chianti in Siena. The wines have a very
distinctive style: aged mainly in barriques,
the modern bottles make few compromises
yet still express a certain personality and a
strong link with their territory of origin. The
delicious Chianti Classico 2011 shows a
flavoursome, nicely-paced progression and
clear, delicate bouquet. The aromas in the
Chianti Classico Vignalparco 2011 are less
defined, with a fresh-tasting palate and
plenty of grip. The abundance of oak in the
ageing of the Chianti Classico Riserva 2010
hinders both nose and palate.

● Chianti Cl. '11	♛♛ 3*
● Chianti Cl. Vignalparco '11	♛♛ 3
● Chianti Cl. Ris. '10	♛ 5
● Chianti Cl. Ris. '95	♛♛♛ 4*
● Chianti Cl. Ris. '93	♛♛♛ 5
● Soloio '94	♛♛♛ 4*
● Chianti Cl. '10	♛♛ 3
● Chianti Cl. '08	♛♛ 3
● Chianti Cl. Ris. '09	♛♛ 5
● Chianti Cl. Ris. '08	♛♛ 5
● Chianti Cl. Ris. '07	♛♛ 5

★Casanova di Neri ✓

POD. FIESOLE
53024 MONTALCINO [SI]
TEL. 0577834455
www.casanovadineri.com

CELLAR SALES
PRE-BOOKED VISITS
ACCOMMODATION
ANNUAL PRODUCTION 225,000 bottles
HECTARES UNDER VINE 55.00

Intensity, concentration, and ripe fruit make
the reds from Casanova di Nero easily
recognizable when compared with all the
other Montalcino wines. These wines
faithfully illustrate the agricultural and
stylistic project carried out in recent years
by Giacomo Neri. This also means taking
into account the location of the vines,
between Seste on the southern slope and
Cava dell'Onice in Castelnuovo dell'Abate,
not to mention the Cerretalto cru with its red
soils to the east. The Pietradonice, a
cabernet, and the Sant'Antimo accompany
three Brunellos and the Rosso di Montalcino
in this range, much appreciated, particularly
abroad. The previous tastings are fully
confirmed, by the Brunello Tenuta Nuova
2008 with its very ripe dark fruit, and the
Pietradonice 2010, a Montalcino Cabernet
that is modern but with well-paced
extraction. The Cerretalto 2007 has far
more impact in the hints of jam and in the
toastiness, but requires further
development.

● Brunello di Montalcino Cerretalto '07	♛♛♛ 8
● Brunello di Montalcino Tenuta Nuova '08	♛♛ 8
● Pietradonice '10	♛♛ 8
● Brunello di Montalcino '08	♛ 6
● Rosso di Montalcino '11	♛ 5
● Brunello di Montalcino '06	♛♛♛ 5
● Brunello di Montalcino Cerretalto '06	♛♛♛ 8
● Brunello di Montalcino Cerretalto '04	♛♛♛ 8
● Brunello di Montalcino Cerretalto '01	♛♛♛ 8
● Brunello di Montalcino Cerretalto '99	♛♛♛ 8
● Brunello di Montalcino Tenuta Nuova '06	♛♛♛ 8
● Brunello di Montalcino Tenuta Nuova '05	♛♛♛ 7
● Brunello di Montalcino Tenuta Nuova '01	♛♛♛ 6
● Pietradonice '05	♛♛♛ 8

Castell'in Villa

LOC. CASTELL'IN VILLA
53019 CASTELNUOVO BERARDENGA [SI]
TEL. 0577359074
www.castellinvilla.com

CELLAR SALES
PRE-BOOKED VISITS
ANNUAL PRODUCTION 100,000 bottles
HECTARES UNDER VINE 54.00

Founded back in 1967 and producing its first Chianti in 1971, Castell'in Villa has now produced its first Chianti Classico. This story of stylistic consistency and precision in production has kept this estate in Castelnuovo Berardenga beyond any passing fashion in the world of wine, yet totally within the greatest tradition of Chianti. Coralia Pignatelli's estate makes uncompromising wines: delicate and pale in colour, with an austere development, full of contrasts, and a complex, subtle aromatic spectrum, all this marked by elegance and balance. The Chianti Classico 2009 is classic and focused in style. Summery fragrances reveal berry fruits, blossom and herbs, followed by an elegant palate: a wine that shows richness, pressure and great length. The Riserva 2008 has to strive harder, with earthiness on the nose and flavour marked by still rigid tannins and grassy notes.

● Chianti Cl. '09	▼▼▼	5
● Chianti Cl. Ris. '08	▼▼	6
● Chianti Cl. '08	♀♀♀	5
● Chianti Cl. Ris. '85	♀♀♀	6
● Chianti Cl. Castell'in Villa '05	♀♀	5
● Chianti Cl. Poggio delle Rose Ris. '06	♀♀	6
● Chianti Cl. Poggio delle Rose Ris. '97	♀♀	8
● Chianti Cl. Poggio delle Rose Ris. '96	♀♀	8
● Chianti Cl. Poggio delle Rose Ris. '95	♀♀	8
● Chianti Cl. Poggio delle Rose Ris. '94	♀♀	8
● Chianti Cl. Ris. '06	♀♀	6
● Chianti Cl. Ris. '04	♀♀	6
● Chianti Cl. Ris. '95	♀♀	6
● Santa Croce '07	♀♀	6
● Santa Croce '90	♀♀	6
○ Vin Santo del Chianti Cl. '95	♀♀	8

★Castellare di Castellina

LOC. CASTELLARE
53011 CASTELLINA IN CHIANTI [SI]
TEL. 0577742903
www.castellare.it

CELLAR SALES
PRE-BOOKED VISITS
ACCOMMODATION
ANNUAL PRODUCTION 200,000 bottles
HECTARES UNDER VINE 28.00

Since its founding in 1968, Castellare di Castellina has wagered on the territory of Chianti Classico; not only by protecting a beautiful corner of Tuscany, but also by adopting production methods totally in line with Chianti winemaking traditions and using mainly local varieties, from the classic sangiovese to the more unusual malvasia nera. The result is a style that is recognizable, consistent and never swayed by passing fashions in winemaking; so much so that the winery's labels have now become one of the most important symbols of this DOC zone. I Sodi di San Niccolò 2009, a sangiovese and malvasia nera blend, has intense, ripe aromas, a soft palate and deep finish. The Chianti Classico Vigneto Il Poggiale Riserva 2010 has nice, peppery aromas and a firm, well-balanced taste. The Chianti Classico Riserva 2010 is fresh and racy. The Chianti Classico 2011 is good.

● I Sodi di S. Niccolò '09	▼▼▼	8
● Chianti Cl. V. Il Poggiale Ris. '10	▼▼	5
● Chianti Cl. '11	▼▼	3
● Chianti Cl. Ris. '10	▼▼	4
● Coniale '09	▼	7
● Chianti Cl. V. Il Poggiale Ris. '01	♀♀♀	5
● I Sodi di S. Niccolò '08	♀♀♀	7
● I Sodi di S. Niccolò '07	♀♀♀	7
● I Sodi di S. Niccolò '06	♀♀♀	7
● I Sodi di S. Niccolò '05	♀♀♀	7
● I Sodi di S. Niccolò '04	♀♀♀	7
● I Sodi di S. Niccolò '03	♀♀♀	7
● I Sodi di S. Niccolò '02	♀♀♀	7
● I Sodi di San Niccolò '01	♀♀♀	7

★Castello Banfi

LOC. SANT'ANGELO SCALO
CASTELLO DI POGGIO ALLE MURA
53024 MONTALCINO [SI]
TEL. 0577840111
www.castellobanfi.com

CELLAR SALES
PRE-BOOKED VISITS
ACCOMMODATION AND RESTAURANT SERVICE
ANNUAL PRODUCTION 10,500,000 bottles
HECTARES UNDER VINE 850.00

Would Montalcino be so world famous
without the work of the Mariani family since
the 1970s? Maybe yes, maybe no, but this
is just speculation. The fact is that Castello
Banfi remains an essential benchmark
when discussing Brunello. This international
brand is primarily an agricultural operation
of approximately 1,000 hectares, managed
for over a decade by cousins Cristina
Mariani-May and James Mariani, under the
supervision of Enrico Viglierchio. Their
wines include those from the Vigne Regali
estate, in the Alessandria area, and the
Banfi Toscana line. The range is always
recognizable by its immediate, easy style.
This year's range confirmed the good
impressions, with various options that know
how to combine both good technique and
substance. The leader is the Poggio alle
Mura Riserva 2007, only a little too open in
the fruit. The 2008 entry-level wine is
relaxed and moreish.

● Brunello di Montalcino Poggio alle Mura Ris. '07	🍷🍷 8
● Brunello di Montalcino '08	🍷🍷 6
● Brunello di Montalcino Poggio all'Oro Ris. '07	🍷🍷 8
● Brunello di Montalcino Poggio alle Mura '08	🍷🍷 7
● Cum Laude '10	🍷🍷 5
● Rosso di Montalcino '11	🍷 3
● Rosso di Montalcino Poggio alle Mura '11	🍷 4
● Summus '10	🍷 6
● Brunello di Montalcino Poggio all'Oro '04	🍷🍷🍷 8
● Sant'Antimo Excelsus '03	🍷🍷🍷 6
● Sant'Antimo Mandrielle '04	🍷🍷🍷 3

Castello d'Albola

LOC. PIAN D'ALBOLA, 31
53017 RADDA IN CHIANTI [SI]
TEL. 0577738019
www.albola.it

CELLAR SALES
PRE-BOOKED VISITS
ANNUAL PRODUCTION 800,000 bottles
HECTARES UNDER VINE 157.00

The Zonin group's estate in Chianti is
situated in one of the most interesting areas
of the Chianti Classico area, the Radda
subzone. The Selvole, Capaccia, Madonnino,
Ellere, Marangole, Mondeggi, Sant'Ilario and
Acciaiolo vineyards are located 350 to 550
metres above sea level, and the Solatio
vineyard at almost 600 metres. This
particular site climate is reflected in the
style of the wines, distinguished by their
supple, almost sharp structure, acid tension
and elegance. Judicious use of large and
small barrels adds to the harmony of these
basic characteristics. Fine scents of flint
and red berries hallmark the Chianti
Classico Riserva 2009, with its lively,
flavoursome and well-balanced mouth. The
aromas of nicely contrasted Chianti Classico
Le Ellere 2010 are a tad closed. The Chianti
Classico 2010 is vertical and good; the pure
sangiovese Solatio 2010 is fluent and soft
in mouth.

● Chianti Cl. Ris. '09	🍷🍷🍷 4*
● Acciaiolo '10	🍷🍷 6
● Chianti Cl. '10	🍷🍷 3
● Chianti Cl. Le Ellere '10	🍷🍷 3
● Il Solatio '11	🍷🍷 5
● Acciaiolo '06	🍷🍷🍷 6
● Acciaiolo '04	🍷🍷🍷 6
● Acciaiolo '01	🍷🍷🍷 6
● Acciaiolo '95	🍷🍷🍷 5
● Chianti Cl. Le Ellere '08	🍷🍷🍷 3
● Chianti Cl. Ris. '08	🍷🍷🍷 4*
● Chianti Cl. '09	🍷🍷 3
● Chianti Cl. Ris. '07	🍷🍷 4

★Castello dei Rampolla

VIA CASE SPARSE, 22
50022 PANZANO [FI]
TEL. 055852001
castellodeirampolla.cast@tin.it

CELLAR SALES
PRE-BOOKED VISITS
ANNUAL PRODUCTION 80,000 bottles
HECTARES UNDER VINE 42.00

Castello di Rampolla and the Di Napoli family have been discussing the so-called renaissance of Chianti Classico and Tuscan wines since the early 1980s. Today the philosophy of this Panzano in Chianti estate still remains firmly at the forefront of the territory's excellence. This is due not only to the strict biodynamic methods applied to growing and vinifying grapes, but also the constant search for the most profound expression of the estate wines, whether made from international varieties or from sangiovese. This year's wines are hard to read. The Chianti Classico 2011's nose is influenced by gamey aromas, vaguely bretty, and mouth-drying, over-intrusive tannin. The Alceo 2009 suffers from the hot summer, very alcoholic both in nose and mouth. Some time in bottle will help the Sanmarco, with its still chafing tannin.

● d'Alceo '09	♀♀ 8
● Chianti Cl. '11	♀ 3
● Sammarco '09	♀ 7
● d'Alceo '03	♀♀♀ 8
● d'Alceo '01	♀♀♀ 8
● d'Alceo '00	♀♀♀ 8
● La Vigna di Alceo '99	♀♀♀ 8
● La Vigna di Alceo '98	♀♀♀ 8
● La Vigna di Alceo '97	♀♀♀ 8
● La Vigna di Alceo '96	♀♀♀ 8
● Sammarco '05	♀♀♀ 8

★Castello del Terriccio

LOC. TERRICCIO
VIA BAGNOLI, 16
56040 CASTELLINA MARITTIMA [PI]
TEL. 050699709
www.terriccio.it

CELLAR SALES
PRE-BOOKED VISITS
ANNUAL PRODUCTION 200,000 bottles
HECTARES UNDER VINE 62.00

Near Castellina Marittima, in a zone bordering the provinces of Pisa, Livorno and the Maremma, this estate occupies an area of land divided between hill and valley where vines, olives and grain are cultivated. In medieval times, the Castello del Terriccio was a look-out tower but was transformed into an agricultural concern when a farm was built here. At the end of the 1980s, it launched an in-depth study of the territory to select the best indigenous and international clones to plant and a new methodology that decreases the yield of every plant to optimize the quality of the wines. Just three wines presented this year but two graced our finals. The Castello del Terriccio 2008 from syrah and petit verdot shows vegetal notes of capsicum softened by hints of spice, including pepper, and forest fruit. Entry on the palate is tasty, compelling and juicy with nice weight and a long, complex finish. The Lupicaia 2009 from cabernet sauvignon, merlot and petit verdot is also good.

● Castello del Terriccio '08	♀♀ 8
● Lupicaia '09	♀♀ 8
● Tassinaia '10	♀♀ 6
● Castello del Terriccio '07	♀♀♀ 8
● Castello del Terriccio '04	♀♀♀ 8
● Castello del Terriccio '03	♀♀♀ 8
● Castello del Terriccio '01	♀♀♀ 8
● Lupicaia '07	♀♀♀ 8
● Lupicaia '06	♀♀♀ 8
● Lupicaia '05	♀♀♀ 8
● Lupicaia '04	♀♀♀ 8
● Lupicaia '01	♀♀♀ 8

Castello di Bolgheri

LOC. BOLGHERI
S.DA LAURETTA, 7
57020 CASTAGNETO CARDUCCI [LI]
TEL. 0565762110
www.castellodibolgheri.eu

CELLAR SALES
PRE-BOOKED VISITS
ACCOMMODATION
ANNUAL PRODUCTION 80,000 bottles
HECTARES UNDER VINE 50.00

Everything about this estate is beautiful and charming, starting with the cellar steeped in a history few in the zone can rival. It dates back to 1500, when the property belonged to the Conti della Gherardesca. Today under the auspices of the Zileri Dal Verme family it has reached the pinnacle of the DOC. The vineyards account for around 50 of the total 130 hectares and sit in sandy, clayey terrains rich in pebbles and limestone. It stands out for a style that is capable of producing refined wines, never excessive or extractive, with a certain elegance. Here are the characteristics that speak to the superb quality of the Bolgheri Superiore Castello di Bolgheri 2010, a wine that rides the vintage and the carousel as it pleases. The nose is wonderful from the outset, intense in its aromas of rose, forest fruit, scrub and very delicate Eastern spices. The palate is just as noble and elegant, silky even, showing elegance and perfect fruit extraction.

● Bolgheri Sup. Castello di Bolgheri '10	▼▼▼	6
● Bolgheri Rosso Varvàra '11	▼	4
● Bolgheri Sup. Castello di Bolgheri '09	♀♀♀	6
● Bolgheri Sup. Castello di Bolgheri '07	♀♀♀	6
● Bolgheri Rosso Varvàra '10	♀♀	4
● Bolgheri Rosso Varvàra '09	♀♀	4
● Bolgheri Rosso Varvàra '08	♀♀	4
● Bolgheri Sup. '05	♀♀	7
● Bolgheri Sup. Castello di Bolgheri '08	♀♀	6
● Bolgheri Sup. Castello di Bolgheri '06	♀♀	7
● Bolgheri Varvàra '07	♀♀	4
● Bolgheri Varvàra '06	♀♀	4

Castello di Bossi

LOC. BOSSI IN CHIANTI
53019 CASTELNUOVO BERARDENGA [SI]
TEL. 0577359330
www.castellodibossi.it

CELLAR SALES
PRE-BOOKED VISITS
ACCOMMODATION
ANNUAL PRODUCTION 702,000 bottles
HECTARES UNDER VINE 124.00

Castello di Bossi in the Chianti Classico, together with Renieri in Montalcino and Terre di Talamo in the Maremma, belongs to the Bacci family. In the area of Castelnuovo Berardenga alone the property amounts to 650 hectares, of which over 120 are planted to vine. The plants grow in rocky terrains made up largely of tufa, yellow clay and silty sand and have a wide aspect that ranges from the south-east all the way to the west. Sangiovese is king here, flanked by cabernet and merlot vines that have grown here for over 40 years. The style favours mature fruit and powerful structure. From sangiovese and cabernet sauvignon, the Corbaio 2010 shows nice concentrated aromas and a fairly dynamic palate ending in a firm, uplifting finish. The Chianti Classico Berardo Riserva 2010 is a tad over-mature; the Merlot Girolamo 2010 is cropped and in thrall to the oak; the Brunello 2008 della Renieri di Montalcino is good, lengthy and well defined.

● Brunello di Montalcino Renieri '08	♀♀	7
● Corbaia '10	♀♀	7
● Chianti Cl. Berardo Ris. '10	▼	5
● Girolamo '10	▼	7
● Corbaia '03	♀♀♀	6
● Corbaia '99	♀♀♀	5
● Chianti Cl. '10	♀♀	4
● Chianti Cl. '08	♀♀	4
● Chianti Cl. Berardo Ris. '07	♀♀	5
● Chianti Cl. Berardo Ris. '06	♀♀	5
● Chianti Cl. Berardo Ris. '04	♀♀	5
● Girolamo '07	♀♀	7
● Girolamo '05	♀♀	7

★★Castello di Fonterutoli

LOC. FONTERUTOLI
VIA OTTONE III DI SASSONIA, 5
53011 CASTELLINA IN CHIANTI [SI]
TEL. 057773571
www.mazzei.it

CELLAR SALES
PRE-BOOKED VISITS
ACCOMMODATION AND RESTAURANT SERVICE
ANNUAL PRODUCTION 700,000 bottles
HECTARES UNDER VINE 117.00

Castello di Fonterutoli is one of the historic Chianti Classico estates, as well as one of the largest in the DOC zone in terms of plots planted to vineyards. These are divided into five basic areas: Fonterutoli, Siepi, Badiola, Belvedere and Caggio. The winery style favours a modern approach that makes soft wines with big structure and sustained length from ageing in small barrels. This same style is found in production from the Belguardo estate in the Maremma. Though wines from here show a more classic, territory-driven profile, particularly those made from mainly sangiovese. The Siepi 2010, a sangiovese and merlot blend, possesses truly wonderful density. Clear, highly concentrated aromas are the prelude to a deep, complex, succulent follow-through. The Mix36 from pure sangiovese is solid and tasty. The Chianti Classico Ser Lapo Riserva 2010 is influenced by its oak-ageing.

● Siepi '10	▼▼▼	8
● Mix36 '10	▼▼	8
● Chianti Cl. Castello di Fonterutoli '10	▼▼	8
● Chianti Cl. Ser Lapo Ris. '10	▼▼	5
○ Belguardo Vermentino '12	▼	4
● Chianti Cl. Fonterutoli '11	▼	5
● Serrata di Belguardo '11	▼	4
● Chianti Cl. Castello di Fonterutoli '07	♀♀♀	6
● Chianti Cl. Castello di Fonterutoli '04	♀♀♀	6
● Mix36 '08	♀♀♀	8
● Siepi '08	♀♀♀	8
● Siepi '06	♀♀♀	8
● Siepi '05	♀♀♀	8

Castello di Monsanto

VIA MONSANTO, 8
50021 BARBERINO VAL D'ELSA [FI]
TEL. 0558059000
www.castellodimonsanto.it

CELLAR SALES
PRE-BOOKED VISITS
ACCOMMODATION
ANNUAL PRODUCTION 450,000 bottles
HECTARES UNDER VINE 72.00

This estate celebrates a half-century of winemaking history, something few can boast, marked by pioneering decisions. First of all, it bottled the first Chianti Classico cru, the Pogo, and at the same time managed to keep intact the eloquence of sangiovese grown in the hills of Barberino Val d'Elsa. These key points show the value of Castello di Monsanto, unanimously recognized as one of the most important estates in the entire DOC zone. These wines are one of the clearest examples of the potential of this region. Very long-lived, austere when first out of the cellar, they are refined and elegant in style. The Chianti Classico 2011 has generous, clear-focused aromas and a taut follow-through on the complex fabulously tasty palate that earns it a Tre Bicchieri trophy. The Chianti Classico Il Poggio Riserva 2009 is more austere and shows the odd trace of over-maturity.

● Chianti Cl. '11	▼▼▼	3*
● Chianti Cl. Il Poggio Ris. '09	▼▼	7
● Chianti Cl. Cinquantenario Ris. '08	♀♀♀	6
● Chianti Cl. Il Poggio Ris. '06	♀♀♀	6
● Chianti Cl. Il Poggio Ris. '88	♀♀♀	5
● Nemo '01	♀♀♀	6
● Chianti Cl. '10	♀♀	3*
● Chianti Cl. Il Poggio Ris. '04	♀♀	6
● Chianti Cl. Ris. '09	♀♀	5
● Chianti Cl. Ris. '08	♀♀	4
● Chianti Cl. Ris. '06	♀♀	4
● Fabrizio Bianchi Sangiovese '99	♀♀	6
● Nemo '00	♀♀	6
● Tinscvil '00	♀♀	5

Castello di Poppiano

FRAZ. POPPIANO
VIA FEZZANA, 45
50025 MONTESPERTOLI [FI]
TEL. 05582315
www.conteguicciardini.it

CELLAR SALES
PRE-BOOKED VISITS
ANNUAL PRODUCTION 270,000 bottles
HECTARES UNDER VINE 130.00

Ferdinando Guicciardini stands at the helm
of Castello di Poppiano with his wife, though
they have been assisted for some time by
their nephews Gabriele and Bernardo.
Together they carry forward the old local
winemaking traditions in a modern key. The
estate is situated on the Florentine hills
where the Guicciardini family have farmed
their own land for centuries. In the 1960s
the estate underwent extensive
transformations with specific dedication of
some of the land to vineyards and olive
groves and modernization of the cellar and
olive oil mill. Today the vineyards are being
replanted with selected native clones. The
castle also boasts an unusually beautiful Vin
Santo cellar. The quality of the production is
on the up. The La Historia 2010, largely from
merlot, is very interesting with its nicely
merged vegetal and fruity aromas. The
palate is full and complex with well-
distributed tannic texture and a tasty finish.
The Syrah 2011 has an intriguing spicy nose
and a smooth under-stated palate that is
pleasant right through the finish.

● Chianti Colli Fiorentini Ris. '10	♟♟ 4
● La Historia '10	♟♟ 5
● Syrah '11	♟♟ 4
● Toscoforte '11	♟♟ 4
● Tricorno '10	♟♟ 6
○ Campo Segreto '12	♟ 3
● Chianti Colli Fiorentini Il Cortile '11	♟ 3
● Morellino di Scansano I Massi '11	♟ 3
● La Historia '09	♟♟ 4
● Morellino di Scansano Carbonile '11	♟♟ 3
● Syrah '10	♟♟ 4

Castello di Radda

LOC. IL BECCO
53017 RADDA IN CHIANTI [SI]
TEL. 0577738992
www.castellodiradda.it

CELLAR SALES
PRE-BOOKED VISITS
ANNUAL PRODUCTION 100,000 bottles
HECTARES UNDER VINE 32.50

The Gussalli Beretta group, the agricultural
firm headed by the Beretta family, includes
Lo Sparviere in Franciacorta, Orlando
Contucci Ponnio in Abruzzo, and Castello di
Radda. This last estate has produced some
definitely interesting wines, though with
some lack of continuity. The traditional style
of this winery comes from a mix of
vineyards planted at different times, and
minimal work in the cellar, producing fine,
elegant wines, nicely reflecting their
territory of origin, and with well-managed
ageing in small barrels. The Chianti
Classico Riserva 2010 presents a
generous, complex nose profile and a
round, dynamic palate. The Chianti Classico
Poggio Selvale lacks focus in the aromas
but comes into its own on the savoury,
complex palate. The Chianti Classico 2010
performs very well, lean, racy and fresh.

● Chianti Cl. Castello di Radda Ris. '10	♟♟ 6
● Chianti Cl. Castello di Radda '10	♟♟ 3
● Chianti Cl. Poggio Selvale '10	♟♟ 3
● Chianti Cl. Ris. '07	♟♟♟ 5
● Chianti Cl. '08	♟♟ 3
● Chianti Cl. Poggio Selvale '05	♟♟ 4
● Chianti Cl. Poggio Selvale Ris. '09	♟♟ 4
● Chianti Cl. Poggio Selvale Ris. '04	♟♟ 4
● Guss '09	♟♟ 6

Castello di San Donato in Perano

LOC. SAN DONATO IN PERANO
53013 GAIOLE IN CHIANTI [SI]
TEL. 0577744121
www.castellosandonato.it

CELLAR SALES
PRE-BOOKED VISITS
ACCOMMODATION AND RESTAURANT SERVICE
ANNUAL PRODUCTION 150,000 bottles
HECTARES UNDER VINE 70.00

The soil and climatic conditions of the vineyards at Castello di San Donato in Perano, between 350 and 500 metres above sea level, on gravelly plots with steep inclines, are ideal for expressing classic Chianti aromas and flavours in the estate wines. Though modern methods are used in the cellar, the link to territory is still solidly there. The balanced mix of large and small barrels and minimal interventions in winemaking produces labels marked by elegance and finesse. The Chianti Classico 2011 shows mature fruitiness and a wonderful follow-through that reveals it to be a well-sustained, rather sumptuous wine. The sweet tones tend to dominate the Chianti Classico Riserva 2010 on both the nose, where the vanilla aromas hold sway, and the palate, where decisive acid verve renders the wine lively and tasty.

Castello di Vicchiomaggio

LOC. LE BOLLE
VIA VICCHIOMAGGIO, 4
50022 GREVE IN CHIANTI [FI]
TEL. 055854079
www.vicchiomaggio.it

CELLAR SALES
PRE-BOOKED VISITS
ACCOMMODATION AND RESTAURANT SERVICE
ANNUAL PRODUCTION 300,000 bottles
HECTARES UNDER VINE 33.00

Castello di Vicchiomaggio has belonged to the Matta family since 1964, and in 1982 steered firmly towards high quality wine production. Today bottles from this winery in Greve di Chianti firmly occupy a top position in the landscape of Chianti Classico production from the section towards Florence. Characterized by a style that is modern, but never excessive, aged in either large or small barrels, depending on the type, these wines show a reassuring continuity in quality marked by balance and expressions of their territory. The Agostino Petri Riserva 2010 is a well-made, modern Chianti Classico with generous aromas and a pleasant palate, if a bit coarse in the finish. The Chianti Classico Vigna La Prima 2010 has nice sensations and edgy tannins. Opulent fruit and a tasty palate mark the Chianti Classico San Jacopo da Vicchiomaggio 2011. The Ripa delle More 2010 from sangiovese, merlot and cabernet sauvignon shows root tones and a gutsy palate.

● Chianti Cl. '11	♛♛ 3
● Chianti Cl. Ris. '10	♛♛ 4
● Chianti Cl. '10	♛♛ 3
● Chianti Cl. '09	♛♛ 3
● Chianti Cl. '07	♛♛ 3*
● Chianti Cl. '06	♛♛ 3*
● Chianti Cl. '05	♛♛ 3*
● Chianti Cl. Ris. '09	♛♛ 4
● Chianti Cl. Ris. '08	♛♛ 5
● Chianti Cl. Ris. '05	♛♛ 5

● Chianti Cl. Agostino Petri da Vicchiomaggio Ris. '10	♛♛ 5
● Chianti Cl. San Jacopo da Vicchiomaggio '11	♛♛ 3
● Chianti Cl. V. La Prima '10	♛♛ 6
● Ripa delle More '10	♛♛ 7
● Campostella Villa Vallemaggiore '12	♛ 3
● Colle Alto Villa Vallemaggiore '11	♛ 3
● FSM '09	♛ 8
● Poggio Re Villa Vallemaggiore '10	♛ 3
● FSM '07	♛♛ 8
● FSM '04	♛♛ 5
● Ripa delle More '97	♛♛ 6
● Ripa delle More '94	♛♛ 7

Castello di Volpaia

LOC. VOLPAIA
P.ZZA DELLA CISTERNA, 1
53017 RADDA IN CHIANTI [SI]
TEL. 0577738066
www.volpaia.com

CELLAR SALES
PRE-BOOKED VISITS
ACCOMMODATION AND RESTAURANT SERVICE
ANNUAL PRODUCTION 200,000 bottles
HECTARES UNDER VINE 46.00
VITICULTURE METHOD Certified Organic

Credit goes to the Mascheroni Stianti family not only for preserving one of the most lovely corners of Chianti Classico, but even more importantly for shaping its wine production to the appearance and character of this village. These flawlessly-made wines have a modern style, but are still capable of showing outstanding personality, with a clearly well-measured contribution of oak, mostly small barrels, and a lively mouthfeel that reveals the origin of the grapes from vineyards at 500 metres, grown with organic methods. The Chianti Classico Riserva 2010 has a fresh balsamic nose and a chewy, complex palate. The agreeable Chianti Classico 2011 reveals a plush palate and warm, concentrated aromas. Both the Balificio 2009 from sangiovese and cabernet sauvignon, and the Riserva Coltassala 2009, are a little too mouth-drying.

● Chianti Cl. Ris. '10	♟♟♟ 5
● Balifico '09	♟♟ 7
● Chianti Cl. '11	♟♟ 3
● Chianti Cl. Coltassala Ris. '09	♟♟ 7
● Balifico '00	♟♟♟ 6
● Chianti Cl. Coltassala Ris. '04	♟♟♟ 6
● Chianti Cl. Coltassala Ris. '01	♟♟♟ 6
● Chianti Cl. Il Puro Vign. Casanova Ris. '08	♟♟♟ 8
● Chianti Cl. Il Puro Vign. Casanova Ris. '06	♟♟♟ 8
● Chianti Cl. Ris. '08	♟♟♟ 5
● Chianti Cl. Ris. '07	♟♟♟ 5
● Balifico '08	♟♟ 6

Castello Romitorio

LOC. ROMITORIO, 279
53024 MONTALCINO [SI]
TEL. 0577847212
www.castelloromitorio.com

CELLAR SALES
PRE-BOOKED VISITS
ACCOMMODATION
ANNUAL PRODUCTION 200,000 bottles
HECTARES UNDER VINE 25.00

Sandro Chia is an internationally famous artist, universally considered one of the greatest representatives of the Transavantgarde movement. For some years now, he has also been owner of the Castello Romitorio estate in Montalcino. The winery was built in 2006 at the foot of the old restored manor. Although several of his original works can be viewed here, those interested solely in the winery will not be disappointed. These Brunellos show the powerful characteristics of the western slope of Montalcino and a clearly modern, yet never excessive, stylistic sensibility. Another brilliant all-round performance. The Rosso 2011 stands out for its iodine delicacy and is well-defined yet not predictable. The Brunello 2008 is more controversial in its aromatic profile, showing hints of forest floor, leather and faint gamey undertones. The structure is sound but the tannins are rather clenched.

● Brunello di Montalcino '08	♟♟ 7
● Brunello di Montalcino Ris. '07	♟♟ 8
● Morellino di Scansano Ghiaccio Forte '11	♟♟ 5
● Rosso di Montalcino '11	♟♟ 4
● Morellino di Scansano Blue Lable '12	♟ 3
● Brunello di Montalcino '05	♟♟♟ 7
● Brunello di Montalcino Ris. '97	♟♟♟ 8
● Brunello di Montalcino '07	♟♟ 7
● Brunello di Montalcino '06	♟♟ 7
● Brunello di Montalcino XXV Vendemmia '06	♟♟ 8
● Rosso di Montalcino '10	♟♟ 4

Castelvecchio

LOC. SAN PANCRAZIO
VIA CERTALDESE, 30
50026 SAN CASCIANO IN VAL DI PESA [FI]
TEL. 0558248032
www.castelvecchio.it

CELLAR SALES
PRE-BOOKED VISITS
ACCOMMODATION
ANNUAL PRODUCTION 100,000 bottles
HECTARES UNDER VINE 22.00

Fattoria Castelvecchio has been owned by the Rocchi family since 1962 and today brother-and-sister team Filippo and Stefania enthusiastically run the farm established by their grandfather. Filippo is in charge of vineyard and winemaking aspects while Stefania focuses mainly on promotion, sales and hospitality facilities. Since 1995 the vineyards have undergone a process of replanting, concerning over half of the total hectares to date, which steadily continues. The winery shows evident willingness to experiment in both the cellar and the vineyards, launching new wines thanks to investments of passion, research and enthusiasm. From sangiovese, merlot and petit verdot, the Il Brecciolino 2009 reaches the finals once again with vegetal tones of green pepper over a fruity base, balanced body and nice pressure leading into a lengthy finish. Always alluring, the Numero Otto 2010 from pure canaiolo displays its refreshing acid vein. The Riserva Vigna la Quercia 2010 is austere and agreeable.

- Il Brecciolino '09 — 🍷🍷 5
- Chianti Colli Fiorentini V. la Quercia Ris. '10 — 🍷🍷 3
- Numero Otto '10 — 🍷🍷 3
- Chianti Colli Fiorentini '11 — 🍷 2
- Chianti Santa Caterina '11 — 🍷 2
- Solo Uno '10 — 🍷 7
- Chianti Colli Fiorentini '09 — 🍸🍸 2
- Il Brecciolino '08 — 🍸🍸 5
- Il Brecciolino '07 — 🍸🍸 5
- Numero Otto '08 — 🍸🍸 3
- Solo Uno '09 — 🍸🍸 7

Famiglia Cecchi

LOC. CASINA DEI PONTI, 56
53011 CASTELLINA IN CHIANTI [SI]
TEL. 057754311
www.cecchi.net

PRE-BOOKED VISITS
ANNUAL PRODUCTION 7,200,000 bottles
HECTARES UNDER VINE 292.00

Since 1893 the Cecchi family has been a prime mover in the world of Tuscan and Italian wine, firstly as a merchant and, then by increasingly undertaking a path towards quality that has seen the gradual acquisition of vineyards and estates such as Castello di Montauto in San Gimignano and Val delle Rose in the Maremma, and these just in Tuscany. Clearly these volumes are still those from a big wine producer, but wines can now be consistently found in the varied product range that are increasingly capable of expressing remarkable personality, outstanding identity, and even total excellence. The Chianti Classico Villa Cerna 2011 tempts with its primary aromas and rich palate showing agreeable hardness. The Chianti Classico Riserva di Famiglia 2010 is a very sound wine with flowery aromas and a lip-smacking, well-paced palate. Obtained from a blend of grapes from the Chianti Classico and Maremma, the very successful Coevo 2010 is elegant and gutsy with nice acidity.

- Coevo '10 — 🍷🍷🍷 7
- Chianti Cl. Riserva di Famiglia '10 — 🍷🍷 4
- Chianti Cl. Villa Cerna '11 — 🍷🍷 3*
- Chianti Cl. Villa Cerna Ris. '10 — 🍷🍷 5
- Morellino di Scansano Val delle Rose Ris. '10 — 🍷🍷 4
- Morellino di Scansano Val delle Rose '11 — 🍷 3
- Chianti Cl. Riserva di Famiglia '07 — 🍸🍸🍸 5
- Chianti Cl. Villa Cerna Ris. '08 — 🍸🍸🍸 5
- Coevo '06 — 🍸🍸🍸 7
- Chianti Cl. Villa Cerna Ris. '09 — 🍸🍸 5
- Coevo '09 — 🍸🍸 7
- Morellino di Scansano Val delle Rose Ris. '09 — 🍸🍸 5

Centolani

LOC. FRIGGIALI
S.DA MAREMMANA
53024 MONTALCINO [SI]
TEL. 0577849454
www.tenutafriggialiepietranera.it

CELLAR SALES
PRE-BOOKED VISITS
ACCOMMODATION
ANNUAL PRODUCTION 260,000 bottles
HECTARES UNDER VINE 70.00

The Centolani operation includes two estates located in different and in some ways complementary areas of Montalcino. In the western part, Tenuta Friggiale has three sizeable plots between 250 and 450 metres above sea level on rather loose soil. In contrast, not far from the Abbey of Sant'Antimo, Tenuta Pietranera has brunello vines more closely spaced due to the combined effect of lower altitude and more compact soil, with marl bound to veins of silt and clay. These differences in terroir are linked by a common thread in the style of work at the cellar managed by the Peluso Centolani family. This line is validated by a group of Brunellos that are advisedly modern in style. Of the 2008s on offer, the Pietranera is chewy and powerful, while the Tenuta Friggiali makes up for its slight lack of support with savoury grip. The Riserva 2007 is half a step behind, a bit pedantic but undeniably possessed of density and spicy thrust.

● Brunello di Montalcino Tenuta Friggiali Ris. '07	♟♟ 6
● Brunello di Montalcino Pietranera '08	♟♟ 5
● Brunello di Montalcino Tenuta Friggiali '08	♟♟ 5
● Brunello di Montalcino Poggiotondo '08	♟ 5
● Brunello di Montalcino Tenuta Friggiali '04	♟♟♟ 5
● Brunello di Montalcino Tenuta Friggiali Ris. '99	♟♟♟ 7
● Brunello di Montalcino Tenuta Friggiali '07	♟♟ 5
● Rosso di Montalcino Tenuta Friggiali '10	♟♟ 2*

Ceralti

VIA DEI CERALTI, 77
57022 CASTAGNETO CARDUCCI [LI]
TEL. 0565763989
www.ceralti.com

CELLAR SALES
PRE-BOOKED VISITS
ACCOMMODATION
ANNUAL PRODUCTION 50,000 bottles
HECTARES UNDER VINE 9.00
VITICULTURE METHOD Certified Organic

This estate is run by the Rutili family who manage the entire production process from cultivation of the vines to vinification to sale of the bottles on the market. The grapes grow on the slopes between Castagneto Carducci and Bolgheri, just one kilometre from the sea and have a high density of vines per hectare. The portfolio of wines is pretty spot-on. The bottles show increasing stylistic definition and good personality, ideally measured in their oak-ageing, and were very coherent when we tasted them. After rather an oaky start, the well-made Bolgheri Scirè 2011 rapidly gives way to more expansive notes of red berry fruit; the palate shows well straight off, young and laid-back in its liveliness. Already coherent and very impressive, the Bolgheri Superiore Alfeo 2010 is graceful, extremely relaxed and never extractive, tasty without meaningless shows of strength.

● Bolgheri Scirè '11	♟♟ 3
● Bolgheri Sup. Alfeo '10	♟♟ 5
○ Bolgheri Bianco '12	♟ 3
● Bolgheri Rosso Alfeo '03	♟♟ 4
○ Bolgheri Vermentino Ceralti '04	♟♟ 2

★La Cerbaiola

P.ZZA CAVOUR, 19
53024 MONTALCINO [SI]
TEL. 0577848499
www.aziendasalvioni.com

CELLAR SALES
PRE-BOOKED VISITS
RESTAURANT SERVICE
ANNUAL PRODUCTION 15,000 bottles
HECTARES UNDER VINE 4.00

La Cerbaiola consists of four hectares in a single plot, 400 metres above sea level, in the north-east quadrant of Montalcino with a southern exposure and soil with a marl base. All of this means little if not related to the work and sensibility of the extraordinary personality that is Giulio Salvioni. His identification with the Montalcino territory goes beyond vineyard management and technical details, and is expressed in Brunellos that are both classic and anarchic in inspiration, outside prefabricated models. These wines are allowed spontaneous fermentation and aged in 20-hectolitre Slavonian oak barrels. Salvioni's Brunello 2008 is without doubt one of the best we tasted, despite the odd expressive inconsistency. The earthy, minerally aromas, savoury texture and crunchy fruit provide a stable element, while the alcoholic pungency and rugged tannins curtail the length and depth. One to keep an eye on in coming years.

● Brunello di Montalcino '08	♥♥ 8
● Brunello di Montalcino '06	♥♥♥ 8
● Brunello di Montalcino '04	♥♥♥ 8
● Brunello di Montalcino '00	♥♥♥ 8
● Brunello di Montalcino '99	♥♥♥ 8
● Brunello di Montalcino '97	♥♥♥ 8
● Brunello di Montalcino '90	♥♥♥ 8
● Brunello di Montalcino '88	♥♥♥ 8
● Brunello di Montalcino '87	♥♥♥ 8

Cerbaiona

LOC. CERBAIONA
53024 MONTALCINO [SI]
TEL. 0577848660

CELLAR SALES
PRE-BOOKED VISITS
ANNUAL PRODUCTION 18,000 bottles
HECTARES UNDER VINE 3.00

We cannot predict what Cerbaiona will become when Diego and Nora Molinari finally take their well-earned retirement, after devoting more than 30 years to one of the most original and best-loved estates in Montalcino. We do know that whoever takes over will inherit a legacy, more human than stylistic, capable of capturing as few others could the mood of these three hectares, almost camouflaged in the far eastern section, with soils full of gravel but little clay. Meanwhile, let us enjoy the present, more authoritative than ever, in the Brunellos and Rossos traditionally vinified in cement with spontaneous fermentation and ageing in 30-hectolitre oak barrels. Cerbaiona placed two of its Sangioveses in the finals. The Rosso di Montalcino 2010 is solid and cheerful, invigorating in its fruit and exhilarating on the palate. The Brunello 2008 is a bit less relaxed, at least in this phase; it offers dark, toasty sensations and is severe rather than austere, lacking that flowery, iodine brilliance that stamps the great versions.

● Brunello di Montalcino '08	♥♥ 8
● Rosso di Montalcino '10	♥♥ 8
● Brunello di Montalcino '06	♥♥♥ 8
● Brunello di Montalcino '04	♥♥♥ 8
● Brunello di Montalcino '01	♥♥♥ 8
● Brunello di Montalcino '99	♥♥♥ 8
● Brunello di Montalcino '97	♥♥♥ 8
● Brunello di Montalcino '90	♥♥♥ 8
● Rosso di Montalcino '07	♥♥♥ 8
● Brunello di Montalcino '07	♥♥ 8
● Brunello di Montalcino '03	♥♥ 8
● Rosso di Montalcino '09	♥♥ 5

Fattoria del Cerro

FRAZ. ACQUAVIVA
VIA GRAZIANELLA, 5
53040 MONTEPULCIANO [SI]
TEL. 0578767722
www.fattoriadelcerro.it

CELLAR SALES
PRE-BOOKED VISITS
ACCOMMODATION AND RESTAURANT SERVICE
ANNUAL PRODUCTION 1,000,000 bottles
HECTARES UNDER VINE 170.00
VITICULTURE METHOD Certified Organic

Saiagricola is the production arm of the insurance group that now belongs to Unipol. It comprises a series of estates in Tuscany, Umbria and Piedmont where the most important wine-growing concern is located. The Fattoria del Cerro is one of the largest and most prestigious Vino Nobile di Montepulciano estates, and this private property has the biggest expanse of vineyards registered in the DOCG. Some of the plots are among the oldest and most significant in the zone and have been chosen to identify and select clones. The estate also produces extra-virgin olive oil and has tourist accommodation. A Tre Bicchieri for the Nobile 2010 and its fresh, complex, lively nose of forest fruit and flowery notes, vibrant palate, tasty acid vein and pleasing drinkability. The powerful Nobile Riserva 2009 offers ripe notes of leather and tobacco with hints of plum, and big structure with savoury, lingering aromas. From sangiovese and merlot, the Manero 2011 is relaxed and enjoyable.

● Nobile di Montepulciano '10	♟♟♟	3*
● Manero '11	♟♟	2*
● Nobile di Montepulciano Ris. '09	♟♟	4
● Nobile di Montepulciano Vign. Antica Chiusina '07	♟♟	6
● Val di Cornia Rosso Poggio Rivivo Villetta di Monterufoli '10	♟♟	2*
● Chianti Colli Senesi '12	♟	2
○ Manero Bianco '12	♟	2
● Rosso di Montalcino La Poderina '11	♟	3
● Rosso di Montepulciano '12	♟	2
○ Spumante Brut La Grazianella '12	♟	2
○ Vermentino '12	♟	2
● Nobile di Montepulciano Ris. '06	♟♟♟	4
● Nobile di Montepulciano Vign. Antica Chiusina '00	♟♟♟	6

Vincenzo Cesani

LOC. PANCOLE, 82D
53037 SAN GIMIGNANO [SI]
TEL. 0577955084
www.cesani.it

CELLAR SALES
PRE-BOOKED VISITS
ACCOMMODATION
ANNUAL PRODUCTION 100,000 bottles
HECTARES UNDER VINE 20.00
VITICULTURE METHOD Certified Organic

The Cesani family winery is a cornerstone of the Vernaccia di San Gimignano DOC zone, not only because of the high quality of all these wines but also because it perfectly interprets the character of the subzone where it is located. In the north of the area, Pancole is distinguished by powerful, mineral-laden whites, dominated by classic flint aromas. They are the product of the local sandy soil and a drier climate than elsewhere. This has led the winery to experiment, successfully with ageing in small oak barrels rather than stainless steel. The very complex Vernaccia di San Gimignano Sanice 2011 offers one of the most original interpretations in the entire DOCG. Ripe, layered aromas hint at peachy fruit and saffron stalks in addition to the classic rock tones. Aromatically consistent, the palate is full and long, precise and characterful. The Vernaccia 2012 is simpler and fresher but extremely tasty.

○ Vernaccia di S. Gimignano Sanice '11	♟♟	2*
○ Vernaccia di S. Gimignano '12	♟♟	2*
● Cellori '09	♟	2
● Chianti Colli Senesi '12	♟	2
● Luenzo '99	♟♟♟	4
● Luenzo '97	♟♟♟	4*
○ Vernaccia di S. Gimignano '11	♟♟	2*
○ Vernaccia di S. Gimignano '09	♟♟	2*
○ Vernaccia di S. Gimignano Pancole '10	♟♟	2*
○ Vernaccia di S. Gimignano Sanice '09	♟♟	3*
○ Vernaccia di S. Gimignano Sanice '08	♟♟	3*

Giovanni Chiappini

LOC. LE PRESELLE
POD. FELCIAINO, 189B
57020 BOLGHERI [LI]
TEL. 0565765201
www.giovannichiappini.it

CELLAR SALES
PRE-BOOKED VISITS
ANNUAL PRODUCTION 40,000 bottles
HECTARES UNDER VINE 7.00

It all started in 1978 when Giovanni Chiappini decided to buy his first hectares in Bolgheri. He has added to these over the years, including the famed Guado de' Gemoli plot. Production volume remains limited but this is one of the best-known small estates in the zone for the high quality of its wines. Giovanni is obsessive in the care of his vines that sit in a semi-hilly position at an altitude of around 100 metres. He practises eco-compatible agriculture that respects the environment. The cellar techniques are precise but never invasive and aim to preserve and enhance the character of the grapes and their zones of origin. The Lienà Cabernet Franc 2010 is on its usual splendid form. This red proposes intense sensations, generous, elegantly grassy aromas with hints of chilli pepper and a balsamic tone that is highly seductive. The Guado de' Gemoli 2010 is still a bit oaky. The Ferrugini 2011 shows well with spicy notes of cumin and a lovely, fresh palate.

Le Chiuse

LOC. PULLERA, 228
53024 MONTALCINO [SI]
TEL. 055597052
www.lechiuse.com

CELLAR SALES
PRE-BOOKED VISITS
ACCOMMODATION
ANNUAL PRODUCTION 25,000 bottles
HECTARES UNDER VINE 8.00
VITICULTURE METHOD Certified Organic

More than just family ties link the name of Simonetta Valiani with the Biondi Santi family. Rather the style and territorial imprint of the Brunellos from Le Chiuse are what mostly suggest these parallels for a winery that seems to grow exponentially from one harvest to the next. The six organically managed hectares on the estate lie on the north-east side of Montalcino facing the hill of Montosoli, around 300 metres above sea level. In the cellar these particular conditions are interpreted to create a style that is now unmistakable, the result of spontaneous fermentation, long maceration and ageing in 20, 30 and 50-hectolitre oak barrels. We found Le Chiuse's Brunellos to be superb. The 2008 and the 2007 Riserva present the same electrifying burst of fresh fruit, medicinal herbs and oriental spices that intermingle in a framework of grace and harmony. The Riserva takes the Tre Bicchieri for its greater richness of flavour.

● Lienà Cabernet Franc '10	♟♟ 7
● Bolgheri Rosso Ferruggini '11	♟♟ 3
● Lienà Cabernet Sauvignon '10	♟♟ 7
● Bolgheri Sup. Guado de' Gemoli '10	♟ 6
○ Bolgheri Vermentino Le Grottine '12	♟ 3
● Bolgheri Rosso Felciaino '09	♟♟ 2*
● Bolgheri Sup. Guado de' Gemoli '09	♟♟ 6
● Bolgheri Sup. Guado de' Gemoli '08	♟♟ 6
● Bolgheri Sup. Guado de' Gemoli '07	♟♟ 6
● Lienà Cabernet Franc '09	♟♟ 7
● Lienà Cabernet Franc '08	♟♟ 7
● Lienà Cabernet Sauvignon '09	♟♟ 7
● Lienà Cabernet Sauvignon '08	♟♟ 7
● Lienà Cabernet Sauvignon '07	♟♟ 7
● Lienà Cabernet Sauvignon '04	♟♟ 7
● Lienà Merlot '04	♟♟ 7

● Brunello di Montalcino Ris. '07	♟♟♟ 8
● Brunello di Montalcino '08	♟♟ 7
● Rosso di Montalcino '11	♟♟ 4
● Brunello di Montalcino '07	♟♟♟ 7
● Brunello di Montalcino '06	♟♟ 6
● Brunello di Montalcino Ris. '06	♟♟ 9
● Rosso di Montalcino '10	♟♟ 3

Cigliano

VIA CIGLIANO, 17
50026 SAN CASCIANO IN VAL DI PESA [FI]
TEL. 055820033
www.villadelcigliano.it

CELLAR SALES
PRE-BOOKED VISITS
ANNUAL PRODUCTION 60,000 bottles
HECTARES UNDER VINE 25.00

The Maccaferri Montecchi family,
descendants of a branch of the Antinori
family, owns this estate in the area of the
Chianti Classico closest to Florence. In
terms of production it has always sought to
convey a close link with the territory. Having
overcome some initial uncertainties, notably
in the aromatic expression of its wines, it
has become one of the most interesting
wineries in the DOCG. The wines are
elegant and slim-bodied with a very classic
style thanks to the fine work in the vineyard
and measured interventions in the cellar,
where ageing takes place in
cement vats and large barrels. The Chianti
Classico 2011 is probably one of the best
we tasted this year. It displays clear,
focused aromas, a taut, tangy, well-paced
palate, well refined with agreeably edgy
tannins. Nor does the Chianti Classico
Riserva 2009 disappoint with its mature,
austere nose and very tasty follow-through,
where it really comes into its own.

● Chianti Cl. Cigliano '11	♥♥ 3
● Chianti Cl. Villa Cigliano Ris. '09	♥♥ 4
● Chianti Cl. '10	♀♀ 2*
● Chianti Cl. '07	♀♀ 2*
● Suganella '06	♀♀ 4

Fattoria di Cinciano

LOC. CINCIANO, 2
53036 POGGIBONSI [SI]
TEL. 0577936588
www.cinciano.it

ANNUAL PRODUCTION 70,000 bottles
HECTARES UNDER VINE 25.00

The Fattoria di Cinciano lies in the area of
the Chianti Classico DOCG next to
Poggibonsi. In the past its wines have
appeared a bit contradictory, but in recent
years the estate seems to have taken a
more determined direction in terms of
quality, consistency and link to its territory
of origin. Credit is due in part to the newly
replanted vineyards and a more measured
use of oak-ageing in mainly small casks.
Today the estate's style is more defined
and shows personality. The Chianti Classico
Riserva 2010 has a clean, very refreshing
nose and a tasty palate with pleasant
hardness and an uplifting finish. The
well-made Chianti Classico 2011 offers
notes of flowers and earth and a delicate,
complex palate. The Pietraforte 2011 from
sangiovese, cabernet sauvignon and merlot
is more concentrated with slightly dominant
oak but good character.

● Chianti Cl. Ris. '10	♥♥ 3*
● Chianti Cl. '11	♥♥ 3
● Pietraforte '11	♥♥ 2*
● Chianti Cl. '06	♀♀ 3
● Chianti Cl. Ris. '06	♀♀ 4
● Chianti Cl. Ris. '05	♀♀ 4
● Pietraforte '07	♀♀ 4

Donatella Cinelli Colombini

LOC. CASATO PRIME DONNE
53024 MONTALCINO [SI]
TEL. 0577662108
www.cinellicolombini.it

CELLAR SALES
PRE-BOOKED VISITS
ACCOMMODATION AND RESTAURANT SERVICE
ANNUAL PRODUCTION 170,000 bottles
HECTARES UNDER VINE 34.00

Founder of the Wine Tourism Movement, creator of the Cantine Aperte event, and university lecturer specialized in wine marketing, Donatella Cinelli Colombini is one of the most well-known faces in what is often termed, not entirely seriously, "women's winemaking". In 1998 she decided to leave the family business and establish Fattoria del Colle in Trequanda and Casato Prime Donne in Montalcino, one of the first production operations run entirely by women. Her Brunellos reveal a modern touch in the ripeness of fruit, and smoke and spice from the oak of various sizes and origin. Although technically well made, we expected a bit more in terms of character and personality from this small range. The two labels we tasted have little to choose between them on these fronts. The Brunello Prime Donne 2008 offers dark, oaky sensations; the Riserva 2007 is more tertiary in character with fairly clenched tannins.

● Brunello di Montalcino Prime Donne '08	♥♥ 6
● Brunello di Montalcino Ris. '07	♥♥ 8
● Orcia Leone Rosso '10	♥ 2
● Brunello di Montalcino Prime Donne '01	♀♀♀ 6
● Brunello di Montalcino '06	♀♀ 5
● Brunello di Montalcino '05	♀♀ 5
● Brunello di Montalcino Prime Donne '07	♀♀ 6
● Brunello di Montalcino Ris. '06	♀♀ 7
● Brunello di Montalcino Ris. '05	♀♀ 6
● Rosso di Montalcino '09	♀♀ 3

Citille di Sopra

FRAZ. TORRENIERI
LOC. CITILLE DI SOPRA, 46
53024 MONTALCINO [SI]
TEL. 0577832749
www.citille.com

CELLAR SALES
PRE-BOOKED VISITS
ANNUAL PRODUCTION 35,000 bottles
HECTARES UNDER VINE 5.50

Despite a winemaking history that not long ago celebrated its tenth harvest, the small estate of Fabio Innocenti is already established as a major player in the Montalcino district. Apart from individual successes, his three house Brunellos (the vintage version, the Poggio Ronconi and the Riserva) display consistent vigour and an austere style, all due to the quality of the Torrenieri plots with clayey soils, rich in limestone, interspersed with large tufaceous areas. These soils mean choices in the cellar must be adjusted in part to the progress of the vintage year, with long fermentation and ageing in oak of various sizes and origin. Our tastings this year revealed rather too much austerity. The Brunello Riserva 2007 has a dark, extractive profile, while the Brunello 2008 is just as severe but shows more energy with refreshing notes of scrub and forest floor. The Vigna Poggio Ronconi 2008 is more complex, full-blooded and substantial.

● Brunello di Montalcino V. Poggio Ronconi '08	♥♥ 5
● Brunello di Montalcino '08	♥♥ 5
● Brunello di Montalcino Ris. '07	♥ 7
● Rosso di Montalcino '11	♥ 3
● Brunello di Montalcino '06	♀♀♀ 5
● Brunello di Montalcino V. Poggio Ronconi '07	♀♀♀ 5
● Brunello di Montalcino Ris. '06	♀♀ 7
● Rosso di Toscana '10	♀♀ 2*

★Tenuta Col d'Orcia

VIA GIUNCHETTI
53020 MONTALCINO [SI]
TEL. 057780891
www.coldorcia.it

CELLAR SALES
PRE-BOOKED VISITS
ANNUAL PRODUCTION 800,000 bottles
HECTARES UNDER VINE 142.00
VITICULTURE METHOD Certified Organic

The nearly 150 hectares of the Col d'Orcia estate are mainly concentrated in the south, forming one of the most important operations in Montalcino in terms of history, continued presence and numbers. The Brunello sangiovese enjoys the beneficial influence of the site climate on nearby Mount Amiata, aided by poor clay soil, rich in limestone and pebbles. These features create the character of the Poggio al Vento, one of the best-known Riserva crus since the 1980s, produced only in the best years after long ageing in oak and bottle. The range is completed by a series of labels made in part with the use of international varieties. The Poggio al Vento Riserva has finally regained the quality and consistency we got to know in the 1980s and 1990s. The 2006 version is at once youthful and moody, offering aromas of cherry and herbs, olive paste and tanned leather that are the prelude to a defined, confident, fresh, savoury palate.

● Brunello di Montalcino Poggio al Vento Ris. '06	▼▼▼ 8
● Brunello di Montalcino '08	▼▼ 7
● Rosso di Montalcino Banditella '10	▼ 5
● Brunello di Montalcino Poggio al Vento Ris. '04	♀♀♀ 8
● Brunello di Montalcino Poggio al Vento Ris. '99	♀♀♀ 8
● Brunello di Montalcino Poggio al Vento Ris. '97	♀♀♀ 7
● Brunello di Montalcino Poggio al Vento Ris. '95	♀♀♀ 7
● Brunello di Montalcino Poggio al Vento Ris. '90	♀♀♀ 7
● Olmaia '01	♀♀♀ 6
● Olmaia '00	♀♀♀ 6
● Olmaia '94	♀♀♀ 6

Col di Bacche

FRAZ. MONTIANO
S.DA DI CUPI
58010 MAGLIANO IN TOSCANA [GR]
TEL. 0564589538
www.coldibacche.com

CELLAR SALES
PRE-BOOKED VISITS
ANNUAL PRODUCTION 80,000 bottles
HECTARES UNDER VINE 13.50

Alberto Carnasciali and his wife founded this estate on the edge of the Parco Naturale dell'Uccellina when they moved here from wine-friendly Chianti Classico in 1997. They decided to start producing wine in a zone that was known for its big reds but had not yet achieved its full potential. Their philosophy focuses on limited production, manual tending of the vineyards, and almost obsessive care for the vines year after year to understand their particular needs. This approach has always given good results, witness the consistent level of quality they have achieved. The Cupinero 2011 from mainly merlot with a little cabernet sauvignon, made it to our final rounds. The nose offers fruity notes of plum and cherry enlivened by balsamic tones and hints of spices like clove. The palate is full and compact with structure that expands lithely to reveal assertive tannins and a lingering, scented finish. We also liked the Riserva Roventa 2010, austere and powerful.

● Cupinero '11	▼▼ 5
● Morellino di Scansano Rovente Ris. '10	▼▼ 5
● Morellino di Scansano '12	▼ 3
○ Vermentino '12	▼ 2
● Cupinero '09	♀♀♀ 5
● Morellino di Scansano Rovente '05	♀♀♀ 4
● Cupinero '08	♀♀ 5
● Maremma Toscana Cupinero '10	♀♀ 5
● Morellino di Scansano '11	♀♀ 3
● Morellino di Scansano Ris. '09	♀♀ 4*
● Morellino di Scansano Rovente '08	♀♀ 5
○ Vermentino '11	♀♀ 2*

Fattoria Collazzi

LOC. TAVARNUZZE
VIA COLLERAMOLE, 101
50029 IMPRUNETA [FI]
TEL. 0552374902
www.collazzi.it

CELLAR SALES
PRE-BOOKED VISITS
ANNUAL PRODUCTION 80,000 bottles
HECTARES UNDER VINE 32.00

The wine and olive oil estate surrounds the prestigious villa of the same name, built to the design of Michelangelo Buonarroti. The Marchi family has owned the farm since the 1930s and has recently shown a renewed spirit of entrepreneurship in their approach, with renovations to the vineyards and cellar, in the pursuit of fine quality wines. Lamberto Frescobaldi is entrusted with the vineyard and winemaking responsibilities, and supervised all the renovations to the buildings and systems. The features of the land dictated the choice to dedicate only part of the vineyards to the traditional sangiovese grapes, adding unusual varieties like greco for the production of white wines. The Collazzi 2010, a Bordeaux blend of cabernet franc and sauvignon, merlot and petit verdot, reached our finals thanks to its balsamic, spicy nose, soft, round, nicely weighty palate, and long, layered finish. The merlot, syrah and sangiovese blend Libertà 2011 is fresh and easy-drinking; the Otto Muri 2012 is refreshing and minerally.

● Collazzi '10	♥♥ 6
● Chianti Cl. I Bastioni '11	♥♥ 3
● Libertà '11	♥♥ 2*
○ Otto Muri '12	♥♥ 3
● Collazzi '09	♀♀ 6
● Collazzi '08	♀♀ 6
● Collazzi '07	♀♀ 6
● Libertà '10	♀♀ 2*
● Libertà '09	♀♀ 2*

Colle Massari

LOC. POGGI DEL SASSO
58044 CINIGIANO [GR]
TEL. 0564990496
www.collemassari.it

CELLAR SALES
PRE-BOOKED VISITS
ACCOMMODATION
ANNUAL PRODUCTION 250,000 bottles
HECTARES UNDER VINE 83.00
VITICULTURE METHOD Certified Organic

Colle Massari owned by Claudio and Maria Iris Tipa is the foundation on which promotion of the value of Montecucco was built, an area which has proved ideal for planting sangiovese. The estate's location enjoys a breezy microclimate with good temperature variation. The vineyards are mainly planted with sangiovese resulting from selections made with the help of the university of Pisa. The cellar is an impressive example of eco-friendly architecture, built on four levels to permit processing of the grapes and must without the use of pumps and mechanical equipment. The Lombrone Riserva 2009 is the jewel in the crown of a production that excels at all levels and takes home a Tre Bicchieri trophy. The complex nose embraces fruity aromas of plum and cherry, minty tones and spicy nuances. The palate is soft and full with perfect tannic pressure and a lip-smacking, leisurely finish.

● Montecucco Sangiovese Lombrone Ris. '09	♥♥♥ 6
● Montecucco Rosso Colle Massari Ris. '10	♥♥ 3*
○ Montecucco Vermentino Le Melacce '12	♥♥ 3
⊙ Grottolo '12	♥ 2
● Montecucco Rosso Rigoleto '11	♥ 2
○ Montecucco Vermentino Irisse '12	♥ 3
● Montecucco Rosso Colle Massari Ris. '08	♀♀♀ 3
● Montecucco Sangiovese Lombrone Ris. '08	♀♀♀ 6
● Montecucco Sangiovese Lombrone Ris. '06	♀♀♀ 6
● Montecucco Sangiovese Lombrone Ris. '05	♀♀♀ 6

Colle Santa Mustiola

VIA DELLE TORRI, 86A
53043 CHIUSI [SI]
TEL. 057820525
www.poggioaichiari.it

CELLAR SALES
PRE-BOOKED VISITS
ANNUAL PRODUCTION 18,000 bottles
HECTARES UNDER VINE 5.00

This historic estate lies in the municipality of Chiusi, in the territory bordering Tuscany and Umbria. Its story is special, born of the link between this place, its history, and the visceral passion of its owner. It is the site of a unique wine-growing project that examined old sangiovese vines and selected several clones, including some pre-phylloxera specimens, and planted them in extremely high density, partly bush-trained. The vines sit in marine terrains composed of sand, pebbles and clay. The wines are produced in an amazing cellar that was once an Etruscan tomb. They are not forced in any way and age in large barrels and barriques. The Poggio ai Chiari is the estate's most important red. It derives from pure sangiovese and is not released on the market until at least seven years after the harvest. The 2006 is a magnificent wine, pale in colour with a complex nose that melds flowery, fruity sensations with tertiary aromas of topsoil, mushrooms and forest floor. The lean, linear palate is a tribute to the territory and to sangiovese. In its most authentic form.

● Poggio ai Chiari '06	♟♟♟ 6
● Vigna Flavia '09	♟♟ 5
● Poggio ai Chiari '05	♟♟ 6
● Poggio ai Chiari '04	♟♟ 6
● Poggio ai Chiari '03	♟♟ 6
● Poggio ai Chiari '02	♟♟ 6
● Poggio ai Chiari '01	♟♟ 6
● Poggio ai Chiari '00	♟♟ 6
● Poggio ai Chiari '99	♟♟ 6
● Poggio ai Chiari '94	♟♟ 6
● Poggio ai Chiari '93	♟♟ 6

Fattoria Colle Verde

FRAZ. MATRAIA
LOC. CASTELLO
55010 LUCCA
TEL. 0583402310
www.colleverde.it

CELLAR SALES
PRE-BOOKED VISITS
ANNUAL PRODUCTION 30,000 bottles
HECTARES UNDER VINE 7.00

When Piero Tartagni and Francesca Pardini opted to leave the city for a life in the country in the 1990s, they chose Matraia as their destination. Francesca's family had owned it for generations and it seemed fitting to launch their wine growing activity here. Today Colle Verde is one of the best-known names in the zone. Originally organic, over time the estate has gone biodynamic. The wines have always been authentic and distinctive, but they have now acquired greater precision and stylistic definition, particularly in their tannins. The very fine Colline Lucchesi Disinòpia 2011 is an elegant, concentrated wine, taut and crisp, complete and precise yet also authentic and full of flavour. The finish is hard and clenched with bags of character but no hint of forward or excessive sensations.

● Colline Lucchesi Disinòpia '11	♟♟ 4
○ Colline Lucchesi Bianco Terre di Matraja '11	♟♟ 2*
● Colline Lucchesi Rosso Brania delle Ghiandaie '09	♟♟ 4
● Colline Lucchesi Rosso Brania delle Ghiandaie '08	♟♟ 5
● Colline Lucchesi Rosso Brania delle Ghiandaie '07	♟♟ 4
● Colline Lucchesi Rosso Brania delle Ghiandaie '06	♟♟ 4
● Colline Lucchesi Rosso Brania delle Ghiandaie '05	♟♟ 4
● Colline Lucchesi Rosso Terre di Matraja '09	♟♟ 2*
● Nero della Spinosa '09	♟♟ 5
● Nero della Spinosa '08	♟♟ 5

Collelceto

LOC. CAMIGLIANO
POD. LA PISANA
53024 MONTALCINO [SI]
TEL. 0577816606
www.collelceto.it

CELLAR SALES
PRE-BOOKED VISITS
ANNUAL PRODUCTION 22,000 bottles
HECTARES UNDER VINE 6.00

Since the early 1900s, the Palazzesi family
has been established at the estate where
Elia today produces some of the most
easily recognizable and characterful
Brunellos. We are in the south-western
corner of the DOC zone, next to the wide
gorge of the Ombrone river, with gravelly
clay loam soil and temperate winds from
the sea. The resulting Sangioveses show a
distinct salty, Mediterranean quality, later
helped along by long ageing in the cellar in
either barriques or medium-sized oak
barrels, for an eclectic style often capable
of appealing to different tastes. Another
very decent performance from this range of
wines, starting with a Brunello 2008 that is
already very approachable, if a tad
over-simple and primary in its fruity
aromas. The Elia Riserva 2007 shows
similar limitations; it is balanced with no
major surprises and notes of candy and
forest fruits.

● Brunello di Montalcino '08	▼▼ 5
● Brunello di Montalcino Elia Ris. '07	▼▼ 6
● Rosso di Montalcino '11	▼ 3
● Brunello di Montalcino '06	▼▼▼ 5
● Brunello di Montalcino '07	▼▼ 5
● Brunello di Montalcino Elia Ris. '06	▼▼ 6
● Rosso di Montalcino '10	▼▼ 3*

Le Colline di Sopra

VIA DELLE COLLINE 17
56040 MONTESCUDAIO [PI]
TEL. 0586650377
www.collinedisopra.com

CELLAR SALES
PRE-BOOKED VISITS
ANNUAL PRODUCTION 4,800 bottles
HECTARES UNDER VINE 5.00
VITICULTURE METHOD Certified Organic

This estate was started from scratch in
2006 with the planting of brand new
vineyards alongside the existing farm
activities that already included two hectares
of olive groves. Right from the start the
philosophy has been rooted in organic
agricultural methods. The varieties are
selected after careful study of the ambient
terrain and microclimate. Particular
attention is paid to the environment; they
employ renewable energy and are
measured in their use of the water
resources. A fine overall showing. The
Ramanto 2011 from cabernet franc and
petit verdot is fresh and vegetal on the
nose with full, inviting structure and a finish
that follows through well. The Larà 2011, a
merlot and syrah blend, has sweet aromas
of chocolate and cinnamon, soft,
harmonious body and a crisp, clean finish.
The Eola 2011 from merlot, cabernet,
sangiovese and syrah has a full, complex
bouquet, a solid, tasty palate and a
lip-smacking finish. The Moscato Lùis 2011
is sweet, appealing, velvety and inviting.

● Eola '11	▼▼ 2*
● Larà '11	▼▼ 2*
○ Moscato Passito Lùis '11	▼▼ 3
● Ramanto '11	▼▼ 4
● Montescusaio Sangiovese '10	▼ 3

Il Colombaio di Santa Chiara

LOC. RACCIANO
SAN DONATO, 1
53037 SAN GIMIGNANO [SI]
TEL. 0577942004
www.colombaiosantachiara.it

CELLAR SALES
PRE-BOOKED VISITS
ACCOMMODATION
ANNUAL PRODUCTION 60,000 bottles
HECTARES UNDER VINE 12.00
VITICULTURE METHOD Certified Organic

The Logi family's estate is among the top wineries in the DOC zone, and clearly following a course of growth and awareness. Colombaio di Santa Chiara lies on the road between San Gimignano and Volterra, though the vineyards are scattered over various areas, all well suited and attractive, capable of expressing the nuances of the local territory. These wines are the product of the potential of this terroir, great care of the vineyards, and a personal commitment to protecting the fruits of nature. The results can be seen in these convincing wines that are certainly among the finest from the DOC zone. What an extraordinary Vernaccia di San Gimignano Campo della Pieve 2011. This very dynamic white alternates aromas of chlorophyll, lime and white peach with rocky, mineral tones. Intensely citrussy, it is shot through with very fresh sensations and vibrant acidity that really draws out the palate. It beats the Vernaccia Selvabianca 2012 by a head.

○ Vernaccia di S. Gimignano Campo della Pieve '11	♥♥♥ 3*
⊙ Rosato Cremisi '12	♥♥ 2*
○ Vernaccia di S. Gimignano Selvabianca '12	♥♥ 2*
● Chianti Colli Senesi Campale '11	♥ 2
● S. Gimignano Rosso Colombaio '06	♀♀ 4
● S. Gimignano Rosso Colombaio '05	♀♀ 4
○ Vernaccia di S. Gimignano Alberta Ris. '10	♀♀ 3
○ Vernaccia di S. Gimignano Alberta Ris. '08	♀♀ 3
○ Vernaccia di S. Gimignano Campo della Pieve '10	♀♀ 3
○ Vernaccia di San Gimignano Selvabianca '11	♀♀ 2*

Il Conventino

FRAZ. GRACCIANO
VIA DELLA CIARLIANA, 25B
53040 MONTEPULCIANO [SI]
TEL. 0578715371
www.ilconventino.it

CELLAR SALES
PRE-BOOKED VISITS
ANNUAL PRODUCTION 55,000 bottles
HECTARES UNDER VINE 12.00
VITICULTURE METHOD Certified Organic

The estate is the property of three brothers, Pino, Duccio and Alessandro Brini, all lawyers, who work in Pontedera but who have always been in love with the territory of Poliziano. They realized their dream of creating a territorial wine that reflected their passion through cultivation methods that respect the environment. In 2003 they bought two properties, Il Conventino and La Casella, and pout their ideas to the test. Two of their children have embraced the project and manage the work in the vineyard, cellar and market. A Tre Bicchieri to the Nobile 2010. Its generous, complex nose mingles aromatic herbs with forest fruits and hints of cinnamon and cloves. The palate is solid, dynamic and wide-ranging with a long, lip-smacking finish. The more austere Riserva 2009 offers notes of blackberry jam, faint traces of aromatic herbs, a sound, balanced body, and a finish that develops well. The Rosso 2012 is fresh and enjoyable.

● Nobile di Montepulciano '10	♥♥♥ 4
● Nobile di Montepulciano Ris. '09	♥♥ 5
● Rosso di Montepulciano '12	♥♥ 2*
● Nobile di Montepulciano '09	♀♀ 4
● Nobile di Montepulciano Ris. '08	♀♀ 5
● Nobile di Montepulciano Ris. '06	♀♀ 5

Fattoria Le Corti

LOC. LE CORTI
VIA SAN PIERO DI SOTTO, 1
50026 SAN CASCIANO IN VAL DI PESA [FI]
TEL. 055829301
www.principecorsini.com

CELLAR SALES
PRE-BOOKED VISITS
ACCOMMODATION
ANNUAL PRODUCTION 150,000 bottles
HECTARES UNDER VINE 50.00

The estate run by Duccio Corsini is one of
the oldest in the Chianti Classico DOCG. It
also has a dépendance in the Maremma,
La Marsiliana. The recent production style
sees wines with rich colour, abundant oak
and powerful structure. As a result, it
skipped a few beats but now seems to
have regained a steady rhythm in a skilful
renewal of the Chianti tradition, above all in
terms of liveliness and drinkability. The
work in the vineyard is precise and always
has been, while cellaring includes what has
proved to be a winning combination of
cement vats, barrels and barriques. The
Chianti Classico Cortevecchia Riserva 2009
has fascinating aromas and a generous,
complex palate. The Chianti Classico 2010
is well-paced with agreeably hardness,
generous and lip-smacking, a very
drinkable wine. The Chianti Classico Don
Tommaso 2009 is over-burdened by its full
oaky expression.

● Chianti Cl. Le Corti '10	♟♟♟	3*
● Chianti Cl. Cortevecchia Ris. '09	♟♟	4
● Chianti Cl. Don Tommaso '09	♟	5
● Chianti Cl. Cortevecchia Ris. '05	♟♟♟	4
● Chianti Cl. Don Tommaso '99	♟♟♟	4*
● Chianti Cl. A-101 Ris. '06	♟♟	3*
● Chianti Cl. Cortevecchia Ris. '07	♟♟	4
● Chianti Cl. Cortevecchia Ris. '06	♟♟	4
● Chianti Cl. Don Tommaso '05	♟♟	5
● Chianti Cl. Don Tommaso '04	♟♟	5
● Marsiliana '04	♟♟	6
● Marsiliana '03	♟♟	6
● Marsiliana '02	♟♟	6

Fattoria Corzano e Paterno

VIA SAN VITO DI SOPRA
50020 SAN CASCIANO IN VAL DI PESA [FI]
TEL. 0558248179
www.corzanoepaterno.com

CELLAR SALES
PRE-BOOKED VISITS
ACCOMMODATION
ANNUAL PRODUCTION 85,000 bottles
HECTARES UNDER VINE 17.00
VITICULTURE METHOD Certified Organic

Since 1969 this estate has belonged to the
Gelpke and Goldschmidt families. The
founder, Swiss architect Wendelin Gelpke,
began business with the Corzano farm
adding the Paterno estate later, in 1974,
and completing the process of union in
1976. The farm produces wine, oil and
sheep's milk cheese, as well as offering
holiday accommodation, all family-run to an
excellent standard. The estate is in the San
Casciano Val di Pesa zone in an area with
Etruscan origins. The wines produced here
since 1972 are made from native grape
varieties, in particular, although international
varieties are also grown. Two finalists from
this estate: the Corzano 2010, a
sangiovese, cabernet and merlot blend,
offers mature, concentrated aromas of jam
and spice, impressive structure with
measured tannins and a lingering,
lip-smacking finish. The Passito 2011 from
trebbiano with a small amount of malvasia
has notes of honey and dried fruit, a soft,
creamy palate and extended length.

● Il Corzano '10	♟♟	5
○ Passito di Corzano '11	♟♟	6
● Chianti Terre di Corzano '11	♟	3
○ Il Corzanello '12	♟	2
● Chianti I Tre Borri Ris. '07	♟♟♟	5
● Il Corzano '05	♟♟♟	5
● Il Corzano '97	♟♟♟	6
● Chianti I Tre Borri Ris. '09	♟♟	5
● Chianti I Tre Borri Ris. '08	♟♟	5
● Il Corzano '09	♟♟	5
● Il Corzano '08	♟♟	5
○ Passito di Corzano '00	♟♟	5

Andrea Costanti

LOC. COLLE AL MATRICHESE
53024 MONTALCINO [SI]
TEL. 0577848195
www.costanti.it

CELLAR SALES
PRE-BOOKED VISITS
ANNUAL PRODUCTION 60,000 bottles
HECTARES UNDER VINE 12.00

Andrea Costanti celebrates his first 30 harvests. In 1983 he took over Colle al Matrichese, inheriting both the honours and duties associated with one of the few historic brands in Montalcino active at that time. His idea of Brunello became immediately visible in a long series of wines with good ageing qualities, perhaps losing something of their eloquent immediacy in order to gain texture, solidity and austerity. These Sangioveses reflect the various vineyard locations to the east of the village at 300 to 450 metres above sea level. They are aged in large casks and 30-hectolitre oak barrels. The Brunello 2008 offers an original, distinctive interpretation of its growing year. Autumn leaf, topsoil, dried flowers with a touch of brine, and the nose abandons all trace of youthful fruity sensations to give way to a refined, moderate palate that is perhaps a tad immature in texture but dynamic and extremely territorial.

● Brunello di Montalcino '08	♥♥	6
● Brunello di Montalcino Ris. '07	♥♥	8
● Rosso di Montalcino '11	♥♥	4
● Brunello di Montalcino '06	♥♥♥	6
● Brunello di Montalcino '88	♥♥♥	6
● Brunello di Montalcino '07	♥♥	6
● Brunello di Montalcino '99	♥♥	6
● Brunello di Montalcino '97	♥♥	6
● Brunello di Montalcino Calbello '00	♥♥	6
● Brunello di Montalcino Calbello '99	♥♥	6
● Brunello di Montalcino Ris. '06	♥♥	8
● Brunello di Montalcino Ris. '01	♥♥	8

La Cura

LOC. CURA NUOVA, 12
58024 MASSA MARITTIMA [GR]
TEL. 0566918094
www.cantinalacura.it

CELLAR SALES
PRE-BOOKED VISITS
ANNUAL PRODUCTION 30,000 bottles
HECTARES UNDER VINE 12.00

This estate was founded in 1968 by Andrea Corsi, father of current owner Enrico. When he bought the property it produced only grain and vegetables, but Andrea had a real passion for wine and so he planted the first two hectares of vines. His son has expanded the area of vineyards to its current size, selecting the varieties according to the terrain. The first wines were bottled between the 1990s and 2000, and the results offer a fine representation of the territory that very distinctive. The entire range shows well led by the Breccerosse 2011 and its concentrated nose, cherry to the fore with hints of aromatic herbs, full, inviting body and succulent finish. Spicy notes with hints of chocolate, soft, relaxed body and tannins nicely integrated with the alcoholic element are the hallmark of the Merlot 2011. The Predicatore Passito 2011 from aleatico and merlot has convincing aromas of cloves and mixed spices and full, soft, lip-smacking entry on the palate.

● Merlot '11	♥♥	5
● Monteregio di Massa Marittima Rosso Breccerosse '11	♥♥	3
● Predicatore '11	♥♥	3
○ Cabernets '11	♥	5
● Cavaliere d'Italia '12	♥	2
● Monteregio di Massa Marittima Rosso Colle Bruno '11	♥	2
○ Valdemàr '12	♥	2
○ La Cura Merlot '08	♥♥	5
● Merlot '09	♥♥	5
● Monteregio di Massa Marittima Rosso Breccerosse '10	♥♥	3
● Monteregio di Massa Marittima Rosso Breccerosse '09	♥♥	2
● Predicatore '10	♥♥	3
○ Trinus '11	♥♥	2*

Maria Caterina Dei

VIA DI MARTIENA, 35
53045 MONTEPULCIANO [SI]
TEL. 0578716878
www.cantinedei.com

CELLAR SALES
PRE-BOOKED VISITS
ACCOMMODATION
ANNUAL PRODUCTION 200,000 bottles
HECTARES UNDER VINE 55.00

The first vines were planted here by
Alibrando Dei, an entrepreneur with a love
for the country, who for a long time sold the
grapes he produced. He made his first Vino
Nobile di Montepulciano, in 1985, in a cellar
rented in the historical centre of
Montepulciano. He later built a big, new,
functional cellar of a very unusual design
using wood, travertine and glass, materials
that blend well into the surrounding
environment. Today the estate is run by his
grand-daughter, Maria Caterina, a lover of
wine, architecture and song. Its elegant nose
mingling thyme and bay leaf with notes of
plum and cherry earns the Nobile 2010 a
place in our finals. The palate is taut,
energetic with fresh sensations that herald
impressive progression and a lip-smacking
finish. The Rosso 2011 is inviting and tasty.
The Vin Santo 2007 is captivating with
pleasing concentration.

● Nobile di Montepulciano '10	▼▼ 4
● Rosso di Montepulciano '11	▼▼ 2*
○ Vin Santo di Montepulciano '07	▼▼ 5
● Nobile di Montepulciano Bossona Ris. '04	▼▼▼ 5
● Nobile di Montepulciano '09	♀♀ 4
● Nobile di Montepulciano '08	♀♀ 4
● Nobile di Montepulciano Bossona Ris. '08	♀♀ 5
● Nobile di Montepulciano Bossona Ris. '07	♀♀ 5
● Nobile di Montepulciano Bossona Ris. '06	♀♀ 5
● Sancta Catharina '09	♀♀ 5

Diadema

VIA IMPRUNETANA PER TAVARNUZZE, 19
50023 IMPRUNETA [FI]
TEL. 0552311330
www.diadema-wine.com

CELLAR SALES
PRE-BOOKED VISITS
ACCOMMODATION
ANNUAL PRODUCTION 170,000 bottles
HECTARES UNDER VINE 15.00

From the footwear sector to hotel
management and finally to wine production:
this is the path of Alberto Giannotti, who
decided to open the Relais Villa L'Olmo in
2000. His first task was restoration of the
houses which were destined for the
accommodation structure, then
reorganization of the vineyards, replanting
those best suited to this area and
completing the process by rebuilding the
cellar and old olive mill. The polished style
of these wines is enhanced by utterly
unique packaging and a newly introduced
line is more traditional in terms of labels
and bottles, while maintaining the same
high level of quality. The Diadema 2011
shows well. This blend of sangiovese with
small amounts of cabernet sauvignon,
merlot and syrah, has cherry and currant
aromas with, spicy nuances of clove,
powerful body and a relaxed finish. The
Rosso D'Amare 2011, the same blend but
with different percentages, is a pleasing
wine, fresh and fruity on the nose, supple
and spirited on the palate.

● D'Amare Rosso '11	▼▼ 5
● D'Vino '11	▼▼ 3
● Diadema Rosso '11	▼▼ 8
○ D'Amare Bianco '12	▼ 4
○ D'Amare Bianco '09	♀♀ 7
● D'Amare Rosso '10	♀♀ 5
● Diadema '10	♀♀ 8
● Diadema '09	♀♀ 8
○ Diadema Bianco '09	♀♀ 7
● Diadema D'Amare '07	♀♀ 7
● Diadema Rosso '08	♀♀ 7

Fabrizio Dionisio

FRAZ. OSSAIA
LOC. IL CASTAGNO
52040 CORTONA [AR]
TEL. 063223541
www.fabriziodionisio.it

PRE-BOOKED VISITS
ANNUAL PRODUCTION 30,000 bottles
HECTARES UNDER VINE 15.00

Since 2003, lawyer-turned-vigneron Fabrizio Dionisio and his wife Alessandra have been producing four wines obtained solely from syrah. This variety has found its ideal growing territory in the zone of Cortona, which some sources claim has flourished here since the Napoleonic occupation. The property was acquired as a country retreat by Fabrizio's father in the 1960s where he could go to relax after the rigours of Rome. It has expanded over time to become a smart, dynamic estate. The property was expanded to its current size through the addition of another farm in 1992. The Cortona Syrah Il Castagno 2010 wins its first Tre Bicchieri, for its lively, aromatic complexity, combining spicy notes of pepper with ripe cherry fruit. On the palate it is soft and balanced, with tannins blending into the alcohol, and fresh notes leading to a tasty, lingering finish.

● Cortona Syrah Il Castagno '10	▼▼▼	5
● Cortona Syrah Cuculaia '09	▼▼	6
● Cortona Syrah Castagnino '12	▼	3
⊙ Rosa del Castagno '12	▼	3
● Cortona Syrah Castagnino '09	♀♀	3*
● Cortona Syrah Cuculaia '08	♀♀	6
● Cortona Syrah Il Castagno '09	♀♀	5
● Cortona Syrah Il Castagno '08	♀♀	5

Donna Olga

LOC. FRIGGIALI
S.DA MAREMMANA
53024 MONTALCINO [SI]
TEL. 0577849454
www.tenutedonnaolga.it

CELLAR SALES
PRE-BOOKED VISITS
ACCOMMODATION
ANNUAL PRODUCTION 25,000 bottles
HECTARES UNDER VINE 11.00

Planted entirely to sangiovese, these four hectares are located on the south-west side of Montalcino, along the road that links the town to the Maremma ports. This is where Olga Peluso has chosen to pursue her personal winemaking project, alongside the work normally carried out at the Centolani family estates. At between 270 and 400 metres above sea level, in an enclave with marl soils rich in gravel, this estate makes a "modern-style" Brunello, placed in quotes here because of the effects of long fermentation and ageing in 30-hectolitre Slavonian oak barrels. They don't quite attain the dizzy heights of the last two years, but Donna Olga's Brunellos retain their welcoming, juicy character. The Riserva 2007 shows rather too-pungent tannins with ripe, balsamic fruit, while the 2008 lacks a bit of lip-smacking, full-bodied support although the palate is close-knit.

● Brunello di Montalcino '08	♀♀	7
● Brunello di Montalcino Ris. '07	♀♀	6
● Brunello di Montalcino '06	♀♀♀	7
● Brunello di Montalcino '01	♀♀♀	6
● Brunello di Montalcino Collezione Arte '06	♀♀♀	7
● Brunello di Montalcino Ris. '01	♀♀♀	6
● Brunello di Montalcino '07	♀♀	7
● Brunello di Montalcino Favorito '07	♀♀	7

Due Mani

LOC. ORTACAVOLI
56046 RIPARBELLA [PI]
TEL. 0583975048
www.duemani.eu

ANNUAL PRODUCTION 40,000 bottles
HECTARES UNDER VINE 10.00
VITICULTURE METHOD Certified Biodynamic

In a barely fertile area with almost extreme features, three zones were identified as suitable for planting three very different vineyards, farmed with biodynamic methods. The estate was established by Elena Celli and Luca D'Attoma, who has over 20 years' experience as an oenologist, in 2000, and immediately became a kind of open-air laboratory for their wine-growing vision. The Altrovino 2011 from cabernet franc and merlot offers relaxed, refined, precise sensations, excellent acidity, and notes of fresh blueberries and black berry fruit. The Syrah Suisassi 2010 is one of the best expressions of its growing year on the coast. Spicy, deep and full of Mediterranean aromas, it brings home a Tre Bicchieri. The excellent Duemani 2010 needs more time.

● Suisassi '10	▼▼▼ 8
● Altrovino '11	▼▼ 5
● Cifra '11	▼▼ 4
● Duemani '10	▼▼ 8
● Duemani '09	♈♈♈ 8
● Altrovino '10	♈♈ 5
● Cifra '10	♈♈ 4
● Duemani '08	♈♈ 8
● Duemani '07	♈♈ 8
● Duemani '05	♈♈ 4
● Suisassi '09	♈♈ 8
● Suisassi '05	♈♈ 4

Eucaliptus

VIA BOLGHERESE, 275A
57022 LIVORNO
TEL. 0565763511
www.agriturismoeucaliptus.com

PRE-BOOKED VISITS
ACCOMMODATION
ANNUAL PRODUCTION 18,000 bottles
HECTARES UNDER VINE 4.00

Vigneron in Bolgheri since the end of the 1960s when wine was sold unbottled, Pasqualino Di Vaira founded this estate now run by his son, Dario. The vineyards occupy barely four hectares along the road to Bolgheri and contain varieties sangiovese, merlot, cabernet sauvignon, petit verdot and syrah for the reds; vermentino and chardonnay for the whites. The top wines on offer are in fine form, well matured, concentrated, yet at the same time lively and deep. We were very pleasantly surprised and our tastings put the wines of this small estate among the best this year. This was perhaps the biggest – positive – surprise of the year. Eucaliptus presents three very well-made wines including a Bolgheri Superiore Ville Rustiche 2010 that can hold its own with the best in the category. The superb nose has a singularly refined elegance; the palate is silky and very long, full of contrasts and changes of pace. A marvel. The Don Clarice 2011 is very good too, a touch toastier and sweeter in its fruity tones.

● Bolgheri Sup. Ville Rustiche '10	▼▼ 5
● Bolgheri Don Clarice '11	▼▼ 3
○ Bolgheri Le Pinete '12	▼ 3

I Fabbri

LOC. LAMOLE
VIA CASOLE, 52
50022 GREVE IN CHIANTI [FI]
TEL. 339412622
www.agricolaifabbri.it

CELLAR SALES
PRE-BOOKED VISITS
ANNUAL PRODUCTION 25,000 bottles
HECTARES UNDER VINE 11.00
VITICULTURE METHOD Certified Organic

I Fabbri, which was named for the smithy in the old village that overlooks the farm, has been making wine since 2000. Located in the subzone of Lamole at an altitude of 500 metres, the estate cultivates its vineyards organically. The cellar processes aim to be as natural as possible and ageing takes place in 900-litre casks, stainless steel and cement. The result is wines with a defined style, very respectful of tradition and the character of this particular territory. They are rigorous and capable of displaying aromas and tastes that touch on the deepest essence of the Chianti Classico DOCG. The Chianti Classico Olinto 2010 is very fresh and tangy with aromatic sensations that in places diminish the intensity of the lovely notes of forest fruit. The Riserva 2010 is splendid, while the linear, austere Chianti Classico Terra di Lamole 2010 shows delicate flowery tones. The Chianti Classico 2010 has intriguing aromas and an essential contrasted palate.

● Chianti Cl. Olinto '10	♟♟ 4
● Chianti Cl. Ris. '10	♟♟ 4
● Chianti Cl. '10	♟♟ 4
● Chianti Cl. Lamole '11	♟♟ 2*
● Chianti Cl. Terra di Lamole '10	♟♟ 2*
● Chianti Cl. '06	♟♟ 3*
● Chianti Cl. Olinto '08	♟♟ 4
● Chianti Cl. Ris. '07	♟♟ 4
● Chianti Cl. Terra di Lamole '06	♟♟ 2*

Fanti

FRAZ. CASTELNUOVO DELL'ABATE
POD. PALAZZO, 14
53020 MONTALCINO [SI]
TEL. 0577835795
www.fantisanfilippo.com

CELLAR SALES
PRE-BOOKED VISITS
ANNUAL PRODUCTION 200,000 bottles
HECTARES UNDER VINE 50.00

With over 300 hectares, 50 of these planted in vineyards, the Fanti family estate is one of the most important agricultural operations in Montalcino. In the past few years, the dynamic Filippo has been helped full-time by his daughter Elisa, bringing a success that also seems to be reflected in the style. Though Fanti Brunellos used to be identified by their distinctly fruity and at times attractively oaky aroma, we now detect greater emphasis on aromatic austerity and finesse. All this depends on the features of this terroir tied to the marly soil and powerful, generous raw materials from the area of Castelnuovo dell'Abate. This range reflects its expressive remodelling again this year, particularly the Riserva 2007. It proposes clear notes of aromatic herbs and dried flowers alongside mature but crunchy fruit, and only lacks a bit of length in the progression. The Brunello 2008 is simpler but already enjoyable.

● Brunello di Montalcino '08	♟♟ 6
● Brunello di Montalcino Ris. '07	♟♟ 8
● Brunello di Montalcino '07	♟♟♟ 5
● Brunello di Montalcino '00	♟♟♟ 6
● Brunello di Montalcino '97	♟♟♟ 5
● Brunello di Montalcino Ris. '95	♟♟♟ 5
● Brunello di Montalcino '06	♟♟ 5
● Brunello di Montalcino '05	♟♟ 5
● Brunello di Montalcino '04	♟♟ 5
● Sant'Antimo Rosso Sassomagno '10	♟♟ 2*
○ Sant'Antimo Vin Santo '06	♟♟ 5

★★Fattoria di Felsina

VIA DEL CHIANTI, 101
53019 CASTELNUOVO BERARDENGA [SI]
TEL. 0577355117
www.felsina.it

CELLAR SALES
PRE-BOOKED VISITS
ANNUAL PRODUCTION 480,000 bottles
HECTARES UNDER VINE 94.00

For several decades the Castelnuovo Berardenga estate has been one of the most illustrious names in the DOC zone, producing long-lived wines with a rigorous, expressive style typical of this entire area. Vineyards are located in the southernmost part of the DOC zone and managed under biodynamic regulations. Interventions in the cellar are reduced and ageing takes place in large oak as well as barriques. Giuseppe Mazzacolin, iconic director of Felsina and clearly responsible for a decade of successful quality, recently handed over the reins of the winery to the daughter of Caterina and Giovanni Poggiali, grandson of the founder, Domenico. The Chianti Classico Rancia Riserva 2010 presents very spicy aromas and a dense, continuous palate that is complex and well-paced. The Fontalloro 2010 shows predominantly sweet aromas from its oak-ageing and a soft, chewy palate. The Chianti Classico 2011 is tasty and very representative of its typology. The Chianti Classico Riserva 2010 has good texture and coherent, elegant progression.

● Fontalloro '10	♥♥♥	6
● Chianti Cl. Rancia Ris. '10	♥♥	6
● Chianti Cl. '11	♥♥	4
● Chianti Cl. Ris. '10	♥♥	4
● Maestro Raro '10	♥	6
● Chianti Cl. Rancia Ris. '07	♥♥♥	6
● Chianti Cl. Rancia Ris. '05	♥♥♥	5
● Chianti Cl. Rancia Ris. '04	♥♥♥	5
● Chianti Cl. Rancia Ris. '03	♥♥♥	5
● Fontalloro '06	♥♥♥	6
● Fontalloro '05	♥♥♥	6
● Fontalloro '01	♥♥♥	5
● Maestro Raro '08	♥♥♥	6
● Maestro Raro '01	♥♥♥	5

Fertuna

LOC. GRILLI
VIA AURELIA VECCHIA KM 205
58040 GAVORRANO [GR]
TEL. 056688138
www.fertuna.it

CELLAR SALES
PRE-BOOKED VISITS
ANNUAL PRODUCTION 300,000 bottles
HECTARES UNDER VINE 50.00

This estate was created from scratch in 1997, devoid of any family tradition linked to the zone. A careful study of the territory identified the terrains best suited to viticulture and the best varieties to plant. Long ago inhabited by the Etruscans and Romans, it is the perfect place to live thanks to its mild climate and ideal farming conditions. The name is pure fantasy, chosen for its assonance with the fortune that can smile on the place and its fruitfulness. The wines are modern in style and suited to an international public. The estate also produces extra-virgin olive oil. A good showing from the Pactio 2011, a blend of sangiovese, cabernet sauvignon and merlot. The complex nose recalls Mediterranean scrub, blackberries and blueberries. The palate is soft with silky, elegant tannins and good length. The Messiio 2009, a similar blend but with syrah, has a fascinating nose, firm body and balanced taste.

● Messiio '09	♥♥	5
● Pactio '11	♥♥	3
○ Droppello '12	♥	3
● Lodai '09	♥	3
○ Plato Bianco '12	♥	2
● Lodai '07	♥♥	1
● Lodai '06	♀♀	4
● Lodai '05	♀♀	4
● Messiio '05	♀♀	5
● Pactio '10	♀♀	2*

Fattoria Fibbiano

FRAZ. TERRICCIOLA
VIA FIBBIANO
56030 TERRICCIOLA [PI]
TEL. 0587635677
www.fattoria-fibbiano.it

CELLAR SALES
PRE-BOOKED VISITS
ACCOMMODATION AND RESTAURANT SERVICE
ANNUAL PRODUCTION 70,000 bottles
HECTARES UNDER VINE 13.90

This is the property of the Cantoni family who originally hail from Lombardy and have always been in agriculture. In the 1960s, owner Giuseppe took an unusual step for that time and left the country to set up in industry. His love for the land was too strong, however, and in 1997 he returned to renovate the farmhouse, turning it into the estate that he runs today with his sons Matteo and Nicola. In addition to the production of wine and extra-virgin olive oil, there is an agriturismo. The Fonte delle Donne 2012, a white blend of colombana and vermentino, does well, offering fresh notes of aromatic herbs like marjoram and lemon verbena, hints of white peach, full, rich, savoury body and a tasty finish. The Le Pianette 2011, a sangiovese and colorino blend, presents intense fruity aromas of cherry and raspberry, energetic structure with well-integrated tannins and full, dynamic body. The Aspetto 2010 from equal parts sangiovese and canaiolo is lively, fruity, round and dynamic.

○ Fonte delle Donne '12	♥♥ 2*
● L'Aspetto '10	♥♥ 3
● Le Pianette '11	♥♥ 2*
● Ceppatella '09	♥ 5
● Chianti Sup. Casalini '11	♥ 2
● Sofia '12	♥ 2
● L'Aspetto '06	♀♀ 3

★Tenute Ambrogio e Giovanni Folonari

LOC. PASSO DEI PECORAI
VIA DI NOZZOLE, 12
50022 GREVE IN CHIANTI [FI]
TEL. 055859811
www.tenutefolonari.com

CELLAR SALES
PRE-BOOKED VISITS
ANNUAL PRODUCTION 1,200,000 bottles
HECTARES UNDER VINE 250.00

Wines from the Nozzole estate in Greve in Chianti, on the Florentine side of Chianti Classico, are made in a modern style, marked by a search for maximum ripeness of fruit and big structure with the small oak showing up front, all produced with flawless technical skill. But wines from Ambrogio and Giovanni Folonari show no lack of stylistic personality, and have frequently reached levels of absolute excellence. This family relies on a well-managed system in the cellar and the best terroirs in Tuscany: Campo al Mare in Bolgheri, La Fuga in Montalcino, Torcalvano in Montepulciano, and Vigne a Porrona in the Maremma. The Cabernet Sauvignon Il Pareto 2010 is a bit curbed by its oak-ageing that limits both the nose and the palate's progression. The Cabreo Il Borgo from sangiovese and cabernet sauvignon is also in thrall to the oak. The Chianti Classico 2011 is enjoyable; the Cabreo La Pietra, a white from chardonnay, is lip-smacking.

● Cabreo Il Borgo '10	♥♥ 5
● Il Pareto '10	♥♥ 7
○ Cabreo La Pietra '11	♥ 5
● Chianti Cl. '11	♥ 4
● Cabreo Il Borgo '06	♀♀♀ 5
● Chianti Cl. La Forra Ris. '90	♀♀♀ 4*
● Il Pareto '09	♀♀♀ 7
● Il Pareto '07	♀♀♀ 7
● Il Pareto '04	♀♀♀ 7
● Il Pareto '01	♀♀♀ 7
● Il Pareto '00	♀♀♀ 7
● Il Pareto '98	♀♀♀ 7
● Il Pareto '97	♀♀♀ 7
● Il Pareto '93	♀♀♀ 7

Fontaleoni

LOC. SANTA MARIA, 39
53037 SAN GIMIGNANO [SI]
TEL. 0577950193
www.fontaleoni.com

★★Fontodi

FRAZ. PANZANO IN CHIANTI
VIA SAN LEOLINO, 89
50020 GREVE IN CHIANTI [FI]
TEL. 055852005
www.fontodi.com

CELLAR SALES
PRE-BOOKED VISITS
ACCOMMODATION AND RESTAURANT SERVICE
ANNUAL PRODUCTION 150,000 bottles
HECTARES UNDER VINE 35.00
VITICULTURE METHOD Certified Organic

The Troiani family's estate is at the top of
the DOCG. Originally viticulturists from the
Marche, they decided to invest their
energies in the territory of San Gimignano
several years ago. From its beginnings in
1959, the estate has expanded to become
a full-blown agricultural concern of 45
hectares divided between cultivated areas
of vineyards, olive groves and arable land,
and the zone's woodland. The vines sit on
the hilly terrains in light soil of medium
texture. The wines offer an authentic,
elegant example of the territory's potential
and are among the best around. 2010 is
clearly a year of grace. Encoring last year's
performance of the Vernaccia Casanova,
this year it is the turn of the Riserva to win
a Tre Bicchieri. This magnificent wine is
aromatically complex and wide-ranging,
offering notes of crusty bread, fresh fruit
and minerally tones enhanced by a chewy,
crunchy, clenched palate with very delicate
texture, delicious in its sweet/acid contrasts.

CELLAR SALES
PRE-BOOKED VISITS
ACCOMMODATION
ANNUAL PRODUCTION 300,000 bottles
HECTARES UNDER VINE 80.00
VITICULTURE METHOD Certified Organic

If the famous Conca d'Oro di Panzano is
universally known as one of the best
Chianti Classico subzones, then credit must
go in large part to this winery, owned by the
Manetti family since 1968, which produces
an absolutely authentic interpretation of
sangiovese from this territory. Fontodi still
has some ways to go along the path to
quality, but is clearly aimed towards an
organic approach in vineyard management,
showing increasing focus on the character
and personality of the wines. The Chianti
Classico 2010 possesses mature but very
clean aromas that are the prelude to
extraordinary wide-ranging, dynamic
progression and a crisp, edgy finish. The
Flaccianello della Pieve 2010 has a
delicate, dark nose and gorgeous, deep
complexity on the palate. The odd
mouth-drying sensation disrupts the Chianti
Classico Vigna del Sorbo Riserva 2010 but
the mouthfeel is superb.

○ Vernaccia di S. Gimignano Ris. '10	▼▼▼ 3*
○ Vernaccia di S. Gimignano '12	▼▼ 2*
○ Vernaccia di S. Gimignano Casanova '11	▼▼ 2*
○ Vernaccia di S. Gimignano Notte di Luna '12	▼ 2
○ Vernaccia di S. Gimignano Casanova '10	♀♀♀ 2*
○ Vernaccia di S. Gimignano '10	♀♀ 2*
○ Vernaccia di S. Gimignano Notte di Luna '11	♀♀ 2*
○ Vernaccia di S. Gimignano Notte di Luna '08	♀♀ 2*
○ Vernaccia di S. Gimignano Ris. '09	♀♀ 3
○ Vernaccia di S. Gimignano Ris. '08	♀♀ 3

● Chianti Cl. '10	▼▼▼ 4*
● Flaccianello della Pieve '10	▼▼ 8
● Chianti Cl. V. del Sorbo Ris. '10	▼▼ 6
● Syrah Case Via '10	▼ 6
● Chianti Cl. V. del Sorbo Ris. '01	♀♀♀ 6
● Flaccianello della Pieve '09	♀♀♀ 8
● Flaccianello della Pieve '08	♀♀♀ 8
● Flaccianello della Pieve '07	♀♀♀ 6
● Flaccianello della Pieve '05	♀♀♀ 6
● Flaccianello della Pieve '03	♀♀♀ 6
● Flaccianello della Pieve '01	♀♀♀ 6
● Flaccianello della Pieve '00	♀♀♀ 6
● Flaccianello della Pieve '97	♀♀♀ 6
● Syrah Case Via '98	♀♀♀ 5
● Syrah Case Via '95	♀♀♀ 5

Podere Forte

Loc. Petrucci, 13
53023 Castiglione d'Orcia [SI]
Tel. 05778885100
www.podereforte.it

CELLAR SALES
PRE-BOOKED VISITS
RESTAURANT SERVICE
ANNUAL PRODUCTION 24,000 bottles
HECTARES UNDER VINE 14.00
VITICULTURE METHOD Certified Biodynamic

Podere Forte, property of Pasquale Forte, is an oenological project centred on a strip of land in Tuscany between Montepulciano and Montalcino, where the terrain is challenging and nothing can be left to chance. Indeed, the estate's production is uncompromisingly efficient and the vineyards are managed using organic and, recently, biodynamic methods. The modern cellar adds to the rigour with the wines ageing in 900-litre casks and barriques. The style is technically irreproachable but perhaps slightly devoid of character and personality. The Orcia Petrucci 2010 presents clean aromas and a succulent, well-paced palate ending in an uplifting finish that is slightly marred by a rather excessive oakiness. The fresh, tasty Orcia Petruccino 2011 does well. The Guardiavigna 2010, a blend of cabernet franc, merlot and petit verdot, has nice grassy notes and a layered palate, although it's a bit weighed down by its oak ageing.

Podere Fortuna

Via San Giusto a Fortuna, 7
50037 San Piero a Sieve [FI]
Tel. 0558487214
www.poderefortuna.com

CELLAR SALES
PRE-BOOKED VISITS
ACCOMMODATION
ANNUAL PRODUCTION 22,000 bottles
HECTARES UNDER VINE 6.00

Historic documents state that Fortuna was producing wines as early as 1465, when the farm belonged to Lorenzo the Magnificent. Various studies of the territory and advice from experts led to the estate being planted mainly to pinot nero in 1998. The variety was unknown in the Mugello zone but it was soon seen to be especially suited to local climate and morphology. The quality in the wine depends on the vine, not on the cellar, and a great Pinot Nero must be the expression of the territory. This is the foundation upon which owner Alessandro Brogi has based his winemaking practices. The MCDLXV 2009 reaches the finals with elegant fruity notes of currant and flowery hints of violet. The palate is relaxed and tasty with a refreshing finish. The pleasant Fortuni 2010 offers more intense aromas of red berry fruit, solid but not oppressive body and a well-positioned acid vein in the finish.

● Orcia Petrucci '10	♥♥ 8
● Guardiavigna '10	♥♥ 8
● Orcia Petruccino '11	♥♥ 8
● Orcia Guardiavigna '01	♥♥♥ 8
● Guardiavigna '09	♀♀ 8
● Guardiavigna '08	♀♀ 8
● Guardiavigna '07	♀♀ 8
● Guardiavigna '05	♀♀ 8
● Orcia Guardiavigna '04	♀♀ 7
● Orcia Guardiavigna '03	♀♀ 7
● Orcia Guardiavigna '02	♀♀ 7
● Orcia Petrucci '02	♀♀ 7
● Orcia Petrucci '01	♀♀ 7
● Orcia Petruccino '06	♀♀ 5
● Orcia Petruccino '05	♀♀ 4

● 1465 MCDLXV '09	♥♥ 8
● Fortuni '10	♥♥ 6
○ Greto alla Macchia '10	♥♥ 5
● Ardito del Mugello '10	♀♀ 3
○ Campo de' Tre Filari '07	♀♀ 6
● Coldaia '09	♀♀ 5
● Coldaia '07	♀♀ 5
● Fortuni '09	♀♀ 6
● Fortuni '07	♀♀ 6
● MCDLXV (1465) '07	♀♀ 8
● Pinot Nero Fortuni '06	♀♀ 5

Tenuta La Fortuna

LOC. LA FORTUNA, 83
53024 MONTALCINO [SI]
TEL. 0577848308
www.tenutalafortuna.it

CELLAR SALES
PRE-BOOKED VISITS
ANNUAL PRODUCTION 60,000 bottles
HECTARES UNDER VINE 18.00

Brother and sister Angelo and Romina Zannoni are the sixth generation working over more than a century at the La Fortuna estate. Together with their father Gioberto, they tend slightly less than 20 hectares in two main areas; the original plot in the area north-east of Montalcino, and recently acquired plots near Castelnuovo dell'Abate. Apart from a few rows of cabernet sauvignon, the star in the vineyard is sangiovese, which creates intense, generous wines, aged mostly in mid-sized barrels, except for some aged in barriques for the Riserva. The Sangioveses we tasted for this edition correspond perfectly to the usual stylistic profile. The Rosso 2011 doesn't have an outstanding nose, but it displays body and pressure. The Brunello Riserva 2007 too is more impressive on the palate than on the nose. The Brunello 2008 is even better, one of the most vigorous interpretations of the vintage, embracing and well sustained despite the odd trace of toastiness that has yet to settle.

● Brunello di Montalcino '08	♼♼ 6
● Brunello di Montalcino Ris. '07	♼♼ 7
● Rosso di Montalcino '11	♼♼ 3
● Brunello di Montalcino '06	♼♼♼ 6
● Brunello di Montalcino '04	♼♼♼ 6
● Brunello di Montalcino '01	♼♼♼ 5
● Brunello di Montalcino '07	♼♼ 6
● Brunello di Montalcino Ris. '06	♼♼ 6

Frascole

LOC. FRASCOLE, 27A
50062 DICOMANO [FI]
TEL. 0558386340
www.frascole.it

CELLAR SALES
PRE-BOOKED VISITS
ACCOMMODATION
ANNUAL PRODUCTION 65,000 bottles
HECTARES UNDER VINE 16.00
VITICULTURE METHOD Certified Organic

The Lippi family, passionate agriculturists, run this estate on the Frascole hill In a zone dotted with ancient Etruscan remains and archaeological digs. Driven by the passion and dedication of the owners, they launched a reconversion project several years ago aimed at improving the quality of the wines based on high-density, low-yield vineyards. They also renovated and extended the cellar to include new vinification and ageing areas. Altitude, ideal aspect and continuous ventilation guarantee healthy plants and wines that are agreeably fresh and far from commonplace. In just a few short years the Vin Santo di Frascole has become a great classic for fans. Intensely scented, continuous, enveloping, very leisurely, this is nectar to be sipped at leisure. The Chianti Rufina 2011 is very good, mineral on the nose with clear notes of forest fruit and blueberry, solid, well-distributed body and freshness that lends it enjoyable drinkability.

○ Vin Santo del Chianti Rufina '04	♼♼ 7
● Chianti Rufina '11	♼♼ 2*
○ Bitornino '11	♼ 2
○ In Albis '11	♼ 2
● Innominato '08	♼ 2
● Chianti Rufina '08	♼♼ 2
● Chianti Rufina Ris. '08	♼♼ 3
● Chianti Rufina Ris. '07	♼♼ 3
○ Vin Santo del Chianti Rufina '03	♼♼ 7
○ Vin Santo del Chianti Rufina '02	♼♼ 7
○ Vin Santo del Chianti Rufina '01	♼♼ 7

Tenuta di Frassineto

S.DA VICINALE DEL DUCA, 14
52100 AREZZO
TEL. 0575367033
www.tenutadifrassineto.com

CELLAR SALES
PRE-BOOKED VISITS
ANNUAL PRODUCTION 38,000 bottles
HECTARES UNDER VINE 30.00

This estate dates back to the 17th century and numbers Giorgio Vasari among its owners. Its winemaking activity was launched by Baroness Favard and reflects her Parisian taste. Along with 25 other estates, it belongs to the Vini senza Solfiti – wines without sulphites – project, which studies techniques for application in the vineyard and cellar to obtain quality wines with the minimum addition of chemical elements. In addition to wine, the estate also produces high-quality durum wheat and other types of grain. A good overall showing led by the Le Fattorie 2011 from pure cabernet franc with fresh aromas of green pepper, balsam and forest fruits. The warm palate shows body, well-structured tannins and a lingering finish. We also liked the Maestro della Chiana 2011, a cabernet franc and petit verdot blend that offers ripe cherry notes, minty nuances, balanced body and a compelling finish. The Vermentino Rancoli 2012 is fresh and enjoyable with citrussy aromas refined by hints of peach.

● Le Fattorie '11	♥♥	4
● Maestro della Chiana '11	♥♥	4
○ Rancoli '12	♥♥	2*
○ Vicinale del Duca V.T. '11	♥	4
● Fontarronco '09	♀♀	2*
○ Rancoli '07	♀♀	2*
○ Vicinale del Duca '07	♀♀	4

★Marchesi de' Frescobaldi

VIA SANTO SPIRITO, 11
50125 FIRENZE
TEL. 05527141
www.frescobaldi.it

CELLAR SALES
PRE-BOOKED VISITS
ANNUAL PRODUCTION 19.000,000 bottles
HECTARES UNDER VINE 1200.00

Lamberto Frescobaldi is the new president of this historic Italian estate that has been going for over 700 years. It operates in several zones in Tuscany including Pomino, Rufina, Maremma, Montalcino, Colli Fiorentini, and also has a property in Friuli. The last few years have seen some new developments, including a greater sensitivity to the concept of eco-sustainability in the vineyard and cellar, a foray into the restaurant business with the wine bar chain De' Frescobaldi, and the Gorgona community project that produces wine on the island in the Tuscan archipelago in collaboration with the correction centre whose inmates work in the vineyards. The Mormoreto 2010, a blend of cabernet franc and sauvignon, merlot and petit verdot, makes the finals with its fresh notes of aromatic herbs, minty tones and forest fruit. The warm palate shows nice weight and balance and a long, tasty finish. The interesting Montesodi 2010 has a spicy nose and a round, harmonious palate. The Nipozzano 2010 has clean aromas and a first-rate palate.

● Mormoreto '10	♥♥	8
● Chianti Rufina Montesodi Ris. '10	♥♥	6
● Chianti Rufina Nipozzano Ris. '10	♥♥	3
● Brunello di Montalcino Castelgiocondo Ris. '07	♥	8
● Morellino di Scansano Pietraregia dell'Ammiraglia Ris. '10	♥	5
● Rosso di Montalcino Campo ai Sassi '11	♥	5
○ Vermentino Ammiraglia '12	♥	3
● Chianti Rufina Montesodi '01	♀♀♀	6
● Chianti Rufina Montesodi '97	♀♀♀	6
● Mormoreto '05	♀♀♀	7
● Mormoreto '01	♀♀♀	7
● Mormoreto '97	♀♀♀	7

Fuligni

VIA SALONI, 33
53024 MONTALCINO [SI]
TEL. 0577848710
www.fuligni.it

CELLAR SALES
PRE-BOOKED VISITS
ANNUAL PRODUCTION 52,000 bottles
HECTARES UNDER VINE 12.00

The Fuligni family winery has existed in Montalcino since the 1920s, and is closely linked to the eastern area known as I Cottimelli. In one of the highest parts of the DOC zone, these vineyards are between 380 and 450 metres above sea level on soils rich in marl and gravel. It is easy to see why these Brunellos, although sometimes intractable and repressed when young, in the best versions still reward the most patient by expressing an airy, graceful profile over time. This is also due to cellar operations marked by a modern classic approach, with ageing in 30-hectolitre oak barrels after a period in large-format casks. We propose our notes again for the Brunellos we tasted this year. The 2008 vintage is endlessly fascinating, offering hints of dried flowers, peach and nutmeg, although the structure is perhaps a little lightweight. The Riserva 2007 is decidedly more powerful with severe tannins to match and offers autumnal, rooty aromas

● Brunello di Montalcino '08	🏆🏆 6
● Brunello di Montalcino Ris. '07	🏆🏆 8
● Rosso di Montalcino Ginestreto '11	🏆 4
● Brunello di Montalcino Ris. '01	🏆🏆🏆 8
● Brunello di Montalcino Ris. '97	🏆🏆🏆 8
● Brunello di Montalcino '07	🏆🏆 6
● Brunello di Montalcino '06	🏆🏆 6
● Brunello di Montalcino '01	🏆🏆 6
● Brunello di Montalcino Ris. '06	🏆🏆 8
● Brunello di Montalcino Ris. '04	🏆🏆 8
● Brunello di Montalcino Ris. '99	🏆🏆 8
● Rosso di Montalcino Ginestreto '10	🏆🏆 3
● Rosso di Montalcino Ginestreto '06	🏆🏆 4

Gattavecchi

LOC. SANTA MARIA
VIA DI COLLAZZI, 74
53045 MONTEPULCIANO [SI]
TEL. 0578757110
www.gattavecchi.it

CELLAR SALES
PRE-BOOKED VISITS
ANNUAL PRODUCTION 280,000 bottles
HECTARES UNDER VINE 40.00

Love of nature and great passion are the secret of this estate's success: 100 years of wine production to celebrate. The family Gattavecchi has reinvented itself over the years, but has never lost sight of tradition. They personally manage all phases of the production. Today sees Luca at the helm. He has thoroughly developed the quality potential of his vineyards and expanded his market overseas. The wines ages in underground caves and rooms in the old Padri Serviti convent, now a historic cellar, at the gates of Montepulciano. The estate's own property of Poggio alla Sala presents the best results. The Nobile Riserva 2009 possesses a varied range of aromas that mingle ripe fruit with tertiary notes, solid, well-defined body and a lingering, succulent finish.

● Nobile di Montepulciano Poggio alla Sala '10	🏆🏆 5
● Nobile di Montepulciano Poggio alla Sala Ris. '09	🏆🏆 5
● Chianti Colli Senesi '12	🏆 2
● Chianti dei Colli Senesi Poggio alla Sala '12	🏆 3
● Nobile di Montepulciano Riserva dei Padri Serviti '09	🏆 4
● Rosso di Montepulciano '12	🏆 2
● Rosso di Montepulciano Poggio alla Sala '12	🏆 2
● Nobile di Montepulciano '09	🏆🏆 4
● Nobile di Montepulciano Parceto Poggio alla Sala '09	🏆🏆 3
● Nobile di Montepulciano Poggio alla Sala '09	🏆🏆 5

Poderi di Ghiaccioforte

LOC. CIVITELLA BASSA, 124A
58024 SCANSANO [GR]
TEL. 0309848311
www.baronepizzini.it

PRE-BOOKED VISITS
ANNUAL PRODUCTION 110,000 bottles
HECTARES UNDER VINE 13.00
VITICULTURE METHOD Certified Biodynamic

Owners Paolo and Christine Endrici,
viticulturists in San Michele all'Adige,
decided to invest in the Maremma in 1999
with Christine's brother Thomas Kessler. It
was no easy task to select the territory in
which to plant their vineyards. The estate
derived its name from a comment about
the challenges of growing vines here made
by the farmer who sold them the land.
Undaunted and determined, the trio did
their research and carefully selected their
cultivars and rootstock. The results are
clear to see. All the wines showed well. The
Serpaiolo 2011, a sangiovese, merlot and
cabernet blend, has concentrated fruity,
spicy aromas and an enveloping, soft
palate with fresh notes and a long finish.
From a similar blend with the addition of
petit verdot, the Meria 2009 is also good.
Vegetal notes recall green pepper and
mixed aromatic herbs; the body is solid and
clearly defined with delicate tannins; the
finish is long and harmonious.

● Meria '09	⚇⚇ 3
● Morellino di Scansano '11	⚇⚇ 4
● Morellino di Scansano Dono Ris. '09	⚇⚇ 4
● Serpaiolo '11	⚇⚇ 2*
● Rosso dei Poderi '10	⚈⚇ 3

★Tenuta di Ghizzano

FRAZ. GHIZZANO
VIA DELLA CHIESA, 4
56037 PECCIOLI [PI]
TEL. 0587630096
www.tenutadighizzano.com

CELLAR SALES
PRE-BOOKED VISITS
ACCOMMODATION
ANNUAL PRODUCTION 80,000 bottles
HECTARES UNDER VINE 20.00
VITICULTURE METHOD Certified Organic

This estate is closely linked to the
charismatic figure of Ginevra Venerosi
Pesciolini, a descendant of the family that
has owned the property for centuries. This
natural beauty comprises 350 hectares, of
which 20 are planted to vine, and offers a
panorama of indescribable splendour. The
terrains are marine in origin, so sandy and
clayey with a high fossil content. This is a
land that commands respect, and after
years of organic agriculture the estate in
fact moved to biodynamic methods some
time ago. The wines are modern but full of
personality and very distinctive. This year
the Nambrot 2010 was absent from the
line-up but a marvellous Veneroso 2010
more than compensated. On the nose
fragrant notes of red berry fruit typical of
Sangiovese mingle with slightly gamey
tones and hints of Mediterranean scrub.
The palate is very juicy, elegant, the
product of a limited growing year that
they have interpreted in an elegant key
at Ghizzano.

● Veneroso '10	⚇⚇⚇ 5
● il Ghizzano '11	⚇⚇ 2*
● Nambrot '09	⚈⚈⚈ 6
● Nambrot '08	⚈⚈⚈ 6
● Nambrot '06	⚈⚈⚈ 6
● Nambrot '05	⚈⚈⚈ 6
● Nambrot '04	⚈⚈⚈ 6
● Nambrot '03	⚈⚈⚈ 6
● Nambrot '01	⚈⚈⚈ 8
● Nambrot '00	⚈⚈⚈ 7
● Veneroso '07	⚈⚈⚈ 5
● Veneroso '04	⚈⚈⚈ 5
● Veneroso '01	⚈⚈⚈ 5
● Nambrot '07	⚈⚈ 6
● Veneroso '09	⚈⚈ 5
● Veneroso '08	⚈⚈ 5

Marchesi Ginori Lisci

FRAZ. PONTEGINORI
LOC. QUERCETO
56040 MONTECATINI VAL DI CECINA [PI]
TEL. 058837443
www.marchesiginorilisci.it

CELLAR SALES
ACCOMMODATION AND RESTAURANT SERVICE
ANNUAL PRODUCTION 35,000 bottles
HECTARES UNDER VINE 17.00
VITICULTURE METHOD Certified Organic

Castle Ginori di Querceto belongs to a
family that has written the story of Florence
and has palaces and streets named after
them. Today the estate is run by Luigi
Malenchini, grandson of Lorenzo Ginori who
started operating in the late 1980s. Towards
the end of the 1990s they uprooted the old
obsolete vineyards and replaced them with
new cultivars that are better suited to the
characteristics of the terroir. They also built
a new cellar using parts of the castle. The
Merlot 2008 reaches the finals showing
evolved tones that mingle chocolate with
leather and ripe fruity notes of cherry jam.
The palate is juicy, solid and lip-smacking
with a lengthy finish. The agreeable
Macchion del Lupo 2009 has fresh,
vegetal notes with undertones of spice and
long length. The Campordigno 2010 is a
simple, well-made wine, lively and fruity on
the nose with flowery nuances and lean but
succulent body.

I Giusti e Zanza

VIA DEI PUNTONI, 9
56043 FAUGLIA [PI]
TEL. 058544354
www.igiustiezanza.it

CELLAR SALES
PRE-BOOKED VISITS
ANNUAL PRODUCTION 100,000 bottles
HECTARES UNDER VINE 17.00
VITICULTURE METHOD Certified Organic

Fuaglia and the hills between Pisa and
Livorno are not new to viticulture; they have
been producing wine here since the end of
the 1800s. This estate in its current form
was established at the beginning of the
1990s and belongs today to Paolo Giusti and
his family. The sandy, clayey terroir with
gravel content, agriculture in tune with
nature and many a nod to organic and
biodynamic methods, meticulous vinifications
and maturation in the cellar all combine to
produce original wines with a decidedly
modern slant. The Dulcamara 2010 does
very well. It opens on fine, elegant toasty
notes that lead into rich, generous aromas of
black berry fruit with delicate and pervasive
nuances of elegant spice. The palate is full,
compact and concentrated right through the
tannic texture. Bottle-ageing is a must; time
will give it greater aromatic definition and a
rounder palate. The excellent Nemorino
Bianco 2012 is intense and juicy with crisp
notes of camomile.

● Montescudaio Merlot '08	▼▼ 2*
● Montescudaio Cabernet Macchion del Lupo '09	▼▼ 3
● Montescudaio Rosso Campordigno '10	▼▼ 2*
⊙ Bacio '12	▼ 2
○ Vermentino Virgola '12	▼ 2
● Castello Ginori '07	♀♀ 4
● Castello Ginori '06	♀♀ 4
● Montescudaio Cabernet Macchion del Lupo '08	♀♀ 3*
● Montescudaio Macchion del Lupo '07	♀♀ 3*
● Montescudaio Rosso Campordigno '08	♀♀ 3*

● Dulcamara '10	▼▼ 5
○ Nemorino Bianco '12	▼▼ 2*
● Belcore '11	▼ 3
● Nemorino Rosso '11	▼ 2
● Belcore '07	♀♀ 3
● Dulcamara '00	▼▼ 5
● Dulcamara '08	♀♀ 5
● Dulcamara '07	♀♀ 5
● Dulcamara '01	♀♀ 5
● Dulcamara '00	♀♀ 5
○ Nemorino Bianco '09	♀♀ 2*
● PerBruno '10	♀♀ 4
● PerBruno '09	♀♀ 4
● PerBruno '06	♀♀ 4
● PerBruno '05	♀♀ 4
● PerBruno '04	♀♀ 4

★Podere Grattamacco

LOC. LUNGAGNANO
57022 CASTAGNETO CARDUCCI [LI]
TEL. 0565765069
www.collemassari.it

CELLAR SALES
PRE-BOOKED VISITS
ANNUAL PRODUCTION 80,000 bottles
HECTARES UNDER VINE 13.00
VITICULTURE METHOD Certified Organic

This absolutely charming estate is a real model for the entire territory. Founded in the 1970s on the eve of the Bolgheri phenomenon when the zone was still a diamond in the rough, it was acquired several years ago by the Tipa brothers. They have kept it much as it was, and if anything they have enhanced the appeal and definition of the wines' elegant style. The bottles express the characteristics of their terroir of origin and are obtained from vines planted among the woods at an altitude of 100 metres in terrains that vary from sandy soil in the low zones to marly limestone higher up. The Bolgheri Superiore Grattamacco 2010 is magnificent. Far removed from the challenges that the growing year brought to the zone, it has weathered and even enhanced the vintage to bring us a red with a lean, fluent character yet mature and never too fine. Notes of red berry fruit and spice accompany herbal, balsamic tones of bay leaf that are echoed on the succulent palate that changes pace continually.

● Bolgheri Rosso Sup. Grattamacco '10	♟♟♟	7
● Bolgheri Sup. L'Alberello '10	♟♟	6
● Bolgheri Rosso '11	♟♟	4
● Bolgheri Rosso Sup. Grattamacco '09	♟♟♟	7
● Bolgheri Rosso Sup. Grattamacco '07	♟♟♟	7
● Bolgheri Rosso Sup. Grattamacco '06	♟♟♟	7
● Bolgheri Rosso Sup. Grattamacco '05	♟♟♟	7
● Bolgheri Rosso Sup. Grattamacco '04	♟♟♟	7
● Bolgheri Rosso Sup. Grattamacco '03	♟♟♟	7
● Bolgheri Rosso Sup. Grattamacco '01	♟♟♟	8
● Bolgheri Rosso Sup. Grattamacco '99	♟♟♟	7
● Grattamacco '85	♟♟♟	7
● Bolgheri Rosso Sup. Grattamacco '08	♟♟	7
● Bolgheri Sup. L'Alberello '09	♟♟	6
● Bolgheri Sup. L'Alberello '06	♟♟	6
● Bolgheri Sup. L'Alberello '04	♟♟	6

Fattoria di Grignano

VIA DI GRIGNANO, 22
50065 PONTASSIEVE [FI]
TEL. 0558398490
www.fattoriadigrignano.com

CELLAR SALES
PRE-BOOKED VISITS
ANNUAL PRODUCTION 250,000 bottles
HECTARES UNDER VINE 49.50
VITICULTURE METHOD Certified Organic

Sitting on the site of a Roman fort, the villa of Grignano was built in 1400 by the Marchesi Gondi on a vast estate that took on its current form in the 1800s. Since 1972 it has belonged to the Inghirami family who work in the fashion industry. Rufina is one of the seven geographic specifications with the Chianti, and its territories produce structured, cellarable wines with a distinctive acid tone. Wine growing is the estate's main agricultural activity, but the over 600 hectares of property are also home to arable land, fruit trees and a large expanse of olive groves. The Riserva Poggio Gualtieri 2008 gives a fine performance. On the nose, tertiary notes of leather and tobacco mix with hints of blackberry jam, while the palate is austere and the tannins well-integrated with the alcoholic element. The Vin Santo 2005 offers an embracing palate, almond and hazelnut aromas and a lengthy finish.

● Chianti Rufina Poggio Gualtieri Ris. '08	♟♟	3
● Chianti Rufina '11	♟	2
○ Pietramaggio Bianco	♟	1*
● Pietramaggio Rosso	♟	1*
○ Vin Santo del Chianti Rufina '05	♟	4
● Chianti Rufina '09	♟♟	2
● Chianti Rufina Poggio Gualtieri Ris. '07	♟♟	3
● Salicaria '05	♟♟	4
○ Vin Santo del Chianti Rufina '04	♟♟	4
○ Vin Santo del Chianti Rufina '03	♟♟	4

Tenuta Guado al Tasso

Loc. Belvedere, 140
57020 Bolgheri [LI]
Tel. 0565749735
www.antinori.it

PRE-BOOKED VISITS
ANNUAL PRODUCTION 800,000 bottles
HECTARES UNDER VINE 300.00

Inherited by the Antinoris in the 1830s, this exceptional estate was part of the Gherardesca holdings. It spans a massive thousand hectares in the most stunning of locations containing beautiful tracts of woodland and Mediterranean scrub in addition to over 300 hectares of vineyards. The wines derive from the classic varieties of the zone, notably merlot and cabernet that grow alongside sangiovese, petit verdot and white cultivars including vermentino. They are modern with a close-focused and impeccable profile, in true estate style. A bit of a low-key year for the wines of this prestigious estate. Our pick of the crop is the Bolgheri Superiore Guado al Tasso 2010, a wine that is still evolving and rather dominated by toasty, grilled sensations of bacon and strong smoky aromas. The palate is clearer, fairly coherent and savoury and well managed in terms of extract. It will grow in the bottle once it has integrated better.

● Bolgheri Rosso Sup. Guado al Tasso '10	🍷🍷 8
○ Bolgheri Vermentino '12	🍷🍷 3
⊙ Bolgheri Rosato Scalabrone '12	🍷 3
● Bolgheri Rosso Bruciato '11	🍷 4
● Bolgheri Rosso Sup. Guado al Tasso '01	🍷🍷🍷 8
● Bolgheri Rosso Sup. Guado al Tasso '90	🍷🍷🍷 8
⊙ Bolgheri Rosato Scalabrone '11	🍷🍷 3
⊙ Bolgheri Rosato Scalabrone '10	🍷🍷 3*
● Bolgheri Rosso Bruciato '02	🍷🍷 4
● Bolgheri Rosso Sup. Guado al Tasso '09	🍷🍷 8
● Bolgheri Rosso Sup. Guado al Tasso '08	🍷🍷 8
● Bolgheri Rosso Sup. Guado al Tasso '00	🍷🍷 8
● Bolgheri Rosso Sup. Guado al Tasso '98	🍷🍷 6
○ Bolgheri Vermentino '11	🍷🍷 3
○ Bolgheri Vermentino '10	🍷🍷 3

Guicciardini Strozzi Fattoria Cusona

Loc. Cusona, 5
53037 San Gimignano [SI]
Tel. 0577950028
www.guicciardinistrozzi.it

CELLAR SALES
PRE-BOOKED VISITS
ANNUAL PRODUCTION 600,000 bottles
HECTARES UNDER VINE 115.00

The Guicciardini Strozzi family is one of the oldest in Italy and boasts an exceptional history in the world of wine. Given its past and the famous admirers of wines from this "chateau", this winery is experiencing a fairly exciting period, thanks mainly to the lively enthusiasm of the new generation. Properties are found in several territories, including the Maremma and Pantelleria, as well as San Gimignano, cornerstone of the estate. Although undergoing a new period of growth and stylistic definition, we felt these wines were focused and well executed. The surprising Vernaccia Titolato Strozzi 2012 is just so good. Minerally, rocky aromas with soft, captivating hints of medicinal herbs give it character and personality. This is an authentic wine, tasty and extraordinarily supple, capable of sharpish development, hard as nails. The Vernaccia Cusona 1933 2011 was less defined when we tasted it, with hesitant and overly aromatic notes.

● Morellino di Scansano Titolato Strozzi '12	🍷🍷 2*
○ Vernaccia di S. Gimignano Titolato Strozzi '12	🍷🍷 2*
○ Arabesque '12	🍷 2
● Chianti Colli Senesi Titolato Strozzi '12	🍷 2
○ Vernaccia di S. Gimignano Cusona 1933 '11	🍷 3
● Millanni '99	🍷🍷🍷 5
● Bolgheri Rosso Sup. VignaRè Villa Le Pavoniere '07	🍷🍷 6
● Sòdole '08	🍷🍷 5
● Sòdole '07	🍷🍷 5
○ Vernaccia di S. Gimignano Cusona 1933 '10	🍷🍷 3
○ Vernaccia di S. Gimignano Titolato Strozzi '11	🍷🍷 2*
○ Vernaccia di S. Gimignano Titolato Strozzi '10	🍷🍷 2*

Fattoria Il Lago

via Campagna, 18
50062 Dicomano [FI]
Tel. 055838047
www.fattoriaillago.com

CELLAR SALES
PRE-BOOKED VISITS
ACCOMMODATION
ANNUAL PRODUCTION 50,000 bottles
HECTARES UNDER VINE 22.00

Now property of the Spagnoli family, this estate was once a farm belonging to the Marchesi Vivai Bartolini Salimbeni. Having renovated all the buildings and created an agriturismo subdivided between two hamlets, the Spagnoli replanted the vineyards and then refurbished the cellar. Viticulture has always been the estate's main activity, as witnessed by the tools unearthed during construction. The Chianti Rufina 2011 makes a good impression with varied aromas including cherries and blackberries, a well-balanced palate with subtle tannins and a pleasant, lingering finish. The interesting Pinot Nero 2010 has fresh hints of aromatic herbs alongside wild berries and a relaxed, velvety texture with a deliciously lip-smacking finish. The spicy, intriguing Syrah 2010 reveals hints of black pepper and curry powder as well as raspberries, while the dynamic palate shows prominent but nicely blended tannin and a juicy, lingering finish.

● Chianti Rufina '11	🍷🍷	2*
● Pinot Nero '10	🍷🍷	5
● Syrah '10	🍷🍷	3
● Chianti Rufina '08	🍷🍷🍷	2*
● Chianti Rufina Ris. '08	🍷🍷	3
● Pian de' Guardi '06	🍷🍷	4
● Pinot Nero '09	🍷🍷	5
● Syrah '08	🍷🍷	3

★Isole e Olena

loc. Isole, 1
50021 Barberino Val d'Elsa [FI]
Tel. 0558072763
www.isoleolena.it

CELLAR SALES
PRE-BOOKED VISITS
ANNUAL PRODUCTION 200,000 bottles
HECTARES UNDER VINE 50.00

Originally from Piedmont but now virtually a native of Chianti, Paolo De Marchi is probably one of the most precise winemakers the Gallo Nero denomination can boast. His work has focused on consistency and reliability, everything aimed of finding a deeper sense of this territory, and so contributing greatly to its revival. As well as the more traditional wines, products from Isole Olena make an intentional digression into so-called "internationals". Aromatically refined and fresh tasting, these wines also show great personality and are clearly above the norm. Once again Cepparello 2010 is one of Chianti's best monovarietal Sangioveses with a really fascinating array of aromas, alternating fruit, flowers and hints of spice. The palate flows with vibrant, creamy elegance into a long, fresh, flavoursome finish. The Chianti Classico 2011 is also a delicious and lively wine, its flavour enhanced by an appetizing contrast of sweetness and acidity.

● Cepparello '10	🍷🍷	8
● Chianti Cl. '11	🍷🍷	5
● Cepparello '09	🍷🍷🍷	8
● Cepparello '07	🍷🍷🍷	8
● Cepparello '06	🍷🍷🍷	8
● Cepparello '05	🍷🍷🍷	8
● Cepparello '03	🍷🍷🍷	7
● Cepparello '01	🍷🍷🍷	6
● Cepparello '00	🍷🍷🍷	6
● Cepparello '99	🍷🍷🍷	6
● Cepparello '98	🍷🍷🍷	6
● Cepparello '97	🍷🍷🍷	6
● Syrah '99	🍷🍷🍷	5
● Cepparello '08	🍷🍷	8

Lamole di Lamole

LOC. VISTARENNI
53013 GAIOLE IN CHIANTI [SI]
TEL. 0577738186
www.lamole.com

CELLAR SALES
PRE-BOOKED VISITS
ANNUAL PRODUCTION 224,000 bottles
HECTARES UNDER VINE 16.00

The Veneto-based group Santa Margherita is one of the most important wine producers in Italy and owns estates in some of the best growing areas. In Tuscany, two are in Chianti, Lamole di Lamole in Greve di Chianti, and Villa Vistarenni in Gaiole, as well as the Sasso Regale estate in the Maremma. Despite the numbers and large quantities, production in Tuscany, especially wines from Lamole, shows a style with good personality and sense of territory. But wines from Villa Vistarenni also maintain a style that is austere and anything but ordinary. Ageing is done in large barrels and small casks. Nicely focused aromas in the Chianti Classico Vigna di Campolungo Riserva 2009 are followed by a weighty, well-coordinated, dynamic palate. The Riserva 2009 Lamole di Lamole is flavoursome if a bit less complex, with soft-focus aromas and a lively, well-balanced mouth. The Chianti Classico 2010 is crisp and refreshing.

La Lastra

FRAZ. SANTA LUCIA
VIA R. DE GRADA, 9
53037 SAN GIMIGNANO [SI]
TEL. 0577941781
www.lalastra.it

CELLAR SALES
PRE-BOOKED VISITS
ANNUAL PRODUCTION 57,600 bottles
HECTARES UNDER VINE 7.00

Founded by a group of vineyard managers and oenologists looking to wager on the potential of Vernaccia and the San Gimignano area, La Lastra has gradually become popular among aficionados. Capable of producing wines that are delicate, linear and vibrant, rather than immediately open and yielding; the winery makes pure, authentic whites, extremely suitable for bottle ageing. The star players here are Renato Spanu, Nadia Betti and Enrico Paternoster; the vineyards plots show clayey silt and are rich in gravel and marine fossils, ideal for the house style and the ideas of the main players at this lovely operation. The Riserva 2011 de La Lastra is one of the best Vernaccias on the market and a benchmark for the whole designation. It was sometimes tricky to grasp when we tasted it, sharpish and linear, the nose far from aggressive but clenched and whispery with lovely minerally hints. Time spent in the bottle will endow this already wonderful wine with complexity.

● Chianti Cl. Vign. di Campolungo Ris. '09	♟♟♟	5
● Chianti Cl. Lamole di Lamole '10	♟♟	3
● Chianti Cl. Lamole di Lamole Ris. '09	♟♟	4
● Chianti Cl. Villa Vistarenni Ris. '09	♟	4
● Chianti Cl. Vign. di Campolungo Ris. '08	♟♟♟	5
● Chianti Cl. Lamole di Lamole '08	♟♟	3*
● Chianti Cl. Lamole di Lamole Et. Blu '09	♟♟	4
● Chianti Cl. Lamole di Lamole Et. Blu '08	♟♟	4
● Chianti Cl. Vign. di Campolungo Ris. '06	♟♟	5
● Chianti Cl. Villa Vistarenni Ris. '08	♟♟	4

○ Vernaccia di S. Gimignano Ris. '11	♟♟	3*
○ Vernaccia di S. Gimignano '12	♟♟	2*
● Chianti Colli Senesi '11	♟	2
○ Vernaccia di S. Gimignano Ris. '09	♟♟♟	3*
● Rovaio '05	♟♟	4
○ Vernaccia di S. Gimignano '11	♟♟	2*
○ Vernaccia di S. Gimignano '10	♟♟	2*
○ Vernaccia di S. Gimignano Ris. '10	♟♟	3*
○ Vernaccia di S. Gimignano Ris. '05	♟♟	3*
○ Vernaccia di S. Gimignano Ris. '03	♟♟	3
○ Vernaccia di S. Gimignano Ris. '02	♟♟	3

La Lecciaia

LOC. VALLAFRICO
53024 MONTALCINO [SI]
TEL. 0583928366
www.lecciaia.it

PRE-BOOKED VISITS
ANNUAL PRODUCTION 200,000 bottles
HECTARES UNDER VINE 30.00

This is a welcome and well-earned return to the main section of our Guide for the estate of Mauro Pacini, one of the most respected winemakers in Montalcino and proprietor of La Lecciaia. Purchased in 1983, the property extends over 60 hectares, 15 of these planted to sangiovese grosso, in the heart of the western sector at 450 metres above sea level, on mixed clayey soils with a good percentage of gravel. These basic conditions explain the youthful severe, dry edge sometimes encountered in the standard, Manapetra and Riserva Brunellos made with long maceration, aged mostly in 50-hectolitre barrels and a small percentage in large casks. We didn't taste much from Lecciaia at Montalcino this year, but a Rosso 2011 with a big solid texture was the prelude to an extremely charming Brunello Vigna Manapetra 2008 with hints of pipe tobacco, damp earth and pot-pourri. Only the over-assertive tannins are holding back a very relaxed flavour.

● Brunello di Montalcino V. Manapetra '08	♥♥ 5
● Brunello di Montalcino '08	♥♥ 5
● Brunello di Montalcino V. Manapetra Ris. '07	♥♥ 6
● Rosso di Montalcino '11	♥♥ 3
● Brunello di Montalcino Ris. '07	♥ 6
● Brunello di Montalcino Ris. '04	♀♀ 6
● Brunello di Montalcino V. Manapetra Ris. '04	♀♀ 7

Cantine Leonardo da Vinci

VIA PROVINCIALE MERCATALE, 291
50059 VINCI [FI]
TEL. 0571902444
www.cantineleonardo.it

CELLAR SALES
PRE-BOOKED VISITS
RESTAURANT SERVICE
ANNUAL PRODUCTION 4,000,000 bottles
HECTARES UNDER VINE 500.00

Cantine Leonardo was set up in the 1960s by a group of about 30 farms, aiming to confront the problems linked to the end of sharecropping. Over the years the number of members has swelled to 160, with consequent enlargement of the range of wines and an increase in quality. The original location in Vinci remains but the growing land is scattered over a large area, ensuring ideal conditions for the various grape varieties planted. One hectare is cared for by students from Florence university's Faculty of Agricultural Science as part of an ongoing research project started several years ago. The co-operative also owns Cantina di Montalcino, now under the supervision of the Caviro group. Chianti Leonardo 2012 is excellent value for money once again, thanks to aromas combining wild berries with hints of spice. The delicious, relaxed palate shows well-judged weight with a refreshing sensation in the finish. A good performance from the Da Vinci Chianti Riserva 2010, well-balanced with weighty structure.

○ Bianco dell'Empolese Vin Santo '07	♥♥ 4
● Chianti Da Vinci Ris. '10	♥♥ 3
● Chianti Leonardo '12	♥♥ 2*
● Rosso di Montalcino Leonardo '11	♥♥ 3
● Brunello di Montalcino Da Vinci '08	♥ 6
● Brunello di Montalcino Da Vinci Ris. '07	♥ 6
● Merlot Poggio del Sasso '12	♥ 2
● Sangiovese Merlot '12	♥ 2
● Sangiovese Poggio del Sasso '12	♥ 2
○ Vermentino Poggio del Sasso Cantina di Montalcino '12	♥ 2
○ Bianco dell'Empolese Vin Santo '06	♀♀ 4
● Chianti Da Vinci '09	♀♀ 2*

Tenuta di Lilliano

LOC. LILLIANO, 8
53011 CASTELLINA IN CHIANTI [SI]
TEL. 0577743070
www.lilliano.com

Lisini

FRAZ. SANT'ANGELO IN COLLE
POD. CASANOVA
53024 MONTALCINO [SI]
TEL. 0577844040
www.lisini.com

CELLAR SALES
PRE-BOOKED VISITS
ANNUAL PRODUCTION 160,000 bottles
HECTARES UNDER VINE 35.00

CELLAR SALES
PRE-BOOKED VISITS
ANNUAL PRODUCTION 90,000 bottles
HECTARES UNDER VINE 21.00

Tenuta di Lilliano lies in the subzone of Castellina in Chianti. Purchased in 1920 by the Ruspoli family, still owner of the property, bottling and marketing began in 1958. The winery is one of the most productive and well-established Chianti Classico production operations. Lilliano produces classic wines with unblemished elegance. Although recently this winery has undertaken a careful shift towards a modern reinterpretation of its wines, it has never lost sight of its own style, based on nuances rather than weight and rigidity. Lovely Mediterranean scrubland aromas in the Chianti Classico Riserva 2010, with a weighty, lingering, well-paced palate. The Chianti Classico 2011 reveals very edgy tannins but is still delicious. Anagallis 2010 is a spicy sangiovese, colorino and merlot blend, still rather stiff in places. The vibrant Vignacatena 2010, a monovarietal Merlot, is back in production after being on hold since 2001.

Active in Montalcino since the late 19th-century, the Lisini family is one of the few who can boast a collection of bottles dating back to the 1960s, which makes this estate historic in the best sense of the word. This legacy that can be felt to this day, resting primarily on ten hectares of vineyards, all planted to sangiovese and mostly located in the area of Sesta, with the notable exception of the Ugolaia cru, recognized by its red, tufaceous soils. This close-knit range is held together by the idea of flavoursome, austere Brunellos, designed to last over time and aged in medium-sized Slavonian oak. As usual the most promising signs come from the Brunellos, starting with Ugolaia 2007: slimmer than usual with vegetal hints confirming the rather raw tannins. The Riserva of the same year shows a similar profile though we enjoyed its very classic expressivity. The Rosso 2011 is also excellent.

● Chianti Cl. Ris. '10	▼▼ 5
● Anagallis '10	▼▼ 5
● Chianti Cl. '11	▼▼ 3
● Vignacatena '10	▼▼ 5
● Chianti Cl. '10	▼▼▼ 3*
● Chianti Cl. '09	▼▼▼ 3
● Anagallis '09	▼▼ 5
● Anagallis '08	▼▼ 5
● Chianti Cl. '08	▼▼ 4
● Chianti Cl. '06	▼▼ 2*
● Chianti Cl. Ris '08	▼▼ 5
● Chianti Cl. Ris. '09	▼▼ 5
● Chianti Cl. Ris. '07	▼▼ 5
● Chianti Cl. Ris. '06	▼▼ 5

● Brunello di Montalcino Ris. '07	▼▼ 7
● Brunello di Montalcino Ugolaia '07	▼▼ 8
● Rosso di Montalcino '11	▼▼ 4
● Brunello di Montalcino '08	▼ 6
● Brunello di Montalcino '90	▼▼▼ 5
● Brunello di Montalcino '88	▼▼▼ 5
● Brunello di Montalcino Ugolaia '06	▼▼▼ 8
● Brunello di Montalcino Ugolaia '04	▼▼▼ 8
● Brunello di Montalcino Ugolaia '01	▼▼▼ 8
● Brunello di Montalcino Ugolaia '00	▼▼▼ 7
● Brunello di Montalcino Ugolaia '91	▼▼▼ 7

Livernano

LOC. LIVERNANO, 67A
53017 RADDA IN CHIANTI [SI]
TEL. 0577738353
www.livernano.it

CELLAR SALES
PRE-BOOKED VISITS
ACCOMMODATION AND RESTAURANT SERVICE
ANNUAL PRODUCTION 50,000 bottles
HECTARES UNDER VINE 20.00

Livernano is the property of Robert Cuillo who in 1990 restored this estate abandoned in 1953 to its former splendour. It lies in the subzone of Radda in Chianti in the Sienese Chianti Classico. The work in the vineyards is extremely meticulous, from the training system that is almost entirely bush-trained, to the absolute respect for the environment. In the cellar maturation is confined to barriques in respect of the estate's style that aims to produce rich, juicy wines that owe much to their oak-ageing. The Chianti Riserva 2010 has well-focused aromas with lovely herbs and light smoky hints. The mouth is flavoursome, vibrant and elegant. Rooty, earthy aromas in the Chianti Classico 2010 are followed by a crisp and succulent palate. The Purosangue 2010, a monovarietal Sangiovese, and the Livernano 2010, a blend of sangiovese, merlot and cabernet sauvignon, are both an elegant glassful with a more powerful, concentrated texture.

● Chianti Cl. '10	♟♟ 3
● Chianti Cl. Ris. '10	♟♟ 4
● Livernano '10	♟♟ 6
● Purosangue '10	♟♟ 5
● Chianti Cl. Ris. '04	♟♟♟ 4
● Livernano '05	♟♟♟ 6
● Livernano '03	♟♟♟ 6
● Livernano '99	♟♟♟ 7
● Livernano '98	♟♟♟ 6
● Livernano '97	♟♟♟ 6
● Chianti Cl. '08	♟♟ 3*
● Chianti Cl. Ris. '09	♟♟ 4
● Livernano '08	♟♟ 6
● Livernano '07	♟♟ 6

Lunadoro

LOC. TERRAROSSA PAGLIERETO
FRAZ. VALIANO
53040 MONTEPULCIANO [SI]
TEL. 0578748154
www.lunadoro.com

CELLAR SALES
PRE-BOOKED VISITS
ACCOMMODATION
ANNUAL PRODUCTION 45,000 bottles
HECTARES UNDER VINE 12.00
VITICULTURE METHOD Certified Organic

After years of running an agriturismo and growing grain in the Val d'Orcia, their home ground, Gigliola Cardinali and Dario Cappelli decided to expand their activity and bought the Pagliareto estate and vineyards in the Poliziano territory. Thus began a new chapter dedicated to wine growing; they renovated the vineyards and reorganized the cellar, both of which they run themselves with care and passion. An excellent performance from the Nobile Riserva Quercione 2009: crisp, clean aromas with well-defined hints of gently spiced fruit. The palate opens broad and consistent, nicely weighty with a delicious long finish. The dynamic, intriguing Rosso Primo Senso 2011 displays fresh wild berries sprinked with hints of spice on the nose and an excellent palate with supple, edgy, lively texture. In the usual style, the Orcia Eclisse 2011 is nicely put together, flavoursome and well-balanced.

● Nobile di Montepulciano Quercione Ris. '09	♟♟ 5
● Orcia Eclisse '11	♟♟ 2*
● Rosso di Montepulciano Primo Senso '11	♟♟ 3
○ Bianco di Toscana '12	♟ 2
● Nobile di Montepulciano Tradizione '10	♟ 4
⊙ Rosato di Toscana '12	♟ 2
● Nobile di Montepulciano '09	♟♟ 4
● Nobile di Montepulciano '08	♟♟ 3
● Nobile di Montepulciano Quercione '05	♟♟ 4
● Nobile di Montepulciano Quercione Ris. '07	♟♟ 4

I Luoghi

LOC. CAMPO AL CAPRIOLO, 201
57022 CASTAGNETO CARDUCCI [LI]
TEL. 0565777379
www.iluoghi.it

CELLAR SALES
PRE-BOOKED VISITS
ANNUAL PRODUCTION 15,000 bottles
HECTARES UNDER VINE 3.50
VITICULTURE METHOD Certified Organic

The story of this estate speaks of love for the land and passion for wine, but it is also unique within the refined Bolgheri wine world. It all began in 1999 when Stefano Granata, a graduate in electronic engineering, decided to change his life and start a small winemaking operation with his wife Paola. It was what came next that makes it unique: a small vineyard divided into two plots ideally suited to their purpose, combined with rigorous yet non-invasive cellar techniques. The result is wines that are very authentic, linear and elegant. This is a shining star in the Maremma firmament. Even in different words than we're used to the Bolgheri Superiore Campo al Fico 2010 still has a lovely story to tell. This vintage presents us with a different wine, even more lean and linear than usual. It will be a real delight for lovers of this type, a Bolgheri red that is almost pinot noiresque, playing on details rather than weight, but those who enter its folds will be enchanted.

● Bolgheri Sup. Campo al Fico '10	♀♀♀	7
● Bolgheri Sup. Podere Ritorti '10	♀♀	5
● Bolgheri Sup. Campo al Fico '09	♀♀♀	7
● Bolgheri Sup. Campo al Fico '08	♀♀♀	7
● Bolgheri Sup. Campo al Fico '07	♀♀	7
● Bolgheri Sup. Campo al Fico '06	♀♀	7
● Bolgheri Sup. Podere Ritorti '09	♀♀	5
● Bolgheri Sup. Podere Ritorti '08	♀♀	5
● Bolgheri Sup. Podere Ritorti '07	♀♀	4

★Le Macchiole

VIA BOLGHERESE, 189A
57020 BOLGHERI [LI]
TEL. 0565766092
www.lemacchiole.it

PRE-BOOKED VISITS
ANNUAL PRODUCTION 150,000 bottles
HECTARES UNDER VINE 22.00

Not just a reference point for the Bolgheri area, this estate is a true Italian wine legend renowned worldwide. Le Macchiole is a model winery, perfect in every way, and capable of producing magnificent wines with exceptional personality, starting with the single varieties vinified and bottled separately. The driving force here is Cinzia Merli, who founded and built the estate with her husband Eugenio. It has always been ahead of its time, from the varieties cultivated, to the vinification, to the high density of vines and the organic methods employed today. The wines pay tribute to the direction taken: today's offerings are splendid; those of the past are memorable. Paleo Rosso 2010 is one of the very small group of wines that most impressed us this year during our Bolgheri tastings. Its extraordinary, almost Indian aromas enfold thick, ripe yet crisp fruit before diving into hints of bay leaves and Mediterranean scrubland. A very fine palate too: a perfect opening, mouthfilling, comforting, sweet and lip-smacking.

● Paleo Rosso '10	♀♀♀	8
● Bolgheri Rosso '11	♀♀	4
● Messorio '10	♀♀	8
● Scrio '10	♀♀	8
● Bolgheri Rosso Sup. Paleo '97	♀♀♀	8
● Messorio '07	♀♀♀	8
● Messorio '06	♀♀♀	8
● Messorio '01	♀♀♀	8
● Messorio '99	♀♀♀	8
● Messorio '98	♀♀♀	8
● Messorio '97	♀♀♀	8
● Paleo Rosso '09	♀♀♀	8
● Paleo Rosso '03	♀♀♀	8
● Paleo Rosso '01	♀♀♀	8
● Scrio '08	♀♀♀	8
● Scrio '01	♀♀♀	8

Le Macioche

SP 55 DI SANT'ANTIMO KM 4,85
53024 MONTALCINO [SI]
TEL. 0577849168
www.lemacioche.it

CELLAR SALES
PRE-BOOKED VISITS
ANNUAL PRODUCTION 18,000 bottles
HECTARES UNDER VINE 3.00

Discovered and restored in the late 1980s by Matilda Zecca and Achille Mazzocchi, Le Macioche is a tiny estate along on the road between Montalcino and Castelnuovo dell'Abate, just over 400 metres above sea level. The almost private production each year is fought over by many fans in love the graceful, almost feminine touch, far removed from showy exhibitions of texture and extract. These Brunellos are original to say the least, involving essential operations in the cellar, which include fermentation with natural yeasts in oak vats and long ageing in 40-hectolitre barrels. Given the underlying of style and terroir, we probably wouldn't have expected to find an outstanding Le Macioche Brunello from a tricky year like 2008. And yet we greatly enjoyed its faithful expression of small red berries, herbs and roots, despite a somewhat over-simple context in terms of flavour.

● Brunello di Montalcino '08	♥♥ 7
● Rosso di Montalcino '10	♥♥ 4
● Brunello di Montalcino '07	♀♀ 7
● Brunello di Montalcino '06	♀♀ 6
● Brunello di Montalcino '04	♀♀ 6
● Brunello di Montalcino '00	♀♀ 5
● Brunello di Montalcino '99	♀♀ 5
● Brunello di Montalcino Ris. '06	♀♀ 8
● Brunello di Montalcino Ris. '01	♀♀ 6

La Mannella

LOC. LA MANNELLA, 322
53024 MONTALCINO [SI]
TEL. 0577848268
www.lamannella.it

PRE-BOOKED VISITS
ANNUAL PRODUCTION 35,000 bottles
HECTARES UNDER VINE 8.00

No fanfares and a lot of work is how Marco Cortonesi made himself known as one of the most reliable and authentic Montalcino winemakers. The Sangiovese de La Mannellas fully respect the special characteristics of the different locations where the almost ten hectares of vines are grown. The sites in the north, close to the winery, are around 250 metres above sea level on clay soils. Those in the south are around 400 metres above sea level in soils mainly rich in gravel. Two Brunellos are produced, the standard-label and Poggiarelli versions, along with the Riserva in the best years. These are aged in mid-sized casks and large barrels. No pinnacle performance compared to previous years but interesting results nonetheless, especially from the 2008 Brunellos. The entry-level version has a strongly Mediterranean feel with plums and salty notes in the foreground while the I Poggiarelli selection is tighter but promises well for the future.

● Brunello di Montalcino '08	♥♥ 5
● Brunello di Montalcino I Poggiarelli '08	♥♥ 5
● Brunello di Montalcino Ris. '07	♥ 6
● Rosso di Montalcino '11	♥ 3
● Brunello di Montalcino '07	♀♀ 5
● Brunello di Montalcino '06	♀♀ 5
● Brunello di Montalcino '05	♀♀ 5
● Brunello di Montalcino '04	♀♀ 5
● Brunello di Montalcino Ris. '06	♀♀ 6
● Brunello di Montalcino I Poggiarelli '07	♀♀ 5
● Brunello di Montalcino I Poggiarelli '06	♀♀ 5
● Brunello di Montalcino I Poggiarelli '05	♀♀ 5
● Brunello di Montalcino I Poggiarelli '04	♀♀ 5

Mannucci Droandi

FRAZ. MERCATALE VALDARNO
VIA ROSSINELLO E CAMPOLUCCI, 79
52020 MONTEVARCHI [AR]
TEL. 0559707276
www.mannuccidroandi.com

CELLAR SALES
PRE-BOOKED VISITS
ANNUAL PRODUCTION 70,000 bottles
HECTARES UNDER VINE 35.00
VITICULTURE METHOD Certified Organic

This estate belongs to Roberto Mannucci Droandi, a viticulturist with a passion for cultivars on the verge of extinction. He has experimented with some of the territory's indigenous varieties and started producing the most successful. The family has been cultivating grapes here the 1800s and before that they worked in the zone of Carmignano. Today Roberto works alongside his wife Mara Grazia and grandsons Andrea and Matteo. Interesting products this year: the Chianti Classico Ceppeto 2010 is on top form with lively, vibrant aromas, well-balanced texture, light tannins and nicely dynamic finish. The austere Campolucci 2008, sangiovese with cabernet sauvignon and merlot, has mature coffee and pipe tobacco aromas, complex structure with no false notes and a tangy finish. The Chianti 2011 is fresh and well-made while the Barsaglina 2009 is unusual, floral and lively.

● Barsaglina '09	♟♟ 4
● Campolucci '08	♟♟ 4
● Chianti Cl. Ceppeto '10	♟♟ 3
● Chianti Colli Aretini '11	♟♟ 2*
● Chianti Cl. Ceppeto Ris. '09	♟ 4
⊙ Rossinello '12	♟ 2
● Barsaglina '08	♟♟ 4
● Chianti Cl. Ceppeto '08	♟♟ 3
● Chianti Cl. Ceppeto Ris. '08	♟♟ 4
● Foglia Tonda '08	♟♟ 4
○ Vin Santo del Chianti Cl. Ceppeto '05	♟♟ 5

Fattoria Mantellassi

LOC. BANDITACCIA, 26
58051 MAGLIANO IN TOSCANA [GR]
TEL. 0564592037
www.fattoriamantellassi.it

CELLAR SALES
PRE-BOOKED VISITS
ANNUAL PRODUCTION 700,000 bottles
HECTARES UNDER VINE 52.00

The Mantellassi family has been involved in wine-growing for generations and the family motto – labor omina vincit – says much about their approach and dedication. Their commitment and passion quickly bore fruit and the founder of the estate in Magliano is remembered as the Ambassador of Morellino. The first vineyard was planted in 1960, in the Maremma area, and it is no coincidence that the family was a founding member of the Consorzio Morellino di Scansano in 1978. Today, brothers Aleardo and Giuseppe run all aspects of the business, participating directly both in the production process and managing the commercial side. The Riserva Le Sentinelle 2009 made the final tastings: its complex aromas highlight mature sensations like tobacco and leather, alongside plums and vegetal hints of aromatic herbs. A mouthfilling entry is followed by fairly muted tannins, a fresh note of acidity and a mouthwatering finish. We recommend the Punton del Sorbo 2010, a monovarietal Cabernet, for its generous aromas.

● Morellino di Scansano Le Sentinelle Ris. '09	♟♟ 4
○ Lucumone '12	♟ 2
● Morellino di Scansano Mentore '12	♟ 2
● Morellino di Scansano San Giuseppe '12	♟ 3
● Punton del Sorbo '10	♟ 3
○ Vermentino Scalandrino '12	♟ 2
● Morellino di Scansano Le Sentinelle Ris. '06	♟♟ 4
● Morellino di Scansano Mentore '11	♟♟ 2*
● Morellino di Scansano Mentore '08	♟♟ 2
● Morellino di Scansano San Giuseppe '09	♟♟ 2
● Morellino di Scansano San Giuseppe '08	♟♟ 2
● Querciolaia '07	♟♟ 4

Il Marroneto

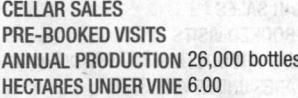

LOC. MADONNA DELLE GRAZIE, 307
53024 MONTALCINO [SI]
TEL. 0577849382
www.ilmarroneto.com

Mastrojanni

FRAZ. CASTELNUOVO DELL'ABATE
POD. LORETO SAN PIO
53024 MONTALCINO [SI]
TEL. 0577835681
www.mastrojanni.com

CELLAR SALES
PRE-BOOKED VISITS
ANNUAL PRODUCTION 26,000 bottles
HECTARES UNDER VINE 6.00

CELLAR SALES
PRE-BOOKED VISITS
ANNUAL PRODUCTION 100,000 bottles
HECTARES UNDER VINE 24.00

Often we recommend patience for wines that can arouse unforgettable emotions given time. In the case of Il Marroneto's Sangioveses this is not only good advice but a requirement. The proof is to be found in a series of simply extraordinary wines which, since the Seventies, have described Alessandro Mori's immense passion for his work and the unmistakeable features of the Montosoli hills, in the northern part of Montalcino. The current vintage and the Madonna delle Grazie cru are aged in large Slavonian oak casks, mostly already used. These Brunellos are more than demonstrative, they are almost elliptical and deserve our careful attention after their release. Fitting nicely into this groove, the Madonna delle Grazie 2008 is extremely youthful and already shows the signs of a real champ with hints of antique wood, dried flowers and oriental spices. We might even term it a lyrical interpretation of Montalcino Sangiovese, offered almost without trace in an unusually beautiful flavour.

Credit is mainly due to Andrea Machetti for fully preserving the stylistic identity of one of Montalcino's classic brands after its purchase a few years ago by the Illy family. His decision to stay on the course already undertaken by the estate is a clear indication of continuity, supported by Brunellos as charismatic, densely textured and flavoursome as we would expect from locations overlooking Castelnuovo dell'Abate, but also proud and down-to-earth. Various cask sizes are used in the cellar: larger for the Vigna Loreto cru, smaller for the estate's other champion, Vigna Schiena d'Asino, not to mention the work that goes into the Rosso which is much more than just an entry-level wine. The 2011 backs this up precisely, a Rosso with an airily broad scope of aromas, and not without weight and length. But this year the real jewel in the crown appears to be the Brunello Vigna Schiena d'Asino 2008, winning Tre Bicchieri for its oriental spices combined with a racy, blended, accomplished palate.

● Brunello di Montalcino Madonna delle Grazie '08	♟♟♟ 8
● Brunello di Montalcino '08	♟♟ 7
● Rosso di Montalcino Ignaccio '09	♟ 3
● Brunello di Montalcino '07	♟♟ 6
● Brunello di Montalcino '06	♟♟ 6
● Brunello di Montalcino Madonna delle Grazie '07	♟♟ 8
● Brunello di Montalcino Madonna delle Grazie '06	♟♟ 8

● Brunello di Montalcino Schiena d'Asino '08	♟♟♟ 8
● Brunello di Montalcino '08	♟♟ 5
● Brunello di Montalcino V. Loreto '08	♟♟ 7
● Rosso di Montalcino '11	♟♟ 3
● Brunello di Montalcino '97	♟♟♟ 7
● Brunello di Montalcino '90	♟♟♟ 7
● Brunello di Montalcino Ris. '88	♟♟♟ 6
● Brunello di Montalcino Schiena d'Asino '93	♟♟♟ 7
● Brunello di Montalcino Schiena d'Asino '90	♟♟♟ 7
● Brunello di Montalcino '07	♟♟ 5
● Brunello di Montalcino Schiena d'Asino '07	♟♟ 8
● Brunello di Montalcino V. Loreto '07	♟♟ 7

Melini

LOC. GAGGIANO
53036 POGGIBONSI [SI]
TEL. 0577998511
www.cantinemelini.it

CELLAR SALES
PRE-BOOKED VISITS
ANNUAL PRODUCTION 4,000,000 bottles
HECTARES UNDER VINE 145.00

The Melini winery in Poggibonsi and Macchiavelli at San Casciano Val di Pesa are Gruppo Italiano Vini's production centres in Chianti Classico, and have played a significant role in the denomination's history. They are probably among the most widespread and best-known Chianti brands in the world and their range of wines represents a steady and consolidated standard of quality. The products are all meticulously put-together with commendable care and are mainly aged in large oak casks. These are characterful wines, favouring elegance over strength and at times achieving absolute excellence. The Chianti Classico Granaio 2011 reveals vibrant, multifaceted aromas and a crisp, tangy flavour. The equally enjoyable Chianti Classico Solatio del Tani 2011 from Fattoria Macchiavelli is well-paced and only slightly less expressive on the nose. The austere La Selvanella Riserva 2010 displays beautifully clean fruity aromas and fresh cherries in the aftertaste.

● Chianti Cl. Granaio '11	♥♥ 3*
● Chianti Cl. La Selvanella Ris. '10	♥♥ 5
● Chianti Cl. Solatio del Tani Fattoria Machiavelli '11	♥♥ 3
● Chianti Cl. V. di Fontalle Fattoria Macchiavelli Ris. '10	♥ 5
● Chianti Governo all'uso Toscano Neocampana '12	♥ 2
● Chianti Cl. La Selvanella Ris. '06	♥♥♥ 5
● Chianti Cl. La Selvanella Ris. '03	♥♥♥ 4
● Chianti Cl. La Selvanella Ris. '01	♥♥♥ 4
● Chianti Cl. La Selvanella Ris. '00	♥♥♥ 4
● Chianti Cl. La Selvanella Ris. '99	♥♥♥ 5
● Chianti Cl. La Selvanella Ris. '90	♥♥♥ 3*
● Chianti Cl. La Selvanella Ris. '86	♥♥♥ 4*

Le Miccine

LOC. LE MICCINE
SS TRAVERSA CHIANTIGIANA, 44
53013 GAIOLE IN CHIANTI [SI]
TEL. 0577749526
www.lemiccine.com

CELLAR SALES
PRE-BOOKED VISITS
ACCOMMODATION
ANNUAL PRODUCTION 30,000 bottles
HECTARES UNDER VINE 7.00

Le Miccine is one of the many artisan family-run estates that dot the Chianti Classico designation. The vines are cultivated naturally and the estate is currently in the process of converting to organic methods. In the cellar, they have pared the process back to the bone and the wines are aged in casks and large oak. The wines are forthright and lean, stylistically rooted in their territory, the Gaiole in Chianti subzone. Their exceptionally slim profile does at times diminish their overall complexity. The Chianti Classico Riserva 2010 shows striking finesse and length: focused aromas in which the hints of citrus herald a fresh-tasting flavour, lipsmacking, conflicted and not without grip. The Chianti Classico 2011 reveals hazy aromas with toasty hints while the palate has relaxed mouthfeel and closes on a nicely flavoursome note.

● Chianti Cl. Ris. '10	♥♥♥ 2*
● Chianti Cl. '11	♥♥ 2*
● Chianti Cl. '09	♀♀ 2*
● Chianti Cl. '07	♀♀ 2
● Chianti Cl. '06	♀♀ 3*
● Chianti Cl. '02	♀♀ 3
● Chianti Cl. '00	♀♀ 3
● Chianti Cl. '97	♀♀ 3
● Chianti Cl. Don Alberto Ris. '07	♀♀ 4
● Chianti Cl. Don Alberto Ris. '06	♀♀ 4
● Chianti Cl. Don Alberto Ris. '02	♀♀ 4
● Chianti Cl. Ris. '09	♀♀ 2*
● La Pricipessa '06	♀♀ 3
○ Vin Santo del Chianti Cl. La Gloria '00	♀♀ 5

Mocali

Loc. Mocali
53024 Montalcino [SI]
Tel. 0577849485
azmocali@tiscali.it

CELLAR SALES
PRE-BOOKED VISITS
ANNUAL PRODUCTION 120,000 bottles
HECTARES UNDER VINE 9.00

Tiziano Ciacci's estate is situated on the south-west slope of Montalcino at altitudes between 350 and 400 metres, covering about 30 hectares, half of which are planted with vineyards and olives. Tiziano, who represents the third generation working at Mocali, continues the task of running a traditional estate which is also able to offer an entirely personal and cliché-free interpretation of Montalcino Sangiovese. While young the Brunellos are sometimes a little austere but are rich in fibre and aged in Slavonian oak, while some wines or particular vintages are matured in smaller casks. A certainly not approachable style is emphasized in the magnificent Brunello Vigna delle Raunate 2008: while the nose acquires greater clarity after the toasty initial impact, the palate dispels all doubts with a juicy, tangy vein through the solid texture, and faultless tannic extract. The Riserva 2007 just shows less grip while the Brunello 2008 lacks character.

● Brunello di Montalcino V. delle Raunate '08	▼▼▼ 6
● Brunello di Montalcino '08	▼▼ 5
● Brunello di Montalcino Ris. '07	▼▼ 7
● I Piaggioni '11	▼ 2
● Rosso di Montalcino '11	▼ 2
● Brunello di Montalcino Poggio Nardone '06	♀♀ 6
● Brunello di Montalcino Ris. '06	♀♀ 7
● Brunello di Montalcino V. delle Raunate '07	♀♀ 6
● Brunello di Montalcino V. delle Raunate '06	♀♀ 6
● Brunello di Montalcino V. delle Raunate Ris. '06	♀♀ 8
● Brunello di Montalcino V. delle Raunate Ris. '04	♀♀ 8

Il Molino di Grace

Loc. Il Volano Lucarelli
50022 Greve in Chianti [FI]
Tel. 0558561010
www.ilmolinodigrace.com

CELLAR SALES
PRE-BOOKED VISITS
ANNUAL PRODUCTION 210,000 bottles
HECTARES UNDER VINE 36.00
VITICULTURE METHOD Certified Organic

In Panzano, an area reputed for the quality of its grapes, Molino di Grace is a relative newcomer, although the estate's vineyards have been established for much longer. Owner Frank Grace and manager Gerhard Hirmer converted an old hayloft into a modern cellar that receives the estate's own organic grapes. There is little intervention in the vineyard, as testified by triennial surfacing ploughing. The wines are cellared in oak of varying sizes, from casks to barrels of up to 25 hectolitres. The Chianti Classico 2011 is really well-made: a generous, fragrant nose, clear hints of strawberries and cherries, dried herbs and gamy notes. The palate is mouthfilling but also graceful and taut. Il Margone Riserva 2009 is more mature with prominent toasty aromas and a relaxed, velvety mouth with a broad finish.

● Chianti Cl. '11	▼▼ 3*
● Chianti Cl. Il Margone Ris. '09	▼▼ 5
● Chianti Cl. Il Margone Ris. '05	♀♀♀ 6
● Chianti Cl. Il Margone Ris. '04	♀♀♀ 6
● Chianti Cl. Ris. '01	♀♀♀ 4
● Gratius '04	♀♀♀ 6
● Chianti Cl. Il Margone Ris. '06	♀♀ 6

Tenuta di Montecucco

LOC. MONTECUCCO
58044 CINIGIANO [GR]
TEL. 0564999029
www.tenutadimontecucco.it

CELLAR SALES
PRE-BOOKED VISITS
ACCOMMODATION
ANNUAL PRODUCTION 60,000 bottles
HECTARES UNDER VINE 10.00
VITICULTURE METHOD Certified Organic

Montecucco is one of two ancient places in the municipality of Cinigiano that were documented as being good wine territory back in the early 12th century and the designation of origin owes its name to this estate. The property has passed through many hands over the centuries and today it is owned by Claudio Tipa, who also owns Colle Massari in the same zone, Grattamacco in Bolgheri and Poggio di Sotto in Montalcino. The vines are now cultivated using integrated pest management, which, combined with top-quality soil and a favourable climate, lend considerable character to their wine and oil. The estate also runs on-site holiday accommodation. An impressive performance from the Riserva Rigomoro 2009 with generous aromas: hints of balsam blending to refine fruity sensations, a pleasant entry on an appreciably firm-bodied palate with fine-grained tannins and refreshing acidity in the finish make a deliciously drinkable wine.

● Montecucco Rigomoro Ris. '09	♥♥ 5
● Canaiolo '12	♥ 2
● Canaiolo '11	♥♥ 2*
● Montecucco Le Coste '09	♥♥ 3
● Montecucco Passonaia '08	♥♥ 2
● Montecucco Rigomoro Ris. '08	♥♥ 4
● Montccucco Rosso Passonaia '09	♥♥ 2*
● Montecucco Rosso Passonaia '08	♥♥ 2*
● Montecucco Sangiovese Le Coste '07	♥♥ 3
● Montecucco Sangiovese Le Coste '06	♥♥ 3
● Montecucco Sangiovese Rigomoro Ris. '07	♥♥ 5
● Montecucco Sangiovese R igomoro Ris. '06	♥♥ 5

Fattoria Montellori

VIA PISTOIESE, 1
50054 FUCECCHIO [FI]
TEL. 0571260641
www.fattoriamontellori.it

CELLAR SALES
PRE-BOOKED VISITS
RESTAURANT SERVICE
ANNUAL PRODUCTION 250,000 bottles
HECTARES UNDER VINE 44.00

Although the property is outside what are generally recognized as the best traditional wine areas, wine has been produced here for over 100 years. The Nieri family has created a range of unusual wines with personality that expresses the terroir while perfectly conveying the family's values, by carefully selection the varieties and analysing the soil. Their love of contemporary art has also transformed the main property into a kind of open-air museum featuring valuable unusual works. The extensive and varied range also includes a top-flight Metodo Tradizionale sparkling wine, conceived back when the type was virtually unheard of in Tuscany. The pleasant Vin Santo 2006 has vibrant aromas of honey, vanilla and citrus zest. The buttery, creamy palate opens out into a flavoursome, lingering finish. The Pas Dosé 2009 sparkling wine reveals a subtle, delicate nose with hints of flowers and breadcrust, followed by a nicely textured, but not weighty, structure with a generous, enjoyable finish.

○ Bianco dell'Empolese Vin Santo '06	♥♥ 5
○ Blanc des Blancs Pas Dosé '09	♥♥ 4
● Chianti '11	♥ 2
● Chianti Sup. Caselle '11	♥ 2
● Dicatum '10	♥ 5
○ Mandorlo '12	♥ 2
● Moro '10	♥ 3
● Salamartano '10	♥ 5
○ Sant'Amato '12	♥ 3
○ Bianco dell'Empolese Vin Santo '05	♥♥ 5
○ Brut Blanc des Blancs Mill. '07	♥♥ 4
● Moro '09	♥♥ 3
● Salamartano '09	♥♥ 6
● Tuttosole '09	♥♥ 4

Montemercurio

VIA DI TOTONA, 25A
53045 MONTEPULCIANO [SI]
TEL. 0578716610
www.montemercurio.com

CELLAR SALES
PRE-BOOKED VISITS
ANNUAL PRODUCTION 40,000 bottles
HECTARES UNDER VINE 10.00

During the 1960s, Damo Anselmi started planting a small vineyard that his family later expanded, taking great care throughout the production process to work on the quality of the wines, which have now reached a level that fully expresses the characteristic flavours and aromas of the territory. In 2000, they began planting new vineyards and, in 2007, they celebrated the newly founded Montemercurio's first harvest. An interesting version of the Caduceo 2012, a white made from malvasia, canaiolo bianco and pulcinculo: floral aromas mix with almonds and hints of apple and white peach fruit, while the delicious entry is followed by an edgy palate showed well-balanced alcohol and freshness and a tangy finish. The Nobile 2010 has intense fruit on the nose, a supple body with well-embedded tannins and a flavoursome finish. The sumptuous, buttery Vin Santo 2009 has a very mature nose and a warm, creamy palate.

○ Caduceo '12	♟♟ 3
● Nobile di Montepulciano Messaggero '10	♟♟ 4
○ Vin Santo di Montepulciano '90	♟♟ 8
● Nobile di Montepulciano Damo '07	♟♟ 8
● Nobile di Montepulciano Messaggero '08	♟♟ 4
○ Vin Santo di Montepulciano '86	♟♟ 8

Montenidoli

LOC. MONTENIDOLI
53037 SAN GIMIGNANO [SI]
TEL. 0577941565
www.montenidoli.com

CELLAR SALES
ACCOMMODATION
ANNUAL PRODUCTION 100,000 bottles
HECTARES UNDER VINE 24.00
VITICULTURE METHOD Certified Organic

This is not only a sensational San Gimignano estate but also a benchmark for the whole of Italy, thanks to its history, style and deep-rooted, radical convictions which rise far above standardization. Montenidoli is an extremely prestigious exponent of the natural movement, producing wines that are both incredibly land-rooted and show outstanding personality. In short, highly original and unique wines, characterful and distinguished without exception, although the Vernaccias paint a particularly multicoloured picture. These are wines to drink and to collect, timeless and above trends. Deep and complex, Vernaccia Carato 2009 speaks volumes about the terroir and particularly the year. Earthy, truffle flavour on a deep, velvety, rich palate with tangy minerally sensations, just lacking the usual touch of finesse. Also in the finals, the Fiore 2011 shows generous fruit, hints of spice and incense, a deliciously juicy palate closing on almondy, smoky notes.

○ Vernaccia di S. Gimignano Carato '09	♟♟ 4
○ Vernaccia di S. Gimignano Fiore '11	♟♟ 3*
○ Vernaccia di S. Gimignano Tradizionale '11	♟♟ 2*
⊙ Canaiuolo '12	♟♟ 3
● Chianti Colli Senesi '10	♟♟ 4
○ Vinbrusco '10	♟♟ 2*
● Chianti Colli Senesi Il Garrulo '11	♟ 2
● Colorino '11	♟ 3
○ Vernaccia di S. Gimignano Carato '05	♟♟♟ 5
○ Vernaccia di S. Gimignano Carato '02	♟♟♟ 5
○ Vernaccia di S. Gimignano Fiore '09	♟♟♟ 3
● Chianti Colli Senesi Ris. '08	♟♟ 4
○ Vernaccia di S. Gimignano Carato '08	♟♟ 4
○ Vernaccia di S. Gimignano Fiore '10	♟♟ 3*

Monteraponi

LOC. MONTERAPONI
53017 RADDA IN CHIANTI [SI]
TEL. 0577738280
www.monteraponi.it

CELLAR SALES
PRE-BOOKED VISITS
ACCOMMODATION
ANNUAL PRODUCTION 30,000 bottles
HECTARES UNDER VINE 10.00
VITICULTURE METHOD Certified Organic

Michele Braganti's estate only entered the
Chianti Classico overview a short time ago
but it has stood out since the beginning for
its strongly traditional wines, offering a real
and irresistibly attractive journey back in
time. The strongpoint of these products is
the pursuit of the best possible expression
of sangiovese from the Radda subzone, and
they stick firmly to this objective. Their
most distinctive feature is aromas
alternating between vibrant sensations and
softer hints, with a taut, flavoursome palate
and bags of energy. Chianti Classico
Baron'Ugo Riserva 2009 is really charming
with hazy, complex aromas and a textured,
well-balanced and lively palate. The Chianti
Classico Il Campitello Riserva 2010 also has
a lively, contrast-rich flavour and alternating
floral hints and aromatic herbs on the nose.
The Chianti Classico 2011 is mature and
mouthwatering.

Montesalario

FRAZ. MONTENERO D'ORCIA
LOC. MONTESALARIO, 27
58040 CASTEL DEL PIANO [GR]
TEL. 0564954173
www.aziendamontesalario.it

CELLAR SALES
PRE-BOOKED VISITS
ANNUAL PRODUCTION 18,000 bottles
HECTARES UNDER VINE 4.50

The estate is owned by the Pasqui brothers,
who decided to establish a winery of high
quality in the Montecucco zone, near
Grosseto. It also produces extra-virgin olive
oil. They have a few hectares on the
west-facing slopes of the mountain, mostly
planted with sangiovese, that here impart
characteristic, never banal aromas and
structure that express the terroir perfectly.
Montecucco Sangiovese 2010 gets
through to the finals thanks to generous,
varied aromas ranging from fresh minty
sensations to ripe cherry fruit and hints of
spice. The palate is mouthwatering, richly
extracted and nicely broad with a delicious
acidic vein creating an appetizing finish. The
Riserva 2009 is well-made with aromas of
fine leather, pipe tobacco and cherry jam
and a firm, well-balanced palate.

● Chianti Cl. Baron'Ugo Ris. '09	♈♈♈ 7
● Chianti Cl. Il Campitello Ris. '10	♈♈ 5
● Chianti Cl. '11	♈♈ 3
● Vin Santo del Chianti Cl. '05	♈♈ 6
● Chianti Cl. Baron'Ugo Ris. '07	♒♒♒ 5
● Chianti Cl. '10	♒♒ 4
● Chianti Cl. '09	♒♒ 3
● Chianti Cl. '03	♒♒ 3*
● Chianti Cl. Il Campitello Ris. '09	♒♒ 5
● Chianti Cl. Ris. Il Campitello '04	♒♒ 5

● Montecucco Sangiovese '10	♈♈♈ 3*
● Montecucco Sangiovese Ris. '09	♈♈ 4
● Montecucco '10	♈ 2
● Montecucco Sangiovese '09	♒♒ 3
● Montecucco Sangiovese '06	♒♒ 3*
● Montecucco Sangiovese '04	♒♒ 3
● Montecucco Sangiovese Ris. '08	♒♒ 4

★Montevertine

LOC. MONTEVERTINE
53017 RADDA IN CHIANTI [SI]
TEL. 0577738009
www.montevertine.it

PRE-BOOKED VISITS
ANNUAL PRODUCTION 85,000 bottles
HECTARES UNDER VINE 15.00

It's hard to find wines as pure as the ones made on this Radda in Chianti estate. It's hard to find wines able to express a concentration of personality and terroir, ageability and accessible flavour. It's hard to find a wine estate that shows such sturdy and steady quality. Hard, but not impossible. Montevertine has been and continues to be the birthplace of probably the most rounded wines in what is, for many, the paradigm of Chianti Sangiovese. Credit goes to Martino Manetti who has continued to follow the path carved out by his father Sergio, without being influenced by the winemaking fashions that have left their mark on this area. As we know, in a characterful year Montevertine wines won't disappoint. The Le Pergole Torte 2010 is simply extraordinary: charming red berries and aromatic herbs, damp earth and leaves on the nose, and palate both edgy and alluring, raring to go and seductive. It's no word of a lie to say that the Montevertine 2010 is equally good.

● Le Pergole Torte '10	▼▼▼	8
● Montevertine '10	▼▼	6
● Pian del Ciampolo '11	▼▼	4
● Le Pergole Torte '09	♈♈♈	8
● Le Pergole Torte '07	♈♈♈	8
● Le Pergole Torte '04	♈♈♈	8
● Le Pergole Torte '03	♈♈♈	7
● Le Pergole Torte '01	♈♈♈	8
● Le Pergole Torte '99	♈♈♈	8
● Le Pergole Torte '92	♈♈♈	8
● Le Pergole Torte '90	♈♈♈	8
● Montevertine '04	♈♈♈	5
● Montevertine '01	♈♈♈	5
● Montevertine '09	♈♈	5

Cantina Vignaioli del Morellino di Scansano

LOC. SARAGIOLO
58054 SCANSANO [GR]
TEL. 0564507288
www.cantinadelmorellino.it

CELLAR SALES
PRE-BOOKED VISITS
ANNUAL PRODUCTION 2,200,000 bottles
HECTARES UNDER VINE 450.00
VITICULTURE METHOD Certified Organic

This co-operative winery has come to be recognized as one of the leading commercial activities in the Tuscan Maremma area. It was founded in 1972 and is dedicated primarily to the production of Morellino di Scansano from grapes supplied by over 150 members. They produce two lines: the Vignaioli del Morellino di Scansano for restaurants, wine bars and wine shops; and Cantina del Morellino di Scansano for supermarkets and large retail chains. Among the countless versions of Morellino this year's best is the Riserva Roggiano 2010, with ripe fruit aromas alongside more evolved hints of leather and pipe tobacco, and a full-bodied, rounded palate with prominent but not excessive tannins and a pleasing finish. The other products are also good: we particularly liked the strikingly rounded flavour of the Capoccia 2012, from Alicante and ciliegiolo, and the Scantianum 2011 from a blend of mainly sangiovese with alicante, colorino and canaiolo and a varied array of aromas.

● Maremma Toscana Rosso Capoccia '12	▼▼	2*
● Morellino di Scansano Roggiano Ris. '10	▼▼	3
● Scantianum '12	▼▼	1*
○ Bianco di Pitigliano Sup. Rasenno '12	▼	2
● Morellino di Scansano Roggiano '12	▼	2
● Morellino di Scansano Sicomoro Ris. '09	▼	3
● Morellino di Scansano Vignabenefizio '12	▼	2
○ Viognier '12	▼	2
● Morellino di Scansano Cantina del Morellino '11	♈♈	2*
● Morellino di Scansano Roggiano '08	♈♈	2*
● Morellino di Scansano Roggiano '07	♈♈	2
● Morellino di Scansano Roggiano Ris. '08	♈♈	3
● Morellino di Scansano Vignabenefizio '06	♈♈	2*
● Morellino di Scansano Vin del Fattore '08	♈♈	2

Morisfarms

LOC. CURA NUOVA
FATTORIA POGGETTI
58024 MASSA MARITTIMA [GR]
TEL. 0566919135
www.morisfarms.it

CELLAR SALES
PRE-BOOKED VISITS
ACCOMMODATION
ANNUAL PRODUCTION 300,000 bottles
HECTARES UNDER VINE 71.00

The Moris family have been farmers for generations and two hundred years ago they decided to move from Spain to Maremma following their dream of making great wine. Some of the vineyards are located in the Morellino di Scansano zone. Here, many vines were replanted from 1995 to 2004. The quality of the wines starts with the harvest and culminates in the ageing process, the result of winemaking techniques that are respectful of the grapes. One of their best-known wines is Avvoltore, named after the Maremma word for falcon, which is often observed in flight above the area. And this is indeed the wine that reaches the finals. A blend of mainly sangiovese with cabernet sauvignon and syrah: generous on the nose with aromas ranging from vegetal hints of aromatic herbs to ripe fruit such as blackberry jam and bottled cherries. A nice entry on the well-rounded palate with well-judged tannin and an appetizing, tangy finish. The Morellino 2012 is fresh-tasting an very drinkable while the Monteregio 2010 is firm-bodied and appetizing.

● Avvoltore '10	🍷🍷 6
● Monteregio di Massa Marittima Rosso '10	🍷🍷 3
● Morellino di Scansano '12	🍷🍷 2*
● Mandriolo '12	🍷 2
○ Monteregio di Massa Marittima Bianco Santa Chiara '12	🍷 2
● Morellino di Scansano Ris. '10	🍷 4
○ Vermentino '12	🍷 2
● Avvoltore '06	🍷🍷🍷 5
● Avvoltore '04	🍷🍷🍷 5
● Avvoltore '01	🍷🍷🍷 5
● Avvoltore '00	🍷🍷🍷 5
● Avvoltore '99	🍷🍷🍷 5

La Mormoraia

LOC. SANT'ANDREA, 15
53037 SAN GIMIGNANO [SI]
TEL. 0577940096
www.mormoraia.it

CELLAR SALES
PRE-BOOKED VISITS
ACCOMMODATION
ANNUAL PRODUCTION 230,000 bottles
HECTARES UNDER VINE 40.00

La Mormoraia is owned by the Passoni family who have succeeded over the years in renovating an extremely beautiful estate, rich in potential, and transforming it into one of the most interesting wine businesses in the San Gimignano area. After the first phase which pursued top quality, the estate turned towards a style that was both increasingly original and faithful to the features of the terroir. For some time skilled vigneron Mattia Barzaghi has been part of the team, contributing his efforts to accelerating the process along with a good helping of sensitivity which is certainly useful in this fascinating journey of development. Without the Vernaccia Riserva, the Ostrea 2012 selection keeps the winery's standard flying. This is a stylish, flavoursome white with aromas opening on notes of ripe fruit with hints of Mediterranean scrubland, catmint and basil and a dry, confident, well-rounded mouth with varietal flavours, closing with fruity hints and an elegant salty sensation. The very interesting Syrah 2011 has juicy hints of yellow peaches and spice.

○ Vernaccia di S. Gimignano Ostrea '12	🍷🍷 3*
● Chianti Colli Senesi '11	🍷🍷 2*
● Syrah '11	🍷🍷 2*
○ Vernaccia di S. Gimignano '12	🍷🍷 2*
○ Vernaccia di S. Gimignano È ReZet Mattia Barzaghi '11	🍷🍷🍷 3*
● Neitea '08	🍷🍷 4
○ Ostrea Grigia '09	🍷🍷 3
● Syrah '08	🍷🍷 2*
○ Vernaccia di S. Gimignano '10	🍷🍷 2*
○ Vernaccia di S. Gimignano '09	🍷🍷 2
○ Vernaccia di S. Gimignano Ostrea Grigia '11	🍷🍷 3
○ Vernaccia di S. Gimignano Ris. '09	🍷🍷 3*
○ Vernaccia di S. Gimignano Ris. '08	🍷🍷 3

Tenuta di Morzano

FRAZ. MORZANO
VIA DI MONTELUPO 69/71
50025 MONTESPERTOLI [FI]
TEL. 0571671021
www.tenutadimorzano.it

CELLAR SALES
PRE-BOOKED VISITS
ACCOMMODATION
ANNUAL PRODUCTION 215,000 bottles
HECTARES UNDER VINE 43.00

The estate was established in 1973 by two brothers, Luciano and Nino Mignolli, who gave life to their grandfather Giovanni's dream. Giovanni was a true wine lover who longed to own his own vineyard and their first plot of around three hectares was named Podere del Nonno Nanni in his honour. Over the years, the estate grew and took on its current name when Tenuta di Morzano was acquired in 1988. They also produce extra-virgin olive oil and run a farm holiday centre. Luciano now owns the estate with his daughter Francesca, who manages it. Through to the finals for the Nicosole 2011, a blend of cabernet and merlot with sangiovese: vibrant fruity aromas of cherries and plums and spicy hints of cinnamon and liquorice with a warm, full-bodied, rounded palate and relaxed finish.

● Nicosole '11	♥♥ 4
○ Bianco di Toscana '12	♥ 1
● Chianti Sup. Emilio '11	♥ 3
● Chianti Montespertoli Ris. '10	♥♥ 3*
● Nicosole '10	♥♥ 4
● Nicosole '09	♥♥ 4
● Nicosole '08	♥♥ 4
● Nicosole '02	♥♥ 4

Tenute Niccolai - Palagetto

VIA MONTEOLIVETO, 46
53037 SAN GIMIGNANO [SI]
TEL. 0577943090
www.tenuteniccolai.it

CELLAR SALES
PRE-BOOKED VISITS
ACCOMMODATION
ANNUAL PRODUCTION 250,000 bottles
HECTARES UNDER VINE 44.00

The estate was founded by Luano Niccolai, an entrepreneur from San Gimignano who was in the caravan business but had always had a passion for agriculture, particularly in terms of wine, that was passed down by his father, a cellarman and master miller during the olive harvest. Today, the business is owned by his daughter Sabrina, who runs the business with her husband Mario. In addition to Fattoria il Palagetto, which was the first property established in San Gimignano, the company also owns the Bellarina estate in Montalcino and the Pian de Cerri vineyards in the Montecucco territory. A good performance from the Niccolò 2011, a blend of vermentino, chardonnay and sauvignon with vibrant, buttery aromas blending yellow peach and apricot fruit with floral hints. A soft, rounded entry and refreshing streak of acidity lead to a lingering finish. We liked the Vernaccia Riserva 2009 with its aromas of almonds, aromatic herbs like aniseed and ripe apples, and firm, well-organized palate with a tangy, lingering flavour.

○ l'Niccolò '12	♥♥ 3
○ Vernaccia di S. Gimignano Ris. '09	♥♥ 3
● Chianti Colli Senesi '10	♥ 2
● Chianti Colli Senesi Ris. '09	♥ 3
○ Vernaccia di S. Gimignano Il Palagetto '12	♥ 2
○ Vernaccia di S. Gimignano V. Santa Chiara '12	♥ 2
● Brunello di Montalcino La Bellarina Ris. '03	♥♥ 6
● San Gimignano Syrah Uno di Quattro '05	♥♥ 6
○ Vernaccia di S. Gimignano '11	♥♥ 2*
○ Vernaccia di S. Gimignano '10	♥♥ 2
○ Vernaccia di S. Gimignano Ris. '07	♥♥ 3
○ Vernaccia di S. Gimignano Ris. '06	♥♥ 3
○ Vernaccia di S. Gimignano Ris. '02	♥♥ 3
○ Vernaccia di S. Gimignano Ris. '01	♥♥ 3

Fattoria Nittardi

LOC. NITTARDI
53011 CASTELLINA IN CHIANTI [SI]
TEL. 0577740269
www.nittardi.com

CELLAR SALES
PRE-BOOKED VISITS
ANNUAL PRODUCTION 94,000 bottles
HECTARES UNDER VINE 29.00 + 37.00

Fattoria Nittarda, owned by the Femfert-Canali family since 1982, is situated near Castellina in Chianti and includes a 37-hectare annex in Maremma, purchased in 1999. The style of these wines is confidently modern: maturation in small casks, pursuit of the ripest possible fruit, weighty structure, full, sweet flavour. All this is presented with elegance and finesse in wines that lack neither depth nor a good dose of personality, and frequently achieve levels of absolute excellence. The Chianti Classico Casanuova di Nittardi 2011 shows a good range of aromas, alternating spicy and fruity hints and heralding a mouthfilling, vibrant palate, with slightly too much oakiness. The Nectar Dei 2010 reveals crystal clear aromas and a firm, compact flavour. The nicely sweet Chianti Classico Riserva 2010 is held back slightly by the toasty sensations from the oak maturation casks.

● Chianti Cl. Casanuova di Nittardi '11	♥♥ 4
● Chianti Cl. Ris. '10	♥♥ 6
● Nectar Dei '10	♥♥ 7
● Ad Astra '11	♥ 3
● Ad Astra '08	♥♥♥ 3
● Chianti Cl. Ris. '98	♥♥♥ 6
● Ad Astra '07	♥♥ 3
● Chianti Cl. Casanuova di Nittardi '09	♥♥ 4
● Chianti Cl. Casanuova di Nittardi '08	♥♥ 4
● Chianti Cl. Ris. '09	♥♥ 6
● Chianti Cl. Ris. '08	♥♥ 6
● Chianti Cl. Ris. '07	♥♥ 6
● Nectar Dei '09	♥♥ 7
● Nectar Dei '07	♥♥ 6

Nottola

FRAZ. GRACCIANO
VIA BIVIO DI NOTTOLA, 9A
53040 MONTEPULCIANO [SI]
TEL. 0578707060
www.cantinanottola.it

CELLAR SALES
PRE-BOOKED VISITS
ACCOMMODATION AND RESTAURANT SERVICE
ANNUAL PRODUCTION 160,000 bottles
HECTARES UNDER VINE 23.00

Nottola is a testimony to Anterivo Giomarelli's passion for country life and good wine. He acquired the property in the late 1980s, expanding and revamping it, while carefully preserving its key characteristics and respecting the surrounding environment. His objective was to make quality wine and so he uses the latest growing and winemaking techniques. His son Giuliano is personally involved in managing the estate, which also produces extra-virgin olive oil and offers farmstay accommodation. The enjoyable Nobile Riserva Il Fattore 2009 has clear cherry aromas with mature hints of tobacco, powerful structure, subtle, fine-grained tannins and tangy, lingering finish. The Rosso 2012 is surprisingly lively and flavoursome, vibrant and juicy with an excellent flavour. The well-made Anterivo 2010 is more modern in style: equal parts sangiovese and merlot, it has spicy aromas and a velvety, elegant structure.

● Nobile di Montepulciano Il Fattore Ris. '09	♥♥ 5
● Anterivo '10	♥♥ 5
● Rosso di Montepulciano '12	♥♥ 2*
● Nobile di Montepulciano '10	♥ 3
○ Vin Santo di Montepulciano '07	♥ 5
● Nobile di Montepulciano '09	♥♥ 3
● Nobile di Montepulciano '07	♥♥ 3
● Nobile di Montepulciano Il Fattore Ris. '07	♥♥ 5
● Rosso di Montepulciano '08	♥♥ 2

Cantine Olivi

LOC. LE BUCHE
VIA CASELFAVA, 25
53047 SARTEANO [SI]
TEL. 0578274066
www.lebuche.eu

CELLAR SALES
PRE-BOOKED VISITS
ACCOMMODATION AND RESTAURANT SERVICE
ANNUAL PRODUCTION 80,000 bottles
HECTARES UNDER VINE 30.00

The heart of the hills around Siena is
particularly suited to wine, as testified by
the cadastral maps showing vineyards here
since ancient times. The Olivi family
acquired their first estate in this area in
1996. With great passion they embarked
upon a new wine project to combine great
Tuscan viticulture traditions with
technological innovations in the vineyard
and the cellar, producing wines with a
distinctive personality and characteristic
flavour. Their respect for tradition is shown
in their recent acquisition of old vineyards
planted to malvasia, trebbiano and
sangiovese. The Coreno 2012, from
trebbiano and malvasia matured in
barriques, is very pleasant with fresh
vegetal and fruity aromas, sturdy, weighty
texture and a mouthwatering minerally
finish. The unusual Orhora 2012 is a blend
of verdicchio and sauvignon blanc, rare in
this area, with citrus and floral aromas and
a lovely well-coordinated palate with a
really delicious fresh sensation in the finish.

○ Coreno '12	♟♟ 3
○ Orhora '12	♟♟ 3
● Chianti Sup. '11	♟ 3
● Le Buche '09	♟ 5
○ Coreno '11	♟♟ 3
● Le Buche '07	♟♟ 5
● Memento '07	♟♟ 6
● Memento '06	♟♟ 6
● Pugnitello '07	♟♟ 5
● Tempore '08	♟♟ 6

Podere Orma

VIA BOLGHERESE
57022 CASTAGNETO CARDUCCI [LI]
TEL. 0575477857
www.tenutasetteponti.it

ANNUAL PRODUCTION 26,000 bottles
HECTARES UNDER VINE 5.50

Antonio Moretti is known for his fascinating
operations. An entrepreneur in the fashion
industry, he decided to move into the wine
world some time ago, discovering an
increasingly passion over the years. After
Sette Ponti near Arezzo and Feudo Maccari
in Sicily, he acquired a little gem that is
stealing the spotlight on the crowded
Bolgheri scene. The estate comprises a
mere five hectares of vines planted in stony
clay soil. He chose to channel his efforts into
one very satisfying, elegant wine, which has
rapidly become one of the best expressions
of the territory. It may not technically be a
Bolgheri wine, because it doesn't belong to
the DOC zone, but Orma 2010 is still a true
child of Bolgheri's terroir and style. This wine
incorporates, encapsulates and highlights
the local winemaking process: a stylish fruity
nose with flashes of ripe cherries,
blackcurrants and mulberries and a precise,
almost sculpted palate that is richly textured
but racy, shrewd and unpredictable. The
tannin in the mouthwatering, endless finish
is evident but well-controlled.

● Orma '10	♟♟♟ 7
● Orma '09	♟♟♟ 6
● Orma '08	♟♟♟ 6
● Orma '07	♟♟♟ 5
● Orma '06	♟♟♟ 6
● Orma '05	♟♟ 6

★★Tenuta dell'Ornellaia

LOC. ORNELLAIA, 191
FRAZ. BOLGHERI
57022 CASTAGNETO CARDUCCI [LI]
TEL. 056571811
www.ornellaia.it

PRE-BOOKED VISITS
ANNUAL PRODUCTION 812,000 bottles
HECTARES UNDER VINE 99.00

One of Italy's most visible companies and a star on the international wine scene, Tenuta dell'Ornellaia has done much to make the nation proud. Founded in the early 1980s, it changed hands several times and is now owned by the Frescobaldi family. This unique winery set in the spectacular Ornellaia estate also owns vines in the Bellaria area in the northern part of the designation. The wines speak the same language as many of the world's great wines. Stylistically and technically impeccable, they are imbued with the history of the company and its makers. The two leading reds from this estate and indeed the whole area are neck and neck but in our opinion the Ornellaia has the edge. So this matchless wine can celebrate its 25th anniversary in the best possible style as a benchmark for the whole Italian winemaking world. It is not just a technical champ, mind, but a giant in flavour and authenticity, developed over spicy, earthy sensations with hugely expressive fruit and a masterly palate in weight and grip.

● Bolgheri Sup. Ornellaia '10	♀♀♀	8
● Masseto '10	♀♀	8
● Bolgheri Rosso Serre Nuove '11	♀	6
● Le Volte '11	♀	3
● Bolgheri Sup. Ornellaia '07	♀♀♀	8
● Bolgheri Sup. Ornellaia '05	♀♀♀	8
● Bolgheri Sup. Ornellaia '04	♀♀♀	8
● Bolgheri Sup. Ornellaia '02	♀♀♀	8
● Bolgheri Sup. Ornellaia '01	♀♀♀	8
● Bolgheri Sup. Ornellaia '99	♀♀♀	8
● Masseto '09	♀♀♀	8
● Masseto '06	♀♀♀	8
● Masseto '04	♀♀♀	8
● Masseto '01	♀♀♀	8
● Masseto '00	♀♀♀	8
● Masseto '99	♀♀♀	8

Siro Pacenti

LOC. PELAGRILLI, 1
53024 MONTALCINO [SI]
TEL. 0577848662
www.siropacenti.it

PRE-BOOKED VISITS
ANNUAL PRODUCTION 60,000 bottles
HECTARES UNDER VINE 22.00

The more time passes, the more we see blurring of the edges of Giancarlo Pacenti the "innovator", one of the first to use small casks in Montalcino. Today his Brunellos are seen as leading contemporary classics above all, in which a dialogue continues between the almost complementary features of his sangiovese plots: Pelagrilli, to the north-east of the town, and Piancornello, a paradigm of the southern district with stony land rich in iron oxide. Small oak casks are still mainly used in the cellar but the range displays some distinctive stylistic features starting with the PS line, which includes a Riserva in the best years. A simply memorable performance from Giancarlo Pacenti. The Pelagrilli 2008 is one of the soundest and best-sustained Brunellos of the vintage, surpassed in attack and authentic flavour by the Rosso PS 2011. But the real champ is the Brunello PS Riserva 2007: a few reductive notes cannot inhibit the solid flavour progression which promises well for the future.

● Brunello di Montalcino PS Ris. '07	♀♀♀	8
● Rosso di Montalcino PS '11	♀♀	5
● Brunello di Montalcino Pelagrilli '08	♀♀	6
● Brunello di Montalcino '97	♀♀♀	7
● Brunello di Montalcino '96	♀♀♀	7
● Brunello di Montalcino '95	♀♀♀	7
● Brunello di Montalcino '88	♀♀♀	7
● Brunello di Montalcino '07	♀♀	8
● Brunello di Montalcino '06	♀♀	8
● Brunello di Montalcino '01	♀♀	7
● Brunello di Montalcino '99	♀♀	8
● Brunello di Montalcino PS '04	♀♀	8
● Brunello di Montalcino PS Ris. '06	♀♀	8
● Rosso di Montalcino '08	♀♀	5

Palazzo

LOC. PALAZZO, 144
53024 MONTALCINO [SI]
TEL. 0577849226
www.aziendapalazzo.it

CELLAR SALES
PRE-BOOKED VISITS
ANNUAL PRODUCTION 20,000 bottles
HECTARES UNDER VINE 4.00
VITICULTURE METHOD Certified Biodynamic

The Palazzo estate covers about 12
hectares in the eastern part of Montalcino,
at just over 300 metres altitude, in an area
with typically dry and stony land of Eocene
origin. Cosimo Loia and his wife Antonietta
Palazzo run the winery alongside their sons
Angelo and Elia. Their task is to carry
forward the 30-year tradition, focusing
confidently on an eclectic and vigorous
style for their Sangiovese, with the two
Brunellos aged in barriques and large
casks and a Rosso matured exclusively in
Slavonian oak. Tenuta Palazzo's
Sangioveses never miss a beat as
demonstrated to great effect by the sweetly
fruity Brunello Riserva 2007, livened up by
hints of Mediterranean scrubland and
shrubs faithfully mirrored in the
flavoursome palate, slightly held back by
tannin. The delicious Rosso 2011 is very
drinkable and full of energy while the
Brunello 2008 is less engaging but
well-supported.

● Brunello di Montalcino '08	♛♛ 6
● Brunello di Montalcino Ris. '07	♛♛ 7
● Rosso di Montalcino '11	♛♛ 3
● Brunello di Montalcino '07	♛♛ 6
● Brunello di Montalcino '06	♛♛ 5
● Brunello di Montalcino Ris. '06	♛♛ 7
● Rosso di Montalcino '10	♛♛ 3
● Rosso di Montalcino '06	♛♛ 3

Panizzi

LOC. SANTA MARGHERITA, 34
53037 SAN GIMIGNANO [SI]
TEL. 0577941576
www.panizzi.it

CELLAR SALES
PRE-BOOKED VISITS
ACCOMMODATION
ANNUAL PRODUCTION 185,000 bottles
HECTARES UNDER VINE 60.00

Panizzi is one of the benchmark names for
San Gimignano wine but also for the area's
history. The name recalls the
accomplishments of a visionary and pioneer
who innovated, and to some extent
revolutionized, the growth of Vernaccia by
exploring unimaginable directions and
potential. Today this prestigious estate is in
the hands of Simone Niccolai and his
helpers who have the task and honour of
carrying on the business. The vineyards are
scattered over various subzones in the area.
The wines are stylistically flawless, skilfully
combining modern features and meticulous
handling with a personal and authentic feel.
The Vernaccia Riserva 2010 is a really
beautifully crafted wine. Extremely subtle
wood grain and toasty sensations hint at
vanilla and country-style butter crisscrossed
with delicious ripe fruit aromas. These are
clearly mirrored on the palate, which only
lacks a little freshness and responsiveness.
Qualities which are to be found in the
Vernaccia 2012, with floral aromas and
citrus hints on the palate.

○ Vernaccia di S. Gimignano Ris. '10	♛♛ 5
○ Vernaccia di S. Gimignano '12	♛♛ 2*
⊙ Ceraso Rosa '12	♛ 2
● Chianti Colli Senesi Vertunno Ris. '10	♛ 2
○ Vernaccia di S. Gimignano Ris. '07	♛♛♛ 5
○ Vernaccia di S. Gimignano Ris. '05	♛♛♛ 5
○ Vernaccia di S. Gimignano Ris. '98	♛♛♛ 4*
○ Vernaccia di S. Gimignano '11	♛♛ 2*
○ Vernaccia di S. Gimignano '10	♛♛ 2*
○ Vernaccia di S. Gimignano Ris. '09	♛♛ 5
○ Vernaccia di San Gimignano V. Santa Margherita '11	♛♛ 3*
○ Vernaccia di San Gimignano V. Santa Margherita '10	♛♛ 3

Pasolini dall'Onda Borghese

P.ZZA MAZZINI, 10
50021 BARBERINO VAL D'ELSA [FI]
TEL. 0558075019
www.pasolinidallonda.com

CELLAR SALES
PRE-BOOKED VISITS
ANNUAL PRODUCTION 90,000 bottles
HECTARES UNDER VINE 17.00

The Pasolini dall'Onda family has been established in Bologna from the 13th century. Wine is produced on the estate in Montericco, near Imola, where sangiovese vines were already grown back in the 1700s, and in the farm in Barberino Val d'Elsa, which has a long tradition of quality wines, with documents proving wine production since 1573. All the processes to craft the Chianti and Vin Santo, from vinification to ageing and bottling, take place in the cellars under the medieval city. There is also guest accommodation and an olive mill, which produces extra-virgin olive oil. A good performance from Montepetri 2011, chardonnay and pinot grigio, with lemon and peach hints alongside various floral aromas. The palate is lively, fresh, tangy and flavoursome with a lipsmacking, lingering finish. Two good versions of Chianti Classico Sicelle: the 2011 is fruitier, supple and delicious while the Riserva 2010 is more austere with well-balanced hints of tobacco and leather.

● Chianti Cl. Sicelle '11	▼▼ 3
● Chianti Cl. Sicelle Ris. '10	▼▼ 4
○ Montepetri Bianco '11	▼▼ 2*
● Chianti Drove '10	▼ 2
● Chianti Cl. Sicelle '05	▽▼ 3*
● Chianti Cl. Sicelle '03	▽▼ 3
○ Montepetri Bianco '10	▽▼ 2*
○ Montepetri Bianco '09	▽▼ 2

Petra

LOC. SAN LORENZO ALTO, 131
57028 SUVERETO [LI]
TEL. 0565845308
www.petrawine.it

CELLAR SALES
PRE-BOOKED VISITS
ANNUAL PRODUCTION 350,000 bottles
HECTARES UNDER VINE 94.00

The estate is part of the diverse stable of Vittorio Moretti, who has invested in red Tuscan wines, specifically in Val di Cornia, south of Bolgheri, on the variegated hillside slopes with rich mineral soil and a microclimate suitable for native varieties, such as sangiovese, and international varieties like merlot and cabernet. The cellar designed by Mario Botta is probably one of the most interesting in the world. Also in Tuscany, in Castiglione della Pescaia, is the other estate, La Badiola, which makes mainly whites. Through to the finals for the Cabernet Potenti 2010: a minty nose with mature hints of plums and spice, generous texture with firm but streamlined tannins and a lingering finish. The enjoyable Ebo 2010 shows a classic nose with cherry aromas and a succulent, fresh-tasting palate. The mouthfilling Quercegobbe 2010 is a velvety, flavoursome Merlot; the Alto 2009, from sangiovese only, has a clean, well-defined nose and a simple, light structure.

● Potenti '10	▼▼ 6
● Alto '09	▼▼ 6
● Quercegobbe '10	▼▼ 6
● Val di Cornia Ebo '10	▼▼ 3
○ Acquadoro Tenuta La Badiola '12	▼ 2
⊙ Acquagiusta Rosato Tenuta La Badiola '12	▼ 2
● Acquagiusta Rosso Tenuta La Badiola '10	▼ 2
○ Acquagiusta Vermentino Tenuta La Badiola '12	▼ 2
● Petra Rosso '04	▽▽▼ 7
● Petra Rosso '09	▽▼ 8
● Potenti '09	▽▼ 6
● Quercegobbe '08	▽▼ 6

Fattoria di Petroio

LOC. QUERCEGROSSA
VIA DI MOCENNI, 7
53019 CASTELNUOVO BERARDENGA [SI]
TEL. 0577328045
www.fattoriapetroio.it

CELLAR SALES
PRE-BOOKED VISITS
ANNUAL PRODUCTION 40,000 bottles
HECTARES UNDER VINE 15.00

The small Fattoria di Petroio estate in Castelnuovo Berardenga has been owned by the Lenzi family since 1961, when Gian Luigi, the current owner, inherited it from his grandfather, Luigi Pallini. It was a time of change and thanks to his great passion, mainly for grapes and vineyard aspects, the standard of the wines started to improve significantly. Today, his daughter Diana runs the business with a focus on quality. The wines have a certain elegance in a style that, while modern, is not over-done, and they are aged in a masterful mix of large and small oak. Just two wines were presented this year, both Chianti Classicos. Very subtle aromas in the 2010 highlight the fruity, earthy sensations with a few smoky hints. Good texture and linear progression on the palate, with some not unpleasant hardness, create a more incisive mouthfeel. At the tastings, the Riserva 2008 seemed less defined, slightly tangy on the nose and lacking vigour on the palate.

● Chianti Cl. '10	♙♙ 2*
● Chianti Cl. Ris. '08	♙ 4
● Chianti Cl. '08	♛♛ 2
● Chianti Cl. '01	♛♛ 3*
● Chianti Cl. Ris. '07	♛♛ 4
● Chianti Cl. Ris. '05	♛♛ 4
● Chianti Cl. Ris. '04	♛♛ 4
● Chianti Cl. Ris. '03	♛♛ 4
● Chianti Cl. Ris. '01	♛♛ 4

★Fattoria Petrolo

LOC. GALATRONA
FRAZ. MERCATALE VALDARNO
VIA PETROLO, 30
52021 BUCINE [AR]
TEL. 0559911322
www.petrolo.it

ACCOMMODATION
ANNUAL PRODUCTION 70,000 bottles
HECTARES UNDER VINE 31.00

Petrolo produces quality wines and extra-virgin olive oil in a beautiful, historic location in the Colli Aretini hills, a zone already basking in the reputation of the quality of its grapes at the time of the edict of Grand Duke Leopold in 1716. The Bazzochi family bought the estate in the 1940s and in the 1980s Lucia Bazzochi Sanjust initiated a series of changes intended to maximize quality. The peculiarities of the soils, combined with careful and selective soil management, organic farming practices and skilled winemakers, have resulted in wines that are both local in character and modern. The estate is currently run by Lucia's son Luca Sanjust. In the absence of Galatrona, the most famous wine, the monovarietal Sangiovese Torrione 2011 wins a Tre Bicchieri. Fruity aromas of cherries and plums, light hints of spice and a pleasant entry on the broad, but not excessive, palate, and fresh acidity in the flavoursome finish. The version of Boggina 2011 marketed in amphora-shaped bottles is interesting and lively.

● Torrione '11	♛♛♛ 5
● Boggina '11	♙♙ 8
● Bogginafora '11	♙♙ 8
● Galatrona '10	♛♛♛ 8
● Galatrona '09	♛♛♛ 8
● Galatrona '08	♛♛♛ 8
● Galatrona '07	♛♛♛ 8
● Galatrona '06	♛♛♛ 8
● Galatrona '05	♛♛♛ 8
● Galatrona '04	♛♛♛ 7
● Galatrona '01	♛♛♛ 8
● Galatrona '00	♛♛♛ 7
● Galatrona '99	♛♛♛ 7
● Galatrona '98	♛♛♛ 7
● Galatrona '97	♛♛♛

Piaggia

LOC. POGGETTO
VIA CEGOLI, 47
59016 POGGIO A CAIANO [PO]
TEL. 0558705401
www.piaggia.com

CELLAR SALES
PRE-BOOKED VISITS
ANNUAL PRODUCTION 75,000 bottles
HECTARES UNDER VINE 15.00

This estate was established in the 1970s by Mauro Vannucci, who was won over by the favourable aspect and the clayey, dry features of the soil. Today Piaggia is the result of teamwork by Mauro and his daughter Silvia, now the owner. Situated about 14 kilometres from Florence, the estate's vineyards are in the Carmignano DOC zone. Since the first Piaggia Carmignano Riserva of 1991, the increasing passion and commitment poured into these wines have demonstrated a high standard of quality. Over time the estate's hectares have increased making it possible to create new wines, thanks to the experience developed in this area, and to produce an excellent extra-virgin olive oil. Two wines through to the finals. Poggio de' Colli 2011, a monovarietal Cabernet Franc, has fresh, alluring vegetal aromas alongside green peppers and wild berries. A pleasing entry on the supple and deliciously fresh palate leads to a crescendo finish. Also excellent, the Riserva 2010 has spicy aromas and a generous, enjoyable body.

● Poggio de' Colli '11	♟♟♟ 7
● Carmignano Ris. '10	♟♟ 6
● Carmignano Il Sasso '11	♟♟ 5
⊙ Vin Ruspo di Carmignano '12	♟ 2
● Carmignano Ris. '08	♟♟♟ 5
● Carmignano Ris. '07	♟♟♟ 5
● Carmignano Ris. '99	♟♟♟ 5
● Carmignano Ris. '98	♟♟♟ 5
● Carmignano Ris. '97	♟♟♟ 5
● Carmignano Sasso '07	♟♟♟ 4
● Il Sasso '01	♟♟♟ 4
● Poggio de' Colli '10	♟♟♟ 6
● Carmignano Sasso '09	♟♟ 4
● Poggio de' Colli '09	♟♟ 6

Piancornello

LOC. PIANCORNELLO
53024 MONTALCINO [SI]
TEL. 0577844105
piancorello@libero.it

CELLAR SALES
PRE-BOOKED VISITS
ANNUAL PRODUCTION 50,000 bottles
HECTARES UNDER VINE 10.00

Piancornello is situated practically opposite Monte Amiata, a short distance from the Asso river at about 250 metres. It was established in 1991 and is well known to enthusiasts as one of the best defined exponents of the southern slope of Montalcino. In this warm area the sangiovese grapes are among the first to ripen, also due to the steep, well-drained land rich in stones and rocks. These conditions pay off in the cellar through careful maceration and extraction procedures, followed by maturation in small oak casks, both barriques and tonneaux. Once again admirers of Piancornello wines will not be disappointed: we found the usual generous, ripe fruit in the Brunello 2008 alongside a very expansive structure. We were even more impressed by the Rosso 2011, a successful blend of weighty texture and verve in a modern style free from over-abundance.

● Brunello di Montalcino '08	♟♟ 6
● Rosso di Montalcino '11	♟♟ 3
● Brunello di Montalcino '06	♟♟♟ 6
● Brunello di Montalcino '99	♟♟♟ 6
● Brunello di Montalcino '07	♟♟ 6
● Brunello di Montalcino Ris. '06	♟♟ 6
● Brunello di Montalcino Ris. '04	♟♟ 6
● Rosso di Montalcino '08	♟♟ 3*

Pianirossi

LOC. PORRONA
POD. SANTA GENOVEFFA, 1
58044 CINIGIANO [GR]
TEL. 0564990573
www.pianirossi.com

CELLAR SALES
PRE-BOOKED VISITS
ACCOMMODATION AND RESTAURANT SERVICE
ANNUAL PRODUCTION 55,000 bottles
HECTARES UNDER VINE 14.00

Located in the part of the province of
Grosseto that faces Montalcino,
Montecucco is considered an emerging
zone where the sangiovese grape can
express itself fully and uniquely. Stefano
Sincini, who owns the Pianerossi winery,
had a vision of the perfect place and, with
perseverance, brought it to fruition,
realizing his dream of creating his own
label to reflect his idea of wine. The
structure is eco-friendly, the vines are
grown using low environmental impact
methods and there is a strong desire to
integrate with nature. This is also reflected
in their visitor facilities. We liked the
Montecucco Sidus 2011: hints of
pencil lead, leather and plum jam on the
nose and a lively, full-bodied, pleasingly
powerful mouth with a flavoursome finish.
The Solus 2010 is also good: sangiovese,
montepulciano and alicante grapes with
spicy aromas, a rounded and well-balanced
palate and long, lingering finish with an
excellent aftertaste.

● Montecucco Sidus '11	♇♇	4
● Solus '10	♇♇	4
● Pianirossi '10	♇	6
● Pianirossi '09	♇♇	6
● Pianirossi '08	♇♇	6
● Pianirossi '07	♇♇	6
● Pianirossi '06	♇♇	6
● Solus '08	♇♇	4

Enrico Pierazzuoli

VIA VALICARDA, 35
50056 CAPRAIA E LIMITE [FI]
TEL. 0571910078
www.enricopierazzuoli.com

CELLAR SALES
PRE-BOOKED VISITS
ACCOMMODATION
ANNUAL PRODUCTION 156,000 bottles
HECTARES UNDER VINE 32.00

Two family-run wineries fall under the
supervision of Enrico Pierazzuoli, vigneron
and chairman of the Carmignano DOC
producers' consortium, and both are
located in areas with historical links to
wine-growing. Tenuta Cantagallo, in the
Chianti Montalbano area, was purchased in
1970 and later joined by Tenuta Farnete.
The estates both make olive oil, honey and
other food products as well as wine, and
offer holiday accommodation too. In order
to guarantee a steady increase in quality,
vineyards were purchased in different areas
or newly planted with clones selected from
native grape varieties that adapt well to the
growing zone's microclimates. An excellent
performance from the Vin Santo 2007 with
a complex nose ranging from dried apricots
and figs to hazelnuts and buttery hints. The
palate is opulent, mouthfilling and buttery
with a lingering flavour. Also excellent, the
two versions of Carmignano, 2011 and
Riserva 2010 and the beautifully drinkable
Barco Reale 2012.

● Carmignano Le Farnete '11	♇♇	3
○ Vin Santo del Chianti Montalbano		
Millarium Ris. '07	♇♇	5
● Barco Reale Le Farnete '12	♇♇	2*
● Carmignano Le Farnete Ris. '10	♇♇	4
● Chianti Montalbano Cantagallo '12	♇	2
● Gioveto Tenuta Cantagallo '10	♇	4
● Carmignano Le Farnete Ris. '97	♇♇♇	6
● Carmignano Le Farnete '10	♇♇	3
● Carmignano Le Farnete Ris. '05	♇♇	5
● Gioveto Tenuta Cantagallo '09	♇♇	4
● Ljatico Le Farnete '11	♇♇	5

Pieve Santo Stefano

LOC. SARDINI
55100 LUCCA
TEL. 0585857996
www.pievedisantostefano.com

CELLAR SALES
PRE-BOOKED VISITS
HECTARES UNDER VINE 10.00

The estate is named after the parish church a few steps away and even the Romans favoured the site for its ideal aspect and soil composition. Among the various owners, the Sardini had the greatest impact on the estate, and indeed the last descendent obtained the noble title of Marchese for the family. Over the years, the various owners continued viticultural work but it was the current owners who introduced specialized cultivation of the vineyards, nurturing them with passion and care. First-time finalist, monovarietal sangiovese, Ludovico Sardini 2011 has a variety of complex and intriguing aromas including vegetal hints and wild berries. The palate is dynamic, full-bodied yet fresh, with a beautifully developing finish. The Villa Sardini 2012 is delicious with uncomplicated fruity aromas and a relaxed flavour. The seductive Lippo 2011, from merlot and cabernet franc, has hints of green peppers on the nose and a complex but well-balanced structure with a tangy, lingering finish.

● Colline Lucchesi Ludovico Sardini '11	♟♟	2*
● Colline Lucchesi Villa Sardini '12	♟♟	2*
● Lippo '11	♟♟	3
● Colline Lucchesi Ludovico '08	♟♟	2
● Lippo '10	♟♟	3

Poggerino

LOC. POGGERINO, 6
53017 RADDA IN CHIANTI [SI]
TEL. 0577738958
www.poggerino.com

CELLAR SALES
PRE-BOOKED VISITS
ACCOMMODATION
ANNUAL PRODUCTION 60,000 bottles
HECTARES UNDER VINE 10.50
VITICULTURE METHOD Certified Organic

Il Poggerino is part of a close-knit group of wine artisans populating the Chianti Classic DOC zone and who often produce very interesting wines. The estate began bottling in the early Eighties and things have changed very little stylistically since then. The Radda in Chianti estate's wines are interpreted in a very personal and sometimes almost surprising style, considering the subzone's microclimate, which highlights the ripeness of the fruit and the pursuit of extreme extract, while never wavering from the royal road of finesse and elegance. The wines are aged both in barriques and in tonneaux. A Tre Bicchieri for the Chianti Classico Bugialla Riserva 2009: intriguing aromas alternating dried flowers, leaves and damp earth while the palate shows nicely contrasting acidity and sweetness and a very long finish. The Chianti Classico 2010 and the Primamateria 2009, from sangiovese and merlot, are both uncomplicated.

● Chianti Cl. Bugialla Ris. '09	♟♟♟	5
● Chianti Cl. '10	♟	3
● Primamateria '09	♟	5
● Chianti Cl. Bugialla Ris. '08	♟♟♟	5
● Chianti Cl. Ris. '90	♟♟♟	4*
● Primamateria '01	♟♟♟	5
● Chianti Cl. '08	♟♟	3
● Chianti Cl. '06	♟♟	3*
● Chianti Cl. '04	♟♟	3
● Chianti Cl. '01	♟♟	3
● Chianti Cl. Bugialla Ris. '04	♟♟	5
● Chianti Cl. Bugialla Ris. '99	♟♟	4
● Primamateria '07	♟♟	5
● Primamateria '06	♟♟	5
● Primamateria '00	♟♟	5
● Primamateria '99	♟♟	5

Poggio ai Lupi

FRAZ. GIUNCARICO
LOC. BARTOLINA
58023 GAVORRANO [GR]
TEL. 056688082
www.poggioailupi.it

CELLAR SALES
ANNUAL PRODUCTION 28,000 bottles
HECTARES UNDER VINE 21.00

The estate is owned by brothers Matteo
and Marco Galtarossa, who carried out a
series of in-depth studies to determine
where to plant the vines when they first
took over the property, which means they
have only planted a section of the land to
vine. Their aim was to produce wines with a
strong local character using new
technologies, starting with a vine density
uncommon in the zone. The resulting wines
are modern in style, produced outside the
designation standard, with a sound respect
for their origins. The very pleasant
Chardonnay Dune Mosse 2011 has citrus
fruit, hints of peaches and aromatic herbs
on the nose with a supple, flavoursome
palate, lively acidity and a lovely clean
finish. We also liked the Monteregio 2011
with spicier aromas on the nose, hints of
leather and ripe fruit. A lovely impact on the
mouthfilling palate with perceptible
close-knit tannins and a refreshing streak
in the fairly flavoursome finish.

○ Chardonnay Dune Mosse '11	♟♟ 4
● Monteregio di Massa Marittima '11	♟♟ 2*
○ Vermentino '12	♟ 2
● Alicante '05	♟♟ 4
○ Chardonnay Dune Mosse '10	♟♟ 4
○ Chardonnay Dune Mosse '09	♟♟ 4
● Syrah '04	♟♟ 2*
● Syrah Luna Matta '09	♟♟ 3

Poggio al Tesoro

LOC. FELCIAINO
VIA BOLGHERESE, 189B
57022 BOLGHERI [LI]
TEL. 0565773051
www.poggioaltesoro.it

CELLAR SALES
PRE-BOOKED VISITS
ANNUAL PRODUCTION 263,000 bottles
HECTARES UNDER VINE 60.00

The operation is the fruit of a partnership
between the Veneto Allegrini family and the
Italo-American importer, Leonardo Lo
Cascio, and has properties in several
zones within the Bolgheri area. This means
that the soils are varied, fluidly going from
red clay rich in pebbles to heavy or even
very sandy soils. Again this year, the wines
were well made and finely tuned, with a
clearly defined style. They are still young,
of course, but promise to age well in the
bottle. In our view the best wine is the
Bolgheri Superiore Sondraia 2010, which
we have raised above the others thanks to
its ability to express the vintage year
without pointless forcing. This is a subtle
wine with light hints of pink grapefruit and
lovely grassy sensations on the nose and a
confident acidic thrust on the palate: a
gamble, especially for possible bottle
ageing. We also liked the Dedicato a
Walter 2010, scattered with darker, more
highly-charged grassy notes.

● Bolgheri Sup. Sondraia '10	♟♟♟ 5
● Dedicato a Walter '10	♟♟ 7
⊙ Bolgheri Rosato Cassiopea '12	♟ 2
○ Bolgheri Vermentino Solosole '12	♟ 3
● Dedicato a Walter '09	♟♟♟ 7
● Bolgheri Sondraia '09	♟♟ 5
● Bolgheri Sondraia '08	♟♟ 5
● Bolgheri Sondraia '07	♟♟ 5
● Bolgheri Sondraia '06	♟♟ 5
○ Bolgheri Vermentino Solosole '11	♟♟ 3
● Dedicato a Walter '08	♟♟ 7
● Dedicato a Walter '07	♟♟ 5
● Dedicato a Walter '06	♟♟ 5
● Mediterra '10	♟♟ 3
● Mediterra '09	♟♟ 3
● Mediterra '08	♟♟ 3

Poggio Antico

LOC. POGGIO ANTICO
53024 MONTALCINO [SI]
TEL. 0577848044
www.poggioantico.com

CELLAR SALES
PRE-BOOKED VISITS
RESTAURANT SERVICE
ANNUAL PRODUCTION 120,000 bottles
HECTARES UNDER VINE 32.00

Only those lucky enough to have tasted the Poggio Antico Brunellos of the Seventies and Eighties can understand why many enthusiasts talk of them with such profound emotion. Things are no different today, because Paola Godler and Alberto Montefiori have a clear idea of that stylistic inspiration and, above all, of the distinctive expressive quality of their vineyards, situated in the southern district of a high and airy growing zone. This is an ideal area for lush, racy Sangioveses, protected from exaggerated extraction and aged in 37 and 55-hectolitre oak casks (for the current vintage and Riservas) and in tonneaux (the Altero selection). A brilliant pair of wines in the finals lead the usual lovely range from Poccio Antico. The Brunello Altero 2008 displays oaky sensations compensated by a beautifully balanced flavour and mature tannins. The Riserva 2007 is more cropped but shows good potential for development: it is more glycerine than usual and could be more expansive but the earthy, smoky sensations are very charming.

● Brunello di Montalcino Altero '08	♥♥ 8
● Brunello di Montalcino Ris. '07	♥♥ 7
● Madre '10	♥♥ 4
● Brunello di Montalcino '08	♥ 7
● Lemartine '11	♥ 4
● Rosso di Montalcino '11	♥ 5
● Brunello di Montalcino '05	♥♥♥ 7
● Brunello di Montalcino Altero '07	♥♥♥ 8
● Brunello di Montalcino Altero '06	♥♥♥ 8
● Brunello di Montalcino Altero '04	♥♥♥ 8
● Brunello di Montalcino Altero '99	♥♥♥ 8
● Brunello di Montalcino Ris. '01	♥♥♥ 7
● Brunello di Montalcino Altero '05	♥♥ 8
● Brunello di Montalcino Altero '03	♥♥ 8
● Brunello di Montalcino Altero '01	♥♥ 6

Poggio Argentiera

LOC. ALBERESE
S.DA BANDITELLA, 2
58010 GROSSETO
TEL. 0564405099
www.poggioargentiera.com

CELLAR SALES
PRE-BOOKED VISITS
ANNUAL PRODUCTION 210,000 bottles
HECTARES UNDER VINE 40.00
VITICULTURE METHOD Certified Organic

Gianpaolo Paglia is an agronomist from the Maremma area who loves his homeland. He started producing Morellino di Scansano in an artisan manner in a small vineyard and later perfected his production with new vineyards. Respect for the vine and minimum intervention have resulted in a perfect balance between the vines and their environment. In accordance with organic regulations, technological intervention is also kept to a minimum in the cellar and the wines are aged in medium-large barrels rather than barriques. Two wines through to the final. Morellino Capatosta 2011 displays a remarkable, generous, varied nose with hints of forest floor, bilberries, blackberries and fresh cherries and a full-bodied mouth, with perceptible well-judged tannin and a tangy, harmonious finish. The Morellino Bellamarsilia 2012 has aromatic herbs, spice and lively plum fruit on the nose and a delicious, forthright palate with a tangy, lingering finish.

● Morellino di Scansano Bellamarsilia '12	♥♥ 2*
● Morellino di Scansano Capatosta '11	♥♥ 5
○ Guazza '12	♥ 2
● Maremmante '12	♥ 2
● Finisterre '07	♥♥♥ 6
● Morellino di Scansano Capatosta '00	♥♥♥ 5*
○ Fonte_40 '10	♥♥ 3
● Maremmante '09	♥♥ 2
● Morellino di Scansano Bellamarsilia '11	♥♥ 2*
● Morellino di Scansano Capatosta '10	♥♥ 5
● Morellino di Scansano Capatosta '08	♥♥ 5
● Morellino di Scansano Capatosta '07	♥♥ 5
● Morellino di Scansano Capatosta '06	♥♥ 5
● Morellino di Scansano Capatosta '05	♥♥ 5
● Morellino di Scansano Capatosta '04	♥♥ 5

Poggio Bonelli

VIA DELL'ARBIA, 2
53019 CASTELNUOVO BERARDENGA [SI]
TEL. 057756661
www.poggiobonelli.it

CELLAR SALES
PRE-BOOKED VISITS
ACCOMMODATION AND RESTAURANT SERVICE
ANNUAL PRODUCTION 124,000 bottles
HECTARES UNDER VINE 83.00

The estate is part of MPS Tenimenti, owned by Gruppo Montepaschi di Siena, which also has another wine-growing estate, Villa Chigi Saracini. The Sienese company took over full management in 2000 from the Landucci and Croci families although Poggio Bonelli has existed as an estate since the Fifties. The vineyards are situated near Castelnuovo Berardenga, in an area where wines are endowed with particular fullness and strength. The winery expresses these features in a faithful and balanced style despite the considerable use of oak, mainly small casks. The Poggiassai 2010, a blend of sangiovese and cabernet sauvignon, displays ripe, sweet red berry fruit and spicy aromas with a rounded, progressive flavour. All about appeal, the Chianti Villa Chigi Saracini 2012 has lovely aromas and a crisp, succulent mouth. The Chianti Classico Riserva 2009 has some oaky sensations that need to settle, while the Chianti Classico 2011 is delicious despite some stiffness.

● Poggiassai '10	♟♟♟ 6
● Chianti Villa Chigi Saracini '12	♟♟ 3
● Chianti Cl. '11	♟ 5
● Chianti Cl. Ris. '09	♟ 6
● Poggiassai '08	♟♟♟ 5
● Poggiassai '07	♟♟♟ 5
● Poggiassai '06	♟♟♟ 5
● Chianti Cl. '10	♟♟ 3
● Chianti Cl. Poggio Bonelli '09	♟♟ 3
● Chianti Cl. Ris. '07	♟♟ 5
● Chianti Cl. Ris. '06	♟♟ 5
● Chianti Cl. Ris. '05	♟♟ 5
● Poggiassai '05	♟♟ 5
● Tramonto d'Oca '04	♟♟ 5
○ Vin Santo del Chianti Cl. Occhio di Pernice '06	♟♟ 8

Poggio Capponi

LOC. SAN DONATO A LIVIZZANO
VIA MONTELUPO, 184
50025 MONTESPERTOLI [FI]
TEL. 0571671914
www.poggiocapponi.it

CELLAR SALES
PRE-BOOKED VISITS
ACCOMMODATION
ANNUAL PRODUCTION 210,000 bottles
HECTARES UNDER VINE 33.00

The farm was built at the end of the 15th century and the historic cellars, which followed a century later, can still be visited today. The estate passed from the hands of the Capponi family to the Rousseau Colzis. Wine took over as the primary product in 1935 and in recent years has taken an interesting leap in quality. They also produce extra-virgin olive oil and run an agriturismo. A good performance from the Tinorso 2010, a blend of merlot and syrah, with clean, well-defined and nicely crafted aromas including spicy hints of cinnamon. The palate delicious palate is light, not too rounded, with a lingering flavoursome finish. The two Chiantis are also both good: the Petriccio 2010 offers pencil lead and leather with hints of plum jam and a broad, firm flavour, while the Chianti 2012 is fresh and lively on the nose with a balanced, relaxed palate.

● Chianti '12	♟♟ 3
● Chianti Montespertoli Petriccio '10	♟♟ 4
● Tinorso '10	♟♟ 5
○ Bianco di Binto '12	♟ 2
● Chianti Poggio Capponi '07	♟♟ 2*
● Tinorso '08	♟♟ 4
● Tinorso '06	♟♟ 4
● Tinorso '05	♟♟ 4

Poggio di Sotto

FRAZ. CASTELNUOVO DELL'ABATE
LOC. POGGIO DI SOTTO
53024 MONTALCINO [SI]
TEL. 0577835502
www.poggiodisotto.com

CELLAR SALES
PRE-BOOKED VISITS
ACCOMMODATION
ANNUAL PRODUCTION 35,000 bottles
HECTARES UNDER VINE 10.00
VITICULTURE METHOD Certified Organic

In many ways this is a transient phase, as we can tell, in the "new life" of Poggio di Sotto. This small Castelnuovo dell'Abate estate was established by Piero Palmucci in the late Eighties and had a profound effect on production in Montalcino before being purchased by the Tipa family in 2011. The family had already notched up some significant achievements in Tuscany with the Grattamacco and Colle Massari estates. They immediately made it clear that they intended to continue in the same style and kept on most of the staff, but we will still have to wait a few months to taste the first vintages from the new management structure. Meanwhile the latest releases fully fit in the expressive groove we expect from Poggio di Sotto. We felt rather lukewarm about the Brunello 2008, which is too unassuming and acidulous but the Riserva 2007 is a pedigree Sangiovese with unmistakeable salty and yeasty sensations flavouring the cheery, lush fruit.

● Brunello di Montalcino Ris. '07	♀♀♀	8
● Brunello di Montalcino '08	♀♀	8
○ Rosso di Montalcino '10	♀♀♀	7
● Brunello di Montalcino '07	♀♀♀	8
● Brunello di Montalcino '04	♀♀♀	8
● Brunello di Montalcino '99	♀♀♀	8
● Brunello di Montalcino Ris. '99	♀♀♀	8
● Brunello di Montalcino Ris. '95	♀♀♀	8
○ Rosso di Montalcino '07	♀♀♀	6
● Brunello di Montalcino '06	♀♀	8
● Brunello di Montalcino '03	♀♀	8
● Brunello di Montalcino '01	♀♀	8
● Brunello di Montalcino Ris. '06	♀♀	8
● Brunello di Montalcino Ris. '04	♀♀	8

Poggio Rubino

LOC. LA SORGENTE, 62
S.DA PROVINCIALE CASTIGLION DEL BOSCO
53024 MONTALCINO [SI]
TEL. 05771698133
www.poggiorubino.it

CELLAR SALES
PRE-BOOKED VISITS
ACCOMMODATION AND RESTAURANT SERVICE
ANNUAL PRODUCTION 32,000 bottles
HECTARES UNDER VINE 6.50

Poggio Rubino, situated on the central western slope of Montalcino at about 470 metres, is a small estate with seven hectares of vineyards run by Edward Corsi and Alessandra Marzocchi. The vineyards, mainly planted with sangiovese, are scattered over various areas in the DOC zone and farmed using biosustainable methods. This winegrowing approach is supported by traditional cellar choices, such as lengthy maceration and ageing in 25 and 30-hectolitre oak casks. The result is a pair of Brunellos in a classic but by no means nostalgic style: these wines are rich in texture and close-knit tannins, and they are worth the wait: we recommend patience. Poggio Rubino's Brunellos reveal a distinct and characteristic common thread. Dried herbs, lavender, thyme: aromas and texture are quickly revealed on the nose of an all-too subtle 2008. Almost mirror-image impressions in the Riserva 2007 which is more rounded and salty but also more mature and evolved.

● Brunello di Montalcino '08	♀♀	6
● Brunello di Montalcino Ris. '07	♀♀	7
● Brunello di Montalcino '07	♀♀	6
● Brunello di Montalcino '06	♀♀	6
● Brunello di Montalcino Ris. '06	♀♀	6

Poggio Trevvalle

LOC. ARCILLE
POD. 348
58042 CAMPAGNATICO [GR]
TEL. 0564998142
www.poggiotrevvalle.it

CELLAR SALES
PRE-BOOKED VISITS
ANNUAL PRODUCTION 65,000 bottles
HECTARES UNDER VINE 13.00
VITICULTURE METHOD Certified Organic

Brothers Umberto and Bernardo Valle purchased the estate in late 1998 with the aim of producing wines with strong local character using organic methods. They initially focused on growing and started planting the vines in 2000, an approach that helped them to adapt comfortably and produced good results from early on. In the cellar, the grapes are vinified following a natural philosophy, without the use of cultured yeasts. Through to the finals for the Morellino Passera 2012, with fresh minty sensations alongside wild berries, hints of cloves and aromatic herbs. The palate opens appetizingly, becoming nicely broad: generous, delicious, moreish with a lively, intriguing finish. We also enjoyed the Morellino 2011 with more run-of-the-mill aromas of recognizable cherries and plums and a firm, well-balanced palate with a crescendo finish.

● Morellino di Scansano Passera '12	♥♥ 2*
● Morellino di Scansano '11	♥♥ 2*
● Montecucco Rosso '10	♥ 3
● Rafele '09	♥ 2
● Morellino di Scansano Fròndina '04	♀♀ 2
● Morellino di Scansano Larcille '03	♀♀ 4
● Morellino di Scansano Larcille '00	♀♀ 3
● Rafele '08	♀♀ 2

Tenuta Il Poggione

FRAZ. SANT'ANGELO IN COLLE
LOC. MONTEANO
53024 MONTALCINO [SI]
TEL. 0577844029
www.tenutailpoggione.it

CELLAR SALES
PRE-BOOKED VISITS
ACCOMMODATION
ANNUAL PRODUCTION 500,000 bottles
HECTARES UNDER VINE 125.00

Not many Montalcino estates can boast over 100 hectares of vineyards but Il Poggione is one of them. Situated in the southernmost strip of the DOC zone, at Sant'Angelo in Colle, the estate has belonged to the Franceschi family since the 19 th century and is managed today by Fabrizio Bindocci. At centre stage in a varied and heterogeneous range is of course Sangiovese, produced with traditional vinification techniques, maceration of around 20 days and maturation in 30 and 50-hectolitre French oak casks. A small quantity of merlot, vermentino and chardonnay complete the chequered range of varieties grown. Another memorable performance from Il Poggione's Sangiovese which just lacks the final high note. To begin with the Rosso 2011 is light, racy and certainly does not lack backbone, a feature shared by the Brunello 2008. The Riserva 2007 shows an even more complete profile: firm-bodied with piquant spice despite the prominent tannin in this phase.

● Brunello di Montalcino V. Paganelli Ris. '07	♥♥ 7
● Brunello di Montalcino '08	♥♥ 6
● Rosso di Montalcino '11	♥♥ 3
● Brunello di Montalcino Ris. '97	♀♀♀ 7
● Brunello di Montalcino '07	♀♀ 6
● Brunello di Montalcino '06	♀♀ 6
● Brunello di Montalcino '05	♀♀ 6
● Brunello di Montalcino '04	♀♀ 6
● Brunello di Montalcino Ris. '04	♀♀ 6
● Brunello di Montalcino Ris. '01	♀♀ 6
● Brunello di Montalcino V. Paganelli Ris. '06	♀♀ 7
● Rosso di Montalcino '10	♀♀ 3

Tenuta Poggiorosso

Loc. Poggio Rosso, 1
57025 Piombino [LI]
Tel. 3485257145
www.tenutapoggiorosso.it

CELLAR SALES
PRE-BOOKED VISITS
ANNUAL PRODUCTION 25,000 bottles
HECTARES UNDER VINE 6.00

The Monelli family acquired the estate in 2002, driven by a love for their land and the desire to create vigorous wines with lots of personality that fully express the character of the territory. They overhauled the estate totally, starting in the vineyard and finishing with the cellars. The estate's name derives from the colour of a strip of land in the vineyards, where the vines thrive particularly well. The wine names and logo are a reference to the ancient Etruscan sovereignty over the area. Tages 2010, a blend of sangiovese and merlot, is a child of Mother Earth, with minerally sensations and aromatic herbs on the nose and a firm, gutsy body with a lively tangy finish. The Velthune 2009 is supreme god of the Earth: a monovarietal cabernet sauvignon with fresh, minty aromas, wild currants and a firm, succulent, well-structured body with subtle tannins and a harmonious finish.

● Tages '10	♥♥ 3
● Velthune '09	♥♥ 5
○ Phylika '12	♥ 3
○ Veive '12	♥ 4
○ Phylika '11	♀♀ 3
○ Veive '11	♀♀ 4

Poggiotondo

via Torribina, 83
50050 Cerreto Guidi [FI]
Tel. 0571559167
www.poggiotondowines.com

PRE-BOOKED VISITS
ACCOMMODATION
ANNUAL PRODUCTION 300,000 bottles
HECTARES UNDER VINE 20.00

Internationally renowned winemaker Alberto Antonini has successfully brought his dream to life. He has restructured his family's estate to make the most of his experience gained making wine in partnership with a variety of producers, which has given him first-hand knowledge of a whole range of grape varieties and winemaking techniques. This synergy has resulted in a series of new wines that beautifully express his winemaking ideology, a philosophy of natural wines that are respectful of their territory, hence the conversion to biodynamic farming methods. An interesting version of Vermentino 2012 with citrus aromas alongside apricot and vegetal hints. The palate is fresh and vibrant with refreshing acidity. The Chianti Superiore 2010 is nicely put-together with complex, generous aromas of spice and wild berries and a supple body with tannins blending into the alcohol and a dynamic finish.

● Chianti Sup. '10	♥♥ 2*
● Chianti V. delle Conchiglie Ris. '10	♥♥ 6
○ Vermentino '12	♥♥ 2*
● Chianti Ris. '10	♥ 5
● Chianti V. delle Conchiglie Ris. '09	♥ 6
● Chianti V. delle Conchiglie Ris. '08	♀♀ 7
● Marmoreccia '09	♀♀ 7

★★Poliziano ✓

LOC. MONTEPULCIANO STAZIONE
VIA FONTAGO, 1
53045 MONTEPULCIANO [SI]
TEL. 0578738171
www.carlettipoliziano.com

CELLAR SALES
PRE-BOOKED VISITS
RESTAURANT SERVICE
ANNUAL PRODUCTION 600,000 bottles
HECTARES UNDER VINE 140.00

It was a love for his land that spurred Dino Carletti to acquire a plot and plant montepulciano vines in the 1960s. The same passion has motivated his son's choices. After a path of targeted training, experience and earlier partnerships with other producers, he has brought a new, continuously evolving drive for quality. The vines, which were all planted in the first 20 years after the vineyard was bought, derive from native 1940s stock and are the expression of their desire to keep close roots in their territory. The Lohsa estate in Maremma was acquired later. Through to the finals for the Nobile Asinone 2010: cherries and strawberries on the nose ennobled by spicy hints and a supple, sinuous, well-paced mouth with tannins blending into the alcohol and a tangy, very concentrated, lingering finish. The Morellino Lohsa 2011 is pleasant, with hints of bay leaves, rosemary and wild berries and a moderate, harmonious structure with fresh acidic sensations on a flavoursome finish.

● Nobile di Montepulciano Asinone '10	♥♥ 6
● Morellino di Scansano Lohsa '11	♥♥ 3
● Mandrone di Lohsa '09	♥ 5
● Nobile di Montepulciano '10	♥ 5
● Rosso di Montepulciano '11	♥ 3
● Le Stanze '03	♥♥♥ 6
● Nobile di Montepulciano '09	♥♥♥ 4*
● Nobile di Montepulciano Asinone '07	♥♥♥ 6
● Nobile di Montepulciano Asinone '06	♥♥♥ 6
● Nobile di Montepulciano Asinone '05	♥♥♥ 6
● Nobile di Montepulciano Asinone '04	♥♥♥ 6
● Nobile di Montepulciano Asinone '03	♥♥♥ 6
● Nobile di Montepulciano Asinone '01	♥♥♥ 6
● Nobile di Montepulciano Asinone '00	♥♥♥ 6
● Nobile di Montepulciano Asinone '99	♥♥♥ 5

Tenuta Le Potazzine ✓

LOC. LE PRATA, 262
53024 MONTALCINO [SI]
TEL. 0577846168
www.lepotazzine.it

CELLAR SALES
PRE-BOOKED VISITS
RESTAURANT SERVICE
ANNUAL PRODUCTION 38,000 bottles
HECTARES UNDER VINE 4.60

Giuseppe Gorelli and Gigliola Giannetti continue to offer an admirably graceful and breezy interpretation from their sangiovese grapes. This is the result of an ideal blend: the Le Prata locations to the west and Sant'Angelo in Colle, in the southern part of Montalcino. With techniques such as spontaneous fermentation, long maceration, maturation in medium-sized Slavonian oak casks, Le Potazzine's Brunellos are recognizable for their crystal clear fruit and their constraint. The standard label versions are particularly striking thanks to a remarkably drinkable flavour and dynamic energy while the Riserva (only made in the very best years) has a more distinctively virile touch. This scenario is fully confirmed by the Brunello 2008 which brings Gorelli's first Tre Bicchieri, thanks to enthralling balsamic and salty development paced by harmonious sensations rather than volume. The Riserva 2006 is red-blooded, very backward in blending the tannins but undeniably characterful and promising well for the future.

● Brunello di Montalcino '08	♥♥♥ 6
● Brunello di Montalcino Ris. '06	♥♥ 7
● Rosso di Montalcino '11	♥ 4
● Brunello di Montalcino '07	♥♥ 6
● Brunello di Montalcino '04	♥♥ 7
● Brunello di Montalcino Ris. '04	♥♥ 7
● Rosso di Montalcino '10	♥♥ 4

Pratesi

LOC. SEANO
VIA RIZZELLI, 10
59011 CARMIGNANO [PO]
TEL. 0558704108
www.pratesivini.it

PRE-BOOKED VISITS
ANNUAL PRODUCTION 60,000 bottles
HECTARES UNDER VINE 7.00

The Carmignano DOC zone has been
considered a good wine-growing area
since the times of the Medici. The Pratesi
family estate has produced wine here for
five generations, since 1875 to be precise,
respecting specific production choices
such as high-density planting in the
vineyards, a highly innovative decision in
an area in which has always preferred a
more traditional method. The wines are
matured in barriques in the new and
completely underground cellar, built with
respect for the environment to preserve
the particular beauty of the surrounding
area. An excellent overall performance: the
Riserva 2010 displays vibrant aromas with
vegetal and spicy hints and generous,
rounded body with a long, tangy finish. The
Carmione 2010 - cabernet sauvignon,
franc and merlot - has striking balsamic
hints, firm structure and a very lingering
finish. The Merlot 2010 has an intriguing
nose and deep mouth.

● Carmignano Circo Rosso Ris. '10	♂♂ 4
● Carmione '10	♂♂ 4
● Merlot Barche di Barchereto '10	♂♂ 3
● Carmignano '08	♀♀ 4
● Carmignano '01	♀♀ 5
● Carmignano '00	♀♀ 5
● Carmignano Circo Rosso Ris. '08	♀♀ 5
● Carmignano V. di Carmio Ris. '07	♀♀ 5
● Carmione '08	♀♀ 5
● Carmione '07	♀♀ 5
● Locorosso Rosso '00	♀♀ 3

★Fattoria Le Pupille

S.DA PIAGGE DEL MAIANO
58100 GROSSETO
TEL. 0564409517
www.fattorialepupille.it

CELLAR SALES
PRE-BOOKED VISITS
ACCOMMODATION
ANNUAL PRODUCTION 500,000 bottles
HECTARES UNDER VINE 70.00

Since 1985, Elisabetta Geppetti has been
the ambassador for the fragrance of
Maremma, a land that she respects, cares
for and loves as a way of life. A founding
member of the Consorzio del Morellino di
Scansano, she was also its first president,
a role to which she was recently nominated
again. She was instrumental in ensuring
that the designation's wine is distinguished
for its elegance and finesse as well as
mirroring its territory beautifully. The estate
is a fine example of how innovation and
tradition can be combined. To this end, an
old farmhouse on the estate has been
renovated and now serves as a guest
house. The 2010 Morellino Riserva made
the finals for its intense currant and
blackberry nose polished by spicy pepper
and liquorice notes. It has a dense palate
with subtle, delicate tannins, a fresh acidic
vein and good continuity in the finish. The
drinkable 2012 Morellino is also good, with
its fresh, lively nose, supple backbone and
crisp, inviting savouriness.

● Morellino di Scansano Ris. '10	♂♂ 3*
● Morellino di Scansano '12	♂♂ 2*
○ Poggio Argentato '12	♂ 2
● Saffredi '10	♂ 8
● Morellino di Scansano Poggio Valente '04	♀♀♀ 5
● Morellino di Scansano Poggio Valente '99	♀♀♀ 5
● Morellino di Scansano Poggio Valente '98	♀♀♀ 5
● Saffredi '05	♀♀♀ 8
● Saffredi '04	♀♀♀ 8
● Saffredi '03	♀♀♀ 8
● Saffredi '02	♀♀♀ 7
● Saffredi '01	♀♀♀ 7
● Saffredi '00	♀♀♀ 7

La Querce

VIA IMPRUNETANA PER TAVARNUZZE, 41
50023 IMPRUNETA [FI]
TEL. 0552011380
www.laquerce.com

CELLAR SALES
PRE-BOOKED VISITS
ACCOMMODATION
ANNUAL PRODUCTION 25,000 bottles
HECTARES UNDER VINE 8.00

The farm is on the road leading from Impruneta to Bagnolo, in a beguilingly beautiful part of the Chianti zone. The estate is owned by the Marchi family, which also owns Villa La Querce, a holiday house nestled amongst the olive groves and vineyards. The land is farmed using both traditional and modern methods and grape varieties, including sangiovese and colorino. Relatively clayey soil, good aspect and a unique site climate combine to produce high-quality grapes. The estate is overseen by Marco Ferretti. The 2010 La Querce made it to the finals. A mix of sangiovese with some colorino, it boasts a balsamic nose and spicy highlights and is full-bodied and plush, with a nice fresh finish and a wild berry aftertaste. We also like the 2009 M, a Merlot monovarietal that is all chocolate and ripe wild berries with a juicy, non-aggressive palate and full-flavoured finish.

Le Querce

LOC. CAMPALTO
57021 CAMPIGLIA MARITTIMA [LI]
TEL. 0565846535
www.agricolalequerce.com

PRE-BOOKED VISITS
ANNUAL PRODUCTION 75,000 bottles
HECTARES UNDER VINE 15.50

Following the winery's decision to produce quality wines, a careful assessment of the features of the territory led them to international varieties, leaving vermentino as the only native representative. Their desire to make wine came from their passion for the land: the estate was well-known for decades for its production of excellent extra-virgin olive oil in the area of Campiglia Marittima, near Livorno. The landscape is extremely varied, from hills to woodland and the seashore, and it is graced with a unique climate ideal for wine-growing. They have achieved impressive results in a few short years and have especially succeeded in creating a distinct character for their products. A blend of the two cabernets, 2010 Calviolo made the finals for its refreshingly charming and balsamic nose with aromas of many wild berries, fresh supple body leading to a juicy, savoury finish. The new 2012 Terre di Paola is interesting, with its citrus and peach aromas, and dense, lively body.

● La Querce '10	♟♟ 5
● M '09	♟♟ 6
● Chianti Colli Fiorentini La Torretta '11	♟ 2
● Chianti Sorrettole '12	♟ 2
● Chianti Colli Fiorentini La Torretta '08	♟♟ 2
● Chianti Colli Fiorentini La Torretta '06	♟♟ 2*
● Chianti Colli Fiorentini La Torretta '05	♟♟ 2
● La Querce '09	♟♟ 5
● La Querce '08	♟♟ 5
● La Querce '07	♟♟ 4
● La Querce '06	♟♟ 4
● M '07	♟♟ 6

● Calviolo '10	♟♟ 2*
○ Vermentino Il Libeccio '12	♟♟ 2*
○ Viognier Terre di Paola '12	♟♟ 2*
○ Il Maestrale '12	♟ 2
● Sancerbone '08	♟♟ 2*

Querce Bettina

LOC CASINA DI MOCALI, 275
53024 MONTALCINO [SI]
TEL. 0577848588
www.quercebettina.it

CELLAR SALES
PRE-BOOKED VISITS
ANNUAL PRODUCTION 15,000 bottles
HECTARES UNDER VINE 2.50

The Brunellos made by husband-and-wife team, the Morettis, are outside the box in many ways, starting with the practically unique productive conditions in an almost unspoilt area in the south-west of the denomination. The two and a half hectares are situated at over 400 metres on clayey soil rich in silty marl mixed with stony material, in one of the lightest, breeziest parts of the DOC zone. These wines progress a great deal in just a few months, which suggests a classic but by no means nostalgic style with long maturation in 25-hectolitre Austrian oak casks. Despite a vintage totally below that of preceding years, the Brunello di Querce Bettina is nevertheless of a very high standard, thanks to an airy, enveloping 2008 upheld by forthright tannins and, most of all, lots of lip-smacking flavour and grip. Although it has a slightly hazy aromatic profile and the finish is bare, the 2007 Riserva does offer nice intact fruit and a well-defined link to its territory.

● Brunello di Montalcino '08	♟♟	6
● Brunello di Montalcino Ris. '07	♟♟	8
● Rosso di Montalcino '10	♟	4
● Brunello di Montalcino '06	♟♟♟	7
● Brunello di Montalcino '07	♟♟	7
● Brunello di Montalcino Ris. '06	♟♟	8
● Rosso di Montalcino '08	♟♟	3

★Querciabella

VIA BARBIANO, 17
50022 GREVE IN CHIANTI [FI]
TEL. 05585927777
www.querciabella.com

CELLAR SALES
PRE-BOOKED VISITS
ANNUAL PRODUCTION 400,000 bottles
HECTARES UNDER VINE 112.00
VITICULTURE METHOD Certified Biodynamic

Querciabella is one of the original pioneers in the renaissance of Chianti Classico spanning the late 1980s to the mid 1990s. Most of the largely organic vineyards cover a vast area and are situated in the hills around Greve in Chianti, one of the most beautiful subzones in the designation. The rest of the vineyards are near Talamone in Maremma. Unfortunately, the wines seem to have lost a little of their lustre in recent years, mainly surrendering a little of their personality. However, they are still exquisitely made. The Turpino is a blend of cabernet franc, merlot and syrah grapes, 50% of which were grown in Maremma. It features a pervasive nose and tasty mouth with a likeable hardness. The 2010 Camartina blend of cabernet sauvignon and sangiovese is decidedly well-made, if possibly a little lacking in personality. The 2011 Mongrana, a sangiovese-merlot-cabernet sauvignon blend, has nice flow.

● Turpino '10	♟♟	6
● Camartina '10	♟♟	8
● Mongrana '11	♟♟	3
● Chianti Cl. '11	♟	3
● Palafreno '10	♟	8
○ Batàr '98	♟♟♟	8
● Camartina '07	♟♟♟	8
● Camartina '06	♟♟♟	7
● Camartina '05	♟♟♟	7
● Camartina '04	♟♟♟	7
● Camartina '03	♟♟♟	8
● Camartina '01	♟♟♟	8
● Camartina '00	♟♟♟	8
● Camartina '99	♟♟♟	8
● Camartina '97	♟♟♟	8
● Camartina '95	♟♟♟	8

Le Ragnaie

LOC. LE RAGNAIE
53024 MONTALCINO [SI]
TEL. 0577848639
www.leragnaie.com

CELLAR SALES
PRE-BOOKED VISITS
ACCOMMODATION
ANNUAL PRODUCTION 80,000 bottles
HECTARES UNDER VINE 15.00
VITICULTURE METHOD Certified Organic

The pace set by Riccardo and Jennifer Campinoti's estate in carving a very prominent niche in the crowded Montalcino area shows no sign of slowing down. The cellar stands on the highest point of the DOC zone, near the Passo del Lume Spento at 600 metres. This is the location of the old vineyard planted in 1968, after which a bottle from the 2007 vintage was named. Other plots are to be found in Castelnuovo dell'Abate and in the central-western sector. Holding it all together is a concept of Brunello consisting of clear-cut fruit, finesse and flavour which is evidently more important than any discussion of working methods and types of oak. In a range with again many highs, the 2008 Brunello Fornace stands out as a "warm" cru, where the cool vintage offers irresistibly nuanced currant, black pepper and Mediterranean scrub, with a palate both compact and full of pressure. The powerful tannins are still settling but it is already worth a Tre Bicchieri.

● Brunello di Montalcino Fornace '08	♥♥♥ 8
● Brunello di Montalcino '08	♥♥ 6
● Brunello di Montalcino V. V. '08	♥♥ 8
● Chianti Colli Senesi '11	♥ 2
● Brunello di Montalcino V. V. '07	♀♀♀ 5
● Rosso di Montalcino '10	♀♀ 4

La Regola

LOC. SAN MARTINO
VIA A. GRAMSCI, 1
56046 RIPARBELLA [PI]
TEL. 058881363
www.laregola.com

CELLAR SALES
PRE-BOOKED VISITS
ANNUAL PRODUCTION 80,000 bottles
HECTARES UNDER VINE 20.00

The estate has been with the Nuti family since the early 20th century, occupying a site where once there was an Etruscan settlement and which was chosen for the fertility of its soils. It was the great-grandfather of the current owners, Luca and Flavio Nuti, who acquired the property to produce wine for his personal use but their grandfather Nilo and father Rolando created an agricultural business. After university, Luca took over the vineyard and cellars with passion and dedication, while his brother Flavio looks after the commercial side. The 2009 La Regola made the finals. This cabernet franc blend topped with a little merlot and petit verdot has a likeable, refreshingly fruity nose with slightly spicy notes, a well-balanced, full body and a juicy palate, leading to a lingering, layered finish. The 2009 Lo Strido, made from merlot grapes, has a sweet, spicy nose and soft body; the 2009 Beloro, from sangiovese grapes, is well-balanced; the cabernet sauvignon-dominated 2009 Vallino is austere and no-nonsense, with good supporting flavour.

● Beloro '09	♥♥ 6
● La Regola '09	♥♥ 6
● Strido '09	♥♥ 8
● Vallino '09	♥♥ 5
○ Lauro Bianco '11	♥ 4
○ Spumante Brut M. Cl.	♥ 4
● Montescudaio Rosso Il Vallino '07	♀♀ 5
● Montescudaio Rosso La Regola '08	♀♀ 6
● Montescudaio Rosso Vallino '08	♀♀ 4
● Strido '08	♀♀ 4

Rocca delle Macìe

LOC. LE MACÌE, 45
53011 CASTELLINA IN CHIANTI [SI]
TEL. 05777321
www.roccadellemacie.com

CELLAR SALES
PRE-BOOKED VISITS
ACCOMMODATION AND RESTAURANT SERVICE
ANNUAL PRODUCTION 4,500,000 bottles
HECTARES UNDER VINE 210.00

Rocca delle Macìe is a solid element in the Castellina subzone, established in 1973 by film producer Italo Zingarelli and managed today by his son Sergio, who is currently President of the Consorzio del Chianti Classico. The impeccably clean workmanship and accessible appeal of the wines confirm that balance and elegance are a priority, avoiding commonplace choices and these specific decisions have sometimes led to absolute excellence, especially recently. But Chianti Classico is not the only focus, because the winery also has two estates in Maremma, Campomaccione and Casamaria. Both the 2010 Chianti Classico Fizzano Riserva and the 2010 Famiglia Zingarelli Riserva are very well-made, although the former is more complex and the oak more pronounced, while the latter is obviously driven by enjoyable mouthfeel. The 2010 Sangiovese Ser Gioveto is nicely supple, although it may be overly tied to the sweetness of the fruit.

● Chianti Cl. Fizzano Ris. '10	♟♟♟ 5
● Chianti Cl. Famiglia Zingarelli Ris. '10	♟♟ 4
● Chianti Cl. Famiglia Zingarelli '11	♟♟ 3
● Chianti Cl. Tenuta S. Alfonso '11	♟♟ 4
● Roccato '10	♟♟ 7
● Ser Gioveto '10	♟♟ 6
● Chianti Vernaiolo '12	♟ 2
● Morellino di Scansano Campomaccione '12	♟ 3
● Chianti Cl. Famiglia Zingarelli Ris. '09	♟♟♟ 3*
● Roccato '00	♟♟♟ 6
● Roccato '99	♟♟♟ 6
● Chianti Cl. Tenuta S. Alfonso '10	♟♟ 4
● Roccato '09	♟♟ 6
● Ser Gioveto '09	♟♟ 6

Rocca di Castagnoli

LOC. CASTAGNOLI
53013 GAIOLE IN CHIANTI [SI]
TEL. 0577731004
www.roccadicastagnoli.com

CELLAR SALES
PRE-BOOKED VISITS
ACCOMMODATION AND RESTAURANT SERVICE
ANNUAL PRODUCTION 450,000 bottles
HECTARES UNDER VINE 132.00

The basic feature of Rocca di Castagnoli wines is their coherent style, which prioritizes balance and perceives and displays the various aspects of the terroir in which they are produced. The winery at Gaiole in Chianti is also the production centre for the Tenuta di Capraia estate in the Castellina subzone and Castello di San Sano, also at Gaiole. This varied productive mosaic has steadily yielded peaks of excellent quality, especially in the recent past. The 2009 Buriano, a monovarietal Cabernet Sauvignon, has a spicy nose and deeply clenched, almost forbidding palate. The elegant 100% merlot 2009 Le Pratola is marked by intense aromas of ripe fruit and well-balanced flavours. The 2011 Chianti Classico del Castello di San Sano has a clean nose, good development in a tangy, juicy palate. The classic 2011 Chianti Classico della Tenuta Capraia is decidedly enjoyable, if very immediate.

● Buriano '09	♟♟ 6
● Chianti Cl. Castello di San Sano '11	♟♟ 3
● Chianti Cl. Tenuta di Capraia '11	♟♟ 3
● Le Pratola '09	♟♟ 5
● Borro al Fumo '09	♟ 5
● Chianti Cl. Guarnellotto Castello di San Sano Ris. '10	♟ 4
● Chianti Cl. Poggio ai Frati Ris. '10	♟ 4
● Chianti Cl. Rocca di Castagnoli '11	♟ 3
● Chianti Cl. Tenuta di Capraia Ris. '10	♟ 5
● Stielle '09	♟ 6
● Chianti Cl. Capraia Ris. '07	♟♟♟ 4
● Chianti Cl. Poggio ai Frati Ris. '08	♟♟♟ 4
● Chianti Cl. Poggio ai Frati Ris. '06	♟♟♟ 4*
● Chianti Cl. Tenuta di Capraia Ris. '06	♟♟♟ 4*

Rocca di Frassinello

LOC. GIUNCARICO
58023 GAVORRANO [GR]
TEL. 056688400
www.roccadifrassinello.it

CELLAR SALES
PRE-BOOKED VISITS
ANNUAL PRODUCTION 200,000 bottles
HECTARES UNDER VINE 80.00

Rocca di Frassinello nestles in the heart of the Tuscan Maremma, between Bolgheri and Scansano and was introduced as an international project to produce the best quality grapes, by combining local characteristics with innovative French techniques. The extremely avant-garde winery was designed by Renzo Piano. Production methods are studied in order to avoid any unnecessary procedures. They even use gravity only to drop the grapes into the vat cellar, without passing through pumps, which provides an additional guarantee of quality. High technology and expert eyes throughout the vinification phases also contribute to the pursuit of excellence. The 100% merlot 2011 Baffo Nero is strongly Mediterranean in character, with an intense and full nose featuring over-ripe berry fruit. It has an opulent mouth, with tar nuances in the finish. The 2011 Rocca di Frassinello, made primarily from sangiovese grapes topped with merlot and cabernet sauvignon, is rich and mature.

● Baffo Nero '11	♟♟♟ 8
● Rocca di Frassinello '11	♟♟♟ 6
● Le Sughere di Frassinello '11	♟♟ 4
● Poggio alla Guardia '11	♟ 3
● Vermentino '12	♟ 3
● Baffo Nero '10	♟♟♟ 8
● Baffo Nero '09	♟♟♟ 8
● Baffo Nero '07	♟♟♟ 8
● Le Sughere di Frassinello '10	♟♟♟ 4*
● Rocca di Frassinello '08	♟♟♟ 5
● Rocca di Frassinello '06	♟♟♟ 5
● Rocca di Frassinello '05	♟♟♟ 5
● Rocca di Frassinello '10	♟♟ 6
● Rocca di Frassinello '09	♟♟ 6

Rocca di Montemassi

FRAZ. MONTEMASSI
VIA SANT'ANNA
58027 ROCCASTRADA [GR]
TEL. 0564579700
www.roccadimontemassi.it

CELLAR SALES
PRE-BOOKED VISITS
ANNUAL PRODUCTION 200,000 bottles
HECTARES UNDER VINE 160.00

Rocca di Montemassi lies between the Tyrrhenian Sea and the metal-rich hills. Gianni Zonin, head of one of Italy's largest wine groups, chose to invest here, with the aim of producing wines of rare excellence that respect the Tuscan Maremma environment. New vines were planted and other plants typically of the area were reinstated with the aim of preserving the existing identity of the landscape. The estate also houses the Museum of Rural Civilization, which features over 3,000 objects and images narrating the story of the place, trades and work on the land. The 2011 Rocca di Montemassi made the finals. This blend of cabernet sauvignon, syrah, merlot and petit verdot has an inviting nose where roast peppers mingle with wild berries and delicate spices, a soft-bodied palate where tannins meld with the alcoholic component leading to a tasty, leisurely finish. The 2011 Monteregio Sassabruna is also good with an inviting nose and enjoyable mouth.

● Rocca di Montemassi '11	♟♟ 5
● Monteregio di Massa Marittima Sassabruna '11	♟♟ 3
○ Astraio '12	♟ 4
○ Calasole '12	♟ 3
● Le Focaie '12	♟ 2
● Rocca di Montemassi '10	♟♟♟ 5
● Rocca di Montemassi '09	♟♟♟ 5
● Monteregio di Massa Marittima Sassabruna '09	♟♟ 3
● Monteregio di Massa Marittima Sassabruna '08	♟♟ 3
● Rocca di Montemassi '08	♟♟ 5

Roccapesta

LOC. MACERETO 9
50854 SCANSANO [GR]
TEL. 0564599252
www.roccapesta.it

PRE-BOOKED VISITS
ANNUAL PRODUCTION 90,000 bottles
HECTARES UNDER VINE 18.00

Between the sea and the mountains, the volcanic and sedimentary soils are rich in minerals that nourish the plants and confer on them well-defined aromatic profiles. Each vineyard was planned following research to optimize the soil, root stock and grape varieties and each is harvested and vinified separately. The grapes undergo a triple selection before destemming and the rest of the vinification process also follows very strict technical criteria. The estate only produces red wines. Alberto Tanzini's estate is doing impressively well and all the wines presented were of a very high standard. The 2009 Riserva Calestaia won its first Tre Bicchieri for its fresh, clean aromas of Mediterranean scrub, dark plum and balsamic hints. The palate is notably well-balanced, with subtle tannins and a rising finish with a fruity aftertaste. The 2011 Morellino Ribero has a lively, powerful nose and well-orchestrated palate.

● Morellino di Scansano Calestaia Ris. '09	♟♟♟ 5
● Morellino di Scansano Ribero '11	♟♟ 3*
● Masca '11	♟♟ 2*
● Morellino di Scansano '11	♟♟ 3
● Morellino di Scansano Ris. '10	♟♟ 4
● Pugnitello '11	♟♟ 5
● Morellino di Scansano '10	♀♀ 3*
● Morellino di Scansano Ribero '10	♀♀ 2*
● Morellino di Scansano Ris. '09	♀♀ 4

Rubbia al Colle

LOC. POGGETTO ALLE PULLEDRE
57028 SUVERETO [LI]
TEL. 0565827026
www.arcipelagomuratori.it

CELLAR SALES
PRE-BOOKED VISITS
ANNUAL PRODUCTION 200,000 bottles
HECTARES UNDER VINE 71.50
VITICULTURE METHOD Certified Organic

The Arcipelago Muratori, as its owners like to call it, comprises a series of estates around Italy in Franciacorta, Sannio and Ischia, all belonging to the same family. This choice followed the desire to grow each grape in the locations best suited to its characteristics. The Rubbia al Colle estate is located in Val di Cornia, extending from the sea to the hills and produces red wines. As well as for aspects linked to the territory, the choice was also determined by sentimental reasons. The 2010 Olpaio is good. It has a spicy nose, with a touch of leather and well-balanced body, while the entry is soft followed by a well expressed liveliness and fresh acidity. The 2010 Le Pulledre is also pleasant. This blend of cabernet sauvignon, petit verdot, syrah, sangiovese and ciliegiolo has a rich set of aromas, with pronounced vegetal notes and a relaxed structure joined by a very enjoyable drinkability.

● Le Pulledre '10	♟♟ 6
● Val di Cornia Olpaio '10	♟♟ 4
● Simbiotico '11	♟ 3
● Val di Cornia Barricoccio '10	♟ 4
● Drumo '03	♀♀ 3
● Rumpotino '01	♀♀ 4
● Val di Cornia V. Molisso '08	♀♀ 5
● Val di Cornia Villa Usilio '08	♀♀ 5

★Tenimenti Ruffino

P.LE RUFFINO, 1
50065 PONTASSIEVE [FI]
TEL. 05583605
www.ruffino.it

CELLAR SALES
PRE-BOOKED VISITS
ANNUAL PRODUCTION 15,000,000 bottles
HECTARES UNDER VINE 600.00

Although it is one of Italy's leading wineries, the estate operates under the stars and stripes (Constellations Brands). In Tuscany it brings together some very important and high profile wine producers such as Greppone Mazzi at Montalcino, Lodola Nuova at Montepulciano, Santedame, Gretolaio, Montemasso and Poggio Casciano in Chianti Classico and La Solatia at Monteriggioni near Siena. The wines are modern in style and also aged in barriques, and offer a high standard of reliable quality across the range. Only a small selection was presented this year. The 2008 Brunello di Montalcino has a fruity nose with hints of cherry jam and is solidly built, offering a full-flavoured finish and good grip. The 2010 Chianti Classico Santedame has a simple nose and develops nicely on the palate, although it is not very structured

● Brunello di Montalcino Greppone Mazzi '08	🍷🍷 7
● Chianti Cl. Santedame '10	🍷 4
● Brunello di Montalcino Greppone Mazzi '05	🍷🍷🍷 6
● Chianti Cl. Ris. Ducale Oro '04	🍷🍷🍷 5
● Chianti Cl. Ris. Ducale Oro '01	🍷🍷🍷 5
● Chianti Cl. Ris. Ducale Oro '00	🍷🍷🍷 5
● Modus '04	🍷🍷🍷 5
● Romitorio di Santedame '00	🍷🍷🍷 7
● Romitorio di Santedame '99	🍷🍷🍷 7
● Romitorio di Santedame '98	🍷🍷🍷 7

Russo

POD. LA METOCCHINA
VIA FORNI, 71
57028 SUVERETO [LI]
TEL. 0565845105
www.vinirusso.it

CELLAR SALES
PRE-BOOKED VISITS
ANNUAL PRODUCTION 80,000 bottles
HECTARES UNDER VINE 14.00

This family-run estate boasts a lengthy history in farming and they established themselves in the area four generations ago. This old-style farm still raises domestic animals and dairy cows and makes its own bread, cheese and cured meats, mostly for personal use, and grows fruit and vegetables. Although wine is the primary activity, olives are also grown. Although wine has always been produced, it was not bottled prior to 1998. The 2011 Ceppitaio performed well. Made mostly from sangiovese with the addition of colorino and canaiolo, it has fresh, lively currant and raspberry notes and a subtle, soft body, refreshed by a nice acidic vein. The powerful 2010 Sassobucato, from merlot and cabernet sauvignon, features sweet chocolate aromas with coffee, toasty notes and mixed spices, followed by a wide, rounded, well-balanced palate with nice length. The vermentino-claret-chardonnay blend 2012 Pietrasca is concentrated and lively.

○ Pietrasca '12	🍷🍷 2*
● Sassobucato '10	🍷🍷 5
● Val di Cornia Rosso Ceppitaio '11	🍷🍷 2*
● Val di Cornia Rosso Barbicone '00	🍷🍷🍷 4*
● Barbicone '05	🍷🍷 4
● Sassobucato '08	🍷🍷 5
● Sassobucato '06	🍷🍷 5
● Val di Cornia Rosso Barbicone '06	🍷🍷 4
● Val di Cornia Rosso Ceppitaio '08	🍷🍷 2

Sada

SP DEI 3 COMUNI
56040 CASALE MARITTIMO [PI]
TEL. 0586650180
www.agricolasada.com

CELLAR SALES
PRE-BOOKED VISITS
ANNUAL PRODUCTION 60,000 bottles
HECTARES UNDER VINE 11.50
VITICULTURE METHOD Certified Organic

The Sada family worked in the food industry
before taking a chance on wine. Their
primary conviction, which became the
estate's philosophy, is that wine should
express its territory through the
characteristics of its grapes. Back in 2000,
they planted their first few hectares in
Casale Marittimo, followed by plots in
Bibbona and Bolgheri, with a head-trained
vineyard of approximately one hectare. The
2011 Baldoro is good. From cabernet
sauvignon, alicante and montepulciano
grapes, it has intense, varied aromas, where
oriental spices and plum jam notes are
followed by a densely rich palate that is
wide, soft and leisurely. The 2010 stylish,
elegant Bolgheri Superiore is well-typed,
with a captivating nose. The plush 2011
Integolo blend of cabernet sauvignon and
montepulciano is sinewy and well-
structured. The 2009 Carpoli blend of
cabernet sauvignon, cabernet franc and
petit verdot has crisply penetrating aromas.

● Baldoro '11	🍷🍷 5
● Bolgheri Sup. '10	🍷🍷 6
● Carpoli '09	🍷🍷 5
● Integolo '11	🍷🍷 6
○ Spumante Brut Versò	🍷 4
● Baldoro '08	🍷🍷 5
● Integolo '10	🍷🍷 6

Salcheto

LOC. SANT'ALBINO
VIA DI VILLA BIANCA, 15
53045 MONTEPULCIANO [SI]
TEL. 0578799031
www.salcheto.it

CELLAR SALES
PRE-BOOKED VISITS
ACCOMMODATION AND RESTAURANT SERVICE
ANNUAL PRODUCTION 230,000 bottles
HECTARES UNDER VINE 50.00
VITICULTURE METHOD Certified Organic

The choice to maintain a balanced
relationship with nature entails production
procedures which are respectful and
non-aggressive towards the land and its
fruits, enabling the wines to give a true
representation of the terroir. Salcheto is the
name of the stream that crosses this area,
along which many willow trees once grew.
In this part of the Montepulciano DOC zone
the challenge is on to produce a great
wine, fully aware that this cannot be
learned from books but in the vineyards,
each of which is managed by a team of
experts in their particular area of
competence, with the least possible impact
on the environment. We have awarded the
prize for sustainable growing to Salcheto, in
recognition of Michele's great work. The
juicy 2010 Nobile takes a Tre Bicchieri for
its lively, penetrating nose featuring fresh
herbs, such as thyme and sage, and
blueberry and redcurrant notes, supported
by a succulent vibrant, firm body and an
inviting, very leisurely finish.

● Nobile di Montepulciano '10	🍷🍷🍷 4*
○ Pigliatello V.T. '09	🍷🍷 5
● Salco 2089	🍷🍷 6
● Chianti Colli Senesi '12	🍷 2
⊙ Rosato di Toscana '12	🍷 2
● Rosso di Montepulciano Obvius '12	🍷 3
● Nobile di Montepulciano '97	🍷🍷🍷 3*
● Nobile di Montepulciano Salco Evoluzione '06	🍷🍷🍷 6
● Nobile di Montepulciano Salco Evoluzione '01	🍷🍷🍷 6
● Nobile di Montepulciano '09	🍷🍷 4
● Nobile di Montepulciano Salco Evoluzione Ris. '07	🍷🍷 6

Salustri

FRAZ. POGGI DEL SASSO
LOC. LA CAVA
58040 CINIGIANO [GR]
TEL. 0564990529
www.salustri.it

CELLAR SALES
PRE-BOOKED VISITS
ACCOMMODATION
ANNUAL PRODUCTION 80,000 bottles
HECTARES UNDER VINE 15.00
VITICULTURE METHOD Certified Organic

For generations the Salustri family has farmed an ideal area for producing fine quality wine and olive oil, according to Maremma tradition. The vineyards have been replanted one by one, with patience and expertise, as owner Leonardo loves to repeat, using the original clones obtained from the vines planted in the late 19th century by his ancestor Secondo Salustri. The estate is committed to safeguarding native local clones, working alongside the Enology Faculty of Pisa University on one of several projects in experimental vineyards. As well as wine, the estate produces olive oil and offers holiday accommodation. The 2010 Sangiovese Grotte Rosse made the finals for its brisk aromatic profile, marked by Mediterranean scrub that mingles with wild berries and fresh mineral notes. The palate has a pleasant entry, where a good tannic weave is well-integrated with the alcohol, followed by a leisurely, well-made finish bursting with flavours.

● Montecucco Grotte Rosse '10	♟♟ 6
● Montecucco Santa Marta '10	♟♟ 4
● Montecucco Marleo '11	♟ 3
○ Narà '12	♟ 3
● Montecucco Grotte Rosse '08	♟♟♟ 6
● Montecucco Grotte Rosse '07	♟♟♟ 5
● Montecucco Santa Marta '06	♟♟♟ 4
● Montecucco Grotte Rosse '06	♟♟ 5
● Montecucco Grotte Rosse '05	♟♟ 5
● Montecucco Santa Marta '09	♟♟ 4
● Montecucco Santa Marta '08	♟♟ 4
● Montecucco Santa Marta '07	♟♟ 4
● Montecucco Santa Marta '05	♟♟ 3

Fattoria San Donato

LOC. SAN DONATO, 6
53037 SAN GIMIGNANO [SI]
TEL. 0577941616
www.sandonato.it

CELLAR SALES
PRE-BOOKED VISITS
ACCOMMODATION AND RESTAURANT SERVICE
ANNUAL PRODUCTION 70,000 bottles
HECTARES UNDER VINE 20.00
VITICULTURE METHOD Certified Organic

The origin of the farm derives from Umberto Fenzi's idea to live in the San Gimignano countryside with his family, in a property purchased by his grandfather in the early 1930s. Today this estate is a leading light in the local area, both for farm holiday facilities and for agricultural products, with grapes and wine at the top of the list. The estate is farmed according to organic methods and, as far as possible, in harmony with the surrounding nature and environment. Judging by our own impressions, the wines benefit from this. The excellent version of Vernaccia di San Gimignano Riserva Benedetta put on a striking performance. While not an easy wine, the 2010 vintage is a nice, well-rounded white with slightly toasted aromas on the nose, which amalgamate with fresher, more vibrant notes in the mouth. The 2012 is simple and slightly evanescent, while the 2011 Angelica is a touch mature and oaky.

○ Vernaccia di S. Gimignano Benedetta Ris. '10	♟♟ 3*
● Chianti Colli Senesi '10	♟ 2
○ Vernaccia di S. Gimignano '12	♟ 2
○ Vernaccia di S. Gimignano Angelica '11	♟ 3
○ San Gimignano Vin Santo '04	♟♟ 5
○ Vernaccia di S. Gimignano '11	♟♟ 1*
○ Vernaccia di S. Gimignano Angelica '07	♟♟ 2*
○ Vernaccia di S. Gimignano Benedetta Ris. '07	♟♟ 3
○ Vin Santo di San Gimignano '05	♟♟ 5

★San Felice

LOC. SAN FELICE
53019 CASTELNUOVO BERARDENGA [SI]
TEL. 05773991
www.agricolasanfelice.it

CELLAR SALES
PRE-BOOKED VISITS
ACCOMMODATION AND RESTAURANT SERVICE
ANNUAL PRODUCTION 1,200,000 bottles
HECTARES UNDER VINE 210.00

San Felice, owned by the Allianz group, has left its mark on the history of Tuscany wine-growing, starting with the Supertuscan phenomenon launched by this Castelnuovo Berardenga winery with its Vigorello wine in 1968. The estate has also pioneered research, especially towards preservation of the genetic heritage of old traditional grape varieties. San Felice has operated in the Chianti Classico zone for over 40 years, and today it can count on the Campogiovanni estate in Montalcino as well as Periolla in Maremma to offer a range of robust and reliable wines. Castelnuovo Berardenga's 2010 Chianti Classico is truly hedonistic, despite its underlying simplicity. The 2011 Contrada San Felice is also good. A sangiovese-cabernet sauvignon-merlot blend, it is not oaked and is both enjoyable and well-paced, with a nice grassy character. The rich and tannic 2010 Vigorello is a classic with its concentrated firm structure and has again won a Tre Bicchieri.

● Vigorello '10	♟♟♟ 6
● Chianti Cl. '10	♟♟ 3
● Chianti Cl. Poggio Rosso Ris. '10	♟♟ 6
● Contrada San Felice '11	♟♟ 3
● Chianti Cl. Il Grigio Ris. '09	♟ 3
● Chianti Cl. Poggio Rosso Ris. '03	♟♟♟ 5
● Chianti Cl. Poggio Rosso Ris. '00	♟♟♟ 5
● Chianti Cl. Poggio Rosso Ris. '95	♟♟♟ 5
● Chianti Cl. Poggio Rosso Ris. '90	♟♟♟ 5
● Pugnitello '07	♟♟♟ 6
● Pugnitello '06	♟♟♟ 6
● Vigorello '08	♟♟♟ 6
● Vigorello '97	♟♟♟ 6
● Vigorello '88	♟♟♟ 6

Fattoria San Felo

LOC. PAGLIATELLI
58051 MAGLIANO IN TOSCANA [GR]
TEL. 056428481
www.fattoriasanfelo.it

PRE-BOOKED VISITS
ANNUAL PRODUCTION 100,000 bottles
HECTARES UNDER VINE 25.00

Any wine produced in Maremma will create great expectations relating to the charm and knowledge of that area. The Vanni family established and run the farm according to traditional values and are autonomous in all production phases, from cultivation of grapes to bottling and shipping the wines, all organized with the utmost precision. The names of these wines echo terms with local significance, old sayings or geographical locations, while the winery's own name derives from the initials of the two brothers who run it. The two whites are intriguing. The 2012 Vermentino Le Stoppie has a striking citrus nose with floral highlights, the palate is edgy with well-balanced alcohol, leading to a long, full-flavoured finish. The 2012 Viognier is also interesting, with vibrant sensations of spring flower and peach and subtle aromatic herb notes. The mouth is pleasantly satisfying and enveloping, with a nice savouriness that prolongs the finish.

○ Le Stoppie '12	♟♟ 2*
● Morellino di Scansano Dicioccatore Ris. '10	♟♟ 4
○ Viognier '12	♟♟ 2*
⊙ Frosali '12	♟ 2
● Morellino di Scansano '11	♟♟ 2*
● Morellino di Scansano Dicioccatore Ris. '08	♟♟ 4
● Morellino di Scansano Lampo '10	♟♟ 2*

San Giusto a Rentennano

LOC. SAN GIUSTO A RENTENNANO, 20
53013 GAIOLE IN CHIANTI [SI]
TEL. 0577747121
www.fattoriasangiusto.it

CELLAR SALES
PRE-BOOKED VISITS
ANNUAL PRODUCTION 80,000 bottles
HECTARES UNDER VINE 29.00
VITICULTURE METHOD Certified Organic

The wines produced on this estate owned by the Martini family of Cigala started attracting attention in the mid-Seventies. Today San Giusto a Rentennano is one of the most prestigious brands in Chianti Classico, with a solid reputation built on authentic, rigorous products whose distinctive features include gutsy style and a strong connection with the terroir. The wines are mainly aged in small casks as demonstrated by a sometimes excessive oakiness, but acquire balance, above all over time. The 2010 Chianti Classico Le Baroncole Riserva is fascinating, starting with its earthy aromas and fresh cherry notes, which evolve into a very tangy, fruity palate. It is really a pity about the slightly overpowering oak. The 2011 has nice red berry fruit notes – a pleasant wine if a little rigid.

● Chianti Cl. Le Baroncole Ris. '10	▼▼ 5
● Chianti Cl. '11	▼▼ 4
● La Ricolma '10	▼ 7
● Percarlo '09	▼ 7
● Chianti Cl. '10	♀♀♀ 4*
● Percarlo '07	♀♀♀ 7
● Percarlo '99	♀♀♀ 7
● Percarlo '97	♀♀♀ 6
● Percarlo '95	♀♀♀ 6
● Percarlo '88	♀♀♀ 6
● Chianti Cl. '09	♀♀ 3
● Chianti Cl. Le Baroncole Ris. '07	♀♀ 5
● La Ricolma '07	♀♀ 7
● Percarlo '06	♀♀ 7

★★Tenuta San Guido

FRAZ. BOLGHERI
LOC. CAPANNE, 27
57022 CASTAGNETO CARDUCCI [LI]
TEL. 0565762003
www.sassicaia.com

PRE-BOOKED VISITS
RESTAURANT SERVICE
ANNUAL PRODUCTION 790,000 bottles
HECTARES UNDER VINE 90.00

Sassicaia is perhaps Italy's best-known wine, proving able to cross national borders and the sector's confines to conquer well-deserved renown all over the world. This wine, and this venture, is of course linked to the land, but also to a dream, an idea, an intuition that could change history, the history of Bolgheri, of course, and largely of Italian winemaking. Untarnished charm and unique style, imitated but inimitable, the ace in Tenuta San Guida's sleeve is the location of its vineyards at Sassicaia, as well as Quercione , Aia Nuova and Castiglioncello. They say that great wines narrate the vintages perfectly, mastering comfortably good or excellent years and coming up with a stroke of genius in the difficult years. Well, this is the umpteenth vintage that proves just how insurmountably classy Sassicaia really is. Hence, an extraordinarily beguiling and wonderfully linear 2010, whose evolution in the bottle deserves to be followed.

● Bolgheri Sassicaia '10	▼▼▼ 8
● Guidalberto '11	▼▼ 6
● Le Difese '11	▼▼ 4
● Bolgheri Sassicaia '09	♀♀♀ 8
● Bolgheri Sassicaia '08	♀♀♀ 8
● Bolgheri Sassicaia '07	♀♀♀ 8
● Bolgheri Sassicaia '06	♀♀♀ 8
● Bolgheri Sassicaia '05	♀♀♀ 8
● Bolgheri Sassicaia '04	♀♀♀ 8
● Bolgheri Sassicaia '03	♀♀♀ 8
● Bolgheri Sassicaia '02	♀♀♀ 8
● Bolgheri Sassicaia '01	♀♀♀ 8
● Bolgheri Sassicaia '00	♀♀♀ 8
● Bolgheri Sassicaia '99	♀♀♀ 8
● Guidalberto '08	♀♀♀ 6
● Guidalberto '04	♀♀♀ 6

Podere San Lorenzo ✓

POD. SANLORENZO, 280
53024 MONTALCINO [SI]
TEL. 3396070930
www.poderesanlorenzo.net

CELLAR SALES
PRE-BOOKED VISITS
ANNUAL PRODUCTION 18,000 bottles
HECTARES UNDER VINE 4.50

The attention focused on San Lorenzo as one of the top wineries in the Montalcino area was in many ways triggered "from below". This certainly did not take place by chance, considering the combined commitment of three generations from founder Bramante to his son Paolo and on to grandson Luciano who is the estate's best-known and most active member today. The vineyards are situated at about 500 metrs altitude in the south-west sector and are a hotbed for Sangioveses that are vigorous and dynamic yet elegant and supple at the same time. This is also due to well-measured cellar techniques with lengthy maceration and ageing in 30-hectolitre Slavonian oak casks. San Lorenzo's star shines brightly again due to a couple of exceptional Brunellos full of character and substance. The 2008 Bramante is marked by a sweet yet sanguine vein, losing pace only slightly in the finish. The 2007 Bramante Riserva, themed around forest floor, is champing at the bit and shows no loss of pace.

● Brunello di Montalcino Bramante Ris. '07	▼▼▼ 8
● Brunello di Montalcino Bramante '08	▼▼ 6
● Rosso di Montalcino '10	▼▼ 3
● Brunello di Montalcino Bramante '07	♀♀♀ 6
● Brunello di Montalcino Bramante '04	♀♀ 6
● Rosso di Montalcino '09	♀♀ 3

San Michele a Torri

VIA SAN MICHELE, 36
50020 SCANDICCI [FI]
TEL. 055769111
www.fattoriasanmichele.it

CELLAR SALES
PRE-BOOKED VISITS
ANNUAL PRODUCTION 200,000 bottles
HECTARES UNDER VINE 55.00
VITICULTURE METHOD Certified Organic

The farm is situated in on the border between the Chianti Colli Fiorentini and Chianti Classico wine-growing zones, although about six hectares are in the Gallo Nero production area. Current owner Paolo Nocentini has brought the property back to life thanks to renewal and extension of the vineyards and organic farming techniques. Arable crops and olive oil are also important, with 30 hectares of olive groves. The strong connection with the local area is clear from activities inside the cellar and those open to the public: as well as direct sales, the estate has opened a shop and restaurant in Florence. The 2011 Murtas is intriguing. This sangiovese-cabernet sauvignon-colorino blend features intense aromas of liquorice and clove mingled with blackberry jam, followed by a supple mouth, with light tannins and a savoury finish. The 2008 Vin Santo offers dried peach, almond and hazelnut, with warmly creamy and enveloping body.

● Murtas '11	▼▼ 5
○ Vin Santo '08	▼▼ 6
● Chicchirossi '11	▼ 3
● Chianti Cl. Tenuta La Gabbiola '07	♀♀ 3*
● Chianti Colli Fiorentini '10	♀♀ 2*
● Chianti Colli Fiorentini '09	♀♀ 2*
● Chianti Colli Fiorentini S. Giovanni Novantasette Ris. '05	♀♀ 3
○ Chianti Colli Fiorentini Vin Santo '07	♀♀ 3
● Murtas '09	♀♀ 5
● Murtas '07	♀♀ 5

San Polino

LOC. CASTELNUOVO DELL'ABATE
POD. SAN POLINO, 163
53024 MONTALCINO [SI]
TEL. 0577835775
www.sanpolino.it

CELLAR SALES
PRE-BOOKED VISITS
ANNUAL PRODUCTION 10,000 bottles
HECTARES UNDER VINE 3.60
VITICULTURE METHOD Certified Biodynamic

We're certain that in the near future a lot more people will be talking about the wines and ideas of San Polino. This is a tiny farm with just over three hectares situated in the eastern part of Montalcino. The vineyards are farmed according to biodynamic methods, thanks also to the local mesoclimate which is extremely windy and to the well-drained land with sandy loam soil and extensive marly areas. This young business is growing exponentially, led by Luigi Fabbro, Katia Nussbaum and Aberto Gjilaska who make Brunellos that are impossible to categorize stylistically, the result of spontaneous fermentation and ageing in a combination of barriques, tonneaux and large Slavonian oak casks. The entire selection of Brunello di San Polino wines was brilliant, with a star performance from the 2007 Riserva, which truly is just a step away from the top rung. This is not an easy wine, with its dark, spicy profile that paves the way to the very close-knit tannins while indicating that it will be some time before it loosens off.

● Brunello di Montalcino Ris. '07	♟♟ 6
● Brunello di Montalcino '08	♟♟ 7
● Brunello di Montalcino Helichrysum '08	♟♟ 7
● Brunello di Montalcino '07	♟♟ 7
● Brunello di Montalcino '05	♟♟ 6
● Brunello di Montalcino '04	♟♟ 7
● Brunello di Montalcino '01	♟♟ 6
● Brunello di Montalcino Helichrysum '06	♟♟ 7
● Brunello di Montalcino Helichrysum '05	♟♟ 7
● Brunello di Montalcino Helichrysum '04	♟♟ 7
● Brunello di Montalcino Ris. '06	♟♟ 6
● Brunello di Montalcino Ris. '01	♟♟ 6
● Rosso di Montalcino '08	♟♟ 4
● Rosso di Montalcino '04	♟♟ 4

San Polo

POD. SAN POLO DI PODERNOVI, 161
53024 MONTALCINO [SI]
TEL. 0577835101
www.poggiosanpolo.com

CELLAR SALES
PRE-BOOKED VISITS
ANNUAL PRODUCTION 160,000 bottles
HECTARES UNDER VINE 17.00

Vintage after vintage this Montalcino estate owned by the Allegrini family, a classic name in Valpolicella, seems to be establishing its own specific identity. The 17 hectares of the San Polo estate are distributed over the south-eastern part of the DOC zone, at 450 metres, on a sort of natural terrace overlooking the Sant'Antimo valley. This area has strongly Mediterranean characteristics, expressed in fairly modern Brunellos which are fermented in concrete vats and aged in both barriques and medium-sized Slavonian and Allier oak casks. We get the impression that we could ask for a bit more personality from San Polo's small range but the two wines tasted this year are already a good start. The 2011 Rosso is meaty and spicy and the 2008 Brunello is well-orchestrated around touches of dark berry fruits, although the texture is a little dusty with slightly too predictable movement in the palate.

● Brunello di Montalcino '08	♟♟ 6
● Rosso di Montalcino '11	♟♟ 3
● Brunello di Montalcino '07	♟♟ 6
● Brunello di Montalcino '06	♟♟ 6
● Brunello di Montalcino '04	♟♟ 6
● Brunello di Montalcino '03	♟♟ 6
● Brunello di Montalcino '99	♟♟ 6
● Brunello di Montalcino '98	♟♟ 6
● Brunello di Montalcino Ris. '06	♟♟ 7
● Brunello di Montalcino Ris. '04	♟♟ 7
● Rosso di Montalcino '07	♟♟ 3
● Rubio '10	♟♟ 2*
● Rubio '08	♟♟ 2

San Quirico

LOC. PANCOLE, 39
53037 SAN GIMIGNANO [SI]
TEL. 0577955007
az.agr.sanquirico@libero.it

CELLAR SALES
PRE-BOOKED VISITS
ANNUAL PRODUCTION 200,000 bottles
HECTARES UNDER VINE 26.00
VITICULTURE METHOD Certified Organic

Andrea Vecchione's historic business has
owned this beautiful estate since the late
19th century. The location is north of San
Gimignano in the well-known and
favourable Pancole terroir which is capable
of producing highly recognizable wines with
strong personality. The vineyards are
planted at a variety of altitudes between
300 and 400 metres, on sandy soil of
marine origin. San Quirico remains faithful
to non-invasive agronomical procedures (in
fact the farm now has organic certification)
and produces authentically artisan wines
that express the very best of their subzone
and the pure features of the grapes used.
Anyone not yet convinced of the ability of
Vernaccia di San Gimignano ability to age
well should try the 2006 La Riserva Isabella
di San Quirico. Seven years after the
harvest, this white is nowhere past its
prime – on the contrary, it is in fine form
and full of flavours.

Sant'Agnese

LOC. CAMPO ALLE FAVE, 1
57025 PIOMBINO [LI]
TEL. 0565277069
www.santagnesefarm.it

CELLAR SALES
PRE-BOOKED VISITS
ANNUAL PRODUCTION 25,000 bottles
HECTARES UNDER VINE 6.00

The Sant'Agata estate is the result of a
great passion. It was established at the
behest of a man who initially chose this
area of Tuscan coastline for its peace and
quiet, and turned into a full-time
commitment. Thus the opportunity to take
over the estate through auction proved to
be an excellent move and led to a solid
productive business. Knowledge of tradition
and the sector, the assistance of skilled
experts and the right equipment
immediately yielded fruits in the form of
fine quality wines. Today the next
generation run the estate, with Paolo in
sales and Alessandro in charge of the
vineyards. The 2008 Spirto, a blend of
cabernet sauvignon and merlot, has a
complex aromatic profile, which combines
vegetal and full fruity aromas with spicy
notes, offering a solid, inviting body and a
finish full of flavours. The 100% sangiovese
2008 Libatio is fresh and lively, where
elegant fruity aromas of cherry and plum
join a stylishly supple and nicely weighted
body leading to a lingering, layered finish.

○ Vernaccia di S. Gimignano Isabella Ris. '06	♟♟♟♟ 4
● Chianti Colli Senesi '11	♟ 2
● San Gimignano Merlot '08	♟ 3
○ Vernaccia di S. Gimignano '12	♟ 2
○ Vernaccia di S. Gimignano Isabella Ris. '04	♟♟♟ 3
○ Vernaccia di S. Gimignano '10	♟♟ 2*
○ Vernaccia di S. Gimignano I Campi Santi Ris. '05	♟♟ 2*
○ Vernaccia di S. Gimignano Isabella Ris. '05	♟♟ 4
○ Vernaccia di S. Gimignano Isabella Ris. '99	♟♟ 3

● Spirto '08	♟♟ 5
● Libatio '08	♟♟ 4
● Val di Cornia Rubido '08	♟♟ 2*
⊙ A Rose is a Rose '12	♟ 2
○ Val di Cornia Kalendamaia '12	♟ 2
● I Fiori Blu '08	♟♟ 6
● I Fiori Blu '07	♟♟ 4
● Spirto '06	♟♟ 5
○ Val di Cornia Kalendamaia '11	♟♟ 2*
● Val di Cornia Rubido '09	♟♟ 2*

Santa Lucia

Fraz. Fonteblanda
via Aurelia, 264
58010 Orbetello [GR]
Tel. 0564885474
www.azsantalucia.it

CELLAR SALES
PRE-BOOKED VISITS
ACCOMMODATION
ANNUAL PRODUCTION 100,000 bottles
HECTARES UNDER VINE 25.00

On the Santa Lucia estate there is a
vineyard, still productive, dating back to
1886, the year in which the Scotto family
began its historic connection with
wine-growing. New vineyards were planted
and production was underway until 1977
when the estate was totally modernized,
new family members entered the business
bringing their own skills alongside love for
the land and recognition of its potential, and
effected changes and improvements to the
quality of the products. Much of the work is
still manual today, as it used to be, due to
the uniquely steep configuration of the land
and the drystone walls The new cellar was
officially opened in 2011. In the pleasant
2011 Morellino Tore del Moro, fruity notes
of currant and blackberry mix with hints of
aromatic herbs. The palate has good impact
but is not invasive, and a well-balanced
roundness leads to a juicy, enjoyable finish.
The easy-drinking 2011 Morellino A Luciano
is subtle, showing currant notes with an
edgy silhouette and inviting body. The 2012
Vermentino Brigante is floral and zesty.

○ Capalbio Vermentino Brigante '12	♥♥ 2*
● Morellino di Scansano A Luciano '11	♥♥ 2*
● Morellino di Scansano Tore del Moro '11	♥♥ 2*
○ Ansonica Costa dell'Argentario '12	♥ 2
○ Ansonica Costa dell'Argentario Santa Lucia '08	♀♀ 2
● Betto '08	♀♀ 3
● Betto '05	♀♀ 3
● Cabernet Sauvignon '04	♀♀ 3
● Capalbio Cabernet Sauvignon '05	♀♀ 5
● Losco '10	♀♀ 2*
● Morellino di Scansano Tore del Moro '10	♀♀ 2*

Fattoria Santa Vittoria

loc. Pozzo
via Piana, 43
52045 Foiano della Chiana [AR]
Tel. 057566807
www.fattoriasantavittoria.com

CELLAR SALES
PRE-BOOKED VISITS
ACCOMMODATION
ANNUAL PRODUCTION 37,000 bottles
HECTARES UNDER VINE 35.00

This typical Tuscan farm, established in the
18th century in the Valdichiana hills,
currently belongs to the Niccolai family and
is run by Marta with her father Francesco,
aided by a team of experts. A variety of
different grapes are grown here ranging
from native local and almost extinct varieties
to others less commonly found in the area,
such as nero d'Avola. The result is a range
of innovative, always interesting wines.
Santa Vittoria also participates in a research
programme with the Tuscan region's
Experimental Wine-growing Institute and in
a project to improve sweet wines promoted
by the province of Arezzo. The estate also
produces olive oil and offers holiday
accommodation. The 100% pugnitello
2010 Leopoldo reaches the finals for the
first time. On the nose, it offers intense
leather and tobacco with liquorice notes,
while a layered body reveals prominent but
not overpowering tannins, a good acid
vein, followed by a progressive finish. The
2008 Vin Santo tempts with dates, dried figs
and honey. Caressingly dense and creamy in
the mouth, it has a leisurely, relaxed finish.

● Leopoldo '10	♥♥ 3*
○ Valdichiana Vin Santo '08	♥♥ 4
● Conforta '11	♥ 4
● Poggio al Tempio '10	♥ 3
⊙ Pugnitello Rosato '12	♥ 2
○ Val di Chiana Grechetto '12	♥ 2
● Leopoldo '08	♀♀ 3
● Poggio al Tempio '09	♀♀ 3
● Poggio del Tempio '08	♀♀ 3
● Scannagallo '09	♀♀ 2*
○ Valdichiana Vin Santo Ris. '07	♀♀ 4

Podere Sapaio

LOC. LO SCOPAIO, 212
57022 CASTAGNETO CARDUCCI [LI]
TEL. 0565765187
www.sapaio.com

PRE-BOOKED VISITS
ANNUAL PRODUCTION 75,000 bottles
HECTARES UNDER VINE 25.00

Podere Sapaio is above all a lovely project, thanks to Massimo Piccini who thought it up and gradually put it into practice, starting in 1999, choosing the right people to build up the business. The location was also a deciding factor of course, and proved ideal for experimentation and the team's innovative ideas. 25 of the estate's 40 hectares are under vine, located on sandy, limestone soil and planted with the classic local grape varieties. The wines reflect a well-focused style, accomplished, precise and modern. The 2010 Bolgheri Rosso Superiore has a tried and true profile, despite a difficult vintage. The nose is dark, revealing black fruits and toasty hints with a hint of coffee and some initial foxy notes. The palate follows in the same vein, with good pulp and plenty of potential, although a few tertiary notes need to be reabsorbed.

● Bolgheri Sup. Sapaio '10	♟♟♟ 6
● Bolgheri Volpolo '11	♟♟ 4
● Bolgheri Sup. Sapaio '09	♟♟♟ 6
● Bolgheri Sup. Sapaio '08	♟♟♟ 6
● Bolgheri Sup. Sapaio '07	♟♟♟ 6
● Bolgheri Sup. Sapaio '06	♟♟♟ 6
● Bolgheri Sup. Sapaio '05	♟♟ 6
● Bolgheri Sup. Sapaio '04	♟♟ 6
● Bolgheri Volpolo '08	♟♟ 4
● Bolgheri Volpolo '07	♟♟ 4
● Bolgheri Volpolo '06	♟♟ 4

Fattoria Sardi Giustiniani

LOC. MONTE SAN QUIRICO
VIA DELLA MAULINA, 747
55100 LUCCA
TEL. 0583341230
www.sardigiustiniani.com

CELLAR SALES
PRE-BOOKED VISITS
ACCOMMODATION AND RESTAURANT SERVICE
ANNUAL PRODUCTION 70,000 bottles
HECTARES UNDER VINE 18.00
VITICULTURE METHOD Certified Organic

Fattoria Sardi Giustiniani is a short distance from the famous walls of Lucca, along the road overlooking the sea. Of the estate's 45 hectares, 18 are under vine. The area has a typically mild, breezy climate and heterogeneous soil features varying from one vineyard to another. Since 2002 Contessa Sardi's nephews Jacopo and Matteo Giustiniani have run the estate, effecting a tangible turning point in the wine-growing activity. The vineyards are currently being converted to organic farming methods and the wines seem worthy of attention: never overly packaged, they show a certain precision and a well-focused profile. The estate has offered a few impressive tastings in recent times. We particularly like two wines, the 2011 Villa Sardi and the 2011 Rosso. They may not be the most complex wines out there but they have fragrance and flavour, and are full of succulent crispness. We like them fractionally better than the 2010 Sebastiano, which may be lovely and mature but is also slightly too sweet.

○ Colline Lucchesi Bianco '12	♟♟ 1*
● Colline Lucchesi Rosso Villa Sardi '11	♟♟ 2*
● Fattoria Sardi Rosso '11	♟ 3
● Colline Lucchesi Merlot Sebastiano '10	♟ 3
⊙ Colline Lucchesi Rosato Villa Sardi '12	♟ 2
○ Colline Lucchesi Sauvignon Fattoria Sardi '12	♟ 3
● Colline Lucchesi Merlot Sebastiano '09	♟♟ 4
● Colline Lucchesi Quinis '06	♟♟ 3
● Colline Lucchesi Quinis '04	♟♟ 3
● Colline Lucchesi Rosso Villa Sardi '10	♟♟ 3
● Colline Lucchesi Sebastiano '06	♟♟ 4
● Colline Lucchesi Sebastiano '04	♟♟ 4
● Colline Lucchesi Sebastiano '03	♟♟ 4
● Fattoria Sardi Rosso '10	♟♟ 4

Michele Satta

LOC. CASONE UGOLINO, 23
57022 CASTAGNETO CARDUCCI [LI]
TEL. 0565773041
www.michelesatta.com

CELLAR SALES
PRE-BOOKED VISITS
ANNUAL PRODUCTION 180,000 bottles
HECTARES UNDER VINE 26.00

Michele Satta started up his Bolgheri winery in the late 1980s, at a favourable and pioneering time for local wine-growing. He is, quite rightly, a well-known character, like his wines, and has succeeded in building a very personal and original wine-growing structure for this area over the years. As well as the usual non-native varieties, like cabernet and merlot, Satta immediately focused on sangiovese as an interesting variety not widely grown in this area. The wines are generally expressive and authentic, with their sharp edges and tannic extraction. We like the 2011 Bolgheri Rosso, which has a lovely nose full of fresh fruit and flowers, with a hint of spice and a lovely fluid mouth. The 2010 Piastraia is on a par, with its nice focus on drinkability and natural expression, rather than concentration, which was not really in keeping with the vintage. The whites are pleasant.

● Bolgheri Rosso '11	♟♟ 3
● Bolgheri Rosso Piastraia '10	♟♟ 5
○ Costa di Giulia '12	♟ 3
○ Giovin Re '12	♟ 6
● Syrah '11	♟ 5
● Bolgheri Rosso Piastraia '02	♟♟♟ 6
● Bolgheri Rosso Piastraia '01	♟♟♟ 6
● Bolgheri Rosso Piastraia '08	♟♟ 6
● Bolgheri Rosso Piastraia '00	♟♟ 6
● Bolgheri Rosso Sup. I Castagni '08	♟♟ 8
● Bolgheri Rosso Sup. I Castagni '03	♟♟ 8
● Bolgheri Rosso Sup. I Castagni '01	♟♟ 7
● Bolgheri Rosso Sup. I Castagni '00	♟♟ 7
● Cavaliere '05	♟♟ 7
● Cavaliere '01	♟♟ 7

Fattoria Selvapiana

LOC. SELVAPIANA, 43
50068 RUFINA [FI]
TEL. 0558369848
www.selvapiana.it

CELLAR SALES
PRE-BOOKED VISITS
ANNUAL PRODUCTION 220,000 bottles
HECTARES UNDER VINE 60.00

This typical Tuscan farm, whose buildings include two medieval towers, has belonged to the Giuntini family for five generations, thanks to Michele who bought it in 1827. Current owner Francesco Giuntini Antinori can take the credit for upholding the name of Chianti Rufina, especially when this subzone risked cancellation. Running the estate are Federico and Silvia Giuntini Masseti. Selvapiana is a traditional farm which prioritizes the cultivation and vinification of the classic sangiovese. Some very old vintages are preserved in the cellar to demonstrate the outstanding ageing capacity of this wine when produced locally. The 2010 Riserva Bucerchiale shows potential in terms of structure and already has a rich and varied nose ranging from mineral notes to leather and tobacco, with a hint of jam. The mouthfeel is powerful, while the tannins are still to expand but are not aggressive. The lip-smacking 2011 Chianti Rufina is full of fresh flavours.

● Chianti Rufina Bucerchiale Ris. '10	♟♟ 5
● Chianti Rufina '11	♟♟ 2*
● Chianti Rufina '10	♟♟ 2*
● Chianti Rufina '09	♟♟ 2
● Chianti Rufina Bucerchiale Ris. '09	♟♟ 5
○ Chianti Rufina Vin Santo '04	♟♟ 5
○ Fornace '09	♟♟ 5
○ Passito '03	♟♟ 5

Sensi

VIA CERBAIA, 107
51035 LAMPORECCHIO [PT]
TEL. 057382910
www.sensivini.com

CELLAR SALES
PRE-BOOKED VISITS
ANNUAL PRODUCTION 2,000,000 bottles
HECTARES UNDER VINE 50.00
VITICULTURE METHOD Certified Organic

The Calappiano farm in Vinci is one of the leading local wine producing estates. It was built around the year 1500 at the behest of Grand Duke Francesco I de' Medici and was once of the first examples of a Tuscan wine- farm with wine production as its primary activity. Today the property is owned by the Sensi family who have worked for many years in the wine sector. Family forefather Pietro Sensi began selling wine in the district markets in the area. Today the estate trades at an international level and a reconstruction project is underway in the cellars, along with revaluation of the vineyards in order to refine a style that favours drinkability and freshness. The wines performed well overall. Of note were the austere 2010 Chianti Dalcampo Riserva, the fresh and enthusiastic 2012 Chianti Campoluce, the elegant sangiovese-colarino blend 2011 Lungarno della Fattoria Calappiano, bursting with mineral notes, the 2011 softly charming Bolgheri Sabbiato, and the impressively structured 2008 Brunello Boscosclvo.

● Bolgheri Sabbiato '11	♟♟ 5
● Brunello di Montalcino Boscoselvo '08	♟♟ 7
● Chianti Campoluce '12	♟♟ 2*
● Chianti Dalcampo Ris. '10	♟♟ 3
● Lungarno Fattoria Calappiano '11	♟♟ 3
● Chianti Dalcampo '12	♟ 2
● Chianti Vinciano Fattoria Calappiano '12	♟ 3
● Chianti Vinciano Fattoria Calappiano Ris. '10	♟ 4
● Mantello '11	♟ 4
● Testardo '11	♟ 4
○ Vernaccia di S. Gimignano Collegiata '12	♟ 2
● Chianti Dalcampo '11	♟♟ 2*
● Chianti Dalcampo Ris. '09	♟♟ 3

Tenuta di Sesta

FRAZ. CASTELNUOVO DELL'ABATE
LOC. SESTA
53024 MONTALCINO [SI]
TEL. 0577835612
www.tenutadisesta.it

CELLAR SALES
PRE-BOOKED VISITS
ANNUAL PRODUCTION 150,000 bottles
HECTARES UNDER VINE 30.00

The very name of this estate is a reference to the terroir implicit in the Ciacci family's Brunellos. This is the Sesta area, an ideal contact point between Sant'Angelo in Colle and Castelnuovo dell'Abate, in the southern part of Montalcino. This has always been considered one of the best suited growing areas in the DOC, especially in cooler years, with generally lean soil, rich in limestone with some seams of tuffstone. Despite its long history the Sangioveses of Tenuta di Sesta have only come into their own in recent years, thanks to their discreet but durable temperament, skilfully underlined by lengthy maceration in medium-sized oak casks. Tenuta di Sesta has a stylistically harmonious range. The 2011 Rosso and 2008 Brunello both have easy drinking appeal, with supporting acidity and nice contrasts. The 2007 Riserva is even better, despite it being a hot year. It is delicate and floral, although a little sterile where the fruit is concerned.

● Brunello di Montalcino Ris. '07	♟♟ 7
● Brunello di Montalcino '08	♟♟ 5
● Poggio d'Arna '11	♟♟ 2*
● Rosso di Montalcino '11	♟♟ 3
● Brunello di Montalcino '07	♟♟ 5
● Brunello di Montalcino '05	♟♟ 5
● Brunello di Montalcino '01	♟♟ 6
● Brunello di Montalcino Ris. '06	♟♟ 7
● Brunello di Montalcino Ris. '01	♟♟ 7
● Brunello di Montalcino Ris. '95	♟♟ 8
● Rosso di Montalcino '10	♟♟ 3*

Sesti - Castello di Argiano

FRAZ. SANT'ANGELO IN COLLE
LOC. CASTELLO DI ARGIANO
53024 MONTALCINO [SI]
TEL. 0577843921
www.sestiwine.com

**CELLAR SALES
PRE-BOOKED VISITS
ANNUAL PRODUCTION 61,000 bottles
HECTARES UNDER VINE 9.00**

Giuseppe and Elisa Sesti usually offer a
well-paced, graceful, strong and characterful
interpretation of the south-western slope of
Montalcino. Their Castello di Argiano is
totally immersed in woodlands and
Mediterranean vegetation in an uncommonly
beautiful area with sea breezes and sandy
soil rich in tuffstone. The variety of this terroir
is in many ways unique, and combines with
an equally particular sensitivity on the part of
the producers, to produce Brunellos
influenced by philosophical and humanistic
inspiration rather than plain technique. This
makes an observation and understanding of
individual vintages more important than the
methods used in the vineyard and cellar.
With its well-thought out set of aromas
conveying peach, pennyroyal and clove, the
2007 Brunello Phenomena Riserva could not
express its territory more fully. On the palate,
it is downright breathtaking combining great
backbone, volume and flavour with subtle
tannins. The 2008 Brunello is only
marginally below.

● Brunello di Montalcino	
Phenomena Ris. '07	▼▼▼ 8
● Brunello di Montalcino '08	▼▼ 6
● Rosso di Montalcino '11	▼▼ 4
● Grangiovese '11	▼ 2
● Brunello di Montalcino '06	▽▽▽ 6
● Brunello di Montalcino	
Phenomena Ris. '01	▽▽▽ 8
● Brunello di Montalcino Ris. '04	▽▽▽ 8
● Brunello di Montalcino '07	▽▽ 6
● Brunello di Montalcino	
Phenomena Ris. '06	▽▽ 8
● Rosso di Montalcino '10	▽▽ 4

Tenuta Sette Ponti

LOC. VIGNA DI PALLINO
52029 CASTIGLION FIBOCCHI [AR]
TEL. 0575477857
www.tenutasetteponti.it

**CELLAR SALES
PRE-BOOKED VISITS
ACCOMMODATION
ANNUAL PRODUCTION 185,000 bottles
HECTARES UNDER VINE 50.00**

The estate was founded here in the land of
sangiovese and Chianti, and was named
after the seven bridges road linking the
banks of the Arno river between Florence
and Arezzo. In the 1950s the Moretti family
bought from the Savoia family these lands
in what had for centuries been a recognized
prime wine-growing location. The current
owner, Antonio Moretti, has combined
passion and dedication for his own sector of
fashion with the same commitment to the
production of elegant wines that also
express the Made in Italy style. As well as
Arezzo, Moretti owns estates in Bolgheri,
Maremma and Sicily. Once again, Oreno
gains a Tre Bicchieri. The 2010 blend of
merlot, cabernet sauvignon and petit verdot
has a subtle nose, with forest floor aromas
over a cherry and blackberry base and
topped with balsamic notes. The entry into
the palate is relaxed and soft, with
well-amalgamated tannins, leading to a
rising finish. The predominantly sangiovese
2011 Crognolo is tangy and lively.

● Oreno '10	▼▼▼ 7
● Crognolo '11	▼▼ 4
○ Anni '12	▼ 3
● Chianti V. di Pallino '11	▼ 2
● Oreno '09	▽▽▽ 7
● Oreno '05	▽▽▽ 7
● Oreno '00	▽▽▽ 5
● Crognolo '10	▽▽ 4
● Crognolo '09	▽▽ 4
● Crognolo '06	▽▽ 4
● Oreno '08	▽▽ 7
● Oreno '07	▽▽ 7
● Oreno '06	▽▽ 7
● Poggio al Lupo '09	▽▽ 4

Fattoria Sorbaiano

LOC. SORBAIANO
56040 MONTECATINI VAL DI CECINA [PI]
TEL. 058830243
www.fattoriasorbaiano.it

CELLAR SALES
PRE-BOOKED VISITS
ACCOMMODATION
ANNUAL PRODUCTION 100,000 bottles
HECTARES UNDER VINE 27.00

Situated not far from the old medieval hamlet of Montecatini Val di Cecina, in the past Sorbaiano was a feudal estate belonging to the Inghirami family of Volterra. It was purchased by the current owners in the 1950s. The fields and vineyards cover land stretching from the sea to the city of Volterra. The farm also produces Vin Santo made employing traditional methods and grape-drying on racks. The cellar was recently rebuilt, with renovations to the storage area and bottling line. The 2010 Rosso delle Miniere is enjoyable. This sangiovese, malvasia nera and cabernet franc blend has a crisp, lively nose, with ripe wild berry notes. The body unfolds slowly into a lovely long, pondered finish. The monovarietal cabernet franc 2010 Velathri has lip-smacking notes of green bell pepper and aromatic herbs in a sound, juicy body, followed by an intensely vibrant finish. The 2007 Vin Santo has evolved aromas of almond and dried fig and a tempting, creamy palate. The two whites boast an intriguing acid vein.

○ Montescudaio Bianco '12	♟♟	2*
○ Montescudaio Bianco Lucestraia '11	♟♟	3
● Montescudaio Rosso delle Miniere '10	♟♟	4
● Velathri '10	♟♟	3
○ Vin Santo di Montescudaio '07	♟♟	4
● Montescudaio Rosso '11	♟	2
● Pian del Conte '10	♟	3
⊙ Rosato di Toscana '12	♟	2
○ Montescudaio Bianco Lucestraia '09	♟♟	3
● Montescudaio Rosso delle Miniere '09	♟♟	4
● Pian del Conte '08	♟♟	3
● Velathri '09	♟♟	3

Tenimenti Angelini

LOC. VAL DI CAVA
53024 MONTALCINO [SI]
TEL. 0577804101
www.tenimentiangelini.it

CELLAR SALES
PRE-BOOKED VISITS
ANNUAL PRODUCTION 250,000 bottles
HECTARES UNDER VINE 55.00

This profile describes the wines produced by the Angelini family in the three Tuscan estates they have owned since 1994: Val di Suga at Montalcino, Tre Rose at Montepulciano and San Leonino at Castellina in Chianti. Their other projects will be described in their respective regional profiles for Veneto, Friuli and Marche. On this occasion, too, we will focus mainly on the work carried out in over 50 hectares planted with Montalcino's sangiovese grosso, distributed over three somewhat complementary areas: Val di Suga and Vigna del Lago to the north-east, Vigneto San Polo to the south-west and Vigna Spuntali to the south-east, after which the cru is named. A range of wines that confirms the successful bridging of classic and modern style: all that's missing is one exceptional feat. The Brunellos are underlined with a Vigna Spuntali 2007 that offers a discreet, succulent expression of the warm, dry year, just lacking a touch of tannic balance.

● Brunello di Montalcino V. Spuntali Val di Suga '07	♟♟	8
● Brunello di Montalcino Val di Suga '08	♟♟	5
● Brunello di Montalcino Val di Suga Ris. '07	♟♟	5
○ Busillis Tenuta Trerose '12	♟♟	3
● Rosso di Montepulciano Tenuta Tre Rose '11	♟♟	2*
○ Vin Santo di Montepulciano Tenuta Tre Rose '05	♟♟	5
● Nobile di Montepulciano Tenuta Trerose '10	♟	3
● Nobile di Montepulciano Villa Romizzi Tenuta Trerose '09	♟	5
⊙ Rosato di Toscana Tenuta Trerose '12	♟	2

Tenimenti Luigi d'Alessandro

VIA MANZANO, 15
52042 CORTONA [AR]
TEL. 0575618667
www.tenimentidalessandro.it

PRE-BOOKED VISITS
ACCOMMODATION
ANNUAL PRODUCTION 130,000 bottles
HECTARES UNDER VINE 37.00

The winery was established in 1967 when the d'Alessandro family purchased 100 hectares in the heart of the huge Manzano estate in Val di Chiana, which dates back to the 18th century. After several years of soil study and experimentation, in 1993 syrah was selected as the preferred variety for this area and was planted at high density. In the intervening years the whole of the Cortona area has been characterized by this grape variety which has found its ideal cradle here. Today the estate is owned by Massimo d'Alessandro and Giuseppe Calabresi who have turned the brand name and quality of the products around since 2007. Into the finals for the Syrah Borgo Vecchie Vigne 2101 with subtle, stylish aromas combining spicy hints of black pepper and cinnamon, lively redcurrants, and pipe tobacco. The palate is generous and rounded with subtle tannins and a pleasant crescendo finish. The Borgo 2011 is captivating while the Fontarca 2011 is citrussy, fresh and edgy.

● Cortona Syrah Borgo V. V. '10	▼▼ 5
● Cortona Syrah Borgo '11	▼▼ 3
○ Fontarca Viognier '11	▼▼ 2*
○ Bianco del Borgo '12	▼ 3
● Cortona Il Bosco '09	▽▽▽ 6
● Cortona Il Bosco '06	▽▽▽ 6
● Cortona Il Bosco '04	▽▽▽ 5
● Cortona Il Bosco '03	▽▽▽ 5
● Cortona Il Bosco '01	▽▽▽ 6
● Cortona Syrah Migliara '08	▽▽▽ 8
● Cortona Syrah Migliara '07	▽▽▽ 8
● Cortona Syrah '10	▽▽ 3
● Cortona Syrah Migliara '09	▽▽ 8
○ Fontarca Sauvignon '10	▽▽ 5

Terenzi

LOC. MONTEDONICO SNC
58054 SCANSANO [GR]
TEL. 0564599601
www.terenzi.eu

CELLAR SALES
PRE-BOOKED VISITS
ACCOMMODATION AND RESTAURANT SERVICE
ANNUAL PRODUCTION 350,000 bottles
HECTARES UNDER VINE 60.00

Maremma is a unique place, wild and rich in vineyards and olive groves, extending from the hills to the sea. The estate's basic wish is to promote this area worldwide and this ambition has led the Terenzi family to express their love for the place through precisely and expertly made wines, following production procedures that respect the habitat and environment. In just a few years they have managed to create wines that fulfil their expectations, providing an accurate impression of the terroir of origin. As well as wine, the estate produces extra-virgin olive oil and grappa, and offers holiday accommodation. Another Tre Bicchieri for the Morellino Riserva Madrechiesa 2010, thanks to fresh, delicate aromas blending bay leaves and sage with balsamic hints and fruity sensations of strawberries and blueberries. The palate is sinuous, stylish and slender with an excellent flavour and extremely pleasing, lingering finish. We also enjoyed the Morellino 2012 with fruity sensations, an edgy, slender mouth and nice clean finish.

● Morellino di Scansano Madrechiesa Ris. '10	▼▼▼ 5
● Morellino di Scansano '12	▼▼ 2*
○ Montedonico '12	▼▼ 3
● Morellino di Scansano Ris. '10	▼▼ 3
○ Balbino '12	▼ 2
● Bramaluce '12	▼ 3
● Morellino di Scansano Madrechiesa Ris. '09	▽▽▽ 5
○ Balbino '11	▽▽ 2*
● Morellino di Scansano '11	▽▽ 2*
● Morellino di Scansano '10	▽▽ 2*
● Morellino di Scansano Ris. '09	▽▽ 3*
● Morellino di Scansano Ris. '08	▽▽ 3*

Terradonnà

Loc. Notri, 78
57028 Suvereto [LI]
Tel. 0565829008
www.terradonna.it

CELLAR SALES
PRE-BOOKED VISITS
ANNUAL PRODUCTION 26,000 bottles
HECTARES UNDER VINE 6.00

Here in the Suvereto DOC zone the Collavari family have owned the estate for over 50 years, but more recently decided to focus more specifically on wine production. The wines are named after minerals, the precious particles present in the earth which endow the wines with particular local characteristics. The grape varieties planted here are the result of precise selections and this, combined with careful production techniques, enables the winery to produce excellent results. The Prasio 2010, cabernet sauvignon and merlot, displays vibrant aromas of blackberry jam and minerally sensations, with a well-rounded, velvety, tasty palate and incisive, succulent flavour. The Gaietto 2010, from a similar blend with the addition of sangiovese, has an uncomplicated, linear, fresh nose with a relaxed, balanced and nicely organized palate. The Okenio 2010 displays subtle aromas with floral sensations and hints of aromatic herbs and black berry fruit. A balanced entry with slightly stiff tannins opening out into a long, pleasant flavour.

● Giaietto '10	▼▼ 2*
● Prasio '10	▼▼ 3
● Val di Cornia Okenio '10	▼▼ 5
○ Faden '12	▼ 2
○ Kalsi '12	▼ 2
● Spato '10	▼ 2
○ Kalsi '11	♈ 3
● Prasio '09	♈ 3
● Spato '09	♈ 3

Teruzzi & Puthod

Loc. Casale, 19
53037 San Gimignano [SI]
Tel. 0577940143
www.teruzzieputhod.it

CELLAR SALES
PRE-BOOKED VISITS
ANNUAL PRODUCTION 1,200,000 bottles
HECTARES UNDER VINE 90.00

Big numbers and general high quality at what might be termed the flagship of San Gimignano wine production. The estate took its first steps way back in the 1970s and grew to be one of the stars in the Campari sky. Breaking into such an important group made it possible for this estate to carry out a significant renewal process in all aspects and workings of the production process. This has been a decisive factor in establishing a quality that takes an authoritative place on the market with fully satisfying results. The wines are well-put together, with stylistic precision, and represent a more than reliable front door into the zone's most classic designations. The Vernaccia Riserva 2010 demonstrates this with aromas combining yeasty and breadcrust sensations with a confident embrace of citrus aromas. A good impact on the palate, maybe a little slender and tight but a very good incisive flavour. The Vernaccia 2012 is simpler but still very pleasant overall.

○ Vernaccia di S. Gimignano '12	▼▼ 2*
○ Vernaccia di S. Gimignano Ris. '10	▼▼ 4
● Arcidiavolo '08	♈ 5
● Arcidiavolo '07	♈ 5
● Peperino '08	♈ 2*
● Peperino '07	♈ 2*
○ Terre di Tufi '09	♈ 4
○ Vernaccia di S. Gimignano '11	♈ 2*
○ Vernaccia di S. Gimignano '09	♈ 2*
○ Vernaccia di S. Gimignano '08	♈ 2*

Testamatta

VIA DI VINCIGLIATA, 19
50014 FIESOLE [FI]
TEL. 055597289
www.bibigraetz.com

PRE-BOOKED VISITS
ANNUAL PRODUCTION 500,000 bottles
HECTARES UNDER VINE 10.00

Italo-Norwegian producer and artist Bibi
Graetz is the owner of her family's
Testamatta estate which produces Tuscan
wines from land on the Fiesole hills.
Production began in the 1990s thanks to the
idea of using modern criteria to value the
rich potential of the vines in their plots,
including sangiovese, canaiolo and colorino
vines between 30 and 60 years old. The
wines are modern in style with distinct
personality. The estate has also begun
making wine on Giglio island, thus
contributing to a renaissance of the local
winemaking tradition. Into the finals for the
Soffocone 2011, mainly sangiovese with a
small addition of colorino and canaiolo: fresh,
lively aromas of forest floor with black berry
fruit and a supple impact on the mouth,
remaining flavoursome and harmonious into
the very satisfying finish. We also liked the
rounded, balanced Testamatta 2010, a
monovarietal sangiovese.

● Soffocone di Vincigliata '11	♟♟ 5
● Grilli del Testamatta '10	♟♟ 5
○ Bugia '12	♟ 6
● Canaiolo '09	♟ 8
○ Casamatta Bianco '12	♟ 2
● Casamatta Rosso '12	♟ 2
● Chianti La Cicala '11	♟ 2
○ Cicala '12	♟ 2
● Colore '07	♟ 8
● It's a Game '11	♟ 4
○ Vermentino '12	♟ 2
○ Casamatta Bianco '11	♟♟ 2*
○ Gigliese '11	♟♟ 3
● It's a Game '10	♟♟ 2*

Tiezzi

VIA DELLE QUERCI
53024 MONTALCINO [SI]
TEL. 0577848187
www.tiezzivini.it

CELLAR SALES
PRE-BOOKED VISITS
ANNUAL PRODUCTION 23,000 bottles
HECTARES UNDER VINE 5,50

Here's another strongly traditional winery
that seems to have shot up in quality in the
last few years. Or perhaps it's just us
paying more attention to the almost
rarefied, yet dynamic and characterful,
atmosphere of the Brunellos moulded by
Enzo Tiezzi. This well-respected agronomist
and oenologist from Montalcino decided to
go it alone in the Eighties, purchasing first
the Cerrino and Cigaleta estates and then
developing Soccorso, after which the cru is
named. This is the location of the winery
headquarters and cellar, with wooden
fermentation vats and 35/40-hectolitre
Slavonian oak casks for maturation. A
well-stocked hand of cards with an
outstanding performance from the Rosso di
Montalcino Poggio Cerrino 2011, a dour
wine with plenty of grip and energy. A
confident finalist like the Brunello Vigna del
Soccorso 2008 whose only shortcoming is
an excessively linear and severe profile
though we fully appreciate its earthy, salty
local character.

● Brunello di Montalcino V. del Soccorso '08	♟♟ 6
● Rosso di Montalcino Poggio Cerrino '11	♟♟ 3*
● Brunello di Montalcino V. del Soccorso Ris. '07	♟♟ 6
● Brunello di Montalcino Poggio Cerrino '08	♟ 5
● Brunello di Montalcino V. del Soccorso '07	♟♟ 5
● Brunello di Montalcino V. del Soccorso '07	♟♟ 6
● Brunello di Montalcino V. del Soccorso '06	♟♟ 6

Tolaini

LOC. VALLENUOVA
SP 9 DI PIEVASCIATA, 28
53019 CASTELNUOVO BERARDENGA [SI]
TEL. 0577356972
www.tolaini.it

CELLAR SALES
PRE-BOOKED VISITS
ANNUAL PRODUCTION 250,000 bottles
HECTARES UNDER VINE 50.00
VITICULTURE METHOD Certified Organic

Pierluigi Tolaini made his fortune as an emigrant to Canada and began his wine-growing project in 1998. He made his first wines in 2002 and having attuned his approach to a rather complex area like Chianti the estate, between Pianella and Vagliagli, set off on the path of absolute excellence. This is achieved thanks to carefully supervised wine-growing procedures and strict cellar techniques which avoid forcing, starting with well-controlled use of mainly small oak casks. The beautifully drinkable Chianti Classico Riserva 2010 owes its pleasing character to velvety tannins and balsamic freshness. Outstanding aromas of red berry fruit on the nose are followed by floral hints and quina, while the palate is mouthwatering and fluid with a deep, very clean finish.

● Chianti Cl. Ris. '10	▼▼5
● Picconero '09	♟♟♟8
● Valdisanti '08	♟♟♟4
● Al Passo '09	♟♟4
● Al Passo '07	♟♟4
● Al Passo '06	♟♟4
● Chianti Cl. Ris. '08	♟♟5
● Picconero '08	♟♟8
● Picconero '07	♟♟8
● Picconero '06	♟♟8
● Valdisanti '09	♟♟8

Fattoria Torre a Cona

LOC. SAN DONATO IN COLLINA
50010 RIGNANO SULL'ARNO [FI]
TEL. 055699000
www.villatorreacona.com

CELLAR SALES
PRE-BOOKED VISITS
ACCOMMODATION
ANNUAL PRODUCTION 30,000 bottles
HECTARES UNDER VINE 14.00

Fattoria Torre a Cona is situated on the hills south of Florence, an area traditionally associated with wine-growing. Work carried out by the Conti Rossi di Montelera includes recently replanting of the vineyards and modernization of the cellars. The oldest nucleus of buildings dates back to the year 1000, and the villa was rebuilt in the 18th century. Today the old barn houses the tasting room while the various houses on the estate have been transformed into holiday apartments. The wines are produced in the Colli Fiorentino designation, and sangiovese is therefore the grape primarily grown here. The Riserva Badia a Corte 2010 is very interesting: marked fresh sensations on the nose of wild black berries perked up by varied hints of aromatic herbs; a pleasant impact on the palate, well-sustained but not excessive, with tannins blending into the alcohol and long, supple finish. The Chianti Colli Fiorentini 2011 is also impressive, with more austere tannins, a faithful child of the vintage year.

● Chianti Colli Fiorentini Badia a Corte Ris. '10	▼▼4
● Chianti Colli Fiorentini Conti Rossi di Montelera '11	▼▼3
● Merlot '11	▼▼3
● Chianti Colli Fiorentini '10	♟♟3
● Chianti Colli Fiorentini '09	♟♟3
● Chianti Colli Fiorentini '08	♟♟1
● Chianti Colli Fiorentini '07	♟♟1
● Chianti Colli Fiorentini Ris. '08	♟♟1*
● R09 '09	♟♟4
● Terre di Cino '09	♟♟3
● Terre di Cino '07	♟♟3
○ Vin Santo del Chianti Merlaia '06	♟♟3
○ Vin Santo del Chianti Merlaia '05	♟♟3
○ Vin Santo del Chianti Merlaia '04	♟♟3

Le Torri di Campiglioni

VIA SAN LORENZO A VIGLIANO, 31
50021 BARBERINO VAL D'ELSA [FI]
TEL. 0558076161
www.letorri.net

CELLAR SALES
PRE-BOOKED VISITS
ACCOMMODATION AND RESTAURANT SERVICE
ANNUAL PRODUCTION 150,000 bottles
HECTARES UNDER VINE 28.00

This estate was created by several friends who wanted to invest in Tuscany, united by a shared passion for wine. This was in 1980, a crucial period for this region when many people fell in love with the area and its landscapes. Farming was the principal interest, so they decided to make olive oil too and purchased an olive mill. The holiday accommodation was built later by restoring the existing farmhouses. No effort has been spared in production: the wines pursue perfect balance of the characteristics of the terroir and have also found success on the international market. An excellent performance from the Magliano 2009 sangiovese, merlot and cabernet sauvignon, with aromatic herbs like mint and sage supporting lovely concentrated fruity sensations. The palate is succulent, generous, with soft tannic texture and an appetizing, flavoursome finish. We also enjoyed the fragrant and nicely drinkable Riserva 2010.

● Magliano '09	♥♥ 5
● Chianti Colli Fiorentini Ris. '10	♥♥ 3
● Chianti Colli Fiorentini '11	♥ 2
● Meridius '11	♥ 2
○ Soleluna '12	♥ 2
● Chianti Colli Fiorentini '10	♥♥ 2*
● Magliano '08	♥♥ 5
● Vigliano '08	♥♥ 5
● Villa San Lorenzo '07	♥♥ 5

Travignoli

VIA TRAVIGNOLI, 78
50060 PELAGO [FI]
TEL. 0558361098
www.travignoli.com

CELLAR SALES
PRE-BOOKED VISITS
ANNUAL PRODUCTION 250,000 bottles
HECTARES UNDER VINE 70.00

The Travignoli farm is situated in the Pelago valley south of Rufina, owned by Giovanni Busi who is currently chairman on the Chianti producers' consortium. This large, historical estate was once a fully fledged farm but later focused solely on wine and extravirgin olive oil combining tradition and experimentation. An Etruscan stele was found on the estate dating back to 500 BC and depicting a banquet with jugs overflowing with wine, proving the area's long history and fame for wine-growing. A good performance from the Riserva Tegolaia 2010: vibrant aromas of blackberries and blueberries and more mature sensations of leather and balsam; a solid, broad, pleasantly velvety mouth with a pleasant, lingering finish. The Chianti Rufina 2011 is simple, fresh and beautifully drinkable while the Gavignano 2012, a blend of chardonnay with a little sauvignon, is edgy and adequately broad.

● Chianti Rufina Tegolaia Ris. '10	♥♥ 3
● Chianti Rufina '11	♥ 2
○ Gavignano '12	♥ 2
● Calice del Conte '08	♥♥ 5
● Chianti Rufina Ris. '05	♥♥ 3
● Chianti Rufina Tegolaia Ris. '09	♥♥ 3
● Chianti Rufina Tegolaia Ris. '08	♥♥ 3
● Chianti Rufina Tegolaia Ris. '07	♥♥ 3
○ Vin Santo Chianti Rufina '01	♥♥ 4

Tenuta di Trinoro

VIA VAL D'ORCIA, 15
53047 SARTEANO [SI]
TEL. 0578267110
www.trinoro.it

CELLAR SALES
PRE-BOOKED VISITS
ANNUAL PRODUCTION 80,000 bottles
HECTARES UNDER VINE 22.00

Andrea Franchetti created his winery in the early Nineties, in Val d'Orcia, a corner of Tuscany that no-one had yet gambled on as a suitable place for prestigious wine production. His rigorous and extreme choices, mainly in the Bordeaux mould, have given this part of the province of Siena one of the most quality-oriented estates in the whole of Tuscany. The wines display a very personal style, with extremely vibrant aromas, fruit ripening almost to the point of lateness and ageing exclusively in small oak casks. The Tenuta di Trinoro 2011, cabernet sauvignon, cabernet franc, petit verdot and merlot, is a well-made wine but lingers too long on sweet sensations. The delicious Le Cupole 2011 is the same blend but from younger vineyards. The Palazzi 2011 is a generous monovarietal merlot while the Cabernet Franc Magnacosta 2011 has oakiness that still needs softening down.

★Tua Rita

LOC. NOTRI, 81
57028 SUVERETO [LI]
TEL. 0565829237
www.tuarita.it

PRE-BOOKED VISITS
ANNUAL PRODUCTION 150,000 bottles
HECTARES UNDER VINE 30.00

This Suvereto estate is a safe bet among those in Val di Cornia, capable of producing wines that offer a perfect interpretation of the area's generous character. Of the estate's 50 hectares, about 30 are under vine, planted on medium-textured clayey soil rich in minerals. The vineyards are planted with the typical local varieties: cabernet sauvignon and franc, merlot, syrah and sangiovese for the red wines and traminer, riesling, chardonnay, trebbiano, ansonica and vermentino for the whites. As usual, a very compact range of wines, with Redigaffi and Syrah, both 2010, leading the pack. The first has a concentrated, almost impenetrable nose with vegetal and balsamic sensations blending together, and looming, slightly bulky tannins from the oak. The Syrah has spicier, peppery aromas with a very vibrant palate, again clenched by tannin.

● Tenuta di Trinoro '11	♔♔ 8	
● Le Cupole di Trinoro '11	♔♔ 5	
● Magnacosta '11	♔♔ 8	
● Palazzi '11	♔♔ 8	
● Tenuta di Trinoro '08	♔♔♔ 8	
● Tenuta di Trinoro '04	♔♔♔ 8	
● Tenuta di Trinoro '03	♔♔♔ 8	
● Palazzi '10	♔♔ 8	
● Palazzi '09	♔♔ 8	
● Tenuta di Trinoro '10	♔♔ 8	
● Tenuta di Trinoro '09	♔♔ 8	
● Tenuta di Trinoro '07	♔♔ 8	
● Tenuta di Trinoro '06	♔♔ 8	
● Tenuta di Trinoro '05	♔♔ 8	

● Redigaffi '10	♔♔ 8	
● Syrah '10	♔♔ 8	
● Giusto di Notri '10	♔♔ 8	
● Perlato del Bosco Rosso '10	♔♔ 5	
● Rosso dei Notri '12	♔♔ 3	
● Tierre '11	♔ 3	
● Redigaffi '08	♔♔♔ 8	
● Redigaffi '07	♔♔♔ 8	
● Redigaffi '06	♔♔♔ 8	
● Redigaffi '04	♔♔♔ 8	
● Redigaffi '03	♔♔♔ 8	
● Redigaffi '02	♔♔♔ 8	
● Redigaffi '01	♔♔♔ 8	
● Redigaffi '00	♔♔♔ 7	
● Giusto di Notri '10	♔♔ 8	
● Perlato del Bosco Rosso '10	♔♔ 5	
● Redigaffi '10	♔♔ 8	

Uccelliera ✓

FRAZ. CASTELNUOVO DELL'ABATE
POD. UCCELLIERA, 45
53020 MONTALCINO [SI]
TEL. 0577835729
www.uccelliera-montalcino.it

CELLAR SALES
PRE-BOOKED VISITS
ANNUAL PRODUCTION 60,000 bottles
HECTARES UNDER VINE 6.00

It is not just a question of excellence that makes Uccelliera Brunellos a benchmark for anyone seeking deeper knowledge of the Montalcino terroir, particularly the southernmost area, the slope that overlooks Castelnuovo dell'Abate. It is also a case of distinctive wines and, above all, work pursued with rare and steadfast passion by the tireless Andrea Cortonesi. As a "layperson" in the best possible sense, his cellar choices display no predefined recipe, just vinification techniques to suit each plot and the particular features of each harvest, with barriques sometimes used alongside the untoasted Slavonian oak. The brilliant encounter between a modest year and the innate firepower of Andrea Cortonesi's Sangioveses produced one of 2008's most impressive and accomplished Brunellos. Calamint, bay leaves, black cherries and spicy, meaty aromas, expanding with lively energy and tangy backbone into a long, pleasantly tannic finish.

● Brunello di Montalcino '08	♟♟♟ 7
● Rosso di Montalcino '11	♟♟ 4
● Brunello di Montalcino Ris. '07	♟♟ 8
● Brunello di Montalcino Ris. '97	♟♟♟ 8
● Brunello di Montalcino '07	♟♟ 7
● Brunello di Montalcino '06	♟♟ 7
● Brunello di Montalcino '05	♟♟ 6
● Brunello di Montalcino '01	♟♟ 6
● Brunello di Montalcino Ris. '06	♟♟ 8
● Brunello di Montalcino Ris. '04	♟♟ 8
● Brunello di Montalcino Ris. '01	♟♟ 8
● Rapace '08	♟♟ 5
● Rosso di Montalcino '10	♟♟ 4
● Rosso di Montalcino '09	♟♟ 4
● Rosso di Montalcino '07	♟♟ 4

Urlari

LOC. URLARI
56046 RIPARBELLA [PI]
TEL. 335215031
www.urlari.com

CELLAR SALES
PRE-BOOKED VISITS
ANNUAL PRODUCTION 30,000 bottles
HECTARES UNDER VINE 6.00

The Urlari estate, in the municipality of Riparbella, is owned by Roberto Cristoforetti, who has managed to integrate the features of Tuscan wine-growing, above all a passion for sangiovese, with a French influence thanks to the selection of some Bordeaux varieties and the help of Jean-Philippe Fort. The French oenologist has put new theories and methods into practice for the first time outside France. The vineyards and harvest are managed by agronomist Francesco Venerini, who shares international experience with the rest of the team. The estate is named after the location which, according to legend, was used as a refuge for soldiers, who could only communicate by shouting. Pervale 2010 is a pleasing blend of sangiovese, cabernet sauvignon and franc, merlot and alicante: a vibrant nose with fresh hints of aromatic herbs alongside red berries and a well-organized, dynamic palate. The Urlo 2010, a monovarietal Merlot, displays very clear wild berry aromas and a harmonious, mouthfilling flavour.

● L'Urlo '10	♟♟ 5
● Pervale '10	♟♟ 3
● L'Urlo '09	♟♟ 4
● Pervale '09	♟♟ 5

F.lli Vagnoni

LOC. PANCOLE, 82
53037 SAN GIMIGNANO [SI]
TEL. 0577955077
www.fratellivagnoni.com

CELLAR SALES
PRE-BOOKED VISITS
ACCOMMODATION
ANNUAL PRODUCTION 120,000 bottles
HECTARES UNDER VINE 20.00
VITICULTURE METHOD Certified Organic

This fully-fledged farm, established in 1955, flanks the village of Pancole, a strong stylistic reference for Vernaccia enthusiasts. This subzone displays specific characteristics of both soil and microclimate, and stands out from the rest of the designation for its slightly denser wines with strongly rocky, yellow-fleshed fruit sensations. The estate covers about 42 hectares of which 20 are under vine and the rest consists of olive groves, orchards, arable land and woods. The wines reflect the strong local imprint and features of the estate. The Vernaccia Riserva 2010 impressed us most of all with a profile that is fresh and mature at the same time, yellow and green, rich in character and shifts in rhythm. A very young palate, despite a period ageing in bottles, with lovely sweet fruit, a fresh streak of acidity and nice deep finish. Also excellent, the Vernaccia 2012 is livelier and jauntier.

○ Vernaccia di S. Gimignano I Mocali Ris. '10	♟♟ 3*	
○ Vernaccia di S. Gimignano '12	♟♟ 2*	
○ Vernaccia di S. Gimignano Fontabuccio '11	♟ 2	
○ Vernaccia di S. Gimignano '11	♟♟ 2*	
○ Vernaccia di S. Gimignano '10	♟♟ 1*	
○ Vernaccia di S. Gimignano '09	♟♟ 1	
○ Vernaccia di S. Gimignano Fontabuccio '09	♟♟ 2*	
○ Vernaccia di S. Gimignano I Mocali Ris. '09	♟♟ 3*	
○ Vernaccia di S. Gimignano I Mocali Ris. '08	♟♟ 3	

Val delle Corti

LOC. CASE SPARSE VAL DELLE CORTI, 144
53017 RADDA IN CHIANTI [SI]
TEL. 0577738215
www.valdellecorti.it

CELLAR SALES
PRE-BOOKED VISITS
ANNUAL PRODUCTION 30,000 bottles
HECTARES UNDER VINE 6.00
VITICULTURE METHOD Certified Organic

Val delle Corti is another of those incredible estates where Chianti-grown sangiovese achieves its most authentic expression. The vineyards in the subzone of Radda in Chianti are organically farmed and cellar procedures are minimal. The result is a range of wines in a style displaying clear-cut aromas and subtle, delicate but beautifully paced structure. A truly admirable interpretation of the terroir, almost unparalleled in Chianti Classico. Alongside these qualities, the pricing policy is spot-on which is a real plus in times like these. A decidedly exemplary Chianti Classico 2010 starting with the initial reductions which gradually give way to beautiful floral aromas and hints of iron filings alongside citrus sensations. The palate is mouthwatering, tangy, lively and very deep. Only just behind it is the Chianti Classico Riserva 2009, with light aromas and a fresh, contrasting flavour.

● Chianti Cl. '10	♟♟♟ 3*	
● Chianti Cl. Ris. '09	♟♟ 5	
● Chianti Cl. '09	♟♟♟ 2*	
● Chianti Cl. '06	♟♟ 2*	
● Chianti Cl. '05	♟♟ 2*	
● Chianti Cl. '04	♟♟ 2*	
● Chianti Cl. '03	♟♟ 2	
● Chianti Cl. Ris. '07	♟♟ 4	
● Chianti Cl. Ris. '00	♟♟ 4	
● Il Campino	♟♟ 2*	

Tenuta Val di Cava

LOC. VAL DI CAVA
53024 MONTALCINO [SI]
TEL. 0577848261
www.valdicava.it

ANNUAL PRODUCTION 80,000 bottles
HECTARES UNDER VINE 27.00

Valdicava wines represent an unusual and
sometimes controversial meeting between
the atmosphere of northern Montalcino,
with the hills of Montosoli historically at its
heart and a concept of Brunello which is
less than traditional, at least in the usual
sense. This is one of the keys to
understanding the work of Vincenzo
Abbruzzese, today at the helm of the estate
taken over by Bramante Martini in 1953,
which began to offer its own brand in 1968.
The recently extended cellar houses oak
casks of various sizes and origins, though
large barrels have been used more in recent
years. Once again our impressions of the
Brunellos were contradictory, aside from
the stylistic consistency. The Madonna del
Piano Riserva 2007 reflects that generous
vintage year with hints of confit
contrasting nicely with a salty, satisfying
mouthfeel, slightly cropped by biting
tannins. The Rosso 20122 is more slender
but equally personal.

Tenuta di Valgiano

VIA DI VALGIANO, 7
55015 LUCCA
TEL. 0583402271
www.valgiano.it

CELLAR SALES
ANNUAL PRODUCTION 70,000 bottles
HECTARES UNDER VINE 21.00
VITICULTURE METHOD Certified Biodynamic

To understand the true scope of the
Valgiano project, you have to visit the
estate, its terrains, vineyards and cellar.
Valgiano is a world unto itself, a microcosm
in tune with nature that enjoys a unique
natural and human richness. Having seen
this magnificent estate, the biodynamic
methods that are universally applied here
seem almost the only choice. 'Almost'
because we cannot overlook the role
played by the sensitivity and intuition of
Moreno Petrini, Laura di Collobiano and
Saverio Petrilli, a leading light in
biodynamic agriculture. The wines are the
result and expression of all these factors;
they thrill as they age and are benchmark
for the zone. Vibrant, minerally, still showing
some sharp edges and all the more exciting
for it, capable of a glowingly brilliant palate,
linear and expansive. That's the Tenuta di
Valgiano 2010, a true child of its vintage
and, above all, of a skilled and sure hand
able to represent and enhance any vintage
without distorting its features.

● Rosso di Montalcino '11	♙♙ 3
● Brunello di Montalcino Madonna del Piano Ris. '07	♙ 6
● Brunello di Montalcino Madonna del Piano Ris. '04	♙♙♙ 8
● Brunello di Montalcino '07	♙♙ 4
● Brunello di Montalcino '06	♙♙ 6
● Brunello di Montalcino '05	♙♙ 6
● Brunello di Montalcino '04	♙♙ 6
● Brunello di Montalcino Madonna del Piano Ris. '05	♙♙ 6
● Rosso di Montalcino '08	♙♙ 3

● Colline Lucchesi Tenuta di Valgiano '10	♙♙♙ 6
● Colline Lucchesi Palistorti Rosso '11	♙♙ 4
● Colline Lucchesi Tenuta di Valgiano '09	♙♙♙ 6
● Colline Lucchesi Tenuta di Valgiano '08	♙♙♙ 6
● Colline Lucchesi Tenuta di Valgiano '07	♙♙♙ 6
● Colline Lucchesi Tenuta di Valgiano '06	♙♙♙ 6
● Colline Lucchesi Tenuta di Valgiano '05	♙♙♙ 6
● Colline Lucchesi Tenuta di Valgiano '04	♙♙♙ 6
● Colline Lucchesi Tenuta di Valgiano '03	♙♙♙ 6
● Colline Lucchesi Tenuta di Valgiano '01	♙♙♙ 8
○ Colline Lucchesi Palistorti Bianco '11	♙♙ 5
○ Colline Lucchesi Palistorti Bianco '09	♙♙ 2*
● Colline Lucchesi Palistorti Rosso '10	♙♙ 4
● Colline Lucchesi Rosso dei Palistorti '03	♙♙ 4

Vecchia Cantina di Montepulciano

VIA PROVINCIALE, 7
53045 MONTEPULCIANO [SI]
TEL. 0578716092
www.vecchiacantina.com

CELLAR SALES
PRE-BOOKED VISITS
ANNUAL PRODUCTION 3,500,000 bottles
HECTARES UNDER VINE 1,000.00

Located near the town of Montepulciano, Vecchia Cantina di Montepulciano is the oldest winery in Tuscany. Its original goal was to produce wines of increasingly high quality across all the types, by paying constant attention to all stages of production. The winery was established in 1937 and the first wines were produced in 1940. Since then the number of grower-members has increased and the production process has been perfected. The members are supervised by the winery's agronomists with the aim of continued grape improvement. As well as the traditional line, Vecchie Cantine have created two commercial lines of a higher standard of quality: Poggio Stella and Cantine Redi. The three 2010 Vino Nobile wines were among the most impressive in the tasting: Poggio Stella shows stylish, sober aromas with a harmonious palate and lovely finish, while Cantina Redi is spicier and more intriguing. The Vecchia Cantina is more classic and traditional but nicely made.

● Nobile di Montepulciano Cantine del Redi '10	♥♥ 4
● Nobile di Montepulciano Poggio Stella '10	♥♥ 3
● Nobile di Montepulciano Vecchia Cantina '10	♥♥ 3
● Chianti dei Colli Senesi Poggio Stella '12	♥ 2
● Chianti Vecchia Cantina '12	♥ 2
● Cortona Merlot '11	♥ 2
● Cortona Merlot Poggio Stella '11	♥ 2
● Orbaio Cantine Redi '09	♥ 4
● Rosso di Montepulciano Poggio Stella '12	♥ 2
● Rosso di Montepulciano Vecchia Cantina '12	♥ 2
● Nobile di Montepulciano '09	♥♥ 3
● Nobile di Montepulciano Poggio Stella Ris. '07	♥♥ 4

I Veroni

LOC. I VERONI
VIA TIFARITI, 5
50065 PONTASSIEVE [FI]
TEL. 0558368886
www.iveroni.it

CELLAR SALES
PRE-BOOKED VISITS
ACCOMMODATION
ANNUAL PRODUCTION 100,000 bottles
HECTARES UNDER VINE 15.00

The property, which includes an old watchtower, has belonged to the Malesci family for over 50 years and is situated in one of Rufina's best locations. The name "verone" once referred to the covered terrace at the top of an outside staircase in old farmhouses. Since the early 1990s the family has worked on replanting the vineyards and today the owner's son, Lorenzo Mariani, runs the operation. Part of the cellar consists of ancient vinification spaces, now renovated and used for barrel ageing, and the rest is of newer construction. The vin santo cellar is preserved inside the 18th-century villa. The Riserva 2010 is very interesting which varied, vibrant aromas including minty, minerally hints and nicely blended wild berries. The palate is firm-bodied, well-organized and has a lingering flavour with a tangy finish. The Vin Santo 1991 has alluring aromas ranging from dried figs to hazelnuts and a sweet, lingering mouth.

● Chianti Rufina '11	♥♥ 2*
● Chianti Rufina Ris. '10	♥♥ 4
○ Vin Santo del Chianti Rufina '05	♥♥ 5
○ Bianco '12	♥ 2
⊙ Rosé '12	♥ 2
● Rosso di Toscana '11	♥ 2
● Chianti Rufina Ris. '09	♥♥ 4
● Chianti Rufina Ris. '08	♥♥ 4
● Chianti Rufina Ris. '07	♥♥ 4
● Chianti Rufina Ris. '06	♥♥ 4
○ Vin Santo del Chianti Rufina '04	♥♥ 5
○ Vin Santo del Chianti Rufina '03	♥♥ 5

Vescine

LOC. VÈSCINE
53017 RADDA IN CHIANTI [SI]
TEL. 0577741144
www.vescine.it

CELLAR SALES
PRE-BOOKED VISITS
ACCOMMODATION AND RESTAURANT SERVICE
ANNUAL PRODUCTION 70,000 bottles
HECTARES UNDER VINE 15.00

Vescine, at Radda in Chianti, is owned by
the Paladin family who play an active role
in the wine sector in both Veneto and
Franciacorta. The vineyards are planted in
two distinct areas: one near the town, to
the south, near the border with Castellina in
Chianti, and the other, Tenuta Castelvecchi,
to the north in the heart of the historical
crus of this particular Chianti Classico
subzone. The wines display well-typed style
that favours balance and finesse with
continual reference to the terroir. Both
small and large casks are put to
well-controlled use for ageing, and the
resulting wines are perfectly judged and
reassuringly dependable in quality. The
Chianti Classico Tenuta Castelvecchi 2010
hinges on balance with aromas divided
between red berries and spices and a
refreshing, flavoursome palate. The Chianti
Classico Tenuta Castelvecchi Riserva 2009
reveals mature hints and a velvety mouth
with a pleasant succession of warm and
fresh sensations.

● Chianti Cl. Tenuta Castelvecchi Ris. '09	♥♥	4
● Chianti Cl. Tenute di Castelvecchi '10	♥♥	5
● Chianti Cl. '07	♥♥	3
● Chianti Cl. Lodolaio Ris. '08	♥♥	6
● Chianti Cl. Lodolaio Ris. '07	♥♥	6
● Chianti Cl. Lodolaio Ris. '06	♥♥	6
● Chianti Cl. Lodolaio Ris. '04	♥♥	7
● Chianti Cl. Tenute di Castelvecchi '09	♥♥	6
● Chianti Cl. Tenute di Castelvecchi '08	♥♥	6

I Vicini

FRAZ. PIETRAIA DI CORTONA
LOC. CASE SPARSE
52038 CORTONA [AR]
TEL. 0575678507
www.ivicinicortona.it

PRE-BOOKED VISITS
HECTARES UNDER VINE 11.00

This estate's interesting backstory brings
together two families with a shared passion
for wine and the local area. Roman lawyer
Romano Antonioli decided to invest in land
suitable for wine cultivation, regrafted the
available vineyards and created a farming
business. Entrepreneur Andy Goldfarb, from
California, was famed for his diffusion of the
airbag when he made a lifestyle choice to
fulfil his dream of living close to nature in
Tuscany. So he settled next-door to
Antonioli's estate, hence the current name.
This encounter led to the founding of an
operation that joined the two men in a
shared objective: to make quality wines in
the area they both loved. A good overall
standard for these wines, with distinctive
clean, well-defined aromas and generally
drinkable flavour. The Syrah 2010 seems
spicier with well-coordinated structure; the
Merlot 2010 is nicely rounded and
harmonious with fruity sensations and the
Cabernet Sauvignon has austere, balsam
aromas and firm, full-bodied texture.

● Cortona Laudario Cabernet Sauvignon '10	♥♥	3
● Cortona Laudario Merlot '10	♥♥	3
● Cortona Laudario Syrah '10	♥♥	3
⊙ Pergolaio '11	♥	2
● Cortona Laudario Cabernet Sauvignon '08	♥♥	3
● Cortona Laudario Syrah '09	♥♥	3

Villa Pillo

VIA VOLTERRANA, 24
50050 GAMBASSI TERME [FI]
TEL. 0571680212
www.villapillo.com

CELLAR SALES
PRE-BOOKED VISITS
ANNUAL PRODUCTION 250,000 bottles
HECTARES UNDER VINE 40.00

The Dysons, a married couple from the US, have owned Villa Pillo since 1989. The farm is situated in the heart of the Chianti Fiorentino area, near the province of Pisa. The old medieval villa was restored when they arrived and most of the vineyards have been completely replanted, resulting in a combination of local tradition and modern Californian techniques applied in loco. This is perceptible in the modern style of the wines that has made their name around the world. As well as sangiovese the estate grows a variety of international grapes which have adapted well to the local climate. The products are consistent and coherent as usual. Cypresses 2011, a monovarietal Sangiovese, has direct aromas and a supple flavour. Sant'Adele 2011, a monovarietal Merlot, is complex on the nose with a fruity, plush, well-balanced palate. Vivaldaia 2011, made from cabernet franc, shows distinctive minty and vegetal aromas and a supple body. All the other wines offer a good drink.

● Cypresses '11	♟♟ 3
● Merlot Sant'Adele '11	♟♟ 5
● Vivaldaia '11	♟♟ 4
● Cingalino '12	♟ 2
● Syrah '11	♟ 5
● Syrah '97	♟♟♟ 5
● Borgoforte '09	♟♟ 3*
● Borgoforte '08	♟♟ 2*
● Cypresses '10	♟♟ 3
● Cypresses '09	♟♟ 3
● Merlot Sant'Adele '10	♟♟ 5
● Merlot Sant'Adele '08	♟♟ 5
● Syrah '07	♟♟ 5
● Syrah '05	♟♟ 5

Villa Sant'Anna

LOC. ABBADIA
VIA DELLA RESISTENZA, 143
53045 MONTEPULCIANO [SI]
TEL. 0578708017
www.villasantanna.it

CELLAR SALES
PRE-BOOKED VISITS
ANNUAL PRODUCTION 80,000 bottles
HECTARES UNDER VINE 18.00

An all-female estate: that's their claim, and it could not be otherwise given that not only the current management but the ownership has followed the family's maternal line. Today Simona Ruggeri Fabroni is at the helm with her daughters Anna and Margherita. Production focuses on local champ Vino Nobile di Montepulciano, but includes an uncomplicated, fragrant Chianti dei Colli Senesi and the jewel in the estate's crown, a weighty Vin Santo. The style is modern and the cellar contains 30-hectolitre casks and barriques. Cream of the crop this year is the Vin Santo di Montepulciano 2004 with dried apricots, dates, almonds and orange zest on the broad, multifaceted nose. The seductive, mouthfilling palate is vibrant and well-balanced with refreshing acidity. The Nobile and the Chianti Colli Senesi, both 2010, are a lovely supple drink.

● Nobile di Montepulciano '10	♟♟ 4
○ Vin Santo di Montepulciano '04	♟♟ 8
● Chianti Colli Senesi '10	♟ 2
● Nobile di Montepulciano Poldo '07	♟ 5
● Nobile di Montepulciano '07	♟♟ 4
● Nobile di Montepulciano '06	♟♟ 4
● Nobile di Montepulciano Poldo '05	♟♟ 5

Villa Vignamaggio

VIA DI PETRIOLO, 5
50022 GREVE IN CHIANTI [FI]
TEL. 055854661
www.vignamaggio.com

CELLAR SALES
PRE-BOOKED VISITS
ACCOMMODATION AND RESTAURANT SERVICE
ANNUAL PRODUCTION 220,000 bottles
HECTARES UNDER VINE 42.00

Giovanni Battista Nunziante established the Villa Vignamaggio estate in 1987. The winery, which belongs to the Florentine part of the DOC zone, in Greve, is now one of Chianti Classico's benchmark estates. The leading role is taken by sangiovese but Vignamaggio owes much of its success to an international grape variety: cabernet franc. The wines display a reassuringly coherent level of quality in a style that pursues elegance and finesse, also thanks to well-judged use of oak in the ageing phase, including large casks and barriques, depending on the type of wine. The 2010 version of the Cabernet Franc Vignamaggio is really very good: elegant aromas ranging from fruity hints to pleasant grassy sensations, and a stylish, well-paced, deep mouth. The Chianti Classico Monna Lisa Riserva 2010 shows lovely texture and clear-cut, characterful aromas. The Chianti Classico Terre di Prenzano 2011 is deliciously succulent.

● Chianti Cl. Monna Lisa Ris. '10	♟♟ 5
● Vignamaggio '10	♟♟ 7
● Chianti Cl. Terre di Prenzano '11	♟♟ 3
● Chianti Cl. Gherardino '11	♟ 3
● Chianti Cl. Monna Lisa Ris. '99	♟♟♟ 5
● Chianti Cl. Monna Lisa Ris. '95	♟♟♟ 5
● Vignamaggio '06	♟♟♟ 7
● Vignamaggio '05	♟♟♟ 7
● Vignamaggio '04	♟♟♟ 6
● Vignamaggio '01	♟♟♟ 6
● Vignamaggio '00	♟♟♟ 6
● Chianti Cl. Gherardino '10	♟♟ 4
● Chianti Cl. Monna Lisa Ris. '09	♟♟ 5
● Vignamaggio '09	♟♟ 7
● Vignamaggio '08	♟♟ 7

Tenuta Vitereta

VIA CASANUOVA, 108/1
52020 LATERINA [AR]
TEL. 057589058
www.tenutavitereta.com

CELLAR SALES
PRE-BOOKED VISITS
ACCOMMODATION AND RESTAURANT SERVICE
ANNUAL PRODUCTION 80,000 bottles
HECTARES UNDER VINE 45.00
VITICULTURE METHOD Certified Organic

A fascinating project brought the Tenuta Vitereta estate to life: 40 years ago two families, the Bidini and the Del Tongo, decided to invest in creating a far-reaching, well-organized agricultural business based on love and respect for the surrounding environment and the passion driving those who worked there. The main products are wine and olive oil, but they also make pecorino cheese and cured meats from their own sheep and pigs, and grow various cereal crops. Hospitality is on offer in the villa, which was renovated upon purchase, and in adjacent holiday accommodation. The Vin Santo Occhio di Pernice 2006 got through to the final tastings with its complex range of aromas blending hints of cloves with plum jam, and a weighty, creamy and mouthfilling palate with a lingering finish. The lipsmacking Ripa della Mozza 2010, from sangiovese, has a fresh, vibrant nose and a dynamic, warm palate. The majestic Villa Bernetti 2009 has fresh aromas with a well-coordinated palate.

○ Vin Santo del Chianti Occhio di Pernice '06	♟♟ 8
● Ripa della Mozza '10	♟♟ 3
○ Trebbiano di Toscana '10	♟♟ 4
● Villa Bernetti '09	♟♟ 4
● Chianti Lo Sterpo '11	♟ 2
● Capitoni '06	♟♟ 3
● Ripa della Mozza '07	♟♟ 3
○ Supremo '03	♟♟ 6
○ Trebbiano di Toscana '08	♟♟ 4
○ Trebbiano di Toscana '07	♟♟ 4
● Villa Bernetti '05	♟♟ 4
○ Vin Santo '03	♟♟ 7
○ Vin Santo del Chianti '04	♟♟ 7
○ Vin Santo del Chianti Occhio di Pernice '05	♟♟ 8

Abbazia di Monte Oliveto

VIA MONTEOLIVETO, 15
53037 SAN GIMIGNANO [SI]
TEL. 0577907136
www.monteoliveto.it

CELLAR SALES
PRE-BOOKED VISITS
ACCOMMODATION
ANNUAL PRODUCTION 120,000 bottles
HECTARES UNDER VINE 18.00

○ Vernaccia di S. Gimignano '12	♥♥ 2*
○ Vernaccia din San Gimignano La Gentilesca '12	♥ 3

Roberto Aglieta

LOC. SCOPETINO
53024 MONTALCINO [SI]
TEL. 0577849442
www.brunelloaglieta.it

● Brunello di Montalcino '08	♥♥ 5

Agrisole

LOC. LA SERRA
VIA SERRA, 64
56028 SAN MINIATO [PI]
TEL. 0571409825
www.agri-sole.it

ANNUAL PRODUCTION 30,000 bottles
HECTARES UNDER VINE 6.00

● Malvasia Nera '11	♥♥ 2*
● Chianti Sanminiatello '12	♥ 2
● Mafefa '12	♥ 2

Altura

LOC. MULINACCIO
58012 GIGLIO
TEL. 0564806041
www.vignetoaltura.it

CELLAR SALES
PRE-BOOKED VISITS
RESTAURANT SERVICE
ANNUAL PRODUCTION 9,000 bottles
HECTARES UNDER VINE 3.50

○ Ansonaco '11	♥♥ 6
● Rosso Saverio '11	♥ 6

Antico Colle

VIA PROVINCIALE, 9
53040 MONTEPULCIANO [SI]
TEL. 0578707828
www.anticocolle.it

CELLAR SALES
PRE-BOOKED VISITS
ANNUAL PRODUCTION 80,000 bottles
HECTARES UNDER VINE 40.00

● Nobile di Montepulciano '10	♥♥ 3
● Rosso di Montepulciano '11	♥ 2

★Avignonesi

FRAZ. VALIANO DI MONTEPULCIANO
VIA COLONICA, 1
53040 MONTEPULCIANO [SI]
TEL. 0578724304
www.avignonesi.it

CELLAR SALES
PRE-BOOKED VISITS
ANNUAL PRODUCTION 700,000 bottles
HECTARES UNDER VINE 119.00

○ Vin Santo di Montepulciano '99	♥♥ 8
● Vin Santo Occhio di Pernice '99	♥♥ 8
○ Cortona Chardonnay Il Marzocco '12	♥♥ 3

Baldetti Alfonso

LOC. PIETRAIA, 71
52044 CORTONA [AR]
TEL. 057567077
www.baldetti.com

CELLAR SALES
ANNUAL PRODUCTION 100,000 bottles
HECTARES UNDER VINE 15.00

● Cortona Crano '11	♙♙ 3
○ Chagrè '11	♙ 2

Erik Banti

LOC. FOSSO DEI MOLINI
58054 SCANSANO [GR]
TEL. 0564508006
www.erikbanti.com

CELLAR SALES
PRE-BOOKED VISITS
ANNUAL PRODUCTION 250,000 bottles
HECTARES UNDER VINE 25.00
VITICULTURE METHOD Certified Organic

● Morellino di Scansano Ciabatta Ris. '10	♙♙ 4
○ Vermentino '12	♙ 2

Barbanera

VIA DEL PALAZZONE, 4
53040 CETONA [SI]
TEL. 0578244174
www.barbaneravini.it

● Nobile di Montepulciano Ris. '09	♙♙ 3
● Nobile di Montepulciano '10	♙ 3
● Rosso di Montepulciano '11	♙ 3
● Vecciano '10	♙ 2

Il Barlettaio

VIA BARLETTAIO, 86
53017 RADDA IN CHIANTI [SI]
TEL. 0577738322
www.barlettaio.it

ANNUAL PRODUCTION 12,600 bottles
HECTARES UNDER VINE 2.20

● Sangiovese '09	♙♙ 3
● Chianti Cl. '10	♙ 2
● Merlot '10	♙ 3

Basile

POD. MONTE MARIO
58044 CINIGIANO [GR]
TEL. 0564993227
www.basilessa.it

CELLAR SALES
PRE-BOOKED VISITS
ANNUAL PRODUCTION 25,000 bottles
HECTARES UNDER VINE 6.00
VITICULTURE METHOD Certified Organic

● Montecucco Sangiovese Ad Agio Ris. '09	♙♙ 3
● Montecucco Cartacanta '10	♙ 2

Pietro Beconcini

FRAZ. LA SCALA
VIA MONTORZO, 13A
56020 SAN MINIATO [PI]
TEL. 0571464570
www.pietrobeconcini.com

CELLAR SALES
PRE-BOOKED VISITS
ANNUAL PRODUCTION 100,000 bottles
HECTARES UNDER VINE 12.00

● Vigna alle Nicchie '09	♙♙ 6
● Chianti Ris. '10	♙ 2
● Maurleo '11	♙ 2
○ Vin Santo del Chianti Caratello '04	♙ 5

Cantine Bellini

VIA PIAVE, 1
50068 RUFINA [FI]
TEL. 0558396025
www.bellinicantine.it

CELLAR SALES
ANNUAL PRODUCTION 900,000 bottles
HECTARES UNDER VINE 7.00

● Chianti Rufina Ris. '09	♟♟ 5
● Chianti '12	♟ 4
● Comedia '09	♟ 5

Belpoggio

FRAZ. CASTELNUOVO DELL'ABATE
LOC. BELLARIA
53024 MONTALCINO [SI]
TEL. 0423982147
www.belpoggio.it

PRE-BOOKED VISITS
ANNUAL PRODUCTION 25,000 bottles
HECTARES UNDER VINE 5.00

● Rosso di Montalcino '11	♟♟ 4
● Brunello di Montalcino '08	♟ 6

Le Bertille

VIA DELLE COLOMBELLE, 7
53045 MONTEPULCIANO [SI]
TEL. 0578758330
www.lebertille.com

● Nobile di Montepulciano '09	♟♟ 3
● Rosso di Montepulciano '11	♟♟ 2*
● Chianti Colli Senesi '09	♟ 2

Il Borro

FRAZ. SAN GIUSTINO VALDARNO
LOC. IL BORRO, 1
52020 LORO CIUFFENNA [AR]
TEL. 055977053
www.ilborro.it

CELLAR SALES
PRE-BOOKED VISITS
ACCOMMODATION AND RESTAURANT SERVICE
ANNUAL PRODUCTION 150,000 bottles
HECTARES UNDER VINE 45.00

○ Vin Santo del Chianti Occhio di Pernice '08	♟♟ 5
● Pian di Nova '11	♟ 3

Brunelli

POD. MARTOCCIA
53024 MONTALCINO [SI]
TEL. 0577848540
www.tenutabrunelli.it

● Brunello di Montalcino '08	♟♟ 7
● Brunello di Montalcino Ris. '07	♟♟ 7
● Rosso di Montalcino '11	♟ 5

Bruni

FRAZ. FONTEBLANDA
LOC. LA MARTA, 6
58010 ORBETELLO [GR]
TEL. 0564885445
www.aziendabruni.it

CELLAR SALES
PRE-BOOKED VISITS
ANNUAL PRODUCTION 400,000 bottles
HECTARES UNDER VINE 36.00

● Morellino di Scansano Marteto '12	♟♟ 2*
● Morellino di Scansano Laire Ris. '11	♟ 4
○ Vermentino Perlaia '12	♟ 3
○ Vermentino Plinio '12	♟ 3

La Buca di Montauto

LOC. MONTAUTO
53037 SAN GIMIGNANO [SI]
TEL. 0577943049
www.labucadimontauto.it

CELLAR SALES
PRE-BOOKED VISITS
ACCOMMODATION
ANNUAL PRODUCTION 30,000 bottles
HECTARES UNDER VINE 5.20

○ Vernaccia di S. Gimignano '12	♥♥ 2*

Ca' del Vispo

LOC. LE VIGNE
VIA DI FUGNANO, 31
53037 SAN GIMIGNANO [SI]
TEL. 0577943053
www.cadelvispo.it

CELLAR SALES
PRE-BOOKED VISITS
ANNUAL PRODUCTION 80,000 bottles
HECTARES UNDER VINE 7.00

○ Vernaccia di San Gimignano '12	♥♥ 2*
● Chianti Colli Senesi '12	♥ 2

Cacciagrande

LOC. TIRLI
S.DA AMPIO -TIRLI
58040 CASTIGLIONE DELLA PESCAIA [GR]
TEL. 0564944168
www.cacciagrande.com

CELLAR SALES
PRE-BOOKED VISITS
ANNUAL PRODUCTION 80,000 bottles
HECTARES UNDER VINE 20.00

● Castiglione '11	♥♥ 4
● Cacciagrande '12	♥ 2
● Cortigliano '11	♥ 3
○ Viognier '12	♥ 3

La Calonica

FRAZ. VALIANO DI MONTEPULCIANO
VIA DELLA STELLA, 27
53045 MONTEPULCIANO [SI]
TEL. 0578724119
www.lacalonica.com

CELLAR SALES
PRE-BOOKED VISITS
ANNUAL PRODUCTION 300,000 bottles
HECTARES UNDER VINE 38.00

● Cortona Syrah Arnth '10	♥♥ 5
● Cortona Sangiovese Calcinaio '12	♥ 3
● Nobile di Montepulciano '10	♥ 4
● Nobile di Montepulciano San Venerio '09	♥ 5

Antonio Camillo

FRAZ. ALBERESE
S.DA BANDITELLA, 2
58100 GROSSETO
TEL. 0564405099
www.poggioargentiera.com

CELLAR SALES
PRE-BOOKED VISITS
ANNUAL PRODUCTION 20,000 bottles
HECTARES UNDER VINE 5.00
VITICULTURE METHOD Certified Organic

● Vallerana Alta '11	♥♥ 3*
● Principio '12	♥ 2

Campo alla Sughera

LOC. CACCIA AL PIANO, 280
57020 BOLGHERI [LI]
TEL. 0565766936
www.campoallasughera.com

CELLAR SALES
PRE-BOOKED VISITS
ANNUAL PRODUCTION 110,000 bottles
HECTARES UNDER VINE 16.50

○ Bolgheri Achenio '12	♥♥ 5
● Bolgheri Arnione '10	♥ 6
● Campo alla Sughera '09	♥ 8

Caparsa

CASE SPARSE CAPARSA, 47
53017 RADDA IN CHIANTI [SI]
TEL. 0577738174
www.caparsa.it

CELLAR SALES
PRE-BOOKED VISITS
ACCOMMODATION
ANNUAL PRODUCTION 20,000 bottles
HECTARES UNDER VINE 11.37
VITICULTURE METHOD Certified Organic

● Chianti Cl. Caparsino Ris. '09   ♟♟ 4

Casa al Vento

LOC. CASA AL VENTO
53013 GAIOLE IN CHIANTI [SI]
TEL. 0577749068
www.borgocasaalvento.com

CELLAR SALES
PRE-BOOKED VISITS
ACCOMMODATION AND RESTAURANT SERVICE
ANNUAL PRODUCTION 40,000 bottles
HECTARES UNDER VINE 5.80
VITICULTURE METHOD Certified Organic

● Chianti Cl. Foho Ris. '10   ♟♟ 4

Casa Dei

LOC. SAN ROCCO
57028 SUVERETO [LI]
TEL. 0558300800
www.tenutacasadei.it

PRE-BOOKED VISITS
ANNUAL PRODUCTION 60,000 bottles
HECTARES UNDER VINE 14.00
VITICULTURE METHOD Certified Organic

● Filare 41 '11   ♟♟ 5
● Armonia '12   ♟ 2
● Filare 18 '11   ♟ 5
● Sogno Mediterraneo '11   ♟ 2

Casa Sola

S.DA DI CORTINE, 5
50021 BARBERINO VAL D'ELSA [FI]
TEL. 0558075028
www.fattoriacasasola.it

CELLAR SALES
PRE-BOOKED VISITS
ACCOMMODATION
ANNUAL PRODUCTION 100,000 bottles
HECTARES UNDER VINE 27.00

● Chianti Cl. Ris. '09   ♟♟ 3
● Chianti Cl. '10   ♟ 4

Fattoria Casabianca

FRAZ. CASCIANO DI MURLO
LOC. MONTEPESCINI
53016 MURLO [SI]
TEL. 0577811033
www.fattoriacasabianca.it

CELLAR SALES
PRE-BOOKED VISITS
ACCOMMODATION AND RESTAURANT SERVICE
ANNUAL PRODUCTION 230,000 bottles
HECTARES UNDER VINE 68.00

● Loccareto '11   ♟♟ 4
● Chianti Colli Senesi Belsedere Ris. '09   ♟ 5

Casale Pozzuolo

LOC. BORGO SANTA RITA
58044 CINIGIANO [GR]
TEL. 0564902019
www.casalepozzuolo.it

CELLAR SALES
ACCOMMODATION
ANNUAL PRODUCTION 15,000 bottles
HECTARES UNDER VINE 4.50

● Montecucco Sangiovese Ris. '09   ♟♟ 4
● Montecucco Rosso della Porticcia '10   ♟ 3

Castellani

FRAZ. SANTA LUCIA, 1
56025 PONTEDERA [PI]
TEL. 0587292900
www.castelwine.com

CELLAR SALES
PRE-BOOKED VISITS
ANNUAL PRODUCTION 22,000,000 bottles
HECTARES UNDER VINE 200.00
VITICULTURE METHOD Certified Organic

● Chianti Cl. Vign. di Campomaggio '10	♟♟	3
● Genius Loci '10	♟	3

Castellinuzza e Piuca

VIA PETRIOLO, 21A
50022 GREVE IN CHIANTI [FI]
TEL. 0558549033
www.castellinuzzaepiuca.it

CELLAR SALES
PRE-BOOKED VISITS
ANNUAL PRODUCTION 10,000 bottles
HECTARES UNDER VINE 2.00

● Chianti Cl. '10	♟♟	3

Castello del Trebbio

VIA SANTA BRIGIDA, 9
50060 PONTASSIEVE [FI]
TEL. 0558304900
www.vinoturismo.it

CELLAR SALES
PRE-BOOKED VISITS
ANNUAL PRODUCTION 250,000 bottles
HECTARES UNDER VINE 52.00

● Vigneti Trebbio '10	♟♟	4
○ Bianco della Congiura '12	♟	3
● Chianti '12	♟	2
○ Vin Santo del Chianti '00	♟	4

Castello di Querceto

LOC. QUERCETO
VIA A. FRANÇOIS, 2
50020 GREVE IN CHIANTI [FI]
TEL. 05585921
www.castellodiquerceto.it

CELLAR SALES
PRE-BOOKED VISITS
ACCOMMODATION
ANNUAL PRODUCTION 600,000 bottles
HECTARES UNDER VINE 60.00

● Il Sole di Alessandro '09	♟♟	7
● Chianti Cl. '11	♟	3
● Chianti Cl. Ris. '10	♟	4
● Cignale '09	♟	7

Castello di Velona

LOC. VELONA
53024 MONTALCINO [SI]
TEL. 0577835700
www.castellodivelonavini.it

● Brunello di Montalcino '08	♟♟	3
● Brunello di Montalcino Ris. '07	♟	3

Castiglion del Bosco

LOC. CASTIGLION DEL BOSCO
53024 MONTALCINO [SI]
TEL. 05771913750
www.castigliondelbosco.com

CELLAR SALES
PRE-BOOKED VISITS
ACCOMMODATION AND RESTAURANT SERVICE
ANNUAL PRODUCTION 20,000 bottles
HECTARES UNDER VINE 67.00

● Rosso di Montalcino '11	♟♟	3
● Brunello di Montalcino '08	♟	6

Cecilia

LOC. LA PILA
POD. LA CASINA, 8
57034 CAMPO NELL'ELBA [LI]
TEL. 024989864
www.aziendacecilia.it

CELLAR SALES
PRE-BOOKED VISITS
ANNUAL PRODUCTION 45,000 bottles
HECTARES UNDER VINE 22.00

● Oglasa '10	♟♟ 4
○ Elba Ansonica '12	♟♟ 2*
● Elba Aleatico Passito '11	♟ 5

Podere La Chiesa

VIA VOLTERRANA, 467
56030 TERRICCIOLA [PI]
TEL. 0587635484
www.poderelachiesa.it

CELLAR SALES
PRE-BOOKED VISITS
ANNUAL PRODUCTION 25,000 bottles
HECTARES UNDER VINE 5.00

● Chianti Terre di Casanova '12	♟♟ 2*
● Le Redole di Casanova '11	♟ 2

Podere il Ciabattino

LOC. CALZALUNGA, 181
57028 SUVERETO [LI]
TEL. 0565829271
calzalunga@gmail.com

ANNUAL PRODUCTION 25,000 bottles
HECTARES UNDER VINE 6.00

● Milia '11	♟♟ 3*
● Calzalunga '11	♟♟ 6
● Podere la Bandita '10	♟♟ 8

Podere Cigli

LOC. CASTEANI
CASA CIGLI, 7
58023 GAVORRANO [GR]
TEL. 056680035
www.poderecigli.com

CELLAR SALES
PRE-BOOKED VISITS
ANNUAL PRODUCTION 20,000 bottles
HECTARES UNDER VINE 7.00

● Monteregio di Massa Marittima CampoMaria '09	♟♟ 4
○ Monteregio di Massa Marittima Vermentino '12	♟ 3

Le Cinciole

VIA CASE SPARSE, 83
50020 PANZANO [FI]
TEL. 055852636
www.lecinciole.it

CELLAR SALES
PRE-BOOKED VISITS
ANNUAL PRODUCTION 45,000 bottles
HECTARES UNDER VINE 11.00
VITICULTURE METHOD Certified Organic

● Chianti Cl. '10	♟♟ 3

Colle di Bordocheo

LOC. SEGROMIGNO IN MONTE
VIA DI PIAGGIORI BASSO, 107
55018 CAPANNORI [LU]
TEL. 0583929821
www.colledibordocheo.com

CELLAR SALES
PRE-BOOKED VISITS
ANNUAL PRODUCTION 30,000 bottles
HECTARES UNDER VINE 10.00

○ Bordocheo Bianco '12	♟♟ 4
○ Colline Lucchesi Bianco dell'Oca '12	♟ 4
● Colline Lucchesi Bordocheo Rosso '11	♟ 5
● Picchio Rosso '10	♟ 4

Collelungo

LOC. COLLELUNGO
53011 CASTELLINA IN CHIANTI [SI]
TEL. 0577740489
www.collelungo.com

CELLAR SALES
PRE-BOOKED VISITS
ACCOMMODATION AND RESTAURANT SERVICE
ANNUAL PRODUCTION 15,000 bottles
HECTARES UNDER VINE 19.00

● Chianti Cl. '11	♥♥ 3
● Chianti Cl. Campo Cerchi Ris. '09	♥♥ 5
● Chianti Cl. Ris. '10	♥ 3

Collemattoni

LOC. SANT'ANGELO IN COLLE
POD. COLLEMATTONI, 100
53020 MONTALCINO [SI]
TEL. 0577844127
www.collemattoni.it

CELLAR SALES
PRE-BOOKED VISITS
ANNUAL PRODUCTION 35,000 bottles
HECTARES UNDER VINE 6.70

● Brunello di Montalcino '08	♥♥ 6
● Rosso di Montalcino '11	♥ 3

Tenuta di Collosorbo

FRAZ. CASTELNUOVO DELL'ABATE
LOC. VILLA A SESTA, 25
53024 MONTALCINO [SI]
TEL. 0577835534
www.collosorbo.com

CELLAR SALES
PRE-BOOKED VISITS
ANNUAL PRODUCTION 100,000 bottles
HECTARES UNDER VINE 27.00

● Brunello di Montalcino Ris. '07	♥♥ 8
● Brunello di Montalcino '08	♥ 6
● Rosso di Montalcino '11	♥ 4

Contucci

VIA DEL TEATRO, 1
53045 MONTEPULCIANO [SI]
TEL. 0578757006
www.contucci.it

CELLAR SALES
PRE-BOOKED VISITS
ACCOMMODATION
ANNUAL PRODUCTION 100,000 bottles
HECTARES UNDER VINE 21.00

● Nobile di Montepulciano Pietra Rossa '10	♥♥ 4
○ Santo	♥♥ 6
● Nobile di Montepulciano '10	♥ 3
● Nobile di Montepulciano Mulinvecchio '10	♥ 5

Corte alla Flora

FRAZ. ACQUAVIVA
VIA DI CERVOGNANO, 23
53040 MONTEPULCIANO [SI]
TEL. 0578766003
www.corteallaflora.it

PRE-BOOKED VISITS
ANNUAL PRODUCTION 200,000 bottles
HECTARES UNDER VINE 35.00

● Nobile di Montepulciano Ris. '09	♥♥ 5
● Rosso di Montepulciano '11	♥♥ 2*
● Nobile di Montepulciano '10	♥ 3
● Pugnitello '11	♥ 5

Croce di Febo

LOC. SANT'ALBINO
VIA DI VILLA BIANCA, 2
53045 MONTEPULCIANO [SI]
TEL. 0578799337
www.crocedifebo.com

CELLAR SALES
PRE-BOOKED VISITS
ACCOMMODATION
ANNUAL PRODUCTION 12,000 bottles
HECTARES UNDER VINE 9.50
VITICULTURE METHOD Certified Organic

● Nobile di Montepulciano '10	♥♥ 4
● Rosso di Montepulciano '11	♥ 3
○ Somaio '12	♥ 3

F.lli Dal Cero

LOC. MONTECCHIO DI CORTONA
SS 403
52044 CORTONA [AR]
TEL. 0457460110
www.vinidalcero.com

CELLAR SALES
PRE-BOOKED VISITS
ANNUAL PRODUCTION 90,000 bottles
HECTARES UNDER VINE 55.00

○ Podere Bianchino '12	♼♼ 2*
● Cortona Syrah '10	♼ 5
● Preziosaterra '11	♼ 3
● Selverello '12	♼ 2

Tenuta degli Dei

VIA SAN LEOLINO, 56
50022 GREVE IN CHIANTI [FI]
TEL. 055852593
www.deglidei.it

PRE-BOOKED VISITS
ANNUAL PRODUCTION 58,000 bottles
HECTARES UNDER VINE 8.70

● Cavalli '10	♼♼ 6
● Le Redini '11	♼♼ 4

Fattoria di Dievole

FRAZ. VIGLIAGLI
VIA DIEVOLE, 6
53010 CASTELNUOVO BERARDENGA [SI]
TEL. 0577322613
www.dievole.it

CELLAR SALES
PRE-BOOKED VISITS
ACCOMMODATION AND RESTAURANT SERVICE
ANNUAL PRODUCTION 550,000 bottles
HECTARES UNDER VINE 91.00

● Chianti Cl. Dieulele Ris. '09	♼♼ 7
● Broccato '09	♼ 5
● Chianti Cl. La Vendemmia '11	♼ 3
● Chianti Cl. Novecento '09	♼ 5

Donna Olimpia 1898

FRAZ. BOLGHERI
LOC. MIGLIARINI, 142
57022 CASTAGNETO CARDUCCI [LI]
TEL. 0565749801
www.donnaolimpia1898.it

CELLAR SALES
ACCOMMODATION
ANNUAL PRODUCTION 160,000 bottles
HECTARES UNDER VINE 42.00

● Bolgheri Rosso '10	♼♼ 5
○ Bolgheri Bianco '11	♼ 5
● Tageto '12	♼ 2

Donne Fittipaldi

LOC. BOLGHERI
VIA BOLGHERESE, 148
57022 CASTAGNETO CARDUCCI [LI]
TEL. 0565762175
www.donnefittipaldi.com

● Bolgheri Rosso Sup. 1S '10	♼♼ 5
○ Bolgheri Bianco '12	♼ 3
● Bolgheri Rosso '11	♼ 3

Fattoi

LOC. SANTA RESTITUTA
POD. CAPANNA, 101
53024 MONTALCINO [SI]
TEL. 0577848613
www.fattoi.it

CELLAR SALES
PRE-BOOKED VISITS
ANNUAL PRODUCTION 50,000 bottles
HECTARES UNDER VINE 9.00

● Brunello di Montalcino Ris. '07	♼♼ 7
● Brunello di Montalcino '08	♼ 5
● Rosso di Montalcino '11	♼ 3

Fattoria di Fiano

LOC. FIANO
VIA FIRENZE, 11
50050 CERTALDO [FI]
TEL. 0571669048
www.fattoriadifiano.it

CELLAR SALES
PRE-BOOKED VISITS
ANNUAL PRODUCTION 150,000 bottles
HECTARES UNDER VINE 22.00

● Fianesco '10	♟♟ 5
● Chianti Colli Fiorentini '11	♟ 2
● Chianti Colli Fiorentini Ris. '09	♟ 2
● Chianti Ris. Fiano '10	♟ 2

Ficomontanino

LOC. FICOMONTANINO
53043 CHIUSI [SI]
TEL. 057821180
www.agricolaficomontanino.it

CELLAR SALES
PRE-BOOKED VISITS
ANNUAL PRODUCTION 50,000 bottles
HECTARES UNDER VINE 8.00

● Chianti Colli Senesi Terre del Fico '10	♟♟ 2*
● Lucumone del Fico '09	♟ 5

Poderi Fontemorsi

VIA DELLE COLLINE
56040 MONTESCUDAIO [PI]
TEL. 3356843438
www.fontemorsi.it

CELLAR SALES
ACCOMMODATION
ANNUAL PRODUCTION 50,000 bottles
HECTARES UNDER VINE 8.50
VITICULTURE METHOD Certified Organic

● Montescudaio Rosso Spazzavento '11	♟♟ 2*
● Guadipiani '10	♟ 4
⊙ Rosato di Fontemorsi '12	♟ 2
○ Tresassi '12	♟ 2

Le Fonti

LOC. LE FONTI
50020 PANZANO [FI]
TEL. 055852194
www.fattorialefonti.it

CELLAR SALES
PRE-BOOKED VISITS
ANNUAL PRODUCTION 45,000 bottles
HECTARES UNDER VINE 9.00

● Chianti Cl. Ris. '09	♟♟ 4
● Chianti Cl. '10	♟ 3
● Fontissimo '09	♟ 5

Fornacina

POD. FORNACINA, 153
53024 MONTALCINO [SI]
TEL. 0577848464
www.cantinafornacina.it

CELLAR SALES
PRE-BOOKED VISITS
ANNUAL PRODUCTION 25,000 bottles
HECTARES UNDER VINE 5.00
VITICULTURE METHOD Certified Organic

● Brunello di Montalcino Ris. '07	♟♟ 7
● Brunello di Montalcino '08	♟ 5
● Rosso di Montalcino '11	♟ 3

La Fralluca

LOC. BARBICONI, 153
57028 SUVERETO [LI]
TEL. 0565829076
www.lafralluca.com

HECTARES UNDER VINE 10.00

● Syrah Pitis '10	♟♟ 3
○ Viognier '11	♟♟ 2*
● Suvereto Sangiovese Ciparisso '10	♟ 3
● Filide '10	♟ 3

Giomi Zannoni

VIA AURELIA NORD, 63
57029 CAMPIGLIA MARITTIMA [LI]
TEL. 0565846416
www.giomi-zannoni.com

ANNUAL PRODUCTION 18,000 bottles
HECTARES UNDER VINE 7.00

● Aldo 917 '11	🍷🍷 5
○ Corniola '12	🍷 3
● Val di Cornia Rodantonio '11	🍷 5
○ Vermentino Ninà 910 '12	🍷 3

Cantina del Giusto

VIA ENEA GACI, 15/17
53045 MONTEPULCIANO [SI]
TEL. 0578767229
www.cantinadelgiusto.it

● Nobile di Montepulciano San Claudio II '10	🍷🍷 3
● Nobile di Montepulciano Purth '10	🍷 5
● Nobile di Montepulciano Purth Ris. '07	🍷 5
● Rosso di Montepulciano Purth '10	🍷 5

Il Grillesino
Compagnia del Vino

LOC. COLLE DI LUPO
58051 MAGLIANO IN TOSCANA [GR]
TEL. 055243101
www.compagniadelvino.it

PRE-BOOKED VISITS
ACCOMMODATION
ANNUAL PRODUCTION 180,000 bottles
HECTARES UNDER VINE 20.00

● Morellino di Scansano Ris. '10	🍷🍷 3
● Ciliegiolo '12	🍷 2
○ Scalavite '12	🍷 2

Podere Gualandi

LOC. POPPIANO
VIA RIPE, 19
50025 MONTESPERTOLI [FI]
TEL. 05582336
www.guidogualandi.com

CELLAR SALES
PRE-BOOKED VISITS
ANNUAL PRODUCTION 25,000 bottles
HECTARES UNDER VINE 3.00
VITICULTURE METHOD Certified Organic

○ Vinum '11	🍷🍷 3
● Chianti Colli Fiorentini Montebetti '11	🍷 2
● Gualandus '08	🍷 5
○ Vinum Porpora '12	🍷 3

Icario

VIA DELLE PIETROSE, 2
53045 MONTEPULCIANO [SI]
TEL. 0578758845
www.icario.it

CELLAR SALES
PRE-BOOKED VISITS
ANNUAL PRODUCTION 140,000 bottles
HECTARES UNDER VINE 20.00

● Nobile di Montepulciano Vitaroccia Ris. '09	🍷🍷 5
● Nobile di Montepulciano '10	🍷 4
● Rosso di Montepulciano '12	🍷 2
● Rosso Icario '11	🍷 2

Istine

VIA ROMA, 11
53017 RADDA IN CHIANTI [SI]
TEL. 0577733684
www.istine.it

● Chianti Cl. '10	🍷🍷 3*
● Chianti Cl. '11	🍷🍷 3

Fattoria Kappa

LOC. LE FABBRICHE
VIA DI GROTTI, 20
57016 ROSIGNANO MARITTIMO [LI]
TEL. 3346619711
www.fattoriakappa.com

CELLAR SALES
PRE-BOOKED VISITS
ANNUAL PRODUCTION 20,000 bottles
HECTARES UNDER VINE 6.00

● Rosso '11	♟♟ 3*
● Kappa '10	♟♟ 3

Fattoria La Striscia

VIA DEI CAPPUCCINI, 3
52100 AREZZO
TEL. 057526740
www.lastriscia.com

ANNUAL PRODUCTION 7,800 bottles
HECTARES UNDER VINE 14.50

● Occhini '11	♟♟ 3
● Chianti '12	♟ 3
● Merlot '09	♟ 3

Maurizio Lambardi

LOC. CANALICCHIO DI SOTTO, 8
53024 MONTALCINO [SI]
TEL. 0577848476
www.lambardimontalcino.it

CELLAR SALES
PRE-BOOKED VISITS
ANNUAL PRODUCTION 17,000 bottles
HECTARES UNDER VINE 6.50

● Brunello di Montalcino '08	♟♟ 5
● Rosso di Montalcino '11	♟ 3

Podere Lamberto

VIA DEI POGGIARDELLI, 16
53045 MONTEPULCIANO [SI]
TEL. 057864601
www.poderelamberto.com

ACCOMMODATION AND RESTAURANT SERVICE
ANNUAL PRODUCTION 5,600 bottles
HECTARES UNDER VINE 1.60
VITICULTURE METHOD Certified Organic

● Nobile di Montepulciano '10	♟♟ 4
● Rosso di Montepulciano '11	♟ 3

Lavacchio

VIA DI MONTEFIESOLE, 55
50065 PONTASSIEVE [FI]
TEL. 0558317472
www.fattorialavacchio.com

CELLAR SALES
PRE-BOOKED VISITS
ACCOMMODATION AND RESTAURANT SERVICE
ANNUAL PRODUCTION 100,000 bottles
HECTARES UNDER VINE 22.00
VITICULTURE METHOD Certified Organic

● Chianti Rufina Cedro Ris. '09	♟♟ 4
○ Vin Santo del Chianti Rufina Ris. '07	♟♟ 5

Il Lebbio

LOC. SAN BENEDETTO, 11c
53037 SAN GIMIGNANO [SI]
TEL. 0577944725
www.illebbio.it

CELLAR SALES
PRE-BOOKED VISITS
ACCOMMODATION
ANNUAL PRODUCTION 60,000 bottles
HECTARES UNDER VINE 23.00

○ Vernaccia di S. Gimignano Tropie '11	♟♟ 3
● Chianti '11	♟ 2
● I Grottoni '12	♟ 3
○ Vernaccia di S. Gimignano '12	♟ 2

Leuta

VIA DI PIETRAIA, 21
52044 CORTONA [AR]
TEL. 3385033560
www.leuta.it

CELLAR SALES
PRE-BOOKED VISITS
ANNUAL PRODUCTION 15,000 bottles
HECTARES UNDER VINE 15.00

● Solitario di Leuta '09	♟♟ 6
● 1,618 Merlot '08	♟ 5
● 2,618 Cabernet Franc '10	♟ 5
● Leuta Rosso '10	♟ 4

La Madonnina - Triacca

LOC. STRADA IN CHIANTI
VIA PALAIA, 39
50027 GREVE IN CHIANTI [FI]
TEL. 055858003
www.triacca.com

PRE-BOOKED VISITS
ANNUAL PRODUCTION 527,000 bottles
HECTARES UNDER VINE 100.00

● Chianti Cl. Bello Stento '11	♟♟ 2*
● Nobile di Montepulciano Fattoria Santa Venere '10	♟♟ 3
● Chianti Cl. Ris. '10	♟ 4

Malenchini

LOC. GRASSINA
VIA LILLIANO E MEOLI, 82
50015 BAGNO A RIPOLI [FI]
TEL. 055642602
www.malenchini.it

CELLAR SALES
PRE-BOOKED VISITS
ANNUAL PRODUCTION 120,000 bottles
HECTARES UNDER VINE 17.00

● Bruzzico '10	♟♟ 4
● Chianti Colli '12	♟ 2
● Chianti Colli Fiorentini '11	♟ 2

Fattoria Lornano

LOC. LORNANO, 11
53035 MONTERIGGIONI [SI]
TEL. 0577309059
www.fattorialornano.it

CELLAR SALES
PRE-BOOKED VISITS
ACCOMMODATION
ANNUAL PRODUCTION 250,000 bottles
HECTARES UNDER VINE 45.00

● Commendator Enrico '10	♟♟ 4
● Chianti Cl. '10	♟ 3
● Chianti Cl. Le Bandite Ris. '10	♟ 4
● Chianti Cl. Ris. '10	♟ 3

Fattoria di Magliano

LOC. STERPETI, 10
58051 MAGLIANO IN TOSCANA [GR]
TEL. 0564593040
www.fattoriadimagliano.it

CELLAR SALES
PRE-BOOKED VISITS
ACCOMMODATION AND RESTAURANT SERVICE
ANNUAL PRODUCTION 300,000 bottles
HECTARES UNDER VINE 50.00

● Poggio Bestiale '11	♟♟ 5
● Morellino di Scansano Heba '12	♟ 2
○ Pagliatura '12	♟ 3
● Sinarra '11	♟ 3

Cosimo Maria Masini

VIA POGGIO AL PINO, 16
56028 SAN MINIATO [PI]
TEL. 0571465032
www.cosimomariamasini.it

CELLAR SALES
PRE-BOOKED VISITS
ANNUAL PRODUCTION 35,000 bottles
HECTARES UNDER VINE 17.00

○ Vin Santo del Chianti Fedardo '06	♟♟ 4
○ Annick '12	♟ 2
○ Daphné '11	♟ 4
● Sincero	♟ 3

Podere Monastero

LOC. MONASTERO
53011 CASTELLINA IN CHIANTI [SI]
TEL. 0577740436
www.poderemonastero.com

CELLAR SALES
PRE-BOOKED VISITS
ACCOMMODATION
ANNUAL PRODUCTION 7,000 bottles
HECTARES UNDER VINE 3.00

● La Pineta '11	♟♟ 6
● Campanaio '11	♟♟ 6

Montebelli

LOC. MOLINETTO CALDANA
58020 GAVORRANO [GR]
TEL. 0566887100
www.montebelli.com

CELLAR SALES
PRE-BOOKED VISITS
ANNUAL PRODUCTION 60,000 bottles
HECTARES UNDER VINE 16.50
VITICULTURE METHOD Certified Organic

● Acantos '09	♟ 5
● Monteregio di Massa Marittima Fabula Ris. '10	♟♟ 4
● Monteregio di Massa Marittima Fabula '10	♟ 2

Fattoria di Montechiari

VIA MONTECHIARI, 27
55015 MONTECARLO [LU]
TEL. 058322189
www.montechiari.com

CELLAR SALES
PRE-BOOKED VISITS
ANNUAL PRODUCTION 7.500 bottles
HECTARES UNDER VINE 6.00

● Montechiari Cabernet '10	♟♟ 5

Montecivoli

LOC. PODERONE DI MONTIANO
58051 MAGLIANO IN TOSCANA [GR]
TEL. 3495349727
www.montecivoli.it

● Morellino di Scansano '10	♟♟ 2*

Montepepe

VIA SFORZA, 76
54038 MONTIGNOSO [MS]
TEL. 0585831042
www.montepepe.com

CELLAR SALES
PRE-BOOKED VISITS
ANNUAL PRODUCTION 15,000 bottles
HECTARES UNDER VINE 5.40

○ Degeres '10	♟♟ 5
○ Montepepe Bianco '11	♟ 3
● Montepepe Rosso '10	♟ 4

Muralia

VIA DEL SUGHERETO
58036 ROCCASTRADA [GR]
TEL. 0564577223
www.muralia.it

CELLAR SALES
PRE-BOOKED VISITS
ANNUAL PRODUCTION 60,000 bottles
HECTARES UNDER VINE 13.00

● Manolibera '11	♟♟ 2*
○ Maremma Toscana Viognier Chiaraluna '12	♟ 4
● Monteregio di Massa Marittima Altana '10	♟ 3
● Muralia '09	♟ 4

Fattoria Ormanni

LOC. ORMANNI, 1
53036 POGGIBONSI [SI]
TEL. 0577937212
www.ormanni.it

CELLAR SALES
PRE-BOOKED VISITS
ACCOMMODATION
ANNUAL PRODUCTION 70,000 bottles
HECTARES UNDER VINE 68.00

● Chianti Cl. '10		♟♟ 3*

Az. Agr. Ornina

S.DA ORNINA, 121
52016 CASTEL FOCOGNANO [AR]
TEL. 3939410053
www.ornina.it

CELLAR SALES
PRE-BOOKED VISITS
ACCOMMODATION
ANNUAL PRODUCTION 7,000 bottles
HECTARES UNDER VINE 3.00

● Ornina '10		♟♟ 3
● Vallechiusa Rosso '11		♟♟ 2*
● Erigono '09		♟ 3
○ Vallechiusa Bianco '11		♟ 2

Padelletti

VIA PADELLETTI, 9
53024 MONTALCINO [SI]
TEL. 0577848314
www.padelletti.it

CELLAR SALES
PRE-BOOKED VISITS
ANNUAL PRODUCTION 30,000 bottles
HECTARES UNDER VINE 6.00

● Brunello di Montalcino '08		♟♟ 8
● Brunello di Montalcino Ris. '07		♟ 8

Pagani de Marchi

LOC. LA NOCERA
VIA DELLA CAMMINATA, 2
56040 CASALE MARITTIMO [PI]
TEL. 0586653016
www.paganidemarchi.com

CELLAR SALES
PRE-BOOKED VISITS
ANNUAL PRODUCTION 30,000 bottles
HECTARES UNDER VINE 6.00

● Olmata '09		♟♟ 4
○ Blumea '12		♟ 3
● Casa Nocera '09		♟ 5

Il Palagio

VIA CASE SPARSE, 38
50022 PANZANO [FI]
TEL. 055852175
www.palagiowineandoil.com

CELLAR SALES
PRE-BOOKED VISITS
ACCOMMODATION
ANNUAL PRODUCTION 25,000 bottles
HECTARES UNDER VINE 7.68

● Chianti Cl. '11		♟♟ 3

Il Palagione

VIA PER CASTEL SAN GIMIGNANO, 36
53037 SAN GIMIGNANO [SI]
TEL. 0577953134
www.ilpalagione.com

CELLAR SALES
PRE-BOOKED VISITS
ANNUAL PRODUCTION 40,000 bottles
HECTARES UNDER VINE 10.00
VITICULTURE METHOD Certified Organic

○ Vernaccia di S. Gimignano Ori Ris. '11		♟♟ 3
● Chianti Colli Senesi Drago Ris. '09		♟ 3

La Palazzetta

FRAZ. CASTELNUOVO DELL'ABATE
VIA BORGO DI SOTTO, 40
53024 MONTALCINO [SI]
TEL. 0577835531
www.fanti.beepworld.it

CELLAR SALES
PRE-BOOKED VISITS
ACCOMMODATION
ANNUAL PRODUCTION 50,000 bottles
HECTARES UNDER VINE 11.00

● Brunello di Montalcino '08	▼ 5
● Brunello di Montalcino Ris. '07	▼ 6
● Rosso di Montalcino '11	▼ 3

Marchesi Pancrazi
Tenuta di Bagnolo

FRAZ. BAGNOLO
VIA MONTALESE, 156
59013 MONTEMURLO [PO]
TEL. 0574652439
www.pancrazi.it

CELLAR SALES
PRE-BOOKED VISITS
ANNUAL PRODUCTION 12,000 bottles
HECTARES UNDER VINE 5.00

● Pinot Nero Villa di Bagnolo '10	▼▼ 5
● Pinot Nero V. Baragazza Villa di Bagnolo '09	▼ 6
● San Donato '12	▼ 2

Perazzeta

LOC. MONTENERO D'ORCIA
VIA DELL'AIA, 14
58040 CASTEL DEL PIANO [GR]
TEL. 0564954158
www.perazzeta.it

CELLAR SALES
PRE-BOOKED VISITS
ANNUAL PRODUCTION 40,000 bottles
HECTARES UNDER VINE 7.50

● Montecucco Rosso Alfeno '11	▼▼ 2*
● Montecucco Terre dei Bocci '10	▼ 3
☉ Rosato '12	▼ 2
● Sara Rosso '12	▼ 2

Peteglia

POD. PETEGLIA
58033 CASTEL DEL PIANO [GR]
TEL. 0564954108
www.peteglia.com

CELLAR SALES
PRE-BOOKED VISITS
ACCOMMODATION AND RESTAURANT SERVICE
ANNUAL PRODUCTION 6,000 bottles
HECTARES UNDER VINE 4.00

● Montecucco Sangiovese Ris. '09	▼▼ 4
○ Montecucco Vermentino '12	▼ 2
☉ Peteglia Rosato '12	▼ 2

Petricci e Del Pianta

LOC. SAN LORENZO, 20
57028 SUVERETO [LI]
TEL. 0565845140
www.petriccidelpianta.it

CELLAR SALES
PRE-BOOKED VISITS
ANNUAL PRODUCTION 40,000 bottles
HECTARES UNDER VINE 11.50

● Cerosecco '10	▼▼ 3
● Val di Cornia Aleatico Passito Stillo '11	▼▼ 5
● Val di Cornia Suvereto Sangiovese Buca di Cleonte '10	▼▼ 4

Pian delle Querci

VIA GIACOMO LEOPARDI, 10
53024 MONTALCINO [SI]
TEL. 0577834174
www.piandellequerci.it

CELLAR SALES
PRE-BOOKED VISITS
ANNUAL PRODUCTION 45,000 bottles
HECTARES UNDER VINE 8.00

● Brunello di Montalcino Ris. '07	▼▼ 8
● Brunello di Montalcino '08	▼ 8
● Rosso di Montalcino '11	▼ 7

Piandaccoli

VIA DI PIANDACCOLI, 7
50055 LASTRA A SIGNA [FI]
TEL. 0550750005
www.piandaccoli.it

● Maiorem '10	♟♟ 2*
● Chianti Cosmus '10	♟ 3
● Imprimis '10	♟ 2

Piandibugnano

LOC. PIAN DI BUGNANO
58038 SEGGIANO [GR]
TEL. 0564950773
www.piandibugnano.com

CELLAR SALES
PRE-BOOKED VISITS
ANNUAL PRODUCTION 27,800 bottles
HECTARES UNDER VINE 3.80

● Nanerone '11	♟♟ 5
● Montecucco Cuccaia '11	♟ 3
○ Montecucco Cuccallegro '12	♟ 2

Pietroso

LOC. PIETROSO
53024 MONTALCINO [SI]
TEL. 0577848573
www.pietroso.it

CELLAR SALES
PRE-BOOKED VISITS
ANNUAL PRODUCTION 30,000 bottles
HECTARES UNDER VINE 4.00

● Rosso di Montalcino '11	♟♟ 3*
● Brunello di Montalcino '08	♟♟ 6

Pieve Vecchia

FRAZ. CAMPAGNATICO
SP LE CONCE, 44
58042 CAMPAGNATICO [GR]
TEL. 0564996452
www.cantinapievevecchia.com

CELLAR SALES
PRE-BOOKED VISITS
ACCOMMODATION AND RESTAURANT SERVICE
ANNUAL PRODUCTION 120,000 bottles
HECTARES UNDER VINE 30.00

● Montecucco Rosso Albatrello '11	♟♟ 2*
○ Montecucco Vermentino Campo del Noce '12	♟ 2
● Pieve dei Monaci '11	♟ 3

La Pievuccia

LOC. LA PIEVUCCIA
VIA SANTA LUCIA, 118
52043 CASTIGLION FIORENTINO [AR]
TEL. 0575651007
www.lapievuccia.it

CELLAR SALES
PRE-BOOKED VISITS
ACCOMMODATION AND RESTAURANT SERVICE
ANNUAL PRODUCTION 20,000 bottles
HECTARES UNDER VINE 5.00
VITICULTURE METHOD Certified Organic

○ Valdichiana Chardonnay 119 '11	♟♟ 2*
⊙ Rosato '12	♟ 2
● Valdichiana Balzanella '10	♟ 2
● Valdichiana Nottelunga '10	♟ 2

Il Pinino

LOC. IL PININO, 327
53024 MONTALCINO [SI]
TEL. 0577849381
www.pinino.com

CELLAR SALES
PRE-BOOKED VISITS
ANNUAL PRODUCTION 90,000 bottles
HECTARES UNDER VINE 16.00

● Brunello di Montalcino Pinone Ris. '07	♟♟ 7
● Rosso di Montalcino '11	♟♟ 3

Podere 414

LOC. MAIANO LAVACCHIO, 10
58051 MAGLIANO IN TOSCANA [GR]
TEL. 0564507818
www.podere414.it

CELLAR SALES
PRE-BOOKED VISITS
ANNUAL PRODUCTION 110,000 bottles
HECTARES UNDER VINE 22.00

● Morellino di Scansano '10	▼▼ 3

Poderi del Paradiso

LOC. STRADA, 21A
53037 SAN GIMIGNANO [SI]
TEL. 0577941500
www.poderidelparadiso.it

CELLAR SALES
PRE-BOOKED VISITS
ACCOMMODATION
ANNUAL PRODUCTION 145,000 bottles
HECTARES UNDER VINE 25.43

○ San Gimignano Vin Santo '07	▼▼ 5
○ Vernaccia di S. Gimignano '12	▼▼ 3

Poderi Firenze

LOC. ABBANDONATO
58031 ARCIDOSSO [GR]
TEL. 0564967271
www.poderifirenze.it

ANNUAL PRODUCTION 120,000 bottles
HECTARES UNDER VINE 18.00

● Scireza '11	▼▼ 2*
● Montecucco Rosso Sottocasa '09	▼ 3

Poggio Alloro

LOC. SANT'ANDREA
53037 SAN GIMIGNANO [SI]
TEL. 0577950276
www. fattoriapoggioalloro.com

ANNUAL PRODUCTION 200,000 bottles
HECTARES UNDER VINE 25.00

○ Vernaccia San Gimignano Nicchiaio '12	▼▼ 2*
⊙ Rosato '12	▼ 2
● San Gimignano Rosso Convivio '11	▼ 2
○ Vernaccia San Gimignano '12	▼ 2

Podere Poggio Bestiale

LOC. POGGIO BESTIALE, 40
58051 MAGLIANO IN TOSCANA [GR]
TEL. 0564509007
www.poggiobestiale.it

CELLAR SALES
ANNUAL PRODUCTION 60,000 bottles
HECTARES UNDER VINE 10.00

● Morellino di Scansano '12	▼▼ 2*
● Morellino di Scansano Capofalco '12	▼ 2
○ Vermentino '12	▼ 2

Poggio Brigante

VIA COLLE DI LUPO, 13
58051 MAGLIANO IN TOSCANA [GR]
TEL. 0564592507
www.poggiobrigante.it

CELLAR SALES
PRE-BOOKED VISITS
ANNUAL PRODUCTION 80,000 bottles
HECTARES UNDER VINE 10.00
VITICULTURE METHOD Certified Organic

○ Guazzalfalco '12	▼▼ 3

Poggio dell'Aquila

LOC. POGGIOLO, 259
53024 MONTALCINO [SI]
TEL. 0577848533
www.poggiodellaquila.it

● Brunello di Montalcino '08	♔♔ 6
● Brunello di Montalcino Ris. '07	♔♔ 8

Poggio Leone

FRAZ. MONTENERO D'ORCIA
LOC. CONIELLA
58033 CASTEL DEL PIANO [GR]
TEL. 0564954203
www.poggioleone.it

CELLAR SALES
PRE-BOOKED VISITS
ANNUAL PRODUCTION 10,000 bottles
HECTARES UNDER VINE 3.00

● Montecucco Rosso '11	♔♔ 2*
● Montecucco Sangiovese '09	♔ 3
● Montecucco Sangiovese Ris. '09	♔ 3

Poggio Nibbiale

LOC. PERETA
58051 MAGLIANO IN TOSCANA [GR]
TEL. 0564505902
www.nibbiale.com

PRE-BOOKED VISITS
ANNUAL PRODUCTION 84,000 bottles
HECTARES UNDER VINE 11.00
VITICULTURE METHOD Certified Organic

● Morellino di Scansano Tommaso Ris. '10	♔♔ 4
● Morellino di Scansano '11	♔ 2

Poggio Rozzi

S.DA ROMITA, 29
50028 TAVARNELLE VAL DI PESA [FI]
TEL. 0558070012
www.toggenburg.it

CELLAR SALES
PRE-BOOKED VISITS
ACCOMMODATION
ANNUAL PRODUCTION 35,000 bottles
HECTARES UNDER VINE 9.00

○ Vin Santo del Chianti 1044 '06	♔♔ 5
● Chianti L'Alano '11	♔ 3
● Eccellenza '11	♔ 6
⊙ Idda '12	♔ 3

Il Poggiolo

LOC. POGGIOLO, 259
53024 MONTALCINO [SI]
TEL. 0577848412
www.ilpoggiolomontalcino.com

CELLAR SALES
PRE-BOOKED VISITS
ANNUAL PRODUCTION 40,000 bottles
HECTARES UNDER VINE 7.00

● Brunello di Montalcino Poggiolo Ris. '07	♔♔ 6
● Rosso di Montalcino Sassello '11	♔♔ 3
● Brunello di Montalcino '08	♔ 6
● Brunello di Montalcino Terra Rossa '08	♔ 6

Poggiopaoli

LOC. POMONTE
VIA LE RAGNAIE, 64
58054 SCANSANO [GR]
TEL. 0564599408
www.poggiopaoli.com

CELLAR SALES
PRE-BOOKED VISITS
ANNUAL PRODUCTION 35,000 bottles
HECTARES UNDER VINE 7.50
VITICULTURE METHOD Certified Organic

● Morellino di Scansano Lorenzolo '11	♔♔ 2*
● Morellino di Scansano Pomonte '11	♔ 3
● Rosso di Brenno '11	♔ 5

Pometti

LOC. LA SELVA, 16
53020 TREQUANDA [SI]
TEL. 057747833
www.pometti.it

CELLAR SALES
PRE-BOOKED VISITS
ACCOMMODATION AND RESTAURANT SERVICE
ANNUAL PRODUCTION 20,000 bottles
HECTARES UNDER VINE 11.00

● Orcia Noi '10	🏆🏆 3
● Tarchun Us '10	🏆 3
● Tinotre '10	🏆 4
● Villa Boscarello '10	🏆 4

Podere Il Pozzo

VIA ARGOMENNA
50065 PONTASSIEVE [FI]
TEL. 0558399102
www.bellinicantine.it

CELLAR SALES
ANNUAL PRODUCTION 40,000 bottles
HECTARES UNDER VINE 10.00

● Chianti Rufina Vignavecchia Ris. '09	🏆🏆 3
● Chianti Rufina '10	🏆 2

Provveditore

LOC. SALAIOLO
POD. PROVVEDITORE, 174
58054 SCANSANO [GR]
TEL. 0564599237
www.provveditore.it

CELLAR SALES
PRE-BOOKED VISITS
ANNUAL PRODUCTION 200,000 bottles
HECTARES UNDER VINE 30.00

● Morellino di Scansano Irio '12	🏆🏆 3
○ Bargaglino '12	🏆 2
● Morellino di Scansano '12	🏆 3

Quercia al Poggio

FRAZ. MONSANTO
S.DA QUERCIA AL POGGIO, 4
50021 BARBERINO VAL D'ELSA [FI]
TEL. 0558075278
www.quercialpoggio.com

CELLAR SALES
PRE-BOOKED VISITS
ACCOMMODATION
ANNUAL PRODUCTION 70,000 bottles
HECTARES UNDER VINE 15.00
VITICULTURE METHOD Certified Organic

● Chianti Cl. Quercia al Poggio '09	🏆🏆 5

Quercia Sola

LOC. STERCOLATI
58044 CINIGIANO [GR]
TEL. 3485602254
www.querciasola.it

HECTARES UNDER VINE 7.00

● Montecucco Sangiovese Solea '11	🏆🏆 2*
● Luvaia '09	🏆 3
● Quercia Sola '09	🏆 3

Rascioni Cecconello

SP SAN DONATO, 73
58010 ORBETELLO [GR]
TEL. 0564884934
www.poggiociliegio.it

● Ciliegiolo '10	🏆🏆 5
● Rotulaia Ciliegiolo '12	🏆 5

La Rasina

LOC. RASINA, 132
53024 MONTALCINO [SI]
TEL. 0577848536
www.larasina.it

CELLAR SALES
PRE-BOOKED VISITS
ACCOMMODATION
ANNUAL PRODUCTION 60,000 bottles
HECTARES UNDER VINE 11.00

● Brunello di Montalcino '08	🍷🍷 6
● Brunello di Montalcino Il Divasco Ris. '07	🍷🍷 7

Renicci

VIA DON MINZONI, 94
57028 SUVERETO [LI]
TEL. 0565828110
www.renicci.it

CELLAR SALES
ANNUAL PRODUCTION 20,000 bottles
HECTARES UNDER VINE 5.00

● Dioré '09	🍷🍷 3
● Il Rosso di Ricci '08	🍷 3
● Sangiovese '09	🍷 2
● Syrah '07	🍷 3

Rietine

LOC. RIETINE, 27
53013 GAIOLE IN CHIANTI [SI]
TEL. 0577731110
www.rietine.com

CELLAR SALES
PRE-BOOKED VISITS
ANNUAL PRODUCTION 70,000 bottles
HECTARES UNDER VINE 12.00

● Chianti Cl. Ris. '09	🍷🍷 4
● Chianti Cl. '10	🍷 2
● Tiziano '09	🍷 4

Fattoria di Rignana

LOC. RIGNANA, 15
50022 GREVE IN CHIANTI [FI]
TEL. 055852065
www.rignana.it

CELLAR SALES
PRE-BOOKED VISITS
ACCOMMODATION AND RESTAURANT SERVICE
ANNUAL PRODUCTION 40,000 bottles
HECTARES UNDER VINE 13.50

● Chianti Cl. '10	🍷🍷 3
● Il Riccio '09	🍷 5

Rigoloccio

LOC. RIGOLOCCIO
VIA PROVINCIALE, 82
58023 GAVORRANO [GR]
TEL. 056645464
www.rigoloccio.it

CELLAR SALES
PRE-BOOKED VISITS
ANNUAL PRODUCTION 40,000 bottles
HECTARES UNDER VINE 9.50

● Abundantia '11	🍷🍷 6
● Cabernet Alicante '10	🍷 2
○ Chardonnay Fiano '12	🍷 3
⊙ Rosato '12	🍷 2

Tenute delle Ripalte

LOC. RIPALTE
57031 CAPOLIVERI [LI]
TEL. 056594211
www.tenutadelleripalte.it

CELLAR SALES
PRE-BOOKED VISITS
ACCOMMODATION AND RESTAURANT SERVICE
ANNUAL PRODUCTION 60,000 bottles
HECTARES UNDER VINE 15.00

● Aleatico dell' Elba Alea Ludendo '11	🍷🍷 6
○ Bianco delle Ripalte '12	🍷 3
⊙ Rosato delle Ripalte '12	🍷 3
● Rosso delle Ripalte '11	🍷 3

Rocca di Montegrossi

FRAZ. MONTI IN CHIANTI
53010 GAIOLE IN CHIANTI [SI]
TEL. 0577747977
www.roccadimontegrossi.it

CELLAR SALES
PRE-BOOKED VISITS
ANNUAL PRODUCTION 80,000 bottles
HECTARES UNDER VINE 18.00
VITICULTURE METHOD Certified Organic

● Chianti Cl. '11	▼▼ 3*
● Chianti Cl. Vign. S. Marcellino '09	▼▼ 5

Rubicini

LOC. SAN BENEDETTO, 17C
53037 SAN GIMIGNANO [SI]
TEL. 0577944816
www.rubicini.com

CELLAR SALES
PRE-BOOKED VISITS
ANNUAL PRODUCTION 60,000 bottles
HECTARES UNDER VINE 10.00

● Pepenero '09	▼▼ 3
○ Vernaccia di S. Gimignano Etherea '11	▼▼ 2*
○ Vernaccia di S. Gimignano '12	▼ 2

La Sala

LOC. PONTEROTTO
VIA SORRIPA, 34
50026 SAN CASCIANO IN VAL DI PESA [FI]
TEL. 055828111
www.lasala.it

CELLAR SALES
PRE-BOOKED VISITS
ANNUAL PRODUCTION 85,000 bottles
HECTARES UNDER VINE 21.00

● Chianti Cl. '11	▼▼ 3
● Campo all'Albero '10	▼ 5
● Chianti Cl. Ris. '10	▼ 5

Podere San Cristoforo

LOC. BAGNO
VIA FORNI
58023 GAVORRANO [GR]
TEL. 3358212413
www.poderesancristoforo.it

CELLAR SALES
PRE-BOOKED VISITS
ACCOMMODATION
ANNUAL PRODUCTION 34,750 bottles
HECTARES UNDER VINE 15.00

● Podere San Cristoforo '12	▼▼ 5
● Amaranto '12	▼ 2
○ Luminoso '12	▼ 3
● Sangiovese Carandelle '12	▼ 3

Fattoria San Fabiano Borghini Baldovinetti

LOC. SAN FABIANO, 33
52100 AREZZO
TEL. 057524566
www.fattoriasanfabiano.it

CELLAR SALES
PRE-BOOKED VISITS
ACCOMMODATION
ANNUAL PRODUCTION 100,000 bottles
HECTARES UNDER VINE 270.00

● Piocaia '10	▼▼ 3
● Chianti '12	▼ 2
● Chianti Et. Nera '11	▼ 2
○ Chiaro di San Fabiano '12	▼ 2

San Ferdinando

LOC. CIGGIANO
VIA DEL GARGAIOLO, 33
52041 CIVITELLA IN VAL DI CHIANA [AR]
TEL. 0575440355
www.sanferdinando.eu

CELLAR SALES
PRE-BOOKED VISITS
ACCOMMODATION
ANNUAL PRODUCTION 20,000 bottles
HECTARES UNDER VINE 9.00

● Ciliegiolo '12	▼▼ 2*
● Chianti Podere Gamba '11	▼ 2
○ Vermentino '12	▼ 2

San Filippo

LOC. SAN FILIPPO, 134
53024 MONTALCINO [SI]
TEL. 0577847176
www.sanfilippomontalcino.com

ANNUAL PRODUCTION 50,000 bottles
HECTARES UNDER VINE 10.50

● Brunello di Montalcino Le Lucere Ris. '07	♛♛ 6
● Brunello di Montalcino '08	♛ 6
● Brunello di Montalcino Le Lucere '08	♛ 6
● Rosso di Montalcino Lo Scorno '11	♛ 5

Tenuta San Jacopo

LOC. CASTIGLIONCELLI, 151
52022 CAVRIGLIA [AR]
TEL. 055966003
www.tenutasanjacopo.it

CELLAR SALES
PRE-BOOKED VISITS
ACCOMMODATION
ANNUAL PRODUCTION 25,000 bottles
HECTARES UNDER VINE 40.00
VITICULTURE METHOD Certified Organic

○ Quarto di Luna '12	♛♛ 2*
● Chianti Cl. Poggio ai Grilli '09	♛ 2
● Orma del Diavolo '08	♛ 3

Santa Maria

LOC. SANTA MARIA, 298
53024 MONTALCINO [SI]
TEL. 0577847081
www.santemarie.it

CELLAR SALES
PRE-BOOKED VISITS
ACCOMMODATION
ANNUAL PRODUCTION 8,000 bottles
HECTARES UNDER VINE 3.00
VITICULTURE METHOD Certified Organic

● Brunello di Montalcino '08	♛♛ 6

Sassotondo

LOC. PIAN DI CONATI, 52
58010 SOVANA [GR]
TEL. 0564614218
www.sassotondo.it

CELLAR SALES
PRE-BOOKED VISITS
ANNUAL PRODUCTION 50,000 bottles
HECTARES UNDER VINE 12.00
VITICULTURE METHOD Certified Organic

● Ciliegiolo '12	♛♛ 2*
○ Bianco di Pitigliano Isolina '12	♛ 3
● Tufo Rosso '12	♛ 2

Sedime

POD. SEDIME, 63
53026 PIENZA [SI]
TEL. 0578748436
capitoni.marco@libero.it

CELLAR SALES
PRE-BOOKED VISITS
ANNUAL PRODUCTION 12,000 bottles
HECTARES UNDER VINE 5.00

● Orcia Rosso Frasi '09	♛♛ 4
● Orcia Rosso Capitoni '10	♛ 3

La Selva

LOC. FONTE BLANDA
SP 81 OSA, 7
58010 ORBETELLO [GR]
TEL. 0564885669
www.laselva-bio.it

CELLAR SALES
PRE-BOOKED VISITS
ACCOMMODATION
ANNUAL PRODUCTION 200,000 bottles
HECTARES UNDER VINE 31.00
VITICULTURE METHOD Certified Organic

● Morellino di Scansano '12	♛♛ 2*
● Ciliegiolo '10	♛ 3
● Maremma Toscana Privo '12	♛ 2
○ Vermentino La Selva '12	♛ 2

Fulvio Luigi Serni

LOC. LE LAME, 237
57022 CASTAGNETO CARDUCCI [LI]
TEL. 0565763585
www.sernifulvioluigi.it

CELLAR SALES
PRE-BOOKED VISITS
ANNUAL PRODUCTION 16,000 bottles
HECTARES UNDER VINE 2.50

● Bolgheri Rosso Tegoleto '11	♟♟ 3
○ Bolgheri Radius '12	♟ 2
● Bolgheri Rosso Acciderba '10	♟ 4
○ Campofitto '12	♟ 2

Serraiola

FRAZ. FRASSINE
LOC. SERRAIOLA
58025 MONTEROTONDO MARITTIMO [GR]
TEL. 0566910026
www.serraiola.it

CELLAR SALES
PRE-BOOKED VISITS
ANNUAL PRODUCTION 40,000 bottles
HECTARES UNDER VINE 12.00

● Monteregio di Massa Marittima Lentisco '11	♟♟ 3
● Campo Montecristo '11	♟ 5
● Shiraz '11	♟ 3

Setriolo

LOC. SETRIOLO, 61
53011 CASTELLINA IN CHIANTI [SI]
TEL. 3385496589
www.setriolo.com

CELLAR SALES
PRE-BOOKED VISITS
ACCOMMODATION
ANNUAL PRODUCTION 20,000 bottles
HECTARES UNDER VINE 3.50

● Chianti Cl. '11	♟♟ 3
● Chianti Cl. Ris. '09	♟ 5

Signano

LOC. SANTA MARGHERITA, 36
53037 SAN GIMIGNANO [SI]
TEL. 0577941085
www.casolaredibucciano.com

CELLAR SALES
PRE-BOOKED VISITS
ANNUAL PRODUCTION 80,000 bottles
HECTARES UNDER VINE 25.00

● Chianti Colli Senesi '11	♟♟ 2*
○ Vernaccia di S. Gimignano '12	♟♟ 2*
○ Vernaccia di S. Gimignano Poggiarelli '11	♟ 2

Solaria
Az. Agr. Cencioni Patrizia

POD. CAPANNA, 102
53024 MONTALCINO [SI]
TEL. 0577849426
www.solariacencioni.com

CELLAR SALES
PRE-BOOKED VISITS
RESTAURANT SERVICE
ANNUAL PRODUCTION 30,000 bottles
HECTARES UNDER VINE 9.00

● Brunello di Montalcino '08	♟♟ 5
● Rosso di Montalcino '11	♟♟ 4
● Brunello di Montalcino 123 Ris. '07	♟ 6

Michele Ventura Vino
Sopra la Ripa

FRAZ. SOVANA
LOC. PODERE SOPRA RIPA
58010 SORANO [GR]
TEL. 0564615579
www.sopralaripa.eu

CELLAR SALES
PRE-BOOKED VISITS
ANNUAL PRODUCTION 43,000 bottles
HECTARES UNDER VINE 10.00
VITICULTURE METHOD Certified Organic

● Ripa '11	♟♟ 3
● San Sebastiano '10	♟ 5

Spadaio e Piecorto

VIA SAN SILVESTRO, 1
50021 BARBERINO VAL D'ELSA [FI]
TEL. 0558072915
www.spadaiopiecorto.it

CELLAR SALES
PRE-BOOKED VISITS
ACCOMMODATION
ANNUAL PRODUCTION 70,000 bottles
HECTARES UNDER VINE 14.00

● Pietrarossa '10	♟♟ 2*
● Il Fratuccio '09	♟ 3

Borgo La Stella

LOC. VAGLIAGLI
B.GO LA STELLA, 60
53017 RADDA IN CHIANTI [SI]
TEL. 0577740699
www.borgolastella.com

● Chianti Cl. '10	♟♟ 3
● Chianti Cl. Ris. '10	♟♟ 4

Il Tagliato

VIA BARBIANO, 22
50022 GREVE IN CHIANTI [FI]
TEL. 3312290822
www.iltagliato.com

CELLAR SALES
PRE-BOOKED VISITS
ANNUAL PRODUCTION 3,000 bottles
HECTARES UNDER VINE 2.00
VITICULTURE METHOD Certified Organic

● Balze d'Istrice '10	♟♟ 6
● Balze d'Istrice '09	♟ 6

Talenti

FRAZ. SANT'ANGELO IN COLLE
LOC. PIAN DI CONTE
53020 MONTALCINO [SI]
TEL. 0577844064
www.talentimontalcino.it

CELLAR SALES
PRE-BOOKED VISITS
ANNUAL PRODUCTION 80,000 bottles
HECTARES UNDER VINE 21.00

● Brunello di Montalcino '08	♟♟ 6
● Rosso di Montalcino '11	♟♟ 3
● Brunello di Montalcino Pian di Conte Ris. '07	♟ 7

Fattoria della Talosa

VIA PIETROSE, 15A
53045 MONTEPULCIANO [SI]
TEL. 0578758277
www.talosa.it

CELLAR SALES
PRE-BOOKED VISITS
ANNUAL PRODUCTION 100,000 bottles
HECTARES UNDER VINE 35.00

● Nobile di Montepulciano '10	♟♟ 3
● Nobile di Montepulciano Ris. '09	♟ 4

Tenuta San Martino

VIA CHIANTIGIANA, 339
50100 BAGNO A RIPOLI [FI]
TEL. 055645588
www.tsanmartino.it

● Chianti Sup. Poggio alle Ripe '10	♟♟ 3
● Chianti Sammartino '11	♟ 2

Terrabianca

LOC. SAN FEDELE A PATERNO
53017 RADDA IN CHIANTI [SI]
TEL. 057754029
www.terrabianca.com

CELLAR SALES
PRE-BOOKED VISITS
ACCOMMODATION AND RESTAURANT SERVICE
ANNUAL PRODUCTION 360,000 bottles
HECTARES UNDER VINE 52.00

● Chianti Cl. San Fedele '10	▼▼ 3
● Chianti Cl. Croce Ris. '09	▼ 5
● Chianti Cl. Scassino '10	▼ 3

Terre dei Fiori Tenute Costa

S.DA GRILLESE UNO VIII
58100 GROSSETO
TEL. 0564405457
www.tenutecosta.it

CELLAR SALES
PRE-BOOKED VISITS
ANNUAL PRODUCTION 100,000 bottles
HECTARES UNDER VINE 30.00

● Morellino di Scansano Ventaio '10	▼▼ 5
● Monteregio di Massa Marittima '11	▼ 3

La Togata

LOC. TAVERNELLE
S.DA DI ARGIANO
53024 MONTALCINO [SI]
TEL. 0668803000
www.brunellolatogata.com

CELLAR SALES
PRE-BOOKED VISITS
ANNUAL PRODUCTION 100,000 bottles
HECTARES UNDER VINE 22.00

● Brunello di Montalcino '08	▼▼ 7
● Rosso di Montalcino '11	▼ 4

Tenuta di Trecciano

SP 52 MONTAGNOLA, 16
53018 SOVICILLE [SI]
TEL. 0577314357
www.trecciano.it

CELLAR SALES
PRE-BOOKED VISITS
ANNUAL PRODUCTION 90,000 bottles
HECTARES UNDER VINE 15.50

● Chianti Colli Senesi Ris. '10	▼▼ 3
● I Campacci '11	▼ 5

Trequanda

LOC. PIAN DELLE FONTI, 100
53020 TREQUANDA [SI]
TEL. 0577662001
www.azienda-trequanda.it

CELLAR SALES
PRE-BOOKED VISITS
ACCOMMODATION AND RESTAURANT SERVICE
ANNUAL PRODUCTION 300,000 bottles
HECTARES UNDER VINE 55.00

● Chianti Alticato Ris. '10	▼▼ 2*
● Orcia Rosso Invidia '10	▼ 3
● Orcia Rosso TreCalici '10	▼ 3

Val di Toro

LOC. POGGIO LA MOZZA
S.DA DELLE CAMPORE, 18
58100 GROSSETO
TEL. 0564409600
www.valditoro.it

CELLAR SALES
PRE-BOOKED VISITS
ANNUAL PRODUCTION 50,000 bottles
HECTARES UNDER VINE 10.00

● Morellino di Scansano '11	▼▼ 2*
○ Auramaris '12	▼ 3

Tenuta Valdipiatta

VIA DELLA CIARLIANA, 25A
53040 MONTEPULCIANO [SI]
TEL. 0578757930
www.valdipiatta.it

CELLAR SALES
PRE-BOOKED VISITS
ACCOMMODATION
ANNUAL PRODUCTION 100,000 bottles
HECTARES UNDER VINE 22.00

● Nobile di Montepulciano '10	🍷🍷 4
● Chianti Colli Senesi Tosca '11	🍷 2
● Nobile di Montepulciano Ris. '08	🍷 6
● Rosso di Montepulciano '11	🍷 3

Valle di Lazzaro

LOC. VALLE DI LAZZARO, 103
57037 PORTOFERRAIO [LI]
TEL. 0565916387
www.valledilazzaro.com

CELLAR SALES
PRE-BOOKED VISITS
ANNUAL PRODUCTION 12,000 bottles
HECTARES UNDER VINE 4.00

● Elba Passito Lazarus '11	🍷🍷 4
○ Chardonnay Lazarus '12	🍷🍷 4
○ Elba Vermentino '12	🍷 3
⊙ Rosato '12	🍷 3

Vignavecchia

VIA SDRUCCIOLO DI PIAZZA, 7
53017 RADDA IN CHIANTI [SI]
TEL. 0577738090
www.vignavecchia.com

CELLAR SALES
PRE-BOOKED VISITS
ANNUAL PRODUCTION 65,000 bottles
HECTARES UNDER VINE 19.00

● Chianti Cl. Ris. '10	🍷🍷 3
● Chianti Cl. Vign. Odoardo Beccari Ris. '10	🍷🍷 4
● Chianti Cl. '11	🍷 3

Villa Calcinaia

FRAZ. GRETI
VIA CITILLE, 84
50022 GREVE IN CHIANTI [FI]
TEL. 055854008
www.villacalcinaia.it

CELLAR SALES
PRE-BOOKED VISITS
ACCOMMODATION AND RESTAURANT SERVICE
ANNUAL PRODUCTION 100,000 bottles
HECTARES UNDER VINE 27.00

● Chianti Cl. '10	🍷🍷 3*
● Chianti Cl. Ris. '10	🍷 3

Villa I Cipressi

LOC. VILLA I CIPRESSI
53024 MONTALCINO [SI]
TEL. 0577848640
www.villacipressi.it

● Rosso di Montalcino '11	🍷🍷 6
● Brunello di Montalcino '08	🍷 7
● Brunello di Montalcino Zebras Ris. '07	🍷 7

Villa La Ripa

LOC. ANTRIA, 38
52100 AREZZO
TEL. 0575315118
www.villalaripa.it

CELLAR SALES
PRE-BOOKED VISITS
ANNUAL PRODUCTION 7,000 bottles
HECTARES UNDER VINE 2.50

● Tiratari '10	🍷🍷 4
⊙ Peconio '10	🍷 2

Villa Loggio

FRAZ. CIGNANO
LOC. IL LOGGIO, 24
52044 CORTONA [AR]
TEL. 0575618306
www.villaloggio.com

PRE-BOOKED VISITS
ANNUAL PRODUCTION 150,000 bottles
HECTARES UNDER VINE 70.00

○ Losna '12	▼▼ 8
● Curtun '09	▼ 8
● Pinot Nero '08	▼ 4
● Thefarie '08	▼ 3

Villa Pinciana

S.DA VILLA PINCIANA, 2/A
58011 CAPALBIO [GR]
TEL. 0564896598
www.villapinciana.com

● Terraria '10	▼▼ 5
● Airali '12	▼ 3
● Tilaria '11	▼ 3

Villa Trasqua

LOC. TRASQUA
53011 CASTELLINA IN CHIANTI [SI]
TEL. 0577743075
www.villatrasqua.it

CELLAR SALES
PRE-BOOKED VISITS
ANNUAL PRODUCTION 200,000 bottles
HECTARES UNDER VINE 54.00

● Trasgaia '09	▼▼ 5
● Chianti Cl. '10	▼ 2
● Chianti Cl. Fanatico Ris. '09	▼ 3

I Vini di Maremma

LOC. IL CRISTO
58046 GROSSETO
TEL. 056434426
www.ivinidimaremma.it

ANNUAL PRODUCTION 600,000 bottles
HECTARES UNDER VINE 400.00

● Maremma Cabernet Sauvignon '09	▼▼ 3
● Lallegro '11	▼ 3
● Monteregio di Massa Marittima Macchiaiolo '09	▼ 2

Tenuta Vitanza

FRAZ. TORRENIERI
POD. BELVEDERE, 145
52024 MONTALCINO [SI]
TEL. 0577832882
www.tenutavitanza.it

CELLAR SALES
PRE-BOOKED VISITS
ANNUAL PRODUCTION 200,000 bottles
HECTARES UNDER VINE 26.00

● Brunello di Montalcino Andreatta '07	▼▼ 7
● Brunello di Montalcino Tradizione '08	▼▼ 5
● Rosso di Montalcino '11	▼▼ 3
● Chianti Colli Senesi '11	▼ 2

Viticcio

VIA SAN CRESCI, 12A
50022 GREVE IN CHIANTI [FI]
TEL. 055854210
www.fattoriaviticcio.com

CELLAR SALES
PRE-BOOKED VISITS
ACCOMMODATION
ANNUAL PRODUCTION 250,000 bottles
HECTARES UNDER VINE 39.00

● Chianti Cl. '11	▼▼ 3*
● Chianti Cl. Ris. '10	▼ 4

MARCHE

The 2010 growing season yielded perfect grapes and the new Castelli di Jesi Verdicchio Classico Riserva designation seized the opportunity to show off the eclectic talent of the quintessential Marche cultivar once again. The vintage has been interpreted in different styles with great expertise and sensitivity, exemplified by the very fresh, focused tone of Leo Felici's Cantico della Figura and the sophistication of Villa Bucci from Ampelio Bucci, as well as Fazi Battaglia's San Sisto, not to mention the intense aromatic profile of Umani Ronchi's Plelo, Plevalta's San Paolo and Moncaro's Vigna Novali. This theory is underpinned and bolstered by Carlo and Gianfranco Garofoli's outstanding La Selezione Gioacchino Garofoli 2008, and the austere elegance of Casalfarneto's Crisio 2011. Poderi Mattioli's Ylice 2012 deserves a special mention, for a masterly interpretation of a current vintage Verdicchio that marks the three-brother team's debut. Matelica performed as well as Jesi, with Alta Vallesina's most representative wineries showing the world the excellence of its terroir. Alongside La Monacesca's Mirum 2011, which displays exceptional consistency even in difficult vintages, three fantastic whites are back at the top this year: Collestefano 2012, Meridia 2010 from Belisario, and Vigneto Fogliano 2010 from Bisci. Piceno area whites are represented by a little-known name already mentioned in past editions of our Guide: Simone Spinelli. His Artemisia 2012 is the flagship of a fine array of excellent-quality Pecorinos. The reds include the solidly consistent Roggio del Filare 2010 from Velenosi and the marvellous Arshura 2011, the best ever produced since the beginning of Valter "La Roccia" Mattoni's venture in far-off 2000, winning him his first ever Tre Bicchieri. Marco Casolanetti is no debutant, but he too can enjoy the excitement of the new with Kupra 2010. The line-up is completed by an exquisite Pollenza 2010 from Aldo Brachetti Peretti, making a total of 18 Tre Bicchieri. This year's tastings also highlighted some excellent sweet wines, mainly from partially dried verdicchio and lacrima di Morro d'Alba grapes. The provinces of Pesaro and Macerata made no waves and no news is good news, as the saying goes, but the situation here is anything but static. One winery in five did not make it into the 2013 Guide, a clear signal that the concept of quality is fluid and that nobody should think of resting on their laurels.

Aurora

LOC. SANTA MARIA IN CARRO
C.DA CIAFONE, 98
63073 OFFIDA [AP]
TEL. 0736810007
www.viniaurora.it

CELLAR SALES
PRE-BOOKED VISITS
ACCOMMODATION
ANNUAL PRODUCTION 50,000 bottles
HECTARES UNDER VINE 9.50
VITICULTURE METHOD Certified Organic

Once an eccentric bastion fighting technical interference and mechanization in the countryside, Aurora is now a proud artisanal model, a trailblazer for mutual solidarity ideals and a distinctive ethical philosophy that rejects any type of chemical pollution of the environment. The key to understanding their temperamental, dramatic wines with their assertive character and sheer sincerity, intentionally yet justifiably flawed, is the combination of many hours in the vineyards, patient ageing, ambient yeasts only, and minimum use of sulphites or other treatments. With no Barricadiero or Rosso Piceno Superiore, both still ageing, Fiobbo 2011 steals the limelight. As usual, it has rather clenched aromas on the nose, then its strength hits the mouth, with a pronounced gastronomic zest, leading to an almost tactile contentment. While a touch countrified, Falerio 2012 and Passerina 2012 flow deliciously across the palate.

Belisario

VIA ARISTIDE MERLONI, 12
62024 MATELICA [MC]
TEL. 0737787247
www.belisario.it

CELLAR SALES
PRE-BOOKED VISITS
ANNUAL PRODUCTION 1,000,000 bottles
HECTARES UNDER VINE 300.00

Every outstanding wine-producing area benefits from the presence of a co-operative winery that is committed to quality. This is the key to understanding Belisario, since 1971 the driving force behind the Verdicchio di Matelica designation and, to date, the efforts to involve this tiny designation in numerous schemes have never dwindled. The calibre of the Cambrugiano and Meridia selections, the striking sense of territory of Cerro, the organic project of the Vigneti Belisario and the irresistibly priced Valbona and L'Anfora are all examples of this work. The splendid Meridia 2010 best reflects the superb qualities of Verdicchio di Matelicas. Citron, almond and aniseed express refined aromas on the nose repeated in the full, soaring mouth, following through an incisive yet very elegant progression. The lip-smacking Cambrugiano 2010 is slightly oaky. Cerro 2012 and Vigneti B. 2012 are as delicious as ever, while the fascinating Carpe Diem 2008 has never been so elegantly charming.

○ Offida Pecorino Fiobbo '11	♀♀ 2*
○ Falerio '12	♀♀ 2*
○ Offida Passerina Passito '10	♀♀ 4
○ Passerina '12	♀♀ 2*
● Marche Rosso '12	♀ 2
● Rosso Piceno '12	♀ 2
● Barricadiero '10	♀♀♀ 4*
● Barricadiero '09	♀♀♀ 4
● Barricadiero '06	♀♀♀ 4
● Barricadiero '04	♀♀♀ 3
● Barricadiero '03	♀♀♀ 3*
● Barricadiero '02	♀♀♀ 3
○ Offida Passerina '11	♀♀ 2*
○ Offida Pecorino Fiobbo '10	♀♀ 2*
● Rosso Piceno '11	♀♀ 2*
● Rosso Piceno Sup. '10	♀♀ 2*

○ Verdicchio di Matelica Meridia '10	♀♀♀ 3*
○ Verdicchio di Matelica Passito Carpe Diem '08	♀♀ 3*
● Enoà '11	♀♀ 3
○ Verdicchio di Matelica Cambrugiano Ris. '10	♀♀ 3
○ Verdicchio di Matelica L'Anfora '12	♀♀ 2*
○ Verdicchio di Matelica Terre di Valbona '12	♀♀ 2*
○ Verdicchio di Matelica Vign. Belisario '12	♀♀ 3
○ Verdicchio di Matelica Vign. del Cerro '12	♀♀ 2*
● Colli Maceratesi Rosso Coll'Amato '12	♀ 2
● Colli Maceratesi Rosso Vigneti B. '12	♀ 2
○ Verdicchio di Matelica Brut Cuvée Nadir '11	♀ 2

Bisci

VIA FOGLIANO, 120
62024 MATELICA [MC]
TEL. 0737787490
www.bisciwines.it

CELLAR SALES
PRE-BOOKED VISITS
ANNUAL PRODUCTION 120,000 bottles
HECTARES UNDER VINE 19.00

Bisci is a classic prestige label thanks to Pierino and Giuseppe, two brothers who set up their aspirational farm between Matelica and Cerreto d'Esi in 1980. True to tradition they also planted red varieties like sangiovese and merlot, although Verdicchio from matelica clones has always been the terroir's best expression. For years, Aroldo Bellelli has skilfully seen to all the vineyard and cellar aspects, fermenting in the most classic style, followed by lengthy ageing in stainless steel or cement tanks. To have the tiniest vision of what a Matelica can offer, you must have a Vigneto Fogliano in your cellar. The 2010 version is a masterpiece, elegantly combining tones of aniseed, toasted almond and aromatic herbs in a perfectly paced mouth, culminating in a deep, slender finish and ending on a salty note. Verdicchio 2012 is equally outstanding. Its crystal-clear almond aromas are backed by a lively vigour extending to clean citrus fruits and stones.

○ Verdicchio di Matelica Vign. Fogliano '10	♟♟♟ 3*
○ Verdicchio di Matelica '12	♟♟ 2*
○ Verdicchio di Matelica Vign. Fogliano '08	♟♟♟ 3*
● Piangifame '07	♟♟ 4
● Rosso Fogliano '10	♟♟ 3
○ Verdicchio di Matelica '11	♟♟ 3
○ Verdicchio di Matelica '10	♟♟ 2*
○ Verdicchio di Matelica '09	♟♟ 2*
○ Verdicchio di Matelica Senex '03	♟♟ 4
○ Verdicchio di Matelica Senex '98	♟♟ 4*
○ Verdicchio di Matelica Vign. Fogliano '07	♟♟ 3*
● Villa Castiglioni '03	♟♟ 3

Boccadigabbia

LOC. FONTESPINA
C.DA CASTELLETTA, 56
62012 CIVITANOVA MARCHE [MC]
TEL. 073370728
www.boccadigabbia.com

CELLAR SALES
PRE-BOOKED VISITS
ANNUAL PRODUCTION 100,000 bottles
HECTARES UNDER VINE 25.00

Under Napoleonic rule, in the late-19th century, the Boccadigabbia estate was planted with French varieties. The Alessandri family acquired the property in the late 1950s and renewed all the vineyards in 1986, remaining loyal to the French spirit, which explains why the most famous varieties of France are grown on the Adriatic shores. Over time, the owners introduced other native grapes, including maceratino, montepulciano and sangiovese. The cellars have recently been given a complete facelift and expanded. The wines are classical along international lines and are distrustful of any modern-day fad. Akronte 2008, from cabernet sauvignon, is austerely Bordeaux in spirit, offering green peppers threaded with toasty, peppery notes. Power, joined to a certain alcoholic strength, also defines the full-bodied merlot-based Pix 2009. La Castelletta 2012, from pinot grigio, has a delicious fruitiness.

● Akronte '08	♟♟ 7
○ La Castelletta Pinot Grigio '12	♟♟ 3
● Pix '09	♟♟ 6
⊙ Roseo '12	♟♟ 2*
● Rosso Piceno Boccadigabbia '10	♟ 3
● Saltapicchio '08	♟ 4
● Akronte '98	♟♟♟ 7
● Akronte '97	♟♟♟ 7
● Akronte '95	♟♟♟ 7
● Akronte '07	♟♟ 7
○ Montalperti '07	♟♟ 4
● Pix Merlot '07	♟♟ 6
● Rosso Piceno Boccadigabbia '08	♟♟ 3
● Rosso Piceno Boccadigabbia '06	♟♟ 3*
● Saltapicchio Sangiovese '07	♟♟ 4

Borgo Paglianetto

LOC. PAGLIANO, 393
62024 MATELICA [MC]
TEL. 073785465
www.borgopaglianetto.it

CELLAR SALES
PRE-BOOKED VISITS
ANNUAL PRODUCTION 60,000 bottles
HECTARES UNDER VINE 18.00

The winery owned by Mario Bassilissi and the Roversi family has slowly consolidated a style where a glass of white accurately expresses its territory. They use stainless steel to kindle the varietal traits of Verdicchio, which at Matelica mean flowers, a stony minerality and depth without excessive alcohol. These characteristics are concentrated in the Vertis selection and are clearly visible in the reasonably-priced Terravignata entry-level wine. The one exception is the rookie Riserva Jera, a blend of various batches, some matured in 900-litre casks and the rest fermented briefly on the skins. Production from red grape varieties is slightly more borderline, despite being well-crafted. Jera 2009 has a striking personality, reflecting the ideal classic Matelica. Dried fruit, spring flowers and aniseed form a refined, neat picture, while the mouth is filled with expansive flavours in a slow, continuous progression. There is a sober lean elegance to the Vertis 2011. Petrara 2012 has the perfect grip.

○ Verdicchio di Matelica Jera Ris. '09	♗♗ 4
○ Verdicchio di Matelica Petrara '12	♗♗ 2*
○ Verdicchio di Matelica Terravignata '12	♗♗ 2*
○ Verdicchio di Matelica Vertis '11	♗♗ 3
○ Verdicchio di Matelica Vertis '09	♗♗♗ 3*
● Terravignata '09	♗♗ 2*
● Terravignata '08	♗♗ 2*
○ Verdicchio di Matelica Aja Lunga '05	♗♗ 2*
○ Verdicchio di Matelica Petrara '10	♗♗ 2*
○ Verdicchio di Matelica Petrara '09	♗♗ 2*
○ Verdicchio di Matelica Petrara '08	♗♗ 2*
○ Verdicchio di Matelica Terravignata '11	♗♗ 2*
○ Verdicchio di Matelica Terravignata '10	♗♗ 2*
○ Verdicchio di Matelica Terravignata '09	♗♗ 2*
○ Verdicchio di Matelica Vertis '10	♗♗ 3*
○ Verdicchio di Matelica Vertis '08	♗♗ 3*

★Bucci

FRAZ. PONGELLI
VIA CONA, 30
60010 OSTRA VETERE [AN]
TEL. 071964179
www.villabucci.com

CELLAR SALES
PRE-BOOKED VISITS
ANNUAL PRODUCTION 120,000 bottles
HECTARES UNDER VINE 31.00
VITICULTURE METHOD Certified Organic

It has certainly been years since Ampelio Bucci jumped a year for its Riserva, probably the top Verdicchio of the whole designation. The box labelled 2011 will not be ticked, after what was undoubtedly a very tough decision, based upon the difficult climatic conditions of the vintage and the firm resolution to only propose a label that is faithfully true to its emblem. The current 2010 version must keep the side up between one vintage and the next. This year, Villa Bucci 2010 is one of the best ever. The familiar sequence of camomile, hay, meadow flowers mixes with fine tones of toasted almond and aniseed; the mouth has a measured pace and, while seductively drinkable, it is layered in complexity. Not to be missed. Bucci 2011, with its sapid suppleness, is delicate yet ready to be enjoyed.

○ Castelli di Jesi Verdicchio Cl. Villa Bucci Ris. '10	♗♗♗ 6
○ Verdicchio dei Castelli di Jesi Cl. Sup. '11	♗♗ 3*
● Rosso Piceno Tenuta Pongelli '11	♗ 3
○ Verdicchio dei Castelli di Jesi Cl. Villa Bucci Ris. '09	♗♗♗ 6
○ Verdicchio dei Castelli di Jesi Cl. Villa Bucci Ris. '07	♗♗♗ 6
○ Verdicchio dei Castelli di Jesi Cl. Villa Bucci Ris. '06	♗♗♗ 6
○ Verdicchio dei Castelli di Jesi Cl. Villa Bucci Ris. '05	♗♗♗ 5
○ Verdicchio dei Castelli di Jesi Cl. Villa Bucci Ris. '04	♗♗♗ 5
○ Verdicchio dei Castelli di Jesi Cl. Villa Bucci Ris. '03	♗♗♗ 5
○ Verdicchio dei Castelli di Jesi Cl. Villa Bucci Ris. '01	♗♗♗ 5

Campo di Maggio

LOC. PAGLIARE DEL TRONTO
VIA ROCCABRIGNOLA
63036 SPINETOLI [AP]
TEL. 07368905590
www.cantinacampodimaggio.it

CELLAR SALES
PRE-BOOKED VISITS
ANNUAL PRODUCTION 20,000 bottles
HECTARES UNDER VINE 9.00

The River Tronto covers about ten kilometres before reaching the Adriatic Sea. Marco Corradetti's estate overlooks the broad, industrialized valley, but up on the hillside things are quite different. No factories, just olive groves, fields of sunflowers and grain, and row upon row of vines. The many small operations that were once growers for co-operative wineries are now a nucleus of little artisanal wineries. Campo di Maggio is only interested in local varieties and makes standard-label wines that cost much less than they are worth. Harvesting by hand and keeping the cellars small means production is monitored at every turn. Of the four labels presented, the most interesting is Pecorino 2012, where aromas of meadow herbs and hints of aniseed meet a vibrant mouth with delicious grassy citrussy tones. More slender, but with no loss of character, is the Passerina 2012. Rosso Piceno 2012 has the fruity succulence of montepulciano grapes mellowed by hints of cherry.

○ Offida Passerina '12	♥♥ 2*
○ Offida Pecorino '12	♥♥ 2*
● Rosso Piceno '12	♥♥ 2*
○ Falerio '12	♥ 2

Le Caniette

C.DA CANALI, 23
63065 RIPATRANSONE [AP]
TEL. 07359200
www.lecaniette.it

CELLAR SALES
PRE-BOOKED VISITS
ANNUAL PRODUCTION 60,000 bottles
HECTARES UNDER VINE 16.00
VITICULTURE METHOD Certified Organic

The Vagnonis are real vignerons with a century of family expertise behind them. Over the years they have developed their own distinctive style of solid wines with vibrant colours and aromas that pour the sunshine accumulated in the vineyards into the bottle. The Constant sea breezes from the nearby Adriatic are the secret of the organic methods long in use here. The artisanal expression of the wines reveals some calculated novelty, also betrayed by a determined use of barriques to age the Offida Pecorino. Small wood is also used for more ambitious reds, while the steel is kept for the early-drinkers. The excellent Morellone 2007 expresses the generous essence of montepulciano in a full body. In the Bordeaux mix Cinabro 2010, oaky tones intersect spices in a well-balanced, weighty mouth, leading to an uplifting finish. In the losonogaia 2011, the oak from small barrels is balanced by a mouth full of evolving flavours.

● Cinabro '10	♥♥ 8
● Rosso Piceno Morellone '07	♥♥ 4
○ Offida Pecorino losonogaia non sono Lucrezia '11	♥♥ 4
○ Offida Pecorino Veronica '12	♥♥ 4
○ Lucrezia '12	♥ 2
● Rosso Piceno Rosso Bello '10	♥ 2
● Cinabro '09	♀♀ 8
○ Offida Passerina Vino Santo Sibilla '06	♀♀ 5
○ Offida Pecorino losonogaia non sono Lucrezia '10	♀♀ 4
○ Offida Pecorino losonogaia non sono Lucrezia '08	♀♀ 4
● Rosso Piceno Morellone '06	♀♀ 4
● Rosso Piceno Rosso Bello '09	♀♀ 2*

La Canosa

C.DA SAN PIETRO, 6
63030 ROTELLA [AP]
TEL. 0736374556
www.lacanosaagricola.it

CELLAR SALES
PRE-BOOKED VISITS
ANNUAL PRODUCTION 150,000 bottles
HECTARES UNDER VINE 28.00

Poggio Canoso is at high altitude, right on the doorstep of Mount Ascensione. Cool nights are an advantage when the sun has the impact of the 43rd parallel. The gentle slopes and open valley bring their own special glow. This is where Riccardo Reina decided to put a crazy idea to the test, making wines that exploit these particular soil and climate characteristics, which are not extreme but are certainly different. No corners were cut. First-class staff is headed up by Carlo Ferrini, and Emidio Felicetti has very attractive, state-of-the-art cellars at his disposal. No master stroke yet, they have still to create the great wine that makes sense of all the hard work of many years. Our tastings of Nullius 2011, from sangiovese, highlighted its elegance, well-ordered tannins, although it does lack complexity. The succulent Nummaria 2011 is well-crafted, as are the two tangy, easy-drinking harvest-year whites: Pekò from pecorino and Servator from passerina.

● Nullius '11	♥♥ 3
○ Pekò '12	♥♥ 2*
● Rosso Piceno Sup. Nummaria '11	♥♥ 2*
○ Servator '12	♥♥ 2*
● Musè '11	♥ 3
● Rosso Piceno Signator '11	♥ 2
● Musé '10	♥♥ 3
● Nullius '10	♥♥ 3
● Nullius '07	♥♥ 3
● Rosso Piceno Sup. Nummaria '10	♥♥ 2*
● Rosso Piceno Sup. Nummaria '05	♥♥ 2*
○ Servator '11	♥♥ 2*

Carminucci

VIA SAN LEONARDO, 39
63013 GROTTAMMARE [AP]
TEL. 0735735869
www.carminucci.com

CELLAR SALES
ANNUAL PRODUCTION 200,000 bottles
HECTARES UNDER VINE 46.00

Giovanni Carminucci is named after his grandfather and now runs the winery founded by him back in 1928. Like his father Piero, Giovanni spends his life among the vines. They are growers, wine and grape merchants, and bottlers. Their shared vision of the wine world can be translated into a single word: experience, which is what the Caminuccis rely on each year to present a solid range of local designations, interpreted in a low-key modern style. Most of the vineyards are located in the classic Piceno area, between Offida and Ripatransone. The large, well-organized cellars are on the hills behind Grottammare, looking over the Tesino Valley. Overall, a great result from all the whites from native grapes, with Pecorino Belato 2012 leading the troop. The best wine is still the Rosso Piceno Superiore Naumachos 2010. Plum, quinine and a subtle gamey trace give character to its weighty energetic mouthfeel.

○ Casta '12	♥♥ 2*
○ Falerio Naumachos '12	♥♥ 2*
○ Offida Pecorino Belato '12	♥♥ 2*
● Rosso Piceno Sup. Naumachos '10	♥♥ 2*
○ Falerio Grotte sul Mare '12	♥ 1*
○ Naumachos '11	♥ 2
● Rosso Piceno Grotte sul Mare '12	♥ 1*
○ Falerio dei Colli Ascolani Grotte sul Mare '11	♥♥ 1*
○ Naumachos '10	♥♥ 2*
○ Offida Pecorino Belato '11	♥♥ 2*
● Paccaosso '09	♥♥ 7
● Paccaosso '04	♥♥ 7
● Rosso Piceno Grotte sul Mare '09	♥♥ 1*
● Rosso Piceno Sup. Naumachos '08	♥♥ 2*
● Rosso Piceno Sup. Naumachos '04	♥♥ 2*

Casalfarneto

VIA FARNETO, 12
60030 SERRA DE' CONTI [AN]
TEL. 0731889001
www.casalfarneto.it

CELLAR SALES
PRE-BOOKED VISITS
ANNUAL PRODUCTION 500,000 bottles
HECTARES UNDER VINE 43.00

The view from the cutting-edge cellars to the vineyards is superb, taking in the neat countryside of colours and crops, dotted with the oak thickets that give the winery its name. The sense of peace seems to infuse the elegance sought by the Tognis for their Verdicchios. The grape's versatility is the key for differentiating the various labels, and a series of hand-harvested vintages impart a fresh, classic style to the drinkable Fontevecchia, to the rich, full-bodied Grancasale fermented by cold skin contact of late-harvest grapes, and to the persuasive finesse of the plush Cimaio from grapes picked after they acquire a mist of noble rot. Their top wine is Crisio 2011, a soberly refined blend offering whiffs of aniseed and lime-blossom, with a fine almondy note emerging clearly in the orderly, pointed finish.

○ Castelli di Jesi Verdicchio Cl. Crisio Ris. '11	♔♔♔ 3*
○ Cimaio '10	♔♔ 5
● Merago '09	♔♔ 3
○ Verdicchio dei Castelli di Jesi Cl. Grancasale '11	♔♔ 3
○ Verdicchio dei Castelli di Jesi Cl. Sup. Fontevecchia '12	♔♔ 2*
○ Verdicchio dei Castelli di Jesi Cl. Crisio Ris. '10	♔♔♔ 3*
○ Cimaio '09	♔♔ 5
● Lacrima di Morro d'Alba Rosae '09	♔♔ 2*
● Merago '08	♔♔ 3
○ Verdicchio dei Castelli di Jesi Cl. Sup. Fontevecchia '11	♔♔ 2*
○ Verdicchio dei Castelli di Jesi Cl. Sup. Fontevecchia '09	♔♔ 2*

Maria Pia Castelli

C.DA SANT'ISIDORO, 22
63015 MONTE URANO [FM]
TEL. 0734841774
www.mariapiacastelli.it

CELLAR SALES
PRE-BOOKED VISITS
ANNUAL PRODUCTION 20,000 bottles
HECTARES UNDER VINE 8.00

Monte Urano is a leading footwear manufacturing town but not all the residents have forgotten their ancient farming heritage. There have always been vegetable gardens, olive groves and rows of vines, their crops often used for personal consumption. Enrico Bartoletti is a firm believer in the potential of his estate, in the Tenna Valley, and at the end of the 1990s he planted the most traditional local varieties. Low yields, organic-style agriculture, natural fermentation, lengthy ageing in small wood all combine to confer a distinctive quality to his wines. Erasmo Castelli 2009 is a monovarietal Montepulciano aged for 24 months in small oak barrels. Dark, with notes of liquorice, iron, fresh meat and capers, it is a layered, close-knit, very complex wine. It needs to breathe. Stella Flora 2011 is a grape-blend of pecorino, passerina, trebbiano and malvasia, fermented on the skins for 25 days and aged for 18 months in small oak barrels. It hints at lemon cream, apricot, aromatic herbs in a softly suffused mouth.

● Erasmo Castelli '09	♔♔ 5
○ Stella Flora '11	♔♔ 5
● Erasmo Castelli '06	♔♔♔ 5
● Erasmo Castelli '07	♔♔ 5
● Erasmo Castelli '05	♔♔ 5
● Orano '11	♔♔ 4
● Orano '10	♔♔ 3
○ Stella Flora '10	♔♔ 5
○ Stella Flora '09	♔♔ 5
○ Stella Flora '07	♔♔ 5

Giacomo Centanni

c.da Aso, 159
63062 Montefiore dell'Aso [AP]
Tel. 0734938530
www.vinicentanni.it

CELLAR SALES
ACCOMMODATION
ANNUAL PRODUCTION 100,000 bottles
HECTARES UNDER VINE 35.00
VITICULTURE METHOD Certified Organic

Giacomo Centanni has just graduated in oenology but he has been active in his family vineyards and cellars for quite a while. The vineyards, planted to traditional varieties, look out over the Aso Valley in a splendid hill setting, with the blue Adriatic in the distance to ensure enough ventilation even on the hottest days and with it the potential for lengthy ageing. The wines are well-defined and express a pleasant fruitiness. Fresh, varietal whites come from cold skin contact and stainless steel; the succulent, invigorating reds come from proper oak ageing. Offida Pecorino is now a fact. The 2012 version offers exceptional drinkability in a citrus key, followed by limpid citrussy tones. Passerina 2012 proved itself with its fresh, invigorating fruit, hinging on immediate enjoyment, as does Profumo di Rosa 2012, a crisp sangiovese rosé. Montepulciano grapes are the source of the polished, neat yet juicy Montefloris 2011.

○ Offida Pecorino '12	♥♥ 2*
● Montefloris '11	♥♥ 2*
○ Offida Passerina '12	♥♥ 2*
☉ Profumo di Rosa '12	♥♥ 2*
○ Falerio dei Colli Ascolani Il Borgo '12	♥ 2
○ Offida Passerina M. Cl. '11	♥ 4
● Montefloris '08	♀♀ 2
○ Offida Passerina '10	♀♀ 2*
○ Offida Passerina '09	♀♀ 2
○ Offida Pecorino '11	♀♀ 2*
● Offida Pecorino '10	♀♀ 2*
● Rosso Piceno Rosso di Forca '10	♀♀ 2*

Cherri d'Acquaviva

via San Francesco, 4
63030 Acquaviva Picena [AP]
Tel. 0735764416
www.vinicherri.it

CELLAR SALES
PRE-BOOKED VISITS
ANNUAL PRODUCTION 160,000 bottles
HECTARES UNDER VINE 32.00

Paolo Cherri's winery is rooted in a long family tradition that started in the early 20th century, but the quality watershed came in 2003, when the new cellars were built. Acquaviva, on its tall hill overlooking the Adriatic, was all set to break away from local shackles, armed with the benefits of wine country set on gentle slopes, blessed with a sunny climate tempered by the constant sea breezes. Here, montepulciano, sangiovese, trebbiano, and passerina ripen without difficulty. The cooler aspects are planted to pecorino. In the cellar, they carry out classical vinification in a reduced environment for the whites, while the more ambitious reds age in small oak barrels. These have given the best results. Tumbulus 2009 has tempting aromas and a mellow, polished tannic weave. Laudi 2009 offers a fruity nature and gutsy tannins, while Falerio 2012 is rounded and full of flavour.

☉ Ancella '12	♥♥ 2*
☉ Falerio '12	♥♥ 2*
● Offida Tumbulus '09	♥♥ 4
● Rosso Piceno Sup. Laudi '09	♥♥ 4
○ Offida Pecorino Altissimo '12	♥ 3
○ Pecorino Brut	♥ 3
● Rosso Piceno '12	♥ 2
○ Offida Passerina Radiosa '11	♀♀ 2*
○ Offida Pecorino Altissimo '09	♀♀ 3
● Offida Tumbulus '07	♀♀ 4
● Offida Tumbulus '06	♀♀ 4
● Rosso Piceno Sup. '09	♀♀ 2*

Ciù Ciù

Loc. Santa Maria in Carro
c.da Ciafone, 106
63035 Offida [AP]
Tel. 0736810001
www.ciuciuvini.it

CELLAR SALES
PRE-BOOKED VISITS
ACCOMMODATION AND RESTAURANT SERVICE
ANNUAL PRODUCTION 600,000 bottles
HECTARES UNDER VINE 130.00
VITICULTURE METHOD Certified Organic

Recent acquisition of top vineyard terrain further enhanced the thriving estate between Offida and Acquaviva Picena, at the heart of the traditional Piceno district. Massimiliano and Walter Bartolomeo also put the finishing touches to an ambitious plan to renew their vineyards, now all under organic management. A young, motivated teams works in the vines and cellars, and the well-equipped operation can cope with growing interest from a market enamoured of the intense, well-focused aromas of wines true to their terroir. The most popular are from the most typical varieties: montepulciano, sangiovese, pecorino and passerina. Merlettaie 2012 steps up the vigour of its usual fruity tones, triggering a harmonious and decidedly tasty mouthfeel. Oppidum 2008, from montepulciano, offers sensations of morello cherry and plum in a round, juicy mouth full of deliciously ripe fruit. Bacchus 2012 and Passerina Evoé 2012 flow fragrantly across the palate.

○ Offida Pecorino Le Merlettaie '12	♟♟ 2*
● Oppidum '08	♟♟ 4
○ Evoé '12	♟ 2
○ Falerio Oris '12	♟ 2
● Offida Rosso Esperanto '08	♟ 5
● Rosso Piceno Bacchus '12	♟ 2
○ Evoé '11	♟♟ 2*
○ Evoé '09	♟♟ 2*
○ Falerio dei Colli Ascolani Oris '11	♟♟ 2*
● Offida Rosso Esperanto '05	♟♟ 5
● Oppidum '07	♟♟ 4
● Rosso Piceno Sup. Gotico '10	♟♟ 2*
● Rosso Piceno Sup. Gotico '09	♟♟ 2*
● Rosso Piceno Sup. Gotico '08	♟♟ 2*
● Saggio '10	♟♟ 2*
● San Carro '09	♟♟ 2*

Tenuta Cocci Grifoni

Loc. San Savino
c.da Messieri, 12
63038 Ripatransone [AP]
Tel. 073590143
www.tenutacoccigrifoni.it

CELLAR SALES
PRE-BOOKED VISITS
ACCOMMODATION
ANNUAL PRODUCTION 330,000 bottles
HECTARES UNDER VINE 50.00

Marilena and Paola Cocci Grifoni follow in the footsteps of their father, Guido, with passion. An icon of local oenology, Guido was a wise and dauntless vigneron, the first to believe in the Rosso Piceno designation, and helped to pluck the pecorino variety from the verge of extinction. If there was ever to be a local hall of fame, the first tile would be his. His daughters have embraced their father's philosophy and today Contrada Messieri still produces wines of impeccable style that include cellarable multi-faceted passerina and pecorino whites, and austere reds, true to tradition, aged at length in medium oak casks. No dashed hopes after waiting so long for a Vigna Messieri 2007 that proudly reveals its severe personality, filling the mouth with typical notes of plum and cherry joined to close-woven, smooth tannins. Le Torri 2008 is austere and spicy. Freshly-cut grass and dry leaves bring charm to the sapid integrity of Colle Vecchio 2012, the most classical Pecorino di Offida.

● Rosso Piceno Sup. V. Messieri '07	♟♟ 4
○ Offida Passerina Adamantea '12	♟♟ 2*
○ Offida Pecorino Podere Colle Vecchio '12	♟♟ 3
● Rosso Piceno Sup. Le Torri '08	♟♟ 3
○ Offida Passerina Brut Gaudio Magno '12	♟ 3
○ Offida Pecorino Podere Colle Vecchio '10	♟♟ 3*
○ Offida Pecorino Podere Colle Vecchio '08	♟♟ 2*
○ Offida Pecorino Podere Colle Vecchio '07	♟♟ 2*
● Offida Rosso Il Grifone '06	♟♟ 3
● Rosso Piceno Rubinio '10	♟♟ 2*
● Rosso Piceno Sup. Le Torri '07	♟♟ 2*
● Rosso Piceno Sup. V. Messieri '06	♟♟ 3

Collestefano

LOC. COLLE STEFANO, 3
62022 CASTELRAIMONDO [MC]
TEL. 0737640439
www.collestefano.com

CELLAR SALES
PRE-BOOKED VISITS
ANNUAL PRODUCTION 60,000 bottles
HECTARES UNDER VINE 17.00
VITICULTURE METHOD Certified Organic

It does not take much to realize that olive trees are very rare in the Upper Esino Valley, as they suffer from the cold. This surely explains why Verdicchio di Matelica has a sharper, more northerly profile than Verdicchio di Jesi. Fabio Marchionni's vineyards are set against the woodland with a backdrop onto Appenine mountain crests. They have always been farmed organically without yielding to idealogical extremes, and his vintage Verdicchio has an unmistakable profile and a character that strengthens with age. Ideally, it should be enjoyed after several years but we already know that its youthful exuberance is impossible to resist. In the 2012 version, the aromatic slant is on cleanly assembled citrus fruit, hawthorn and pebbles; backed by an electrifying acidity, the mouth releases a sensational progression underpinned by salty tones that gradually turn into full-blown minerality. The sangiovese Rosa di Elena 2012 is equally fascinating.

○ Verdicchio di Matelica Collestefano '12	♟♟♟	2*
⊙ Rosa di Elena '12	♟♟	2*
○ Verdicchio di Matelica Collestefano '07	♟♟♟	2*
○ Verdicchio di Matelica Collestefano '06	♟♟♟	2*
⊙ Rosa di Elena '10	♟♟	2*
⊙ Rosa di Elena '08	♟♟	2*
○ Sauvignon '09	♟♟	2*
○ Verdicchio di Matelica Collestefano '11	♟♟	2*
○ Verdicchio di Matelica Collestefano '10	♟♟	2*
○ Verdicchio di Matelica Collestefano '09	♟♟	2*
○ Verdicchio di Matelica Collestefano '08	♟♟	2*

Colli di Serrapetrona

VIA COLLI, 7/8
62020 SERRAPETRONA [MC]
TEL. 0733908329
www.collidiserrapetrona.it

CELLAR SALES
PRE-BOOKED VISITS
ACCOMMODATION AND RESTAURANT SERVICE
ANNUAL PRODUCTION 80,000 bottles
HECTARES UNDER VINE 20.00

Serrapetrona is a unique terroir on the Marche landscape, with tall hills verging on the Apennines. This is home to the native vernaccia nera, a robust grape with a rustic temperament traditionally used to make a sweetish sparkling wine. Founded about ten years ago, Colli di Serrapetrona aimed to call into question this system and used the variety as the base for producing some still, quite textured, reds. The winery developed various protocols, observing phenolic ageing closely and setting aside the barriques of the past, replaced by larger wood. The results are thrilling. All the monovarietal Vernaccias are impressive. Robbione 2008 has fruity, spicy aromas upheld by a sound tannic weave; the fresh Collequanto 2011 has clean peppery overtones and a moreish drinkability; Sommo 2009 is an unusual sweet wine. We were blown over by the Pinot Nero 2009, with its salty tones and elegantly lean profile.

● Pinot Nero '09	♟♟	5
● Serrapetrona Collequanto '11	♟♟	3
● Serrapetrona Robbione '08	♟♟	5
● Sommo '09	♟♟	4
⊙ Serrarosa '12	♟	2
● Serrapetrona Collequanto '08	♟♟	2*
● Serrapetrona Collequanto '07	♟♟	2*
● Serrapetrona Robbione '06	♟♟	4
● Sommo '06	♟♟	4

Cantina Cològnola

LOC. COLÒGNOLA
62011 CINGOLI [MC]
TEL. 0733616438
www.agrarialombardi.it

CELLAR SALES
PRE-BOOKED VISITS
ANNUAL PRODUCTION 65,000 bottles
HECTARES UNDER VINE 20.00

Attentive readers will recall that Cantina Cològnola is no newcomer to the Guide although much has changed since entrepreneur Walter Darini acquired the property from the Lombardi family in 2011. Firstly, the cellars were completely refurbished to cutting-edge standards. A new technical team came aboard, headed by young oenologist Gabriele Villani. The past lingers in some of the vineyards, waiting for newcomers to reach the production stage, and in some of the wine names. Above all, the perfect, unspoilt territory, a stone's throw from Staffolo, has not changed and has already shown it can bring forth charismatic wines. During our tastings, we were impressed by the restrained elegance of Ghiffa 2011, where aromas of aniseed and aromatic herbs are replicated in a tidy, precise mouth. With a touch more vigour, denied by the over-hot year, it would have made the grade. Labieno Riserva 2010 elegantly features the tangy, bitterish language of Verdicchio.

○ Verdicchio dei Castelli di Jesi Cl. Ghiffa '11	♥♥ 2*
○ Castelli di Jesi Verdicchio Cl. Labieno Ris. '10	♥♥ 3
○ Brut M. Cl. Tango Brut '09	♥ 5
○ Brut Musa Verde '12	♥ 5
○ Verdicchio dei Castelli di Jesi Cl. Via Condotto '12	♥ 2
○ Esino Bianco Condotto '07	♥♥ 2*
● Sestiere '06	♥♥ 3
○ Verdicchio dei Castelli di Jesi Cl. Ghiffa '08	♥♥ 2*
○ Verdicchio dei Castelli di Jesi Cl. Labieno Ris. '07	♥♥ 3
○ Verdicchio dei Castelli di Jesi Cl. Sup. San Michele della Ghiffa '07	♥♥ 3*
○ Verdicchio dei Castelli di Jesi Passito Cingulum '08	♥♥ 5

Colonnara

VIA MANDRIOLE, 6
60034 CUPRAMONTANA [AN]
TEL. 0731780273
www.colonnara.it

CELLAR SALES
PRE-BOOKED VISITS
ANNUAL PRODUCTION 1,000,000 bottles
HECTARES UNDER VINE 120.00
VITICULTURE METHOD Certified Organic

Colonnara has been operating for 55 years and is the oldest co-operative winery in the Marche and the cellars, with their enormous tanks installed in the striking tower, are the reminder of that. The basement levels keep jealous guard over entire vintages of Cuprese: a real treasure, a liquid memory that captures the wealth of the Verdicchio world from 1991. Alongside shelves of vintage bottles, the cool rooms contain dozens of riddling racks, icon of the winery's other flagship, its sparkling wines. Once again, Ubaldo Rosi 2007 is the best Metodo Classico in the region, elegantly revealing balsamic tones, fine herbs and aniseed. A pinch too much softness keeps it a step away from the top award. We did taste the best Cuprese in years, back to its clear classical form where dried fruit, flowers and meadow flowers melt in a supple, elegant mouth that fades to a delicious bitterish finish, the seal of a pure-bred Verdicchio.

○ Verdicchio dei Castelli di Jesi Brut M. Cl. Ubaldo Rosi '07	♥♥ 5
○ Verdicchio dei Castelli di Jesi Cl. Sup. Cuprese '12	♥♥ 2*
○ Verdicchio dei Castelli di Jesi Cl. Brut Luigi Ghislieri	♥♥ 4
● Tornamagno '09	♥ 3
○ Verdicchio dei Castelli di Jesi Spumante Cuvée Tradition	♥ 4
○ Verdicchio dei Castelli di Jesi M. Cl. Brut Ubaldo Rosi Ris. '06	♥♥♥ 5
○ Verdicchio dei Castelli di Jesi Cl. Portonuovo '10	♥♥ 2*
○ Verdicchio dei Castelli di Jesi Cl. Sup. Cuprese '11	♥♥ 2*
○ Verdicchio dei Castelli di Jesi Cl. Sup. Cuprese '10	♥♥ 2*

Conti di Buscareto

FRAZ. PIANELLO
VIA SAN GREGORIO, 66
60010 OSTRA [AN]
TEL. 0717988020
www.contidibuscareto.com

CELLAR SALES
PRE-BOOKED VISITS
ANNUAL PRODUCTION 220,000 bottles
HECTARES UNDER VINE 70.00

Enrico Giacomelli and Claudio Gabellini's operation has three main production sites. The main variety is a lacrima nera, concentrated in the vineyards surrounding the winery; montepulciano and sangiovese come from plots further south, situated in the heart of the Ancona district; verdicchio is grown in the vast Arcevia vineyard, set high on hills at the northernmost border of the designation. The cellars are large and well equipped to produce wines in a relaxed, up-to-the-minute style that keeps a close eye on the market but the right vintage can drum up more interest for some labels. Lacrima Passito 2010 is a masterpiece. Mulberry, mineral whiffs, dried rose petals, bottled black cherries blend into intense aromas and reappear in a perfectly-balanced dense, creamy mouth. This wine would never bore. The typical, well-structured yet flowing Lacrima 2012 is excellent, and so is the Verdicchio 2012, which is lean but vaunts a savoury progression.

● Lacrima di Morro d'Alba Passito '10	🍷🍷	3*
● Lacrima di Morro d'Alba '12	🍷🍷	2*
● Lacrima di Morro d'Alba		
Compagnia della Rosa '07	🍷🍷	3
● Rosso Piceno '11	🍷🍷	2*
○ Verdicchio dei Castelli di Jesi '12	🍷🍷	2*
○ Crimà '12	🍷	2
☉ Rosé '12	🍷	3
○ Tyche '12	🍷	2
● Bisaccione '08	🍷🍷	5
● Bisaccione '07	🍷🍷	5
● Lacrima di Morro d'Alba '10	🍷🍷	2*
● Lacrima di Morro d'Alba '09	🍷🍷	2*
● Lacrima di Morro d'Alba Passito '08	🍷🍷	3
● Rosso Piceno '08	🍷🍷	2*
○ Verdicchio dei Castelli di Jesi '09	🍷🍷	2*

Coroncino

C.DA CORONCINO, 7
60039 STAFFOLO [AN]
TEL. 0731779494
coroncino@libero.it

CELLAR SALES
PRE-BOOKED VISITS
ANNUAL PRODUCTION 45,000 bottles
HECTARES UNDER VINE 9.50

If anyone asks Lucio Canestrari which farming methods he prefers, his laconic reply is "Sensible ones". Which may seem evasive but those who know him also know how much time he spends in his vineyards. The main plot is located in Spescia, between Staffolo and Cupramontana, closed to any use of synthetic chemicals and even the use of heavy metals is restricted. His judgement makes him prefer ripe grapes, which he then converts into wines of generous profile, extractive, and high in alcohol glycerine. In the cellars, intervention is kept to a minimum and so are levels of sulphur dioxide. Musts are housed mainly in stainless steel, but the selections that go into Gaiospino age in small used barrels. Despite being nearly too soft and caressing, Gaiospino 2010 can be summed up into an overflowing personality, with complex, oxidized aromas on the nose, boosted by a powerful mouth where flavours linger for minutes. Il Coroncino 2011 is similar.

○ Verdicchio dei Castelli di Jesi Cl. Sup.		
Gaiospino '10	🍷🍷	4
○ Verdicchio dei Castelli di Jesi Cl. Sup.		
Il Coroncino '11	🍷🍷	2*
○ Verdicchio dei Castelli di Jesi Cl. Sup.		
Il Bacco '11	🍷	2
○ Verdicchio dei Castelli di Jesi Cl. Sup.		
Gaiospino '03	🍷🍷🍷	4
○ Verdicchio dei Castelli di Jesi Cl. Sup.		
Gaiospino '97	🍷🍷🍷	4*
○ Verdicchio dei Castelli di Jesi Cl. Sup.		
Gaiospino '09	🍷🍷	4
○ Verdicchio dei Castelli di Jesi Passito		
Bambulè '10	🍷🍷	3
○ Verdicchio dei Castelli di Jesi Passito		
Oracacio '10	🍷🍷	3

Tenuta De Angelis

VIA SAN FRANCESCO, 10
63030 CASTEL DI LAMA [AP]
TEL. 073687429
www.tenutadeangelis.it

CELLAR SALES
PRE-BOOKED VISITS
ANNUAL PRODUCTION 500,000 bottles
HECTARES UNDER VINE 50.00

Quinto Fausti runs one of the Piceno district's best-known operations, with a compact mantle of vineyards sited in excellent wine country right in the traditional heart of Offida. Here he exploits the generous solidity of montepulciano for full-bodied, mature Rosso Picenos of striking fruit and subtle tannins. Whites come from typical passerina and pecorino varieties but Quinto has never given up on trebbiano in his Falerios, or monovarietal Chardonnays. The large cellars are the base for classic fermentation, in a reductive environment for the whites so popular with the locals, and in ever-smaller wood depending on the destination of the reds for international clientele. Pecorino 2012 is lovely, full of fine flavours in balance between zesty grip and lavish juiciness; Passerina 2012 has a fresh vitality. The Rosso Picenos are well-crafted: the 2012 version has a fragrant drinkability with hints of cherry. Superiore 2011 has structure and a fruity lustre.

○ Offida Pecorino '12	♟♟ 2*
● Anghelos '11	♟♟ 3
○ Offida Passerina '12	♟♟ 2*
● Rosso Piceno '12	♟♟ 1*
● Rosso Piceno Sup. '11	♟♟ 2*
● Rosso Piceno Sup. Oro '09	♟ 3
● Anghelos '01	♟♟♟ 4
● Anghelos '99	♟♟♟ 4*
● Anghelos '10	♟♟ 3
● Anghelos '09	♟♟ 3
● Anghelos '07	♟♟ 3
● Rosso Piceno Sup. '10	♟♟ 2*

Fattoria Dezi

C.DA FONTEMAGGIO, 14
63029 SERVIGLIANO [FM]
TEL. 0734710090
fattoriadezi@hotmail.com

CELLAR SALES
PRE-BOOKED VISITS
ACCOMMODATION
ANNUAL PRODUCTION 50,000 bottles
HECTARES UNDER VINE 15.00

Elfish Stefano Dezi travels round Italy and Europe to introduce his wines to the market. A quintessential Marche man, he is practical and proud of his origins, and when at home in Contrada Fontemaggio, he is the winemaker, king of the cellars, meandering around the steel tanks that house the pecorino, verdicchio and malvasia-based whites, and the small wood used for the monovarietal montepulciano Regina del Bosco and sangiovese Solo. The other side of the coin is his brother Davide, a vigneron to the bone, who spends his time in the vineyards around the winery, all with different aspects and altitudes, and all as manicured as a lawn. Regina 2010 is forbidding and gutsy. It needs decanting to free its aromatic intensity, where morello cherry mixes with spices and a pronounced note of liquorice. Dezio 2011 is close-focused, offering a succulent drink.

● Regina del Bosco '10	♟♟ 6
● Dezio '11	♟♟ 3
○ Falerio Pecorino P. '11	♟♟ 3
● Solo '11	♟ 6
● Regina del Bosco '06	♟♟♟ 6
● Regina del Bosco '05	♟♟♟ 6
● Regina del Bosco '03	♟♟♟ 6
● Solo Sangiovese '05	♟♟♟ 6
● Solo Sangiovese '01	♟♟♟ 5
● Solo Sangiovese '00	♟♟♟ 6
○ Le Solagne '10	♟♟ 3
● Regina del Bosco '09	♟♟ 6
● Solo '10	♟♟ 6

Fazi Battaglia

VIA ROMA, 117
60031 CASTELPLANIO [AN]
TEL. 073181591
www.fazibattaglia.it

CELLAR SALES
PRE-BOOKED VISITS
ANNUAL PRODUCTION 2,000,000 bottles
HECTARES UNDER VINE 210.00

Despite its position as the prime exporter of Verdicchio throughout the world since the post-war years, the remarkable Fazi Battaglia has been making profound changes. The most evident is to its technical direction, entrusted to Lorenzo Landi, and distribution structure, in the hands of the experienced Campari group. Attention is centred on the white grapes of Jesi, in its many interpretations. While San Sisto remains, as always, a deep white, Massaccio is now more refined and Le Moie and Ekeos focus on pleasantly fresh aromas. Firm efforts are directed towards improving the famous amphora Titulus as in the past it has harboured many unduly anonymous wines. The refined San Sisto 2010, with its supple and coherent take on the best values of Verdicchio, deserves the highest honour. Bewitching sensations emerge from the honey and candied fruit in Arkezia, from botrytized verdicchio grapes. Acclaim resounds for the powerful, supple Massaccio 2010, last year in the guide instead of the 2009 version.

○ Castelli di Jesi Verdicchio Cl.
  San Sisto Ris. '10 ♟♟♟ 4*
○ Arkezia '10 ♟♟ 5
○ Verdicchio dei Castelli di Jesi Cl. Sup.
  Massaccio '10 ♟♟ 3*
● Rosso Conero Ekeos '12 ♟♟ 3
○ Verdicchio dei Castelli di Jesi Cl. Sup.
  Ekeos '12 ♟♟ 3
○ Verdicchio dei Castelli di Jesi Cl. Sup.
  Le Moie '12 ♟♟ 2*
● Conero Passo del Lupo Ris. '10 ♟ 4
○ Verdicchio dei Castelli di Jesi Cl.
  Titulus '12 ♟ 2
○ Verdicchio dei Castelli di Jesi Cl.
  San Sisto Ris. '09 ♟♟♟ 4*
○ Verdicchio dei Castelli di Jesi Cl.
  San Sisto Ris. '07 ♟♟♟ 4

Andrea Felici

VIA SANT'ISIDORO, 28
62021 APIRO [MC]
TEL. 0733611431
www.andreafelici.it

CELLAR SALES
PRE-BOOKED VISITS
ANNUAL PRODUCTION 35,000 bottles
HECTARES UNDER VINE 7.00
VITICULTURE METHOD Certified Organic

Leo Felici is a marvel. Endowed with exhilarating energy and fuelled by a deep love for his work as grower, he slips nonchalantly out of work overalls peppered with holes and into the latest sartorial elegance, or off a tractor and onto a plane en route to Japan. His Verdicchios, worked in stainless steel only, are rooted in tradition but imbued with a modern sensitivity where organic practices are employed without excessive fuss to obtain crystalline wines. In this, he is helped by the fantastic mountain territory of Apiro where the strength of Jesi meets the deep mineral tones of Matelica. The mix of amazing vigour, very fresh aromas and pervasive flavours allow Il Cantico 2010 to replicate the giddy heights of 2009. This is a wine not to be missed, overflowing with personality and with great potential. The younger Andrea Felici 2012 is an irresistible wine to drink now, dipping into its limpid aromas and vibrant salty acidity.

○ Castelli di Jesi Verdicchio Cl.
  Il Cantico della Figura Ris. '10 ♟♟♟ 4*
○ Verdicchio dei Castelli di Jesi Cl. Sup.
  Andrea Felici '12 ♟♟ 2*
○ Verdicchio dei Castelli di Jesi Cl.
  Il Cantico della Figura Ris. '09 ♟♟♟ 4*
○ Verdicchio dei Castelli di Jesi Cl.
  Il Cantico della Figura Ris. '08 ♟♟ 4
○ Verdicchio dei Castelli di Jesi Cl.
  Il Cantico della Figura Ris. '07 ♟♟ 4
○ Verdicchio dei Castelli di Jesi Cl.
  Andrea Felici '11 ♟♟ 2*
○ Verdicchio dei Castelli di Jesi Cl. Sup.
  Andrea Felici '10 ♟♟ 2*
○ Verdicchio dei Castelli di Jesi Cl. Sup.
  Andrea Felici '09 ♟♟ 2

Fiorano

C.DA FIORANO, 19
63030 COSSIGNANO [AP]
TEL. 073598446
www.agrifiorano.it

CELLAR SALES
PRE-BOOKED VISITS
ACCOMMODATION
ANNUAL PRODUCTION 30,000 bottles
HECTARES UNDER VINE 5.00
VITICULTURE METHOD Certified Organic

Small is beautiful because it means Paolo Beretta can adopt an organic approach for his little montepulciano, sangiovese and pecorino vineyards. He can also supervise all the phases of vinification and subsequent ageing in the well-designed cellars just a stone's throw from the vines. Of course this is artisan-style production and true to varietal expression, tending to interpret the vintage and effects of any unsettling climate variations, especially for reds. The winery's only white is a monovarietal pecorino produced in reduction. Our tastings confirm the goodness of Donna Orgilla 2012, with its juicy peachy fruitiness, energetic progression and citrussy finish. It may have lost some of its past brilliance, but Terre di Giobbe 2010 always puts on a good show. Temperamental, its ripe fruit offers cherry notes and a fleshy, weighty mouth. The young-drinking Sangiovese 2012 is simple and cherry-crisp.

Cantine Fontezoppa

C.DA SAN DOMENICO, 38
62012 CIVITANOVA MARCHE [MC]
TEL. 0733790504
www.cantinefontezoppa.it

CELLAR SALES
PRE-BOOKED VISITS
ACCOMMODATION AND RESTAURANT SERVICE
ANNUAL PRODUCTION 290,000 bottles
HECTARES UNDER VINE 38.00

Fontezoppa wines are a fusion of Macerata's various terroirs. The Civitanova Alta vineyards by the sea, are variously aspected and grow cabernet, merlot, sangiovese, pecorino, and maceratino. Serrapetrona's pre-Apennine vineyards are planted to vernaccia nera and pinot nero, while the verdicchio comes from Matelica. Giovanni Basso, an experienced oenologist, knows exactly how to handle each variety to retain varietal differences by separate fermentation, followed by ageing in small wood of different passages. Grapes from the Serrapetrona territory provided the best testings. Vernaccia gave origin to the unusual, delicately fragrant Rosé Metodo Classico 2010 and the peppery, tannic Falcotto 2009, held back by a looming grassy note. Pinot nero conveys elegance and severity to Dedicato a Piero 2008. Among the rest, Marche Rosso 2011, half sangiovese plus cabernet sauvignon and merlot, has rounded tannins and is ready to drink.

○ Offida Pecorino Donna Orgilla '12	▼▼ 3
● Rosso Piceno Sup. Terre di Giobbe '10	▼▼ 3
● Sangiovese '12	▼ 2
● Fiorano Sangiovese '10	♈♈ 2*
○ Offida Pecorino Donna Orgilla '11	♈♈ 3
○ Offida Pecorino Donna Orgilla '10	♈♈ 3*
○ Offida Pecorino Donna Orgilla '09	♈♈ 3*
● Rosso Piceno Sup. Terre di Giobbe '09	♈♈ 2*
● Rosso Piceno Sup. Terre di Giobbe '08	♈♈ 2*
● Rosso Piceno Sup. Terre di Giobbe '06	♈♈ 3*
● Sangiovese '11	♈♈ 2*

● Dedicato a Piero '08	▼▼ 6
● Marche Rosso '11	▼▼ 2*
⊙ Rosé M. Cl. '10	▼▼ 5
● Serrapetrona Falcotto '09	▼▼ 4
● Carapetto '10	▼ 5
○ Marche Bianco '12	▼ 2
● Mariné '09	▼ 3
○ Colli Maceratesi Ribona '10	♈♈ 4
○ Colli Maceratesi Ribona '09	♈♈ 2*
⊙ Frapicci '11	♈♈ 3
● Marche Rosso '10	♈♈ 3
● Marche Rosso '09	♈♈ 2*
● Serrapetrona Falcotto '08	♈♈ 5
○ Verdicchio di Matelica '11	♈♈ 3
○ Verdicchio di Matelica '10	♈♈ 2*

★Gioacchino Garofoli

VIA CARLO MARX, 123
60022 CASTELFIDARDO [AN]
TEL. 0717820162
www.garofolivini.it

CELLAR SALES
PRE-BOOKED VISITS
ANNUAL PRODUCTION 2,000,000 bottles
HECTARES UNDER VINE 42.00

The strength of Carlo and Gianfranco Garofoli lies in a complete range of wines where quality is set at a high bar throughout, and many of their labels can shake hands with the best in the region. The lion's share is taken by Verdicchio, sourcing grapes from the vineyards of Serra de' Conti, to obtain, alongside the famous Podium - aged in stainless steel - and Serra Fiorese - aged in small oak barrels - an elegant, sparkly Blanc de Blancs. The other cornerstone grape is montepulciano, cultivated by the winery on the calcareous soils of Mount Conero and from which they produce the Conero, the sapid rosé Kòmaros and a fascinating and particularly interesting Metodo Classico Rosé. Podium 2011 is excellent: despite a poor growing year, it reproduces its finest style, where balsamic notes and orange peel blend in a tidy, rigorous mouth. Selezione GG 2008 is a sign of the future, where power, vigour and salty creaminess meet and contrast in a long finish of immense style. A special mention goes to Delis 2010, a new Metodo Classico with soft bubbles.

○ Verdicchio dei Castelli di Jesi Cl. Sel. GG Ris. '08	♟♟♟ 6
○ Verdicchio dei Castelli di Jesi Cl. Sup. Podium '11	♟♟ 4
⊙ Kòmaros '12	♟♟ 2*
○ Verdicchio dei Castelli di Jesi Brut Delis '10	♟♟ 4
○ Verdicchio dei Castelli di Jesi Cl. Serra Fiorese '08	♟♟ 4
○ Verdicchio dei Castelli di Jesi Cl. Sup. Macrina '12	♟♟ 2*
○ Brut Charmat	♟ 3
○ Verdicchio dei Castelli di Jesi Cl. Sup. Podium '10	♟♟♟ 4*
○ Verdicchio dei Castelli di Jesi Cl. Sup. Podium '08	♟♟♟ 3
○ Verdicchio dei Castelli di Jesi Cl. Sup. Podium '04	♟♟♟ 3*

Fattoria Laila

VIA SAN FILIPPO SUL CESANO, 27
61040 MONDAVIO [PU]
TEL. 0721979353
www.fattorialaila.it

CELLAR SALES
PRE-BOOKED VISITS
ANNUAL PRODUCTION 140,000 bottles
HECTARES UNDER VINE 42.00

The Libenzi family has its winery in Mondavio, province of Pesaro, while the verdicchio, montepulciano and sangiovese vineyards are in the province of Ancona. After lengthy renovation work the nearby Corinaldo vineyards are beginning to give the best results. The cellars, built by Artide Libenzi, after whose daughter Laila the enterprise is named, are quite dated but still efficient. Steel tanks are used for the younger wines and small wood reserved for the more ambitious labels. Verdicchio Lailum 2011 is really good, with crisp aromas blending citrus fruit, apple and almond while, in the mouth, it has energy despite moderate alcohol content, leading to an open finish with the perfectly integrated smokiness of wood and tones of citron peel. Eklektikos 2012 is well-crafted. Rosso Piceno is an interesting harvest-year red, with a full, clear fruitiness.

○ Verdicchio dei Castelli di Jesi Cl. Lailum '11	♟♟ 4
● Rosso Conero Fattoria Laila '12	♟♟ 3
● Rosso Piceno Fattoria Laila '12	♟♟ 3
○ Verdicchio dei Castelli di Jesi Cl. Eklektikos '12	♟♟ 3
○ Verdicchio dei Castelli di Jesi Cl. Sup. Fattoria Laila '12	♟♟ 2*
● Rosso Piceno Lailum '11	♟ 5
● Rosso Conero Fattoria Laila '11	♟♟ 2*
● Rosso Piceno Fattoria Laila '11	♟♟ 2*
● Rosso Piceno Lailum '10	♟♟ 3
○ Verdicchio dei Castelli di Jesi Cl. Eklektikos '11	♟♟ 2*
○ Verdicchio dei Castelli di Jesi Cl. Sup. Fattoria Laila '11	♟♟ 2*

Conte Leopardi Dittajuti

VIA MARINA II, 24
60026 NUMANA [AN]
TEL. 0717390116
www.conteleopardi.com

CELLAR SALES
PRE-BOOKED VISITS
ANNUAL PRODUCTION 250,000 bottles
HECTARES UNDER VINE 44.00

Piervittorio Leopardi runs a complex operation with four production sites. The sovereign variety, montepulciano, is found mainly on the chalky soil at Coppo di Sirolo and Svarchi di Numana, near the Adriatic, along with some sauvignon. More montepulciano comes from the Monte Camillone vineyards around Castelfidardo. The verdicchio is cultivated at Cupramontana, the only rented estate. All the vineyards are well-aspected and benefit from the warm climate and good ventilation, so plant treatments are minimal. A wide range of cellar techniques are applied but all with a modern approach. Small oak casks are preferred for ageing the reds. The Rosso Conero Villa Marina 2010 is amazing, full of fresh fruit and flavours and strengthened by a close weave of docile tannins. The temperamental mouth-drying Fructus 2012 and the two soft-hearted, fruity Verdicchios are well-crafted.

● Rosso Conero Villa Marina '10	♀♀ 3*
⊙ Rosé del Coppo '12	♀♀ 2*
● Rosso Conero Fructus '12	♀♀ 2*
○ Verdicchio dei Castelli di Jesi Cl. Artemano '11	♀♀ 2*
○ Verdicchio dei Castelli di Jesi Cl. Castelverde '12	♀♀ 2*
○ Calcare '12	♀ 3
● Conero Pigmento Ris. '10	♀ 5
● Rosso Conero Casirano '11	♀ 3
○ Villamarina Brut	♀ 3
○ Calcare '11	♀♀ 3*
● Conero Pigmento Ris. '09	♀♀ 5
● Conero Pigmento Ris. '08	♀♀ 5
● Rosso Conero Casirano '10	♀♀ 3
○ Verdicchio dei Castelli di Jesi Cl. Castelverde '11	♀♀ 2*

Roberto Lucarelli

LOC. RIPALTA
VIA PIANA, 20
61030 CARTOCETO [PU]
TEL. 0721893019
www.laripe.com

CELLAR SALES
PRE-BOOKED VISITS
ANNUAL PRODUCTION 200,000 bottles
HECTARES UNDER VINE 26.00

Olive oil is stellar at Cartoceto and the only Marche PDO is named after it, but the rolling greenery of this landscape is not just from the olive trees. Here vines also play an important role, especially for Roberto Lucarelli, whose plots are planted mainly to local bianchello and sangiovese varieties, along with international types used in easy-drinking monovarietals or to blend with sangiovese. The cellars are modern, well-equipped, with steel tanks and barrels of different sizes. The two Bianchellos offer their own slants on how to do citrus fruit. La Ripe is refreshingly supple and flowing, while the tempting Rocho, part vinified in barrique, is juicy and full of flavour, but the finish lacks breadth. The Chardonnay 2012 drinks very well. Insieme Riserva 2011 is the best red; it offers elegant and fairly complex nuances in taste. SamuFe, from over-ripe grapes, is well-balanced with notes of saffron and lemon cream.

○ Bianchello del Metauro La Ripe '12	♀♀ 2*
○ Bianchello del Metauro Rocho '11	♀♀ 2*
○ Chardonnay '12	♀♀ 2*
● Colli Pesaresi Sangiovese Insieme Ris. '11	♀♀ 4
○ SamuFè	♀♀ 4
● Colli Pesaresi Sangiovese Goccione '09	♀ 3
○ Esther Brut	♀ 2
○ Sauvignon '12	♀ 2
○ Bianchello del Metauro La Ripe '10	♀♀ 2*
○ Bianchello del Metauro La Ripe '09	♀♀ 2*
○ Bianchello del Metauro Rocho '10	♀♀ 2*
○ Bianchello del Metauro Rocho '09	♀♀ 2*

Mario Lucchetti

VIA SANTA MARIA DEL FIORE, 17
60030 MORRO D'ALBA [AN]
TEL. 073163314
www.mariolucchetti.it

Ma.Ri.Ca.

VIA ACQUASANTA, 7
60030 BELVEDERE OSTRENSE [AN]
TEL. 0731290091
www.cantinamarica.it

CELLAR SALES
PRE-BOOKED VISITS
ANNUAL PRODUCTION 150,000 bottles
HECTARES UNDER VINE 25.00

CELLAR SALES
PRE-BOOKED VISITS
ANNUAL PRODUCTION 70,000 bottles
HECTARES UNDER VINE 15.00

Mario Lucchetti is a landmark figure in the small yet dynamic world of Morro d'Alba, a town at the back of Senigallia, and home to lacrima nera, a native grape with very distinctive aromatics. Mario's secret is sheer experience, dating back to the mid-1970s, working plots of just the right age with different aspects. His son Paolo has now joined the business and brings new energy to the winery. The three Lacrima labels are very distinct, from the fresh, fragrant style of the harvest-year wines to the firmly structured presence of the Guardengo. The Amarone-style Mariasole is made from fully raisined grapes. As usual, they produce two monovarietal whites from verdicchio, as the typical grape of nearby Jesi has always grown in their vineyards. Tastings reward the delicious Guardengo 2011, juicy and perfectly conveying the intense floweriness of the grape. Verdicchio Classico Superiore 2012 is slim and vegetal but has vigour.

The Moriconi family winery, between Jesi and Morro d'Alba, has been in operation for 20 years, applying the same care to vinification of both verdicchio and lacrima nera varieties. Indeed, the two productions are perfectly complementary and the quality expressed by both types proves they are in their element on the gently rolling, marl-based hills. The cellars are large and installed mainly with stainless steel tanks. The wines undergo classic fermentation, with brief ageing. We have seen in past years that Tosius, their flagship wine, can easily spend several years improving in the bottle. The 2012 version has the same solid nature, with a full, juicy drink followed by pronounced length on the palate to reveal the grape's typical features. Tregaso 2012, though, should be enjoyed for its youthful exuberance full of a zesty drinkability. Among the Lacrimas, our votes go to the base version, with its precise meeting between florality and a smooth palate.

● Lacrima di Morro d'Alba '12	♟♟ 2*
● Lacrima di Morro d'Alba Sup. Guardengo '11	♟♟ 3
○ Verdicchio dei Castelli di Jesi Cl. Sup. '12	♟♟ 3
● Lacrima di Morro d'Alba Mariasole '10	♟ 6
○ Verdicchio dei Castelli di Jesi Cl. '12	♟ 2
● Lacrima di Morro d'Alba '08	♟♟ 2*
● Lacrima di Morro d'Alba Passito '07	♟♟ 5
● Lacrima di Morro d'Alba Sup. Guardengo '10	♟♟ 3
○ Verdicchio dei Castelli di Jesi Cl. '11	♟♟ 2*
○ Verdicchio dei Castelli di Jesi Cl. Sup. '11	♟♟ 3
○ Verdicchio dei Castelli di Jesi Cl. Sup. '08	♟♟ 2*

○ Verdicchio dei Castelli di Jesi Cl. Sup. Tosius '12	♟♟ 3*
● Lacrima di Morro d'Alba Ramosceto '12	♟♟ 2*
○ Verdicchio dei Castelli di Jesi Cl. Tregaso '12	♟♟ 1*
● Baroncesco '11	♟ 2
● Lacrima di Morro d'Alba Sup. Castello di Ramosceto '11	♟ 2
● Lacrima di Morro d'Alba Ramosceto '09	♟♟ 2*
● Lacrima di Morro d'Alba Sup. Castello di Ramosceto '09	♟♟ 2*
○ Verdicchio dei Castelli di Jesi Cl. Sup. Aurato Ris. '09	♟♟ 3
○ Verdicchio dei Castelli di Jesi Cl. Sup. Tosius '10	♟♟ 2*
○ Verdicchio dei Castelli di Jesi Cl. Tregaso '10	♟♟ 1*

Stefano Mancinelli

VIA ROMA, 62
60030 MORRO D'ALBA [AN]
TEL. 073163021
www.mancinellivini.it

CELLAR SALES
PRE-BOOKED VISITS
ACCOMMODATION
ANNUAL PRODUCTION 150,000 bottles
HECTARES UNDER VINE 25.00

The hills behind Senigallia, at about ten kilometres from the sea, are the cradle of the rare, inimitable and challenging lacrima nera grape. The marked floral notes, and robust, edgy tannins brand some unique reds. The Mancinelli family was the first to push this wine to recognition beyond local confines, researching its genetic features, adaptability to different growing conditions, and raisining prospects. In the cellar they have even used carbonic maceration to boost the aromatic profile, and partial wood ageing improve phenolic staying power. So it comes as no surprise that the Mancinellis are a byword for Lacrima di Morro d'Alba. The floral Lacrima Superiore 2011 is well-balanced and supple. Terre dei Goti, a dry wine from dried grapes lacks the same agility but it has heady aromas and a marked density. The real gems are three sweet wines, led by a fantastic glycerine-rich and caressing Stell 2008 that is never over-sweet.

Filippo Maraviglia

LOC. PIANNÉ, 584
62024 MATELICA [MC]
TEL. 0737786340
www.vinimaraviglia.com

CELLAR SALES
PRE-BOOKED VISITS
ANNUAL PRODUCTION 30,000 bottles
HECTARES UNDER VINE 27.00

In the Upper Vallesina winemaking may seem placid but nothing could be further from the truth, and new operations are popping up, drawn by the unique terroir. Filippo Maraviglia started up in 2004 and we watched with interest for a few years as he got his sea legs before he finally came up with the goods. His approach is underpinned by an artisan spirit and he works on a family scale. His vineyards are at altitudes of 350 to 450 metres, planted to verdicchio, sangiovese, and Bordeaux varieties used to make Bosco, his only red. The 2011 version rings with red berry fruits and is very drinkable, but we are more interested in the Matelicas. Alarico, aged in stainless steel, offers typical Matelica notes of dried fruit and spring flowers, while a long elegant sapidity explodes in the mouth. Grappoli d'Oro 2009 is a late-harvest wine, 20% aged in barrique, with aniseed and saffron in an elegant mouth leading to a resounding finish.

○ Cu de Cu Passito		5
● Lacrima di Morro d'Alba Passito Re Sole '07		5
○ Verdicchio dei Castelli di Jesi Passito Stell '08		5
● Lacrima di Morro d'Alba Santa Maria del Fiore '11		2*
● Lacrima di Morro d'Alba Sup. '11		3
● Terre dei Goti '08		5
● Lacrima di Morro d'Alba Sensazioni di Frutto '12		2
○ Verdicchio dei Castelli di Jesi Cl. '12		2
○ Verdicchio dei Castelli di Jesi Cl. Sup. '12		2
● Lacrima di Morro d'Alba Passito Re Sole '06		4
● Lacrima di Morro d'Alba Sup. '10		3*
● Lacrima di Morro d'Alba Sup. '09		3

○ Verdicchio di Matelica Alarico '12		2*
○ Verdicchio di Matelica Grappoli d'Oro Ris. '09		3*
● Colli Maceratesi Rosso Bosco '11		2*

Marotti Campi

VIA SANT'AMICO, 14
60030 MORRO D'ALBA [AN]
TEL. 0731618027
www.marotticampi.it

CELLAR SALES
PRE-BOOKED VISITS
ACCOMMODATION
ANNUAL PRODUCTION 185,000 bottles
HECTARES UNDER VINE 56.00

This winery, based in Morro d'Alba, was always destined to produce lacrima. A grape with a rustic temperament, it is full of exciting aromas and biting tannins. Lorenzo Marotti and his oenologist Roberto Potentini have worked hard to smooth away its most crotchety aspects and open it to the world market. In the meantime, they are not resigned to treating Verdicchio simply as an addition to their range, turning it rather into a valuable asset, a white capable of defying the years with composure. The excellence of the Orgiolo and Salmariano selections, some aged in small oak barrels, certainly repays all the hard work and the line is encouragingly reliable across the board. The two Lacrimas are peerless. The spicy Orgiolo 2011 is complex and layered with good tannins. Rubico 2012 is flowery with a supple, fragrant mouthfeel. Aniseed, orange peel and ginger are revealed in Salmariano 2010, softly powerful but a bit inert in the finish. The Rosato from lacrima is surprising with a rich, tangy taste and flowery notes.

Poderi Mattioli

VIA FARNETO, 17A
60030 SERRA DE' CONTI [AN]
TEL. 0731878676
www.poderimattioli.it

ANNUAL PRODUCTION 13,500 bottles
HECTARES UNDER VINE 5.00

The walls of the new, well-organized winery are lined with large photographs of special family moments. They capture the essence of how verdicchio is an integral part of Mattioli life, as it is for every other grower in Serra De' Conti, one of the most extensive and intensive terroirs. The three siblings, aged from 30 to 40, move with the confidence of people fully versed in the complex mechanisms of this zone. Giordano and Letizia manage the vines while Giacomo tends to fermentation and ageing, using steel. For the time being the operation only produces a still white but the future holds a sparkling Metodo Classico and a red. Ylice 2012 is a dream. Aromas of aniseed, almond and aromatic herbs like fennel and basil chase around a mouth that blends crispness and complexity into a refined, energetic progression. Lauro 2010 is more restrained, with a calm elegance. Ylice 2011 is generous and relaxed, and very enjoyable.

○ Castelli di Jesi Verdicchio Cl. Salmariano Ris. '10	♟♟ 3
● Donderè '10	♟♟ 3
● Lacrima di Morro d'Alba Orgiolo '11	♟♟ 3
● Lacrima di Morro d'Alba Rùbico '12	♟♟ 2*
⊙ Rosato '12	♟♟ 2*
○ Verdicchio dei Castelli di Jesi Cl. Sup. Luzano '12	♟♟ 2*
● Xyris '12	♟♟ 2*
⊙ Brut Rosé '12	♟ 3
○ Verdicchio dei Castelli di Jesi Cl. Albiano '12	♟ 1*
○ Verdicchio dei Castelli di Jesi Cl. Salmariano Ris. '08	♟♟♟ 3*
○ Verdicchio dei Castelli di Jesi Cl. Salmariano Ris. '07	♟♟♟ 2*

○ Verdicchio dei Castelli di Jesi Cl. Sup. Ylice '12	♟♟♟ 2*
○ Verdicchio dei Castelli di Jesi Cl. Sup. Lauro '10	♟♟ 3*
○ Verdicchio dei Castelli di Jesi Cl. Sup. Ylice '11	♟♟ 2*

Valter Mattoni

C.DA PESCOLLA
63030 CASTORANO [AP]
TEL. 073687329

CELLAR SALES
ANNUAL PRODUCTION 5,500 bottles
HECTARES UNDER VINE 3.00

His ID card says he is called Valter Mattoni but for everyone he is La Roccia. Anyone involved in Piceno winemaking knows of his passion, his outgoing character, and can describe his solid shape and distinctive head of hair, once fair but now increasingly snowy. His wines are interpreted with a natural artisan spirit and his few hectares under vine are planted to ancient local varieties. La Roccia does everything himself, with Marco Casonetti always on hand to offer friendly advice. Marketing is strictly by word of mouth, guaranteed in full by his sincerity. Arshura 2011 is the masterpiece we were waiting for. Montepulciano to its core, it reflects the best features in its dark colour and wild cherry aromas, leading to a generous drink of gutsy energy and powerful fruity intenseness. The elegantly rare Rosso Bordò 2010 is a Bordeaux blend. The very drinkable Trebbien 2012 has a rustic heart.

● Arshura '11	♈♈♈ 3*
● Rosso Bordò '10	♈♈ 8
⊙ Cose Cose '12	♈♈ 2*
○ Trebbien '12	♈♈ 2*
● Arshura '10	♈♈ 3*
● Arshura '09	♈♈ 3
● Arshura '08	♈♈ 3
⊙ Cose Cose '11	♈♈ 2*

★La Monacesca

C.DA MONACESCA
62024 MATELICA [MC]
TEL. 0733672641
www.monacesca.it

CELLAR SALES
PRE-BOOKED VISITS
ANNUAL PRODUCTION 160,000 bottles
HECTARES UNDER VINE 30.00

In 1966, Casimiro Cifola bought the chapel and convent built by the monks of Farfa, and several years later the vineyards of verdicchio produced their first fruit, vinified according to an ethos of high quality unusual for that time. In 1982, the young Aldo joined the winery and made it his profession. Casimiro, who died in 2012, saw his brand strengthen, bringing credit to the entire designation. Mirum, a wonderful Matelica aged in stainless steel, is named as a homage to his intuition, which flourished through the great entrepreneurial skills of his son. Even in an unsettled year like 2011, Mirum can replicate its opulent style, underpinned by a residual sweetness balanced by a vibrant acidity and completed by an appealing aromatic wealth, from aniseed flowers to liquorice and distant peaty echoes. Its performance does not overshadow one of the best harvest-year Verdicchios, a tactile wine full of character.

○ Verdicchio di Matelica Mirum Ris. '11	♈♈♈ 5
○ Verdicchio di Matelica '12	♈♈ 3*
● Camerte '10	♈ 4
● Camerte '99	♈♈♈ 5
○ Mirum '94	♈♈♈ 3*
○ Mirus '91	♈♈♈ 5
○ Verdicchio di Matelica '94	♈♈♈ 3
○ Verdicchio di Matelica Mirum Ris. '10	♈♈♈ 4*
○ Verdicchio di Matelica Mirum Ris. '09	♈♈♈ 4
○ Verdicchio di Matelica Mirum Ris. '08	♈♈♈ 4
○ Verdicchio di Matelica Mirum Ris. '07	♈♈♈ 4*
○ Verdicchio di Matelica Mirum Ris. '06	♈♈♈ 4
○ Verdicchio di Matelica Mirum Ris. '04	♈♈♈ 4
○ Verdicchio di Matelica Mirum Ris. '02	♈♈♈ 3

Monte Schiavo

FRAZ. MONTESCHIAVO
VIA VIVAIO
60030 MAIOLATI SPONTINI [AN]
TEL. 0731700385
www.monteschiavo.it

CELLAR SALES
PRE-BOOKED VISITS
ANNUAL PRODUCTION 1,500,000 bottles
HECTARES UNDER VINE 115.00

The Pieralisi family spent a lifetime bringing olive farming methods into the present and they organized their winery with the same philosophy, giving it the cutting-edge apparatus while never underrating the immense value of agronomy. This reflects in the well-tended vineyards planted in some of the most prestigious sites. Apart from the 1990s legacy of cabernet and merlot, most of the plots are dominated by native grapes. The operation's excellent Verdicchios are interpreted in a low-key, modern style; the reds are refined and fragrant, but lack a hint of character. Le Giuncare Riserva 2010 is outstanding: tempting aromas of lemon peel and almond lead to a mouth seeking balance between softness and the varietal zest of its structure. It lacks a little complexity, which may emerge with further ageing in bottle. Pallio 2012 offers the same experience, harnessed by its youth but provided with a good mouthfeel and mineral vibrations.

○ Verdicchio dei Castelli di Jesi Cl. Le Giuncare Ris. '10	🏆🏆 3*
● Rosso Piceno Sassaiolo '10	🏆🏆 2*
○ Verdicchio dei Castelli di Jesi Cl. Coste del Molino '12	🏆🏆 2*
○ Verdicchio dei Castelli di Jesi Cl. Sup. Pallio di S. Floriano '12	🏆🏆 3
● Lacrima di Morro d'Alba Marzaiola '12	🏆 2
○ Verdicchio dei Castelli di Jesi Brut V. Tassanare	🏆 2
○ Verdicchio dei Castelli di Jesi Cl. Sup. Vino dell'Imperatore '11	🏆 3
● Rosso Conero Adeodato '00	🏆🏆🏆 5
○ Verdicchio dei Castelli di Jesi Cl. Sup. Pallio di S. Floriano '11	🏆🏆🏆 2*
○ Verdicchio dei Castelli di Jesi Cl. Sup. Pallio di S. Floriano '10	🏆🏆🏆 2*

Montecappone

VIA COLLE OLIVO, 2
60035 JESI [AN]
TEL. 0731205761
www.montecappone.com

CELLAR SALES
PRE-BOOKED VISITS
ANNUAL PRODUCTION 120,000 bottles
HECTARES UNDER VINE 70.00

Gianluca Mirizzi has very clear ideas about his Verdicchios. They have to burst at the seams with a crisp intensity. Following Lorenzo Landi's advice, Gianluca set up a careful farming programme, and in the hottest years he is quite happy to harvest slightly ahead of time. In the cellar he applies various forms of cold techniques including carbon dioxide snow, controlled temperatures and ageing in steel, used to help retain aromatic precursors. The reds take full advantage of montepulciano's typically rich, fruity vein. Verdicchio Utopia 2011 may not impress with its solid backbone of acidity and rigorous style but younger brother Federico II 2012 does just that, and its crisp juiciness and saline tones place it among the best of the vintage. All the reds are good, headed by Utopia Rosso 2010, from montepulciano, with red fruit, spices and coffee in a juicy mouth, underpinned by smooth tannins. A special mention goes to La Breccia 2012, from sauvignon, with a fruity stamp and light-hearted drinkability.

○ Castelli di Jesi Verdicchio Cl. Utopia Ris. '11	🏆🏆 4
○ Verdicchio dei Castelli di Jesi Cl. Sup. Federico II A.D. 1194 '12	🏆🏆 3*
○ La Breccia '12	🏆🏆 3
● Rosso Piceno '12	🏆🏆 2*
● Tabano Rosso '11	🏆🏆 4
● Utopia '10	🏆🏆 5
○ Verdicchio dei Castelli di Jesi Cl. '12	🏆🏆 2*
⊙ Pergolesi 1710 '12	🏆 2
○ Tabano Bianco '12	🏆 3
○ Verdicchio dei Castelli di Jesi Cl. Utopia Ris. '08	🏆🏆🏆 4
○ Verdicchio dei Castelli di Jesi Cl. Utopia Ris. '07	🏆🏆🏆 4*
○ Castelli di Jesi Verdicchio Cl. Utopia Ris. '10	🏆🏆 4

Alessandro Moroder

VIA MONTACUTO, 121
60029 ANCONA
TEL. 071898232
www.moroder-vini.it

CELLAR SALES
PRE-BOOKED VISITS
ANNUAL PRODUCTION 130,000 bottles
HECTARES UNDER VINE 18.00
VITICULTURE METHOD Certified Organic

The most important step taken by
Alessandro Moroder over the years was to
go organic. With the European law on
organic wines coming into force in time for
his 2012 vintage, he presented his first
certified organic wines. This was just the
latest step in the long path he began to
walk in 1984, becoming the driving force
behind the promotion of the montepulciano
grapes grown on the Conero promontory's
chalky soils. The key factor for this
operation has always been care of the
vineyards. Cellar intervention is limited. The
reds age in small and medium-sized wood,
and time ensures the variety's exuberant
character is nicely tamed. A couple of
rather poor years have sapped the
performance of the better reds. Dorico
Riserva 2009 reveals some evolved notes
among the flowers and balms but in the
mouth there is a sound acid vigour and
plenty of tannin. Moroder 2010 is decently
made but is lazy in character.

○ BianConero '12	♥♥ 2*
⊙ Brut Rosé '12	♥♥ 2*
● Conero Dorico Ris. '09	♥♥♥ 5
○ Elleno '12	♥ 2
⊙ Rosa di Montacuto '12	♥ 2
● Rosso Conero Aiòn '11	♥ 2
● Rosso Conero Moroder '10	♥ 2
● Conero Dorico Ris. '05	♥♥♥ 5
● Rosso Conero Dorico '93	♥♥♥ 5
● Rosso Conero Dorico '90	♥♥♥ 5
● Rosso Conero Dorico '88	♥♥♥ 5
● Conero Dorico Ris. '08	♥♥ 5
● Conero Dorico Ris. '07	♥♥ 5
● Rosso Conero Moroder '09	♥♥ 2*
● Rosso Conero Moroder '08	♥♥ 2*

★Oasi degli Angeli

C.DA SANT'EGIDIO, 50
63012 CUPRA MARITTIMA [AP]
TEL. 0735778569
www.kurni.it

CELLAR SALES
PRE-BOOKED VISITS
ANNUAL PRODUCTION 5,000 bottles
HECTARES UNDER VINE 16.00

Marco Casolanetti studied engineering but
initially his love of wine led him to a career
as an expert wine critic. As a producer,
with his life partner Eleonora, he uses his
critical skills to observe, extrapolate and
re-invent, while never bowing to
convention. His intuition about planting
density, an overwhelming use of barriques,
and tenacious studies and research have
led to a new way of understanding
viticulture and oenology. The rare aromatic
perceptions offered by his wines - Kurni
from montepulciano and Kupra from
grenache - are that rare thing: human
talent tapping into the delicate balance
between climate, soil and grape. The
fantastic Kupra 2010 has overwhelmingly
complex aromas: raspberry syrup, white
chocolate, lavender, gentian and wild
thyme interweave into an elegant blend,
repeated in an incredibly well-balanced,
dense and taut palate. Kurni 2011 is the
usual fruit-laden bomb but with a slightly
more creamy structure.

● Kupra '10	♥♥♥ 8
● Kurni '11	♥♥ 8
● Kurni '10	♥♥♥ 8
● Kurni '09	♥♥♥ 8
● Kurni '08	♥♥♥ 8
● Kurni '07	♥♥♥ 8
● Kurni '04	♥♥♥ 8
● Kurni '03	♥♥♥ 8
● Kurni '02	♥♥♥ 8
● Kurni '01	♥♥♥ 8
● Kurni '00	♥♥♥ 8
● Kurni '98	♥♥♥ 8
● Kurni '97	♥♥♥ 8
● Kupra '09	♥♥ 8
● Kurni '06	♥♥ 8
● Kurni '05	♥♥ 8

Pievalta

via Monteschiavo, 18
60030 Maiolati Spontini [AN]
Tel. 0731705199
www.baronepizzini.it

CELLAR SALES
PRE-BOOKED VISITS
ANNUAL PRODUCTION 125,000 bottles
HECTARES UNDER VINE 26.50
VITICULTURE METHOD Certified Biodynamic

A healthy artisan spirit permeates the
Pievalta wines, fruit of the meticulous work
carried out by Alessandro Fenino, in
charge of the Marche-based operations of
the Barone Pizzini winery. He supervises
the entire outfit personally, in particular
looking after the vineyards where
verdicchio is cultivated together with the
odd row of montepulciano. Total loyalty
towards biodynamic practices is
moderated by their previous experience, so
that they employ selected yeasts and have
stopped using wood. Wines of considerable
character follow a style that is direct and
spontaneous. San Paolo 2010 carries Tre
Bicchieri back home. The only wine
fermented using exclusively indigenous
yeasts, it has a wonderful character full of
a thousand expressions and aromas,
above all grapefruit and basil, and mouth
full of great vitality, adorned by a deep
salty finish. The austere verdicchio-based
Perlugo and the complex, creamy and
leisurely Curina 2011 have never been so
good. The lean Pievalta 2012 offers a
great drink.

○ Castelli di Jesi Verdicchio Cl. San Paolo Ris. '10	♥♥♥ 3*
○ Verdicchio dei Castelli di Jesi Passito Curina '11	♥♥ 3*
○ Perlugo Extra Brut M. Cl.	♥♥ 3
○ Verdicchio dei Castelli di Jesi Cl. Sup. Pievalta '12	♥♥ 2*
● Rosso di Pievalta '12	♥ 2
○ Verdicchio dei Castelli di Jesi Cl. Sup. Pievalta '09	♥♥♥ 2*
○ San Paolo '06	♥♥ 3*
○ Verdicchio dei Castelli di Jesi Cl. Sup. Dominè '11	♥♥ 2*
○ Verdicchio dei Castelli di Jesi Cl. Sup. Pievalta '11	♥♥ 2*
○ Verdicchio dei Castelli di Jesi Cl. Sup. Pievalta '10	♥♥ 2*

Il Pollenza

via Casone, 4
62029 Tolentino [MC]
Tel. 0733961989
www.ilpollenza.it

PRE-BOOKED VISITS
ANNUAL PRODUCTION 130,000 bottles
HECTARES UNDER VINE 60.00

The estate is splendid. Aldo Brachetti
Peretti's home and his cellar occupy
outstandingly beautiful villas surrounded by
extremely well-tended vineyards. It looks
like the Bordeaux countryside rather than a
corner of provincial Macerata. That the
chateaux are the source of inspiration is
clear from the two cabernets, merlot and
petit verdot planted, the use of small
barrels in expensive woods, the shape of
the bottles and the style of the labels. For
less ambitious products, they make use of
local grapes like maceratino and age the
wines in embellished cement barrels.
Offspring of a polished style with care for
every detail, the wines have a distinctive
international breadth. Pollenza 2010, 60%
sauvignon plus merlot, cabernet franc and
petit verdot, is rivetingly austere with a true
Bordeaux spirit and paced elegance.
Pollenza Metodo Classico Rosé 2009, from
pinot nero, after 30 months on the lees
offers the fragrance of crusty bread and
wild strawberries leading to a fine creamy
progression with a salty finish.

● Il Pollenza '10	♥♥♥ 7
○ Colli Maceratesi Bianco Angera '12	♥♥ 3
● Cosmino '10	♥♥ 5
⊙ Extra Brut M. Cl. Il Pollenza '09	♥♥ 5
○ Pius IX Mastai '11	♥♥ 6
⊙ Didi '12	♥ 3
● Porpora '10	♥ 3
● Il Pollenza '09	♥♥♥ 7
● Il Pollenza '07	♥♥♥ 7
● Cosmino '09	♥♥ 5
⊙ Didi '11	♥♥ 3
● Il Pollenza '08	♥♥ 7
○ Pius IX '10	♥♥ 6

San Giovanni

c.da Ciafone, 41
63035 Offida [AP]
Tel. 0736889032
www.vinisangiovanni.it

PRE-BOOKED VISITS
ANNUAL PRODUCTION 100,000 bottles
HECTARES UNDER VINE 30.00
VITICULTURE METHOD Certified Organic

The extensive area under vine in the great
Ciafone terroir provides the San Giovanni
winery with a huge grape heritage derived
mainly from typical montepulciano,
sangiovese, passerina, pecorino, and
trebbiano varieties. In recent years, Gianni
Di Lorenzo has converted all his vineyards
to organic methods and dedicated the new
Geo line to this mission. Nicely ripe grapes
give a significant rich palate to tannic,
mouth-filling reds. Steel is used for the
whites, which have a greater freshness and
are enjoyed best when young. The one
exception is Zagros, an attempt to give
stature to the old trebbiano vineyards, which
is part-aged in wood. Indeed, Zagros 2011
was one of the best wines we tasted, in
terms of complexity, strength and taste
detail. Pecorino Kiara 2012 confirms the
quality of its elegant tones of meadow
flowers and aniseed and its slimness in
the mouth. Rosso Piceno Geo 2012 is a
head above the other reds, with its
approachable fruitiness.

○ Offida Pecorino Kiara '12	♟♟ 3
● Rosso Piceno Geo '12	♟♟ 3
○ Zagros '11	♟♟ 3
○ Brut Passerina Marta	♟ 3
○ Falerio Pecorino Geo '12	♟ 2
○ Marta '12	♟ 3
● Offida Rosso Zeii '09	♟ 3
○ Passerina Geo '12	♟ 2
● Rosso Piceno Sup. Leo Guelfus '10	♟ 3
○ Falerio dei Colli Ascolani Leo Guelfus '10	♟♟ 2*
○ Marta '11	♟♟ 3
○ Offida Pecorino Kiara '11	♟♟ 3
○ Offida Pecorino Kiara '10	♟♟ 2*
● Rosso Piceno Sup. Leo Guelfus '07	♟♟ 2*

Poderi San Lazzaro

c.da San Lazzaro, 88
63035 Offida [AP]
Tel. 0736889189
www.poderisanlazzaro.it

CELLAR SALES
PRE-BOOKED VISITS
ANNUAL PRODUCTION 45,000 bottles
HECTARES UNDER VINE 7.50
VITICULTURE METHOD Certified Organic

With his new cellar finally up and running,
Paolo Capriotti can now spend his time
doing what he does best, producing wines
that exude true territoriality, with an artisan
slant and a commitment to local
designations. And all without haste. Grifola,
a powerful montepulciano red aged in
small oak barrels, is back after missing a
turn, and so is Pecorino Pistillo, which was
granted a longer ageing process. The
hottest news features the rare bottles of
the monovarietal Grenache, following a joint
project with Marco Casolanetti to
re-introduce the grape - known here as
bórdò - into the area. Bordò 2011 is rare
and fascinating. The nose is continually
seduced by aromatic herbs, red fruit,
smoky traits and clear overtones of oriental
spices, while the ample, pervasive mouth
has a precise progression and an expansive
finish. Grifola 2010 is veined by gamey
whiffs but fleshy fruit and alcoholic energy
also emerge. Passerina 2012 is fruity on
the nose and salty in the mouth.

● Bordò '11	♟♟ 7
● Grifola '10	♟♟ 4
○ Offida Passerina '12	♟♟ 2*
○ Offida Pecorino Pistillo '11	♟ 2
● Polesio '12	♟ 2
● Grifola '07	♟♟ 3
○ Offida Passerina '11	♟♟ 2*
○ Offida Pecorino Pistillo '09	♟♟ 2*
● Polesio '11	♟♟ 2*
● Rosso Piceno Sup. Podere 72 '10	♟♟ 2*
● Rosso Piceno Sup. Podere 72 '08	♟♟ 2*

Fattoria San Lorenzo

VIA SAN LORENZO, 6
60036 MONTECAROTTO [AN]
TEL. 073189656
az-crognaletti@libero.it

CELLAR SALES
PRE-BOOKED VISITS
ACCOMMODATION AND RESTAURANT SERVICE
ANNUAL PRODUCTION 100,000 bottles
HECTARES UNDER VINE 30.00
VITICULTURE METHOD Certified Organic

Natalino Crognaletti is a genuine Verdicchio craftsman. A tireless worker, he personally takes care of every phase, adamantly refusing the use of systemic products. In line with this, he practises a low intervention approach in the cellar. His style is spontaneous and, as its origins lie in ripening the grapes at length, it is decisively rich and full of flavour, producing wines where the aromas are never masked. Montepulciano, sangiovese and lacrima bring a flourish of red to a project inspired by tradition and fully committed to the territory. Campo delle Oche 2010 shows great potential, obtained from over-ripe grapes; it reveals aromas of orange peel and badly disguised minerals behind traits of peach and honey, while the long progression is tender yet solid and full of flavours. San Lorenzo 2001, from verdicchio, has oxidized tones and tangy aromas, while saline notes and dried fruit meet in a mature mouth that is fascinating in its own way. The montepulciano Solleone '08 is gamey, moody and mineral.

○ Verdicchio dei Castelli di Jesi Cl. Sup. Campo delle Oche '10	♟♟ 4
● Il Solleone '08	♟♟ 5
● Rosso Piceno Vign. Burello '09	♟♟ 3
● Vigna Paradiso '08	♟♟ 4
○ Il San Lorenzo '01	♟ 6
● Rosso Conero Artù '09	♟ 3
○ Verdicchio dei Castelli di Jesi Cl. ...Le Oche... '11	♟ 3
○ Verdicchio dei Castelli di Jesi ...di Gino... '12	♟ 2
○ Verdicchio dei Castelli di Jesi Cl. Vign. delle Oche Ris. '01	♟♟♟ 3
● Rosso Conero Vign. La Gattara '07	♟♟ 2*
○ Verdicchio dei Castelli di Jesi Cl. ...Le Oche... '10	♟♟ 3*

San Savino - Poderi Capecci

LOC. SAN SAVINO
VIA SANTA MARIA IN CARRO, 13
63038 RIPATRANSONE [AP]
TEL. 073590107
www.sansavino.com

CELLAR SALES
PRE-BOOKED VISITS
ANNUAL PRODUCTION 120,000 bottles
HECTARES UNDER VINE 22.00
VITICULTURE METHOD Certified Organic

Simone Capecci has never abandoned the artisanal approach that gives his wines that extra nuance of style. The register varies significantly from reds to whites, with pecorino and passerina grown on fresh soils, harvested early if possible, and managed with cold and steel to preserve the aromatic precursors. All the reds, both designation wines and the montepulciano and sangiovese monovarietals, benefit from well-aspected vineyards, full ripening, long maceration, and barrels of varying sizes. Bitter orange and a clear backbone of acidity define one of the best versions of Ciprea of the last years, only held back by its youth. It will evolve magnificently. We are equally convinced by the montepulciano Quinta Regio 2008, altogether more complex and mature, with its fine-grained tannins and full power. Fedus 2011 is made from sangiovese and tastes of cherry and dried leaves, with a solid structure and well-balanced extracts.

○ Offida Pecorino Ciprea '12	♟♟ 3*
● Quinta Regio '08	♟♟ 5
● Fedus '11	♟♟ 4
● Rosso Piceno Sup. Picus '11	♟♟ 2*
○ Tufilla '12	♟♟ 2*
● Rosso Piceno Collemura '12	♟ 2
● Fedus Sangiovese '06	♟♟♟ 4
○ Offida Pecorino Ciprea '10	♟♟♟ 3*
○ Offida Pecorino Ciprea '09	♟♟♟ 3*
○ Offida Pecorino Ciprea '08	♟♟♟ 3*
● Quinta Regio '01	♟♟♟ 5
● Quinta Regio '00	♟♟♟ 5
● Fedus '10	♟♟ 4
○ Offida Pecorino Ciprea '11	♟♟ 3*

Santa Barbara

B.GO MAZZINI, 35
60010 BARBARA [AN]
TEL. 0719674249
www.vinisantabarbara.it

CELLAR SALES
PRE-BOOKED VISITS
ANNUAL PRODUCTION 650,000 bottles
HECTARES UNDER VINE 45.00

Stefano Antonucci believes in the values of beauty and pleasure, which he carefully pursues in his wines. He knows the market inside out, hitting the bull's eye at every step and creating direct, fragrant wines that are simple to understand and flexible when matched with food. His wide production range vaunts elegantly supple Verdicchios, full of lip-smacking flavours and easily able to weather the years. The rest of the range is crafted with care and speaks with an international tongue. The full, tasty Verdicchio Stefano Antonucci 2011 stands out from the range as usual, with hints of yellow-fleshed fruit and saffron; while marginally less complex, this is balanced by its free and easy drinkability. The varietal Verdicchio Pignocco 2012 is surprisingly good, with marked vigour and tangy stylish aromatics. Just below the best, the Bordeaux blend Stefano Antonucci Rosso 2011 has an open character and well-gauged body. Le Vaglie 2012 is denoted by a flowing citrussy taste.

● Stefano Antonucci Rosso '11	♚♚ 3*
○ Verdicchio dei Castelli di Jesi Cl. Pignocco '12	♚♚ 2*
○ Verdicchio dei Castelli di Jesi Cl. Stefano Antonucci Ris. '11	♚♚ 3*
● Brut Rosé Stefano Antonucci	♚♚ 5
● Colleravara '11	♚♚ 3
● Pathos '11	♚♚ 6
● San Bartolo '11	♚♚ 2*
☉ Sensuade '12	♚♚ 3
○ Verdicchio dei Castelli di Jesi Cl. Le Vaglie '12	♚♚ 3
○ Verdicchio dei Castelli di Jesi Cl. Tardivo Ma non Tardo '10	♚♚ 5
○ Verdicchio dei Castelli di Jesi Passito Lina '10	♚♚ 5
○ Anima Celeste '12	♚ 3

Sartarelli

VIA COSTE DEL MOLINO, 24
60030 POGGIO SAN MARCELLO [AN]
TEL. 073189732
www.sartarelli.it

CELLAR SALES
PRE-BOOKED VISITS
ANNUAL PRODUCTION 280,000 bottles
HECTARES UNDER VINE 55.00

Sartarelli means verdicchio, lovingly cultivated in several different vineyards all set on the left bank of the Esino River. The most famous are in Contrada Balciana at Poggio San Marcello - for the Balciana wines - and those in Coste del Molino and Le Busche at Montecarotto for Tralivio. For their Classico, grapes are sourced from the vineyards at Castelbellino and Serra de' Conti. Harvest is carried out plot by plot and in several stages to make sure that the grapes are truly ripe while, in the cellar, only stainless steel is used in order to retain the grapes' varietal traits. Mineral, fully-evolved and elegant: three terms describe Tralivio 2011, hanging on even in a poor year. Its legacy is a certain softness due to a fragile backbone of acidity but the finish finds the strength to soar, releasing positive vibrations. Classico 2012 is the usual blaze of almondy typicity and lip-smacking mouthfeel. Balciana 2011 offers a lesser version, pleasing but imprecise aromatically.

○ Verdicchio dei Castelli di Jesi Cl. Sup. Tralivio '11	♚♚ 3*
○ Verdicchio dei Castelli di Jesi Cl. '12	♚♚ 2*
○ Verdicchio dei Castelli di Jesi Cl. Sup. Balciana Ris. '11	♚ 5
○ Verdicchio dei Castelli di Jesi Cl. Sup. Balciana '09	♚♚♚ 5
○ Verdicchio dei Castelli di Jesi Cl. Sup. Balciana '04	♚♚♚ 5
○ Verdicchio dei Castelli di Jesi Cl. Sup. Contrada Balciana '98	♚♚♚ 5
○ Verdicchio dei Castelli di Jesi Cl. Sup. Contrada Balciana '97	♚♚♚ 5
○ Verdicchio dei Castelli di Jesi Cl. Sup. Contrada Balciana '95	♚♚♚ 5
○ Verdicchio dei Castelli di Jesi Cl. Sup. Contrada Balciana '94	♚♚♚ 5

Selvagrossa

s.da Selvagrossa, 37
61020 Pesaro
Tel. 0721202923
www.selvagrossa.it

CELLAR SALES
PRE-BOOKED VISITS
ANNUAL PRODUCTION 32,000 bottles
HECTARES UNDER VINE 4.00

Brothers Alberto and Alessandro Taddei took on a great challenge as the area around Pesaro is patently not the cradle of internationally-renowned reds. And yet, their ambition is just that: to make prestigious wines. They only have a few hectares but everything is studied to perfection, from the composition of the soils to the best grapes to plant, from the use of special clones to the quality of the small barrels used to coax the wines along their way. In only a few years, Poveriano - from cabernet franc - and Tripilin - from sangiovese and a touch of ciliegiolo - have become iconic jewels, enjoyed for their elegant personality and, in part at least, for their delightfully designed labels. An interesting debut for Cappitano 2009, an international style Merlot that features a subtle oakiness and certain intensity to its structure, linked to compact, sweet tannins. Poveriano 2010 is more expressive and the oak does not disguise the spices and raspberries reflected with graceful energy in the mouth.

● Cappitano '09	♥♥ 7
● Poveriano '10	♥♥ 5
● Muschèn '11	♥ 2
● Trimpilin '10	♥ 4
● Muschèn '09	♀♀ 2*
● Muschèn '08	♀♀ 1*
● Poveriano '09	♀♀ 5
● Poveriano '08	♀♀ 5
● Poveriano '07	♀♀ 3
● Selva Rosso '09	♀♀ 1*
● Trimpilin '09	♀♀ 4
● Trimpilin '08	♀♀ 4

Tenuta Spinelli

via Lago, 2
63032 Castignano [AP]
Tel. 0736821489
simonespinelli@tiscali.it

CELLAR SALES
PRE-BOOKED VISITS
ANNUAL PRODUCTION 22,000 bottles
HECTARES UNDER VINE 5.00

Simone Spinelli belongs to the legion of young growers who know how to fuse passion, rigour and sense of duty. He believes deeply in his territory and will use only traditional varieties. His only break with custom is to work just with white grapes, ignoring the red varieties abundant in the Piceno area. This choice is perfectly understandable as his vineyards feel the influence of Mount Ascensione, with the Montemisio plot on a rock bed at 600 metres of altitude. The pecorino used for the Artemisia is grown here. The cellars are small and efficient, with steel equipment and a few riddling racks used for the Méroe, a monovarietal Metodo Classico pecorino. Artemisia 2012 has crystalline aromas of citrus fruit, meadow flowers and broom, great character full of deep sapidity in the mouth and a juicy, flavoursome progression leading to an open and refreshing finish. Eden 2012 offers ripe fruit in a soft mouth.

○ Offida Pecorino Artemisia '12	♥♥♥ 2*
○ Méroe Pecorino M. Cl. '10	♥ 3
○ Offida Passerina Eden '12	♥ 2
○ Eden '11	♀♀ 2*
○ Méroe Pecorino M. Cl. '09	♀♀ 3
○ Offida Pecorino Artemisia '11	♀♀ 2*

La Staffa

Via Castellaretta, 19
60039 Staffolo [AN]
Tel. 0731779810
www.vinilastaffa.it

CELLAR SALES
PRE-BOOKED VISITS
ANNUAL PRODUCTION 30,000 bottles
HECTARES UNDER VINE 6.00

Riccardo Baldi was faced with a dilemma. Sell his small winery on the Staffolo hills and pay for his university studies, or take it over himself and turn his parents' costly hobby into a professional operation. Riccardo had no doubts and decided to tend the old vineyards of verdicchio and montepulciano, add more, then take the biggest step of all by building new cellars overlooking the vineyards in the Salmàgina and Castellaretta districts. Thanks to the support given by Lucio Canestrari, the young vigneron has clear ideas and talent, and is working on building up his experience. The harvest of 2012 was the watershed between the old and the new. We tasted a good Verdicchio 2012 with all the flavoursome robustness of the right bank of the River Esino. The Rincrocca 2010 selection was equally powerful, while Rincrocca 2011 appeared rather inert and mature.

○ Verdicchio dei Castelli di Jesi Cl. '12	♟♟ 2*
○ Verdicchio dei Castelli di Jesi Cl. Sup. La Rincrocca '10	♟♟ 3
● Rubinia '08	♟ 5
○ Verdicchio dei Castelli di Jesi Cl. Sup. La Rincrocca '11	♟ 3
● Esino Rosso Vivinaja '08	♟♟ 1*
● Rubinia '06	♟♟ 3
○ Verdicchio dei Castelli di Jesi Cl. '08	♟♟ 2*
○ Verdicchio dei Castelli di Jesi Cl. Sup. La Rincrocca '06	♟♟ 2*
○ Verdicchio dei Castelli di Jesi Cl. Sup. Rincrocca '08	♟♟ 2*

Tenuta di Tavignano

Loc. Tavignano
62011 Cingoli [MC]
Tel. 0733617303
www.tenutaditavignano.it

CELLAR SALES
PRE-BOOKED VISITS
ANNUAL PRODUCTION 100,000 bottles
HECTARES UNDER VINE 30.00

Tavignano is in a splendid panoramic position, midway between the Adriatic and the Apennines. The estate stands above the Musone valley to the south and the Esino valley to the north, on a typical clay and limestone hill. The oldest part of the vineyards, given over completely to verdicchio, was planted over 20 years ago. These plots are surrounded by others planted to smaller amounts of montepulciano, sangiovese and lacrima. In the cellar, the whites and rosés are aged in steel while the reds are aged in wood of different sizes. Misco Riserva 2011 is a step away from the top award, brilliant on the nose and with lively flavours, hindered only by its small production of 1,500 bottles. Misco 2012 is altogether pleasant, harmoniously blending youthful exuberance and a fruity softness. Villa Torre 2012 is more typical and flowing with a clean varietal stamp. Cervidoni 2011, with its strong character, has a good set of tannins.

○ Castelli di Jesi Verdicchio Cl. Misco Ris. '11	♟♟ 4
● Rosso Piceno Cervidoni '11	♟♟ 2*
○ Verdicchio dei Castelli di Jesi Cl. Sup. Misco '12	♟♟ 3
○ Verdicchio dei Castelli di Jesi Cl. Sup. Villa Torre '12	♟♟ 2*
⊙ Rosato '12	♟ 2
● Rosso Piceno Libenter '10	♟ 3
○ Verdicchio dei Castelli di Jesi Cl. Vigna Verde '12	♟ 2
○ Verdicchio dei Castelli di Jesi Cl. Misco Ris. '06	♟♟♟ 3*
○ Verdicchio dei Castelli di Jesi Cl. Sup. Misco '10	♟♟♟ 3*
○ Verdicchio dei Castelli di Jesi Cl. Sup. Misco '06	♟♟♟ 3*

MARCHE

Fattoria Le Terrazze

VIA MUSONE, 4
60026 NUMANA [AN]
TEL. 0717390352
www.fattorialeterrazze.it

CELLAR SALES
PRE-BOOKED VISITS
ANNUAL PRODUCTION 90,000 bottles
HECTARES UNDER VINE 20.00

From Fattoria Le Terrazze, your gaze can sweep from the Adriatic Sea as far as the cupola of the Basilica of Loreto. The nearness of the sea explains the large amount of sand found in the soil. Although vineyards have been here for a century, they were all renewed recently, the earliest in 1995. The largest areas have fittingly been kept for montepulciano but this is backed by the international grape varieties merlot, syrah and chardonnay. The style is soberly modern, rich but not overly ripe, where character is carefully retained without giving in to current fads. Sassi Neri 2008 proposes sweet toasty notes but a few evolved whiffs have slipped in, while the mouth is polished and alcohol-rich, harnessed by its own structure. We actually prefer the Rosso Conero 2011, with its crisp fruit, taut and juicy to the last drop. The contrast between tropical fruit and saltiness in the chardonnay Le Cave '12 is lovely.

○ Le Cave Chardonnay '12	♥♥ 2*
● Rosso Conero Le Terrazze '11	♥♥ 2*
● Rosso Conero Sassi Neri Ris. '08	♥♥ 5
● Rosso Conero Praeludium '12	♥ 2
● Chaos '04	♥♥♥ 5
● Chaos '01	♥♥♥ 6
● Conero Sassi Neri Ris. '04	♥♥♥ 5
● Rosso Conero Sassi Neri '02	♥♥♥ 5
● Rosso Conero Sassi Neri '99	♥♥♥ 5
● Rosso Conero Sassi Neri '98	♥♥♥ 5
● Rosso Conero Visions of J '01	♥♥♥ 7
● Chaos '08	♥♥ 5
● Conero Sassi Neri Ris. '06	♥♥ 5
● Rosso Conero Le Terrazze '10	♥♥ 2*
● Rosso Conero Praeludium '11	♥♥ 2*
● Rosso Conero Visions of J '06	♥♥ 6

Terre Cortesi Moncaro

VIA PIANOLE, 7A
63036 MONTECAROTTO [AN]
TEL. 073189245
www.moncaro.com

CELLAR SALES
PRE-BOOKED VISITS
RESTAURANT SERVICE
ANNUAL PRODUCTION 7,500,000 bottles
HECTARES UNDER VINE 1,618.00

The strength of the Moncaro co-operative winery is its enormous vineyard estate, extending across three exceptional Marche growing districts: Castelli di Jesi, Conero and Piceno. This means only the best grapes make it into production, interpreted in a consolidated modern style to deliver a series of labels clearly defined by fruit-infused aromas, a refined weave with no rough edges, and overall pleasurability that is pure drinking delight in the most successful wines. Vigna Novali Riserva 2010 is magnificent, revealing a kaleidoscope of aromas, where citron, fines herbes, aniseed and yellow peach resound in an expansive mouth, leading to an assertive, creamy progression where the tangy tones become nearly mineral in the finish. Following in its footsteps is Fondije 2012, where the progression is less intrusive. Among the reds, the best is Vigneto del Parco 2010, with overtones of plums and wild cherries in a virtually tactile structure.

○ Castelli di Jesi Verdicchio Cl. V. Novali Ris. '10	♥♥♥ 3*
● Conero Nerone Ris. '09	♥♥ 5
● Conero Vign. del Parco '10	♥♥ 4
● Rosso Piceno Sup. Roccaviva '10	♥♥ 2*
○ Verdicchio dei Castelli di Jesi Cl. Sup. Fondije '12	♥♥ 3
● Conero Montescuro Ris. '10	♥ 3
○ Madreperla Gran Cuvée	♥ 5
○ Offida Pecorino Ofithe '12	♥ 3
○ Verdicchio dei Castelli di Jesi Cl. Le Vele '12	♥ 2
○ Verdicchio dei Castelli di Jesi Cl. Sup. Verde Ca' Ruptae '12	♥ 3
○ Castelli di Jesi Verdicchio Cl. V. Novali Ris. '09	♥♥♥ 3*
○ Verdicchio dei Castelli di Jesi Cl. V. Novali Ris. '08	♥♥♥ 3*

Tenuta dell'Ugolino

LOC. MACINE
VIA COPPARONI, 32
60031 CASTELPLANIO [AN]
TEL. 360487114
www.tenutaugolino.it

CELLAR SALES
PRE-BOOKED VISITS
ANNUAL PRODUCTION 33,000 bottles
HECTARES UNDER VINE 6.00

Small producers may linger unseen in the complex Jesi landscape, with their efforts based on artisanal methods and endless passion overlooked in silence. We do not think this is the case for Andrea Petrini, a grower we have been watching for years and who embodies these qualities perfectly. From only a few hectares planted near the winery he makes two young Verdicchios: Vigneto del Balluccio, obtained from a vineyard selection set on siliceous soil with large amounts of sand and pebbles; Le Piaole, which scoops up the rest. Grapes are picked by hand, in several stages, and the cellar work uses only steel, to retain varietal freshness. Not to be missed is Balluccio 2012, which perfectly combines grace, strength and depth with clear aromas of almond, aniseed and lime blossom. Le Piaole is a real bargain: a few coins can buy a white that reflects the qualities of the Balluccio, with just a bit less intensity and elegance.

○ Verdicchio dei Castelli di Jesi Cl. Sup. Vign. del Balluccio '12	♥♥ 3*
○ Verdicchio dei Castelli di Jesi Cl. Le Piaole '12	♥♥ 2*
○ Verdicchio dei Castelli di Jesi Cl. '10	♀♀ 2*
○ Verdicchio dei Castelli di Jesi Cl. '07	♀♀ 2*
○ Verdicchio dei Castelli di Jesi Cl. '06	♀♀ 2*
○ Verdicchio dei Castelli di Jesi Cl. Sup. Vign. del Balluccio '11	♀♀ 3*
○ Verdicchio dei Castelli di Jesi Cl. Sup. Vign. del Balluccio '10	♀♀ 3
○ Verdicchio dei Castelli di Jesi Cl. Sup. Vigneto del Balluccio '07	♀♀ 3*
○ Verdicchio dei Castelli di Jesi Cl. Sup. Vigneto del Balluccio '06	♀♀ 3
○ Verdicchio dei Castelli di Jesi Cl. Sup. Vigneto del Balluccio '06	♀♀ 3

★Umani Ronchi

VIA ADRIATICA, 12
60027 OSIMO [AN]
TEL. 0717108019
www.umanironchi.com

CELLAR SALES
PRE-BOOKED VISITS
ANNUAL PRODUCTION 2,800,000 bottles
HECTARES UNDER VINE 230.00

Umani Ronchi is a private operation boasting one of the largest vineyard estates, suggesting that the winery has never forgotten its origins in grape production, reinforced by a recent decision to initiate organic management in over half its vineyards, starting from the top terroirs, between Jesi and the Conero promontory. Cellar approach respects the grape's varietal characteristics in a low-key modern style, and aims for a universally pleasing message, while sidestepping the most damaging effects like loss of territorial identity. Vecchie Vigne 2011, despite its sober elegance and closeness to its variety, passes the sceptre to the opulent Plenio 2010, a refined Verdicchio part-aged in oak and from it acquiring character and complexity blended into a generous mouthfeel. Maximo 2010, made from botrytized sauvignon, has fine nose marked by wild thyme, oregano and peach, while the mouth is a whisper of sweetness.

○ Castelli di Jesi Verdicchio Cl. Plenio Ris. '10	♥♥♥ 4*
○ Maximo '10	♥♥ 4
○ Verdicchio dei Castelli di Jesi Cl. Sup. V. V. '11	♥♥ 4
● Montepulciano d'Abruzzo Jorio '11	♥♥ 3
○ Vellodoro '12	♥♥ 2*
○ Verdicchio dei Castelli di Jesi Cl. Sup. Casal di Serra '12	♥♥ 3
○ Extra Brut M. Cl. Umani Ronchi	♥ 4
● Rosso Conero Serrano '12	♥ 2
○ Verdicchio dei Castelli di Jesi Cl. Villa Bianchi '12	♥ 2
○ Verdicchio dei Castelli di Jesi Cl. Sup. Vecchie Vigne '10	♀♀♀ 4*
○ Verdicchio dei Castelli di Jesi Cl. Sup. Vecchie Vigne '09	♀♀♀ 4

Vallerosa Bonci

VIA TORRE, 15
60034 CUPRAMONTANA [AN]
TEL. 0731789129
www.vallerosa-bonci.com

CELLAR SALES
PRE-BOOKED VISITS
ANNUAL PRODUCTION 250,000 bottles
HECTARES UNDER VINE 26.00

For many, Bonci means Verdicchio, but be well advised that this is a special type of Verdicchio, one that is varietal, flavoursome and almost always crafted in a style that prefers muscle to lightness. An approach embodying the magic of obstinate tradition, put in place with grapes imprinted with the Cupramontana terroir, extensive wine country rich in history. Concrete tank fermentation for all and, for the more prized labels, the path of lengthy bottle ageing. San Michele feels the very hot years as its grapes are sourced from the south-facing San Michele vineyard. All in all, despite 2011 being a scorcher, the wine has a flicker of vitality and the alcohol content, by no means low, is not overbearing and blends with a flavoursome driving power. It may not have a long life but, while it lasts, it is very pleasant. Manciano 2012 reveals the typical notes of almond and aniseed. The rich, inert Pietrone 2009 is slightly evolved.

○ Verdicchio dei Castelli di Jesi Cl. Sup. S. Michele '11	♟♟ 3*
○ Verdicchio dei Castelli di Jesi Cl. Manciano '12	♟♟ 2*
○ Verdicchio dei Castelli di Jesi Cl. Pietrone Ris. '09	♟ 5
○ Verdicchio dei Castelli di Jesi Cl. Pietrone Ris. '04	♟♟♟ 3
○ Verdicchio dei Castelli di Jesi Cl. Sup. Le Case '04	♟♟♟ 3*
○ Verdicchio dei Castelli di Jesi Cl. Sup. S. Michele '10	♟♟♟ 3*
○ Verdicchio dei Castelli di Jesi Cl. Sup. S. Michele '06	♟♟♟ 3
○ Verdicchio dei Castelli di Jesi Cl. Sup. S. Michele '00	♟♟♟ 3*

★Velenosi

LOC. MONTICELLI
VIA DEI BIANCOSPINI, 11
63100 ASCOLI PICENO
TEL. 0736341218
www.velenosivini.com

CELLAR SALES
ANNUAL PRODUCTION 2,500,000 bottles
HECTARES UNDER VINE 140.00

Velenosi never misses a wine fair or tasting: Angela knows that she needs to do more than bask in the fame of the terroir and its famous designations. She knows the only way to convince people is if they taste the wines. At the cellar, the close-knit group of leading professionals produce her wines of a dazzling aromatic focus and completely true to type. These polyglot wines are often made from native varieties but speak to many cultures and palates. This talented entrepreneur's personal dedication has taken Marche wines halfway around the world. Roggio del Filare 2010 is still at the head of a long line, invigorating and juicy in the mouth, the finish reveals rich fruity sensations, while intense spices and toasty aromas fill the nose. The same aromas, in a key of yellow-flesh fruit and field flowers, are found in the Rêve 2010, a modern Pecorino that is enjoyably weighty in the mouth. The two 2012 Lacrimas are very varietal.

● Rosso Piceno Sup. Roggio del Filare '10	♟♟♟ 5
○ Offida Pecorino Rêve '11	♟♟ 4
○ Falerio V. Solaria '12	♟♟ 3
● Lacrima di Morro d'Alba Querciantica '12	♟♟ 3
● Lacrima di Morro d'Alba Sup. Querciantica '12	♟♟ 4
● Offida Rosso Ludi '10	♟♟ 5
● Rosso Piceno Sup. Il Brecciarolo Gold '10	♟♟ 4
○ Chardonnay Villa Angela '12	♟ 2
○ Offida Pecorino Villa Angela '12	♟ 3
○ Passerina Villa Angela '12	♟ 3
● Rosso Piceno Sup. Brecciarolo '10	♟ 4
○ Verdicchio dei Castelli di Jesi Cl. Querciantica '12	♟ 2
● Rosso Piceno Sup. Roggio del Filare '09	♟♟♟ 5

Vicari

VIA POZZO BUONO, 3
60030 MORRO D'ALBA [AN]
TEL. 073163164
www.vicarivini.it

CELLAR SALES
PRE-BOOKED VISITS
ANNUAL PRODUCTION 90,000 bottles
HECTARES UNDER VINE 20.00

Almost a mantra, every Vicari label
mentions Pozzo Buono. On first sight, it
looks like a geographical indication, as it is
a place name for vineyard terrain, a grape
drying loft, the winery and the home. In
reality, it refers to a deep, proud sense of
belonging. Although the wines are
interpreted with a modern style approach,
applying all sorts of cellar techniques to
produce very diverse wines, the vineyards
accept the presence of lacrima nera and
verdicchio only. The only exception is some
moscatello, which, after raisining,
generates the voluptuous Amabile 2011.
Equally fascinating is its red alter ego
Amaranto 2011, a glycerine-rich wine with
an impressive set of blackberry aromas.
Among the dry wines, Verdicchio 2012 has
grip in the mouth and a convincingly salty
finish. Dasempre, the simplest of the
Lacrimas, gave a good display. Its main
strength lies in its balance combined with
fragrant suppleness.

○ Amabile del Pozzo Buono '11	♟♟ 3
● Lacrima di Morro d'Alba Amaranto del Pozzo Buono '11	♟♟ 4
● Lacrima di Morro d'Alba Dasempre del Pozzo Buono '12	♟♟ 2*
○ Verdicchio dei Castelli di Jesi Cl. del Pozzo Buono '12	♟♟ 2*
● Lacrima di Morro d'Alba Essenza del Pozzo Buono '12	♟ 3
● Lacrima di Morro d'Alba Sup. del Pozzo Buono '11	♟ 3
● Lacrima di Morro d'Alba Amaranto del Pozzo Buono '10	♟♟ 4
● Lacrima di Morro d'Alba Sup. del Pozzo Buono '10	♟♟ 3
○ Verdicchio dei Castelli di Jesi Cl. Sup. Insolito del Pozzo Buono '11	♟♟ 3

Le Vigne di Clementina Fabi

VIA FRANILE, 3
63069 MONTEDINOVE [AP]
TEL. 0736828217
www.levignediclementinafabi.it

CELLAR SALES
PRE-BOOKED VISITS
ANNUAL PRODUCTION 25,000 bottles
HECTARES UNDER VINE 9.00

Montedinove is a small town, perched at
500 metres above sea level and despite
climate changes, not all varieties thrive at
these altitudes, especially when Mount
Ascensione looms so close, with its cold
night breezes. Marco Fabi was smart
enough to invest in passerina and pecorino,
white varieties that work well with
significant day-night temperature
fluctuations. For his reds, Marco preferred
merlot, an early-ripener that wards off the
risk of unripe phenolics. His wines respond,
interpreting the terroir and expressing
richness of flavour, a solid acid backbone,
and snappy aromas. The greatest
beneficiary is Merlot 2011, far removed
from the classical cliché, with taut aromas
of orange blossom and berries and
engagingly juicy and energetic progression.
Between the two Offidas, we prefer a
Pecorino that joins depth and fullness, while
the Passerina focuses on tasting delicious.
Passerina Brut is very good, a rare case
when charmat method winemaking is
carried out in one's own cellar.

● Merlot '11	♟♟ 2*
○ Offida Passerina '12	♟♟ 2*
○ Offida Pecorino '12	♟♟ 2*
○ Passerina Brut '11	♟♟ 3

Angeli di Varano

FRAZ. VARANO, 228
60131 ANCONA
TEL. 0718046019
www.angelidivarano.it

CELLAR SALES
PRE-BOOKED VISITS
ACCOMMODATION
ANNUAL PRODUCTION 15,000 bottles
HECTARES UNDER VINE 3.20

● Conero Stile Libero Ris. '10	♥♥	4
● MeMoS '11	♥	4
● Rosso Conero Primo di Tre '11	♥	2

Cantine di Castignano

C.DA SAN VENANZO, 31
63032 CASTIGNANO [AP]
TEL. 0736822216
www.cantinedicastignano.com

CELLAR SALES
PRE-BOOKED VISITS
ANNUAL PRODUCTION 450,000 bottles
HECTARES UNDER VINE 520,00
VITICULTURE METHOD Certified Organic

○ Offida Pecorino Montemisio '12	♥♥	2*
● Offida Rosso Gran Maestro '09	♥♥	3
○ Offida Passerina '12	♥	1*
● Rosso Piceno Sup. Destriero '11	♥	1*

La Cantina dei Colli Ripani

C.DA TOSCIANO, 28
63038 RIPATRANSONE [AP]
TEL. 07359505
www.colliripani.it

CELLAR SALES
PRE-BOOKED VISITS
ANNUAL PRODUCTION 1,000,000 bottles
HECTARES UNDER VINE 700.00
VITICULTURE METHOD Certified Organic

○ Falerio Brezzolino '12	♥♥	2*
○ Offida Passerina Passito Anima Mundi '07	♥♥	5
○ Offida Pecorino Rugaro Gold '12	♥	3
● Offida Rosso Leo Ripanus '08	♥	4

Costadoro

VIA MONTE AQUILINO, 2
63039 SAN BENEDETTO DEL TRONTO [AP]
TEL. 073581781
www.vinicostadoro.com

CELLAR SALES
PRE-BOOKED VISITS
ANNUAL PRODUCTION 1,500,000 bottles
HECTARES UNDER VINE 87.00

○ Offida Pecorino Danù '12	♥♥	4
● Rosso Piceno Sup. Il Cardinale '08	♥♥	3
○ La Feròla '12	♥	1*
● Rosso Piceno '12	♥	2

Cristina Fausti

C.DA CASTELLETTA, 15
63023 FERMO
TEL. 0734620492
www.faustivini.it

CELLAR SALES
PRE-BOOKED VISITS
ANNUAL PRODUCTION 65,000 bottles
HECTARES UNDER VINE 11.00
VITICULTURE METHOD Certified Organic

○ Falerio Pecorino Ale '12	♥♥	3
● Per Domenico Syrah '10	♥♥	4
⊙ Rosato '12	♥	2
● Vespro '11	♥	4

Fiorini

VIA GIARDINO CAMPIOLI, 5
61040 BARCHI [PU]
TEL. 072197151
www.fioriniwines.it

CELLAR SALES
PRE-BOOKED VISITS
ACCOMMODATION AND RESTAURANT SERVICE
ANNUAL PRODUCTION 200,000 bottles
HECTARES UNDER VINE 45.00

○ Bianchello del Metauro Tenuta Campioli '12	♥♥	2*
● Colli Pesaresi Rosso Bartis '11	♥♥	3

Fosso dei Ronchi

VIA ZONGO, 9
61100 PESARO
TEL. 3395312093
www.fossodeironchi.it

ANNUAL PRODUCTION 2,500 bottles
HECTARES UNDER VINE 2.50

● Colli Pesaresi Focara Pinot Nero Costa del Picchio Ris. '11	♥♥ 3*
● Colli Pesaresi Focara Pinot Nero Costa del Riccio Ris. '11	♥♥ 3

Piergiovanni Giusti

LOC. MONTIGNANO
VIA CASTELLARO, 97
60019 SENIGALLIA [AN]
TEL. 071918031
www.lacrimagiusti.it

CELLAR SALES
PRE-BOOKED VISITS
ANNUAL PRODUCTION 51,000 bottles
HECTARES UNDER VINE 13.00

● Lacrima di Morro d'Alba Sup. Luigino '09	♥♥ 4
● L'Intruso '10	♥ 7
● Lacrima di Morro d'Alba '12	♥ 2
⊙ Le Rose di Settembre '12	♥ 2

Luca Guerrieri

VIA SAN FILIPPO, 24
61030 PIAGGE [PU]
TEL. 0721890152
www.aziendaguerrieri.it

CELLAR SALES
PRE-BOOKED VISITS
ACCOMMODATION AND RESTAURANT SERVICE
ANNUAL PRODUCTION 250,000 bottles
HECTARES UNDER VINE 35.00

● Colli Pesaresi Sangiovese Galileo Ris. '10	♥♥ 3
○ Bianchello del Metauro '12	♥ 2
○ Bianchello del Metauro Celso '12	♥ 2
● Rosa dei 20 '12	♥ 2

Esther Hauser

C.DA CORONCINO, 1A
60039 STAFFOLO [AN]
TEL. 0731770203
zara.hauser@gmail.com

CELLAR SALES
PRE-BOOKED VISITS
ANNUAL PRODUCTION 6,000 bottles
HECTARES UNDER VINE 1.00

● Il Ceppo '10	♥♥ 4
● Il Cupo '10	♥♥ 5

Lanari

FRAZ. VARANO
VIA POZZO, 142
60029 ANCONA
TEL. 0712861343
cantinalanari@libero.it

CELLAR SALES
PRE-BOOKED VISITS
ANNUAL PRODUCTION 50,000 bottles
HECTARES UNDER VINE 12.00

● Conero Fibbio Ris. '09	♥♥ 5
● Rosso Conero '11	♥♥ 2*
● Maria Sole '12	♥ 2

Luciano Landi

VIA GAVIGLIANO, 16
60030 BELVEDERE OSTRENSE [AN]
TEL. 073162353
www.aziendalandi.it

CELLAR SALES
PRE-BOOKED VISITS
ANNUAL PRODUCTION 100,000 bottles
HECTARES UNDER VINE 18.00

● Lacrima di Morro d'Alba Sup. Gavigliano '11	♥♥ 3
● Lacrima di Morro d'Alba '12	♥ 2
○ Verdicchio dei Castelli di Jesi Cl. '12	♥ 2

La Marca di San Michele

VIA TORRE, 13
60034 CUPRAMONTANA [AN]
TEL. 0731781183
www.lamarcadisanmichele.com

CELLAR SALES
ACCOMMODATION
ANNUAL PRODUCTION 12,000 bottles
HECTARES UNDER VINE 6.00
VITICULTURE METHOD Certified Organic

○ Capovolto '12	♥♥ 3
○ Verdicchio dei Castelli di Jesi Cl.Sup. Capovolto '11	♥ 3

Clara Marcelli

VIA FONTE VECCHIA, 8
63030 CASTORANO [AP]
TEL. 073687289
www.claramarcelli.it

PRE-BOOKED VISITS
ANNUAL PRODUCTION 40,000 bottles
HECTARES UNDER VINE 14.00
VITICULTURE METHOD Certified Organic

● K'un '11	♥♥ 3
○ Offida Passerina Raffa '12	♥ 2
○ Offida Pecorino Irata '12	♥ 2

Marchetti

FRAZ. PINOCCHIO
VIA DI PONTELUNGO, 166
60131 ANCONA
TEL. 071897386
www.marchettiwines.it

CELLAR SALES
PRE-BOOKED VISITS
ANNUAL PRODUCTION 60,000 bottles
HECTARES UNDER VINE 20,00

● Conero Villa Bonomi Ris. '10	♥♥ 4
● Rosso Conero Castro di San Silvestro '12	♥ 2
○ Verdicchio dei Castelli di Jesi Cl. '12	♥ 2

Federico Mencaroni

VIA OLMIGRANDI, 72
60013 CORINALDO [AN]
TEL. 0717975625
www.mencaroni.eu

HECTARES UNDER VINE 4.50

○ Verdicchio dei Castelli di Jesi Brut Apollonia '09	♥♥ 5
○ Verdicchio dei Castelli di Jesi Isola '10	♥♥ 2*
○ Flora '12	♥ 2

Muròla

C.DA VILLAMAGNA, 9
62010 URBISAGLIA [MC]
TEL. 0733506843
www.murola.it

CELLAR SALES
PRE-BOOKED VISITS
ANNUAL PRODUCTION 200,000 bottles
HECTARES UNDER VINE 55.00

● Camà '10	♥♥ 4
○ Colli Maceratesi Ribona '12	♥♥ 2*
○ Jurek M.Cl. '09	♥ 2
☉ Millerose '12	♥ 2

Cantina Offida

VIA DELLA REPUBBLICA , 70
63073 OFFIDA [AP]
TEL. 0736880104
www.cantinaoffida.com

ANNUAL PRODUCTION 210,000 bottles
HECTARES UNDER VINE 300.00

● Rosso Piceno Sup. '10	♥♥ 2*
● Rosso Piceno Sup. Podestà '09	♥♥ 3
○ Offida Pecorino '12	♥ 2
● Rosso Piceno '11	♥ 2

Pantaleone

VIA COLONNATA ALTA, 118
63100 ASCOLI PICENO
TEL. 3478757476
www.pantaleonewine.com

ANNUAL PRODUCTION 60,000 bottles
HECTARES UNDER VINE 11.00

● La Ribalta '10	♟♟ 8
○ Onirocep '11	♟♟ 3
● Sipario '10	♟ 2

Piersanti

B.GO SANTA MARIA, 60
60038 SAN PAOLO DI JESI [AN]
TEL. 0731703214
www.piersantivini.com

CELLAR SALES
PRE-BOOKED VISITS
ANNUAL PRODUCTION 3,500,000 bottles
HECTARES UNDER VINE 3.50

○ Verdicchio dei Castelli di Jesi Cl. Sup. Terre di Sampaolo '12	♟♟ 2*
○ Verdicchio dei Castelli di Jesi Cl. Sup. Bachero '12	♟ 2

Elio Polenta

LOC. COLLINA DI PORTONOVO
VIA CAMPANA, 146
60129 ANCONA
TEL. 071801070
www.cantinapolenta.it

CELLAR SALES
PRE-BOOKED VISITS
ACCOMMODATION AND RESTAURANT SERVICE
ANNUAL PRODUCTION 12,000 bottles
HECTARES UNDER VINE 3.00

● Rosso Conero Accipicchia '09	♟♟ 2*
● Rosso Conero Poy Ris. '09	♟♟ 4
● Rosso Conero Gianco Ris. '09	♟ 5

Rio Maggio

C.DA VALLONE, 41
63014 MONTEGRANARO [FM]
TEL. 0734889587
www.riomaggio.it

CELLAR SALES
PRE-BOOKED VISITS
ANNUAL PRODUCTION 100,000 bottles
HECTARES UNDER VINE 18.00

● Colle Monteverde Pinot Nero '10	♟♟ 4
● Rosso Piceno Rubeo '08	♟♟ 3
● Rosso Piceno Vign. Contrada Vallone '10	♟♟ 4

Ripa Marchetti

VIA FONDE SANTA LIBERATA
60030 MAIOLATI SPONTINI [AN]
TEL. 3337376888
www.ripamarchetti.it

ANNUAL PRODUCTION 18,000 bottles
HECTARES UNDER VINE 6.00

○ Castelli di Jesi Verdicchio V. Roncone Ris. '10	♟♟ 2*
○ Verdicchio dei Castelli di Jesi Cl. Sup. Apicus '11	♟♟ 2*

Saladini Pilastri

VIA SALADINI, 5
63078 SPINETOLI [AP]
TEL. 0736899534
www.saladinipilastri.it

CELLAR SALES
PRE-BOOKED VISITS
ANNUAL PRODUCTION 1,000,000 bottles
HECTARES UNDER VINE 150.00
VITICULTURE METHOD Certified Organic

● Rosso Piceno V. Piediprato '11	♟♟ 3
○ Falerio V. Palazzi '12	♟ 2
● Rosso Piceno V. Monteprandone '11	♟ 5

Santa Cassella

c.DA SANTA CASSELLA, 7
62018 POTENZA PICENA [MC]
TEL. 0733671507
www.santacassella.it

CELLAR SALES
PRE-BOOKED VISITS
ANNUAL PRODUCTION 70,000 bottles
HECTARES UNDER VINE 32.00

● Conte Leopoldo '10	♟♟ 3*
● Rosso Piceno '11	♟♟ 2*
○ Donna Angela '12	♟ 3
○ Donna Eleonora '12	♟ 3

Podere Santa Lucia

VIA SANTA LUCIA, 65
60037 MONTE SAN VITO [AN]
TEL. 0717489179
www.poderesantalucia.com

ANNUAL PRODUCTION 70,000 bottles
HECTARES UNDER VINE 13.00

○ Verdicchio dei Castelli di Jesi Cl. Sup. Gianni Balducci '11	♟♟ 3*
○ Verdicchio dei Castelli di Jesi Cl. Fonte della Romita '12	♟♟ 2*

Fattoria Serra San Martino

VIA SAN MARTINO, 1
60030 SERRA DE' CONTI [AN]
TEL. 0731878025
www.serrasanmartino.com

CELLAR SALES
PRE-BOOKED VISITS
ANNUAL PRODUCTION 10,000 bottles
HECTARES UNDER VINE 3.00

● Costa dei Zoppi '10	♟♟ 4
● Lo Sconosciuto '09	♟♟ 5
● Lysipp '09	♟♟ 5
● Roccuccio '10	♟♟ 3

Silvano Strologo

VIA OSIMANA, 89
60021 CAMERANO [AN]
TEL. 071731104
www.vinorossoconero.com

CELLAR SALES
PRE-BOOKED VISITS
ANNUAL PRODUCTION 70,000 bottles
HECTARES UNDER VINE 33.00

● Rosso Conero Julius '11	♟♟ 2*
● Conero Decebalo Ris. '08	♟ 4
● Rosso Conero Traiano '08	♟ 4

Vigneti Vallorani

c.DA LA ROCCA, 28
63079 COLLI DEL TRONTO [AP]
TEL. 0736890892
www.vignetivallorani.com

CELLAR SALES
PRE-BOOKED VISITS
ANNUAL PRODUCTION 20,000 bottles
HECTARES UNDER VINE 7.00

○ Falerio Avora '11	♟♟ 2*
○ Offida Passerina Zaccarì '11	♟ 2
● Rosso Piceno Polisia '11	♟ 2

Valturio

VIA DEI PELASGI, 10
61023 MACERATA FELTRIA [PU]
TEL. 0722728049
www.valturio.com

CELLAR SALES
PRE-BOOKED VISITS
ACCOMMODATION
ANNUAL PRODUCTION 40,000 bottles
HECTARES UNDER VINE 10.00

● Olmo '11	♟♟ 2*
○ Tamerice '12	♟ 2

UMBRIA

We disagree with the popular image of Umbria as a static wine region, with largely standardized production based on just a few native varieties and a predictable, simplistic style. While it is true that the area has replicated the winning strategy of international cultivars in the past, importing "foreign" winemaking models, sometimes abandoning the classic designations or reworking them to meet the demands of a new trend, it is equally undeniable that things have changed over the years, and more than may be evident at first glance. Reading between the lines of the progress underway, particularly in the past few years, it is impossible not to notice that the picture is far more complex than it was. The merit for this goes to growers and wine entrepreneurs, some young or even very young, who have embarked upon some very interesting paths that are very modern but capable of drawing on the lessons of the past. It is also the merit of a land that has proven its flexibility and is ready to give good results on the most diverse fronts. In ampelographic terms too, the situation in Umbria appears much more interesting than just a few years ago. While the region may not boast dozens of traditional grape varieties, there are enough considering Umbria's size. The scene is no longer dominated solely by sangiovese, grechetto and sagrantino, but also confidently features rediscovered cultivars like trebbiano spoletino, ciliegiolo, particularly in the area around Narni and along the Tuscan border, and Trasimeno gamay similar to grenache. There are also some totally forgotten varieties, including very recent experiments with grero, a kind of grechetto nero that was once grown in the Todi area. These are just a few examples, which will undoubtedly encounter developing styles and banish a single approach, offering instead a wide array of scenarios in terms of both ageing methods and the final identity of the wines. In other words, there is work in progress, or better still it is a workshop that promises an even more interesting future for a region that has never failed to live up to expectations and has always played an important role in the world of Italian wine. We invite readers to pursue the tips found in this Guide, not stopping at the top wines, but instead seeking to appreciate the progress of a very dynamic region in all respects.

Adanti

LOC. ARQUATA
VIA BELVEDERE, 2
06031 BEVAGNA [PG]
TEL. 0742360295
www.cantineadanti.com

CELLAR SALES
PRE-BOOKED VISITS
ANNUAL PRODUCTION 160,000 bottles
HECTARES UNDER VINE 30.00

Just outside stunning Bevagna, heading for Montefalco, we will find one of the zone's oldest estates. Adanti produces some very interesting wines and gives Sagrantino fans a classical expression of this varietal, thanks to the use of traditional growing and cellar methods, like spontaneous fermentation, long maceration, and ageing in quite large oak casks. All technical details we can use to get an idea of what the winery is like, but at the end of the day the essence of its success lies in its old-world charm and the ability of its wines to defy time and trends. These are all traits inherent to the estate's 2008 Montefalco Sagrantino. Less intense in colour than many of its peers in the designation, with a garnet rim. The nose features leather, dried flowers, tar and Mediterranean scrub over a gentle fruit core, with hints of tawny orange. The powerful palate, with incisive but not overpowering tannic weave, is elegant and deep.

● Montefalco Sagrantino Arquata '08	♟♟♟ 6
○ Colli Martani Grechetto '12	♟♟ 2*
○ Montefalco Bianco '11	♟ 2
● Montefalco Rosso '09	♟ 3
● Montefalco Sagrantino Arquata '06	♟♟♟ 5
● Montefalco Sagrantino Arquata '05	♟♟♟ 5
○ Montefalco Bianco Arquata '10	♟♟ 2*
● Montefalco Rosso '08	♟♟ 2*
● Montefalco Rosso Ris. '08	♟♟ 3
● Montefalco Sagrantino Arquata '07	♟♟ 5
● Montefalco Sagrantino Il Domenico '07	♟♟ 6
● Montefalco Sagrantino Il Domenico '06	♟♟ 6
● Montefalco Sagrantino Il Domenico '05	♟♟ 6

Antonelli - San Marco

LOC. SAN MARCO, 60
06036 MONTEFALCO [PG]
TEL. 0742379158
www.antonellisanmarco.it

CELLAR SALES
PRE-BOOKED VISITS
ACCOMMODATION
ANNUAL PRODUCTION 300,000 bottles
HECTARES UNDER VINE 40.00

The Antonelli family's gorgeous historic estate lies in one of the designation's best subzones. Medieval documents talk about San Marco de Corticellis as one of the finest areas for the cultivation of grapes and olives. The estate was owned by the Bishop of Spoleto from the 13th to the 19th century, and was acquired in 1881 by Spoleto lawyer, Francesco Antonelli, whose family still owns it. A lengthy history and a fine terroir enhanced by organic farming practices, all conveyed to the bottle by one of the most sensitive winemakers here, capable of producing elegant, cellarable wines with a strong local identity. The 2007 Montefalco Sagrantino Chiusa di Pannone, a proper cru with obvious potential, follows in the same vein. This well-made version has a relaxed, seductive aromatic profile, with a few lovely mineral hints. The nicely elegant palate has depth even though a held back a tad by somewhat overblown tannins. The very good 2010 Rosso di Montefalco is elegant and compelling.

● Montefalco Sagrantino Chiusa di Pannone '07	♟♟ 6
○ Colli Martani Grechetto '12	♟♟ 2*
● Montefalco Rosso '10	♟♟ 3
● Montefalco Rosso Ris. '08	♟♟ 4
○ Trebbiano Spoletino Trebuim '11	♟♟ 3
● Baiocco '11	♟ 2
● Contrario '10	♟ 3
● Montefalco Sagrantino '08	♟♟♟ 5
● Montefalco Sagrantino Chiusa di Pannone '04	♟♟♟ 6
○ Colli Martani Grechetto '11	♟♟ 2*
● Montefalco Rosso Ris. '07	♟♟ 4
● Montefalco Sagrantino '07	♟♟ 5
● Montefalco Sagrantino Chiusa di Pannone '06	♟♟ 6

Barberani

LOC. CERRETO
05023 BASCHI [TR]
TEL. 0763341820
www.barberani.it

CELLAR SALES
PRE-BOOKED VISITS
ACCOMMODATION
ANNUAL PRODUCTION 350,000 bottles
HECTARES UNDER VINE 55.00
VITICULTURE METHOD Certified Organic

The Barberani family's historic Orvieto estate is one of the more convincing producers in the zone. The vineyards and winery lie on the stunning hills above Lake Corbara, the underlying reason for their wonderful Noble Rot wine. Their entire range is convincing and testifies to their active approach and increasingly original styling. From the vineyard to the cellar, the operation is increasingly focused on natural, environmentally friendly methods that allow the wines to express themselves fully. The fantastic 2008 Villa Monticelli Polvento is one of the region's best reds. A classy, deep wine that is chewy, delicately grassy, crisp and silky. The stellar 2010 Muffa Nobile Calcaia is memorable, a spectacularly elegant, complex and leisurely white, with delicious dried fruit and saffron notes.

○ Orvieto Cl. Sup. Muffa Nobile Calcaia '10	🍷🍷🍷 5
● Lago di Corbara Rosso Polvento Villa Monticelli '08	🍷🍷 5
○ Orvieto Cl. Sup. Castagnolo '12	🍷🍷 3
○ Orvieto Cl. Sup. Vinoso '12	🍷🍷 4
● Aleatico Passito Villa Monticelli '08	🍷 6
○ Grechetto '12	🍷 3
○ Vermentino '12	🍷 3
● Lago di Corbara Rosso Villa Monticelli '04	🍷🍷🍷 4
● Lago di Corbara Rosso Polvento '06	🍷🍷 5
● Lago di Corbara Rosso Villa Monticelli '05	🍷🍷 4
○ Orvieto Cl. Sup. Calcaia '08	🍷🍷 5
○ Orvieto Cl. Sup. Calcaia '07	🍷🍷 5
○ Orvieto Cl. Sup. Calcaia '06	🍷🍷 5
○ Orvieto Cl. Sup. Vinoso '11	🍷🍷 3*

Tenuta Bellafonte

LOC. TORRE DEL COLLE
VIA COLLE NOTTOLO, 2
06031 BEVAGNA [PG]
TEL. 0742710019
www.tenutabellafonte.it

PRE-BOOKED VISITS
ACCOMMODATION
ANNUAL PRODUCTION 5,500 bottles
HECTARES UNDER VINE 7.00

Tenuta Bellafonte is the dream of Peter Heilbron, a Milanese manager who travelled all over Italy before settling in this stunning part of Umbria, close to Torre del Colle and Bevagna. In the unspoilt countryside, sagrantino vines alternate with woods and olive groves. The operation is run with care and almost obsessive attention to detail, and rare concern for the environment. Nothing is left to chance in the vineyard or the fine cellars. Spontaneous fermentation, large wood, and winemaking that channels lively sangrantino into the most elegant, authentic wine. All factors elevating this newcomer to star status for the designation, the area and Umbria overall. The estate made a big entrance last year and its style has matured to the point of a sublime 2009 Montefalco Sagrantino. It is the only wine but it is stellar, with Mediterranean scrub, fresh cut flower and berry fruit aromas uplifted by unusual mineral overtones. The elegant mouth is silky, gracefully powerful, effortlessly long and vibrantly well-orchestrated.

● Montefalco Sagrantino '09	🍷🍷🍷 6
● Montefalco Sagrantino '08	🍷🍷 5

Bigi

LOC. PONTE GIULIO
05018 ORVIETO [TR]
TEL. 0763315888
www.cantinebigi.it

PRE-BOOKED VISITS
ANNUAL PRODUCTION 4,000,000 bottles
HECTARES UNDER VINE 196.00

In Umbria, the name Bigi comes with a hefty legacy, dating back to the late 1800s. As the story goes, the passion and vision of the estate's founder, Luigi Bigi, produced some lovely interpretations of classic Orvieto wines, initially produced in the former monastery of La Trinità, but now made nearby, in Ponte Giulio. This romantic past, so closely tied to the territory, has since been superseded by a more modern approach, after the estate joined Gruppo Italiano Vini, and now produces impeccable modern wines of outstanding consistency. The range is generally well made throughout, with a couple of interesting wines standing out in both the classical and the more experimental lines. The 2012 Vipra Rossa sangiovese and merlot blend is good, a fresh, racy wine with a pleasantly earthy palate. The stalwart 2011 Sartiano is austere, with torrefaction and redcurrant notes. The surprising 2012 Vipra Rosa rosé has an elegant nose and subtle, very stylish palate with white rose aromas.

● Sartiano '11	♟♟ 3
○ Strozzavolpe '12	♟♟ 2*
⊙ Vipra Rosa '12	♟♟ 2*
● Vipra Rossa '12	♟♟ 2*
○ Orvieto Cl. Vign. Torricella '12	♟ 2
○ Orvieto Cl. Torricella '11	♟♟ 3
○ Orvieto Cl. Vign. Torricella '10	♟♟ 2*
● Sartiano '08	♟♟ 3
○ Strozzavolpe '11	♟♟ 2*
○ Strozzavolpe Grechetto '09	♟♟ 2

Bocale

LOC. MADONNA DELLA STELLA
VIA FRATTA ALZATURA
06036 MONTEFALCO [PG]
TEL. 0742399233
www.bocale.it

CELLAR SALES
PRE-BOOKED VISITS
ANNUAL PRODUCTION 20,000 bottles
HECTARES UNDER VINE 4.20

The small, but impeccably run Bocale winery is a new producer with ancient roots. Bocale itself is a term used as a nickname for the Valentina family and leaves no doubt as to the owners' agricultural origins. The estate is situated a few kilometres from the heart of Montefalco, in the locality of Fratta Alzatura, not far from the Madonna della Stella sanctuary. The well-made wines communicate a strong local character and testify nicely to the zone's potential. The operation cultivates four hectares of vines itself and has achieved good results with red wines over the last few vintages. In our opinion, this little winery has produced one of the best Montefalco Sagrantino Passitos this year. It is beautifully intense and full, outstandingly harmonious, and the classic sweet sensations are tamed by perfectly balanced tannins and acidity. Also excellent is the firm, mouthfilling 2010 Sagrantino.

● Montefalco Sagrantino Passito '09	♟♟ 5
● Montefalco Sagrantino '10	♟♟ 5
● Montefalco Rosso '11	♟ 2
● Montefalco Rosso '09	♟♟ 4
● Montefalco Rosso '08	♟♟ 4
● Montefalco Sagrantino '09	♟♟ 5
● Montefalco Sagrantino '07	♟♟ 5

Leonardo Bussoletti

S.DA DELLE PRETARE, 62
05035 NARNI [TR]
TEL. 0744715687
www.leonardobussoletti.it

PRE-BOOKED VISITS
ANNUAL PRODUCTION 15,000 bottles
HECTARES UNDER VINE 7.00
VITICULTURE METHOD Certified Organic

Leonard Bussoletti has been involved with wine professionally for many years, but it was only recently that he decided to produce his own, with immediate results. An attentive, sensitive grower with a competent, well-trained palate, Bussoletti has successfully channelled his ideas into a project that is original, well founded, and focused in every way. Artisanal by vocation, the winery originally chose ciliegiolo di Narni as its prime variety, including a small number of old vines, but has also shown that it is capable of producing good whites, headed by grechetto. The estate style is direct, with an unmistakable focus on drinkability and finesse. What a lovely Ciliegiolo, or should we say what lovely Ciliegiolos as this year there are two. The relaxed, juicy, deep 2010 Vigna Vecchia is so good that it fully deserved a place in the finals for the sheer fruit lushness in a distinctly mature yet crisp vein. This archetypical wine is a varietal benchmark in Umbria. The other Ciliegiolo is also excellent, as is the delicious vibrant, mineral 2012 Grechetto Colle Ozio.

● Ciliegiolo di Narni Vigna Vecchia '10	♈♈	7
● Brecciaro '11	♈♈	3
○ Colle Ozio '12	♈♈	3
● Brecciaro '10	♈♈	3

★Arnaldo Caprai

LOC. TORRE
06036 MONTEFALCO [PG]
TEL. 0742378802
www.arnaldocaprai.it

CELLAR SALES
PRE-BOOKED VISITS
ANNUAL PRODUCTION 750,000 bottles
HECTARES UNDER VINE 136.00

The way in which Caprai mastered entry to the wine scene was astonishing enough, transforming as the face of Sagrantino and the Montefalco zone. However, the way the operation is writing its own story is nothing less than mind-blowing, progressing from chapter to exciting new chapter. In short, not only is this leading winery a local milestone, but it is also capable of uniting managerial savoir-faire, hard work and passion as few can. What is more, the wines have a unique style that it would not only be difficult, but almost perilous, to imitate. They are intense and concentrated, but also promote the natural exuberance of the territory and its native varieties. Once again, the monumental Montefalco Sagrantino 25 Anni selection, possibly the region's most famous wine, stands out by a mile. The 2009 harvest produced a red of matchless depth, with assertive concentration and plenty of tannins. As always time will soften its youthful exuberance. The 2009 Collepiano comes a close second and the rest of the range is also first-rate.

● Montefalco Sagrantino 25 Anni '09	♈♈♈	8
● Montefalco Sagrantino Collepiano '09	♈♈	6
○ Colli Martani Grechetto Grecante '12	♈♈	4
● Montefalco Rosso '11	♈♈	4
● Montefalco Rosso Ris. '09	♈♈	6
● Montefalco Sagrantino Passito '09	♈♈	7
● Montefalco V. Flaminia Maremmana '10	♈♈	3
● Montefalco Sagrantino 25 Anni '08	♈♈♈	8
● Montefalco Sagrantino 25 Anni '07	♈♈♈	8
● Montefalco Sagrantino 25 Anni '06	♈♈♈	8
● Montefalco Sagrantino 25 Anni '05	♈♈♈	8
● Montefalco Sagrantino 25 Anni '04	♈♈♈	8
● Montefalco Sagrantino Collepiano '08	♈♈♈	6
● Montefalco Sagrantino Collepiano '03	♈♈♈	6
● Rosso Outsider '03	♈♈♈	8

UMBRIA

Carini

LOC. CANNETO
FRAZ. COLLE UMBERTO
S.DA DEL TEGOLARO
06133 PERUGIA
TEL. 0756059495
www.agrariacarini.it

CELLAR SALES
PRE-BOOKED VISITS
ANNUAL PRODUCTION 40,000 bottles
HECTARES UNDER VINE 10.00

One of the smaller Umbrian wineries, the estate of brothers Carlo and Marco Carini is a real gem. Situated in a stunning corner of Umbria, between Mount Tezio and Lake Trasimeno, not far from the provincial capital, it represents a kind of rural microcosm where wine takes centre stage. We might call it a modern farm whose core product is wine. The grapes are fermented in the lovely cellars and the wine is aged in barrels. The entire range of reds and whites has a modern, well-defined style, with a predominance of big international varieties. I Colli del Trasimeno Oscano also speaks an international language but its roots are clearly local. The wine is mainly Trasimeno gamay, a variety similar to grenache and now a classic in the lake area. The 2012 vintage is a treat, with its incredibly intense red robe, a rich, dark fruit, and liquorice aromas. A real character that has a dense yet vibrant palate. Our favourite white was the easier Rile rather than the overly vegetal Poggio Canneto.

● C. del Trasimeno Òscano '12	♟♟	2*
○ C. del Trasimeno Rile '12	♟♟	2*
○ Poggio Canneto '11	♟	3
○ C. del Trasimeno Rile '11	♟♟	2*
● Òscano '09	♟♟	2
● Òscano '08	♟♟	2*
○ Poggio Canneto '09	♟♟	3
○ Poggio Canneto '08	♟♟	3*
○ Poggio Canneto '07	♟♟	3*
● Tegolaro '08	♟♟	5
● Tegolaro '07	♟♟	5
● Tegolaro '06	♟♟	5
● Tegolaro '05	♟♟	5
● Tegolaro Selezione Armando '08	♟♟	5

La Carraia

LOC. TORDIMONTE, 56
05018 ORVIETO [TR]
TEL. 0763304013
www.lacarraia.it

CELLAR SALES
PRE-BOOKED VISITS
ANNUAL PRODUCTION 550,000 bottles
HECTARES UNDER VINE 119.00

The prize-winning Gialletti-Cotarella team is steadfastly pursuing its quest for quality and each year produces stylistically well-defined and technically irreproachable wines. These wines are definitely worth tasting and sharing. The operation is located in the Orvieto area and the estate is planted to local and international varieties. The wines are modern in style and convey the personality and imprint of the various varieties perfectly as well as allowing the terroir to shine through. The 2010 Fobiano has a dark, toasty profile, with pervasive spicy, smoky notes that enhance the black berry fruit sensations. The mouth is warm, slightly alcoholic, and tannic. The 2012 Cabernet Sauvignon has black and red forest fruit aromas, with contrasting leather and vanilla notes. The entry is soft and clean, and closes with low-key tannins. The 2012 Sangiovese is equally good, with spicy, rose water, and black berry notes.

● Fobiano '10	♟♟	4
● Cabernet Sauvignon '12	♟♟	2*
○ Orvieto Cl. Sup. Poggio Calvelli '12	♟♟	2*
● Sangiovese '12	♟♟	2*
● Giro di Vite '11	♟	4
○ Le Basque '12	♟	3
● Tizzonero '11	♟	3
● Fobiano '03	♟♟♟	4
● Fobiano '99	♟♟♟	4*
● Cabernet Sauvignon '11	♟♟	2*
● Giro di Vite '10	♟♟	4
○ Orvieto Cl. Sup. Poggio Calvelli '11	♟♟	2*

Tenuta Castelbuono

LOC. BEVAGNA
VOC. FOSSATO, 54
06031 PERUGIA
TEL. 0742361670
www.tenutacastelbuono.it

ANNUAL PRODUCTION 100,000 bottles
HECTARES UNDER VINE 32.00

Owned by the Lunelli family, Tenuta Castelbuono is one of the most interesting new producers in the region in many respects. The winery, designed by artist Arnaldo Pomodorro, is a local gem. It focuses almost exclusively on the terroir and elegance for top-quality wines that have also forged ahead in exploration of style. The vineyards are located in two different zones, the first around the winery itself, near Bevagna; the second located in the municipality of Montefalco. Our latest tasting confirms that the Lunellis and their staff are applying a sound, yet original reading of the terroir. The wine is not easy to read in a comparative tasting, but it is beguiling, with a strong local, varietal character. That is the 2008 Montefalco Rosso Riserva in a nutshell. Earthy, almost bony and at times spiky, but it is also truly genuine and great with food. The 2008 Sagrantino is good and the 2010 Montefalco Rosso is racy and juicy.

● Montefalco Rosso Ris. '08	♥♥♥ 5
● Montefalco Rosso '10	♥♥ 3
● Montefalco Sagrantino '08	♥♥♥ 5
● Montefalco Rosso '09	♥♥ 3
● Montefalco Rosso '07	♥♥ 3*
● Montefalco Rosso '06	♥♥ 3*
● Montefalco Sagrantino '07	♥♥ 5
● Montefalco Sagrantino '06	♥♥ 5
● Montefalco Sagrantino '05	♥♥ 5
● Montefalco Sagrantino '04	♥♥ 5
● Montefalco Sagrantino '03	♥♥ 5
● Montefalco Sagrantino '01	♥♥ 5

★★Castello della Sala

LOC. SALA
05016 FICULLE [TR]
TEL. 076386051
www.antinori.it

PRE-BOOKED VISITS
HECTARES UNDER VINE 140.00

When a great wine territory meets with the ideas, expertise and visionary spirit of a great family of winemakers, it is highly likely that the product will be fascinating. This is what happened when the Antinori family set out to create a great white wine in the tufa hills that rise up to 500 metres above Ficulle, near Orvieto. After the first few experimental vintages in the late 1980s, they began achieving quite astounding results and we can safely say that the endeavour has greatly exceeded expectations. The wonderful white Cervaro is international in both character and stature, as striking when young as it is when aged. The 2011 vintage lives up to expectations with very tight-grained oaky, toasted notes blending perfectly with the fruity, floral and chlorophyll aromas. In the mouth it is full, and in some respects powerful, but it is also vibrant and fluid, with good supporting pulp and a finely-tuned acidic vein.

○ Cervaro della Sala '11	♥♥♥ 6
○ Orvieto Cl. Sup. San Giovanni della Sala '12	♥♥ 3
● Pinot Nero '11	♥ 5
○ Cervaro della Sala '10	♥♥♥ 6
○ Cervaro della Sala '09	♥♥♥ 6
○ Cervaro della Sala '08	♥♥♥ 6
○ Cervaro della Sala '07	♥♥♥ 6
○ Cervaro della Sala '06	♥♥♥ 6
○ Cervaro della Sala '05	♥♥♥ 6
○ Cervaro della Sala '04	♥♥♥ 6
○ Cervaro della Sala '03	♥♥♥ 5
○ Cervaro della Sala '02	♥♥♥ 5
○ Cervaro della Sala '01	♥♥♥ 5
○ Cervaro della Sala '00	♥♥♥ 5
○ Cervaro della Sala '99	♥♥♥ 5

Castello di Magione

VIA DEI CAVALIERI DI MALTA, 31
06063 MAGIONE [PG]
TEL. 075843542
www.castellodimagione.it

CELLAR SALES
PRE-BOOKED VISITS
ANNUAL PRODUCTION 150,000 bottles
HECTARES UNDER VINE 44.00

The castle belongs to the Prince and Grand Master of the Sovereign Military Order of Malta and dates back to 1150–70, when it was used as a hospitium for pilgrims travelling to and from Rome and Jerusalem on the nearby Via Francigena, on their way to Santiago de Compostela. The castle dominates the Trasimeno valley and the vines perch on the surrounding hillsides, arranged to a very clearly defined cru classification. In contrast to this very traditional view of winemaking, the cellars are resolutely modern. Despite the predominance of red varieties, like cabernet sauvignon, merlot, sangiovese, Trasimeno gamay and pinot nero, grechetto is the real jewel in the crown. Once again, the Colli del Trasimeno Grechetto Monterone provides a stunning interpretation of Umbria's most traditional white variety. Very well made, elegant and mineral, with a palate balanced perfectly between savoury and acidic sensations, just the right amount of body, and floral nuancing. Of the reds, the 2010 Novecento stands out by a mile interpreted as a weave of modern verve, attitude, and personality.

○ C. del Trasimeno Grechetto Monterone '12	⬙⬙ 2*
● Novecento '10	⬙⬙ 3
● Sangiovese '12	⬙⬙ 2*
● Carpaneto '11	⬙ 3
○ C. del Trasimeno Grechetto Monterone '11	⬙⬙ 2*
○ C. del Trasimeno Grechetto Monterone '10	⬙⬙ 2
○ C. del Trasimeno Grechetto Monterone '08	⬙⬙ 2*
● Carpaneto '10	⬙⬙ 3
● Carpaneto '08	⬙⬙ 3

Cantina Castello Monte Vibiano Vecchio

LOC. MONTE VIBIANO VECCHIO DI MERCATELLO
VOC. PALOMBARO, 22
06072 MARSCIANO [PG]
TEL. 0758783386
www.montevibiano.it

CELLAR SALES
PRE-BOOKED VISITS
HECTARES UNDER VINE 35.00

This estate has experienced exponential growth and is well worth noting. Behind the winery's picturesque façade there is a strong, very interesting modern vision of winemaking, through which the estate has successfully achieved zero CO_2 emissions. Close to Perugia, the hillside castle boasts magnificent old walls, its own stunning marble chapel, and ancient trees that grace the surrounding landscape. Over the years, the wines have grown considerably, both in overall quality and in style, and now play a key role on the Umbrian wine scene. The 2009 Colli Perugini Rosso L'Andrea confirmed its reputation this year and while it may be slightly less captivating than the previous vintage, it is still on top form. This upright red, a 50% sangiovese with merlot, cabernet sauvignon, and syrah blend, is meaty and blood-rich, at times sweet and spicy, with a nice savoury sign-off and subtle oak hints.

● Colli Perugini Rosso L'Andrea '09	⬙⬙ 5
● Colli Perugini Rosso Monvì '10	⬙⬙ 2*
⊙ Maryam '12	⬙⬙ 3
○ Maria Camilla '12	⬙ 3
● Villa Monte Vibiano Rosso '12	⬙ 1*
● Colli Perugini Rosso L'Andrea '08	⬙⬙⬙ 5
● Colli Perugini Rosso Monvì '09	⬙⬙ 2*

Fattoria Colleallodole

LOC. COLLE ALLODOLE
06031 BEVAGNA [PG]
TEL. 0742361897
www.fattoriacolleallodole.it

CELLAR SALES
PRE-BOOKED VISITS
ANNUAL PRODUCTION 60,000 bottles
HECTARES UNDER VINE 12.00

The charming estate named after Milziade Antano, the sorely missed pioneer of the Sagrantino movement, was established many moons ago, but in recent times it has taken some surprising turns. The winery is near Bevagna, as are the vineyards, including the star Colleallodole cru. The wines capture the essence of their native terroir and bear the stamp of an inspired winemaker. Opulent and classical, yet easy to read, these wines show unquestionable attention to detail, great expressive ability, and exceptional ageing potential. Could we ask for more? The Sagrantinos are all equally good and singling one out is very subjective, although the Colleallodole cru might just win out in terms of complexity. But we might well change our minds after tasting some well-aged bottles. The wine is magnificent, nuanced, very classy, with a kaleidoscopic aromatic profile ranging from blackberries to bitter chocolate, tobacco, and liquorice. Stratospherically long despite young tannins.

● Montefalco Sagrantino Colleallodole '10	♟♟♟ 8
● Montefalco Sagrantino '10	♟♟ 5
● Montefalco Rosso '11	♟♟ 3
● Montefalco Rosso Ris. '10	♟♟ 5
○ Bianco di Milziade '12	♟ 3
● Montefalco Rosso Ris. '08	♟♟♟ 5
● Montefalco Sagrantino Colleallodole '09	♟♟♟ 8
● Montefalco Sagrantino Colleallodole '06	♟♟♟ 6
● Montefalco Sagrantino Colleallodole '05	♟♟♟ 6
● Montefalco Rosso '10	♟♟ 2
● Montefalco Rosso Ris. '09	♟♟ 5
● Montefalco Sagrantino '09	♟♟ 5
● Montefalco Sagrantino '08	♟♟ 8

★Còlpetrone

LOC. MARCELLANO
VIA PONTE LA MANDRIA, 8/1
06035 GUALDO CATTANEO [PG]
TEL. 074299827
www.colpetrone.it

CELLAR SALES
PRE-BOOKED VISITS
ANNUAL PRODUCTION 200,000 bottles
HECTARES UNDER VINE 63.00

When history evolves without losing sight of its roots or its role, the result will necessarily be significant. Naturally, this also applies to wine and Còlpetrone is a fine example. In short, this estate has been skilful in reading the terroir and interpreting it masterfully from the outset, starting with the Montefalco Sagrantino, which was and is one of its top wines. Today, after numerous changes and a thorough technical and managerial revamping, Còlpetrone is still a leading player, with a future-oriented vision. The wines are a continuation of recent tradition but they also look to the future. They are modern and concentrated, with a clearly defined winemaking style. Born as the estate's super selection, the Montefalco Sagrantino Gold confirms itself as being a thoroughbred and benchmark for its type. The 2007 vintage treats fans to plenty of pulp and a certain sweetness in both nose and mouth, carried by the oak ageing.

● Montefalco Sagrantino Gold '07	♟♟ 8
● Montefalco Rosso '11	♟ 3
● Montefalco Sagrantino '07	♟♟♟ 5
● Montefalco Sagrantino '04	♟♟♟ 5
● Montefalco Sagrantino '03	♟♟♟ 5
● Montefalco Sagrantino '02	♟♟♟ 5
● Montefalco Sagrantino '01	♟♟♟ 5
● Montefalco Sagrantino '00	♟♟♟ 5
● Montefalco Sagrantino '99	♟♟♟ 5
● Montefalco Sagrantino '98	♟♟♟ 5
● Montefalco Sagrantino '97	♟♟♟ 5
● Montefalco Sagrantino '96	♟♟♟ 5
● Montefalco Sagrantino Gold '05	♟♟♟ 8
● Montefalco Sagrantino Gold '04	♟♟♟ 8

Fattoria Colsanto

LOC. MONTARONE
06031 BEVAGNA [PG]
TEL. 0742360412
www.livon.it

CELLAR SALES
ANNUAL PRODUCTION 30,000 bottles
HECTARES UNDER VINE 20.00

Colsanto is owned by the Livon family, who
have indissoluble ties with growing and
winemaking with success in Friuli and other
vineyard country around Italy. From year to
year, the estate is growing a reputation with
critics and wine lovers alike, for a very
simple reason: the wines produced in the
gorgeous Bevagna property get better and
more original with each vintage, as well as
being stylistically interesting. Everything
starts in the vineyard, naturally, and follows
through with what are now classic
vinification techniques. Over time, the
ageing process has been modified and now
takes place primarily in large barrels. As we
said, all the wines are good, especially the
robust, characterful 2009 Montefalco
Sagrantino, with a slight gaminess that
slowly opens into dark fruit aromas with
floral, earthy, and sanguine overtones. The
deep, pulpy palate is also memorable,
although the tannins are still young. The
2010 Montefalco Rosso is not bad either, a
wine with a similar stylistic imprint but
different varietal characteristics.

● Montefalco Sagrantino '09	♟♟ 5
● Montefalco Rosso '10	♟♟ 3
● Ruris Rosso '11	♟ 2
● Montefalco Rosso '09	♟♟ 3*
● Montefalco Sagrantino '08	♟♟ 5
● Montefalco Sagrantino '07	♟♟ 5
● Montefalco Sagrantino '03	♟♟ 5

Custodi

LOC. CANALE
V.LE VENERE
05018 ORVIETO [TR]
TEL. 076329053
www.cantinacustodi.com

CELLAR SALES
PRE-BOOKED VISITS
ANNUAL PRODUCTION 60,000 bottles
HECTARES UNDER VINE 40.00

We recommend Custodi's wines for quality
and style, offering one of the best
expressions of Orvieto wines, at least with
respect to their originality and finesse. The
vineyards and cellars are in Canale. The
property spans around 70 hectares in total,
half of which are planted to vines. Of these,
a good number are devoted to the zone's
main designation, Orvieto Classico. The
other vines are largely sangiovese and
international varieties. We were most
impressed by their whites, which we would
not hesitate to classify as some of the best
in the zone. The 2012 Orvieto Classico
Belloro is very worthy with delicate floral
aromas and good fresh fruit and citrus
notes. The easy mouth lives up to
expectation, with a nice mid-palate and
decisive finish that reiterates the nose. The
2012 Vendemmia Tardiva Petrusa is also
excellent, with rich apricot and dried fig
aromas. The 2012 Merlot Piancoleto is less
complex.

○ Orvieto Cl. Belloro '12	♟♟ 1*
○ Orvieto Cl. Sup. Pertusa V. T. '12	♟♟ 4
● Piancoleto '12	♟ 2
● Austero '07	♟♟ 3*
○ Orvieto Cl. Belloro '11	♟♟ 1*
○ Orvieto Cl. Belloro '10	♟♟ 1*
○ Orvieto Cl. Belloro '09	♟♟ 1
○ Orvieto Cl. Belloro '08	♟♟ 1*
○ Orvieto Cl. Belloro '07	♟♟ 1*
○ Orvieto Cl. Sup. Pertusa V. T. '07	♟♟ 4
● Piancoleto '11	♟♟ 2*
● Piancoleto '09	♟♟ 2

Decugnano dei Barbi

LOC. FOSSATELLO, 50
05019 ORVIETO [TR]
TEL. 0763308255
www.decugnano.it

CELLAR SALES
PRE-BOOKED VISITS
ANNUAL PRODUCTION 120,000 bottles
HECTARES UNDER VINE 32.00

This is one of the most prestigious estates in the region and a flagship for Orvieto wines. From their classic whites to a couple of spot-on reds, Decugnano is making some seriously good stuff again after a few less glorious years. The setting is superb; the estate lies on perfect wine-growing slopes that have always been devoted to viticulture. The soils are of marine origin and rich in fossils, the best a vigneron could hope for to make great white wines that are scented, vibrant, with a distinctly mineral character. The range includes a tasty Metodo Classico, which undergoes second fermentation in the area's evocative tufa grottos. The Orvieto Classico Superiore Il Bianco is again the estate's top wine and one of the best in the designation. The 2012 version may be slightly more aromatic and the nose gains some intensity at the expense of a little complexity. A truly a great white that is both tangy and drinkable, once again marked by savoury sensations that fit perfectly into the overall framework. The other wines are all well made.

○ Orvieto Cl. Sup. Il Bianco '12	♟♟♟ 3*
● Il Rosso '11	♟♟ 4
● Villa Barbi Rosso '11	♟♟ 2*
○ Decugnano Brut '07	♟ 4
○ Orvieto Cl. Villa Barbi Bianco '12	♟ 2
● "IL" Rosso '98	♟♟♟ 5
○ Orvieto Cl. Sup. "IL" '11	♟♟♟ 3*
○ Orvieto Cl. Sup. Il Bianco '10	♟♟♟ 3
○ Orvieto Cl. Sup. Il Bianco '09	♟♟♟ 4
○ Decugnano Brut '06	♟♟ 4
● Il Rosso di Decugnano '09	♟♟ 3
● Lago di Corbara "IL" '02	♟♟ 5
● Lago di Corbara "IL" '01	♟♟ 5
○ Maris '09	♟♟ 5
○ Orvieto Cl. Sup. "IL" '01	♟♟ 3

Di Filippo

VOC. CONVERSINO, 153
06033 CANNARA [PG]
TEL. 0742731242
www.vinidifilippo.com

CELLAR SALES
PRE-BOOKED VISITS
ANNUAL PRODUCTION 200,000 bottles
HECTARES UNDER VINE 30.00
VITICULTURE METHOD Certified Organic

This appealing estate, in the Cannara area, lies in a kind of border zone between territories that are very different from both a historic and a winemaking perspective. In recent years the quest to work the land as naturally as possible and produce natural wines seems to have opened interesting new avenues. The wines have also taken a leap in quality and style. We had excellent impressions across the board, both from the classic range of whites, with trebbiano spoletino-based wines now accompanying Grechettos. The reds, starting with Sagrantinos, are also fantastic. The most widespread Montefalco variety underpins the new 2009 Etnico, an original red with distinctive Mediterranean scrub, currants and wild strawberry on the nose, opening to a lean, deep, silky, and slightly smoky palate. The 2010 Terre di San Nicola is even better, unbelievably spicy, with cypress and juniper aromas, a leisurely palate and great follow-through.

● Montefalco Sagrantino Etnico '09	♟♟ 5
○ Colli Martani Grechetto '12	♟♟ 2*
○ Colli Martani Grechetto Sassi d'Arenaria '11	♟♟ 3
● Colli Martani Sangiovese '12	♟♟ 2*
○ Farandola Trebbiano Spoletino '12	♟♟ 2*
● Montefalco Sagrantino Passito '07	♟♟ 5
● Terre di S. Nicola Rosso '10	♟♟ 3
● Vernaccia di Cannara '11	♟♟ 4
☉ Villa Conversino Rosato '12	♟♟ 2*
● Montefalco Rosso Sallustio '10	♟ 3
○ Colli Martani Grechetto '11	♟♟ 2*
○ Colli Martani Grechetto Sassi d'Arenaria '10	♟♟ 2*
● Montefalco Rosso Sallustio '09	♟♟ 3
● Vernaccia di Cannara '10	♟♟ 3
○ Villa Conversino Bianco '11	♟♟ 1*

Duca della Corgna

VIA ROMA, 236
06061 CASTIGLIONE DEL LAGO [PG]
TEL. 0759652493
www.ducadellacorgna.it

CELLAR SALES
PRE-BOOKED VISITS
ANNUAL PRODUCTION 280,000 bottles
HECTARES UNDER VINE 55.00

For some years now, Cantina del Trasimeno has been involved in a highly commendable project to raise the profile of the typical wines of the lake area. The top wines of this co-operative winery bear the Duca della Corgna label. The operation sources its grapes from many hectares of vines of numerous varieties. The winemaking facility is located in Castiglione del Lago, as is the point-of-purchase, while the beautiful old cellars are located in lovely Città della Pieve. The vines grow on a limestone promontory and the winery is particularly interested in trasimeno gamay, a now classic variety similar to grenache. This monovarietal, matured for a short period in small oak barrels, provided the best tasting of the year for the lakeside estate. The 2011 Divina Villa Etichetta Nera is a fascinating wine, with black cherry, vanilla, and currant notes, and faintly herbaceous overtones. It is fleshy yet crisp, juicy and vibrant, despite the round, mature tendencies of the variety.

● C. del Trasimeno Baccio del Rosso '12	♀♀ 2*
● C. del Trasimeno Gamay Divina Villa Et. Nera '11	♀♀ 3
● C. del Trasimeno Rosso Corniolo Ris. '10	♀♀ 4
○ Ascanio '12	♀ 2
○ C. del Trasimeno Baccio del Bianco '12	♀ 2
● C. del Trasimeno Gamay Divina Villa Et. Bianca '12	♀ 2
☉ Martavello Rosato '12	♀ 2
● C. del Trasimeno Baccio del Rosso '11	♀♀ 2*
● C. del Trasimeno Gamay Divina Villa Et. Bianca '11	♀♀ 2*
○ C. del Trasimeno Grechetto Nuricante '11	♀♀ 2*
● C. del Trasimeno Rosso Corniolo '05	♀♀ 3
● C. del Trasimeno Rosso Corniolo Ris. '09	♀♀ 4
● C. del Trasimeno Rosso Corniolo Ris. '07	♀♀ 3

Podere Fontesecca

VOC. FONTESECCA, 30
06062 CITTÀ DELLA PIEVE [PG]
TEL. 0763835008
www.fontesecca.it

CELLAR SALES
PRE-BOOKED VISITS
ACCOMMODATION
ANNUAL PRODUCTION 10,000 bottles
HECTARES UNDER VINE 3.50
VITICULTURE METHOD Certified Organic

In recent years Umbria has offered few surprises for lovers of everyday wines, by no means ordinary but very easy to drink, with plenty of flavour and detail. So in this respect, the winery is quite out of the ordinary. Owned by Paolo Bolla, who moved lock, stock and barrel to the stunning hills of Città della Pieve. Here he makes flavoursome, authentic wines that express the terroir. The estate is probably best summed up by its fossil-rich soils of marine origin, organic farming practices, use only of local varieties, and attention to detail, all of which provide a fairly accurate key to understanding Fontesecca wines. The 2012 Elso has a rich robe and persuasive, layered aromas. The nose expresses almonds, spring flowers and yellow-fleshed fruit, with a wisp of honey. The mouth is savoury, slightly buttery, full of personality and nuances. The tried and tested 2011 Ciliegiolo is also excellent, although it may be a tad more concentrated than usual, while there is nothing prosaic about the juicy, all-embracing 2012 Canaiolo rosé.

○ Elso '12	♀♀ 2*
☉ Canaiolo '12	♀♀ 3
● Ciliegiolo '11	♀♀ 3
○ Bianco Fontesecca '09	♀♀ 3
● Canaiolo '10	♀♀ 3
● Ciliegiolo '10	♀♀ 3*
● Pino Sangiovese '09	♀♀ 3*
● Pino Sangiovese '08	♀♀ 4

Goretti

LOC. PILA
S.DA DEL PINO, 4
06132 PERUGIA
TEL. 075607316
www.vinigoretti.com

PRE-BOOKED VISITS
ANNUAL PRODUCTION 400,000 bottles
HECTARES UNDER VINE 50.00

Goretti is a typical family-run business, with its roots in agriculture and a solid background in quality wines. The estate is run by several generations that continue to work hand in hand, ensuring an ideal mix of experience and youthful enthusiasm. The estate straddles two zones. The historic winery just outside the town of Pila, in the Perugia hills, watched over by its beautiful iconic tower, has been with the family since the start. Their more recent property in Montefalco is home to the Le Mura Saracene label and is devoted to Sagrantino and other wines typical of that area. A well-nuanced performance from the two estates and we took note of the 2012 Fontanelle, both for price and category. This is definitely an easy but by no means ordinary wine, well-orchestrated over red berry fruit sensations and with elegant gunpowder and bay leaf notes. The 2010 Sagrantino is good, although the toasted notes tend to dominate. The 2012 Grechetto is tangy.

★Lungarotti

V.LE GIORGIO LUNGAROTTI, 2
06089 TORGIANO [PG]
TEL. 075988661
www.lungarotti.it

CELLAR SALES
PRE-BOOKED VISITS
ACCOMMODATION AND RESTAURANT SERVICE
ANNUAL PRODUCTION 2,200,000 bottles
HECTARES UNDER VINE 250.00
VITICULTURE METHOD Certified Organic

Lungarotti is one of Umbria's best-known brands, appreciated the world over, and it holds a special place in the region's quality wine scene. History, tradition and a pioneering spirit are the cornerstones of this winery, which succeeds in being quintessentially modern while retaining a healthy respect for the past. The extensive range features historic Torgianos (including several from some of the best crus) and more recent wines from the property in Montefalco. All are capable of exceptional results, with several gems that have made this one of Italy's star producers. Of these, the Vigna Monticchio cru is unrivalled. This Riserva has done much for the reputation of Italian wine over the years, lauded by critics the world over, and it continues to be an icon for many a wine lover. The 2008 vintage is no less legendary and may even turn out better than recent vintages. A graceful and definitely complex wine that is still young but dense and deep. With its underlying character already well defined it is truly exceptional.

● Fontanella Rosso '12	♈♈ 2*
● Montefalco Sagrantino Le Mure Saracene '10	♈♈ 3
○ Grechetto '12	♈ 1*
○ Il Moggio '12	♈ 3
○ Colli Perugini Chardonnay '11	♈♈ 2*
● Colli Perugini Rosso L'Arringatore '08	♈♈ 3
● Colli Perugini Rosso L'Arringatore '07	♈♈ 3
● Colli Perugini Rosso L'Arringatore '05	♈♈ 3
● Fontanella Rosso '09	♈♈ 2
○ Il Moggio '09	♈♈ 3
● Montefalco Sagrantino Le Mure Saracene '06	♈♈ 5

● Torgiano Rosso V. Monticchio Ris. '08	♈♈♈ 6
● Torgiano Rosso Rubesco '10	♈♈ 3*
● Montefalco Sagrantino '10	♈♈ 5
○ Torgiano Bianco Torre di Giano V. il Pino Ris. '12	♈♈ 4
○ Torgiano Vin Santo '09	♈♈ 5
○ Torre di Giano '12	♈♈ 2*
○ Torgiano Bianco Torre di Giano V. il Pino Ris. '08	♈♈♈ 3*
● Torgiano Rosso Rubesco V. Monticchio Ris. '07	♈♈♈ 6
● Torgiano Rosso V. Monticchio Ris. '06	♈♈♈ 5
● Torgiano Rosso V. Monticchio Ris. '05	♈♈♈ 5*
● Torgiano Rosso V. Monticchio Ris. '04	♈♈♈ 5

Moretti Omero

LOC. SAN SABINO, 19
06030 GIANO DELL'UMBRIA [PG]
TEL. 074290433
www.morettiomero.it

CELLAR SALES
PRE-BOOKED VISITS
ANNUAL PRODUCTION 45,000 bottles
HECTARES UNDER VINE 11.00
VITICULTURE METHOD Certified Organic

Certified organic from the outset, this lovely estate owned by Omero Moretti, has continued to improve in quality to the point that it is now one of the most interesting producers in the Sagrantino zone. A word of warning, however as the enterprise takes an extremely artisanal approach, with all the twists and turns that this implies. Technical purists may turn up their noses at their lack of concern for winemaking grammar. We, on the other hand, think the wines of this small winery, whose vineyards nestle at the base of Mount Martani, have lots of charm and rare authenticity, and this applies as much to their whites as to their reds. Even so, the elegant 2010 Montefalco Rosso is worth lingering over, its soul best expressed by tobacco notes followed by fine spice and soft, silky tannins, signing off with a delicate bitter orange that begs a return visit. Then there is Nessuno, a very enjoyable 2012 white, primarily grechetto, which is aromatic and fine, with a lovely acid backbone that promises good cellaring potential.

○ Grechetto '12	▼▼ 2*
● Montefalco Rosso '10	▼▼ 3
○ Nessuno '12	▼▼ 2*
● Terre di Giano '12	▼ 2
○ Grechetto dell'Umbria '10	♀♀ 2
● Montefalco Rosso '09	♀♀ 5
● Montefalco Sagrantino '08	♀♀ 5
● Montefalco Sagrantino '07	♀♀ 5
● Montefalco Sagrantino '06	♀♀ 5
● Montefalco Sagrantino '05	♀♀ 5
● Montefalco Sagrantino '02	♀♀ 5
● Montefalco Sagrantino Vignalunga '06	♀♀ 7
○ Nessuno '09	♀♀ 2*
● Sagrantino di Montefalco '01	♀♀ 5

La Palazzola

LOC. VASCIGLIANO
05039 STRONCONE [TR]
TEL. 0744609091
www.lapalazzola.it

ANNUAL PRODUCTION 150,000 bottles
HECTARES UNDER VINE 28.00

Stefano Grilli has personality in spades, a passionate, pioneering vigneron and an inspired, if eccentric and slightly rustic, producer. This historic representative of the Umbrian scene is all this and more, and his wines continue to astound. His winery is located in Vascigliano, near Terni, and is a veritable breeding ground for wines and interpretations of every kind. He alternates structured reds and sweet wines with disarming nonchalance, and the estate also produces an irresistibly seductive range of Metodo Ancestrale sparkling wines. In short, what his artisanal wines lose in terms of constancy, they make up for in terms of flavour and authenticity. The selection of wines presented this year was convincing on all levels. Alongside the usual Metodo Ancestrales and a convincing Rubino, marred by a whisper too many wood notes, we preferred the 2008 Umbria Passito, with its date, noble oak, and candied peel aromas. The fleshy mouth is very deep, with an incredibly long finish.

● Umbria Passito '08	▼▼ 4
○ Riesling Brut Metodo Ancestrale '09	▼▼ 3
○ Riesling Extra Dry Metodo Ancestrale '08	▼▼ 4
● Rubino '09	▼▼ 5
● Syrah '11	▼▼ 3
● Merlot '97	♀♀♀ 4*
○ Gran Cuvée Brut '08	♀♀ 4
○ Riesling Brut M. Cl. '05	♀♀ 3
○ Riesling Brut Metodo Ancestrale '08	♀♀ 3
⊙ Rosé Brut '06	♀♀ 4
⊙ Rosé Brut Metodo Ancestrale '10	♀♀ 4
⊙ Rosé Brut Metodo Ancestrale '09	♀♀ 4
● Rubino '07	♀♀ 5
● Uve Gelate '09	♀♀ 6
○ Vin Santo '06	♀♀ 4

Palazzone

loc. Rocca Ripesena, 68
05019 Orvieto [TR]
Tel. 0763344921
www.palazzone.com

CELLAR SALES
PRE-BOOKED VISITS
ACCOMMODATION AND RESTAURANT SERVICE
ANNUAL PRODUCTION 130,000 bottles
HECTARES UNDER VINE 24.00

Giovanni Dubini's wines are testimony to
the Orvieto terroir, or rather certain parts of
the terroir, as winemaking country and
make no mistake: Orvieto has long been
considered one of Italy's top white zones.
The stunning hills of the Rocca Ripesana
area serve as a podium for the sensitive,
personal touch and experience of a
vigneron who has also shown himself to be
exceptionally skilled. This stalwart of the
designation is a real character, a beacon
for the younger generations, who has done
much for Umbrian wine. His wines,
especially the whites, embody the essence
of their territory, along with being strikingly
typed and natural. We feel the 2011
vintage of the Campo del Guardiano is
quite something, and possibly slightly more
readable than others at this stage, oozing
grip and complexity. The nose bewitches
with rock and wild herb aromas blending
well into the fruit. The succulent mouth has
a surprising fine texture, and is very long
and savoury. A well-made wine that is
lively, with sheer Mediterranean impact and
a typical almond finish.

○ Orvieto Cl. Sup. Campo del Guardiano '11	♀♀♀ 2*
○ Grek '12	♀♀ 2*
○ Orvieto Cl. Sup. Terre Vineate '12	♀♀ 2*
○ Viognier '12	♀♀ 3
● Armaleo '09	♀ 5
● Piviere '11	♀ 3
● Armaleo '00	♀♀♀ 5
○ Orvieto Cl. Sup. Campo del Guardiano '09	♀♀♀ 3
○ Orvieto Cl. Sup. Campo del Guardiano '07	♀♀♀ 3
○ Orvieto Cl. Sup. Terre Vineate '11	♀♀♀ 2*
○ Grechetto '10	♀♀ 2*
○ Orvieto Cl. Sup. Campo del Guardiano '10	♀♀ 3*
○ Orvieto Cl. Sup. Terre Vineate '10	♀♀ 2*

F.lli Pardi

via Giovanni Pascoli, 7/9
06036 Montefalco [PG]
Tel. 0742379023
www.cantinapardi.it

CELLAR SALES
PRE-BOOKED VISITS
ANNUAL PRODUCTION 60,000 bottles
HECTARES UNDER VINE 11.00

This estate was founded in 1919, when
Sagrantino was usually produced as a
sweet wine from raisined grapes. Over time
the business developed and even closed for
a time, before the younger generations of a
family that has made some great
contributions to Montefalco wine history
revived it in 2002. The business was
handed down by great-grandfathers
Alfredo, Francesco and Alberto Pardi, and is
now run by Francesco, Gianluca Rio and
Alberto Mario. The bond between past and
present seen here is the key to some fine
wines with personality, shaped by a long
and positive history. We particularly like the
easy drinkability of wines that also manage
to be nicely complex. The 2008 Montefalco
Sagrantino Sacrantino is a good
interpretation of the zone's flagship variety,
with lovely, gently acidulous berry fruit
aromas and a generous, meaty, sanguine
palate with hints of sea salt. The 2012 Colli
Martani Grechetto is also convincing with a
summery, citrus nose and nicely acidic,
savoury palate.

○ Colli Martani Grechetto '12	♀♀ 2*
● Montefalco Rosso '11	♀♀ 2*
● Montefalco Sagrantino Sacrantino '08	♀♀ 6
● Montefalco Bianco Colle di Giove '12	♀ 2
○ Spoleto Trebbiano Spoletino '12	♀ 2
○ Colli Martani Grechetto '11	♀♀ 2*
○ Montefalco Bianco Colle di Giove '10	♀♀ 2
● Montefalco Rosso '10	♀♀ 2*
● Montefalco Sagrantino '09	♀♀ 5
● Montefalco Sagrantino '04	♀♀ 5
● Montefalco Sagrantino Passito '09	♀♀ 5
● Montefalco Sagrantino Sacrantino '06	♀♀ 6
● Rosso di Montefalco '09	♀♀ 2*
○ Spoleto Trebbiano Spoletino '11	♀♀ 2*

Domenico Pennacchi

FRAZ. MARCELLANO
VIA SANT'ANGELO, 10
06035 GUALDO CATTANEO [PG]
TEL. 0742920069
pennacchidomenico@tiscalinet.it

CELLAR SALES
PRE-BOOKED VISITS
ANNUAL PRODUCTION 12,000 bottles
HECTARES UNDER VINE 6.00

Domenico Pennacchi is a passionate grower in Marcellano, in the municipality of Gualdo Cattaneo, part of the Sagrantino designation. The estate was founded in the early 1990s and the vines are planted in the lignite-rich peaty soil typical of the zone, at elevations of up to 400 metres. Pennacchi's home and winery, which is almost entirely underground, are in the same building and somehow seem to sum up the estate's family-run, artisanal approach. The vinification process is predominantly traditional, with long maceration on the skins and ageing in French barriques. We enjoyed Pennacchi's wines more than ever this year. This outstanding performance is crowned by a sumptuous 2007 Montefalco Sagrantino. This gorgeous, spacious, elegant wine has finesse, depth and a silky texture. The slightly exuberant tannic weave makes it no less fascinating or drinkable, and it will develop further in the bottle. The 2007 Montefalco Rosso Riserva is also excellent.

● Montefalco Rosso Ris. '07	♥♥ 4
● Montefalco Sagrantino '07	♥♥ 5
● Colli di Fontivecchie Rosso '10	♥♥ 2*
● Montefalco Rosso '08	♥♥ 3
● Colli di Fontivecchie Rosso '01	♀♀ 2*
● Montefalco Sagrantino Terre dei Capitani '05	♀♀ 5

Cantina Peppucci

LOC. SANT'ANTIMO
FRAZ. PETRORO, 4
06059 TODI [PG]
TEL. 0758947439
www.cantinapeppucci.com

CELLAR SALES
PRE-BOOKED VISITS
ACCOMMODATION
ANNUAL PRODUCTION 70,000 bottles
HECTARES UNDER VINE 12.50

The Peppucci family estate, which young Filippo manages with enthusiasm and passion, is one of the more interesting emerging wineries in the region. The property is situated in an idyllic landscape, populated with vines facing the Todi peak, and the winery itself sits atop one of the area's typical hills. The wines convey all this and whether based on traditional or non-native varieties, they are modern, but rooted in the history of the terroir. Both the whites and the reds are surely improving, which testifies to the soundness of recent, promising innovations, confirmed by this year's tasting. The 2010 Altro Io is made from sagrantino grapes grown a stone's throw from the Montefalco designation and the great red variety's influence is unavoidable. This wine easily holds its own against the best expressions of the variety, with a nose that is still very woody but a palate promising a glorious future, showing dried mint, bay leaves, currants, and black tea. This wine is definitely a deep, tasty Mediterranean, with a lovely incisive tannic weave.

● Altro Io '10	♥♥ 5
● Giovanni '10	♥♥ 4
○ Todi Grechetto Montorsolo '12	♥♥ 2*
○ Todi Petroro 4 '12	♥♥ 2*
● Alter Ego '06	♀♀ 5
● Alter Ego '05	♀♀ 5
○ Colli Martani Grechetto di Todi Montorsolo '10	♀♀ 2
● Giovanni '09	♀♀ 4
● Giovanni '08	♀♀ 4
● Petroro 4 '11	♀♀ 2*
● Petroro 4 '09	♀♀ 3*
● Petroro 4 '08	♀♀ 3*
● Petroro 4 '06	♀♀ 3
○ Todi Grechetto Montorsolo '11	♀♀ 2*

Perticaia

LOC.CASALE
06035 MONTEFALCO [PG]
TEL. 0742379014
www.perticaia.it

CELLAR SALES
PRE-BOOKED VISITS
ANNUAL PRODUCTION 100,000 bottles
HECTARES UNDER VINE 15.00

Perticaia, whose very name testifies to its strong ties to the land and to agriculture, is one of the brightest stars in the Sagrantino constellation. The guiding light of this estate, founded in the late 1990s-early 2000s, is a skilled, knowledgeable and experienced vigneron called Guido Guardigli, who launched his winery on the local stage with absolute confidence. The winery and vineyards are all located in Casale di Montefalco, a terroir that has proven itself to have an inherent finesse, transposed to the bottle by a rigorous vinification process but allowing the natural expressiveness of the grapes to emerge. After what we felt was a slightly patchy version last year, Perticaia's Sagrantino is back at the top of the designation, with a sumptuous interpretation of the 2009 vintage. The wine is absolutely wonderful, with a few toasty notes still to be tamed, but palate finesse and texture leave no room for doubt. This great wine is destined to become a highlight of the estate's prestigious selection.

● Montefalco Sagrantino '09	♛♛♛ 5
● Montefalco Rosso '10	♛♛ 3
● Montefalco Rosso Ris. '10	♛♛ 4
○ Trebbiano Spoletino '12	♛♛ 2*
● Montefalco Sagrantino '07	♛♛♛ 5
● Montefalco Sagrantino '06	♛♛♛ 5
● Montefalco Sagrantino '05	♛♛♛ 5
● Montefalco Sagrantino '04	♛♛♛ 5
● Montefalco Rosso Ris. '09	♛♛ 4
● Montefalco Sagrantino '08	♛♛ 5
○ Trebbiano Spoletino '11	♛♛ 2*

Pucciarella

LOC. VILLA
VIA CASE SPARSE, 39
06063 MAGIONE [PG]
TEL. 0758409147
www.pucciarella.it

CELLAR SALES
PRE-BOOKED VISITS
ACCOMMODATION
ANNUAL PRODUCTION 200,000 bottles
HECTARES UNDER VINE 58.00

Here, in the heart of the Colli del Trasimeno designation, between Magione and Corciano, Pucciarella's 58 hectares under vines spread along the best hillsides for growing quality grapes. The vineyards climb to an elevation of 300 metres in places and are typically stony with moderately loose terrain. Technically speaking, this is one of the top estates in the Trasimeno area, capable of producing top-flight wines, and with a business-like approach encouraged by the company's owners, Fondo Pensioni Cariplo. As a direct result, the wines are finely tuned and impeccably made, with a focus on quality, drawing much from local and international varieties. This year we found the 2010 Colli del Trasimeno Rosso Riserva Sant'Anna red to be eloquent, with a perky aromatic profile and succulent mouth that is full of enjoyable, crisp, fresh fruit. On a par, although more toasty and concentrated, is the 2010 Empireo. The classic 2009 Vin Santo is also very good.

● C. del Trasimeno Rosso Sant'Anna Ris. '10	♛♛ 2*
○ C. del Trasimeno Vin Santo '09	♛♛ 3
● Empireo '10	♛♛ 3
○ Arsiccio '12	♛ 3
○ C. del Trasimeno Bianco Agnolo '12	♛ 2
○ Arsiccio '11	♛♛ 3
○ Arsiccio '08	♛♛ 2*
● Buggea Trequanda '10	♛♛ 1*
● C. del Trasimeno Rosso Sant'Anna Ris. '09	♛♛ 2*
○ C. del Trasimeno Vin Santo '08	♛♛ 3
● Empireo '07	♛♛ 3*

Raina

LOC. TURRI
VIA CASE SPARSE, 42
06036 MONTEFALCO [PG]
TEL. 0742621356
www.raina.it

CELLAR SALES
PRE-BOOKED VISITS
RESTAURANT SERVICE
ANNUAL PRODUCTION 40,000 bottles
HECTARES UNDER VINE 10.00

Young vigneron Francesco Mariani has clear ideas and continues to prove that he can be a star player with his typical Montefalco wines. Founded in 2001, Raina is a relatively recent arrival on the scene and from the outset has shown it can play a unique role, at least with respect to style. The estate is located in Turri di Montefalco and the vines are planted on moderately loose-packed, somewhat rocky limestone soils at 200–300 metres in altitude. As far as these exemplary wines go, we can safely say that the entire range is testimony to Francesco's quest for finesse and easy-drinking appeal, rather than a single-minded emphasis on the terroir's natural exuberance. This year's tastings confirm the Raina style is here to stay and that this young estate knows where it is headed. All the wines tasted, from the bigger reds to the basic range, and a selection of whites and sweet wines, were of a very high standard. Of these, the 2009 Montefalco Sagrantino Campo di Raina stood out for its abundant spicy, citrus notes, hint of dryness, and slightly warm finish.

● Montefalco Sagrantino Campo di Raina '09	♟♟♟ 4
● Montefalco Rosso '11	♟♟ 2*
○ Trebbiano Spoletino '12	♟♟ 2*
● Montefalco Sagrantino Passito '09	♟ 4
● Montefalco Rosso '10	♟♟ 3
● Montefalco Rosso '09	♟♟ 3
● Montefalco Sagrantino '08	♟♟ 5
● Montefalco Sagrantino Passito '07	♟♟ 5
● Sagrantino di Montefalco '07	♟♟ 5

Roccafiore

FRAZ. CHIOANO
VOC. COLLINA 110A
06059 TODI [PG]
TEL. 0758942416
www.roccafiorewines.com

CELLAR SALES
PRE-BOOKED VISITS
ACCOMMODATION AND RESTAURANT SERVICE
ANNUAL PRODUCTION 90,000 bottles
HECTARES UNDER VINE 11.00
VITICULTURE METHOD Certified Organic

The young Roccafiore estate is a brilliant operation that has made its mark on the Todi wine scene in no time at all. Conceived and created by the Baccarelli family, which counts some outstanding wine professionals among its number, it has become a benchmark for anyone who wants solid insight into the wines of the zone. Modern, yet personal, relaxed, flavourful, and fragrant, without ever falling prey to technique, the winery's whites and reds demonstrate a natural expressivity that is perfectly in line with their rigorous organic growing methods. The Todi Grechetto Superiore Fior Fiore is top of its league. While not typical of either the variety or the region, this wine has a very attractive stylistic imprint. The course is well and truly set and the 2011 vintage looks like it is on the verge of getting to destination. This original white is expressive and rich in detail, with a hazelnut, soft toffee, and liquorice nose, followed by a dense, warm, but possibly slightly over-alcoholic palate. The 2012 Fiordaliso and 2010 Sangiovese are also very good.

○ Todi Grechetto Sup. Fiorfiore '11	♟♟ 3*
○ Fiordaliso '12	♟♟ 2*
● Todi Rosso Melograno '11	♟♟ 2*
● Todi Sangiovese Rosso '10	♟♟ 2*
○ Colli Martani Grechetto di Todi Fiorfiore '08	♟♟ 3
○ Colli Martani Grechetto di Todi Fiorfiore '07	♟♟ 3*
○ Collina d'Oro Passito '11	♟♟ 5
○ Collina d'Oro Passito '07	♟♟ 4
○ Fiordaliso '11	♟♟ 2*
○ Fiordaliso '09	♟♟ 2
○ Fiordaliso '08	♟♟ 2*
○ Fiorfiore Bianco '09	♟♟ 3
● Prova d'Autore '08	♟♟ 4
● Roccafiore Rosso '09	♟♟ 2*
○ Todi Grechetto Sup. Fiordaliso '10	♟♟ 3

Romanelli

LOC. COLLE SAN CLEMENTE 129A
06036 MONTEFALCO [PG]
TEL. 3479065613
www.romanelli.se

CELLAR SALES
PRE-BOOKED VISITS
ANNUAL PRODUCTION 40,000 bottles
HECTARES UNDER VINE 7.00

Another young operation here, although the owners have an extensive background in agriculture. This small artisanal estate also embraces organic farming methods and fitting together all the pieces of the puzzle, we get a clear, very fascinating picture of the Romanelli estate. The vineyards are planted in silty, clayey soil at an elevation of around 350 metres, and the family also produces oil. Cellaring practices have a traditional imprint, with long maceration on the skins and ageing in barrels of varying sizes. The result is territorial wines with personality. Ever since we tasted the Montefalco Rosso, we have have preferred it to the Sagrantinos and this vintage is no different. Not so much for any lack on the part of the most famous designation in the zone, but rather because of the merits of the Montefalco Rosso. Suffice it to say that the 2009 Rosso is a great wine, tapered, mineral, crunchy, with elegant blackberry and cigar box aromas.

● Montefalco Rosso '09	♥♥ 3*
○ Colli Martani Grechetto '12	♥♥ 2*
● Montefalco Rosso Ris. '09	♥♥ 3
● Montefalco Sagrantino '09	♥ 5
● Montefalco Sagrantino Passito '09	♥ 5
○ Colli Martani Grechetto '11	♀♀ 2*
○ Colli Martani Grechetto '08	♀♀ 2
● Montefalco Rosso '08	♀♀ 3
● Montefalco Rosso '07	♀♀ 3
● Montefalco Sagrantino Passito '08	♀♀ 5

Scacciadiavoli

LOC. CANTINONE, 31
06036 MONTEFALCO [PG]
TEL. 0742371210
www.scacciadiavoli.it

CELLAR SALES
PRE-BOOKED VISITS
ANNUAL PRODUCTION 220,000 bottles
HECTARES UNDER VINE 32.00

The esteemed Scacciadiavoli operation not only boasts a wealth of charm and a beautifully designed winery, it is also a very dynamic, modern business that skilfully interprets the current trend in Montefalco wines. Indeed, since the extensive revamping initiated in the early 2000s, the wines are increasingly contemporary in style and there seems to be a steady focus on balance and territory. The estate produces several labels and experiments widely in addition to producing the stalwart Sagrantino and Montefalco Rosso. Scacciadiavoli's wines show restyling and growth in full swing. All the wines tasted were centred, of good quality and capable of expressing both local and varietal character. The 2008 Sagrantino is one of the best the estate has produced, despite being slightly hindered by a few toasty notes, both in the nose and tannins. We recommend watching it evolve in the bottle and meanwhile enjoy an already very tasty 2010 Montefalco Rosso.

● Montefalco Sagrantino '08	♥♥ 5
● Montefalco Rosso '10	♥♥ 3
● Montefalco Sagrantino Passito '07	♥♥ 5
○ Grechetto '12	♥ 2
⊙ Brut Rosé M. Cl. '09	♀♀ 4
○ Brut Scacciadiavoli M. Cl. '08	♀♀ 4
● Montefalco Rosso '09	♀♀ 3*
● Montefalco Rosso '05	♀♀ 3
● Montefalco Sagrantino '07	♀♀ 5
● Montefalco Sagrantino '06	♀♀ 5
● Montefalco Sagrantino '05	♀♀ 5
● Montefalco Sagrantino '04	♀♀ 5
● Montefalco Sagrantino Passito '06	♀♀ 5
● Montefalco Sagrantino Passito '05	♀♀ 5
● Montefalco Sagrantino Passito '04	♀♀ 5

Sportoletti

LOC. CAPITAN LORETO
VIA LOMBARDIA, 1
06038 SPELLO [PG]
TEL. 0742651461
www.sportoletti.com

CELLAR SALES
PRE-BOOKED VISITS
ANNUAL PRODUCTION 220,000 bottles
HECTARES UNDER VINE 30.00

This leading winery has developed into a sound business. Despite both the family and the area having an extensive agricultural background, Sportoletti wines only became known in the 1990s, when operations were brought up-to-date. Modernization covered everything from the vineyards on the stunning Spello hillside, near renowned Assisi after which the designation is named, to the varieties grown, the cellars and the wine style. The estate has since produced concentrated quality reds and whites full of soft tones, very well defined, with plenty of personality. Bottles that contributed handsomely to Umbria's wine renaissance and the recent history of this beautiful region. Once again Villa Fidelia Rosso proves to be the winery flagship and a veritable Super Umbrian. This Bordeaux blend brilliantly encapsulates the key aromas and sensations of the varieties in its make-up. Intensely fruity in the nose, it has a meaty, full palate with plenty of stuffing, and lovely spicy notes.

● Villa Fidelia Rosso '11	🍷🍷 4
○ Assisi Grechetto '12	🍷🍷 1*
● Assisi Rosso '12	🍷🍷 2*
○ Villa Fidelia Bianco '11	🍷🍷 3
○ Villa Fidelia Passito '11	🍷🍷 4
● Villa Fidelia Rosso '98	🍷🍷🍷 4*
○ Assisi Grechetto '11	🍷🍷 1*
● Assisi Rosso '11	🍷🍷 2*
○ Villa Fidelia Bianco '10	🍷🍷 3
● Villa Fidelia Rosso '10	🍷🍷 4
● Villa Fidelia Rosso '09	🍷🍷 4
● Villa Fidelia Rosso '08	🍷🍷 5
● Villa Fidelia Rosso '07	🍷🍷 5

Giampaolo Tabarrini

FRAZ. TURRITA
06036 MONTEFALCO [PG]
TEL. 0742379351
www.tabarrini.com

CELLAR SALES
PRE-BOOKED VISITS
ANNUAL PRODUCTION 70,000 bottles
HECTARES UNDER VINE 18.00

Giampaolo Tabarrini is a force to be reckoned with, incredibly passionate about his winemaking and feeling the winery to be his personal creation. There is no explanation for his unfaltering devotion and almost missionary-like zeal. Impeccable organization, love for the everyday work in excellent vineyards, whose character shines in every bottle, and meticulous care in the cellars, explain in part the well-deserved popularity of this young winery, which is already a huge success. Tabarrini is supported by a large staff and the rest of his family also chip in but at the end of the day, without him, the estate would not be what it is. The estate's Sagrantinos have taken the path of crus for several years now and vary according to the vineyard and the cellaring techniques used. This year, we once again favoured a splendid, intensely spicy and unmistakably Mediterranean 2009 Colle alle Macchie. The white 2011 Adarmando is also sensational.

● Montefalco Sagrantino Colle alle Macchie '09	🍷🍷🍷 6
○ Adarmando '11	🍷🍷 3*
● Montefalco Sagrantino Campo alla Cerqua '09	🍷🍷 6
● Il Padrone delle Vigne '12	🍷🍷 2*
● Montefalco Rosso '10	🍷🍷 3
● Montefalco Rosso Colle Grimaldesco '09	🍷🍷 5
● Montefalco Sagrantino Colle alle Macchie '08	🍷🍷 6
● Montefalco Sagrantino Colle alle Macchie '07	🍷🍷 6
● Montefalco Sagrantino Passito '08	🍷🍷 6
○ Adarmando '07	🍷🍷🍷 3*
● Montefalco Sagrantino Campo alla Cerqua '08	🍷🍷🍷 6
● Montefalco Sagrantino Campo alla Cerqua '07	🍷🍷🍷 6

Terre de La Custodia

LOC. PALOMBARA
06035 GUALDO CATTANEO [PG]
TEL. 0742929586
www.terredelacustodia.it

CELLAR SALES
PRE-BOOKED VISITS
ANNUAL PRODUCTION 1,000,000 bottles
HECTARES UNDER VINE 128.00

The Farchionis are internationally reputed and highly successful entrepreneurs with a broad background in farming, producing everything from olive oil to cereals, beer and wine. Their winemaking venture started around ten years ago, with a brand new operation and vineyards straddling the municipalities of Gualdo Cattaneo, primarily for reds, and Todi, where white varieties grow. Both the whites and the reds are modern, and carefully managed, with a very well-defined style. The top labels are often aged in oak. We were utterly convinced by the Metodo Classico Brut Glaudius. Supported by muscled acidity, it opens on the palate with plenty of personality and velvety body, and yeasty, candied fruit highlights. The 2012 Colli Martani Rosso Collezione is simpler and younger, but very enjoyable, with its lovely juicy fruit, lively character, and fleshy finish. The whites are also very good.

○ Brut Glaudius	♟♟	4
⊙ Brut Rosé	♟♟	5
● Colli Martani Collezione '12	♟♟	2*
○ Colli Martani Grechetto Plentis '12	♟♟	3
○ Colli Martani Grechetto '12	♟	2
⊙ Brut Rosé '08	♕♕	5
○ Colli Martani Glaudius '08	♕♕	4
○ Colli Martani Grechetto '11	♕♕	2*
○ Colli Martani Grechetto Plentis '11	♕♕	3
○ Colli Martani Grechetto Plentis '09	♕♕	3
● Montefalco Rosso '10	♕♕	4
● Montefalco Sagrantino '09	♕♕	6
● Montefalco Sagrantino '06	♕♕	5
● Montefalco Sagrantino '04	♕♕	5

Todini

FRAZ. ROSCETO
VIA COLLINA, 29
06059 TODI [PG]
TEL. 075887122
www.cantinafrancotodini.com

CELLAR SALES
PRE-BOOKED VISITS
ACCOMMODATION AND RESTAURANT SERVICE
ANNUAL PRODUCTION 300,000 bottles
HECTARES UNDER VINE 53.00

The Todini winery is one of the largest and most highly structured in the Collevalenza area of Todi. Here, the rolling hills map out a stunning and very harmonious landscape. That said, we should also add that the operation is the result of significant investment and boasts many hectares under vine, with modern cellars that have lovely views of the surrounding area, a magnificent tasting room, and lovely guest accommodation. The wines come from local and international grape varieties, interpreted with a modern approach and styling, offering a widely comprehensible reading of the territory. Todini's wines are even better than usual. The Bianco del Cavaliere is really very good and offers up an equally enjoyable nose and mouth. A lustrous bright straw yellow with golden highlights, it has a touch of iodine and clear hints of broom, on a deep, pulpy mouth, slightly predominant tannins, and lots of flavour. The 2012 Relais Rosso is excellent both in its own right and in the category.

● Colli Martani Sangiovese Rubro '11	♟♟	4
○ Grechetto Riesling '12	♟♟	2*
○ Relais Rosso '12	♟♟	2*
○ Todi Bianco del Cavaliere '12	♟♟	2*
○ Colli Martani Grechetto di Todi Bianco del Cavaliere '09	♕♕	3
○ Colli Martani Grechetto di Todi Bianco del Cavaliere '08	♕♕	3*
● Colli Martani Sangiovese Rubro '06	♕♕	4
○ Eteria '08	♕♕	2*
○ Grechetto di Todi Bianco del Cavaliere '10	♕♕	3
○ Grechetto di Todi Bianco del Cavaliere Sup. '11	♕♕	3
● Nero della Cervara '08	♕♕	5
● Nero della Cervara '07	♕♕	5
● Nero della Cervara '05	♕♕	5

Tudernum

LOC. PIAN DI PORTO, 146
06059 TODI [PG]
TEL. 0758989403
www.tudernum.it

Villa Mongalli

VIA DELLA CIMA, 52
06031 BEVAGNA [PG]
TEL. 3485110506
www.villamongalli.com

CELLAR SALES
PRE-BOOKED VISITS
ACCOMMODATION AND RESTAURANT SERVICE
ANNUAL PRODUCTION 2,000,000 bottles
HECTARES UNDER VINE 7.00

OSPITALITÀ
ANNUAL PRODUCTION 70,000 bottles
HECTARES UNDER VINE 15.00

Long gone are the days when this co-operative winery was a mass producer of insignificant wines. Today Tudernum is a worthy operation, located at the foot of Todi itself, collecting from growers with sizeable plots both in local and other zones, especially Sagrantino. Both the reds and the whites were of merit again this year, from flagships to the many other labels offering exceptional value for money. While Tudernum does use international varieties, it is focused on local varieties and, of course, mainly grechetto. White or red at heart? Both, if the truth be told, although this year it was a stunning 2011 Rojano that stole the limelight. This intense wine has a dense nose and palate, fascinating aromatic weave where dark fruit and more markedly herby notes cohabit comfortably. Fresh and mature, juicy and precise, full and fleshy, it has a very complex, decidedly original palate. The 2012 Grechetto Colle Nobile is fantastic.

Few Umbrian wineries can boast such lovely vineyards in wine country as excellent as Villa Mongalli. This partly explains the quality of the wines produced by this small operation, which has rapidly become a benchmark for the designation. The rest is the work of Pierpaolo Menghini, a committed vigneron who has been achieving impressive results with the fruit from the vines he so lovingly tends. Villa Mongalli's wines are not just good, they are authentic, personal, and flavoursome, with naturally pleasant yet complex development. In just a few short years, the winery has become a benchmark for its style and unwavering authenticity. Both Sagrantinos presented this year are delicious and on the verge of excellence. We preferred the 2010 Colcimino, born of one of the designation's top vineyards. With well-orchestrated, bewitching development, this exceptionally elegant wine is possibly a fraction stiff in the tannic finish. Lip-smacking and well above average for the category, the 2011 Rosso Le Grazie is all-embracing and complex, with a few elegant herby notes.

● Todi Rosso Sup. Rojano '11	♥♥ 3*
● Montefalco Rosso '09	♥♥ 3
○ Todi Grechetto '12	♥♥ 2*
○ Todi Grechetto Sup. Colle Nobile '12	♥♥ 2*
● Todi Sangiovese '12	♥♥ 2*
○ Grechetto di Todi '10	♀♀ 2*
○ Grechetto di Todi Sup. '10	♀♀ 2*
○ Le Lucrezie '10	♀♀ 1*
● Merlot '07	♀♀ 2*
● Montefalco Sagrantino '07	♀♀ 5
● Montefalco Sagrantino Fidenzio '08	♀♀ 5
● Montefalco Sagrantino Tudernum '04	♀♀ 5
○ Todi Grechetto Sup. Colle Nobile '11	♀♀ 2*
● Todi Rosso Sup. Rojano '09	♀♀ 3

● Montefalco Rosso Le Grazie '11	♥♥ 5
● Montefalco Sagrantino Colcimino '10	♥♥ 3*
○ Calicanto '12	♥♥ 5
● Montefalco Sagrantino Della Cima '09	♥♥ 8
● Montefalco Sagrantino Colcimino '08	♀♀♀ 3*
● Montefalco Sagrantino Della Cima '06	♀♀♀ 6
● Montefalco Sagrantino Pozzo del Curato '09	♀♀♀ 6
● Montefalco Sagrantino Colcimino '07	♀♀ 3*
● Montefalco Sagrantino Della Cima '08	♀♀ 3*
● Montefalco Sagrantino Della Cima '05	♀♀ 6
● Montefalco Sagrantino Pozzo del Curato '08	♀♀ 6

Tenuta Alzatura

LOC. FRATTA ALZATURA, 108
06036 MONTEFALCO [PG]
TEL. 0742399435
www.tenuta-alzatura.it

PRE-BOOKED VISITS
ANNUAL PRODUCTION 36,000 bottles
HECTARES UNDER VINE 18.28

● Montefalco Sagrantino Uno di Dodici '09	♟♟	5
● Montefalco Rosso '11	♟♟	3

Argillae

VOC. POMARRO, 45
05010 ALLERONA [TR]
TEL. 0763624604
www.argillae.eu

CELLAR SALES
PRE-BOOKED VISITS
ANNUAL PRODUCTION 65,000 bottles
HECTARES UNDER VINE 70.00

○ Grechetto '12	♟♟	2*
○ Orvieto '12	♟♟	2*

Berioli

LOC. CASE SPARSE, 21
06063 MAGIONE [PG]
TEL. 3355490173
www.cantinaberioli.it

ANNUAL PRODUCTION 15,000 bottles
HECTARES UNDER VINE 12.00

● Colli del Trasimeno Merlot Spiridione Ris. '09	♟♟	3
○ Colli del Trasimeno Vercanto '12	♟♟	3
○ Colli del Trasimeno Vin Santo Sperello '08	♟♟	3

Briziarelli

VIA COLLE ALLODOLE, 10
06031 BEVAGNA [PG]
TEL. 07587461
www.cantinebriziarelli.it

CELLAR SALES
PRE-BOOKED VISITS
ACCOMMODATION AND RESTAURANT SERVICE
ANNUAL PRODUCTION 70,000 bottles
HECTARES UNDER VINE 18.50

● Montefalco Rosso '10	♟♟	2*
● Dunarobba '11	♟	2

Brogal Vini

LOC. BASTIA UMBRA
VIA DEGLI OLMI, 9
06083 PERUGIA
TEL. 0758001501
www.brogalvini.com

CELLAR SALES
PRE-BOOKED VISITS
ACCOMMODATION AND RESTAURANT SERVICE
ANNUAL PRODUCTION 3,000,000 bottles
HECTARES UNDER VINE 75.00

○ Bizante Bianco '12	♟♟	4
○ Grechetto Noi '12	♟♟	2*
● Arteo '10	♟	3
● Ligajo '10	♟	3

Cardeto

FRAZ. SFERRACAVALLO
LOC. CARDETO
05018 ORVIETO [TR]
TEL. 0763341286
www.cardeto.com

CELLAR SALES
PRE-BOOKED VISITS
ANNUAL PRODUCTION 4,000,000 bottles
HECTARES UNDER VINE 800.00

○ Grechetto '12	♟♟	2*
○ Orvieto Cl. Sup. '12	♟	2

Castello delle Regine

LOC. LE REGINE
VIA DI CASTELLUCCIO
05022 AMELIA [TR]
TEL. 0744702005
www.castellodelleregine.com

CELLAR SALES
PRE-BOOKED VISITS
ACCOMMODATION AND RESTAURANT SERVICE
ANNUAL PRODUCTION 400,000 bottles
HECTARES UNDER VINE 65.00

○ Poggio delle Regine Grechetto '12	♟♟ 2*
⊘ Rosé delle Regine '12	♟♟ 2*

Castello di Corbara

LOC. CORBARA, 7
05018 ORVIETO [TR]
TEL. 0763304035
www.castellodicorbara.it

CELLAR SALES
PRE-BOOKED VISITS
ANNUAL PRODUCTION 200,000 bottles
HECTARES UNDER VINE 200.00

● Lago di Corbara Cabernet Sauvignon '12	♟♟ 3
● Lago di Corbara Merlot De Coronis '10	♟♟ 2*
○ Orzalume '11	♟♟ 3

Chiorri

LOC. SANT'ENEA
VIA TODI, 100
06132 PERUGIA
TEL. 075607141
www.chiorri.it

CELLAR SALES
PRE-BOOKED VISITS
ACCOMMODATION AND RESTAURANT SERVICE
ANNUAL PRODUCTION 100,000 bottles
HECTARES UNDER VINE 25.00

○ Colli Perugini Bianco '10	♟♟ 1*
● Colli Perugini Saliato '10	♟♟ 3
○ Grechetto '12	♟♟ 2*
○ Colli Perugini Bianco '12	♟ 2

Le Cimate

LOC. CECAPECORE, 41
06036 MONTEFALCO [PG]
TEL. 0742290136
www.lecimate.it

CELLAR SALES
ANNUAL PRODUCTION 300,000 bottles
HECTARES UNDER VINE 20.00

○ Aragon '12	♟♟ 3
● Montefalco Sagrantino '09	♟♟ 5

Col di Betto

LOC. COLLE UMBERTO
VOC. COL DI BETTO
06133 PERUGIA
TEL. 3355779228
www.coldibetto.com

ANNUAL PRODUCTION 50,000 bottles
HECTARES UNDER VINE 5.00

● Terre del Cardinale '09	♟♟ 2*

Col Falco

LOC. BELVEDERE
VIA MONTEPENNINO, 5
06036 MONTEFALCO [PG]
TEL. 0742379294
www.viniruggeri.it

CELLAR SALES
PRE-BOOKED VISITS
ANNUAL PRODUCTION 20,000 bottles
HECTARES UNDER VINE 5.00

○ Grechetto '12	♟ 2

Cantina Dionigi

voc. Madonna della Pia, 92
06031 Bevagna [PG]
Tel. 0742360395
www.cantinadionigi.it

CELLAR SALES
PRE-BOOKED VISITS
ACCOMMODATION
ANNUAL PRODUCTION 40,000 bottles
HECTARES UNDER VINE 6.00

○ Colli Matrani Grechetto Colle Sorragani '12	🍷🍷 3
● Merlot Passito Civico 92 '11	🍷🍷 3

Il Gheppio

fraz. Fratta
voc. Argentella, 1
06036 Montefalco [PG]
Tel. 3298467868
www.cantineilgheppio.it

CELLAR SALES
PRE-BOOKED VISITS
ANNUAL PRODUCTION 5,500 bottles
HECTARES UNDER VINE 2.30

● Montefalco Sagrantino '09	🍷🍷 4
● Montefalco Sagrantino Passito '09	🍷🍷 4
● Umbria Rosso '11	🍷🍷 2*

Giro di Vento

loc. Schifanoia
s.da Collespino, 39
05035 Narni [TR]
Tel. 3356136353
www.fattoriagirodivento.it

ANNUAL PRODUCTION 30,000 bottles
HECTARES UNDER VINE 10.50

● Ciliegiolo di Narni Spiffero '12	🍷🍷 2*
● Ciliegiolo di Narni Spiffero '11	🍷🍷 2*
○ Lunaria '12	🍷 2
○ Raggio Vermentino '12	🍷 2

Cantina La Spina

fraz. Spina
via Emilio Alessandrini, 1
06055 Marsciano [PG]
Tel. 0758738120
www.cantinalaspina.it

CELLAR SALES
PRE-BOOKED VISITS
ANNUAL PRODUCTION 16,000 bottles
HECTARES UNDER VINE 2.20

● Polimante '11	🍷🍷 3
● Rosso Spina '11	🍷🍷 3
○ V. Maiore '12	🍷🍷 2*
○ Cimaàlta '12	🍷 2

Lamborghini

loc. Soderi, 1
06064 Panicale [PG]
Tel. 0758350029
www.lamborghinionline.it

CELLAR SALES
PRE-BOOKED VISITS
ACCOMMODATION AND RESTAURANT SERVICE
ANNUAL PRODUCTION 140,000 bottles
HECTARES UNDER VINE 32.00

● Campoleone '10	🍷🍷 5
● Era '11	🍷 3
● Torami '10	🍷 4

Madrevite

via Cimbano, 36
06061 Castiglione del Lago [PG]
Tel. 0759527220
www.madrevite.com

PRE-BOOKED VISITS
ANNUAL PRODUCTION 30,000 bottles
HECTARES UNDER VINE 7.50

● Colli del Trasimeno Glanio '11	🍷🍷 3
○ Re Minore '12	🍷🍷 2*

Sabrina Morami

FRAZ. PANICAROLA
VOC. MORAMI
06060 CASTIGLIONE DEL LAGO [PG]
TEL. 0759589107
www.morami.it

CELLAR SALES
PRE-BOOKED VISITS
ACCOMMODATION
ANNUAL PRODUCTION 10,000 bottles
HECTARES UNDER VINE 10.50

● Renaia '10	🍷🍷 6
○ Pratolungo '10	🍷 3

Pomario

LOC. PIEGARO
06066 PIEGARO [PG]
TEL. 064818418
www.pomario.it

CELLAR SALES
PRE-BOOKED VISITS
ANNUAL PRODUCTION 6,000 bottles
HECTARES UNDER VINE 4.00
VITICULTURE METHOD Certified Organic

○ Arale '12	🍷🍷 4
● Sariano '10	🍷🍷 3

Terre del Carpine

VIA FORMANUOVA, 87
06063 MAGIONE [PG]
TEL. 075840298
www.terredelcarpine.it

CELLAR SALES
PRE-BOOKED VISITS
ANNUAL PRODUCTION 200,000 bottles
HECTARES UNDER VINE 250.00

○ C. del Trasimeno Grechetto Grìeco '12	🍷🍷 2*
● C. del Trasimeno Rosso Erceo '11	🍷🍷 1*
● Poggio Villano Merlot '12	🍷🍷 2*

Terre Margaritelli

FRAZ. CHIUSACCIA
LOC. MIRALDUOLO
06089 TORGIANO [PG]
TEL. 0757824668
www.terremargaritelli.com

CELLAR SALES
PRE-BOOKED VISITS
ANNUAL PRODUCTION 130,000 bottles
HECTARES UNDER VINE 52.00
VITICULTURE METHOD Certified Organic

● Roccascossa '11	🍷🍷 2*
● Torgiano Freccia degli Scacchi '10	🍷🍷 5
○ Greco di Renabianca '11	🍷 3
○ Torgiano Costellato '12	🍷 2

Tenuta Vitalonga

LOC. MONTIANO
05016 FICULLE [TR]
TEL. 0763836722
www.vitalonga.it

CELLAR SALES
PRE-BOOKED VISITS
ACCOMMODATION AND RESTAURANT SERVICE
ANNUAL PRODUCTION 130,000 bottles
HECTARES UNDER VINE 19.00

● Elcione '11	🍷🍷 2*
⊙ Rosé '12	🍷🍷 2*
● Terra di Confine '11	🍷 4

Zanchi

VIA ORTANA, 122
05022 AMELIA [TR]
TEL. 0744970011
www.cantinezanchi.it

CELLAR SALES
PRE-BOOKED VISITS
ANNUAL PRODUCTION 100,000 bottles
HECTARES UNDER VINE 33.00

○ V. Vecchia Trebbiano '10	🍷🍷 5
● Amelia Armané '10	🍷🍷 2*
○ Amelia Grechetto Arvore '12	🍷🍷 2*

LAZIO

Lazio winemaking proceeds without major spikes in the cruising speed, underpinned mainly by good quality and the right price, which keep consumers happy. This does not mean there are no changes taking place. The recovery of the area's typical native grapes continues and greater attention is now being paid to them, from malvasia puntinata to bellone, nero buono di Cori, the various cesanese varieties, aleatico and grechetto. There is also an increasing number of estates working with organic or biodynamic methods. Several small producers have been brave enough to propose wines with strong characters, sometimes as an interpretation of a designation or a grape variety, sometimes as a personal, original interpretation of an area whose winemaking tradition may appear a little under par. Of the production areas, Viterbo vaunts some of the region's best growers but is struggling to achieve a successful model, perhaps because the producers themselves do not fully believe in the potential of the terroir, with its denominations and grape varieties. This is true even of the most prestigious, like grechetto, and there are still few wineries that really invest in this grape despite the example of Sergio Mottura. Moreover, it is very difficult to re-position designations that have long been synonymous with cheap, everyday wine like Montefiascone Est! Est! Est! or Orvieto, so the leading wineries much prefer to propose and promote corporate brands. The Castelli Romani zone is home to several prominent estates seeking a way to recover their markets, but at the same time some of the area's evergreen labels seem not to be on top form, and we hope this is a passing moment. While the province of Latina has not shown anything much to talk about apart from Ponza and a positive consolidation of overall results from Cori to Terracina, the home of cesanese, between the provinces of Frosinone and Rome is on a quest for a style that will convince the reluctant Roman market of the goodness of the grape and the land where it grows. We will conclude with two observations, the first concerning the new Roma DOC, and having seen the first bottle with this label, we hope that it is at least a marketing success because in production terms it is inexplicable. Our second observation refers to a very small area but one that could be particularly interesting in coming years. Just last year we celebrated a Guide newcomer, a winery from the island of Ponza, but this year we can pinpoint the excellent results from biancolella, a grape now beginning to bear very satisfying fruit for those who decided to believe in it and make it a key variety for this island. We will just have to wait and see.

Marco Carpineti

LOC. CAPO LE MOLE
SP VELLETRI-ANZIO, KM 14,300
04010 CORI [LT]
TEL. 069679860
www.marcocarpineti.it

CELLAR SALES
PRE-BOOKED VISITS
ANNUAL PRODUCTION 200,000 bottles
HECTARES UNDER VINE 37.00
VITICOLTURA Biologico Certificato

Producers like Marco Carpineti deserve nothing but praise for believing passionately in their territory, and for the skill with which they bring the best out of its products, whether wine or oil, year after year. The new vineyards are almost at full capacity, and continual improvements are being made to the cellar. As in the past, the range stands out for consistent quality across the board, not to mention the return to top form of the winery's two champions, the Dithyrambus 2009 and the Moro 2011. The former marries Mediterranean aromas with sweet spice, offering pleasurable drinking now, but also good ageing potential. The latter shows rich mineral and iodine notes, giving length and depth on the palate. For its part, the pure bellone Brut 2010 was as impressive as always, and is surely one of Lazio's best sparklers. The Bellone Capolemole Bianco 2012 and the Nero Buono Apolide 2009 round off nicely a range that aims to promote native varieties.

Casale del Giglio

LOC. LE FERRIERE
S.DA CISTERNA-NETTUNO KM 13
04100 LATINA
TEL. 0692902530
www.casaledelgiglio.it

CELLAR SALES
PRE-BOOKED VISITS
ANNUAL PRODUCTION 1,200,000 bottles
HECTARES UNDER VINE 164.00

Our congratulations go to the Santarelli family, with 2014 marking a century in the wine business for them. The owner, Antonio, is celebrating the occasion by embarking on an ambitious new project on the island of Ponza, aimed at promoting the local biancolella variety. The first year of production has already brought impressive results and the promise of more to come. Nor should we forget the winery's other new arrival, the Tempranijo 2011. Although the variety sounds exotic, this wine is the result of over a decade of experimentation by the oenologist Paolo Tiefenthaler, aimed at getting the best out of Pontine Marshes growing conditions. On another note, the Mater Matuta 2010 made the finals with a complex and balanced version, one of the best ever. In a quality range dominated by whites, a special mention must also go to the Satrico 2012, yet again excellent value for money.

● Dithyrambus '09	♥♥ 5
● Apolide '09	♥♥ 5
○ Capolemole Bianco '12	♥♥ 2*
○ Marco Carpineti Brut '10	♥♥ 3
○ Moro '11	♥♥ 3
● Capolemole Rosso '11	♥ 2
○ Ludum '10	♥ 4
⊙ Os Rosae '12	♥ 2
● Tufaliccio '12	♥ 2
○ Capolemole Rosso '10	♀♀ 2*
○ Marco Carpineti Brut '09	♀♀ 3*
○ Marco Carpineti Brut Trentamesi '07	♀♀ 4

○ Faro della Guardia '12	♥♥ 3
● Mater Matuta '10	♥♥ 6
● Tempranijo '11	♥♥ 4*
○ Antinoo '11	♥♥ 3
○ Aphrodisium '12	♥♥ 5
○ Petit Manseng '12	♥♥ 3
○ Satrico '12	♥♥ 2*
● Cabernet Sauvignon '10	♥ 4
○ Chardonnay '12	♥ 3
● Madreselva '10	♥ 4
● Petit Verdot '11	♥ 3
○ Sauvignon '12	♥ 3
● Shiraz '11	♥ 3
○ Viognier '12	♥ 3
○ Antinoo '10	♀♀ 3*
● Cabernet Sauvignon '09	♀♀ 4
○ Petit Manseng '11	♀♀ 3*

Casale della Ioria

P.ZZA REGINA MARGHERITA, 1
03010 ACUTO [FR]
TEL. 077556031
www.casaledellaioria.com

CELLAR SALES
PRE-BOOKED VISITS
ANNUAL PRODUCTION 65,000 bottles
HECTARES UNDER VINE 38.00

Paolo Perinelli's merits in promoting cesanese are legendary, but this producer also continues to believe in the potential of another local grape, olivella, and we have no doubts that his dedication will soon bear fruit. This year, the result was an impressive trio of Cesanese del Piglios. After being dethroned by last year's superb Campo Novo 2010, Torre del Piano 2011 is back in pole position, with a warm, sumptuous palate showing notes of morello cherry. Balance is provided by a solid acid backbone and polished, forthright tannins. The Tenuta della Ioria 2011 is more approachable, with international tastes in mind, while the Campo Novo 2011 fully confirms its potential, already clearly visible despite the youthfulness of the vineyard. Last off, the Passerina Colle Bianco 2012 is as pleasurable as ever, despite less complexity on the nose than in previous years.

● Cesanese del Piglio Sup. Torre del Piano Ris. '11	♀♀ 4
● Cesanese del Piglio Campo Novo '11	♀♀ 2*
● Cesanese del Piglio Sup. Tenuta della Ioria '11	♀ 3
○ Passerina Colle Bianco '12	♀ 2
● Cesanese del Piglio Campo Novo '10	♀♀ 2*
● Cesanese del Piglio Torre del Piano '08	♀♀ 4
○ Colle Bianco '11	♀♀ 2*

Casale Marchese

VIA DI VERMICINO, 68
00044 FRASCATI [RM]
TEL. 069408932
www.casalemarchese.it

CELLAR SALES
PRE-BOOKED VISITS
ANNUAL PRODUCTION 150,000 bottles
HECTARES UNDER VINE 40.00

One of the most evocative views in Tuscolana can be enjoyed from the historic winery of the brothers Alessandro and Ferdinando Carletti, who work the 40 hectares of vineyard around their farmhouse. Pride of place goes to the traditional white grape varieties of the Frascati zone, mentioned as far back as 230 BC by the illustrious citizen of the Castelli area, Cato the Censor: malvasia, trebbiano, bombino and bellone, here joined by international varieties. The vineyards, for the most part cordon-trained and spur-pruned, lie on volcanic hills to the south-east of Rome. The high vine density, at 4,000 to 5,000 plants per hectare, short pruning and low yields are aimed at concentrating minerality and aromatics. We loved both the Clemens 2011, an aromatic, supple blend of 50% chardonnay and 50% malvasia, with notes of tropical fruit and saffron, and the well-textured, focused Frascati Superiore 2012, offering citrus and spice aromas, and one of the DOC zone's best.

○ Clemens '11	♀♀ 4
○ Frascati Sup. '12	♀♀ 2*
● Novum '12	♀ 3
● Rosso Eminenza '12	♀ 3
○ Clemens '09	♀♀♀ 3
○ Clemens '10	♀♀ 3
○ Clemens '07	♀♀ 3*
○ Clemens '06	♀♀ 2*
○ Clemens '05	♀♀ 4
○ Frascati Sup. '11	♀♀ 2*
○ Frascati Sup. '10	♀♀ 2*
○ Frascati Sup. '09	♀♀ 2
○ Frascati Sup. '08	♀♀ 2*
○ Frascati Sup. '06	♀♀ 2*
● Rosso di Casale Marchese '03	♀♀ 2
● Vigna del Cavaliere '00	♀♀ 4

Cincinnato

VIA CORI-CISTERNA KM 2
04010 CORI [LT]
TEL. 069679380
www.cantinacincinnato.it

CELLAR SALES
PRE-BOOKED VISITS
ANNUAL PRODUCTION 3,000,000 bottles
HECTARES UNDER VINE 400.00

Cincinnato has become a benchmark for co-operative wineries not in Lazio, but also farther afield, thanks to the passion of its growers and the professionalism of its management. Although varieties from neighbouring areas, such as cesanese or greco, are not neglected, the main focus is on the native Cori varieties, nero buono and bellone. In this year's range, the latter steals the limelight and actually with wines at very tempting prices. The full-flavoured, almost salty Castore 2012 was on top form, with a citrus nose and good structure, proving to be complex yet also highly drinkable. We also enjoyed the Charmat version, perfect proof of the variety's versatility. The Raverosse 2009, which was included by mistake in the Guide last year, when we actually tasted the 2008, confirms its reputation as a fine Montepulciano, while the best of the Nero Buonos was the Ercole 2010.

○ Castore '12	♟♟	1*
○ Brut Cincinnato Spumante	♟♟	1*
○ Cori Bianco Illirio '12	♟♟	2*
● Cori Rosso Raverosse '09	♟♟	2
● Ercole Nero Buono '10	♟♟	3
○ Pozzodorico Bellone '11	♟♟	2*
● Arcatura '11	♟	3
○ Pantaleo '12	♟	2
○ Pollùce '11	♟	2
○ Castore '11	♟♟	1*
● Ercole Nero Buono '09	♟♟	3*

Antonello Coletti Conti

VIA VITTORIO EMANUELE, 116
03012 ANAGNI [FR]
TEL. 0775728610
www.coletticonti.it

CELLAR SALES
PRE-BOOKED VISITS
ANNUAL PRODUCTION 20,000 bottles
HECTARES UNDER VINE 20.00

When a grower has the courage to release only two wines out of a possible five, it is indicative of a categorical pursuit of quality and real self-confidence. A case in point is Antonello Coletti Conti, who decided not to bottle Cosmato or Arcadia for various reasons, and left his Cesanese Hernicus to mature for an extra year. It clearly paid off, with both the wines presented making the finals. The first of these, the Cesanese Romanico, is a contemporary classic, and the 2011 version matches the heights of the 2007, earning a fully-deserved Tre Bicchieri with its combination of finesse and character, and notes of cherry, red berry fruit, pomegranate and rhubarb. We were pleasantly surprised by the Passerina Hernicus 2012 which in only its second year of production already looks set to become a benchmark for the variety. Intriguing notes of tropical fruit are harmoniously integrated within a well-typed profile, for a rounded, satisfying wine of great cleanliness.

● Cesanese del Piglio Romanico '11	♟♟♟	5
○ Passerina del Frusinate Hernicus '12	♟♟	3*
● Cesanese del Piglio Romanico '07	♟♟♟	5
● Cesanese del Piglio Hernicus '11	♟♟	3*
● Cesanese del Piglio Hernicus '10	♟♟	3
● Cesanese del Piglio Romanico '10	♟♟	5
● Cesanese del Piglio Romanico '09	♟♟	5
● Cesanese del Piglio Romanico '08	♟♟	5
● Cosmato '08	♟♟	5

Paolo e Noemia D'Amico

FRAZ. VAIANO
LOC. PALOMBARO
01024 CASTIGLIONE IN TEVERINA [VT]
TEL. 0761948034
www.paoloenoemiadamico.it

CELLAR SALES
PRE-BOOKED VISITS
ANNUAL PRODUCTION 150,000 bottles
HECTARES UNDER VINE 25.00

For 25 years now, Paolo and Noemia D'Amico have been producing quality wines in this corner of northern Lazio, characterized by its volcanic soils and picturesque gullies. The vineyards, situated on clay and limestone soils at elevations of between 420 and 550 metres, are mainly planted to international varieties, such as chardonnay, sauvignon, pinot nero and merlot, although the native sangiovese, procanico, grechetto and malvasia are well represented. The wines display superb technical execution and a modern style. The Chardonnay Calanchi di Vaiano 2011, aged almost exclusively in steel, once more proved to be one of Lazio's best whites, showing an intense, floral nose with notes of white-fleshed fruit, leading into a tangy, vibrant palate. Also excellent was the other Chardonnay, the Falesia 2011, although its flowery nose and aromas of peach and apricot were somewhat overwhelmed by the butter and vanilla notes from barrique ageing.

○ Calanchi di Vaiano '11	🏆🏆🏆 3*
○ Falesia '11	🏆🏆 4
● Notturno dei Calanchi '09	🏆 5
○ Orvieto Noe '12	🏆 2
○ Seiano Bianco '12	🏆 2
● Seiano Rosso '12	🏆 2
● Villa Tirrena '09	🏆 3
○ Calanchi di Vaiano '09	🏆🏆 3
○ Calanchi di Vaiano '08	🏆🏆 3
○ Falesia '10	🏆🏆 4
○ Falesia '09	🏆🏆 4

★Falesco

LOC. SAN PIETRO
05020 MONTECCHIO [TR]
TEL. 07449556
www.falesco.it

CELLAR SALES
PRE-BOOKED VISITS
ACCOMMODATION
ANNUAL PRODUCTION 2,600,000 bottles
HECTARES UNDER VINE 370.00

The estate on the Umbria-Lazio border continues to prove its worth. Riccardo Cotarella, the new president of the Italian association of oenology and oenotechnology, runs the operation with his brother Renzo. Together the Cotarellas have pursued the same philosophy of territory, science and vitality for some 30 years now. The vineyards roll over the hills from Lake Bolsena to Lake Corbara, from Montefiascone to Montecchio, on the varied sandy, clayey and calcareous terrain. The estate has done extensive work in support of micro-varieties and old clones, but also works with classic international vines with positive results and the range continues to be of a very high standard. The Montiano earns another Tre Bicchieri with a 2011 vintage of spice, tobacco and forest floor aromas, a full palate with good body, and a lengthy, balsamic finish. The 2011 Ferentano is no less and the savoury, leisurely Roscetto takes its first Tre Bicchieri. A debut in the finals for the 2011 Trentanni, a 50% merlot and 50% sangiovese blend of rich fruit and fine balance.

○ Ferentano '11	🏆🏆🏆 4*
● Montiano '11	🏆🏆🏆 6
● Trentanni '11	🏆🏆 3*
○ Est Est Est di Montefiascone Poggio dei Gelsi '12	🏆🏆 2*
● Marciliano '10	🏆🏆 6
● Montefalco Sagrantino 2R '09	🏆🏆 6
● Pomele '12	🏆🏆 3
○ Soente '12	🏆🏆 3
● Tellus '12	🏆🏆 2*
● Marciliano '04	🏆🏆🏆 5
● Montiano '10	🏆🏆🏆 6
● Montiano '09	🏆🏆🏆 5
● Montiano '08	🏆🏆🏆 5
● Montiano '07	🏆🏆🏆 5
● Montiano '06	🏆🏆🏆 5
● Montiano '05	🏆🏆🏆 5

Fontana Candida

VIA FONTANA CANDIDA, 11
00040 MONTE PORZIO CATONE [RM]
TEL. 069401881
www.fontanacandida.it

CELLAR SALES
PRE-BOOKED VISITS
RESTAURANT SERVICE
ANNUAL PRODUCTION 4,000,000 bottles
HECTARES UNDER VINE 97.00

This iconic Frascati producer is situated in
the Agro Tuscolano area, straddling the
districts of Grottaferrata, Frascati and
Monteporzio Catone. Its 97 hectares of
vineyards lie on volcanic hills at elevations
of between 200 and 400 metres. The
winery, which became a commercial
concern in 1958, is headed by Mauro
Merz, the new vice-chairman of the
Consorzio di Tutela dei vini Frascati. The
grapes, mainly native varieties, give a range
of wines with a strong sense of
place: Malvasia di Candia, Trebbiano
Toscano, Greco and Malvasia del Lazio, all
bursting with flavour and minerality. The
Frascati Superiore Luna Mater Riserva
finally took home a Tre Bicchieri thanks to
the beautifully focused 2012 version,
displaying a fine balance of aromatic notes
and fruit. The other Frascatis, both the
tangy, linear Superiore Santa Teresa 2012,
and the Terre dei Grifi 2012, with notes of
sage and citrus, were well managed.

○ Frascati Sup. Luna Mater Ris. '12	🍷🍷 3*
○ Frascati Sup. Santa Teresa '12	🍷🍷 2*
○ Frascati Sup. Terre dei Grifi '12	🍷🍷 2*
● Kron '09	🍷 4
○ Roma Malvasia Puntinata '12	🍷 3
● Siroe '12	🍷 2
○ Frascati Sup. Luna Mater '11	🍷🍷 3*
○ Frascati Sup. Luna Mater '10	🍷🍷 3
○ Frascati Sup. Luna Mater '09	🍷🍷 3
○ Frascati Sup. Luna Mater '08	🍷🍷 3
○ Frascati Sup. Luna Mater '07	🍷🍷 5
○ Frascati Sup. Santa Teresa '11	🍷🍷 2*
○ Frascati Sup. Santa Teresa '01	🍷🍷 2*
● Kron '01	🍷🍷 5
● Sesto 21 Syrah '10	🍷🍷 4

Antica Cantina Leonardi

VIA DEL PINO, 12
01027 MONTEFIASCONE [VT]
TEL. 0761826028
www.cantinaleonardi.it

CELLAR SALES
PRE-BOOKED VISITS
ACCOMMODATION
ANNUAL PRODUCTION 100,000 bottles
HECTARES UNDER VINE 37.00
VITICOLTURA Biologico Certificato

The Leonardi winery, established early last
century, is now run by Ugo and Maria
Vittoria, the third generation of the family.
The winery's holdings are divided into two
estates, one situated at an elevation of
around 450 metres on the volcanic and tuff
soils of the hills around Lake Bolsena, the
other in the district of Graffignano, on the
border with Umbria, at around 400 metres
on a small plateau overlooking the Tiber
Valley. All the wines in the range are rooted
in local tradition, with a particular focus on
white wines from native varieties. Once
again, the Grechetto Pensiero leads the
way. The 2012 version, brimming with citrus
and white-fleshed fruit, displays aromas of
garden vegetables, followed by full flavour
in the mouth and good length. We also
enjoyed the fresh, tangy Est! Est!! Est!!! with
its lingering, gutsy finish. The other wines
presented were all well managed.

○ Est! Est!! Est!!! di Montefiascone Poggio del Cardinale '12	🍷🍷 2*
○ Pensiero '12	🍷🍷 2*
○ Luce di Lago '12	🍷 2
○ Vivi '12	🍷 2
● Don Carlo '09	🍷🍷 2*
● Don Carlo '08	🍷🍷 2*
○ Est! Est!! Est!!! di Montefiascone Poggio del Cardinale '11	🍷🍷 2*
○ Le Muffe '10	🍷🍷 3*
○ Le Muffe '09	🍷🍷 4
○ Pensiero '11	🍷🍷 2*

Sergio Mottura

LOC. POGGIO DELLA COSTA, 1
01020 CIVITELLA D'AGLIANO [VT]
TEL. 0761914533
www.motturasergio.it

CELLAR SALES
PRE-BOOKED VISITS
ACCOMMODATION AND RESTAURANT SERVICE
ANNUAL PRODUCTION 95,000 bottles
HECTARES UNDER VINE 37.00
VITICOLTURA Biologico Certificato

This estate enjoys iconic status, not only in the province of Viterbo, but at a regional level, with its excellent organic wines. The owner, Sergio, arrived here in 1964, and continues to play an active role both in the rows and the cellar, assisted by his wife Alessandra and their children. The 37 hectares under vine are planted mainly to the native varieties of grechetto, verdello, procanico, and montepulciano, but the clay gullies of the Tiber Valley have also proved to be an excellent habitat for sauvignon, chardonnay, pinot nero and merlot. The result, once again, is a range of fine wines. The fresh, pleasurable Poggio della Costa confirms its reputation as one of Italy's great white wines, with aromas of Mediterranean scrub, white-fleshed fruit and elderflower, followed by a tangy, taut palate and impressive minerality. The rest of the range shows excellent quality, with the Sergio Mottura Brut 2007 worth a special mention.

○ Poggio della Costa '12	♔♔♔ 3*
○ Muffo '10	♔♔ 5
● Nenfro '10	♔♔ 4
○ Orvieto V. Tragugnano '12	♔♔ 3
○ Sergio Mottura Brut '07	♔♔ 5
● Magone '11	♔ 5
● Syracide '10	♔ 4
○ Grechetto Latour a Civitella '06	♕♕♕ 4*
○ Grechetto Latour a Civitella '05	♕♕♕ 4*
○ Grechetto Latour a Civitella '04	♕♕♕ 4*
○ Grechetto Latour a Civitella '01	♕♕♕ 3
○ Grechetto Poggio della Costa '10	♕♕♕ 3*
○ Grechetto Poggio della Costa '09	♕♕♕ 3*
○ Grechetto Poggio della Costa '08	♕♕♕ 3*
○ Poggio della Costa '11	♕♕♕ 3*

Principe Pallavicini

VIA CASILINA KM 25,500
00030 COLONNA [RM]
TEL. 069438816
www.vinipallavicini.com

CELLAR SALES
PRE-BOOKED VISITS
RESTAURANT SERVICE
ANNUAL PRODUCTION 556,500 bottles
HECTARES UNDER VINE 80.00

The Principe Pallavicini winery owns two estates. The most important is the historic Colonna vineyard of 65 hectares, comprising the Colonna, Pasolina and Marmorelle plots at elevations of 100 to 300 metres, on volcanic and calcareous-clay soils. Frascati is home to another 50 hectares, making this the largest privately-owned vineyard in the DOC zone, planted above all to white grape varieties. The other estate, planted to red grape varieties, lies on rocky limestone soils at Cerveteri, at an elevation of around 150 metres. This major Castelli Romani winery is back in the main section with a fine overall performance. We loved the Frascati Superiore Poggio Verde 2012, with sage and citrus aromas and zesty freshness on the supple palate. The late harvest Stillato 2012, from malvasia puntinata, also impressed us with a cinnamon and rosemary nose and well-dosed sweetness, underpinned by attractive acid sinew, as did the Amarasco 2011, a Cesanese with good fruit and backbone.

○ Frascati Sup. Poggio Verde '12	♔♔ 2*
● Amarasco '11	♔♔ 3
● Stillato '12	♔♔ 3
○ 1670 '11	♔ 3
● Moroello '11	♔ 5
● Rubillo '12	♔ 2
● Syrah '11	♔ 2
● Moroello '05	♕♕ 5
● Soleggio '10	♕♕ 3
● Soleggio '08	♕♕ 3
○ Stillato '10	♕♕ 3

La Pazzaglia

S.DA DI BAGNOREGIO, 4
01024 CASTIGLIONE IN TEVERINA [VT]
TEL. 0761947114
www.tenutalapazzaglia.it

CELLAR SALES
PRE-BOOKED VISITS
ACCOMMODATION
ANNUAL PRODUCTION 44,000 bottles
HECTARES UNDER VINE 12.00

Tenuta la Pazzaglia, owned by the Verdecchia family, has been a leading name in the Tuscia Viterbese viticultural area for some years now. The vineyards, planted around the winery headquarters, are home to a wide range of varieties, including montepulciano, sangiovese, ciliegiolo, canaiolo, aleatico, syrah, chardonnay, and pinot bianco, although particular attention is reserved for grechetto and merlot. Vinification is supervised by Maria Teresa, one of Randolfo and Agnese Verdecchia's daughters. The enjoyable wines are in a modern, drinkable style. They earn a full-length profile in this year's Guide thanks to Il Corno 2012, a gutsy, supple blend of 70% grechetto and 20% chardonnay, topped up with pinot bianco, with peach, apricot and floral hints, that flows nicely across the palate, and to the attractively zesty, full-bodied Orvieto 2012, one of the DOC zone's best. The reds are also well managed.

○ Il Corno '12	♟♟	2*
○ Orvieto '12	♟♟	2*
● Montijone '11	♟	4
● Palagio '12	♟	2
○ Il Corno '10	♟♟	2
● Montijone '08	♟♟	4
○ Orvieto '11	♟♟	2*

Poggio Le Volpi

VIA COLLE PISANO, 27
00040 MONTE PORZIO CATONE [RM]
TEL. 069426980
www.poggiolevolpi.it

CELLAR SALES
PRE-BOOKED VISITS
ANNUAL PRODUCTION 230,000 bottles
HECTARES UNDER VINE 35.00

When Felice Mergè established his winery in 1996 he began to focus solely on native varieties. The passion of this young oenologist, however, has its roots in the work of his grandfather Mario, a grower back in the 1920s. The success of what is one of the most representative wineries in the Castelli Romani area, especially known for its Frascati Epos, relies on its malvasia di candia, malvasia puntinata, trebbiano, greco, cesanese, and nero buono varieties. The vines are planted at an elevation of 400 metres on the volcanic soils typical of the area. In the absence of the Frascati Epos, solid reliability was provided by the Baccarossa 2011, a balsamic, earthy Nero Buono with notes of bramble and dark berry fruit, and a close-woven, impressive backbone, and the citrus-infused Donnaluce 2012, a pleasurable, full-flavoured blend of 60% malvasia puntinata and 30% greco topped up with chardonnay.

● Baccarossa '11	♟♟♟	4
○ Donnaluce '12	♟♟	3
○ Frascati Sup. Epos '11	♟♟♟	2*
○ Frascati Sup. Epos '10	♟♟♟	2*
○ Frascati Sup. Epos '09	♟♟♟	2*
● Baccarossa '10	♟♟	4
● Baccarossa '09	♟♟	4
● Baccarossa '07	♟♟	4
● Baccarossa '06	♟♟	4
● Baccarossa '05	♟♟	5
● Baccarossa '04	♟♟	5
○ Donnaluce '10	♟♟	3
○ Donnaluce '09	♟♟	3
○ Donnaluce '05	♟♟	3
○ Frascati Sup. Epos '08	♟♟	2*
○ Frascati Sup. Epos '06	♟♟	3

Sant'Andrea

Loc. Borgo Vodice
via Renibbio, 1720
04010 Terracina [LT]
Tel. 0773755028
www.cantinasantandrea.it

CELLAR SALES
PRE-BOOKED VISITS
ANNUAL PRODUCTION 500,000 bottles
HECTARES UNDER VINE 80.00

The history of Moscato di Terracina, both the variety and the DOC zone, goes hand in hand with that of the Pandolfo family winery, where Andrea now provides his father Gabriele with expert assistance. It thus comes as no surprise that their five Moscatos have been joined by a sixth, the ambitious Hum. The first bottles failed to live up to expectations, but it should be noted that 2012 was not a great year for this variety, underscored by the classic Oppidum, less complex and, above all, less aromatic than in previous versions. The best performance was provided by Oppidum Brut 2012, whose fizz helped show off its attractive aromas and nose-palate harmony. The excellent Capitolium 2011, with hints of almond and hazelnut, proved to be attractively sweet while not cloying, and displayed marked varietal character. Last of all, the Circeos were, as ever, interesting, with Incontro al Circeo 2011 standing out for its intrinsic quality and value for money.

● Circeo Rosso Incontro al Circeo '11	♟♟ 2*
○ Moscato di Terracina Passito Capitolium '11	♟♟ 4
○ Moscato di Terracina Secco Oppidum Spumante '12	♟♟ 2*
○ Circeo Bianco Dune '11	♟ 2
● Circeo Rosso Il Sogno '09	♟ 3
○ Moscato di Terracina Amabile Templum '12	♟ 2
○ Moscato di Terracina Hum '12	♟ 2
○ Moscato di Terracina Secco Oppidum '12	♟ 2
⊘ Riflessi Rosé Extra Dry	♟ 2
○ Circeo Bianco Dune '09	♟♟ 2*
● Circeo Rosso Il Sogno '08	♟♟ 3
○ Moscato di Terracina Secco Oppidum '11	♟♟ 2*
○ Moscato di Terracina Secco Oppidum '10	♟♟ 2*

Tenuta di Fiorano

via di Fioranello, 19/31
00134 Roma
Tel. 0679340093
info@tenutadifiorano.it

CELLAR SALES
PRE-BOOKED VISITS
ANNUAL PRODUCTION 12,000 bottles
HECTARES UNDER VINE 5.00

This legendary operation, renowned for its long-lived wines, has been in business since the post-war years, when Alberico Boncompagni Ludovisi, Prince of Venosa, planted international varieties such as merlot, cabernet sauvignon and semillon alongside the local malvasia di Candia. Since his death in 2005 his cousin, Principe Alessandrojacopo Boncompagni, has been producing wines of great quality from the 5 hectares under vine. The Bordeaux blend Fiorano Rosso and the Fiorano Bianco take their names from the winery's location at Fioranello, near the Appian Way to the south of Rome. The oxidative Fiorano Bianco 2011, a blend of grechetto e viogner, confirms its worth, offering notes of sage and saffron over a long, complex palate. The Fiorano Rosso 2008, from a blend of 60% cabernet sauvignon topped up with merlot, shows good stuffing and staying power.

○ Fiorano Bianco '11	♟♟ 4
● Fiorano Rosso '08	♟♟ 4
○ Fiorano Bianco '10	♟♟♟ 5
● Fiorano Rosso '06	♟♟ 6

Giovanni Terenzi

LOC. LA FORMA
VIA FORESE, 13
03010 SERRONE [FR]
TEL. 0775594286
www.viniterenzi.com

CELLAR SALES
PRE-BOOKED VISITS
ANNUAL PRODUCTION 60,000 bottles
HECTARES UNDER VINE 10.00

A well-deserved full-length profile this time round for the winery established over half a century ago by Giovanni Terenzi, and still a family business, also thanks to the dedication of his three children. In the vineyards, all attentively tended and superbly aspected, the prized Affile clone of cesanese dominates, but there is also sangiovese grosso, used for the Querciarossa, and some passerina. It was the last of these that gave the best showing, in a version whose excellent aromatic profile was matched by its length and finesse. The four expressions of Cesanese were equally impressive, and their diversity epitomises the versatility of the variety: from the drinkable entry-level wine and the modern-styled Vajoscuro 2010, to a contemporary classic such as the Velobra 2011 and the Colle Forma 2011, a potential future classic that becomes more interesting every year. We were also won over by the Rosato, whose attractive cleanliness makes it one of the best of its type.

Trappolini

VIA DEL RIVELLINO, 65
01024 CASTIGLIONE IN TEVERINA [VT]
TEL. 0761948381
www.trappolini.com

CELLAR SALES
PRE-BOOKED VISITS
ANNUAL PRODUCTION 150,000 bottles
HECTARES UNDER VINE 25.00

Since he started out in the 1960s with much lower production figures, Mario Trappolini has expanded significantly, investing in the acquisition of new vineyards. Nevertheless, he is still driven by the same passion and respect for the territory, and gives pride of place to the local varieties of the Tiber Valley, both red and white: aleatico, sangiovese, montepulciano, canaiolo, grechetto, trebbiano and malvasia. The winery is now run by Roberto and Paolo, Mario's sons, who took the road less travelled, deciding to focus on red wines in what is particularly good white wine country. The market has proved them right. The Sangiovese Paterno 2011 remains the winery's champion, offering good structure swathed in spice and ripe red berry fruit, but this year was joined by a deliciously refreshing Est! Est!! Est!!! di Montefiascone 2012, with aromas of white-fleshed fruit and hints of resin, and the supple, citrus-infused Orvieto 2012.

○ Passerina Villa Santa '12	♥♥ 2*
● Cesanese del Piglio Sup. Colle Forma '11	♥♥ 4
● Cesanese del Piglio Vajoscuro '10	♥♥ 5
● Cesanese del Piglio Velobra '11	♥♥ 2*
● Cesanese del Piglio '12	♥ 2
● Quercia Rossa '11	♥ 3
⊙ Rosato '12	♥ 2
● Cesanese del Piglio Sup. Vajoscuro Ris. '09	♀♀ 4
● Cesanese del Piglio Velobra '08	♀♀ 2*
○ Passerina Villa Santa '11	♀♀ 2*

● Paterno '11	♥♥ 3
○ Est! Est!! Est!!! di Montefiascone '12	♥♥ 2*
○ Orvieto '12	♥♥ 2*
○ Brecceto '12	♥ 3
● Cenereto '12	♥ 2
○ Grechetto '12	♥ 2
● Idea '12	♥ 3
○ Sartei '12	♥ 2
○ Est! Est!! Est!!! di Montefiascone '11	♀♀ 2*
● Paterno '10	♀♀ 3*
● Paterno '08	♀♀ 3*
● Paterno '07	♀♀ 3*
● Paterno '06	♀♀ 3*
● Paterno '03	♀♀ 3*
● Paterno '99	♀♀ 3*
○ Sartei '11	♀♀ 1*

Antiche Cantine Migliaccio

VIA PIZZICATO
04027 PONZA [LT]
TEL. 3392822252
www.fienodiponza.com

CELLAR SALES
PRE-BOOKED VISITS
ANNUAL PRODUCTION 8,000 bottles
HECTARES UNDER VINE 2.00

○ Biancolella di Ponza '12	♥♥ 5
○ Fieno Bianco '12	♥ 4
⊙ Fieno Rosato '12	♥ 4
● Fieno Rosso '10	♥ 2

Casale Cento Corvi

VIA AURELIA KM 45,500
00052 CERVETERI [RM]
TEL. 069903902
www.casalecentocorvi.com

CELLAR SALES
PRE-BOOKED VISITS
ANNUAL PRODUCTION 300,000 bottles
HECTARES UNDER VINE 35.00

● Giacché Rosso '11	♥♥ 6
● Kantharos Rosso '11	♥ 4
○ Kottabos Bianco '12	♥ 2
○ Malvasia '12	♥ 2

Castel de Paolis

VIA VAL DE PAOLIS
00046 GROTTAFERRATA [RM]
TEL. 069413648
www.casteldepaolis.it

CELLAR SALES
PRE-BOOKED VISITS
RESTAURANT SERVICE
ANNUAL PRODUCTION 90,000 bottles
HECTARES UNDER VINE 12.00

○ Frascati Sup. '12	♥♥ 3
● Campo Vecchio Rosso '10	♥ 3
○ Frascati Campo Vecchio '12	♥ 2
● Quattro Mori '09	♥ 5

Cantina Sociale Cesanese del Piglio

VIA PRENESTINA, KM 42
03010 PIGLIO [FR]
TEL. 0775502356
www.cesanesedelpiglio.it

CELLAR SALES
PRE-BOOKED VISITS
ANNUAL PRODUCTION 450,000 bottles
HECTARES UNDER VINE 18.00

● Cesanese del Piglio Sup. Diverso '11	♥♥ 3
● Cesanese del Piglio Et. Oro '10	♥ 2

Damiano Ciolli

VIA DEL CORSO
00035 OLEVANO ROMANO [RM]
TEL. 069564547
www.damianociolli.it

CELLAR SALES
PRE-BOOKED VISITS
ANNUAL PRODUCTION 23,000 bottles
HECTARES UNDER VINE 5.00

● Cesanese di Olevano Silene '11	♥♥ 3*

Colle Picchioni Paola Di Mauro

LOC. FRATTOCCHIE
VIA COLLE PICCHIONE, 46
00040 MARINO [RM]
TEL. 0693546329
www.collepicchioni.it

CELLAR SALES
PRE-BOOKED VISITS
ANNUAL PRODUCTION 90,000 bottles
HECTARES UNDER VINE 15.00

● Collerosso '12	♥♥ 2*
○ Donna Paola '12	♥ 3
○ Marino Coste Rotonde '11	♥ 2
● Perlaia '12	♥ 3

Cominium

VIA RITINTO
03041 ALVITO [FR]
TEL. 0776510683
www.cantinacominium.it

HECTARES UNDER VINE 13,00

● Atina Cabernet Satur '09	♥♥ 4
○ Maturano '12	♥♥ 2*
● Colle Alto '10	♥ 3

Cordeschi

LOC. ACQUAPENDENTE
VIA CASSIA KM 137,400
00121 VITERBO
TEL. 3356953547
www.cantinacordeschi.it

CELLAR SALES
ANNUAL PRODUCTION 30,000 bottles
HECTARES UNDER VINE 8.50

● Ost '11	♥♥ 3
○ Palea '12	♥ 2
⊙ Siele '12	♥ 2

Corte dei Papi

LOC. COLLETONNO
03012 ANAGNI [FR]
TEL. 0775769271
www.cortedeipapi.it

CELLAR SALES
PRE-BOOKED VISITS
ANNUAL PRODUCTION 75,000 bottles
HECTARES UNDER VINE 25.00

○ Passerina '12	♥♥ 2*
● Cesanese del Piglio Ottavo Cielo '11	♥ 3
● Cesanese del Piglio San Magno '10	♥ 3

Donato Giangirolami

LOC. BORGO MONTELLO
VIA DEL CAVALIERE, 1414
04100 LATINA
TEL. 3358394890
www.donatogiangirolami.it

CELLAR SALES
PRE-BOOKED VISITS
ANNUAL PRODUCTION 70,000 bottles
HECTARES UNDER VINE 38.00
VITICULTURE METHOD Certified Organic

○ Apricor Passito '11	♥♥ 4
○ Propizio '12	♥♥ 2*
○ Cardito '12	♥ 2
○ Regius '12	♥ 2

Marcella Giuliani

LOC. VICO MORICINO
VIA ANTICOLANA, KM 5
03012 ANAGNI [FR]
TEL. 0644235908
www.aziendaagricolamarcellagiuliani.it

CELLAR SALES
PRE-BOOKED VISITS
ANNUAL PRODUCTION 35,000 bottles
HECTARES UNDER VINE 10.70
VITICULTURE METHOD Certified Organic

● Cesanese del Piglio Dives Riserva del Fondatore '07	♥♥ 4
○ Alagna Bianco Passerina '12	♥ 2
⊙ Alagna Rosato '12	♥ 2

Gotto d'Oro

LOC. FRATTOCCHIE
VIA DEL DIVINO AMORE, 115
00040 MARINO [RM]
TEL. 0693022211
www.gottodoro.it

CELLAR SALES
PRE-BOOKED VISITS
ANNUAL PRODUCTION 9,000,000 bottles
HECTARES UNDER VINE 1,400.00

○ Mitreo Sol '11	♥♥ 2*
● Castelli Romani Rosso '12	♥ 2
○ Chardonnay '12	♥ 2
● Mitreo Mithra '11	♥ 2

Podere Grecchi

S.DA SAMMARTINESE, 8
01100 VITERBO
TEL. 0761305671
www.poderegrecchi.com

CELLAR SALES
PRE-BOOKED VISITS
ANNUAL PRODUCTION 45,000 bottles
HECTARES UNDER VINE 10.50

○ San Silvestro '12	♟♟ 2*
● CEV Poggio Ferrone '11	♟ 2
● CEV Poggio Santirossi '12	♟ 2
○ Poggio Grecchi '12	♟ 2

Le Lase

LOC. RESANO
01028 ORTE [VT]
TEL. 0761281460
www.lelase.com

CELLAR SALES
PRE-BOOKED VISITS
ACCOMMODATION
ANNUAL PRODUCTION 28,000 bottles
HECTARES UNDER VINE 12.00

● Cautha '10	♟♟ 3
○ Goccia '11	♟ 3
● Thesan '10	♟ 3
○ Zefiro '11	♟ 2

Cantine Lupo

VIA MEDIANA CISTERNA, 27
04011 LATINA
TEL. 0668309520
www.cantinelupo.com

PRE-BOOKED VISITS
ANNUAL PRODUCTION 50,000 bottles
HECTARES UNDER VINE 18.00

● Primolupo Merlot '11	♟♟ 2*
● Syranto '11	♟♟ 2*
● Perseide '10	♟ 4
○ Terra Marique '12	♟ 2

Occhipinti

LOC. MONTEMAGGIORE
01010 GRADOLI [VT]
TEL. 0633249347
www.occhipintiagricola.it

CELLAR SALES
PRE-BOOKED VISITS
ANNUAL PRODUCTION 15,000 bottles
HECTARES UNDER VINE 4.00

○ Alter Ego '12	♟♟ 2*
● Caldera '11	♟♟ 2*

I Pampini

LOC. ACCIARELLA
S.DA FOGLINO, 1126
04010 LATINA
TEL. 0773643144
www.ipampini.it

CELLAR SALES
PRE-BOOKED VISITS
ANNUAL PRODUCTION 20,000 bottles
HECTARES UNDER VINE 6.50
VITICULTURE METHOD Certified Organic

○ Bellone '12	♟♟ 2*
● Il Capitano '08	♟♟ 3
● Kubizzo '10	♟♟ 2*
● Coboldo '11	♟ 2

Pietra Pinta

SP PASTINE KM 20,200
04010 CORI [LT]
TEL. 069678001
www.pietrapinta.com

CELLAR SALES
PRE-BOOKED VISITS
ACCOMMODATION AND RESTAURANT SERVICE
ANNUAL PRODUCTION 300,000 bottles
HECTARES UNDER VINE 34.00
VITICULTURE METHOD Certified Organic

○ Carinthia '12	♟♟ 2*
● Costa Vecchia Rosso '11	♟♟ 2*
● Shiraz '11	♟♟ 2*
○ Viognier '12	♟ 2

Pileum

VIA DEL CASALOTTO
03010 PIGLIO [FR]
TEL. 3663129910
www.pileum.it

PRE-BOOKED VISITS
ANNUAL PRODUCTION 56,000 bottles
HECTARES UNDER VINE 9.00

● Cesanese del Piglio Sup. Bolla di Urbano Ris. '10	▼▼ 4
● Cesanese del Piglio Sup. Pila Rocca Ris. '09	▼▼ 4

Poggio alla Meta

VIA VALLONI
03034 CASALVIERI [FR]
www.poggioallameta.it

● Atina Cabernet Il Giovane '11	▼▼ 3
○ Maturano '12	▼▼ 2*
○ Piluc '12	▼▼ 2*
● Lot '11	▼ 3

Il Quadrifoglio

LOC. DOGANELLA DI NINFA
VIA ALESSANDRO III, 5
04012 CISTERNA DI LATINA [LT]
TEL. 069601530
ilquadrifoglio.ss@libero.it

PRE-BOOKED VISITS
ANNUAL PRODUCTION 60,000 bottles
HECTARES UNDER VINE 30.00

○ Pezze di Ninfa '12	▼▼ 2*
○ Doganella '12	▼ 2
● Syrah '11	▼ 2

La Rasenna

LOC. CERVETERI
VIA DELLA NECROPOLI, 2
00059 SANTA SEVERA [RM]
TEL. 3924974478
www.larasenna.it

ANNUAL PRODUCTION 60,000 bottles
HECTARES UNDER VINE 8.00

○ Moss '12	▼▼ 2*
● Cabernet Franc '10	▼ 3
○ Costa Marina Vermentino '12	▼ 2
● Petit Verdot '11	▼ 2

Riserva della Cascina

LOC. FIORANO
VIA APPIA ANTICA, 560
00134 ROMA
TEL. 067917221
riservadellacascina.blogspot.com

CELLAR SALES
PRE-BOOKED VISITS
ANNUAL PRODUCTION 45,000 bottles
HECTARES UNDER VINE 23.50
VITICULTURE METHOD Certified Organic

● Castelli Romani Rosso IX Miglio '11	▼▼ 2*
○ Marino Sup. '12	▼ 2

San Giovenale

LOC. LA MACCIA
01010 BLERA [VT]
TEL. 066877877
www.sangiovenale.it

CELLAR SALES
PRE-BOOKED VISITS
ANNUAL PRODUCTION 7,000 bottles
HECTARES UNDER VINE 9.00
VITICULTURE METHOD Certified Organic

● Habemus '11	▼▼ 7

Cantine San Marco

LOC. VERMICINO
VIA DI MOLA CAVONA, 26/28
00044 FRASCATI [RM]
TEL. 069409403
www.sanmarcofrascati.it

CELLAR SALES
PRE-BOOKED VISITS
ANNUAL PRODUCTION 1,800,000 bottles
HECTARES UNDER VINE 32.00

○ Frascati Sup. Crio 12 '12	♟♟ 3
○ Frascati Sup. Crio 8 '12	♟ 2
● Solomerlot '12	♟ 2
● Soloshiraz '12	♟ 3

Sant'Isidoro

LOC. PORTACCIA
01016 TARQUINIA [VT]
TEL. 0766869716
www.santisidoro.net

CELLAR SALES
PRE-BOOKED VISITS
ANNUAL PRODUCTION 65,000 bottles
HECTARES UNDER VINE 57,00

○ Forca di Palma '12	♟♟ 2*
● Soremidio '10	♟♟ 4
● Corithus '11	♟ 3

Tenuta Santa Lucia

LOC. SANTA LUCIA
02047 POGGIO MIRTETO [RI]
TEL. 076524616
www.tenutasantalucia.com

CELLAR SALES
PRE-BOOKED VISITS
RESTAURANT SERVICE
ANNUAL PRODUCTION 200,000 bottles
HECTARES UNDER VINE 43.00

○ Falanghina '12	♟♟ 2*
● Colli della Sabina Collis Pollionis Rosso '11	♟ 3
○ Pecorino '12	♟ 2

Tenuta Le Quinte

VIA DELLE MARMORELLE, 71
00040 MONTECOMPATRI [RM]
TEL. 069438756

○ Malvasia Orchidea '12	♟♟ 2*
● Nasyr '11	♟♟ 3
○ Canestraro '12	♟ 2

Terra delle Ginestre

SS 630 AUSONIA, 59
04020 SPIGNO SATURNIA [LT]
TEL. 3495617153
www.terradelleginestre.it

CELLAR SALES
PRE-BOOKED VISITS
ANNUAL PRODUCTION 13,000 bottles
HECTARES UNDER VINE 4.00

○ Invito Senza Solfiti Aggiunti '12	♟♟ 4
○ Lentisco '10	♟♟ 2*
○ Letizia '12	♟♟ 2*
○ Invito '12	♟ 2

Tre Botti

S.DA DELLA POGGETTA, 10
01024 CASTIGLIONE IN TEVERINA [VT]
TEL. 0761948930
www.trebotti.it

CELLAR SALES
ANNUAL PRODUCTION 40,000 bottles
HECTARES UNDER VINE 10.00
VITICULTURE METHOD Certified Organic

● Bludom '12	♟♟ 3
○ Orvieto Incanthus '12	♟ 2

Tenuta Tre Cancelli

VIA DELLA PISCINA, 3
00053 CERVETERI [RM]
TEL. 0699060008
tenutatrecancelli@tiscali.it

CELLAR SALES
PRE-BOOKED VISITS
ANNUAL PRODUCTION 25,000 bottles
HECTARES UNDER VINE 10.00

○ Flere '12	♟♟ 2*
● Cerveteri Rosso Pacha '11	♟ 2
● Lituo '10	♟ 3
○ Zio Carlo '10	♟ 3

Vigneti Iucci

FRAZ. SANT'ELIA FIUMERAPIDO
LOC. LA CRETA
03043 CASSINO [FR]
TEL. 0776311883
www.vignetiiucci.it

● Atina Cabernet Sammichele '11	♟♟ 3
● Merlot La Creta '11	♟♟ 2*
● Sant'Elia '11	♟ 2
○ Tenuta La Creta Bianco '11	♟ 2

Villa Caviciana

LOC. TOJENA CAVICIANA
01025 GROTTE DI CASTRO [VT]
TEL. 0763798212
www.villacaviciana.com

CELLAR SALES
PRE-BOOKED VISITS
ANNUAL PRODUCTION 25,000 bottles
HECTARES UNDER VINE 15.00
VITICULTURE METHOD Certified Biodynamic

● Eleonora '11	♟♟ 3
● Faustina '11	♟♟ 6
● Letizia '11	♟ 5
⊙ Tadzio '12	♟ 3

Villa Gianna

FRAZ. B.GO SAN DONATO
S.DA MAREMMANA
04010 SABAUDIA [LT]
TEL. 0773250034
www.villagianna.it

CELLAR SALES
PRE-BOOKED VISITS
ANNUAL PRODUCTION 865,000 bottles
HECTARES UNDER VINE 50.00
VITICULTURE METHOD Certified Organic

○ Elogio Mediterraneo '10	♟♟ 3
○ Moscato di Terracina Amabile '12	♟♟ 1*
○ Circeo Bianco Innato '12	♟ 2
○ Circeo Bianco NobilVite '12	♟ 1*

Villa Simone

VIA FRASCATI COLONNA, 29
00040 MONTE PORZIO CATONE [RM]
TEL. 069449717
www.villasimone.com

CELLAR SALES
PRE-BOOKED VISITS
ANNUAL PRODUCTION 299,000 bottles
HECTARES UNDER VINE 33.00

○ Frascati Sup. Villa dei Preti '12	♟♟ 2*
○ Frascati '12	♟ 2
○ Frascati Sup. Vign. Filonardi '12	♟ 3
● La Torraccia '11	♟ 3

Cantine Volpetti

VIA NETTUNENSE, 21
00040 ARICCIA [RM]
TEL. 069342000
www.cantinevolpetti.it

CELLAR SALES
PRE-BOOKED VISITS
ANNUAL PRODUCTION 450,000 bottles
HECTARES UNDER VINE 40.00

○ Malvasia del Lazio V.T. '09	♟♟ 3
○ Chardonnay Le Piantate '12	♟ 2
○ Frascati Sup. Feudi dei Papi '12	♟ 1*
● Sangiovese Le Piantate '12	♟ 2

ABRUZZO

Abruzzo is no longer simply Italy's fourth-largest wine-producing region. It is now also a well-established scenario of top-quality wines and it is not unusual to find Abruzzo's best labels on the world's foremost store shelves. The flagship is certainly Montepulciano d'Abruzzo, Italy's number-two type, but there are also Trebbiano, Cerasuolo and the flourishing native wines. All at amazing value for money and displaying their undeniable quality, a heritage built on the value of the vines and the production, but also on a style that has never succumbed to the temptation of international varieties, focusing instead on traditional grapes and territorial identity. The variety of the Abruzzo landscape plays a significant role, from its glaciers to the Adriatic coast: just a few kilometres yet with a great variety of habitats and soil and climate conditions, which yield wines very different aromas and flavours, reflecting the different terroirs. The Guide became aware of this phenomenon years ago and believed in it with enthusiasm and conviction, rewarding an increasing number of wineries with a Tre Bicchieri, reflecting the importance of regional growth. The number of newcomers and new cellars in evidence, from competitive wine co-operatives with impressive figures to small artisans of distinctive characteristics, prove quality and impact at national level. The most recent development is certainly due to the focus on a simpler, more discreet style for wines with a distinct traditional, natural feel, never too flashy or flaunted. Cantina Tollo confirms its role as a fascinating lead player, this year presenting its C'Incanta 2010 Trebbiano, an old-school white made with age-old vinification techniques. Then all the evergreens like Valentini's stunningly pleasing Trebbiano 2011 and Masciarelli's Marina Cvetic Montepulciano 2010. Cataldi Madonna confirms L'Aquila as one of the region's great wine areas with his 2011 Pecorino, at its usual amazing standard. Valle Reale convinces with its Vigne di Capestrano 2011 Trebbiano and the exuberant scents bestowed by the mountains. Loreto-based Torre dei Beati is confirmed as a great artisan cellar and its Cocciapazza 2010 is getting better and better. Tiberio, on the hills of Pescara, no longer rouses any doubts, just certainties, and the same can be said for Castorani, which has staked everything on a revival of winemaking in concrete. In the Teramo zone, Barba confirms its Vasari 2010 and Nicodemi and Villa Medoro express two different but equally valid ways of recounting the Mediterranean Colline Teramane designation. Last but not least, there's newcomer Tenuta Ulisse, now established on the market with well-made wines and a fabulous 2012 Montepulciano from the spontaneously fermented Nativae line.

Agriverde

LOC. CALDARI
VIA STORTINI, 32A
66020 ORTONA [CH]
TEL. 0859032101
www.agriverde.it

CELLAR SALES
PRE-BOOKED VISITS
ACCOMMODATION AND RESTAURANT SERVICE
ANNUAL PRODUCTION 900,000 bottles
HECTARES UNDER VINE 65.00
VITICULTURE METHOD Certified Organic

A true pioneer of organic systems, this worthy Ortona winery has been a certified producer for decades. The location is a nook of southernmost Abruzzo, where constant sun and clay soils have made this the homeland of mighty wines and plentiful yields exploited by large co-operative wineries. Giannicola took a different approach and got certification for his entire 65 hectares under vine. The winery was designed to bioarchitecture criteria and he added a charming agritourism facility with its own spa. Agriverde produces a respectable range of wines for quality and quantity, from simple, affordable whites to muscular Montepulciano crus that are a traditional expression of this zone. The battery of remarkable labels includes the winery's new offshoot Vigna Madre, and the wines are as interesting and persuasive as ever. The 2008 Plateo that just missed a ranking because of the difficult vintage is complex and richly extracted, remaining a benchmark for opulent, Mediterranean-style Montepulcianos.

● Montepulciano d'Abruzzo Plateo '08	♟♟ 6
● Montepulciano d'Abruzzo Vignamadre '12	♟♟ 1*
○ Trebbiano d'Abruzzo Solarea '11	♟♟ 3*
● Montepulciano d'Abruzzo Natum '12	♟♟ 2*
● Montepulciano d'Abruzzo Piane di Maggio '12	♟♟ 2*
● Montepulciano d'Abruzzo Solàrea '09	♟♟ 4
● Montepulciano d'Abruzzo Villa Roscià Vignamadre '10	♟♟ 2*
○ Trebbiano d'Abruzzo Natum '12	♟♟ 2*
○ Passerina Riseis '12	♟ 3
○ Pecorino Eikos '12	♟ 3
○ Pecorino Riseis '12	♟ 3
○ Trebbiano d'Abruzzo Piane di Maggio '12	♟ 2
○ Trebbiano d'Abruzzo Vignamadre '12	♟ 1*
○ Trebbiano d'Abruzzo Villa Roscià Vignamadre '12	♟ 2

F.lli Barba

LOC. SCERNE DI PINETO
S.DA ROTABILE PER CASOLI
64020 PINETO [TE]
TEL. 0859461020
www.fratellibarba.it

CELLAR SALES
PRE-BOOKED VISITS
ACCOMMODATION
ANNUAL PRODUCTION 350,000 bottles
HECTARES UNDER VINE 68.00

This solid, reputed Teramo winery is part of a farm that produces a full range of vegetables, fruit, bulk wine, and oil. The limited number of bottles made from the 70 hectares of estate by the coast at Scerne and Pineto, are much respected in the region and are the expression of this unique wine country. The traditional style is flanked by the revival of age-old techniques to shape a very appreciable range, which runs from the affordable but prodigious entry-level wines to the interesting efforts with Trebbiano fermented in amphorae, and amazing Montepulciano crus. The compact range of pleasing, quality wines includes Vasari 2010, an ambitious Montepulciano that earned another Tre Bicchieri award with its old-school smoky nose and very young, full, tightly woven palate, supported by prominent tannins and savoury verve. Hats off to Moreno too, a small, sound Montepulciano at a small, small price.

● Montepulciano d'Abruzzo I Vasari '10	♟♟♟ 5
● Montepulciano d'Abruzzo Colle Morino Et. Bianca '11	♟♟ 2*
○ Vignafranca Bianco '11	♟♟ 3*
● Montepulciano d'Abruzzo Colle Morino '12	♟♟ 2*
● Montepulciano d'Abruzzo Vignafranca '10	♟♟ 3
○ Trebbiano d'Abruzzo '10	♟♟ 4
○ Trebbiano d'Abruzzo Colle Morino '12	♟♟ 1*
● Montepulciano d'Abruzzo I Vasari '09	♟♟♟ 5
● Montepulciano d'Abruzzo Vignafranca '09	♟♟ 3*
○ Vignafranca Bianco '10	♟♟ 3*

Barone Cornacchia

VILLA TORRI, 19
64010 TORANO NUOVO [TE]
TEL. 0861887412
www.baronecornacchia.it

CELLAR SALES
PRE-BOOKED VISITS
ACCOMMODATION
ANNUAL PRODUCTION 300,000 bottles
HECTARES UNDER VINE 42.00
VITICULTURE METHOD Certified Organic

Barone Cornacchia, the evergreen
Controguerra winery, a byword for quality
in the competitive Colline Teramane DOC
district, is also a local stalwart and the
driving force behind the designation itself.
The estate is made up of a single
30-hectare plot, one of the most stunning
vineyards in the area, managed with the
care and passion of venerable tradition.
The classic wines are muscular and
sometimes lose balance in endeavours for
rich extraction. This year's battery of
tastings was numerous and at times fell
short of its reputation. The classic red
Montepulciano 2011 comes from certified
organic vineyards. It stands out for its nose
of supercharged fruit and full, tightly-
woven palate, underpinned by superbly
controlled body. The Cerasuolo 2012, also
organic, is a juicy, food-friendly wine with a
well-typed nose of strawberries and
almonds followed by a crisp, well-paced
palate. The ambitious crus are less
convincing, bogged down at times by
exaggerated super-ripeness.

● Montepulciano d'Abruzzo '11	♟♟ 2*
☉ Montepulciano d'Abruzzo Cerasuolo '12	♟♟ 1*
● Montepulciano d'Abruzzo V. Le Coste '10	♟♟ 3
● Montepulciano d'Abruzzo Colline Teramane Vizzarro '08	♟ 5
● Montepulciano d'Abruzzo Poggio Varano '10	♟ 3
○ Trebbiano d'Abruzzo Sup. '12	♟ 2
☉ Montepulciano d'Abruzzo Cerasuolo '11	♟♟ 1*
● Montepulciano d'Abruzzo Poggio Varano '09	♟♟ 2*
● Montepulciano d'Abruzzo Poggio Varano '08	♟♟ 2*
● Montepulciano d'Abruzzo V. Le Coste '09	♟♟ 2*

Tenute Barone di Valforte

C.DA PIOMBA, 11
64029 SILVI MARINA [TE]
TEL. 0859353432
www.baronedivalforte.it

CELLAR SALES
PRE-BOOKED VISITS
ANNUAL PRODUCTION 270,000 bottles
HECTARES UNDER VINE 50.00

This large winery on the border between
Pescara and Teramo has over 50 hectares
under vine in Silvi Marina, right on the
Adriatic. The enterprise comprises several
estates, each with its own traits. The
Sorricchio family have always been
vignerons and run their operation with a
determination befitting modern
winemaking. They produce interesting,
competent wines that reap success for
their fresh, clean style. Their drinkable
native whites are as technically
accomplished and stylish as their ambitious
Colline Teramane reds. This operation just
gets better, with increasingly good wines
reconciling tradition and modernity. The
2010 Montepulciano Riserva is very sound,
with a well-typed varietal nose supported
by an alluring citrus note. Its impressive
palate shows well-controlled body and
good acidity that ensures fresh drinkability
and good progression. Colle Sale 2009, an
ambitious Colline Teramane, is very
recognizable for its acidity and alluring
old-fashioned smoky note.

● Montepulciano d'Abruzzo Colline Teramane Colle Sale '09	♟♟ 3*
● Montepulciano d'Abruzzo Ris. '10	♟♟ 3*
● Montepulciano d'Abruzzo '12	♟♟ 2*
○ Passerina '12	♟♟ 2*
☉ Montepulciano d'Abruzzo Cerasuolo '12	♟ 2
○ Pecorino '12	♟ 2
○ Trebbiano d'Abruzzo Villa Chiara '12	♟ 2
○ Colle Sale Bianco '10	♟♟ 3
● Montepulciano d'Abruzzo '11	♟♟ 2*
○ Passerina '10	♟♟ 2*
○ Trebbiano d'Abruzzo '10	♟♟ 2*

Nestore Bosco

c.da Casali, 147
65010 Nocciano [PE]
Tel. 085847345
www.nestorebosco.com

CELLAR SALES
PRE-BOOKED VISITS
ANNUAL PRODUCTION 600,000 bottles
HECTARES UNDER VINE 75.00

One of Abruzzo's oldest wineries can be found on the Pescara hills, right on the Adriatic coast. In a territory that has always been dedicated wine country, the operation took its first steps more than a century ago, and was the first to export its wines to competitive international markets. The Nocciano estate, 70 hectares under vine, produces sophisticated raw materials. We have no doubts about the Montepulciano 2010, whose well-typed pleasantly rustic nose offers keen gamey hints against a background of austere, close-focused fruit. The elegant palate is rich and full with lively suppleness. Trebbiano 2012 is a great classic interpretation of the grape, with a fresh varietal nose of grass and citrus fruit, and a hint of rocky minerality on the palate, destined to emerge with ageing.

● Montepulciano d'Abruzzo R '10	🍷🍷 3*
● Montepulciano d'Abruzzo '10	🍷🍷 2*
● Montepulciano d'Abruzzo Don Bosco '09	🍷🍷 4
● Montepulciano d'Abruzzo Pan '09	🍷🍷 4
○ Trebbiano d'Abruzzo Sup. '12	🍷🍷 2*
○ Pecorino '12	🍷 2
● Montepulciano d'Abruzzo '09	🍷🍷 2*
● Montepulciano d'Abruzzo Don Bosco '08	🍷🍷 4
● Montepulciano d'Abruzzo Pan '08	🍷🍷 4

Castorani

loc. c.da Oratorio
via Castorani, 5
65020 Alanno [PE]
Tel. 3466355635
www.castorani.it

CELLAR SALES
PRE-BOOKED VISITS
ANNUAL PRODUCTION 1.000,000 bottles
HECTARES UNDER VINE 75.00
VITICULTURE METHOD Certified Organic

With its unique site between the mountains and the sea on the Pescara hills, Alanno enjoys both frequent coastal breezes and cool air from higher altitudes. The winery owns a single vineyard plot of nearly 75 hectares and regularly produces wines striking for technical merit and appeal, skilfully walking the tightrope between tradition and modernity. This is also the result of some gutsy decisions like fermentation in concrete, a winemaking method used extensively here in the past but never applied to contemporary, precise wines. The battery boasts impressive quality and quantity. Another Tre Bicchieri went to the ambitious Podere Castorani Riserva 2009, a vineyard selection with a sound varietal nose and the typical relaxed notes of concrete-fermented Montepulciano. Although still very young, the tight-knit palate is already enjoyable, releasing a juicy swathe of savoury marine notes on the finish. The simpler Amorino 2009 is another relaxed Montepulciano with an extremely pleasant, gutsy palate.

● Montepulciano d'Abruzzo Ris. '09	🍷🍷🍷 5
● Montepulciano d'Abruzzo Amorino '09	🍷🍷 3*
⊙ Montepulciano d'Abruzzo Cerasuolo Costa delle Plaie '12	🍷🍷 3*
● Montepulciano d'Abruzzo Cadetto '11	🍷🍷 2*
● Montepulciano d'Abruzzo Costa delle Plaie '10	🍷🍷 3
○ Pecorino Amorino '12	🍷🍷 3
○ Pecorino Le Paranze '12	🍷🍷 2*
○ Trebbiano d'Abruzzo Cadetto '12	🍷🍷 2*
○ Trebbiano d'Abruzzo Sup. Costa delle Plaie '12	🍷🍷 3
⊙ Montepulciano d'Abruzzo Cerasuolo Cadetto '12	🍷 2
○ Passerina Le Paranze '12	🍷 2
○ Pecorino Costa delle Plaje '12	🍷 3
● Rocco '10	🍷 4

★Luigi Cataldi Madonna

LOC. PIANO
67025 OFENA [AQ]
TEL. 0862954252
www.cataldimadonna.it

CELLAR SALES
PRE-BOOKED VISITS
ANNUAL PRODUCTION 230,000 bottles
HECTARES UNDER VINE 27.00

Ofena is home to one of Abruzzo's first artisan wineries, whose range of labels never fails to impress thanks to a very personal and distinctive reading of Abruzzo varieties. The unique location is a small plateau in the province of L'Aquila, completely embraced by mountains. Daytime temperatures are high, earning the place the title of "Furnace of Abruzzo", while at night temperatures can fall by as much as 20 °C, influenced by Calderone, the only glacier in the Apennines. Which explains why aromas are preserved and why the wines have the kind of attitude revealed by the famous Pecorino. The compact and very convincing battery of labels confirms Tonì as one of the region's top Montepulcianos. Its complex, layered nose offers crisp fruit with edgy mineral notes, and is accompanied by a still young, tightly knit palate. The wondrous 2011 Pecorino confirms its Tre Bicchieri with a nose of medicinal herbs and bitter orange and a palate that already hints at the minerality that it's destined to develop.

○ Pecorino '11	♟♟♟ 5
● Montepulciano d'Abruzzo Tonì '10	♟♟ 5
● Montepulciano d'Abruzzo '11	♟♟ 2*
○ Montepulciano d'Abruzzo Cerasuolo '12	♟♟ 2*
● Montepulciano d'Abruzzo Malandrino '11	♟♟ 3
○ Pecorino Giulia '12	♟♟ 3
○ Trebbiano d'Abruzzo '12	♟ 2
○ Pecorino '10	♟♟♟ 5
○ Montepulciano d'Abruzzo Cerasuolo Piè delle Vigne '10	♟♟ 3*
○ Pecorino Giulia '11	♟♟ 3*

Cerulli Irelli Spinozzi

LOC. CASALE 26
SS 150 DEL VOMANO KM 17,600
64020 CANZANO [TE]
TEL. 086157193
www.cerullispinozzi.it

CELLAR SALES
PRE-BOOKED VISITS
ACCOMMODATION AND RESTAURANT SERVICE
ANNUAL PRODUCTION 180,000 bottles
HECTARES UNDER VINE 45.00
VITICULTURE METHOD Certified Organic

The operation's 45 hectares under vine are all managed with certified organic methods. Here, along the River Tronto, whose course is on the border between Abruzzo and the Marche, the terrain by the sea is fertile and sandy, producing rich, concentrated wines. This expert winery interprets the climate with wines that are an interesting fusion of tradition with a modern slant. The single estate guarantees carefully tended grapes for wines in a contemporary, fuss-free style. The range was small in number but big on quality. Sadly there is no sign of the virtuoso we hope to taste sooner or later from this laudable Teramo winery. Torre Migliori 2008 is a classy, powerful, tightly knit Colline Teramane, with fine typical notes of soot and Mediterranean scrubland on the nose. On the palate the fruity attack is followed by alluring tangy acidity. The uncomplicated Montepulciano d'Abruzzo 2012 is also sound.

○ Cortalto '12	♟♟ 2*
● Montepulciano d'Abruzzo '12	♟♟ 2*
● Montepulciano d'Abruzzo Colline Teramane Torre Migliori '08	♟♟ 4
○ Trebbiano d'Abruzzo '12	♟ 2
○ Montepulciano d'Abruzzo Cerasuolo '11	♟♟ 2*
● Montepulciano d'Abruzzo Colline Teramane Torre Migliori '07	♟♟ 4
● Montepulciano d'Abruzzo Colline Teramane Torre Migliori '06	♟♟ 4

Cirelli

LOC. TRECIMINIERE
VIA COLLE SAN GIOVANNI, 1
64032 ATRI [TE]
TEL. 0858700106
www.agricolacirelli.com

CELLAR SALES
PRE-BOOKED VISITS
ACCOMMODATION AND RESTAURANT SERVICE
ANNUAL PRODUCTION 26,000 bottles
HECTARES UNDER VINE 5.00
VITICULTURE METHOD Certified Organic

The enterprise is managed with confidence by two siblings who may be young but have very clear ideas about producing sound, distinctive wines in a natural, traditional style. The estate lies on the lovely hills near Atri, the Teramo district's historic heartland, known for increasingly compelling, interesting wines. The fragrant, approachable entry-level range is affordable and always pleasing. A new line is being produced in amphorae. The five hectares of estate are managed with organic methods and make interesting wines that flank the farm's other crops and produce. The fabulous Montepulciano d'Abruzzo Anfora 2012 has none of the weightiness to which we have been accustomed by some amphora-fermented wines. The nose has the supercharged, pleasantly husky aromas typical of the variety, while the fruity attack rapidly veers towards acidity on the palate. The Cerasuolo of the same line is very enjoyable, with plenty of spirit and fruit, making it a perfect everyday food wine.

● Montepulciano d'Abruzzo Amphora '12	♥♥	5
☉ Montepulciano d'Abruzzo Cerasuolo Amphora '12	♥♥	5
● Montepulciano d'Abruzzo '12	♥♥	2*
☉ Montepulciano d'Abruzzo Cerasuolo '12	♥♥	2*
○ Trebbiano d'Abruzzo '12	♥♥	2*
○ Trebbiano d'Abruzzo Amphora '12	♥	5
● Montepulciano d'Abruzzo '11	♀♀	2*
○ Trebbiano d'Abruzzo '11	♀♀	2*

Citra

C.DA CUCULLO
66026 ORTONA [CH]
TEL. 0859031342
www.citra.it

CELLAR SALES
PRE-BOOKED VISITS
ANNUAL PRODUCTION 18,000,000 bottles
HECTARES UNDER VINE 8,000.00

This second-level cooperative racks up some impressive numbers and aims to reconcile quantity and quality. Its frank wines travel the globe and are a huge success on competitive international markets. Citra is an umbrella for the work of nine wineries dotted around the Chieti area, from the foothills of Mount Majella to the sunny slopes of Ortona, right on the Adriatic Sea. A wide-ranging territory that has always been dedicated to vines that the Ortona-based co-operative interprets in a confident, modern style. This impressive array of wines is characterized by a very modern, well-groomed style. They're all very well made, albeit sometimes rather conventional. Montepulciano Palio 2011 has a typical, edgy nose and prominent fruit on the palate, supported by the grape's varietal acidity and attractive close-knit tannins. The Niro 2011 is a stylish Montepulciano with vintage notes of soot and a juicy palate, despite the oak, while Laus Vitae 2006 is powerful but quite well paced.

● Merlot '12	♥♥	2*
● Montepulciano d'Abruzzo Laus Vitae '06	♥♥	5
● Montepulciano d'Abruzzo Niro '11	♥♥	2*
● Montepulciano d'Abruzzo Palio '11	♥♥	2*
○ Pecorino Palio '12	♥♥	2*
○ Trebbiano d'Abruzzo Citra '12	♥♥	1*
○ Aer '12	♥	2
☉ Montepulciano d'Abruzzo Cerasuolo Palio '06	♥	2
● Montepulciano d'Abruzzo Quis '11	♥	2
○ Moscardello	♥	2
☉ Primae Lucis Brut Rosé	♥	2
● Sangiovese Terre di Chieti '12	♥	1*
○ Trebbiano d'Abruzzo Palio '12	♥	2

Collebello

VIA DEL LAGO, 19
64081 TORTORETO [TE]
TEL. 0861786056
www.collebello.it

CELLAR SALES
PRE-BOOKED VISITS
ANNUAL PRODUCTION 40,000 bottles
HECTARES UNDER VINE 18.00
VITICULTURE METHOD Certified Organic

The unique scenario of the sunny Tortoreto hills, on the Adriatic coast with Gran Sasso behind, is fertile and thriving, perfect for close-knit Mediterranean wines that go the extra mile thanks to old vines recovered with a countryman's care and little interference in the natural fermentation, although the method can be overstated at times. The wines are generally interesting, distinctive and improve year after year. This full profile is well-earned, thanks to wines that bode well for the future. Luì 2010 is a lively organic Montepulciano with a well-typed nose of soot and concentrated, well-paced fruit. The tightly knit, husky palate opens on animal-skin notes before progressing to scrubland and ending with a good tannic weave. The 2011 vintage of the seductive white Mario's 39 is a Trebbiano from old vineyards, with a varietal nose of citrus fruit and grass, and a very tidy, delicate palate despite its terse acidity.

● Montepulciano d'Abruzzo Luì Terraviva '10	♈♈ 2*
○ Ekwo Terraviva '12	♈♈ 2*
○ Trebbiano d'Abruzzo Mario's 39 Terraviva '11	♈♈ 2*
● Solorosso Terraviva '11	♈ 2
○ Declivio '11	♈♈ 2*
● Montepulciano d'Abruzzo Borgo Gaio '07	♈♈ 2*
○ Trebbiano d'Abruzzo Fonte del Lago '11	♈♈ 2*

Collefrisio

LOC. PIANE DI MAGGIO
66030 FRISA [CH]
TEL. 0859039074
www.collefrisio.it

CELLAR SALES
PRE-BOOKED VISITS
HECTARES UNDER VINE 36.00
VITICULTURE METHOD Certified Organic

The winery, on the sunny Ortona hills, has two estates. One looks out over the Adriatic and the other can be found on the Chieti slopes of the Majella foothills, both areas with lengthy winemaking history. Collefrisio is a poised producer of pondered, uncluttered, modern wines with a contemporary feel, very popular with the market. The wines coming out of the smart, cutting-edge Frisa cellars aim to bring tradition and innovation together, and often succeed nicely. The battery we received was varied and quite convincing. Montepulciano Zero 2011 is fresh and edgy, true to type, successfully interpreted without the use of oak. The traditional-style Morreccine 2011 is made from organic montepulciano grapes with long maceration, and displays charming old-fashioned notes of dark fruit and burnt embers. Trebbiano Zero 2012 is well typed and very drinkable, a perfect food wine with impressive tight aromas of wild flowers and citrus fruit.

● Montepulciano d'Abruzzo Zero '11	♈♈ 2*
● Montepulciano d'Abruzzo Morreccine '11	♈♈ 2*
● Montepulciano d'Abruzzo Uno '10	♈♈ 3
○ Pecorino '12	♈♈ 3
○ Trebbiano d'Abruzzo Zero '12	♈♈ 2*
● Montepulciano d'Abruzzo Collefrisio di Collefrisio '09	♈ 5
○ Trebbiano d'Abruzzo Uno '12	♈ 3
● Montepulciano d'Abruzzo Collefrisio di Collefrisio '08	♈♈ 5
○ Trebbiano d'Abruzzo Zero '11	♈♈ 2*

Contesa

c.da Caparrone, 4
65010 Collecorvino [PE]
Tel. 0858205078
www.contesa.it

CELLAR SALES
PRE-BOOKED VISITS
RESTAURANT SERVICE
ANNUAL PRODUCTION 240,000 bottles
HECTARES UNDER VINE 13.00

Rocco Pasetti is an institution on the Abruzzo viticulture horizon, a leading winemaker with endless knowledge of the region and its traditions. His striking Collecorvino winery on the sunny Pescara hills produces quantities of interesting wines that weave a contemporary feel of past and present. The 13-hectare estate rolls seamlessly across the Colle Corvino slopes, overlooking the sea and providing the operation with stunning grapes for a skilful interpretation of persuasive wines that are also a success on international markets. The Pescara winery delivered a text-book performance this year. Its red Montepulciano Riserva 2008 offers very close-focused juicy fruit on the nose and rhythmic progression on the dynamic palate, sustained by typical acidity. The Pecorino 2012, traditionally one of the region's best, also put up an excellent show, with a charming clean, grassy nose and a complex, but already delightful, palate.

● Montepulciano d'Abruzzo Ris. '08	♟♟♟ 3*
● Montepulciano d'Abruzzo Amir Ris. '08	♟♟ 5
☉ Montepulciano d'Abruzzo V. Corvino '12	♟♟ 2*
○ Pecorino '12	♟♟ 3
○ Trebbiano d'Abruzzo '12	♟♟ 2*
● Montepulciano d'Abruzzo Amir '07	♟♟ 3*
☉ Montepulciano d'Abruzzo Cerasuolo '11	♟♟ 2*
● Montepulciano d'Abruzzo V. Corvino '11	♟♟ 2*

Nicoletta De Fermo

65014 Loreto Aprutino [PE]
Tel. 0858289136
www.defermo.it

PRE-BOOKED VISITS
ANNUAL PRODUCTION 10,000 bottles
HECTARES UNDER VINE 17.00
VITICULTURE METHOD Certified Organic

A small operation, in Loreto Aprutino, that quickly managed to scale Guide heights with traditional wines in a marked artisanal style. The winery's 17 hectares under vine are managed with biodynamic methods, a card played close to its chest in the charmed Loreto district. The old vaulted cellar is home to concrete fermentation tanks and some large oak used for ageing when required. The rest is the handiwork of former lawyer turned vigneron, Stefano Papetti, who oversees and tends the limited number of bottles produced with meticulous craftsmanship. This year the estate earned our full profile with an exemplary tasting of a few well-made wines. Prologo 2011 is a charismatic Montepulciano with a nose of soot and close-focused fruit, accompanied by a juicy, supple palate derived from vinification in concrete, which smoothes the variety's roughness. Its tight-knit tannic weave supports good progression. Le Cince is the best Cerasuolo we tasted this year, delicious with food, displaying amazing freshness and notes of wild flowers.

☉ Montepulciano d'Abruzzo Cerasuolo Le Cince '12	♟♟ 4
● Montepulciano d'Abruzzo Prologo '11	♟♟ 5
○ Launegild '12	♟♟ 5
● Montepulciano d'Abruzzo Prologo '10	♟♟ 2*

Filomusi Guelfi

via F. Filomusi Guelfi, 11
65028 Tocco da Casauria [PE]
Tel. 085986908
elleffegi@tiscali.it

CELLAR SALES
PRE-BOOKED VISITS
ANNUAL PRODUCTION 60,000 bottles
HECTARES UNDER VINE 9,60

Lorenzo Filomusi Guelfi's Tocco a Causaria winery goes back a long way in the Abruzzo winegrowing past. Based inland of the region, where the Majella hills are a terroir for taut, stylish wines, this smart, striking operation is as venerable and fascinating as its solid wines. The winery is right in the old town, true to the traditional belief that making wine is a trade like any other, so customers refilled their bottles when they did the rest of their errands. This year the selection is limited but quality is very high. The Fonte Dei 2007 is the usual appealing Montepulciano with charming old-style contrasts. On the nose it offers typical notes of burnt embers and good rugged fruit, while the dynamic palate is full-flavoured, approachable and mature. Thumbs up for the Montepulciano 2010, a racy varietal red with lots of character and elegance.

Cantina Frentana

via Perazza, 32
66020 Rocca San Giovanni [CH]
Tel. 087260152
www.cantinafrentana.it

CELLAR SALES
PRE-BOOKED VISITS
ACCOMMODATION
ANNUAL PRODUCTION 650,000 bottles
HECTARES UNDER VINE 22.00
VITICULTURE METHOD Certified Organic

Cantina Frentana, like many large co-operative wineries, has had a landslide success on international markets thanks to the competitive prices of its wines. Here, on the Costa dei Trabocchi, a slice of hills overlooking the sea on the fragment of the Abruzzo coast that leads down to Molise, the area has always crafted muscular wines, moulded by sunlight and a rich, calcareous soil. A significant district, subject to meticulous zoning and selection of the top winery vines, with individual fermentation, to achieve a successful battery of unfailingly interesting labels at amazing value for money. The wines presented were only slightly less dazzling than last year. Panarda 2010 is the usual rich, delicious Montepulciano. Its powerful, tightly knit palate has a fruity attack followed by good acidity, and is marred only by a slightly bitterish finish. Pecorino 2012 is well made and exuberant.

● Montepulciano d'Abruzzo '10	▼▼ 2*
● Montepulciano d'Abruzzo Fonte Dei '07	▼▼ 5
○ Le Scuderie del Cielo '12	▼▼ 2*
● Montepulciano d'Abruzzo Ris. '07	▼▼ 2*
○ Casa Scamolla '11	▼ 2
⊙ Montepulciano d'Abruzzo Cerasuolo '08	▼ 2
○ Le Scuderie del Cielo '11	♈ 2*
● Montepulciano d'Abruzzo '08	♈ 2*
● Montepulciano d'Abruzzo Ris. '06	♈ 2*

○ Cococciola Costa del Mulino '12	▼▼ 1*
○ Donna Greta '11	▼▼ 2*
● Montepulciano d'Abruzzo Panarda '10	▼▼ 2*
● Montepulciano d'Abruzzo Rubesto '11	▼▼ 2*
○ Passerina Costa del Mulino '12	▼▼ 1*
○ Pecorino '12	▼▼ 2*
● Montepulciano d'Abruzzo '11	▼ 2
○ Donna Greta '10	♈ 3*
⊙ Montepulciano d'Abruzzo Cerasuolo Colle del Mulino '11	♈ 1*
● Montepulciano d'Abruzzo Rubesto '10	♈ 2*

Gentile

VIA DEL GIARDINO, 7
67025 OFENA [AQ]
TEL. 0862956618
www.gentilevini.it

CELLAR SALES
PRE-BOOKED VISITS
ANNUAL PRODUCTION 90,000 bottles
HECTARES UNDER VINE 12.00

Inland Abruzzo is experiencing a revival, the rediscovery of a fascinating area that infuses its wines with heady aromas. Gentile is a small artisan winery based in Ofena, located on a plateau encircled by mountains and where the Calderone glacier, with its perpetual snow, sits right opposite. During the day the sun beats down on the vines while night-time mountain breezes push the thermometer down to create temperature ranges that chisel flavour and acidity, for a battery of persuasive, accomplished wines. The Trebbiano 2012 Vigne di Ofena is a delicious white with varietal wild flowers and hazelnut aromas, on a spirited, tangy palate, with good stuffing and a captivating, bitterish hint of mountain herbs. Montepulciano 2011 convinces with the typical, boisterous aromas of a fresh, dynamic, high-altitude red, with sound, rustic progression.

○ Trebbiano d'Abruzzo V. di Ofena '12	♥♥	2*
● Montepulciano d'Abruzzo V. di Ofena '11	♥♥	4
● Pecorino Vigne di Ofena '11	♥♥	2*
⊙ Vigne di Ofena Rosato '12	♥♥	2*
● Montepulciano d'Abruzzo V. V. Ris. '10	♥	4
○ Pecorino Vigne di Ofelia '11	♥♥	2*
○ Trebbiano d'Abruzzo V. di Ofena '11	♥♥	2*

★Dino Illuminati

C.DA SAN BIAGIO, 18
64010 CONTROGUERRA [TE]
TEL. 0861808008
www.illuminativini.it

CELLAR SALES
PRE-BOOKED VISITS
ANNUAL PRODUCTION 1,100,000 bottles
HECTARES UNDER VINE 130.00

A venerable Abruzzo winery that dates back to the 1800s, as is proudly declared on its labels, and which has made its mark on the history of Teramo's competitive world of wine. The style is classic, handed down over the generations, with mighty Mediterranean wines whose main aim is to interpret the terroir, crafted from the landscape and human tradition. From rich, close-knit Montepulciano crus to drinkable everyday reds and simpler whites, the battery excels every year in a classic, competent rendering of the region's vines. A prestige tasting this year for the Teramo winery, although there was no Zanna and the Riparosso and Pieluni did not quite make up for that. The first is the best entry-level Montepulciano 2012 we tasted this year, typical and spirited, sustained by amazing grip. The Pieluni is a solid, Mediterranean-style Colline Teramane Riserva 2008 with pleasant citrus notes.

● Montepulciano d'Abruzzo Colline Teramane Pieluni Ris. '08	♥♥	6
● Montepulciano d'Abruzzo Riparosso '12	♥♥	2*
○ Controguerra Pecorino '12	♥♥	2*
○ Illuminati Brut '07	♥♥	4
⊙ Montepulciano d'Abruzzo Cerasuolo Campirosa '12	♥♥	2*
● Montepulciano d'Abruzzo Ilico '11	♥♥	2*
● Montepulciano d'Abruzzo Spiano '12	♥♥	2*
○ Controguerra Bianco Pligia '12	♥	2
○ Controguerra Passerina '12	♥	2
● Montepulciano d'Abruzzo Colline Teramane Pieluni Ris. '07	♥♥♥	6
● Montepulciano d'Abruzzo Colline Teramane Zanna Ris. '08	♥♥♥	4*
● Montepulciano d'Abruzzo Colline Teramane Zanna Ris. '07	♥♥♥	5

★★Masciarelli

VIA GAMBERALE, 1
66010 SAN MARTINO SULLA MARRUCINA [CH]
TEL. 087185241
www.masciarelli.it

CELLAR SALES
PRE-BOOKED VISITS
ACCOMMODATION
ANNUAL PRODUCTION 2,500,000 bottles
HECTARES UNDER VINE 420.00

The 400 hectares under vine are located in all four of the Abruzzo provinces, a truly remarkable selection of environment, soil and climate for vineyards that start at the Adriatic Sea and reach the slopes of Gran Sasso. This lavish setting brings forth the wines we are accustomed to receiving from this winery: rich, powerful, meticulous, in a stimulating fusion of territory and innovation. A battery of labels that has marked a revival of memorable Abruzzo wines on world markets. From the delicious, affordable entry-level wines, produced in large quantities, to the high-flying crus with their unwavering quality, Masciarelli style is a given. Another Tre Bicchieri goes to the classic Montepulciano Marina Cvetic 2010, a great wine with high production figures. The nose is bursting with close-focused notes of fruit and Mediterranean herbs, and is accompanied by a pleasant, tidy, well-defined palate. La Botte di Gianni is a sound, varietal 2010 Trebbiano, which is still very young.

● Montepulciano d'Abruzzo Marina Cvetic '10	♛♛♛ 4*
○ Chardonnay Marina Cvetic '11	♛♛ 5
○ Trebbiano d'Abruzzo La Botte di Gianni Ris. '10	♛♛ 5
○ Trebbiano d'Abruzzo Marina Cvetic Ris. '11	♛♛ 5
● Castello di Semivicoli '11	♛♛ 3
● Merlot Marina Cvetic '10	♛♛ 4
● Montepulciano d'Abruzzo '11	♛♛ 2*
⊙ Montepulciano d'Abruzzo Cerasuolo Villa Gemma '12	♛♛ 2*
○ Trebbiano d'Abruzzo '12	♛♛ 2*
○ Villa Gemma Bianco '12	♛ 2
● Montepulciano d'Abruzzo Villa Gemma '06	♛♛♛ 7
○ Trebbiano d'Abruzzo Marina Cvetic '10	♛♛♛ 5
○ Trebbiano d'Abruzzo Marina Cvetic '09	♛♛♛ 5

Camillo Montori

LOC. PIANE TRONTO, 80
64010 CONTROGUERRA [TE]
TEL. 0861809900
www.montorivini.it

CELLAR SALES
PRE-BOOKED VISITS
ACCOMMODATION AND RESTAURANT SERVICE
ANNUAL PRODUCTION 600,000 bottles
HECTARES UNDER VINE 50.00

The historic Notaresco winery is located deep in the Colline Teramane, where Camillo Montori and Illuminati laid the foundations for the designation, convinced of the unique features of an area whose hills overlook the Adriatic Sea, with Gran Sasso at their back. Grapes come from over 50 hectares of vineyards on the Abruzzo border with the Marche, managed with traditional tenacity, long macerations and large oak. The solid, well-typed wines often cellar very well and the battery is always appealing for its classic, winning style. The popular base lines flank a native Pecorino that Montori was one of the first to replant, and mighty Colline Teramane reds. This year's tasting was good, confirming some great classic wines. Pecorino 2012 is a top-notch white, with a well-typed Mediterranean nose of scrubland and bitter oranges, and a fresh, supple palate that will improve with age, shaping the mineral profile that can already be glimpsed. The classic Trebbiano Fonte Cupa 2012 is also very good.

○ Pecorino Fonte Cupa '12	♛♛ 3*
○ Trebbiano d'Abruzzo Fonte Cupa '12	♛♛ 2*
● Montepulciano d'Abruzzo Colline Teramane '09	♛♛ 2*
⊙ Montepulciano d'Abruzzo Cerasuolo Fonte Cupa '12	♛ 2
○ Trend '12	♛ 2
○ Colli Aprutini Pecorino Trend '11	♛♛ 2*
⊙ Montepulciano d'Abruzzo Cerasuolo Fonte Cupa '10	♛♛ 2*
● Montepulciano d'Abruzzo Fonte Cupa '07	♛♛ 2*
● Montepulciano d'Abruzzo Fonte Cupa '06	♛♛ 3
○ Pecorino Fonte Cupa '11	♛♛ 3*
○ Trebbiano d'Abruzzo Fonte Cupa '11	♛♛ 2*

Bruno Nicodemi

C.DA VENIGLIO
64024 NOTARESCO [TE]
TEL. 085895493
www.nicodemi.com

CELLAR SALES
PRE-BOOKED VISITS
ANNUAL PRODUCTION 250,000 bottles
HECTARES UNDER VINE 30.00

An artisanal winery that has always been a leader in the competitive Colline Teramane wine world, located in classic wine country on the sunny Notaresco plain. The 30 hectares of estate under vine produce grapes that are tended with passion by Elena and Alessandro, the winery's second generation. Their recipe has been perfected over the years and has never changed, preferring traditional cultivation methods and cellar techniques that combine the past with the present. The rich, muscular wines are typically Mediterranean in style and the range is always persuasive, from the incisive base lines to the aspirational Colline Teramane DOCs. This year saw a range of classy wines. The Neromoro 2009 had no trouble earning a Tre Bicchieri, with its distinctive spicy, Mediterranean aromas, and nicely controlled body sustained by acidity and hints of scrubland. The rhythmic 2012 Notàri Trebbiano balances complexity and herbaceous freshness very well.

● Montepulciano d'Abruzzo	
Colline Teramane Neromoro Ris. '09	♆♆♆ 5
● Montepulciano d'Abruzzo	
Colline Teramane Notàri '10	♆♆ 3*
● Montepulciano d'Abruzzo '11	♆♆ 2*
○ Trebbiano d'Abruzzo '12	♆♆ 2*
○ Trebbiano d'Abruzzo Notàri '12	♆♆ 2*
⊙ Montepulciano d'Abruzzo Cerasuolo '12	♆ 4
● Montepulciano d'Abruzzo	
Colline Teramane Neromoro Ris. '08	♈♈ 5
● Montepulciano d'Abruzzo	
Colline Teramane Neromoro Ris. '07	♈♈ 5
● Montepulciano d'Abruzzo	
Colline Teramane Notàri '09	♈♈ 3*
● Montepulciano d'Abruzzo	
Colline Teramane Notàri '08	♈♈ 3
○ Trebbiano d'Abruzzo Notàri '10	♈♈ 2*

Pasetti

LOC. C.DA PRETARO
VIA SAN PAOLO, 21
66023 FRANCAVILLA AL MARE [CH]
TEL. 08561875
www.pasettivini.it

CELLAR SALES
PRE-BOOKED VISITS
ACCOMMODATION AND RESTAURANT SERVICE
ANNUAL PRODUCTION 600,000 bottles
HECTARES UNDER VINE 65.00

Pasetti is the private winery that has been most successful on the Abruzzo wine scene in reconciling quantity and quality. Their wines are popular while keeping faith with the territory and its typical style. The operation owns two mountain estates, with the original site at Pescosansonesco, on Majella's Pescara slopes, and the newly- acquired Capestrano unit, in L'Aquila, at the foot of Gran Sasso. The prized grapes are processed with true modern grit and contemporary style in the historic cellars at Francavilla al Mare. The wines are enjoyable and well made, from the fresh natives to the challenging Montepulciano crus. This admirable Chieti winery was slightly lacklustre this year. The classic Montepulciano 2010 has very ripe, warm fruit on the nose, but also dense, powerful body nicely controlled and refreshed by typical acidity. Vigne Capestrano 2012 is an aromatic Cerasuolo with hints of berry fruits, shaped by altitude and climate.

○ Gesmino '10	♆♆ 4
● Montepulciano d'Abruzzo '10	♆♆ 2*
⊙ Montepulciano d'Abruzzo Cerasuolo	
V. Capestrano '12	♆♆ 2*
○ Testarossa Bianco '11	♆♆ 4
○ Trebbiano d'Abruzzo Zarachè '12	♆♆ 2*
● Montepulciano d'Abruzzo	
Testarossa Rosso '09	♆ 4
○ Pecorino '12	♆ 2
⊙ Montepulciano d'Abruzzo Cerasuolo V.	
Capestrano '11	♈♈ 2*
● Montepulciano d'Abruzzo Pasetti '09	♈♈ 2*
● Montepulciano d'Abruzzo Testarossa '08	♈♈ 4

Emidio Pepe

VIA CHIESI, 10
64010 TORANO NUOVO [TE]
TEL. 0861856493
www.emidiopepe.com

CELLAR SALES
PRE-BOOKED VISITS
ACCOMMODATION AND RESTAURANT SERVICE
ANNUAL PRODUCTION 80,000 bottles
HECTARES UNDER VINE 15.00
VITICULTURE METHOD Certified Biodynamic

Few wineries have left their mark on Abruzzo viticulture like Pepe, whose well-typed, familiar wines with their distinctive artisanal style, were made famous 50 years ago by the author Mario Soldati. Since then, little or nothing has changed at this lovely Torano estate. The generations pass on but the approach to the 15 hectares of vineyards is always the same. It was inevitable that the most natural, least invasive style of management would lead to biodynamic methods, while the cellar prefers concrete fermentation tanks. The wines produced are unusual, individual and juicy, with a typical, rustic taste. The battery was limited but persuasive. The Montepulciano 2010 is gutsy and typical, with rustic aromas and a supple, juicy palate with notes of sage that develop into vibrant fruit, while the 2011 Trebbiano is attractively fuzzy with a pleasant, lively palate.

● Montepulciano d'Abruzzo '10	♟♟	6
○ Trebbiano d'Abruzzo '11	♟♟	5
○ Montepulciano d'Abruzzo Cerasuolo '12	♟♟	5
● Montepulciano d'Abruzzo '98	♟♟♟	8
● Montepulciano d'Abruzzo '09	♟♟	5
● Montepulciano d'Abruzzo '08	♟♟	5
○ Trebbiano d'Abruzzo '10	♟♟	6
○ Trebbiano d'Abruzzo '09	♟♟	5

Pietrantonj

VIA SAN SEBASTIANO, 38
67030 VITTORITO [AQ]
TEL. 0864727102
www.vinipietrantonj.it

CELLAR SALES
PRE-BOOKED VISITS
ANNUAL PRODUCTION 650,000 bottles
HECTARES UNDER VINE 60.00

Vittorito, in deepest Abruzzo, is on the slopes of Mount Majella, a tough area for winegrowing, with its temperature variations and mountainous terrain. Here the classic cellar style interprets typical, solid wines, some pleasantly rustic, but with a consistently incisive, slim-bodied acid profile conferred by the territory itself. Time seems to stand still in this beautiful, ancient L'Aquila winery, and despite the effects of the recent earthquake, it is business as usual for making wines with a strong traditional impact. Cerano 2009 is a Montepulciano with a spirited, edgy nose of smoky, fruity notes and a dynamic, tightly knit palate sustained by the taut, invigorating acidity that drives it. Cerasuolo Cerano 2012 has always been one of the region's best, with strawberries and medicinal herbs on the nose and a lively, juicy palate, making it a perfect food rosé.

● Montepulciano d'Abruzzo Cerano Ris. '09	♟♟	3*
⊙ Montepulciano d'Abruzzo Sup. Cerasuolo Cerano '12	♟♟	3*
● Montepulciano d'Abruzzo Cerano '10	♟♟	2*
⊙ Montepulciano d'Abruzzo Cerasuolo Arboreo '12	♟♟	2*
⊙ Montepulciano d'Abruzzo Cerasuolo Sup. Cerano '11	♟♟	3
● Passito Rosso Valle Peligna '09	♟♟	4

San Lorenzo

c.da Plavignano, 2
64035 Castilenti [TE]
Tel. 0861999325
www.sanlorenzovini.com

CELLAR SALES
PRE-BOOKED VISITS
ANNUAL PRODUCTION 800,000 bottles
HECTARES UNDER VINE 150.00
VITICULTURE METHOD Certified Biodynamic

A superb, large-scale winery on the border between the provinces of Teramo and Pescara, which combines a modern style with ambitious quality standards. The 150-hectare Castilenti estate makes truly rich, weighty wines, often tamed thanks to some contemporary winemaking techniques to meet the preferences of international markets. San Lorenzo wines, whether classic Abruzzo natives, international varieties or lush Montepulciano crus, are always an explosion of Mediterranean richness and pleasure. The wines did not disappoint and tasting was a pleasure. Although a star has yet to emerge, we believe it to be a matter of time. The Casabianca spontaneous fermentation line is very interesting, with fresh, pleasant food wines, in a deliberately low-key natural style. Oinos is its usual powerful self and this 2010 vintage has the additional appeal of edgy, well-defined fruit.

● Montepulciano d'Abruzzo Casabianca '11	♀♀ 2*
● Montepulciano d'Abruzzo Colline Teramane Oinos '10	♀♀ 4
○ Trebbiano d'Abruzzo Casabianca '12	♀♀ 2*
● Montepulciano d'Abruzzo Colline Teramane Escol Ris. '09	♀♀ 4
● Montepulciano d'Abruzzo Sirio '12	♀♀ 1*
○ Pecorino '12	♀♀ 2*
○ Trebbiano d'Abruzzo Sirio '12	♀♀ 1*
○ Trebbiano d'Abruzzo Zerosolfiti '12	♀♀ 3
● Montepulciano d'Abruzzo Antares '10	♀♀ 2*
● Montepulciano d'Abruzzo Colline Teramane Escol Ris. '08	♀♀ 4
● Montepulciano d'Abruzzo Colline Teramane Oinos '09	♀♀ 4

Nicola Santoleri

via dei Cavalieri, 20
66016 Guardiagrele [CH]
Tel. 0871893301
www.nicolasantoleri.it

ANNUAL PRODUCTION 40,000 bottles
HECTARES UNDER VINE 30.00

The name Santoleri has always been linked with viticulture in Abruzzo and the Guardiagrele winery pursues the commitment to tradition of its founder, Nicola. The 30 hectares of property on the Chieti hills, at the foot of Majella, are managed with a countryman's resolve and produce stunning fruit that this second generation of vignerons process with artisanal care and attention, preferring long maceration, large oak, and little interference, sustaining nature's own slow work. The finishing touch is long bottle ageing for the ultra-classic wines we like so much. The range is small but highly convincing. Vigna Ladra is always a linear, easy-drinking Montepulciano but the 2011 vintage is a cut above, with a pervasive nose of cherries and herbs, and a gutsy palate showing fresh acidity and well-paced tanginess. The classic Trebbiano Crognaleto 2012 is also very good, with a supple palate and fine rustic notes of grass and citrus fruit, making it a perfect, food-friendly white.

● Montepulciano d'Abruzzo V. Ladra '11	♀♀ 2*
⊙ Montepulciano d'Abruzzo Cerasuolo Crognaleto '12	♀♀ 2*
○ Trebbiano d'Abruzzo Crognaleto '12	♀♀ 2*
⊙ Montepulciano d'Abruzzo Cerasuolo Crognaleto '11	♀♀ 2*
⊙ Montepulciano d'Abruzzo Cerasuolo Crognaleto '10	♀♀ 2*
● Montepulciano d'Abruzzo Crognaleto '06	♀♀ 2*
● Montepulciano d'Abruzzo Crognaleto '04	♀♀ 2*
● Montepulciano d'Abruzzo V. Ladra '08	♀♀ 2*
● Montepulciano d'Abruzzo V. Ladra '07	♀♀ 2*
○ Trebbiano d'Abruzzo Crognaleto '11	♀♀ 2*

Strappelli

LOC. TORRI, 15
64010 TORANO NUOVO [TE]
TEL. 0861887402
www.cantinastrappelli.it

CELLAR SALES
PRE-BOOKED VISITS
ANNUAL PRODUCTION 60,000 bottles
HECTARES UNDER VINE 10.00
VITICULTURE METHOD Certified Organic

The ten hectares, managed with certified organic methods, are tended with traditional rural determination. Strappelli and the lovely Villa Torri estate wedged between the Adriatic Sea and the Gran Sasso, are now firmly established as one of the most interesting wineries in the competitive Colline Teramane DOC zone. The method is always one of long maceration, large oak and minimum winemaking interference for wines of discernible traditional flavour and lots of character, defying time as they age gracefully. Colle Trà Cerasuolo 2012 is a food rosé with a varietal, organic, sanguine nose that is accompanied by a dynamic, juicy palate of lively, racy fruit and Mediterranean scrubland with a swathe of fresh marine notes. The 2011 Montepulciano is dense and powerful, with a nose of exuberant red berries and a well-typed supple palate that is still very close knit and will open up with age.

⊙ Montepulciano d'Abruzzo Cerasuolo Colle Trà Sup. '12	🍷🍷 2*
● Montepulciano d'Abruzzo '11	🍷🍷 2*
⊙ Montepulciano d'Abruzzo Cerasuolo '12	🍷🍷 2*
○ Pecorino Soprano '12	🍷🍷 2*
○ Trebbiano d'Abruzzo '12	🍷🍷 2*
● Montepulciano d'Abruzzo '08	🍷🍷 2*
● Montepulciano d'Abruzzo '07	🍷🍷 2*
⊙ Montepulciano d'Abruzzo Cerasuolo '11	🍷🍷 2*
⊙ Montepulciano d'Abruzzo Cerasuolo '10	🍷🍷 2*
● Montepulciano d'Abruzzo Colline Teramane Celibe Ris. '07	🍷🍷 5
● Montepulciano d'Abruzzo Colline Teramane Colle Trà '07	🍷🍷 3*
○ Pecorino Soprano '11	🍷🍷 2*
○ Trebbiano d'Abruzzo '11	🍷🍷 2*

Tiberio

C.DA LA VOTA
65020 CUGNOLI [PE]
TEL. 0858576744
www.tiberio.it

CELLAR SALES
PRE-BOOKED VISITS
ANNUAL PRODUCTION 90,000 bottles
HECTARES UNDER VINE 30.00

This new Cugnoli winery leaves us in no doubt that it is now a fully-fledged operation. The 30 hectares of vineyards form a single estate and are tended with a countryman's care and contemporary enthusiasm, set against the stunning backdrop of the Pescara hills, wedged between Majella and Gran Sasso, cooled by breezes that come both from the mountains and the sea. Hence the superb wines that show no fear of acidity, indeed they store it up and make it their trump card. Every wine is worthy of note, from scented native whites to spirited Montepulcianos. The talented Cristiana Tiberio has deployed a truly remarkable range this year. Her 2012 Pecorino is stellar, with the vintage providing richer body. Although the nose has the usual notes of medicinal herbs and bitter orange, the palate already shows amazing mineral complexity. Fonte Canale 2012 is a spontaneously fermented Trebbiano, whose production method ensures complexity and rhythm.

○ Pecorino '12	🍷🍷🍷 3*
○ Trebbiano d'Abruzzo Fonte Canale '12	🍷🍷 2*
● Montepulciano d'Abruzzo '11	🍷🍷 2*
⊙ Montepulciano d'Abruzzo Cerasuolo '12	🍷🍷 2*
○ Trebbiano d'Abruzzo '12	🍷🍷 2*
○ Pecorino '11	🍷🍷🍷 3*
○ Pecorino '10	🍷🍷🍷 3
● Montepulciano d'Abruzzo '10	🍷🍷 2*
● Montepulciano d'Abruzzo Althea '09	🍷🍷 4
● Montepulciano d'Abruzzo Althea '08	🍷🍷 4
⊙ Montepulciano d'Abruzzo Cerasuolo '10	🍷🍷 2
○ Trebbiano d'Abruzzo '11	🍷🍷 2*
○ Trebbiano d'Abruzzo '10	🍷🍷 2
○ Trebbiano d'Abruzzo Fonte Canale '11	🍷🍷 2*

Cantina Tollo

VIA GARIBALDI, 68
66010 TOLLO [CH]
TEL. 087196251
www.cantinatollo.it

CELLAR SALES
PRE-BOOKED VISITS
ANNUAL PRODUCTION 11,000,000 bottles
HECTARES UNDER VINE 3,200.00
VITICULTURE METHOD Certified Organic

This co-operative, on the Chieti hills between the Adriatic and Majella, wrote a chapter in Abruzzo viticulture history. Its numerous growers, 3,500 hectares under vine and 11,000,000 bottles produced come from some venerable wine country. These figures underpin an extensive battery of impressive wines for quantity and quality, with a striking compromise of tradition and modern winemaking techniques that makes an unfussy, respectable product. From simple everyday Montepulcianos to some aspirational crus, the Tollo style is well-made, well-typed wines that can also satisfy an international palate. C'Incanta really did enchant us. It's a traditional, old-school Trebbiano that easily earned a Tre Bicchieri with its expansive, organic nose, which is pleasantly rustic and accompanies the taut, zesty, thoroughly enjoyable palate. The Cagiòlo is what we expect from an elegant, complex, dense Montepulciano.

○ Trebbiano d'Abruzzo C'Incanta '10	♔♔♔	4*
● Montepulciano d'Abruzzo Cagiòlo Ris. '10	♔♔	4
● Montepulciano d'Abruzzo Aldiano Ris. '09	♔♔	3
● Montepulciano d'Abruzzo Colle Secco Ris. '09	♔♔	2*
● Montepulciano d'Abruzzo Rubì '09	♔♔	2*
○ Trebbiano d'Abruzzo Biologico '12	♔♔	2*
○ Trebbiano d'Abruzzo Senza Solfiti '12	♔♔	3
○ Abruzzo Cococciola '12	♔	2
○ Pecorino '12	♔	3
○ Trebbiano d'Abruzzo Aldiano '12	♔	2
● Montepulciano d'Abruzzo Cagiòlo Ris. '09	♔♔♔	4*
● Montepulciano d'Abruzzo Cagiòlo Ris. '08	♔♔	4

Torre dei Beati

C.DA POGGIORAGONE, 56
65014 LORETO APRUTINO [PE]
TEL. 0854916069
www.torredeibeati.it

CELLAR SALES
PRE-BOOKED VISITS
ANNUAL PRODUCTION 100,000 bottles
HECTARES UNDER VINE 18.00
VITICULTURE METHOD Certified Organic

Adriana Galasso and Fausto Albanese are life and work partners who manage their winery with drive and passion. They have fast become one of the most interesting operations on the Abruzzo winemaking scene with a winning recipe of certified organic vineyard management, native grapes only, and a light, respectful touch in the cellar for true artisanal wines. The terroir also plays a role since noble Loreto, stretched across the Pescara hills, is traditionally a land of great wines. The battery of labels presented each year is always impressive for some well-typed, distinctive wines. Cocciapazza 2010 is a classic old-school Montepulciano with an alluring nose of soot and topsoil, accompanied by lively, well-defined fruit. On the palate it is very young, showing unfettered and full flavoured, already very good and on its way to amazing. Mazzamurello is the winery's second cru, generally with more intervention in the cellar. This 2010 version has ultra-pleasant contrasts of Mediterranean scrubland and grass.

● Montepulciano d'Abruzzo Cocciapazza '10	♔♔♔	4*
● Montepulciano d'Abruzzo Mazzamurello '10	♔♔	5
● Montepulciano d'Abruzzo '11	♔♔	2*
☉ Montepulciano d'Abruzzo Cerasuolo Rosa-ae '12	♔♔	2*
○ Pecorino Giocheremo con i Fiori '12	♔♔	3
● Montepulciano d'Abruzzo Cocciapazza '09	♔♔♔	4*
● Montepulciano d'Abruzzo Mazzamurello '09	♔♔	5
○ Pecorino Giocheremo con i Fiori '11	♔♔	3*

Tenuta Ulisse

VIA SAN POLO, 40
66014 CRECCHIO [CH]
TEL. 0871407733
www.tenutaulisse.it

CELLAR SALES
PRE-BOOKED VISITS
ANNUAL PRODUCTION 470,000 bottles
HECTARES UNDER VINE 60.00

This young winery, run by three generations of the stalwart Ulisse family, has come of age. The location is Crecchio, in the Ortona area of the Chieti hills, and the 60 hectares under vine spread across a rich, varied district. Ulisse manages both the sturdy vines near the sea and those climbing towards Mount Majella at higher altitude, in the same traditional rustic style to achieve a raw material rich in fragrance preserved through reductive winemaking. This synthesis of past and present obtains interesting, fresh, pleasant wines. Nativae is a well-defined Montepulciano with exuberant varietal notes of burnt embers and red berries, sustained by fresh acidity. It vaunts a very pleasant, close-knit tannic weave. The wine fast-tracked to a Tre Bicchieri thanks to the rhythmic, lively tone derived from spontaneous fermentation. Pecorino Unico 2012 is confirmed as one of the most interesting in the region.

● Montepulciano d'Abruzzo Nativae '12	♚♚♚ 4*
○ Trebbiano d'Abruzzo Nativae '12	♚♚ 4
○ Cococciola Unico '12	♚♚ 3
● Montepulciano d'Abruzzo Amaranta '11	♚♚ 4
● Montepulciano d'Abruzzo Sogno di Ulisse '11	♚♚ 2*
○ Pecorino Brut Unico	♚♚ 3
○ Pecorino Unico '12	♚♚ 3
○ Trebbiano d'Abruzzo Unico '12	♚♚ 3
○ Chardonnay Unico '12	♚ 3
○ Pecorino Amaranta '12	♚ 4
● Montepulciano d'Abruzzo Amaranta '10	♛♛ 4
● Montepulciano d'Abruzzo Cerasuolo Unico '11	♛♛ 3
● Montepulciano d'Abruzzo Unico '10	♛♛ 3
○ Pecorino Unico '11	♛♛ 3

La Valentina

VIA TORRETTA, 52
65010 SPOLTORE [PE]
TEL. 0854478158
www.fattorialavalentina.it

CELLAR SALES
PRE-BOOKED VISITS
ANNUAL PRODUCTION 350,000 bottles
HECTARES UNDER VINE 40.00

A stellar Abruzzo winemaking concern, with 40 hectares under vine, this winery operates from two superb but quite different sites. The main unit is in Spoltore, on Pescara's sunlit hills between the Adriatic and Majella; the other perches on the Pescara side of Majella at San Valentino. The different climates produce a fruit of rich, aromatic complexity, which la Valentina interprets in a fragrant, recognizable style, expressing the interaction of past and present. The battery of wines is interesting and always up to par, with a special mention for the amazing base range of great, very affordable bottles. The wonderful tasting revealed convincing, fascinating wines. Spelt 2012 is a richly extracted, full-bodied Montepulciano with a Mediterranean nose and savoury marine notes that ensure rhythmic progression. The uncomplicated Montepulciano 2011 is a big red at a small price that had no trouble reaching the finals with its complex, stylish balsamic aromas, and the Binomio 2009 is simply the best so far.

● Montepulciano d'Abruzzo '11	♚♚ 2*
● Montepulciano d'Abruzzo Binomio '09	♚♚ 5
⊙ Montepulciano d'Abruzzo Cerasuolo Spelt '12	♚♚ 3*
● Montepulciano d'Abruzzo Spelt '09	♚♚ 3*
○ Bianco Fiano '12	♚♚ 3
● Montepulciano d'Abruzzo Bellovedere '08	♚♚ 6
⊙ Montepulciano d'Abruzzo Cerasuolo '12	♚♚ 2*
○ Trebbiano d'Abruzzo '12	♚♚ 2*
○ Trebbiano d'Abruzzo Sup. Spelt '12	♚♚ 3
○ Pecorino '12	♚ 2
● Montepulciano d'Abruzzo Bellovedere '05	♛♛♛ 6
● Montepulciano d'Abruzzo Spelt '08	♛♛♛ 3*
● Montepulciano d'Abruzzo Spelt '07	♛♛♛ 3
● Montepulciano d'Abruzzo Spelt '05	♛♛♛ 3

★★Valentini

VIA DEL BAIO, 2
65014 LORETO APRUTINO [PE]
TEL. 0858291138

ANNUAL PRODUCTION 30,000 bottles
HECTARES UNDER VINE 60.00

Valentini wines keep faith to their
traditional charisma and amazing talent for
ageing. For years Francesco Paolo has
battled to defend artisanal wines made
with characteristic, time-honoured care
and age-old winemaking techniques,
brought up to date by contemporary
know-how and expertise. Loreto Aprutino,
in the heart of the Pescara hills, is a land
of vines and olive trees. The winery's 60
hectares of Abruzzo-style pergola produce
only 30,000 bottles over and above the
bulk wine that is a legend in itself. The
cellar houses only the largest oak and
bottle ageing is lengthy to ensure quite
exquisite results. Trebbiano 2011 is very
good, already delicious, available and
highly drinkable, while we wait for the
2010 to bottle age, in the winery's familiar
unique style. The nose has grassy notes of
wild flowers, and the juicy palate is
accessible and very well paced. The
Cerasuolo 2012 is still young but already a
convincing food wine.

○ Trebbiano d'Abruzzo '11	▼▼▼ 6
⊙ Montepulciano d'Abruzzo Cerasuolo '12	▼▼ 6
● Montepulciano d'Abruzzo '06	♀♀♀ 8
● Montepulciano d'Abruzzo '02	♀♀♀ 8
● Montepulciano d'Abruzzo '01	♀♀♀ 8
⊙ Montepulciano d'Abruzzo Cerasuolo '09	♀♀♀ 6
⊙ Montepulciano d'Abruzzo Cerasuolo '08	♀♀♀ 6
⊙ Montepulciano d'Abruzzo Cerasuolo '06	♀♀♀ 6
○ Trebbiano d'Abruzzo '09	♀♀♀ 6
○ Trebbiano d'Abruzzo '08	♀♀♀ 6
○ Trebbiano d'Abruzzo '07	♀♀♀ 6
○ Trebbiano d'Abruzzo '05	♀♀♀ 6
○ Trebbiano d'Abruzzo '04	♀♀♀ 6
○ Trebbiano d'Abruzzo '02	♀♀♀ 6

Valle Reale

LOC. SAN CALISTO
65026 POPOLI [PE]
TEL. 0859871039
www.vallereale.it

CELLAR SALES
PRE-BOOKED VISITS
ANNUAL PRODUCTION 300,000 bottles
HECTARES UNDER VINE 49.00
VITICULTURE METHOD Certified Organic

The Pescara hills, at the point where they
become the mountains of the Majella range
ascending to the perennial Blockhaus
snows, are a piece of unsullied inland
Abruzzo and home to Valle Reale. There are
almost 50 hectares of vineyards in two
estates, one around the winery in Popoli,
the other nearby, on the Capestrano
plateau in the province of L'Aquila.
Mountain viticulture is forged by the climate
and the territory, and the elegant wines
have distinctive aromas, derived from
house preferences for certified organic
vineyard management , with spontaneous
fermentation doing the rest in an artisanal
approach applied with a modern touch.
This year's brilliant tasting saw the
Trebbiano Vigne di Capestrano 2011
confirm a Tre Bicchieri with its boisterous
nose of gentian and toasted hazelnut,
followed by a complex, layered palate that
will improve further with age. The San
Calisto is the usual stylish Montepulciano
whose spontaneous fermentation gives it
an edge.

○ Trebbiano d'Abruzzo V. di Capestrano '11	▼▼▼ 5
● Montepulciano d'Abruzzo San Calisto '10	▼▼ 5
● Montepulciano d'Abruzzo Sant'Eusanio '12	▼▼ 3*
● Montepulciano d'Abruzzo Vign. di Popoli '11	▼▼ 3*
● Montepulciano d'Abruzzo '11	▼▼ 2*
⊙ Montepulciano d'Abruzzo Cerasuolo '12	▼▼ 2*
○ Trebbiano d'Abruzzo '12	▼▼ 2*
○ Trebbiano d'Abruzzo Vign. di Popoli '11	▼▼ 5
● Montepulciano d'Abruzzo San Calisto '08	♀♀♀ 5
● Montepulciano d'Abruzzo San Calisto '07	♀♀♀ 5
○ Trebbiano d'Abruzzo V. di Capestrano '10	♀♀♀ 5

Villa Medoro

C.DA MEDORO
64030 ATRI [TE]
TEL. 0858708142
www.villamedoro.it

CELLAR SALES
PRE-BOOKED VISITS
ACCOMMODATION
ANNUAL PRODUCTION 300,000 bottles
HECTARES UNDER VINE 100.00

Federica Morricone, the region's vivacious wine doyenne, has finally made her dream come true with this enticing, impressive operation. The all-glass, white designer space capsule merges perfectly into the landscape of low hills between the Adriatic Sea and Gran Sasso of Fontanelle di Atri, in the Teramo area. She has 100 hectares of vineyards, tended with meticulous care, in one of the top Colline Teramane zones, producing a battery of wines that grows annually in quality and quantity. Much thought and care goes into the wines, aiming to give a contemporary slant to tradition. Adrano is now a classic Colline Teramane wine and confirms its Tre Bicchieri status with this 2010 version, which displays concentrated fruit and notes of Mediterranean scrubland. Its tightly knit, rounded palate is surprisingly gutsy and full flavoured. The Montepulciano d'Abruzzo 2011 is the usual great wine at an amazing price that only this area can forge.

● Montepulciano d'Abruzzo Colline Teramane Adrano '10	♥♥♥ 4*
● Montepulciano d'Abruzzo '11	♥♥ 2*
⊙ Montepulciano d'Abruzzo Cerasuolo '11	♥♥ 2*
● Montepulciano d'Abruzzo Rosso del Duca '10	♥♥ 3
○ Pecorino '12	♥♥ 2*
○ Trebbiano d'Abruzzo '12	♥♥ 2*
○ Passerina '11	♥ 2
○ Trebbiano d'Abruzzo Chimera '12	♥ 2
● Montepulciano d'Abruzzo '08	♥♥♥ 2*
● Montepulciano d'Abruzzo Colline Teramane Adrano '09	♥♥♥ 4*
● Montepulciano d'Abruzzo Colline Teramane Adrano '08	♥♥♥ 2*
● Montepulciano d'Abruzzo Colline Teramane Adrano '06	♥♥♥ 2*

Ciccio Zaccagnini

C.DA POZZO
65020 BOLOGNANO [PE]
TEL. 0858880195
www.cantinazaccagnini.it

CELLAR SALES
PRE-BOOKED VISITS
ANNUAL PRODUCTION 1,500,000 bottles
HECTARES UNDER VINE 180.00

The eminent winery that has always played a key role in the Abruzzo wine world is located in Bolognano. Steinerian artist Beuys, a leading figure in Land Art, gave one of his most important speeches here on Majella's Pescara foothills, and traces of a bond with art are visible throughout the stylish winery, which has developed over the years. This wonderful wine country is home to over 150 hectares of estate, plus more on lease, for an operation that produces an impressive selection of labels each year. The range goes from simple, well-made base wines to the ambitious and muscular Montepulciano crus that seek to reconcile Abruzzo's varietal stamping with international tastes. Trebbiano d'Abruzzo San Clemente 2011 is vigorous and juicy despite the layer of oak. The palate is well typed and pleasantly rustic, with edgy fruit and wild flower notes. The Rosso di Ciccio 2011 is an uncomplicated Montepulciano, with strikingly well-defined fruit with very good texture.

● Plaisir Passito Rosso '12	♥♥ 3*
⊙ Montepulciano d'Abruzzo Cerasuolo Myosotis '12	♥♥ 2*
● Montepulciano d'Abruzzo Cuvée dell'Abate '11	♥♥ 2*
● Montepulciano d'Abruzzo Rosso di Ciccio Vino del Tralcetto '11	♥♥ 2*
○ Plaisir Bianco '12	♥♥ 3
○ Bianco di Ciccio '12	♥ 2
● Clematis '08	♥ 7
● Montepulciano d'Abruzzo Chronicon '10	♥ 3
● Montepulciano d'Abruzzo S. Clemente Ris. '10	♥ 5
○ Yamada '12	♥ 2
● Montepulciano d'Abruzzo Chronicon '09	♥♥ 3*
● Montepulciano d'Abruzzo S. Clemente Ris. '09	♥♥ 5

Angelucci

c.da VICENNE, 7
65020 CASTIGLIONE A CASAURIA [PE]
TEL. 0857998193
www.angeluccivini.it

CELLAR SALES
PRE-BOOKED VISITS
ANNUAL PRODUCTION 150,000 bottles
HECTARES UNDER VINE 24.00

○ Moscatello Travertine '12	🏆 3
○ Leonate Pecorino '12	🏆 3

Centorame

LOC. CASOLI DI ATRI
VIA DELLE FORNACI, 15
64030 ATRI [TE]
TEL. 0858709115
www.centorame.it

CELLAR SALES
PRE-BOOKED VISITS
ANNUAL PRODUCTION 90,000 bottles
HECTARES UNDER VINE 11.00

● Montepulciano d'Abruzzo San Michele '11	🏆 2*
● Montepulciano d'Abruzzo Colline Teramane Castellum Vetus '09	🏆 4

Col del Mondo

c.da CAMPOTINO, 35c
65010 COLLECORVINO [PE]
TEL. 0858207831
www.coldelmondo.com

CELLAR SALES
PRE-BOOKED VISITS
ANNUAL PRODUCTION 50,000 bottles
HECTARES UNDER VINE 9.00

● Montepulciano d'Abruzzo Sunnae '11	🏆 2*
● Montepulciano d'Abruzzo '10	🏆 3
○ Kerrias Pecorino '09	🏆 2
○ Trebbiano d'Abruzzo Sunnae '12	🏆 2

Antonio Costantini

c.da MADONNA DELLA PACE, 36
65013 CITTA SANT'ANGELO [PE]
TEL. 0859699169
www.costantinivini.it

CELLAR SALES
PRE-BOOKED VISITS
ACCOMMODATION AND RESTAURANT SERVICE
ANNUAL PRODUCTION 130,000 bottles
HECTARES UNDER VINE 50.00

● Montepulciano d'Abruzzo '08	🏆 2*
● Montepulciano d'Abruzzo Tornese '07	🏆 3
○ Pecorino '12	🏆 2*
○ Trebbiano d'Abruzzo '09	🏆 2

Coste di Brenta

c.da CAMICIE, 50
66034 LANCIANO [CH]
TEL. 0872895280
www.costedibrenta.it

CELLAR SALES
PRE-BOOKED VISITS
ANNUAL PRODUCTION 50,000 bottles
HECTARES UNDER VINE 15.00
VITICULTURE METHOD Certified Organic

○ Elisio Pecorino '12	🏆 2*
● Montepulciano d'Abruzzo '11	🏆 2*
○ Trebbiano d'Abruzzo '12	🏆 2*
○ Gocce di Passione Passito '07	🏆 5

De Angelis Corvi

c.da PIGNOTTO
64010 CONTROGUERRA [TE]
TEL. 086189475
www.deangeliscorvi.it

CELLAR SALES
PRE-BOOKED VISITS
ANNUAL PRODUCTION 40,000 bottles
HECTARES UNDER VINE 8.00
VITICULTURE METHOD Certified Organic

● Montepulciano d'Abruzzo Colline Teramane Elevito Ris. '09	🏆 5
○ Trebbiano d'Abruzzo Sup. Fonte Raviliano '12	🏆 2

Faraone

LOC. COLLERANESCO
VIA NAZIONALE PER TERAMO, 290
64020 GIULIANOVA [TE]
TEL. 0858071804
www.faraonevini.it

CELLAR SALES
PRE-BOOKED VISITS
ANNUAL PRODUCTION 50,000 bottles
HECTARES UNDER VINE 7.00

⊙ Montepulciano d'Abruzzo Cerasuolo Le Vigne '12		�♛ 2*
○ Passerina Colle Pietro '12		♛♛ 2*

Tenuta I Fauri

S.DA CORTA, 9
66100 CHIETI
TEL. 0871332627
www.tenutaifauri.it

CELLAR SALES
PRE-BOOKED VISITS
ANNUAL PRODUCTION 150,000 bottles
HECTARES UNDER VINE 35.00

● Montepulciano d'Abruzzo Baldovino '12		♛♛ 2*
● Montepulciano d'Abruzzo Ottobre Rosso '12		♛♛ 2*
● Montepulciano d'Abruzzo Santa Cecilia '10		♛♛ 4

Feudo Antico

VIA PERRUNA, 35
66010 TOLLO [CH]
TEL. 0871969128
www.feudoantico.it

CELLAR SALES
ANNUAL PRODUCTION 55,000 bottles
HECTARES UNDER VINE 20.00

○ Tullum Pecorino '12		♛♛ 3*
⊙ Rosato '12		♛♛ 2*

Lidia e Amato

C.DA SAN BIAGIO, 2
64010 CONTROGUERRA [TE]
TEL. 0861817041
www.lidiaeamatoviticoltori.com

CELLAR SALES
PRE-BOOKED VISITS
ANNUAL PRODUCTION 50,000 bottles
HECTARES UNDER VINE 12.00

○ Controguerra Elena '12		♛♛ 2*
● Montepulciano d'Abruzzo Colline Teramane Amato Ris. '09		♛♛ 4
● Montepulciano d'Abruzzo Forty '12		♛♛ 2*

Mastrangelo

VIA ISTONIA, 81
66054 VASTO [CH]
TEL. 3358390720
www.vinimastrangelo.com

CELLAR SALES
PRE-BOOKED VISITS
ACCOMMODATION
ANNUAL PRODUCTION 35,000 bottles
HECTARES UNDER VINE 5.50

○ Trebbiano d'Abruzzo Monsignore '12		♛♛ 2*
● Montepulciano d'Abruzzo Alma Dei '11		♛ 3
○ Nunthius '12		♛ 3

Antonio e Elio Monti

VIA PIGNOTTO, 62
64010 CONTROGUERRA [TE]
TEL. 086189042
www.vinimonti.it

CELLAR SALES
PRE-BOOKED VISITS
ANNUAL PRODUCTION 80,000 bottles
HECTARES UNDER VINE 9.00

● Montepulciano d'Abruzzo Voluptas '10		♛♛ 2*
● Montepulciano d'Abruzzo Colline Teramane Pignotto Ris. '08		♛♛ 4

Cantine Mucci

C.DA VALLONE DI NANNI, 65
66020 TORINO DI SANGRO [CH]
TEL. 0873913366
www.cantinemucci.com

PRE-BOOKED VISITS
ANNUAL PRODUCTION 250,000 bottles
HECTARES UNDER VINE 24.00

● Montepulciano d'Abruzzo Santo Stefano '11	♟♟ 3
○ Pecorino Valentino '12	♟ 2
○ Trebbiano d'Abruzzo Valentino '12	♟ 2

Orlandi Contucci Ponno

LOC. PIANA DEGLI ULIVI, 1
64026 ROSETO DEGLI ABRUZZI [TE]
TEL. 0858944049
www.orlandicontucci.com

CELLAR SALES
PRE-BOOKED VISITS
ANNUAL PRODUCTION 180,000 bottles
HECTARES UNDER VINE 31.00

● Montepulciano d'Abruzzo Colline Teramane Podere La Regia Specula '10	♟♟ 3
● Montepulciano d'Abruzzo Colline Teramane Ris. '09	♟♟ 5

Praesidium

VIA GIOVANNUCCI, 24
67030 PREZZA [AQ]
TEL. 086445103
www.vinipraesidium.it

CELLAR SALES
PRE-BOOKED VISITS
ANNUAL PRODUCTION 26,000 bottles
HECTARES UNDER VINE 5.00

⊙ Montepulciano d'Abruzzo Cerasuolo Sup. '12	♟♟ 3
● Montepulciano d'Abruzzo Ris. '08	♟♟ 5

La Quercia

C.DA COLLE CROCE
64020 MORRO D'ORO [TE]
TEL. 0858959110
www.vinilaquercia.it

CELLAR SALES
PRE-BOOKED VISITS
ANNUAL PRODUCTION 120,000 bottles
HECTARES UNDER VINE 13.00

● Montepulciano d'Abruzzo '11	♟♟ 2*
● Montepulciano d'Abruzzo Colline Teramane Primamadre '08	♟♟ 3
○ Abruzzo Montonico Santapupa '12	♟ 2

Talamonti

C.DA PALAZZO
65014 LORETO APRUTINO [PE]
TEL. 0858289039
www.cantinetalamonti.it

CELLAR SALES
PRE-BOOKED VISITS
ANNUAL PRODUCTION 371,000 bottles
HECTARES UNDER VINE 32.00

● Montepulciano d'Abruzzo Modà '12	♟♟ 2*
● Montepulciano d'Abruzzo Tre Saggi '11	♟♟ 3
● Pecorino Trabocchetto '12	♟♟ 3
○ Trebbiano d'Abruzzo Trebì '12	♟ 2

Valori

VIA TORQUATO AL SALINELLO, 8
64027 SANT'OMERO [TE]
TEL. 086188461
www.masciarellidistribuzione.it

PRE-BOOKED VISITS
ANNUAL PRODUCTION 200,000 bottles
HECTARES UNDER VINE 20.00
VITICULTURE METHOD Certified Organic

● Montepulciano d'Abruzzo '12	♟♟ 2*
● Montepulciano d'Abruzzo Bio '12	♟♟ 2*
○ Trebbiano d'Abruzzo '12	♟♟ 2*

MOLISE

This little region, set between the Adriatic and the Apennines, is a fabulous area of verdant hills gently sloping down to the sea, a few kilometres that have always been eminently suited for growing the quintessential Mediterranean crops of grapes and olives. In this region, wedged between Campania and Abruzzo, traditional cultivars are grown, with montepulciano, aglianico, falanghina and trebbiano accounting for the lion's share. These varietals have always been grown here and are well acclimatized, producing grapes with different nuances according to soil and climate conditions. The region is also home to tintilia, a native red grape variety with exuberant aromas of fruit and herbs, a fine edgy cultivar that deserves greater attention and different treatment. With these traits, Molise could produce highly distinctive wines, and so we become increasingly frustrated in each year's tastings when we see that the region's production does not reflect its soil and climate conditions. The wines presented frequently display rustic traits, associated with an old-fashioned style based on power and overripe fruit that certainly does the local grape varieties no favours. Only a very few wineries, with a carefully crafted modern style, are an exception to this rule. The finest of these is Di Majo Norante, whose wines have strong international inspiration, like Aglianico 2012 Biorganic. In short, the history and terroir of Molise wines make them worthy of greater attention, which would rid them of a style rendering them commonplace and relegating them to a secondary role. Tintilia offers a great opportunity, if only its rhythmic, vital nature were respected, instead of weighed down with pointless cellar processes, and both aglianico and montepulciano have the potential for distinctive expression, but are instead fossilized in the quest for power through super-ripeness. So come on Molise: we believe in you and are waiting for you to prove us right!

Borgo di Colloredo

LOC. NUOVA CLITERNIA
VIA COLLOREDO, 15
86042 CAMPOMARINO [CB]
TEL. 087557453
www.borgodicolloredo.com

CELLAR SALES
PRE-BOOKED VISITS
ACCOMMODATION AND RESTAURANT SERVICE
ANNUAL PRODUCTION 300,000 bottles
HECTARES UNDER VINE 60.00

This artisan winery is in Campomarino, a classic area for Molise vine cultivation. The 60 hectares overlook the sea, and are ably managed by the Di Giulio family, whose agricultural expertise is now renowned across the region. They use only local varieties and traditional management. The lovely vines produce remarkable raw material that is processed in a traditional, slightly rustic, but unfailingly effective way. The wines are light on the wallet but extremely pleasing and truly drinkable. The spirited 2012 Gironia is a food-friendly white with a crisp, taut citrus palate attack veering adroitly to grass and chlorophyll. The well-typed, varietal 2010 Montepulciano has brisk fruit on the nose, and a round, compact palate. The 2012 Falanghina is surprisingly deep and vibrant for a wine of this price.

○ Biferno Bianco Gironia '12	♥♥	2*
○ Molise Falanghina '12	♥♥	2*
● Molise Montepulciano '10	♥♥	2*
☉ Biferno Rosato Gironia '12	♥	2
● Aglianico '07	♀♀	2*
○ Biferno Bianco Gironia '09	♀♀	2*
● Biferno Rosso Gironia '08	♀♀	3
● Molise Rosso '09	♀♀	2*
○ Terre degli Osci Greco '11	♀♀	2*

★Di Majo Norante

FRAZ. NUOVA CLITERNIA
C.DA RAMITELLI, 4
86042 CAMPOMARINO [CB]
TEL. 087557208
www.dimajonorante.com

CELLAR SALES
PRE-BOOKED VISITS
ANNUAL PRODUCTION 800,000 bottles
HECTARES UNDER VINE 90.00
VITICULTURE METHOD Certified Organic

In the winemaking world, when you say Di Majo Norante you mean Molise. This long-established winery has always been a regional leader and is based in Campomarino wine country, an endless chain of mountains and hills that roll right down to the sea. The estate of almost 90 hectares is a fully-fledged certified organic enterprise whose ship-shape range of wines is traditionally very well made and offers excellent value for money. From pleasing, easy-drinking native whites, to plush reds blended from montepulciano aglianico, always aiming for the best mix of modernity and tradition, this array of labels shows impressive average quantity and quality. The new varietal, vibrant 2011 Aglianico Biorganic has an eager, husky, heady nose, and a well-paced palate with austere, nicely astringent fruit. The fresh, dynamic 2011 version of the Apianae is not your usual sweet Moscato del Molise.

● Molise Aglianico Biorganic '11	♥♥♥	2*
● Molise Apianae '11	♥♥	4
● Biferno Rosso Ramitello '11	♥♥	3
● Molì Rosso '12	♥♥	2*
● Molise Don Luigi '10	♥♥	5
● Molise Tintilia '10	♥♥	3
○ Molì Bianco '12	♥	2
● Molise Aglianico Contado Ris. '11	♥	3
○ Molise Falanghina '12	♥	2
○ Molise Falanghina Biorganic '12	♥	2
○ Molise Falanghina Ramì '12	♥	2
● Sangiovese '12	♥	2
● Molise Aglianico Contado Ris. '10	♀♀♀	3*
● Molise Aglianico Contado Ris. '09	♀♀♀	3*
● Molise Don Luigi Ris. '08	♀♀♀	5

Cantine Salvatore

C.DA VIGNE
86049 URURI [CB]
TEL. 0874830656
www.cantinesalvatore.it

CELLAR SALES
PRE-BOOKED VISITS
ANNUAL PRODUCTION 80,000 bottles
HECTARES UNDER VINE 15.00

The Ururi winery makes persuasive, precise, contemporary wines, designed to please international markets. Here, in lower Molise, the area is still wild, and these 15 hectares are carefully managed with a modern approach, producing a range of exciting, aspirational wines. Pasquale Salvatore is a firm believer in reviving tintilia, a native red variety, and interprets this grape with the same pleasant, velvety feel typical of all his wines, clean and well crafted, yet lacking a bit of varietal imprint on occasion. Cantine Salvatore was not on top form this year. The 2011 Rutilia, a rashly aged Tintilia, revealed a heady varietal fruit on the nose and the brooding, Mediterranean palate was overly muscular and rich in extract. The 2012 IndoVINO stunned us with its intense nose of citrus and wild flowers.

○ L'IndoVINO Bianco '12	♟♟ 2*
● Molise Tintilia Rutilia '11	♟♟ 3
● L'IndoVINO Rosso '11	♟ 2
○ Molise Falanghina Nysias '12	♟ 3
● Molise Rosso Don Donà '10	♟ 3
⊙ Ros Is '12	♟ 2
○ Molise Falanghina Nysias '11	♟♟ 2*
○ Molise Falanghina Nysias '09	♟♟ 3*
● Molise Rosso Biberius '09	♟♟ 2*
● Molise Tintilia Rutilia '10	♟♟ 3*
● Molise Tintilia Rutilia '09	♟♟ 3

Terresacre

C.DA MONTEBELLO
86036 MONTENERO DI BISACCIA [CB]
TEL. 0875960191
www.terresacre.net

CELLAR SALES
PRE-BOOKED VISITS
ACCOMMODATION AND RESTAURANT SERVICE
ANNUAL PRODUCTION 100,000 bottles
HECTARES UNDER VINE 35.00

The winery is in Montenero di Bisaccia, on the border between Abruzzo and Molise, in the hills facing the Adriatic Sea. The 50-hectare estate is divided equally between olive groves and vineyards. The wines are well made, but maybe a bit too pat as they strive to reconcile tradition and modern winemaking techniques. The range produced increases in number and quality with each passing year. The persuasive array of wines runs from laidback Trebbianos to powerful, ambitious Tintilias. A 2009 Tintilia, all potent extract and well-crafted nose, nearly made the podium. Its intense berry aromas hint at super ripeness, and the spirited palate is a delight. The 2012 Rosavite is a varietal Montepulciano of brisk fruit, aptly well paced and feisty. The spirited, food-friendly 2012 Falanghina is nicely made.

● Molise Tintilia '09	♟♟ 5
● Molise Falanghina '12	♟♟ 3
● Molise Rosso Rispetto '09	♟♟ 4
⊙ Rosavite '12	♟♟ 2*
○ Molise Trebbiano Orovite '12	♟ 2
● Molise Rosso Neravite '10	♟♟ 2*
● Molise Rosso Rispetto '07	♟♟ 4
● Molise Rosso Tempora '06	♟♟ 4
● Molise Tintilia '08	♟♟ 5
○ Molise Trebbiano Orovite '08	♟♟ 2

Cantina Catabbo

C.DA PETRIERA
86046 SAN MARTINO IN PENSILIS [CB]
TEL. 0875604945
www.catabbo.it

CELLAR SALES
ANNUAL PRODUCTION 160,000 bottles
HECTARES UNDER VINE 54.00

● Molise Tintilia '10	♚ 4
● Molise Tintilia Ris. '09	♚ 5

Cantine Cipressi

C.DA MONTAGNA
86030 SAN FELICE DEL MOLISE [CB]
TEL. 0874874535
www.cantinecipressi.it

CELLAR SALES
PRE-BOOKED VISITS
ANNUAL PRODUCTION 150,000 bottles
HECTARES UNDER VINE 24.00
VITICULTURE METHOD Certified Organic

● Molise Rosso Mekan '11	♚♚ 3*
○ Falanghina '12	♚♚ 2*

D'Uva

C.DA RICUPO, 13
86035 LARINO [CB]
TEL. 0874822320
www.cantineduva.com

CELLAR SALES
PRE-BOOKED VISITS
ACCOMMODATION AND RESTAURANT SERVICE
ANNUAL PRODUCTION 80,000 bottles
HECTARES UNDER VINE 15.00

● Molise Tintilia '11	♚♚ 2*
○ Molise Trebbiano Kantharos '12	♚♚ 2*
● Gavio '09	♚ 2
○ Keres '12	♚ 2

Valerio Vini - San Nazzaro

LOC. SELVOTTA
86075 MONTERODUNI [IS]
TEL. 0865493043
www.valeriovini.it

CELLAR SALES
PRE-BOOKED VISITS
ANNUAL PRODUCTION 70,000 bottles
HECTARES UNDER VINE 5.00

● Pentro di Isernia '10	♚♚ 5
○ Lare Brut M. Cl. '12	♚ 6

CAMPANIA

We hardly needed a crystal ball to predict that
sooner or later Campania would take its rightful
place on the Italian wine-growing stage. The
region is an outright compendium of varieties and
styles, sustained by the availability of some quite
thrilling contemporary wines: tasty, perfect for food pairing,
and, most importantly, suiting every pocket. A general trend that can be seen in
the regional map of excellence. For the first time, all five of Campania's provinces
took home Tre Bicchieri awards and there were over 60 selected finalists, from
almost 1,000 tastings, in a formidable true-to-vintage group of innovative
expression. Firstly, the warm summer of 2012 left less of a mark than might
have been expected on a lovely range of crisp, racy whites that still have room to
grow. Fiano di Avellino is still the benchmark for this type and three newcomers
were singled out for our top award: Pietracupa's entry-level wine, Pietramara
de I Favati, and Michele Contrada's Selvecorte. Greco di Tufo responds with two
stunners like Gabriella Ferrara's Vigna Cicogna and San Gregorio's Cutizzi di
Feudi. Moreover, 2012 is a vintage to remember for Ischia, making a comeback
after nearly two decades, with a Tre Bicchieri for Casa d'Ambra's Biancolella
Tenuta Frassitelli, and for the province of Benevento, with its first-ever award
going to Fontanavecchia's Falanghina del Sannio. We might also mention
some authentically lovely Mediterranean atmospheres expressed by two Fiano
del Cilentos: San Salvatore's Pian di Stio and San Giovanni's Tresinus. For
Campania's solid, tasty reds, however, we find that 2011 was an almost perfect
vintage. The Campi Flegrei Piedirossos bear watching carefully, while Colline
Caiatine Pallagrellos and Casavecchias like Terre del Principe's Centomoggia
2011, Nanni Copè's Sabbie di Sopra il Bosco 2011, and Alois's Trebulanum
2010 are great expressions of grape varieties literally saved from extinction. And
then there's Aglianico. Its powerful, smoky chords resound in Galardi's Terra di
Lavoro 2011 and Masseria Felicia's Falerno Rosso Etichetta Bronzo 2010; while
La Rivolta's Aglianico del Taburno 2010 and Cantina del Taburno's Delius 2009
have the variety's tobacco hints, while more austere, spirited notes can be found
in Contrade di Taurasi's 2008 Taurasi Coste, Terredora's 2008 Fatica Contadina,
and Mastroberardino's 2007 Radici Riserva. We close with yet another award for
Silvia Imparato, going to her 2011 Montevetrano.

A Casa

LOC. PIANODARDINE
VIA FILANDE, 6
83100 AVELLINO
TEL. 0825626406
www.cantineacasa.it

CELLAR SALES
PRE-BOOKED VISITS
ANNUAL PRODUCTION 200,000 bottles
HECTARES UNDER VINE 40.00

A few months back, Sergio Iavarone, still to reach the age of 30, took over the helm of A Casa, a project started by his father Tommaso in 2007, together with a group of partners and friends, some who are leading names from the last 20 years of politics and business in Campania. Its headquarters and cellars are based in the old cotton mill in Borgo Ferrovia, near Avellino, where grapes arrive from around 40 hectares of vineyards in the main districts of Irpinia and Sannio. They are still trying to find their style, but their soft, fruity whites and sumptuous reds show greater character with every passing year. In a more limited range than usual due to the absence of new red vintages ready for tasting, the best performance came from the main white Irpinian designations. The Fiano di Avellino Oro del Passo 2012 and the Greco di Tufo Bussi 2012 share the same rounded, fermentative style, together with good structure.

○ Fiano di Avellino Oro del Passo '12	♀♀ 3
○ Greco di Tufo Bussi '12	♀♀ 3
○ Sannio Coda di Volpe Bebiana '12	♀ 2
○ Sannio Falanghina Cortenuda '12	♀ 3
○ Greco di Tufo Bussi '11	♀♀ 3
● Irpinia Aglianico Vecchio Postale '09	♀♀ 4
● Sannio Piedirosso Fiore dell'Isca '10	♀♀ 2*
● Taurasi V. di Noè Ris. '07	♀♀ 5

Alois

LOC. AUDELINO
VIA RAGAZZANO
81040 PONTELATONE [CE]
TEL. 0823876710
www.vinialois.it

CELLAR SALES
PRE-BOOKED VISITS
ANNUAL PRODUCTION 160,000 bottles
HECTARES UNDER VINE 30.00

The productive and stylistic shift sought in recent vintages by Michele and Massimo Alois, assisted by Carmine Valentino, clearly seems to have been achieved. New vineyard acquisitions have moved the heart of the estate to higher elevations, where we find the traditional varieties of the Caiazzo hills, such as pallagrello, casavecchia, aglianico and falanghina. We also see clearly that vinification processes have focused on endowing the wines with a far more classic style, with ageing techniques aimed above all at ensuring definition and drinkability. The change has been marked by a surprising Trebulanum 2010, one of the most original reds tasted this year in Campania. This monovarietal Casavecchia, aged in large barrels, lacks aromatic intensity, but in compensation boasts a racy, expansive palate, with sweet fruit in the long watermelon and liquorice finish. It has excellent prospects.

● Trebulanum '10	♀♀♀ 5
○ Pallagrello Bianco Caiatì '12	♀♀ 2*
● Settimo '10	♀♀ 2*
● Campole '11	♀ 2
○ Caulino '12	♀ 2
● Campole '10	♀♀ 2*
● Campole '08	♀♀ 2*
● Cunto '10	♀♀ 4
● Cunto '09	♀♀ 4

Antonio Caggiano

C.DA SALA
83030 TAURASI [AV]
TEL. 082774723
www.cantinecaggiano.it

CELLAR SALES
PRE-BOOKED VISITS
RESTAURANT SERVICE
ANNUAL PRODUCTION 155,000 bottles
HECTARES UNDER VINE 25.00

Contrada Sala, Piano di Montevergine, Pezza dei Preti, San Pietro and Coste: some of the best wine country in Taurasi, and home for almost 20 years to the aglianico grown by Antonio Caggiano, now assisted full time by his son Pino. Their iconic wine is still the Vigna Macchia dei Goti, one of Irpinia's first vineyard selections to be bottled separately, and also one of the first experiments here with a Bordeaux-style wine, based on malolactic fermentation and ageing solely in barriques. The range is completed with buttery, rounded versions of Fiano and Greco, made using grapes from tried-and-tested growers at Lapio and Tufo. The vintages presented were not strong, but we nevertheless saw good performance. Even though the difficult 2009 growing year compromised its usual vibrant fruit and complexity, the Taurasi Vigna Macchia dei Goti was nevertheless pleasing. The close-knit, salty Fiano di Avellino Béchar 2012 was also on form, displaying assured expressiveness.

○ Fiano di Avellino Béchar '12	♟♟	3
● Taurasi V. Macchia dei Goti '09	♟♟	5
○ Greco di Tufo Devon '12	♟	3
● Irpinia Aglianico Taurì '11	♟	2
● Taurasi V. Macchia dei Goti '08	♟♟♟	5
● Taurasi V. Macchia dei Goti '04	♟♟♟	5
● Taurasi V. Macchia dei Goti '99	♟♟♟	5
● Irpinia Aglianico Taurì '10	♟♟	2*
● Irpinia Campi Taurasini Salae Domini '09	♟♟	5
○ Mel '09	♟♟	5
● Taurasi V. Macchia dei Goti '07	♟♟	5

Cantina del Taburno

VIA SALA, 16
82030 FOGLIANISE [BN]
TEL. 0824871338
www.cantinadeltaburno.it

CELLAR SALES
PRE-BOOKED VISITS
ANNUAL PRODUCTION 1,200,000 bottles
HECTARES UNDER VINE 600.00

After being absent for a few editions, Cantina del Taburno, which officially changed its name to Consorzio Agrario Provinciale di Benevento in 2008, is back in the main section of the Guide. This co-operative accounts for around 600 hectares and hundreds of growers, and vinifies all the main Sannio varieties at the Foglianise facility, including aglianico, falanghina, piedirosso, greco, fiano, and coda di volpe. Its vast range brings together entry-level labels aged in steel at extremely attractive prices, and more ambitious selections, released after long barrel maturation. Nor should we forget its sparklers, rosés, late harvest wines, and raisin wines. We loved the two versions of Aglianico, one an extraordinarily long Bue Apis 2008, a limited production from age-old vines, the other a Delius 2009, with a complex nose of red berry fruit, tobacco, pencil lead and spices swathed in elegant balsam. The palate showed potent and velvety with elegant tannins and superb length: Tre Bicchieri.

● Aglianico del Taburno Delius '09	♟♟♟	4
● Bue Apis '08	♟♟	6
○ Falanghina del Sannio Taburno '12	♟♟	2*
○ Greco del Beneventano '12	♟♟	2*
● Taburno Aglianico '10	♟♟	2*
○ Coda di Volpe Amineo '12	♟	2
● Falanghina Cesco Dell'Eremo V.T. '12	♟	3
○ Fiano del Beneventano '12	♟	2
● Bue Apis '00	♟♟♟	6
● Bue Apis '99	♟♟♟	6
● Taburno Aglianico Bue Apis '04	♟♟♟	8
○ Falanghina del Sannio Taburno '11	♟♟	2*

Tenuta del Cavalier Pepe

VIA SANTA VARA
83040 SANT'ANGELO ALL'ESCA [AV]
TEL. 082773766
www.tenutacavalierpepe.it

CELLAR SALES
PRE-BOOKED VISITS
ACCOMMODATION AND RESTAURANT SERVICE
ANNUAL PRODUCTION 300,000 bottles
HECTARES UNDER VINE 45.00

Although she grew up in Belgium, Milena Pepe is now a fully-fledged Irpinian, and one of the most determined women in the world of Campanian wine. With her father Angelo she has established a leading estate and winery in the historic patchwork of small plots at the heart of the Calore Valley. Their 45 hectares or so are distributed mainly between Luogosano and Sant'Angelo all'Esca, and above all planted to aglianico and coda di volpe, topped up by targeted purchases of fiano and greco. The result is a varied range, comprising selections and experimental wines, approachable easy-drinkers and austere reds, aged in barrels of various sizes and provenance. The 2007 vintage once more proves to be lucky for the reds of Tenuta Cavalier Pepe: after reaching the final a couple of years ago with the Taurasi Opera Mia, this year is the turn of La Loggia del Cavaliere Riserva. Dark but reactive, it combines flavour and vitality, pleasurableness and tannic austerity.

● Taurasi La Loggia del Cavaliere Ris. '07	♟♟ 6
○ Greco di Tufo Nestor '12	♟♟ 3
● Irpinia Aglianico Terra del Varo '10	♟♟ 2*
○ Irpinia Coda di Volpe Bianco di Bellona '12	♟♟ 2*
○ Falanghina Lila '12	♟ 2
○ Fiano di Avellino Brancato '11	♟ 4
○ Fiano di Avellino Refiano '12	♟ 3
○ Irpinia Fiano Passito Chicco d'Oro '10	♟ 4
⊙ Irpinia Rosato Napoli 2012 '12	♟ 2
○ Greco di Tufo Nestor '11	♟♟ 3
● Irpinia Campi Taurasini Santo Stefano '08	♟♟ 3
○ Irpinia Coda di Volpe Bianco di Bellona '11	♟♟ 2*
● Taurasi Opera Mia '08	♟♟ 5

Colli di Castelfranci

C.DA BRAUDIANO
83040 CASTELFRANCI [AV]
TEL. 082772392
www.collidicastelfranci.com

CELLAR SALES
PRE-BOOKED VISITS
ACCOMMODATION
ANNUAL PRODUCTION 160,000 bottles
HECTARES UNDER VINE 25.00

We feel the winery of brothers-in-law Luciano Gregorio and Gerardo Colucci has only partly realized its potential. Castelfranci is one of the best zones for aglianico in Irpinia, and the source of Taurasis whose high levels of acidity and extract ensure long life. Here Colli di Castelfranci produces two versions, the vintage Alta Valle and the Riserva, matured in small barrels for around a year before a further period in Slavonian oak and in the bottle. They are gradually finding the character and identity that has always distinguished their whites, vinified exclusively in steel to boost freshness and sinew. Among the recent reds we particularly liked the Taurasi Alta Valle 2009, a solid, potent wine just slightly lacking in depth from what was a difficult growing year. Less successful was the Alta Valle Riserva 2008. Although opening to intriguing iodine aromas, in the mouth intrusive tannins were overpowering, despite weighty stuffing.

● Taurasi Alta Valle '09	♟♟ 5
○ Greco di Tufo Grotte '12	♟♟ 3
○ Irpinia Greco Vallicelli '11	♟♟ 4
● Taurasi Alta Valle Ris. '08	♟♟ 7
○ Fiano di Avellino Pendino '12	♟ 3
● Taurasi Alta Valle '08	♟♟ 4
● Taurasi Alta Valle '06	♟♟ 4
● Taurasi Alta Valle Ris. '07	♟♟ 7

Colli di Lapio

VIA ARIANIELLO, 47
83030 LAPIO [AV]
TEL. 0825982184
www.collidilapio.it

CELLAR SALES
PRE-BOOKED VISITS
ANNUAL PRODUCTION 50,000 bottles
HECTARES UNDER VINE 6.00
VITICULTURE METHOD Certified Organic

On restaurant wine lists you will often find it listed as Fiano di Romano Clelia rather than under its brand name Colli di Lapio. This is indicative of its perception as a highly artisanal wine, able to offer a masterful interpretation of the northern feel of the vineyards at Arianiello, Stazzone and Scarpone, at elevations of 600 metres. Technical intervention is limited to late harvesting, generally in the second half of October, ageing in steel on the lees, and staggered bottlings between spring and the autumn following harvest. The result is wines which are extremely faithful to the character of their vintages. This effect of the growing year is evident in the Fiano di Avellino 2012. Like many other wines from the DOC zone, it lacks something both on the nose, dominated by primary fruit aromas, and in the mouth, compromised by alcoholic warmth and vibrant acidity that has yet to be translated into flavour.

○ Fiano di Avellino '12	♟♟ 4
○ Greco di Tufo Alèxandros '12	♟ 3
○ Fiano di Avellino '10	♟♟♟ 4
○ Fiano di Avellino '09	♟♟♟ 4
○ Fiano di Avellino '08	♟♟♟ 4*
○ Fiano di Avellino '07	♟♟♟ 4
○ Fiano di Avellino '05	♟♟♟ 4
○ Fiano di Avellino '04	♟♟♟ 4
○ Fiano di Avellino '11	♟♟ 4
○ Greco di Tufo Alexandros '11	♟♟ 4
● Irpinia Campi Taurasini Donna Chiara '09	♟♟ 4
● Taurasi V. Andrea '08	♟♟ 5
● Taurasi V. Andrea '07	♟♟ 5
● Taurasi V. Andrea '06	♟♟ 5

Michele Contrada

C.DA TAVERNA, 31
83040 CANDIDA [AV]
TEL. 0825988434
www.vinicontrada.it

CELLAR SALES
PRE-BOOKED VISITS
ANNUAL PRODUCTION 50,000 bottles
HECTARES UNDER VINE 10.00

New arrivals and veterans are not the only cause for enthusiasm in the Campanian wine scene, as the family-run winery of Contrada, established in 2003, clearly shows. It initially made a reputation for characterful but somewhat inconsistent wines until, only a few years back, it made a quantum leap in terms of quality. What has made the difference is its holdings at Candida, an area where Fiano di Avellino seems to bring together the more mountain styles of Lapio and Montefredane's mineral character. Greco and coda di volpe complete the range of white varieties, all vinified in steel, while aglianico comes from Candida and Castelfranci. This journey of growth is reflected in the splendid Fiano di Avellino Selvecorte 2012, which took home a Tre Bicchieri. Although still slightly closed, the nose shows elegant notes of summer fruit, citrus and dried herbs; the solid backbone and energy on the palate are the real source of its expressive complexity and depth.

○ Fiano di Avellino Selvecorte '12	♟♟♟ 3*
○ Greco di Tufo Gaudioso '12	♟♟ 3
○ Irpinia Coda di Volpe Taberna '12	♟ 2
○ Fiano di Avellino Selvecorte '11	♟♟ 3*
○ Greco di Tufo Gaudioso '07	♟♟ 3*
○ Greco di Tufo Gaudioso '06	♟♟ 3*
○ Irpinia Coda di Volpe Taberna '11	♟♟ 2*
○ Irpinia Coda di Volpe Taberna '10	♟♟ 2*

Contrada Salandra

LOC. CUMA
80078 POZZUOLI [NA]
TEL. 0815265258
www.dolciqualita.com

CELLAR SALES
PRE-BOOKED VISITS
ANNUAL PRODUCTION 15,000 bottles
HECTARES UNDER VINE 4.00

Peppino Fortunato is much more than a talented grower and apiarist. His every word reveals knowledge and sensitivity, but above all his utmost respect for the still largely undiscovered territory of Campi Flegrei. Helped by his wife Sandra Castaldo, his limited production comes from around four hectares spread over Coste di Cuma, Monte Sant'Angelo and Monteruscello, planted to falanghina, piedirosso and other, as yet unidentified local varieties. Maceration on the skins also for the whites, and long periods in steel resting on the fine lees result in wines that are only apparently subtle, with a marked mineral accent. They are not released until at least two years after harvest. Even in a more approachable vintage such as 2011, the wines of Contrada Salandra require patience. The Falanghina is still closed on the nose of apple and iodine, and shows natural progression, while lacking a certain focus. Equally introverted, but with greater thrust and clarity, is the Piedirosso.

● Campi Flegrei Piedirosso '11	♛♛ 3*
○ Campi Flegrei Falanghina '11	♛♛ 2*
○ Campi Flegrei Falanghina '10	♛♛ 2*
○ Campi Flegrei Falanghina '09	♛♛ 2*
● Campi Flegrei Piedirosso '09	♛♛ 2*

Contrade di Taurasi

VIA MUNICIPIO, 39
83030 TAURASI [AV]
TEL. 082774483
www.cantinelonardo.it

CELLAR SALES
PRE-BOOKED VISITS
ANNUAL PRODUCTION 20,000 bottles
HECTARES UNDER VINE 5.00
VITICULTURE METHOD Certified Organic

We always predicted an exciting future for the Lonardo family's project at the Contrade di Taurasi property. After research and stylistic remodelling, their Aglianicos are now the epitome of naturally styled wines with real territorial character. This is particularly evident in the vineyard selections Vigne d'Alto and Coste, vinified separately since 2007, using controlled natural fermentation and ageing in medium-sized barrels. The old, organically farmed plots in north-eastern Taurasi have been joined by century-old starseta-trained vines of roviello, known locally as greco musc', one of the most distinctive white varieties in the whole province. This time round we were excited by the selections of Taurasi, bringing extra brightness and tannic definition to the character we already appreciated back in 2007. We slightly preferred the Coste 2008, with spectacular spicy brightness and marked minerality, although Vigne d'Alto 2008, with its volcanic, earthy profile, is also attractive.

● Taurasi Coste '08	♛♛♛ 7
○ Greco Musc' '11	♛♛ 4
● Taurasi Vigne d'Alto '08	♛♛ 7
● Taurasi '08	♛♛ 5
○ Greco Musc' '10	♛♛♛ 4*
● Taurasi '04	♛♛♛ 6
○ Greco Musc' '09	♛♛ 4
● Taurasi '07	♛♛ 5
● Taurasi Coste '07	♛♛ 7
● Taurasi Vigne d'Alto '07	♛♛ 7

Marisa Cuomo

VIA G. B. LAMA, 16/18
84010 FURORE [SA]
TEL. 089830348
www.marisacuomo.com

CELLAR SALES
PRE-BOOKED VISITS
RESTAURANT SERVICE
ANNUAL PRODUCTION 109,000 bottles
HECTARES UNDER VINE 18.00

It is above all generational expansion that has dictated progress in recent years at what is an iconic winery for Furore and the Amalfi Coast. Andrea Ferraioli and Marisa Cuomo are in fact now assisted by their children Raffaele and Dora, who have inherited their parents' energy for tackling the numerous difficulties of an area that is as enchantingly beautiful as it is extreme. In the small plots of land clawed from the rock, dozens of local varieties with widely differing characteristics and ripening times come together smoothly to create an impeccable range. The whites are aged in steel, with the exception of the Fiorduva. This is an impeccable range, with numerous labels combining substance and drinkability, starting with the Ravello Bianco 2012, a full-flavoured, warm, complex wine with aromas of blossom and moss, which just needs to make a leap of faith. The sweet, toasty Fiorduva, meanwhile, paid the price of the hot 2011 growing year.

D'Ambra Vini d'Ischia

FRAZ. PANZA
VIA MARIO D'AMBRA, 16
80077 FORIO [NA]
TEL. 081907210
www.dambravini.com

CELLAR SALES
PRE-BOOKED VISITS
ANNUAL PRODUCTION 500,000 bottles
HECTARES UNDER VINE 12.00

We are so used to remembering the role that Casa D'Ambra has played in the history of wine in Campania and southern Italy, that we risk forgetting its glorious present. Without bowing to changing fashions, this iconic Ischia winery has been producing a faultless range of traditional varieties for years, combining territorial character, competitive prices and impressive production figures. Merit goes to the commitment and passion of Andrea D'Ambra and daughters, Sara and Marina, for their management of a vast patchwork of plots and over 150 growers in targeted purchases of grapes and rented vineyards. A sunny, yet variably tempered growing year, 2012 promised a thoroughbred Frassitelli. Its youth is evident above all on the nose, hinging on typical aromas of white melon and broom, while its gentle Mediterranean character is already evident on the palate. As a result, after over 20 years, Casa d'Ambra once again takes home a Tre Bicchieri.

○ Costa d'Amalfi Ravello Bianco '12	♟♟ 3*
○ Costa d'Amalfi Furore Bianco '12	♟♟ 4
○ Costa d'Amalfi Furore Bianco Fiorduva '11	♟♟ 6
● Costa d'Amalfi Ravello Rosso Ris. '10	♟♟ 5
⊙ Costa d'Amalfi Rosato '12	♟♟ 3
● Costa d'Amalfi Furore Rosso '12	♟ 3
○ Costa d'Amalfi Fiorduva '08	♟♟♟ 6
○ Costa d'Amalfi Fiorduva '05	♟♟♟ 6
○ Costa d'Amalfi Fiorduva '04	♟♟♟ 6
○ Costa d'Amalfi Furore Bianco '10	♟♟♟ 4
○ Costa d'Amalfi Furore Bianco Fiorduva '10	♟♟♟ 6
○ Costa d'Amalfi Furore Bianco '11	♟♟ 4
○ Costa d'Amalfi Ravello Bianco '11	♟♟ 3

○ Ischia Biancolella Tenuta Frassitelli '12	♟♟♟ 3*
○ Ischia Biancolella '12	♟♟ 3
● Ischia Per' 'e Palummo '12	♟♟ 3
○ Gocce D'Ambra	♟ 5
○ Ischia Bianco '12	♟ 2
○ Ischia Forastera Euposia '12	♟ 3
● Ischia Rosso Dedicato a Mario D'Ambra '09	♟ 4
○ Ischia Biancolella Tenuta Frassitelli '90	♟♟♟ 3*
○ Ischia Biancolella '11	♟♟ 2*
○ Ischia Biancolella Tenuta Frassitelli '11	♟♟ 3*
● Ischia Per"e Palummo '11	♟♟ 3

D'Antiche Terre - Vega

C.DA LO PIANO - SS 7 BIS
83030 MANOCALZATI [AV]
TEL. 0825675358
www.danticheterre.it

CELLAR SALES
PRE-BOOKED VISITS
ACCOMMODATION AND RESTAURANT SERVICE
ANNUAL PRODUCTION 450,000 bottles
HECTARES UNDER VINE 40.00

With over 25 years in the business, D'Antiche Terre is an icon in Irpinian winemaking. Led by Gaetano Ciccarella, the Manocalzati winery boasts one of the largest and most variegated vineyard holdings in the province, offering Greco from Tufo, Santa Paolina, Prata and Montefusco; Fiano from Pratola Serra and Manocalzati; and Aglianico from Pietradefusi and Torre le Nocelle. Its extensive, territorial range is at times inconsistent, but often achieves peaks of excellence in wines with an essential, lustrous style. Thanks to outstanding performance across the board, D'Antiche Terre once more earns a full profile this year. The range is led by a superb Fiano di Avellino 2012, which sailed into the finals with its invigorating yet delicate progression. Although lacking some density, it shows balanced progression in the mouth. We also loved the Taurasi 2008, the Greco 2012 and the Coriliano 2011.

○ Fiano di Avellino '12	♟♟	3*
● Coriliano '11	♟♟	2*
○ Greco di Tufo '12	♟♟	3
● Taurasi '08	♟♟	5
☉ Irpinia Aglianico Rosato Elbe '12	♟	2
○ Irpinia Coda di Volpe '12	♟	2
○ Sannio Falanghina '12	♟	2
○ Fiano di Avellino '10	♟♟	3
○ Greco di Tufo '10	♟♟	3
○ Sannio Falanghina '10	♟♟	2*
● Taurasi '07	♟♟	5
● Taurasi Il Vicario Ris. '05	♟♟	6

Viticoltori De Conciliis

LOC. QUERCE, 1
84060 PRIGNANO CILENTO [SA]
TEL. 0974831390
www.viticoltorideconciliis.it

CELLAR SALES
PRE-BOOKED VISITS
ANNUAL PRODUCTION 200,000 bottles
HECTARES UNDER VINE 25.00

What the De Conciliis family has achieved in almost 20 years of work at Prignano is of sociocultural as much as production value. They have driven the prospects and frontiers of Cilento viticulture, developing unexplored territories in the hilly interior to the south of the zone, at Morigerati, San Giovanni a Piro, and Acciaroli. Moreover, they have produced a range whose constantly evolving style is the result of experiments and influences. They are like a rock band, as the fiery Bruno puts it, producing a different sound each time, depending on the labels and growing years, without ever forgetting the central role played by fiano and aglianico. The Donnaluna Fiano confirms its place as the stylistically most impressive label at De Conciliis: the 2012 version reveals a juicy, Mediterranean soul, with notes of shrubs, broom and peach in a somewhat flat yet invigorating profile. With greater grip and depth, it would be perfect.

○ Donnaluna Fiano '12	♟♟	3*
● Cilento Aglianico Donna Luna '11	♟♟	3
● Bacioilcielo Rosso '12	♟	2
○ Selim Brut	♟	2
● Naima '01	♟♟♟	5
○ Bacioilcielo Bianco '11	♟♟	2*
● Naima '07	♟♟	6
● Zero '07	♟♟	8

Di Marzo

VIA GAETANO DI MARZO, 2
83010 TUFO [AV]
TEL. 0825998022
www.cantinedimarzo.it

CELLAR SALES
PRE-BOOKED VISITS
ANNUAL PRODUCTION 150,000 bottles
HECTARES UNDER VINE 26.00

Can we talk of innovation when we are
dealing with one of Italy's oldest wineries?
We clearly can in the case of Di Marzo,
awoken from its long slumber by Filippo Di
Somma and his children Ferrante and
Maria Giovanna, today at the helm of the
operation. Its natural focus is on Greco di
Tufo, of which Scipione Di Marzo is to some
extent considered the forefather, with
vineyards spread over the districts of Santa
Lucia and San Paolo di Tufo, as well as
plots at Santa Paolina. No fewer than five
versions are produced, including a metodo
classico sparkler, all aged in steel. Changes
in production techniques and style were
evident in our tastings, and took the Greco
di Tufo Scipio 2011 to the finals. This
surprising white shows no signs of the hot
growing year, and instead boasts an
attractively lustrous, salty, even reductive
nature, suggesting character and youth.

○ Greco di Tufo Scipio '11	♟♟ 4
○ Fiano di Avellino Donatus '12	♟♟ 3
● Taurasi Albertus '09	♟♟ 3
○ Extra Brut M. Cl. Anni Venti	♟ 5
● Irpinia Aglianico Cantine Storiche '11	♟ 3
○ Greco di Tufo Franciscus '11	♟♟ 3

Di Prisco

C.DA ROTOLE, 27
83040 FONTANAROSA [AV]
TEL. 0825475738
www.cantinadiprisco.it

CELLAR SALES
PRE-BOOKED VISITS
ANNUAL PRODUCTION 100,000 bottles
HECTARES UNDER VINE 10.00

Few artisanal wineries in the province of
Avellino manage to achieve consistently
high quality in both whites and reds. One
that does is the operation run by
Pasqualino Di Prisco at Fontanarosa, where
limestone soils generally give lean, mineral,
saline Aglianico di Taurasi. The winery can
also count on its plots of fiano and coda di
volpe, as well as grapes from the vineyards
tended by growers at Montefusco, used in
the Greco di Tufo and the Pietrarosa
selection. Both are aged in steel and
instantly recognizable with their markedly
northern, lustrous, almost salty profile.
Once again, the greco-based whites were
the best of the range. The 2012 shows a
complex, incisive profile, with cereal traits
and a solid palate that would benefit from
just a touch more minerality. We found the
Pietrarosa 2010 to be more complex and
racy, with its notes of citrus and peat, and
long, tasty finish.

○ Greco di Tufo Pietrarosa '10	♟♟ 3*
○ Greco di Tufo '12	♟♟ 2*
○ Fiano di Avellino '11	♟ 2
● Taurasi '08	♟ 5
○ Greco di Tufo '11	♟♟♟ 2*
● Taurasi '06	♟♟♟ 5
● Taurasi '05	♟♟♟ 5*
○ Greco di Tufo Pietrarosa '09	♟♟ 3*
● Taurasi '07	♟♟ 5

DonnaChiara

LOC. PIETRACUPA
VIA STAZIONE
83030 MONTEFALCIONE [AV]
TEL. 0825977135
www.donnachiara.it

CELLAR SALES
PRE-BOOKED VISITS
RESTAURANT SERVICE
ANNUAL PRODUCTION 200,000 bottles
HECTARES UNDER VINE 30.00

Thanks to consistent performance, the Petitto family has managed to consolidate its presence in the competitive Avellino area. The merit goes to the strong-willed Ilaria, the daughter of Umberto and Chiara, aided by Angelo Valentino to interpret Irpinian varieties and designations which are consciously but not excessively modern. The whites are aged in steel, with long periods on the lees, while barrel maturation, mainly in small oak, is reserved for the Taurasis. The estate owns vineyards covering around 23 hectares, mostly dedicated to aglianico, but also rents three hectares and buys in some fiano, greco and falanghina grapes. We would first of all like to stress the excellent average level seen in the range presented by Donnachiara, now joined by two new raisined wines, an Esoterico from fiano and an Ostinato from greco, both 2011s. The best performance came, however, from the DOC wines, led by the Fiano di Avellino 2012.

○ Fiano di Avellino '12	♟♟ 3
○ Greco di Tufo '12	♟♟ 3
● Taurasi '09	♟♟ 5
● Taurasi Ris. '08	♟♟ 6
○ Esoterico Fiano Passito '11	♟ 3
● Irpinia Coda di Volpe '12	♟ 3
○ Ostinato Greco Passito '11	♟ 4
○ Greco di Tufo '11	♀♀ 3
● Irpinia Aglianico '09	♀♀ 3
● Irpinia Aglianico '08	♀♀ 3
● Taurasi '08	♀♀ 5
● Taurasi Ris. '07	♀♀ 6

I Favati

P.ZZA DI DONATO
83020 CESINALI [AV]
TEL. 0825666898
www.cantineifavati.it

CELLAR SALES
PRE-BOOKED VISITS
ANNUAL PRODUCTION 80,000 bottles
HECTARES UNDER VINE 10.00

I Favati is a family operation, run by brothers Piersabino and Giancarlo, and Giancarlo's wife Rosanna Petrozziello, with technical support from Vincenzo Mercurio. The headquarters are at Cesinali, in the Sabato Valley, known for fiano, although purchases and rented plots allow them to cover a comprehensive range of Irpinian wines. The classic line comprises Fiano Pietramara, Greco Terrantica and Taurasi Terzotratto, which are mirrored by labels in the second line, Etichette Bianche, from selected grapes picked late and vinified using different methods, with pre-fermentation maceration for whites and ageing in small oak for the reds. They have often come close and finally I Favati can take home their first well-deserved Tre Bicchieri with the Fiano di Avellino Pietramara 2012, one of the most approachable, rounded versions of the vintage, and better than the corresponding Etichetta Bianca. Varietal notes of mimosa, chalk and spring herbs lead into a subtle, persistent palate.

○ Fiano di Avellino Pietramara '12	♟♟♟ 3*
○ Fiano di Avellino Pietramara Et. Bianca '12	♟♟ 5
○ Greco di Tufo Terrantica '12	♟♟ 3
○ Greco di Tufo Terrantica Et. Bianca '12	♟♟ 5
● Irpinia Campi Taurasini Cretarossa '10	♟ 3
○ Fiano di Avellino Pietramara '11	♀♀ 3*
○ Fiano di Avellino Pietramara '10	♀♀ 3
○ Fiano di Avellino Pietramara Et. Bianca '11	♀♀ 5
○ Greco di Tufo Terrantica '11	♀♀ 3
○ Greco di Tufo Terrantica Et. Bianca '11	♀♀ 5

Benito Ferrara

FRAZ. SAN PAOLO, 14A
83010 TUFO [AV]
TEL. 0825998194
www.benitoferrara.it

CELLAR SALES
PRE-BOOKED VISITS
ANNUAL PRODUCTION 45,000 bottles
HECTARES UNDER VINE 9.50

There are always a smile and a glass of good wine to reward those who decide to climb the 500 metres to the top of the San Paolo di Tufo hill to visit Gabriella Ferrara and her husband Sergio. There may even be the treat of a Vigna Cicogna, one of the first selections of Greco bottled separately in the 1990s, and still today one of its best known, most typical incarnations. Recent vintages from the two hectares of south-facing clayey, sulphur-rich soil have given lighter, brighter wines, especially on the nose, without compromising their proverbial minerality and stuffing. Vinification is solely in steel, also for the basic wine and the Fiano di Avellino. 2012 is a vintage to remember for the Ferrara family's Greco wines. The "village" is already a champion of territorial style, with its sulphurous, mossy notes and crisp palate, but the real star is the Vigna Cicogna, which should be decanted to appreciate its magnificent structure and spicy complexity.

○ Greco di Tufo V. Cicogna '12	🍷🍷🍷 4*
○ Greco di Tufo '12	🍷🍷 3*
○ Fiano di Avellino '12	🍷🍷 4
● Irpinia Aglianico V. Quattro Confini '11	🍷 3
○ Greco di Tufo V. Cicogna '10	🍸🍸🍸 4
○ Greco di Tufo V. Cicogna '09	🍸🍸🍸 4
○ Greco di Tufo V. Cicogna '11	🍸🍸 4
● Taurasi V. Quattro Confini '08	🍸🍸 5

★★Feudi di San Gregorio

LOC. CERZA GROSSA
83050 SORBO SERPICO [AV]
TEL. 0825986683
www.feudi.it

CELLAR SALES
PRE-BOOKED VISITS
RESTAURANT SERVICE
ANNUAL PRODUCTION 3,500,000 bottles
HECTARES UNDER VINE 250.00
VITICULTURE METHOD Certified Organic

A new era has clearly begun for Feudi di San Gregorio, thanks to the drive of its dynamic chairman Antonio Capaldo, assisted by Pierpaolo Sirch and his staff, many of whom are new. The renaissance has been made possible thanks to extraordinary vineyards and the rediscovery of a style based on territorial identity more than ever before, but also to a drastic review of certain projects, such as that involving sparklers. The reds tend increasingly towards an approachable, relaxed style, while restyling already seems to be complete in a range of whites that now offer much more than just technical and varietal precision, in both the basic wines and the selections. A quick glance at the grid below gives a clear idea of form across the range, led by the Greco di Tufo Cutizzi 2012. But the label that best embodies the recent production revolution has to be the basic Greco 2012, with production figures of almost 1,000,000 bottles, showing textbook aromas of nectarine and a savoury, almost cutting profile.

○ Greco di Tufo Cutizzi '12	🍷🍷🍷 3*
○ Fiano di Avellino Pietracalda '12	🍷🍷 3*
○ Greco di Tufo '12	🍷🍷 3*
● Taurasi Piano di Montevergine Ris. '08	🍷🍷 6
● Aglianico del Vulture '10	🍷🍷 3
○ Dubl Brut M.Cl.	🍷🍷 5
⊙ Dubl Rosato Brut M.Cl.	🍷🍷 5
○ Fiano di Avellino '12	🍷🍷 3
● Irpinia Aglianico Dal Re '11	🍷🍷 3
○ Irpinia Fiano Passito Privilegio '11	🍷🍷 6
● Irpinia Rosso Sirica '10	🍷🍷 5
○ Sannio Falanghina Serrocielo '12	🍷🍷 3
● Taurasi '09	🍷🍷 5
● Irpinia Aglianico Rubrato '11	🍷 3
○ Sannio Falanghina '12	🍷 3

Fontanavecchia

VIA FONTANAVECCHIA
82030 TORRECUSO [BN]
TEL. 0824876275
www.fontanavecchia.info

CELLAR SALES
PRE-BOOKED VISITS
ANNUAL PRODUCTION 160,000 bottles
HECTARES UNDER VINE 18.00

Fontanavecchia is one of the best known brands in Sannio, and Libero Rillo one of those most convinced of the area's potential, not only for falanghina and aglianico, but also for other regional varieties such as fiano, greco and piedirosso. This is the spirit behind his extremely varied range, in which we find drinkable basic wines aged in steel alongside selections that undergo long barrel maturation, mainly in small oak. While the former prove to be consistent, the latter could benefit from greater cohesion and a lighter style, along the lines of the great, late-1990s versions like Vigna Cataratte and Facetus. This hope was reinforced by the latest tastings, graced with a Falanghina del Sannio Taburno 2012 that beautifully married primary aromas with linear verve. The Aglianico del Taburno Vigna Cataratte Riserva 2007, meanwhile, is sustained by ripe fruit and oak, and displays solid structure.

○ Taburno Falanghina '12	♀♀♀ 2*	
● Aglianico del Taburno V. Cataratte Ris. '07	♀♀ 4	
○ Sannio Fiano '12	♀♀ 2*	
● Aglianico del Taburno Grave Mora '07	♀ 5	
● Aglianico del Taburno '07	♀♀ 2	
○ Sannio Fiano '11	♀♀ 2*	
● Sannio Piedirosso '11	♀♀ 2*	
○ Taburno Falanghina '11	♀♀ 2*	
○ Taburno Falanghina '10	♀♀ 2	

★Galardi

FRAZ. SAN CARLO
SP SESSA-MIGNANO
81037 SESSA AURUNCA [CE]
TEL. 0823708900
www.terradilavoro.com

PRE-BOOKED VISITS
ANNUAL PRODUCTION 33,000 bottles
HECTARES UNDER VINE 10.00
VITICULTURE METHOD Certified Organic

Fontana Galardi is synonymous with Terra di Lavoro, the only label the winery has ever produced since it was set up at San Carlo di Sessa Aurunca by Luisa Murena, Francesco Catello, Arturo and Dora Celentano, with the help of Riccardo Cotarella. This blend of aglianico topped up with piedirosso, rapidly made a name for itself, especially abroad, for its unmistakable smoky aromas and the great ageing potential provided by its weighty stuffing and extract. The initial semi-experimental productions have resulted in new plantings, today bringing the winery's holdings to around ten hectares, but its soul clearly remains artisanal. Thanks also to increasingly sunny, generous growing years, the recent releases from Terra di Lavoro emphasize its Mediterranean credentials, fully confirmed in the 2011 version, in which plum jam, grass and blood-rich meat over a toasty oak backdrop pave the way for a warm, mature palate with a masculine tannic backbone.

● Terra di Lavoro '11	♀♀♀ 7
● Terra di Lavoro '10	♀♀♀ 7
● Terra di Lavoro '09	♀♀♀ 7
● Terra di Lavoro '08	♀♀♀ 7
● Terra di Lavoro '07	♀♀♀ 7
● Terra di Lavoro '06	♀♀♀ 7
● Terra di Lavoro '05	♀♀♀ 7
● Terra di Lavoro '04	♀♀♀ 7
● Terra di Lavoro '03	♀♀♀ 6
● Terra di Lavoro '02	♀♀♀ 6
● Terra di Lavoro '99	♀♀♀ 6

Cantine Grotta del Sole

VIA SPINELLI, 2
80010 QUARTO [NA]
TEL. 0818762566
www.grottadelsole.it

CELLAR SALES
PRE-BOOKED VISITS
ANNUAL PRODUCTION 700,000 bottles
HECTARES UNDER VINE 42.00

A day with the Martusciello family is a full immersion in the history and geography of Campanian wine. The winery at Quarto, in the heart of the Campi Flegrei, is actually only the hub of a project that involves a series of small estates in the region's main winemaking districts, from Irpinia and Aversa to Vesuvius and the Sorrento peninsula. The winery's range represents all the region's main traditional varieties, many of which have indeed been rediscovered and developed by Grotta del Sole, like falanghina flegrea and an asprinio used mainly sparklers, without forgetting those used for Gragnano and Lettere. Once again, we saw a range full of potential and great value for money. This time we would like to focus on the delicious, racy Vesuvio Lacryma Christi Rosso 2012, with a tidy nose of wild berries, burnt chaff and roots, over a lean, focused palate. We also liked the fine version of the Gragnano 2012.

○ Campi Flegrei Falanghina Coste di Cuma '11	♟♟ 3
● Campi Flegrei Piedirosso '12	♟♟ 2*
○ Fiano di Avellino Tenuta Vicario '12	♟♟ 3
● Penisola Sorrentina Gragnano '12	♟♟ 2*
● Vesuvio Lacryma Christi Rosso '12	♟♟ 3
○ Asprinio d'Aversa Extra Brut M. Cl.	♟ 4
○ Campi Flegrei Falanghina '12	♟ 2
○ Falanghina Spumante Malia Extra Dry	♟ 2
○ Greco di Tufo Tenuta Vicario '12	♟ 3
○ Vesuvio Lacryma Christi Bianco '12	♟ 2
○ Vesuvio Lacryma Christi Dolce	♟ 2
● Aglianico Tenuta Vicario '10	♟♟ 2*
○ Greco di Tufo Tenuta Vicario '11	♟♟ 3
● Quarto di Sole '09	♟♟ 4

La Guardiense

C.DA SANTA LUCIA, 104/106
82034 GUARDIA SANFRAMONDI [BN]
TEL. 0824864034
www.laguardiense.it

CELLAR SALES
PRE-BOOKED VISITS
RESTAURANT SERVICE
ANNUAL PRODUCTION 3,000,000 bottles
HECTARES UNDER VINE 1900.00

The work that has transformed La Guardiense from a colossus on weak foundations into a modern co-operative continues unabated. The operation, headed by Domizio Pigna, with oenological consultancy from Riccardo Cotarella, is above all one of the best wineries in Sannio, with almost 1,000 member-growers, close on 2,000 hectares under vine, and potential production of 3,000,000 bottles. The range comprises both an entry-level line, that shows outstanding value for money, and the Janare line, including more ambitious selections and reds with a more modern touch in terms of density and use of oak. As often happens, however, one of the entry-level wines made the most impression and in this case it was the Guardiolo Aglianico 2011, with crunchy, clear fruit on the nose, echoed on the taut palate with surprisingly relaxed tannins and good breadth. The fuller, darker, mouthfilling Guardiolo Rosso Riserva 2011 shows more extract and attractive oak.

○ Sannio Falanghina Le Janare Senete '12	♟♟ 2*
● Sannio Guardiolo Aglianico '11	♟♟ 2*
● Sannio Guardiolo Rosso Ris. '11	♟♟ 2*
● Guardiolo Aglianico Cantari Ris. '10	♟ 3
○ Sannio Fiano '12	♟ 2
○ Sannio Fiano Colle di Tilio '12	♟ 3
○ Sannio Greco '12	♟ 2
○ Sannio Greco Pietralata '12	♟ 3
● Guardiolo Aglianico Lùcchero '10	♟♟ 2*
● Guardiolo Aglianico Lùcchero '09	♟♟ 2*
● Guardiolo Aglianico Sel. '10	♟♟ 2*
● Guardiolo Rosso Ris. '08	♟♟ 2*

Luigi Maffini

FRAZ. SAN MARCO
LOC. CENITO
84048 CASTELLABATE [SA]
TEL. 0974966345
www.maffini-vini.com

CELLAR SALES
PRE-BOOKED VISITS
ANNUAL PRODUCTION 95,000 bottles
HECTARES UNDER VINE 11.00
VITICULTURE METHOD Certified Organic

The new headquarters of Luigi Maffini and his family are taking shape in the Giungano hills, on a single plot of over 30 hectares, of which 11 are under vine and already in production. The change of address has not stopped here, though, with the winery looking for sites better suited to bringing out the qualities of tautness, measure and drinkability that have always distinguished its versions of Fiano and Aglianico. Unlike the vineyards at San Marco, which will not be abandoned, the new sites lie at higher elevations, of between 250 and 350 metres, on marly limestone soils. As always, Luigi Maffini presented an excellent range, headed by Fiano Pietraincatenata. The 2011 is an admirable version, especially considering the growing year, in which judiciously dosed oak combines with rich, ripe fruit and a firm, complex weave. All it lacks is a hint more flavour.

○ Cilento Fiano Pietraincatenata '11	♟♟	5
● Cilento Aglianico Cenito '09	♟♟	5
○ Kràtos '12	♟♟	3
● Klèos '11	♟	3
● Cilento Aglianico Cenito '03	♟♟♟	5
○ Cilento Fiano Pietraincatenata '10	♟♟♟	4*
○ Pietraincatenata '07	♟♟♟	4
○ Pietraincatenata '04	♟♟♟	4

Masseria Felicia

FRAZ. CARANO
LOC. SAN TERENZANO
81037 SESSA AURUNCA [CE]
TEL. 0823935095
www.masseriafelicia.it

CELLAR SALES
PRE-BOOKED VISITS
ANNUAL PRODUCTION 25,000 bottles
HECTARES UNDER VINE 5.00

The identity of contemporary Falerno is also a result of the aglianico- and piedirosso-based wines produced by the Brini family at their Sessa Aurunca estate at Carano. This small artisanal operation, run by the young Felicia and father Alessandro, has always enjoyed an excellent reputation, both at home and abroad, while also showing a constantly evolving style. Fully expressing the volcanic soils of the north-western slopes of Massico, the winery's three versions of Falerno combine mouthfilling density with tangy contrast, and generally require time in the bottle to unbend. It is by no means a Tre Bicchieri that marks the coming-of-age of a winery of great importance for its territory, but it is surely no coincidence that the first award for Masseria Felicia arrives with the Falerno Etichetta Bronzo 2010. It has the same full-flavoured, smoky energy of the best versions, but also graceful tannins and a more spontaneous, gamey character.

● Falerno del Massico Rosso Et. Bronzo '10	♟♟♟	5
○ Falerno del Massico Bianco Anthologia '12	♟♟	3
● Falerno del Massico Rosso '11	♟♟	2*
● Falerno del Massico Rosso Ariapetrina '10	♟♟	3
⊙ Rosalice '12	♟	3
○ Sinopea '12	♟	2
● Falerno del Massico Rosso '09	♟♟	2
● Falerno del Massico Rosso Ariapetrina '09	♟♟	3
● Falerno del Massico Rosso Ariapetrina '08	♟♟	3
● Falerno del Massico Rosso Et. Bronzo '09	♟♟	5
● Falerno del Massico Rosso Et. Bronzo '08	♟♟	5

★Mastroberardino

VIA MANFREDI, 75/81
83042 ATRIPALDA [AV]
TEL. 0825614111
www.mastroberardino.com

CELLAR SALES
PRE-BOOKED VISITS
ACCOMMODATION AND RESTAURANT SERVICE
ANNUAL PRODUCTION 2,000,000 bottles
HECTARES UNDER VINE 200.00

Few Italian wineries can count on cellars like those of the Mastroberardino family, whose many rarities include bottles of Taurasi from the 1920s and 1930s, still in fine fettle. These memories of the past paved the way for what is now a distinctly modern style, supported above all by various estates in Irpinia's best wine country. The winery is still at Atripalda, but the operation is now run from the estate at Radici di Mirabella, the province's largest single vineyard, as well as being home to an experimental farm, a resort and spa, the Morabianca restaurant and a golf club. As usual, we saw impressive quality across the board, with some peaks of excellence in the white selections, which were fine and gutsy, despite their fermentative edge, and in the Taurasi versions, including a juicy Radici 2009, authoritative despite the difficult year, and a proudly classic Radici Riserva 2007, that earned a Tre Bicchieri.

Salvatore Molettieri

C.DA MUSANNI, 19B
83040 MONTEMARANO [AV]
TEL. 082763424
www.salvatoremolettieri.it

CELLAR SALES
PRE-BOOKED VISITS
ANNUAL PRODUCTION 65,000 bottles
HECTARES UNDER VINE 13.00

It has been 30 years since Salvatore Molettieri decided to stop working solely as a grower and to start producing his own wine, in a sense making him the first vigneron of modern Irpinian viticulture. His Taurasis have become a benchmark for those who associate Aglianico from Montemarano with a dense, rustic character, but at the same time one bursting with mineral energy. His style may divide opinion, especially considering current fashions, but should be considered in the light of the Cinque Querce vineyard and the long harvesting, almost always in November, rather than in terms of strictly technical and oenological choices. The capricious growing year prevented a repeat performance of last year's success for the Taurasi Renonno 2009, whose delicate, variegated nose is followed by a somewhat green, unsubstantial palate. To make up for it, the intense, austere Vigna Cinque Querce 2008 offered masses of extract.

● Taurasi Radici Ris. '07	♀♀♀ 5
○ Fiano di Avellino Radici '12	♀♀ 3*
○ Greco di Tufo Novaserra '12	♀♀ 3*
● Taurasi Radici '09	♀♀ 4
● Aglianico '11	♀♀ 2*
○ Greco di Tufo '12	♀♀ 2*
● Irpinia Aglianico Redimore '11	♀♀ 2*
○ Irpinia Fiano Passito Melizie '11	♀♀ 3
● Taurasi Naturalis Historia '07	♀ 5
○ Fiano di Avellino '12	♀ 2
● Irpinia Aglianico Passito Antheres '10	♀ 5
⊙ Lacrimarosa '12	♀ 2
○ Sannio Falanghina '12	♀ 2
○ Vesuvio Lacryma Christi Bianco '12	♀ 2
● Vesuvio Lacryma Christi Rosso '12	♀ 2

● Taurasi V. Cinque Querce '08	♀♀ 6
○ Greco di Tufo '11	♀♀ 3
● Taurasi Renonno '09	♀♀ 5
○ Fiano di Avellino '11	♀ 3
● Taurasi Renonno '08	♀♀♀ 5
● Taurasi V. Cinque Querce '05	♀♀♀ 6
● Taurasi V. Cinque Querce '04	♀♀♀ 6
● Taurasi V. Cinque Querce Ris. '05	♀♀♀ 7
● Taurasi V. Cinque Querce Ris. '04	♀♀♀ 7
● Taurasi V. Cinque Querce Ris. '01	♀♀♀ 7
● Irpinia Aglianico O'Calice Rosso '10	♀♀ 3
● Taurasi V. Cinque Querce '07	♀♀ 6

Montesole

LOC. SERRA DI MONTEFUSCO
VIA SERRA
83030 MONTEFUSCO [AV]
TEL. 0825963972
www.montesole.it

PRE-BOOKED VISITS
ANNUAL PRODUCTION 1,200,000 bottles
HECTARES UNDER VINE 120.00

We can count on one hand the wineries in the province of Avellino that combine high average quality, impressive production figures, and attractive pricing. One of them is Montesole, which takes its name from the old name of Montefusco, where the winery is situated. Despite not having vineyards of its own, it manages an area of almost 200 hectares with long-term leases and targeted outsourcing, for a comprehensive range dedicated to the main varieties of Irpinia and Sannio. Significant attention is reserved for sparklers and a series of selections, representing more complex versions of the invigorating, racy basic wines. The grid below gives a better idea of Montesole's excellent wines than words ever could. Various labels combine expressive identity and substance, especially the 2012 versions of Greco, but for us the best all-rounder was the mouthfilling, creamy Taurasi Vigna Vinieri 2007, with serious extract and persistent floral aromas.

★Montevetrano

LOC. NIDO
VIA MONTEVETRANO, 3
84099 SAN CIPRIANO PICENTINO [SA]
TEL. 089882285
www.montevetrano.it

CELLAR SALES
PRE-BOOKED VISITS
ACCOMMODATION
ANNUAL PRODUCTION 30,000 bottles
HECTARES UNDER VINE 5.00

For over 20 years, a single name embodied Silvia Imparato's adventure in the world of wine. Montevetrano, the district of San Cipriano Picentino where it all began; Montevetrano, the winery that decided to focus on a single label, from the initial limited productions to today's 30,000 bottles; and Montevetrano, the world's most famous blend of cabernet, merlot and aglianico, which became a cult wine thanks to a coherence that withstood changing fashions and style debates. Now there's another name to remember: since the 2011 harvest, the monovarietal Aglianico Core from the same hills, comes to the range. We saw a good début from the Core 2011, which impressed with its fruit, despite being somewhat schematic. The Montevetrano from the same year, meanwhile, is different from usual, also due to the higher percentage of aglianico, this time at 30%, and shows a Mediterranean nature based more on body than stylistic details.

● Taurasi V. Vinieri '07	♟♟ 6
○ Fiano di Avellino Sirios '12	♟♟ 4
○ Greco di Tufo '12	♟♟ 3
○ Greco di Tufo Serapis '12	♟♟ 3
○ Greco di Tufo V. Breccia '12	♟♟ 4
○ Greco Spumante Brut	♟♟ 3
○ Fiano di Avellino '12	♟ 3
○ Fiano di Avellino V. Acquaviva '12	♟ 4
○ Sannio Falanghina '12	♟ 3
○ Sannio Falanghina V. Zampino '12	♟ 3
○ Spumante Fiano Demi Sec	♟ 3
● Taurasi '08	♟ 4
○ Fiano di Avellino V. Acquaviva '11	♟♟ 4
○ Greco di Tufo V. Breccia '11	♟♟ 4
● Taurasi '07	♟♟ 4

● Montevetrano '11	♟♟♟ 7
● Core '11	♟♟ 3
● Montevetrano '10	♟♟♟ 7
● Montevetrano '09	♟♟♟ 7
● Montevetrano '08	♟♟♟ 7
● Montevetrano '07	♟♟♟ 7
● Montevetrano '06	♟♟♟ 7
● Montevetrano '05	♟♟♟ 7
● Montevetrano '04	♟♟♟ 7
● Montevetrano '03	♟♟♟ 7
● Montevetrano '02	♟♟♟ 7
● Montevetrano '01	♟♟♟ 7
● Montevetrano '00	♟♟♟ 6
● Montevetrano '99	♟♟♟ 7
● Montevetrano '98	♟♟♟ 7
● Montevetrano '97	♟♟♟ 7

Nanni Copè

VIA TUFO, 3
81041 VITULAZIO [CE]
TEL. 0823990529
www.nannicope.it

CELLAR SALES
PRE-BOOKED VISITS
ANNUAL PRODUCTION 7,000 bottles
HECTARES UNDER VINE 2.50

Giovanni Ascione, alias Nanni Copè, started out as a grower in 2008, on a plot of two and a half hectares created about 30 years ago at Monticelli di Castel Campagnano, in the heart of the Colline Caiatine. His single vineyard, planted with modified pergola-trained vines of pallagrello nero and some aglianico, supplies a single label, the Sabbie di Sopra il Bosco, whose name is a geological reference to the Caiazzo sandstone that provides these rolling slopes with such excellent drainage. Work in the cellar is based on staggered harvesting, gentle extraction and ageing in medium-sized oak, aimed at bringing out the grace and full flavour of this characterful wine. It is precisely in terms of vintage identity that the Sabbie di Sopra il Bosco 2011 reaches new heights compared to previous versions. Although somewhat reductive, this time it boasts more focused aromas of grape skin and blossom, followed by an attractive play of contrasts on the delicious, caressing palate.

● Sabbie di Sopra il Bosco '11	▼▼▼	5
● Sabbie di Sopra il Bosco '10	♀♀♀	5
● Sabbie di Sopra il Bosco '09	♀♀♀	5
● Sabbie di Sopra il Bosco '08	♀♀	5

Perillo

C.DA VALLE, 19
83040 CASTELFRANCI [AV]
TEL. 082772252
cantinaperillo@libero.it

CELLAR SALES
PRE-BOOKED VISITS
ANNUAL PRODUCTION 20,000 bottles
HECTARES UNDER VINE 5.00

There are still real treasures waiting to be discovered in the garage winery of Michele Perillo at Castelfranci. This untiring, quiet yet hospitable grower clearly prefers the old, raggiera-trained vines behind his house to banquets and tastings. It is here, on light clay and marine sand at an elevation of 500 metres that he tends the aglianico clone known as coda di cavallo. But his best means of expression remains his Taurasi, rustic in the best sense of the word, aged in partly new barriques and Slavonian oak, that can be laid down and left in the cellar without any worries. Long bottle-ageing is one of the keys to fully understanding and appreciating the Taurasis of Michele Perillo. The 2004 and 2005 are currently available, and in a few months will be joined by the 2006, a racy, austere wine, reminiscent of nebbiolo in its aromatic profile, yet more Mediterranean in terms of body and depth of flavour.

● Taurasi '06	▼▼	4
● Taurasi '05	♀♀♀	4
● Irpinia Campi Taurasini '07	♀♀	4
● Irpinia Campi Taurasini '06	♀♀	4
● Taurasi Ris. '05	♀♀	5

Ciro Picariello

VIA MARRONI
83010 SUMMONTE [AV]
TEL. 0825702516
www.ciropicariello.com

CELLAR SALES
PRE-BOOKED VISITS
ANNUAL PRODUCTION 50,000 bottles
HECTARES UNDER VINE 7.00

Ciro Picariello's success is not only a question of talent. This Irpinia grower also has the ability to sense like few others which way the wind is blowing in terms of winemaking philosophy and style, leading him to adopt a natural, low-impact approach to viticulture. He eschews the help of consultant oenologists, to focus on a pared-down style of vinification, with malolactic fermentation reduced to the bare minimum, maturation in steel, and the release of wines to the market no sooner than a year after harvest. Pigeon-holing apart, his Fianos are always at the top of their league, and reflect perfectly the complementary traits of his vineyards at Summonte and Montefredane. As we often say, the award of top honours is not the only sign of our appreciation. For example, Picariello's Fiano 2011 is a masterful interpretation of a complicated growing year, and little does it matter that it shows some limitations, opening to a deep, complex nose, but followed by a warm palate and an abrupt finish.

○ Fiano di Avellino '11	♥♥ 3*
○ Fiano di Avellino '10	♥♥♥ 3*
○ Fiano di Avellino '08	♥♥♥ 3*
○ Fiano di Avellino '09	♥♥ 3
○ Fiano di Avellino '07	♥♥ 3*
○ Fiano di Avellino '06	♥♥ 3*
○ Fiano di Avellino '05	♥♥ 3*

★Pietracupa

C.DA VADIAPERTI, 17
83030 MONTEFREDANE [AV]
TEL. 0825607418
pietracupa@email.it

CELLAR SALES
PRE-BOOKED VISITS
ANNUAL PRODUCTION 50,000 bottles
HECTARES UNDER VINE 7,50

Sabino Loffredo is not content with being universally considered one of the best old-world producers of whites. His instinctive, restless nature naturally leads him to look for new challenges, and one of the latest is his desire to produce a Taurasi to match the territorial purity and stylistic originality of his splendid Fianos and Grecos. With this in mind, in 2008 he acquired a plot of around two hectares at Torre le Nocelle, the perfect subzone for Aglianicos hinging on harmony and flavour rather than muscle, which he ages in medium-sized barrels and used 20-hectolitre oak. The first Taurasi produced using entirely their own grapes is a racy, lean 2008, but as always it was the whites that really excited us. It was no easy task to choose between the crystalline austerity of the Greco 2012 and the flinty elegance of the Fiano 2012. The latter came first by a whisker, but both of them are a fine match for the fantastic 2010s.

○ Fiano di Avellino '12	♥♥♥ 3*
○ Greco di Tufo '12	♥♥ 3*
● Taurasi '08	♥♥ 5
● Quirico '11	♥ 3
○ Cupo '10	♥♥♥ 5
○ Cupo '08	♥♥♥ 5
○ Cupo '05	♥♥♥ 5
○ Cupo '03	♥♥♥ 3*
○ Greco di Tufo '10	♥♥♥ 3*
○ Greco di Tufo '09	♥♥♥ 3*
○ Greco di Tufo '08	♥♥♥ 3*
○ Greco di Tufo '07	♥♥♥ 3*
○ Greco di Tufo '06	♥♥♥ 3*

Quintodecimo

VIA SAN LEONARDO, 27
83036 MIRABELLA ECLANO [AV]
TEL. 0825449321
www.quintodecimo.it

CELLAR SALES
PRE-BOOKED VISITS
ACCOMMODATION
ANNUAL PRODUCTION 36,000 bottles
HECTARES UNDER VINE 15.00

In many ways the project set up at
Mirabella by Luigi Moio and his partner
Laura Di Marzio is just what Irpinia was
missing. Quintodecimo is the province of
Avellino's chateau approach, focusing on a
complete range of wines based on
aglianico, from vineyards planted around
the winery. In addition, greco, fiano and
falanghina come from targeted purchases
and rented plots. Harvested when fully ripe
and aged in small oak, the grapes give
modern, at times attractively oaky wines,
designed to maintain structure and
substance over time. This openly haute
couture approach is also reflected in
attention to detail and prices. In many ways
this was not the best possible formation
that Quintodecimo could have hoped for,
with the new Taurasis still ageing and all of
the whites coming from the variable 2011
vintage. Nevertheless, it gave us an
opportunity to appreciate the excellent
Terra d'Eclano 2010, a small, yet vigorous,
crunchy Taurasi.

● Irpinia Aglianico Terra d'Eclano '10	♟♟ 6
○ Fiano di Avellino Exultet '11	♟♟ 6
○ Greco di Tufo Giallo D'Arles '11	♟♟ 6
○ Via Del Campo Falanghina '11	♟♟ 5
○ Fiano di Avellino Exultet '09	♟♟♟ 6
○ Fiano di Avellino Exultet '10	♟♟ 6
○ Greco di Tufo Giallo D'Arles '10	♟♟ 6
● Irpinia Aglianico Terra d'Eclano '09	♟♟ 6
● Taurasi V. Quintodecimo Ris. '07	♟♟ 8

Fattoria La Rivolta

C.DA RIVOLTA
82030 TORRECUSO [BN]
TEL. 0824872921
www.fattorialarivolta.com

CELLAR SALES
PRE-BOOKED VISITS
ACCOMMODATION
ANNUAL PRODUCTION 150,000 bottles
HECTARES UNDER VINE 29.00
VITICULTURE METHOD Certified Organic

Purchased in the 1990s by the Cotroneo
family in the district of the same name at
Torrecuso, La Rivolta covers 29 hectares,
farmed using organic techniques and
dedicated to all Campania's main traditional
varieties. For some years we have
appreciated the close-knit, lustrous style,
seen above all in the whites and rosé, all
aged in steel after brief cold maceration,
with the exception of Sogno di Rivolta. There
are two Aglianico del Taburnos, somewhat
different in form but increasingly similar in
terms of performance. The basic wine is
aged in large, mostly second-passage
barrels, while new barriques are used for
the Terra di Rivolta Riserva. The 2012
whites are lustrous, dense varietal
interpretations, while among the Aglianico
del Taburnos, we preferred the lean,
dynamic drinkability of the 2010
extraordinary wine to the somewhat
restrained, lean Terra di Rivolta Riserva
2010.

● Aglianico del Taburno '10	♟♟♟ 3*
● Aglianico del Taburno Terra di Rivolta Ris. '10	♟♟ 5
○ Sannio Fiano '12	♟♟ 3
○ Taburno Coda di Volpe '12	♟♟ 2*
○ Taburno Falanghina '12	♟♟ 2*
○ Sannio Taburno Greco '12	♟ 2
● Taburno Piedirosso '12	♟ 2
● Aglianico del Taburno Terra di Rivolta Ris. '08	♟♟♟ 5
● Aglianico del Taburno Terra di Rivolta Ris. '09	♟♟ 5
○ Sogno di Rivolta '11	♟♟ 3
○ Taburno Falanghina '11	♟♟ 2*
● Taburno Piedirosso '11	♟♟ 2*

Rocca del Principe

VIA ARIANIELLO, 9
83030 LAPIO [AV]
TEL. 0825982435
www.roccadelprincipe.it

CELLAR SALES
PRE-BOOKED VISITS
ANNUAL PRODUCTION 23,000 bottles
HECTARES UNDER VINE 10.00

Although Lapio has always been known in the province of Avellino as the home of Fiano, it is only recently that a significant group of growers here has been able to express its identity to the full. Among the leaders of this renaissance are husband-and-wife team Aurelia Fabrizio and Ercole Zarrella, the owners of Rocca del Principe. Their sole Fiano, which brings together grapes from Lenze, Arianiello, Tognano and Campore, spends a long time in steel on the fine lees, and is released over a year after harvest. Their second label, the Taurasi Materdomini, is made using outsourced grapes, and aged in barrique, tonneau and large barrels. The Fiano di Avellino 2011 presented by Rocca del Principe was one of the very best in its category. Attempts to limit the problems caused by a torrid growing year seem to have worked on the nose, with its citrus, wild flowers and new-mown grass, while the palate clearly suffered in depth of flavour and thrust.

○ Fiano di Avellino '11	♀♀ 3*
● Taurasi Mater Domini '09	♀♀ 5
○ Fiano di Avellino '10	♀♀♀ 3*
○ Fiano di Avellino '08	♀♀♀ 2*
○ Fiano di Avellino '07	♀♀♀ 2*
● Taurasi Master Domini '07	♀♀ 5
● Taurasi Mater Domini '08	♀♀ 5

Tenuta San Francesco

FRAZ. CORSANO
VIA SOFILCIANO, 18
84010 TRAMONTI [SA]
TEL. 089876748
www.vinitenutasanfrancesco.it

CELLAR SALES
PRE-BOOKED VISITS
ACCOMMODATION
ANNUAL PRODUCTION 40,000 bottles
HECTARES UNDER VINE 10.00

Few areas compete with the Amalfi Coast when it comes to attracting expert wine lovers looking not just for good wines but for unique, inimitable bottles. This is thanks to projects like Tenuta San Francesco, established in 2004 by four partners and now covering just under ten hectares, of which a third is owned by the winery. We are in Tramonti, a subzone of extraordinary ampelographical interest, with its age-old ungrafted tintore vines that give austere, Mediterranean reds like the Quattrospine Riserva and the E' Iss Vigna Paradiso. Steel alone is used for the two white falanghina, pepella and ginestra blends. There were many excellent labels from a winery that has seen exponential growth in consistency and stylistic focus in recent years. We hoped for more from the E' Iss Vigna Paradiso 2010 and the Per Eva 2011, but to compensate, the Tramonti Bianco 2012 was one of the year's best blends from the Amalfi Coast: subtle, lively and progressive.

○ Costa d'Amalfi Tramonti Bianco '12	♀♀ 3*
● Costa d'Amalfi Tramonti Rosso '11	♀♀ 3
● Costa d'Amalfi Tramonti Rosso Quattrospine Ris. '09	♀♀ 5
● E' Iss V. Paradiso '10	♀♀ 5
○ Costa d'Amalfi Bianco Per Eva '11	♀ 4
⊙ Costa d'Amalfi Tramonti Rosato '12	♀ 3
○ Costa d'Amalfi Bianco Per Eva '10	♀♀ 3
○ Costa d'Amalfi Tramonti Bianco '11	♀♀ 2*
○ Costa d'Amalfi Tramonti Bianco '10	♀♀ 2*
● Costa d'Amalfi Tramonti Rosso Quattrospine Ris. '08	♀♀ 5
● Costa d'Amalfi Tramonti Rosso Quattrospine Ris. '07	♀♀ 5
○ E' Iss V. Paradiso '09	♀♀ 3*

San Giovanni

C.DA TRESINO
84048 CASTELLABATE [SA]
TEL. 0974965136
www.agricolasangiovanni.it

CELLAR SALES
PRE-BOOKED VISITS
ACCOMMODATION
ANNUAL PRODUCTION 20,000 bottles
HECTARES UNDER VINE 4.00

Until recently the place even lacked mains electricity. A single detail that suffices to render the idea of the enchanted, unspoilt place that Mario and Ida Corrado chose as their home and winery in 1993, when they established Agricola San Giovanni at Punta Tresino di Castellabate. Literally a stone's throw from the cliffs, in a protected area of the Cilento National Park, the views are stunning, but the wines have a beauty all their own. The four-hectare plot is planted almost exclusively to fiano and aglianico, with some piedirosso, which become wines of a lustrous, spirited style that intensifies their inherently Mediterranean, salty nature. This was exactly the expressive profile found in the Tresinus 2012, one of the most exciting Fianos ever tasted outside Irpinia, with a stratified Mediterranean nose of aniseed, flint, melon, bread, and wood resin, paving the way for a palate modulated more by flavour than linearity, with a lovely camomile finish.

○ Fiano Tresinus '12	♟♟♟	3*
● Castellabate '11	♟♟	3
● Ficonera '11	♟♟	5
● Maroccia '09	♟	5
○ Paestum Bianco '12	♟	3
○ Fiano '11	♟♟	2*
○ Fiano Tresinus '11	♟♟	3
○ Fiano Tresinus '10	♟♟	3*
● Maroccia '07	♟♟	5

San Salvatore

VIA DIONISIO
84050 GIUNGANO [SA]
TEL. 08281990900
www.sansalvatore1988.it

CELLAR SALES
ACCOMMODATION AND RESTAURANT SERVICE
ANNUAL PRODUCTION 120,000 bottles
HECTARES UNDER VINE 16.50
VITICULTURE METHOD Certified Organic

The headquarters of San Salvatore are situated in the hills overlooking Paestum, Stio and Giungano in the Cilento National Park. The organic winery created by Giuseppe Pagano has 16 hectares under vine and is only the latest part of a project that includes market gardening, oil production and buffalo farming, aimed at provisioning the family's restaurants and hotels using a self-sufficient system. The vineyard includes plantings of Campania's main varieties, interpreted in a modern style, with a focus on rounded, aromatic whites, and well-extracted, toasty reds. These style features emerged in our tastings, dominated by the Pian di Stio 2012. The temperature-controlled vinification of this pure Fiano emphasizes its terpenic, almost sauvignon-like traits, mirrored on the off-dry palate, finishing with lime and white-fleshed fruit. The Omaggio a Gillo Dorfles 2010 showed a modern style, with berry fruit and coffee aromas.

○ Pian di Stio '12	♟♟♟	3*
● Omaggio a Gillo Dorfles '10	♟♟	6
○ Joi Brut Rosé '10	♟♟	5
○ Calpazio '12	♟	3
○ Cecerale Senza Solfiti Aggiunti '12	♟	3
○ Trentenare '12	♟	3
● Jungano '10	♟♟	3
○ Pian di Stio '11	♟♟	3*

Sanpaolo - Magistravini

C.DA SAN PAOLO
83042 ATRIPALDA [AV]
TEL. 0832704398
www.magistravini.it

CELLAR SALES
PRE-BOOKED VISITS
ANNUAL PRODUCTION 250,000 bottles
HECTARES UNDER VINE 15.00

After only a year down in the ranks, Sanpaolo is back in Campania's main section. Owned by the Puglia group Magistravini, this is one of the few projects set up by investors from outside the province of Avellino. The company is named for one of the districts of Torrioni, in the heart of the Greco di Tufo DOC zone, and offers a complete range of wine types from Irpinia and Sannio. They are interpreted with a real sense of place, as can be seen in the vineyard selections: Lapio and Montefredane for Fiano di Avellino, Montefusco for Greco di Tufo, and no fewer than four versions of Falanghina del Beneventano, all differing from each other in terms of soil composition. The return to the full profiles was due to labels, the whites especially, that often went well beyond mere technical correctness. An austere, vibrant interpretation of the 2012 growing year can be seen in the delicate, flowery Fiano di Avellino Lapio, and even more so in the Montefredane, with greater backbone and minerality.

○ Falanghina Acqua '12	♟♟	3
○ Fiano di Avellino Lapio '12	♟♟	3
○ Fiano di Avellino Montefredane '12	♟♟	3
○ Greco di Tufo '12	♟♟	2*
○ Greco di Tufo Montefusco '12	♟♟	3
● Taurasi '08	♟♟	5
● Taurasi Ris. '08	♟♟	5
○ Falanghina Aria '12	♟	3
○ Falanghina Fuoco '12	♟	3
○ Falanghina Terra '12	♟	3
○ Fiano di Avellino '12	♟	2
○ Falanghina Fuoco '10	♟♟	3
○ Fiano di Avellino Lapio '10	♟♟	3
○ Fiano di Avellino Montefredane '11	♟♟	3
○ Greco di Tufo Montefusco '11	♟♟	3

Tenuta Sarno 1860

C.DA SERRONI, 4B
83100 AVELLINO
TEL. 082526161
www.tenutasarno1860.it

CELLAR SALES
ANNUAL PRODUCTION 15,000 bottles
HECTARES UNDER VINE 7.00

It has only taken a few harvests for Maura Sarno to scale the ranks of Fiano di Avellino with her sole wine. The heart of it all is the family estate, a single seven-hectare plot in the Candida uplands, at elevations of 500 metres. Here, plantings began in 2004 on clayey-limestone soils, where the cellar is currently being built. Although the facility itself is unfinished, the estate's style has been clear and defined since the very first vintage in 2009, with temperature-controlled fermentation in steel and a few months on the lees giving lustrous, aromatically exuberant Fianos that play on focus rather than power. Tenuta Sarno's Fiano di Avellino makes the main section of our Guide thanks to the promising 2012 version. Intense aromas of aniseed, citrus and bouquet garni come immediately to the fore, and are set against the iodine, mineral backdrop running through a well-sustained palate that lacks only a final shift of gear.

○ Fiano di Avellino '12	♟♟	3*
○ Fiano di Avellino '11	♟♟	3
○ Fiano di Avellino '10	♟♟	3*

La Sibilla

FRAZ. BAIA
VIA OTTAVIANO AUGUSTO, 19
80070 BACOLI [NA]
TEL. 0818688778
www.sibillavini.it

CELLAR SALES
PRE-BOOKED VISITS
ANNUAL PRODUCTION 70,000 bottles
HECTARES UNDER VINE 9.50

Young Vincenzo Di Meo now works full time at the family winery, whose links with the Campi Flegrei are even in its logo, depicting the Cumaean Sybil mentioned by Virgil. The operation is witnessing impressive growth and has managed to combine the untamed nature of the terroir with a focused, juicy style, especially in the selections that flank the line of fragrant basic wines. The Falanghina Cruna deLago spends nine months in steel on the lees and is released over a year after harvest. The Piedirosso Vigne Storiche is aged in third-passage medium-sized oak after fermentation with native yeasts and an initial period resting on toasted grape pips. An important part of the growth of La Sibilla has been the Piedirosso Vigne Storiche 2011. Fermented in steel, it already displays expressive maturity, offering a combination of fruit and smoky tones on the nose, but its real racy spirit is found on the richly flavoured, luxuriant, stratified palate with its long citrus finish.

● Campi Flegrei Piedirosso Vigne Storiche '11	♟♟ 4
○ Campi Flegrei Falanghina Cruna deLago '11	♟♟ 4
● Campi Flegrei Piedirosso '12	♟♟ 3
● Marsiliano '10	♟♟ 5
● Marsiliano '09	♟♟ 5
○ Campi Flegrei Falanghina '12	♟ 2
⊙ Pedirosa '12	♟ 3
○ Campi Flegrei Falanghina '10	♟♟ 2*
○ Campi Flegrei Falanghina Cruna deLago '10	♟♟ 4
● Marsiliano '07	♟♟ 5

Sorrentino

VIA RIO, 26
80042 BOSCOTRECASE [NA]
TEL. 0818584963
www.sorrentinovini.com

CELLAR SALES
PRE-BOOKED VISITS
ACCOMMODATION AND RESTAURANT SERVICE
ANNUAL PRODUCTION 220,000 bottles
HECTARES UNDER VINE 30.00
VITICULTURE METHOD Certified Organic

If wine on Vesuvius is slowly waking from a long slumber, this is also thanks to the commitment of the Sorrentino family. Situated at Boscotrecase, on the southern slopes of the sleeping volcano at elevations of 400 – 500 metres, the family-owned estate is a magnificent laboratory of biodiversity, whose 20 hectares are mainly planted to piedirosso, falanghina, caprettone and catalanesca. The result is an extensive range of labels with a constantly evolving style. The Prodivi line comprises the more ambitious wines, designed to age well with their unmistakably spirited, smoky character. Whether we are talking about old or new labels, once again this year the wines of Sorrentino impressed above all as a group. A special mention should go both to the Vigna Lapillo Rosso 2011, with bright, attractively almondy fruit, and the Frupa 2011, a monovarietal piedirosso that shows more stuffing and toasty oak but also good minerality.

● Don Paolo '11	♟♟ 4
● Frupa '11	♟♟ 5
○ Nati '11	♟♟ 4
⊙ Vesuvio Lacryma Christi Rosato Versacrum '12	♟♟ 2*
● Vesuvio Lacryma Christi Rosso V. Lapillo '11	♟♟ 3
○ Falanghina Versacrum '12	♟ 2
○ Vesuvio Lacryma Christi Bianco V. Lapillo '12	♟ 3
○ Vesuvio Lacryma Christi Bianco Versacrum '12	♟ 2
● Don Paolo '10	♟♟ 4
● Don Paolo '09	♟♟ 3
○ Nati '10	♟♟ 3
● Vesuvio Lacryma Christi Rosso Ver Sacrum '11	♟♟ 2*

Luigi Tecce

C.DA TRINITÀ, 6
83052 PATERNOPOLI [AV]
TEL. 082771375
ltecce@libero.it

CELLAR SALES
PRE-BOOKED VISITS
ANNUAL PRODUCTION 10,000 bottles
HECTARES UNDER VINE 4.00

The crucial role played by Luigi Tecce's Taurasi in the competitive Irpinia district cannot be seen just in terms of performance, scores and tasting notes. Above all, he has shown that a different approach is possible with aglianico, that it does not always need to be reined in to offer thrills and originality. The old raggiera-trained vines at Paternopoli and Castelfranci are the only thing that has remained unchanged, with work in the rows and winery adjusting to the growing year's conditions. This renders superfluous any considerations on the type of maceration or size and origin of the containers used for ageing. The style here is unique, in the best sense of the term. Unsurprisingly, Luigi Tecce's interpretation of the capricious 2009 growing year showed a certain courage. His Poliphemo plays on roots, liquorice, dark berry fruit and almost charcoally notes, leading to impetuous, full flavour on the palate, sustained by a weighty tannic weave.

● Taurasi Poliphemo '09	♟♟ 7
● Irpinia Campi Taurasini Satyricon '10	♟♟ 5
● Taurasi Poliphemo '08	♟♟♟ 6
● Taurasi Poliphemo '07	♟♟♟ 6
● Irpinia Campi Taurasini Satyricon '09	♟♟ 4
● Taurasi Poliphemo '06	♟♟ 6

Terre del Principe

FRAZ. SQUILLE
VIA SS. GIOVANNI E PAOLO, 30
81010 CASTEL CAMPAGNANO [CE]
TEL. 0823867126
www.terredelprincipe.com

CELLAR SALES
PRE-BOOKED VISITS
ACCOMMODATION AND RESTAURANT SERVICE
ANNUAL PRODUCTION 55,000 bottles
HECTARES UNDER VINE 11.00

Terre del Principe represents the second phase of the project begun by Peppe Mancini and Manuela Piancastelli in the 1990s, thanks to which we are now aware of pallagrello and casavecchia. Their job was made easier by the fact that they owned important vineyard holdings, spread over the various slopes of the Castel Campagnano hills, where both the Squille production facility and the tuff barrel cellar for the reds are situated. Their take on local Caiazzo varieties involves maturation in small, mainly new barrels for the Ambruco, Centomoggia, Piancastelli and Le Sérole selections, while the vintage Pallagrello Bianco, Fontanavigna, is aged in steel. Independently of its Tre Bicchieri, the Casavecchia Centomoggia 2011 was stylistically the most convincing of those we tasted at Terre del Principe. We liked the relaxed profile of this multifaceted middleweight, brimming with herbs and roots, that plays more on iodine suppleness than tannic backbone.

● Casavecchia Centomoggia '11	♟♟♟ 5
○ Le Serole '11	♟♟ 5
● Ambruco '11	♟♟ 5
● Castello delle Femmine '11	♟♟ 3
○ Fontanavigna '12	♟♟ 3
● Piancastelli '10	♟♟ 6
⊙ Roseto del Volturno '12	♟ 3
● Ambruco '06	♟♟♟ 5
● Ambruco Pallagrello Nero '10	♟♟♟ 5
● Centomoggia '08	♟♟♟ 5
● Centomoggia '07	♟♟♟ 5

Terredora

VIA SERRA
83030 MONTEFUSCO [AV]
TEL. 0825968215
www.terredora.com

CELLAR SALES
PRE-BOOKED VISITS
ACCOMMODATION
ANNUAL PRODUCTION 1,200,000 bottles
HECTARES UNDER VINE 200.00

The sudden loss of Lucio Mastroberardino left a deep mark on the world of wine in Campania, and further afield. A former chairman of Federvini and of the Consorzio di Tutela Vini d'Irpinia, he also spent almost 20 years as the technical manager at Terredora, the company he established in 1993 with his father Walter and siblings Paolo and Daniela, to whom we express our heartfelt condolences. They are left with the task of managing a series of strategically positioned estates in Irpinia, at Montefusco and Santa Paolina for Greco; Lapio for fiano and aglianico; Pietradefusi for Taurasi. All underpinning an extremely variegated, composite range. There can be no better way of commemorating Lucio Mastroberardino than opening a bottle of Taurasi Fatica Contadina 2008. This fantastic thoroughbred Aglianico displays stripped down fruit but wonderful complexity: despite its youthful stiffness, it is earthy, gutsy, and satisfying, as well as classical to the core.

● Taurasi Fatica Contadina '08	♥♥♥	5
○ Fiano di Avellino Campo Re '10	♥♥	5
○ Fiano di Avellino Terre Dora '12	♥♥	3
○ Greco di Tufo Terre degli Angeli '12	♥♥	3
○ Coda di Volpe '12	♥	2
○ Falanghina '12	♥	3
○ Greco di Tufo Loggia della Serra '12	♥	3
○ Fiano di Avellino Terre di Dora '10	♀♀	3
○ Greco di Tufo Loggia della Serra '10	♀♀	3
○ Greco di Tufo Terre degli Angeli '10	♀♀	3

Urciuolo

FRAZ. CELZI
VIA DUE PRINCIPATI, 9
83020 FORINO [AV]
TEL. 0825761649
www.fratelliurciuolo.it

CELLAR SALES
PRE-BOOKED VISITS
ANNUAL PRODUCTION 120,000 bottles
HECTARES UNDER VINE 22.00

The project developed over recent years by brothers Ciro and Antonello Urciuolo seems to be going through a period of transition in many ways. Over time, rising production figures and a growing range of wines have required new investments both in the rows and in the winery. We will see in coming seasons whether they focus on distribution and prices or whether they prefer to try and attract demanding wine lovers with increasingly original, characterful interpretations. With the 2008 vintage we have their first Taurasi Riserva, from the Mirabella vineyard, while the Castelfranci and Montemarano grapes are used for the basic wine. Precisely the Taurasi 2009 seems to be one of the most effective interpretations of a difficult vintage, despite lacking some complexity. We were also convinced by the Fiano di Avellino 2012, as usual playing on rich fruit and density, whose buttery swathes nicely counterpoint its stiff backbone.

○ Fiano di Avellino '12	♥♥	2*
● Taurasi '09	♥♥	4
● Taurasi Ris. '08	♥♥	5
● Aglianico '11	♥	1*
○ Greco di Tufo '12	♥	2
● Taurasi '07	♀♀♀	5
● Taurasi '06	♀♀♀	5*
● Taurasi '05	♀♀♀	5
● Taurasi '08	♀♀	5

CAMPANIA

Vestini Campagnano Poderi Foglia

FRAZ. SAN GIOVANNI E PAOLO
VIA BARRACCONE, 5
81013 CAIAZZO [CE]
TEL. 0823679087
www.vestinicampagnano.it

CELLAR SALES
PRE-BOOKED VISITS
ANNUAL PRODUCTION 70,000 bottles
HECTARES UNDER VINE 8.00
VITICULTURE METHOD Certified Organic

This historic Caiazzo winery, run by the Barletta and Quaranta families, owns two estates. Five hectares near Caiazzo at Vestini Campagnano are dedicated to pallagrello and casavecchia, while three more are situated in Podere Foglia at Conca della Campania, in the area of Galluccio, with large plantings of aglianico and falanghina. It is difficult to identify a single style in a range in which international interpretations, especially in the reds, rich in oak and extract, rub shoulders with more unpredictable wines that play on tertiary and gamey notes. Our impressions were confirmed in our tastings, among the most convincing in recent years, and it had been some time since we sampled a Galluccio as personal and expressive as the Concarosso 2011. This blend of aglianico and pallagrello nero aged in steel combines delicious fruit with full-flavoured, austere volcanic notes. The Concabianco 2012 is also excellent.

Villa Diamante

VIA TOPPOLE, 16
83030 MONTEFREDANE [AV]
TEL. 0825670014
www.villadiamante.eu

CELLAR SALES
PRE-BOOKED VISITS
ANNUAL PRODUCTION 10,000 bottles
HECTARES UNDER VINE 2.90
VITICULTURE METHOD Certified Organic

The small Villa Diamante operation, with its three or so hectares of Vigna Congregazione vines, can be found on the Toppole di Montefredane hill, at just over 400 metres of altitude. Partially north-facing on clayey, stony soils, this is one of the best vineyards for Fiano di Avellino, whose unmistakable flinty, smoky traits are lifted by the light hand of Antoine Gaita and Diamante Renna, who shun clarification and filtration to focus on long maturation in steel. The Greco di Tufo Vigna del Ciamillo and the Taurasi Pater Nobilis are produced using outsourced grapes, and are aged for two years in new barrels and third-passage barriques. For us, the 2011 is one of the best odd-numbered vintages of Vigna della Congregazione, and above all the most successful Fiano di Avellino from a difficult year. This was not quite enough for top honours, but this is one to watch, with more Mediterranean character than usual and its trademark saline thrust.

● Galluccio Rosso Concarosso '11		▼▼ 2*
○ Galluccio Bianco Concabianco '12		▼▼ 2*
● Galluccio Rosso Concarosso Ris. '10		▼▼ 2*
● Pallagrello Nero '10		▼▼ 5
○ Asprinio da Viti Maritate '12		▼ 2
● Casa Vecchia '10		▼ 5
● Kajanero '12		▼ 2
○ Le Ortole '11		▼ 4
○ Pallagrello Bianco '12		▼ 3
⊙ Vado Ceraso '12		▼ 3
● Casa Vecchia '01		▼▼▼ 4*
○ Asprinio '11		▼▼ 2*
● Kajanero '11		▼▼ 2*

○ Fiano di Avellino Vigna della Congregazione '11	▼▼ 5
○ Fiano di Avellino Vigna della Congregazione '10	▼▼▼ 5
○ Fiano di Avellino Vigna della Congregazione '08	▼▼▼ 4
○ Fiano di Avellino Vigna della Congregazione '06	▼▼▼ 4
○ Fiano di Avellino Vigna della Congregazione '04	▼▼▼ 4
○ Fiano di Avellino Vigna della Congregazione '09	▼▼ 5
● Taurasi Pater Nobilis '07	▼▼ 5

★Villa Matilde

SS Domitiana, 18
81030 Cellole [CE]
Tel. 0823932088
www.villamatilde.it

CELLAR SALES
PRE-BOOKED VISITS
ACCOMMODATION AND RESTAURANT SERVICE
ANNUAL PRODUCTION 700,000 bottles
HECTARES UNDER VINE 130.00

It is somewhat simplistic to refer to Villa
Matilde as the mother winery of
contemporary Falerno, rescued with
difficulty by Francesco Avallone and his
worthy heirs Maria Ida and Salvatore, today
at the helm. With its acquisitions of Tenuta
Rocca dei Leoni, in Sannio, and Tenute
d'Altavilla, in Irpinia, they have transformed
the Cellole operation into a regional
colossus, with a varied but stylistically
coherent range based on falanghina,
aglianico, piedirosso, primitivo, fiano, and
greco. The basic wines display fantastic
value for money and intriguing vitality, while
the Camarato and Caracci selections show
greater extract and intensity. As always, we
were won over by the reliability of an
extensive range of wines at attractive prices,
such as the Falerno Bianco and Falanghina
Rocca dei Leoni 2012. Among the more
ambitious labels, the Cecubo 2009 is on
great form, attractively reminiscent of a
Rhone wine and offering full flavour with
good supporting tannins.

● Cecubo '09	▼▼ 4
○ Falanghina Tenuta Rocca dei Leoni '12	▼▼ 2*
○ Falerno del Massico Bianco '12	▼▼ 3
● Falerno del Massico Rosso V. Camarato Ris. '07	▼▼ 7
● Aglianico Tenuta Rocca dei Leoni '11	▼ 2
● Deira Aglianico Passito '05	▼ 8
○ Falanghina di Roccamonfina '12	▼ 2
● Falerno del Massico Rosso '10	▼ 3
○ Fiano di Avellino Tenute di Altavilla '12	▼ 3
○ Greco di Tufo Tenute di Altavilla '12	▼ 3
○ Falerno del Massico Bianco V. Caracci '08	▽▽▽ 3
○ Falerno del Massico Bianco V. Caracci '05	▽▽▽ 3
○ Falerno del Massico Bianco V. Caracci '04	▽▽▽ 3*

Villa Raiano

loc. San Michele di Serino
via Bosco Satrano, 1
83020 Serino [AV]
Tel. 0825595550
www.villaraiano.com

CELLAR SALES
PRE-BOOKED VISITS
ANNUAL PRODUCTION 300,000 bottles
HECTARES UNDER VINE 26.00

The growth of Irpinia is also based on
projects such as that developed at Villa
Raiano by brothers Sabino and Simone
Basso, and the latter's brother-in-law, Paolo
Sibillo. This winery played a leading role in
the 1990s boom but managed to reinvent
its style, acquiring important vineyards and
placing increasing emphasis on the
territorial aspects of a range that was
already solid and reliable. The focus is still
on whites, as seen in the vineyard
selections Marotta di Montefrusco for
Greco, and Alimata di Montefredane and
Ventidue di Lapio for Fiano, although the
sites at Castelfranci lead us to believe that
Taurasi will soon be given similar attention.
The latest tastings also impressed, despite
the reduced range. We will have to wait
until next year to try the selections, but
once again were amazed by the entry-level
whites: the Fiano di Avellino 2012 displays
closely-knit citrus while the Greco di Tufo
from the same year plays on cereal traits
and a lean palate.

○ Fiano di Avellino '12	▼▼ 3
○ Greco di Tufo '12	▼▼ 3
● Taurasi '09	▼▼ 5
● Aglianico '11	▼ 2
○ Fiano di Avellino Alimata '10	▽▽▽ 4
○ Fiano di Avellino '11	▽▽ 3
○ Fiano di Avellino Alimata '11	▽▽ 4
○ Fiano di Avellino Ventidue '11	▽▽ 4
○ Greco di Tufo '11	▽▽ 3
● Taurasi Raiano '08	▽▽ 5

Abbazia di Crapolla

Loc. Avigliano
via San Filippo, 2
80069 Vico Equense [NA]
Tel. 3383517280
www.abbaziadicrapolla.it

ANNUAL PRODUCTION 12,000 bottles
HECTARES UNDER VINE 2.00

● Pinot Nero '11	♟♟ 5
○ Sireo Bianco '11	♟♟ 5
● Sireo Rosso '11	♟♟ 5

Aia dei Colombi

c.da Sapenzie
82034 Guardia Sanframondi [BN]
Tel. 0824817384
www.aiadeicolombi.it

CELLAR SALES
PRE-BOOKED VISITS
ANNUAL PRODUCTION 60,000 bottles
HECTARES UNDER VINE 18.00

○ Falanghina del Sannio Guardia Sanframondi '12	♟♟ 2*
○ Falanghina del Sannio Guardia Sanframondi Vignasuprema '11	♟ 2

Alepa

via Barraccone
81013 Caiazzo [CE]
Tel. 0823862755
www.alepa.it

PRE-BOOKED VISITS
ACCOMMODATION
ANNUAL PRODUCTION 15,000 bottles
HECTARES UNDER VINE 4.00

○ Maria Carolina '11	♟♟ 5
○ Riccio Bianco '11	♟♟ 3
● Riccio Nero '09	♟ 4

Amarano

c.da Torre, 32
83040 Montemarano [AV]
Tel. 082763351
www.amarano.it

CELLAR SALES
PRE-BOOKED VISITS
ANNUAL PRODUCTION 20,000 bottles
HECTARES UNDER VINE 3.00

● Irpinia Campi Taurasini Malambruno '10	♟♟ 3
● Taurasi Principe Lagonessa '09	♟♟ 5

Antichi Coloni

c.da Salici
83052 Paternopoli [AV]
Tel. 3472563997
www.antichicoloni.com

CELLAR SALES
ANNUAL PRODUCTION 10,000 bottles
HECTARES UNDER VINE 1.73

● Taurasi Centaurus '08	♟♟ 5
● Vinicius '11	♟ 2

Antico Castello

c.da Poppano, 11
83050 San Mango sul Calore [AV]
Tel. 3408062830
www.anticocastello.com

CELLAR SALES
PRE-BOOKED VISITS
ANNUAL PRODUCTION 40,000 bottles
HECTARES UNDER VINE 10.00

● Irpinia Aglianico Magis '09	♟♟ 3
○ Irpinia Fiano '12	♟ 3
○ Irpinia Greco '12	♟ 3

Giuseppe Apicella

FRAZ. CAPITIGNANO
VIA CASTELLO SANTA MARIA, 1
84010 TRAMONTI [SA]
TEL. 089856209
www.giuseppeapicella.it

CELLAR SALES
PRE-BOOKED VISITS
ANNUAL PRODUCTION 70,000 bottles
HECTARES UNDER VINE 7.00
VITICULTURE METHOD Certified Organic

● Costa d'Amalfi Tramonti Rosso '09	♀♀ 3
● Costa d'Amalfi Tramonti Rosso A' Scippata Ris. '08	♀♀ 5
○ Costa d'Amalfi Tramonti Bianco '12	♀ 2

Cantine Astroni

FRAZ. ASTRONI
VIA SARTANIA, 48
80126 NAPOLI
TEL. 0815884182
www.cantineastroni.com

CELLAR SALES
PRE-BOOKED VISITS
RESTAURANT SERVICE
ANNUAL PRODUCTION 360,000 bottles
HECTARES UNDER VINE 25.00

● Campi Flegrei Piedirosso Colle Rotondella '12	♀♀ 2*
● Campi Flegrei Piedirosso Tenuta Camaldoli '11	♀♀ 2*

Bambinuto

VIA CERRO
83030 SANTA PAOLINA [AV]
TEL. 0825964634
info@cantinabambinuto.com

PRE-BOOKED VISITS
ANNUAL PRODUCTION 30,000 bottles
HECTARES UNDER VINE 4.00

○ Greco di Tufo '12	♀♀ 3
○ Falanghina '12	♀ 2

Boccella

VIA SANT'EUSTACHIO
83040 CASTELFRANCI [AV]
TEL. 082772574
www.boccellavini.it

CELLAR SALES
PRE-BOOKED VISITS
ANNUAL PRODUCTION 10,000 bottles
HECTARES UNDER VINE 5.00
VITICULTURE METHOD Certified Organic

● Taurasi Sant'Eustachio '08	♀♀ 5

Il Cancelliere

C.DA IAMPENNE, 45
83040 MONTEMARANO [AV]
TEL. 082763557
www.ilcancelliere.it

CELLAR SALES
PRE-BOOKED VISITS
ANNUAL PRODUCTION 18,000 bottles
HECTARES UNDER VINE 7.00
VITICULTURE METHOD Certified Organic

● Irpinia Aglianico Gioviano '09	♀♀ 2*

Cantina dei Monaci

FRAZ. SANTA LUCIA, 206
83030 SANTA PAOLINA [AV]
TEL. 0825964350
www.cantinadeimonaci.it

CELLAR SALES
PRE-BOOKED VISITS
ANNUAL PRODUCTION 80,000 bottles
HECTARES UNDER VINE 9.50

○ Greco di Tufo '12	♀♀ 3

Alexia Capolino Perlingieri

VIA MARRAIOLI, 58
82037 CASTELVENERE [BN]
TEL. 0824971541
www.capolinoperlingieri.com

CELLAR SALES
PRE-BOOKED VISITS
ANNUAL PRODUCTION 30,000 bottles
HECTARES UNDER VINE 13.00
VITICULTURE METHOD Certified Organic

○ Sannio Falanghina Preta '12	♙♙ 2*
○ Sannio Fiano Nembo '12	♙ 3
● Sannio Rosso Sciascì '09	♙ 3

La Casa dell'Orco

FRAZ. SAN MICHELE
VIA LIMATURO, 52
83039 PRATOLA SERRA [AV]
TEL. 0825967038
www.lacasadellorco.it

CELLAR SALES
PRE-BOOKED VISITS
ANNUAL PRODUCTION 200,000 bottles
HECTARES UNDER VINE 30.00

○ Fiano di Avellino '12	♙♙ 3
○ Irpinia Coda di Volpe '12	♙♙ 2*
○ Greco di Tufo '12	♙ 3

Casa Di Baal

LOC. MACCHIA
VIA TIZIANO, 14
84096 MONTECORVINO ROVELLA [SA]
TEL. 089981143
www.casadibaal.it

CELLAR SALES
PRE-BOOKED VISITS
ANNUAL PRODUCTION 23,000 bottles
HECTARES UNDER VINE 5.00
VITICULTURE METHOD Certified Organic

○ Fiano di Baal '11	♙♙ 3*
● Rosso di Baal '11	♙♙ 2*
● Aglianico di Baal '10	♙ 3
○ Bianco di Baal '12	♙ 2

Viticoltori del Casavecchia

VIA MADONNA DELLE GRAZIE, 28
81040 PONTELATONE [CE]
TEL. 3289726688
www.viticoltoridelcasavecchia.it

CELLAR SALES
PRE-BOOKED VISITS
ANNUAL PRODUCTION 18,000 bottles
HECTARES UNDER VINE 3.00

● Erta dei Ciliegi '11	♙♙ 2*
● Pallagrello Bianco '12	♙♙ 2*
● Vigna Prea '10	♙♙ 4
◉ Sfizio Rosa '12	♙ 2

Casebianche

VIA CASE BIANCHE, 8
84076 TORCHIARA [SA]
TEL. 0974843244
www.casebianche.eu

CELLAR SALES
PRE-BOOKED VISITS
ANNUAL PRODUCTION 30,000 bottles
HECTARES UNDER VINE 5.50
VITICULTURE METHOD Certified Organic

○ Cilento Fiano Cumalè '12	♙♙ 2*
○ La Matta Dosaggio Zero '12	♙♙ 3
● Cilento Aglianico Cupersito '11	♙ 3
● Delle More '11	♙ 2

Casula Vinaria

VIA MATTINELLE, 109
84022 CAMPAGNA [SA]
TEL. 3485437133
www.casulavinaria.com

CELLAR SALES
PRE-BOOKED VISITS
ANNUAL PRODUCTION 20,000 bottles
HECTARES UNDER VINE 2.00

○ Melodia '12	♙♙ 2*
● Brigante '11	♙ 2

Cautiero

c.da Arbusti
82030 Frasso Telesino [BN]
Tel. 3387640641
www.cautiero.it

CELLAR SALES
ACCOMMODATION
ANNUAL PRODUCTION 16,000 bottles
HECTARES UNDER VINE 4.00
VITICULTURE METHOD Certified Organic

○ Sannio Falanghina Fois '12	♟♟ 2*
● Sannio Aglianico Donna Candida '10	♟♟ 4
○ Erba Bianca '12	♟ 2
● Piedirosso '12	♟ 2

Carlo Centrella

via Guardie, 115
83010 Torrioni [AV]
Tel. 0825998098
www.centrellavino.it

CELLAR SALES
PRE-BOOKED VISITS
ANNUAL PRODUCTION 6,000 bottles
HECTARES UNDER VINE 1.00

○ Greco di Tufo Selvetelle '12	♟♟ 3

Colle di San Domenico

SS Ofantina km 7,500
83040 Chiusano di San Domenico [AV]
Tel. 0825985423
www.cantinecolledisandomenico.it

CELLAR SALES
PRE-BOOKED VISITS
ANNUAL PRODUCTION 100,000 bottles
HECTARES UNDER VINE 20.00

○ Fiano di Avellino '12	♟♟ 3
○ Greco di Tufo '12	♟ 3
● Irpinia Aglianico '11	♟ 2

Di Meo

c.da Coccovoni, 1
83050 Salza Irpina [AV]
Tel. 0825981419
www.dimeo.it

CELLAR SALES
PRE-BOOKED VISITS
RESTAURANT SERVICE
ANNUAL PRODUCTION 500,000 bottles
HECTARES UNDER VINE 30.00

○ Fiano di Avellino Alessandra '10	♟♟ 3
○ Greco di Tufo Sel. Roberto Di Meo '10	♟♟ 4
● Aglianico '10	♟ 3
● Isso '11	♟ 2

Cantina Farro

loc. Fusaro
fraz. Bacoli
via Virgilio, 16/24
80070 Napoli
Tel. 0818545555
www.cantinefarro.it

CELLAR SALES
PRE-BOOKED VISITS
ANNUAL PRODUCTION 207,000 bottles
HECTARES UNDER VINE 20.00

○ Campi Flegrei Falanghina '12	♟♟ 2*
○ Campi Flegrei Le Cigliate '11	♟♟ 3
● Campi Flegrei Piedirosso '12	♟ 2

Feudo Apiano

via Casale Monaci, 8
83030 Lapio [AV]
Tel. 0825982181
www.feudoapiano.it

CELLAR SALES
ANNUAL PRODUCTION 15,000 bottles
HECTARES UNDER VINE 6.00

○ Fiano di Avellino '12	♟♟ 3
● Taurasi '05	♟♟ 5
○ Fiano di Avellino '11	♟ 3

Fonzone Caccese

Loc. Scorzagalline
83052 Paternopoli [AV]
Tel. 0810511118
www.fonzone.it

PRE-BOOKED VISITS
ANNUAL PRODUCTION 50,000 bottles
HECTARES UNDER VINE 30.00

○ Fiano di Avellino '12	♟♟ 3
○ Greco di Tufo '12	♟♟ 2*
● Irpinia Campi Taurasini '10	♟♟ 4
○ Irpinia Fiano Sequoia '11	♟ 3

Historia Antiqua

via Variante Est SS 7Bis, 75
83030 Monocalzati [AV]
Tel. 0825675179
www.historiaantiqua.it

CELLAR SALES
PRE-BOOKED VISITS
ANNUAL PRODUCTION 90,000 bottles
HECTARES UNDER VINE 30.00

○ Greco di Tufo '12	♟♟ 3
● Taurasi '09	♟♟ 6
○ Fiano di Avellino '12	♟ 3
● Taurasi '08	♟ 6

Il Verro

Loc. Acquavalle, Lautoni
81040 Formicola [CE]
Tel. 3456416200
www.ilverro.it

CELLAR SALES
ANNUAL PRODUCTION 18,000 bottles
HECTARES UNDER VINE 3.00

○ Sheep '12	♟♟ 2*
● Casavecchia Lautonis '12	♟ 2
○ Pallagrello Bianco Verginiano '12	♟ 2
● Pallagrello Nero '12	♟ 2

Lunarossa

via V. Fortunato Lotto, 10
84095 Giffoni Valle Piana [SA]
Tel. 0898021016
www.viniepassione.it

PRE-BOOKED VISITS
ANNUAL PRODUCTION 55,000 bottles
HECTARES UNDER VINE 4.50

● Aglianico Camporeale '12	♟♟ 2*
● Borgomastro '07	♟♟ 6
● Rossomarea '08	♟♟ 2
○ Costacielo Bianco '11	♟ 2

Salvatore Magnoni

via Fratelli Magnoni, 11
84070 Rutino [SA]
Tel. 0974830018
www.primalaterra.it

CELLAR SALES
PRE-BOOKED VISITS
ANNUAL PRODUCTION 50,000 bottles
HECTARES UNDER VINE 2.00

● Cilento Aglianico Primalaterra '11	♟♟ 4

Guido Marsella

via Marone, 1
83010 Summonte [AV]
Tel. 0825691005
cantine@guidomarsella.com

CELLAR SALES
PRE-BOOKED VISITS
ANNUAL PRODUCTION 25,000 bottles
HECTARES UNDER VINE 8.00

○ Fiano di Avellino '11	♟♟ 2*
○ Greco di Tufo Poggi Reali '11	♟ 2

Le Masciare

c.da Barbassano
83052 Paternopoli [AV]
Tel. 3486412799
www.lemasciare.com

ANNUAL PRODUCTION 70,000 bottles
HECTARES UNDER VINE 9.00

○ Greco di Tufo Settepietre '12	♥♥	2*
○ Fiano di Avellino Ambra '12	♥	2
● Irpinia Campi Taurasini '11	♥	2

Masseria Frattasi

via Torre Varoni, 15
82016 Montesarchio [BN]
Tel. 0823351740
www.masseriafrattasi.it

CELLAR SALES
PRE-BOOKED VISITS
ANNUAL PRODUCTION 150,000 bottles
HECTARES UNDER VINE 10.00
VITICULTURE METHOD Certified Biodynamic

○ Taburno Falanghina '12	♥♥	2*
○ Taburno Falanghina di Bonea '12	♥♥	3

Mustilli

via Caudina, 10
82019 Sant'Agata de' Goti [BN]
Tel. 0823718142
www.mustilli.com

CELLAR SALES
PRE-BOOKED VISITS
ACCOMMODATION AND RESTAURANT SERVICE
ANNUAL PRODUCTION 150,000 bottles
HECTARES UNDER VINE 35.00
VITICULTURE METHOD Certified Organic

● Sannio Piedirosso '12	♥♥	3
● Sant'Agata dei Goti Aglianico Cesco di Nece '10	♥♥	3
○ Sant'Agata dei Goti Falanghina '12	♥♥	3

Lorenzo Nifo Sarrapochiello

via Piana
82030 Ponte [BN]
Tel. 0824876450
www.nifo.eu

CELLAR SALES
PRE-BOOKED VISITS
ANNUAL PRODUCTION 70,000 bottles
HECTARES UNDER VINE 16.00
VITICULTURE METHOD Certified Organic

● Aglianico del Taburno '10	♥♥	2*
○ Falanghina del Sannio Taburno '12	♥♥	2*
○ Falanghina del Sannio Alenta V.T. '12	♥	3
○ Sannio Taburno Fiano '12	♥	2

Ocone

loc. La Madonnella
via del Monte, 56
82030 Ponte [BN]
Tel. 0824874040
www.oconevini.it

CELLAR SALES
PRE-BOOKED VISITS
ANNUAL PRODUCTION 250,000 bottles
HECTARES UNDER VINE 49.00
VITICULTURE METHOD Certified Organic

● Aglianico del Taburno V. Pezza la Corte '07	♥♥	3
● Aglianico del Taburno Diomede '07	♥	4
○ Falanghina del Sannio Taburno Flora '12	♥	2

Gennaro Papa

p.zza Limata, 2
81030 Falciano del Massico [CE]
Tel. 0823931267
www.gennaropapa.it

CELLAR SALES
PRE-BOOKED VISITS
ANNUAL PRODUCTION 18,000 bottles
HECTARES UNDER VINE 6.00

● Falerno del Massico Conclave '11	♥♥	3

La Pietra di Tommasone

VIA PROVINCIALE FANGO, 98
80076 LACCO AMENO [NA]
TEL. 0813330330
www.tommasonevini.it

CELLAR SALES
PRE-BOOKED VISITS
ANNUAL PRODUCTION 100,000 bottles
HECTARES UNDER VINE 11.00

○ Ischia Biancolella '12	♥♥ 2*
○ Ischia Biancolella V. dei Preti '11	♥ 4
● Ischia Per'e Palummo '12	♥ 3

Tenuta Ponte

VIA CARAZITA, 1
83040 LUOGOSANO [AV]
TEL. 082773564
www.tenutaponte.it

CELLAR SALES
PRE-BOOKED VISITS
ANNUAL PRODUCTION 180,000 bottles
HECTARES UNDER VINE 25.00

○ Fiano di Avellino '12	♥♥ 3
○ Greco di Tufo '12	♥ 3
● Irpinia Campi Taurasini Carazita '09	♥ 2

Andrea Reale

LOC. BORGO DI GETE
VIA CARDAMONE, 75
84010 TRAMONTI [SA]
TEL. 089856144
www.aziendaagricolareale.it

CELLAR SALES
PRE-BOOKED VISITS
ACCOMMODATION AND RESTAURANT SERVICE
ANNUAL PRODUCTION 1,200 bottles
HECTARES UNDER VINE 2.50

⊙ Costa d'Amalfi Tramonti Getis Rosato '12	♥♥ 4
○ Costa d'Amalfi Tramonti Rosso Cardamone '11	♥♥ 4
● Borgo di Gete '09	♥ 6

Regina Viarum

LOC. FALCIANO DEL MASSICO
VIA VELLARIA
81030 FALCIANO DEL MASSICO [CE]
TEL. 0823931299
www.reginaviarum.it

CELLAR SALES
PRE-BOOKED VISITS
ANNUAL PRODUCTION 19,000 bottles
HECTARES UNDER VINE 5.00
VITICULTURE METHOD Certified Organic

● Falerno del Massico Barone '10	♥♥ 5
● Falerno del Massico Zero5 '10	♥♥ 3

Ettore Sammarco

VIA CIVITA, 9
84010 RAVELLO [SA]
TEL. 089872774
www.ettoresammarco.it

CELLAR SALES
PRE-BOOKED VISITS
ANNUAL PRODUCTION 62,000 bottles
HECTARES UNDER VINE 13.00

○ Costa d'Amalfi Ravello Bianco Selva delle Monache '12	♥♥ 3
○ Costa d'Amalfi Ravello Bianco V. Grotta Piana '12	♥♥ 3

Terra di Vento

VIA TEVERE
84090 MONTECORVINO PUGLIANO [SA]
TEL. 0828354597
www.terradivento.it

CELLAR SALES
PRE-BOOKED VISITS
ACCOMMODATION AND RESTAURANT SERVICE
ANNUAL PRODUCTION 15,000 bottles
HECTARES UNDER VINE 10.00
VITICULTURE METHOD Certified Organic

● Petrale '09	♥♥ 3
○ Faiano '12	♥ 2

Terre Stregate

VIA MUNICIPIO, 105
82034 GUARDIA SANFRAMONDI [BN]
TEL. 0824817857
www.terrestregate.it

CELLAR SALES
PRE-BOOKED VISITS
ANNUAL PRODUCTION 50,000 bottles
HECTARES UNDER VINE 20.00
VITICULTURE METHOD Certified Organic

○ Falanghina del Sannio Svelato '12	♟♟ 2*
● Guardiolo Aglianico Scrypta '10	♟♟ 3
○ Sannio Greco Aurora '12	♟♟ 2*
○ Falanghina del Beneventano Trama '12	♟ 2

Torre a Oriente

LOC. MERCURI I, 19
82030 TORRECUSO [BN]
TEL. 0824874376
www.torreaoriente.eu

CELLAR SALES
PRE-BOOKED VISITS
ACCOMMODATION AND RESTAURANT SERVICE
ANNUAL PRODUCTION 40,000 bottles
HECTARES UNDER VINE 10.00

● Janico '10	♟♟ 2*
○ Falanghina del Sannio Taburno Siriana '11	♟ 2

Torricino

LOC. TORRICINO
VIA NAZIONALE
83010 TUFO [AV]
TEL. 0825998119
www.torricino.it

CELLAR SALES
PRE-BOOKED VISITS
ANNUAL PRODUCTION 40,000 bottles
HECTARES UNDER VINE 10.00
VITICULTURE METHOD Certified Organic

○ Fiano di Avellino '12	♟♟ 3
○ Greco di Tufo '12	♟ 3

Trabucco

VIA VITTORIO EMANUELE, 1
81030 CARINOLA [CE]
TEL. 0823737345
www.trabucconicola.it

CELLAR SALES
PRE-BOOKED VISITS
ANNUAL PRODUCTION 12,000 bottles
HECTARES UNDER VINE 2.00

● Falerno del Massico Rosso Erre '10	♟♟ 2*
○ Falerno del Massico Bianco 16 Marzo '12	♟ 2
● Falerno del Massico Rosso Rapicano '10	♟ 4

Traerte

C.DA VADIAPERTI
83030 MONTEFREDANE [AV]
TEL. 0825607270
info@traerte.it

○ Greco di Tufo Tornante '12	♟♟ 5
○ Fiano di Avellino Aipierti '12	♟♟ 5
○ Greco di Tufo '12	♟♟ 4
○ Irpinia Coda di Volpe Torama '12	♟♟ 2*

Verrone Antonio

C.DA CANNETIELLO
84043 AGROPOLI [SA]
TEL. 089236306
verrone.viticoltori@gmail.com

CELLAR SALES
PRE-BOOKED VISITS
ANNUAL PRODUCTION 30,000 bottles
HECTARES UNDER VINE 16.00

○ Cilento Fiano V. Girapoggio '12	♟♟ 3
● Cilento Aglianico V. Girapoggio '10	♟ 3

Le Vigne di Raito

FRAZ. RAITO
VIA SAN VITO, 9
84019 VIETRI SUL MARE [SA]
TEL. 089233428
www.levignediraito.com

CELLAR SALES
PRE-BOOKED VISITS
RESTAURANT SERVICE
ANNUAL PRODUCTION 6,000 bottles
HECTARES UNDER VINE 1.70
VITICULTURE METHOD Certified Organic

● Ragis '10	♟♟ 5
⊙ Vitamenia '12	♟ 4

Vigne Guadagno - Vistabella

VIA SANT'ANIELLO
83030 MONTEFREDANE [AV]
TEL. 08251686278
www.vigneguadagno.it

PRE-BOOKED VISITS
ANNUAL PRODUCTION 47,000 bottles
HECTARES UNDER VINE 10.00

○ Greco di Tufo '12	♟♟ 8
○ Fiano di Avellino '12	♟ 8
● Irpinia Aglianico '11	♟ 2

Vigne Sannite

LOC. SALELLA
82037 CASTELVENERE [BN]
TEL. 0824941494
www.cesas.it

CELLAR SALES
ANNUAL PRODUCTION 300,000 bottles
HECTARES UNDER VINE 150.00
VITICULTURE METHOD Certified Organic

○ Falanghina del Sannio '12	♟♟ 2*
● Sannio Barbera '11	♟♟ 2*

Vinosia

VIA APPIA, 150
83042 ATRIPALDA [AV]
TEL. 0825628185
www.vinosia.com

RESTAURANT SERVICE
ANNUAL PRODUCTION 850,000 bottles
HECTARES UNDER VINE 40.00

● Taurasi Marziacanale '08	♟♟ 5
● Taurasi Santandrea '07	♟♟ 4
● Irpinia Campi Taurasini Neromora '11	♟ 2
● Taurasi Rajamagra Ris. '05	♟ 5

Votino

VIA FIZZO, 14
82013 BONEA [BN]
TEL. 0824834762
www.aziendavotino.com

CELLAR SALES
ANNUAL PRODUCTION 40,000 bottles
HECTARES UNDER VINE 5.00

● Aglianico del Taburno Furius '08	♟♟ 3
○ Falanghina Taburno Cocceius '12	♟♟ 2*
○ Sannio Fiano '12	♟ 2

Vuolo

LOC. PASSIONE
84135 SALERNO
TEL. 089282178
www.milavuolo.it

CELLAR SALES
ANNUAL PRODUCTION 1,000 bottles
HECTARES UNDER VINE 3.50
VITICULTURE METHOD Certified Organic

○ Fiano '11	♟♟ 3
● Aglianico '09	♟ 5

BASILICATA

Basilicata vaunts four award-winning wines this year, so one more than in the last Guide, offering proof of the commitment made in such trying times by the region's best wineries. Winemaking Basilicata has visibility thanks to the Vulture district, which accounts for 80% of regional production and is substantially represented by only one wine: Aglianico del Vulture. The big news at this difficult time was the commitment of Vulture producers in seeking and obtaining DOCG status for their labels. From the 2011 vintage, Aglianico del Vulture Superiore will have a mandatory two years of maturation and ageing in the cellar, while the Superiore Riserva will require four, with two in wood and two in bottle. These are ambitious decisions that on the surface seem to clash with a contingent reality that prefers low-cost, easy-drinkers, but they are almost obligatory for Vulture's vignerons, who are in no doubt about the potential of their great wines, which are the aristocrats of Italy's southern labels. Cantine del Notaio's Aglianico Vulture la Firma is back on top form with a sumptuous interpretation of the 2010 vintage, while Fucci's 2011 Titolo simply confirms its excellence yet again. A Tre Bicchieri also goes to GIV's Terre degli Svevi for an elegant, layered Re Manfredi 2009. Another was on the cards for an enthralling version of the 2009 Don Anselmo, by the Paternoster family cellars. Despite the current economic climate, new wineries are springing up and confirm just how much these winemakers believe in the excellence of their products, while co-operative structures, with the Cantina di Venosa in the front line, do an important job for the territory and, most importantly, for quality. Big smoke signals are to be seen above the province of Matera, where a few cellars with ambitious objectives are setting up technical and technological facilities to achieve quality production. Primitivo is a frequent denizen of the sunny hills overlooking the Ionian Sea, expressing itself with personality and a distinctive character, which is beginning to emerge in our tastings. So pick up the next edition of the Guide to find out how the first bottle of Aglianico del Vulture DOCG fares.

Basilisco

VIA DELLE CANTINE, 22
85022 BARILE [PZ]
TEL. 0972771033
www.basiliscovini.it

CELLAR SALES
PRE-BOOKED VISITS
ACCOMMODATION
ANNUAL PRODUCTION 50,000 bottles
HECTARES UNDER VINE 27.00
VITICULTURE METHOD Certified Organic

Irpinia-based Feudi di San Gregorio
pursues its Vulture operation with passion.
After buying valuable vineyards and
buildings, it built a state-of-the-art cellar at
Barile and has now acquired Michele
Cutolo's Basilisco operation. Distributing
this respected southern Italian red will
certainly be easier with an enterprise like
Feudi on board. The estate comprises 27
hectares in the Macarico and Gelosia
districts, also in Barile. Consultant
oenologist Lorenzo Landi is still in charge of
technical operations. The Basilisco 2010
just missed our top award. This potent,
structured, austere red shows character,
rich fruit, full flavour, and a lovely spice and
black berry finish. The rich, balanced
second label, a Teodosio 2011, has a hint
of rigid tannins. The interesting Sophia is
from fiano, malvasia bianca and traminer.

Cantine del Notaio

VIA ROMA, 159
85028 RIONERO IN VULTURE [PZ]
TEL. 0972723689
www.cantinedelnotaio.com

CELLAR SALES
PRE-BOOKED VISITS
RESTAURANT SERVICE
ANNUAL PRODUCTION 230,000 bottles
HECTARES UNDER VINE 30.00
VITICULTURE METHOD Certified Biodynamic

Gerardo Giuratrabocchetti has dedicated his
life to his family winery. We know he believes
deeply in this terroir as has invested two
decades in promoting it to build up the
visibility it lacked. A former researcher,
Gerardo is an enthusiastic agronomist who
has total respect for the environment, and
manages his 30 hectares with certified
organic and biodynamic methods. Rionero's
venerable cellars are dug out of the tufa. The
riddling racks are stacked with classic
method sparklers, while the rest of the wines
produced can be found in the state-of-the-
art Ripacandida cellars. Estate flagship, the
lush, stylish Aglianico La Firma 2010 has
texture, and red berry, balsam, summer and
spice aromas; the compact, rounded palate
is well behaved and dynamic, and closes on
pencil lead and oak. The Aglianico Il Sigillo
2009 has eucalyptus, cherry and morello
cherry. The mature Repertorio 2010 shows
beefy tannins.

● Aglianico del Vulture Basilisco '10	♟♟ 5
● Aglianico del Vulture Teodosio '11	♟♟ 3
○ Sophia '12	♟ 3
● Aglianico del Vulture Basilisco '09	♟♟♟ 5
● Aglianico del Vulture Basilisco '08	♟♟♟ 5
● Aglianico del Vulture Basilisco '07	♟♟♟ 5
● Aglianico del Vulture Basilisco '06	♟♟♟ 5
● Aglianico del Vulture Basilisco '04	♟♟♟ 5
● Aglianico del Vulture Basilisco '01	♟♟♟ 5
● Aglianico del Vulture Basilisco '05	♟♟ 5
● Aglianico del Vulture Teodosio '10	♟♟ 3*
● Aglianico del Vulture Teodosio '08	♟♟ 3
● Aglianico del Vulture Teodosio '07	♟♟ 3

● Aglianico del Vulture La Firma '10	♟♟♟ 6
● Aglianico del Vulture Il Repertorio '10	♟♟ 4
● Aglianico del Vulture Il Sigillo '09	♟♟ 6
○ Il Preliminare '12	♟♟ 3
○ L'Autentica '11	♟♟ 5
☉ Il Rogito '11	♟ 3
● L'Atto '11	♟ 3
☉ La Stipula Brut Rosé	♟ 4
● Aglianico del Vulture La Firma '00	♟♟♟ 5
● Aglianico del Vulture Il Sigillo '07	♟♟ 6
● Aglianico del Vulture La Firma '09	♟♟ 6
● Aglianico del Vulture La Firma '08	♟♟ 6
○ L'Autentica '10	♟♟ 5

Carbone

VIA NITTI, 48
85025 MELFI [PZ]
TEL. 0972237866
www.carbonevini.it

CELLAR SALES
PRE-BOOKED VISITS
ANNUAL PRODUCTION 45,000 bottles
HECTARES UNDER VINE 18.00

Siblings Luca and Sara Carbone have been passionately involved in the family business since the mid-1970s, working with Sergio Paternoster on 18 hectares of lovely vines in the Melfi area to produce an excellent range of labels. The old ageing cellar in the historic centre of Melfi is used as a venue for cultural events and conferences aimed at a revival of this area. An overall ambitious project, vines are managed with low-impact methods while a cutting-edge fermentation cellar is located in the Braide district. The red Aglianico 400 Some is dedicated to Charles of Anjou, King of Naples, who ordered 400 "some", or loads, for court cellars after he tasted Aglianico. The full-flavoured 2011 made our finals for its structure, depth and profusion of smooth tannins. The Fiano 2012 is probably the region's best white.

Casa Maschito

VIA F. S. NITTI
85020 MASCHITO [PZ]
TEL. 097233101
www.casamaschito.it

CELLAR SALES
PRE-BOOKED VISITS
ACCOMMODATION AND RESTAURANT SERVICE
ANNUAL PRODUCTION 60,000 bottles
HECTARES UNDER VINE 10.00

In 1999 a group of young entrepreneurs opened this winery, adding more vineyards year by year to achieve the current ten hectares in the municipality of Maschito. Quality has also been a priority, and the winery now generates 60,000 bottles annually. The complete, excellent range obviously centres on the leading local wine, Aglianico del Vulture. The complex, structured Aglianico La Terrazza 2005 is stunning, showing lively morello cherry and red berries, balanced oak, polished tannins, and a finish of morello cherry and aromatic herbs. The compact, invigorating Aglianico Portale Adduca 2009 is admirable, showing stylish chocolate and Virginia tobacco.

● Aglianico del Vulture 400 Some '11	▼▼ 4
○ Fiano '12	▼▼ 3
● Aglianico del Vulture Terra dei Fuochi '11	▼ 2
⊙ Rosa Carbone '12	▼ 3
● Aglianico del Vulture 400 Some '09	♀♀ 4
● Aglianico del Vulture 400 Some '08	♀♀ 4
● Aglianico del Vulture Stupor Mundi '08	♀♀ 5
● Aglianico del Vulture Stupor Mundi '07	♀♀ 5
● Aglianico del Vulture Terra dei Fuochi '09	♀♀ 2

● Aglianico del Vulture Portale Adduca '09	▼▼ 2*
● Aglianico del Vulture Ris. La Terrazza '05	▼▼ 6
○ Malvasia Lucana '12	▼▼ 2*
○ Moscato Passito Majsor '11	▼▼ 3
● Aglianico del Vulture La Bottaia '09	▼ 3
○ Biancospino '12	▼ 2
● Aglianico del Vulture La Bottaia '08	♀♀ 3
● Aglianico del Vulture Portale Adduca '08	♀♀ 2*
● Aglianico del Vulture Portale Adduca '05	♀♀ 2

Casa Vinicola D'Angelo

VIA PROVINCIALE, 8
85028 RIONERO IN VULTURE [PZ]
TEL. 0972721517
www.dangelowine.it

CELLAR SALES
PRE-BOOKED VISITS
ANNUAL PRODUCTION 300,000 bottles
HECTARES UNDER VINE 35.00

This well-established Vulture winery, in business since the 1930s, has certainly contributed to showcasing Aglianico del Vulture outside regional boundaries. Today siblings Erminia and Rocco d'Angelo run this operation, producing local wines from their own plots located in the Rionero, Barile, Rapolla, and Ripacandida districts. The products are true to the winery's austere, poised style, and the result of long maceration and ageing, almost always in large oak. The bright ruby Aglianico Vigna Caselle Riserva 2008 flagship wine has a complex nose of red berries, cherry, morello cherry, spice, and Mediterranean herbs; the austere, full-flavoured palate is warm and rich, with elegant tannins. The stylish Valle del Noce 2011 is fleshy and fruity, with a tobacco and spice finish.

D'Angelo di Filomena Ruppi

VIA PADRE PIO, 10
85028 RIONERO IN VULTURE [PZ]
TEL. 0972724602
www.agrida.com

CELLAR SALES
ANNUAL PRODUCTION 50,000 bottles
HECTARES UNDER VINE 12.00

Donato D'Angelo is an icon of Vulture winemaking that recently left the parent winery to set up his own operation with his wife, Filomena Ruppi. The 15 hectares of vineyards are mainly dedicated to aglianico, which Donato uses to make stylish reds in his traditionally austere, complex style. Filomena directly manages Tenuta del Portale, but her husband is on hand during the vinification process. The Donato d'Angelo 2009 was not up to the superb Balconara of the same year but Portale's brisk Aglianico Le Vigne a Capanno 2011 made up for it thanks to a clean style with sound, taut, crisp fruit and a solid tannin underpinning, closing elegantly in a long finish. The Aglianico Riserva 2008 is also good.

● Aglianico del Vulture V. Caselle Ris. '08	♟♟ 4
● Aglianico del Vulture Valle del Noce '11	♟♟ 5
● Aglianico del Vulture '11	♟ 2
● Canneto '11	♟ 4
● Aglianico del Vulture V. Caselle Ris. '01	♟♟♟ 3*
● Aglianico del Vulture '09	♟♟ 2*
● Aglianico del Vulture V. Caselle Ris. '07	♟♟ 4
● Aglianico del Vulture V. Caselle Ris. '06	♟♟ 4
● Aglianico del Vulture Valle del Noce '10	♟♟ 5
● Aglianico del Vulture Valle del Noce '09	♟♟ 5
● Canneto '09	♟♟ 4

● Aglianico del Vulture Ris. '08	♟♟ 3
● Tenuta del Portale Aglianico del Vulture Le Vigne a Capanno '11	♟♟ 3
● Balconara '09	♟♟♟ 4*
● Aglianico del Vulture Donato D'Angelo '08	♟♟ 3
● Balconara '08	♟♟ 4

Elena Fucci

c.da Solagna del Titolo
85022 Barile [PZ]
Tel. 0972770736
www.elenafuccivini.com

CELLAR SALES
PRE-BOOKED VISITS
ANNUAL PRODUCTION 18,000 bottles
HECTARES UNDER VINE 6.00

If any winery can tell the story of the Vulture district and its excellent Aglianico, there is none better than Salvatore Fucci's family business. Surprisingly, Salvatore and daughter Elena, an oenologist who now owns the winery and manages the cellaring side, make just one label, the Aglianico Titolo, which takes its name from the eponymous Barile district where the Fuccis have almost seven hectares under vine. The secret is a core of 50-year-old bush-trained vines that produce superb grapes. A great dense, brooding ruby red, the Titolo 2011 again wins a Tre Bicchieri. A nose of rich cherry, morello cherry and plum makes way for oak, tobacco and spice. The warm, fruity palate is mouthfilling and rounded, with elegant tannins. Long, balanced and still young, it fades out on echoes of smoke and pencil lead.

Grifalco della Lucania

loc. Pian di Camera
85029 Venosa [PZ]
Tel. 097231002
grifalcodellalucania@email.it

CELLAR SALES
PRE-BOOKED VISITS
ANNUAL PRODUCTION 65,000 bottles
HECTARES UNDER VINE 16.00
VITICULTURE METHOD Certified Organic

Fabrizio and Cecilia Piccin spent many years in Tuscany, both in Chianti and Montepulciano. About ten years ago they decided to move to Lucania and chose Venosa to start up their commendable Grifalco winery. The large area under vine includes carefully tended plots located in Venosa, Maschito, Rapolla, and Ginestra. They barrel age their distinctive fresh, stylish wines, created with a minimal approach and respect for the environment. The Aglianico Gricos 2011, one of the top labels for this DOC, came up trumps in the finals. This brooding ruby red opens on an intense nose layered with red berry, blackberry, plum, lots of morello cherry, and crisp hints of mountain herbs. The full juicy palate has intact fruit and a nice aromatic length.

● Aglianico del Vulture Titolo '11	♟♟♟ 5
● Aglianico del Vulture Titolo '10	♟♟♟ 5
● Aglianico del Vulture Titolo '09	♟♟♟ 5
● Aglianico del Vulture Titolo '08	♟♟♟ 6
● Aglianico del Vulture Titolo '07	♟♟♟ 6
● Aglianico del Vulture Titolo '06	♟♟♟ 5
● Aglianico del Vulture Titolo '05	♟♟♟ 5
● Aglianico del Vulture Titolo '02	♟♟♟ 5
● Aglianico del Vulture Titolo '04	♟♟ 5
● Aglianico del Vulture Titolo '03	♟♟ 5

● Aglianico del Vulture Gricos '11	♟♟ 2*
● Aglianico del Vulture Grifalco '11	♟♟ 3
● Aglianico del Vulture Damaschito '09	♟ 4
● Aglianico del Vulture Bosco del Falco '07	♟♟ 4
● Aglianico del Vulture Damaschito '08	♟♟ 4
● Aglianico del Vulture Damaschito '07	♟♟ 3
● Aglianico del Vulture Gricos '09	♟♟ 2*
● Aglianico del Vulture Gricos '08	♟♟ 2*
● Aglianico del Vulture Grifalco '10	♟♟ 3
● Aglianico del Vulture Grifalco '09	♟♟ 3
● Aglianico del Vulture Grifalco '08	♟♟ 3
● Aglianico del Vulture Grifalco '07	♟♟ 3

Paternoster

C.DA VALLE DEL TITOLO
85022 BARILE [PZ]
TEL. 0972770224
www.paternostervini.it

CELLAR SALES
PRE-BOOKED VISITS
ANNUAL PRODUCTION 150,000 bottles
HECTARES UNDER VINE 20.00
VITICULTURE METHOD Certified Organic

Founded in 1925, Paternoster is definitely a leading name in Lucania winemaking, with smart state-of-the-art cellars located in Rotondo, on the outskirts of Barile, and seven vineyard plots scattered around the district's best sites, including Valle del Titolo, Macarico and Gelosia. Today Vito Paternoster skilfully runs the company, with winemaking assistance from Fabio Mecca. A Tre Bicchieri goes to the balanced, refined Aglianico Don Anselmo 2009, with magical depth, finesse and velvety tannins, then a long, caressing finish of liquorice, fruit and pencil lead. The concentrated, rich Rotondo 2010, from the eponymous cru, shows hints of scrub and oak. The juicy Synthesi 2009 has nice pressure.

● Aglianico del Vulture Don Anselmo '09	♟♟♟ 6
● Aglianico del Vulture Rotondo '10	♟♟ 5
● Aglianico del Vulture Synthesi '10	♟♟ 3
○ Biancorte Fiano '12	♟ 3
○ Klino '12	♟ 2
● Aglianico del Vulture Don Anselmo '94	♟♟♟ 6
● Aglianico del Vulture Don Anselmo Ris. '05	♟♟♟ 6
● Aglianico del Vulture Rotondo '01	♟♟♟ 5
● Aglianico del Vulture Rotondo '00	♟♟♟ 5

Taverna

C.DA TAVERNA, 15
75020 NOVA SIRI [MT]
TEL. 0835877083
www.aataverna.com

CELLAR SALES
PRE-BOOKED VISITS
ACCOMMODATION AND RESTAURANT SERVICE
ANNUAL PRODUCTION 150,000 bottles
HECTARES UNDER VINE 17.00

Today this commendable Lucania winemaking enterprise has espoused innovation and environmental awareness. The winery, owned by Pasquale Lunati, was established in 1947 by his grandfather, another Pasquale, who bought a vineyard and started a thriving business producing and selling wine. Taverna now boasts 280 hectares, with 17 under vine and the rest planted to organic fruit, vegetables and olives. The operation is based in Nova Siri, 200 metres above sea level and close to the Ionian coast. The Venosa vines produce the grapes for the winery's Aglianico del Vulture. The two finalists are the deep, elegant Aglianico Loukania 2011, all flavour, fruit, smooth tannins and Mediterranean shades, and the Matera Moro I Sassi 2011, a primitivo, cabernet sauvignon, merlot blend that combines full body, structure and spicy opulence for total appeal. The other labels are also worthy.

● Aglianico del Vulture Loukania '11	♟♟ 4
● Matera Moro I Sassi '11	♟♟ 3*
○ Dry Muscat	♟♟ 2*
○ Matera San Basile '12	♟♟ 3
● Il Lagarino di Dioniso '11	♟ 4
⊙ Matera Maddalena '12	♟ 3
● Syrah '11	♟ 3
● Aglianico del Vulture '07	♟♟ 2*
● Aglianico del Vulture '04	♟♟ 2*
● Aglianico del Vulture Loukania '08	♟♟ 2*
● Il Lagarino di Dioniso '08	♟♟ 2
● Lagarino di Dioniso '06	♟♟ 3

Terre degli Svevi

LOC. PIAN DI CAMERA
85029 VENOSA [PZ]
TEL. 097231263
www.giv.it

CELLAR SALES
PRE-BOOKED VISITS
ACCOMMODATION
ANNUAL PRODUCTION 230,000 bottles
HECTARES UNDER VINE 120.00

In 1998 Gruppo Italiano Vini made the decision to invest in Lucania, an emerging and very promising area, setting up Terre degli Svevi, a large, successful winery. Based in Venosa, with 120 hectares under vine, this estate is also home to a modern cellar and an old farmhouse used as a reception area. Here aglianico reigns supreme, but there are also aromatic white varieties, like those used for the fragrant Re Manfredi Bianco. Terre degli Svevi has more vineyards at superb sites in Barile and Maschito. Successful labels and a clean style are nicely summed up in this year's Re Manfredi 2010, striking for its overall rich elegance, brisk red berries and medicinal herbs, appealing spice and striking pressure. The dense, oaky Aglianico Taglio del Tralcio 2011 is interesting, from grapes lightly dried on the vine.

Cantina di Venosa

LOC. VIGNALI
VIA APPIA
85029 VENOSA [PZ]
TEL. 097236702
www.cantinadivenosa.it

CELLAR SALES
PRE-BOOKED VISITS
ANNUAL PRODUCTION 800,000 bottles
HECTARES UNDER VINE 800.00

This well-known co-operative was founded in 1947 by 27 members. Nowadays, thanks to the hard work of management over the years, it has become the region's leading winemaking enterprise, with 500 member-growers and 800 hectares under vine. Currently chaired by enthusiastic, go-getting Francesco Perillo, this co-operative now offers a vast range of labels, all at unbeatable value for money. A place in the finals goes to the winery flagship, the barrique-aged Aglianico del Vulture Terre di Orazio 2011. We liked its modern approach, rich extract, and overall balance. The elegant finish hints at morello cherry and iodine notes. The Dry Muscat and malvasia-based white D'Avalos are also respectable.

● Aglianico del Vulture Re Manfredi '10	♟♟♟ 4*
● Aglianico del Vulture	
Taglio del Tralcio '11	♟♟ 4
○ Re Manfredi Bianco '12	♟ 3
⊙ Re Manfredi Rosato '12	♟ 3
● Aglianico del Vulture Re Manfredi '05	♀♀♀ 4
● Aglianico del Vulture Re Manfredi '99	♀♀♀ 4*
● Aglianico del Vulture Vign. Serpara '03	♀♀♀ 4*
● Aglianico del Vulture '09	♀♀ 3
● Aglianico del Vulture Re Manfredi '09	♀♀ 4
● Aglianico del Vulture Serpara '08	♀♀ 5
● Aglianico del Vulture Serpara '07	♀♀ 5

● Aglianico del Vulture Terre di Orazio '11	♟♟ 3*
○ D'Avalos di Gesualdo '12	♟♟ 3
○ Dry Muscat Terre di Orazio '12	♟♟ 2*
● Aglianico del Vulture Bali'Aggio '11	♟ 2
⊙ Terre di Orazio Rosé '12	♟ 3
● Aglianico del Vulture Carato Venusio '08	♀♀ 5
● Aglianico del Vulture	
Gesualdo da Venosa '08	♀♀ 4
● Aglianico del Vulture	
Gesualdo da Venosa '07	♀♀ 4
● Aglianico del Vulture Terre di Orazio '09	♀♀ 3
● Aglianico del Vulture Vignali '09	♀♀ 2*
○ Dry Muscat Terre di Orazio '11	♀♀ 2*

Colli Cerentino

VIA MATTEOTTI, 10
85025 RIONERO IN VULTURE [PZ]
TEL. 0972720329
www.collicerentino.com

CELLAR SALES
PRE-BOOKED VISITS
ANNUAL PRODUCTION 40,000 bottles
HECTARES UNDER VINE 9.00

● Aglianico del Vulture Cerentino '06 ♟♟ 5
● Aglianico del Vulture Masquito '06 ♟♟ 6

Cantine Cerrolongo

C.DA CERROLONGO, 1
75020 NOVA SIRI [MT]
TEL. 0835536174
www.cerrolongo.it

CELLAR SALES
PRE-BOOKED VISITS
ANNUAL PRODUCTION 20,000 bottles
HECTARES UNDER VINE 25.00

● Matera Primitivo Akratos '11 ♟♟ 2*
☉ Cerrolongo Rosé '12 ♟ 2
● Passito Il Patrimonio '11 ♟ 4

Tenute D'Auria

C.DA PIANO DI CROCE
85022 BARILE [PZ]
TEL. 0972536029
www.tenutedauria.com

CELLAR SALES
ANNUAL PRODUCTION 40,000 bottles
VITICULTURE METHOD Certified Organic

● Aglianico del Vulture Rupe di Apollo '07 ♟♟ 5
● Aglianico del Vulture Rupe di Apollo '09 ♟ 5
● Aglianico del Vulture Strapellum '10 ♟ 4

Eleano

FRAZ. PIAN DELL'ALTARE
SP 8
85028 RIPACANDIDA [PZ]
TEL. 0972722273
www.eleano.it

CELLAR SALES
PRE-BOOKED VISITS
ACCOMMODATION
ANNUAL PRODUCTION 35,000 bottles
HECTARES UNDER VINE 7.50

● Aglianico del Vulture Dioniso '11 ♟♟ 3
● Aglianico del Vulture Pian dell'Altare '09 ♟♟ 4
● Teseo '11 ♟ 2

Eubea

SP 8
85020 RIPACANDIDA [PZ]
TEL. 3284312789
www.agricolaeubea.com

CELLAR SALES
PRE-BOOKED VISITS
ANNUAL PRODUCTION 50,000 bottles
HECTARES UNDER VINE 16.00
VITICULTURE METHOD Certified Organic

● Aglianico del Vulture Roinos '11 ♟♟ 5
● Aglianico del Vulture Il Covo dei Briganti '11 ♟ 3
☉ Covo dei Briganti '12 ♟ 2

Lagala Viticoltori in Vulture

C.DA LA MADDALENA
85029 VENOSA [PZ]
TEL. 0972375007
www.lagala.it

CELLAR SALES
PRE-BOOKED VISITS
ANNUAL PRODUCTION 40,000 bottles
HECTARES UNDER VINE 7.00

● Aglianico del Vulture Massaro'n Ris. '05 ♟♟ 5
☉ Maddalena '12 ♟♟ 3
● Aglianico del Vulture Nero degli Orsini '07 ♟ 4
● Aglianico del Vulture Rosso del Balzo '07 ♟ 3

Michele Laluce
VIA ROMA, 21
85020 GINESTRA [PZ]
TEL. 3476386630
www.vinilaluce.com

CELLAR SALES
PRE-BOOKED VISITS
ANNUAL PRODUCTION 40,000 bottles
HECTARES UNDER VINE 7.00

○ Morbino Bianco '12	♟3
● S'Adatt '09	♟2

Cantine Madonna delle Grazie
LOC. VIGNALI
VIA APPIA
85029 VENOSA [PZ]
TEL. 097235704
www.cantinemadonnadellegrazie.it

CELLAR SALES
PRE-BOOKED VISITS
ANNUAL PRODUCTION 18,000 bottles
HECTARES UNDER VINE 8.00
VITICULTURE METHOD Certified Organic

● Aglianico del Vulture Bauccio '08	♟♟4
● Aglianico del Vulture Liscone '09	♟♟3

Armando Martino
VIA LUIGI LA VISTA, 2A
85028 RIONERO IN VULTURE [PZ]
TEL. 0972721422
www.martinovini.com

CELLAR SALES
PRE-BOOKED VISITS
ANNUAL PRODUCTION 300,000 bottles

● Aglianico del Vulture Oraziano '08	♟♟5
● Aglianico del Vulture '10	♟3
● Aglianico del Vulture Pretoriano '08	♟5

Mastrodomenico
V.LE EUROPA, 5
85022 MATERA
TEL. 0972770108
www.vignemastrodomenico.com

HECTARES UNDER VINE 10.00

● Aglianico del Vulture Likos '09	♟♟4
● Aglianico del Vulture Mos '09	♟3
● Passito Shekar '11	♟3

Musto Carmelitano
VIA PIETRO NENNI, 23
85020 MASCHITO [PZ]
TEL. 097233312
www.mustocarmelitano.it

CELLAR SALES
PRE-BOOKED VISITS
ACCOMMODATION AND RESTAURANT SERVICE
ANNUAL PRODUCTION 22,000 bottles
HECTARES UNDER VINE 9.00
VITICULTURE METHOD Certified Organic

○ Maschitano Bianco '12	♟3
◉ Maschitano Rosato '12	♟3
● Maschitano Rosso '11	♟3

Tenuta Parco dei Monaci
C.DA PARCO DEI MONACI
75100 MATERA
TEL. 0835259546
www.tenutaparcodeimonaci.it

PRE-BOOKED VISITS
ACCOMMODATION
ANNUAL PRODUCTION 20,000 bottles
HECTARES UNDER VINE 5.00

● Matera Moro Spaccasassi '11	♟♟6
● Matera Primitivo Monacello '11	♟♟5
◉ Matera Rosa per Sempre '12	♟4

Regio Cantina

loc. Piano Regio
85029 Venosa [PZ]
Tel. 3346966263
www.regiocantina.it

CELLAR SALES
PRE-BOOKED VISITS
ANNUAL PRODUCTION 38,000 bottles
HECTARES UNDER VINE 18.00

- ● Aglianico del Vulture Genesi '10 — 🍷🍷 3
- ● Aglianico del Vulture Solagna '10 — 🍷🍷 2*
- ● Aglianico del Vulture Donpà '10 — 🍷 4

Tenute Serra del Prete

loc.Serra del Prete
85020 Maschito [PZ]
Tel. 3341971231
www.tenuteserradelprete.it

ANNUAL PRODUCTION 8,000 bottles
HECTARES UNDER VINE 4.00

- ● Aglianico del Vulture Amaranthus '10 — 🍷🍷 4

I Talenti - Padri Trinitari

p.zza Don Bosco, 3
85029 Venosa [PZ]
Tel. 097234221
www.trinitarivenosa.it

CELLAR SALES
PRE-BOOKED VISITS
ANNUAL PRODUCTION 6,000 bottles
HECTARES UNDER VINE 4.00

- ● Aglianico del Vulture Cripta Sant'Agostino '08 — 🍷🍷 5
- ● Aglianico del Vulture Meracius '08 — 🍷 4

Terra dei Re

via Monticchio s. s. 167 Km 2,700
85028 Rionero in Vulture [PZ]
Tel. 0972725116
www.terradeire.com

CELLAR SALES
PRE-BOOKED VISITS
ACCOMMODATION AND RESTAURANT SERVICE
ANNUAL PRODUCTION 80,000 bottles
HECTARES UNDER VINE 31.00
VITICULTURE METHOD Certified Organic

- ● Aglianico del Vulture Nocte '10 — 🍷🍷 4
- ● Aglianico del Vulture Vultur '10 — 🍷 2
- ● Pacus '10 — 🍷 3

Vigneti del Vulture

c.da Pipoli
85011 Acerenza [PZ]
Tel. 0971285061
www.vignetidelvulture.it

PRE-BOOKED VISITS
ANNUAL PRODUCTION 100,000 bottles
HECTARES UNDER VINE 56.00

- ● Aglianico del Vulture Piano del Cerro Ris. '08 — 🍷🍷 3
- ○ Greco Fiano Pipoli '12 — 🍷🍷 2*

Vulcano & Vini

c.da Finocchiaro
85024 Lavello [PZ]
Tel. 0972877033
www.vulcanoevini.com

CELLAR SALES
PRE-BOOKED VISITS
ANNUAL PRODUCTION 400,000 bottles
HECTARES UNDER VINE 55.00

- ● Aglianico del Vulture Gudarrà Ris. '05 — 🍷🍷 5
- ● Aglianico del Vulture Terra di Vulcano '11 — 🍷 2
- ○ Fiano Terre di Vulcano '12 — 🍷 2

PUGLIA

Puglia has become one of the favourite regions of wine consumers, both at home, with a Nomisma survey placing it sixth among the regions producing the wines most popular with Italians, and abroad, with the value of its wine exports practically doubling since 2008. Its new status is confirmed again this year with an ever-more convincing series of wines giving the region's production the consistent quality unheard of just a few years ago. This growth and consistency appear to go hand in hand with the increasingly decisive rise of primitivo as the benchmark grape variety for the entire region, due to a series of labels at the pinnacle of Puglia's wine production. However, the improvements are not merely limited to good interpretation of the variety. As we already noted last year, the decisive step that the most far-sighted producers are taking consists of the progressive discovery and enhancement of the characteristics of the various terroirs. The clearest and most successful examples are represented by Gioia del Colle and Manduria. Here, in addition to the search for and protection of the old bush-trained vines, the main battle that Puglia viticulture must fight and win to make the most of its traditions and distinctive traits, knowledge of the different characteristics of the various areas is being extended with a view to making wines that are an increasing expression of the terroir and not just the grapes used. Nonetheless, not everything is perfect. Castel del Monte is struggling far more than expected to find its identity, and the same can be said of almost the whole of Salento, where the various minor designations are fraught and the most important, Salice Salentino, is failing to find either a shared aim for promotion of its wines or a stylistic definition able to give at least a general idea of its salient characteristics. The white wines continue to oscillate between international and native grape varieties, with an increasingly significant presence of fiano, without managing to offer an original model or production of a comparable level to the reds. While the rosé wines are designed and made to be pleasant, early-drinkers, we consider them an asset and a speciality of Puglia production, which could reach even loftier quality heights if only the producers themselves were more convinced. Finally, we extend our welcome to a new arrival in the exclusive club of Puglia's Tre Bicchieri winners: Plantamura, which has achieved the rare feat of making its debut in our Guide coincide with a Tre Bicchieri, awarded for its Gioia del Colle Primitivo Etichetta Rossa 2011. Good show!

A Mano

VIA SERGIO LEONE, 8C
70023 GIOIA DEL COLLE [BA]
TEL. 0803434872
www.amanowine.it

PRE-BOOKED VISITS
ANNUAL PRODUCTION 165,000 bottles
VITICULTURE METHOD Certified Organic

Elvezia Sbalchiero and Mark Shannon have
lived in Puglia for the past 15 years and
have created one of the most reliable,
high-quality wineries in the region, despite
not having vines of their own. Working like
real grower-producers, they oversee a
patchwork of old vineyards tended by small
growers in the most interesting areas for
each variety: Manduria, Sava, Torricella and
Maruggio for primitivo; San Pietro Vernotico
for negroamaro; and Putignano and
Acquaviva for fiano and greco. Their wines
combine pleasing drinkability with aromatic
precision to offer an authentic expression
of the territory. Elvezia and Mark presented
a new wine this year, the 2012 Imprint, a
raisined Primitivo with berry fruit aromas.
This wine is refreshing and enjoyable in
spite of being slightly high in alcohol. As
always, the supple, fruity 2011 Primitivo,
the enjoyable, floral 2012 Rosato, which
features 75% primitivo and 25% aleatico,
and the well-bodied, leisurely 2012
Fiano-Greco are all well made and focused.

● Imprint '12		♈♈ 2*
○ Fiano Greco '12		♈♈ 2*
● Primitivo '11		♈♈ 2*
⊙ Rosato '12		♈♈ 2*
● Aleatico Passito '09		♈ 2
⊙ Brut A Mano Rosa		♈ 2
● Negroamaro A Mano '08		♈♈ 2*
● Prima Mano '09		♈♈ 3*
● Prima Mano Primitivo '08		♈♈ 2*
● Primitivo A Mano '08		♈♈ 2*

Cantina Albea

VIA DUE MACELLI, 8
70011 ALBEROBELLO [BA]
TEL. 0804323548
www.albeavini.com

CELLAR SALES
PRE-BOOKED VISITS
ANNUAL PRODUCTION 380,000 bottles
HECTARES UNDER VINE 40.00

Dante Renzini masterfully runs this
gorgeous winery, which was established in
the early 20th century. The stone buildings
and troughs carved out of the rock are
reminiscent of ancient trullo cisterns. The
modern, internationally styled wines are the
result of scrupulous attention to technical
detail. The many labels are organized into
three ranges - Albea for the key selections,
Due Trulli, and Terre del Sole - and are
based primarily on local varieties, with nero
di Troia playing a star role. However, this
year the 2010 Riservato, a 60%
negroamaro, 40% primitivo blend,
impressed most. This fruity wine starts with
a Mediterranean scrub and spice nose,
followed by a rich and juicy, if slightly
alcoholic palate. The 2011 Nero di Troia
again presents good structure and fruit,
although slightly less deep and complex
than usual. The rest of the range is also
well made.

● Riservato '10		♈♈ 3*
● Lui '11		♈♈ 5
● Petranera '11		♈ 3
⊙ Petrarosa '12		♈ 3
● Raro '11		♈ 3
● Terra Lucente '12		♈ 2
● Lui '06		♈♈♈ 5
● Lui '05		♈♈♈ 5
● Lui '10		♈♈ 5
● Lui '09		♈♈ 5
● Petranera '10		♈♈ 3
● Petranera '09		♈♈ 3
● Raro '09		♈♈ 3

Antica Enotria

C.DA RISICATA
SP 65
71042 CERIGNOLA [FG]
TEL. 0885418462
www.anticaenotria.it

CELLAR SALES
PRE-BOOKED VISITS
ANNUAL PRODUCTION 100,000 bottles
HECTARES UNDER VINE 13.00
VITICULTURE METHOD Certified Organic

For 20 years now, Raffaele Di Tuccio has been using organic methods in his vineyards and, together with his wife Antonia and son Luigi, has created a winery whose products are a true expression of the territory. Highly drinkable and well made, the wines also have an experimental side, with no added sulphites, vinification in amphorae, and the use of maceration on the skins for white grapes. The vineyards are located between Cerignola and the sea, in a windy, arid area with medium-textured limestone and clay soils. The 2010 Nero di Troia is of a good standard with its berry fruit and liquorice notes, and relaxed, classic palate. The 2012 Contessa Staffa, a Rosato made with montepulciano grapes, features fruity yellow peach and sweet citrus notes, while the 2008 Dieci Ottobre offers an interesting reinterpretation of the traditional style. This equal blend of nero di Troia and aglianico, which ages in steel for 18 months and large barrels for a further 18 months, is mature and supple.

⊙ Contessa Staffa '12	♥♥ 2*
● Dieci Ottobre '08	♥♥ 3
● Nero di Troia '10	♥♥ 3
○ Falanghina '12	♥ 2
● Vriccio '12	♥ 2
● Falù Rosso '08	♀♀ 2*
● Puglia Rosso '09	♀♀ 1*
● Vriccio '11	♀♀ 2*
● Vriccio '10	♀♀ 2*

Cantele

SP SALICE SALENTINO-SAN DONACI KM 35,600
73010 GUAGNANO [LE]
TEL. 0832705010
www.cantele.it

CELLAR SALES
PRE-BOOKED VISITS
ANNUAL PRODUCTION 16,000,000 bottles
HECTARES UNDER VINE 150.00

The Cantele family has been attracting attention from the wine world for years, with their modern, technically precise range, in which quantity and quality come together in well-typed, drinkable wines. Cantele has 50 hectares of its own vineyards situated mainly at Guagnano, Montemesola and San Pietro Vernotico, on predominantly red earth, and another 100 in various localities, such as Sava for primitivo, Alberobello for verdeca, and the north-eastern Murge plateau for aglianico. These are farmed by a group of growers who receive extensive support from the winery's technicians. Alongside the well-made 2010 Salice Salentino Rosso Riserva, which is well made if less brilliant than last year, the 2011 Amativo makes a comeback. This classical 60% primitivo and negroamaro blend is a taut, well-orchestrated, typically Mediterranean wine. The elegant, supple 2011 Primitivo is also very pleasant. However, the Teresa Manara line does not quite live up to its usual standard.

● Amativo '11	♥♥ 4
● Primitivo '11	♥♥ 2*
⊙ Negroamaro Rosato '12	♥♥ 2*
● Salice Salentino Rosso Ris. '10	♥♥ 2*
○ Alticelli Fiano '12	♥ 2
● Negroamaro '12	♥ 2
○ Teresa Manara Chardonnay '12	♥ 3
● Amativo '07	♀♀♀ 4*
● Amativo '03	♀♀♀ 3*
● Salice Salentino Rosso Ris. '09	♀♀♀ 2*
● Amativo '10	♀♀ 4
● Salice Salentino Rosso Ris. '08	♀♀ 2*
● Teresa Manara Negroamaro '09	♀♀ 3
● Varius Syrah '10	♀♀ 2*

Carvinea

VIA PER SERRANOVA, 1
72012 CAROVIGNO [BR]
TEL. 0805862345
www.carvinea.com

CELLAR SALES
ACCOMMODATION AND RESTAURANT SERVICE
ANNUAL PRODUCTION 34,000 bottles
HECTARES UNDER VINE 8.75
VITICULTURE METHOD Certified Organic

Beppe di Maria is a strong-willed, passionate man, and his decision to produce a range of wines from varieties such as montepulciano, aglianico and petit verdot, not usually found in the Altosalento area, seems to have paid off. Despite the vines being less than ten years old, his impressive work in the vineyard – with deliberately low yields per vine – and back in the cellar, has enabled Carvinea to produce internationally styled, technically flawless wines showing dense concentration and rich fruit. This year, it was the 2011 Merula Montepulciano monovarietal that most stood out in Carvinea's offerings, with its liquorice and wild fennel aromas and attractive fresh fruit palate. The 2011 Aglianico Sierma, with its berry fruit aromas, has great backbone, although the oak is still a little too evident. This was, however, as always a well-managed wine, as were the spicy 2011 Frauma, from 60% aglianco and petit verdot, and the citrusy 2012 Fiano Lucerna.

Castello Monaci

C. DA DEI MONACI
VIA CASE SPARSE
73015 SALICE SALENTINO [LE]
TEL. 0831665700
www.castellomonaci.it

CELLAR SALES
PRE-BOOKED VISITS
RESTAURANT SERVICE
ANNUAL PRODUCTION 2,000,000 bottles
HECTARES UNDER VINE 200.00

Castello Monaci, owned by Gruppo Italiano Vini, is rightly considered one of the most reliable and emblematic estates in the region. Situated a stone's throw from Salice Salentino, the operation boasts vineyards at Lecce, Taranto and Brindisi, primarily planted to local varieties on fertile topsoil that sits on a rocky base with good drainage. Their reliable, well-made wines combine quality and quantity, and are available in two lines: Castello Monaci and Feudo Monaci. We really liked the 2010 Salentino Rosso Aiace Riserva, which is one of the best in the DOC zone. This lengthy and complex, but also fresh and fruity wine has plenty of spirit. The 2011 Primitivo Artas, with notes of chocolate and dark berry jam, is also excellent. The well-orchestrated 2012 Pilùna Primitivo is enjoyable and juicy, with good structure, while the equally well-made 2012 Negroamaro Maru features plum and damp-earth aromas.

● Merula '11	♟♟♟ 3*
● Frauma '11	♟♟ 5
○ Lucerna '12	♟♟ 2*
● Sierma '11	♟♟ 5
⊙ Merularosa '12	♟ 2
● Frauma '08	♟♟♟ 4
● Sierma '09	♟♟♟ 5
● Lunachiena '09	♟♟ 2*
● Sierma '07	♟♟ 5

● Artas '11	♟♟ 5
● Salice Salentino Aiace Ris. '10	♟♟ 3*
● Maru '12	♟♟ 2*
● Pilùna '12	♟♟ 2*
○ Acante '12	♟ 2
⊙ Kreos '12	♟ 2
● Medòs '12	♟ 3
● Salice Salentino Liante '12	♟ 2
○ Simera '12	♟ 2
● Artas '07	♟♟♟ 5
● Artas '06	♟♟♟ 4
● Artas '05	♟♟♟ 4*
● Artas '04	♟♟♟ 3*
⊙ Kreos '11	♟♟ 2*

Chiaromonte

VICO MURO SANT'ANGELO, 6
70021 ACQUAVIVA DELLE FONTI [BA]
TEL. 0803050432
www.vinichiaromonte.it

CELLAR SALES
PRE-BOOKED VISITS
ANNUAL PRODUCTION 60,000 bottles
HECTARES UNDER VINE 27.00
VITICULTURE METHOD Certified Organic

Nicola Chiaromonte carries out his work with passion and curiosity, and the results are having a positive impact on not only the wines, but also the Gioia del Colle area in general. In this vein, he recently acquired an old vineyard of about a hectare of century-old head-trained vines which, despite being one of the few remaining of its kind, was set to be uprooted by the previous owners. His Primitivos have become a benchmark for Puglian wine, and offer an astonishing balance of fullness, freshness, rich flavour and fruit. The 2010 Gioia del Colle Primitivo Muro Sant'Angelo Contrada Barbatto is still one of the top wines in Puglia. This gorgeous Mediterranean wine offers up fresh dark berry fruit, rosemary and bay leaf aromas, with a savoury, textured palate and lengthy finish. The 2010 Gioia del Colle Primitivo Muro Sant'Angelo 2010 is also well made with its sweet spice and chocolate aromas. We should mention that Nicola has decided to hold the Riserva back for a year.

● Gioia del Colle Muro Sant'Angelo Contrada Barbatto '10	♥♥♥ 7
● Gioia del Colle Muro Sant'Angelo '10	♥♥ 3*
● Nigredo '10	♥♥ 5
● Elè '11	♥ 4
○ Kimìa '12	♥ 4
● Gioia del Colle Muro Sant'Angelo Contrada Barbatto '09	♀♀♀ 5
● Gioia del Colle Muro Sant'Angelo Contrada Barbatto '08	♀♀♀ 5
● Gioia del Colle Muro Sant'Angelo Contrada Barbatto '07	♀♀♀ 5
● Gioia del Colle Primitivo Ris. '06	♀♀♀ 7
● Gioia del Colle Muro Sant'Angelo '09	♀♀ 3
● Gioia del Colle Primitivo Ris. '09	♀♀ 8

Cantine Due Palme

VIA SAN MARCO, 130
72020 CELLINO SAN MARCO [BR]
TEL. 0831617865
www.cantineduepalme.it

CELLAR SALES
PRE-BOOKED VISITS
ACCOMMODATION AND RESTAURANT SERVICE
ANNUAL PRODUCTION 10.000,000 bottles
HECTARES UNDER VINE 2,500.00

Cantine Due Palme now counts over 1,200 members. This operation is a fine example of how hard work and conviction can make a cooperative winery a sound option for a large number of small growers. There is an underlying emphasis on quality, but also a strong regional focus and an effort to bring out the local character in the wines, through the preservation of traditional head-training systems and predominant use of local varieties. The resulting wines are modern in both technique and concentration, while also offering a more classical sweet, ripe fruitiness. The 2010 Salice Salentino Rosso Selvarossa Riserva, with its fruit-rich personality defined by a blueberry, blackberry and Mediterranean scrub nose, and a pleasing, velvety, but gutsy palate, unquestionably remains the point of reference for the designation as a whole. Of note is the successful 2012 Susumaniello Serre, which is at once supple and fresh, with attractive spicy notes.

● Salice Salentino Rosso Selvarossa Ris. '10	♥♥♥ 4*
● Serre '12	♥♥ 3*
● Canonico '12	♥♥ 2*
○ Anthea '12	♥ 3
● Ettamiano '11	♥ 3
● Primitivo di Manduria San Gaetano '12	♥ 3
○ Salice Salentino Bianco Tinaia '12	♥ 3
● Salice Salentino Rosso Selvarossa Ris. '09	♀♀♀ 4*
● Salice Salentino Rosso Selvarossa Ris. '08	♀♀♀ 4
● Salice Salentino Rosso Selvarossa Ris. '07	♀♀♀ 4*

Felline - Pervini

VIA SANTO STASI PRIMO
74024 MANDURIA [TA]
TEL. 0999711660
www.racemi.it

CELLAR SALES
PRE-BOOKED VISITS
ANNUAL PRODUCTION 300,000 bottles
HECTARES UNDER VINE 60.00
VITICULTURE METHOD Certified Organic

Gregory Perrucci's estate, Felline-Pervini, was founded in 1994 and was a leader in the revolution that raised primitivo to the level of quality and international success it now enjoys. This revolution was played out both through the wines, which are distinguished by their bright fruitiness and pure aromatics, and through the protection and rehabilitation of old Puglian-style head-trained vines. The estate produces a range of well-balanced, pleasant everyday wines and more exclusive labels from the older vines. The 2009 Vigna del Feudo, an equal blend of primitivo, malvasia nera and ottavianello, is making a comeback, and reached the finals this year. Gutsy and fresh, the wine has thrust and structure, with a dark berry fruit finish. The savoury, supple 2012 Primitivo di Manduria Archidamo, and the complex, well-balanced 2011 Alberello with mature dark berry fruit notes are both pleasant and well orchestrated.

● Vigna del Feudo '09	♟♟ 4
● Alberello '11	♟♟ 2*
● Primitivo di Manduria Archidamo '12	♟♟ 2*
● I Monili Primitivo '11	♟ 1*
● Primitivo di Manduria Felline '10	♟ 2
● Primitivo di Manduria Segnavento '12	♟ 2
○ Rufiano '12	♟ 2
⊙ Vigna Rosa '12	♟ 2
● Vigna del Feudo '97	♟♟♟ 4*
● Primitivo di Manduria Archidamo '09	♟♟ 2*
● Primitivo di Manduria Segnavento '10	♟♟ 2*
● Vigna del Feudo '08	♟♟ 4

Gianfranco Fino

VIA PIAVE, 12
74028 SAVA [TA]
TEL. 0997773970
www.gianfrancofino.it

PRE-BOOKED VISITS
ANNUAL PRODUCTION 12,000 bottles
HECTARES UNDER VINE 14.50

Gianfranco and Simona have come a long way from their first vineyard and first 2,800 bottles of Es, making Manduria famous nationally and internationally above all by creating a wine that has established itself as one of Italy's best. Today, Gianfranco produces wines from 12 limy, red-earthed vineyards between Manduria and Sava, which are all planted to head-trained vines over 50 years old. In addition to Primitivo, he now also produces a Negroamaro called Jo, made in the same style and with the same passion as its big brother. The only wine presented this year, the 2011 Primitivo di Manduria Es, has done the impossible. Its intense nose, which features black cherry and Mediterranean scrub notes, is coupled with a palate rich in sweet fruit that is also savoury, lingering, dynamic and wonderfully fresh.

● Primitivo di Manduria Es '11	♟♟♟ 7
● Primitivo di Manduria Es '10	♟♟♟ 6
● Primitivo di Manduria Es '09	♟♟♟ 6
● Primitivo di Manduria Es '08	♟♟♟ 6
● Primitivo di Manduria Es '07	♟♟♟ 6
● Primitivo di Manduria Es '06	♟♟♟ 5
● Jo '08	♟♟ 6
● Jo '07	♟♟ 6

Leone de Castris

VIA SENATORE DE CASTRIS, 26
73015 SALICE SALENTINO [LE]
TEL. 0832731112
www.leonedecastris.com

CELLAR SALES
PRE-BOOKED VISITS
ACCOMMODATION AND RESTAURANT SERVICE
ANNUAL PRODUCTION 2,500,000 bottles
HECTARES UNDER VINE 250.00

Leone de Castris's story is tightly woven with that of Puglian wine. Founded in 1665, the estate only started producing its own wines in 1925, and in 1943 released Italy's first rosé, under the name Five Roses. Most of the estate's vineyards are located between Salice Salentino, Campi and Guagnano, and are planted to traditional varieties, such as negroamaro, malvasia nera and sussumaniello, alongside international cultivars, including cabernet sauvignon, chardonnay and petit verdot. The estate offers an extensive range of reliable, modern wines produced with international markets in mind. The 2010 Salice Salentino Rosso Riserva is again at the top of the estate's production, with its spicy, black cherry aromas and pleasant, balanced palate with good acidity. The two Five Roses are again good, although we had a slight preference for the basic wine, which is fresher and more aromatic than the Anniversario. The 2012 Primitivo di Manduria Villa Santera is juicy and pleasant.

● Salice Salentino Rosso Ris. '10	♛♛♛ 2*
⊙ Five Roses '12	♛♛ 2*
⊙ Five Roses 69° Anniversario '12	♛♛ 3
● Primitivo di Manduria Villa Santera '12	♛♛ 2*
● Salice Salentino Rosso Donna Lisa Ris. '10	♛♛ 6
○ Don Piero Brut	♛ 2
● Elo Veni '12	♛ 2
○ Imago '12	♛ 2
○ Messapia '12	♛ 2
● Salice Salentino Rosso Donna Lisa Ris. '06	♕♕♕ 5
● Salice Salentino Rosso Donna Lisa Ris. '05	♕♕♕ 5
● Salice Salentino Rosso Ris. '09	♕♕♕ 2*

Masseria Li Veli

SP CELLINO-CAMPI, KM 1
72020 CELLINO SAN MARCO [BR]
TEL. 0831618259
www.liveli.it

CELLAR SALES
PRE-BOOKED VISITS
ANNUAL PRODUCTION 350,000 bottles
HECTARES UNDER VINE 33.00
VITICULTURE METHOD Certified Organic

Masseria Li Veli, which is owned by the Falvo family, has made a noticeable leap in quality in recent years. The estate-owned vineyards largely feature sandy, red soil over a water-rich subsoil, and contain almost exclusively head-trained vines planted in a septunx pattern. Local red varieties dominate. The white grapes come from rented vineyards in Vallet d'Itria, in one of Puglia's best zones for these varieties. The wines are technically sound, with a strong local character. This year the estate earned a Tre Bicchieri for its 2010 Masseria Li Veli, a blend of 60% negroamaro and cabernet sauvignon, with sour cherry and damp-earth aromas, complemented by a nicely complex, textured palate. The 2008 Aleatico Passito is also excellent, with its cinnamon, dried fig and toasted almond notes.

● Masseria Li Veli '10	♛♛♛ 5
● Aleatico Passito '08	♛♛ 6
● Primonero '12	♛♛ 2*
● Susumaniello Askos '12	♛♛ 3
○ Fiano '12	♛ 2
● Malvasia Nera Askos '12	♛ 3
● Orion '12	♛ 2
● Salice Salentino Rosso Passamante '12	♛ 2
○ Verdeca Askos '12	♛ 3
● Aleatico Passito '07	♕♕ 6
● Masseria Li Veli '09	♕♕ 5
● MLV '08	♕♕ 5
● Salice Salentino Rosso Pezzo Morgana Ris. '08	♕♕ 3

Tenute Mater Domini

VIA DEI MARTIRI, 17/19
73012 CAMPI SALENTINA [LE]
TEL. 0832792442
www.tenutematerdomini.it

CELLAR SALES
PRE-BOOKED VISITS
ANNUAL PRODUCTION 100,000 bottles
HECTARES UNDER VINE 50.00

Ten years down the track, Tenute Mater Domini continues to combine innovative farming techniques with modern winemaking technologies and traditional Salento methods. The company is divided into two main estates: Borgo Mater Domini in Arnesano, and Tenute Mater Domini between Salice Salentino and Veglie. The latter is further divided into marly, stony Masseria Casili, where the more recent vineyards have been planted, and Masseria Fontanelle, which boasts silty clay soils and has been planted with new spur-pruned vines and old head-trained negroamaro and primitivo vines over 60 years old. The 2010 Salice Salentino Rosso Casili Riserva was less impressive than in recent editions, due to a lack of aromatic focus and excessive oak. On the other hand, the 2012 Marangi Primitivo is juicy and enjoyable, with bright berry fruit notes. Likewise the leisurely 2011 Marangi Negroamaro, with spice and Mediterranean scrub aromas.

● Marangi Negroamaro '11	♥♥	3
● Marangi Primitivo '12	♥♥	2*
● Salice Salentino Casili Ris. '10	♥♥	3
⊙ La Nova Rosato '12	♥	1*
● La Nova Rosso '10	♥	1*
○ Marangi Bianco '12	♥	2
⊙ Marangi Rosato '12	♥	2
● Salice Salentino Casili Ris. '09	♥♥♥	5
● Salice Salentino Casili Ris. '08	♥♥♥	5
○ Marangi Bianco '11	♥♥	3
● Marangi Rosso '09	♥♥	3
● Salice Salentino Casili Ris. '07	♥♥	5

Morella

VIA PER UGGIANO, 147
74024 MANDURIA [TA]
TEL. 0999791482
www.morellavini.com

CELLAR SALES
PRE-BOOKED VISITS
ANNUAL PRODUCTION 18,000 bottles
HECTARES UNDER VINE 16.00

Lisa Gilbee and Gaetano Morella are as passionate as ever about making wines that are 100% typical of the territory, while offering a savoury, fresh fruitiness that is difficult to achieve in this area. They went biodynamic four years ago and have made some fairly unconventional choices in the cellar, such as the use of unlined concrete vats. They are adding other old vineyards beside their existing plots planted to 50–80-year-old head-trained vines, and have recently rented a genuine clos with vines over 100 years old. It may seem strange that the maker of one of the most Mediterranean of wines is Australian, but her 2010 La Signora leaves no room for doubt. Deep, savoury, tangy and gutsy, with Mediterranean scrub and sea notes, this is truly an extraordinary Primitivo. The other Primitivo, the 2010 Old Vines, is not far behind. This wine has more focused berry fruit aromas and shows balsamic, dynamic and juicy.

● Primitivo La Signora '10	♥♥♥	6
● Old Vines Primitivo '10	♥♥	6
● Mezzanotte '11	♥	3
● Primitivo Malbek '10	♥	4
● Primitivo La Signora '07	♥♥♥	5
● Primitivo Old Vines '09	♥♥♥	5
● Primitivo Old Vines '08	♥♥♥	5
● Primitivo Old Vines '07	♥♥♥	5

Cosimo Palamà

VIA A. DIAZ, 6
73020 CUTROFIANO [LE]
TEL. 0836542865
www.vinicolapalama.com

CELLAR SALES
PRE-BOOKED VISITS
ANNUAL PRODUCTION 250,000 bottles
HECTARES UNDER VINE 15.00

The Palamà family's winery is typically Puglian. The estate was founded in 1936, and in 1990 Cosimo decided to bottle his own wine and begin to focus on quality, with positive results, particularly in recent years. The four lines beautifully express the local terroir and varieties while offering great value for money. The estate-owned vineyards are largely situated in Cutrofiano and Matino, on moderately loose, mainly limestone soil. The 75 Vendemmie 2012 obtained good results again this year. This Negroamaro marked by damp-earth and liquorice notes offers an intriguing interpretation of Puglian tradition. However, we were also very impressed by the 2012 Metiusco Rosato from negroamaro grapes. In our opinion, this is the best rosé in Puglia, with its berry fruit, peach and spice aromas, pleasant, harmonious palate and long, savoury, fresh finish.

● 75 Vendemmie '12	🍷🍷 4
⊙ Metiusco Rosato '12	🍷🍷 2*
● Mavro '11	🍷🍷 3
● Albarossa Primitivo '11	🍷 2
● Metiusco Oro Passito '11	🍷 3
● Metiusco Rosso '12	🍷 2
● Salice Salentino Rosso Albarossa '11	🍷 1*
● 75 Vendemmie '11	🍷🍷🍷 4*
● Il Vino d'Arcangelo '08	🍷🍷 3
● Mavro '09	🍷🍷 3*

Pietraventosa

C.DA PARCO LARGO
70023 GIOIA DEL COLLE [BA]
TEL. 0805034436
www.pietraventosa.it

CELLAR SALES
ANNUAL PRODUCTION 12,000 bottles
HECTARES UNDER VINE 5.40
VITICULTURE METHOD Certified Organic

Year after year Marianna, Annio and Raffaele Leo's small estate reinforces its position as one of the region's more substantial and interesting producers. The vines are planted at an elevation of around 380 metres in mineral-rich limestone soil with rock less than a metre below the surface. The vineyards are divided into two plots, one planted with old head-trained vines and the other with young cordon-trained and spur-pruned vines. This year Marianna and Raffaele only presented two wines. The 2012 EstRosa is a highly drinkable Rosato made with primitivo grapes that features a floral nose and rich fruit palate with a good acid backbone. The 2010 Gioia del Colle Primitivo Riserva is, as always, one of the DOC zone's best, offering a dark berry nose and a balanced fresh, savoury palate with good texture and fruit.

● Gioia del Colle Primitivo Ris. '10	🍷🍷 5
⊙ EstRosa '12	🍷🍷 3
● Gioia del Colle Primitivo Ris. '06	🍷🍷🍷 4
● Gioia del Colle Primitivo Allegoria '08	🍷🍷 3
● Gioia del Colle Primitivo Riserva di Pietraventosa '08	🍷🍷 5
● Gioia del Colle Primitivo Riserva di Pietraventosa '07	🍷🍷 5
● Ossimoro '08	🍷🍷 3

Plantamura

VIA SANTA CANDIDA, 1
70023 GIOIA DEL COLLE [BA]
TEL. 3474711027
www.viniplantamura.it

CELLAR SALES
ANNUAL PRODUCTION 50,000 bottles
HECTARES UNDER VINE 8.00
VITICULTURE METHOD Certified Organic

Founded in the early 1900s, the estate run by Mariangela Plantamura and her husband Vincenzo is devoted entirely to the primitivo variety across three labels. All the vineyards are located in the countryside around Gioia del Colle, at an elevation of around 360 metres. The vines are partly vertical-trellised and partly head-trained, and planted on clay and limestone soil, fed by aquifers that prevent water stress during dry periods. Plantamura made a grand entrance this year. The 2011 Gioia del Colle Primitivo Etichetta Rossa won us over entirely. In theory it should be a less imposing wine, given that it is produced with grapes from the youngest vines and is aged exclusively in stainless steel. However, it is elegant and rich yet tangy, gutsy and juicy, with berry fruit and pomegranate aromas: a true delight. The 2010 Gioia del Colle Primitivo Riserva is also gorgeous. Although showing more structure, it is also wonderfully fresh and savoury.

● Gioia del Colle Primitivo Et. Rossa '11	♔♔♔	4*
● Gioia del Colle Primitivo Ris. '10	♔♔	5
● Gioia del Colle Primitivo Et. Nera '11	♔♔	4

Polvanera

S.DA VICINALE LAMIE MARCHESANA, 601
70023 GIOIA DEL COLLE [BA]
TEL. 080758900
www.cantinepolvanera.it

CELLAR SALES
RESTAURANT SERVICE
ANNUAL PRODUCTION 200,000 bottles
HECTARES UNDER VINE 60.00
VITICULTURE METHOD Certified Organic

Polvanera was founded in 2003 and since then, along with a handful of other producers, has literally reinvented Primitivo di Gioia del Colle, offering powerful, richly alcoholic wines that are balanced by a freshness and savouriness unthinkable even a few years ago. The vineyards are located between Acquaviva and Gioia del Colle, on the typical karst terrain of the Murgia ranges, which consists in a thin layer of soil on a base of solid rock. In addition to the young estate-owned vineyards, Polvanera also manages plots of 60-year-old head-trained vines, which provide grapes for its top wines. The 2010 vintage was definitely a success. The Gioia del Colle Primitivo 17 is rich and taut, with aromas of black berry fruit, Mediterranean scrub, and chestnut honey. It is also savoury and well balanced, despite its high alcohol content. The other two Gioia del Colle Primitivo's presented are also excellent. The 16 is distinguished by brilliant fresh fruit and the 14, while less complex, is juicy and very enjoyable.

● Gioia del Colle Primitivo 17 '10	♔♔♔	5
● Gioia del Colle Primitivo 14 '10	♔♔	3*
● Gioia del Colle Primitivo 16 '10	♔♔	5
⊙ Rosato '12	♔♔	2*
○ Minutolo '12	♔	3
● Gioia del Colle Primitivo 16 '07	♔♔♔	2*
● Gioia del Colle Primitivo 17 '09	♔♔♔	5
● Gioia del Colle Primitivo 17 '08	♔♔♔	4*
● Gioia del Colle Primitivo Vign. Marchesana 14 '09	♔♔	3

Primis

VIA G. SCIREA
71048 STORNARELLA [FG]
TEL. 0885433333
www.primisvini.com

CELLAR SALES
PRE-BOOKED VISITS
ANNUAL PRODUCTION 160,000 bottles
HECTARES UNDER VINE 24.00

Gianni Mauriello and Nicola Selano's young estate is now considered one of the most interesting in Puglia. They grow numerous varieties and produce a range of monovarietals, the majority of which are vinified and aged exclusively in stainless steel. The estate's vineyards are situated in the countryside around Stornarella, on moderately loose calcareous clay. The wines are resolutely modern in style, with plenty of fruit freshness – a characteristic that also applies to their few barrel-aged wines. The 2009 Crusta, a splendid Montepulciano monovarietal, has black berry fruit, plum and liquorice aromas, with hints of Peruvian bark, and a dense, fruit-rich palate that is also fresh, leisurely and taut. In our opinion, this is the best version ever presented. The 2012 Monrose is also very good. This floral Nero di Troia Rosato with apricot and peach notes is incredibly enjoyable, despite its light structure and forthright tannins. Lastly, the 2011 Negroamaro is well orchestrated, nicely fleshy and long.

● Crusta '09	♈♈ 3*
☉ Monrose '12	♈♈ 2*
● Negroamaro '11	♈♈ 2*
○ Bombino Bianco '12	♈ 2
● Nero di Troia '11	♈ 2
○ Bombino Bianco '11	♈♈ 2*
○ Cenerata '10	♈♈ 2*
● Crusta '08	♈♈ 3
● Syrah '09	♈♈ 2*

Racemi

VIA SANTO STASI PRIMO, 42
74024 MANDURIA [TA]
TEL. 0999711660
www.racemi.it

CELLAR SALES
PRE-BOOKED VISITS
ANNUAL PRODUCTION 1,200,000 bottles
HECTARES UNDER VINE 120.00
VITICULTURE METHOD Certified Organic

Gregory Perrucci's Racemi project has played a leading role in shaping the Puglian wine industry and in preserving Salento's wine-growing traditions and landscape. The restoration of old head-trained vines, careful winemaking, and a focus on highlighting the character of individual areas has made Racemi's wines a benchmark for understanding Salento's viticultural traditions. The vineyards are planted on a variety of soil types, ranging from sandy near the sea to red, black or stony soils, resulting in a range of intriguing, high-quality wines. They take Tre Bicchieri again this year with the tangy and savoury 2010 Primitivo di Manduria Dunico Masseria Pepe, which features crunchy red berry fruits with spicy nuances. The other Primitivo di Manduria wines presented were also very good. The 2011 Sinfarosa Zinfandel is richer and more structured, but slightly less tangy, and the 2011 Giravolta Tenuta Pozzopalo is very enjoyable.

● Primitivo di Manduria Dunico Masseria Pepe '10	♈♈♈ 5
● Primitivo di Manduria Giravolta Tenuta Pozzopalo '11	♈♈ 3*
● Primitivo di Manduria Zinfandel Sinfarosa '11	♈♈ 3*
● Pietraluna Torre Guaceto '12	♈ 2
● Susumaniello Sum Torre Guaceto '11	♈ 4
● Primitivo di Manduria Dunico Masseria Pepe '05	♈♈♈ 5*
● Primitivo di Manduria Zinfandel Sinfarosa '06	♈♈♈ 3*
● Primitivo di Manduria Zinfandel Sinfarosa '98	♈♈♈ 3*
● Anarkos '09	♈♈ 2*
● Primitivo di Manduria Dunico Masseria Pepe '09	♈♈ 5

Rasciatano

C.DA RASCIATANO
76121 BARLETTA
TEL. 0883510999
www.rasciatano.com

CELLAR SALES
PRE-BOOKED VISITS
ANNUAL PRODUCTION 90,000 bottles
HECTARES UNDER VINE 18.00

Tenuta Rasciatano is located in the countryside of Murgia, halfway between the sea and the hills, and enjoys a long-standing reputation on the local winemaking scene. However, it was only in 2005 that the Porro family decided to focus their energies on quality wines, redeveloping the winery to achieve better results from their estate-grown grapes. The vineyards, most planted between 1992 and 2002, stand around the main buildings on sandy soil over layers of limestone rock. There is clear attention to quality in the winemaking, and the wines all tend towards an attractive combination of fruit, structure and elegance. Without their star wine, the Rasciatano Nero di Troia, the estate presented a mixed bag this year. However, we liked the 2010 Tenute Nero di Troia, with its floral berry fruit nose and pleasant, fresh, lingering palate, and the fresh, citrusy 2012 Rasciatano Malvasia Bianca, which showed good grip.

○ Rasciatano Malvasia Bianca '12	♟♟ 3
● Tenute Nero di Troia '10	♟♟ 2*
⊙ Rasciatano Rosé '12	♟ 3
● Rasciatano Rosso '11	♟ 4
○ Tenute Chardonnay '12	♟ 2
● Rasciatano Nero di Troia '08	♟♟♟ 6
● Rasciatano Nero di Troia '07	♟♟♟ 6
● Rasciatano Nero di Troia '10	♟♟ 4
● Rasciatano Rosso '09	♟♟ 4

Rivera

C.DA RIVERA, SP 231 KM 60,500
76123 ANDRIA [BT]
TEL. 0883569510
www.rivera.it

CELLAR SALES
PRE-BOOKED VISITS
ANNUAL PRODUCTION 1,200,000 bottles
HECTARES UNDER VINE 95.00

The De Corato family's estate is one of the leading names in the Castel del Monte zone. The black varieties are planted on tuffaceous limestone soil between 200 and 220 metres above sea level, and the white varieties on the typical karst soil of the Murgia hills at elevations of between 300 and 350 metres. The climate is a lot cooler than the rest of the region, and produces noticeably more acidic grapes, resulting in richly aromatic, technically well-made wines. This year's tastings revealed a reasonable series of Castel del Montes, but no stars. The traditional 2008 Castel del Monte Rosso Il Falcone Riserva is a fresh, gutsy wine, produced with 70% nero di Troia and montepulciano grapes, showing good structure with Peruvian bark and dark berry aromas. The 2007 Castel del Monte Aglianico Cappellaccio Riserva is expansive and well-defined, and the 2012 Castel del Monte Bombino Nero Pungirosa, an enjoyable, floral rosé.

● Castel del Monte Aglianico Cappellaccio Ris. '07	♟♟ 2*
⊙ Castel del Monte Bombino Nero Pungirosa '12	♟♟ 2*
● Castel del Monte Rosso Il Falcone Ris. '08	♟♟ 4
○ Castel del Monte Bianco Fedora '12	♟ 2
○ Castel del Monte Bombino Bianco Marese '12	♟ 2
● Castel del Monte Nero di Troia Puer Apuliae '08	♟ 5
● Castel del Monte Rosso Rupicolo '11	♟ 2
○ Scariazzo '12	♟ 2
● Castel del Monte Nero di Troia Puer Apuliae '04	♟♟♟ 6
● Castel del Monte Nero di Troia Puer Apuliae '03	♟♟♟ 6

Tenute Rubino

VIA E. FERMI, 50
72100 BRINDISI
TEL. 0831571955
www.tenuterubino.it

CELLAR SALES
PRE-BOOKED VISITS
ANNUAL PRODUCTION 1,000,000 bottles
HECTARES UNDER VINE 200.00

Over the past decade, the Rubino family estate has become one of the key players on the Puglian wine scene, for both the quality of its wines and its energetic work to develop and raise awareness of the region's wines. The vineyards are divided into four main holdings, ranging from the coast to the tablelands above Brindisi, and the vast range is almost entirely produced from local varieties, with a particular focus on giving new life to sussumaniello. The wines are technically well managed, and show strong local identity. The Susumaniello Torre Testa has once again taken Tre Bicchieri. Due to a printing error last year, the 2010 vintage was published as 2011. We actually tasted the 2011 this year. It is juicy, complex, rich in fruit, and plush yet fresh. The 2012 Oltremé consolidates Rubino's success with this grape. The wine is simple yet vibrant, and extraordinarily enjoyable.

Schola Sarmenti

VIA GENERALE CANTORE, 37
73048 NARDÒ [LE]
TEL. 0833567247
www.scholasarmenti.it

PRE-BOOKED VISITS
ANNUAL PRODUCTION 240,000 bottles
HECTARES UNDER VINE 41.00
VITICULTURE METHOD Certified Organic

In a time of crisis, during which the vines in the Nardò area were being severely culled, Schola Sarmenti's Carlo Marra and Benedetto Lorusso rallied to defend and restore this zone's wine-growing traditions and cultural heritage. Not coincidentally, 85% of the estate's holdings are planted to head-trained vines, which account for 40% of the 70 hectares remaining in the entire designation. Their wines have a strong local identity, with a studied richness and sweet fruit. The 2011 Diciotto really impressed us when it first came out. This Primitivo is made with grapes from the estate's 80-year-old head-trained vines – their oldest. Made in the new Primitivo style, it is rich in dark fruit, with chocolate notes, a complex, dense palate, and lingering finish. The well-managed 2009 Nardò Riserva shows Mediterranean scrub and cherry on the nose. The fruit-rich 2010 Cubardi is a doughy Primitivo.

● Torre Testa '11	▼▼▼ 6
● Oltremé '12	▼▼ 2*
● Punta Aquila '11	▼▼ 2*
● Visellio '11	▼▼ 4
○ Giancola '12	▼ 2
○ Libens Extra Dry	▼ 2
○ Marmorelle Bianco '12	▼ 2
● Marmorelle Rosso '11	▼ 2
☉ Saturnino '12	▼ 2
● Primitivo Visellio '01	♈♈♈ 3*
● Torre Testa '02	♈♈♈ 5
● Torre Testa '01	♈♈♈ 5
● Visellio '10	♈♈♈ 4*

● Diciotto '11	▼▼ 7
● Cubardi '10	▼▼ 3
● Nardò Nerìo Ris. '09	▼▼ 3
○ Fiano '12	▼ 2
● Nardò Rosso Roccamora '10	▼ 2
● Nauna '11	▼ 4
● Artetica '08	♈♈ 5
● Nardò Rosso Roccamora '09	♈♈ 2*
● Primitivo Diciotto '08	♈♈ 7
○ Salento Fiano '11	♈♈ 2*

Cantine Soloperto

SS 7
74024 Manduria [TA]
Tel. 0999794286
www.soloperto.it

CELLAR SALES
PRE-BOOKED VISITS
ANNUAL PRODUCTION 2,000,000 bottles
HECTARES UNDER VINE 50.00

This estate is run by the Soloperto family and heads the registry of vineyards for the Primitivo di Manduria designation. It has successfully increased its vineyard holdings in recent years to produce wines of ever-higher quality from head-trained vines such as those found in the historic century-old vineyards in Bagnolo and the new vineyards replanted in ideally suited zones such as Petrose. The extensive range features not only early-drinkers, but also more structured, long-lived wines, all traditional in style with impressive aromatic focus. This year the 2011 Primitivo di Manduria Centofuochi Tenuta Bagnolo confirmed that it is one of the best in the designation when it again reached the finals. Spicy, fresh fruit and Mediterranean scrub aromas are complemented by an elegant, pleasant palate. The 2011 Primitivo di Manduria Rubinum Etichetta Blu 14° is more supple, with predominant dark fruit aromas and richness of flavour.

● Primitivo di Manduria Centofuochi Tenuta Bagnolo '11	♟♟ 4
● Primitivo di Manduria Rubinum Et. Blu 14° '11	♟♟ 2*
● Primitivo di Manduria '12	♟ 2
● Primitivo di Manduria Passulentu '11	♟ 4
● Primitivo di Manduria Patriarca '11	♟ 4
⊙ Rosato Salento '12	♟ 2
● Vintia '11	♟ 3
● Primitivo di Manduria Centofuochi Tenuta Bagnolo '10	♟♟ 4
● Primitivo di Manduria Centofuochi Tenuta Bagnolo '09	♟♟ 4

Cosimo Taurino

SS 605
73010 Guagnano [LE]
Tel. 0832706490
www.taurinovini.it

CELLAR SALES
PRE-BOOKED VISITS
ANNUAL PRODUCTION 600,000 bottles
HECTARES UNDER VINE 85.00

Founded 40 years ago, Cosimo Taurino is one of the best-known Puglian wineries both in Italy and abroad, thanks particularly to their red negroamaro wines, such as the legendary Patriglione and Notarpanaro, which dominate the region's winemaking history. Most of the estate's vineyards are located in Guagnano on sandy limestone, and almost 90% of them are devoted to negroamaro, producing traditional, long-cellaring wines with strong local character, while the white wines are mainly produced from international varieties. We have to admit that we were a little baffled by the direction taken by this historic estate over recent years. Our expectations are still high and although the absence of the Patriglione has a part to play, the overall standard did not entirely convince. The best wine this year was the 2006 Cosimo Taurino, which shows good fruit and attractive density.

● A64 Cosimo Taurino '06	♟♟ 4
● 7° Ceppo '11	♟ 3
⊙ I Sierri '12	♟ 2
● Notarpanaro '07	♟ 3
⊙ Scaloti '12	♟ 2
● Patriglione '94	♟♟♟ 7
⊙ I Sierri '10	♟♟ 2*
● Patriglione '07	♟♟ 7
● Salice Salentino Rosso Ris. '08	♟♟ 2*
⊙ Scaloti '11	♟♟ 2*

★Tormaresca

C.DA TORRE D'ISOLA
LOC. TOFANO
70055 MINERVINO MURGE [BT]
TEL. 0883692631
www.tormaresca.it

Torrevento

LOC. CASTEL DEL MONTE
SP 234 KM 10,600
70033 CORATO [BA]
TEL. 0808980923
www.torrevento.it

CELLAR SALES
PRE-BOOKED VISITS
ACCOMMODATION
ANNUAL PRODUCTION 3,000,000 bottles
HECTARES UNDER VINE 348.00
VITICULTURE METHOD Certified Organic

CELLAR SALES
ACCOMMODATION AND RESTAURANT SERVICE
ANNUAL PRODUCTION 2,500,000 bottles
HECTARES UNDER VINE 450.00
VITICULTURE METHOD Certified Organic

The Antinoris started out in Puglia in 1998 and in the space of 15 years Tormaresca has become one of the most successful wineries in the region. The vineyards are divided into two estates: Bocca di Lupo in the Murgia hills, in the Castel del Monte designation, and Masseria Maime in San Pietro Vernotico, in the Upper Salento zone, not far from the Adriatic coast. Aglianico, nero di Troia and most of the estate's white grapes are grown at Bocca di Lupo, with the negroamaro and primitivo coming primarily from Masseria Maime. The wines are modern in style, with an emphasis on pleasurableness and balance. The Primitivo Torcicoda attained Tre Bicchieri for the third year running. The 2011 version is textured and generous, juicy and dynamic, rich in fruit and highly enjoyable. In the absence of the Masseria Maime and the Castel del Monte Pietrabianca, we particularly liked the 2012 Calafuria, an easy-drinking, floral Rosato made from negroamaro grapes.

Set in the heart of the Parco Rurale della Murgia, Francesco Liantonio's winery is a fine example of sustainable, environmentally friendly wine-growing. A flagship for the Castel del Monte designation, Torrevento's vineyards are planted on the typically rocky limestone soils of the karst Murgia plateau. The estate's vast range is produced almost exclusively from native varieties, with a marked predominance of nero di Troia. A focus on finesse, crisp fruitiness and drinkability is the common denominator here. The Castel del Monte Rosso Vigna Pedale Riserva is something of a regular in the Tre Bicchieri listing. The 2010 version of this Nero di Troia is again fresh, expansive, and well balanced – in short, highly drinkable. The fruity 2011 Castel del Monte Nero di Troia Ottagono Riserva, with smoky nuances, the spicy, mouthfilling 2009 Kebir, an equal blend of nero di Troia and cabernet sauvignon, and the 2008 Salice Salentino Rosso Sine Nomine Riserva, with its cherry and coffee aromas, are all well orchestrated.

● Torcicoda '11	▼▼▼ 4*
⊙ Calafuria '12	▼▼ 3
● Fichimori '12	▼ 2
● Morgicchio '11	▼ 3
○ Roycello '12	▼ 3
● Masseria Maime '08	♈♈♈ 5
● Masseria Maime '07	♈♈♈ 4
● Masseria Maime '06	♈♈♈ 4
● Masseria Maime '05	♈♈♈ 4*
● Masseria Maime '04	♈♈♈ 4*
● Masseria Maime '02	♈♈♈ 4
● Torcicoda '10	♈♈♈ 3*
● Torcicoda '09	♈♈♈ 3
○ Moscato di Trani Kaloro '10	♈♈ 4

● Castel del Monte Rosso V. Pedale Ris. '10	▼▼▼ 3*
● Castel del Monte Nero di Troia Ottagono Ris. '11	▼▼ 4
● Kebir '09	▼▼ 5
● Matervitae Negroamaro '11	▼▼ 2*
● Salice Salentino Rosso Sine Nomine Ris. '08	▼▼ 3
● Castel del Monte Rosso Bolonero '11	▼ 2
● Matervitae Primitivo '11	▼ 2
● Primitivo di Manduria Ghenos '11	▼ 3
● Torre del Falco '11	▼ 3
● Castel del Monte Rosso V. Pedale Ris. '09	♈♈♈ 3*
● Castel del Monte Rosso V. Pedale Ris. '08	♈♈♈ 3

Agricole Vallone

via XXV Luglio, 5
73100 Lecce
Tel. 0832308041
www.agricolevallone.it

PRE-BOOKED VISITS
ANNUAL PRODUCTION 397,000 bottles
HECTARES UNDER VINE 161.00
VITICULTURE METHOD Certified Organic

Owned by sisters Vittoria and Maria Teresa Vallone, this winery is an historic name in the Puglian winemaking scene. There are three holdings: Flaminio, where the cellars are located, totally within the Brindisi designation; lore, which is home to their best-known wine, Graticciaia, in the countryside around San Pancrazio Salentino in the Salice Salentino DOC zone; and Castelserranova, which is set in the area around Carovigno, within shouting distance of the Adriatic, and constitutes the heart of the winery. Their wines are all traditional in style, with sweet overtones and plenty of fruit. After a series of problem bottles, we decided to put off evaluating the 2009 Graticciaia until next year. We were, however, impressed with the wonderfully fresh 2009 Brindisi Rosso Vigna Flaminio Riserva, with its fruit and garden vegetable aromas. Likewise, the 2012 Corte Valesio, a blend of 70% sauvignon and chardonnay, was pleasantly aromatic, with citrus notes and good acid grip.

● Brindisi Rosso V. Flaminio Ris. '09	▼▼ 3
○ Salento Corte Valesio '12	▼▼ 2*
⊙ Brindisi Rosato V. Flaminio '12	▼ 2
○ Passo delle Viscarde '10	▼ 4
● Graticciaia '03	▽▽▽ 6
● Graticciaia '01	▽▽▽ 6
⊙ Brindisi Rosato V. Flaminio '11	▽▽ 2*
● Brindisi Rosso V. Flaminio '10	▽▽ 2*
● Brindisi Rosso V. Flaminio Ris. '06	▽▽ 2
○ Passo delle Viscarde '07	▽▽ 4

Cantina Sociale Cooperativa Vecchia Torre

via Marche, 1
73045 Leverano [LE]
Tel. 0832925053
www.cantinavecchiatorre.it

CELLAR SALES
PRE-BOOKED VISITS
ANNUAL PRODUCTION 2,200,000 bottles
HECTARES UNDER VINE 1300.00

For over fifty years, the Vecchia Torre cooperative winery has offered its members, of which there are now over 1300, support in the vineyard and quality wine-making services. Most of the growers are situated in the municipality of Leverano and here – thanks largely to the winery – things are very different from the dramatic situation to be seen in the rest of the Salento area, which is marked by abandoned or decommissioned vineyards, particularly those planted with head-trained vines. The wines offer exemplary value for money. The Leveranos remedied a less than brilliant year with a series of sound, well-orchestrated wines, such as the soft and juicy 2011 Negroamaro with its sweet fruit aromas, the spicy 2009 Salice Salentino Rosso Riserva, which has good acidity and well-blended tannins, the fresh, enjoyable 2012 Rosato, also from negroamaro, with a berry fruit, pomegranate and mint nose, and, lastly the citrusy, floral 2012 Vermentino.

⊙ Leverano Rosato '12	▼▼ 2*
● Negroamaro '11	▼▼ 2*
● Salice Salentino Rosso Ris. '09	▼▼ 2*
○ Vermentino '12	▼▼ 2*
● Arneide '09	▼ 3
● Leverano Rosso '11	▼ 2
● Leverano Rosso Ris. '08	▼ 2
● 50° Anniversario '08	▽▽ 3*
● Arneide '08	▽▽ 3
● Leverano Rosso '10	▽▽ 2*
● Leverano Rosso Ris. '07	▽▽ 2*
● Leverano Rosso Ris. '06	▽▽ 2*

Tenuta Viglione

via Carlo Marx, 44p
70029 Santeramo in Colle [BA]
Tel. 0803023927
www.tenutaviglione.it

CELLAR SALES
PRE-BOOKED VISITS
ANNUAL PRODUCTION 200,000 bottles
HECTARES UNDER VINE 40.00
VITICULTURE METHOD Certified Organic

Giovanni Zullo represents the third generation at Tenuta Viglione and is part of the new wave of wine-making in the Gioia del Colle designation, which is swelling in both number and quality. The estate cultivates a number of varieties, headed by primitivo, followed by aleatico, merlot, sangiovese, montepulciano, falanghina, trebbiano, malvasia, minutolo and chardonnay. The vineyards are planted in moderately loose, stony, mineral-rich calcareous clay, which is the typical karst soil of the Murge ranges. Impressively, two wines reached the finals. The 2009 Gioia del Colle Primitivo Marpione Riserva has balsamic, slightly toasted almond notes. It is rich, dense, juicy, and nicely savoury, with good length. The 2011 Gioia del Colle Pri-mit-ivo is more supple, but also has a very-well-defined nose, with black cherry, damp-earth and spicy notes. On the other hand, the tangy 2011 Johe, a 50-50 blend of primitivo and aleatico, offers berry fruit aromas.

● Gioia del Colle Pri-mit-ivo '11	🍷🍷 5
● Gioia del Colle Rosso Marpione Ris. '09	🍷🍷 3*
● Johe '11	🍷🍷 2*
○ Gioia del Colle Bianco Paglione '12	🍷 2
⊙ Nisia '12	🍷 2
● Gioia del Colle Primitivo '09	🍷🍷 2*
● Gioia del Colle Rosso Marpione Ris. '08	🍷🍷 3
● Gioia del Colle Rosso Rupestre '07	🍷🍷 2*
● Johe '11	🍷🍷 2*

★Conti Zecca

via Cesarea
73045 Leverano [LE]
Tel. 0832925613
www.contizecca.it

CELLAR SALES
PRE-BOOKED VISITS
ANNUAL PRODUCTION 2,000,000 bottles
HECTARES UNDER VINE 320.00

The aristocratic Neapolitan Zecca family settled in Leverano over five centuries ago, and Conti Zecca has since become a flagship for the Puglian wine industry. Its four estates are Saracena, Donna Marzia and Santo Stefano at Leverano, and Cantalupi at Salice Salentino. Their extensive, attractively priced range is consistently of a high quality, and the modern-styled wines reflect the best possible combination of strong local character and easy drinkability. The range presented by Conti Zecca is again of a good standard, although this year they did not achieve a Tre Bicchieri. We found the 2010 Nero to have good fruit and structure, but it was less complex than other versions and slightly over-oaked. We loved the intense, aromatic 2012 Fiano, the best white tasted in Puglia this year in fact, with sage and citrus aromas, a fresh palate and a nice long finish.

○ Fiano '12	🍷🍷 2*
● Nero '10	🍷🍷 5
● Cantalupi Negroamaro '11	🍷🍷 2*
● Salice Salentino Cantalupi Ris. '10	🍷🍷 2*
○ Donna Marzia Malvasia Bianca '12	🍷 2
● Donna Marzia Primitivo '11	🍷 2
● Donna Marzia Rosso '11	🍷 1*
○ Luna '12	🍷 3
○ Saraceno Vermentino '12	🍷 1*
● Nero '09	🍷🍷🍷 5
● Nero '08	🍷🍷🍷 5
● Nero '07	🍷🍷🍷 5
● Nero '06	🍷🍷🍷 5
● Nero '03	🍷🍷🍷 5

Masseria Altemura

c.da Palombara - SP 69
72028 Torre Santa Susanna [BR]
Tel. 0831740485
www.masseriaaltemura.it

CELLAR SALES
PRE-BOOKED VISITS
ACCOMMODATION
ANNUAL PRODUCTION 400,000 bottles
HECTARES UNDER VINE 130.00

● Primitivo di Manduria Altemura di Altemura '10	♥♥ 4
● Sasseo '11	♥♥ 3
⊙ Rosato '12	♥ 3

Amastuola

via Martina Franca, 80
74016 Massafra [TA]
Tel. 0998805668
www.amastuola.it

CELLAR SALES
ANNUAL PRODUCTION 300,000 bottles
HECTARES UNDER VINE 101.89
VITICULTURE METHOD Certified Organic

● Vignatorta '10	♥♥ 2*
○ Calaprice '12	♥ 2
● Onda del Tempo '10	♥ 2
● Primitivo '11	♥ 2

Apollonio

via San Pietro in Lama, 7
73047 Monteroni di Lecce [LE]
Tel. 0832327182
www.apolloniovini.it

CELLAR SALES
PRE-BOOKED VISITS
ANNUAL PRODUCTION 1,500,000 bottles
HECTARES UNDER VINE 50.00

● Elfo Rosso '12	♥♥ 2*
● Elfo Susumaniello '11	♥♥ 2*
● Copertino Divoto Ris. '08	♥ 5
● Salice Salentino Rosso '11	♥ 3

Michele Biancardi

s.da Provinciale, 68
71042 Cerignola [FG]
Tel. 3394912659
www.michelebiancardi.it

CELLAR SALES
PRE-BOOKED VISITS
ANNUAL PRODUCTION 30,000 bottles
HECTARES UNDER VINE 4.00
VITICULTURE METHOD Certified Organic

○ Solo Fiano '12	♥♥ 2*
● L'Insolito '12	♥ 3
● Ponte Viro '11	♥ 3

Cantine Botromagno

via Archimede, 24
70024 Gravina in Puglia [BA]
Tel. 0803265865
www.botromagno.it

CELLAR SALES
PRE-BOOKED VISITS
ACCOMMODATION AND RESTAURANT SERVICE
ANNUAL PRODUCTION 300,000 bottles
HECTARES UNDER VINE 50.00

● Gioia del Colle Primitivo Dedicato a Franco e Lucia '10	♥♥ 6
● 5 Uve Rosse '10	♥ 2
● Nero di Troia '12	♥ 2

I Buongiorno

c.so Vittorio Emanuele II, 71
72012 Carovigno [BR]
Tel. 0831996286
www.giasottolarco.it

ANNUAL PRODUCTION 50,000 bottles
HECTARES UNDER VINE 10.00

● Primitivo '10	♥♥
○ Fiano '12	♥
● Negramaro '10	♥

C.a.l.o.s.m.

VIA PIETRO SICILIANI, 8
73058 TUGLIE [LE]
TEL. 0833598051
www.calosm.it

CELLAR SALES
PRE-BOOKED VISITS
ANNUAL PRODUCTION 75,000 bottles
HECTARES UNDER VINE 22.00

● Donna Stracca '09	♟♟ 3
● Tisciano '12	♟♟ 2*
● Villa Valentino Don Carlo '12	♟♟ 1*

Vini Classici Cardone

VIA MARTIRI DELLA LIBERTÀ, 32
70010 LOCOROTONDO [BA]
TEL. 0804312561
www.cardonevini.com

CELLAR SALES
PRE-BOOKED VISITS
ANNUAL PRODUCTION 100,000 bottles
HECTARES UNDER VINE 6.00

● Primaio '12	♟♟ 3
○ Falera '12	♟ 3
○ Locorotondo Il Castillo '12	♟ 2
⊙ Nausica '12	♟ 2

Giancarlo Ceci

C.DA SANT'AGOSTINO
76123 ANDRIA [BT]
TEL. 0883565220
www.agrinatura.net

ANNUAL PRODUCTION 520,000 bottles
HECTARES UNDER VINE 70.00
VITICULTURE METHOD Certified Biodynamic

○ Castel del Monte Bianco '12	♟♟ 2*
○ Moscato di Trani Dolce Rosalia '12	♟♟ 3
● Castel del Monte Rosso Felice Ceci '10	♟ 4

Francesco Candido

VIA A. DIAZ, 46
72025 SAN DONACI [BR]
TEL. 0831635674
www.candidowines.it

CELLAR SALES
PRE-BOOKED VISITS
ANNUAL PRODUCTION 1,600,000 bottles
HECTARES UNDER VINE 142.00

● Immensum '09	♟♟ 3
● Duca d'Aragona '07	♟♟ 5
● Cappello di Prete '08	♟ 3
○ Salice Salentino Bianco Portafalsa '12	♟ 2

Castel di Salve

FRAZ. DEPRESSA
VIA SALVEMINI, 30
73026 TRICASE [LE]
TEL. 0833771041
www.casteldisalve.com

CELLAR SALES
PRE-BOOKED VISITS
ANNUAL PRODUCTION 150,000 bottles
HECTARES UNDER VINE 40.00

● Cento su Cento '11	♟♟ 4
● Armecolo '11	♟ 2
○ Santi Medici Bianco '12	♟ 2
⊙ Santi Medici Rosato '12	♟ 2

Centovignali

P.ZZA ALDO MORO, 10
70010 SAMMICHELE DI BARI [BA]
TEL. 0805768215
www.centovignali.it

CELLAR SALES
PRE-BOOKED VISITS
ANNUAL PRODUCTION 35,000 bottles
HECTARES UNDER VINE 19.00
VITICULTURE METHOD Certified Organic

● Gioia del Colle Primitivo Indellicato '10	♟♟ 4
○ Albiore '12	♟ 3

Masseria Cuturi

LOC. CUTURI
VIA XX SETTEMBRE, 75
74024 MANDURIA [TA]
TEL. 3382800744
www.masseriacuturi.it

CELLAR SALES
PRE-BOOKED VISITS
ANNUAL PRODUCTION 15,000 bottles
HECTARES UNDER VINE 22.00
VITICULTURE METHOD Certified Organic

● Primitivo di Manduria Il 1° '11	♥♥	4
⊙ Rosa di Cuturi '12	♥	3
○ Vento di Cuturi '12	♥	3

D'Alfonso del Sordo

C.DA SANT'ANTONINO
71016 SAN SEVERO [FG]
TEL. 0882221444
www.dalfonsodelsordo.it

CELLAR SALES
PRE-BOOKED VISITS
ANNUAL PRODUCTION 350,000 bottles
HECTARES UNDER VINE 80.00

⊙ San Severo Rosato Posta Arignano '12	♥♥	2*
● Casteldrione '10	♥	2
○ Dammisole '12	♥	2

De Falco

VIA MILANO, 25
73051 NOVOLI [LE]
TEL. 0832711597
www.cantinedefalco.it

CELLAR SALES
PRE-BOOKED VISITS
ANNUAL PRODUCTION 200,000 bottles
HECTARES UNDER VINE 20.00

● Artiglio Rosso '08	♥♥	4
● Squinzano Rosso Serre di Sant'Elia '11	♥♥	2*
● Salice Salentino Rosso Falconero Ris. '08	♥	3
● Salice Salentino Rosso Salore '10	♥	2

Eméra

VIA PROVINCIALE, 222
73010 GUAGNANO [LE]
TEL. 0832704398
www.magistravini.it

CELLAR SALES
PRE-BOOKED VISITS
ANNUAL PRODUCTION 200,000 bottles
HECTARES UNDER VINE 46.00

● Primitivo di Manduria Anima di Primitivo '11	♥♥	2*
⊙ Lizzano Rosato Rosé '12	♥	2
● Sud del Sud '12	♥	3

Feudi di Guagnano

VIA CELLINO, 3
73010 GUAGNANO [LE]
TEL. 0832705422
www.feudiguagnano.com

CELLAR SALES
PRE-BOOKED VISITS
ANNUAL PRODUCTION 100,000 bottles
HECTARES UNDER VINE 15.00

● Le Camarde '10	♥♥	2*
● Miralde '12	♥	1*
● Salice Salentino Rosso '11	♥	1
● Salice Salentino Rosso Cupone Ris. '10	♥	2

Feudi di Terra D'Otranto

VIA ARNEO MARE
73010 VEGLIE [LE]
TEL. 0832966467
www.feudidotranto.com

CELLAR SALES
PRE-BOOKED VISITS
ANNUAL PRODUCTION 80,000 bottles
HECTARES UNDER VINE 25.00

● Ardentius '10	♥♥	4
⊙ Passerose '12	♥♥	3
● Le Maschere Primitivo '12	♥	3
● Le Maschere Syrah '12	♥	3

Tenuta Fujanera

C.DA QUADRONE DELLE VIGNE KM 2,500
VIA BARI
71100 FOGGIA
TEL. 0881652619
www.fujanera.it

PRE-BOOKED VISITS
RESTAURANT SERVICE
ANNUAL PRODUCTION 60,000 bottles
HECTARES UNDER VINE 10.00

● L'Angelo Ribelle '10	♟♟ 4
● Arrocco '12	♟ 3
○ Bellalma '12	♟ 2
⊙ Re del Cuore '12	♟ 2

Duca Carlo Guarini

L.GO FRISARI, 1
73020 SCORRANO [LE]
TEL. 0836460288
www.ducacarloguarini.it

CELLAR SALES
PRE-BOOKED VISITS
ACCOMMODATION AND RESTAURANT SERVICE
ANNUAL PRODUCTION 250,000 bottles
HECTARES UNDER VINE 70.00
VITICULTURE METHOD Certified Organic

● Piutri '10	♟♟ 2*
● Primitivo Vigne Vecchie '10	♟♟ 3
⊙ Campo di Mare '12	♟ 2
● Nativo '11	♟ 3

Hiso Telaray - Libera Terra Puglia

VICO DEI CANTELMO, 1
72023 MESAGNE [BR]
TEL. 0831775981
www.hisotelaray.it

CELLAR SALES
ANNUAL PRODUCTION 120,000 bottles
HECTARES UNDER VINE 25.00
VITICULTURE METHOD Certified Organic

● Renata Fonte '11	♟♟ 3
⊙ Alberelli De La Santa '12	♟ 2
● Filari de Sant'Antonii '12	♟ 2
● Primitivo Antò '11	♟ 3

Masseria L'Astore

LOC. L'ASTORE
VIA G. DI VITTORIO, 1
73020 CUTROFIANO [LE]
TEL. 0836542020
www.lastoremasseria.it

CELLAR SALES
PRE-BOOKED VISITS
ANNUAL PRODUCTION 100,000 bottles
HECTARES UNDER VINE 25.00
VITICULTURE METHOD Certified Organic

● Alberelli di Negramaro '09	♟♟ 5
⊙ Massaro Rosa '12	♟♟ 2*
● Jèma '11	♟ 2
○ Krita '12	♟ 2

Paolo Leo

VIA TUTURANO, 21
72025 SAN DONACI [BR]
TEL. 0831635073
www.paololeo.it

CELLAR SALES
PRE-BOOKED VISITS
ANNUAL PRODUCTION 1,300,000 bottles
HECTARES UNDER VINE 35.00

● Orfeo '11	♟♟ 4
⊙ Grecia Rosé '12	♟ 3
○ Numen '12	♟ 4

Alberto Longo

C.DA PADULECCHIA
SP 5 LUCERA-PIETRAMONTECORVINO KM 4
71036 LUCERA [FG]
TEL. 0881539057
www.albertolongo.it

CELLAR SALES
PRE-BOOKED VISITS
ANNUAL PRODUCTION 120,000 bottles
HECTARES UNDER VINE 35.00

● Cacc'e Mmitte di Lucera '11	♟♟ 3
● Le Cruste '11	♟♟ 4
● Capoposto '11	♟ 3

Produttori Vini Manduria

VIA FABIO MASSIMO, 19
74024 MANDURIA [TA]
TEL. 0999735332
www.cpvini.com

CELLAR SALES
PRE-BOOKED VISITS
ANNUAL PRODUCTION 700,000 bottles
HECTARES UNDER VINE 900.00

● Primitivo di Manduria Sonetto Ris. '10	♟♟ 6
● Neama '12	♟ 2
● Primitivo di Manduria Memoria '12	♟ 2

Cantine Miali

VIA MADONNINA, 1
74015 MARTINA FRANCA [TA]
TEL. 0804303222
www.cantinemiali.com

CELLAR SALES
PRE-BOOKED VISITS
ANNUAL PRODUCTION 400,000 bottles
HECTARES UNDER VINE 17.00

⊙ Ametys Rosato '12	♟♟ 2*
○ Firr '12	♟♟ 2*
○ Martina Dolcimèlo '12	♟ 2
● Mater '08	♟ 3

Mille Una

L.GO CHIESA, 11
74020 LIZZANO [TA]
TEL. 0996414541
www.milleuna.it

CELLAR SALES
PRE-BOOKED VISITS
ACCOMMODATION
ANNUAL PRODUCTION 70,000 bottles
HECTARES UNDER VINE 33.00

● Primitivo di Manduria Tre Tarante '09	♟♟ 3
● Aladino '07	♟ 3
● Bacmione '09	♟ 6
● Negroamaro Ori di Taranto '11	♟ 3

Mocavero

VIA MALLACCA ZUMMARI
73010 ARNESANO [LE]
TEL. 0832327194
www.mocaverovini.it

CELLAR SALES
PRE-BOOKED VISITS
RESTAURANT SERVICE
ANNUAL PRODUCTION 600,000 bottles
HECTARES UNDER VINE 65.00

● Salice Salentino Rosso '11	♟♟ 3
● Curtirussi Negramaro '09	♟ 3
● Primitivo '10	♟ 3
● Sjre Primitivo '11	♟ 2

Mottura

P.ZZA MELICA, 4
73058 TUGLIE [LE]
TEL. 0833596601
www.motturavini.it

CELLAR SALES
PRE-BOOKED VISITS
ANNUAL PRODUCTION 2,500,000 bottles
HECTARES UNDER VINE 200.00

● Negroamaro Le Pitre '11	♟♟ 5
● Primitivo Le Pitre '11	♟♟ 6
○ Fiano Le Pitre '12	♟ 4
⊙ Rosato Le Pitre '12	♟ 4

Paradiso

V.LE MANFREDONIA, 39
71042 CERIGNOLA [FG]
TEL. 0885428720
www.cantineparadiso.it

ANNUAL PRODUCTION 130,000 bottles
HECTARES UNDER VINE 16.00

⊙ Posta Piana Rosato '12	♟♟ 2*
● Angelo Primo '10	♟ 4
● Posta Piana Negroamaro '10	♟ 2

Pichierri - Vinicola Savese

VIA IPPOLITA PRATO, 3
74028 SAVA [TA]
TEL. 0999726232
www.vinipichierri.com

CELLAR SALES
PRE-BOOKED VISITS
ANNUAL PRODUCTION 350,000 bottles
HECTARES UNDER VINE 21.00

● Primitivo di Manduria Dolce Naturale Il Sava '07	♔♔ 5

Pirro Varone

VIA SENATORE LACAITA, 90
74024 MANDURIA [TA]
TEL. 3397429098
www.pirrovarone.com

CELLAR SALES
PRE-BOOKED VISITS
ANNUAL PRODUCTION 90,000 bottles
HECTARES UNDER VINE 16.00
VITICULTURE METHOD Certified Organic

● Le Vigne Rare Primitivo '09	♔♔ 3
● Primitivo di Manduria '11	♔ 3
● Terre Nere '09	♔ 4

Podere 29

VIA RAFFAELLO, 4
76016 MARGHERITA DI SAVOIA [BT]
TEL. 3471917291
www.podere29.it

ANNUAL PRODUCTION 46,000 bottles
HECTARES UNDER VINE 6.00

● Gelso D'Oro '11	♔♔ 4
● Gelso Nero '12	♔♔ 2*

Risveglio Agricolo

C.DA TORRE MOZZA
72100 BRINDISI
TEL. 0831519948
www.cantinerisveglio.it

CELLAR SALES
PRE-BOOKED VISITS
ANNUAL PRODUCTION 100,000 bottles
HECTARES UNDER VINE 44.00

● 72100 '10	♔♔ 2*
● Brindisi Rosso Simposio Ris. '07	♔ 2

Rosa del Golfo

VIA GARIBALDI, 56
73011 ALEZIO [LE]
TEL. 0833281045
www.rosadelgolfo.com

CELLAR SALES
PRE-BOOKED VISITS
ANNUAL PRODUCTION 300,000 bottles
HECTARES UNDER VINE 40,00

● Quarantale '08	♔♔ 5
● Portulano '10	♔ 2
● Scaliere '11	♔ 2

Cantina Cooperativa di San Donaci

VIA MESAGNE, 62
72025 SAN DONACI [BR]
TEL. 0831681085
www.cantinasandonaci.it

CELLAR SALES
PRE-BOOKED VISITS
ANNUAL PRODUCTION 350,000 bottles
HECTARES UNDER VINE 543.00

● Fulgeo '10	♔♔ 2*
● Contrada del Falco '11	♔ 2
● Posta Vecchia '11	♔ 2
● Salice Salentino Anticaia '11	♔ 2

Santi Dimitri

C.DA SANTI DIMITRI
VIA GUIDANO
73013 GALATINA [LE]
TEL. 0836565866
www.santidimitri.it

CELLAR SALES
PRE-BOOKED VISITS
ACCOMMODATION
ANNUAL PRODUCTION 130,000 bottles
HECTARES UNDER VINE 60.00

● Ruvezzo Rosso '11	♟♟ 2*
● Aruca Rosso '10	♟ 2
⊙ Rosato Aruca '12	♟ 2
● Sharav Primitivo '10	♟ 3

Spelonga

VIA MENOLA
71047 STORNARA [FG]
TEL. 0885431048
www.cantinespelonga.altervista.org

CELLAR SALES
PRE-BOOKED VISITS
ANNUAL PRODUCTION 40,000 bottles
HECTARES UNDER VINE 10.00
VITICULTURE METHOD Certified Organic

● Nero di Troia '12	♟♟ 3
● Samà Rosso '12	♟♟ 2*
○ Samà Bianco '12	♟ 2

Vetrere

FRAZ. VETRERE
SP MONTEIASI-MONTEMESOLA KM 16
74100 TARANTO
TEL. 0995661054
www.vetrere.it

CELLAR SALES
PRE-BOOKED VISITS
ACCOMMODATION
ANNUAL PRODUCTION 230,000 bottles
HECTARES UNDER VINE 37.00

○ Cré '12	♟♟ 3
● Passaturo '12	♟♟ 2*
○ Cré Vendemmia Tardiva '12	♟ 3
○ Laureato '12	♟ 3

Vigne & Vini

VIA AMENDOLA, 36
74020 LEPORANO [TA]
TEL. 0995315370
www.vigneevini.it

CELLAR SALES
PRE-BOOKED VISITS
ANNUAL PRODUCTION 600,000 bottles
HECTARES UNDER VINE 155.00
VITICULTURE METHOD Certified Organic

● Primitivo di Manduria Papale Linea Oro '11	♟♟ 5
● 12 e Mezzo Negroamaro '11	♟♟ 2*
● Primitivo di Manduria Papale '11	♟ 3

Vigneti Reale

VIA EGIDIO REALE, 55
73100 LECCE
TEL. 0832248433
www.vignetireale.it

PRE-BOOKED VISITS
ACCOMMODATION AND RESTAURANT SERVICE
ANNUAL PRODUCTION 100,000 bottles
HECTARES UNDER VINE 84.00

● Salice Salentino Santa Croce Ris. '10	♟♟ 4
○ Blasi '12	♟ 2
○ Malvasia '12	♟ 2
● Norie '11	♟ 2

Vinicola Imperatore

VIA MARCONI, 36
70010 ADELFIA [BA]
TEL. 0804594041
www.cantineimperatore.it

CELLAR SALES
PRE-BOOKED VISITS
ANNUAL PRODUCTION 4,000 bottles
HECTARES UNDER VINE 1,80

● Gioia del Colle Primitivo Il Sogno '09	♟♟ 5
● Cabernet '11	♟ 2
⊙ Rosato '11	♟ 2
● Sonya '12	♟ 2

CALABRIA

Despite Calabria's venerable history and long tradition in winemaking, by the end of the 20th century the region was certainly not at the forefront of the Italian scenario. Slowly but surely, however, something started to move at the start of the new millennium, when many new wineries appeared in a territory and on a local market that had been bogged down for years, making an impact in an area that may have been resting on its laurels for too long. Most of the old estates reacted positively to this phenomenon, investing heavily both in the vineyard and in the cellar, thus setting in motion a virtuous circle that has brought the region to a truly magical moment. Indeed four of Calabria's wineries earned a Tre Bicchieri this year and we are especially pleased that one of them went to Roberto Ceraudo of Strongoli, who was one of the first, 20 years ago, to convert to organic methods and is now geared up to a biodynamic system. The region's driving force from a commercial standpoint is, as always, the Cirò zone, embracing the entire province of Crotone, where the greater part of Calabria's production is concentrated. Here the quality curve is improving constantly and apart from the aforementioned Ceraudo, we also gave a Tre Bicchieri to Librandi and iGreco, but they are not isolated cases. The other wineries performed well too and we hope to acknowledge more labels in the near future. We lack the space to mention all those deserving cellars whose wines clocked up interesting scores, like Enotria, Scala, Capoano, and Termine Grosso. The Cosenza area continues to develop and each year an increasing number of wineries send bottles in for our regional selections. While Terre Nobili, Marini and Serracavallo are now well-established operations, and known even outside regional boundaries, others are emerging, like Ferrocinto and Falvo, for example, or the young Casa Comerci winery whose inclusion in this Guide is only a matter of time. The fourth Tre Bicchieri was awarded to Saracena, another stunning version of Luigi Viola's Moscato Passito. We are happy to see the return to full capacity of Barbara and Gregorio Odoardi's cellar, finally confirming the quality standards to which we had become accustomed in recent years.

Roberto Ceraudo

LOC. MARINA DI STRONGOLI
C.DA DATTILO
88815 CROTONE
TEL. 0962865613
www.dattilo.it

CELLAR SALES
PRE-BOOKED VISITS
ACCOMMODATION AND RESTAURANT SERVICE
ANNUAL PRODUCTION 60,000 bottles
HECTARES UNDER VINE 20.00
VITICULTURE METHOD Certified Organic

Roberto Ceraudo's estate is a dream come true for this enterprising farmer who had the energy and courage to invest in local varieties and green farming methods. Now, the vineyard – and pretty much everything at Dattilo – is managed biodynamically. These days, Roberto is assisted by his children: Giuseppe, who looks after the vines; Susy, who runs the estate's popular restaurant; and Caterina, the youngest, who manages the cellar. The wines have character, a unique personality, and a strong local identity. We awarded a Tre Bicchieri to the 2012 Grisara, a white of rare elegance from pecorello grapes, featuring spicy and Mediterranean scrub aromas. The wine is savoury and tangy, with a good fleshy palate. The 2010 Dattilo, a pure gaglioppo, made the finals for its compact, elegant nose and a plush palate, with plenty of fruit supported by the tannins.

○ Grisara '12	🍷🍷🍷 3*
● Dattilo '10	🍷🍷 3*
⊙ Grayasusi Et. Rame '12	🍷🍷 3
○ Imyr '12	🍷🍷 5
⊙ Grayasusi Et. Argento '12	🍷 4
○ Petelia '12	🍷 3
⊙ Grayasusi Et. Rame '11	🍷🍷 3
○ Grisara '11	🍷🍷 3
○ Imyr '11	🍷🍷 5
● Petraro '09	🍷🍷 5

iGreco

LOC. SALICE
C.DA GUARDAPIEDI
87062 CARIATI [CS]
TEL. 0983969441
www.igreco.it

CELLAR SALES
PRE-BOOKED VISITS
ACCOMMODATION AND RESTAURANT SERVICE
ANNUAL PRODUCTION 250,000 bottles
HECTARES UNDER VINE 80.00
VITICULTURE METHOD Certified Organic

The Greco brothers' estate was founded by their father, Tommaso, who started with the family's olive oil mill in Cariati and within a few decades had 1,000 hectares dotted around Cirò, Cirò Marina, Crucoli, Scala Coeli, Camigliatello Silano, Terravecchia and Cariati. Despite its size, the Greco estate is still a family-run business and is now managed by Tommaso's seven children: Cataldo, Ernesto, Filomena, Natale Francesco, Saverio, Marilena and Giancarlo. Their elegant, modern wines are produced primarily from local varieties such as calabrese, greco and gaglioppo, using organic methods. The 2011 Masino earned the Tre Bicchieri for its tight-knit, complex nose, with spice and wood notes that combine elegantly with berry fruit and fresher balsamic and minty overtones. It has a leisurely palate, well sustained by good acidity and tannins that boost the full, juicy fruit.

● Masino '11	🍷🍷🍷 5
● Catà '11	🍷🍷 2*
○ Filù '12	🍷 2
○ Riticella '10	🍷 4
⊙ Savù '12	🍷 2
● Masino '10	🍷🍷🍷 5
● Catà '10	🍷🍷 2*
⊙ Savù '11	🍷🍷 2*

Ippolito 1845

VIA TIRONE, 118
88811 CIRÒ MARINA [KR]
TEL. 096231106
www.ippolito1845.it

CELLAR SALES
PRE-BOOKED VISITS
ANNUAL PRODUCTION 1,000,000 bottles
HECTARES UNDER VINE 100.00

Gianluca and Vincenzo Ippolito are the latest generation of the wine-growing family that founded this stunning estate in 1845. The 100-plus hectares of vineyards are situated in the Cirò Classico zone and fall pretty much into two groups: the whites down at sea level at Punta Alice and the reds on the hills at Tenuta del Mancuso, which is approximately 250 metres above sea level. They follow a simple recipe to produce successful, long-lasting wines, taking great care in the vineyard to ensure that the healthy grapes will produce sound, enjoyable wines with good market appeal and a strong local identity based on authoctonous varieties. A national finalist this year, the 160 Anni 2010 is a pure gaglioppo, with part of the grapes fermented after a lengthy period of loft drying well into late November. The harmonious 2011 Cirò Liber Pater reveals a very pleasing nose with distinctive spicy and balsamic notes, and a gutsy, fruit-rich mouth.

● 160 Anni '10	▼▼ 5
● Cirò Rosso Cl. Sup. Liber Pater '11	▼▼ 2*
● Cirò Rosso Cl. Sup. Ripe del Falco Ris. '02	▼▼ 5
● Calabrise '12	▼ 2
○ Cirò Bianco Res Dei '12	▼ 2
⊙ Cirò Rosato Mabilia '12	▼ 2
● Cirò Rosso Cl. '11	▼ 2
● Cirò Rosso Cl. Sup. Colli del Mancuso Ris. '10	▼ 3
○ Gemma Del Sole '08	▼ 4
● I Mori '11	▼ 2
● 160 Anni '09	♈♈ 5
● 160 Anni '08	♈♈ 5
● Calabrise '11	♈♈ 2*
● Cirò Rosso Cl. Sup. Colli del Mancuso Ris. '09	♈♈ 3

★Librandi

LOC. SAN GENNARO
SS JONICA 106
88811 CIRÒ MARINA [KR]
TEL. 096231518
www.librandi.it

CELLAR SALES
PRE-BOOKED VISITS
ANNUAL PRODUCTION 2,200,000 bottles
HECTARES UNDER VINE 232.00

The early passing of the estate's founder, Tonino Librandi, has accelerated the handover to younger generations. Now Teresa and Francesco manage the family's lovely winery with their cousins Raffaele and Paolo. This has given Nicodemo more time to focus on the revolutionizing project he holds dear and which, in less than a decade, has completely transformed the winery's philosophy, turning it from a commercial concern into a modern agricultural business that cares greatly about the Calabrian region and its native varieties. The wines are consistently reliable, elegant and original, and in a short space of time have become a veritable benchmark for the area. This commendable Cirò winery's 2011 Duca Sanfelice Riserva takes a Tre Bicchieri award. This most classic of wines, despite a reticent attack, opens up in few minutes to reveal its class and elegance, with cherry jam, rose, cigar, and herb on the nose, and a seductive, silky, mineral palate.

● Cirò Rosso Duca Sanfelice Ris. '11	▼▼▼ 3*
● Gravello '11	▼▼ 5
● Cirò Rosso Cl. '12	▼▼ 2*
○ Critone '12	▼▼ 2*
○ Efeso '12	▼▼ 4
○ Le Passule '11	▼▼ 5
● Magno Megonio '11	▼▼ 4
● Melissa Asylia Rosso '12	▼▼ 2*
⊙ Cirò Rosato '12	▼ 2
○ Melissa Asylia Bianco '12	▼ 2
⊙ Terre Lontane '12	▼ 2
● Cirò Rosso Duca Sanfelice Ris. '08	♈♈♈ 3*
● Gravello '10	♈♈♈ 5
● Gravello '09	♈♈♈ 5

Salvatore Marini

LOC. SANT'AGATA
VIA TERMOPILI, 47
87069 SAN DEMETRIO CORONE [CS]
TEL. 0984947868
www.vinimarini.it

CELLAR SALES
ANNUAL PRODUCTION 35,000 bottles
HECTARES UNDER VINE 7.00
VITICULTURE METHOD Certified Organic

San Demetrio Corone is a small township
at the foot of the Sila ranges in an area
best known historically for its olive oil and
citrus, where the language and traditions of
the Arberesh are still strong. The
brother-and-sister team of Salvatore and
Maria Paola Marini owns one of the oldest
farms in the area. A while ago they added
wine to their production, focusing primarily
on regional varieties, especially magliocco.
Until now their organic production has been
limited to seven hectares of hillside vines.
Stylistically they aim for well-structured, yet
elegant, attractive wines. Of the many
worthy wines that made it into our regional
selection this year, we particularly like the
2012 Collimarini Passito blend of
chardonnay and sauvignon blanc. The wine
is delicate and stylish, with candied citrus,
nut and lavender aromas, and a sweet,
fresh, lingering palate.

○ Collimarini Passito '12	♟♟	6
● Basileus '11	♟♟	5
● Elaphe '11	♟♟	4
● Koronè '11	♟♟	2*
☉ Brigantino Rosato '12	♟	2
○ Sandolino '12	♟	2
● Basileus '10	♟♟	5
● Basileus '09	♟♟	5
● Elaphe '10	♟♟	4

G.B. Odoardi

C.DA CAMPODORATO, 35
88047 NOCERA TERINESE [CZ]
TEL. 098429961
odoardi@tin.it

PRE-BOOKED VISITS
ANNUAL PRODUCTION 200,000 bottles
HECTARES UNDER VINE 80.00

After a long pause for reflection and a
low-key return to last year's Guide, Barbara
and Gregorio Odoardi's winery is finally
back in full swing with a range of excellent
wines with plenty of promise. Most of the
80-hectare estate is planted to vine, with a
density of around 10,000 vines each. The
wines are made in the kind of modern style
that aims for great elegance but also wants
good extractive weight and concentration.
The 2011 Odoardi G.B., a variable blend of
gaglioppo, magliocco, nerello cappuccino,
and greco nero, is a vibrant, almost
impenetrable, ruby colour, with a balsamic
nose marked by berry jam, chocolate, and
coffee notes, and a full, tannic, lengthy
palate. The 2012 Terra Damia is the same
blend, but more mature, with elegant red
berry, spice, and mint aromas, supported a
polished tannic weave on the palate.

● G.B. Odoardi '11	♟♟	6
● Savuto '12	♟♟	2*
● Terra Damia '12	♟♟	3
○ Scavigna Bianco '12	♟	2
○ Scavigna Pian della Corte '12	♟	3
☉ Scavigna Rosato '12	♟	2
● G.B. Odoardi '09	♟♟	6
● Terra Damia '09	♟♟	3

Santa Venere

LOC. TENUTA VOLTAGRANDE
SP 04 KM 10,00
88813 CIRÒ [KR]
TEL. 096238519
www.santavenere.com

CELLAR SALES
PRE-BOOKED VISITS
ANNUAL PRODUCTION 125,000 bottles
HECTARES UNDER VINE 25.00
VITICULTURE METHOD Certified Organic

The Scala family runs an all-round farming operation on an estate of over 150 hectares of which 25 are under vine, while the rest are given over to olives and prized breeds of cattle. There has always been a focus on the environment and the winery was one of the first in Calabria to go 100% organic, while they are now experimenting with biodynamic methods to try and make the farm even more environmentally friendly. Santa Venere wines have a stylish, up-to-the-minute feel, are true to their varietal origins, and are eminently drinkable. The 2011 Cirò Rosso Classico, which easily reached national finals, is a perfect example, with floral notes and rich Mediterranean nuances on the nose, full and invigorating on the palate, with plenty of juicy fruit and a stunning tangy, very leisurely finish. The 2011 Vurgadà, an elegant blend of nerello, cappuccio, gaglioppo, and merlot in almost equal amounts, has intriguing berry fruit and herb notes.

● Cirò Rosso Cl. '11	🍷🍷 2*
⊙ Rosé Brut SP 1 '11	🍷🍷 4
● Vurgadà '11	🍷🍷 3
○ Cirò Bianco '12	🍷 2
⊙ Cirò Rosato '12	🍷 2
○ Vescovado '12	🍷 3
● Cirò Rosso Cl. Sup. Federico Scala Ris. '09	🍷🍷 5
● Vurgadà '10	🍷🍷 3

Senatore Vini

LOC. SAN LORENZO
88811 CIRÒ MARINA [KR]
TEL. 096232350
www.senatorevini.com

CELLAR SALES
PRE-BOOKED VISITS
ANNUAL PRODUCTION 250,000 bottles
HECTARES UNDER VINE 29.00

The Senatore family had long owned vines in Cirò but, like many local producers, until recently had limited themselves to growing the grapes and selling them on. A few years ago they finally decided to produce wine under their own brand. They wanted to do things properly, so first they renovated all the old vines and then planted new ones in San Lorenzo, where they also built new modern cellars. Their extensive range highlights their efforts to balance innovation and tradition and features a selection of reliable, well-made, elegant, and pleasantly drinkable wines. The 2010 Ehos finalist is a cabernet sauvignon, merlot, and gaglioppo blend in almost equal amounts, always enjoyable, steadfast, and technically well made. The 2010 Cirò Arcano is an outstanding classic with a balsamic nose, fresh acidity, and plenty of close-knit tannins that will soften with time.

● Ehos '10	🍷🍷 2*
○ Alikia '12	🍷🍷 3
⊙ Cirò Rosato Puntalice '12	🍷🍷 3
● Cirò Rosso Cl. Arcano Ris. '10	🍷🍷 2*
○ Cirò Bianco Alaei '12	🍷 2
● Cirò Rosso Cl. Arcano '10	🍷 3
○ Eukè '12	🍷 3
● Nerello '09	🍷 4
○ Silò '12	🍷 3
⊙ Cirò Rosato Puntalice '11	🍷🍷 2*
● Cirò Rosso Cl. Arcano '09	🍷🍷 3
● Ehos '09	🍷🍷 2*
● Unico S '08	🍷🍷 4

CALABRIA

Serracavallo

C.DA SERRACAVALLO
87043 BISIGNANO [CS]
TEL. 098421144
www.viniserracavallo.it

CELLAR SALES
PRE-BOOKED VISITS
RESTAURANT SERVICE
ANNUAL PRODUCTION 80,000 bottles
HECTARES UNDER VINE 32.00

Demetrio Stancati was one of the first to believe in the potential of varieties such as magliocco and pecorello and he now manages 18 hectares of vines, planted mostly in small blocks on steep terraced vineyards that climb to 700 metres above sea level. His philosophy is simple: harvest healthy, perfectly mature grapes and do as little as possible to them during the vinification process. This is made much easier by the marked difference between daytime and night-time temperatures. This plays a significant role in refining the wines, which are consistently well structured with plenty of substance, and nicely balanced by good acidity and tannins. The 2009 Magliocco Vigna Savuco made it to the finals again for its nicely full, muscular structure, well balanced by a tangy acidic vein, but chiefly for the tightly-woven, intense nose profile of ripe berry fruits, spices, and savoury iodine notes.

● Vigna Savuco '09	♥♥ 6
● Terraccia '11	♥♥ 3
○ Besidiae '12	♥ 2
⊙ Don Filì '11	♥ 3
● Settechiese '12	♥ 2
● Terraccia '10	♀♀ 3
● Vigna Savuco '08	♀♀ 6

Statti

C.DA LENTI
88046 LAMEZIA TERME [CZ]
TEL. 0968456138
www.statti.com

CELLAR SALES
PRE-BOOKED VISITS
RESTAURANT SERVICE
ANNUAL PRODUCTION 300,000 bottles
HECTARES UNDER VINE 55.00

This exquisite, long-standing estate was founded in 1700 and is still managed with great care by the Statti family. Originally, the 500-hectare property was devoted mostly to olives and citrus, with only a tiny portion dedicated to grapes. Current owners Antonio and Alberto decided to increase the estate's wine production. They made a major investment in a new winery and expanded the vineyard to around 100 hectares. The quality of all their wines, whether top flight or produced on a larger scale, is rising steadily. An outstanding 2011 Gaglioppo Batassarro has generous, intense nose, with hints of violet, sweet spice, and berry fruit, and a tannic, varietal palate. The tangy 2011 Arvino blend of gaglioppo and cabernet is also good, with a leisurely palate and marked fruit and balsam on the nose.

● Batassarro '11	♥♥ 4
● Arvino '11	♥♥ 2*
○ Greco '12	♥♥ 2*
● Gaglioppo '12	♥ 2
○ I Gelsi Bianco '12	♥ 1*
⊙ I Gelsi Rosato '12	♥ 2
● I Gelsi Rosso '12	♥ 1*
● Arvino '10	♀♀ 2*
● Batassarro '10	♀♀ 4

Tenuta Terre Nobili

VIA CARIGLIALTO
87046 MONTALTO UFFUGO [CS]
TEL. 0984934005
www.tenutaterrenobili.it

CELLAR SALES
PRE-BOOKED VISITS
ACCOMMODATION
ANNUAL PRODUCTION 37,000 bottles
HECTARES UNDER VINE 16.00
VITICULTURE METHOD Certified Organic

Lidia Matera's lovely hillside estate, at an elevation of around 400 metres, enjoys excellent exposure. These organically-managed vineyards account for 16 of the 36 hectares of property. In recent years Lidia has turned more towards local wine-making traditions, replacing many of the international vines with local varieties like magliocco, greco, and nerello, and she now produces wines with a strong local character, but which are also considerably more elegant and appealing. She achieves a modern style without crushing the varietal character of the grape, with an eye to international markets. The magliocco dolce and canino blend 2012 Cariglio made it to the finals. It is elegant, with a fresh Mediterranean herb, tobacco and berry fruit nose, and savoury, well-balanced palate. The 2012 Alarico is also very drinkable, with a balsamic, oaky nose and a savoury palate balanced nicely with plenty of juicy, ripe fruit.

Luigi Viola

VIA ROMA, 18
87010 SARACENA [CS]
TEL. 0981349099
www.cantineviola.it

CELLAR SALES
PRE-BOOKED VISITS
ANNUAL PRODUCTION 7,000 bottles
HECTARES UNDER VINE 3.00
VITICULTURE METHOD Certified Organic

The estate that Luigi Viola has managed for many years now with the assistance of his three children comprises several hectares of vines at the foot of the Pollino ranges and a small cellar in Saracena's historic centre. However, this limited description does not really do it justice, because behind the amber nectar that goes by the name of Moscato di Saracena lie many years of financial sacrifice and battles with bureaucracy that Luigi has fought to save this ancient wine, which was first recognized and classified in the 16th century. His latest project, a red wine from magliocco vines over 50 years old, is also off to a good start. The 2012 Moscato Passito has earned yet another well-deserved Tre Bicchieri award. The delicate, elegant nose has apricot, candied mandarin and fresh Mediterranean herb aromas, followed by a fresh, deep palate, with a full, yet supple backbone, and long, fruity finish.

● Cariglio '12	♀♀ 3*
● Alarico '12	♀♀ 3
☉ Donn'Eleonò '12	♀ 2
○ Santa Chiara '12	♀ 2
● Alarico '11	♀♀ 3
● Cariglio '10	♀♀ 3
☉ Donn'Eleonò '11	♀♀ 2*

○ Moscato Passito '12	♀♀♀ 6
○ Rossoviola '11	♀♀ 4
○ Moscato Passito '11	♀♀♀ 6
○ Moscato Passito '10	♀♀♀ 6
○ Moscato Passito '09	♀♀♀ 6
○ Moscato Passito '08	♀♀♀ 6
○ Moscato Passito '07	♀♀♀ 6

'A Vita

FRAZ. CIRÒ MARINA
SS 106 KM 279,800
88811 CROTONE
TEL. 3290732473
www.avitavini.it

CELLAR SALES
PRE-BOOKED VISITS
ANNUAL PRODUCTION 15,000 bottles
HECTARES UNDER VINE 8.00

● Cirò Rosso Cl. '09	♟♟ 3*
☉ Rosato 'A Vita '12	♟ 2
● Rosso 'A Vita '09	♟ 3

Caparra & Siciliani

BIVIO SS JONICA, 106
88811 CIRÒ MARINA [KR]
TEL. 0962373319
www.caparraesiciliani.it

CELLAR SALES
PRE-BOOKED VISITS
ANNUAL PRODUCTION 1,000,000 bottles
HECTARES UNDER VINE 200.00
VITICULTURE METHOD Certified Organic

● Mastrogiurato '09	♟♟ 3*
☉ Cirò Rosato Le Formelle '12	♟♟ 2*
● Cirò Rosso Cl. Sup. Volvito '10	♟ 3
○ Curiale '12	♟ 2

Capo Zefirio

VIA LUNGOFERROVIA, 20
89032 BIANCO [RC]
TEL. 0964911446
www.capozefirio.com

○ Greco di Bianco '09	♟♟ 7

Colacino

VIA COLLE MANCO
87054 ROGLIANO [CS]
TEL. 09841900252
www.colacino.it

CELLAR SALES
PRE-BOOKED VISITS
ANNUAL PRODUCTION 80,000 bottles
HECTARES UNDER VINE 21.00

● Savuto Sup. Britto '10	♟♟ 4
● Amanzio '12	♟ 2
☉ Savuto Rosato '12	♟ 2

Tenuta del Conte

VIA TIRONE, 131
88811 CIRÒ MARINA [KR]
TEL. 096236239
www.tenutadelconte.it

PRE-BOOKED VISITS
ANNUAL PRODUCTION 90,000 bottles
HECTARES UNDER VINE 20.00

☉ Cirò Rosato '12	♟♟ 2*
○ Cirò Bianco '12	♟ 2
● Cirò Rosso Cl. Sup. '11	♟ 2

Du Cropio

VIA SELE, 5
88811 CIRÒ MARINA [KR]
TEL. 096231322
www.viniducropio.it

CELLAR SALES
PRE-BOOKED VISITS
ACCOMMODATION AND RESTAURANT SERVICE
ANNUAL PRODUCTION 90,000 bottles
HECTARES UNDER VINE 30.00
VITICULTURE METHOD Certified Organic

● Serra Sanguigna '12	♟♟ 3*
● Cirò Cl. Sup. Damis '10	♟♟ 5
● Cirò Cl. Sup. Don Giuvà '12	♟♟ 3

Masseria Falvo 1727

LOC. GARGA
87010 SARACENA [CS]
TEL. 098127968
www.masseriafalvo.it

CELLAR SALES
ANNUAL PRODUCTION 50,000 bottles
HECTARES UNDER VINE 26.00
VITICULTURE METHOD Certified Organic

● Graneta '11	🍷🍷 3
○ Donna Filomena '12	🍷 3
○ Pircoca '12	🍷 3

Tenute Ferrocinto

C.DA FERROCINTO
87012 CASTROVILLARI [CS]
TEL. 0981415122
www.cantinecampoverde.it

CELLAR SALES
PRE-BOOKED VISITS
ANNUAL PRODUCTION 700,000 bottles
HECTARES UNDER VINE 45.00
VITICULTURE METHOD Certified Organic

● Pollino Magliocco '11	🍷🍷 3
⊙ Dolcedorme '12	🍷 2
○ Dovì Brut '10	🍷 5
○ Pollino Passito 1658 '11	🍷 3

Feudo dei Sanseverino

VIA VITTORIO EMANUELE, 108/110
87010 SARACENA [CS]
TEL. 098121461
www.feudodeisanseverino.it

CELLAR SALES
PRE-BOOKED VISITS
ANNUAL PRODUCTION 20,000 bottles
HECTARES UNDER VINE 6.00
VITICULTURE METHOD Certified Organic

○ Mastro Terenzio '10	🍷🍷 5

Cantine Lento

VIA DEL PROGRESSO, 1
88046 LAMEZIA TERME [CZ]
TEL. 096828028
www.cantinelento.it

CELLAR SALES
PRE-BOOKED VISITS
ANNUAL PRODUCTION 500,000 bottles
HECTARES UNDER VINE 70.00

● Federico II '09	🍷🍷 5
● Magliocco '09	🍷🍷 4
○ Contessa Emburga '12	🍷 4
○ Lamezia Greco '12	🍷 4

Le Moire

VIA C.M. TALLARIGO, 12
88040 MOTTA SANTA LUCIA [CZ]
TEL. 3385739758
www.lemoire.it

CELLAR SALES
PRE-BOOKED VISITS
ACCOMMODATION
ANNUAL PRODUCTION 13,000 bottles
HECTARES UNDER VINE 8.00

● Savuto Mute '12	🍷🍷 3
● Annibale '12	🍷 2
⊙ Savuto Shemale '12	🍷 3

La Pizzuta del Principe

C.DA LA PIZZUTA, 1
88816 STRONGOLI [KR]
TEL. 096288252
www.lapizzutadelprincipe.it

CELLAR SALES
PRE-BOOKED VISITS
ACCOMMODATION AND RESTAURANT SERVICE
ANNUAL PRODUCTION 80,000 bottles
HECTARES UNDER VINE 110.00

⊙ Calastrazza '12	🍷🍷 2*
○ Melissa Santa Foca '12	🍷 2
○ Molarella '12	🍷 2

Fattoria San Francesco

LOC. QUATTROMANI
88813 CIRÒ [KR]
TEL. 096232228
www.fattoriasanfrancesco.it

CELLAR SALES
PRE-BOOKED VISITS
ANNUAL PRODUCTION 250,000 bottles
HECTARES UNDER VINE 40.00

⊙ Cirò Rosato San Francesco '12	♀♀ 2*
○ Cirò Bianco San Francesco '12	♀ 2
● Cirò Rosso Cl. Ronco dei Quattro Venti '11	♀ 5
● Cirò Rosso Cl. San Francesco '12	♀ 2

Cantine Spadafora 1915

ZONA IND. PIANO LAGO, 18
87050 MANGONE [CS]
TEL. 0984969080
www.cantinespadafora.it

CELLAR SALES
PRE-BOOKED VISITS
ANNUAL PRODUCTION 600,000 bottles
HECTARES UNDER VINE 40.00

● Donnici Rosso V. Fiego '11	♀♀ 3
⊙ Donnici Rosato V. Fiego '12	♀ 3
● Donnici Telesio Ris. '09	♀ 5
● Nerello '09	♀ 3

Terre del Gufo - Muzzillo

FRAZ. DONNICI INFERIORE
C.DA ALBO SAN MARTINO
87100 COSENZA
TEL. 3357725614
www.terredelgufo.com

CELLAR SALES
ANNUAL PRODUCTION 22,000 bottles
HECTARES UNDER VINE 3.00

● Timpamara '11	♀♀ 5
● Donnici Portapiana '11	♀♀ 3
⊙ Donnici Kaulòs '12	♀ 3
⊙ Donnici Rosato Chiaroscuro '12	♀ 2

Terre di Balbia

C.DA MONTINO
87042 ALTOMONTE [CS]
TEL. 048161264
www.terredibalbia.it

CELLAR SALES
PRE-BOOKED VISITS
ANNUAL PRODUCTION 15,100 bottles
HECTARES UNDER VINE 23.00

● SerraMonte '08	♀♀ 6
● Balbium The Empero's Wine '11	♀ 3

Vignaioli del Pollino

C.DA FERROCINTO, 151
87012 CASTROVILLARI [CS]
TEL. 098138035
www.vinopollino.com

PRE-BOOKED VISITS
ANNUAL PRODUCTION 300,000 bottles
HECTARES UNDER VINE 32.00
VITICULTURE METHOD Certified Organic

● Pollino Rosso '12	♀♀ 2*
● Pollino Sup. Harè '08	♀♀ 5
⊙ Pollino Ceraso '12	♀ 2

Vinicola Zito

FRAZ. PUNTA ALICE
VIA SCALARETTO
88811 CIRÒ MARINA [KR]
TEL. 096231853
www.cantinezito.it

CELLAR SALES
PRE-BOOKED VISITS
ANNUAL PRODUCTION 800,000 bottles
HECTARES UNDER VINE 70.00
VITICULTURE METHOD Certified Organic

● Cirò Rosso Cl. '11	♀♀ 2*
● Macalla '10	♀♀ 2*
○ Cirò Bianco Nosside '12	♀ 2
● Cirò Rosso Cl. Ris. '10	♀ 3

SICILY

This year's tastings reconfirmed the region's 19 Tre Bicchieri awards, underscoring the excellent health of the island's wine industry, which is rapidly opening up to both the new DOC and DOP Sicilia designations. At the same time, we noted the propensity of established and upcoming producers alike to focus greater attention on the island's wealth of native grape varieties, often adopting innovative stylistic solutions. And all of this is taking place within a framework of increasingly eco-sustainable agriculture. A well-deserved Tre Bicchieri went to Rallo's Bianco Maggiore 2012, an elegant Grillo that has brought this extraordinary but neglected variety back into the limelight. Feudi del Pisciotto's Frappato Carolina Marengo 2011 is excellent, as is the Frappato 2011 from Arianna Occhipinti, who follows her own personal path in the production of natural wines. Nero d'Avola plays a leading role, as always, with the terroir-true Saia 2011 from Feudo Maccari, the deep Sàgana 2011 from Cusumano and Planeta's vibrant Santa Cecilia 2011. Firriato's exemplary 2011 vintage of Santagostino Baglio Soria, from nero d'Avola and syrah, also caused a stir. In the absence of its Faro, Salvatore Geraci's elegant Rosso del Soprano 2011 repeated last year's success. Tasca d'Almerita's fabulous Cabernet Sauvignon 2010 also won our top accolade, and Donnafugata's classic Passito di Pantelleria Ben Ryè 2011 collected yet another. Marsala Superiore Ambra Riserva 1985 from Pellegrino is simply alluring, once again showing the extraordinary personality of this legendary wine. Then there's a great return, in the form of what is perhaps the best version ever of Malvasia delle Lipari Passito Carlo Hauner 2010, which is an explosion of Mediterranean aromas. The extraordinary terroir around Mount Etna remains true to form, bringing home an impressive seven Tre Bicchieri awards to three Etna Biancos, including Graci's Arcuria 2011, Fessina's 'A Puddara 2011, and Benanti's Superiore Pietramarina 2009, and to four reds: Passopisciaro's Contrada Guardiola 2011 and three Etna Rossos, namely Pietradolce's Vigna Barbagalli 2010, Tenuta delle Terre Nere's Santo Spirito 2011, and Girolamo Russo's Feudo 2011. These 19 award-winning wines are jewels in the crown of one of Italy's most seductive winegrowing regions.

Abbazia Santa Anastasia

C.DA SANTA ANASTASIA
90013 CASTELBUONO [PA]
TEL. 091671959
www.abbaziasantanastasia.it

CELLAR SALES
PRE-BOOKED VISITS
ACCOMMODATION AND RESTAURANT SERVICE
ANNUAL PRODUCTION 250,000 bottles
HECTARES UNDER VINE 65.00
VITICULTURE METHOD Certified Biodynamic

The vineyards are part of a splendid estate of over 300 hectares, set in the Madonie national park, whose fertile hills slope down to the sea, benefiting from the altitude and strong coastal winds. The Lena family, owners since the 1980s, have built modern cellars with service facilities, which also encompass the abbey founded in 1100 by Ruggero d'Altavilla, from which the winery takes its name. The estate already adopts organic farming practices, but is well on the way to converting to biodynamic methods, with the declared intent of producing wines with a strong territorial character. The graceful Nero d'Avola Il Moro 2010 boasts typical Mediterranean notes, while sweet spice and incense combine with a mature, crisp palate in the Tanè 2010, from nero d'Avola and syrah. The Cerasuolo di Vittoria Classico 2010 is pleasing, while the Il Frappato 2012 offers fresh, fragrant fruit.

Alessandro di Camporeale

C.DA MANDRANOVA
90043 CAMPOREALE [PA]
TEL. 092437038
www.alessandrodicamporeale.it

CELLAR SALES
PRE-BOOKED VISITS
ANNUAL PRODUCTION 150,000 bottles
HECTARES UNDER VINE 35.00
VITICULTURE METHOD Certified Organic

This family-run boutique winery has over a century's experience of viticulture, spanning four generations of the Alessandro family, and is widely appreciated for the quality of its territory-dedicated wines and its great respect for the environment. Today, the estate is run with passion by the dynamic brothers Nino, Natale and Rosolino, who each deal with a specific aspect of the business. The fine estate, with sandy soil rich in clay and limestone, lies on a hillside site at Mandranova, near Camporeale, and benefits not only from its altitude, but also from wide diurnal temperature ranges and the frequent winds typical of the area. Kaid 2011, a classic of its type from a selection of syrah, made the finals, winning us over with intense cherry and sweet spice, paving the way for a dynamic, silkily satisfying palate. The fruit-infused Grillo Vigna di Mandranova 2012 proved to be attractively fresh and aromatic.

● Litra '11	♟♟ 6
● Montenero '11	♟♟ 4
● Passomaggio '11	♟♟ 3
● Sens(i)nverso Cabernet Sauvignon '10	♟♟ 4
● Sens(i)nverso Nero d'Avola '10	♟♟ 4
● Sens(i)nverso Syrah '11	♟♟ 4
○ Sens(i)nverso Chardonnay '12	♟ 4
○ Sinestesia '12	♟ 3
● Litra '04	♟♟♟ 6
● Litra '01	♟♟♟ 7
● Litra '00	♟♟♟ 7
● Litra '99	♟♟♟ 7
● Montenero '04	♟♟♟ 4

● Kaid '11	♟♟ 3*
● DonnaTà '12	♟♟ 2*
○ Grillo V. di Mandranova '12	♟♟ 3
○ Benedè '12	♟ 2
○ Kaid Sauvignon Blanc '12	♟ 3
● Kaid '10	♟♟ 3*
● Kaid '09	♟♟ 3
● Kaid '08	♟♟ 3*
● Kaid '07	♟♟ 3
● Kaid '06	♟♟ 3
● Kaid '02	♟♟ 4
● Kaid '01	♟♟ 3

Baglio del Cristo di Campobello

C.DA FAVAROTTA, SS 123 KM 19,200
92023 CAMPOBELLO DI LICATA [AG]
TEL. 0922 877709
www.cristodicampobello.it

CELLAR SALES
PRE-BOOKED VISITS
ANNUAL PRODUCTION 300,000 bottles
HECTARES UNDER VINE 30.00

The dependable, easy-going trio of Angelo Bonetta and his sons Carmelo and Domenico embody a passionate dedication to wine-making, and an uncompromising type of Sicilian wine-grower, strongly rooted in tradition. Their fine estate covers 50 hectares, 30 of which are under vine, in excellent wine country in the hills near Campobello di Licata, whose deep, chalky, limestone soils are lashed by the salty, sometimes violent winds from the nearby coast. At its heart is an 18th-century enclosed farmstead and modern winery, while amidst the vines stands the statue of Christ that gives its name to the winery and has been an object of popular worship for centuries. The excellent Lu Patri 2011, a monovarietal Nero d'Avola with real personality, boasts elegant, intense hints of damson and black cherry, topsoil and chocolate, over a lively palate with a lingering finish. The balsamic Syrah Lusirà 2011 is soft and juicy. We also liked the winery's other labels.

○ C'D'C' Bianco Cristo di Campobello '12	🍷🍷 2*
● C'D'C' Rosso Cristo di Campobello '12	🍷🍷 2*
○ Laudàri '11	🍷🍷 4
● Lu Patri '11	🍷🍷 5
● Lusirà '11	🍷🍷 5
○ Adènzia Bianco '12	🍷 3
● Adènzia Rosso '11	🍷 3
○ Lalùci '12	🍷 3
● Lu Patri '09	🍷🍷🍷 5
● Adènzia Rosso '10	🍷🍷 3
● C'D'C' Rosso Cristo di Campobello '11	🍷🍷 2*
○ Lalùci '11	🍷🍷 3

Baglio di Pianetto

VIA FRANCIA
90030 SANTA CRISTINA GELA [PA]
TEL. 0918570002
www.bagliodipianetto.com

CELLAR SALES
PRE-BOOKED VISITS
ANNUAL PRODUCTION 400,000 bottles
HECTARES UNDER VINE 95.00

Established in 1997, the winery is the result of Conte Paolo Marzotto's passion for Sicily, which he explored as a "gentleman driver" in memorable 1950s motoring competitions. The headquarters near Santa Cristina Gela are fitted with large, modern cellars and include a 19th-century enclosed farmstead, now restored and converted into an elegant boutique agritourism. In addition to 65 hectares of vineyards on the hills of Santa Cristina, there are 90 more near Siracusa, in the heart of the Eloro and Moscato di Noto DOC zones, at Contrada Baroni. Noto is home to the operation's nero d'Avola, syrah and moscato bianco, while viognier, inzolia, merlot and petit verdot grow at Santa Cristina. Ramione 2011, from nero d'Avola and merlot, made our finals with its complex, stylish nose, leading into a close-knit, rounded palate. Ra'is 2010, a raisin wine from moscato bianco, combines gracefulness with intense citrus and lavender aromas. The Shymer 2011 is a spirited, spicy syrah-merlot blend .

● Ramione '11	🍷🍷 3*
● Piana dei Cembali '10	🍷🍷 5
○ Ra'is '10	🍷🍷 4
● Salici '10	🍷🍷 4
● Shymer '11	🍷🍷 2*
● Carduni '07	🍷 5
○ Ficiligno '12	🍷 3
○ Ginolfo '11	🍷 4
● Ramione '04	🍷🍷🍷 3*
○ Ra'is '09	🍷🍷 4
● Ramione '06	🍷🍷 3*
● Salici '07	🍷🍷 4

Cantine Barbera

C.DA TORRENOVA, SP 79
92013 MENFI [AG]
TEL. 0925570442
www.cantinebarbera.it

CELLAR SALES
PRE-BOOKED VISITS
RESTAURANT SERVICE
ANNUAL PRODUCTION 80,000 bottles
HECTARES UNDER VINE 15.00

Their proximity to the River Belice and the sea endows the Barbera family's vineyards with an ecosystem of spectacular beauty as well as unique soil and climate conditions. This is inevitably reflected in the grapes, which are transformed into wines with a marked Mediterranean personality. Also of interest is the wide variety of labels on offer, reflecting different choices made according to the age of the vine stock. Marilena, the current owner, can in fact choose from the inzolia planted by her grandfather 90 years ago, the international varieties introduced by her father Pietro, and, coming full circle, the native varieties she has decided to return to. The Alba Marina Vendemmia Tardiva 2012, from catarratto partially dried on the vine, impressed with its elegant, invigorating citrus notes. The Microcosmo 2011, from perricone and nerello, showed generous fresh fruit and texture. We also liked the Sicilia Nero d'Avola 2012 and Sicilia Inzolia 2012.

○ Alba Marina V. T. '12	♥♥ 3
● Microcosmo '11	♥♥ 3
● Sicilia Inzolia '12	♥♥ 2*
● Sicilia Nero d'Avola '12	♥♥ 2*
● Coste al Vento '12	♥ 4
⊙ La Bambina '12	♥ 2
● Menfi Cabernet Sauvignon La Vota '11	♥ 4
○ Menfi Inzolia Dietro le Case '12	♥ 4
● Menfi Rosso Coda della Foce Ris. '11	♥ 4
○ Albamarina Passito '11	♀♀ 4
● Menfi Cabernet Sauvignon La Vota '10	♀♀ 4
● Menfi Merlot Azimut '10	♀♀ 4
● Microcosmo '10	♀♀ 3

Barone di Villagrande

VIA DEL BOSCO, 25
95025 MILO [CT]
TEL. 0957082175
www.villagrande.it

CELLAR SALES
PRE-BOOKED VISITS
ACCOMMODATION AND RESTAURANT SERVICE
ANNUAL PRODUCTION 180,000 bottles
HECTARES UNDER VINE 19.00

The winery of the Nicolosi Asmundo family has a long history, and the first mentions of wine production at the current site date back to the mid-18th century. The current owner, Carlo Nicolosi Asmundo, drafted the first production protocol for the Etna designation, back in 1968. The operation has 16 hectares under vine on Etna, at an elevation of around 700 metres, and two hectares on the island of Salina, where it produces Malvasia delle Lipari. Production is now dealt with by Carlo's son, Marco, who in recent years has focused his energies on producing modern, elegantly styled wines that also respect tradition. The Etna Bianco Superiore 2012, from carricante, boasts great personality, offering a mineral, citrus nose, and a fresh, zesty palate with a long, clean finish. We also liked the fruity, floral Etna Rosso 2011, from nerello mascalese and cappuccio, which was generous and elegant with good acidic balance.

○ Etna Bianco Sup. '12	♥♥ 4
● Etna Rosso '11	♥♥ 4
○ Fiore di Villagrande '11	♥♥ 4
○ Etna Bianco Legno di Conzo Sup. '10	♥ 6
⊙ Etna Rosato '12	♥ 3
○ Salina Bianco '12	♥ 3
○ Etna Bianco Legno di Conzo Sup. '08	♀♀ 6
○ Etna Bianco Legno di Conzo Sup. '07	♀♀ 6
○ Etna Bianco Sup. '11	♀♀ 2*
○ Etna Bianco Sup. '10	♀♀ 3
○ Etna Bianco Sup. '09	♀♀ 2*
○ Etna Bianco Sup. '08	♀♀ 2*
○ Etna Bianco Sup. '07	♀♀ 2*
● Etna Rosso Lanza di Mannera '08	♀♀ 6
○ Fiore '06	♀♀ 4
● Sciara '05	♀♀ 4

★Benanti

VIA G. GARIBALDI, 475
95029 VIAGRANDE [CT]
TEL. 0957893399
www.vinicolabenanti.it

CELLAR SALES
PRE-BOOKED VISITS
ANNUAL PRODUCTION 120,000 bottles
HECTARES UNDER VINE 45.00

Giuseppe Benanti, honoured with the title of Cavaliere del Lavoro, is now assisted with passion by his sons Antonio and Salvino. For some time he was the sole champion of Etna wine making, and he deserves credit for its rediscovery by wine writers and consumers. His model, in keeping with tradition and fiercely loyal to the history of the area, has been an inspiration for many other growers. What's more, it is based on indisputable scientific premises and decades of experimentation, as seen in his patented ambient yeasts, which have helped unleash much of the potential of local varieties. A return to Tre Bicchieri form for the potent, racy Pietramarina 2009, from carricante, which convinced with its bright pale green hue and intense notes of flint and mimosa blossom.

○ Etna Bianco Sup. Pietramarina '09	♙♙♙	5
○ Etna Bianco di Caselle '11	♙♙	3
● Etna Rosso Rosso di Verzella '10	♙♙	3
○ Noblesse	♙	6
○ Etna Bianco Sup. Pietramarina '04	♛♛♛	6
○ Etna Bianco Sup. Pietramarina '02	♛♛♛	5
○ Etna Bianco Sup. Pietramarina '01	♛♛♛	5
○ Etna Bianco Sup. Pietramarina '00	♛♛♛	5
○ Etna Bianco Sup. Pietramarina '99	♛♛♛	4
○ Etna Bianco Sup. Pietramarina '97	♛♛♛	4*
● Etna Rosso Serra della Contessa '06	♛♛♛	7
● Etna Rosso Serra della Contessa '04	♛♛♛	7
● Etna Rosso Serra della Contessa '03	♛♛♛	7
● Il Drappo '04	♛♛♛	5

Centopassi

VIA PORTA PALERMO, 132
90048 SAN GIUSEPPE JATO [PA]
TEL. 0918577655
www.centopassisicilia.it

CELLAR SALES
PRE-BOOKED VISITS
ACCOMMODATION AND RESTAURANT SERVICE
ANNUAL PRODUCTION 300,000 bottles
HECTARES UNDER VINE 90.00
VITICULTURE METHOD Certified Organic

The name Centopassi refers to the story of Peppino Impastato, and shows how the redemption of an area can also be achieved through an estate run by the three young co-operatives, Placido Rizzotto, Pio La Torre and Lavoro, which farm an overall 400 hectares of land confiscated from local Mafia families. The area under vine amounts to 90 hectares, mainly planted to the native varieties of grillo, catarratto and nero d'Avola. After a couple of years of trial vinifications, many of the Centopassi labels are now produced using grapes from the individual vineyards, a choice that has had a significant impact on the personality and originality of the entire range. Once again, the Centopassi winery turned out a range of outstanding wines. The superb Nero d'Avola Argille di Tagghia Via 2012, with its marvellous deep ruby hue, is an intense, racy wine, with spice and notes of fruit and citrus.

● Argille di Tagghia Via '12	♙♙	3
● Argille di Tagghia Via di Sutta '11	♙♙	3
○ Catarratto Terre Rosse di Giabbascio '12	♙♙	3
● Centopassi Rosso '12	♙♙	2*
○ Tendoni di Trebbiano '11	♙♙	4
○ Centopassi Bianco '12	♙	2
○ Cimento di Perricone '11	♙	4
○ Grillo Rocce di Pietra Longa '12	♙	3
● Argille di Tagghia Via '11	♛♛	3
● Argille di Tagghia Via '10	♛♛	3
○ Grillo Rocce di Pietra Longa '11	♛♛	3
○ Grillo Rocce di Pietra Longa '10	♛♛	3*
● Marne di Saladino '10	♛♛	4
● Marne di Saladino '09	♛♛	3
○ Terre Rosse di Giabbascio '10	♛♛	3*

Frank Cornelissen

FRAZ. SOLICCHIATA
VIA NAZIONALE, 297
95012 CASTIGLIONE DI SICILIA [CT]
TEL. 0942986315
www.frankcornelissen.it

PRE-BOOKED VISITS
ANNUAL PRODUCTION 40,000 bottles
HECTARES UNDER VINE 12.00
VITICULTURE METHOD Certified Organic

Some years ago Dutchman Frank
Cornelissen decided to settle on Mount
Etna, where he lives in harmony with nature
and farms the land. Frank rejects labels like
organic and biodynamic, and he avoids this
type of schematic intervention. His
viticulture is natural in the broadest sense
and he does not mow fields and vineyards,
or practice monoculture. He has 8.5
hectares of bush-trained vines on his
12-hectare estate, often ungrafted, and
growing alongside fruit trees, cereals,
vegetables, and wild herbs. The same
occurs for the remaining plots, where other
crops alternate among his olive trees
according to the season, and the bees are
custodians of a valuable environmental
equilibrium. The wines ferment in amphorae
and concrete vats, and both the whites and
reds are the result of long maceration on
the skins, without the use of sulphites. The
2012 Munjebel Vigne Alte 9, from vineyards
at an altitude of over 1,000 metres, is
extraordinarily intense, mineral and
compact, showing fruit-rich, full-flavoured
and vibrant.

● Magma Barbabecchi '10	♟♟ 8
● Munjebel Vigne Alte 9 '12	♟♟ 7
● Contadino 10 '12	♟♟ 4
○ Munjebel Bianco 9 '12	♟♟ 5
● Munjebel Chiusa Spagnola 9 '12	♟♟ 7
● Munjebel Monte Colla 9 '12	♟♟ 7
● Munjebel Rosso 9 '12	♟♟ 6
☉ Susucaru '12	♟♟ 4

Cottanera

LOC. IANNAZZO
SP 89
95030 CASTIGLIONE DI SICILIA [CT]
TEL. 0942963601
www.cottanera.it

CELLAR SALES
PRE-BOOKED VISITS
ANNUAL PRODUCTION 300,000 bottles
HECTARES UNDER VINE 55.00

It all began back in the 1990s, when
Guglielmo Cambria, the winery's
unforgettable founder, planted vines on land
owned by the family on Etna's northern
slopes, along the banks of the Alcantara. In
addition to native varieties, he introduced the
major international varieties on sites with
suitable soil and climate conditions, as well
as mondeuse, on its Sicilian debut. The first
reds met with critical acclaim, and Cottanera
went from strength to strength, culminating
in the triumphant return of traditional DOC
wines. Both of the lines perfectly reflect the
volcanic terroir, and are underpinned by
attentive viticultural and oenological
practices based on respect for the raw
materials. Attractive grapefruit and herbs
with fresh, tangy fruit took the elegant,
mineral Etna Bianco 2012 into the finals.
Hard on its heels were the Etna Rosso 2010,
whose good structure underpins dense,
chewy fruit, and the fleshy, fragrant
Barbazzale Bianco 2012, with intense peach
and mint, and good length.

○ Etna Bianco '12	♟♟ 3*
● Etna Rosso '10	♟♟ 5
○ Barbazzale Bianco '12	♟♟ 2*
● Barbazzale Rosso '12	♟♟ 2*
● Fatagione '11	♟♟ 3
● Sole di Sesta '10	♟♟ 4
○ Etna Bianco '11	♟♟♟ 3*
● Etna Rosso '07	♟♟♟ 5
● Etna Rosso '06	♟♟♟ 5
● Etna Rosso '05	♟♟♟ 5
○ Etna Bianco '10	♟♟ 3
● Etna Rosso '09	♟♟ 5
● Etna Rosso '08	♟♟ 5
● L'Ardenza '09	♟♟ 4

★Cusumano

c.da San Carlo SS 113
90047 Partinico [PA]
Tel. 0918908713
www.cusumano.it

Marco De Bartoli

c.da Fornara Samperi, 292
91025 Marsala [TP]
Tel. 0923962093
www.marcodebartoli.com

PRE-BOOKED VISITS
ANNUAL PRODUCTION 2,500,000 bottles
HECTARES UNDER VINE 400.00

CELLAR SALES
PRE-BOOKED VISITS
ANNUAL PRODUCTION 100,000 bottles
HECTARES UNDER VINE 19.00

Alberto and Diego Cusumano's winery, launched in the early 2000s, wasted no time in making a name for itself on international markets with innovative, extremely drinkable products, faithfully reflecting the terroir of the estates from which they originate at Salemi, Pachino, Piana degli Albanesi and Butera. These are stylish, modern wines, designed to respond to consumers' needs and supported by a marketing campaign with Sicily at its heart. They have recently also acquired various plots on Etna, at Verzella, Guardiola and Pietramarina. Fleshy and spicy, velvet-soft yet racy, the elegant Sàgana 2011, from nero d'Avola grapes of outstanding quality, confidently collects yet another Tre Bicchieri. In what is an exceptional range of wines, we should also mention the exquisite Moscato dello Zucco 2009.

Marco De Bartoli left his beloved children Renato, Giuseppina and Sebastiano a difficult inheritance, an uncompromising philosophy based on morality and respect for one's roots. This unsurpassed interpreter and custodian of Marsala, a larger-than-life figure in modern winemaking on the island, had no time for hypocrisy or pretence. He was an old-school vigneron, clear-sighted and determined, proud of his Sicilian heritage, and this was always evident in his sought-after wines. The labels show continuity of style and character, while the youthful enthusiasm of his three children has also resulted in an inspired new line of natural wines, Terza Via, supervised personally by Renato. The stylish Rosso di Marco 2011, from pignatello, sailed straight into the finals. A deep garnet hue ushers in this mature, leisurely wine, with intense, focused aromas of cherry, white pepper, cardamom and thyme. The new Passito Sole d'Agosto Bukkuram 2011, from zibibbo, is elegant and smooth.

● Sàgana '11	￦￦￦ 4*
● Noà '11	￦￦ 4
● Benuara '12	￦￦ 3
○ Cubìa '12	￦￦ 3
○ Inzolia '12	￦￦ 2*
○ Jalé '12	￦￦ 3
○ Moscato dello Zucco '09	￦￦ 5
● Ramusa '12	￦￦ 3
● Syrah '12	￦￦ 2*
● Noà '10	￦￦￦ 4*
● Sàgana '09	￦￦￦ 4
● Sàgana '08	￦￦￦ 4
● Sàgana '07	￦￦￦ 4

● Rosso di Marco '11	￦￦ 3*
○ Passito di Pantelleria Bukkuram '08	￦￦ 7
○ Passito di Pantelleria Bukkuram Sole d'Agosto '11	￦￦ 6
○ Grappoli del Grillo '11	￦ 5
○ Lucido '12	￦ 3
○ Marsala Sup. 10 Anni	￦￦￦ 6
○ Grappoli del Grillo '05	￦￦ 4
○ Marsala Sup. 10 Anni Ris.	￦￦ 6
○ Marsala Sup. Ris. 1986 '86	￦￦ 6
○ Passito di Pantelleria Bukkuram '05	￦￦ 7
○ Passito di Pantelleria Bukkuram '03	￦￦ 8
○ Vecchio Samperi Ventennale	￦￦ 6

Disisa

LOC. C.DA DISISA
FRAZ. GRISÌ
SP 30 KM 6
90046 MONREALE [PA]
TEL. 0919127109
www.vinidisisa.it

CELLAR SALES
PRE-BOOKED VISITS
ANNUAL PRODUCTION 120,000 bottles
HECTARES UNDER VINE 400.00
VITICULTURE METHOD Certified Organic

Disisa is a 400-hectare feudal estate straddling the hills between the Jato and Belice valleys, whose history dates back to Arab rule. Later it was donated by King William II the Good to the Archbishop of Monreale and was finally acquired by its current owners, the Di Lorenzo family, in the 1800s. Since the 1970s, the family has upgraded the vineyards and was the first to introduce chardonnay to Sicily, followed by the main international varieties, as well as fiano and müller thurgau, integrating native types such as inzolia, catarratto, nero d'Avola and grillo. In 2004, the winery began producing its own wines and the technical side is entrusted to a brilliant Sicilian winemaker. The plush, fruit-infused and balsamic Tornamira 2008, from syrah, merlot and cabernet sauvignon, almost made the finals. The captivating Syrah Adhara 2010 opens to subtle cherry, spice and chocolate, followed by a grassy, rounded palate. The pleasingly fresh Grillo 2012 offers focused herb aromas.

● Adhara '10		♟♟ 2*
○ Chara '12		♟♟ 2*
○ Grillo '12		♟♟ 2*
● Tornamira '08		♟♟ 4
● Monreale Vuaria '09		♟ 3
○ Terra delle Fate '11		♟ 3
● Tornamira '06		♟♟ 4
● Tornamira '04		♟♟ 4

★Donnafugata

VIA SEBASTIANO LIPARI, 18
91025 MARSALA [TP]
TEL. 0923724200
www.donnafugata.it

CELLAR SALES
PRE-BOOKED VISITS
ANNUAL PRODUCTION 2,200,000 bottles
HECTARES UNDER VINE 270.00

This leading Italian wine producer is a fine combination of family tradition and modernity, and one of the champions of Sicilian winemaking on the international stage. Giacomo and Gabriella Rallo managed to create their own innovative, and highly successful business model, which effectively combined the undisputed quality of their wines with marketing savvy, communicated with engaging charm, and inspired by culture, sustainability and respect for the environment. Their sons Antonio and José, now at the helm of the winery, have added the finishing touches. A Tre Bicchieri went to this year's Ben Ryé, the 2011, from moscato d'Alessandria. Sensual and bewitching as never before, it proffers fresh notes of lavender, apricot and citrus, over a plush, lingering palate. The Tancredi 2009, from nero d'Avola and cabernet sauvignon, is elegant and austere.

○ Passito di Pantelleria Ben Ryé '11		♟♟♟ 7
● Tancredi '09		♟♟ 5
○ Contessa Entellina Chardonnay La Fuga '12		♟♟ 3
○ Contessa Entellina Chiarandà '10		♟♟ 5
○ Lighea '12		♟♟ 3
● Sherazade '12		♟♟ 3
○ Sursur '12		♟♟ 3
● Contessa Entellina Milleunanotte '06		♟♟♟ 7
● Contessa Entellina Milleunanotte '05		♟♟♟ 7
○ Passito di Pantelleria Ben Ryé '10		♟♟♟ 7
○ Passito di Pantelleria Ben Ryé '09		♟♟♟ 7
● Tancredi '07		♟♟♟ 4

Duca di Salaparuta
Vini Corvo

VIA NAZIONALE, SS 113
90014 CASTELDACCIA [PA]
TEL. 091945201
www.duca.it

CELLAR SALES
PRE-BOOKED VISITS
ANNUAL PRODUCTION 15,000,000 bottles
HECTARES UNDER VINE 155.00

The three brands Duca di Salaparuta, Corvo and Florio, owned by Augusto Reina's Illva In Saronno, are part of the history of quality Sicilian wine-making, recognized and appreciated throughout the world. They also embody a system of entrepreneurial values, based on respect for consumers' needs, foresight and the ability to interpret a wine's present and future evolution that has few equals. All the labels, from raisin wine to sparklers, from entry-level products to those at the top of the range, are well-managed, technically impeccable expressions of the territory and its native varieties, as well as perfect combinations of tradition and modernity. This prestigious winery offers excellence across the board. The gracefully contoured Nero d'Avola Duca Enrico 2010 sailed into the finals with focused varietal notes of ripe fruit and topsoil, and superb structure, displaying a perfect balance of softness, acidity and polished tannins.

● Duca Enrico '10	❦❦ 7	
○ Bianca di Valguarnera '11	❦❦ 5	
○ Calanica Insolia e Chardonnay '12	❦❦ 2*	
● Corvo Irmana '12	❦❦ 4	
○ Kados Risignolo '12	❦❦ 3	
● Lavico '10	❦❦ 4	
○ Malvasia delle Lipari Passito '11	❦❦ 6	
○ Marsala Sup.Targa 1840 Ris. '02	❦❦ 4	
○ Marsala Vergine Baglio Florio '00	❦❦ 6	
○ Marsala Vergine Terre Arse '02	❦❦ 5	
○ Passito di Pantelleria '11	❦❦ 5	
● Duca Enrico '03	❦❦❦ 6	
● Duca Enrico '01	❦❦❦ 6	
● Duca Enrico '84	❦❦❦ 6	

Tenuta di Fessina

LOC. C.DA ROVITTELLO
VIA NAZIONALE 120, 22
95012 CASTIGLIONE DI SICILIA [CT]
TEL. 057155284
www.cuntu.it

CELLAR SALES
PRE-BOOKED VISITS
ANNUAL PRODUCTION 65,000 bottles
HECTARES UNDER VINE 12.00

Silvia Maestrelli and Federico Curtaz have done much for the renaissance of viticulture on Etna, and have made a significant contribution to raising awareness and appreciation of the wines of Santa Maria di Licodia, a little-known zone on the south-western slopes of the volcano, where they produce their Etna Bianco, 'A Puddara. Recent acquisitions at Milo, on the eastern slopes of the volcano, are blessed with ideal growing conditions for carricante, and mean that the estate's wines are now produced on three different sides of the mountain. The reds hark from the north, the whites from the south and east, and all stand out for their elegance, sense of place and impressive varietal typing. A well-deserved Tre Bicchieri went to the Carricante A' Puddara 2011, a wine of rare elegance, offering focused mineral and citrus notes, that manages to combine a compact, fleshy palate with a fresh, racy style. The Nerello Cappuccio Laeneo 2012 is clean with a lingering finish.

○ Etna Bianco A' Puddara '11	❦❦❦ 5	
○ Etna Bianco Erse '12	❦❦ 3	
● Etna Rosso Erse '11	❦❦ 4	
● Sicilia Ero '12	❦❦ 3	
● Sicilia Laeneo '12	❦❦ 3	
○ Etna Bianco A' Puddara '10	❦❦❦ 5	
○ Etna Bianco A' Puddara '09	❦❦❦ 5	
● Etna Rosso Musmeci '07	❦❦❦ 6	
● Ero '09	❦❦ 3*	
○ Etna Rosso Erse '10	❦❦ 4	
● Etna Rosso Musmeci '09	❦❦ 6	
● Etna Rosso Musmeci '08	❦❦ 6	
● Laeneo '11	❦❦ 3	
● Laeneo '09	❦❦ 3	
○ Nakone '11	❦❦ 3	
○ Nakone '10	❦❦ 3	

Feudi del Pisciotto

C.DA PISCIOTTO
93015 NISCEMI [CL]
TEL. 09331930280
www.castellare.it

CELLAR SALES
PRE-BOOKED VISITS
ACCOMMODATION
ANNUAL PRODUCTION 200,000 bottles
HECTARES UNDER VINE 45.00

On the beautiful Sicilian estate of Paolo Panerai wine was already being produced three centuries ago, when its beautiful wine press was built. Boasting eight large tanks that work in parallel, the press is now the symbolic link between the original buildings and the state-of-the-art winery beneath. The vineyard, covering around 50 hectares, is dominated by the old town at its centre, which has been totally redeveloped to create an elegant resort. The Carolina Marengo 2011, from frappato, earned a Tre Bicchieri, showing wild berries and sweet spice with well-integrated oak and fresh cedar, over a caressing palate buttressed by fresh acidity. We saw a fine debut from L'Eterno 2011, a fruit-driven Pinot Nero.

● Frappato Carolina Marengo '11	♥♥♥ 4*
○ Passito Gianfranco Ferrè '11	♥♥ 5
● Baglio del Sole Merlot Syrah '11	♥♥ 2*
● Baglio del Sole Nero d'Avola '11	♥♥ 2*
○ Chardonnay Alberta Ferretti '11	♥♥ 4
○ Grillo Carolina Marengo '11	♥♥ 4
○ Gurra di Mare Tirsat '12	♥♥ 4
● L'Eterno '11	♥♥ 7
● Merlot Valentino '11	♥♥ 4
● Nero d'Avola Versace '11	♥♥ 4
● Cerasuolo di Vittoria Giambattista Valli Paris '09	♥♥♥ 6
● Nero d'Avola Versace '08	♥♥♥ 4*
● Nero d'Avola Versace '07	♥♥♥ 4*
○ Passito Gianfranco Ferrè '09	♥♥♥ 4

Feudo Maccari

C.DA MACCARI SP PACHINO-NOTO, KM 13,500
96017 NOTO [SR]
TEL. 0931596894
www.feudomaccari.it

CELLAR SALES
PRE-BOOKED VISITS
ANNUAL PRODUCTION 166,000 bottles
HECTARES UNDER VINE 50.00

The Moretti family's estate covers around 100 hectares between Noto and Pachino, half of which are planted to the bush vines typical of eastern Sicily. We are in what may rightly be considered the birthplace of nero d'Avola, a variety that here achieves its most typical expression. The particular site climate of the estate, only a couple of kilometres from the sea, and the painstaking care lavished on the vineyard in all the growing phases, means that the cellar receives healthy, perfectly ripe grapes, resulting in elegant, well-typed wines that require little intervention. A Tre Bicchieri went to the Saia 2011, a Nero d'Avola of rare elegance and depth with an admirable sense of place. Its complex nose, swathed in mineral and floral notes, offers plenty of fruit nicely underpinned by fresh balsam. We also liked the silky Moscato di Noto Sultana 2011.

● Saia '11	♥♥♥ 4*
● Nero d'Avola '12	♥♥ 2*
○ Sicilia Sultana '11	♥♥ 5
○ Grillo '12	♥ 2
● Saia '10	♥♥♥ 4*
● Saia '08	♥♥♥ 4*
● Saia '07	♥♥♥ 4*
● Saia '06	♥♥♥ 4
● Mahâris '08	♥♥ 6
● Mahâris '07	♥♥ 6
● Mahâris '06	♥♥ 6
● Mahâris '05	♥♥ 5
○ Moscato di Noto Sultana '10	♥♥ 5
● Saia '09	♥♥ 4
● Saia '05	♥♥ 3
● Saia '03	♥♥ 4

Feudo Principi di Butera

C.DA DELIELLA
93011 BUTERA [CL]
TEL. 0934347726
www.feudobutera.it

CELLAR SALES
PRE-BOOKED VISITS
ANNUAL PRODUCTION 900,000 bottles
HECTARES UNDER VINE 180.00

The new team at Feudo, led by Domenico
Zonin, who has always had a particular love
for his family's Sicilian estate, has
successfully consolidated production at the
high-quality standards to which we have
become accustomed since its spectacular
début a decade ago. The estate's vineyards
are located on a hilltop site, at elevations of
between 250 and 350 metres, on chalky
white, rocky soil, particularly suited to wine-
growing. Feudo's wines display great
drinkability, but also boast real personality,
especially towards the top of the range. The
potent Nero d'Avola Deliella 2011 is at the
top of its category, and made our finals
with its great opulence and character. But a
winery should also be judged on the quality
of its entry-level wines, such as the
ambrosial Cabernet Sauvignon 2011, which
offers outstanding value for money.

● Cabernet Sauvignon '11	♥♥ 3*
● Deliella '11	♥♥ 6
○ Chardonnay '12	♥♥ 3
○ Insolia '12	♥♥ 3
● Nero d'Avola '11	♥♥ 3
● Riesi '11	♥♥ 3
● Symposio '11	♥♥ 5
● Syrah '11	♥♥ 3
● Cabernet Sauvignon '00	♥♥♥ 5
● Deliella '05	♥♥♥ 6
● Deliella '02	♥♥♥ 7
● Deliella '00	♥♥♥ 6
● Deliella '08	♥♥ 6
● Deliella '06	♥♥ 6
● Symposio '10	♥♥ 4
● Symposio '08	♥♥ 4

★Firriato

VIA TRAPANI, 4
91027 PACECO [TP]
TEL. 0923882755
www.firriato.it

CELLAR SALES
PRE-BOOKED VISITS
ANNUAL PRODUCTION 4,250,000 bottles
HECTARES UNDER VINE 320.00
VITICULTURE METHOD Certified Organic

This brand, whose quality, quantity and
reliability give it international clout, has been
built up with dedication and vision since the
mid-1980s by Salvatore and Vinzia Di
Gaetano, who fell in love with Sicily, its
agriculture and its wines. This love is behind
their respect for the environment, the
meticulous fine-tuning of every label, and
the pursuit of wines with a sense of place
and the grapes that compose them. The
operation's fine, well-tended estates include
recent acquisitions at Cavanera Etnea,
Castiglione di Sicilia, and Calamoni, on the
island of Favignana, a gem of five hectares
planted to bush vines, caressed by the sea,
amidst tuff and red sand. Santagostino
Baglio Soria 2011 celebrates almost 25
years among Italy's classics with a
well-deserved Tre Bicchieri. This blend of
nero d'Avola and syrah charmed us with its
depth, elegance and great
pleasureableness. The rest of the range is
quite simply superb.

● Santagostino Rosso Baglio Sorìa '11	♥♥♥ 3
● Ribeca '11	♥♥ 5*
● Camelot '11	♥♥ 5
● Chiaramonte Nero d'Avola '11	♥♥ 2*
● Etna Rosso Cavanera '11	♥♥ 5
● Harmonium '11	♥♥ 5
● Maharajà '11	♥♥ 3*
○ Passito L'Ecrù '11	♥♥ 5
○ Quater Bianco '12	♥♥ 4
● Quater Rosso '11	♥♥ 5
○ Santagostino Bianco Baglio Sorìa '11	♥♥ 3
● Etna Rosso Cavanera Rovo delle Coturnie '09	♥♥♥ 5
● Harmonium '08	♥♥♥ 5*
● Ribeca '10	♥♥♥ 5

Geraci

VIA CORSICA,18
90146 PALERMO
TEL. 0916154146
www.tarucco.com

CELLAR SALES
PRE-BOOKED VISITS
ANNUAL PRODUCTION 120,000 bottles
HECTARES UNDER VINE 15.00
VITICULTURE METHOD Certified Organic

The huge Tarucco feudal estate dates to 1382, when King Martin assigned it to the parish of Monreale. Since 1920 a fraction of it, about 20 hectares, located at an altitude of 400–500 metres, has belonged to the Geraci family who have developed the terrain's natural vocation for cultivation of vines and olive trees. In 2000, Stefano Geraci, a famous civil lawyer with a love of the countryside, decided to involve himself personally and made some changes to estate management, replanting 15 hectares with vines that are now farmed with certified organic methods. The impressive state-of-the-art cellar is the icon of this dedication and upgrading.Intense and deep, with focused red berry fruit, capers and Mediterranean wild herbs, Tarucco Alicante 2011 is pleasing, juicy and satisfying. The Tarucco Nero d'Avola 2010 is savoury and refreshing, while the Tarucco Grillo 2012 shows notes of sea breeze with well-balanced softness and acidity.

● Tarucco Alicante '11	🍷🍷 3
○ Tarucco Colonna Chardonnay Grillo '12	🍷🍷 3
○ Tarucco Grillo '12	🍷🍷 3
● Tarucco Nero d'Avola '10	🍷🍷 3
● Tarucco Peralta '09	🍷🍷 3
○ Tarucco Chardonnay '11	🍷 3
● Tarucco Syrah '09	🍷 3
● Tarucco Alicante '05	🍸🍸 3*
○ Tarucco Chardonnay '05	🍸🍸 3
○ Tarucco Colonna Bianco '07	🍸🍸 2*
● Tarucco Nero d'Avola '05	🍸🍸 3*
● Tarucco Nero d'Avola '04	🍸🍸 2*

Tenuta Gorghi Tondi

C.DA SAN NICOLA
91026 MARSALA [TP]
TEL. 0923719741
www.gorghitondi.com

CELLAR SALES
PRE-BOOKED VISITS
ACCOMMODATION
ANNUAL PRODUCTION 1,300,000 bottles
HECTARES UNDER VINE 130.00

In 2000 Annamaria and Clara Sala decided to establish a new winery to exploit the vineyards bought in the late 19th century by their great-grandfather, located near the sea in the WWF reserve of Preola and Gorghi Tondi, a place of dazzling beauty near Mazara del Vallo. The traditional varieties grown in the area are grillo, catarratto and zibibbo, now integrated with nero d'Avola and the main international varieties. At the same time they built a large, well-equipped cellar whose style and proportions are reminiscent of a traditional enclosed farmstead. This attractive blend of modernity and Mediterranean tradition is echoed in their wines. Coste a Preola 2011, a monovarietal nero d'Avola, once more makes the finals with its focused, fleshy fruit and notes of balsam. The Syrah Segreante 2011 shows wonderful varietal character and a Mediterranean soul. Summery sensuality and botrytis aromas distinguish the Grillo d'Oro 2010.

● Coste a Preola Rosso '11	🍷🍷 2*
○ Grillo d'Oro '10	🍷🍷 7
○ Kheirè '12	🍷🍷 4
○ Rajah '12	🍷🍷 4
● Segreante '11	🍷🍷 4
○ Coste a Preola Bianco '12	🍷 2
○ Coste a Preola Bianco '10	🍸🍸 2*
● Coste a Preola Rosso '10	🍸🍸 2*
● Nero d'Avola '08	🍸🍸 3
● Segreante '07	🍸🍸 3

Graci

LOC. PASSOPISCIARO
C.DA ARCURIA
95012 CASTIGLIONE DI SICILIA [CT]
TEL. 3487016773
www.graci.eu

CELLAR SALES
PRE-BOOKED VISITS
ANNUAL PRODUCTION 13,000 bottles
HECTARES UNDER VINE 18.00

With the new bottling line up and running, Elena and Alberto Aiello Graci's winery is now fully self-sufficient. To keep the wines as faithful as possible to their varietal traits without sacrificing the strong imprint endowed by a territory such as Etna, the rows of wooden truncated cone tanks have this year been joined by a similar number of concrete tanks designed and built by Nico Velo for ageing the wines. To emphasize their link with the volcano, from this vintage onwards the precise district of origin will be specified on the label. Top honours went to the Etna Bianco Arcuria 2011, a classic Carricante, whose mineral notes and fresh citrus aromas pave the way for full flavour and acidity in the mouth, nicely counterpointed by lots of delicious, juicy fruit. The 2011 Etna Rosso Quota 600 was leisurely and polished.

○ Etna Bianco Arcuria '11	♈♈♈ 5
● Etna Rosso Quota 600 '11	♈♈ 5
● Etna Rosso '11	♈♈ 3*
○ Etna Bianco '12	♈ 4
○ Etna Bianco '10	♈♈♈ 4*
○ Etna Bianco Quota 600 '10	♈♈♈ 5
○ Etna Bianco '11	♈♈ 4
● Etna Rosso '10	♈♈ 3
● Etna Rosso '09	♈♈ 3
● Etna Rosso '07	♈♈ 3
● Etna Rosso Quota 600 '10	♈♈ 5
● Etna Rosso Quota 600 '09	♈♈ 5
● Etna Rosso Quota 600 '08	♈♈ 5
● Etna Rosso Quota 600 '07	♈♈ 5
● Etna Rosso Quota 600 '06	♈♈ 5

Gulfi

C.DA PATRIA
97012 CHIARAMONTE GULFI [RG]
TEL. 0932921654
www.gulfi.it

CELLAR SALES
PRE-BOOKED VISITS
ACCOMMODATION AND RESTAURANT SERVICE
ANNUAL PRODUCTION 300,000 bottles
HECTARES UNDER VINE 75.00
VITICULTURE METHOD Certified Organic

Since his first harvest, the farsighted Vito Catania has based his winery's philosophy on three key concepts: organic farming methods, native varieties, and bringing out the best of the territory. The 75 hectares of vineyards, all planted to bush vines, are farmed using natural irrigation methods, and fertilized solely with animal and green manure. This is probably why these extremely seductive wines display a marked, unmistakable style, and are clearly affected by the climatic conditions of the growing year, which can sometimes make them slightly unapproachable. The Valcanzjria 2012, an invigorating blend of carricante, albanello and chardonnay, made our finals with its fresh, vibrant character, and finishes attractively with well-balanced fruit and zestiness. The best of the reds is the Nero d'Avola Nerobaronj 2009, with its jammy berry fruit and spice.

○ Valcanzjria '12	♈♈ 3*
● Nerobaronj '09	♈♈ 5
● Neromàccarj '09	♈♈ 6
○ Carjcanti '11	♈ 5
● Cerasuolo di Vittoria '12	♈ 3
● Rossojbleo '12	♈ 3
● Nerobufaleffj '07	♈♈♈ 5
● Neromàccarj '08	♈♈♈ 6
● Neromàccarj '07	♈♈♈ 5
● Neromàccarj '04	♈♈♈ 5
● Nerosanlorè '05	♈♈♈ 5
● Nerobaronj '06	♈♈ 5
● Nerosanlorè '08	♈♈ 5
● Nerosanlorè '07	♈♈ 5

Hauner

LOC. SANTA MARIA
VIA G.GRILLO, 61
98123 MESSINA
TEL. 0906413029
www.hauner.it

CELLAR SALES
PRE-BOOKED VISITS
ANNUAL PRODUCTION 80,000 bottles
HECTARES UNDER VINE 18.00

One of Italy's oldest, most celebrated sweet wines, Malvasia delle Lipari, risked disappearing in the middle of the last century, when farming on the Aeolian Islands was gradually abandoned as the islanders emigrated en masse to mainland Italy. Not yet a popular summer tourist destination, in the 1960s Salina saw the arrival of a young artist from Brescia, Carlo Hauner. It was love at first sight. He decided to settle on the island and to restore Malvasia to its ancient splendour, renovating vineyards and building a winery. Hauner's passion and hard work reaped the hoped-for rewards, and his work is now continued by his son and heir, Carlo Junior. The Passito Riserva Carlo Hauner 2010, a joyous explosion of summery, Mediterranean aromas, spellbound us with its seductive, velvety palate and impressive length, earning Tre Bicchieri in the process. We also loved the Passito 2011 and the Rosso Hierà 2011, from nero d'Avola, alicante and nocera.

○ Malvasia delle Lipari Passito Ris. '10	♥♥♥ 8
● Hierà Rosso '11	♥♥ 3
○ Malvasia delle Lipari '11	♥♥ 5
○ Malvasia delle Lipari Passito '11	♥♥ 6
● Rosso Antonello '09	♥♥ 4
○ Salina Bianco '12	♥♥ 2*
☉ Hierà Rosato '12	♥ 3
● Salina Rosso '11	♥ 2
○ Malvasia delle Lipari '10	♀♀ 5
○ Malvasia delle Lipari Passito '10	♀♀ 5
○ Malvasia Passito Carlo Hauner '09	♀♀ 8

Marabino

C.DA BUONIVINI, SP ROSOLINI - PACHINO KM 8,5
97017 NOTO [SR]
TEL. 3355284101
www.marabino.it

CELLAR SALES
PRE-BOOKED VISITS
ACCOMMODATION AND RESTAURANT SERVICE
ANNUAL PRODUCTION 100,000 bottles
HECTARES UNDER VINE 27.00
VITICULTURE METHOD Certified Organic

The entrepreneur Nello Messina established this impressive winery in 2002, and immediately handed over its management to his young son Pierpaolo, who has shown foresight, a clear vision, enthusiasm and skill. The winery's philosophy hinges on respect for the environment, and organic farming methods were adopted from the start. The estate, which straddles the prestigious DOC zones of Eloro and Noto, is now well on its way to completing conversion to biodynamic methods. Worthy of note is the modern cellar and visitors' centre, built in the characteristic style of a traditional south-eastern Sicilian farm. We saw an excellent 2012 version of the Moscato della Torre, reaching our finals with its seductive deep golden hue and elegant nose of candied fruit, acacia honey and citrus, over a silky, invigorating palate with good length. The Eloro Rosato Rosa Nera 2012 is savoury, fresh and pleasurable.

○ Moscato di Noto Moscato della Torre '12	♥♥ 5
☉ Eloro Rosato Rosa Nera '12	♥♥ 3
○ Eureka '12	♥♥ 3
○ Moscato di Noto Muscatedda '12	♥ 3
● Noto Rosso '11	♥ 3
● Eloro Archimede '08	♀♀ 5
● Eloro Archimede '07	♀♀ 4
● Eloro Pachino Archimede Ris. '10	♀♀ 5
○ Moscato di Noto Moscato della Torre '10	♀♀ 5
○ Moscato di Noto Moscato della Torre '09	♀♀ 5
○ Moscato di Noto Moscato della Torre '08	♀♀ 5
○ Moscato di Noto Moscato della Torre '07	♀♀ 5

Occhipinti

c.da Fossa di Lupo via dei Mille, 55
97019 Vittoria [RG]
Tel. 0932868222
www.agricolaocchipinti.it

CELLAR SALES
PRE-BOOKED VISITS
ANNUAL PRODUCTION 120,000 bottles
HECTARES UNDER VINE 18.00
VITICULTURE METHOD Certified Organic

Arianna Occhipinti began to produce wine
when she was barely 20, on a small plot of
land covering less than two hectares. Now
she is 30, and has 18 hectares under vine.
In the meantime, the small cellar, with
barrels stacked on top of each other due to
lack of space, has become a large facility
employing cutting-edge technology.
Arianna's wines manage to combine a
fresh, dynamic, personal style with a sense
of tradition. With Il Frappato 2011 Arianna
Occhipinti wins her first Tre Bicchieri. The
spicy, elegant nose beautifully combines
bags of red berry fruit with fresh herbal
and floral notes, and is followed by good
progression on the graceful but vibrant
palate, with fresh, dynamic tannins and
terrific length.

● Il Frappato '11	♟♟♟ 5
● Cerasuolo di Vittoria Cl. Grotte Alte '08	♟♟ 6
● SP 68 Bianco '12	♟♟ 4
● SP 68 Rosso '12	♟♟ 3
● Frappato '07	♟♟ 5
● Frappato '06	♟♟ 4
● Frappato '05	♟♟ 4
● Il Frappato '10	♟♟ 4
● Il Frappato '08	♟♟ 4
● Siccagno '09	♟♟ 5
● Siccagno '08	♟♟ 5
● Siccagno '06	♟♟ 4
● Siccagno '05	♟♟ 5
● SP 68 '09	♟♟ 3*
● SP 68 Rosso '11	♟♟ 3
● Vittoria Rosso SP 68 '08	♟♟ 3*

★Palari

loc. Santo Stefano Briga
c.da Barna
98137 Messina
Tel. 090630194
www.palari.it

ANNUAL PRODUCTION 50,000 bottles
HECTARES UNDER VINE 7.00

This unique estate lies on a few hectares of
steep, inhospitable terrain, with inclines of
over 80%, contained with difficulty by stone
terraces and their twisted bush vines, some
very old, bearing just a few clusters of
grapes. A charming 18th-century villa
houses the cellar, and offers breathtaking
views over the Straits of Messina and the
Calabrian coast. There is an artisanal,
almost sartorial air about the prestigious,
renowned winery of Salvatore Geraci,
architect and globetrotter, and his brother
Giampiero, a great "man of action". Their
limited production is appreciated by critics
and wine lovers for its elegance and sense
of place, and enjoys an international cult
following. This year the Faro Palari 2011
will be left to rest in the cellar. Its many
fans will console themselves with what is
perhaps the best ever version of the Rosso
del Soprano, the 2011. This marvellously
fresh, nerello mascalese-heavy blend is
sublimely stylish, and romps off with a Tre
Bicchieri.

● Rosso del Soprano '11	♟♟♟ 4*
● Faro Palari '09	♟♟♟ 6
● Faro Palari '08	♟♟♟ 6
● Faro Palari '07	♟♟♟ 6
● Faro Palari '06	♟♟♟ 6
● Faro Palari '05	♟♟♟ 6*
● Faro Palari '04	♟♟♟ 7
● Faro Palari '03	♟♟♟ 6
● Faro Palari '02	♟♟♟ 6
● Faro Palari '01	♟♟♟ 6
● Faro Palari '00	♟♟♟ 6
● Rosso del Soprano '10	♟♟♟ 4*
● Rosso del Soprano '07	♟♟♟ 4

Tenuta Palmeri

C.DA BOCHINI - FIUMARELLA
96012 AVOLA [SR]
TEL. 3345646866
www.cantinapalmeri.it

ANNUAL PRODUCTION 28,000 bottles
HECTARES UNDER VINE 11.00

The story of German-Swiss couple Ueli and
Erika Breitschmid is quite touching. They fell
in love with Sicily back in 2001 and decided
to put down roots here. Ueli, a businessman
who speaks perfect Italian, worldwide
interests, and other wine estates in Europe,
bought ten hectares in the homeland of
nero d'Avola. A full refurbishment was
implemented and winery buildings
recovered, with the addition of a
state-of-the-art cellar. The rules of
engagement for oenologists and
agronomists are inflexible: no more than
four clusters per vine, hand-picked in crates
of a few kilos, constant use of cold
temperatures to avoid pre-fermentation, and
vinification only of perfect fruit.Purplish and
inky-hued, the balsamic Palmeri Blu 2010,
from nero d'Avola and cabernet sauvignon,
shows uncontainable energy alongside
admirably balanced acidity, softness and
tannins. The Grillo Chardonnay 2009
opens to a lovely nose of fruit and spring
flowers, and finishes long. The rest of the
range impressed.

○ Palmeri Bianco Grillo Chardonnay '09	♟♟ 4
● Palmeri Blu '10	♟♟ 5
● Palmeri Rosso '10	♟♟ 6
● Palmeri Rosso '09	♟♟ 6
○ Palmeri Bianco '11	♟ 4
● Palmeri Rosso '10	♟♟ 6

Passopisciaro

LOC. PASSOPISCIARO
VIA SANTO SPIRITO
95030 CASTIGLIONE DI SICILIA [CT]
TEL. 0578267110
www.passopisciaro.com

CELLAR SALES
ANNUAL PRODUCTION 60,000 bottles
HECTARES UNDER VINE 26.00

Although hailing from Tuscany, Andrea
Franchetti can be considered one of the
founding fathers of Etna's wine-making
renaissance. His arrival on the volcano
effectively paved the way for many other
producers, who subsequently invested in
this unique terroir where the same variety,
nerello mascalese, gives widely varying
results depending on where it is grown.
This is why Franchetti, in addition to the
main estate where he has also planted
non-native varieties such as cesanese
d'Affile, petit verdot and chardonnay, has
over time acquired vineyards in five other
areas, each possessing different altitudes
and soil composition. Andrea Franchetti got
the best out of the 2011 vintage in a
difficult growing year on Etna. His Contrada
G, a monovarietal nerello mascalese, wins
a Tre Bicchieri for its subtle, elegant
balsamic and mineral notes, over a velvety,
dynamic palate with incredible length. The
other labels, all from 2011, are very good.

● Contrada G '11	♟♟♟ 6
● Contrada R '11	♟♟ 6
● Contrada C '11	♟♟ 6
● Contrada P '11	♟♟ 7
● Contrada S '11	♟♟ 6
● Franchetti '11	♟♟ 8
● Passopisciaro '11	♟♟ 5
● Contrada P '10	♟♟♟ 7
● Contrada P '09	♟♟♟ 7
● Contrada C '09	♟♟ 6
● Contrada Porcaria '08	♟♟ 7
● Contrada R '10	♟♟ 6
● Passopisciaro '08	♟♟ 5
● Passopisciaro '07	♟♟ 5

Carlo Pellegrino

VIA DEL FANTE, 39
91025 MARSALA [TP]
TEL. 0923719911
www.carlopellegrino.it

CELLAR SALES
PRE-BOOKED VISITS
ANNUAL PRODUCTION 7,000,000 bottles
HECTARES UNDER VINE 100.00

The quality of its wines and its capable management has made this one of Sicily's leading wineries since its establishment in 1880. Today, it is in the capable hands of Pietro Alagna and Benedetto Renda, Chairman and CEO respectively, who have brought it international acclaim. The fascinating historical cellars in the centre of Marsala testify to a tradition originally based on Marsala wine, which over time was joined by other products, all admirably well-typed, faithful expressions of the various zones where the winery's vast estates are situated. They have also done exceptional work on Pantelleria, bringing the best out of moscato d'Alessandria, known in Sicily as zibibbo. This historic operation proved its worth, easily winning a Tre Bicchieri for its excellent Marsala Superiore Ambra Semisecco Riserva 1985, the epitome of finesse, character and sweetness. The exquisite Zibibbo Secco Gibelè 2012 is also on great form, and made our finals. The rest of the range is impeccable.

○ Marsala Sup. Ambra Semisecco Ris. '85	♈♈♈ 4*
○ Duca di Castelmonte Gibelè '12	♈♈ 3*
● Duca di Castelmonte Dinari del Duca Syrah '11	♈♈ 3
○ Duca di Castelmonte Tripudium Bianco '12	♈♈ 3
● Duca di Castelmonte Tripudium Rosso '10	♈♈ 4
● Marsala Fine Rubino	♈♈ 3
○ Marsala Sup. Oro Dolce Ris.	♈♈ 3
● Alicante Incarrozza '10	♈ 3
● Syrah Incarrozza '08	♈ 3
○ Marsala Vergine Ris. '81	♈♈♈ 6
○ Passito di Pantelleria Nes '09	♈♈♈ 5
● Tripudium Rosso Duca di Castelmonte '09	♈♈♈ 4*

Pietradolce

FRAZ. SOLICCHIATA
C.DA RAMPANTE
95012 CASTIGLIONE DI SICILIA [CT]
TEL. 3474037792
www.pietradolce.it

ANNUAL PRODUCTION 24,000 bottles
HECTARES UNDER VINE 11.00

When they decided to turn their few hectares of vineyard into a fully fledged winery, the dynamic duo of Michele and Mario Faro set themselves a precise schedule for completion of the project. So far they are right on time, and recent acquisitions have brought their vineyard holdings to almost a dozen hectares, three of which at Rampante have now commenced production. New to the range are a rosé and an extraordinary selection of Nerello Mascalese, named after the pre-phylloxera Barbagalli vineyard at Rampante lying at an altitude of 900 metres. The supremely elegant Etna Rosso Vigna Barbagalli 2011, from nerello mascalese, took top honours for its fine combination of jammy, red berry fruit, spices and mineral notes. The Etna Rosso Pietradolce 2012 made the finals with its silky tannins. We loved the tangy Etna Bianco Archineri 2012, from carricante.

● Etna Rosso V. Barbagalli '10	♈♈♈ 8
● Etna Rosso Pietradolce '12	♈♈ 5
○ Etna Bianco Archineri '12	♈♈ 5
○ Etna Rosato '12	♈♈ 5
● Etna Rosso Archineri '11	♈♈ 5
● Etna Rosso Archineri '10	♈♈♈ 5
● Etna Rosso Archineri '08	♈♈♈ 3*
● Etna Rosso Archineri '07	♈♈♈ 3*
○ Etna Bianco Archineri '11	♈♈ 5
● Etna Rosso Archineri '09	♈♈ 3

★★Planeta

C.DA DISPENSA
92013 MENFI [AG]
TEL. 091327965
www.planeta.it

PRE-BOOKED VISITS
ACCOMMODATION AND RESTAURANT SERVICE
ANNUAL PRODUCTION 2,300,000 bottles
HECTARES UNDER VINE 364.00

With the new cellar at Castiglione di Sicilia on Etna, a beautiful, well-proportioned lava stone construction perfectly integrated into the landscape, Planeta now owns five estates in what are traditionally considered the best wine-growing zones in Sicily. The company philosophy strives to keep the environmental impact of its production facilities to a minimum, to fully respect the area's historically established wine-making tradition and, above all, to work on building personal relations and synergies with other local growers, convinced that this is the best way to foster the territory's positive growth. We were bowled over by the quality of the wines sent by Planeta for this year's tastings. An epitome of elegance, the Nero d'Avola Santa Cecilia 2010 won a Tre Bicchieri, offering a perfect interpretation of what is some of the island's best wine country, near Noto.

● Noto Santa Cecilia '10	▼▼▼ 5
○ Cometa '12	▼▼ 5
○ Alastro '12	▼▼ 2*
● Burdese '10	▼▼ 4
○ Carricante Eruzione 1614 '12	▼▼ 3
● Cerasuolo di Vittoria Cl. Dorilli '11	▼▼ 3
○ Chardonnay '11	▼▼ 5
● Nerello Mascalese Eruzione 1614 '11	▼▼ 4
○ Passito di Noto '11	▼▼ 5
● Plumbago '11	▼▼ 2*
● Sito dell'Ulmo '10	▼▼ 4
○ Chardonnay '10	♀♀♀ 5
○ Cometa '09	♀♀♀ 5
○ Cometa '08	♀♀♀ 5
● Plumbago '09	♀♀♀ 2*

Poggio di Bortolone

FRAZ. ROCCAZZO
VIA BORTOLONE, 19
97010 CHIARAMONTE GULFI [RG]
TEL. 0932921161
www.poggiodibortolone.it

CELLAR SALES
PRE-BOOKED VISITS
ACCOMMODATION AND RESTAURANT SERVICE
ANNUAL PRODUCTION 80,000 bottles
HECTARES UNDER VINE 15.00

For over two centuries the Cosenza family has cultivated its lands in the heart of the Cerasuolo di Vittoria terroir, in Chiaramonte Gulfi, where the Para Para and Mazzarronello streams meet, and Mediterranean scrub alternates with vines, olive groves and wheat. The modern winery was founded in the early 1970s by Ignazio Cosenza, father of the current owner, Pierluigi. Some 20 years later, international varieties such as cabernet sauvignon, syrah and petit verdot were introduced alongside traditional local vines of frappato and nero d'Avola. The cellar also has some grosso nero, a local wine and table variety that is almost extinct. The Frappato 2011 almost made the finals, with charming fruit and spice over a pleasing palate. The mature, silky Cerasuolo Contessa Costanza 2010 showed great length, and perfectly embodied the winery's style. The vineyard selection Vigna Para Para 2010 was a tad rustic on the nose, but pleasing in the mouth.

● Addamanera '11	▼▼ 2*
● Cerasuolo di Vittoria Contessa Costanza '10	▼▼ 3
● Cerasuolo di Vittoria Poggio di Bortolone '10	▼▼ 3
● Cerasuolo di Vittoria V. Para Para '10	▼▼ 4
● Frappato '11	▼▼ 2*
● Cerasuolo di Vittoria V. Para Para '05	♀♀♀ 4
● Cerasuolo di Vittoria Poggio di Bortolone '08	♀♀ 3
● Cerasuolo di Vittoria V. Para Para '08	♀♀ 4
● Pigi Rosso '07	♀♀ 5
● Pigi Rosso '06	♀♀ 5

Cantine Rallo

VIA VINCENZO FLORIO, 2
91025 MARSALA [TP]
TEL. 0923721633
www.cantinerallo.it

CELLAR SALES
PRE-BOOKED VISITS
ANNUAL PRODUCTION 250,000 bottles
HECTARES UNDER VINE 100.00
VITICULTURE METHOD Certified Organic

The fine winery of Andrea Vesco, whose dedication and clear vision are all-consuming, was one of the first in Sicily to go organic and seriously take into account the concept of biodiversity. Environmental compatibility is thus ensured by alternating vineyards with woodland – although the estate also contains olive groves, orchards and arable land – and using green manure to fertilize the land planted to vine. Grillo, catarratto, nero d'Avola and syrah, the four most widely planted varieties, give focused, uncompromising, yet appealingly drinkable wines with intact fruit that perfectly reflect the terroir. Andrea Vesco's winery has made a quantum leap in terms of quality, as the excellent wines presented this year proved. A Tre Bicchieri goes to the wonderfully stylish Bianco Maggiore 2012, vaunting floral aromas alongside tropical fruit and citrus, with a fresh, zesty palate and lingering finish.

○ Bianco Maggiore '12	♟♟♟ 3*
○ Alcamo Beleda '12	♟♟ 2*
○ Passito di Pantelleria Bugeber '10	♟♟ 5
○ Al Quasar '12	♟♟ 3
○ Marsala Soleras Venti Anni Ris. '80	♟♟ 6
● Nero d'Avola Il Principe '12	♟♟ 2*
● Syrah La Clarissa '12	♟♟ 2*
● Alcamo Nero d'Avola '09	♟♟ 2*
○ Beleda '11	♟♟ 4
○ Bianco Maggiore '11	♟♟ 3
● Nero d'Avola Il Principe '11	♟♟ 2*
● Nero d'Avola Il Principe '09	♟♟ 2*
● Syrah La Clarissa '11	♟♟ 2*
● Syrah La Clarissa '08	♟♟ 2*

Tenute Rapitalà

C.DA RAPITALÀ
90043 CAMPOREALE [PA]
TEL. 092437233
www.rapitala.it

CELLAR SALES
PRE-BOOKED VISITS
ANNUAL PRODUCTION 2,800,000 bottles
HECTARES UNDER VINE 175.00

Rapitalà, one of Sicily's most famous wine houses, was established 45 years ago as a result of the enduring love affair between Gigi Guarrasi and Hugues Bernard de la Gatinais. They shared a passion for their wine and the territory it embodies – the hills that gently slope down from Camporeale to Alcamo and the sea. Here, reflecting their own bond, they planted catarratto alongside chardonnay, and nero d'Avola next to pinot noir, aiming to create attractive, richly nuanced wines with an unmistakable style and a noble, generous character. Their dream lives on in the capable hands of their son Laurent, who now heads the winery, which for some time has been part of Gruppo Italiano Vini. The Chardonnay Grand Cru 2011 made the finals thanks to its subtle aromas and vibrant, focused structure, accompanied by an exemplary use of oak. It was joined by the balsamic, smooth Hugonis 2011, from cabernet sauvignon and nero d'Avola. We were also pleased with the rest of the range.

○ Conte Hugues Bernard de la Gatinais Grand Cru '11	♟♟ 4
● Hugonis '11	♟♟ 5
○ Conte Hugues Bernard de la Gatinais Grand Cru '10	♟♟♟ 4*
● Hugonis '01	♟♟♟ 6
● Solinero '03	♟♟♟ 5
● Hugonis '10	♟♟ 5
● Hugonis '09	♟♟ 5
● Nadir '10	♟♟ 3
● Nuhar '10	♟♟ 3
● Nuhar '09	♟♟ 3
● Solinero '10	♟♟ 5

Riofavara

c.da Favara SP 49 Ispica - Pachino
97014 Ispica [RG]
Tel. 0932705130
www.riofavara.it

CELLAR SALES
PRE-BOOKED VISITS
ACCOMMODATION AND RESTAURANT SERVICE
ANNUAL PRODUCTION 70,000 bottles
HECTARES UNDER VINE 21.00
VITICULTURE METHOD Certified Organic

This small family company was established in 1920 and for almost three-quarters of a century focused solely on viticulture. In 1994 wine production began at the initiative of Massimo and Marianta Padova, who own 16 hectares of vineyards in excellent wine country, distributed over six plots in the Eloro and Moscato di Noto DOC zones. Marked by a distinctive adherence to territorial values, Riofavara's wines are made exclusively from organically grown grapes vinified using self-selected ambient yeasts in order to keep their sensory profile intact. Pending release of the Sciavè 2011, we tried the excellent, attractively mineral Nero d'Avola San Basilio 2011. The Moscato di Noto Notissimo 2012 nearly made the finals, showing sweet, fresh and leisurely, with captivating lavender aromas. The white blend, Marzaiolo 2012, is zesty and crisp.

○ Marzaiolo '12	♟♟	3
○ Moscato di Noto Notissimo '12	♟♟	3
● San Basilio '11	♟♟	3
● Eloro Nero d'Avola Sciavé '10	♟♟	4
● Eloro Nero d'Avola Sciavé '09	♟♟	4
○ Marzaiolo '11	♟♟	2*
○ Moscato di Noto Notissimo '11	♟♟	3
○ Moscato di Noto Notissimo '09	♟♟	3
● San Basilio '10	♟♟	2*

Girolamo Russo

loc. Passopisciaro
via Regina Margherita, 78
95012 Castiglione di Sicilia [CT]
Tel. 3283840247
www.girolamorusso.it

CELLAR SALES
PRE-BOOKED VISITS
ANNUAL PRODUCTION 35,000 bottles
HECTARES UNDER VINE 15.00
VITICULTURE METHOD Certified Organic

In recent years many have described Etna as Italy's Burgundy. Although such a comparison may seem a little far-fetched to some, the volcano is nevertheless home to extraordinary winemakers like Giuseppe Russo, who would feel entirely at home as a vigneron in Beaune. He shows a deep attachment to his land and vineyards, that he tends personally with dedication and painstaking care, separately vinifying grapes from each plot. The work of a year in the rows always translates into bewitching, original wines, with a marked sense of place and rare elegance. The austerely deep, elegant Etna Rosso Feudo 2011, from nerello mascalese and cappuccio, wins a Tre Bicchieri, with blood-rich meat, iron filings and floral notes, followed by a soft, fresh palate. The Etna Rosso 'A Rina 2011 shows territorial aromas of minerals and iodine, but is still a touch edgy and sharp.

● Etna Rosso Feudo '11	♟♟♟	5
● Etna Rosso 'A Rina '11	♟♟	5
● Etna Rosso Feudo '11	♟♟	5
● Etna Rosso San Lorenzo '11	♟♟	5
○ Etna Bianco Nerina '12	♟	6
● Etna Rosso Feudo '10	♟♟♟	5
● Etna Rosso Feudo '07	♟♟♟	5
● Etna Rosso San Lorenzo '09	♟♟♟	5
○ Etna Bianco Nerina '11	♟♟	5
● Etna Rosso 'A Rina '10	♟♟	4
● Etna Rosso Feudo '08	♟♟	5
● Etna Rosso San Lorenzo '10	♟♟	5
● Etna Rosso San Lorenzo '07	♟♟	5
● Etna Rosso San Lorenzo '06	♟♟	5

Settesoli

SS 115
92013 Menfi [AG]
Tel. 092577111
www.cantinesettesoli.it

CELLAR SALES
PRE-BOOKED VISITS
ANNUAL PRODUCTION 20,000,000 bottles
HECTARES UNDER VINE 6500.00
VITICULTURE METHOD Certified Organic

This colossal co-operative winery boasts 2,300 growers and 6,000 hectares under vine, and for decades was expanded and run with great skill by its chairman Diego Planeta, who took it to unimagined heights. Its philosophy is based on two concepts, simple yet difficult to put into practice: thinking, seeing and acting in unison, and encouraging among the members a sense of responsibility for their vineyards, rewarding quality and "healthy" viticulture. At the end of 2011 Diego Planeta stepped down, making way for Vito Varvaro, for some years a member of his illustrious predecessor's team. Since the late 1990s the Mandrarossa line has included the winery's best labels and its vineyard selections. The Nero d'Avola Cartagho 2011 nearly won top honours with its character, stuffing and harmonious fullness. The Sauvignon Blanc Urra di Mare 2012 showed fresh and stylish. Settesoli released two excellent Seligo 2012s, one from nero d'Avola and syrah, the other from grillo and chardonnay.

● Cartagho Mandrarossa '11	♟♟ 3*
○ Seligo Bianco '12	♟♟ 3
● Seligo Rosso '12	♟♟ 2*
○ Urra di Mare Mandrarossa '12	♟♟ 3
● Cavadiserpe Mandrarossa '12	♟ 4
○ Grillo Isola '12	♟ 2
● Nero d'Avola Isola '12	♟ 2
○ Santannella Mandrarossa '12	♟ 3
● Cartagho Mandrarossa '09	♟♟♟ 3*
● Cartagho Mandrarossa '08	♟♟♟ 3*
● Cartagho Mandrarossa '06	♟♟♟ 3
● Mandrarossa Cavadiserpe '09	♟♟ 4
● Seligo Rosso '11	♟♟ 2*

Spadafora

via Ausonia, 90
90144 Palermo
Tel. 091514952
www.spadafora.com

CELLAR SALES
PRE-BOOKED VISITS
ACCOMMODATION AND RESTAURANT SERVICE
ANNUAL PRODUCTION 280,000 bottles
HECTARES UNDER VINE 95.00

In the early 1970s, Don Pietro Spadafora decided to devote himself to the family's land at Virzì, in the sun-kissed hills between Alcamo and the Monreale DOC zone. He repaired the farmhouses damaged by the 1968 earthquake and renovated the olive groves and vineyards, also planting international varieties such as cabernet, chardonnay and syrah. In 1993 he began to produce his own wine, converting some of the farmhouses into a modernly equipped cellar, while furnishing others for holiday accommodation. Francesco, who succeeded his father Pietro in 1988, personally supervises every phase of the production cycle, from the use of organic farming methods in the rows to vinification. The well-coordinated Schietto Nero d'Avola 2010 is an expression of austere elegance, with plush, juicy fruit. Stylish maturity and a pleasantly weighty palate are the hallmarks of the Schietto Syrah 2008, while the fresh, zesty Don Pietro Bianco 2012, from catarratto, grillo and inzolia, shows good focus.

○ Don Pietro Bianco '12	♟♟ 2*
● Schietto Nero d'Avola '10	♟♟ 4
● Schietto Syrah '08	♟♟ 3
○ Alhambra Bianco '12	♟ 2
● Alhambra Rosso '11	♟ 2
● Don Pietro Rosso '10	♟ 3
⊙ Nero d'Avola Rosato '12	♟ 2
● Syrah '11	♟ 2
● Don Pietro Rosso '09	♟♟ 3
● Don Pietro Rosso '08	♟♟ 3
⊙ Nero d'Avola Rosato '11	♟♟ 2*
● Schietto Cabernet Sauvignon '08	♟♟ 4
● Sole dei Padri '08	♟♟ 6
● Syrah '09	♟♟ 2

★★Tasca d'Almerita

C.DA REGALEALI
90129 SCLAFANI BAGNI [PA]
TEL. 0916459711
www.tascadalmerita.it

CELLAR SALES
PRE-BOOKED VISITS
ACCOMMODATION AND RESTAURANT SERVICE
ANNUAL PRODUCTION 3,000,000 bottles
HECTARES UNDER VINE 346.00

This great family has an indissoluble bond with its land, in particular the magnificent Regaleali estate in the heart of Sicily. In the space of only a few years, the energy and astute management of Conte Giuseppe Tasca d'Almerita led to the creation of a recognizable Sicilian brand in a different league to the few other quality wineries around at the time, small islands in an ocean of unbottled wine. Above all, it was able to compete with the big names in the rest of Italy and further afield. Giuseppe's work continues through Lucio and his sons Giuseppe and Alberto, who have consolidated past success as well as investing in new wine-growing areas on the island of Salina and Etna. A Tre Bicchieri goes to the magnificent Cabernet Sauvignon 2010. Extraordinary fruit, well-focused balsam and mineral notes are followed by majestic, ethereal grace on the palate and a leisurely finish. The soft, summery Chardonnay 2011 also made the finals. The Buonora 2012, a Carricante, made a fine debut.

● Contea di Sclafani Cabernet Sauvignon '10	♛♛♛	5
○ Chardonnay '11	♛♛	5
⊙ Almerita Rosé Brut '08	♛♛	6
○ Buonora '12	♛♛	3
○ Cavallo delle Fate '12	♛♛	3
○ Contea di Sclafani Almerita Brut '10	♛♛	5
○ Contea di Sclafani Almerita Extra Brut '08	♛♛	6
○ Diamante d'Almerita '12	♛♛	5
● Ghiaia Nera '11	♛♛	3
● Cabernet Sauvignon '07	♛♛♛	5
○ Chardonnay '06	♛♛♛	5
● Contea di Sclafani Rosso del Conte '07	♛♛♛	6
● Contea di Sclafani Rosso del Conte '05	♛♛♛	6
● Contea di Sclafani Rosso del Conte '04	♛♛♛	6
● Contea di Sclafani Rosso del Conte '03	♛♛♛	5

Terrazze dell'Etna

C.DA BOCCA D'ORZO
95036 RANDAZZO [CT]
TEL. 0916236343
www.terrazzedelletna.it

CELLAR SALES
PRE-BOOKED VISITS
ANNUAL PRODUCTION 120,000 bottles
HECTARES UNDER VINE 23.00

In the municipality of Randazzo, on the north-western slopes of Etna, at elevations of between 700 and 800 metres, we find Nino Bevilacqua's estate, on a site where until a few years ago brambles and weeds reigned undisturbed. This respected engineer and wine lover built a splendid winery here in record time, restoring an extraordinary site to its former beauty, and at the same time bringing out the best of the area's breathtaking landscape with admirable skill and respect. His modern-styled wines stand out for their clear focus. The Etna Rosso Cirneco 2010, from nerello mascalese and cappuccio, offers intense black berry fruit and pencil lead, with a soft, lively weave and a slightly clenched finish. The stylish, fruity, mineral Carusu 2011 comes from nerello mascalese and cappuccio.

● Etna Rosso Cirneco '10	♛♛	6
○ Ciuri '12	♛♛	3
● Etna Rosso Carusu '11	♛♛	4
⊙ Rosé Brut '10	♛♛	5
○ Cuvée Brut '09	♛	5
● Etna Rosso Cirneco '09	♛♛♛	6
● Etna Rosso Cirneco '08	♛♛♛	5
○ Cuvée Brut '08	♛♛	5
⊙ Rosé Brut '09	♛♛	5
⊙ Rosé Brut '08	♛♛	5

Tenuta delle Terre Nere

C.DA CALDERARA
95036 RANDAZZO [CT]
TEL. 095924002
www.tenutaterrenere.com

CELLAR SALES
PRE-BOOKED VISITS
ANNUAL PRODUCTION 200,000 bottles
HECTARES UNDER VINE 28.00
VITICULTURE METHOD Certified Organic

It is no coincidence that once Marc De Grazia decided to producc his own wine, after a life spent selecting and exporting Italian wines all over the world, he chose Etna. This expert of Langhe and Burgundy was one of the first to produce wines that faithfully reflected their various zones of provenance. This decision was undoubtedly justified by the extraordinary diversity of soils on Etna, in which hundreds of lava flows stratified over centuries have created a unique terroir. Marc's direct, uncompromising wines are characterized by a fresh, elegant style, and although capable of superb evolution over the years, can be enjoyed right away. Once again, the Etna Rosso Santo Spirito 2011, from nerello mascalese and cappuccio, took home a Tre Bicchieri. This complex, elegant wine vaunts close-knit, vibrant tannins and a seemingly endless finish. The multifaceted, rich and lingering Prephylloxera 2011 was also extremely pleasing.

● Etna Rosso Santo Spirito '11	♥♥♥ 6
● Etna Rosso Prephylloxera La V. di Don Peppino '11	♥♥ 8
○ Etna Bianco '12	♥♥ 3
○ Etna Bianco Le Vigne Niche '11	♥♥ 6
⊙ Etna Rosato '12	♥♥ 3*
● Etna Rosso Calderara Sottana '11	♥♥ 6
● Etna Rosso Feudo di Mezzo Quadro delle Rose '11	♥♥ 6
● Etna Rosso Guardiola '11	♥♥ 6
● Etna Rosso Feudo di Mezzo Quadro delle Rose '05	♀♀♀ 6
● Etna Rosso Prephylloxera La V. di Don Peppino '07	♀♀♀ 8
● Etna Rosso Prephylloxera La V. di Don Peppino '06	♀♀♀ 8
● Etna Rosso Santo Spirito '10	♀♀♀ 6

Valle dell'Acate

C.DA BIDINI
97011 ACATE [RG]
TEL. 0932874166
www.valledellacate.it

CELLAR SALES
PRE-BOOKED VISITS
ANNUAL PRODUCTION 400,000 bottles
HECTARES UNDER VINE 100.00

Feudo Bidini covers over 100 hectares in the valley of the River Dirillo, whose agate-rich waters led the Greeks and Romans to call it Achates. The local calcareous clay hillside soils in fact have a history of viticulture going back to ancient times. The winery dates back to the 19th century, when it was established by the Jacono family, now in its sixth generation of growers, represented by the energetic Gaetana, responsible for the winery's international success, as well as for restoring the cellar and modernizing the equipment. Her production philosophy focuses on bringing the best out of local grapes skilfully blended with non-native varieties, using sustainable farming practices. The graceful Nero d'Avola Il Moro 2010 boasts typical Mediterranean notes, while sweet spice and incense combine with a mature, crisp palate in the Tanè 2010, from nero d'Avola and syrah. The Cerasuolo di Vittoria Classico 2010 is pleasing, while the Il Frappato 2012 offers fresh, fragrant fruit.

○ Bidis '11	♥♥ 4
● Cerasuolo di Vittoria Cl. '10	♥♥ 3
● Il Moro '10	♥♥ 3
● Tanè '10	♥♥ 5
● Vittoria Il Frappato '12	♥♥ 2*
○ Bidis '10	♥ 4
● Rusciano '10	♥ 4
○ Vittoria Inzolia '12	♥ 2
○ Zagra '12	♥ 2
○ Bidis '09	♀♀ 3
● Cerasuolo di Vittoria Cl. '09	♀♀ 3
● Il Moro '09	♀♀ 3
● Vittoria Il Frappato '11	♀♀ 2*
○ Zagra '11	♀♀ 2*

Alliata

VIA ARCHI 9
91100 TRAPANI
TEL. 0923547267
www.alliatavini.com

ANNUAL PRODUCTION 100,000 bottles
HECTARES UNDER VINE 82.00

○ Daxia '11	♥♥ 3
● Kaspar '10	♥♥ 5
○ Taya '11	♥♥ 3
○ Insola '12	♥ 3

Avide

C.DA MASTRELLA, 346
97013 COMISO [RG]
TEL. 0932967456
www.avide.it

CELLAR SALES
PRE-BOOKED VISITS
ANNUAL PRODUCTION 250,000 bottles
HECTARES UNDER VINE 68.00

● Cerasuolo di Vittoria Cl. Barocco '07	♥♥ 6
● Sigillo '07	♥♥ 6
● Cerasuolo di Vittoria Et. Nera '10	♥ 4
○ Maria Stella Inzolia '12	♥ 4

Biondi

C.SO SICILIA, 20
95039 TRECASTAGNI [CT]
TEL. 0957633933
www.levignebiondi.it

CELLAR SALES
PRE-BOOKED VISITS
ANNUAL PRODUCTION 20,000 bottles
HECTARES UNDER VINE 14.00

○ Carricante Chianta '11	♥♥ 5
● Cisterna Fuori '11	♥♥ 5

Biscaris

VIA MARESCIALLO GIUDICE, 52
97011 ACATE [RG]
TEL. 0932990762
www.biscaris.it

CELLAR SALES
ANNUAL PRODUCTION 80,000 bottles
HECTARES UNDER VINE 10.00
VITICULTURE METHOD Certified Biodynamic

● Cerasuolo di Vittoria Pricipuzzu '11	♥♥ 3
● Frappato Baruneddu '12	♥♥ 2
● Nero d'Avola Cavalieri '12	♥ 2

Bonavita

LOC. FARO SUPERIORE
C.DA CORSO
98158 MESSINA
TEL. 3471754983
www.bonavitafaro.it

PRE-BOOKED VISITS
ANNUAL PRODUCTION 5,000 bottles
HECTARES UNDER VINE 2.00

● Faro '11	♥♥ 5
⊙ Rosato '12	♥♥ 4

Brugnano

C.DA SAN CARLO, SS 113, KM 307
90047 PARTINICO [PA]
TEL. 0918783360
www.brugnano.it

CELLAR SALES
PRE-BOOKED VISITS
ANNUAL PRODUCTION 120,000 bottles
HECTARES UNDER VINE 45.00

● Lunario Rosso '10	♥♥ 3
○ V90 Bianco '12	♥ 2
● V90 Nero d'Avola '11	♥ 2
● V90 Syrah '12	♥ 2

Buceci

LOC. C.DA ROCCABIANCA
VIA UNITÀ D'ITALIA, 3
90035 MARINEO [PA]
TEL. 0918726367
www.bucecivini.it

CELLAR SALES
PRE-BOOKED VISITS
ANNUAL PRODUCTION 100,000 bottles
HECTARES UNDER VINE 150.00
VITICULTURE METHOD Certified Organic

● Buceci Rosso '09	♟♟ 3
● Doncarmè Rosso '08	♟ 3
○ Inzolia '12	♟ 2
● Nero D'Avola '12	♟ 3

Calatrasi

C.DA PIANO PIRAINO
90040 SAN CIPIRELLO [PA]
TEL. 0918576767
www.calatrasi.it

CELLAR SALES
PRE-BOOKED VISITS
RESTAURANT SERVICE
ANNUAL PRODUCTION 2.000,000 bottles
HECTARES UNDER VINE 650.00
VITICULTURE METHOD Certified Organic

● Terre di Ginestra 651 Nero d'Avola Syrah '11	♟♟ 4
● Terre di Ginestra Magnifico Syrah '11	♟♟ 3
○ Terre di Ginestra 651 Chardonnay '11	♟ 3

Calcagno

FRAZ. PASSOPISCIARO
VIA REGINA MARGHERITA
95012 CASTIGLIONE DI SICILIA [CT]
TEL. 3387772780
www.vinicalcagno.it

CELLAR SALES
PRE-BOOKED VISITS
ANNUAL PRODUCTION 10,000 bottles
HECTARES UNDER VINE 2.00

● Etna Rosso Arcuria '11	♟♟ 4
○ Carricante '12	♟ 3

Paolo Calì

LOC. C.DA SALMÈ
SP VITTORIA PEDALINO, KM 2,500
VIA DEL FRAPPA
97019 VITTORIA [RG]
TEL. 0932510082

ANNUAL PRODUCTION 50,000 bottles
HECTARES UNDER VINE 14.00

● Vittoria Nero d'Avola Violino '10	♟♟ 3*
● Cerasuolo di Vittoria Cl. Manene '11	♟ 4
⊙ Frappato Rosato Osa '12	♟ 2
● Vittoria Frappato Mandragola '12	♟ 3

Cantina Viticoltori Associati Canicattì

C.DA AQUILATA
92024 CANICATTÌ [AG]
TEL. 0922829371
www.cvacanicatti.it

CELLAR SALES
PRE-BOOKED VISITS
ANNUAL PRODUCTION 900,000 bottles
HECTARES UNDER VINE 1000.00

● Aquilae Cabernet Sauvignon '11	♟♟ 2*
○ Aquilae Catarratto '12	♟ 2
● Aquilae Nero d'Avola '11	♟ 2
○ Fileno '12	♟ 2

Caruso & Minini

VIA SALEMI, 3
91025 MARSALA [TP]
TEL. 0923982356
www.carusoeminini.it

CELLAR SALES
PRE-BOOKED VISITS
ANNUAL PRODUCTION 530,000 bottles
HECTARES UNDER VINE 120.00

○ Inzolia '12	♟♟ 3*
○ Corte Ferro '12	♟ 3
● Cutaja '11	♟ 3
○ Timpune Grillo '12	♟ 3

La Casa di Filippo

C.DA ARRIGO SP 59 LINGUAGLOSSA ZAFFERANA KM 2,2
95015 LINGUAGLOSSA [CT]
TEL. 3472347826
www.lacasadifilippo.it

ANNUAL PRODUCTION 3,000 bottles
HECTARES UNDER VINE 1.50

● Etna Rosso '11	♥♥ 4

Le Casematte

LOC. FARO SUPERIORE
C.DA CORSO
98163 MESSINA
TEL. 0906409427
www.lecasematte.it

● Faro Quattroenne '11	♥♥ 5
● Figliodiennenne '11	♥♥ 2*

Ceuso

LOC. SEGESTA
C.DA VIVIGNATO
91013 CALATAFIMI [TP]
TEL. 092422836
www.ceuso.it

PRE-BOOKED VISITS
ANNUAL PRODUCTION 130,000 bottles
HECTARES UNDER VINE 50.00

● Ceuso '10	♥♥ 5
● Fastaia '11	♥♥ 3
○ Scurati Grillo '12	♥ 2
● Scurati Rosso '12	♥ 2

Tenuta Chiuse del Signore

C.DA CHIUSE DEL SIGNORE
SP LINGUAGLOSSA-ZAFFERANA KM 2
95015 LINGUAGLOSSA [CT]
TEL. 0942611340
www.gaishotels.com

CELLAR SALES
PRE-BOOKED VISITS
ANNUAL PRODUCTION 45,000 bottles
HECTARES UNDER VINE 50.00

⊙ Rasule Alte Rosato '12	♥♥ 2
● Rasule Alte Rosso '12	♥♥ 2*
○ Rasule Alte Bianco '12	♥ 3

COS

SP 3 AGATE-CHIARAMONTE KM 14,300
97019 VITTORIA [RG]
TEL. 0932876145
www.cosvittoria.it

CELLAR SALES
PRE-BOOKED VISITS
ANNUAL PRODUCTION 160,000 bottles
HECTARES UNDER VINE 30.00
VITICULTURE METHOD Certified Organic

● Cerasuolo di Vittoria Cl. '10	♥♥ 4
● Nero di Lupo '12	♥♥ 3
● Pithos Rosso '11	♥ 4

Curto

SS 115 ISPICA - ROSOLINI KM 358
97014 ISPICA [RG]
TEL. 0932950161
www.curto.it

CELLAR SALES
PRE-BOOKED VISITS
ANNUAL PRODUCTION 70,000 bottles
HECTARES UNDER VINE 36.00

● Eloro Nero d'Avola '10	♥♥ 2*
⊙ Eloro Nero d'Avola Eos '12	♥ 2
● Ikano '09	♥ 3
○ Poiano '12	♥ 2

D'Alessandro

C.DA MANDRASCAVA
92100 AGRIGENTO
TEL. 0633623175
www.dalmin.it

CELLAR SALES
PRE-BOOKED VISITS
ANNUAL PRODUCTION 120,000 bottles
HECTARES UNDER VINE 20.00

○ Catarratto '12	♟♟ 3
○ Inzolia '12	♟ 2
● Nero d'Avola '12	♟ 2
● Nero dei Templi '10	♟ 5

Gianfranco Daino

VIA CROCE DEL VICARIO, 115
95041 CALTAGIRONE [CT]
TEL. 093358226
www.vinidaino.it

CELLAR SALES
PRE-BOOKED VISITS
ANNUAL PRODUCTION 18,000 bottles
HECTARES UNDER VINE 2,44

● Suber '11	♟♟ 5

De Gregorio

C.DA RAGANA
92019 SCIACCA [AG]
TEL. 0925991299
www.cantinedegregorio.it

CELLAR SALES
PRE-BOOKED VISITS
ACCOMMODATION AND RESTAURANT SERVICE
ANNUAL PRODUCTION 90,000 bottles
HECTARES UNDER VINE 15.00

○ Dragonara Bianco Grillo '12	♟♟ 2*
○ Bianco di San Lorenzo '12	♟ 3
● Haris '11	♟ 2
○ Rahana Inzolia '12	♟ 2

Destro

LOC. MONTELAGUARDIA
95036 RANDAZZO [CT]
TEL. 095937060
www.destrovini.com

● Etna Rosso Aspide '09	♟♟ 5
○ Etna Bianco Isolanuda '12	♟ 4
● Etna Rosso Sciarakè '09	♟ 5
○ Nausìca '12	♟ 4

Di Giovanna

C.DA SAN GIACOMO
92017 SAMBUCA DI SICILIA [AG]
TEL. 09251955675
www.digiovanna-vini.it

CELLAR SALES
PRE-BOOKED VISITS
ANNUAL PRODUCTION 250,000 bottles
HECTARES UNDER VINE 53.00
VITICULTURE METHOD Certified Organic

○ Grillo '12	♟♟ 2*
○ Helios '12	♟♟ 3*
⊙ Gerbino Rosato Nero d'Avola '12	♟ 2
● Nero d'Avola '11	♟ 3

Gaspare Di Prima

VIA G. GUASTO, 27
92017 SAMBUCA DI SICILIA [AG]
TEL. 0925941201
www.diprimavini.it

CELLAR SALES
PRE-BOOKED VISITS
ANNUAL PRODUCTION 50,000 bottles
HECTARES UNDER VINE 38.00
VITICULTURE METHOD Certified Organic

○ Grillo del Lago '12	♟♟ 2*
● Villamaura Syrah '08	♟♟ 6
● Gibilmoro Merlot '10	♟ 3
⊙ Rosé del Lago '12	♟ 2

Fazio Wines

FRAZ. FULGATORE
VIA CAPITAN RIZZO, 39
91010 ERICE [TP]
TEL. 0923811700
www.faziowines.com

ANNUAL PRODUCTION 750,000 bottles
HECTARES UNDER VINE 100.00

○ Erice Catarratto Calebianche '12	♟♟ 3*
○ Erice Grillo Aegades '12	♟♟ 3
○ Erice Levantio '12	♟ 3
● Erice Torre dei Venti '11	♟ 3

Ferreri

C.DA SALINELLA
91029 SANTA NINFA [TP]
TEL. 092461871
www.ferrerivini.it

CELLAR SALES
PRE-BOOKED VISITS
ANNUAL PRODUCTION 100,000 bottles
HECTARES UNDER VINE 50.00

● Nero d'Avola '12	♟♟ 2*
○ Zibibbo '12	♟♟ 3
○ Catarratto '12	♟ 2
○ Inzolia '12	♟ 2

Feudo Arancio

C.DA PORTELLA MISILBESI
92017 SAMBUCA DI SICILIA [AG]
TEL. 0925579000
www.feudoarancio.it

CELLAR SALES
PRE-BOOKED VISITS
ANNUAL PRODUCTION 800,000 bottles
HECTARES UNDER VINE 650.00

● Cantodoro '11	♟♟ 3
○ Hekate Passito '11	♟♟ 5
○ Dalila '11	♟ 3
● Syrah '11	♟ 3

Feudo di Santa Tresa

S.DA COMUNALE MARANGIO, 35
97019 VITTORIA [RG]
TEL. 0932513126
www.santatresa.it

PRE-BOOKED VISITS
ANNUAL PRODUCTION 250,000 bottles
HECTARES UNDER VINE 38.00
VITICULTURE METHOD Certified Organic

● Frappato '12	♟♟ 2*
● Nìvuro '10	♟♟ 2*
● Cerasuolo di Vittoria Cl. '11	♟ 2
○ Rina Ianca '12	♟ 2

Feudo Montoni

C.DA MONTONI VECCHI
90144 CAMMARATA [AG]
TEL. 091513106
www.feudomontoni.it

CELLAR SALES
PRE-BOOKED VISITS
ANNUAL PRODUCTION 180,000 bottles
HECTARES UNDER VINE 23.00
VITICULTURE METHOD Certified Organic

● Nero d'Avola V. Lagnusa '11	♟♟ 3*
● Nero d'Avola Vrucara '10	♟♟ 5
○ Catarratto V. del Masso '12	♟ 3
○ Grillo V. della Timpa '12	♟ 3

Feudo Ramaddini

FRAZ. MARZAMENI
C.DA LETTIERA
96018 PACHINO [SR]
TEL. 09311847100
www.feudoramaddini.com

CELLAR SALES
PRE-BOOKED VISITS
ANNUAL PRODUCTION 35,000 bottles
HECTARES UNDER VINE 17.00

○ Passito di Noto Al Hamen '12	♟♟ 5
○ 420 quattroventi '12	♟ 3
○ Nassa '12	♟ 2
● Note Nere Nero d'Avola '11	♟ 2

Fondo Antico

FRAZ. RILIEVO
VIA FIORAME, 54A
91100 TRAPANI
TEL. 0923864339
www.fondoantico.it

CELLAR SALES
PRE-BOOKED VISITS
ANNUAL PRODUCTION 400,000 bottles
HECTARES UNDER VINE 35.00

● Baccadoro	♚♚ 3
○ Grillo Parlante '12	♚ 2
● Il Canto di Fondo Antico '10	♚ 3
● Nero d'Avola '12	♚ 2

Giasira

C.DA RITILLINI
96019 ROSOLINI [SR]
TEL. 0931501700
www.lagiasira.it

● Giasira Rosso '11	♚♚ 3
● Rosso Isabella '11	♚♚ 4
○ Aurantium '12	♚ 4
○ Keration Catarratto Lucido '12	♚ 3

Giovi

VIA VALDINA, 30
98040 VALDINA [ME]
TEL. 0909942256
www.distilleriagiovi.it

ANNUAL PRODUCTION 8,000 bottles
HECTARES UNDER VINE 4,50

● Etna Rosso Akraton '10	♚♚ 3
● Pirao '10	♚ 4

Tenuta Enza La Fauci

C.DA MEZZANA-SPARTÀ
98163 MESSINA
TEL. 3476854318
www.tenutaenzalafauci.com

CELLAR SALES
ACCOMMODATION
ANNUAL PRODUCTION 14,000 bottles
HECTARES UNDER VINE 5.00

● Faro Obli '11	♚♚ 5
● Terra di Vento '11	♚ 5

Maggiovini

LOC. VITTORIA
S.DA COMUNALE MARANGIO, 35
97019 VITTORIA [RG]
TEL. 0932984771
www.maggiovini.it

CELLAR SALES
PRE-BOOKED VISITS
ACCOMMODATION
ANNUAL PRODUCTION 210,000 bottles
HECTARES UNDER VINE 35.00
VITICULTURE METHOD Certified Organic

● Amongae '11	♚♚ 2*
● Cerasuolo di Vittoria V. di Pettineo '12	♚ 2
● Rasula Nero d'Avola '11	♚ 1*
● V. di Pettineo Nero d'Avola '11	♚ 2

Miceli

C.DA PIANA SCUNCHIPANI, 190
92019 SCIACCA [AG]
TEL. 092580188
www.miceli.net

PRE-BOOKED VISITS
ANNUAL PRODUCTION 800,000 bottles
HECTARES UNDER VINE 60.00

○ Passito di Pantelleria Yrnm '11	♚♚ 3
○ Shahar Adonay '12	♚ 4
● Smodato '11	♚ 5
○ Verver '12	♚ 3

Cantina Modica di San Giovanni

C.DA BUFALEFI
96017 NOTO [SR]
TEL. 09311805181
www.olioevinobufalefi.it

CELLAR SALES
PRE-BOOKED VISITS
RESTAURANT SERVICE
ANNUAL PRODUCTION 60,000 bottles
HECTARES UNDER VINE 40.00

● Eloro Nero d' Avola Filinona '09	♟♟ 4
○ Moscato di Noto Dolcenoto '12	♟♟ 5
○ Lupara '12	♟ 3
⊙ Mamma Draja '12	♟ 4

Morgante

C.DA RACALMARE
92020 GROTTE [AG]
TEL. 0922945579
www.morgantevini.it

CELLAR SALES
PRE-BOOKED VISITS
ANNUAL PRODUCTION 283,000 bottles
HECTARES UNDER VINE 52.00

● Don Antonio '11	♟♟ 5
○ Bianco di Morgante '12	♟ 2
● Schinthili '12	♟ 2

Cantine Nicosia

VIA LUIGI CAPUANA
95039 TRECASTAGNI [CT]
TEL. 0957806767
www.cantinenicosia.it

CELLAR SALES
PRE-BOOKED VISITS
ANNUAL PRODUCTION 2.000.000 bottles
HECTARES UNDER VINE 260.00

○ Etna Bianco Fondo Filara '12	♟♟ 3*
● Fondo Filara Sosta Tre Santi Nero d'Avola '09	♟♟ 6

Orestiadi

LOC. C.DA SALINELLA
FRAZ. SANTA NINFA
VIA A. GAGINI, 41
91029 GIBELLINA [TP]
TEL. 092469124
www.orestiadivini.it

CELLAR SALES
PRE-BOOKED VISITS
ANNUAL PRODUCTION 1.300.000 bottles
HECTARES UNDER VINE 160.00
VITICULTURE METHOD Certified Organic

● Agamennone '12	♟♟ 2*
● Cassandra '12	♟ 3
● Molino a Vento Cabernet Sauvignon '12	♟ 2
○ Molino a Vento Inzolia '12	♟ 1*

Ottoventi

C.DA TORREBIANCA - FICO
91019 VALDERICE [TP]
TEL. 0923 1892880
www.cantinaottoventi.it

CELLAR SALES
PRE-BOOKED VISITS
ANNUAL PRODUCTION 80,000 bottles
HECTARES UNDER VINE 35.00

○ Grillo .8 '12	♟♟ 2*
○ Ottoventi Bianco '12	♟♟ 3
○ Grillo '12	♟ 4
● Ottoventi Nero d'Avola '10	♟ 3

Pollara

C.DA MALVELLO
90046 MONREALE [PA]
TEL. 0918462922
www.principedicorleone.it

CELLAR SALES
PRE-BOOKED VISITS
ACCOMMODATION AND RESTAURANT SERVICE
ANNUAL PRODUCTION 1,300,000 bottles
HECTARES UNDER VINE 60.00

● Principe di Corleone Sophia '12	♟♟ 2*
○ Grillo Principe di Corleone '12	♟ 2
○ Principe di Corleone Chardonnay '12	♟ 2
○ Principe di Corleone Rosato '12	♟ 2

Porta del Vento

C.DA VALDIBELLA
90043 CAMPOREALE [PA]
TEL. 0916116531
www.portadelvento.it

ANNUAL PRODUCTION 40,000 bottles
HECTARES UNDER VINE 12.00
VITICULTURE METHOD Certified Organic

○ Porta del Vento Catarratto '12	♥♥ 3
○ Saray '09	♥♥ 4
⊙ MaQuè Rosé '12	♥ 2
● MaQuè Rosso '11	♥ 3

Rizzuto Guccione

C.DA PICONELLO
92011 CATTOLICA ERACLEA [AG]
TEL. 091333081
www.rizzutoguccione.com

CELLAR SALES
PRE-BOOKED VISITS
ACCOMMODATION
ANNUAL PRODUCTION 60,000 bottles
HECTARES UNDER VINE 53.00

● Ibisco '06	♥♥ 5
○ Enzo '12	♥ 3
⊙ Piconello Cabernet Sauvignon Chiaro '12	♥ 3
○ Piconello Grillo '12	♥ 3

Sallier de la Tour

C.DA PERNICE
90144 MONREALE [PA]
TEL. 0916459711
www.tascadalmerita.it

PRE-BOOKED VISITS
ANNUAL PRODUCTION 250,000 bottles
HECTARES UNDER VINE 41.00

● Syrah '11	♥♥ 2*
○ Grillo '12	♥ 2
○ Inzolia '12	♥ 2
● Nero d'Avola '11	♥ 2

Emanuele Scammacca del Murgo

VIA ZAFFERANA, 13
95010 SANTA VENERINA [CT]
TEL. 095950520
www.murgo.it

CELLAR SALES
PRE-BOOKED VISITS
ACCOMMODATION AND RESTAURANT SERVICE
ANNUAL PRODUCTION 230,000 bottles
HECTARES UNDER VINE 35.00

○ Etna Bianco '12	♥♥ 2*
○ Lapilli '12	♥♥ 2*
⊙ Etna Rosato '12	♥ 2
⊙ Murgo Brut Rosé '10	♥ 4

Scilio

V.LE DELLE PROVINCIE, 52
95015 GIARRE [CT]
TEL. 095932822
www.scilio.com

CELLAR SALES
PRE-BOOKED VISITS
ACCOMMODATION AND RESTAURANT SERVICE
ANNUAL PRODUCTION 95,000 bottles
HECTARES UNDER VINE 22.00
VITICULTURE METHOD Certified Organic

● Sikélios Rosso '07	♥♥ 4
○ Etna Bianco Valle Galfina '12	♥ 2
⊙ Etna Rosato Valle Galfina '12	♥ 2
● Etna Rosso Orphéus '10	♥ 4

Solidea

C.DA KADDIUGGIA
91017 PANTELLERIA [TP]
TEL. 0923913016
www.solideavini.it

ANNUAL PRODUCTION 12,000 bottles
HECTARES UNDER VINE 1.80

○ Ilios '12	♥♥ 3
○ Passito di Pantelleria '12	♥♥ 5

Terre di Giurfo

VIA PALESTRO, 536
97019 VITTORIA [RG]
TEL. 0957221551
www.terredigiurfo.it

CELLAR SALES
PRE-BOOKED VISITS
ANNUAL PRODUCTION 100,000 bottles
HECTARES UNDER VINE 40.00

● Ronna '11	♟♟ 2*
● Cerasuolo di Vittoria Maskaria '09	♟ 3
● Kudyah '12	♟ 2
● Kuntari '11	♟ 3

Terre di Trente

C.DA MOLLARELLA, 1
95015 LINGUAGLOSSA [CT]
TEL. 3403075433
www.terreditrente.com

ACCOMMODATION
ANNUAL PRODUCTION 6,000 bottles
HECTARES UNDER VINE 4.00

○ Etna Bianco Dayini '12	♟♟ 5
● Nerello Mascalese '10	♟ 4

Valenti

FRAZ. PASSOPISCIARO
VIA ROMA, 42
95012 CASTIGLIONE DI SICILIA [CT]
TEL. 0942983016
www.vinicolavalenti.com

CELLAR SALES
ANNUAL PRODUCTION 36.500 bottles
HECTARES UNDER VINE 17.00

● Puritani '10	♟♟ 6
○ Etna Bianco Enrico IV '12	♟ 5
● Etna Rosso Norma '10	♟ 5

Vasari

C.DA CASALE
98046 SANTA LUCIA DEL MELA [ME]
TEL. 0909359956
www.biovinivasari.it

CELLAR SALES
PRE-BOOKED VISITS
ACCOMMODATION
ANNUAL PRODUCTION 60,000 bottles
HECTARES UNDER VINE 13.00
VITICULTURE METHOD Certified Organic

● Mamertino Cru Timpanara '10	♟♟ 5
○ Mamertino Bianco Pianeta '12	♟ 5
● Mamertino Nero d'Avola '09	♟ 3
● Mamertino Rosso '09	♟ 3

Vivera

C.DA MARTINELLA SP 59/IV
95015 LINGUAGLOSSA [CT]
TEL. 095643837
www.vivera.it

PRE-BOOKED VISITS
ANNUAL PRODUCTION 120,000 bottles
HECTARES UNDER VINE 39.00
VITICULTURE METHOD Certified Organic

○ A'mami '11	♟♟ 4
○ Altrove '12	♟♟ 2*
○ Etna Bianco Salisire '11	♟♟ 3*
● Terra dei Sogni '10	♟ 2

Zisola

C.DA ZISOLA
96017 NOTO [SR]
TEL. 057773571
www.mazzei.it

ANNUAL PRODUCTION 120,000 bottles
HECTARES UNDER VINE 21.00

● Zisola Nero d'Avola '11	♟♟ 5
● Doppiozeta '10	♟♟ 6

SARDEGNA

Although the number of Tre Bicchieri awards won by Sardinian wineries has remained practically unchanged in recent years, we must mention the further step forward made by wine-growing throughout the region. Additionally, this year a large number of new operations presented their wines for the first time and many of them managed to get into our Guide, despite increasingly stringent entry requirements due to the high quality of production, confirming that today those who decide to produce wine do so meticulously and with great expertise. They are often small producers who tend just a few hectares, with artisanal methods, but they do make fascinating wines full of character, which are the result of an experience and a calling that is handed down from father to son. Turning our attention now to the latest vintage presented, the 2012, we can see that, while better than the hot 2011, it was not a great year, particularly for the most prestigious whites, like Vermentino di Gallura. Once again the temperature took its toll and its effect on the wines is evident, particularly in the case of the finest labels, which lacked that glimmer of vibrancy that would have earned them our top accolade. However, the reds are a different story, commencing with Cannonau. The producers who decided to release the standard-label red, often fermented exclusively in steel or concrete, presented succulent, balanced, highly drinkable wines with an authentic flavour: characteristics that we find increasingly appealing. A great leap forward in quality is also evident among the Cannonau Riservas, where it seems that the focus is on the quest for extreme finesse, avoiding over-ripeness and excessive alcohol, to offer magnificent acid backbone that balances the distinctive traits of Mediterranean wines. Indeed, it is no coincidence that we gave an impressive five Tre Bicchieri awards to Cannonaus. Two were debutants to the podium: the first vintage for Pala's Riserva, and Deiana's Sileno Riserva. The high quality of Carignano from the Sulcis area is confirmed once again, as is the customary excellent performance of three long-standing wineries: Argiolas, Capichera and Sella & Mosca. We end with a note about the award-winning Semidano di Mogoro Superiore Puistèris 2010 from Cantina di Mogoro, a great wine made from a traditional grape variety found only in this designation, which demonstrates how certain Mediterranean whites, made with a specific production vision, are capable of cellaring well.

6Mura

LOC. FUNATANONA
09010 GIBA [CI]
TEL. 0781689718
www.6mura.com

CELLAR SALES
ACCOMMODATION
ANNUAL PRODUCTION 100,000 bottles
HECTARES UNDER VINE 30.00

6Mura was founded a decade ago at Giba, in the heart of Sulcis, and within a few years became one of the island's most renowned wineries, adopting a precise approach to producing wine, starting with old vines, some ungrafted, and culminating in the cellar, where vinification involves the use of large barrels and native yeasts. Vincenzo Aru and Carlo Locci, two of the members, are above all great wine enthusiasts, and their passion translates into well-typed, captivating reds. In addition to Carignano del Sulcis, the winery also produces a Mediterranean Vermentino di Sardegna reminiscent of a salty sea breeze. Once again this year, the Giba winery presented a solid, appealing range of wines, led by a well-typed, territorial Carignano del Sulcis 2010, from a selection of old vines. It opens to Mediterranean scrub and autumn leaves, followed by a fresh, tangy palate with creamy tannins, all held together by good stuffing. We also loved the Vermentino di Sardegna 2012.

● Carignano del Sulcis Giba '11	♈♈ 2*
○ Vermentino di Sardegna '12	♈♈ 4
○ Vermentino di Sardegna Giba '12	♈♈ 2*
● Carignano del Sulcis '09	♈♈♈ 5
● Carignano del Sulcis Giba '10	♈♈ 2*
○ Vermentino di Sardegna '11	♈♈ 4

Agricola Punica

LOC. BARRUA
09010 SANTADI [CI]
TEL. 0781941012
www.agripunica.it

PRE-BOOKED VISITS
ANNUAL PRODUCTION 306,000 bottles
HECTARES UNDER VINE 65.00

The Agricola Punica winery in Sulcis boasts 65 hectares under vine, with the lion's share going to carignano, the heart and soul of their two reds. This year they have also added a vermentino-based white to the range. Production methods focus on low yields and attentive selection of the grapes, and are managed by Sebastiano Rosa, known above all for running Tenuta San Guido. He owns the estate along with Giacomo Tachis, the Santadi winery, Tenuta San Guido, and Antonello Pilloni. In addition to carignano, plantings include international varieties, mainly cabernet and smaller amounts of merlot and syrah. The Barrua 2010, from carignano topped up with international varieties, was one of the most charming versions ever. Its finesse and glossy, caressing tannins, with textbook freshness, combine with depth and creaminess in the mouth to earn it a Tre Bicchieri. The Montessu 2011 also pleased.

● Barrua '10	♈♈♈ 6
● Montessu '11	♈♈ 4
○ Samas '12	♈ 2
● Barrua '07	♈♈♈ 6
● Barrua '05	♈♈♈ 5
● Barrua '09	♈♈ 6
● Barrua '08	♈♈ 6
● Montessu '10	♈♈ 4
● Montessu '09	♈♈ 4

★★Argiolas

VIA ROMA, 28
09040 SERDIANA [CA]
TEL. 070740606
www.argiolas.it

Cantina di Calasetta

VIA ROMA, 134
09011 CALASETTA [CI]
TEL. 078188413
www.cantinadicalasetta.it

CELLAR SALES
PRE-BOOKED VISITS
ACCOMMODATION
ANNUAL PRODUCTION 2,200,000 bottles
HECTARES UNDER VINE 230.00

CELLAR SALES
PRE-BOOKED VISITS
ANNUAL PRODUCTION 100,000 bottles
HECTARES UNDER VINE 300.00

The traditional, close-knit Argiolas family undoubtedly has one of the Island's most prestigious, largest wineries. Franco and Pepetto still run the company, even though the practical side of things is now dealt with by their children Valentina, Francesca and Antonio, and Valentina's husband, Elia. A constant presence throughout their history has been the oenologist Mariano Murru, considered one of the family, with whom they share research and projects. The result is an impressive range with a wide variety of labels. All are convincing, from young, early-drinkers to selections whose ageing potential has few rivals on the island. A new vintage and new sources of satisfaction for the range produced by Serdiana. Once again, Turriga, a blend of cannonau, carignano, bovale and malvasia nera, enchanted the tasting panel and took home a Tre Bicchieri. The 2009 boasts intense aromas of Mediterranean scrub and tobacco leaves, cocoa and bark. The close-knit, austere palate shows stiff, yet well-integrated tannins and good stuffing.

Among Sardinia's many co-operative wineries, that of Calasetta, situated on the island of Sant'Antioco, is one of the smallest in terms of its number of member growers and bottles produced. As far as the quality of the wines goes however, it is a different story, and especially in recent years a string of successes and awards have proved its ability to produce excellent labels. Various declinations of Carignano del Sulcis obviously lead the way, especially the versions vinified solely in stainless steel, which transmit all the typical traits of this important variety. Lastly, we should mention excellent value for money across the whole range. Once again, this small Sulcis co-operative winery rolled out some terrific Carignanos. We were particularly taken with Aina, a Riserva 2009 boasting a focused nose of intense dark fruit and myrtle. In the mouth, it shows freshness and rich flavour, along with amazing length, and tannins that are never mouth-drying. The other three Carignanos were all excellent, as well as being superb value for money.

● Turriga '09	♈♈♈ 8
○ Angialis '10	♈♈ 6
● Cannonau di Sardegna Costera '11	♈♈ 3*
● Is Selis Rosso '11	♈♈ 5
● Monica di Sardegna Perdera '11	♈♈ 3
○ Vermentino di Sardegna Merì '12	♈♈ 3
○ Is Selis Bianco '12	♈ 3
○ Nuragus di Cagliari S'Elegas '12	♈ 2
○ Vermentino di Sardegna Costamolino '12	♈ 2
○ Vermentino di Sardegna Is Argiolas '12	♈ 3
● Turriga '08	♈♈♈ 8
● Turriga '07	♈♈♈ 8
● Turriga '06	♈♈♈ 6

● Carignano del Sulcis Aina Ris. '09	♈♈ 4
● Carignano del Sulcis Maccòri '11	♈♈ 2*
● Carignano del Sulcis Piede Franco '11	♈♈ 2*
● Carignano del Sulcis Tupei '11	♈♈ 2*
○ Moscato di Cagliari In Fundu '11	♈ 3
● Carignano del Sulcis Tupei '10	♈♈♈ 2*
● Carignano del Sulcis Maccòri '10	♈♈ 2*
● Carignano del Sulcis Piede Franco '10	♈♈ 2*

Capichera

SS Arzachena-Sant'Antonio, km 4
07021 Arzachena [OT]
Tel. 078980612
www.capichera.it

CELLAR SALES
PRE-BOOKED VISITS
ANNUAL PRODUCTION 250,000 bottles
HECTARES UNDER VINE 50.00

When someone mentions Capichera we immediately think of grand, long-lived white wines that can hold their heads high on the international stage. The winery is owned by the Ragnedda family, who have always focused on the quality that can be achieved by vermentino here in Gallura. We feel that the standard has improved even further in recent years, with their decision to produce wines that retain the body and structure typical of Mediterranean whites without sacrificing finesse, freshness and elegance. This approach to production is increasingly found across the range and helps maintain Vermentino's international reputation. This stunning range shows quality across the board. We particularly liked the Capichera 2011, a monovarietal vermentino vaunting a nose of herbs, citrus, peach and apricots. In the mouth, it is bursting with freshness and flavour, and a Tre Bicchieri was a foregone conclusion. The other wines were close behind, in particular Mantenghja and Vigna'ngena, that continue to charm us with their finesse and drinkability.

○ Capichera '11	♟♟♟6
● Mantenghja '08	♟♟8
○ Vermentino di Gallura Vigna'ngena '12	♟♟5
○ Capichera V.T. '11	♟♟7
● Carignano del Sulcis Assajè '10	♟♟6
● Liànti '11	♟♟4
○ Santigaini '09	♟♟8
○ Vermentino di Sardegna Lintori '12	♟♟3
○ Vermentino di Gallura Vigna'ngena '10	♟♟♟5
○ Vermentino di Gallura Vigna'ngena '09	♟♟♟5

Giovanni Cherchi

loc. Sa Pala e Sa Chessa
07049 Usini [SS]
Tel. 079380273
www.vinicolacherchi.it

CELLAR SALES
PRE-BOOKED VISITS
ANNUAL PRODUCTION 170,000 bottles
HECTARES UNDER VINE 30.00

The historic Cherchi winery has been a constant presence in the Guide, and deserves credit for promoting the territory of Usini in the Sassari area through traditional varieties. In addition to cannonau and vermentino we should note its investment in cagnulari, an interesting native variety only found in this area. But the winery is also working on other new projects, such as its superb new vermentino-based Metodo Classico, which joins its range of classic labels, including Tuvaoes, always a benchmark for the island's white DOC wine. This year saw a top performance, particularly from Cannonau di Sardegna 2011, opening to intense berry fruit, cherries and tobacco leaves, followed on the palate by freshness and a clean, satisfying finish. Another interesting red is the Cagnulari, this year also released in a Billia version, while the Tuvaoes remains one of the best of Vermentino di Sardegna labels in the DOC zone.

● Cannonau di Sardegna '11	♟♟3*
● Billia Cagnulari '11	♟♟3
● Cagnulari '11	♟♟3
● Luzzana '11	♟♟4
○ Vermentino di Sardegna Tuvaoes '12	♟♟3
○ Vermentino di Sardegna Billia '12	♟2
○ Vermentino di Sardegna Pigalva '12	♟2
○ Vermentino di Sardegna Tuvaoes '88	♟♟♟3
● Cagnulari '10	♟♟3
○ Vermentino di Sardegna Pigalva '11	♟♟2*

Chessa

VIA SAN GIORGIO
07049 USINI [SS]
TEL. 3283747069
www.cantinechessa.it

CELLAR SALES
PRE-BOOKED VISITS
ANNUAL PRODUCTION 43,000 bottles
HECTARES UNDER VINE 15.00

For some years, we have been closely following the meticulous work of Giovanna Chessa, who owns around 12 hectares in the Usini area. She has always opted to focus on the traditional varieties that give of their best in the zones of north-western Sardinia. This means vermentino among the whites and cagnulari among the reds. As far as regards the latter, Giovanna has worked on bringing out the elegance and finesse of a difficult variety, so often marked by huskiness on the nose and palate. There is also room in the range for a sweet Moscato obtained from naturally raisined grapes. Usini presented two wines, and both were excellent. The Cagnulari 2012, despite the variety's poor reputation, is fine and elegant, with aromas of rosemary, sage and pennyroyal over a fruity backdrop and a fresh, juicy palate. We were also impressed with the full-flavoured, aromatic Vermentino di Sardegna Mattariga 2012.

● Cagnulari '12	♟♟ 3
○ Vermentino di Sardegna Mattariga '12	♟♟ 3
● Cagnulari '11	♟♟ 3
● Cagnulari '10	♟♟ 3*
● Cagnulari '09	♟♟ 3*
● Lugherra '10	♟♟ 5

Attilio Contini

VIA GENOVA, 48/50
09072 CABRAS [OR]
TEL. 0783290806
www.vinicontini.it

CELLAR SALES
PRE-BOOKED VISITS
ANNUAL PRODUCTION 800,000 bottles
HECTARES UNDER VINE 70.00

In Sardinia, Contini is synonymous with Vernaccia di Oristano, an exceptional wine that unfortunately risks disappearing due to its failure to find favour with contemporary consumers. Despite this, the winery at Cabras, established in the late 1800s, continues to produce this unusual oxidative wine, releasing Riservas over 20 years old, special, charming wines we will never tire of. The rest of the range comprises labels from traditional varieties produced in the area around Oristano and other zones of the island's best wine country. Every year Contini presents a vast range, including some outstanding wines of various types. The Barrile 2010, a blend of nieddera and muristellu, made our finals, impressing us with its depth and concentration. The 2010 follows cocoa and autumn leaves on the nose with a slightly drying finish. We also enjoyed the Pontis, a dessert wine from vernaccia, with honeyed notes and dried fruit.

● Barrile '10	♟♟ 6
● Cannonau di Sardegna Inu Ris. '10	♟♟ 4
○ Karmis '12	♟♟ 3
● Nieddera Rosso '10	♟♟ 3
○ Pontis '12	♟♟ 5
○ Vermentino di Gallura Elibaria '12	♟♟ 3
○ Brut Attilio	♟ 3
● Cannonau di Sardegna Tonaghe '11	♟ 3
⊙ Nieddera Rosato '12	♟ 2
○ Vermentino di Sardegna Pariglia '12	♟ 2
○ Vermentino di Sardegna Tyrsos '12	♟ 2
○ Vernaccia di Oristano Antico Gregori	♟♟♟ 7
○ Vernaccia di Oristano Ris. '88	♟♟♟ 4*
○ Vernaccia di Oristano Antico Gregori	♟♟ 7

Ferruccio Deiana

LOC. SU LEUNAXI
VIA GIALETO, 7
09040 SETTIMO SAN PIETRO [CA]
TEL. 070749117
www.ferrucciodeiana.it

CELLAR SALES
PRE-BOOKED VISITS
ANNUAL PRODUCTION 520,000 bottles
HECTARES UNDER VINE 74.00
VITICULTURE METHOD Certified Organic

Ferruccio Deiana is a capable oenologist, who, after important experience abroad, some time ago decided to establish himself in his native land. His winery, based a few kilometres from Cagliari, produces around 500,000 bottles a year, and focuses on local varieties, grown in vineyards surrounding the modern, functional cellar. Many of the vineyards are already farmed using organic methods, and some plots are in the process of being converted. The resulting wines, stylish and complex, reflect the peculiarities of the territory, and all show well-focused finesse on the palate. We have always praised the quality of Ferruccio Deiana's wines, and this year they are joined by a red, the Cannonau di Sardegna Sileno Riserva 2010, that exceeded all expectations for a well-deserved Tre Bicchieri. It offers aromas of Mediterranean scrub and dark berry fruit, with menthol and balsamic notes on the palate, leaving a tangy freshness in the mouth. The Ajana 2010, from cannonau, carignano and cabernet, is also superb.

● Cannonau di Sardegna Sileno Ris. '10	♟♟♟ 3*
● Ajana '10	♟♟ 6
● Cannonau di Sardegna Sileno '10	♟♟ 3
○ Oirad '11	♟♟ 5
○ Vermentino di Sardegna Donnikalia '12	♟♟ 2*
● Monica di Sardegna Karel '11	♟ 2
● Monica di Sardegna Sanremy '12	♟ 2
○ Pluminus '10	♟ 6
○ Vermentino di Sardegna Sanremy '12	♟ 2
● Ajana '02	♟♟♟ 6
● Ajana '09	♟♟ 6
● Cannonau di Sardegna Sileno '09	♟♟ 3
● Cannonau di Sardegna Sileno Ris. '09	♟♟ 3
○ Oirad '10	♟♟ 5

Cantine Dolianova

LOC. SANT'ESU
SS 387 KM 17,150
09041 DOLIANOVA [CA]
TEL. 070744101
www.cantinedidolianova.it

CELLAR SALES
PRE-BOOKED VISITS
ANNUAL PRODUCTION 4,000,000 bottles
HECTARES UNDER VINE 1200.00

The historic Dolianova co-operative winery in Parteolla is an important operation that brings together over 400 member growers, providing grapes from their 1,200 hectares of vineyards. The new pursuit of quality common to so many Sardinian co-operative wineries can also be seen here, with a range of wines that becomes more convincing with every passing year. Pride of place goes to Cannonau and Vermentino, but wines such as Nuragus di Cagliari and Nasco are also worthy of attention. The vast range includes Metodo Charmat sparklers and sweet wines, all offered at attractive prices. Tastings of some of the winery's top labels, including the Falconaro, are postponed until next year. In the meantime, we tried a captivating Cannonau di Sardegna Blasio Riserva 2009, whose fragrant notes of cherry and autumn leaves usher in a fresh, compact palate with well-balanced tannins. The other wines are all well-executed, especially a dessert wine from moscato.

● Cannonau di Sardegna Blasio Ris. '09	♟♟ 3
○ Moscato di Cagliari '10	♟♟ 3
○ Nuragus di Cagliari Perlas '12	♟♟ 2*
● Terresicci '08	♟♟ 5
○ Vermentino di Sardegna Prendas San Pantaleo '12	♟♟ 2*
○ Caralis Brut	♟ 2
○ Malvasia Scaleri	♟ 3
○ Vermentino di Sardegna Naeli '12	♟ 2
● Cannonau di Sardegna Anzenas '09	♟♟ 2*
● Cannonau di Sardegna Blasio Ris. '08	♟♟ 3
● Falconaro '09	♟♟ 3
● Terresicci '07	♟♟ 5

Cantina Dorgali

VIA PIEMONTE, 11
08022 DORGALI [NU]
TEL. 078496143
www.csdorgali.com

CELLAR SALES
PRE-BOOKED VISITS
ANNUAL PRODUCTION 1,500,000 bottles
HECTARES UNDER VINE 750.00

The Dorgali co-operative winery has always specialized in the production of Cannonau, and operates in one of the areas best suited to growing this traditional variety. Especially in recent years, quality has increased significantly, thanks to the staff's ability to involve the growers, whose contribution in the rows is crucial. Most of the vineyards are situated in the breathtaking Valle di Oddoenne, with some very old vineyards still planted to bush vines. Vermentino, alongside international varieties such as syrah, which clearly appreciates the soils and climate of the Dorgali area, account for most of the plantings. Among the various Cannonaus presented this year, all superb, the Vinìola una Riserva 2010 stands out, taking a Tre Bicchieri with its intense, crunchy red berry fruit and notes of eucalyptus and myrtle. In the mouth it shows smooth and graceful, with the merest hint of well-integrated tannins and a satisfying finish backed up by thrusting freshness. We also loved the Hortos 2009, from cannonau and syrah.

● Cannonau di Sardegna Vinìola Ris. '10	♥♥♥ 4*
● Hortos '09	♥♥ 6
● Cannonau di Sardegna V. di Isalle '12	♥♥ 3
● Fùili '09	♥♥ 5
● Norìolo '10	♥♥ 4
● Cannonau di Sardegna Filieri '12	♥ 2
☉ Cannonau di Sardegna Rosato Filieri '12	♥ 2
☉ Nues Brut	♥ 3
● Cannonau di Sardegna Vinìola Ris. '07	♥♥♥ 3*
● Cannonau di Sardegna Vinìola Ris. '06	♥♥♥ 3*
● Hortos '08	♥♥♥ 6

Giuseppe Gabbas

VIA TRIESTE, 59
08100 NUORO
TEL. 078433745
www.gabbas.it

CELLAR SALES
PRE-BOOKED VISITS
ANNUAL PRODUCTION 80,000 bottles
HECTARES UNDER VINE 20.00

Giuseppe Gabbas is a true vigneron who loves the vineyard and the country, a man of few words dedicated to his work, on which he lavishes meticulous care. This starts with the selection of the clusters, aimed at getting the best out of the cannonau grapes that occupy most of the winery's vineyards. Of the five labels produced, no fewer than three are Cannonau di Sardegna, and Gabbas's interpretations of Sardinia's most renowned wine express finesse, freshness and elegance, while preserving its Mediterranean soul. The range is completed by a raisin wine from local red grapes, in which cannonau also plays an important role, and the latest arrival, a convincing Vermentino di Sardegna. Gabbas has accustomed us to outstanding Cannonaus, and this year proved to be no exception, with the Dule Riserva 2010 earning a Tre Bicchieri for a finesse and elegance rarely found in Sardinia's most widely grown variety. Opening to red berry fruit, it moves into a fresh, juicy palate backed up by supple tannins.

● Cannonau di Sardegna Dule Ris. '10	♥♥♥ 4*
● Cannonau di Sardegna Arbòre Ris. '10	♥♥ 4
● Cannonau di Sardegna Lillové '12	♥♥ 2*
☉ Vermentino di Sardegna Manzanile '12	♥♥ 3
● Cannonau di Sardegna Dule Ris. '09	♥♥♥ 3*
● Cannonau di Sardegna Dule Ris. '08	♥♥♥ 3*
● Cannonau di Sardegna Dule Ris. '07	♥♥♥ 3*
● Cannonau di Sardegna Dule Ris. '06	♥♥♥ 3*
● Cannonau di Sardegna Dule Ris. '05	♥♥♥ 3*
● Cannonau di Sardegna Arbòre Ris. '09	♥♥ 3*

Cantina Gallura

VIA VAL DI COSSU, 9
07029 TEMPIO PAUSANIA
TEL. 079631241
www.cantinagallura.com

CELLAR SALES
PRE-BOOKED VISITS
ANNUAL PRODUCTION 1,300,000 bottles
HECTARES UNDER VINE 350.00

Cantina Gallura, the large historic
co-operative at Tempio Pausania, is run by
the capable oenologist Dino Addis. The level
of quality achieved, especially in recent
years, is down to his untiring
experimentation, starting in the rows, where
he creates vineyard selections and chooses
the best clusters to take to the cellar. This
policy has resulted in a wide range of labels,
all distinguished by cleanliness on the nose
and palate and a strong sense of place. The
granite-based soils and old vineyards also
make a difference, and are an added bonus
for producers of Vermentino di Gallura. This
year, it was once again the range of
Vermentino di Galluras that impressed,
and some are also excellent value for
money, such as the Piras 2012 and the
Canayli 2012. The former offers citrus,
floral notes; the latter, peach and apricots.
But the star of the show is the full-
flavoured selection Genesi 2012, dynamic
despite the hot growing year.

○ Vermentino di Gallura Sup. Genesi '12	▼▼ 5
○ Vermentino di Gallura Piras '12	▼▼ 2*
○ Vermentino di Gallura Sup. Canayli '12	▼▼ 2*
○ Balajana '10	▼ 3
⊙ Campos '12	▼ 2
● Dolmen '09	▼ 3
● Gemellae '11	▼ 2
● Karana '12	▼ 2
○ Moscato di Tempio Pausania	▼ 3
○ Vermentino di Gallura Gemellae '12	▼ 2
○ Vermentino di Gallura Mavriana '12	▼ 2
○ Vermentino di Gallura Sup. Genesi '10	♟♟♟ 5
○ Vermentino di Gallura Sup. Genesi '08	♟♟♟ 5
○ Vermentino di Gallura Sup. Canayli '11	♟♟ 2*

Antichi Poderi Jerzu

VIA UMBERTO I, 1
08044 JERZU [OG]
TEL. 078270028
www.jerzuantichipoderi.it

CELLAR SALES
PRE-BOOKED VISITS
ANNUAL PRODUCTION 1,500,000 bottles
HECTARES UNDER VINE 750.00

Jerzu is quintessential cannonau territory,
so much so that the Cannonau di Sardegna
DOC regulations list it as a subzone. Antichi
Poderi's dedication to the island's
prestigious variety has involved careful
zoning, with the aim of selecting the best
vineyards, and obtaining wines that offer
freshness, drinkability and ageing potential
without betraying the grape's varietal traits.
The excellent results are evident when you
taste the two Riservas, Josto Miglior and
Chuerra, but also the vintage Bantu, a
concentration of typicity and finesse. The
range includes a large number of other
labels, all produced from local varieties. And
it was in fact the two Riservas that most
convinced, in particular the Chuerra 2010,
with earthy notes of forest floor and bark,
and a close-knit, creamily satisfying palate.
It may lack a little finesse, but has masses
of charm and local character. The Josto
Miglior, another 2010 Cannonau Riserva, is
also excellent, while we were pleasantly
surprised by the Akratos, a sweet wine
from overripe grapes.

● Cannonau di Sardegna Chuerra Ris. '10	▼▼ 5
● Akratos '07	▼▼ 5
● Cannonau di Sardegna Bantu '12	▼▼ 2*
● Cannonau di Sardegna Josto Miglior Ris. '10	▼▼ 5
● Cannonau di Sardegna Marghìa '11	▼▼ 4
⊙ Cannonau di Sardegna Rosato Isara '12	▼ 2
● Monica di Sardegna Camalda '12	▼ 2
○ Vermentino di Sardegna Lucean Le Stelle '12	▼ 3
○ Vermentino di Sardegna Telavè '12	▼ 2
● Cannonau di Sardegna Josto Miglior Ris. '09	♟♟♟ 4*
● Cannonau di Sardegna Josto Miglior Ris. '05	♟♟♟ 4
● Radames '01	♟♟♟ 5

Alberto Loi

SS 125 km 124,1
08040 Cardedu [OG]
Tel. 070240866
www.albertoloi.it

CELLAR SALES
PRE-BOOKED VISITS
ACCOMMODATION
ANNUAL PRODUCTION 250,000 bottles
HECTARES UNDER VINE 53.00

Now in its third generation of growers, the Loi family continues to produce well typed, territorial wines, almost exclusively based on cannonau. With intervention kept to a minimum, the use of large barrels and long maturation, the resulting wines show great charm, and perfectly express the variety and local flavour of this area in the Jerzu subzone. The Cannonau di Sardegna selections in particular need time in the bottle to express themselves fully, and some versions clearly have no fear of ageing. The range is completed by a Monica, a Vermentino, and an extremely interesting, not to say unique, white Cannonau from grapes fermented off the skins. All the Cannonaus produced were excellent. The Cardedo 2010 is our favourite Riserva: combining great drinkability with real Mediterranean character, brimming with aromas of rose and black berry fruit, but also iron filings and blood-rich meat. The fresh, supple palate signs off with a touch of balsam.

● Astangia '10	♟♟ 4
● Cannonau di Sardegna Jerzu Cardedo Ris. '10	♟♟ 3
● Cannonau di Sardegna Jerzu Sa Mola '11	♟♟ 2*
● Cannonau di Sardegna Ris. '09	♟♟ 3
● Loi Corona '09	♟♟ 5
● Tuvara '09	♟♟ 5
○ Leila '11	♟ 4
● Monica di Sardegna Nibaru '12	♟ 2
○ Vermentino di Sardegna Theria '12	♟ 2
● Astangia '06	♟♟ 4
● Cannonau di Sardegna Jerzu Sa Mola '07	♟♟ 2*

Masone Mannu

loc. Su Canale
SS 199 km 48
07020 Olbia
Tel. 078947140
www.masonemannu.com

CELLAR SALES
PRE-BOOKED VISITS
ANNUAL PRODUCTION 100,000 bottles
HECTARES UNDER VINE 18.50

Masone Mannu was established a decade ago, and immediately set itself the goal of pursuing quality in an area, Gallura, particularly well suited for the production of white wines from vermentino. The estate covers around 18 hectares and produces 100,000 bottles. Aromatic cleanness and extreme finesse distinguish the two Galluras produced, and every year the Superiore exhibits good ageing potential. The rest of the range is completed by reds from local and international varieties that share a fresh, drinkable style. We saw yet another convincing performance from the Masone Mannu winery, even if Costarenas, its Vermentino di Gallura Superiore was not on its usual form. The hot 2011 growing year did nothing to help, and although excellent, with ripe peachy fruit and candied peel, it lacks a certain vitality and freshness. There is however lots of flavour on the palate, and an attractive salty finish. The other wines are all well-managed.

○ Vermentino di Gallura Sup. Costarenas '11	♟♟ 4
● Entu '10	♟♟ 4
○ Vermentino di Gallura Petrizza '12	♟♟ 3
● Zurria '12	♟♟ 2*
○ Ammentu '12	♟ 5
⊙ Rena Rosa '12	♟ 3
● Cannonau di Sardegna '09	♟♟ 3*
● Mannu '10	♟♟ 8
○ Vermentino di Gallura Petrizza '11	♟♟ 3
○ Vermentino di Gallura Sup. Costarenas '10	♟♟ 4

908

SARDINIA

Mesa

LOC. SU BARONI
09010 SANT'ANNA ARRESI [CA]
TEL. 0781965057
www.cantinamesa.it

Cantina di Mogoro Il Nuraghe

SS 131 KM 62
09095 MOGORO [OR]
TEL. 0783990285
www.ilnuraghe.it

CELLAR SALES
PRE-BOOKED VISITS
ANNUAL PRODUCTION 750,000 bottles
HECTARES UNDER VINE 70.00

CELLAR SALES
PRE-BOOKED VISITS
ANNUAL PRODUCTION 850,000 bottles
HECTARES UNDER VINE 480.00

Mesa is one of the few private wineries operating in Sulcis, and is owned by the advertising agent Gavino Sanna. Considering the area, the winery naturally decided to concentrate on Carignano, a wine that for some years it has also produced in a raisin version, as permitted by the DOC regulations. Recent years have seen a focus on attractively drinkable wines, most of which exhibit a fresh, elegant style. In addition to the Carignano del Sulcis, the Vermentino di Sardegna and the wines from international varieties are also worthy of mention. Mesa presented an impressive range, led by the Carignano del Sulcis Buio Buio Riserva 2011, outstanding for its aromas of Mediterranean scrub, myrtle and blackberry. It also convinces on the austere, harmonious palate, despite lacking a little depth. We also loved the other Carignanos, especially the Forte Rosso Passito, offering scents of rose and wild cherry over a sweet, fresh palate with nuances of balsam.

We are happy to see that Nuraghe, Mogoro's historic co-operative winery, has in recent years become one the most important operations in the Guide. The merit goes to the entire staff, starting with the chairman and the capable young oenologist Daniele Manca, right down to the dozens of growers who passionately tend around 400 hectares under vine. Of the many labels produced, we should mention Semidano di Mogoro, from the homonymous native variety produced only here, and Bovale, from another traditional variety which gives of its best in the Campidano di Terralba area. The former in particular is proving to be an outstanding white with a good few years' ageing potential. There have been significant improvements at the Mogoro winery in recent years, as is evident in its range of top-quality labels based mainly on Sardinia's traditional varieties and historic designations. A good example is the Semidano di Mogoro Superiore Puistèris 2010, a captivating white that still shows vitality and freshness even after some years' ageing.

● Carignano del Sulcis Buio Buio Ris. '11	♥♥ 5
● Cannonau di Sardegna Moro '11	♥♥ 5
● Carignano del Sulcis Buio '12	♥♥ 3
● Carignano del Sulcis Passito Forte Rosso '11	♥♥ 5
● Carignano del Sulcis Primo Rosso '12	♥♥ 2*
● Malombra '10	♥♥ 6
● Cannonau di Sardegna Primo Scuro '11	♥ 2
○ Carignano del Sulcis Rosa Grande '12	♥ 3
○ Vermentino di Sardegna Giunco '12	♥ 3
○ Vermentino di Sardegna Primo Bianco '12	♥ 2
● Buio Buio '10	♥♥♥ 4*
● Carignano del Sulcis Primo Rosso '11	♀♀ 2*
● Malombra '09	♀♀ 6
○ Vermentino di Sardegna Giunco '11	♀♀ 3

○ Semidano di Mogoro Sup. Puistèris '10	♥♥♥ 4*
● Campidano di Terralba Tiernu '10	♥♥ 2*
● Cannonau di Sardegna Nero Sardo '11	♥♥ 2*
○ Sardegna Semidano Mogoro Anastasia '12	♥♥ 2*
● Monica di Sardegna San Bernardino '10	♥ 2
○ Nuragus di Cagliari Ajò '12	♥ 2
○ Vermentino di Sardegna Don Giovanni '12	♥ 2
● Cannonau di Sardegna Vignaruja '08	♀♀ 2*
○ Semidano di Mogoro Sup. Puistèris '09	♀♀ 4
○ Vermentino di Sardegna Don Giovanni '11	♀♀ 2*

Mura

Loc. Azzanidò, 1
07020 Loiri Porto San Paolo [OT]
Tel. 078941070
www.vinimura.it

CELLAR SALES
PRE-BOOKED VISITS
RESTAURANT SERVICE
ANNUAL PRODUCTION 50,000 bottles
HECTARES UNDER VINE 12.00

The fine Mura winery is a family business, capably run by the oenologist Marianna Mura and her brother, assisted by their father, the founder of the winery. The operation, based in the heart of Gallura, at Loiri Porto San Paolo, self-evidently specializes in vermentino, and in recent years has strived to obtain fresh, mineral wines, unique expressions of north-eastern Sardinia's wine country. As recent vintages show, they have clearly achieved their goal. In addition to selections of whites, the range is completed by a Cannonau di Sardegna and two labels from local varieties. Once again, this year's range from Mura shows marvellous quality. Our favourite was the Vermentino di Gallura Superiore Sienda 2012, with its intense aromas of herb, aniseed and pennyroyal, over a fresh, full-flavoured and beautifully plush palate. The Baja 2011, a blend of cannonau and other traditional varieties, was extremely drinkable.

● Vermentino di Gallura Sup. Sienda '12	♀♀♀ 3*
● Baja '11	♀♀ 5
○ Vermentino di Gallura Cheremi '12	♀♀ 3
● Cannonau di Sardegna Prisma '11	♀ 2
○ Vermentino di Sardegna Prisma '12	♀ 2
● Cannonau di Sardegna Cortes '10	♀♀ 2*
○ Vermentino di Gallura Cheremi '11	♀♀ 2*
○ Vermentino di Gallura Sup. Sienda Il Decennio '11	♀♀ 3*

Pala

via Verdi, 7
09040 Serdiana [CA]
Tel. 070740284
www.pala.it

CELLAR SALES
PRE-BOOKED VISITS
ANNUAL PRODUCTION 450,000 bottles
HECTARES UNDER VINE 88.00

The forthright yet reserved Mario Pala is an old-school grower who loves his work in the rows and cellar. He dedicates his time to achieving well-typed wines with a sense of place, exclusively using local varieties. His winery is one of Sardinia's most successful on international markets, the result of years of work pursuing the highest quality. The vineyards, some extremely old, provide aromatic wines with great cleanliness on the nose and saline notes on the palate, a feature that makes the whites in particular extremely attractive and ensures longevity. Alongside the classic vermentino and cannonau, the estate has concentrated its efforts on the traditional varieties nuragus and bovale. The long years of work have borne fruit, and the latest wine from Pala was the one that most surprised us during our tastings. This Cannonau di Sardegna Riserva 2011, aged in large oak, displays blackberries and tobacco leaves over a supple and caressing, yet fresh palate.

● Cannonau di Sardegna Ris. '11	♀♀♀ 3*
● S'Arai '10	♀♀ 5
● Assoluto '12	♀♀ 5
⊙ Chiaro di Stelle '12	♀♀ 3
● Siray '10	♀♀ 3
● Thesys '12	♀♀ 3
○ Vermentino di Sardegna I Fiori '12	♀♀ 2*
○ Vermentino di Sardegna Stellato '12	♀♀ 3
● Monica di Sardegna I Fiori '12	♀ 2
○ Nuragus di Cagliari I Fiori '12	♀ 2
○ Silenzi Bianco '12	♀ 2
⊙ Silenzi Rosato '12	♀ 2
● Silenzi Rosso '12	♀ 2
● S'Arai '08	♀♀ 5
● Siray '09	♀♀ 3*

Cantina Pedres

ZONA IND. SETTORE 7
07026 OLBIA
TEL. 0789595075
www.cantinapedres.it

CELLAR SALES
PRE-BOOKED VISITS
ANNUAL PRODUCTION 290,000 bottles
HECTARES UNDER VINE 40.00

The Pedres winery in Gallura covers around 40 hectares and is run by Antonella Mancini, heir of the Mancini family, who have been producing wine in Sardinia since the late 1800s. Their best results are without doubt to be found in their versions of Vermentino di Gallura, which like few others manage to transmit the whole essence of northern Sardinia's granite-based soils, while remaining true to the peculiarities of this variety. This means tangy, fresh, mineral wines, ready for drinking now, but, we are sure, able to give satisfaction for some years to come. The range is completed by a Cannonau and Metodo Charmat sparklers, with pride of place going to an excellent Moscato di Tempio. The most convincing wines we tasted were a Vermentino and a Cannonau. The former, the Thilibas 2012, is a perfect expression of its Gallura origins, a lean-bodied wine with vertical development and upfront herbal notes. The latter is the juicy, highly drinkable Cerasio, a Cannonau di Sardegna 2011, with cherries and blackcurrants on the nose.

● Cannonau di Sardegna Cerasio '11	♟♟ 4
○ Vermentino di Gallura Sup. Thilibas '12	♟♟ 4
● Cannonau di Sardegna Sulità i '10	♟♟ 3
● Maranto '11	♟♟ 2*
○ Vermentino di Gallura Brino '12	♟♟ 3
○ Vermentino di Gallura Colline '12	♟♟ 2*
○ Moscato di Sardegna Spumante	♟ 3
● Muros '11	♟ 4
⊙ Pedres Brut Rosé	♟ 3
○ Vermentino di Gallura Sup. Thilibas '10	♟♟♟ 3*
○ Vermentino di Gallura Sup. Thilibas '09	♟♟♟ 3*

★Cantina di Santadi

VIA CAGLIARI, 78
09010 SANTADI [CI]
TEL. 0781950127
www.cantinadisantadi.it

CELLAR SALES
PRE-BOOKED VISITS
ANNUAL PRODUCTION 1,700,000 bottles
HECTARES UNDER VINE 606.00

Santadi deserves credit not only for having produced wine of the highest quality since the 1980s, but also for having made many co-operative wineries on the island aware that they too can achieve excellent results through attentive, meticulous work, starting with educating growers about the importance of quality in the rows. This is all thanks to the chairman Antonello Pilloni and his staff, who have brought Sardinian wine, and in particular Carignano del Sulcis into the limelight. They also benefit from a particularly well-suited territory, with a large number of ungrafted, century-old vineyards growing on the sand, a stone's throw from the sea. We could do with more space, seeing how many of Santadi's wines deserve a mention. Terre Brune nevertheless remains a symbol of the winery and the whole territory, and thoroughly deserves its Tre Bicchieri. The 2009 offers an intense nose of blackberry, morello cherry, autumn leaves and wood resin. Sumptuous and mouthfilling, yet at the same time elegant and lean, this is yet another masterpiece.

● Carignano del Sulcis Sup. Terre Brune '09	♟♟♟ 7
○ Latinia '08	♟♟ 5
● Shardana '09	♟♟ 5
● Araja '11	♟♟ 3
● Carignano del Sulcis Grotta Rossa '11	♟♟ 2*
● Carignano del Sulcis Rocca Rubia Ris. '10	♟♟ 4
⊙ Carignano del Sulcis Rosato Tre Torri '12	♟ 2
● Monica di Sardegna Antigua '12	♟ 2
○ Nuragus di Cagliari Pedraia '12	♟ 2
○ Vermentino di Sardegna Cala Silente '12	♟ 3
○ Vermentino di Sardegna Villa Solais '12	♟ 2
○ Villa di Chiesa '11	♟ 5
● Carignano del Sulcis Sup. Terre Brune '08	♟♟♟ 7

Sardus Pater

VIA RINASCITA, 46
09017 SANT'ANTIOCO [CI]
TEL. 0781800274
www.cantinesarduspater.com

CELLAR SALES
PRE-BOOKED VISITS
ANNUAL PRODUCTION 500,000 bottles
HECTARES UNDER VINE 295.00

Sardus Pater, one of the three co-operative wineries working in the south-west of the island, is situated at Sant'Antioco, where production naturally focuses on Carignano del Sulcis. For some years it has been producing excellent wines, some of the region's best, with even the more prestigious selections representing superb value for money. The best results are obviously given by the wines from century-old vineyards, many of which are ungrafted and grown on sand. The range is completed by labels obtained from local varieties, including an excellent raisin wine from moscato grapes and a Metodo Classico in the Vermentino di Sardegna DOC zone. This year we tasted a wide range of wines, all convincing. The best were two first-rate versions of Carignano del Sulcis: the austere, close-knit Arruga 2008, with aromas of black berry fruit and scrubland, and the deep, full-flavoured Is Arenas Riserva 2009, which took home a Tre Bicchieri, combining extreme drinkability with good structure and a complex nose of red berry fruit.

● Carignano del Sulcis Is Arenas Ris. '09	♟♟♟	4*
● Carignano del Sulcis Sup. Arruga '08	♟♟	6
● Cannonau di Sardegna Foras '11	♟♟	2*
● Carignano del Sulcis Is Solus '10	♟♟	2*
● Carignano del Sulcis Nur '11	♟♟	2*
○ Moscato di Cagliari Amentos '11	♟♟	4
○ Vermentino di Sardegna Brut AD 49	♟♟	5
○ Vermentino di Sardegna Lugore '12	♟♟	3
● Carignano del Sulcis Rosato Horus '12	♟	2
● Monica di Sardegna Insula '12	♟	2
○ Nasco di Cagliari Amentos '10	♟	4
○ Vermentino di Sardegna Terre Fenicie '12	♟	2
● Carignano del Sulcis Is Arenas Ris. '08	♟♟♟	4*
● Carignano del Sulcis Is Arenas Ris. '07	♟♟♟	3*
● Carignano del Sulcis Sup. Arruga '07	♟♟♟	5

Giuseppe Sedilesu

VIA VITTORIO EMANUELE II, 64
08024 MAMOIADA [NU]
TEL. 078456791
www.giuseppesedilesu.com

CELLAR SALES
PRE-BOOKED VISITS
ANNUAL PRODUCTION 120,000 bottles
HECTARES UNDER VINE 17.00

Mamoiada is a town in Barbagia with a rich cultural heritage, where Cannonau has been produced since time immemorial. The Sedilesus are a great wine family, now in their third generation, who over the years have invested and moved with the times, pursuing excellence with Sardinia's most important variety. The results have not been long coming, and are mainly down to the beautiful plots of old bush vines at high elevations, regaling wines with impressive structure that remain fresh and fragrant. In addition to various declinations of Cannonau, we would like to mention an extremely unusual white from granazza di Mamoiada grapes. This was a great year for the reds of Sedilesu, with two wines making the final. A well-deserved Tre Bicchieri went to the Mamuthone 2011, a well-typed, territorial Cannonau di Sardegna, with a glycerine-rich palate and enfolding body behind forest floor aromas, dark, crunchy fruit, bark and bramble. The Ballu Tundu, a Riserva 2010, was also exceptional, combining drinkability with serious structure.

● Cannonau di Sardegna Mamuthone '11	♟♟♟	3*
● Cannonau di Sardegna Ballu Tundu Ris. '10	♟♟	6
● Cannonau di Sardegna Carnevale Ris. '10	♟♟	5
⊙ Cannonau di Sardegna Erèssia '12	♟♟	3
○ Perda Pintà '11	♟♟	5
● Cannonau di Sardegna S'Annada '11	♟	3
● Cannonau di Sardegna Mamuthone '08	♟♟♟	3*
○ Perda Pintà '09	♟♟♟	4
○ Perda Pintà '07	♟♟♟	5
● Cannonau di Sardegna Ballu Tundu Ris. '07	♟♟	6
● Cannonau di Sardegna Carnevale Ris. '08	♟♟	5
● Cannonau di Sardegna Gràssia '09	♟♟	3
● Cannonau di Sardegna S'Annada '09	♟♟	3
● Cannonau di Sardegna S'Annada '08	♟♟	3*

★Tenute Sella & Mosca

LOC. I PIANI
07041 ALGHERO [SS]
TEL. 079997700
www.sellaemosca.com

CELLAR SALES
PRE-BOOKED VISITS
ANNUAL PRODUCTION 7,600,000 bottles
HECTARES UNDER VINE 571.00

To give an idea of the reputation this winery from Alghero has earned in recent years, we need merely mention that in our last edition Sella & Mosca was Winery of the Year. This is not only one of the island's largest private operations, with over 500 hectares under vine, but also one able to make ongoing investments, convinced that the constant quest for outstanding quality is the only way to survive in a global market. Their investment in the native variety torbato is just one of the examples of this policy. The vast range of labels show convincing performance across the board, including the vintages, always sold at competitive prices. Once again this year, the large number of labels produced by this Alghero winery show quality across the board. Among the best is a masterfully-executed Marchese di Villamarina 2008, a dense, Mediterranean wine showing grassy notes and black berry fruit, accompanied by hints of scrub and forest floor.

Siddura

LOC. SIDDURA
07020 LUOGOSANTO [OT]
TEL. 0796513027
www.siddura.com

CELLAR SALES
PRE-BOOKED VISITS
ANNUAL PRODUCTION 30,000 bottles
HECTARES UNDER VINE 17.00

One of the most pleasant surprises in recent years, the recently established Siddura winery in Gallura, has already earned a prime position among the Guide's top names. The merit goes to impeccable management, with clear ideas on vinification and style, and an estate boasting spectacular vineyards on sandy, granite-based soils. The extremely drinkable yet complex wines all display impressive linearity, hinging on mineral elegance and finesse. As we said, the winery earned a full-length profile this time, thanks to a surprising range, including some excellent wines. One of these is the Maìa 2012, a Vermentino di Gallura Superiore with an intense nose of aromatic herbs, pennyroyal and helichrysum. In the mouth, fresh flavours accompany good depth and superb supporting acidity. The Vermentino di Gallura Spèra and the Cannonau di Sardegna Fòla also impressed.

● Alghero Rosso Marchese di Villamarina '08	♥♥♥ 6
○ Alghero Torbato Terre Bianche Cuvée 161 '12	♥♥ 3*
○ Vermentino di Gallura Sup. Monteoro '12	♥♥ 3*
● Alghero Anghelu Ruju Ris. '04	♥♥ 6
⊙ Alghero Oleandro '12	♥♥ 3
● Alghero Rosso Tanca Farrà '09	♥♥ 4
○ Alghero Torbato Terre Bianche '12	♥♥ 3
● Cannonau di Sardegna Dimonios Ris. '09	♥♥ 3
● Carignano del Sulcis Terre Rare '10	♥♥ 3
● Carignano del Sulcis Terre Rare Ris. '09	♥♥ 4
○ Alghero Thìlion '12	♥ 4
○ Vermentino di Sardegna Cala Reale '12	♥ 3
○ Vermentino di Sardegna La Cala '12	♥ 3
● Alghero Marchese di Villamarina '07	♥♥♥ 6
● Alghero Marchese di Villamarina '06	♥♥♥ 6

○ Vermentino di Gallura Sup. Maìa '12	♥♥ 5
● Cannonau di Sardegna Fòla '12	♥♥ 5
● Èrema '12	♥♥ 4
○ Vermentino di Gallura Spèra '12	♥♥ 3

Tenute Soletta

LOC. SIGNOR'ANNA
07040 CODRONGIANOS [SS]
TEL. 079435067
www.tenutesoletta.it

CELLAR SALES
PRE-BOOKED VISITS
ANNUAL PRODUCTION 100,000 bottles
HECTARES UNDER VINE 15.00

Umberto Soletta is both the brains and the brawn of the Codrongianus winery, whose 15-or-so hectares produce around 100,000 bottles a year. We are in the north-west of the island, on interesting, lean soils, perfect for winegrowing. Both cannonau and vermentino give flattering results here, and Umberto's aim is to produce well typed wines with a real sense of place and good ageing potential, while also achieving elegance and finesse on the palate. The Riservas of Canonau convince us more with every passing year, as does the raisin wine from aromatic grapes, one of Sardinia's best. We saw a fine performance from Soletta, with two Cannonau di Sardegnas reaching the finals: the long, drinkable Corona Majore 2010, and the Keramos 2009, a close-woven, austere Riserva with serious structure, just a tad clenched due to its austere, weighty tannins. The whites include the Kianos 2012, a blend of vermentino and incrocio Manzoni.

● Cannonau di Sardegna Corona Majore '10	♀♀ 4
● Cannonau di Sardegna Keramos Ris. '09	♀♀ 5
○ Kianos '12	♀♀ 4
○ Vermentino di Sardegna Chimera '12	♀♀ 3
○ Vermentino di Sardegna Sardo '12	♀ 2
● Cannonau di Sardegna Keramos Ris. '07	♀♀♀ 5
● Cannonau di Sardegna Keramos Ris. '04	♀♀♀ 4
● Cannonau di Sardegna Corona Majore '09	♀♀ 3*
● Cannonau di Sardegna Corona Majore '08	♀♀ 3*
● Cannonau di Sardegna Keramos Ris. '08	♀♀ 5
● Cannonau di Sardegna Keramos Ris. '06	♀♀ 4

Vigne Surrau

SP ARZACHENA - PORTO CERVO
07021 ARZACHENA [OT]
TEL. 078982933
www.vignesurrau.it

PRE-BOOKED VISITS
ANNUAL PRODUCTION 250,000 bottles
HECTARES UNDER VINE 40.00

Although a fairly new operation, Surrau has already shown that it can consistently produce a convincing range, with some excellent bottles, both amongst the vermentino-based whites and the reds. The fresh, mineral, zesty Galluras, faithful expressions of the Arzachena territory, show that whites too, if made the right way, need have no fear of ageing. The red wines, meanwhile, from local grapes, sometimes blended with international varieties, display excellent drinkability and finesse. For some years the range has also included an interesting, flavoursome metodo classico Vermentino Spumante. Two of the wines made our final tastings, and the Vermentino di Gallura Superiore Sciala earned a Tre Bicchieri. The Sciala 2012 remains one of the DOC zone's best, with its apple and helichrysum aromas, and fresh, tasty palate. The Barriu 2010, a well-structured red from cannonau, carignano, cabernet sauvignon and muristellu, shows admirable length.

○ Vermentino di Gallura Sup. Sciala '12	♀♀♀ 5
● Barriu '10	♀♀ 5
● Cannonau di Sardegna Sincaru '10	♀♀ 5
● Cannonau di Sardegna Sincaru Ris. '09	♀♀ 5
● Surrau '11	♀♀ 4
○ Vermentino di Gallura Branu '12	♀♀ 4
○ Vermentino di Gallura Sup. Sciala V.T. '12	♀♀ 5
● Surrau '09	♀♀♀ 4*
● Barriu '08	♀♀ 5
○ Vermentino di Gallura Branu '11	♀♀ 4
○ Vermentino di Gallura Sciala V.T. '11	♀♀ 5
○ Vermentino di Gallura Sup. Sciala '11	♀♀ 5

Cantina Trexenta

V.LE PIEMONTE, 40
09040 SENORBÌ [CA]
TEL. 0709808863
www.cantinatrexenta.it

CELLAR SALES
PRE-BOOKED VISITS
ANNUAL PRODUCTION 1,000,000 bottles
HECTARES UNDER VINE 350.00

The Trexenta co-operative winery, based in
Senorbì, can rely on dozens of growers,
who farm around 350 hectares of
vineyards. Like the majority of co-operative
wineries, it was established in the 1950s,
with production focusing for much of its
early life on whites, a natural choice in this
territory particularly well-suited to
vermentino, nuragus and moscato.
However, in recent decades the reds have
taken over, and with cannonau in particular
the winery has shown its mettle, offering
well typed, Mediterranean, highly drinkable
wines at consistently attractive prices. The
versions of Cannonau di Sardegna in
particular impressed, especially the
graceful Corte Adua 2011, which was juicy,
yet complex and deep, with notes of black
berry fruit and bark paving the way for
excellent tannic structure on the palate.

● Cannonau di Sardegna Corte Adua '11	▼▼	2*
● Cannonau di Sardegna Baione '11	▼▼	2*
● Cannonau di Sardegna Bingias '11	▼▼	2*
● Cannonau di Sardegna Goimajor '11	▼▼	2*
● Monica di Sardegna Duca di Mandas '11	▼▼	2*
○ Vermentino di Sardegna Bingias '12	▼▼	2*
● Antigu '12	▼	4
● Monica di Sardegna Bingias '11	▼	2
○ Nuragus di Cagliari Tenute San Mauro '12	▼	2
○ Vermentino di Sardegna Donna Leonora '12	▼	2
● Antigu '08	♆♆	4
● Cannonau di Sardegna Corte Adua '10	♆♆	2*
● Cannonau di Sardegna Tanca su Conti Ris. '09	♆♆	4
● Monica di Sardegna Duca di Mandas '10	♆♆	2*

Cantina del Vermentino Monti

VIA SAN PAOLO, 2
07020 MONTI [SS]
TEL. 078944012
www.vermentinomonti.it

CELLAR SALES
PRE-BOOKED VISITS
ANNUAL PRODUCTION 2,500,000 bottles
HECTARES UNDER VINE 500.00

In the heart of Gallura, less than 30
kilometres from Olbia, lies Monti, a small
town immersed among vineyards and cork
plantations, that lends its name to the local
co-operative winery. It has always been
associated with vermentino, the territory's
main grape, and a wine that displays
unique traits on these granite-based soils,
at elevations of up to 500 metres with a
wide day-to-night temperature range.
Monti's wines exhibit a unique stylistic
focus, showing clean on the nose and
fresh and graceful on the palate. But
Vermentino is not the sole performer here,
and the vineyards are also home to local
red varieties such as cagnulari, mu It was
above all the versions of Vermentino di
Gallura that made a mark in our final
tastings. The Funtanaliras Oro 2012 offers
spring flowers and savoury herbs with a
touch of fruit, leading to freshness and
masses of flavour on the deep, mineral
palate. The softer, more Mediterranean
Arakena 2011, from late-harvested
grapes, shows apricot and minty notes.
ristellu and cannonau.

● Galana '06	▼▼	4
○ Vermentino di Gallura Funtanaliras Oro '12	▼▼	3
○ Vermentino di Gallura Sup. Arakena V.T. '11	▼▼	4
● Cannonau di Sardegna Tàmara '11	▼	3
● Kiri '11	▼	3
● Cannonau di Sardegna Kiri '11	♆♆	3
○ Vermentino di Gallura Funtanaliras '11	♆♆	3*
○ Vermentino di Gallura Sup. Arakena V.T. '10	♆♆	4

Angelo Angioi

LOC. COLORAS
09079 TRESNURAGHES [OR]
TEL. 3409357227
saltodicoloras@gmail.com

CELLAR SALES
PRE-BOOKED VISITS
ANNUAL PRODUCTION 5,000 bottles
HECTARES UNDER VINE 2.80

○ Malvasia di Bosa Dolce Salto di Coloras '12	♥♥ 4

Poderi Atha Ruja

VIA EMILIA, 45
08022 DORGALI [NU]
TEL. 3475387127
www.atharuja.com

CELLAR SALES
ACCOMMODATION AND RESTAURANT SERVICE
ANNUAL PRODUCTION 25,000 bottles
HECTARES UNDER VINE 5.00

● Cannonau di Sardegna '10	♥♥ 3*
● Cannonau di Sardegna Kuentu Ris. '09	♥♥ 5

Berritta

VIA KENNEDY, 108
08022 DORGALI [NU]
TEL. 078495372
www.cantinaberitta.it

ANNUAL PRODUCTION 5,000 bottles
HECTARES UNDER VINE 2.00

● Cannonau di Sardegna Thurcalesu '11	♥♥ 2*
● Cannonau di Sardegna Nostranu '12	♥ 2
● Panzale '12	♥ 2

Cantina del Bovale

LOC. S'ISCA
09098 TERRALBA [OR]
TEL. 3460573346
www.cantinadelbovale.it

CELLAR SALES
ACCOMMODATION
ANNUAL PRODUCTION 35,000 bottles
HECTARES UNDER VINE 9.00

● Terralba Majorale '10	♥♥ 5
○ Vermentino di Sardegna Sabbie d'Oro '12	♥♥ 2*
● Sinnos '11	♥ 2
● Terralba Arcuentu '10	♥ 3

Cantina delle Vigne Piero Mancini

LOC. CALA SACCAIA
VIA MADAGASCAR, 17
07026 OLBIA
TEL. 078950717
www.pieromancini.it

CELLAR SALES
PRE-BOOKED VISITS
ANNUAL PRODUCTION 1,500,000 bottles
HECTARES UNDER VINE 100,00

● Cannonau di Sardegna Falcale '11	♥♥ 2*
○ Vermentino di Gallura Sup. Mancini Primo '12	♥♥ 4
○ Vermentino di Gallura Sup. Cucaione '12	♥ 2

Carpante

VIA GARIBALDI, 151
07049 USINI [SS]
TEL. 079380614
www.carpante.it

CELLAR SALES
PRE-BOOKED VISITS
ANNUAL PRODUCTION 30,000 bottles
HECTARES UNDER VINE 8.00

● Carpante '10	♥♥ 4
● Disizzu '12	♥♥ 4
○ Vermentino di Sardegna Frinas '12	♥♥ 4
● Cagnulari '12	♥ 3

Cantina di Castiadas

LOC. OLIA SPECIOSA
09040 CASTIADAS [CA]
TEL. 0709949004
www.cantinacastiadas.com

CELLAR SALES
PRE-BOOKED VISITS
ANNUAL PRODUCTION 150,000 bottles
HECTARES UNDER VINE 150.00

● Cannonau di Sardegna Capo Ferrato Ris. '09	♟♟ 3
● Parolto '09	♟♟ 3
○ Vermentino di Sardegna Notteri '12	♟ 2

Nino Castiglia

VIA MOSCA, 3
07023 CALANGIANUS [OT]
TEL. 079670530
www.cantinacastiglia.it

CELLAR SALES
ANNUAL PRODUCTION 30,000 bottles
HECTARES UNDER VINE 5.00

● Intentu '10	♟♟ 5
● Pergula '10	♟♟ 3
● Incimbrà '10	♟ 5
○ Vermentino di Gallura Myali '12	♟ 3

Colle Nivera

VIA VENETO, 14
08100 NUORO
TEL. 0784294037
www.collenivera.com

CELLAR SALES
PRE-BOOKED VISITS
HECTARES UNDER VINE 15.00

● Cannonau di Sardegna '10	♟♟ 4
● Cannonau di Sardegna I Monili di Colle Nivera '11	♟♟ 4
○ Vermentino di Sardegna Talai '12	♟ 3

Columbu

VIA MARCONI, 1
08013 BOSA [OR]
TEL. 0785373380
www.vinibosa.com

CELLAR SALES
PRE-BOOKED VISITS
ANNUAL PRODUCTION 4,000 bottles
HECTARES UNDER VINE 3.40

○ Malvasia di Bosa Alvarega '12	♟♟ 2*

Gianluigi Deaddis

LOC. SAN PIETRO
SS 134 KM 2,2
07030 BULZI [SS]
TEL. 079588314
www.cantinadeaddis.com

CELLAR SALES
PRE-BOOKED VISITS
ANNUAL PRODUCTION 14,900 bottles
HECTARES UNDER VINE 6.00

● Ultana '10	♟♟ 5
○ Vermentino di Sardegna Narami '12	♟♟ 3

Vigne Deriu

LOC. SIGNORANNA
07040 CODRONGIANOS [SS]
TEL. 079435101
www.vignederiu.it

CELLAR SALES
PRE-BOOKED VISITS
ANNUAL PRODUCTION 30,000 bottles
HECTARES UNDER VINE 6.00

● Cannonau di Sardegna '11	♟♟ 3
● Tiu Filippu '09	♟ 5

Fradiles

VIA SANDRO PERTINI, 2
08030 ATZARA [NU]
TEL. 3331761683
www.fradiles.it

CELLAR SALES
PRE-BOOKED VISITS
ANNUAL PRODUCTION 12,000 bottles
HECTARES UNDER VINE 10.00

● Bagadiu '11	♟♟ 3
● Mandrolisai Antiogu '10	♟♟ 4

Cantina Giogantinu

VIA MILANO, 30
07022 BERCHIDDA [OT]
TEL. 079704163
www.giogantinu.it

CELLAR SALES
PRE-BOOKED VISITS
ANNUAL PRODUCTION 1,500,000 bottles
HECTARES UNDER VINE 320.00

○ Vermentino di Gallura Lunghente '12	♟♟ 3
○ Vermentino di Gallura Sup. Aldia '12	♟ 2
○ Vermentino di Gallura Sup. Vigne Storiche '11	♟ 4

Andrea Ledda

VIA MUSIO, 13
07043 BONNANARO [SS]
TEL. 079845060
agriledda@tiscali.it

CELLAR SALES
PRE-BOOKED VISITS
ANNUAL PRODUCTION 25,000 bottles
HECTARES UNDER VINE 13.00

● Cannonau di Sardegna Mogano '10	♟♟ 4
● Ebano '10	♟♟ 5

Pietro Lilliu

VIA SARDEGNA, 13
09020 USSARAMANNA [VS]
TEL. 3939787352
www.cantinalilliu.it

CELLAR SALES
PRE-BOOKED VISITS
ANNUAL PRODUCTION 20,000 bottles
HECTARES UNDER VINE 4.00

● Biazzu '11	♟♟ 3
● Cannonau di Sardegna Dicciosu '11	♟♟ 3
● Presciu '10	♟♟ 3
⊙ Cannonau di Sardegna Pantumas '12	♟ 3

Tenute Massidda

LOC. GIUANNI PORCU
09040 DONORI [CA]
TEL. 3478088683
massiddavini@tiscali.it

CELLAR SALES
PRE-BOOKED VISITS
ANNUAL PRODUCTION 200,000 bottles
HECTARES UNDER VINE 45.00

● L'Orizzonte si Colorava di Rosso '10	♟♟ 4
○ Vermentino di Sardegna Cannisonis '12	♟♟ 4

Abele Melis

VIA SANTA SUINA, 3
09098 TERRALBA [OR]
TEL. 0783851090
melis.vini@tiscali.it

CELLAR SALES
PRE-BOOKED VISITS
ANNUAL PRODUCTION 100,000 bottles
HECTARES UNDER VINE 35.00

● Bovale '12	♟♟ 2*
○ Vermentino di Sardegna Ereb '12	♟ 3
○ Vermentino di Sardegna localia '12	♟ 2

Meloni Vini

VIA GALLUS, 79
09047 SELARGIUS [CA]
TEL. 070852822
www.melonivini.com

CELLAR SALES
PRE-BOOKED VISITS
ANNUAL PRODUCTION 1,000,000 bottles
HECTARES UNDER VINE 200.00
VITICULTURE METHOD Certified Organic

● Cannonau di Sardegna Terreforru '10	🍷🍷 2*
● Nue Rosso '11	🍷🍷 2*
● Monica di Sardegna Jaccia '11	🍷 2
● Monica di Sardegna Sup. Kre'u '09	🍷 4

Giovanni Montisci

VIA ASIAGO, 7B
08024 MAMOIADA [NU]
TEL. 0784569021
www.barrosu.it

CELLAR SALES
PRE-BOOKED VISITS
ANNUAL PRODUCTION 6,000 bottles
HECTARES UNDER VINE 2.00

● Cannonau di Sardegna Franzisca Ris. '10	🍷🍷 6
○ Barrosu Bianco Dolce	🍷🍷 5
● Cannonau di Sardegna Barrosu Ris. '10	🍷🍷 6
● Cannonau di Sardegna Rosato '12	🍷🍷 3

Mora&Memo

VIA CIUSA, 13
09040 SERDIANA [CA]
TEL. 3311972266
www.moraememo.it

CELLAR SALES
ANNUAL PRODUCTION 28,000 bottles
HECTARES UNDER VINE 30.00

● Nau&Co. '12	🍷🍷 4
○ Tino Sur Lie '12	🍷 4
○ Vermentino di Sardegna Tino '12	🍷 3

Murales

LOC. PILIEZZU, 1
07026 OLBIA
TEL. 3929059400
www.vinimurales.it

ANNUAL PRODUCTION 100,000 bottles
HECTARES UNDER VINE 15.00

○ Vermentino di Gallura Miradas '12	🍷🍷 3*
○ Vermentino di Sardegna Tutti i Venti '11	🍷🍷 3

Tenute Olbios

LOC. VENAFIORITA
VIA LOIRI, 83
07026 OLBIA
TEL. 0789641003
info@tenuteolbios.com

HECTARES UNDER VINE 60.00

○ Vermentino di Gallura Sup. Lupus in Fabula '12	🍷🍷 5
○ Vermentino di Sardegna M. Cl. Blanc de Blancs Dosaggio Zero '08	🍷🍷 5

Olianas

LOC. PORRUDDU
09031 GERGEI [CA]
TEL. 0558300800
www.olianas.it

CELLAR SALES
PRE-BOOKED VISITS
ANNUAL PRODUCTION 50,000 bottles
HECTARES UNDER VINE 13.00

● Cannonau di Sardegna '12	🍷🍷 3
● Perdixi '11	🍷 4
⊙ Rosato '12	🍷 3
○ Vermentino di Sardegna '12	🍷 3

Cantina Cooperativa di Oliena

VIA NUORO, 112
08025 OLIENA [NU]
TEL. 0784287509
www.cantinasocialeoliena.it

ANNUAL PRODUCTION 300,000 bottles
HECTARES UNDER VINE 180.00

● Cannonau di Sardegna Nepente '11		♟♟ 2*

Cantine di Orgosolo

VIA SANTA LUCIA
08027 ORGOSOLO [NU]
TEL. 0784403096
www.cantinediorgosolo.it

CELLAR SALES
PRE-BOOKED VISITS
RESTAURANT SERVICE
ANNUAL PRODUCTION 17,000 bottles
HECTARES UNDER VINE 16.00

● Cannonau di Sardegna Neale '12		♟♟ 3

Gabriele Palmas

V.LE ITALIA, 3
07100 SASSARI
TEL. 079233721
gabrielepalmas@tiscali.it

CELLAR SALES
PRE-BOOKED VISITS
ANNUAL PRODUCTION 20,000 bottles
HECTARES UNDER VINE 10.00

● Syrah '11		♟♟ 3
○ Vermentino di Sardegna '12		♟ 4

Poderosa

VIA E. TOTI, 14
07047 THIESI [SS]
TEL. 3283237413
www.agricolapoderosa.it

CELLAR SALES
PRE-BOOKED VISITS
ANNUAL PRODUCTION 15,000 bottles
HECTARES UNDER VINE 6.00

● Lierra '09		♟ 5
○ Vermentino di Sardegna Lunadu '12		♟♟ 4
○ Gainu '12		♟ 4
● Monte Santu '10		♟ 3

Giampietro Puggioni

VIA NUORO, 11
08024 MAMOIADA [NU]
TEL. 0784203516
www.cantinagiampietropuggioni.it

CELLAR SALES
PRE-BOOKED VISITS
ANNUAL PRODUCTION 60,000 bottles
HECTARES UNDER VINE 15.00
VITICULTURE METHOD Certified Organic

● Cannonau di Sardegna Isula '10		♟♟ 3
● Cannonau di Sardegna Lakana '11		♟♟ 3
● Cannonau di Sardegna Mamuthone '11		♟♟ 3

Quartomoro di Sardegna

VIA PORCELLA, 107
09092 ARBOREA [OR]
TEL. 3467643552
www.quartomoro.it

CELLAR SALES
PRE-BOOKED VISITS
ANNUAL PRODUCTION 6,500 bottles
HECTARES UNDER VINE 2.00

● Memorie di Vite CRG '12		♟♟ 3*
● Memorie di Vite CGN '12		♟♟ 3
○ Memorie di Vite NRG '12		♟♟ 3
○ Memorie di Vite Q Brut M. Cl.		♟♟ 3

Rigatteri

LOC. SANTA MARIA LA PALMA
REG. FLUMELONGU, 56
07041 ALGHERO [SS]
TEL. 3408636375
www.rigatteri.com

CELLAR SALES
PRE-BOOKED VISITS
ANNUAL PRODUCTION 15,000 bottles
HECTARES UNDER VINE 10.00

● Cannonau di Sardegna Mirau '12	♥♥ 2*
● Alghero Rosso Graffiante '12	♥ 3
○ Vermentino di Sardegna Ardelia '12	♥ 3
○ Vermentino di Sardegna Yiòs '12	♥ 2

Santa Maria La Palma

LOC. SANTA MARIA LA PALMA
07041 ALGHERO [SS]
TEL. 079999008
www.santamarialapalma.it

CELLAR SALES
PRE-BOOKED VISITS
ANNUAL PRODUCTION 3,800,000 bottles
HECTARES UNDER VINE 700,00

● Cannonau di Sardegna Valmell '12	♥♥ 2*
● Alghero Cagnulari '10	♥ 3
● Cannonau di Sardegna Le Bombarde '12	♥ 2
○ Vermentino di Sardegna I Papiri '12	♥ 3

Su Entu

SP 48 KM 1,800
09025 SANLURI [CA]
TEL. 07093571200
www.cantinesuentu.com

CELLAR SALES
PRE-BOOKED VISITS
ANNUAL PRODUCTION 30,000 bottles
HECTARES UNDER VINE 32.00

● Cannonau di Sardegna '11	♥♥ 3
○ Spumante Brut '12	♥ 3
⊙ Spumante Brut Rosé '12	♥ 3
○ Vermentino di Sardegna '12	♥ 3

Tanca Gioia Carloforte

LOC. GIOIA
09014 CARLOFORTE [CI]
TEL. 3356359329
www.u-tabarka.com

CELLAR SALES
PRE-BOOKED VISITS
ANNUAL PRODUCTION 30,000 bottles
HECTARES UNDER VINE 7.00

● Carignano del Sulcis Roussou '11	♥♥ 3
○ Giancu '12	♥♥ 3
○ Perdigiournou '12	♥♥ 3
● Ciù Roussou '11	♥ 3

Cantina Sociale della Vernaccia

LOC. RIMEDIO
VIA ORISTANO, 6A
09170 ORISTANO
TEL. 078333383
www.vinovernaccia.com

CELLAR SALES
PRE-BOOKED VISITS
ANNUAL PRODUCTION 260,000 bottles
HECTARES UNDER VINE 120.00

○ Terresinis '12	♥♥ 2*
● Cannonau di Sardegna Korash Ris. '10	♥♥ 3
● Monica di Sardegna Don Efisio '11	♥ 2

Zarelli Vini

VIA VITTORIO EMANUELE, 36
08010 MAGOMADAS [OR]
TEL. 078535311
www.zarellivini.it

CELLAR SALES
PRE-BOOKED VISITS
ANNUAL PRODUCTION 20,000 bottles
HECTARES UNDER VINE 7,00

○ Andula	♥♥ 5
● Cannonau di Sardegna Sa Costa '11	♥♥ 2*
○ Inachis '12	♥ 3

INDICE
wineries in alphabetical order
wineries by region

La Carraia	724	Michele Castellani	341
Tenuta Carretta	181	Castellare di Castellina	549
Caruso & Minini	891	Castellari Bergaglio	77
Carussin	181	Maria Pia Castelli	687
Carvinea	836	Castellinuzza e Piuca	658
Casa al Vento	657	Castello Banfi	550
Casa alle Vacche	547	Castello Bonomi	226
Casa Cecchin	340	Castello d'Albola	550
Casa Dei	657	Castello dei Rampolla	551
La Casa dell'Orco	816	Castello del Poggio	183
Casa Di Baal	816	Castello del Terriccio	551
La Casa di Filippo	892	Castello del Trebbio	658
Casa Emma	548	Castello della Sala	725
Casa Geretto	397	Castello delle Regine	742
Casa Maschito	825	Castello di Bolgheri	552
Casa Roma	340	Castello di Bossi	552
Casa Sola	657	Castello di Buttrio	415
Casa Zuliani	414	Castello di Cigognola	226
Fattoria Casabianca	657	Castello di Corbara	742
La Casaccia	67	Castello di Fonterutoli	553
Casale Cento Corvi	755	Castello di Gabiano	77
Casale del Giglio	746	Castello di Gussago	256
Casale della Ioria	747	Castello di Lispida	397
Casale Marchese	747	Castello di Luzzano	256
Casale Pozzuolo	657	Castello di Magione	726
Casalfarneto	687	Castello di Monsanto	553
Casalone	68	Castello di Neive	78
Casanova di Neri	548	Castello di Poppiano	554
Viticoltori del Casavecchia	816	Castello di Querceto	658
Cascina Adelaide	181	Castello di Radda	554
Cascina Barisél	68	Tenuta Castello di Razzano	78
Cascina Belmonte	256	Castello di San Donato in Perano	555
Cascina Bertolotto	181	Castello di Spessa	416
Cascina Ca' Rossa	69	Castello di Tassarolo	79
Cascina Castlet	182	Castello di Uviglie	79
Cascina Chicco	69	Castello di Velona	658
Cascina Corte	70	Castello di Verduno	80
Cascina Cucco	70	Castello di Vicchiomaggio	555
Cascina del Monastero	182	Castello di Volpaia	556
Cascina Flino	182	Castello Monaci	836
Cascina Fonda	71	Cantina Castello Monte Vibiano Vecchio	726
Cascina Fontana	71	Castello Romitorio	556
Cascina Garitina	182	Castello Sant'Anna	416
Cascina Gilli	72	Castelluccio	490
Cascina Giovinale	72	Castelvecchio	417
Cascina La Barbatella	73	Castelvecchio	557
Cascina La Maddalena	73	Castelveder	256
Cascina la Pertica	256	Cantina di Castiadas	916
Cascina Montagnola	74	Nino Castiglia	916
Cascina Morassino	74	Castiglion del Bosco	658
Cascina Nirasca	199	Cantine di Castignano	714
Cascina Pellerino	75	Castorani	764
Cascina Salicetti	75	Casula Vinaria	816
Cascina Tavijn	182	Cantina Catabbo	786
Cascina Val del Prete	76	Luigi Cataldi Madonna	765
Cascina Zoina	182	La Caudrina	80
Case Paolin	341	Cautiero	817
Casebianche	816	Cavalchina	342
Lino Casella	476	Tenuta del Cavalier Pepe	790
Le Casematte	892	Cavalleri	227
La Casetta dei Frati	518	F.lli Cavallotto – Tenuta Bricco Boschis	81
Casetto dei Mandorli	489	Domenico Cavazza & F.lli	342
Francesca Castaldi	76	Cavicchioli U. & Figli	490
Castel de Paolis	755	Cavim - Cantina Viticoltori Imolesi	518
Castel di Salve	851	Caviro	518
Castel Sallegg	291	Cavit	271
Tenuta Castelbuono	725	Le Cecche	183
CastelFaglia - Monogram	225	Giorgio Cecchetto	343
Castelfeder	291	Famiglia Cecchi	557
Castell'in Villa	549	Marco Cecchini	417
Renzo Castella	183	Giancarlo Ceci	851
La Castellada	415	Cecilia	659
Castellani	658	Celli	491